a canonical and synthetic approach

THEOLOGY *of the* NEW TESTAMENT

a canonical and synthetic approach

THEOLOGY *of the* NEW TESTAMENT

FRANK THIELMAN

GRAND RAPIDS, MICHIGAN 49530 USA

ZONDERVAN™

Theology of the New Testament

Requests for information should be addressed to:
Zondervan, *Grand Rapids, Michigan 49530*

Library of Congress Cataloging-in-Publication Data

Thielman, Frank.
Theology of the New Testament : a canonical and synthetic approach / Frank Thielman.
p. cm.
Summary: "A basic resource for serious teachers, pastors, scholars, or lay people interested in learning about the theology of the New Testament"—Provided by publisher.
Includes bibliographical references and index.
ISBN-10: 0-310-21132-8 (alk. paper)
ISBN-13: 978-0310-21132-7
1. Bible. N.T.—Theology. 2. Bible. N.T.—Canonical criticism. I. Title.
BS2397.T445 2005
230'.0415—dc22 2004030070
CIP

This edition printed on acid-free paper.

Interior design by Sherri Hoffman

Printed in the United States of America

05 06 07 08 09 10 11 12 /❖ DCI/ 10 9 8 7 6 5 4 3 2

In loving memory of
Calvin Thielman
δίκαιος τετελειωμένος

CONTENTS

THREE

THE NON-PAULINE LETTERS AND THE REVELATION OF JOHN

CONCLUSION

PREFACE

I have written this book for two reasons: to provide a service and to make a case. I hope that the book will serve the needs of serious students of the New Testament for a brief theological orientation to each New Testament text. I also hope to have made a persuasive argument that although each text is rooted in its own cultural world, all twenty-seven texts, when read sympathetically, are theologically unified. At one level, therefore, I hope the book will provide a theological introduction to the single New Testament text that interests the reader, whether a student beginning a course on John's gospel, a pastor beginning a sermon series on Romans, or a teacher preparing a course on Revelation. At a second level, I hope that the book will be helpful to the reader in gaining an overview of the theological concerns of the entire New Testament, in seeing its theological coherence, and in appreciating the compelling nature of its worldview.

My approach to the subject lies somewhere between those whose New Testament theologies are basically theological histories of early Christianity and those who stick closely to the theological concerns of the New Testament canon.[1] I have tried to take to heart the criticism of William Wrede that merely discussing what the New Testament texts say about a variety of topics stands in danger of cutting these texts free from the cultures, politics, and religious traditions that anchor them in real life. But I have also taken to heart the perspective of Adolf Schlatter and many others that it is neither irrational nor unreasonable to read these texts sympathetically—as they want to be read—and from the perspective of a Christian faith that acknowledges them to be the Word of God. I have, therefore, tried to produce a theology of the New Testament rather than a theological history of early Christianity, but I have also tried to describe the theological concerns of each New Testament book, and of the New Testament as a whole, from the perspective of the times and circumstances in which each text was written.

My approach also lies somewhere between those who have written synthetic theologies in which the various New Testament authors are in constant conversation with one another and those whose theological studies focus on one author or one text only.[2] Perhaps unwisely, I have tried to do both. In an effort to show the fundamental theological unity of the New Testament texts, I have treated each of the three major parts of the New Testament canon as a theological unit. In introductory chapters to each unit I orient the reader to the leading question that affects the theological description of these three sections, whether the problem of a fourfold gospel, the

1 See respectively, e.g., Klaus Berger, *Theologiegeschichte des Urchristentums: Theologie des Neuen Testaments*, 2nd ed. (Tübingen: Francke, 1995), and Georg Strecker, *Theology of the New Testament*, ed. and completed by Friedrich Wilhelm Horn (New York: Walter de Gruyter/Louisville, Ky.: Westminster John Knox, 2000).

2 For the synthetic approach, see, e.g., G. B. Caird, *New Testament Theology*, ed. and completed by L. D. Hurst (Oxford: Oxford Univ. Press, 1994), and François Vouga, *Une théologie du Nouveau Testament* (Le Monde de la Bible 43; Genève: Labor et Fides, 2001), and for the individual book or author approach, see, e.g., the volumes in the series "New Testament Theology," ed. James D. G. Dunn (Cambridge: Cambridge Univ. Press, 1991–2003).

coherence and center of Paul's theology, or "early catholicism" in the New Testament. I then provide a synthetic chapter at the conclusion to each of the three major sections in which I try to place the various texts in that section in conversation with one another. In the book's final chapter I attempt to outline briefly the basic theological unity of the entire New Testament.

In an effort to give attention to the historical contingencies of each text and to allow each text its own theological voice, I have given each New Testament document its own chapter. The hobgoblin of consistency has driven me to provide separate chapters for Philemon, Titus, and 3 John, for example, but not for Acts, which Luke, I believe, wrote together with his gospel as a single, two-part work.

The question of how to arrange these chapters on each New Testament document posed something of a problem. It seemed possible to walk one of two paths. I could follow a strictly chronological order, beginning with the Pauline letters and ending with the Johannine literature. In reality, however, the chronology of the New Testament texts is uncertain, and assigning John's gospel a place before Revelation or 2 Timothy a place before 2 Peter, for example, seemed almost arbitrary. Alternatively, I could follow the canonical order of the texts as it appears in modern printed Bibles, but that seemed to privilege this order over other equally sensible and ancient arrangements of the texts found in some of the earliest editions of the New Testament.

In the end, I decided to follow a roughly chronological approach, not so much to the texts themselves as to the history of early Christianity that they presuppose. Thus, I begin with Jesus as we know him from the four gospels, move to Paul, and then to the non-Pauline texts that treat the problems of heresy and persecution in the developing church. Within each of the first two sections, where the relative chronology of the texts can be something more than a guess, I have treated them in the order that I think they were written.

- In the case of the gospels, I have assumed that Mark wrote first, that Matthew and Luke used Mark, and that John wrote last, perhaps with a knowledge of the other three.
- I have arranged the Pauline letters in a chronological order that takes into account evidence for Paul's ministry both from the letters themselves and from Acts.
- In the third part of the canon almost any attempt to follow a chronological scheme fails for lack of evidence, and so here I drop the concern with chronology (the chapter on 2 Peter, for example, precedes the chapter on 1 Peter, despite 2 Peter 3:1) and arrange the texts thematically—treating first those in which a concern for heresy seems dominant and then those in which persecution is a primary theme.

I have tried to write at a level intelligible to students whose primary focus is theology and to pastors with theological training. I have assumed that the reader has read the biblical text under discussion carefully and has an open text close at hand.

I do not, therefore, quote extensively from the biblical text.[3] I have also assumed a basic knowledge of the discipline of New Testament "introduction" and so have only occasionally touched on issues such as the authorship, date, and provenance of the New Testament documents.

I am deeply grateful to the many friends who have taken an interest in this book and provided substantial help to me in writing it. Dr. Timothy George, Dean of the Beeson Divinity School of Samford University, provided much encouragement along the way and enthusiastically supported my application to the Board of Trustees of the University for a sabbatical leave during the fall semester of 2002 to work on the book. I wish to thank the Board of Trustees for granting this leave. Professors Mark Strauss of Bethel Seminary, Sigurd Grindheim of Trinity Evangelical Divinity School, and Thomas R. Schreiner of Southern Baptist Theological Seminary read through all or most of the manuscript with great care and provided pages of helpful, written comments on a host of issues. Professor Edward P. Meadors of Taylor University, Professor Karen Jobes of Westmont College, Professor Jeffrey A. D. Weima of Calvin Theological Seminary, my brother Samuel B. Thielman, M.D., Ph.D., the members of Samford University's Workshop on Religion in Antiquity, and four semesters of students at Beeson Divinity School read parts of the manuscript and gave generous amounts of both help and encouragement. Mr. Michael Garrett and Ms. Cheryl Cecil of Davis Library at Samford University tirelessly located numerous necessary books and articles. The editors at Zondervan, including Stan Gundry, Jack Kuhatschek, Katya Corvett, and Verlyn Verbrugge, were kind to ask me to write this volume and extraordinarily helpful in seeing the manuscript through the final stages of production.

Dr. Bruce Winter, Warden of Tyndale House, Cambridge, England, discussed parts of the manuscript with me on many occasions during his several visits to Beeson Divinity School and found a desk for me among the bibliographical treasures of the Tyndale House Library when I made a week-long visit there. Dr. Richard and Mrs. Martha Burnett of Erskine Theological Seminary, Emeritus Professor Martin Hengel of the University of Tübingen, Germany, and Dr. Rolfe Hille, Director of the Albrecht Bengel Haus in Tübingen, arranged accommodations for me and showed me the kindest hospitality during a research visit there. Ms. Beate Martin provided a study desk for me at the Evangelische Stift with its incomparable library and located a number of books for me cheerfully and efficiently. These generous friends, and many others, gave freely of their time and energy to make this a much better book than it could possibly have been without their aid. My heartfelt thanks to each of them.

3 When I do quote, I use the New International Version where possible, although I also provide my own translations or modify the NIV when the discussion requires a more literal rendering of the text. I indicate where I have done this with the abbreviation "aut." Quotations from the Apocrypha come from the New Revised Standard Version. Quotations from non-Christian Greek and Roman sources, unless otherwise noted, come from the corresponding translation in the Loeb Classical Library. Quotations from the early church fathers, unless otherwise noted, come from Alexander Roberts and James Donaldson, eds., *The Anti-Nicene Fathers*, 1885–1887, 10 vols. (repr. Peabody, Mass.: Hendrickson, 1994), except for quotations from the Apostolic Fathers and Eusebius, where I have used the translations of Kirsopp Lake and J. E. L. Oulton in the Loeb editions. Quotations from Celsus' *On the True Doctrine* are from Henry Chadwick's translation of Origen's *Contra Celsum* (Cambridge: Cambridge Univ. Press, 1953).

I am also profoundly grateful to my immediate and extended family, including my mother, Dorothy Thielman, and my three children, Jonathan (who gave invaluable help with the computer), Sarah Jane, and Rebekah. With their warmth and cheer, especially when the work at various points grew difficult, they helped put the task in perspective.

Most helpful of all was my wonderful wife and dearest friend, Abigail. She frequently gave wise counsel not to become burdened with other smaller tasks so that I could finish this large one. She also provided much needed reminders to view my work on this book through the lens of life's most important issues—loving God and loving others. The theology that I talk so much about here and in my classes, she lives out day to day, reminding me that, as James says, what counts is not intellectual assent to correct doctrine, but staking one's life on the truth of the gospel. It would take another book to count the many specific ways in which she has herself been an example of this kind of faith in action to me and our three children. I had intended to dedicate the book to her.

After my father passed from this life into the visible presence of God on August 17, 2002, however, Abby and I agreed that I should dedicate the book to his memory. He was simply a wonderful father. In his eyes my very meager attempts at New Testament scholarship made me a giant in the field. In our weekly telephone conversations, he was free with his advice about this project, lavish with his encouragement, and eager to write checks to buy the books I needed to progress. I was in the middle of a sentence in the chapter on 3 John when news came that he had collapsed and lost consciousness. As I moved into Revelation, it was encouraging to think that Dad stood among the great multitude from every nation, tribe, people, and language praising the God whom he had faithfully served for so many years. May this book lead those who read it to understand the God of the New Testament better and to add their voices to that praise.

Frank Thielman
Lent, 2004

ABBREVIATIONS

AB	Anchor Bible
ABR	*Australian Biblical Review*
ABD	*Anchor Bible Dictionary*
ABRL	Anchor Bible Reference Library
ACCS	*Ancient Christian Commentary on Scripture*, New Testament. Edited by Thomas C. Oden
AGJU	Arbeiten zur Geschichte des antiken Judentums und des Urchristentums
AJP	*American Journal of Philology*
AnBib	Analecta biblica
ANTC	Abingdon New Testament Commentaries
ANRW	*Aufstieg und Niedergang der römischen Welt*
ASNU	Acta seminarii neotestamentici upsaliensis
aut.	author's translation
BBB	Bonner biblische Beiträge
BBR	*Bulletin for Biblical Research*
BBET	Beiträge zur biblischen Exegese und Theologie
BDAG	*A Greek English Lexicon of the New Testament and Other Early Christian Literature*, 3rd ed. By Walter Bauer. Revised and edited by Frederick William Danker.
BECNT	Baker Exegetical Commentary on the New Testament
BETL	Bibliotheca ephemeridum theologicarum lovaniensium
BSac	*Bibliotheca sacra*
BJRL	*Bulletin of the John Rylands Papyrus Library*
BNTC	Black's New Testament Commentary
BTB	*Biblical Theology Bulletin*
BZET	Beiträge zur evangelischen Theologie
BZNW	Beihefte zur Zeitschrift für die neutestamentliche Wissenschaft
CBQ	*Catholic Biblical Quarterly*
CJA	Christianity and Judaism in Antiquity
ConBNT	Coniectanea neotestamentica
CSEL	Corpus scriptorum ecclesiasticorum latinorum
CST	Contemporary Studies in Theology
CSHJ	Chicago Studies in the History of Judaism
CGTC	Cambridge Greek Testament Commentary
DCB	*Dictionary of Christian Biography*. Edited by Henry Wace and William C. Piercy.
DDD	*Dictionary of Deities and Demons in the Bible*. Edited by Karel van der Toorn, Bob Becking, and Pieter W. Van der Horst.

EBib	Études bibliques
EDNT	*Exegetical Dictionary of the New Testament.* Edited by Horst Balz and Gerhard Schneider.
EKK	Evangelisch-katholischer Kommentar zum Neuen Testament
ESV	English Standard Version
FF	Foundations and Facets
FRLANT	Forschungen zur Religion und Literatur des Alten und Neuen Testaments
GGBB	*Greek Grammar Beyond the Basics: An Exegetical Syntax of the New Testament.* By Daniel B. Wallace.
GNS	Good News Studies
HBT	*Horizons in Biblical Theology*
HNT	Handbuch zum Neuen Testament
HNTC	Harper's New Testament Commentaries
HTKNT	Herders theologischer Kommentar zum Neuen Testament
HTKNTSup	Herders theologischer Kommentar zum Neuen Testament: Supplementband
HTR	*Harvard Theological Review*
HTS	Harvard Theological Studies
HUT	Hermeneutische Untersuchungen zur Theologie
ICC	International Critical Commentary
Interp	*Interpretation*
IRT	Issues in Religion and Theology
ISBE	*The International Standard Bible Encyclopedia*, rev. ed., 4 vols. Ed. Geoffrey Bromiley et al.
ITC	International Theological Commentary
JBL	*Journal of Biblical Literature*
JPSTC	Jewish Publication Society Torah Commentary
JR	*Journal of Religion*
JRS	*Journal of Roman Studies*
JSJSup	*Journal for the Study of Judaism in the Persian, Hellenistic, and Roman Periods, Supplements*
JSNT	*Journal for the Study of the New Testament*
JSNTSup	Journal for the Study of the New Testament: Supplement
JTS	*Journal of Theological Studies*
LCC	Library of Christian Classics
LCL	Loeb Classical Library
LEC	Library of Early Christianity
LSJ	*A Greek-English Lexicon*, by Henry G. Liddell and Robert Scott. Rev. and augmented by Henry S. Jones
LuthB	Lutherbibel. Revised 1984.
LW	*Luther's Works.* Edited by Jaroslav Pelikan.
LXX	Septuagint

MdB	*Le Monde de la Bible*
MeyerK	Meyers kritisch-exegetischer Kommentar über das Neue Testament
MM	*The Vocabulary of the Greek Testament.* By James Hope Moulton and George Milligan.
MNTC	Moffatt New Testament Commentary
MStud	Monographien und Studienbücher
MT	Masoretic Text
MTS	Marburger theologische Studien
NA[25]	*Novum Testamentum Graece.* Edited by Eberhard Nestle, Erwin Nestle, and Kurt Aland. 25th ed.
NA[27]	*Novum Testamentum Graece.* Edited by Barbara Aland, Kurt Aland, et al. 27th ed.
NAB	New American Bible
NAC	New American Commentary
NASB	New American Standard Bible
NCB	New Century Bible
NHL	*Nag Hammadi Library in English.* Edited by James M. Robinson.
NICNT	New International Commentary on the New Testament
NICOT	New International Commentary on the Old Testament
NIGTC	New International Greek Testament Commentary
NIV	New International Version
NJB	New Jerusalem Bible
NovT	*Novum Testamentum*
NovTSup	Novum Testamentum Supplement
NRSV	New Revised Standard Version
NTAbh	Neutestamentliche Abhandlungen
NTD	Das Neue Testament Deutsch
NTL	New Testament Library
NTS	*New Testament Studies*
NTTS	New Testament Tools and Studies
OBT	Overtures to Biblical Theology
OTL	Old Testament Library
OTP	*The Old Testament Pseudepigrapha.* 2 vols. Edited by James H. Charlesworth.
PG	Patrologia graeca. Edited by J.-P. Migne.
PL	Patrologia latina. Edited by J.-P. Migne.
PNTC	Pillar New Testament Commentary
PRSt	*Perspectives in Religious Studies*
REB	Revised English Bible
RNT	Regensburger Neues Testament
SBEC	Studies in the Bible and Early Christianity
SBT	Studies in Biblical Theology
SCH	Studies in Church History

SJLA	Studies in Judaism and Late Antiquity
SJT	*Scottish Journal of Theology*
SAC	Studies in Antiquity and Christianity
SANT	Studien zum Alten und Neuen Testaments
SBLDS	Society of Biblical Literature Dissertation Series
SBLMS	Society of Biblical Literature Monograph Series
SBLSBS	Society of Biblical Literature Sources for Biblical Study
SBLSymS	Society of Biblical Literature Symposium Series
SBLTT	Society of Biblical Literature Texts and Translations
SCHNT	Studia ad corpus hellenisticum Novi Testamenti
SFSHJ	South Florida Studies in the History of Judaism
SJLA	Studies in Judaism in Late Antiquity
SNT	Studien zum Neuen Testament
SNTSMS	Society for New Testament Studies Monograph Series
SNTW	Studies of the New Testament and Its World
SP	Sacra Pagina
Str-B	*Kommentar zum Neuen Testament aus Talmud und Midrasch.* By Hermann Leberecht Strack and Paul Billerbeck.
StudBib	Studia Biblica
SubBi	*Subsidia biblica*
TANZ	Texte und Arbeiten zum neutestamentlichen Zeitalter
TDNT	*Theological Dictionary of the New Testament.* Edited by G. Kittel and G. Friedrich.
THKNT	Theologischer Handkommentar zum Neuen Testament
TLG	*Thesaurus linguae graecae: Canon of Greek Authors and Works.* Edited by L. Berkowitz and K. A. Squitier.
TLNT	*Theological Lexicon of the New Testament.* By Ceslas Spiq.
TNIV	Today's New International Version
TNTC	The New Testament in Context
TynNTC	Tyndale New Testament Commentaries
TRu	*Theologische Rundschau*
TynB	*Tyndale Bulletin*
TZ	*Theologische Zeitschrift*
VCSup	Vigiliae christianae Supplement
WBC	Word Biblical Commentary
WUNT	Wissenschaftliche Untersuchungen zum Alten und Neuen Testament
ZNW	*Zeitschrift für die neutestamentliche Wissenschaft und die Kunde der älteren Kirche*
ZTK	*Zeitschrift für Theologie und Kirche*

Abbreviations of ancient texts follow the conventions of Patrick H. Alexander et al., eds., *The SBL Handbook of Style: For Ancient Near Eastern, Biblical, and Early Christian Studies* (Peabody, Mass.: Hendrickson, 1999) and, for classical sources not mentioned there, Henry George Liddell and Robert Scott, *A Greek English Lexicon*, rev. and aug. Henry Stuart Jones, 2 vols. (Oxford: Oxford Univ. Press, 1940). The Other Ancient Literature Index also contains a comprehensive list of the abbreviations of classical works used in the book together with their full titles and, where necessary, English translations of those titles.

INTRODUCTION

Chapter 1

THE THEOLOGY OF THE NEW TESTAMENT: THE BASIC QUESTIONS

Since the eighteenth century, the discipline of New Testament theology has come under close scrutiny. Should the discipline be abandoned? Some have said so. Does it only need to be restructured? Some have offered new models. In the discussion, two problems with the discipline have repeatedly emerged as most significant.

The first problem, it is said, is an unhealthy blend in the discipline of dogmatics with historical concerns. On the one hand, theological convictions influence New Testament theologians both in the conclusions they draw about the meaning of the New Testament texts and in their insistence on examining only the canonical documents. On the other hand, since the church values these documents largely for the historical claims made in them, New Testament theologians find that they must work as historians in much the same way that any historian would work with ancient texts. Is it possible to bring together faith and reason in this way, or must New Testament theologians bracket their own dogmatic presuppositions about the importance of the New Testament and place the canonical texts on a level with all other ancient texts? If so, then they should shift their attention away from the theologically biased investigation of "New Testament theology" to the more objective and universally useful task of describing the history of early Christian thought.

The second problem arises from the theological diversity of the New Testament texts. The New Testament documents not only express a variety of theological themes, but sometimes they speak in different ways on the same theme. Do these differences sometimes amount to contradiction? If not, why is the theological coherence of the New Testament sometimes so hard to detect? If so, is it accurate to speak of "New Testament theology" at all, as if we are speaking of some coherent whole?

THEOLOGY OR HISTORY?

Since the sixteenth century, biblical theologians have struggled with the relationship between interpreting the Bible to find support for the church's traditional theological teachings and interpreting the Bible within its own historical context without consideration for the theological convictions of the church. Because the church has traditionally held to the primacy of Scripture over its traditions (even if extrabiblical tradition is given great weight), ideally no conflict should arise. In fact, the church's traditions and the theological emphases of the Bible have often been incompatible, and so any study of biblical theology has often been characterized by the tension between theological conviction and historical analysis.

Biblical theology arose early in the Reformation era as a discipline intended to chasten the church's unbiblical theological speculations and to hasten its reform. The emphasis at this time was more on theological reform than on sensitivity to the historical situations in which the biblical documents were composed. Later, biblical theology fell under the spell of Enlightenment rationalism, and some of its practitioners began to define the discipline in terms of a historically motivated and theologically independent study of the Bible that could use human reason to sit in judgment not only on the teachings of the church, but on the content of the Bible itself.

Out of this link between biblical theology and the Enlightenment arose a criticism of the discipline itself. Why speak of "biblical" theology at all? If the student of the biblical texts is to be truly an historian, then it is necessary to speak only of the history of Jewish and Christian thought and religion—to speak of the Bible, or of the New Testament, is already to speak in dogmatic language that the historian interested in the objective study of the past must find unacceptable.

Over the last three centuries, three criticisms of the discipline as theologically rather than historically grounded have been particularly influential. J. P. Gabler, William Wrede, and Heikki Räisänen, writing at the turn of the nineteenth, twentieth, and twenty-first centuries respectively, called for the liberation of the historical study of the Bible or early Christianity from the dogmatic concerns of the church. Gabler's seminal challenge differs from that of Wrede and Räisänen because it is simply a call for methodological clarity in the theological enterprise rather than a disparagement of the theologically motivated study of the Bible. Nevertheless, both Wrede and Räisänen understand themselves to be standing on the shoulders of Gabler. It is important, therefore, to consider Gabler's challenge to the discipline before evaluating the more direct attacks of Wrede and Räisäinen. In order to understand all three thinkers and to put our criticisms of their challenges in historical perspective, it is necessary first to survey briefly the historical roots of biblical, and specifically New Testament, theology.

The Early History of the Discipline

The development of a "biblical theology" had its roots in the age-old commitment of the church to govern its theology and practice by the canonical writings of the Old and New Testaments. One of the most important concerns of the Reformation was that the church reform its doctrine and worship so that it might be more faithful to the standards laid down in the Bible. In 1521, Luther's close friend and colleague at the University of Wittenburg, Philip Melancthon, published one of the earliest theological treatises of the Reformation—a brief treatment of important theological topics based on Luther's lectures on Paul's letter to the Romans given in the summer of 1519 and repeated the following year.[1]

1 See the note of Wilhelm Pauck in his edition of *Loci Communes Theologici* in *Melanchthon and Bucer* (LCC 19; Philadelphia: Westminster, 1969), 18 n. 2. All further references to the *Loci communes* are to this edition. On the importance of the *Loci communes* for the origins of biblical theology see the historical survey in Ferdinand Christian Baur, *Vorlesungen über neutestamentliche Theologie*, ed. F. F. Baur (Darmstadt: Wissenschaftliche Buchgesellschaft, 1973; orig. ed. 1864), 2, and Otto Merk, *Biblische Theologie des Neuen Testaments in ihrer Anfangszeit* (MTS 9; Marburg: N. G. Elwert Verlag, 1972), 12.

This treatment of *Loci communes rerum theologicarum* ("Fundamental Theological Themes") provided a list of important theological topics and then briefly explained the teaching of Scripture, and Scripture alone, on each topic.[2] Melancthon was weary of reading the lengthy speculations of medieval scholastic theologians on Christian theology and wanted instead to discover how the Bible itself, and particularly "Paul's own compendium of Christian doctrine" in Romans, described the Christian religion.[3] This urge to tap speculative theologians on the shoulder and point them back to the Bible remained a constant theme in the early history of biblical theology as a discrete discipline. Melancthon puts it this way:

> I am discussing everything sparingly and briefly because the book is to function more as an index than a commentary. I am therefore merely stating a list of the topics to which a person roaming through Scripture should be directed. Further, I am setting forth in only a few words the elements on which the main points of Christian doctrine are based. I do this not to call students away from the Scriptures to obscure and complicated arguments but, rather, to summon them to the Scriptures if I can.[4]

As the Reformation matured into Protestantism, however, Protestant thinkers began to refine their theological commitments and to develop complicated theological arguments of their own. In their works, Scripture was often used not so much to set the theological agenda but to demonstrate that the various theological principles that Protestants considered important, and which were now growing increasingly complex, were, in fact, biblical. Those who first used the term "biblical theology" to describe their theological studies made this proof-texting of preexisting theological systems their goal.[5] A new Protestant brand of scholasticism began to develop with "biblical theology" as its handmaid.

Under the influence of German pietism on one hand and rationalism on the other, biblical theology began to break away from this role as a prop for systematic theology. Pietism sought to remind Protestant orthodoxy both of the preeminence of the Bible in Christian belief and practice and of the place of religious experience in Christian commitment. It viewed a return to the study of the Bible for its own sake as a necessary antidote to the sterile theological debates that seemed to dominate Protestant scholasticism, much in the way they had dominated the theological scene prior to the Reformation.[6] In 1758, Anton Friderich Büsching made a complaint in a pamphlet

2 The translation "Fundamental Theological Themes" belongs to Wilhelm Pauck. See his introduction to *Loci Communes Theologici*, 3.

3 *Loci communes*, 22.

4 Ibid., 19.

5 Again, see Baur, *Neutestamentliche Theologie*, 2–3, and in addition, the historical survey of Martin Kähler, "Biblische Theologie," *Realencyklopädie für protestantische Theologie und Kirche*, 3rd ed., 24 vols. (Leipzig: J. C. Hinrichs'sche Buchhandlung, 1896–1913), 3:192–200, here at 193; Merk, *Biblische Theologie*, 15–17; Gerhard Hasel, *New Testament Theology: Basic Issues in the Current Debate* (Grand Rapids: Eerdmans, 1978), 17.

6 Kähler, "Biblische Theologie," 193; Merk, *Biblische Theologie*, 18–20. The famous Pietist leader Philipp Jacob Spener (1635–1705) in the third part of his manifesto, *Pia desideria*, published in 1675, laid out a six-point program for the reform of the German church. His first point called for the renewed reading and study of the whole Bible—not merely the set lectionary texts—by individuals, groups, and families. See Philipp Jacob Spener, *Pia desideria*, ed. Kurt Aland (Kleine Texte für Vorlesungen und Übungen 170; Berlin: Walter de Gruyter, 1964), 53–58.

that was typical of Pietist concerns at the time. Young ministers returning to their village pulpits from their theological education, he wrote, were disabled as preachers. They were bringing to the pulpit not "the pure biblical theology" but a "school theology which neither they nor their churches understand."[7]

At about the same time, rationalism began to influence the study of the Bible.[8] In England, philosophers such as John Locke (1632–1704) and John Toland (1670–1722) had elevated reason above faith, claiming that only those elements of the Scriptures and of Christianity that passed the test of rational inquiry should be retained.[9] In Germany, this thinking influenced biblical scholars such as Johann Salomo Semler (1725–1791), who began to say forthrightly that parts of the canonical Scriptures were theologically inferior and therefore not inspired.[10] Along with this conviction went the insistence that the historical analysis of each biblical writing should precede any theological treatment of it. Although Semler himself was an opponent of Pietism because he thought that it encouraged a personal, subjective reading of Scripture unaffected by historical exegesis, both the pietists and Semler agreed that the study of the Scriptures themselves must precede theological speculation.[11]

The work of Gotthilf Traugott Zachariä (1729–1777), professor of theology at Göttingen and Kiel, reveals the concerns of both pietism and rationalism to some extent.[12] Zachariä was not a rationalist in the ordinary sense of the term—he believed that the miracles recorded in the Bible actually happened and that the Bible was the Word of God—nor did he intend to engage in polemics against systematic theology when he wrote his biblical theology.[13] Still, he was convinced that the study of systematic theology needed the salutary correction of careful biblical exegesis.[14] This exegesis, he argued, should be anchored in the time and place in which each biblical author wrote and should be sensitive to the historical differences between the situation of the biblical writers and the situation of the modern church.[15] The presentation of a biblical theology, moreover, should not follow the familiar systematic categories or the headings of the theological compendia but should follow a plan that arises out of Scripture itself and the order of salvation that unfolds from it.[16]

7 Anton Friedrich Büsching, "Gedanken von der Beschaffenheit und dem Vorzug der biblisch-dogmatischen Theologie vor der alten und neuen Scholastichen, und von theologischen Aufgaben" (Lemod: Meyerschen Buchhandlung, 1758), 15.

8 See esp. Baur, *Neutestamentliche Theologie*, 3–4, who does not even mention Pietism, although he does briefly mention Büsching.

9 See Werner Georg Kümmel, *The New Testament: The History of the Investigation of Its Problems* (Nashville: Abingdon, 1972), 51–61; W. Neil, "The Criticism and Theological Use of the Bible, 1700–1950," in *The Cambridge History of the Bible*, ed. S. L. Greenslade, G. W. H. Lampe, P. R. Ackroyd, and C. F. Evans, 3 vols. (Cambridge: Cambridge Univ. Press, 1963–70), 3:238–93, here at 238–41; and William Baird, *History of New Testament Research*, 2 vols. (Minneapolis: Fortress, 1992), 1:31–43.

10 Semler read the deistic literature of England and had even translated some of it into German. On this, see Kümmel, *History*, 415 n. 63, and Baird, *History*, 1:118.

11 On Semler, who was reared in a pietist home, see Kümmel, *History*, 62–69; Baird, *History* 1:117–27; and G. Hornig, "Semler, Johann Salomo," in *Dictionary of Biblical Interpretation*, ed. John H. Hayes, 2 vols. (Nashville: Abingdon, 1999), 2:456–57.

12 *Biblischer Theologie, oder Untersuchung des biblischen Grundes der vornehmsten theologischen Lehren*, 4 pts. (Göttingen und Kiel: Verlage Victorinus Bospiegel und Sohn, 1771–75).

13 Merk, *Biblische Theologie*, 24–25.

14 Baur, *Neutestamentliche Theologie*, 4–6, while recognizing Zachariä's work as "the most significant of this first period of biblical theology," implicitly criticizes its failure to lead the discipline into independence from systematic theology. The critical service that it provided to systematic theology in Zachariä's view means that it was, despite its critical stance, still dependent on systematic theology for its legitimacy.

15 Heinrich Hoffmann, "Zachariä, Gotthilf Traugott," *Realencyklopädie für protestantische Theologie und Kirche*, 3rd ed., 24 vols. (Leipzig: J. C. Hinrichs'sche Buchhandlung, 1896–1913), 21:587–88.

16 Zachariä, *Biblischer Theologie*, 1:xcvii–xcviii.

The Challenges of Gabler, Wrede, and Räisänen

Johann Philipp Gabler

The stage was now set for a highly significant statement by Johann Philipp Gabler (1753–1826), a devoted student of the New Testament scholar Johann Jakob Griesbach and professor of theology at Altdorf and then at Jena.[17] Gabler's historical significance for the discipline of biblical theology is out of proportion to the physical size of his published work on the subject. Unlike Zachariä, whose *Biblischer Theologie* consumes four thick volumes, Gabler produced no biblical theology at all but merely gave a lecture on the subject on the occasion of his appointment to the faculty of the German academy at Altdorf on March 31, 1787.[18] Evidently this lecture put in precisely the right words something that many others believed needed to be addressed.[19] The lecture functioned as a kind of declaration of independence for the historical study of the Bible, insisting that it be freed from the shackles that systematic theology had clamped on it.

Gabler attempted to describe the difference between biblical and dogmatic theology and to argue that each had its own aims. By "biblical theology" Gabler meant the historical study of the religious convictions of the biblical authors, and by "dogmatic theology" Gabler meant the theological and philosophical systems of more modern times. Gabler believed that dogmatic theologians had been reading their modern theological systems back into the biblical texts and were thus distorting the meaning of those texts. This had resulted in a multitude of different dogmatic systems, all claiming the authority of the Bible, and had therefore contributed to the disunity of the church. Dogmatic theologians, said Gabler, should leave the historical task of investigating the meaning of the biblical texts to biblical theologians and should await the results of the theologically unfettered investigation of the texts in their original historical and cultural contexts before constructing modern theological systems.[20]

Biblical theologians, said Gabler, must shoulder a two-part task. They must first investigate the meaning of the biblical texts within their original, primitive contexts and come to their conclusions apart from any dogmatic considerations. They must then search their historical results for the pure and universal truths expressed within them. These truths they must carefully extract from the grit and grime of the biblical authors' prescientific world, and then they must deliver these purified doctrines to the systematic theologian.[21] The systematic theologian could then use

17 For the details of Gabler's life, see the substantial article by E. L. T. Henke, "Gabler, Johann Philipp," in *Realencyklopädie für protestantische Theologie und Kirche*, 3rd ed., 24 vols. (Leipzig: J. C. Hinrichs'sche Buchhandlung, 1896–1913), 4:720–22, and for a full analysis of Gabler's intellectual roots and commitments, see Merk, *Biblische Theologie*, 29–140.

18 An English translation of Gabler's Latin lecture, "On the Proper Distinction between Biblical and Dogmatic Theology and the Specific Objectives of Each," appears in John Sandys-Wunsch and Laurence Eldredge, "J. P. Gabler and the Distinction between Biblical and Dogmatic Theology: Translation, Commentary, and Discussion of His Originality," *SJT* 33 (1980): 133–58.

19 Already in 1825, F. A. Lossius could say in his *Biblische Theologie des Neuen Testaments oder die Lehren des Christenthums aus einzelnen Schriften des N. T. entwickelt* (Leipzig: C. G. Kayser, 1825), 8, that "Gabler was the first to understand the idea of a biblical theology."

20 "Distinction," 142.

21 Cf. Martin Kähler, *The So-called Historical Jesus and the Historic Biblical Christ* (Philadelphia: Fortress, 1988; orig. ed. 1896), 67: "Dogmatics is in a very real sense the mediator between past and present; it puts what is genuine and indispensable in the past at the service of the present. This task of mediation, then, belongs to dogmatics, after it has made a thorough and serious study of

this precious distillate to construct a modern theology.[22] Since everything would be done according to clearly delineated and widely recognized rational principles, the results both of the biblical theologian and of the systematic theologian ought to be acceptable to all, and the church would be able to present a united front against its detractors.[23]

William Wrede

Slightly over a century later, in 1897, William Wrede composed another famous essay in which he attempted to resurrect Gabler's distinction between biblical and dogmatic theology, this time with reference specifically to New Testament theology.[24] Between Gabler and Wrede a number of New Testament theologies had appeared, but they had failed, at least in Wrede's opinion, to preserve Gabler's distinction between biblical and dogmatic theology. Most New Testament theologians, Wrede insisted, pay lip service to Gabler's call for a distinction between biblical and dogmatic theology. But in reality, he complained, the method that New Testament theologians follow betrays their awareness that the systematic theologians are looking over their shoulders.[25] Only their concern for the watchful eye of the systematic theologians can explain why they limit their investigations to the New Testament canon rather than using all the evidence at their disposal to construct a complete history of early Christianity.[26] Only this concern for dogmatics can explain why their New Testament theologies are hardly more than tedious commentaries on a list of doctrinal concepts.[27]

Wrede concluded his essay with a sentence that has become famous: "The name New Testament theology is wrong in both its terms." Historians of early Christianity should not limit their investigative efforts to the canonical New Testament, and they should not be concerned with the supposed expression of theological concepts within the New Testament. Instead, they should aim at describing the "early Christian history of religion," by which Wrede meant "*what was believed, thought, taught, hoped, required and striven for* in the earliest period of Christianity."[28] If the spicy meal that historians dish up according to this recipe does not suit the taste of the systematic theologians, then that, for a change, is the problem of the systematic theologians. Historians must be left alone to pursue their own agenda without any requirement that the church find the results of their work palatable.

what historical study can accomplish and has learned from history what is important enough to warrant consideration by dogmatics."

22 "Distinction," 140–44. See the discussion of Gabler's distinction between "true Biblical theology" and "pure Biblical theology" in Hendrikus Boers, *What Is New Testament Theology: The Rise of Criticism and the Problem of a Theology of the New Testament* (Philadelphia: Fortress, 1979), 33–35.

23 "Distinction," 134–38.

24 William Wrede, *Über Aufgabe und Methode der sogenannten neutestamentlichen Theologie* (Göttingen: Vandenhoeck & Ruprecht, 1897). Wrede was professor of New Testament exegesis at Breslau at the time.

25 William Wrede, "The Task and Methods of 'New Testament Theology,'" in *The Nature of New Testament Theology: The Contribution of William Wrede and Adolf Schlatter*, ed. Robert Morgan (SBT 25; London: SCM, 1973), 68–116, here at 69. Again, cf. Baur, *Neutestamentliche Theologie*, 8–10, who comments that Bauer's concern to show the rational essence of the Christian faith had prevented him from producing a New Testament theology that was oriented to historical concerns alone.

26 Wrede, "Task and Methods," 70–73.

27 Ibid., 73–84.

28 See ibid., 116 and 84, respectively.

Heikki Räisänen

Just as Wrede took up Gabler's cause a century later, so Heikki Räisänen has done the same for William Wrede in a work that has gone through two editions in ten years. In the first edition of *Beyond New Testament Theology*, Räisänen complained, in a manner reminiscent of Wrede, that no one had produced the kind of historical study of early Christian religion that Wrede envisioned.[29] In the second edition of his work he was able to modify this complaint—works that fulfilled Wrede's vision in important ways had now appeared—but he still found that much of his original case needed to be heard.[30]

Unlike Wrede, who saw no legitimacy, theological or historical, in limiting one's efforts to the New Testament canon, Räisänen concedes that within the confines of the church, studying the theological ideas in the twenty-seven New Testament books may have some value for preaching or catachesis. Historians who do not limit their audience to the church, however, cannot restrict their analytical efforts to the New Testament canon. Because of their broader humanitarian vision and their independence of the church, they must focus on the history of early Christianity generally, not merely the haphazard glimpses of that history available in the New Testament.[31] Although the encroachment of presuppositions on historical investigation is inevitable, Gabler and Wrede were correct in their emphasis on the dangers of allowing theological presuppositions to determine the results of historical investigation.[32] The New Testament scholar, therefore, should be concerned not with proclamation but with a historical description of New Testament thought and experience and with the influence of the canon in history.[33] The humanitarian value of this will emerge as texts once thought to be authoritative are exposed as oppressive and people are liberated from them.[34]

The Common Elements in the Three Challenges

Gabler at the turn of the nineteenth century, Wrede at the turn of the twentieth, and Räisänen at the turn of the twenty-first all call for the separation of historical analysis from theological proclamation in the study of the New Testament.

- Gabler was optimistic that once the eternal, universal, and consequently divine elements of the Scriptures had been separated from the contingent, specific, and human elements, theology would forever be safe from attack: "Exactly thus will our theology be made more certain and more firm, and there will be nothing further to be feared for it from the most savage attack from its enemies."[35]

29 Heikki Räisänen, *Beyond New Testament Theology: A Story and a Programme* (London and Philadelphia: SCM and Trinity Press International, 1990; 2nd ed., 2000). On the absence of a truly historical approach such as Wrede envisioned, see the first edition, 89–90. Räisänen is hopeful (78–79), however, that Klaus Berger will produce the needed fulfillment of Wrede's program, a hope that was fulfilled to some extent, although also with some disappointments, in Berger's eventual publication of *Theologiegeschichte des Urchristentums: Theologie des Neuen Testaments* (Tübingen: Francke, 1994). See Räisänen's review of Berger's book in *Beyond New Testament Theology*, 2nd ed., 134–36.

30 Räisänen, *Beyond New Testament Theology*, 2nd ed., 134–47.

31 Ibid., 1st ed., 100–103, 121; 2nd ed. 154–56, 160–62.

32 Ibid., 106; 2nd ed., 166.

33 Ibid., 97–100, 103–4; 2nd ed. 157–59, 162–64.

34 Ibid., 112; 2nd ed., 178–79.

35 Gabler, "Distinction," 138.

- Wrede was certainly not concerned about attacks on the Christian religion, but he too was optimistic that once dogmatic concerns were laid to rest, a purely historical account of early Christian religion could be composed.[36]
- Räisänen, aware of the presence of presuppositions in all historical work, describes the separation more cautiously; but, like Wrede, he is concerned that Christian faith not distort the texts, for "an unwary interpreter will tend to discover his own image at possible and impossible points in the sources."[37]

All three scholars argue that this separation of the historical from the theological task implies the priority of the historical task. Gabler puts it this way:

> When these opinions of the holy men have been carefully collected from Holy Scripture and suitably digested, carefully referred to the universal notions, and cautiously compared among themselves, the question of their dogmatic use may then profitably be established, and the goals of both biblical and dogmatic theology correctly assigned.[38]

In other words, once the historian has painstakingly analyzed the text, theologians can use the results.

Wrede is not so explicit; but he too claims that if Christian theologians feel for theological reasons that they must also be historians, then they must recognize that historians follow their own principles. Theologically motivated historians, then, can only do their historical work after setting aside their theological convictions:

> On the whole it is not within the historical researcher's power to serve the church through his work. The theologian who obeys the historical object as his master is not in a position to serve the church through his properly scientific-historical work, even if he were personally interested in doing so.[39]

This implies that the theologian who wants to stand in some continuity with early Christianity must wait until the historians (and he may be one of them) have finished analyzing early Christian history before engaging in the theological task.

Räisänen similarly believes that the danger of distorting the historical significance of the biblical texts is too great when the believing historian attempts to perform the historical and the "actualizing" tasks at the same time. Historians of early Christianity may select texts on which to concentrate on the basis of modern concerns, or they may arrange their presentations in order to make them accessible to those who want to put modern men and women in contact with early Christianity, but they must take their interaction with modern concerns at the historical stage of their work no further:

> All this moves on the level of historical interpretation (Gabler's 'true' biblical theology). It depends on the scholar himself whether he wants to move, following

36 Wrede, "Task and Methods," 69.

37 Räisänen, *Beyond New Testament Theology*, 1st ed., 111; 2nd ed., 177.

38 Gabler, "Distinction," 142.

39 Wrede, "Task and Methods," 73.

> Gabler's lead, *at a second stage of the work*, to theological questions proper, i.e. to reflections on what his historical findings can mean for men and women of today.[40]

Another implication of the separation of the theological from the historical task, at least for Wrede and Räisänen, is the illegitimacy of confining one's historical efforts to the Christian canon. Wrede argued that the twenty-seven books comprising the New Testament canon have no historical claim to priority over other literary evidence for early Christian religion. The notion of the canon is a dogmatic assertion of Christian bishops and councils from the second to the fourth centuries. "So," Wrede concluded, "anyone who accepts without question the idea of the canon places himself under the authority of the bishops and theologians of those centuries."[41] Since historians are hardly bound by such decisions, they should not confine their efforts to those books.

Räisänen also believes that those who limit their efforts to the theology of the New Testament and do not apply equal effort to the study of early Christian religion generally have allowed the church to define their work. While this is "meaningful" from the perspective of Christian faith, "in historical work it is, by contrast, arbitrary."[42] Räisänen works hard to be fair to Christian theologians by acknowledging that within the church their efforts to explain New Testament theology may be legitimate. Nevertheless, he also argues that Christian scholars who attempt to combine the historical with the theological analysis of the New Testament often insist on breaking out of the boundaries of the church and claiming that their theologically motivated exegetical work on the canonical text has implications for all of life. "With astonishing ease," he complains, "'life' is simply narrowed down to 'Christian life' or 'life in the church.'"[43] If one's concerns encompass the wider society and all of humanity, says Räisänen, such a perspective is too narrow. By providing accurate information about early Christianity, the historian can explode myths that have been used in the service of oppression, increase understanding and tolerance among various cultures, and make a positive future for humanity more likely.[44]

In summary, over the last three centuries, Gabler, Wrede, and Räisänen have presented a significant challenge to those who attempt to understand the New Testament historically and theologically at the same time. All three argued for the separation of the historical task from the theological enterprise, and all three gave history priority over theology. For Wrede and Räisänen, this meant that Christians who restricted their work to the New Testament canon endangered its historical accuracy and, at least for Räisänen, lowered its humanitarian value.

40 Räisänen, *Beyond New Testament Theology*, 1st ed., 109; 2nd. ed., 171.

41 Wrede, "Task and Methods," 71.

42 Räisänen, *Beyond New Testament Theology*, 1st ed., 100; 2nd ed., 160.

43 Ibid., 1st ed., 94; 2nd ed., 152.

44 Ibid., 1st ed., 97–100; 2nd ed., 156–59.

A Response to the Challenges of Gabler, Wrede, and Räisänen

The Issue of the Canon

Wrede and Räisänen are surely right to say that the methodological decision to study New Testament theology rather than the history of early Christian religion reflects the perspective of Christian faith. Historians of early Christianity will use every text at their disposal for the reconstruction of the beliefs, thoughts, teachings, hopes, requirements, and goals of early Christians. Moreover, they will value the texts not for their theological perspective but for the raw data they can provide in reconstructing this complex world. The canonicity of certain texts has no meaning for the historian of early Christianity until the authoritative status of the canonical texts themselves becomes important for early Christianity. At that point, however, the historian's interest shifts from the historical context in which the texts were first produced and read to the history of their influence as authoritative Scripture.[45]

By contrast, theologians who give priority to the New Testament documents do so because they speak about God with an authority that other texts do not possess. The selection of the theology of the canonical texts for special attention, therefore, results from the Christian commitment of the interpreter, as Christians have recognized for centuries. The *French Confession of Faith* (1559) puts it this way:

> We know these books to be canonical, and the sure rule of our faith, not so much by the common accord and consent of the Church, as by the testimony and inward illumination of the Holy Spirit, which enables us to distinguish them from other ecclesiastical books upon which, however useful, we can not found any articles of faith.[46]

Some New Testament scholars, however, have attempted to justify the study of New Testament theology from a historical perspective. Peter Balla has produced the most thorough defense of this approach.[47] Balla argues that the authors of at least some New Testament documents, at the time that they wrote their texts, may have intended for them to function alongside the Jewish canon as authoritative Scripture. The New Testament authors, he argues, quote the Old Testament in a way that reveals a "canonical awareness."[48] If the Qumran covenanters could produce their own canon in addition to the Jewish Scriptures, and if the author of *4 Ezra* could place certain secret books of eschatology on the same level of authority with the Jewish Scriptures, then why should it seem improbable that Christians from earliest times understood certain documents to have canonical status?[49] He concludes that historians may legitimately choose the

45 Ibid., 1st ed., 103–4; 2nd ed., 162–64.

46 Art. 4; Philip Schaff, *The Creeds of Christendom*, 3 vols. (New York: Harper & Brothers, 1877), 3:361–62. Cf. John Calvin, *Institutes of the Christian Religion* (1559), 1.7.5; the *Belgic Confession of Faith* (1561), art. 5; *Westminster Confession of Faith* (1647), 1.5.

47 Peter Balla, *Challenges to New Testament Theology: An Attempt to Justify the Enterprise* (WUNT 2.95; Tübingen: Mohr, 1997). Other, weaker cases, include claims that the New Testament documents are the oldest witnesses to Christian history or that they are the most influential documents in Christian history. See, e. g., Christian Friedrich Schmid, *Biblical Theology of the New Testament* (Edinburgh: T. & T. Clark, 1882), 8–9, and Leonard Goppelt, *Theology of the New Testament*, 2 vols. (Grand Rapids: Eerdmans, 1981–82), 1:271–72. Cf. the comments of Räisänen, *Beyond New Testament Theology*, 1st ed., 72, 103.

48 Balla, *Challenges*, 101.

49 Ibid., 106–14.

canon of a particular ancient group for historical study; they may choose the canon of Marcion, for example, or they may choose the canon of orthodox Christianity.[50]

Although Balla makes a perceptive contribution to the discussion with his insight about how early some of the New Testament authors considered their texts to be Scripture, it is difficult to see how this point—which deals with individual authors and their texts—can justify the study of the entire New Testament canon as a discrete body of literature. No one denies the historical legitimacy of investigating the theology of single New Testament authors. The question is whether the twenty-seven texts that comprise the New Testament canon have a basic theological unity.

Second, Balla helpfully argues that we can learn something about ancient religious groups from studying their canons. The Samaritan Pentateuch will say much about the beliefs of the Samaritans, and the Marcionite canon will yield valuable information about Marcionite religion. But this merely legitimates the study of the influence of a particular canon, not the study of individual canonical authors (and no others) in their original historical contexts. In other words, New Testament theologians are not typically interested in discovering the theology of the group of early Christians that held the New Testament documents as a whole to be canonical. They are usually interested in describing the theologies of the individual authors of the canonical documents and then, because of their faith commitments, finding some inner coherence to those theologies.[51] Wrede and Räisänen are therefore correct: The need to study New Testament theology arises from within the Christian community, not from outside it.

Räisänen is less helpful, however, when he criticizes New Testament theologians, bound as they are to the canon, for their narrow, ecclesiastical focus. Although willing to concede that scholarly work on the New Testament in the service of the church may be helpful for those in the church, he appeals to all New Testament scholars to avoid identifying the life of the church with life generally and to raise their eyes to focus on a global horizon. "Theology and exegesis," he pleads, "need a global perspective, an 'ecumenical' horizon, in the original sense of the word."[52]

This would be a valid criticism except that many New Testament theologians understand their service to the church as service to the wider world as well. By helping the church to understand the claims of the New Testament on the people of God and on the world that God created, they aid the church in its efforts to proclaim the gospel. The gospel, many New Testament theologians believe, is what the world needs to hear. This may seem imperialistic, depending on one's perspective, but the horizon of these scholars is not narrow.

Wrede too has misunderstood the nature of the decision among Christian scholars to limit their efforts to the New Testament canon. Wrede imagines that this decision implies submission to the bishops and councils of "the second-to-fourth-century

50 Ibid., 116.

51 Brevard S. Childs, *The New Testament as Canon: An Introduction* (Philadelphia: Fortress, 1985), 39, observes that someone who does not share the theological perspective of the canonical text can nevertheless describe the witness of the canon to the Christian faith, but, he admits, "it is rare to find penetrating theological exegesis of the New Testament by one who shares little or nothing of the faith reflected by the literature."

52 Räisänen, *Beyond New Testament Theology*, 1st ed., 95–96; 2nd ed., 155.

church" since only their pronouncements led to the selection of the books that now comprise the New Testament canon. This image, however, reflects a misunderstanding of the process that created the canon. It is true that the fourth-century synod of Laodicea (ca. 363) and fourth-century bishops such as Cyril of Jerusalem, Athanasius, Gregory of Nazianzen, Rufinus, and Augustine declared that only certain books were canonical.[53] But for at least four-fifths of the material involved, these lists and pronouncements merely recognized officially books whose authority was already well established in the communities over which these authorities presided.[54] New Testament theologians who observe the limits of the canon are not therefore bowing to the authority of bishops and councils but to the will of Christian communities for centuries past that these writings should shape the identity of the church.[55]

The Issue of Presuppositions

Gabler, Wrede, and Räisänen have each called for the separation of the historical from the theological task. The merger of the two tasks, they argued, would result in a distortion of the results of historical investigation. Thus, Gabler scourged a scholar of his own time, whose name he did not reveal, for "heedlessly" daring "to attribute some of his own most insubstantial opinions to the sacred writers themselves."[56] Wrede believed that as long as New Testament theologians regarded the writings that they analyzed as "normative," they would be psychologically inclined to work over the texts until the texts met their theological expectations.[57] Räisänen is aware of the hermeneutical and philosophical problems in following the claims of some nineteenth-century biblical scholars that the historian can describe a pure history, free of personal bias, but he believes that their instincts were right:

> The scholar presumably thinks both of the past and of the present all (or most of) the time. But it is still possible to keep the horizons distinct. And it would be helpful to keep them apart when presenting the results to readers.[58]

The New Testament theologian can only applaud this concern. Like the historian of early Christianity, the New Testament theologian is interested both in the historical events to which the New Testament texts provide partial access and in listening attentively to the texts themselves with as little personal bias as possible. The New Testament itself links its theological claims to historical claims. If the historical claims are untrue, the theological edifice must necessarily crumble.[59] Moreover, New Testament

53 Metzger, *The Canon of the New Testament: Its Origin, Significance, and Development* (New York: Oxford Univ. Press, 1987), 209–47.

54 See Kurt Aland, *The Problem of the New Testament Canon* (CST 2; London: Mowbray, 1962), 18–24, and the researches of Franz Stuhlhofer, *Der Gebrauch der Bibel von Jesus bis Euseb: eine statistische Untersuchung zur Kanonsgeschichte* (Monographien und Studienbücher 335; Wuppertal: Brockhaus, 1988).

55 See Luke Timothy Johnson, *The Writings of the New Testament: An Interpretation* (Philadelphia: Fortress, 1986), 542, and cf. Childs, *New Testament as Canon*, 3–33, 39–40. Ultimately, the authority of these writings comes from Jesus himself, who commissioned the apostles to preach the gospel. The tradition of their preaching, witness, and teaching is contained in the New Testament, and thus that tradition carries their apostolic authority. On this, see Herman N. Ridderbos, *Redemptive History and the New Testament Scriptures* (Phillipsburg, N.J.: Presbyterian and Reformed, 1963).

56 Gabler, "Distinction," 135.

57 Wrede, "Task and Methods," 69.

58 Räisänen, *Beyond New Testament Theology*, 1st ed., 106; 2nd ed., 166. Cf. idem, "Liberating Exegesis," *BJRL* 78 (1996): 193–204.

59 Cf. James Barr, *The Scope and Authority of the Bible* (Philadelphia: Westminster, 1980), 28–29.

theologians who believe that the New Testament texts are theologically authoritative have a stake in listening carefully to the texts themselves and not imposing on them some predetermined meaning. Krister Stendahl has put it this way:

> The more intensive the expectation of normative guidance, and the more exacting the claims for the holiness of the Scriptures, the more indispensable is the attention to the meaning of Scripture at the time of its conception and to an examination of the possible intentions of the authors.[60]

Gabler, Wrede, and Räisänen were all justified in pointing out how often New Testament scholars failed to live up to these ideals, but none of the three seemed to recognize that the theological convictions of New Testament theologians demand that they also be good historians. Both the German pietists who wrote biblical theologies in the seventeenth and eighteenth centuries and the participants in the Biblical Theology Movement of the mid-twentieth century wanted to avoid the imposition of predetermined, systematic theological convictions on the biblical texts.[61] They may have continued to impose their theology on the texts without realizing it, but they tried to avoid doing this. They recognized that the person who honestly wants to sit under the authority of Scripture must listen to Scripture regardless of how disturbing its message might be to inherited norms. To this extent, Wrede was wrong to say that theologians and historians do their work on the basis of different principles. Theologians, because of the historical claims of the texts with which they work and because they must submit to the texts as the Word of God, must be historians and therefore must work with the historian's tools.[62]

At the same time, a vast difference exists between the unbelieving historian of early Christianity and the New Testament theologian who does historical work in the service of the church. Whereas both the New Testament theologian and the secular historian are interested in the history to which the canonical texts give access, they differ on the importance that they grant to the perspectives of the texts themselves. Historians who stand outside the church employ every means at their disposal to render the perspectives of the canonical texts inoperative in their thinking. The texts then provide the raw data with which the secular historian attempts to reconstruct the story of early Christianity according to another perspective. The New Testament theologian, however, through the basic insight of faith, wants to embrace the perspectives of the texts on the events that provoked their composition.[63] The perspectives of the texts on the history of early Christianity are not husks to be peeled away so that the

60 Krister Stendahl, *Meanings: The Bible as Document and as Guide* (Philadelphia: Fortress, 1984), 7.

61 On the role of German pietism in the development of biblical theology see Hasel, *New Testament Theology*, 17–18; on the goals and shortfalls of the Biblical Theology Movement see Steven J. Kraftchick, "Facing Janus: Reviewing the Biblical Theology Movement," in *Biblical Theology: Problems and Perspectives: In Honor of J. Christiaan Beker*, ed. Steven J. Kraftchick, Charles D. Myers Jr., and Ben C. Ollenburger (Nashville: Abingdon, 1995), 54–77.

62 The synthesis of the historical and theological task proposed by James Barr in his inaugural lecture as Oriel Professor of the Interpretation of Holy Scripture at Oxford University ("Does Biblical Study Still Belong to Theology") is more satisfactory. For the text of this lecture, see Barr's *Scope and Authority of the Bible*, 18–29.

63 That such a basic insight, although operating in a different way from reason, is nevertheless not irrational, has been recognized by a wide variety of philosophers. See, e.g., William James, "The Will to Believe" in *William James: Writings: 1878—1899* (Library of America; New York: Library Classics of the United States, 1992), 457–79; C. Stephen Evans, *Faith Beyond Reason: A*

historian might see more clearly. They are not merely historical data that provide information about early Christian religion. For New Testament theologians who regard the texts as authoritative, the perspectives of the texts speak of their true significance. They are, in other words, objects of faith.

Is the faith of a New Testament theologian at the same time a crippling prejudice that prevents plausible historical analysis of the New Testament texts? It is not necessarily any more crippling than the perspectives of secular historians are to their own attempts at historical analysis. Gabler, Wrede, and Räisänen dis not seem to grasp this. For Gabler and Wrede, who wrote from within the hermeneutically unsophisticated contexts of the eighteenth and nineteenth century, this is understandable. It is more distressing to see Räisänen, who is careful to acknowledge the inevitable influence of presuppositions on the historical reconstruction of early Christianity, nevertheless claiming that scholars of religion should separate the transmission of information about Christian origins from any attempt at proclamation.[64] The goal of this transmission of information about Christianity, he says, is to pave the way for understanding, to clarify the identity of the modern Westerner, and generally to improve society.[65] Since this is the goal, it is difficult to understand in what sense this is not itself proclamation.[66] Every historian has a perspective, and every historian who writes or teaches about history proclaims that perspective.[67] The New Testament theologian proclaims the perspective of the texts, but that does not mean that he or she is any less a historian for doing so. Adolf Schlatter put it this way:

> It is clear that without the honest attempt to lay aside all personal concerns and the opinions of one's school or party, and seriously to *see*, academic work degenerates into hypocrisy. But even this honest attempt cannot overcome the fact that an observer sees with his own eyes only what the certainties which internally determine him allow him to perceive.[68]

Kierkegaardian Account (Reason & Religion; Grand Rapids: Eerdmans, 1998); and Alvin Plantinga, *Warranted Christian Belief* (Oxford: Oxford Univ. Press, 2000).

64 Räisänen, *Beyond New Testament Theology*, 1st ed., 97–100; 2nd ed., 156–59. Francis Watson attributes the curious notion in scholarly circles that biblical interpretation and theological concerns should be kept separate to "the enforced privatization of religious commitment in modern western societies," "the belief that theological concerns inevitably distort the autonomous processes of biblical exegesis," and "an unwillingness to accept the existence and the significance of theology as a discipline in its own right." See his *Text and Truth: Redefining Biblical Theology* (Grand Rapids: Eerdmans, 1997), 4. Räisänen, *Beyond New Testament Theology*, 2nd ed., 116–17, can only mourn the conversion of Watson, once a brilliant critical historian, to "dogmatism," but seems unaware that even prior to his shift Watson operated from a set of basic insights dictated by the rationalistic culture of the academy. On the failure of this culture to recognize its own presuppositions, see Evans, *Faith beyond Reason*, 32, and the related material on 94 and 121–22.

65 Räisänen, *Beyond New Testament Theology*, 1st ed., 96; 2nd ed., 155; cf. "Liberating Exegesis," 199. Räisänen's attempt in the second edition (155) to explain that because "the results of the analyses are not to be adapted even to global needs," no proclamation is involved, does not adequately answer the concern.

66 There are some parallels here to William James' argument in "Will to Believe" against the well-known essay of W. K. Clifford, "The Ethics of Belief," *The Contemporary Review* 29 (1877): 289–309. Clifford had claimed that to believe something without adequate empirical grounds for doing so was immoral. James showed successfully that this position itself rested on the unproved assumption that it was better to withhold a decision about a matter of faith than to be a dupe.

67 See Rudolf Bultmann, "Is Exegesis without Presuppositions Possible?," in *Existence and Faith: Shorter Writings of Rudolf Bultmann*, ed. Schubert M. Ogden (Cleveland: World Publishing, 1960), 289–96, here at 292.

68 "The Theology of the New Testament and Dogmatics" in *The Nature of New Testament Theology: The Contribution of William Wrede and Adolf Schlatter*, ed. Robert Morgan (London: SCM, 1973), 122–23. Rudolf Bultmann agreed with Schlatter that the New Testament theologian cannot be expected to separate think-

There is, furthermore, no reason to think that the perspective of faith, or any other perspective for that matter, is a hindrance to historical investigation. The uninterested party is rarely the best candidate for discovering the truth about any issue. William James put it this way:

> If you want an absolute duffer in an investigation, you must, after all, take the man who has no interest whatever in its results: he is the warranted incapable, the positive fool. The most useful investigator, because the most sensitive observer, is always he whose eager interest in one side of the question is balanced by an equally keen nervousness lest he become deceived.[69]

Students of New Testament theology have an enthusiastic interest in "one side of the question"—the side that informs and instructs their faith. They need to be cautious that they are not deceived into reading the New Testament in ways that only support their preconceived notions, though the need for this caution arises from their interest in the New Testament as a text under whose authority they should sit.

The Legitimacy of New Testament Theology

To summarize, the challenges that Gabler, Wrede, and Räisänen present to the New Testament theologian helpfully clarify why it is possible to study New Testament theology and the purpose for which such study should be undertaken. Wrede and Räisänen argue forcefully that studying New Testament theology, because its primary focus is the canon of Christian Scripture, is fundamentally a Christian enterprise, undertaken from within the church.

This does not mean, however, that the study of New Testament theology is an act of submission to the fourth-century councils and bishops who canonized the New Testament documents. Christians who study New Testament theology stand in continuity with the Christian communities that have valued these books since ancient times as the touchstone of Christian identity. Their decision to treat precisely these books also flows from an inner, spiritual conviction that they are the Word of God.

The decision to work with the canon and for the church also does not betray a less than global focus. New Testament theologians often believe that the gospel they proclaim through their work can aid those outside the church by making the Scriptures intelligible to them and leading them to an encounter with God.

Gabler, Wrede, and Räisänen also argue forcefully that in order to listen attentively to the New Testament texts, interpreters must work to overcome their preconceived notions about what the texts should say. This is a principle with which New Testament theologians should agree, although for different reasons than those of the unbelieving historian who is interested in early Christianity. Historians of early Christianity hope to bracket their presuppositions in an attempt to listen to the text so that they might discover historical information with which to construct the history of early Christianity.

---

ing from living. He sided with the history-of-religions school against Schlatter, however, on the issue of whether the perspective of the texts ought to be an object of faith. The texts, he said, give sometimes a faltering and culturally encumbered witness to the *kerygma*, and the *kerygma* ought to be the object of faith. See *Theology of the New Testament*, 2 vols. (New York: Charles Scribner's Sons, 1951–55), 2:248–51.

69 James, "Will to Believe," 471.

New Testament theologians who work within and for the church hope to hear the text rather than echoes of their own voices because they believe the perspective of the text, and not their own presuppositions, should shape the identity of the church.

Wrede and Räisänen are skeptical that New Testament theologians writing in the service of the church and with the purpose of proclamation could restrict the influence of their presuppositions enough to lend their efforts historical legitimacy, and justly point out examples of the many failures of New Testament theologians to do this. There is nevertheless no reason in principle why New Testament theologians cannot be as successful at listening to the texts as secular historians. Every historian, including one who argues against theological bias, is engaged to some extent in proclamation.

The study of New Testament theology is, therefore, not a narrow and self-defeating enterprise. When pursued within the church and under the authority of the texts, it can provide the means through which the prophetic voice of the texts is heard clearly in the modern church and, through the church, in the world.

Even if it is possible in principle to analyze the New Testament theologically, however, do competing theological tendencies within the New Testament itself make writing a "Theology of the New Testament" impossible?

DIVERSITY OR CONTRADICTION?

The Problem

Every Christian who has engaged in the serious study of the New Testament has puzzled over the diversity of its theological statements, a diversity that sometimes appears, at least on a first reading, to reach the point of contradiction. How can Peter say that God does not want anyone to perish whereas Mark claims that Jesus told his parables to prevent the repentance of some who heard them (2 Peter 3:9; Mark 4:12)? How can Jesus nullify the Mosaic dietary commandments in Mark's gospel (Mark 7:15, 19) but claim in both Matthew and Luke that not even a dot of the law will become void (Matt. 5:18; Luke 16:17)? How can James use Genesis 15:6 ("Abraham believed God, and it was credited to him as righteousness") to show that Abraham's "faith was made complete by what he did" (James 2:22), when Paul uses the same text to show that "God . . . justifies the wicked" (Rom. 4:5)? How can Paul say that there is neither slave nor free in Galatians 3:28 but that slaves should obey their earthly masters with fear and trembling in Ephesians 6:5?

New Testament scholars have produced a more sophisticated and lengthier list. The theology of the historical Jesus is at odds with the theology that the gospel authors placed in his mouth. The theology of glory advocated in Luke–Acts contradicts the theology of the cross found in Paul. The theology of John's "signs source" contradicts the theology of John himself. Paul contradicts himself in many ways on the subject of the Mosaic law. The institutionalized, "early catholic" picture of the church in the Pastoral Letters contradicts the loosely organized, Spirit-driven picture of the church in the authentic letters. And this is only the tip of a large iceberg.

As we will see in the pages that follow, many of the theological "problems" in the New Testament evaporate under careful historical and literary scrutiny. Even so, it is clear that the New Testament is a collection of writings characterized by theological diversity. How should Christians handle this diversity?

A Canon within the Canon?

Since the Enlightenment, it has become common to solve the problem of theological diversity in the New Testament by identifying a "canon within the canon." This approach specifies a core of theological teaching within the New Testament that all Christians should embrace and that serves as a theological standard against which competing theologies within the New Testament can then be measured. This approach to theological diversity within the New Testament has a long history, but its modern roots seem to lie in Martin Luther's claim that "justification by faith" is the touchstone of all theology, including the theology expressed in the Christian canon.[70] Luther found four canonical books—Hebrews, James, Jude, and Revelation—deficient by this standard and relegated them to an appendix in his translation of the Bible. He was especially hostile toward James with its claim that faith without works is dead and its apparent lack of teaching about Christ. Speaking to students at the university in Wittenberg, he commented, "We should throw the Epistle of James out of this school."[71] John's gospel, Paul's letters, and 1 Peter, by contrast, formed "the true kernel and marrow of all the books."[72]

This approach blossomed during the eighteenth century, especially in Germany, and reappeared in Gabler's famous inaugural lecture. As we have seen, Gabler argued that after biblical scholars have understood the biblical material in its original context, they must separate what is culturally conditioned, time-bound, and useless in the Scriptures from the universal theological truths that can be mined from its pages. Once these universal truths have been carefully harvested from the grit and grime of their original historical setting, they can be delivered to the systematic theologian, who should then use them to construct a universally acceptable modern theology. This is not simply a matter of transferring the theological principle behind certain culturally conditioned texts into the modern world, but may involve distinguishing between "the opinions of the Apostles" and the "truly divine," dogmatically useful truths of Scripture.[73]

Much later, Rudolf Bultmann maintained that New Testament writers frequently obscured their deepest theological insights behind ancient mythologies and cultural

70 Interpreters as different as Rudolf Bultmann, *Theology of the New Testament*, 2 vols. (New York: Charles Scribners' Sons, 1951–55), 2:238, and Luke Timothy Johnson, *The Real Jesus: The Misguided Quest for the Historical Jesus and the Truth of the Traditional Gospels* (San Francisco: HarperSanFrancisco, 1996), 69, recognize this. Luther also differed, however, from more recent advocates of a canon within the canon in significant ways. Paul Althaus, *The Theology of Martin Luther* (Philadelphia: Fortress, 1966), 82–86, points out that Luther's criterion for discriminating between canonical documents was not reason, science, or a theory of human existence but the gospel of God's grace in Christ, which he found in Scripture itself. I am grateful to Dr. Sigurd Grindheim for drawing this point to my attention.

71 *LW*, 54:424–25.

72 Martin Brecht, *Martin Luther*, 2 vols. (Minneapolis: Fortress, 1990), 2:50–52.

73 Gabler, "Distinction," 143.

trappings. New Testament theologians, he said, must use an encyclopedic knowledge of ancient culture and a sensitive understanding of the perennial problem of human existence to separate myth from insight in the New Testament.[74] Bultmann called this procedure "content criticism" (*Sachkritik*) and believed that through its careful implementation one could actually understand the New Testament writers better than they had understood themselves.

Thus, for example, Bultmann believed that when Paul spoke of the resurrection of the dead in 1 Corinthians 15, he inevitably wrapped the real content of what he intended to say in "the oriental salvation myth of the Original Man."[75] Although we can no longer accept this myth in the way Paul did, we can penetrate beneath the myth to Paul's basic point: "When Paul speaks of the resurrection of the dead, it is clear that he means to speak of *us*, of our reality, of our existence, of a reality in which *we* stand."[76] Occasionally Paul strays from the path of such transcendent insights, as when he mounts an apologetic for the resurrection of Jesus from the dead as a credible historical fact (1 Cor. 15:3–8). These detours from Paul's real content should be set aside—along with the cultural trappings in which his real meaning is expressed—as irrelevant for the church today.[77]

Bultmann's student Ernst Käsemann put his teacher's approach to the text in even more radical terms and came to more radical conclusions. He claimed that the New Testament contains "irreconcilable theological contradictions."[78] Because of this, he urged that some important theological tendencies within the New Testament, such as the movement toward institutional structure and unquestioning acceptance of authority ("early catholicism"), be rejected.[79]

Some feminist and liberation theologians have followed this trend by claiming that the experience of the oppressed should take on the status of divine revelation and that this new revelation should sit in judgment on the supposedly patriarchal, elitist, and homophobic elements of the canon.[80] Thus Neil Elliott has argued that the six letters falsely attributed to Paul in the New Testament depict a "gentrified" apostle who advocates slavery and the oppression of women. Paul himself taught the liberation of the socially oppressed, but the church has often allowed the pseudo-Paul of these pseudepigrapha to control its understanding of the real Paul of the authentic letters. The church should therefore reject the "gentrified" Paul of

74 See, e.g., Bultmann's 1926 review of Karl Barth's *Die Auferstehung der Toten* in *Faith and Understanding*, ed. Robert W. Funk (Philadelphia: Fortress, 1987), 66–94, esp. 72, 86, 92–93. A succinct summary of this element of Bultmann's hermeneutic appears in Erich Grässer, "Der Schatz in irdenen Gefässen (2 Kor 4,7): Existentiale Interpretation im 2. Korintherbrief," *ZTK* 97 (2000): 300–316, here at 301–3.

75 Bultmann, *Faith and Understanding*, 82.

76 Ibid., 81

77 Ibid., 83–84.

78 Käsemann, *Essays on New Testament Themes*, 100. Cf. idem, "The Problem of a New Testament Theology," *NTS* 19 (1972–73): 235–45, here at 242, and *The Testament of Jesus: A Study of the Gospel of John in the Light of Chapter 17* (Philadelphia: Fortress, 1968), 76.

79 Ernst Käsemann, *New Testament Questions of Today* (Philadelphia: Fortress, 1969), 236–51. A similar perspective appears in, e.g., W. G. Kümmel, "Notwendigkeit und Grenze des neutestamentlichen Kanons," *ZTK* 47 (1950): 227–313; Herbert Braun, "Hebt die heutige neutestamentliche-exegetische Forschung den Kanon auf?" *Fuldaer Hefte* 12 (1960): 9–24; and the comments of Robert Morgan on the necessity of *Sachkritik* for the theological interpretation of John's gospel in "Can the Critical Study of Scripture Provide a Doctrinal Norm?" *JR* 76 (1996): 206–32, here at 221.

80 See the appreciative survey of some of these approaches in John Riches, *A Century of New Testament Study* (Valley Forge, Penn.: Trinity Press International, 1993), 219–22.

the Pastoral Letters and return to the original Paul with his program of radical social change.[81]

This long-standing method of handling theological diversity within the canon is unsatisfactory, however, for two reasons. First, it is subjective and individualistic. It can claim no higher authority than the judgment of an individual or a group that a particular text should not be authoritative.[82] Thus it is difficult to know how advocates of a canon within the canon would answer interpreters who regard as their canon precisely those texts that others have rejected as prescientific or oppressive. What would Rudolf Bultmann say to the person who would rather adopt Paul's ancient mythology than Bultmann's existentialism? What would Ernst Käsemann say to the person who wanted to make the "early catholicism" of the New Testament normative? And on what grounds would Neil Elliott claim that the historical Paul is more authentically Christian than the gentrified Paul of the Pastorals?

One person's husk will always be another person's kernel, and it is difficult to say how the canon-within-the-canon approach to Scripture can legitimately elevate one theological strain within the text as authentically Christian but discard another as offensive.[83] Käsemann's claim that "the authority of the canon is never greater than the authority of the Gospel which should be heard from it" does not solve the problem.[84] This assertion only prompts the question, "Whose definition of the gospel should we accept, and on what authority should we accept it?"

Second, this approach fails to recognize the antiquity and universality of the canon. A part of the canon that may appear to one generation of Christians or to Christians in a certain setting as useless may be the prophetic voice of God to another generation of Christians or to those in other settings. As Luke Timothy Johnson says, "A measure that can be altered by addition or subtraction at any time and place cannot have the capacity to address every time and place."[85] The exclusion of supposedly primitive or oppressive texts in the New Testament, therefore, is not an adequate answer to the problem of theological diversity within it.

In summary, focusing on some irreducible theological core within the New Testament and then rejecting elements that fail to cohere with this core is not a successful strategy for coping with the theological diversity of the New Testament. It is both subjective and myopic. It is necessary to follow another path.

81 Neil Elliott, *Liberating Paul: The Justice of God and the Politics of the Apostle* (Maryknoll, N.Y.: Orbis, 1994), 25–90.

82 This is a common, and legitimate, Roman Catholic criticism. See, e.g., the careful analysis of Käsemann's position in Hans Küng, *Structures of the Church* (New York: T. Nelson, 1964), 152–67, esp. his comments on 162.

83 Cf. Wayne A. Meeks, "The 'Haustafeln' and American Slavery: A Hermeneutical Challenge" in *Theology and Ethics in Paul and His Interpreters: Essays in Honor of Victor Paul Furnish*, ed. Eugene H. Lovering Jr. and Jerry L. Sumney (Nashville: Abingdon, 1996), 232–53, at 248: "The trouble is, if all is ideology, then it is hard to see how the oppressor is to be persuaded by any moral compunction that might be shared with the revisionists. The pessimist might conclude that finally only power counts. The abolitionists did not persuade the slave owners; slavery ceased to have an ethical claim in American society because a war was won and lost."

84 Käsemann, *The Testament of Jesus*, 76.

85 Johnson, *Writings of the New Testament*, 545. Cf. Metzger, *Canon of the New Testament*, 279–82, and Childs, *The New Testament as Canon*, 30.

A Way Forward

A more promising strategy for handling the diversity within the New Testament is to recognize its principal theological themes and then to follow two paths when significant deviations from those themes arise. Sometimes it is necessary to look closely at the texts that supposedly run counter to the dominant theological trend. Often these texts have been too quickly dismissed without taking adequate account of their literary or historical contexts. On close inspection, and for good historical reasons, these texts can often be found not to swerve away from the dominant theological trend of the New Testament after all. Claims that the New Testament contains fundamental theological contradictions can be met with reasonable counter-arguments. These arguments are based both on the basic insight that the New Testament texts are the Word of God and on good historical-critical procedures.

At other times, however, the best historical reconstruction of the text seems to yield a meaning that is contradictory to the canon's dominant theological tendency. When this happens, it seems necessary to view the apparent divergence as itself theologically significant. If we try to minimize it either by trimming the canon down to a size that fits us theologically or by advancing implausible harmonizations, we impoverish our understanding of God. The theological diversity of the New Testament shows us that at the same time God is near us he is also beyond our comprehension.

The Tension as Evidence of God's Nearness

It shows us that God is near us because apparent theological divergence in the canon is often the result of the profoundly contingent nature of the New Testament writings. If Luke and Mark had coauthored a treatise on the Mosaic law, we would probably know with certainty how Jesus did not invalidate any part of the Mosaic law yet declared the Mosaic food laws invalid. If Paul had written a book on eschatology, we would probably understand clearly how Jesus can come unexpectedly—like a thief in the night—and yet certain signs can precede his coming. But Luke and Mark wrote gospels and Paul wrote letters to early Christian communities. Their purpose was not theoretical reflection but calling people to repentance and providing pastoral oversight for various local churches. Because of this, certainty about how their sometimes tensive theological statements cohere must sometimes elude us. We are missing the wider body of knowledge that provides the key to this coherence.

It would be easy to bemoan our loss. Before we do this, however, we should recall the theological gain of having a body of Scriptures that are fundamentally evangelistic and pastoral in nature. That God revealed himself to us in this way shows us that he is a gracious God who comes to his people of his own initiative and in the midst of their day-to-day existence. He is interested in the problems faced by the runaway slave Onesimus, the sick messenger Epaphroditus, and marginalized social groups like the poor in whom Luke and James express such interest.

The Tension as Evidence of God's Otherness

At the same time that the diversity of New Testament theology should show us the nearness of God, however, it should also show us that people are incapable of understanding him fully. The resolution to some theological tensions within the New Testament probably lies beyond the comprehension of the Christian who believes that the New Testament is God's Word. This does not mean that the tensions have no comprehensible explanation, only that the explanation lies beyond the ability of human reasoning, tainted as it is by sin and infirmity, to understand. If this is fideism, then it is what the philosopher C. Stephen Evans calls a "responsible fideism"—the idea that although reason has an important role to play in understanding God and his Word, it is reasonable to recognize that it has limitations only faith can overcome.[86]

This way of understanding aspects of God's revelation that appear to be in tension with one another has precedent in the New Testament itself. In Romans 9–11, for example, Paul addresses a problem that seems to set God's promises to Israel in the Scriptures against the gospel as Paul has explained it in Romans 1–8. Paul has argued at length in those chapters that both Jews and Gentiles are sinful and fall under the just condemnation of God. Because of this, Paul says, the Jew has no privilege over the Gentile at the day of judgment—apart from faith in Christ Jesus both will stand condemned. Moreover, the gospel has had its greatest success among the Gentiles rather than among the Jews. This means that not only do Jews stand condemned alongside godless Gentiles, but that many Gentiles have experienced God's grace and become part of his people at the same time that many Jews have been cut off from God's people and experienced his condemnation. But if this is true, what has become of God's promises, particularly in the prophetic books, that he would give his people a new heart, make with them a new covenant, and restore their fortunes? Paul's letter seems to stand in irreconcilable contradiction to the prophetic promises of God.

Paul's explanation of this tension is both complex and, on the basis of Israel's Scriptures, unexpected. Paul claims in Romans 11:7–32 that although it may not appear that way, God still plans to be faithful to his people Israel and that one day all Israel will be saved through faith in Christ. Contrary to expectations, God has planned to do this by bringing such large numbers of Gentiles into the company of his people that they will outnumber the Jews. This does not mean, however, that the Jews will be excluded. Rather, the Gentiles will provoke them to jealousy for the promises that God gave to them in their Scriptures, and this in turn will lead them to embrace the gospel. No one could have predicted, on the basis of Paul's Scriptures, that God would work in this way to fulfill his promises, but he revealed to Paul the mystery that this is his intended way of working. It is the unexpected nature of

86 Evans, *Faith beyond Reason*. Evans argues that although the term "fideism" is often used pejoratively, philosophers as diverse as Thomas Aquinas, William James, and Immanuel Kant find a role for faith in arriving at truth that goes beyond anything reason is capable of accomplishing by itself. Conversely, Kierkegaard, who is often seen as an advocate of an irrational form of fideism, reveals a concern that reason should play some role in the search for truth. All of these thinkers then can be described as advocates of "responsible fideism."

this plan that leads Paul to the doxology of praise at the end of this section of his letter to the Romans:

> Oh, the depth of the riches of the wisdom and knowledge of God!
> How unsearchable his judgments,
> and his paths beyond tracing out!
> "Who has known the mind of the Lord?
> Or who has been his counselor?
> Who has ever given to God,
> that God should repay him?"
> For from him and through him and to him are all things.
> To him be glory forever! Amen.

Paul is not claiming here that God is irrational, but that God's rationality is at times above human comprehension until he shows his hand more clearly.[87] When we encounter apparently irreconcilable theological tensions in the New Testament, therefore, we should be reminded of "the depth of the riches of the wisdom and knowledge of God."

If such a profound tension between the prophet's promises and the outworking of the gospel can be resolved in so surprising a way, then we should expect that other difficult tensions within the New Testament itself may have a similarly surprising solution. Students of the New Testament should therefore resist the temptation to flatten the theological diversity of the New Testament into a series of logical statements so tight that the mystery of God's greatness is missing from them.

New Testament Theology and Theological Diversity: A Summary

The theological diversity of the New Testament cannot be used as a weapon in the hands of human reason to force Christian interpreters of the New Testament to abandon their study of New Testament theology. Reason itself should recognize both its own usefulness and its limitations and realize that faith addresses its limitations. Christian interpreters have sound philosophical reasons, therefore, for giving their authoritative texts the benefit of the doubt. Christians should not explain the theological diversity of the New Testament by conceding that it contains incompatible theological tendencies and by using one of those tendencies to disfranchise others.

At the same time, Christians should honor the ancient commitment of the church to the theological diversity of its authoritative texts, a commitment that was well established by the late second century through the important place accorded the four gospels, as we will see in the next chapter. Those who skirted the scandal of the text's diversity by means of harmonizing the texts were rejected as soundly, if not as quickly, as those who radically reduced the number of the texts. It is necessary for the diversity of the canon to stand as a witness both to the nearness and to the otherness of God, who, despite his infinite wisdom, has met us where we are through his Word.

87 Carson, "Unity and Diversity in the New Testament: The Possibility of Systematic Theology," in *Scripture and Truth*, ed. D. A. Carson and John D. Woodbridge (Grand Rapids: Zondervan, 1983), 93–94.

HISTORY, THEOLOGY, UNITY, AND DIVERSITY IN THE STUDY OF NEW TESTAMENT THEOLOGY

The student of New Testament theology faces two critical challenges: the challenge of the historian who believes that the historical work of New Testament theologians is hopelessly biased and the challenge of those who believe that the New Testament's theology is hopelessly diverse.

Many opponents of the discipline of New Testament theology, at least as it is practiced by professing Christians, claim that it is methodologically flawed. It makes historical claims but is so laced with theological presuppositions that its historical claims are of little value except perhaps to those who are already convinced of them. This is a serious criticism because if it has merit, the New Testament theologian is reduced to arguing one of Christianity's most important convictions—that its truth claims are based in historical occurrences—on grounds that no unbelieving historian would accept.

In this chapter we have seen that the Christian does accept through the basic insight of faith that the New Testament is the Word of God and therefore a special body of literature whose own theological perspectives are worth studying. This does not mean, however, that New Testament theology is an irrational discipline or is crippled from the start by its unreasonable presuppositions. Several important philosophers have recognized that a basic insight, such as faith, can play a rational role, alongside reason, in arriving at the truth. Reason has limitations that it "reasonably" must recognize.

Most historians, moreover, recognize that even the most objective unbeliever approaches historical analysis for particular purposes and with particular presuppositions. The possession of presuppositions is inevitable and should not hinder historical study, whether for the believer or for the unbeliever. Believers have a good reason for carefully bracketing presuppositions that do not call into question the basic insight that the New Testament is the Word of God; they are motivated by a desire to listen, not to an echo of their own prejudices when they read the New Testament, but to the voice of the text itself. Only by doing this will they hear the Word of God.

For much the same reason, the believer who is a student of New Testament theology must honor the theological diversity within it. Although the basic insight of faith can warrant the conclusion that the theological emphases of the New Testament documents are not ultimately contradictory, that same conviction prohibits solving the problem of theological diversity either by reducing the witness of the texts to a harmonious core or by offering implausible harmonizations.

The basic insight of faith dictates that the twenty-seven New Testament documents comprise an appropriate subject for study. The crucial role of history in Christian belief dictates that students of New Testament theology understand these documents in their historical contexts, that they understand them as objectively as possible within the boundaries of Christian commitment, and that they attempt to honor both the theological unity and the theological diversity of these twenty-seven texts.

In the chapters that follow, we will attempt to honor the theological diversity of the New Testament by describing the theological emphases of each of its twenty-seven discrete texts. We will also attempt to honor the theological connections between these different texts by summarizing them, both in groups with similar historical and literary characteristics (the Gospels and Acts, the Pauline letters, the non-Pauline letters, and Revelation) and, at the end, in a concluding theological overview.

Part One

THE GOSPELS AND ACTS

Chapter 2

THE PERSISTENCE AND IMPORTANCE OF A FOURFOLD GOSPEL

The New Testament contains four narrative witnesses to the ministry of Jesus, each of which describes the theological significance of Christ in distinctive ways. Since Acts is an integral part of Luke's two-part narrative, it is also part of the fourfold narrative witness to Jesus. Much common theological ground unites these books—they all describe "the gospel of Jesus Christ, the Son of God" (Mark 1:1)—but they are also, as their titles suggest, the discrete witnesses of four separate authors (whoever they might be) to this one gospel. The unwillingness of many early Christians, at least from the third century, to consider more or fewer gospels than these four as primary narrative witnesses to the significance of Jesus has posed, and continues to pose, an apologetic problem for the church. Similarly, the plurality and diversity of these four witnesses has over the centuries been the delight of the church's critics.

Despite intense pressure from opponents of Christianity, from heretical movements that wanted to identify with historic Christianity, and from orthodox Christians themselves, however, the church eventually decided against either accepting more than these gospel narratives or reducing the offensive plurality of the gospels to a single, manageable narrative. The majority of Christians over the centuries has insisted that these four, in all their diversity, but only these four gospel narratives, bear a wholly truthful witness to the one gospel of Jesus Christ. Before investigating the discrete theological intentions of these four narratives and discussing what unites them in the following chapters, therefore, it will be helpful to reflect on the ancient church's reasons for its commitment to these four gospels and the relevance of its reasoning to more recent challenges to their authority.

DIVERSITY AMONG THE GOSPELS AS A PROBLEM IN THE EARLY CHURCH

Efforts to Reduce or Harmonize the Gospels

As early as the second century, some people who followed Jesus felt the diversity of the four most widely accepted gospels to be a problem. In the middle of the century, Marcion claimed that the four gospels reflected the corrupt Judaizing tendencies of those who wrote them. He tried to restore the single, Pauline gospel in all its purity by radically editing Luke's gospel, the one of the four most closely linked with Paul.[1] In later years, Marcion's followers claimed that the differences between their

1 Martin Hengel, *The Four Gospels and the One Gospel of Jesus Christ* (Harrisburg, Pa.: Trinity Press International, 2000), 31–33.

own gospel and the gospels of the orthodox church signaled the falsity of the orthodox gospels.[2]

The *Gospel of Peter* also appeared about this time, and although we neither have its text in its entirety nor do we know the motives for its production, it may have been an attempt to combine elements of the four widely accepted gospels (in addition to material from other sources) into a single narrative.[3] This single narrative is then attributed to the preeminent apostle Peter. Although it is impossible to say for certain, the editor of this text may have wanted to produce a single, authoritative gospel that would replace the four widely known gospels of the church.[4]

More orthodox attempts at harmonizing may have occurred with Justin Martyr and Theophilus of Antioch, but the effort of Justin's pupil Tatian was the most thoroughgoing and widely known of such attempts.[5] Tatian wove a lengthy and rich narrative of Jesus' life out of the four widely accepted gospels and called it "the gospel from the four," or, in Greek, *[to] dia tessarōn [euangelion]*: the *Diatessaron*.[6] Although we cannot speak precisely of Tatian's motives, we know from his *Oration to the Greeks* that he valued simplicity and unity as signs of truth in both religion and historical narrative. This philosophical commitment may have led him to try to advance the cause of the church by creating a harmony of its four diverse, but widely accepted, narratives of Jesus' ministry.[7]

Tatian's effort evidently struck a resonant cord with many Christians. His *Diatressaron* became so popular in the Syriac-speaking church that it was read in worship, and the four separate gospels were not translated into Syriac until the end of the third or the beginning of the fourth century.[8] Eusebius, writing in the early fourth century, said that copies of the *Diatessaron* were still in circulation in his own time, and the fifth-century Bishop of Cyrrhus, Theodoret, felt compelled to insist that copies of the work be destroyed and replaced with the four gospels. Both manuscript discoveries and literary inferences show that the *Diatessaron* existed in Arabic, Persian, Armenian, Latin, Old High German, Middle Dutch, and Middle English.[9]

2 Tjitze Baarda, "ΔΙΑΦΩΝΙΑ–ΣΥΜΦΩΝΙΑ: Factors in the Harmonization of the Gospels, Especially in the Diatessaron of Tatian," in *Gospel Traditions in the Second Century: Origins, Recensions, Text, and Transmission*, ed. William L. Petersen (CJA 3; Notre Dame, Ind.: Univ. of Notre Dame Press, 1989), 133–54, here at 127, citing *Dial. Adam.* 7.1.

3 Ibid., 141. Cf. Hengel, *Four Gospels*, 13. Against the idea that the *Gospel of Peter* or part of it may be older than the canonical gospels, see R. E. Brown, "The Gospel of Peter and Canonical Gospel Priority," *NTS* 33 (1987): 321–43; John P. Meier, *A Marginal Jew: Rethinking the Historical Jesus*, 3 vols. (ABRL; New York: Doubleday, 1991–2001), 1:116–18; and James D. G. Dunn, *Jesus Remembered* (Grand Rapids: Eerdmans, 2003), 164, 170.

4 See Oscar Cullmann, *The Early Church*, ed. A. J. B. Higgins (London: SCM, 1956), 47, who also suggests that the "Gospel according to Basilides" and the "Gospel of the Twelve" referred to by Origen (*Hom. Luc.* 1 on Luke 9:5) were produced with the same intention. On the "Gospel according to Basilides," see also Hengel, *Four Gospels*, 57–58.

5 For the harmonizing activity of Theophilus and for the possibility that Justin was also engaged in creating a harmony of at least the Synoptic Gospels, see Baarda, "ΔΙΑΦΩΝΙΑ–ΣΥΜΦΩΝΙΑ," 142; William L. Petersen, "Textual Evidence of Tatian's Dependence upon Justin's 'ΑΠΟΜΝΗΜΟΝΕΥΜΑΤΙΑ," *NTS* 36 (1990): 512–34, here at 512–15; idem, *Tatian's Diatessaron: Its Creation, Dissemination, Significance, and History in Scholarship*, (VCSup 25; Leiden: Brill, 1994), 32, 346–48; and Hengel, *Four Gospels*, 24, 55–56, 245 n. 229. For the debate over whether or not these early harmonies existed see Helmut Merkel, *Die Widersprüche zwischen den Evangelien: Ihre polemische und apologetische Behandlung in der alten Kirche bis zu Augustin* (WUNT 13; Tübingen: J. C. B. Mohr [Paul Siebeck]: 1971), 68 n. 92.

6 Cf. Hengel, *Four Gospels*, 25.

7 This is the burden of Baarda's essay. Cf. Merkel, *Widersprüche zwischen den Evangelien*, 68–69, and Stanton, "The Fourfold Gospel," *NTS* 43 (1997): 317–46, here at 344.

8 Hengel, *Four Gospels*, 25.

9 Cullman, *Early Church*, 49; Petersen, *Tatian's Diatessaron*, 1–2; Hengel, *Four Gospels*, 25–26.

While all this was happening overtly, a few of the scribes who preserved the texts of the four gospels supplied a steady undercurrent of harmonizing readings. Those given to harmonizing tendencies found particularly offensive the differences between these gospels in the passion and resurrection narratives and devised often subtle means for smoothing out what they took to be discrepancies.[10] The longer ending of Mark is one of the earlier and bolder attempts to harmonize the ending of the gospels. It was probably constructed in the early second century in part from the accounts of Jesus' resurrection appearances in the other three gospels.[11] This addition to Mark must have repaired what many felt was a major discrepancy between Mark and its three companions: the absence of resurrection appearances of the Lord.

The Use of Gospel Differences in Anti-Christian Polemic

Coinciding with this evidence of discomfort with the fourfold gospel among many early Christians is evidence that opponents of Christianity regularly pointed to supposed discrepancies between the gospels as proof that Christianity was false. Celsus, writing about A.D. 180, knew of Christian efforts to harmonize their gospels and made merry over it:

> Some believers, as though from a drinking bout, go so far as to oppose themselves and alter the original text of the gospel three or four or several times over, and they change its character to enable them to deny difficulties in face of criticism.[12]

Whether Celsus was thinking of Marcion, Tatian, the harmonizing work of scribes, or simply the diversity of the gospels themselves remains obscure.[13] It is clear, however, that he saw the variations in the three (or four) gospels as an embarrassment for Christians and charged them with attempting to remove this stumbling block by tampering with their texts.

About a century later, the philosopher Porphyry produced his book *Against the Christians*, which engaged in a much more detailed critique of the inconsistencies that he thought plagued the four gospels. He pointed out, for example, the differences that a minute comparison of their accounts of Jesus' death revealed. Especially telling for Porphyry were the differences in Jesus' final words and the absence from the Synoptics of John's reference to the piercing of Jesus' side.[14] The problem that Porphyry's detailed criticism of the differences between the four gospels posed for Christian apologists is clear from Augustine's laborious attempt a whole century later to refute him.

10 See Baarda, "ΔΙΑΦΩΝΙΑ–ΣΥΜΦΩΝΙΑ," 138–40.

11 Ibid., 138–40; Hengel, *Four Gospels*, 26–27.

12 Origen, *Cels.* 2.27. On the date of Celsus' *On the True Doctrine*, see Henry Chadwick's introduction to Origen's *Contra Celsum*, trans. and ed. Henry Chadwick (Cambridge: Cambridge Univ. Press, 1953), xxviii, and on the mid-third century date of Origen's reply, see ibid., xiv–xv.

13 Origen thinks that Celsus may have been familiar with Marcion's handling of the gospels. He also mentions Valentinus or the quasi-Marcionite Lucan as possibly engaged in the activity that Celsus describes.

14 Porphyry was a student and biographer of the Neoplatonic philosopher Plotinus. On his use of the differences between the four gospels in his case against Christianity, see Merkel, *Widersprüche zwischen den Evangelien*, 13–18, and Robert L. Wilken, *The Christians as the Romans Saw Them* (New Haven, Conn.: Yale Univ. Press, 1984), 144–47. Graham Stanton, "Fourfold Gospel," 321, also points out that the gnostic Valentinians, according to Irenaeus, *Haer.* 3.2.1, also accused the Scriptures of error, and Stanton believes that this is a reference to "the errors and contradictions of the gospels."

In his treatise *On the Harmony of the Gospels*, Augustine says that he undertook this work because the adversaries of Christianity "are in the habit of adducing" as their primary evidence "that the evangelists are not in harmony with one another" (1.10; cf. 1.52; 2.1). Throughout his treatise, he seems to be thinking primarily of Porphyry.[15]

The Response of the Orthodox Church

Despite the pressure exerted by these forces, both from within orthodoxy and outside its bounds, and despite the high quality of Tatian's carefully constructed mega-gospel, most Christians refused to abandon the four ancient witnesses to the founding events of their faith. Marcion's insistence on a single gospel was rejected. The *Gospel of Peter*, although it enjoyed acceptance in the church at Rhossus in Syria and although Serapion, the early third-century bishop of Antioch, tolerated it for a time, was evidently not widely known even during Serapion's time and was never widely accepted.[16] Tatian's *Diatessaron* was rejected eventually even in Syria as an unfit substitute for the four gospels. The very subtlety with which the scribes who made harmonizing changes to the gospels tried to hide their repairs also demonstrates their awareness that most Christians frowned on the practice. Origen considered scribes who purposely harmonized the gospels to be rascals: "Villainous recklessness" drove them to harmonize the text (*Comm. Matt.* 15.14).[17] Jerome, writing to Pope Damasus in the late fourth century, was also deeply annoyed:

> The numerous errors in our manuscripts result first and foremost from the fact that those passages in the gospels which record the same event have been filled out from one another. To avoid the difficulties in the four gospels, men have taken as a model the first account they have read, and then corrected the others to bring them into line with it.[18]

Most Christians wanted their four ancient witnesses to the one gospel to stand as they were, in all their "offensive" diversity. Even Augustine, although writing specifically to explain how the four gospels can be historically credible despite supposed discrepancies, affirmed the need for their separate witness to "the gospel" and did not wish to replace them with a single, harmonious narrative (*Cons.* 1.1–9).

The Reasons for This Response

The reasons for this reaction to attempts to remove the offensive diversity of the four gospels were theological. Three reasons seem to have been particularly important.

The Theological Necessity of Truthful History

The early Christians had a theological stake in an accurate historical record of the ministry, death, and resurrection of Jesus Christ. Their one gospel made historical

15 Wilken, *Christians*, 144–45.

16 Serapion's letter to the church at Rhossus, quoted in Eusebius, *Hist. eccl.* 6.12.3–4, implies that the bishop was unfamiliar with the work and that it was not widely known. See Hengel, *Four Gospels*, 13.

17 They change the text, says Origen, *apo tolmēs ... mochthēras.* On this, see Xavier Léon-Dufour, *The Gospels and the Jesus of History* (London: Collins, 1968), 46.

18 Léon-Dufour, *Gospels*, 46–47, translating a letter of Jerome to Pope Damasus on the difficulty of using Greek manuscripts of the gospels to correct the Latin manuscripts (PL 29.560).

claims, and fraudulent forms of that gospel also made historical claims. It was critical, therefore, that orthodox early Christians plant their own theological convictions firmly in the earliest witnesses to Jesus and his significance. The efforts of Marcion, Tatian, and harmonizing scribes were useless for this purpose—they simply did not have antiquity on their side. Matthew, Mark, Luke, and John, however, were from an early date and considered by a wide variety of parties to be the best witnesses to the historical Jesus.

Irenaeus, writing in the second half of the second century, claimed that both orthodox and heretical Christians grappled for control of the four gospels because of the widespread conviction that these gospels were the best witnesses to the historical Jesus and his teaching:

> So firm is the ground upon which these Gospels rest, that the very heretics themselves bear witness to them, and, starting from these [documents], each one of them endeavours to establish his own peculiar doctrine.[19]

Irenaeus then listed four heretical groups, each of which had attached itself to a particular gospel: the Ebionites to Matthew, Marcionites to Luke, docetists to Mark, and Valentinians to John. He concluded this section with this observation: "Since, then, our opponents do bear testimony to us, and make use of these [documents], our proof derived from them is firm and true."

Everyone, in other words, had to appeal to these four texts because they were commonly accepted as the best witnesses to the real Jesus. Whatever the theological battle, it had to be fought on the battlefield of the gospels because they were considered the authoritative voices on Jesus.

The validity of Irenaeus's claim about the widespread recognition of the four gospels is confirmed when we move back into the first half of the second century. Justin Martyr, writing around A.D. 136, can speak of "the memoirs which I say were drawn up by His apostles and those who followed them."[20] This implies that Justin knew at least four gospels, at least two by apostles and two by followers.[21] It seems reasonable to conclude that he was speaking of Matthew and John (both apostles) and of Luke and Mark (both followers of apostles), and doing so in an order that corresponds to the sequence in which the four gospels appear in many ancient gospel collections.[22]

This conclusion becomes all but certain when we realize that Justin quotes from all three Synoptics and probably alludes to John's gospel, but never from noncanonical gospels. He feels, moreover, no need to argue for the authority of these gospels but takes their authority for granted. Statistical analysis of the actual use of the gospels in early Christian literature shows why Justin could do this: From the time of the

19 Irenaeus, *Haer.* 3.11.7.

20 Justin Martyr, *Dial.* 103.8.

21 Martin Hengel, *Studies in the Gospel of Mark* (Philadelphia: Fortress, 1985), 68; idem, *Four Gospels*, 19–20; Stanton, "Fourfold Gospel," 330.

22 This "Western" order (Matthew, John, Luke, and Mark) is not more common than the "chronological" order (Matthew, Mark, Luke, and John). It is, nevertheless, found in P45, some manuscripts of the Old Latin, the Apostolic Constitutions, Codex Bezae, Codex Washingtonianus, and Codex Monacensis. On the order of the gospels in various ancient lists, see Hengel, *Four Gospels*, 42.

Apostolic Fathers on, the four gospels that later became canonical were quoted and alluded to far more frequently than other gospel literature.[23] The respective intensity with which the Christian literature of the second and third centuries quotes and alludes to the canonical gospels also basically corresponds to the ordering of the gospels that Justin implies: Matthew appears most often, then John, then Luke and Mark.[24]

The widespread authority of the four canonical gospels is also tacitly confirmed by the production of noncanonical gospels in the second century, such as the *Gospel of Peter* and the *Gospel of Thomas*. These gospels mimicked the titles of the four commonly accepted gospels and used much of their content because Matthew, John, Luke, and Mark were simply the best and most widely accepted sources for the historical Jesus available.[25] The only hope that the authors and editors of these texts had for gaining them acceptance lay in imitating the commonly accepted gospels.

Both orthodox Christians and heretics alike, therefore, acknowledged the importance of the four gospels. A wide swath of Christianity acknowledged these texts to be the most ancient witnesses to Jesus, and those who hoped to trace their theological convictions back to the Jesus of history had somehow to come to grips with these gospels. Because its theology had to be anchored in truthful historical accounts, therefore, the early church could not shift its attention from the four gospels either to one of the four or to a harmony of the four. All four, in their offensive plurality, had to be retained.

The Theological Unity of the Fourfold Gospel

It is possible to exaggerate the offense of the gospels' plurality. Most early Christians were impressed not with the divergences among the gospels but with their theological unity. For all their diversity, these four voices speak in unison on the theological principles that early orthodox Christians valued most highly.[26] From its earliest days, the church called those principles "the gospel."

In what is probably the earliest extant Christian text, Paul can already speak of "the gospel of God" (1 Thess. 2:2, 8, 9), "the gospel of Christ" (1 Thess. 3:2), and of "our gospel" (1 Thess. 1:5; cf. 1 Cor. 15:1–2). A few years later, Paul is deeply distressed because troublemakers in Galatia have "changed the gospel of Christ" into something that is no gospel at all (Gal. 1:6–7). To this, Paul responds, "even if we or an angel from heaven should preach a gospel other than the one we preached to you, let him be eternally condemned!" (Gal. 1:8–9; cf. 2 Cor. 11:4). The gospel, in other words, both has

23 John Barton, *Holy Writings, Sacred Text: The Canon in Early Christianity* (Louisville: Westminster John Knox, 1997), 17, relying on the statistical analysis of Franz Stuhlhofer, *Der Gebrauch der Bibel von Jesus bis Euseb: Eine statistische Untersuchung zur Kanonsgeschichte* (Monographien und Studienbücher 335; Wuppertal: Brockhaus, 1988).

24 Stuhlhofer, *Der Gebrauch der Bibel*, 19–20, 98.

25 Cf. Hengel, *Four Gospels*, 59–60. Some—e.g., Ron Cameron, *The Other Gospels: Non-Canonical Gospel Texts* (Philadelphia: Westminster, 1982), 24–25; John Dominic Crossan, *Four Other Gospels: Shadows on the Contours of Canon* (Minneapolis: Winston, 1985), 35–37; and Richard Valantasis, *The Gospel of Thomas* (New Testament Readings; London: Routledge, 1997)—believe that the *Gospel of Thomas* often preserves a form of Jesus' sayings and parables independent of and as primitive as what we find in the four canonical gospels. It is more likely, however, that *Thomas* is dependent upon at least Matthew and Luke, as a comparison, for example, of Mark 3:35; Luke 8:21; Matt. 12:50; and *Gos. Thom.* 99 shows. See Michael Fieger, *Das Thomasevangelium: Einleitung, Kommentar, und Systematik* (NTAbh 22; Münster: Aschendorffsche Verlagsbuchhandlung, 1991), 6–8, and Meier, *Marginal Jew*, 1:134–36.

26 Cf. Cullmann, *Early Church*, 53.

a firm and unalterable core and must be preached through human instruments. Some of these messengers get it right, and some of them perversely change it so that their message can no longer be identified with the truth of the gospel (Gal. 2:5, 14).

This idea of a single gospel that people can render in several versions probably reappears not long after Paul's death in the title of Mark's gospel. Martin Hengel has suggested plausibly that whoever first copied the gospel of Mark for wide circulation affixed to it the title "the gospel according to Mark," borrowing the term "gospel" from Mark's first line (1:1). If so, then from the time Mark's gospel began to circulate widely, Christians recognized that "the gospel of Jesus Christ" could be rendered faithfully in more than one form and that this particular narrative contained "the gospel according to Mark."[27] The same can be said of the other gospels: to speak of "the gospel according to Matthew," "the gospel according to Luke," and "the gospel according to John" implies that one unalterable gospel lies at the foundation of their various expressions.[28]

This conviction breaks into the open in the second and third centuries. The late second-century Muratorian Canon could say that "the one Spirit informs" the four gospels. Irenaeus, writing toward the end of the second century, said similarly that "he who was manifested to men has given us the Gospel under four aspects, but bound together by one Spirit."[29] Origen, writing in the third century, could answer Marcion's disparagement of the orthodox attachment to four different gospels with the comment that "there is one who is preached by all, thus the gospel written down by many is one in power, and the gospel that comes by means of four (*to*... *dia tessarōn*) is truly one."[30]

Irenaeus insisted that a common witness to the one gospel unifies the four gospels and that no other gospel can add to or supplant this common witness. The Valentinians, by adding to the number of the gospels with "their own compositions" and by producing their own *Gospel of Truth*, deviated from the one gospel that all four widely accepted gospels uphold. The *Gospel of Truth*, wrote Irenaeus, "agrees in nothing with the Gospels of the Apostles, so that [the Valentinians] have really no Gospel which is not full of blasphemy."[31]

At this point, Irenaeus introduced into his argument the witness of the second part of Luke's two-part work. The Acts of the Apostles is valuable because it shows that the common theological ground uniting the four gospels also represents the preaching of the earliest Christians. Peter, John, Philip, Paul, Stephen, and James join the witness of the four gospels to present a united front against the theological claims of Marcion and Valentinus.[32]

From the time of Paul, Christians have agreed that orthodoxy is measured by how closely those who claim to know who Jesus is and what he taught conform to the

27 Hengel, *Studies in the Gospel of Mark*, 83.

28 This is a common observation. See, e.g., Cullmann, *Early Church*, 40; Brevard S. Childs, *The New Testament as Canon: An Introduction* (Philadelphia: Fortress, 1984), 152; Stanton, "Fourfold Gospel," 332; Hengel, *Studies in the Gospel of Mark*, 64–84; and idem, *Four Gospels*, 48.

29 Irenaeus, *Haer.* 3.11.8.

30 Origen, *Comm. Jo.* 5.7. I am indebted to Cullmann, *Early Church*, 48 n. 26 and 53 n. 38 for drawing this important paragraph in Origen to my attention.

31 Irenaeus, *Haer.* 3.11.9.

32 Ibid., 3.12.1–14.

one gospel of Jesus Christ. At least by the time that the titles were affixed to Mark, Matthew, Luke, and John, many Christians believed that these gospels were different renderings of this one, unalterable core. By the time of Irenaeus, and probably earlier, the common ground among precisely these traditional four witnesses was the standard against which Christians measured religious claims. Attempts to add other compositions to their number or to trump their significance with a single composition was the method of those who taught theological error.

The Theological Advantage of a Pluriform Witness

The early church believed that the manifold ramifications of the gospel could not be adequately appreciated by accepting any fewer than the generally accepted four gospels. Although they viewed the theological variation in the fourfold gospel as in some ways a stumbling block, they also saw its advantages.

First, the plurality of the gospels was just as important in preventing heresy as acknowledging the one gospel that lay behind all four gospels. Irenaeus commented that the heretics err not only in adding their own deviant texts to the four gospels but also in focusing on one gospel narrative to the exclusion of the others.[33] Marcion had done this by accepting only a truncated form of Luke's gospel[34] and by separating Luke's gospel from the Acts of the Apostles, which clearly demonstrates that Paul was not the only apostle who preached the truth of the gospel.[35] The Valentinians and anti-Paulinists made the same mistake in that they used Luke's gospel but ignored his second volume. If they attended to the truth expressed in the continuation of Luke's gospel, however, they would stand corrected and be saved from their error. According to Irenaeus, a fully orbed and therefore correct theology demands that we accept not merely those gospels we find most congenial to our preconceived notions, but also those that challenge and correct these notions. Narrowing our focus to one gospel only, or tailoring the existing gospels to fit our preconceived ideas, therefore, is theologically perilous.

Second, some early Christians probably understood the theological variation among the four gospels as advantageous because it demonstrated that the one gospel of Jesus Christ was richer in its implications than any single expression of it could fully grasp. At least two, and perhaps three, of the four gospels may themselves imply this. By incorporating Mark into the texts of their own gospels, Matthew and Luke implied that they agreed with Mark. They accepted his witness as valid (otherwise they would not have included it in their own texts) but they did not believe it was adequate by itself, and so, to paraphrase Luke, it seemed good to them also to write their own orderly accounts (Luke 1:3). John's knowledge of the Synoptic Gospels is a hotly disputed point, but if he knew them, as Clement of Alexandria assumed on the basis of an ancient tradition,[36] then he too felt there was more to be said (cf. John 20:30; 21:25).

In later years, Origen celebrated what he understood to be discrepancies between the gospels because they pointed to the immense spiritual treasures that lay beneath

33 Ibid., 3.11.9.

34 Ibid., 3.11.7, 9; 3.14.4.

35 Ibid., 3.13.1–3; 3.14.4.

36 See Eusebius, *Hist. eccl.* 6.14.5–7.

the surface of a literal reading of the text. Although this hermeneutic was in many ways misguided, an element of truth lay beneath it: Origen saw the diversity of the gospels as a witness to the inability of any single writer to grasp the full significance of the one gospel.[37]

Many early Christians believed, therefore, that the attempt to sum up the one gospel in a single, neat package was ill advised. They understood, as Oscar Cullmann put it, that "the faith cries out for manifold witness."[38]

THE CONTINUING RELEVANCE OF THE EARLY CHURCH'S RESPONSE

Over the last two centuries the pressure has again intensified to reduce the four primary witnesses to a single metanarrative that then replaces the Jesus of the four commonly accepted gospels. Scholars have done this primarily in the form of the so-called "quest for the historical Jesus." The beginning of the quest is usually dated to 1778 with the posthumous publication of Hermann Samuel Reimarus's work, "On the Intention of Jesus and His Disciples."[39] Reimarus believed that Jesus had been a religious reformer who became convinced that he could release the Jews from Roman captivity and set up a "secular kingdom." He succeeded only in angering the authorities, however, who captured, tried, and crucified him, putting his political goals to a disillusioning end. It was left to his disciples to pick up the pieces, and they rehabilitated their teacher as a spiritual figure who died for human sin, was resurrected, and would return. The gospels, said Reimarus, are the deposit of this reconstruction. In other words, they are tendentious documents that can supply useful historical information, but only after the historian takes account of their authors' deceptive intentions.

In the initial phases of the Jesus quest, this two-sided approach to the gospels emerged as a constant theme. On the one hand the gospels were the most valuable historical witnesses to the life and ministry of Jesus, and therefore the historian had to use them. On the other hand, those engaged in the effort to recover the historical Jesus were deeply suspicious that the religious faith permeating these gospels from beginning to end had masked the real Jesus from view. The history of the "quest for the historical Jesus" in its early phases was largely the story of the attempt, through the use of various critical tools, to purify the gospels of their theological tendentiousness so that they might yield historical data useful for reconstructing Jesus as he actually existed.

37 On Origen's approach to discrepancies among the gospels, see Merkel, *Widersprüche zwischen den Evangelien*, 94–121, and for the theological value of diverse witnesses, see Luke Timothy Johnson, *The Real Jesus: The Misguided Quest for the Historical Jesus and the Truth of the Traditional Gospels* (San Francisco: HarperSanFrancisco, 1996), 149.

38 Cullmann, *Early Church*, 54. Cullmann's article, "Die Pluralität der Evangelien als theologisches Problem im Altertum," originally appeared in *TZ* 1 (1945): 23–42.

39 This, at least, is where Albert Schweitzer starts his famous analysis of *The Quest of the Historical Jesus* (New York: Macmillan, 1968; orig. ed. 1906), 13–26. George Wesley Buchanan has translated Reimarus's essay into English under the title, *The Goal of Jesus and His Disciples* (Leiden: Brill, 1970). Originally, the essay was part of a much larger unpublished work, *Apologie oder Schutzchrift für die vernüftigen Verehrer Gottes*, to which G. E. Lessing gained access. Lessing published "fragments" of the larger work in seven installments between 1774 and 1778. "On the Intention of Jesus and His Disciples" was the seventh of these. Reimarus's complete manuscript remained unpublished until 1972.

The "lives of Jesus" that these early phases of the Jesus quest spawned bear a resemblance to the efforts of Marcion, Tatian, and others to overcome the offensive plurality of the gospels by supplying in their place a single account of Jesus.[40] Just as Marcion and Tatian constructed from one or more of the commonly accepted gospels a single narrative that fit their philosophical presuppositions, so the lives of Jesus that arose out of the Enlightenment and modernism often purged the gospel accounts of their miraculous element in accord with the rationalistic and ethical presuppositions of their authors.

Martin Kähler had already noticed this in 1892 in his book *The So-Called Historical Jesus and the Historic Biblical Christ*. There he observed that since those who wrote lives of Jesus found sparse material for a historical biography in the gospels, they tended to fit the available evidence together in ways that reflected their own ideological presuppositions. "Some outside force must rework the fragments of the tradition," said Kähler. "This force is nothing other than the theologian's imagination—an imagination that has been shaped and nourished by the analogy of his own life and of human life in general."[41] For Kähler, it was impossible to get to the real Jesus by going behind the gospels. Those who tried to do so only succeeded in constructing a "fifth gospel" patterned after themselves.[42]

More recent, postmodern efforts to describe the "real" Jesus have given a more prominent place to various noncanonical texts than did previous forms of the Jesus quest. The hypothetical literary source that Matthew and Luke both used (often called Q), the *Gospel of Thomas*, at least parts of the *Gospel of Peter*, and the so-called *Secret Gospel of Mark* are sometimes added to the witness of the Synoptic Gospels, and occasionally privileged over them, in the effort to describe Jesus as he really was rather than Jesus as the canonical gospels portray him. The result of this expansion of admissible evidence for Jesus to texts beyond the four gospels is then sometimes used to produce an account of Jesus intended to replace the accounts in the four gospels and in traditional Christian belief.[43]

The early church's argument that the real Jesus is the Jesus of the four gospels is almost as relevant to these modern and postmodern quests for the historical Jesus as it was to ancient efforts to multiply or reduce the number of narrative witnesses to Jesus. To the extent that the quest for the historical Jesus in its various forms claims to give us a real Jesus that stands over against the Jesus of the gospels, these claims need to be evaluated historically, just as Irenaeus evaluated the historical method of Marcion, the Valentinians, and the anti-Paulinists in his time.

40 Cf. Johnson, *Real Jesus*, 146–51.

41 Martin Kähler, *The So-Called Historical Jesus and the Historic Biblical Christ* (Fortress Texts in Modern Theology; Philadelphia: Fortress, 1964; orig. ed. 1896), 55.

42 See Carl E. Braaten, "Revelation, History, and Faith in Martin Kähler," in Kähler, *So-Called Historical Jesus*, 1–38, here at 20, and reflecting the comments of Kähler, *So-Called Historical Jesus*, 57 and 62.

43 See, e.g., Morton Smith, *Clement of Alexandria and a Secret Gospel of Mark* (Cambridge, Mass.: Harvard Univ. Press, 1973); idem, *The Secret Gospel: The Discovery and Interpretation of the Secret Gospel according to Mark* (New York: Harper & Row, 1973); idem, *Jesus the Magician* (New York: Harper & Row, 1978); John Dominic Crossan, *The Historical Jesus: The Life of a Mediterranean Jewish Peasant* (New York: HarperCollins, 1991); idem, *Jesus: A Revolutionary Biography* (New York: HarperCollins, 1994); Burton Mack, *The Lost Gospel: The Book of Q and Christian Origins* (Shaftesbury, Dorset, U.K.: Element, 1993); and Robert W. Funk, *Honest to Jesus: Jesus for a New Millennium* (New York: HarperCollins, 1996).

The Christian commitment to the truthfulness of the one gospel that lies behind the gospel's four diverse witnesses, therefore, should caution Christians against a flight from inquiry into the historical Jesus or a denial that the historical-critical method can be used to write Jesus' biography.[44] In the words of N. T. Wright's witty paraphrase of Festus, "Christianity appeals to history; to history it must go."[45] Since for Christians historical study is theologically important, they can and should meet the challenge of the Jesus quest on the battlefield of historiography, just as Irenaeus and Augustine tried to do in answer to the historiographical challenges of heretics and skeptics in their own time.

The results of this kind of historical-critical investigation tend to confirm the judgments of the early church about the historical value of the gospels. The various noncanonical texts that those involved in the Jesus quest have brought into the discussion cannot stand shoulder to shoulder with the canonical gospels in their usefulness as sources for the historical Jesus. Except in the case of Q, which itself is only known from the canonical texts, reasonable historical investigation points to the conclusion that these noncanonical texts are not equal to or more valuable than the canonical gospels in their witness to the historical Jesus and may in fact be dependent on them.[46]

As important as this kind of historical study is, however, it is also important that Christians who engage in the Jesus quest avoid the tendency of its participants to produce metanarratives that supplant the gospels. Even a robust historical account of Jesus that is theologically faithful to the gospels and takes account of faith as well as historical method as a way of knowing cannot replace the four gospels as a guide to the real Jesus. Tatian's *Diatessaron*, unlike Marcion's edition of Luke's gospel or Valentinus' *Gospel of Truth*, apparently taught nothing explicit that was theologically offensive to most Christians. The unitary form of the *Diatessaron* implied, however, that Tatian could fix a deficiency in the fourfold form of the gospel—the tensions that existed between the various accounts—and was therefore superior to that traditional form. Eventually, Christians concluded that only the four gospel narratives, each written from a particular perspective, could bear adequate witness to the one gospel of Jesus Christ.

To the extent that the study of the historical Jesus shows the plausibility of the Christian claim that "God was reconciling the world to himself" (2 Cor. 5:19) not

44 Although they have much that is wise to say about the misuse of the historical-critical method in the "life of Jesus" movement, both Kähler, *So-Called Historical Jesus*, 57–71, and Johnson, *Real Jesus*, 105–40, move in this direction, as does Étienne Nodet, *Histoire de Jésus? Nécessité et limites d'une enquête* (Lire la Bible; Paris: Cerf, 2003). For an epistemology that strikes the correct balance between the necessity of both historical plausibility and faith commitment for arriving at theological truth see, e.g., C. Stephen Evans, *The Historical Christ and the Jesus of Faith: The Incarnational Narrative as History* (Oxford: Oxford Univ. Press, 1996); Carl E. Braaten, *Mother Church: Ecclesiology and Ecumenism* (Minneapolis: Fortress, 1998), 98–116; Rainer Riesner, "Sollen wir das Neue Testament unhistorisch-unkritisch auslegen?" in *Gotteswort im Menschenwort? Zum Verstehen und Auslegen der Bibel*, ed. Sven Grosse and Jochen Walldorf (Porta-Studien 30; Marburg: Studentenmission in Deutschland, 1999), 22–41; and Alvin Plantinga, *Warranted Christian Belief* (Oxford: Oxford Univ. Press, 2000), 374–421, esp. 420–21.

45 N. T. Wright, *Jesus and the Victory of God* (Minneapolis: Fortress, 1996), 11.

46 See, e.g., Brown, "Gospel of Peter," 321–43; C. M. Tuckett, "Thomas and the Synoptics," *NovT* 30 (1988): 132–57; idem, *Nag Hammadi and the Gospel Tradition: Synoptic Tradition in the Nag Hammadi Library* (Studies in the New Testament and Its World; Edinburgh: T. & T. Clark, 1986); Meier, *Marginal Jew*, 1:112–41; and Dunn, *Jesus Remembered*, 139–72.

merely in the Christ of faith but also in the Jesus of history, it is a useful enterprise. To the extent that it participates in a quest to find the "real" Jesus behind the tendentious mask of the four gospels or seeks to replace the four gospels with even a pious harmony of them, then from the perspective of traditional Christian commitment to the gospel in fourfold form, it is misguided.[47]

THE THEOLOGICAL IMPORTANCE OF THE FOURFOLD GOSPEL

From ancient times to the present, the insistence among most Christians that the real Jesus is the Jesus described in Mark, Matthew, Luke, and John has both posed an apologetic challenge and made an important theological contribution. The challenge has arisen from the differences among the four gospels. Do these differences rise to the level of contradictions? If so, are the contradictions so serious that they impugn the historical claims of the Christian faith?

The contribution that the four gospels make arises from their antiquity, unity, and diversity. The historical claims of Christianity are so important that the very antiquity of the gospels in their present form demands their preservation as witnesses to Jesus, whatever the differences among them might be. The large measure of common theological ground among the four, and between the four and the apostolic witness contained in the rest of the New Testament, shows that their antiquity is matched by their fundamental theological unity. Their diversity attests to the richness of the gospel. It reminds Christians that the gospel is not the possession of any particular sectarian group and that the gospel is more profound than human schemes to harmonize it and manage it are able to comprehend.

For all these reasons, an account of the separate testimonies of each of the four gospels to the significance of Jesus is an important aspect of the study of New Testament theology. Since the separate testimonies of the gospels possess a unity that Christians have recognized as the one gospel of Jesus Christ at least since the gospels received their titles, it is also important to describe this common ground. In the chapters that follow, we look first at the separate theological witnesses of Mark, Matthew, Luke–Acts, and John, and then at the common theological ground that unites them.

47 It is the great merit of the analyses of Kähler, *So-Called Historical Jesus*, and Johnson, *Real Jesus*, that they see this clearly.

Chapter 3

MARK: THE DEATH OF GOD'S SON AS GOOD NEWS

Mark's gospel is a puzzling gospel. Its first line says that it tells the glad tidings about Jesus the Messiah and Son of God, but Jesus consistently silences those who identify him this way in the narrative. When Jesus calls his disciples, they immediately leave everything to follow him, but throughout the narrative they fail to comprehend his teaching. Despite Jesus' identity as the Christ and the Son of God, the leaders of the Jewish people, almost without exception, reject him, and some of them plot his death. Mark makes it clear that Jesus rose from the dead, but in a final mysterious stroke, those who first discover his resurrection flee from his tomb in fear and say nothing to anyone. Oddly, that is how Mark's gospel ends. What is "glad" about these tidings?[1]

The puzzling nature of Mark's gospel may have contributed to its neglect in the early centuries of the church. It may be one reason why Matthew and Luke both made use of Mark to write gospels of their own. While they valued Mark's witness and so included it in their own accounts, they wisely realized that Mark was too enigmatic to function as the sole available narrative about the "gospel of Jesus Christ, the Son of God."

The early church was also wise, however, not to supplant Mark's gospel with other accounts. This gospel's curious character is part of a profound theological statement about who Jesus is, what he came to do, and how God promises to restore through him people with even the hardest hearts. For Mark, Jesus is the human manifestation of the God of the Jewish Scriptures. He came to fulfill the eschatological expectations expressed in those Scriptures, particularly in Isaiah, that God would one day visit and restore his people. Jesus proclaimed the reign of God anticipated in Isaiah's prophecy, and like Isaiah's Servant of the Lord, he died an atoning death for God's people. Mark wants his readers to know that this death can effectively atone for any sin, even the sin of those who abandoned Jesus in his hour of greatest need and even the sin of those who plotted his death, for Jesus came not to call the righteous but sinners to repentance.

THE IDENTITY OF JESUS

The Importance of Jesus' Identity in Mark

Jesus' identity is a central concern of Mark's gospel. This is clear from a number of considerations. One of the most important of these is the frequency with which all sorts of people in the gospel ask, in various ways, who Jesus is.[2]

1 The puzzling character of Mark's gospel can be exaggerated, however, as happens in Frank Kermode, *The Genesis of Secrecy: On the Interpretation of Narrative* (Cambridge, Mass.: Harvard Univ. Press, 1979). See the response to Kermode in Francis Watson, *Text and Truth: Redefining Biblical Theology* (Grand Rapids: Eerdmans, 1997), 71–93.

2 Cf. Jack Dean Kingsbury, *The Christology of Mark's Gospel* (Philadelphia: Fortress, 1983), 80–85.

- "What is this?" everyone asks in 1:27, "A new teaching—and with authority! He even gives orders to evil spirits and they obey him."[3]
- "Why does this fellow talk like that?" ask the scribes in 2:7. "He's blaspheming! Who can forgive sins but God alone?"
- "Who is this?" ask Jesus' awe-struck disciples in 4:41. "Even the wind and the waves obey him!"
- "Where did this man get these things?" ask the people from Jesus' hometown in 6:2–3. "What's this wisdom that has been given him, that he even does miracles! Isn't this the carpenter? Isn't this Mary's son and the brother of James, Joseph, Judas and Simon? Aren't his sisters here with us?"
- "Who do people say I am?" Jesus himself asks of his disciples in 8:27, and again in 8:29, "Who do you say I am?"
- "Why do you call me good?" he asks a rich man in 10:18. "No one is good—except God alone."
- "Are you the Christ, the Son of the Blessed One?" the high priest asks of Jesus in 14:61.

All three major groups in the gospel—the populace, the antagonistic Jewish leaders, and the disciples—from the beginning of the gospel to its conclusion want to know who Jesus is. Mark's gospel was written, in part, to provide an answer.

Why did Mark want to answer this question? One influential proposal claims that Mark was faced with contradictory traditions about Jesus—some of which supported the notion that he had never made any supernatural claims for himself and others of which assumed that he was a glorious being from God. If so, then perhaps Mark constructed his gospel to show that Jesus was the glorious Messiah and Son of God during his lifetime, yet he silenced and hid this truth in various ways from people around him.[4] That much of his gospel nevertheless contradicts this notion with the breaking of the "messianic secret" and other public demonstrations of his identity was no deterrent to Mark—he was a "painfully naïve" author and, in any case, his theological ideas about Jesus, not a plausible story, were his main concern.[5]

Another proposal claims that Mark disagreed with a vision current in his community of Jesus as a wonder-working "divine man" who transferred his powers to his disciples. Perhaps, it is said, he refuted this vision of Jesus and his followers by reproducing it alongside a competing vision of Jesus as the Suffering Servant who called on his disciples to suffer.[6] On this theory, all the excitement over Jesus' miracle-working activity in Mark 1:1–8:29 is presented in the hope that readers will learn from Jesus himself in Mark 8:29–16:8 not to take this miracle-working activity seriously.[7]

3 *Pace* Robert H. Gundry, *Mark: A Commentary on His Apology for the Cross* (Grand Rapids: Eerdmans, 1993), 77, 83, this is a question primarily about Jesus' identity, not about the nature of his teaching. As Kingsbury, *Christology*, 82, points out, the comment after the question focuses on who Jesus is.

4 William Wrede, *The Messianic Secret* (Cambridge: James Clarke, 1971; orig. German ed. 1901). Cf. Joel Marcus, *Mark 1–8: A New Translation and Commentary* (AB 27; New York: Doubleday, 2000), 525–27, and idem, "Mark—Interpreter of Paul," *NTS* 46 (2000): 473–87, here at 478–79.

5 Wrede, *Messianic Secret*, 124–45.

6 Theodore J. Weeden, *Mark: Traditions in Conflict* (Philadelphia: Fortress, 1971).

7 Ibid., 52–69.

Neither of these understandings of the reasons for Mark's focus on Jesus' identity is plausible, nor are other explanations likely that require both Mark and his readers to be either unusually gullible or unusually sophisticated. Mark's narrative, although puzzling, is not as odd as these readings would make it.[8] He says in the first several sentences of his gospel why he concentrates on Jesus' identity. He wants to tell anyone who will listen to him that Jesus is the Messiah, the Son of God, whom the prophets Isaiah and Malachi said would come. In other words, he wants to define Jesus' identity in scriptural terms and to show that Jesus fulfills the expectations of the prophets that God would one day come to his people for deliverance and judgment.

Who, then, is Jesus? Mark tells us in the first line of his gospel that he is both Messiah and Son of God.

Jesus' Messiahship and Divine Sonship in Historical Context

Like many first-century Jews, Mark believed that the Scriptures told of a future king who would come and rule God's people Israel with justice and establish Israel's hegemony over the Gentiles who so often oppressed them. The Scriptures implied that this great king would be a descendent of David both physically and in spirit. As 2 Samuel 7:9b–16 said, God would establish David's throne forever through a son of David whom God would also consider his own son.[9] In this way, God would rescue his people from the oppression of their wicked enemies.

Psalm 2 picks up this theme, describing how God will give his king victory over all the nations who oppose him and his people. This king is described as God's son and the "anointed one" of God's people.[10] In the Hebrew text, "anointed one" translates the Hebrew word "messiah," and when this psalm was rendered into Greek, its translator put this word down as *christos*.[11] Jeremiah and Ezekiel remembered that David had been Israel's shepherd king, taken, as Psalm 78:70–71 says, from "the sheep pens ... to be the shepherd of his people Jacob," and they both envisioned a time when God would replace the wicked "shepherds," or kings, of his people with a king from David's line (Jer. 23:1–6; Ezek. 34:1–6, 15–16, 23–24).[12] Through this king, they claimed, God himself would shepherd his people. According to Jeremiah, these days would be so happy for God's people that God's deliverance of them from Egypt would pale in significance by comparison (Jer. 23:7–8).

By the first century B.C. these ideas had coalesced into a firm belief, at least among some Jews, in a coming king called both "the son of David" and "the Lord Messiah" (*Pss. Sol.* 17:21, 32).[13] According to one articulation of the vision, this king would

8 Cf. Gundry, *Mark*, 1.

9 Cf. 1 Chron. 17:8b–14; Ps. 89:3–4, 20, 35–37, 49. On the currency in the first century of expectations for a Davidic king, see Mark L. Strauss, *The Davidic Messiah in Luke–Acts: The Promise and Its Fulfillment in Lukan Christology* (JSNTSup 110; Sheffield: Sheffield Academic Press, 1995), 35–74.

10 Cf. Ps. 89:26–27.

11 Cf. Ps. 89:20, which, in the Hebrew and in the Greek translation respectively, uses the verbal forms of these nouns. Joseph A. Fitzmyer, *A Wandering Aramean: Collected Aramaic Essays* (Chico, Calif.: Scholars Press, 1979), 105, is right to say that Ps. 2 refers to a historical king of the time in which it was written, not to a future Messiah. Cf. idem, *The Gospel according to Luke I–IX* (AB 28; Garden City, N.Y.: Doubleday, 1981), 206. The question here, however, is how the psalm might have been read in Mark's time; on this see Rikki E. Watts, *Isaiah's New Exodus in Mark* (WUNT 2.88; Tübingen: J.C.B. Mohr [Paul Siebeck], 1997), 111.

12 Cf. 2 Sam. 7:8; 1 Chron. 17:7.

13 Cf. Luke 2:11. The translation "Lord Messiah" for *christos kyrios* in *Pss. Sol.* 17:32 is controversial because some scholars are

answer the prophecy of 2 Samuel 7:12 and 16 that God would raise up "offspring" (lit., in the LXX, *sperma,* "seed") for David who would establish his throne forever (*Pss. Sol.* 17:4). The Messiah would come to a nation previously purified of its sins (*Pss. Sol.* 18:5) and, when he arrived, would purge Jerusalem and the land of their Gentile oppressors (*Pss. Sol.* 17:22–25) and of any remaining unrighteous Israelites (*Pss. Sol.* 17:26–27, 32). Here too the Davidic Messiah is a shepherd of God's people:

> Faithfully and righteously shepherding the Lord's flock, he will not let any of them stumble in their pasture. (*Pss. Sol.* 17:40)

> Fortunate are those who live in those days to see the good things of the Lord. (*Pss. Sol.* 18:6; cf. 17:44).

John 7:42 indicates that speculation about the Messiah, based on 2 Samuel 7:9b–16, was common in the first century. There John tells us that when the crowds in Jerusalem for the Feast of Booths heard Jesus' teaching, a debate broke out about whether Jesus was the Messiah. Some of the debaters, ignorant of Jesus' real birthplace, weighed in against the idea with the comment, "Does not the Scripture say that the Christ will come from David's family [lit., seed] and from Bethlehem, the town where David lived?" Their reference to David's "seed" could only come from 2 Samuel 7:12.[14]

Mark's Understanding of Jesus' Messiahship and Divine Sonship

Mark wants his readers to know that Jesus fulfills many of these current messianic expectations. This understanding of Jesus' identity appears explicitly at the beginning, in the middle, and near the end of Mark's narrative. His first line, with its designation of Jesus as the Christ, the Son of God, echoes the language of Psalm 2, which calls the king both God's "christ" (2:2) and his "son" (2:7, 12).[15] In the middle of the narrative, and at the climax of the various questions about Jesus' identity, Peter confesses him to be the "Christ." Jesus, who only silences correct understandings of his identity in the narrative, indicates his acceptance of this title with a warning for his disciples not to tell anyone about him (Mark 8:29–30).[16] Near the gospel's conclusion, Jesus affirms again that this understanding of his identity is correct when the high priest asks him, "Are you the Christ, the Son of the Blessed One?" (14:61). Jesus responds with an unambiguous, "I am" (14:62).

Mark also reveals the importance of this identification for Jesus in more subtle ways. In the account of Jesus' baptism, the Spirit of God descends on Jesus, indicating that God has "anointed" him king (1:10), and immediately following this, God himself speaks from heaven to identify Jesus specifically as his Son (1:11).[17] Again,

suspicious that it reflects an anachronistic, specifically Christian, understanding of the phrase. There is, however, no textual evidence for the frequently suggested alternative translation "Lord's Messiah" (which would require *christos kyriou*). See the comments of R. B. Wright in *OTP*, 2:667–68.

14 Cf. 4 QFlor, frag. 1, col. 1, line 10, which interprets 2 Sam. 7:12–14 as a reference to "the branch of David, who will arise with the Interpreter of the law who will rise up in Zion in the last days" (Martínez, *DSST*, 136), and the comments of William L. Lane, *Hebrews 1–8* (WBC 47A; Dallas: Word, 1991), 25.

15 Cf. Ps. 89:20, 26–27.

16 Kingsbury, *Christology*, 94.

17 Cf. ibid., 60–68. Confirmation of this interpretation comes from 11Q13, which sees the "messenger" of Isa. 52:7 as "the anointed of the spirit about whom Daniel spoke" (l. 18; *DSST*, 140). Apparently the eschatological deliverer of Isa. 52 is here

Jesus is both Messiah and Son of God in the sense of 2 Samuel 7 and Psalm 2.[18] Later, just before Jesus feeds the five thousand on the shore of the Sea of Galilee, Mark tells us that Jesus surveyed the crowd and "had compassion on them, because they were like sheep without a shepherd" (Mark 6:34; cf. 14:27). Here, Jesus takes the role of the Davidic shepherd king. As Jesus' passion draws closer, the title "Son of David" emerges, first on the lips of blind Bartimaeus as he shouts to get Jesus' attention so that he might be healed (10:47–48), and then, a few paragraphs later, when the crowds greet Jesus' arrival in Jerusalem with the cry, "Blessed is the coming kingdom of our father David!" (11:10).

The passion narrative itself demonstrates, however, that Mark was not fully satisfied with casting Jesus in the role of the Davidic Messiah, and also shows us why this is true. When Pilate asks Jesus whether he is "the king of the Jews," Jesus responds hesitantly, "so you say" (*sy legeis*, 15:2). This is a way of affirming the correctness of the designation without embracing it fully.[19]

The reason for this hesitation becomes clear as the narrative proceeds. Both the Roman soldiers who carry out the crucifixion and the Jewish elders, scribes, and Sanhedrin who want Jesus crucified believe that Jesus claims to be "the king of the Jews," but they misunderstand the sense in which he fills this role. The Roman soldiers demonstrate their confusion about what it means that Jesus is the Messiah when they mock him by dressing him in a parody of royal garb (15:17–18). Clearly they think that he is claiming the power of some political office. The chief priests and scribes similarly mock Jesus as he suffers on the cross with the taunt, "He saved others ... but he can't save himself! Let this Christ, this King of Israel, come down now from the cross, that we may see and believe" (15:31–32). They too believe that if he is the Messiah, he must fulfill this role by asserting his power to his own benefit, and presumably in order to triumph over his enemies.

Mark, however, wants his readers to understand that Jesus' messiahship is both less and more than these common expectations imply. It is less, because Jesus did not intend to use his messianic identity to save himself or the "righteous" within his own people. As his teaching and healing activity demonstrated, he came for the benefit of the demon-possessed, the perpetually unclean, Gentiles, and any who understood themselves to be sinners. He came, moreover, not to be served but to serve and to give his life as a ransom for many (10:45; cf. 14:24). Ironically, had he saved himself from the cross (15:31), in that action he would have failed also to save others.[20]

understood to be one whom God will anoint with his Spirit.

18 Mark also alludes to Isa. 42:1 ("Here is my servant ... my chosen one in whom I delight ... I will put my Spirit on him") in Mark 1:10–11 ("Jesus ... saw ... the Spirit descending on him ... and a voice came from heaven ... with you I am well pleased"). This allusion anticipates his development of Jesus' identity as the Suffering Servant of Isaiah later in the gospel. See Howard Clark Kee, "The Function of Scriptural Quotations and Allusions in Mark 11–16," in *Jesus und Paulus: Festschrift für Werner Georg Kümmel zum 70. Geburtstag*, ed. E. Earle Ellis and Erich Grässer (Göttingen: Vandenhoeck & Ruprecht, 1975), 165–88, here at 177.

19 So many commentators. See, e.g., Henry Barclay Swete, *The Gospel according to St. Mark* (London: Macmillan, 1898), 347; Vincent Taylor, *The Gospel according to St. Mark* (London: Macmillan, 1957), 579; and Joachim Gnilka, *Das Evangelium nach Markus*, 2 vols., 3rd ed. (EKK 2; Zürich/Neukirchen-Vluyn: Benziger/Neukirchener, 1989), 1:300.

20 William L. Lane, *The Gospel according to Mark* (NICNT; Grand Rapids: Eerdmans, 1974), 569–70.

In the political sense, therefore, his messianic role failed to fill contemporary expectations.

In another sense, however, Jesus was far more than a righteous king and specially designated "son" of God. Mark wants his readers to understand that Jesus is the Messiah who is "Son of God" in a unique sense that goes beyond what we might expect simply by merging 2 Samuel 7 with Psalm 2.[21]

The importance of the title "Son of God" to Mark is immediately apparent from the number of times it appears in his gospel and from the crucial places at which it appears in the flow of the narrative. The designation appears nine times—in the opening line, at Jesus' baptism, three times on the lips of demon-possessed people, at the transfiguration, in the parable of the wicked tenants, as a part of the charges leveled against Jesus at his trial, and on the mouth of the Roman centurion who confesses that Jesus "truly . . . was the Son of God."[22] Like the designation "Christ," therefore, it appears at the beginning, in the middle, and near the end of the gospel.[23]

"Son of God," however, takes on greater importance than "Christ" as a title for Jesus. This becomes clear from four considerations. First, it is the title for Jesus on which both God and Jesus agree in the narrative. Twice the voice of God himself breaks into Mark's account of Jesus' ministry to say that Jesus is his Son (1:11; 9:7), and, in Jesus' telling of the parable of the wicked tenants, he uses this designation of himself (12:6).[24]

Second, the title appears at the narrative's most important point—the moment of Jesus' death. This is the point toward which everything has been moving since Jesus' prediction of his death in 2:20, and, by Jesus own testimony in 10:45, is a major reason for his coming. At precisely this most important moment, the centurion in attendance at Jesus' crucifixion confesses what God, the demons, and Jesus himself, but no other person in the narrative, has understood—that Jesus is the Son of God (15:39).[25]

Third, during the period of Jesus' teaching in the temple area just before his passion, he makes a point of showing his hearers that the Messiah is more than merely the Son of David by referring to Psalm 110:1: "The Lord said to my Lord, 'Sit at my right hand until I put your enemies under your feet'" (Mark 12:36). Jesus and his hearers take this to be a psalm of David. They also believe that the first "Lord" refers to God and that the second "Lord" refers to the Messiah, whom God will make victorious over his enemies (12:35). If all this is true, says Jesus, then in this passage David calls the Messiah his "Lord," and this means that the Messiah must be more than simply David's descendent (12:37). Within the context of Mark's gospel, the solution to this mystery, as 1:1 states and 1:10–11 and 14:61 imply, is that Jesus is not only the Davidic Messiah but also, and more importantly, the Son of God.[26]

---

21 Cf. Rudolf Schnackenburg, *Jesus in the Gospels: A Biblical Christology* (Louisville: Westminster John Knox, 1995), 48.

22 See 1:1, 11, 24; 3:11; 5:7; 9:7; 12:6; 14:61; 15:39. At 1:24, the man with the unclean spirit calls Jesus "the Holy One of God," but the title is synonymous with "the Son of God." On this see Kingsbury, *Christology*, 160 n. 2, and Lane, *Mark*, 74.

23 Gnilka, *Markus*, 1:60.

24 Cf. G. H. Boobyer, "The Secrecy Motif in St. Mark's Gospel," *NTS* 6 (1959–60): 225–35, here at 228, and Kingsbury, *Christology*, 56, 65–68.

25 Kingsbury, *Christology*, 132–33, 152–53.

26 Ibid., 108–14.

Fourth, the primary importance of this title for Jesus is visible in the questions the high priest and Pilate ask at his two trials. When the high priest asks Jesus whether he is the Christ, the Son of the Blessed One, he unambiguously says, "I am" (*egō eimi*, 14:61). But when Pilate asks Jesus whether he is "the king of the Jews," with no reference to his divine sonship, Jesus responds with reserve, "so you say" (*sy legeis*, 15:2). Jesus is the Messiah, but in a special sense that the phrase "Son of God" helps to define.[27]

The term "Son of God," however, is itself subject to a variety of meanings. Not only did Mark's Scriptures recognize the special relationship between God and his appointed monarch in Jewish tradition, but they called all Israel God's "firstborn son" (Ex. 4:22–23; Hos. 11:1) and sometimes referred to angelic beings as "sons of God" (e.g., Gen. 6:2, 4; Job 1:6; 38:7; Dan. 3:25).[28] Mark was probably also aware that in Greek tradition, Zeus was considered to be "father of both men and gods" (*Iliad* 1.544; cf. Epictetus, *Diatr.* 3.24.14–16) and that in Roman tradition, the emperor could be described as the "son of a god."[29]

Perhaps because of this potential ambiguity, Mark wanted his readers to know that Jesus was "the Son of God" in a unique sense. Thus, when God announces that Jesus is his Son in 1:11 and 9:7, Mark's Greek reveals the unique nature of his sonship. In each instance, Mark uses the Greek adjective *agapētos* ("only beloved") in what Greek grammarians call the "second attributive position." An adjective in this position receives particular stress. In both 1:11 and 9:7, therefore, God says that Jesus is "my son—the uniquely beloved one."[30] The high priest at Jesus' trial seems to understand the unusual connotations of Jesus' claim to divine sonship in the parable of the wicked tenants (12:6). Looking for a conviction, he asks Jesus the apparently astounding question, "Are you the Christ, the Son of the Blessed One?" (14:61).

The unique nature of Jesus' relationship to God is evident throughout Mark's narrative. When Jesus forgives the sins of the paralytic in 2:5, the scribes think disapprovingly, "Who can forgive sins but God alone?" Although the question is rhetorical—the scribes intend it to be a statement of the obvious truth that Jesus has usurped a divine prerogative—it prompts the Christian reader to think of Jesus as acting in the way God acts. Mark has led us to think of Jesus as God. This impression is confirmed in 4:41 when, after stilling the raging storm, the disciples ask, "Who is this that even the wind and the waves obey him?" The disciples know that the stilling of raging storms is the business of Yahweh (Ps. 65:7; 89:9; 107:28–30), and their question implies the unthinkable—that when they are in the presence of Jesus, they are in the presence of God himself.[31]

27 Cf. ibid., 125–26, 151–52.

28 It is likely that these understandings of the phrase were current in Mark's time. The author of 4Q246 (first century B.C.) refers to a powerful king as the "son of God" and "son of the Most High God," and the authors of Pss. Sol. 18:4 (first century B.C.) and 4 Ezra 6:58 (first century A.D.) speak of Israel as God's "firstborn" and "only begotten" son. In 11Q13 (first century B.C.), the author refers to heavenly beings as "sons of God" (l. 14).

29 For example, an inscription from Magnesia in Asia Minor, created shortly before Nero became emperor, calls him the "son of the greatest of the gods." See Adolf Deissmann, *Light from the Ancient East: The New Testament Illustrated by Recently Discovered Texts of the Graeco-Roman World* (London: Hodder & Stoughton, 1923), 346–48; W. v. Martitz, "υἱός (κτλ)," *TDNT*, 8:334–340; and Martin Hengel, *The Son of God: The Origin of Christology and the History of Jewish–Hellenistic Religion* (Philadelphia: Fortress, 1976), 21–24, 30.

30 See *BDAG*, 7, and Daniel B. Wallace, *GGBB*, 306. When Jesus refers to himself as God's Son in 12:6, he does not use this construction, perhaps because the title appears within the context of a story.

31 Cf. Gnilka, *Markus*, 1:196. Sverre Aalen, *Guds Sønn og Guds Rike: Nytestamentlige Studier* (Oslo: Universitetsforlaget, 1973), 270–88, argues that Jesus' actions in the gospels often imitate the

The same implication arises from Jesus' question to the rich man. Jesus asks, "Why do you call me good? No one is good—except God alone" (10:18). We know by this time in the narrative that Jesus is good; as the people of the Decapolis have said, "He has done everything well" (7:37). But if Jesus is good and no one is good but God alone, then this implies that Jesus is God.[32]

This does not mean that Mark somehow thought either that God and his Son were identical persons or that they were two separate gods. The most important commandment in the Mosaic law for Jesus and for Mark was, "the Lord our God, the Lord is one," which means that "there is no other but him" (Mark 12:29, 32). Moreover, Jesus is subordinate to and submissive to his Father, who alone knows the time of the end (13:32) and whose purpose includes the suffering and death of his Son (14:36).[33] Still, for Mark, where Jesus was present, God was present, and Mark wanted his readers to feel the impact of this astounding claim.

THE MISSION OF JESUS

If it is true that where Jesus was present, God was present, then what had God, in Jesus, come to do? Mark punctuates his narrative with several explicit references to the reasons for Jesus' coming. He "came" to destroy the power of demons (1:24), to preach the good news that God's kingdom was near (1:38; cf. 1:14–15), to call sinners and not "the righteous" (2:17), and to die as a ransom "for many" (10:45).[34] These four statements of purpose comprehend the two principal purposes for Jesus' coming in Mark's gospel—to bring in the long-awaited reign of God and to die for sinners.

Jesus Proclaims and Establishes the Reign of God

Mark shows in a number of ways, both overt and subtle, that he believed Jesus fulfilled the promises in Isaiah that God would restore the fortunes of his people and reign over them in righteousness. Mark begins his gospel with a collage of biblical quotations from Exodus 23:20, Malachi 3:1, and Isaiah 40:3, but Mark attributes the entire collection to Isaiah. In this way, he alerts the reader to the importance of Isaiah's depiction of God's return of his people from exile to Jerusalem for understanding the significance of the events that he is about to narrate. John the Baptist will fulfill the role of Elijah in Malachi 4:5 and will prepare the way for God to lead his people, in a new exodus, out of their exile into a restored Jerusalem.[35] As Isaiah 40:1–5 puts it:

actions of God in the Old Testament. Mark's gospel figures largely in Aalen's case. I am grateful to Dr. Sigurd Grindheim for bringing this book to my attention and providing me both with a copy of the relevant portion and an English summary of it.

32 *Pace* Schnackenburg, *Jesus in the Gospels*, 46.

33 Cf. 10:40, where Jesus indicates that the authority to assign places of honor at the time of his glorification belongs not to him but to God the Father.

34 Following, e.g., C. E. B. Cranfield, *The Gospel according to Saint Mark* (CGTC; Cambridge: Cambridge Univ. Press, 1959), 89–90, 106, and Marcus, *Mark 1–8*, 203–4, rather than, e.g., Robert A. Guelich, *Mark 1–8:26* (WBC 34A; Dallas: Word, 1989), 70, and Gundry, *Mark*, 100.

35 Watts, *Isaiah's New Exodus*, 53–90; cf. Joel Marcus, *The Way of the Lord: Christological Exegesis of the Old Testament in the Gospel of Mark* (Louisville: Westminster John Knox, 1992), 12–47, and Martin Hengel, *The Four Gospels and the One Gospel of Jesus Christ* (Harrisburg, Pa.: Trinity Press International, 2000), 158–61.

Comfort, comfort my people,
says your God.
Speak tenderly to Jerusalem,
and proclaim to her
that her hard service has been completed,
that her sin has been paid for,
that she has received from the LORD's hand
double for all her sins.
A voice of one calling:
"In the desert prepare
the way for the LORD;
make straight in the wilderness
a highway for our God.
Every valley shall be raised up,
every mountain and hill made low;
the rough ground shall become level,
the rugged places a plain.
And the glory of the LORD will be revealed,
and all people[36] will see it together."

In Jesus, God was accomplishing this eschatological deliverance of his people. Mark shows this in many ways. At Jesus' baptism God rends the heavens and comes down as the lament in Isaiah 64:1 urges him to do (Mark 1:10); when he does this, he recognizes Jesus as his Son in words that recall the description in Isaiah 42:1 of God's Servant who would deliver Israel: "Here is my servant, whom I uphold, my chosen one in whom I delight; I will put my Spirit on him and he will bring justice to the nations" (cf. Mark 1:11).[37]

Jesus then immediately spends forty days in the desert (1:13)—the place where, according to Isaiah 40, God will appear to restore his people—and, as if to put into action the "new exodus" that Isaiah prophesied, he emerges from the desert, like the messenger of Isaiah 52:7 (cf. 62:1), to bring good news from God (Mark 1:14).[38]

Mark summarizes the "good news" (*euangelion*) that Jesus "came forth" to preach (1:38) in terms of the arrival or nearness of "the kingdom [*basileia*] of God" (1:15). Precisely what this phrase means and the sense in which the kingdom "is near" (*ēngiken*) have been the subjects of a virtual library of scholarly discussion.[39] In light of the explicit quotation from Isaiah with which Mark begins his gospel and the clear allusions to Isaiah throughout his gospel's prologue, however, there can be little doubt that he understood Jesus' proclamation of the kingdom of God in Isaianic terms.

36 Throughout this book, I will be making minor modifications to the NIV text, using such words as "people" instead of the NIV's "mankind." For the most part, these will be based on the NRSV.

37 Watts, *Isaiah's New Exodus*, 102–18.

38 On the Isaianic significance of Jesus' temptation in the desert, see Guelich, *Mark 1–8:26*, 39–40.

39 See the survey in G. R. Beasley-Murray, *Jesus and the Kingdom of God* (Grand Rapids: Eerdmans, 1986), 71–75.

When Isaiah spoke of God's restoration of his people, he sometimes used language similar to the language Mark uses to summarize Jesus' preaching.[40] Isaiah 52:7–10 summarizes the deliverance of God's people from the Babylonians, which has been the prophet's focus since 40:1. In 52:7 he depicts a messenger who announces the "good news" (LXX, *euangelizomenou*) that Zion's God "reigns" (LXX, *basileusei*).[41] In Isaiah, God can also speak of the imminent restoration of his people as "bringing my righteousness near" (LXX, *ēngisa*; Isa. 46:13; cf. 51:5; 56:1). Mark seems to have understood Jesus' proclamation of the kingdom's nearness in these terms. Jesus announced that the time of waiting for Isaiah's prophesied restoration had been completed—God's reign had drawn near in Jesus' preaching.[42]

It was not enough for Jesus merely to "preach" this good news, however; his mission was also to put this long-expected restoration into effect. Therefore, like God in Isaiah 40–66, whose arm is bared as a warrior's to do battle against the enemies of his people (Isa. 40:10; 42:13–17; 49:24–26; 51:9–11; 52:10) and to lead them along "the way" out of exile and back to Jerusalem (Isa. 35:8–10; 40:3; 42:16; 43:16, 19; 49:9, 11; 57:14), Jesus conquers the demons in 1:16–8:26 and then in 8:27–11:1 leads his disciples along "the way" to Jerusalem.[43] Similarly, just as God in Isaiah 35:5–10 restores sight to the blind, hearing to the deaf, and strength to the lame prior to the jubilant return of Israel to Zion along the "Way of Holiness," Jesus gives sight to the blind (8:22–26; 10:46–52), hearing to the deaf (Mark 7:31–37; 9:13–29), and strength to the lame (2:1–12) prior to and during his journey with his followers along the "way" to Jerusalem.[44]

For Mark, therefore, Jesus' proclamation of the kingdom of God and his establishment of this reign through exorcisms, healings, and feedings were all signs that through Jesus, God had visited his people to effect the restoration Isaiah had promised.

Jesus Dies for Sinners

Although it is an exaggeration to say that Mark's gospel is a passion narrative with a long introduction, no sensitive reader of Mark's gospel can miss the emphasis that Mark places on the death of Jesus.[45] Already in 1:14, the imprisonment of John the Baptist casts a shadow over the divine Son whom he has baptized. In 2:7, the scribes believe that Jesus has blasphemed God—a capital crime (Lev. 2:16). By 3:6, the Pharisees and the Herodians begin to plot Jesus' death. And like the tolling of a bell, in 8:31, 9:31, and 10:33–34 Jesus sounds a clear and repetitive warning of his impending death.

40 Watts, *Isaiah's New Exodus*, 96–102.

41 Although Mark uses nouns where the LXX uses verbs, the conceptual similarity between Mark 1:14–15 and Isa. 52:7 is still clear.

42 Thoughts of Isaiah's prophesied restoration were apparently on the minds of others during Mark's era also. See, e.g., Pss. Sol. 11:1, produced during the first century B.C.

43 Marcus, *Way*, 29–33. The significance of "the way" that Jesus clears for God's restoring purposes is evident from 1:3; 8:27; 9:33–34; 10:17, 32, 46, 52. On Mark's use of the image of God as warrior in Isaiah, see Kee, "Function of Scriptural Quotations," 184.

44 Watts, *Isaiah's New Exodus*, 137–82.

45 Martin Kähler, *The So-Called Historical Jesus and the Historic Biblical Christ* (Fortress Texts in Modern Theology; Philadelphia: Fortress, 1964), 80 n. 11, "To state the matter somewhat provocatively, one could call the Gospels passion narratives with extended introductions."

Finally, it happens: Jesus is arrested, tried, convicted, and executed. Mark underlines the details of his suffering. In Gethsemane, as he ponders his fate, he is "deeply distressed and troubled" (14:33). After Jesus' arrest, Mark wants his readers to appreciate that Jesus was abandoned by every one of his followers (14:50). One was so desperate to get away from him that he left his clothes in the grasp of Jesus' enemies and fled naked (14:51). Jesus' trial was a sham of false testimony (14:57), and in the end Jesus was convicted of making a false and therefore blasphemous claim about his relationship with God—a claim that was in fact true (14:61–64). Peter, who alone among his disciples had correctly confessed him to be "the Christ" (8:29), denied in the strongest possible terms that he knew anything at all about "that Nazarene, Jesus" (14:68, 70–71).

The Roman governor, who knew Jesus had committed no crime (14:14), nevertheless handed him over for flogging and crucifixion at the same time that he released from custody an insurrectionist and murderer (15:7, 15). Jesus was repeatedly mocked, beaten, and spat upon (14:65; 15:16–20). Finally, he was crucified between two thieves and died amid the jeers of his enemies (15:29–32). His last articulate words came from Psalm 22:1, "My God, my God, why have you forsaken me?" (Mark 15:34)—an appropriate reminiscence, since he had experienced the horrors of which this Psalm spoke (Ps. 22:6–8, 16, 18).

Mark's focus on Jesus' death is also clear from the brevity of the attention he gives to the resurrection (16:1–8).[46] The resurrection is important for Mark (8:31; 9:9, 31; 10:34; 16:6), but he recounts no resurrection appearances, and even in the one verse that he devotes to the resurrection (16:6), the focus is somehow still on the crucifixion when the young man at the tomb describes Jesus as "the crucified one," using the emphatic perfect tense (*estaurōmenon*).[47] This is the equivalent in modern English of putting the word "crucified" in italics.[48]

As if to prevent anyone from missing the paradox contained in this point, Mark brings his account of Jesus' suffering to a climax in the centurion's confession of Jesus' identity at the moment of his death (15:39). Here, for the first time in the narrative, someone finally confesses what the reader has known, what God himself has confirmed, and what the demonic world has fearfully recognized, but what everyone else has either failed to perceive or completely rejected—that Jesus was the Son of God.[49] The centurion utters this confession not, as is sometimes said, because Jesus died on the cross and Mark wanted somehow to define his sonship in terms of suffering, but, as Mark's Greek implies, because he saw how Jesus breathed his last—with a "great shout" (15:37).[50]

46 *Pace* Karl Kertelge, "The Epiphany of Jesus in the Gospel (Mark)," in *The Interpretation of Mark*, ed. William R. Telford, 2nd ed. (Studies in New Testament Interpretation; Edinburgh: T. & T. Clark, 1995), 105–23, here at 115–21. Kertelge believes that the resurrection shines back through the entire gospel and is evident particularly in Jesus' miracles.

47 Since it is a transitive verb, the term *estaurōmenon* is probably an "extensive perfect," which means that although the emphasis lies on the completed action, the verb also refers to the continuing condition that results from this completed action. See Daniel B. Wallace *GGBB*, 577, and Marcus, "Mark—Interpreter of Paul," 483.

48 See the comments of Stanley Porter, *Idioms of the Greek New Testament* (Biblical Languages: Greek Series, 2; Sheffield: Sheffield Academic Press, 1992), 22, on the "stative aspect" (covering the perfect and pluperfect tenses) as the "most heavily weighted" verbal aspect.

49 On this point, see Kingsbury, *Christology*, 132–33, 152–53.

50 For examples of the common view that Jesus' death somehow defines his divine sonship, see C. Clifton Black, "Christ Crucified in Paul and in Mark: Reflections on an Intracanonical Conversation," in *Theology and Ethics in Paul and His Interpreters: Essays in Honor of Victor Paul Furnish*, ed. Eugene H. Lovering and

In other words, as the great shout showed, while Jesus hung on the cross, he had lost nothing of the immense power that he had exhibited throughout Mark's narrative.[51] In his dying moment, this power was so clear that someone finally recognized who he was. The contrast could hardly be starker: Jesus is the powerful Son of God, who could have easily come down from the cross both to save himself and to shame his accusers, but he refused to use his divine sonship for his own advantage.

This bold contrast forcefully raises the question "why": Why did "Christ, the Son of God" (1:1) submit to such a shameful death? Mark gives his readers two clear reasons. First, Jesus had to die because he was the Son of Man, and the Scriptures indicated that the Son of Man must suffer. Second, Jesus submitted to death in order to serve as a vicarious sacrifice for the sins of God's people, and specifically as the Suffering Servant of Isaiah's prophecy.

Jesus Dies as the Son of Man

In Mark's narrative, Jesus says three times that he, as the Son of Man, must suffer in order to fulfill the Scriptures.[52] In 8:31, after Peter has confessed him to be the Christ, Mark tells us that Jesus taught his disciples, "The Son of Man must suffer many things and be rejected by the elders, chief priests and teachers of the law, and that he must be killed and after three days rise again." If we want to know why these things "must" (*dei*) happen, the answer comes a few paragraphs later when Jesus tells Peter, James, and John that "it is written that the Son of Man must [*dei*] suffer much and be rejected" (9:12), and again during Jesus' Passover meal with his disciples when he gives them the disturbing news that one of them will betray him "because [*hoti*] the Son of Man will go just as it is written about him" (14:21; cf. 14:49). These things "must" happen because Scripture says that they must happen.[53]

But where does Scripture indicate that someone called "the Son of Man" must suffer? In two places, Mark shows his readers exactly which passage of Scripture he has in mind. In 13:26 Jesus tells his disciples that at an unknown future day and hour the Son of Man will come in "clouds with great power and glory," and in 14:62 he tells the high priest at his Jewish trial that the Son of Man will come "on the clouds of heaven." This can only refer to Daniel 7, which speaks of "one like a son of man" who comes "with the clouds of heaven" and receives "authority, glory and sovereign power" from God (Dan. 7:13–14).[54]

Jerry L. Sumney (Nashville: Abingdon, 1996), 184–206, here at 200 n. 57; Marcus, "Mark—Interpreter of Paul," 480; and Gnilka, *Markus*, 2:324. For the understanding of 15:39 adopted here, see Swete, *Mark*, 366; Taylor, *Mark*, 597; and especially Gundry, *Mark*, 950, 974, although without endorsing his view that the cry of Jesus split the temple veil.

51 Scholars sometimes claim that the "great shout" implies that Jesus was possessed by a demon as he hung on the cross since the only uses of the phrase "great shout" (*phōnē megalē*) other than 15:34 and 37 appear in connection with demoniacs (1:26; 5:7). See, e.g., Marcus, "Mark—Interpreter of Paul," 486. It is difficult to know, however, why a demon would prompt Jesus to quote Scripture "with a great shout," as happens in 15:34. See Robert H. Gundry, "A Response to Joel Marcus's 'Mark and Paul,'" a paper given at the 1998 meeting of the Studiorum Novi Testamenti Societas in Copenhagen, Denmark, 5 n. 2.

52 In Mark, the title "Son of Man" speaks not so much of Jesus' identity as of the nature of his mission—he will act on earth with authority, suffer, and be vindicated. On this, see Kingsbury, *Christology*, 157–73. Cf. Douglas R. A. Hare, *The Son of Man Tradition* (Minneapolis: Fortress, 1990), 194, 210–11.

53 Cf. Kee, "Function of Scriptural Quotations," 174–75, 182.

54 "The Son of Man" also appears in *4 Ezra* 13 and in *1 Enoch* 46–48, 62–71, which are apparently dependent on Dan. 7. The description of the figure in Mark is closer to Dan. 7:13 in its details than to the portrait of the Son of Man in either of these texts. On this, see Marcus, *Way*, 164–65. The parallel between Dan. 7:13 and Mark 13:26 and 14:62 is not exact: In Daniel the Son of Man

Daniel 7 is the record of a dream in which Daniel saw four beasts, the first three of which resembled different, recognizable animals—a lion, a bear, and a leopard. The final beast, however, was so terrifying that it resembled no known animal. It had large iron teeth, ten horns, and among the ten horns, one "had eyes like the eyes of a man and a mouth that spoke boastfully" (7:8). After the emergence of this final beast, God's eschatological court was convened, and "the Ancient of Days" sat down to render judgment. As a result of this judgment, the fourth beast "was slain and its body destroyed and thrown into the blazing fire" (7:9–11). At this point "the one like a son of man" entered Daniel's dream. He rode from earth to heaven on the clouds and approached "the Ancient of Days" as he sat in the seat of judgment (7:13). Unlike the terrifying fourth beast who was condemned, the "son of man" was vindicated:

> He was given authority, glory and sovereign power; all peoples, nations and human beings of every language worshiped him. His dominion is an everlasting dominion that will not pass away, and his kingdom is one that will never be destroyed. (Dan. 7:14)

When the dream is interpreted, the four beasts turn out to be Gentile nations, and the beast with the boastful horn is a nation that persecutes the people of God—"waging war against the saints and defeating them" (Dan. 7:21), speaking against "the Most High," oppressing his people, and trying to change their sacred calendar and laws (7:25). Although God hands "the saints" over to this oppressor for a time (7:25), eventually God's court convenes, and he forever destroys the power of the oppressor (7:26). After that,

> the sovereignty, power and greatness of the kingdoms under the whole heaven will be handed over to the saints, the people of the Most High. His kingdom will be an everlasting kingdom, and all rulers will worship and obey him. (Dan. 7:27; cf. 7:18)

In Daniel, therefore, the four beasts and "one like a son of man" stand for nations. Just as God gave human beings authority over the beasts (Gen. 1:28; 2:19–20), so the "son of man," a symbol for God's people, should properly have authority over the nations, because they are the saints of the Most High.[55] Before that authority is conferred, however, they must pass through a period of suffering at the hands of a particularly fierce Gentile oppressor. At the end of that period, "the one like a son of man" will be vindicated by the Ancient of Days and will assume his rightful hegemony over the nations in a "kingdom that will never be destroyed."

The vision and its interpretation, therefore, follow a threefold pattern. The "one like a son of man" is (1) characterized by authority that is (2) hidden for a time by the oppression of God's enemies but (3) is eventually vindicated by God.

---

travels on the clouds up to heaven, whereas in Mark, he comes to earth "in" (*en*) or "with" (*meta*) the clouds.

55 Morna D. Hooker, *The Son of Man in Mark* (Montreal: McGill Univ. Press, 1967), 18–20, 27. On the "humanity" of the Son of Man as an indication of authority, see John E. Goldingay, *Daniel* (WBC 30; Dallas: Word, 1989), 168.

When Mark applies the term "Son of Man" to Jesus, he implies that Jesus' ministry followed this threefold pattern.[56] Mark uses the phrase "Son of Man" to refer to Jesus fourteen times. He uses it twice at the beginning of his gospel to indicate Jesus' authority to take the role of God in forgiving sins and deciding how the Sabbath ought to be observed (2:10, 28).[57] This authority is soundly rejected by Jesus' enemies, however, as the response of the scribes and Pharisees to Jesus' claims of authority in both instances reveals.[58] This response reaches its terrible climax in Jesus' passion, and Jesus forewarns his disciples of his suffering many times, referring to himself each time as "the Son of Man" (8:31; 9:12, 31; 10:33, 45; 14:21, 41). Three times Jesus speaks of his glorious coming as the coming of "the Son of Man" in the company of God (8:38; 13:26; 14:62). The last of these uses occurs during Jesus' trial before the hostile Jewish authorities and provides an implicit declaration of his future vindication by God.

Mark probably also intends for his readers to see another correlation between Jesus and the "one like a son of man" in Daniel 7.[59] In Daniel, this figure has both an individual and a corporate character. When we first meet him, he is an individual who receives the worship of all peoples, nations, and human beings (7:13–14), but then in the dream's interpretation he becomes "the saints, the people of the Most High" (7:18, 22, 25, 27). The interplay between the corporate and the individual is especially visible in 7:27, where the interpretation of the figure "like a son of man" is given. In the first half of the verse, this figure is "the people of the saints of the Most High," just as in 7:18, but in the second half of the verse this people seems to be conceived as an individual to whom all nations will give obedience:

> Then the sovereignty, power and greatness of the kingdoms under the whole heaven will be handed over to the saints, the people of the Most High. His kingdom will be an everlasting kingdom, and all rulers will worship and obey him. (Dan. 7:27)[60]

In the same way, both a corporate and an individual dimension emerges from Jesus' ministry as Mark depicts it. When he comes "in his Father's glory with the holy angels" and "in the clouds with great power," he will come as a judge (Mark 8:38) and as the one who gathers "his elect from the four winds" (13:27).[61] The criterion for judgment on that day will be whether one has been willing to deny one's self and follow Jesus to the cross (8:34–37). Just as Jesus, as the Son of Man, "must suffer many things" and then rise from the dead (8:31–33a), so his followers will experience vindication only if they are faithful to follow him in suffering (8:33b–38).[62] His suffering and vindication and their suffering and vindication are therefore intertwined.

---

56 Hooker, *Son of Man*, 180–82, 192. Cf. Schnackenburg, *Jesus in the Gospels*, 52–58, 60.

57 Hooker, *Son of Man*, 90, 99. Cf. Kingsbury, *Christology*, 169. *Pace* Hare, *Son of Man Tradition*, 189–90, who concludes that the authority of which Mark speaks in 2:10 does not attach to the title "Son of Man." This conclusion is puzzling, since the "son of man" in Dan. 7:13–14 is given authority, just as the "Son of Man" is given authority here.

58 Hooker, *Son of Man*, 80, 99.

59 Ibid., 181–82.

60 The antecedent of "his" is "people," not "the Most High." See Edward J. Young, *The Prophecy of Daniel: An Introduction and Commentary* (Grand Rapids: Eerdmans, 1949), 162.

61 On the connotations of eschatological judgment contained in the word "to be ashamed" (*epaischynesthai*) in 8:38, see Marcus, *Way*, 166.

62 Ibid., 171.

To summarize, as the Son of Man, Jesus followed the pattern laid out for the "one like a son of man" in Daniel 7:13. He had authority; he suffered at the hands of his enemies; and he was vindicated and exalted by God. As the Son of Man he also called on his followers to follow him in this pattern of life. (1) They were God's chosen people and possessed the authority God gave to his people. (2) Now they must suffer faithfully in their commitment to Jesus. (3) When God brings his purposes to an end and executes judgment on all peoples, they will be vindicated and restored to their rightful place of authority.

Jesus Dies as Isaiah's Suffering Servant

The picture sketched above of Jesus' death is far from complete. In Mark's view Jesus did not merely lead his followers through the pain of suffering to final vindication at the judgment. He died as an atoning sacrifice for those who had failed to follow God faithfully. Almost as if to say that the normal Son of Man pattern in Daniel 7 cannot tell the whole story of Jesus' death, Mark records a saying of Jesus in which Jesus summarizes his mission as Son of Man by describing the atoning character of his death: ". . . the Son of Man did not come to be served, but to serve, and to give his life as a ransom for many [*anti pollōn*]" (Mark 10:45).

Here the "Son of Man" stands apart from his followers, doing something for them that they cannot do for themselves.[63] Similarly, at the end of the Passover meal with his disciples, Jesus lifts the cup of wine and says, "This is my blood of the covenant, which is poured out for many [*hyper pollōn*]" (14:24).

If we give the preposition *anti* in 10:45 its proper meaning and interpret the more ambiguous *hyper* in 14:24 in light of it, then Jesus died "as a ransom *in the place of* many," and in this sense he poured out his blood "*for* many."[64] For Mark, then, Jesus willingly submitted to suffering and death as an atoning sacrifice for the transgressions of God's people. In this role Jesus suffered not as the Son of Man but as the Suffering Servant of Isaiah's third and fourth "Servant Songs."[65] Like Jesus in Mark 10:45 and 14:24, Isaiah's Servant bears the sins of "many" by dying for them. The correspondence is more conceptual than verbal, but the conceptual correspondence is striking:[66]

63 Cf. Schnackenburg, *Jesus in the Gospels*, 58–59, who observes that although Jesus presents himself in 10:45 as a model of self-sacrifice for the disciples to follow, the saving significance of Jesus' death for others "is reserved for Jesus" alone.

64 See the definitive argument for this understanding of *anti* in 10:45 in Daniel B. Wallace, *GGBB*, 365–67.

65 The "Servant Songs" were first isolated by Bernhard Duhm. See his *Das Buch Jesaia*, 4th ed. (Göttingen: Vandenhoeck & Ruprecht, 1922; orig ed. 1892), 311, as passages that "attract notice above all through their style, through their tranquil speech, and through the symmetry of their lines and stanzas." The exact boundaries of the Servant Songs, and even whether it is appropriate to separate these references to the Servant from other Servant passages, are matters of scholarly dispute. The traditional terminology is retained here for convenience and follows the numbering of Duhm: (1) 42:1–4 [1–9]; (2) 49:1–6 [1–13]; (3) 50:4–9 [1–11]; and (4) 52:13–53:12. The suffering of the Servant appears most clearly in the third and fourth Songs.

66 The closest correspondences appear in italics in the table (on the next page).

Isa. 53:11b–12	Mark 10:45	Mark 14:24
By his knowledge my righteous servant will justify *many*, and he will *bear their iniquities*. Therefore I will give him a portion among the great ... because he *poured out his life* unto death, and was numbered with the transgressors. For he *bore the sins of many*, and made intercession for the transgressors.	For even the Son of Man did not come to be served, but to serve, and to give his life as a ransom *for many*.	This is my blood of the covenant, which is poured out *for many*.

Since Mark has already quietly identified Jesus with Isaiah's Servant at his baptism, it seems reasonable to see in Mark 10:45 and 14:24 an understanding of Jesus' death in light of the Servant's vicarious suffering. That we are on the right track here becomes clear as Mark's narrative of Jesus' passion proceeds.[67]

Just as the Servant offered his back to those who beat him and did not hide his face "from mocking and spitting" (Isa. 50:6), so Mark tells us that after the Sanhedrin condemned Jesus to death, "some began to spit at him; they blindfolded him, struck him with their fists, and said, 'Prophesy!' And the guards took him and beat him" (Mark 14:65). The Roman soldiers charged with carrying out Jesus' crucifixion similarly mocked him, beat him, and spat on him (15:17–19). Passers-by "hurled insults at him" (15:29).

In the fourth Servant Song, the Servant "did not open his mouth" despite his oppression and affliction but was silent, "as a sheep before her shearers is silent" (Isa. 53:7). In the same way, when false charges were brought against Jesus at both his Jewish and his Roman trial, Mark emphasizes that he remained silent (Mark 14:60–61; 15:3–5).[68]

These correlations make it likely that Mark also saw parallels between the vicarious nature of the Servant's suffering and the vicarious nature of Jesus' death. The Servant himself was blameless (Isa. 53:9), and yet "he poured out his life unto death,

67 It is true, as Kee ("Function of Scriptural Quotations," 174) observes, that Mark does not explicitly develop a view of the atonement based on Isa. 53, but Kee's unwillingness to say that Mark intended to make the connection between Jesus' death and the fourth Servant Song fails to give sufficient weight to the power of allusion in Mark's narrative. Mark is not writing an abstract treatise on the doctrine of the atonement but the story of Jesus' death, and in a story, just as in a poem, allusion to rather than explicit exegesis of well-known, traditional texts is appropriate. See John Hollander, *The Figure of Echo: A Mode of Allusion in Milton and After* (Berkeley: Univ. of California Press, 1981), and Richard B. Hays, *Echoes of Scripture in the Letters of Paul* (New Haven, Conn.: Yale Univ. Press, 1989), 14–21. The same objection applies to the argument of Morna Hooker, *Jesus and the Servant* (London: SPCK, 1959), which is primarily terminological.

68 Cf. Watts, *Isaiah's New Exodus*, 349–65, who mounts a persuasive counter-argument to Hooker's case in *Jesus and the Servant* that Mark's passion narrative does not cast Jesus as Isaiah's Suffering Servant.

and was numbered among the transgressors." He did not, therefore, suffer for his own sins, but the Lord made "his life a guilt offering" (53:10) through which he "bore the sins of many" (53:12). He "took up our infirmities and carried our sorrows" (53:4). He "was pierced for our transgressions" and "crushed for our iniquities" (53:5). "The LORD has laid on him the iniquity of us all" (53:6). He was stricken "for the transgression of [the Servant's] people" (53:8).[69] As a result of his vicarious punishment, the Servant's people have "peace" (53:5), and because he will bear their iniquities, the Servant "will justify many" (53:11).

In the same way, Mark wants us to know that Jesus was blameless in the affair of his arrest, trial, and death. Although many witnessed against him, they testified falsely (Mark 14:56–57). Pilate himself understood that "it was out of envy that the chief priests had handed Jesus over to him" (15:10). When the crowds shout that Jesus should be crucified, Pilate affirms Jesus' innocence by asking, "Why? What crime has he committed?" (15:14). This means that his death, like the death of the Suffering Servant, was a vicarious death (as 10:45 and 14:24 imply). Jesus' enemies unknowingly acknowledge this when they taunt him with the statement, "He saved others ... but he can't save himself!" (15:31). By refusing to exercise his power as the Son of God to "save himself" and instead giving his life "as a ransom in the place of many," Jesus was "saving others."[70] He was therefore fulfilling the role of Isaiah's Suffering Servant.

This understanding of the effect of Jesus' death helps us to see the sense in which Jesus did "not come to call the righteous, but sinners" (2:17). This statement appears in Mark's narrative as the climax to Mark's account of Jesus' invitation to Levi, a tax collector, to follow him. After Levi left his tax office to follow Jesus, Jesus ate a meal at his house with a large group of "tax collectors and sinners." Aware of this, some scribes who belonged to the party of the Pharisees criticized Jesus to his disciples for eating with such people (2:13–16). Jesus responded this way: "It is not the healthy who need a doctor, but the sick. I have not come to call the righteous, but sinners" (2:17).

The tax collectors and sinners described here were not merely, as has often been thought, untutored "people of the land" who failed to conform to the strict purity observances of the Pharisees.[71] Legal impurity, even in the Pharisees' eyes, involved people in "sin" only rarely.[72] The problem with Jesus was that he had called wicked people to follow him—quislings of the oppressive Roman government and people whose "sexual immorality, theft, murder, greed, malice, deceit, lewdness, envy, slander, arrogance and folly" arose from "unclean" hearts (7:20–23).[73] He extended forgiveness to them prior to any attempt of their own to reform their lives.[74]

69 Here I take the enigmatic first person pronoun "my" to refer to the Servant. Cf. Brevard S. Childs, *Isaiah* (OTL; Louisville: Westminster John Knox, 2001), 417, who cites the reading "his people" in 1QIsa.

70 Cf. Lane, *Mark*, 569–70.

71 See, e.g., Joachim Jeremias, *New Testament Theology*, (London: SCM, 1971), 1:118–19, and the summary both of Jeremias's position and that of many other New Testament scholars in E. P. Sanders, *Jesus and Judaism* (Philadelphia: Fortress, 1985), 176–77.

72 Sanders, *Jesus and Judaism*, 182–85.

73 Ibid., 203, 206–8. See also Marcus, *Mark 1–8*, 230–31.

74 Cf. 2:5, where Jesus forgives the paralytic merely on the basis of his and his friends' faith without asking questions about the paralytic's intentions to reform his life. Sanders, *Jesus and Judaism*, 204–8, believes that Jesus "may have offered [the wicked] inclusion in the kingdom not only *while they were still sinners* but also *without* requiring repentance as normally understood" (emphasis in the original). The phrase "as normally understood" is important.

Jesus had the authority to extend God's forgiveness because he was acting as God. God had the authority to extend such forgiveness because his Son would die "in the place of many" and "for" their transgressions. To put it in a nutshell, Mark sees Jesus as the physician who heals the sick because he is the Servant "who was pierced for our transgressions ... crushed for our iniquities ... and by [whose] wounds we are healed" (Isa. 53:5).

THE RESPONSE TO JESUS

Mark is especially interested in the responses of two groups of people to Jesus and his mission: Jesus' disciples and his antagonists. Jesus' disciples are those who respond positively to his call and follow him. They appear throughout the narrative, from the time that Simon, Andrew, James, John, and Levi leave their occupations to "follow" Jesus to the end of the narrative when the young man at the empty tomb tells the women to report to "the disciples" and Peter that they will see Jesus in Galilee. This group is primarily "the twelve" whom Jesus appointed as apostles, but some texts hint that Mark included others within this circle also (3:34; 4:10; 10:32).[75] Since Mark knew that his readers would also identify themselves as followers of Jesus, this group is especially important to him.[76]

Jesus' antagonists are also important. They are comprised of the scribes, the Pharisees, the Herodians, the chief priests (including the high priest), the elders, and (once) the Sadducees. They are, in other words, the political and religious leadership of the Jewish people. They too appear throughout the narrative, and they are important because their rejection of Jesus from the beginning to the end of his ministry is so surprising. Why would the leadership of the Jewish people want to kill the Jewish Messiah, the royal descendant of David?

Mark's portrait of these two groups is complex. The disciples are chiefly, but far from consistently, faithful followers of Jesus. Similarly, the Jewish leaders are chiefly, but not entirely, against him. Each group is plagued with hard-heartedness, and Mark extends the promise of restoration to both. The basis for this restoration can only be the atoning death of Jesus, as the Suffering Servant, for the unfaithful among God's people.

Jesus' Disciples

Interpreters of Mark have often puzzled over why the gospel puts the disciples in such an intensely negative light. They fail to understand even simple parables (4:13; 7:18; cf. 9:6). Jesus wonders whether they have any faith at all (4:40). They cannot

Jesus, as Mark describes him, required repentance of those who followed him (1:15; 6:12; cf. 4:12), but not a repentance defined by the Mosaic law as it was "normally understood" (7:1–23; cf. 2:21–22). For Mark, repentance is closely connected with belief in the good news that God, in Jesus, is establishing his long-expected reign (1:15).

75 Cf. Robert C. Tannehill, "The Disciples in Mark: The Function of a Narrative Role," in *The Interpretation of Mark*, ed. William R. Telford, 2nd ed. (Studies in New Testament Interpretation; Edinburgh: T. & T. Clark, 1995), 169–95, here at 171.

76 Ibid., 175.

perceive the significance of Jesus' miracles because their hearts are hardened (6:52; cf. 4:41; 8:17). They seem to be unable to "see" and to "hear" the significance of Jesus and his teachings, and, if so, this aligns them with those whom Jesus has said are "on the outside" (8:17–21; cf. 4:11–12). The disciples neglect prayer and so fail to drive out a harmful spirit (9:18). They argue about who is the greatest (9:33–37; cf. 10:35–45). They mistakenly try to stop an exorcist who is not part of their group (9:38–41).

They adopt a patronizing attitude toward Jesus and give him wrong-headed advice (5:31; 6:36; 8:4, 32; cf. 1:37; 10:35), a procedure that once draws a shocking rebuke from Jesus—"Get behind me, Satan!" he says to Peter, "For you are setting your mind not on divine things but on human things" (8:33, NRSV). Worst of all, in Jesus' moment of greatest need and despite protests of loyalty (14:19), one of them betrays Jesus to the authorities (14:10), another denies that he knows him (14:68, 70, 71), and everyone abandons him (14:50). Even the women who followed Jesus and were more loyal to him than the twelve disciples (15:40–41) failed to obey the instructions of the young man at Jesus' tomb to tell the disciples and Peter that Jesus will meet them again in Galilee (16:7). Instead, they flee in fear and bewilderment (16:8).[77]

One common explanation of this feature of Mark's gospel is that the disciples in Mark represent Mark's own theological opponents. He paints them in such dark tones because he wants to warn his reader against their error.[78] This explanation does not work, however, because Mark's picture of the disciples is not universally negative. They promptly follow Jesus when he calls them to do so (1:18, 20; 3:14). Jesus designates the twelve to be apostles (3:14) and commissions them to imitate his own preaching and exorcising activity (6:7–13). The disciples obediently undertake this mission and report "to him all they [have] done and taught" (6:30).

Mark's picture of the disciples becomes more negative after 6:30, but even here the disciples are not Jesus' enemies.[79] As their protests of loyalty during the Last Supper (14:19, 29, 31) and their willingness to follow Jesus to Gethsemane demonstrate (14:32–41), Mark wants his readers to sympathize with the disciples at the same time that he wants his readers to see their weakness (14:37–38, 40–41). Perhaps most important of all, Jesus indicates unambiguously that although his disciples are uncomprehending and unfaithful to him, they "will see" Jesus again in Galilee after his death (16:7; cf. 14:28), and they will be faithful to him in their own moment of trial (13:11). Jesus' comment in 14:38 seems to summarize Mark's picture of the disciples throughout the narrative. "The spirit is willing," he says, "but the flesh is weak."

Why did Mark shape his record of the disciples' response to Jesus in this way? By presenting the disciples basically in a positive light in 1:16–6:30, Mark draws his readers into the narrative and encourages them to identify with the disciples. By then exposing the disciples' weakness clearly after 6:30, he urges his readers to examine their own response to and faithfulness to Jesus.[80]

77 On this, see Andrew T. Lincoln, "The Promise and the Failure: Mark 16:7, 8" in *The Interpretation of Mark,* ed. William R. Telford, 2nd ed. (Studies in New Testament Interpretation; Edinburgh: T. & T. Clark, 1995), 229–51, here at 233–36.

78 One of the best known arguments to this effect is that of Weeden, *Mark: Traditions in Conflict.*

79 On 6:30 as the dividing point in Mark's portrait of the disciples, see Tannehill, "Disciples in Mark," 182.

80 Ibid., 175–76, 182, 189–91.

Jesus' Enemies

Mark presents a picture of the Jewish leadership that is almost unrelievedly negative. As early as 1:16–17, when the scribes and the Pharisees question Jesus' association with "tax collectors and sinners," we begin to understand that the religious leaders of the Jewish people are against him because he associates with the wicked. By 2:6, it becomes clear that they think Jesus is wicked too—he has blasphemed God, they believe. Already by 3:6, after Jesus heals a man on the Sabbath, their hostility is so intense that they begin to plot Jesus' death.

From this point forward, the response of the Jewish religious and political leadership to Jesus cuts an almost undeviating path toward the sham trial that results in Jesus' death. They claim that Jesus is possessed by the prince of demons (3:22). They argue with Jesus (7:5; 8:11) and "test" him by asking him to produce some heavenly sign, apparently to prove his claims to authority (8:11; 10:2). Afraid and envious of his popularity with "the crowd," they look "for a way to kill him" (11:18; cf. 12:12, 13, 18; 15:10). When at last their efforts succeed, they celebrate their achievement by gleefully mocking Jesus as he hangs on the cross (15:31; cf. 14:65).

Ironically, at the same time that the religious and political leadership of the Jews repudiates Jesus, petty collaborators with the Roman government, wicked Jews, and Gentiles follow him. Mark places special emphasis on the response of Gentiles to Jesus. Jesus heals a man possessed with a legion of unclean spirits in the Gentile region surrounding the city of Gerasa. The man then tells throughout the Gentile region of the Decapolis "how much Jesus had done for him." Mark says that as a result, "all the people were amazed" (5:1–20).

Similarly, when Jesus travels to the Gentile region surrounding Tyre and is approached by a woman who seeks healing for her demon-possessed daughter, the woman shows an unusual level of insight into Jesus' identity and mission. At first Jesus refuses her request, saying, "First, let the children eat all they want, for it is not right to take the children's bread and toss it to their dogs." He is referring here to the Jews' biblically mandated priority in experiencing the reign of God. The woman understands this priority, but also somehow appreciates that Gentiles are included in the blessings that come to the Jews. "Yes, Lord," she says, "but even the dogs under the table eat the children's crumbs." In response, Jesus heals the woman's daughter (7:24–30). Finally, at the climax of Mark's narrative, at the moment of Jesus' death, the one who finally recognizes Jesus as "the Son of God" is a Roman centurion (15:39).

For Mark, whose subtle use of the Hebrew Scriptures probably indicates that he too is a Jew, the Jewish leaders' rejection of Jesus at the same time that Jewish outcasts and Gentiles accepted him must have clamored for an explanation. Mark provides this explanation in the form of what many scholars have labeled "the messianic secret."[81]

81 Johannes Weiss, *Das älteste Evangelium: Ein Beitrag zum Verständnis des Markus-Evangeliums und der ältesten evangelischen Überlieferung* (Göttingen: Vandenhoeck & Ruprecht, 1903), 52, 58.

The Messianic Secret

The "messianic secret" is a label sometimes fixed to a list of puzzling characteristics of Mark's gospel that have in common an emphasis on the hidden nature of Jesus' identity and teaching. He prohibits demons from speaking when they reveal his identity (1:25, 34; 3:12). He commands those whom he heals not to recount their healing to others (1:43–45; 5:43; 7:36; 8:26). After Peter's confession of his identity, Jesus prohibits his disciples from telling others that he is the Christ (8:30; cf. 9:9). He hides himself from people (7:24; 9:30–31). Even the crowd silences blind Bartimaeus when he identifies Jesus as the Son of David (10:47–48). He purposefully uses obscure speech (4:10–13). When he does speak clearly of his coming death and resurrection, the disciples fail to understand him (9:9–10, 31–32). In addition, some scholars include the failure of the disciples to comprehend Jesus throughout the gospel in the messianic secret.[82] As if Jesus' desire to conceal his identity is not puzzling enough, Mark also says that Jesus was unsuccessful in his efforts at concealment.[83]

Scholars have offered a long list of possible explanations for this feature of Mark's gospel. Three explanations of it have become particularly influential. First, some scholars believe that Mark sits at the confluence of two rivers of tradition: the historical memory that Jesus made no messianic claims during his lifetime and the desire of the early church to read their belief that he was the Messiah back into his historical existence. The messianic secret would then be a fairly crude effort to explain why the supernatural Messiah remained unrecognized until after his resurrection.[84]

Second, others claim that Mark used the messianic secret as a literary device to alert the reader to the glory that surrounds Jesus. He did not intend for his readers to understand the device historically but only as an indicator of how glorious the revelation about Jesus was: Even commands to silence his glory could not succeed![85]

Third, some interpreters think that Mark was embracing a "theology of the cross" and correcting the notion that following Jesus means power and success. If so, then the commands not to reveal Jesus' identity, particularly the silencing in 8:31 of Peter's confession, may provide a corrective to a "divine man" Christology that viewed Jesus as a miracle worker whose disciples should be powerful miracle workers also.[86]

A fourth explanation of the messianic secret holds more promise than these three ideas. Mark himself seems to provide two separate explanations for two different types of material that are often placed together under the heading of the messianic secret. First, Mark offers a clear explanation for Jesus' frequent commands to silence after his healings—Jesus simply did not want to be impeded in his movements by

82 Wrede, *Messianic Secret*, 34–36, 53–66, 82–114.

83 Ibid., 126–29.

84 Ibid., 228–29. The basic features of Wrede's explanation, if not the details, remain popular. See, e.g., Georg Strecker, *Theology of the New Testament* (Berlin: Walter de Gruyter, 2000), 350–51; Marcus, *Mark 1–8*, 525–27.

85 Hans Jürgen Ebling, *Das Messiasgeheimnis und die Botschaft des Marcus-Evangelisten* (BZNW 19; Berlin: A. Töpelmann, 1939). See the summary and analysis of Ebeling's thesis in Christopher Tuckett, "Introduction," in *The Messianic Secret*, ed. Christopher Tuckett (Philadelphia: Fortress, 1983), 1–28, here at 13–15, and Heikki Räisänen, *The "Messianic Secret" in Mark* (Edinburgh: T. & T. Clark, 1990), 60–62.

86 See esp. Weeden, *Mark: Traditions in Conflict.* Weeden's position, and the positions of others who hold a similar view, are summarized and analyzed in Tuckett, "Introduction," 17–19, and Räisänen, *"Messianic Secret,"* 62–68.

swarms of people seeking healing. Mark begins to develop this explanation for Jesus' commands to silence in his first two healing stories. After recounting the healing of Simon's mother-in-law, Mark says that by evening of the day on which she was healed, "the whole town" was at the door of Simon's house (1:33). Although Jesus arose before sun-up the next morning to find a quiet place for prayer, Mark tells us that the disciples found him to tell him that "everyone" was looking for him (1:37). Jesus responded with the suggestion that he and his disciples should leave that village and go to other villages so that Jesus could preach there too. "That," he says, "is why I have come" (1:38–39).

Mark then records Jesus' healing of a leper, and after this healing we find Jesus' first command that the healed person not reveal to others what has happened to him (1:43–44). Instead, the man spreads the news, and "as a result [*hōste*] Jesus could no longer enter a town openly but stayed outside in lonely places" (1:45).

Mark therefore prepares the way for the first appearance of the so-called "miracle secret" by telling his readers that Jesus was so besieged by people wanting to be healed that he could not accomplish his purpose of preaching widely in various Galilean villages. When the first command is disobeyed, he then says that Jesus' plan was frustrated—Jesus was forced to retreat to "lonely places," and still people came "to him from everywhere" (1:45). Mark gives the clear impression, by the context in which he places it, that Jesus' command to the healed leper to be quiet about his healing was intended to keep mobs of people from coming to him and impeding his movement.

This impression is confirmed elsewhere in the narrative. In Capernaum, we read that "so many gathered that there was no room left, not even outside the door" (2:2). Elsewhere, crowds flock to Jesus from distant regions so that he has to tell his disciples "to have a small boat ready for him, to keep the people from crowding him" next to the lake (3:9; cf. 4:1). These crowds, Mark tells us, came specifically for healing: "For he had healed so many, that those with diseases were pushing forward to touch him" (3:10). Eventually the crowds became so thick around the house where Jesus was staying that "he and his disciples were not even able to eat" (3:20; cf. 6:30–34, 53–56).

Although this explanation seems pedestrian when compared to the complicated historical and theological theories often floated about the messianic secret, the conclusion seems unavoidable that Mark wanted his readers to understand Jesus' commands to silence after healings (1:43–45; 5:43; 7:36; 8:26), his occasional efforts to seek privacy for his healings (5:37; 7:33; 8:23), and his occasional retreat from the crowds (1:35; 3:7; 6:31–32; 7:24) in this way. Jesus did not want mobs seeking healing to impede his movement around Galilee, and he tried to control the crowds by hindering the spread of news about his healing abilities.[87]

The only theological point here is that Jesus' healing powers were so great and so obviously authentic that people crowded around him hoping to receive some relief

87 Jesus' concern seems to be both that the crowds will physically impede his movement and the movement of his disciples (1:37–38; 3:9–10; 4:1) and that his goal of preaching widely will be frustrated by the physical exhaustion of ministering to the needs of such great numbers (3:20; 6:30–32).

for their suffering. That people do not always obey Jesus' commands to silence (1:45; 7:36) merely underscores this point.[88]

Second, much of the material in Mark often lumped into the category of the messianic secret seems intended to emphasize the reason for Jesus' rejection by the Jewish authorities, his family, and eventually by a "crowd" (15:11) who came under the authorities' influence. These are "the outsiders" (4:11), whose hearts are hard toward Jesus (3:5; 10:5) and for whom Jesus' teaching is not revelation but judgment. Mark wants his readers to appreciate the similarity between Israel's spiritual condition when its leaders and many of its people rejected Jesus and its condition during Isaiah's time.

In Isaiah's time Israel had been an undesirable vineyard because it replaced justice with bloodshed, righteousness with cries of distress, and respect for the work of the Lord with lack of understanding (Isa. 5:7, 13). In a similar way, when Israel's leaders rejected Jesus, they revealed themselves to be a vineyard with wicked tenants who failed to produce fruit for God by treating the prophets, and God's Son himself, with contempt (12:1–9). Just as God called Isaiah to preach to his disobedient people as a means of clouding their ears, eyes, and understanding until their country lay ruined by defeat and exile (Isa. 6:9–13; cf. 5:5–6, 8–30), so Jesus only explains "the mystery of the kingdom of God" to his disciples.[89]

> But to those on the outside everything is said in parables so that, "they may be ever seeing but never perceiving, and ever hearing but never understanding; otherwise they might turn and be forgiven!" (4:11–12, paraphrasing Isa. 6:9–10)

The outsiders, in other words, will reject Jesus' teaching about the kingdom of God according to God's own design and as an act of God's judgment on them for their hard-heartedness.

Although Jesus' quotation of Isaiah, strictly speaking, applies only to his parables, it supplies the simplest explanation from the narrative itself for Jesus' private instruction of his disciples (4:11, 34; 7:17; 9:2, 30–31) and for his silencing of those, including the demons, who know his identity (1:25, 34; 3:12; 8:30; 9:9). That this is the function of these features of the narrative seems evident from hints that Mark gives about their purpose. In 4:34, Mark implies that Jesus taught openly in parables to fulfill the prophetic judgment of 4:12 but, in contrast to this open and obscure teaching, "when he was alone with his own disciples, he explained everything." This means that elsewhere, when Jesus seeks privacy with his disciples, this theme of judgment on those outside is probably also present (7:17; 9:2, 28, 30–31; 10:10; 13:3).[90]

---

88 This does not mean, *pace* Francis Watson, "The Social Function of Mark's Secrecy Theme," *JSNT* 24 (1985): 49–69, here at 51–52, that "the 'miracle secret' is thus part of the 'messianic secret'" and that commands to silence about the miracles should be understood in the same way as commands to silence about Jesus' identity. Such a connection is not consistent with the explanation that Mark provides in his narrative of the "miracle secret."

89 On the link between Isaiah 5 and 6 and the theological significance of Isa. 6:9–10, see Childs, *Isaiah*, 54–57.

90 Cf. Watson, "Social Function," 58–59. Watson places 7:24 (where Jesus seeks privacy in the region of Tyre and Sidon) in this category, but neither the disciples nor Jesus' teaching are mentioned, so Mark probably intends for his readers to understand this statement as part of the first theme: the search for relief from the mobs.

Similarly, in 5:19–30 Jesus tells the Gentile Gerasene demoniac to proclaim to his family what Jesus has done for him with the result that "all the people" in the Gentile Decapolis were amazed. In 15:39, the climactic revelation of Jesus' identity by a human character in the narrative occurs on the lips of a Gentile. In these places, Mark seems to be inviting the reader to compare Jesus' willingness for his identity to be proclaimed among the Gentiles and the readiness of Gentiles to embrace his identity with his frequent cloaking of his identity among the Jews.

Since Mark understands Jesus' shrouding of his identity and private tutoring of his disciples as acts of prophetic symbolism, there is no need for perfect consistency. Indeed, in the passion narrative Jesus or those around him sometimes speak openly of his identity, even to the Jewish leaders, who reject him (10:47–48; 11:10; 12:6; 14:61–62). Once a "large crowd" listens to a broad hint about his identity "with delight" (12:35–37). These, however, are exceptions to the trend of his ministry, and they are counterbalanced by Jesus' statement to the Jewish leaders, "Neither will I tell you by what authority I am doing these things" (11:33; cf. 8:12).[91] The trend of Jesus' ministry in Galilee and Judea is concealment, especially from the Jewish leaders, and the purpose for the trend seems clear: Through Jesus' frequent refusal to proclaim his identity openly and persuasively in Jewish regions, God is, in the words of the parable of the wicked tenants, giving "the vineyard to others" (12:9).[92] Jesus is putting into practice the principle that "whoever has will be given more; whoever does not have, even what he has will be taken from him" (4:25).[93]

Will Jesus' Disciples Become His Enemies?

In 8:14–21, Mark raises forcefully the question of whether Jesus' disciples will also become his enemies. As we have seen, Mark presents the disciples in a basically positive light through 6:30.[94] His picture of the disciples takes a decidedly negative turn, however, after Jesus feeds five thousand people, and the disciples, who failed to comprehend the magnitude of Jesus' power as it was displayed in the feeding, become terrified when they see Jesus walk on water—they think he is an apparition (6:49). They are afraid, Mark tells us, because "they had not understood about the loaves; their hearts were hardened" (6:52). The disciples then fail to understand Jesus' claim that what comes out of people, not the food that goes into them, makes them unclean (7:15, 17). When they ask Jesus what he meant by this remark, he responds, "Are you so dull?" (7:18). It is hard not to think of the hardened hearts of the Pharisees in 3:5 and the lack of understanding of "the outsiders" in 4:12.

A few paragraphs later, Jesus miraculously feeds four thousand people and then leaves for the other side of the lake with his disciples (8:1–13). On the way, Jesus and his disciples engage in a dialogue in which the question of the disciples' hard-heartedness toward

91 Boobyer, "Secrecy Motif," 232.

92 Cf. Weiss, *Das älteste Evangelium*, 52–60; Martin Dibelius, *From Tradition to Gospel* (Cambridge: James Clarke, 1971; orig. German ed., 1919), 297; Boobyer, "Secrecy Motif," 232–35. Jesus' command to silence about his healing of the deaf and mute man in the Gentile Decapolis (8:36) is not an exception to the trend since it fits with the first set of prohibitions designed to curtail the numbers of people who crowded around Jesus.

93 Cf. Watson, "Social Function," 58.

94 But see 4:13, 40–41.

Jesus breaks into the open. Jesus warns them against the "yeast of the Pharisees and that of Herod," a statement that reminds us that the Pharisees and the Herodians were plotting to kill Jesus (3:6; cf. 12:13) and that Herod himself had killed John the Baptist (6:14–29). Jesus' disciples take his reference to yeast to refer to literal bread and wonder if he is commenting on their failure to bring more than one loaf of bread with them in the boat. Just as they had failed to understand the miraculous power of Jesus when he fed the five thousand and, because of this failure, became terrified when they saw him walk on the water, so now they have failed to appreciate the feeding of the four thousand and imagine that Jesus would worry about a lack of bread. Since Jesus has just fed nine thousand people with bread to spare, it is obvious that finding enough food would not concern him and should not concern his disciples.

Ironically, the disciples' dullness up to this point reveals precisely the danger that they are becoming like the Pharisees and Herod: "Why are you talking about having no bread? Do you still not see or understand? Are your hearts hardened? Do you have eyes but fail to see, and ears but fail to hear?" (8:17–18). The echo of Jesus' prophetic judgment against "outsiders" a few chapters earlier could hardly be clearer: "To those on the outside everything is said in parables so that 'they may be ever seeing but never perceiving, and ever hearing but never understanding; otherwise they might turn and be forgiven!'" (4:11–12). Jesus then reminds them of the enormous excess of bread that he had produced at the two feedings—twelve baskets full on one occasion and seven on the other. Amazed at their inability to comprehend the significance of his power, he concludes with the question, "Do you still not understand?" (8:21).

As the narrative proceeds, the disciples continue to follow Jesus and to be positively disposed toward him, but their comprehension of his identity and of his mission does not improve. Finally, as we have already seen, they abandon Jesus in his hour of greatest need, and even his women followers (whose faithfulness to Jesus lasts longer than that of the twelve) in the end disobey the command to take the news of Jesus' resurrection to the disciples and, like the disciples themselves, are led by fear to failure (16:7–8).[95]

If this were all, we would have to conclude that Jesus' followers had become like his enemies, not only failing to see, hear, and understand, but finally failing to follow him as well. But Mark's narrative prevents us from drawing this conclusion. Mark's readers know from Jesus' prophecy in 13:9–11 that his disciples will proclaim the gospel to the nations and will follow Jesus' path of suffering in doing so (cf. 8:34–38).[96] Even as the women fail to obey the young man's commission at the gospel's conclusion, Mark's readers learn that Jesus' disciples, including Peter who denied him, "will see" him, risen from the dead in Galilee, in fulfillment of Jesus' prophecy on the night of his arrest (16:7; cf. 14:27–28). Although Mark's gospel encourages its readers to examine whether their hearts are hard like the disciples' hearts in the

95 Lincoln, "The Promise and the Failure," 234–35; cf. Martin Hengel, *The Atonement: The Origins of the Doctrine in the New Testament* (Philadelphia: Fortress, 1981), 67.

96 Lincoln, "The Promise and the Failure," 237.

narrative, it also holds out the promise of restoration for disciples whose failure to follow Jesus faithfully has been exposed.[97]

Will Jesus' Enemies Become His Disciples?

Does Mark intend for his readers to carry the promise of restoration even further to include Jesus' enemies in the narrative? Is it possible that just as Jesus' disciples were in danger of becoming his enemies, so his enemies might also become his disciples? If Mark holds out the promise of restoration for unperceptive and hard-hearted followers of Jesus, does he also hold out the promise of restoration for Jesus' hard-hearted Jewish antagonists?

Several irregularities in the otherwise seamless robe of opposition to Jesus among the Jewish leaders hint that Mark does extend the promise of restoration to them also.

- The synagogue ruler Jairus comes to Jesus on behalf of his dying daughter. He is obviously a Jewish leader, but his openness to Jesus and the possibility that he will obey Jesus' command, "Do not fear; only believe" (5:36), are real.
- In the midst of Jesus' antagonistic theological debates with the Jewish leaders shortly before his death, "one of the scribes" who questions Jesus answers him "wisely," and the account concludes with Jesus' pronouncement, "You are not far from the kingdom of God" (12:34).
- Joseph of Arimathea, who, Mark points out, was a prominent member of the "Council"—the very judicial body that had condemned Jesus to death—was himself awaiting the kingdom of God and went boldly to Pilate to ask for Jesus' body so that he might give it an appropriate burial (15:43–46).

If these Jewish leaders could break with the trend of vigorous opposition among their colleagues in the narrative, and if the promise of restoration could be extended to Jesus' hard-hearted disciples in the midst of their failure, then Mark probably intends for his readers to know that even those who had plotted Jesus' death could be restored as well.

If so, then Mark has faithfully reproduced the theology implied by Isaiah 6:9–13. Not only does that passage pronounce God's bitter judgment of making the sinful hearts of his people calloused to his prophetic word, their ears dull, their eyes closed, and their utter destruction as a result, but it ends on a note of promise: "Though a tenth remains there, it will again be laid waste, like a terebinth or an oak, whose stump is left over even when felled. Holy seed is its stump."[98]

This final sentence of the oracle pictures a green sprig of life breaking through the barren ground left behind by destruction. It points forward to "the shoot that will come up from the stump of Jesse," on whom the Spirit of the Lord will rest (Isa. 11:1–16).[99]

97 Ibid., 242–43.

98 The translation belongs to Childs, *Isaiah*, 50.

99 Ibid., 58.

In the same way, Mark shows that God's word of promise extends to those whose hard hearts have led them to reject Jesus. Jesus gave his life as a ransom for them (10:45; cf. 14:24). Like Isaiah's Suffering Servant, he died in their place and as an atoning sacrifice for their sin. Because of his death, hearts that God has hardened in prophetic judgment can become soft, and on the barren soil of disobedience, the green leaf of eyes that see, ears that hear, and hearts that understand can come to life.

THE DEATH OF GOD'S SON AS GOOD NEWS

It is now clear why Mark's story of Jesus is good news. Mark tells us that God's Son, Jesus, the anointed, royal Son of David, inaugurated the long-expected reign of God over his people. Where Jesus went, God's reign was present. To paraphrase Isaiah, the eyes of the blind were opened and the ears of the deaf unstopped, the lame leaped like deer, and the mute tongue shouted for joy (cf. Isa. 29:5–6). At the same time the insensitivity of Israel's leadership and of Jesus' disciples to the presence of God in their midst led them to reject Jesus, albeit in different ways and at different levels. As Jeremiah might have said, they had eyes but did not see and ears but did not hear that the God who made the sea and the dry land was among them (cf. Jer. 5:21–22; Mark 8:18). Enigmatically, the hard-hearted rejection of God and the eschatological presence of God had not followed each other but were present at the same time in Jesus' ministry. Their clash eventually brought Jesus to the cross.

For Mark, however, the clash of the ages and the crucifixion of Jesus did not take God by surprise. The Scriptures decreed Jesus' death, and Jesus himself understood its necessity from the beginning of his ministry. Indeed this was a primary purpose for his coming. Jesus' death was necessary, like the death of the Suffering Servant, to atone for "the sins of many," including the disciples who had failed him and others who had rejected him.

The clash of the ages continued into Mark's own time. Thus, Mark made clear to his readers that they were called to arrive at final vindication through the path of suffering, just as the Son of Man was called to suffer and, only then, to rise from the dead. Mark also wanted his readers to understand that if, in the midst of suffering, they should fail Jesus as his disciples had failed him, the promise of restoration was available to them just as it was to "his disciples and Peter." It was available because of the atoning death of God's Son—and that is good news.

Chapter 4

MATTHEW: NEW WINE IN OLD SKINS

When Matthew wrote his gospel, he was engaged in an intense and polemical dialogue with unbelieving Jews. He himself was a Jew, but by the time he wrote his gospel, he could speak of "their synagogues" and of "the Jews" as if he were no longer part of Jewish society (4:23; 9:35; 10:17; 12:9; 13:54; 28:15).[1] The references in his gospel to Jewish persecution of and polemic against Christians probably mean that his break with Judaism did not come at his own initiative (10:17; 23:34; 28:15). Matthew's understanding of Christianity was still within the hearing of Jewish society, and Jewish society did not like what it heard: Christians were setting aside the authority of Moses in favor of Jesus' authority and were overturning Jewish tradition.

In this situation, Matthew articulated three concerns. First, he wanted to show that although the gospel did bring changes, these changes were a fulfillment of the Jewish Scriptures, not their betrayal. To use the words of a parable that Matthew found important: New wine only ruins old wineskins, but if new wine is placed in new skins, "both are preserved" (9:17).[2]

Second, Matthew wanted to demonstrate that for the Jews who had rejected Jesus, both wine and skins had been ruined. God had judged them for their complacency and hypocrisy by forming a new multiethnic people and, as in the sixth century B.C., by destroying Jerusalem.

Third, Matthew understood that God's new people could themselves fall into the same trap of complacency and hypocrisy. Because he understood this danger, he told of severe judgment for false Christians and urged a winsome approach toward vulnerable Christians with a tendency to stray from the fold.

In this chapter we will look at each of these theological themes.

JESUS' FULFILLMENT OF JEWISH BIBLICAL TRADITION

Matthew knew that to make a plausible case against his Jewish detractors for their rejection of Jesus as a magician (9:34; 10:25; 12:24, 27) and a deceiver (27:63–64), he had to explain how Jesus fulfilled Israel's Scriptures and why Jesus had the authority to change the Mosaic law.[3] Matthew's gospel is steeped in this concern, and it is visible in five strands woven into the fabric of his narrative: Jesus' fulfillment of Israel's

1 Graham Stanton, *A Gospel for a New People: Studies in Matthew* (Edinburgh: T. & T. Clark, 1992), 119–20, 131.

2 The phrase "both are preserved" is unique to Matthew's telling of the parable (cf. Mark 2:22; Luke 5:37–39). For the approach to the parable taken here see, e.g., W. D. Davies and Dale C. Allison, *The Gospel according to Matthew*, 3 vols. (ICC; Edinburgh: T. & T. Clark, 1988–1997), 2:115; Donald A. Hagner, *Matthew 1–13* (WBC 33A; Dallas: Word, 1993), 244; and Craig S. Keener, *A Commentary on the Gospel of Matthew* (Grand Rapids: Eerdmans, 1999), 301.

3 On the probability that Matthew knew of Jewish claims that Jesus was a magician and deceiver, see Stanton, *A Gospel for a New People*, 171–80.

Scriptures, his embodiment of the Law and of Wisdom, his identity as the new and greater Moses, his identity as the messianic son of David and Son of God, and his personification of Israel.

Jesus' Fulfillment of Israel's Scriptures

One of the most prominent theological themes in Matthew is that Jesus' life and teaching correspond to various statements in the Jewish Scriptures that Matthew took as predictions of the Messiah. Fifteen times Matthew says that some aspect of Jesus' life "fulfilled" the Scriptures:

1. his virgin birth (1:22–23; cf. Isa. 7:14 LXX)
2. his birth in Bethlehem (2:3–6; cf. Micah 5:2)[4]
3. his move with his family from Egypt to Israel (2:14–15; cf. Hos. 11:1)
4. Herod's slaughter of children under two in Bethlehem in an effort to kill Jesus (2:16–18; cf. Jer. 31:15)
5. his family's choice of Nazareth in Galilee over Judea as a place to live (2:23)
6. his own decision to live in Capernaum beside the sea of Galilee (4:13–16; cf. Isa. 9:1–2)
7. his teaching (5:17)
8. his healing ministry (8:16–17; cf. Isa. 53:4)
9. his silencing of those whom he healed (12:17; cf. Isa. 42:1–4)
10. the use of parables to obscure his teaching for those who rejected him (13:13–14; cf. Isa. 6:9–10)
11. his use of parables in his teaching generally (13:34–35; cf. Ps. 78:2)
12. his decision to ride into Jerusalem on a donkey and her foal (21:4–7; cf. Isa. 62:11; Zech. 9:9)
13. his refusal to call on the army of heaven to rescue him at his arrest (26:53–54)
14. the arrest itself (26:55–56)
15. the purchase of "the potter's field" with Judas's thirty pieces of silver (27:6–10; cf. Jer. 18:2–6; 19:1–2, 4, 6, 11; 32:6–15; Zech. 11:13)

Ten of these references introduce their quotations in virtually the same way—"in order that what was spoken through the prophet might be fulfilled, saying . . ."[5] Matthew went to considerable trouble to incorporate this material into his gospel. He inserted four of these "formula quotations" into passages that he took over from Mark's gospel, and eight of his citations appear nowhere else in the New Testament.[6]

The formula quotations show that Jesus' life and ministry from his conception to his death mesh with the expectations of Israel's prophets for the eschatological

4 Here Matthew does not use the term "fulfill" (*plēroō*), but the idea that Jesus' birth in Bethlehem fulfilled the prophecy of Micah 5:2 is clearly present. See R. T. France, *Matthew: Evangelist and Teacher* (Grand Rapids: Zondervan, 1989), 171.

5 See 1:22–23; 2:14–15, 17–18, 23; 4:14–16; 8:17; 12:17–21; 13:35; 21:4–5; 27:9–10. These "formula quotations" vary from each other slightly, but they all share a common pattern. For an exact account of the variations, see Davies and Allison, *Matthew*, 3:574. If we include 2:3–6, which does not contain the crucial word "fulfill" (*plēroō*) but fits the pattern in other ways, the count increases to eleven.

6 Ibid., 3:576.

restoration of Israel.[7] Jesus' birth to a virgin is the ultimate fulfillment of the sign that, according to Isaiah, God would give to Ahaz (no. 1). Jesus' birth in Bethlehem shows that he is the Davidic king whom Micah prophesied would bring security and peace to Israel (no. 2). Herod's slaughter of the infants in Bethlehem sets the stage for the restoration of Israel that Jeremiah promised (no. 4). Jesus' decision to settle by the sea of Galilee shows that he fulfills Isaiah's expectation for a "Wonderful Counselor" who would reign on David's throne (no. 6). Jesus' willingness to heal the sick and his silencing of those whom he healed shows that he is the Suffering Servant whom Isaiah described (nos. 9 and 10). The way in which he entered Jerusalem during the final week of his life shows that he is the messianic king whom Zechariah expected and who would thus usher in the age of Israel's restoration for which Isaiah longed (no. 12).

Matthew also wanted his readers to understand that Jesus' teaching fulfilled the Mosaic law. This is the burden of 5:17–20, a passage whose importance is signaled by its location near the beginning of the first major block of Jesus' teaching, the Sermon on the Mount. This position tells the reader that 5:17–20 is the lens through which at least 5:21–48 should be read. Jesus is speaking:

> Do not think that I have come to abolish the Law or the Prophets; I have not come to abolish them but to fulfill them. I tell you the truth, until heaven and earth disappear, not the smallest letter, not the least stroke of a pen, will by any means disappear from the Law until everything is accomplished. Anyone who breaks one of the least of these commandments and teaches others to do the same will be called least in the kingdom of heaven, but whoever practices and teaches these commands will be called great in the kingdom of heaven. For I tell you that unless your righteousness surpasses that of the Pharisees and the teachers of the law, you will certainly not enter the kingdom of heaven.

Interpreters sometimes describe this paragraph as evidence that Matthew was a legal rigorist who never broke with Judaism and whose Christian community functioned as a sect within Judaism. Matthew's Jesus, they say, set aside nothing of the Mosaic law, and even Gentiles who wanted to join Matthew's church had to be circumcised and follow the Jewish dietary laws. On this reading, Matthew's gospel expresses the view of the Judaizers whom Paul opposed in Galatians—Jesus is the Jewish Messiah, and Gentiles who want to follow him must first become Jews by means of submission to the Torah.[8]

7 *Pace* Raymond E. Brown, *The Birth of the Messiah*, 2nd ed. (ABRL; New York: Doubleday, 1997), 97, most of the formula citations reveal a general awareness of the biblical context from which they are taken.

8 David C. Sim, *The Gospel of Matthew and Christian Judaism: The History and Social Setting of the Matthean Community* (SNTW; Edinburgh: T. & T. Clark, 1998), 188–211; idem, "Matthew's Anti-Paulinism: A Neglected Feature of Matthean Studies" (paper presented at the annual meeting of the Studiorum Novi Testamenti Societas, Montreal, Quebec, Aug. 2, 2001). In his paper, Sim comments that the understanding of Matthew's church as "a small sectarian group within Judaism ... is clearly gaining momentum in the field." See also Amy-Jill Levine, *The Social and Ethnic Dimensions of Matthean Salvation History: "Go Nowhere among the Gentiles (Matt. 10:5b),"* (SBEC 14; Lewiston, N.Y.: Mellen, 1988), 180–85, and the similar positions of J. Andrew Overman, *Matthew's Gospel and Formative Judaism: The Social World of the Matthean Community* (Minneapolis: Fortress, 1990), 86–89, and Anthony J. Saldarini, *Matthew's Christian-Jewish Community* (CSHJ; Chicago: Univ. of Chicago Press, 1994), 124–64.

This understanding of the passage cannot work, however, for two reasons.[9] First, it fails to recognize that when Jesus illustrates what he means by these words in the paragraphs that follow (5:21–48), he contrasts his own teaching with the teaching given to "the people long ago" (5:21, 33) who heard Moses say, "Do not murder," "do not commit adultery," and "eye for eye, and tooth for tooth."[10] In other words, there is an unambiguous element of discontinuity between Jesus' ethical teaching and the ethical teaching enshrined in the Mosaic law.

Second, elsewhere in Matthew's gospel, Jesus sets aside elements of the Mosaic law. Instead of agreeing that all work is forbidden on the Sabbath, as the law states, Jesus asserts his authority over the Sabbath as the Son of Man who is greater than the temple, and he claims that "it is lawful to do good on the Sabbath" (12:6, 8, 12).[11] Similarly, although Matthew omits Mark's explicit statement that "Jesus declared all foods 'clean'" (Mark 7:19) and focuses the discussion on the washing of hands (15:20), the implications of Jesus' statement about food are as clear in Matthew as they are in Mark:

> Do you not see that whatever enters the mouth goes into the stomach and then out of the body? But the things that come out of the mouth come from the heart, and these defile you. (15:17–18; cf. Mark 7:18–20)[12]

On the issue of divorce, again Jesus could not be clearer: Moses permitted divorce and remarriage (Deut. 24:1, 3), but Jesus does not permit it, except on the grounds of sexual infidelity (5:31–32; 19:3–12). Jesus is not taking the strict position of Shammai rather than the lenient position of Hillel on the interpretation of Moses here.[13] He is doing something that combatants in the debate between these two schools of thought would never do: He *contrasts* his teaching with that of Moses by appealing to God's own intentions in creating the institution of marriage.

The notion that Matthew's gospel teaches strict fidelity to the Mosaic law, therefore, is wrong. The first gospel teaches fidelity to Jesus' teaching, something that even Gentiles can do (28:20) because Jesus abrogated the food laws and never reaffirmed the necessity of circumcision.[14]

---

9 A more detailed discussion of this issue appears in Frank Thielman, *The Law and the New Testament: The Question of Continuity* (Companions to the New Testament; New York: Crossroad, 1999), 47–77.

10 Murder: Ex. 20:13; Deut. 5:17; adultery: Ex 20:14; Deut. 5:18; Lev. 18:20; retaliation: Ex. 21:23–24; Lev. 24:19–20; Deut. 19:21. *Pace* William R. G. Loader, *Jesus' Attitude towards the Law: A Study of the Gospels* (WUNT 2.97; Tübingen: J.C.B. Mohr [Paul Siebeck], 1997), 172, 181, "it was said to the people long ago" does not refer to the "commandments as they were being heard, i.e. interpreted." The phrase "it was said" (5:21, 27, 31, 33, 38, 43) translates the Greek term *errethē*, which is in the aorist tense and passive voice. Matthew's frequent use of this verb in this tense and voice refers in every instance outside 5:18–48 to the words of God. Moreover, because what "was said" in three of the antitheses is a *verbatim* quotation of the Mosaic law (5:21, 27, 38), it is likely that the phrase "to the generations of old" refers to the generation who received the law at Mount Sinai. See John P. Meier, *Law and History in Matthew's Gospel* (AnBib 71; Rome: Biblical Institute, 1976), 132; Robert A. Guelich, *The Sermon on the Mount: A Foundation for Understanding* (Waco, Tex.: Word, 1982), 179–82; and Davies and Allison, *Matthew*, 1:506–7, 510–11.

11 *Pace* Saldarini, *Matthew's Christian-Jewish Community*, 126–34, who fails to see that for Matthew the ultimate justification for Jesus' approach to the Sabbath lies in his authority, not in his ability to muster arguments that he has not actually violated the Sabbath. Cf. France, *Matthew: Evangelist and Teacher*, 169–71, and for an expansion of this point, see Thielman, *Law and the New Testament*, 63–66. The Mosaic law prohibits work on the Sabbath in Ex. 16:22–30; 20:10; 35:3; Num. 15:32–36; and Deut. 5:14; cf. Neh. 10:31; 13:15–22; Isa. 58:13; and Jer. 17:19–27.

12 Thielman, *Law and the New Testament*, 66–68.

13 As Saldarini, *Matthew's Jewish-Christian Community*, 159–51, maintains.

14 *Pace*, e.g., Levine, *Social and Ethnic Dimensions*, 180–85, and Sim, "Anti-Paulinism," 10.

What, then, could Matthew mean when he says that Jesus' disciples must not relax even the least of the law's commandments but should instead teach those commandments (5:19)? The answer to this question is found in 5:17, where Jesus says that he has not "come to abolish the Law or the Prophets" but "to fulfill them." Here Matthew couples the law with the prophets and uses his special term "fulfill" (*plēroō*) to describe what Jesus does to the law and the prophets.[15] We have already seen that Jesus "fulfills" the prophets by meeting their expectations for a Messiah who would bring the eschatological restoration of God's people. Is it possible that Matthew thought of Jesus' teaching as somehow bringing the law to its eschatological fulfillment also? Since Matthew could speak of the law as something that "prophesied" (11:13), it seems likely that this was precisely his understanding of the relationship between Jesus' teaching and the Mosaic law. The Mosaic law was incomplete as it stood, and Jesus brought it to its eschatological fulfillment.[16]

How did he do this? Matthew seems to have understood Jesus' teaching to be the completion of tendencies already latent in the Mosaic law. The Mosaic law provided legislation for the functioning of a society that would inevitably include people uninterested in the humane impulses that lay beneath the law. In this situation, the law could not address the condition of a person's heart. Thus, murder could be forbidden as a way of reducing the number of people killed by other people, but there could be no witness to or visible evidence of the smoldering anger that gave rise to murder, and therefore this interior emotion could not be addressed by the courts. Certain adulterous actions could be forbidden as a way of preventing men from abusing their wives, but the emotional abandonment that lay at the heart of these adulterous actions was known only to God and to those guilty of it. The sinful motivations that give rise to murder and adultery lay out of reach of the rules of evidence required by the courts.

Within the nation of Israel, rules had to be enacted to place some restraint on less than perfect situations. Divorce was inevitable, so the woman who became its victim might at least receive a certificate indicating her unmarried status so that she could marry again. Violence was unavoidable, so retribution for the injury one had incurred might at least be limited to nothing more harmful than what one had experienced—an eye (and no more) for an eye; a tooth (and no more) for a tooth. The "law of the LORD" was indeed "perfect" for these less than perfect situations in a theocracy that included both the godly and those whose hearts were corrupt.

15 In Matthew, the verb *plēroō* normally refers to the fulfillment of the prophetic element in Scripture. The one exception to this pattern is 3:15, where Jesus says that his baptism will "fulfill all righteousness." Even here, however, Jesus is not merely saying that his baptism is the "right thing to do" but that it fulfills the will of God in a general and profound sense. Cf. Daniel Marguerat, *Le jugement dans l'évangile de Matthieu*, 2nd ed. (*MdB* 6; Geneva: Labor et Fides, 1995), 126–27.

16 Cf. Meier, *Law and History*, 123–24; Donald A. Carson, "Matthew," in *The Expositor's Bible Commentary*, ed. Frank E. Gaebelein, 12 vols. (Grand Rapids: Zondervan, 1976–92), 8:140–47; France, *Matthew: Evangelist and Teacher*, 194–95. Marguerat, *Le jugement dans l'évangile de Matthieu*, who argues that 5:17–20 "is not the expression of an allegiance of Jesus to the Torah, but of his authority over it" (140), and that Jesus "fulfills the Law and the prophets by his teaching and his deeds" (127). Despite this, Marguerat believes that Matthew's Jesus does not establish a new law but considers the Mosaic law to be common ground between himself and Judaism (139).

In contrast, Matthew believed that Jesus was assembling a new people who were "pure in heart" (5:8). For such a people the humane foundation that lay beneath the Mosaic law could be brought to the surface and the Mosaic law brought to its fulfillment. In the situation Jesus envisioned, the only court would be the eschatological judgment of God, and the maximum punishment would not be physical death but hell itself (5:22, 29–30). Evidence in this court would not be the outward, physical violations of normal societal statutes but the intentions of the heart (5:22, 28; cf. 6:21; 12:34; 13:15; 15:8, 18; 19:8).

Since Jesus did not define this new people as a political entity, the only standard that mattered would be God's ultimate standard. There should not only be no murder, but none of the hate-filled anger that produces murder (5:21–22). There should not only be no adultery, but there should be no lust, which leads to adultery (5:27–30). Marriage should be the institutionalization of the permanent bonding of two people into one flesh through sexual intercourse, and one's marriage should only be declared a failure if one's spouse was sexually unfaithful (19:3–9; cf. 5:31–32). Disciples of Jesus must not merely limit to a reasonable level the vengeance that they take against those who harm them, but they must do their enemies no violence at all (5:38–42).

This is the sense, therefore, in which Jesus fulfilled the law and in which none of it passed away in his teaching. The Mosaic law had legislated love for God and neighbor in the less than perfect situation of a theocracy. With the coming of Jesus, God's law could be reduced to its fundamental principles since Jesus' disciples were called upon to "be perfect . . . as your heavenly Father is perfect" (5:48). Gregory of Nyssa captured this element of the Sermon on the Mount when he wrote:

> One can divide wickedness under two headings, one concerned with works, the other with thoughts. The former, the iniquity which shows itself in works, he [God] has punished through the old law. Now, however, he has given the law regarding the other form of sin, which punishes not so much the evil deed itself, as guards against even the beginning of it.[17]

In summary, Matthew showed throughout his gospel that Jesus "fulfilled the Law and the Prophets." Many aspects of his life and ministry from his conception to his death matched the expectations of the prophets for the coming Messianic King and Suffering Servant, who would usher in the eschatological restoration of God's people. In a similar way, his ethical teaching brought the ethical tendencies of the Mosaic law to completion for God's newly constituted people.

Jesus as the Embodiment of the Law and of Wisdom

Matthew not only wanted to show that Jesus' ethical teaching fulfilled the law but also that Jesus himself replaced the law as the revelation of God's will. He does

17 Gregory of Nyssa, *Homilies on the Beatitudes* 6.6. I am indebted for this quotation to Dale C. Allison, *The New Moses: A Matthean Typology* (Minneapolis: Fortress, 1993), 188. Allison (182–90) also believes that the Sermon on the Mount functions as the Messiah's eschatological Torah, but he is less willing than I am to see discontinuity between Jesus' new Torah and the law of Moses.

this in two ways. First, he issues his own teaching as a new law, comparable to the law of Moses in authority, but different from that law because it is now his own teaching. The Sermon on the Mount is modeled on the Mosaic law: Its promulgation is connected with a mountain (5:1), it contains a programmatic passage demonstrating how it brings the Mosaic law to its divinely appointed fulfillment (and therefore end, 5:17–48), and it concludes, like the Mosaic law, with a blessing on those who obey it and a curse on those who disobey it (7:24–27).[18] The same idea appears at the end of Matthew's gospel when Jesus, again speaking from a mountain, urges the eleven to make disciples of all nations by baptizing them and by "teaching them to obey everything I have commanded you" (28:16–20). Jesus' teachings, not the Mosaic law, now form the standard for God's will.

Second, Matthew shows that Jesus' teaching and actions were integrated. He embodied what he taught. Not only did he urge his disciples to be merciful (5:7), but he showed mercy to others (9:27; 15:22; 20:30). Not only did he bless those who were persecuted for righteousness' sake (5:10), but he himself died unjustly, despite his innocence (27:23). Not only did he tell others to turn the other cheek (5:39), but he refused to strike back at those who arrested him (26:52–53). He urged his followers to deny themselves, take up their crosses, and follow him (16:24), and he took up the cross to suffer death for the forgiveness of others' sins (26:28, 39, 42; 27:26).[19] Not merely Jesus' teaching, therefore, but Jesus himself is the expression—in deed as well as word—of God's will. Because of this Jesus replaces the Mosaic law.

Matthew also understood Jesus as the embodiment of Wisdom. He makes this most explicit in 11:1–30. Here Matthew says that John the Baptist heard, while he was in prison, of "the works of the Messiah" (NIV "what Christ was doing," 11:2).[20] Curious about the significance of the works for understanding the identity of Jesus, John sent his disciples to ask Jesus if he was the Christ. Jesus responded with a summary of his miraculous healings and of his preaching (11:3–6). He then praised John and criticized "this generation" for rejecting both John and Jesus himself. "But," he concludes, "wisdom is justified by her works" (11:19, aut.).[21] Matthew shows how Jesus justifies his messianic status by reference to his works and then claims that wisdom is justified by her works.[22] This gives the impression that Matthew considered Jesus to be the embodiment of Wisdom.[23]

This impression receives confirmation in Jesus' thanksgiving prayer and call for people to come to him a few sentences later (11:28–30). Here Jesus' relationship to God is put in terms that customarily described the relationship between Wisdom

18 Cf. Allison, *New Moses*, 172–94.

19 Davies and Allison, *Matthew*, 3:715–16. Cf. Allison, *New Moses*, 228.

20 At this point, Luke has simply "all these things" (7:18).

21 Luke reads here, "and wisdom is proved right by all her children" (7:35).

22 See also 23:34, where Matthew probably changed the source that he and Luke had in common (Q) from an original "Because of this, the wisdom of God also said, 'I am sending to them prophets and apostles ...'" (Luke 11:49) to "Because of this, behold I am sending to you prophets and wise men and scribes...." In Luke, and probably in Q, Wisdom sends messengers, but Matthew attributes this function specifically to Jesus.

23 Many commentators understand the passage this way. See, e.g., Hagner, *Matthew 1–13*, 311; Davies-Allison, *Matthew*, 2:264–65; Joachim Gnilka, *Das Matthäusevangelium*, 2 vols. (HTKNT; Freiburg: Herder, 1988), 1:424–25.

and God.[24] God has a unique knowledge of Wisdom, just as the Father has a unique knowledge of the Son (e.g. Bar. 3:32). Similarly, Wisdom has a unique understanding of God, just as Jesus has a unique understanding of his Father (e.g., Wisd. 9:9). Jesus' call for the weary and burdened to come to him and take his yoke is also reminiscent of the traditional call of Wisdom to the simple to come and learn from her:

"Come to me, you who desire me,
and eat your fill of my fruits.
For the memory of me is sweeter than honey,
and the possession of me sweeter than the honeycomb.
Those who eat of me will hunger for more,
and those who drink of me will thirst for more.
Whoever obeys me will not be put to shame,
and those who work with me will not sin." (Sir. 24:19–22 NRSV)[25]

This identification of Jesus with Wisdom is in some ways not surprising since Jewish literature from the second temple period often portrays the Messiah as a teacher of Wisdom, and a Christian tradition identifying Jesus with Wisdom already surrounded Matthew.[26] For Matthew, however, this identification may have assumed special importance because he may have been familiar with a Jewish tendency to view the law of God as the embodiment of the Wisdom of God on earth. Ben Sira, for example, includes in a lengthy discussion of Wisdom the following judgment:

All this is the book of the covenant of the Most High God,
the law that Moses commanded us
as an inheritance for the congregations of Jacob. (Sir. 24:23)[27]

For Matthew, therefore, Jesus is the embodiment of God's will, sometimes conceived as God's law and sometimes conceived as Wisdom. Matthew expresses this motif subtly rather than explicitly, so it is important not to exaggerate its importance. It would also be a mistake, however, to miss the contribution that it makes to one of Matthew's most important themes. Just as Jesus' life fulfills the prophets' expectations for the Messiah and just as Jesus' teaching perfects the Mosaic law, so Jesus himself has replaced the Mosaic law as the perfect revelation of God's will. If many Jews of Matthew's time understood the law to be the embodiment of Wisdom, then Matthew wants his readers to see that Jesus was the embodiment of both.

Jesus as the New and Greater Moses

As readers of his gospel have often observed, Matthew makes an implicit comparison between Jesus and Moses.[28] Allusions to Moses are most frequent in the birth

24 See Davies-Allison, *Matthew*, 2:272, and Ben Witherington, *Jesus the Sage: The Pilgrimage of Wisdom* (Minneapolis: Fortress, 1994), 360–61.

25 Cf. Bar. 3:12, which calls the Mosaic law "the fountain of Wisdom."

26 See, e.g., Pss. Sol. 17: 25–26, 31, 39–40; 42; Mark 6:2; Luke 11:49 (cf. Isa. 11:2; *Tg. Isa.* 53:5, 11) and the discussion in Martin Hengel, *Studies in Early Christology* (Edinburgh: T. & T. Clark, 1995), 93–104.

27 Cf. Bar. 3:37–4:1, "She [Wisdom] is the book of the commandments of God, the law that endures forever." See also Allison, *New Moses*, 228–29.

28 See, e.g., W. D. Davies, *The Setting of the Sermon on the Mount* (Cambridge: Cambridge Univ. Press, 1964), 25–108, who

and infancy narratives (1:18–2:21). Just as Pharaoh, king of Egypt, tried to kill every male infant in Egypt (Ex. 1:15–16), so Herod, king of Judea, ordered that male infants in Bethlehem should be killed (Matt. 2:16–18). Just as Moses was forced from Egypt because Pharaoh wanted to kill him (Ex. 2:15), so Jesus had to leave Judea because Herod wanted to kill him (Matt. 2:13–14). Just as God commanded Moses to return to Egypt since "those seeking your life have died" (Ex. 4:19), so God's angel ordered Joseph to return to Israel since "those seeking the child's life have died" (Matt. 2:19–20).[29] Just as Moses took his wife and sons back to his native land (Ex. 4:20), so Joseph took Mary and Jesus back to the place of Jesus' birth.

The parallels continue, although in a less concentrated way, as the narrative proceeds. When Matthew wrote that Jesus "went up into the mountain [*anebē eis to oros*]" and "sat" (*kathisantos*) to teach his disciples a set of ethical precepts that fulfilled the Mosaic law (5:1, 17), he probably intended to evoke the image of Moses "going up into the mountain" (LXX: *anabainontos . . . eis to oros*) to receive from God the tablets of the covenant and "sitting" (MT: *yāšab*) there "forty days and forty nights" (Deut. 9:9; cf. Matt. 4:2).[30]

In Matthew's mind, other instances of Jesus going "up into the mountain" (14:23; cf. 17:1; 28:16) or going up into the mountain and sitting (15:29; cf. 24:3) may also have echoed this connection between Moses and "the mountain" in the Pentateuch.[31] In his account of Jesus' transfiguration (17:1–9), Matthew followed Mark in saying that Jesus brought Peter, James, and John "up into a mountain," but then he deviated from Mark in commenting that Jesus' face shone and in placing Moses before Elijah when he listed Jesus' companions during the transfiguration. These slight changes seem to underline Jesus' similarity to Moses, whose face also shone on a mountain (Ex. 34:29).[32] Finally, at the end of the gospel Jesus again goes to a mountain and there recalls "everything" he has "commanded" (28:19–20). His disciples, he says, should teach these things to all nations. It is difficult not to think of the connection between Moses, Mount Sinai, and the commandments of the law when reading this passage.[33]

Here too, however, Jesus is not simply like Moses but is greater than Moses.[34] Unlike Moses, Jesus was conceived by the intervention of God's Holy Spirit (1:18–25).[35] Unlike Moses, Jesus gives the eschatological fulfillment of God's law, not its provisional expression. Unlike Moses, the transfiguration of Jesus' face leads his followers to address him as "Lord" (17:4; cf. Mark 9:5, "Rabbi," and Luke 9:33, "Master") and is followed by God's announcement that Jesus is his beloved Son and the

holds that Matthew expressed the motif cautiously and with an emphasis on Jesus' transcendence of Mosaic categories, and Allison, *New Moses*, who says that although Matthew believed Jesus to be greater than Moses, he stressed Jesus' imitation of and similarity to Moses, the great lawgiver.

29 Ex. 4:19 (LXX): *tethnēkasin gar pantes hoi zētountes sou tēn psychēn*; Matt. 2:20: *tethnēkasin gar hoi zētountes tēn psychēn tou paidiou.*

30 Allison, *New Moses*, 174–75.

31 In 14:23, Matthew has apparently changed Mark's "*departed* into the mountain" to "*went up* into the mountain," but in 17:1, he follows Mark's "he brought them into a high mountain" word for word. Allison, *New Moses*, 174, comments that "in the LXX *anabainō + eis to oros* ['I go up' + 'into the mountain'] occurs twenty-four times. Of these, a full eighteen belong to the Pentateuch, and most refer to Moses."

32 Ibid., 243–48.

33 *Pace* Gnilka, *Matthäusevangelium*, 2:510.

34 *Pace* Allison, *New Moses*, 247, 267.

35 Allison, *New Moses*, 146–50, discusses several ancient texts that speak of unusual circumstances surrounding Moses' birth, but he is appropriately cautious about saying that any of these influenced Matthew.

Servant of whom Isaiah spoke (17:5).[36] Not surprisingly, then, Jesus commissions his disciples at the gospel's conclusion to teach the nations everything that he has commanded, not everything that Moses has commanded (28:16–20). Jesus is like Moses, but is greater than Moses and supersedes him.[37]

Jesus as the Messiah, Son of David, and Son of God

Like Mark before him (see chapter 3, above), Matthew wants his readers to know that Jesus fulfilled Jewish expectations about "the Christ"—the descendent of the shepherd king, David, who would be anointed king and would rescue Israel from the wicked shepherds of God's people. Jeremiah put the expectation this way:

> "The days are coming," declares the LORD,
> "when I will raise up to David a righteous Branch,
> a King who will reign wisely
> and do what is just and right in the land.
> In his days Judah will be saved
> and Israel will live in safety." (Jer. 23:5–6a)

Matthew began the opening section of his gospel (1:1–2:23), which is unique to him, by identifying Jesus as the "Christ the son of David" and then by emphasizing to his readers that Jesus was "the Christ" (1:16, 18), "the one who has been born king of the Jews" (2:2) in accord with the expectations of the prophets that "a ruler" would come who would "shepherd my people Israel" (2:5–6). Matthew underlines Jesus' Davidic descent by explicitly referring to him as David's son (1:1), by repeating the name "David" in his genealogy of Jesus more often than any other name (1:1, 6, 17), and by telling readers that Joseph too was the "son of David" (1:20). Matthew emphasizes Jesus' royal status in the tragic account of "the king" Herod's murder of children in Bethlehem in an effort to snuff out the one "who has been born king of the Jews" (2:2, 9). The position of all this at the beginning of the narrative shows that Matthew wanted to portray Jesus as the messianic king of prophetic expectation.

This emphasis continues throughout the gospel in statements that are unique to Matthew. In 11:2–6, John the Baptist, in prison, learns about the deeds of the Christ. In 16:16–20 Jesus commands his disciples not to tell to others what his Father in heaven has revealed to them, namely, that he is the Christ (cf. 11:27). In 23:10 Jesus tells his disciples that they should not be called "teacher" because they have "one Teacher, the Christ." In his account of Jesus' trial before Pilate, Matthew twice replaces Mark's title "king of the Jews" with the title "Christ" (Matt. 27:17, 22; cf. Mark 15:9, 12).

In a similar way, Matthew multiplies references to Jesus as the "son of David."[38] He incorporates two accounts of blind men approaching Jesus for healing with a plea for Jesus as "Son of David" to have mercy on them (9:27–31; 20:29–34). Only the

36 Cf. Davies, *Setting*, 55–56.
37 See esp. ibid., 93–108.
38 On the importance of this title to Matthew, see esp. Reinhart Hummel, *Die Auseinandersetzung zwischen Kirche und Judentum im Matthäusevangelium* (BZET 33; München: Kaiser, 1966), 116–22.

second of these accounts appears in Mark, and there only one blind man acclaims Jesus with this title (Mark 10:46–52). Only in Matthew do the crowds inquire, "Could this be the Son of David?" after Jesus heals a blind and mute man (Matt. 12:23).

In addition, Matthew alters Mark's account of the Syro-Phoenician woman so that she approaches Jesus with the plea, "Lord, Son of David, have mercy on me!" (15:22). Similarly, when Jesus enters Jerusalem amid the praises of the people gathered for Passover, Matthew rephrases Mark so that the people shout not, "Hosanna! . . . Blessed is the coming kingdom of our father David" (Mark 11:10), but, "Hosanna to the Son of David!" (21:9). A few sentences later, Matthew adds to Mark an account of the chief priests and scribes rebuking Jesus for accepting from the lips of children the same acclamation: "Hosanna to the Son of David!" (21:15).[39]

As if to complete the picture, Matthew emphasizes Jesus' role as the one like King David who, according to the prophet Ezekiel, would come to the scattered flock of God's people and "tend them and be their shepherd" (Ezek. 34:23–24). Not only does he preserve Mark's shepherding metaphors and the parable of the lost sheep, which also appears in Luke, but he uses this imagery in ways that are unique to his gospel. Matthew says that the chief priests and scribes assembled by the troubled Herod knew that, according to Micah, the Messiah would be born in Bethlehem because from that small town would come a leader who would "be the shepherd of my people Israel" (2:6; cf. Mic. 5:2, 4). In addition, Matthew says that when Jesus sent out his disciples, they went "to the lost sheep of Israel" (10:6), and that Jesus himself was sent "only to the lost sheep of Israel" (15:24). At the final judgment Jesus, who is both "Son of Man" and "king," will judge the nations, separating "the people one from another as a shepherd separates the sheep from the goats" (25:32).[40]

Like Mark, Matthew linked Jesus' messiahship with the idea that Jesus was God's Son.[41] Thus Peter's confession of Jesus' identity binds the two designations together: "You are the Christ [Messiah]," says Peter, "the Son of the living God" (16:16). As we have seen in our study of Mark's theology, the notion that Israel's anointed king was also God's Son appears in Psalm 2:7 and 2 Samuel 7:14. These Old Testament passages did not imply that God and the anointed king were qualitatively unified. Matthew joins Mark, however, in implying precisely this when he links Jesus' messiahship with his divine sonship. Matthew's opening genealogical record of "Jesus Christ the son of David" (1:1), for example, ends by referring to Jesus specifically as "the Christ [Messiah]" (1:17), and a line introducing "the birth of Jesus the Messiah" (1:18, aut.) immediately follows this ending.

39 This account is similar to Luke 19:39–40, where, at Jesus' triumphal entry, some Pharisees tell Jesus to rebuke his disciples' cries of praise. In Luke, however, those ascribing praise to Jesus are disciples rather than children, there is no reference to the Son of David, and Jesus' response to the Pharisees (not the chief priests and scribes, as in Matthew), is not to quote Ps. 8:3 but to say that if his disciples were silent, the stones would cry out.

40 Ancient Jews frequently used the metaphor of a shepherd for the leader of the nation. See Num. 27:15–17; 1 Kings 22:17 (2 Chron. 18:16); Judith 11:19, and the discussion in Allison, *New Moses*, 213–14. Because the metaphor was particularly appropriate for David (Ps. 78:70–72), the shepherd king, and because Matthew's interest in Jesus' Davidic sonship is so intense, it seems likely that Matthew connected the shepherding metaphor in his gospel with the theme of Jesus' Davidic sonship.

41 Cf. Jack Dean Kingsbury, *Matthew: Structure, Christology, Kingdom*, 2nd ed. (Minneapolis: Fortress, 1989), 40–83, 96–99.

The account of this birth then reveals that the action of God's Spirit created the Messiah Jesus in Mary's womb (1:20) and that this Messiah would fulfill Isaiah's prophecy of the birth of one whose name would be "Immanuel" (cf. Isa. 7:14). Matthew translates this name for his readers as "God with us" (Matt. 1:23).

By weaving Jesus' messiahship into the account of Jesus' birth and by telling his readers that Jesus' real father was God, Matthew implies that Jesus' messianic sonship broke the boundaries of Jewish expectations. At the beginning of his gospel, therefore, Matthew defines Jesus' sonship in a way that implies the unity of Jesus with God. He probably intends this initial definition of Jesus' divine sonship to inform his readers' understanding of the sixteen places in his narrative, fifteen of them unique to his gospel, in which Jesus refers to God as "my Father."

To summarize, Matthew considers Jesus to be the messianic son of David and Son of God. At the same time, he joins Mark in moving beyond this traditional category to define Jesus' messianic divine sonship in terms of union with God. As God's Son, he is also "Immanuel ... God with us." For Matthew, if Jesus is present "with us," then, in Jesus, "God" is present "with us" also (18:20; 28:20).

Jesus as the Personification of Israel

Although this theme is not prominent, Matthew implies in several passages that Jesus himself embodies the nation of Israel, recapitulating its temptations and suffering its fate. As he develops this theme, Matthew subtly makes the case that Jesus succeeded in obeying God whereas Israel failed.

The theme begins in 2:14–23, where Matthew says that an angel of the Lord warned Joseph in a dream to flee the wrath of Herod who would soon "search for the child to kill him." The angel told Joseph to flee to Egypt and to stay there until the Lord signaled him that it was safe to return to Israel. Matthew says that this happened to fulfill the prophecy of Hosea 11:1, "Out of Egypt I called my son." The "son" to whom Hosea referred here was the nation of Israel itself, whom God called out of slavery in Egypt during the Exodus but who rebelled against God's love by falling into idolatry.

The theme continues in Matthew's account of Jesus' testing in the desert (4:1–11), which he patterns after the account of Israel's wandering in the desert as Deuteronomy 6–8 describe and allude to it.[42] According to Deuteronomy 8:2–3 (LXX), God "harmed," "tested," and "examined" Israel in the desert for forty years, and, more specifically, "weakened them through hunger." He did this to show them that "a human being shall not live on bread alone, but on every word that comes from the mouth of God." Israel did not pass the test but instead grumbled about their lack of food (Ex. 16:1–36), and themselves put God to the test by insisting that their lack of water in the desert called into question whether the Lord was among them (Deut. 6:16; cf. Ex. 17:1–7).

42 Allison, *New Moses*, 165–66, 169; Hagner, *Matthew 1–13*, 61–62.

They also committed idolatry, and Moses had to remind them that they should "fear the Lord your God, and serve him, and cling to him" (Deut. 6:13, LXX). In Matthew's gospel, Jesus, too, faces these tests, but unlike Israel, he remains obedient to God, answering the devil in the words of Deuteronomy 8:3 ("[A human being] does not live on bread alone, but on every word that comes from the mouth of God"), 6:16 ("Do not put the LORD your God to the test"), and 6:13 ("Worship the LORD your God, and serve him only"; cf. Matt. 4:1–11). For Matthew, Jesus recapitulated the history of Israel, but at the points in Israel's story where the nation failed to obey God, Jesus succeeded.

This made Jesus the ideal candidate for fulfilling the role of the Servant in Isaiah's four Servant Songs. Isaiah imagines the Servant as both an individual and the nation of Israel.[43] His character as an individual is clear. He would not come as a military conqueror but would establish justice in a gentle way (Isa. 42:1–4). His justice would not be limited to one people but would extend to the whole earth (Isa. 42:4; 49:6; 52:15). He would suffer, but not for his own sins (Isa. 50:5–6). Instead, his suffering would atone for the sins of others (Isa. 52:13–53:12). At the same time, the context of the first Servant Song, which uses the term "servant" unambiguously of Israel (41:8–9), and the explicit statement within the second Servant Song that God's servant is Israel (Isa. 49:3), reveal that the image has a corporate, national dimension.[44]

When he describes Jesus' ministry prior to his passion, Matthew emphasizes the identification of Jesus with the Servant that he found before him in Mark, bringing it more clearly into the open. He follows Mark in recording God's commendation of Jesus at his baptism in words reminiscent of Isaiah 42:1, but then repeats precisely these words in his narrative of Jesus' transfiguration (Matt. 3:15; 17:5). In addition to this, he interprets Jesus' healing ministry as a fulfillment of the Servant's role in Isaiah 53:4 and 11 (Matt. 8:17), and he correlates Jesus' nonviolent approach to his enemies with the description of the Servant in Isaiah 42:1–4 (Matt. 12:18–21). This last instance is the longest biblical quotation in Matthew's gospel.[45]

He follows this pattern of bringing out into the open Mark's more allusive correlation between Jesus and the Servant when he speaks of Jesus' death. He follows Mark 10:45 ("as a ransom for many") precisely in 20:28, but in Jesus' words over the cup at the Last Supper, he makes more explicit than Mark that Jesus' death corresponded to the vicarious, atoning nature of the Servant's suffering:[46]

43 Here I follow in its basic outline the position of Harold Henry Rowley, *The Servant of the Lord and Other Essays on the Old Testament* (London: Lutterworth, 1952), 51–52, without adopting his now discredited notion that ancient Jews possessed a special concept of "corporate personality." Rowley argues convincingly that the metaphor of the Servant in Isaiah oscillates between corporate and individual conceptions.

44 Brevard Childs, *Isaiah: A Commentary* (OTL; Louisville: Westminster John Knox, 2001), 325.

45 See David Hill, "Son and Servant: An Essay on Matthean Christology," *JSNT* 6 (1980): 2–16.

46 In the table on the nexxt page, the closest correspondences appear in italics, and Matthew's crucial addition in bold italics.

Isa. 53:11b–12	**Mark 14:24**	**Matt. 26:28**
By his knowledge my righteous servant will justify *many*, and he will *bear their iniquities*. Therefore I will give him a portion among the great. . .because he *poured out his life* unto death, and was numbered with the transgressors. For he *bore the sin of many*, and made intercession for the transgressors.	This is my blood of the covenant, which is *poured out for many*.	This is my blood of the covenant, which is *poured out for many for the* ***forgiveness of sins***.

Of the Synoptic Gospels only Matthew has the reference to the "forgiveness of sins" here, a reference that is conceptually parallel to the Suffering Servant's role in bearing the "iniquities" and "sins" of God's people (cf. 1:21).[47] As we move through Matthew's passion narrative, we find that he meticulously followed Mark's detailed correlation of the circumstances of Jesus' passion with the passion of the Servant. Everything is here: the beating (26:67; 27:30), mocking (26:68; 27:29), spitting (26:67; 27:30), and insults from passers-by (27:40)—all received in silence (26:62; 27:14) and all heaped on a blameless victim (27:23).

Matthew, therefore, makes a more explicit identification of Jesus with Isaiah's Suffering Servant than does Mark. Since in other ways he emphasizes that Jesus personified Israel, he may have been especially interested in this category for understanding Jesus because in Isaiah the Servant is both an individual and the whole people. Like the Servant, Jesus was everything that Israel should have been but was nevertheless numbered among the transgressors. His suffering, therefore, was not for his own sin but for the sins of others.

Summary

Much of Matthew's gospel is devoted to the demonstration that Jesus fulfilled the eschatological tendencies of Israel's Scriptures. Jesus brought the teaching of the law and the prophets to completion, fulfilling them through his person, his deeds, and his words. He perfected the ethical tendencies of the Mosaic law, modifying it so that it governed not a theocracy but the eschatological people of God. Just as the law embodied "Wisdom" in Jewish tradition, so Jesus embodied the law, revealing a perfect integrity between his teaching and his actions. He was like Moses, yet was greater than Moses. He fulfilled and went beyond the expectations of Israel for a Davidic King who would be God's anointed Son. His ministry and death fulfilled the role of the Isaianic Servant, who both faithfully discharged Israel's commission and bore the sins of unfaithful Israel through an atoning death.

The completeness with which Jesus fulfilled and exceeded the expectations of Israel's Scriptures for the nation's deliverance highlights for Matthew the tragedy of

47 On the allusion to Isa. 53:12, see Gnilka, *Matthäusevangelium*, 2:401, and Davies and Allison, *Matthew*, 3:474.

Jesus' clash with the Jewish leaders over his identity and his teaching. If the theme that Jesus fulfilled the Scriptures dominates Matthew's gospel, the theme that the hard-heartedness and hypocrisy of the Jewish leaders led them to reject Jesus dominates it also.

THE CLASH BETWEEN JESUS AND THE JEWISH LEADERSHIP

Like Mark, Matthew viewed the Jewish leadership's rejection of Jesus as profoundly tragic.[48] Matthew's development of this theme, however, is more polemical than Mark's approach to it, perhaps in response to Jewish persecution of Christians (10:17; 23:34) and Jewish polemics against Christian claims (28:15).[49] In any case, Matthew wanted his readers to know that opposition to Jesus came from a broad spectrum of the Jewish leadership and from many of the common people. He also wanted to show that Jesus had pronounced God's judgment on the Jews who rejected his Son. This judgment would come in two forms: Their city and temple would be destroyed and God's saving purposes would move beyond the Jewish people to a new people, composed of both Jews and Gentiles who had decided to follow Jesus.

The Jewish Leaders' Rejection of Jesus

The comprehensiveness of Jesus' fulfillment of the Scriptures is matched ironically by the comprehensiveness of his rejection by the Jewish leadership. Matthew used a variety of terms for this leadership—scribes, Pharisees, Sadducees, elders of the people, and chief priests—and this variety leaves the reader with the impression that every type and rank of leader opposed Jesus. They opposed him, moreover, not sporadically or gradually, but unremittingly and from cradle to grave. "All Jerusalem"—including the chief priests and scribes—are troubled together with the notoriously cruel Herod when they hear that the king of the Jews has been born (2:3).[50] The scribes believe that when Jesus forgives the sins of a paralytic, he is blaspheming (9:3). The Pharisees say twice that he casts out demons "by the prince of demons" (9:34; 12:24) and seek ways to destroy Jesus because they believe he has broken the Sabbath (12:14). As part of their plot to kill him, they frequently "test" Jesus (16:1; 19:3; 22:18; cf. 22:35), hoping to snare him in his words (22:15).

The scribes and the Pharisees are disturbed that Jesus' disciples transgress their legal traditions (15:2). The chief priests and scribes are angry when children in the temple hail Jesus as the Son of David (21:15–16). The chief priests and the elders of the people are skeptical that Jesus has any authority to act and teach like a prophet (21:23). The chief priests and the Pharisees take offense at his parables (21:45). The Sadducees argue with him over the resurrection (22:23).

48 Cf. Lloyd Gaston, "The Messiah of Israel as Teacher of the Gentiles: The Setting of Matthew's Christology," *Interp* 29 (1975): 24–40, here at 27.

49 On this, see esp. Stanton, *Gospel for a New People*, 171–80.

50 Jack Dean Kingsbury, *Matthew as Story*, 2nd ed. (Philadelphia: Fortress, 1988), 5.

Finally, the chief priests and the elders of the people plot to arrest Jesus (26:3–5). They hire Judas to betray Jesus (26:14); they arrest Jesus (26:47); they convict him of blasphemy (26:65); and they see to it that Pilate carries out their death sentence (27:12, 20). Joined by the scribes, they mock Jesus as he suffers on the cross (27:41). Anticipating reports of Jesus' resurrection, the chief priests place guards at his tomb (27:62–66), and after Jesus has risen from the dead, they bribe their guards to say that Jesus' disciples stole his body. "This story," comments Matthew, "has been widely circulated among the Jews to this very day" (28:15).

This is a bleak picture of total opposition to Jesus. A broad spectrum of the Jewish leadership repudiates his person, claims, and teaching throughout his life and into Matthew's own time. What could account for such resistance from the leaders of Israel to the Messiah, the Son of the living God?

Matthew has no doubt about the answer to this question. The outward display of piety among the Jewish leaders disguises hearts full of corruption. Their claims to be descendants of Abraham (3:9), their ostentatious display of almsgiving (6:2), their public prayers (6:5), their obvious fasts (6:16), their unwillingness to associate with sinners (9:10–13), their concern that people keep the Mosaic law in meticulous detail (12:1–14; 23:5, 23, 25), their zeal for making proselytes (23:15), their displays of devotion to the temple (15:3–6), and their care for their ancestors' monuments (23:29) comprise a pious veneer over impure hearts. This outward piety is often merely intended to win the applause of others (6:2, 5, 16; 23:5–7), to mask greed (15:5–6; 23:25), or to find a way to break one's word legally (23:16–22). The Jewish leaders are therefore like whitewashed tombs—beautiful on the outside but inside full of dead, and ritually impure, bones (23:27–28). Their lips mouth pious language, but their hearts are far from God (15:7–8).

Matthew singles out for particular criticism the failure of the Jewish leadership to match their words with their deeds. They claim to be Abraham's children but do not bear the fruits of repentance (3:7–10). They claim to be devoted to God's law but have failed to appreciate its weightier matters of justice, mercy, and faith (9:13; 12:7; 23:23). They possess copies of the Mosaic law and therefore control the access of many others to it, but they fail to obey the very law that they teach to others (23:1–3). In a word, they are hypocrites.[51]

If one looks beyond their theatrical displays of piety, however, one discovers that the wicked deeds of the Jewish leaders are consistent with the corrupt hearts from which these deeds flow. For example, Matthew follows Mark in recounting Jesus' forgiveness and healing of a paralytic (9:1–8; cf. Mark 2:1–12), but where Mark records Jesus' rebuke to the scribes as, "Why are you thinking these things?" (Mark 2:8), Matthew puts, "Why do you entertain *evil thoughts in your hearts*?" (9:4). Matthew does something similar with words that he apparently found without any narrative context in the source that he shared with Luke (Q) and that he had already

51 The term *hypocritēs* ("hypocrite") appears in the New Testament eighteen times. Thirteen of these belong to Matthew.

included in the Sermon on the Mount (7:15–20; cf. Luke 6:43–45).[52] He paraphrases these words and uses them to explain why the Pharisees have blasphemed the Holy Spirit by accusing Jesus of casting out demons by the power of Beelzebub, the prince of demons (12:22–32):

> Either make a tree good, and its fruit good; or make a tree bad, and its fruit bad; for the tree is known by its fruit. You brood of vipers! How can you speak good things, when you are evil? For out of the abundance of the heart the mouth speaks. The good person brings good things out of a good treasure, and the evil person brings evil things out of an evil treasure. (12:33–35; cf. 15:18)

The Pharisees have spoken unpardonably evil words against the Holy Spirit because their hearts are evil. They need to clean the inside of their cup, which is full of greed and self-indulgence (23:26), of hypocrisy and wickedness (23:28), and only then will the outside be clean also (23:26).

God's Judgment on the Jewish Leaders' Rejection of Jesus

For Matthew, this comprehensive rejection of Jesus by the corrupt leaders of the Jewish people leads inexorably to God's judgment on his people. This judgment takes two forms: the destruction of Jerusalem and the movement of God's saving purposes beyond the ethnic boundaries of Israel.[53] Matthew brings these two themes to the surface in several places.

In his account of the healing of the centurion's servant (8:5–13), Matthew makes three changes that emphasize these themes. These changes become visible when we compare Matthew's version of the story with the one in Luke 7:1–10, which probably reproduces more exactly their (hypothetical) common source Q. First, in Luke, a group of Jews tells Jesus that the centurion deserves to have his request for the healing of his servant granted because "he loves our nation and has built our synagogue" (Luke 7:5). Matthew omits this positive reference to the connection between the centurion, the Jewish people, and their institutions.

Second, in Luke, Jesus' amazed response to the centurion's faith runs, "I tell you, I have not found such great faith *even* in Israel" (Luke 7:9). Matthew, however, highlights the lack of faith in Israel by rendering Jesus' words, "I have not found *anyone* in Israel with such great faith" (Matt. 8:10).

Third, and most significant, Matthew moves a comment he has found at another place in Q (Luke 13:22–30; cf. Matt. 7:21–23) to give it a place in this story:

> I say to you that many will come from the east and the west, and will take their places at the feast with Abraham, Isaac and Jacob in the kingdom of heaven. But the subjects of the kingdom will be thrown outside, in the darkness, where there will be weeping and gnashing of teeth. (8:11–12; cf. Luke 13:28–29)

---

52 Cf. Hagner, *Matthew 1–13*, 349; Hans Dieter Betz, *The Sermon on the Mount* (Hermeneia; Minneapolis: Fortress, 1995), 532; Ulrich Luz, *Matthew 8–20: A Commentary* (Hermeneia; Minneapolis, Minn.: Fortress, 2001), 202.

53 Cf. Gnilka, *Matthäusevangelium*, 2:459, and Scot McKnight, "A Loyal Critic: Matthew's Polemic with Judaism in Theological Perspective," in *Anti-Semitism and Early Christianity: Issues of Polemic and Faith*, ed. Craig A. Evans and Donald A. Hagner (Minneapolis: Fortress, 1993), 55–79, here at 71–76.

Matthew intends his readers to understand that the lack of faith in Jesus within Israel has led to God's judgment, and this judgment has expressed itself in the extension of God's saving purposes beyond Israel to include Gentiles.

Similarly, Matthew shapes his version of Jesus' teaching about the people of Nineveh, the Queen of the South, and the return of the unclean spirit in chapter 12 to emphasize the theme of judgment on God's people. This again becomes visible when we compare Matthew's account with its counterpart in Luke. Luke, who probably followed the order of Q here, placed Jesus' teaching on the return of the unclean spirit (Luke 11:24–26) directly after his response to the hostile charge that he could cast out demons because he was an ally of Beelzebub (11:14–23).[54] This is a natural place for the paragraph since it seems to warn those who have benefited from Jesus' exorcisms to follow this experience with faith rather than leaving unfilled the spiritual vacuum that the departed evil spirit left behind.[55] For Luke, this is the sense in which "the final condition of that person is worse than the first" (11:26).

In contrast, Matthew, who was probably also following Q, shifts the position of this paragraph (Matt. 12:43–45) so that it forms the climax to Jesus' teaching on the people of Nineveh and the Queen of the South (12:41–42). Jesus contrasts the penitent hearts and godly devotion of these Gentiles with "the Pharisees and scribes," whose insistence on a sign from Jesus to prove his identity is evidence that they are part of a "wicked and adulterous generation" (12:38–39). In this context, the story of the returning spirit refers to the nation of Israel, which has benefited from Jesus' exorcisms and other compassionate activity but whose rejection of Jesus will result in a "final condition ... worse than the first" (12:45). As if to remove any ambiguity that this is how he reads Jesus' teaching on the return of the unclean spirit, Matthew adds to his version, "That is how it will be with this wicked generation" (12:45).[56] Once again, Matthew has spoken of the two facets of God's judgment of Israel for their rejection of Jesus: He will devastate their nation and move his purposes beyond its boundaries to include the Gentiles.

This theme becomes crystal clear in two back-to-back parables strategically located near the end of Matthew's gospel as the plot of the Jewish leaders against Jesus reaches its climax. In the parable of the wicked tenants (21:33–43), Jesus recalls Isaiah's parable of an unfruitful vineyard—"the house of Israel"—to which God brings judgment (Isa. 5:1–7). In Matthew's version, the action focuses less on the vineyard than on the tenants who rent the vineyard from a landowner and then brazenly mistreat two successive groups of servants who come to collect the owner's rent. Finally, the vineyard owner sends his own son to the tenants, thinking that they will surely respect him. Instead, blinded by greed, they kill the owner's son. The owner's natural reaction to these events, as the chief priests and Pharisees themselves comment, is to put the

54 I. Howard Marshall, *Commentary on Luke* (NIGTC; Grand Rapids: Eerdmans: 1978), 479.

55 For this meaning of the paragraph, see Marshall, ibid., and Darrell L. Bock, *Luke 9:21–24:53* (BECNT 3B; Grand Rapids: Baker, 1996), 1092.

56 Davies and Allison, *Matthew*, 2:360.

wretched tenants to a fittingly miserable death and rent the vineyard to others "who will give him his share of the crop at harvest time" (Matt. 21:41).[57]

In the parable of the wedding banquet (22:1–14), Jesus makes the same two points of destruction for Israel and extension of God's saving purposes to other peoples. The story speaks of a king who prepared a banquet "for his son" (22:2) and sent out servants to invite his subjects. Those to whom these servants went, however, snubbed, mistreated, and killed them. As a result,

> the king was enraged. He sent his army and destroyed those murderers and burned their city.
>
> Then he said to his servants, "The wedding banquet is ready, but those I invited did not deserve to come. Go to the street corners and invite to the banquet anyone you find." (22:7–9)

It is difficult not to see allusions to the destruction of Jerusalem and the extension of the gospel to the Gentiles in both of these parables.

In a similar way, any doubt that Matthew understands God's judgment to include the destruction of Jerusalem is laid to rest when we consider the final paragraph of Jesus' "woes" against the scribes and Pharisees in chapter 23.[58] The seventh and final woe accuses the scribes and Pharisees of standing at the end of a long line of persecutors of God's prophets, wise men, and scribes. God's judgment for all this mayhem, Jesus says, will fall "upon this generation" (23:36). Jesus then laments the recalcitrance of Jerusalem and pronounces its doom: "Look, your house is left to you desolate" (23:38). He next gives a detailed prophecy of the destruction of the temple (24:1–2) and of great suffering in Judea (24:15–25).

Anti-Judaism in Matthew?

Matthew's criticism of the Jewish leadership and his implication of many other Jews in the rejection and death of Jesus have led some interpreters of his gospel to conclude that he was anti-Jewish, perhaps even an anti-Jewish Gentile.[59] Three considerations make this an unfair reading of Matthew's gospel.

First, Matthew is a member of a minority group that is being threatened by an unbelieving Jewish majority (10:17; 23:34; cf. 5:11–12). In later centuries the tables were reversed on a massive scale so that the first-century Jewish persecution of Christians paled in comparison with the horrors perpetrated against Jewish people under the banner of a false Christianity. Matthew, however, wrote before this turn of events,

57 Matthew's placement of the description of the wicked tenants' punishment on the lips of the chief priests and Pharisees is reminiscent of the self-condemning words of the Jewish crowds in 27:25. Among the three accounts of this parable in the gospels, this feature is unique to him. The final phrase of the parable is also unique to Matthew's version (cf. Mark 12:9; Luke 20:16).

58 France, *Matthew: Evangelist and Teacher*, 214–18, esp. 216.

59 See, e.g., Gaston's rejection of what he considers to be anti-Semitic elements in Matthew's gospel in "The Messiah of Israel," 40: "If the redaction critics are right, then the redactor Matthew, as distinguished from the tradition he transmits, can no longer be part of the personal canon of many. As Luther once put it, '*urgemus Christum contra scripturam* ('We urge Christ against Scripture').'" For others who hold a similar view, see the survey in McKnight, "A Loyal Critic," 58 n. 9. On the claim that Matthew was a Gentile, see the survey in Gaston, ibid., 33–34, and Stanton, *Gospel for a New People*, 131–35.

and if we are to read his gospel in a historically sensitive way, then his criticism must be understood not as an instrument of oppression but as a response to his own (and Jesus') experience of oppression at the hands of a powerful majority.

Second, although Matthew's own context of persecution at the hands of unbelieving Jews understandably makes a critique of unbelieving Judaism his first concern, he occasionally reveals that, if asked to do so, he could have produced an equally withering critique of unbelieving Gentiles. In the Sermon on the Mount, Jesus not only criticizes hypocritical Jews who pray in ostentatious ways "to be seen by others" (6:5), but Gentiles as well, "for they think they will be heard because of their many words" (6:7). Jesus' disciples should not be like them any more than they should be like Jewish hypocrites (6:5, 8). Moreover, Matthew does not imagine that unbelieving Gentiles will receive Christians any more warmly than unbelieving Jews. Not only will Jesus' disciples be flogged in synagogues, but they will be dragged "before governors and kings as witnesses to them and to the Gentiles" (10:17–18), and they "will be hated by all nations" (24:9).

In addition, as we will see more fully below, Matthew tolerates hypocrites within the church no more than hypocrites among unbelieving Jews. For Matthew, the church is a mixed body of authentic followers of Jesus and those who only pay lip service to the Lord. This second group, whom Matthew makes a point of calling "hypocrites" (24:51; cf. 7:5), will face eschatological judgment and banishment from the kingdom just as assuredly as the hypocrites among the Jews will experience the destruction of their temple and their own ejection from the people of God.

Third, and most important for understanding the theology of Matthew, he interprets Jesus' role (and perhaps his own) against the background of Jeremiah's difficult career during the late seventh and early sixth centuries B.C. In his great temple speech, Jeremiah spoke against the hypocrisy of Israel's leaders who oppressed the alien, the fatherless, and the widow (Jer. 7:6), violated the ten commandments (Jer. 7:9), and engaged in perverse worship (Jer. 7:9, 16–18), but who thought that by their burnt offerings in the Jerusalem temple they would escape God's wrath (Jer. 7:22; cf. 26:1–24).[60] In a similar way, in Matthew Jesus speaks against those whose hypocrisy has driven them to place sacrifice above mercy (Matt. 9:13; 12:7; 23:23). Just as Jeremiah predicted rejection for "this generation that is under [God's] wrath" (Jer. 7:29) and destruction for Jerusalem and its temple (Jer. 7:12–15, 32–34; 26:6), so Jesus in Matthew's gospel speaks of "this generation" as if it is rejected (Matt. 11:16; 12:41–45; 23:36; 24:34) and warns of the impending destruction of Jerusalem and its temple (Matt. 21:12–22; 23:1–24:35).[61]

60 On the historical circumstances and purpose of Jeremiah's temple speech see J. A. Thompson, *The Book of Jeremiah* (NICOT; Grand Rapids: Eerdmans, 1980), 274, and William L. Holladay, *Jeremiah*, 2 vols. (Hermeneia; Philadelphia: Fortress, 1986–89), 1:639–40.

61 In Matthew, the cleansing of the temple and the withering of the fig tree (Matt. 21:12–22) are reminiscent of Jeremiah's temple speech in Jer. 7:1–15, which Jesus quotes in 21:13 (Jer. 7:11), and of the lament over Israel's disobedience in Jer. 8:13. In Jeremiah, these passages stress the destruction of the temple (Jer. 7:14) or of Israel (8:14) for disobedience, just as they do in Matthew. In Matthew, moreover, the cleansing of the temple and the withering of the fig tree occur directly after the crowds at the Triumphal Entry call Jesus "the prophet from Nazareth" (21:11). On this see Michael Knowles, *Jeremiah in Matthew's Gospel: The Rejected Prophet Motif in Matthean Redaction* (JSNTSup 68; Sheffield: Sheffield Academic Press, 1993), 173–80.

It seems likely, therefore, that when in Matthew's gospel "all the people" take responsibility for Jesus' death with the words, "His blood is on us and on our children!" (27:25), they are echoing Jeremiah's defense against the religious officials that nearly succeeded in having him condemned to death for blasphemy against the temple:

> As for me, I am in your hands; do with me whatever you think is good and right. Be assured, however, that if you put me to death, you will bring the guilt of innocent blood on yourselves and on this city and on those who live in it. . . . (Jer. 26:14–15)

Wiser heads prevailed and Jeremiah was spared, but Uriah the son of Shemaiah, who spoke a message similar to Jeremiah's, was not so fortunate. He was caught and brought before Jehoiakim, who executed him (Jer. 26:20–23).

Incidents like this are probably in Matthew's mind when he records Jesus' claim that the scribes and Pharisees are "descendants of those who murdered the prophets" (23:31). Jesus stands in the tradition of such prophets, and the Jewish leaders stand in the tradition of those who murdered them; but Matthew makes this correlation as a wounded and rejected Jew, like Jeremiah. He shares the traditions of the unbelieving Jews he criticizes and speaks out of those traditions.[62]

Summary

The religious leaders clashed with Jesus over a variety of issues: his authority to contravene the Mosaic law, his right to forgive sins, his willingness to associate with "tax collectors and sinners," and his implicit claims to be the Davidic Messiah and Son of God. Their rejection of Jesus was comprehensive: A broad range of the Jewish leadership participated in it, and it lasted from his infancy until Matthew's own day. Led astray by their leaders (15:14; 27:20), many of the Jewish people rejected Jesus also. The people of Bethsaida, Korazin, and Capernaum in Galilee rejected Jesus (11:21–23), and the crowds at Jesus' hearing before Pilate insisted that his death was their responsibility and that of their children (27:25).[63] At least among the leaders, this wholesale rejection of Jesus arose from corrupted hearts. They displayed forms of piety and taught pious precepts, but they only did so for the applause of people as their wicked deeds testified. Unlike Jesus, whose life and teaching were perfectly coordinated, the Jewish leaders failed to practice what they preached (23:3).

As a result, God will bring judgment on his people: Their rejection of God will bring destruction to their country, and God will extend his saving purposes beyond the Jewish people to include the Gentiles. This does not mean that Matthew is anti-Jewish. He speaks from within a powerless and persecuted minority, and although he speaks in one sense from outside the structures of Judaism as it was organized in

62 That Matthew was a Jew seems clear from his subtle use of the Jewish Scriptures (which he seems to have occasionally paraphrased from the Hebrew) and from the level of his interaction with Judaism. On his use of Scripture, see esp. Allison, *New Moses*, 137–270. On the whole question of whether Matthew was a Gentile, see Stanton, *Gospel for a New People*, 135–39.

63 Cf. Gaston, "Messiah of Israel," 32, and McKnight, "Loyal Critic," 60.

his time, he also speaks from within the prophetic traditions that Judaism embraced. He understands Jesus' role as consistent with the role of Jeremiah in the late seventh and early sixth centuries B.C. Both proclaimed the destruction of Jerusalem and the temple as the consequence for rejecting the message of God's prophet. For Matthew, however, Jesus goes beyond Jeremiah in announcing the beginning of a new people, comprised of both Jews and Gentiles, to whom God will give the kingdom and who will produce the fruit of righteousness that God requires (21:43).[64]

JESUS' ADMONITION TO THE CHURCH

Matthew has a special interest in preserving Jesus' teaching about the church. Only in his gospel does Jesus use the term "church" (*ekklēsia*, 16:18; 18:17) and express an interest in the church's authority (16:18–19; 18:18), discipline (18:15–18), and offices (23:8–10).[65] When Matthew considers the church, however, most of his attention is focused on a single concern: The church should not repeat the errors of the "wicked and adulterous generation" who have rejected Jesus and persecuted his followers. He hopes to prevent this both by recording warnings of Jesus against the hypocrisy that characterizes unbelieving Judaism and by urging the church to shepherd vulnerable Christians with special care.

The Certainty of Judgment against Hypocrisy within the Church

Matthew is keenly aware that people within the church are not innocent of the faults that he has attributed to the Jews who rejected Jesus.[66] Everyone, whether Jew or Gentile, falls under his indictment. This is apparent in many passages. For example, Matthew's inclusion of criticisms of "the hypocrites ... in the synagogues" in 6:1–18 and of Jesus' denunciations of the scribes and Pharisees in 23:1–39 assume that followers of Jesus are subject to the same tendencies as the Jewish leaders and need to work against them. Matthew punctuates both passages with imperatives directed to his Christian readers:

- "Be careful not to do your 'acts of righteousness' before people to be seen by them" (6:1).
- "So when you give to the needy, do not announce it with trumpets ... but ... do not let your left hand know what your right hand is doing." (6:2–3).
- "And when you pray, do not be like the hypocrites ... but ... go into your room, close the door and pray to your Father, who is unseen" (6:5–6).
- "When you fast, do not look somber as the hypocrites do ... but ... put oil on your head and wash your face" (6:16–17).

64 Cf. Hagner, *Matthew 14–28*, 623.

65 See esp. Eduard Schweizer, "Matthew's Church," in *The Interpretation of Matthew*, ed. Graham N. Stanton, 2nd ed. (Edinburgh: T. & T. Clark, 1995), 149–77.

66 John P. Meier, *The Vision of Matthew: Christ, Church, and Morality in the First Gospel* (New York: Paulist, 1979), 129; Stanton, *New People*, 149; France, *Matthew: Evangelist and Teacher*, 255–56, 275.

- "So you must obey and do everything [the scribes and Pharisees] tell you. But do not do what they do" (23:3).
- "You are not to be called 'Rabbi' . . . and do not call anyone on earth 'father' . . . nor are you to be called 'teacher'" (23:8–10).

The intention of these passages is not merely to point out the faults of the Jewish leaders who rejected Jesus but to warn Christians that they should avoid falling into the same destructive attitudes. The underlying assumption is that they are capable of doing so.

The possibility that the corrupt hearts of people within the church will lead them astray is for Matthew more than merely theoretical. He considers the church a *corpus mixtum* of authentic Christians and those who only play the part.[67] This understanding of the church is already evident in the Sermon on the Mount when Jesus warns against "false prophets" who appear to be sheep but are only wolves in disguise (7:15). Like the Pharisees and Sadducees who came to John for baptism (3:8; cf. 12:33), the failure of these Christians to produce "fruit" in keeping with their pious claims marks them as fake (7:16–20).[68] These fruits do not consist of professing Jesus to be Lord, prophesying, exorcising demons, and working miracles, but doing the will of God (7:21–23).

These hypocritical Christians appear not only among prophets but also within the church generally, as the parables of the weeds among the wheat (13:24–30, 36–43), the good and bad fish (13:47–50), the wedding banquet (22:1–14), the good and wicked servants (24:45–51), and the ten virgins (25:1–13) demonstrate.[69] According to the parable of the weeds among the wheat, which is unique to Matthew, the kingdom of heaven contains both wheat (the sons of the kingdom) and weeds (the sons of the evil one) growing together prior to the eschatological harvest. At harvest time, however, the angels of the Son of Man "will weed out of his kingdom everything that causes sin and all who do evil" (13:41).[70] The parable of the good and bad fish, also unique to Matthew, follows a similar pattern: A dragnet collects all kinds of fish from the sea (13:47), but in the end the good fish go into baskets and the bad fish are thrown away (13:48), just as angels will separate the wicked from the righteous at the end of the age (13:49–50).

This understanding of the church corresponds with the action of the servants of the king and of the king himself in parts of the parable of the wedding banquet that

67 This is a common view of Matthew's understanding of the church. It has come under attack from Petri Luomanen, "*Corpus Mixtum*—An Appropriate Description of Matthew's Community?" *JBL* 117 (1998): 469–80, but Luomanen's argument has been persuasively refuted by Robert H. Gundry, "In Defense of the Church in Matthew as a *Corpus Mixtum*," *ZNW* 91 (2000): 153–65.

68 Cf. Günther Bornkamm, "End-Expectation and Church in Matthew," in *Tradition and Interpretation in Matthew*, ed. Günther Bornkamm, Gerhard Barth, and Heinz Joachim Held (NTL; Philadelphia: Westminster, 1963), 15–51, here at 16.

69 *Pace* Luomanen, "*Corpus Mixtum*," 476, who also fails to see the significance of the phrases "not everyone who says to me" (7:21) and "many will say to me" (7:22) in 7:15–23. These phrases show that although false prophets dominate the first part of the passage (7:15–20), in the second part, Matthew expanded his warning to cover Christians generally (7:21–23).

70 It is true, as Davies and Allison, *Matthew*, 2:408–9, point out, that in the parable's interpretation, "the field is the world" (13:38), but this only means that the church, consisting of both tares and wheat, is spread throughout the world (cf. 24:14; 26:13; 28:19). See Gundry, *Matthew*, 275; idem, "*Corpus Mixtum*," 161.

are unique to Matthew (cf. Luke 14:16–24). When those invited at first fail to respond to the invitation, the servants search the streets and gather "both good and bad" (22:10).[71] The king, when he spots a guest without wedding clothes, asks, "Friend, how did you get in here without wedding clothes?" and has him thrown into the outer darkness (22:11–13).[72]

Similarly, in the parable of the good and wicked servants, both servants work in the master's house (24:45), but when the master returns to find the wicked servant beating his fellow servants and getting drunk (24:48–50), the master cuts him to pieces and assigns him a place with "the hypocrites" (24:51). The term "hypocrites" is Matthew's contribution to this parable (cf. Luke 12:46) and demonstrates that he sees no qualitative difference between the "hypocrites" among the Jewish leaders he has described so harshly a few paragraphs earlier in chapter 23 and the false Christians depicted in this parable.[73]

Finally, in the parable of the ten virgins, again a parable unique to Matthew, all the virgins go out to meet the bridegroom (25:1), but those who are unready at his arrival find themselves shut out of the wedding banquet (25:10). Their cries of "Lord! Lord!" (25:11, aut.) like the cries of the false Christians in 7:21–23, are futile, and they hear the Lord say in response, "I tell you the truth, I don't know you" (25:12).

Matthew faces the reality of hypocrisy and corruption within the church and warns his readers to examine their lives to see whether they are bearing good fruit. Eschatological judgment awaits those whose only evidence of faith in Christ is the confession of Jesus as Lord. Matthew is a realist: Such offenses will come, but woe to the person through whom they come (18:7).

The Need to Shepherd Vulnerable Sheep

Although Matthew's picture of the eschatological fate of such false Christians is unsparing, Matthew believes that this fate is only sealed at the eschatological judgment. Before that time Matthew advocates a gently persuasive approach to those who seem to totter on the edge of authentic Christianity. This aspect of Matthew's understanding of the church comes to the fore in chapter 18. Here Matthew collects a body of Jesus' teaching on the church whose purpose is to encourage followers of Jesus to be humble toward and welcoming of one another (18:1–5, 10), to avoid behavior that might cause another Christian to sin (18:6–9), to seek to return to the fold those straying from their commitment to follow Jesus (18:12–13), to seek reconciliation with one another (18:15–20), and to forgive each other (18:21–35).

Matthew introduces this discourse by recounting a question that the disciples pose to Jesus about who will be the greatest person in the kingdom of heaven (18:1).

71 *Pace* Luomanen, "*Corpus Mixtum*," 475; this gathering of good and bad is not a gathering for the judgment and therefore a general gathering of those in the world, but an eschatological celebration of the Messiah with his people (cf. 26:29). See also Gundry, "*Corpus Mixtum*," 155.

72 Gundry, "*Corpus Mixtum*," observes that Jesus also addresses Judas "the betrayer" as "friend" in 26:50 and 26:25. Both designations of Judas are unique to Matthew and cohere with the notion that hypocrites exist even within the church.

73 Gundry, *Matthew*, 497; Davies and Allison, *Matthew*, 3:391; Ulrich Luz, *Das Evangelium nach Matthäus (Mt 18–25)* (EKK 1.3; Zurich/Neukirchen–Vluyn: Benziger Verlag/Neukirchener Verlag, 1997), 464.

Jesus responds by calling a child over to stand among them. He then tells the disciples that all who enter the kingdom of heaven must turn and become like little children, and that whoever does this is the greatest in the kingdom of heaven (18:4). Those who welcome little children, he continues, welcome him (18:5).

Jesus then shifts from discussing "children" (*paidia*, 18:2–5) to discussing "these little ones" (*tōn mikrōn toutōn*, 18:6, 10, 14). Jesus' disciples must avoid causing "these little ones" to stumble and looking down on them. Within the immediate context, "these little ones" appear to be children like the little child standing among Jesus and the disciples. Most interpreters observe, however, that elsewhere in his gospel Matthew conceives of the disciples generally as "these little ones" (*tōn mikrōn toutōn*, 10:42) and "babies" (*nēpiois*, 11:25). This means, according to these interpreters, that Jesus has broadened his remarks to include disciples generally.[74]

Although this seems to be true, the context and the diminutive terms also show that Matthew means to say more than simply that disciples of Jesus should welcome one another, avoid causing one another to stumble, and pursue fellow disciples who have strayed. By beginning the section with a reference to a literal child and by using diminutive language, Matthew shows that he understands Jesus' teaching in this section to be particularly applicable to vulnerable believers—those who are especially prone to stumbling (18:6–9), to straying from faith in Jesus (18:12–14), and to sinning against others (18:15–17)—those, in other words, whom other believers, in their misdirected quest for the highest place in the kingdom (18:1), might be tempted to despise (18:10) and to refuse to forgive (18:21–35).[75]

In Matthew's vision of the church, the church needs to welcome precisely these vulnerable believers (18:5), return them to the fold when they stray (18:12–14), win them back to fellowship with those against whom they have sinned (18:15–16), and forgive them (18:35). Only if "one of these little ones" should refuse to listen to the church should the church finally think of him or her as a "Gentile or a tax collector" (18:17). Even then, however, presumably the church will simply treat that person as someone who needs to hear afresh the call of Jesus to "tax collectors" (9:9–11; 11:19) and as someone in need of forgiveness from the one who has come "to save his people from their sins" (1:21; cf. 26:28).

Perhaps this understanding of the church's need to deal winsomely with the vulnerable in its midst prior to the final judgment explains why Matthew includes Jesus' parable of the wheat and the weeds (13:24–30) in his gospel. When the farmer's slaves ask their master in that parable whether they should pull up the weeds that the enemy has sown in the wheat field, the master responds this way:

> "No . . . because while you are pulling the weeds, you may root up the wheat with them. Let both grow together until the harvest. At that time I will tell the

74 See, e.g., Carson, "Matthew," 398; Hagner, *Matthew 14–28*, 520, 521–22; Luz, *Matthew 8–20*, 432–34.

75 For a similar understanding of the passage, see William G. Thompson, *Matthew's Advice to a Divided Community: Mt. 17,22–18,35* (AnBib 44; Rome: Biblical Institute Press, 1970), 163–64; Meier, *Vision*, 129–31; and Gundry, *Matthew*, 361, 367. *Pace* Luz, *Matthew 8–20*, 434.

harvesters: First collect the weeds and tie them in bundles to be burned; then gather the wheat and bring it into my barn." (13:29–30)

Matthew is aware that both false and true Christians inhabit the church, and he believes that the church can often tell one from the other by their fruits (7:15–20), but he also believes that the church should be slow to excommunicate the erring (18:16–17), gentle toward the vulnerable (18:5–10), and eager to pursue those who have strayed (18:12–14), lest in its haste to exclude false Christians the church uproot genuine but vulnerable Christians as well.[76]

Some interpreters of Matthew have concluded from the emphasis in his gospel on ethical demands that he had a less pessimistic view than Paul of sin's hold on the human heart.[77] Matthew's understanding of the nature and vocation of the church shows that such an interpretation of his gospel is wrong. Matthew takes seriously the grip of evil on the human heart. The hardened hearts of unbelieving Jews have led them to reject Jesus and to persecute his followers. Even among Jesus' followers, however, some only mouth their commitment to him as Lord and fail to produce fruit that is consistent with their confession. Others whose confession is sincere are prone to wander like sheep from the fold and are in need of the church's pastoral care to help them in their vulnerability. Matthew believes, therefore, that he must warn the church against hypocrisy as much as the Jews who have rejected Jesus. He must also admonish them to welcome, seek, persuade, and forgive those within its fold whose faith is weak.

MATTHEW'S GOSPEL AND THE PROBLEM OF WINESKINS

Matthew wants any who read his gospel to know that the Jewish majority who have rejected Jesus and his followers have failed to see Jesus as the fulfillment of the Jewish Scriptures. With this fulfillment has come change, and because the hearts of those who have rejected Jesus and his Jewish Christian followers are hard and evil, they have refused to accept the change, failed to perceive the fulfillment, and brought the judgment of God on themselves. Like the old wineskins in the parable, their temple has been ruined and God has begun to work among a new, multiethnic people.

Matthew believes that within this new community, the old biblical traditions of Israel have been truly preserved. In important details, the structure of obedience to these Scriptures have changed—one no longer needs to keep the food laws and the Sabbath—but change has happened as a positive fulfillment of the tendencies of the Mosaic law and of the expectations of the prophets, not as a negative disavowal of them. As understood through the lens of the fulfillment that Jesus' life and teaching provided, the Mosaic law will continue to stand "until everything [is] accomplished" (5:18).

76 It is unclear why the tension between 13:30 and 18:17 should be thought to betray a lack of coherence in Matthew's theology, as, for example, Stanton, *A Gospel for New People*, 43, argues. Matthew believes in the necessity of church discipline, but he also holds that the church should be cautious about using it and careful not to foreclose the possibility of repentance and restoration prior to the eschatological judgment.

77 Marguerat, *Le jugement dans l'évangile de Matthieu*, 230–35.

Before that eschatological day, Matthew believes God's new community must remain alert to the danger of developing the same patterns of corruption and hypocrisy that led to judgment and ruin for unbelieving Jews. The church is a mixed body of weeds and tares that includes false prophets and false claimants to the lordship of Christ as well as "little ones" in need of special care, and so there is no place for complacency. Merely mouthing the words "Lord! Lord!" will count for as little at the final judgment as the cry, "The temple of the LORD! The temple of the LORD! The temple of the LORD!" in Jeremiah's time (Jer. 7:4). Fruit in keeping with repentance is as necessary for the new people of God as it was for the Jewish people and their leaders. For Matthew, God has placed the new wine of the gospel into the new wineskins of the church, but now it is imperative that the church keep the new skins themselves undamaged.

Chapter 5

LUKE–ACTS: THE PLACE OF CHRISTIANS IN THE PROGRESS OF SALVATION HISTORY

Luke provides his readers with an explicit statement of his purpose for composing his two-volume work: "that you may know the certainty of the things you have been taught" (Luke 1:4).[1] This statement may imply that Luke's patron, Theophilus, was a recent convert to Christianity. The phrase "you have been instructed" translates a word (*katēcheō*) that Luke uses elsewhere in a similar context to speak of instruction in "the way of the Lord" (Acts 18:25), and Luke can use the word "things" or "matters" (*logōn*) elsewhere in the singular to mean the teachings of Jesus (Luke 4:32; 10:39).[2] It seems reasonable, therefore, to think of Luke writing to assure recent converts like Theophilus of the certainty of the basic precepts of the faith to which they have committed themselves.[3]

Why might people like Theophilus need such assurance? Conversion to Christianity in antiquity, as Luke's second volume amply attests, frequently met with persecution. Religious commitments in the Greco-Roman world were also social commitments, and commitment to a religion that dissolved the social boundaries between one religion and another or denied the validity of other religions led inevitably to social tensions.[4]

Yet early Christianity represented precisely this kind of commitment. It proclaimed the dissolution of the Mosaic law's "impregnable palisades" of food laws, festival keeping, and circumcision that for centuries had distinguished Jew from Gentile.[5] It also claimed, to the astonishment of many, that every god but the God

1 The "you" in this sentence refers most immediately to Luke's patron, the "most excellent Theophilus." Loveday Alexander, however, has suggested that Luke–Acts, like other works dedicated to a patron, was published through Theophilus, who made it available in his house for anyone to read or copy. If this is true, the "you may know" (*epignōs*) probably also refers to anyone who reads the work or who hears it read. See Alexander's essay, "Ancient Book Production and the Circulation of the Gospels," in *The Gospels for All Christians: Rethinking the Gospel Audiences*, ed. Richard Bauckham (Grand Rapids: Eerdmans, 1998), 71–111, here at 103–4.

2 Cf. Luke 6:47; 9:26, 28, 44; 20:20; 24:19; 24:44; Joseph Fitzmyer, *The Gospel according to Luke (I–IX)* (AB 28; Garden City, N. Y.: Doubleday, 1981), 301, and Ceslas Spicq, *TLNT*, 2:293.

3 Fitzmyer, *Luke (I–IX)*, 301.

4 Paul W. Walasky, *'And So We Came to Rome': The Political Perspective of St. Luke* (SNTSMS 49; Cambridge: Cambridge Univ. Press, 1983), 64, believes that Luke wrote during "the enlightened reign of the Flavians" and therefore during "a period of relative tranquillity and tolerance throughout the empire." Whatever the attitude of the emperor toward Christianity may have been, however, harassment of Christians at the local and provincial level was probably frequent during the last half of the first century as 1 Thess. 1:6–7; 2 Thess. 1:4–7; Phil. 1:28; and 1 Peter 1:6; 4:12–19 show.

5 *Let. Aris.* 139 (2nd cent. B.C.): "When therefore our lawgiver, equipped by God for insight into all things, had surveyed each particular, he fenced us about with impregnable palisades and with walls of iron, to the end that we should mingle in no way with any of the other nations, remaining pure in body and in spirit, emancipated from vain opinions, revering the one and mighty God above the whole of creation." See Moses Hadas, ed. and trans., *Aristeas to Philocrates (Letter of Aristeas)* (New York: Harper, 1951), 157.

of Abraham, Isaac, Jacob, and Jesus was a false god.[6] It was not a coincidence that the Jewish mob who tried to kill Paul on the temple steps fell quiet when he addressed them in Hebrew, but, when he spoke of his commission to go to the Gentiles, "raised their voices and shouted, 'Rid the earth of him! He is not fit to live!'" (Acts 22:22; cf. Luke 4:28).

Nor was it a coincidence that Demetrius the Ephesian silversmith succeeded in stirring up the wrath of his fellow silversmiths with the charge that Paul had led huge numbers of Ephesians astray by saying "that handmade gods are no gods at all" (Acts 19:26). Were such a message to go unchecked, says Demetrius,

> there is danger not only that our trade will lose its good name, but also that the temple of the great goddess Artemis will be discredited, and the goddess herself, who is worshiped throughout the province of Asia and the world, will be robbed of her divine majesty. (Acts 19:27)

In other words, there was danger that "the word of the Lord," which had permeated all the province of Asia, "both Jews and Greeks" (Acts 19:10), would disturb the peace and security that Rome guarded so closely in all its provinces.

To believe the gospel in spite of all this was often to break the social boundaries that defined one's family, guild, or tribe. It frequently meant severing ties with father, mother, wife, and children (Luke 14:26). It meant going by a new name, "Christian" (Acts 11:26; 26:28). It meant persecution from both Jewish and Gentile unbelievers (Luke 21:12). In short, it meant suffering extreme social dislocation. If new believers like Theophilus and the class of readers he represented were to survive this trauma, they needed assurance that what they believed was true. They needed to have a new social location and needed to understand their corporate identity.

Luke provides this new social location and corporate identity in his two-volume account of the earliest Christians and their founder.[7] He makes the case that this new people called "Christians" represents the fulfillment of God's purpose for his people Israel, and for all humanity, as Israel's Scriptures describe it.[8] In the course of his narrative he makes clear what that purpose is. He shows his readers how the Messiah Jesus and the assembly of a group of people who believed the message about him fulfilled this purpose. He assures his readers that God's purpose, although unfinished in the present, will inevitably triumph, and he teaches Christians how they should live as they proceed along the often difficult way toward this triumph. In this chapter we will investigate how Luke develops each of these themes in his effort to supply "an account of the things that have been fulfilled among us" (Luke 1:1).

---

6 Celsus (2nd cent. A.D.), for example, was thoroughly puzzled why Christians would rather endure torture and death than worship other gods than their own, "for," he says, "the worship of God becomes more perfect by going through them all." See Origen, *Cels.* 8.66.

7 Gregory Sterling, *Historiography and Self-Definition: Josephus, Luke–Acts and Apologetic Historiography* (NovTSup LXIV; Leiden: Brill, 1992). Although she understands the genre of Luke–Acts differently, the proposal of Marianne Palmer Bonz, *The Past as Legacy: Luke–Acts and Ancient Epic* (Minneapolis: Fortress, 2000), that Luke has constructed a foundational epic, like Vergil's *Aeneid*, for a new people is compatible with the argument that Luke's primary purpose was identity formation.

8 Cf. Joel B. Green, *The Theology of the Gospel of Luke* (New Testament Theology; Cambridge: Cambridge Univ. Press, 1995), 24–28, who helpfully points out that Luke believed the Scriptures of Israel set the direction for God's purpose but that this purpose was still being worked out in the church.

SALVATION HISTORY AS LUKE'S ORGANIZING THEOLOGICAL PRINCIPLE

Interpreters of Luke–Acts commonly describe the dominant theological perspective of the work as a concern with "salvation history." The first scholars to use this term of Luke's theology used it pejoratively. For them, Luke had removed from his sources the fervently held conviction that the end of the world had arrived in the life, death, and resurrection of Jesus and transformed these eschatological events into episodes that occurred along a chronological continuum stretching into Luke's own day and beyond. The problem with this, in the view of these scholars, was that Luke had handled historiographically what can be properly understood only in existential categories, or, put differently, he had subordinated the encounter of the individual with the preached word of the gospel to the authority of an institutionalized church. He had done this in an effort to resist on the one hand the excesses of religious extremists and on the other hand to defend the church against persecution from an empire that saw the church as a threat to social stability.[9]

The term "salvation history" need only imply a theological criticism of Luke, however, if the interpreter adopts the following questionable premises:

- Virtually all Christians of the first generation, like Jesus himself, expected the end of the space-time universe well within their lifetimes.[10]
- This fervent expectation prevented the earliest Christians from writing the historical record of Jesus' place in whatever remained of the world's history.[11]
- Luke "corrected" this enthusiasm for the end by emphasizing the delay of Jesus' return, removing Jesus from present experience into the historical past, and domesticating many of the socially radical elements of primitive Christianity, particularly its emphasis on Jesus' crucifixion.[12]

Since good arguments can be sustained against each of these premises, we can dispense with pejorative evaluations of Luke's theological perspective and ask the more important question of whether "salvation history" is a useful description, from Luke's own perspective, of his primary theological concern.[13]

9 See, e.g., Rudolf Bultmann, *Theology of the New Testament*, 2 vols. (New York: Scribner's, 1951–55), 2:116–18; Philipp Vielhauer, "On the 'Paulinism' of Acts," in *Studies in Luke–Acts*, ed. Leander E. Keck and J. Louis Martin (Philadelphia: Fortress, 1966), 33–50; Hans Conzelmann, *The Theology of St. Luke* (Philadelphia: Fortress, 1961), 137–69; and Ernst Käsemann, *Essays on New Testament Themes* (Philadelphia: Fortress, 1964), 28–29; and idem, *New Testament Questions of Today* (Philadelphia: Fortress, 1969), 21–22.

10 See, e.g., Bultmann, *Theology of the New Testament*, 1:4, 37; Vielhauer, "'Paulinism' of Acts," 45–46; Conzelmann, *Theology of St. Luke*, 97–99.

11 See, e.g., Vielhauer, "'Paulinism' of Acts," 47; Käsemann, *Essays*, 28; and cf. Bultmann, *Theology of the New Testament*, 1:35–36; 2:123.

12 Bultmann, *Theology of the New Testament*, 2:117, 123, 126; Vielhauer, "'Paulinsim' of Acts," 42–43, 45–49; Conzelmann, *Theology of St. Luke*, 95–136; Käsemann, *Essays*, 29. Cf. Walasky, *'And So We Came to Rome,'* who believes that Luke sought to quell apocalyptic fervor within his church by commending the Roman empire as an instrument of God's purposes.

13 Against the first premise, see Ben Witherington, *Jesus, Paul and the End of the World: A Comparative Study in New Testament Eschatology* (Downers Grove, Ill.: InterVarsity Press, 1992). Against the second premise, see Martin Hengel, *Acts and the History of Earliest Christianity* (London: SCM, 1979), 43–46. Against the third premise, see Green, *Theology of the Gospel of Luke*, 119–21, and cf. the comments of Robert Maddox, *The Purpose of Luke–Acts* (Edinburgh: T. & T. Clark, 1982), 95, on Luke's realistic evaluation of the susceptibility of Roman power to corruption.

There is much to be said for examining Luke's theology under this rubric.[14] Luke–Acts contains a pronounced emphasis on the existence of a divine plan for the unfolding of history and on the goal of that plan as the salvation of God's people.[15] Although the Greek noun for "plan, purpose, intention" (*boulē*) appears only twelve times in the New Testament, Luke uses it five times to refer to God's "purpose"—a purpose that the Pharisees rejected (Luke 7:30), that God predetermined and foreknew to include the crucifixion of Jesus (Acts 2:23; 4:28; cf. Luke 22:22), that incorporated the preaching and healing activity of the apostles (Acts 5:38–39), and that stretched back to King David, who "served God's purpose in his own generation" (Acts 13:36).[16]

In addition, Luke can speak of God's setting "times or dates ... by his own authority" (Acts 1:7), of his setting both the chronological and geographical boundaries of the world's nations (17:26), and of a wide variety of events occurring because "it was necessary" for them to happen (e.g., Luke 4:43; 13:33; 19:5; 22:37; 24:44; Acts 3:21; 9:6, 16). The past events of Jesus' life, the circumstances of the church since then, and future events also represent the "fulfillment" of God's intention, whether that intention was expressed beforehand in Scripture (Luke 4:21; 21:22; 22:37; 24:44; Acts 1:16; 3:18; 13:27, 29; 13:32–33; cf. Luke 1:20, 45) or only in the occurrence of the events themselves (Luke 1:1; 2:16; 12:50; 21:24; Acts 14:26).[17]

That the purpose of God is the salvation of his people also becomes evident from the important role that the themes of salvation, and of Jesus Christ as Savior, play in Luke–Acts.[18] The infancy narratives set the stage for the theme when Mary refers to God as her "Savior" (Luke 1:47) because he has visited her in her humble position. Mary takes God's concern for her as a paradigm for his mercy to Israel in its oppression (1:48–55). These themes continue but become more specific when Zechariah refers to the one to be born from the house of David as "a horn of salvation" (1:69), who will redeem Israel by saving it from the oppression of its enemies according to the promises that God made in his covenant with Abraham (1:68–75).

When the angel of the Lord announces Jesus' birth to the shepherds, Luke even more specifically identifies the baby born in David's city as "a Savior ... Christ the Lord" (Luke 2:11). Finally, Simeon reveals that Jesus is the means of "salvation" that God has "prepared in the sight of all people" (2:30–31). Later in the gospel, when Jesus comes to Zacchaeus' house, salvation is present there (19:9).

In Luke's second volume, apostles and evangelists describe Jesus as the "Savior" when they preach the good news about him (Acts 5:31; 13:23). They also claim that "salvation is found in no one else" (4:12) and call their preaching "this message of salvation" (13:26; cf. 16:17; 28:28). The term "salvation history," therefore, is a useful way of describing the theological content of Luke–Acts.

---

14 Fitzmyer, *Luke I–IX*, 179–81.

15 Cf. Robert C. Tannehill, "The Story of Israel within the Lukan Narrative" in David P. Moessner, ed., *Jesus and the Heritage of Israel: Luke's Narrative Claim upon Israel's Legacy*, Luke the Interpreter of Israel 1 (Harrisburg, Penn.: Trinity Press International, 1999), 325–39, here at 325–26.

16 On the definition of *boulē*, see BDAG, 181–82.

17 Fitzmyer, *Luke I–IX*, 179–80; Green, *Theology of the Gospel of Luke*, 29; Jacob Jervell, *The Theology of the Acts of the Apostles* (Cambridge: Cambridge Univ. Press, 1996), 20.

18 I. Howard Marshall, *Luke: Historian and Theologian* (Grand Rapids: Zondervan, 1970), 94–102; Fitzmyer, *Luke I–IX*, 181.

This term can only be useful as a global description of Luke's theology, however, if we understand "salvation" as Luke understood the term. Luke could have easily developed the notion that Jesus was a "Savior" in the commonly accepted Hellenistic and Greco-Roman sense of a king who brings peace and restores order.[19] Yet Luke's concept of Jesus as "Savior" comes instead from Israel's Scriptures, particularly from the prophecies of Isaiah.[20] In Isaiah 25:1–12, for example, the prophet looks forward to the future deliverance of God's people from their enemies as a time when God will prepare a rich banquet "for all peoples" (25:6), death will be destroyed (25:7–8), and God's people will say: "Surely this is our God; we trusted in him, and he saved us. This is the LORD, we trusted in him; let us rejoice and be glad in his salvation" (Isa. 25:9).

In Isaiah 26:1–19, the prophet rejoices in God's past acts of deliverance at the same time that he recognizes God's people to be standing under God's wrath for their sins. "We have not brought salvation to the earth," God's people say (26:18), but they look forward to a time when salvation will come through the resurrection of the dead (26:19).[21] In Isaiah 40:1–5, the prophet speaks of a coming time in which God's punishment of his people for their sins will end. Israel will be at peace and God's glory will be present among them. Not only will Israel see his glory, but "all people shall see it together," or, in the words of the LXX, "all flesh shall see the salvation of God." In Isaiah 45:14–25, the prophet envisions the restoration of Israel as a period when the nations will recognize that God is with Israel (45:14). These nations will forsake their idolatry (45:22) and see in the God who created the heavens and the earth (45:18) a "Savior" (45:21; cf. 45:17, 22).

The convergence in these passages of the notion that God is Savior of his people and the notion that his salvation in some way extends to all the peoples of creation reappears in Luke–Acts. In a passage reminiscent of the LXX's rendering of Isaiah 40:1–5, Simeon says that in Jesus God has extended his glory to Israel, a light to the Gentiles, and salvation "in the sight of all people" (Luke 2:31–32).[22] In John the Baptist, Luke, like Matthew and Mark, found the fulfillment of this same passage, but unlike Matthew and Mark, Luke extended the quotation of Isaiah 40:3–5 to include the LXX's statement that "all flesh shall see the salvation of God" (Luke 3:4–6).

Similarly, when Paul says in the synagogue in Pisidian Antioch that Jesus was the promised Savior (Acts 13:23; cf. Luke 1:47, 54–55), it is difficult to know what promises he is referring to if not to those in Isaiah that depict God as the future "Savior" of his people.[23] When he experienced opposition to his message from unbelieving Jews

---

19 On this use of the term see Ceslas Spicq, *TLNT*, 3:351–54. I. H. Marshall, *Commentary on Luke* (NIGTC; Grand Rapids: Eerdmans, 1978), 110, believes that in Luke's use of the title "Savior" for Jesus we may detect an expectation that his readers would "see a contrast with rival Hellenistic statements."

20 Fitzmyer, *Luke I–IX*, 181; Tannehill, "Story of Israel," 325–27, 329–30.

21 The varying chronological perspectives in this passage make it especially difficult. For the interpretation adopted here, see Brevard S. Childs, *Isaiah* (OTL; Louisville: Westminster John Knox, 2001), 188–90.

22 On the significance of this passage for Luke's understanding of the relationship between Israel and the extension of salvation to the Gentiles, see esp. Petr Pokorný, *Theologie der lukanischen Schriften* (FRLANT 174; Göttingen: Vandenhoeck & Ruprecht, 1998), 55–56.

23 In addition to the passages referred to above, see Isa. 43:3; 49:26; 60:16; cf. 63:8.

a week later, he and Barnabas told them that they would go to the Gentiles with their message instead, for "this is what the Lord has commanded us, 'I have made you a light for the Gentiles, that you may bring salvation to the ends of the earth'" (Acts 13:47). These words are spoken to the Servant of the Lord in Isaiah 49:6b, but in its own context the preceding sentence speaks also of Israel's restoration (49:5–6a). Indeed, despite Paul's harsh condemnation of unbelieving Jews in Pisidian Antioch, he continues to preach the gospel to Jews until the conclusion of Acts.

For Luke, therefore, "salvation" refers specifically to Isaiah's promises that one day God will restore his people and that, at the same time, since he is Creator of heaven and earth, God will extend his saving work to all peoples.[24] The time of Jesus' birth, ministry, resurrection, heavenly exaltation, and of the proclamation of the good news about him through his witnesses fulfills God's purpose for the salvation of both Jews and Gentiles as Israel's Scriptures describe it. If we think of "salvation history" in these terms, the phrase is a suitable description of the organizing principle of Luke's theology.

THE PROGRESS OF SALVATION HISTORY

The Unfolding of Salvation History in Luke–Acts

Most scholars have recognized that Luke possesses a coherent outline of the progress of salvation history. Some have organized this outline into three parts: the period of Israel, the period of Jesus' ministry, and the period of the church under duress. Others have thought that Luke understands salvation history as a simple two-part story consisting of God's promises in the Scriptures and their fulfillment in Jesus and the church.[25]

Advocates of the threefold pattern point to Luke 16:16, which uses John the Baptist as the boundary line between the law and the prophets on one hand and the preaching of the kingdom of God as a boundary on the other hand. Here, these scholars say, we find evidence of Luke's first two historical periods. The disappearance of Satan during the time of Jesus' ministry and his reappearance at Jesus' passion (Luke 4:13; 10:4; 22:3; 22:35) demarcate the second of these periods from a third period in which the church continues its existence under duress. Scholars debate the precise points at which one period gives way to another (where do John and the ascension fit into the scheme?), but the basic outline continues to be useful to many interpreters for understanding Luke–Acts.[26]

Others have insisted that the threefold scheme is a figment of the scholarly imagination. Luke himself, they argue, only explicitly refers to two periods, the time of the law and the prophets and the time of the gospel's proclamation (Luke 16:16).

24 Cf. Hans Hübner, *Biblische Theologie des Neuen Testaments*, 3 vols. (Göttingen: Vandenhoeck & Ruprecht, 1990–95), 3:122–23, 127.

25 Stephen F. Plymale, "Luke's Theology of Prayer," *Society of Biblical Literature 1990 Seminar Papers*, ed. David J. Lull (Atlanta, Ga.: Scholars Press, 1990), 529–51, speaks of four periods of salvation history (including the future coming of the kingdom in all its fullness), but this proposal has not been widely accepted.

26 See, e.g., Conzelmann, *Theology of St. Luke*, 16–17; Fitzmyer, *Luke I–IX*, 181–87.

Luke 7:27–28, it is said, supports the twofold promise-fulfillment scheme since it speaks of two periods, one far greater than the other, and describes John the Baptist in his role as forerunner of Jesus as the end of the first period.[27]

Both positions reveal important aspects of Luke's perspective. If we take as our guide Luke's explicit references to the relationship between "the things that have been fulfilled among us" (Luke 1:1) and God's past activity, then the twofold scheme seems to be Luke's dominant paradigm. Not only do 16:16 and 7:27–28 (cf. 10:24) support this understanding of Luke's historical viewpoint, but Luke's many references to the anticipation of the Messiah's suffering, death, resurrection, and proclamation in Israel's Scriptures also reveal its importance (Luke 24:25–27, 44–47; Acts 3:18–26; 17:2–3; 18:28; 24:14; 26:6–7; 26:22–23, 27; 28:20). Since the perspective of promise and fulfillment is common to many New Testament authors, however, to say that it is also present in Luke is of limited usefulness in understanding the distinctive elements of Luke's theology.[28]

Although the boundaries of the period of Jesus are more subtly expressed than those of the other two periods, Luke appears to have understood the time of Jesus' ministry as a discrete period in salvation history. On one side of this period, the careful dating of John's preaching in Luke 3:1–3 and the mention of John's imprisonment already in 3:20 (cf. Matt. 14:1–12; Mark 6:14–26) hint that Luke conceives of the period of Jesus as separate from the period of preparation, and Luke 16:16 confirms this. On the other side, Luke implies that the period of the church is separate from the period of Jesus by his repetition of the story of Jesus' ascension, once at the end of the gospel (Luke 24:50–51) and once at the beginning of Acts (1:9–11). Luke again subtly expresses the importance of Jesus' baptism and ascension as temporal markers in the statement of Peter that Judas's replacement should be one who was with the Twelve "from John's baptism to the time when Jesus was taken up from us" (Acts 1:22).[29]

There is, therefore, some reason for thinking that Luke understood salvation history to have unfolded in three distinct stages. The first stage was a period of promise, and the last two stages were times of fulfillment.[30]

The Biblical Shape of Salvation History and Its Fulfillment in Jesus and the Church

How does Luke understand the link between promise and fulfillment? To put the question another way, why does Luke assume that the Christians for whom he is writing, most of them Gentiles, can consider themselves to be participants in the

27 See, e.g., Werner Georg Kümmel, "Current Theological Accusations against Luke," *Andover Newton Quarterly* 16 (1975): 131–45, here at 137–38; Darrell L. Bock, *Luke 1:1–9:50* (BECNT 3A; Grand Rapids: Baker, 1994), 28; idem, *Luke 9:51–24:53* (BECNT 3B; Grand Rapids: Baker, 1996), 1351.

28 Fitzmyer, *Luke I–IX*, 181.

29 Ibid., 184. Cf. Conzelmann, *Theology of St. Luke*, 21.

30 Kümmel, "Current Theological Accusations," 138, does not seem far from this understanding of Luke–Acts when he subdivides the period of fulfillment into the time in which "the message of final salvation" is "proclaimed *first of all* in Jesus, and *then* through the apostles" [emphasis added]. Cf. Hübner, *Biblische Theologie*, 3:123, who agrees in principle with Kümmel's critique of Conzelmann's three-part scheme but still believes that the phrase "the middle of time" is useful; also Rudolf Schnackenburg, *Jesus in the Gospels: A Biblical Christology* (Louisville: Westminster John Knox, 1995), 132–33.

eschatological fulfillment of the promises of Israel's Scriptures? If we can assume that Luke's own theology matches that expressed by Jesus and the earliest Christians, then a reasonably clear picture emerges of how, in Luke's thinking, the periods of Jesus and the church constitute the fulfillment of the period of Israel.

Creation and Idolatry

Luke's understanding of salvation history begins where the Bible begins—with the Genesis account of God's creation of the universe and of all peoples on the earth. Not only does he trace Jesus' lineage back to Adam (Luke 3:38), but he frequently emphasizes that God was the Creator of "heaven and earth and sea and everything in them" (Acts 4:24; 14:15; 17:24; cf. Gen. 1:1–25). God made the first man (Acts 17:26; cf. Gen. 1:26–27; 2:7), and just as Adam was God's offspring (Luke 3:38), so all people are the offspring of God (Acts 17:28). God produced every ethnic group from Adam and provided these peoples with the earth as their dwelling place, with its chronological seasons and geographical boundaries (Acts 17:26; cf. Ps. 74:17).[31] God provided to all people rain, crops, food, and the pleasures of life (Acts 14:17; 17:25; cf. Gen. 1:28–30). These signs of his providence and sovereignty should have led people to worship him (Acts 17:27), but instead they worshiped idols (Acts 14:15; 17:23, 29; cf. Wisd. 13:1–9).

Israel's Rebellion and God's Saving Purpose

Luke also knows that according to Genesis God focused his saving purpose on one ethnic group, the descendants of Abraham, with whom he made a covenant (Acts 3:25; cf. Luke 1:54–55, 73; Acts 7:2–5; 13:17).[32] According to Genesis 22:18 and 26:4, this covenant had three terms: (1) that God would give Abraham many descendants, (2) that these descendants would possess "the cities of their enemies," and (3) that through these descendants "all nations on the earth" would be "blessed." Luke is interested primarily in the third term of this covenant because it provides a decisive link between Gentile Christians, whom God blessed by including them within his people through the gospel, and the Jewish people, with whom God had initially made his covenant and whose prophets spoke of a Messiah that could only be identified with Jesus.

Luke believes that the story of God's relationship with his covenant people reveals both their persistent rejection of his messengers and God's constant work, despite these rejections, to accomplish his goal of blessing all the nations of the earth through Israel. Stephen tells the story of Israel's rejection of God's saving purpose in his lengthy speech in Acts 7:2–53. After the period of the patriarchs, Stephen says, the story of Israel is the account of a downward spiral of rejection of God's attempts to save them. Joseph's brothers sold him into Egypt. In Egypt, the enslaved children of Israel thrust aside their savior Moses, questioning his justice, disobeying his instructions, and yearning to return to slavery in Egypt (cf. 13:18). After they received God's promise of the land and built for him a temple, they mistakenly concluded that God lived in the temple.[33] They also persecuted and killed the prophets.

31 Ernst Haenchen, *The Acts of the Apostles: A Commentary* (Philadelphia: Westminster, 1971), 523.

32 Cf. Tannehill, "Story of Israel," 327–28.

33 Luke does not say this explicity, but it is implied.

This pessimistic perspective on Israel's history in Stephen's speech coincides with Jesus' perspective in Luke's gospel. Using material that he may have taken over from the hypothetical source Q, Luke twice records a warning of Jesus that Jerusalem and its leaders stand in the tradition of their "fathers" who killed the prophets (Luke 11:47–51; 13:34; cf. Matt. 23:29–37). Similarly, in a passage unique to Luke's gospel, Jesus refuses to interrupt his journey to Jerusalem with the statement, "Surely no prophet can die outside Jerusalem!" (Luke 13:31–33).

Alongside this account of disobedience to God and rejection of his saving purpose, however, Luke also tells the heartening story of the onward march of God's intention to accomplish this purpose. The first part of Paul's synagogue sermon in Pisidian Antioch in Acts 13:16b–22 is the positive counterpart to Stephen's speech.[34] Paul reminds his audience that God chose the patriarchs, increased the population of his people in Egypt, powerfully led them out of slavery in that land, and brought them to Canaan, where he destroyed the occupants and settled his people. There he provided leaders for them in the land: judges, the prophet Samuel, and kings. Among the kings the most notable was David, a man wholly devoted to God.

Luke matches this positive account of God's relationship with a positive assessment of Israel's history in the two main prayers of praise in the infancy narrative. In her prayer, Mary speaks of God's mercy from generation to generation (Luke 1:50), of the mighty deeds that his arm has performed (1:52–53), and of how he has done all this for his "servant Israel," the descendants of Abraham (1:54–55). Similarly, Zechariah's benediction tells of the "holy covenant" that "the Lord, the God of Israel" made by means of an oath with Abraham to rescue his people from their enemies (1:68, 72–75).

Jesus as the Convergence Point of the Two Stories

These two paths, one positive and one negative—one that follows God's saving purpose for his people and the other that follows Israel's rejection of God's purpose—intersect in Jesus of Nazareth, whom Luke has a special interest in portraying as Israel's royal Messiah, Suffering Servant, and eschatological prophet.

Israel's Royal Messiah

Jesus is both the "Son of the Most High" and the promised "Son of David" who, according to the prophecies of 2 Samuel 7:11b–16 and Isaiah 9:7, will "reign over the house of Jacob forever" (Luke 1:31–33, 69–70; 2:30; Acts 13:23). He is therefore the Messiah whom Jews commonly expected to come as God's primary instrument of his people's salvation (Luke 2:11, 26; 4:41; 9:20; Acts 2:36; 3:20; 5:42; 8:5; 9:22; 17:3; 18:5, 28). At this high point of God's saving work on behalf of his people, however, their rejection of his merciful purpose reaches its lowest ebb. In Paul's synagogue sermon in Pisidian Antioch, he concludes his otherwise positive overview of salvation history with the following indictment:

34 On the importance of these two speeches for understanding Luke's approach to salvation history (but without dividing them as they are divided here into a positive and a negative portrayal), see Jervell, *Theology of the Acts*, 19, 24.

> The people of Jerusalem and their rulers did not recognize Jesus, yet in condemning him they fulfilled the words of the prophets that are read every Sabbath. Though they found no proper ground for a death sentence, they asked Pilate to have him executed. (Acts 13:27–28; cf. 2:23b; 3:13b–15, 17; 4:10, 27; 5:30; 10:38–39)

Jesus as Suffering Servant

Luke also understands Jesus to be the Servant of the Lord, whom Isaiah the prophet described.[35] In a series of passages that find no parallels in the other gospels, Luke identifies Jesus with the Servant in both explicit and subtle ways. Simeon speaks of the infant Jesus as "a light for revelation to the Gentiles and for glory to your people Israel" (Luke 2:32), recalling the role of Isaiah's servant according to Isaiah 49:6:

> It is too small a thing for you to be my servant
> to restore the tribes of Jacob
> and bring back those of Israel I have kept.
> I will also make you a light for the Gentiles,
> that you may bring my salvation to the ends of the earth. (cf. Isa. 42:6)

Shortly before his arrest, Jesus himself says that the description of the Servant's plight in Isaiah 53:12 ("he was numbered with the transgressors") finds its fulfillment in him (Luke 22:37). Later, Philip explains to the Ethiopian eunuch that Jesus fulfilled another aspect of the Servant's plight:

> He was led like a sheep to the slaughter,
> and as a lamb before the shearer is silent,
> so he did not open his mouth.
> In his humiliation he was deprived of justice.
> Who can speak of his descendants?
> For his life was taken from the earth. (Acts 8:32–33; cf. Isa. 53:7–8 LXX)

These explicit identifications of Jesus with Isaiah's Servant should probably lead us to understand the references to Jesus as God's "servant" in Acts 3–4 (3:13, 26; 4:27, 30) as echoes of Isaiah's Servant Songs also.

Luke 4:16–22, another ambiguous passage, is probably also a claim that Jesus fulfills the role of the Servant in Isaiah. Here Jesus preaches a sermon on Isaiah 61:1–2 in his hometown synagogue in Nazareth:

> The Spirit of the Lord is on me,
> because he has anointed me
> to preach good news to the poor.
> He has sent me to proclaim freedom for the prisoners
> and recovery of sight for the blind,
> to release the oppressed,
> to proclaim the year of the Lord's favor.

35 Cf. Marshall, *Luke*, 178, 183, and Bock, *Luke 1:1–9:50*, 406.

Jesus claims to be the one who fulfills the expectations of this passage. Although Luke never identifies the "me" of the passage explicitly as the Lord's Servant, it rings with echoes of the first Servant Song.[36] In the first song, God says that he will put his Spirit on the Servant (Isa. 42:1), that the Servant will "open eyes that are blind," and that the Servant will "free captives from prison" (42:7). Since Luke was familiar with the first Servant Song and considered it important for understanding Jesus' mission (Luke 2:32), he probably also understands Isaiah 61:1–2 in light of Jesus' Servant role.[37]

This passage may also be the place where messianic conceptions and the role of the Servant converge in Luke's thinking.[38] In Isaiah 61:1 the speaker claims that the Lord "anointed" him, and in the LXX the word "anointed" becomes *echrisen*, a verb that Luke uses elsewhere of Jesus (Acts 4:27; 10:38). Luke is well aware of the connection between this verb and the noun "Christ," which translates the Hebrew "Messiah" (Acts 4:26–27). In light of this, Luke may have understood Jesus' fulfillment of the role of the "anointed" one of Isaiah 61:1 to be the fulfillment of a messianic role.[39]

If Luke also thinks of the speaker in Isaiah 61:1–2 as the Servant, and if suffering is an important part of the Servant's mission (Luke 22:37; Acts 8:32–33), then it is easy to see how Luke can say that, according to the Scriptures, the Messiah will suffer (Luke 24:26; Acts 3:18; 17:3; 26:23).[40] From Luke's perspective, Isaiah demonstrated the identity of the Servant and the Messiah, and this means that in his descriptions of the Servant's suffering Isaiah had also foretold the suffering of the Messiah.[41]

Once again, however, at the climactic point in salvation history when the long-awaited Servant arrived, Israel rejected rather than embraced him. Immediately after happily identifying the infant Jesus as God's Servant, Simeon utters this ominous pronouncement:

> This child is destined to cause the falling and rising of many in Israel, and to be a sign that will be spoken against, so that the thoughts of many hearts will be revealed. And a sword will pierce your [Mary's] own soul too. (Luke 2:34–35)

Similarly, just after identifying himself with the speaker of Isaiah 61:1–3, the people of Jesus' hometown are so enraged by his positive comments about non-Israelites that they attempt to lynch him (Luke 4:24–30). Jesus must be "numbered among the transgressors" because the chief priests and officers of the temple guard

36 See the discussions in C. H. Dodd, *According to the Scriptures: The Substructure of New Testament Theology* (London: Nisbet, 1952), 94; Edward P. Meadors, "The Orthodoxy of the 'Q' Sayings of Jesus," *TynB* 43 (1992): 233–57, here at 254; Childs, *Isaiah*, 502–6; and esp. John N. Oswalt, *The Book of Isaiah: Chapters 40–66* (NICOT; Grand Rapids: Eerdmans, 1998), 562–63.

37 *Pace* Fitzmyer, *Luke I–IX*, 529–30.

38 Although, as Dr. Edward Meadors reminds me, the convergence of Servant and Messiah also occurs when God announces at Jesus' baptism (Luke 3:22 [Matt. 3:17]; cf. Luke 9:35; Matt. 17:5) that Jesus is God's "Son" (cf. 2 Sam. 7:14) with whom he is "pleased" (cf. Isa. 42:1).

39 Cf. Isa. 11:1–2, where the Spirit of the Lord is said to rest on the "shoot . . . from the stump of Jesse."

40 Again, *pace* Fitzmyer, *Luke I–IX*, 200–201, but in agreement with Oswalt, *Isaiah: Chapters 40–66*, 563.

41 Cf. Mark L. Strauss, *The Davidic Messiah in Luke–Acts: The Promise and Its Fulfillment in Lukan Christology* (JSNTSup 110; Sheffield: Sheffield Academic Press, 1995), 341, who suggests that Luke, reading Isaiah as a unity, merged the figure of "the prophet-herald of Isaiah 61, the servant of the Isaianic servant songs and the coming of the Davidic king of Isaiah 9 and 11."

will shortly arrest him (22:37). The "men of Israel" handed God's "servant Jesus" over to be killed (Acts 3:13; cf. 4:27).

Jesus as Eschatological Prophet

Jesus was not only the expected Messiah and Servant but also the prophet about whom Moses spoke when he said to the people of Israel in Deuteronomy 18:15–19:

> The LORD your God will raise up for you a prophet like me from among your own brothers. You must listen to him. For this is what you asked of the LORD your God at Horeb on the day of the assembly when you said, "Let us not hear the voice of the LORD our God nor see this great fire anymore, or we will die."
>
> The LORD said to me: "What they say is good. I will raise up for them a prophet like you from among their brothers; I will put my words in his mouth, and he will tell them everything I command him. If anyone does not listen to my words that the prophet speaks in my name, I myself will call him to account."

Although Luke thinks of Jesus as a prophet in the generic sense of the term (Luke 7:16; 9:8, 19; 24:19; 13:33), and as "a great prophet" (7:13) like Elijah and Elisha (4:25–27), he has a special interest in Jesus' fulfillment of the role of the prophet like Moses.[42] Like the other Synoptic Gospels, Luke implies this identification when, at the transfiguration, God tells Peter, John, and James to "listen to" (Luke 9:35; cf. Matt. 17:5; Mark 9:7; also Deut. 18:15, 19) Jesus, who is standing in the presence of Moses. Luke gives the motif special emphasis, however, when he identifies the topic of Jesus' discussion with Elijah and Moses as Jesus' "departure [*exodos*], which he was about to bring to fulfillment at Jerusalem" (9:31). Like Moses, Jesus led an exodus of God's people when "he resolutely set out for Jerusalem" only a few paragraphs later (9:51).[43]

The identification of Jesus as this eschatological prophet and its significance for Luke becomes more explicit in Acts, where Peter paraphrases Deuteronomy 18:15–19 and claims that to reject Jesus is to become liable to the curse pronounced on those who reject God's prophet according to Deuteronomy 18:19 (Acts 3:22–23).[44] Stephen is also interested in Jesus' fulfillment of this role. In his indictment of Israel, he dwells at length on Moses (7:20–44) and identifies Moses as the one "who told the Israelites, 'God will send you a prophet like me from your own people'" (7:37), a clear allusion to Jesus. Here too God's saving purpose and Israel's rejection of that purpose intersect. Jesus is not merely another prophet who dies in Jerusalem (Luke 13:33–34; Acts 7:52) but the prophet like Moses, who, like Moses himself, was "pushed ... aside" by God's people (Acts 7:27, 35, 39).

This very rejection of God's Messiah, Servant, and prophet, however, was part of God's "set purpose" (Acts 2:23) to extend the opportunity for repentance and forgiveness not only to Israel but to all people everywhere. Jesus' rejection aided this purpose

42 Fitzmyer, *Luke I–IX*, 213–14, and David P. Moessner, *The Lord of the Banquet: The Literary and Theological Significance of the Lukan Travel Narrative* (Minneapolis: Fortress, 1989), 45–79.

43 Moessner, *Lord of the Banquet*, 46, 66.

44 Peter apparently merges Deut. 18:19 with Lev. 23:29. See C. K. Barrett, *The Acts of the Apostles*, 2 vols. (ICC; Edinburgh: T. & T. Clark, 1994–98), 1:209–10.

by providing irrefutable proof that Jesus was the Messiah, for the prophets had predicted the Messiah's suffering (Luke 22:22; 24:26, 46; Acts 3:18; 17:2–3; 26:23, 27), and David had said that people would plot against the Lord's anointed one (Acts 4:25–26; cf. Ps. 2:1–2). Such a correspondence between what the Scriptures prophesied and what happened in the death of Jesus, once explained, can dispel the ignorance of those who rejected Jesus, and it can pave the way both to their repentance and to God's forgiveness of their sins (Acts 3:17–19). At the same time, this correspondence can create certainty in the hearts of followers of Jesus—followers like Theophilus—that their faith in Jesus is well placed (Luke 1:3–4; 24:25–27, 32).

Jesus' Resurrection and Exaltation

Although claims that Luke plays down the significance of Jesus' death are exaggerated, there can be no question that the most important event in salvation history for Luke was Jesus' resurrection and his exaltation to the right hand of God. These events are important to Luke for several reasons. Like the death of Jesus, they fulfill expectations expressed in various psalms and Isaiah and therefore offer confirmation that Jesus is the Messiah (Luke 24:26–27, 45–46; Acts 2:24–36; 13:32–38; 17:2–3; 26:22–23, 27).[45] Such correspondences help Luke's readers to develop a sense of "certainty of the things" they have "been taught" (Luke 1:4). In addition, Luke conceives of Jesus as offering repentance and forgiveness of sins to Israel from his position of exaltation at God's right hand (Acts 5:30–31; 13:37–39).

Above all, however, Jesus' resurrection and exaltation are important because they demonstrate that "in Jesus" the era of the general "resurrection from the dead" has begun (Acts 4:2). He is "the first to rise from the dead" (26:23), and thus his resurrection inaugurates the epoch of Israel's restoration.[46] This is the primary point of Paul's preaching in Acts. Luke can summarize Paul's preaching as "the good news about Jesus and the resurrection" (17:18; cf. 13:32). In the judicial hearings that dominate the final quarter of Acts, Paul insists that the central issue is his "hope in the resurrection of the dead" (23:6; 24:21), a hope that corresponds both with "what God has promised to our fathers" (26:6; cf. 24:14) and with the present expectations of "our twelve tribes" (26:7–8; cf. 24:15). With the resurrection of Jesus, the period of the general resurrection has begun in which God will fulfill "the hope of Israel" (28:20).

Luke knows well the picture that the biblical prophets painted of this period of Israel's restoration. It was a time when not only would God raise the dead but give sight to the blind, cleanse lepers, make the lame walk, and reverse the fortunes of the oppressed (Luke 7:22; cf. Isa. 26:19; 35:5–6; 29:18–19; 61:1). It was a time when God would establish a new covenant with his people and forgive their sins (Luke 22:20; cf. Jer. 31:31, 34). It was a time when God would pour out his Spirit on all

45 In Acts 17:31, where Paul preaches to a Greek audience, the resurrection of Jesus serves not as proof of Jesus' correspondence to the expectations of the Scriptures but simply as proof that God "has set a day when he will judge the world with justice by the man he has appointed."

46 *Pace* Georg Strecker, *Theology of the New Testament* (New York: Walter de Gruyter/Louisville: Westminster John Knox, 2000), 410, who says that Jesus' death and resurrection are for Luke no longer the decisive saving events but simply two saving events on a long historical continuum of other, similar events.

his people and would be powerfully present among them (Acts 2:17; 5:1–11; 9:31; cf. Joel 2:28–29; Ezek. 11:19; 36:22–37:14; Zech. 2:11).[47]

As we have already seen in our examination of Luke's understanding of salvation, he is convinced that the period of Israel's restoration is also a time when God will reconfigure his people to include all the peoples of the earth. It is a time when the marginalized and oppressed within Israel will find acceptance and relief: The poor will hear the good news, prisoners will be freed, the blind will see, and the eschatological year of Jubilee will release the oppressed from their plight (Luke 4:18–19; 7:22; 14:21; cf. Isa. 61:1–3). It is also a time when Israel's restoration will expand beyond Israel itself to include "all who are far off" (Acts 2:39; 3:25–26; 13:46; 26:23). The word of the Lord will expand from Jerusalem, to Judea, to Samaria, to the ends of the earth to include within God's restored people everyone who believes without regard to their ethnic affiliation (Luke 24:46–47; Acts 1:8; cf. 10:36–39). Thus, Peter argues twice before the astonished Jewish leadership of the church in Jerusalem that the place of Gentiles within the people of God is unimpeachable, for they too have received God's eschatologically given Spirit (Acts 10:1–11:18; 15:8).

Luke claims that this vision comes from Israel's Scriptures (Luke 24:46–47; Acts 10:42–43; 26:22–23). At times he reveals the Scriptures that inform this vision, quoting from and alluding to Isaiah 61:1–2a (Luke 4:18–19; 7:22; 14:21), Isaiah 42:6 (Luke 2:29–32), Isaiah 49:6 (Acts 13:47), and Amos 9:11–12 (LXX, Acts 15:13–21). Perhaps in addition to these texts, he had in mind the pattern reflected in Isaiah 2:3 and Micah 4:2, where in the last days:

> Many peoples will come and say,
> "Come, let us go up to the mountain of the LORD,
> to the house of the God of Jacob.
> He will teach us his ways,
> so that we may walk in his paths."
> The law will go out from Zion,
> the word of the LORD from Jerusalem.

This movement of God's Word outward from Jerusalem to the nations articulates precisely the pattern we find at the end of Luke's gospel and the beginning of Acts. At these two critical places in Luke's narrative, Jesus says the Scriptures testify that "repentance and forgiveness of sins will be preached in his name to all the nations, beginning at Jerusalem" (Luke 24:47), and then that the apostles will be his witnesses "in Jerusalem, and in all Judea and Samaria, and to the ends of the earth" (Acts 1:8).[48]

Once "all whom the Lord our God will call" (Acts 2:39) have heard the gospel, repented, and received forgiveness of their sins, Luke believes that Jesus the Messiah

47 Luke and other early Christians were not the only ones who read the prophets in this way. Edward P. Meadors, "The 'Messianic' Implications of the Q Material," *JBL* 118 (1999): 253–77, here at 257–64, observes that 4Q521 expects the eschatological release of captives, restoration of sight to the blind, the resurrection of the dead, and the Lord's proclamation of good news to the poor.

48 Cf. David W. Pao, *Acts and the Isaianic New Exodus* (WUNT 2.130; Tübingen: J. C. B. Mohr [Paul Siebeck], 2000), 156–59, who also observes that this theme is present in Isa. 40:1–2, 9; 49:13–18; and 51:3.

will come from his place of exaltation in heaven and "restore everything, as he promised long ago through the prophets" (Acts 3:21). At that time God will judge the entire world, whether the Jews in Jerusalem or the Greeks in Athens, whether living or resurrected dead, on the basis of the response that they have made to the proclamation about Jesus (17:18, 31; 24:15). For the Jews he is the prophet like Moses whose rejection means being "completely cut off" from God's people (3:23). For the Greeks, he is perhaps only the appointed judge whose position God confirms through the astounding miracle of his resurrection from the dead (17:31). In either case "both Jews and Greeks . . . must turn to God in repentance and have faith in [the] Lord Jesus" (20:21).

In this way Luke believed that God will finally fulfill the terms of the covenant that he made with Abraham when he promised, "Through your offspring all peoples on earth will be blessed" (Acts 3:25). Apparently the fulfillment of this promise will also signal the fulfillment of God's intention to "restore the kingdom to Israel" (1:6; cf. 3:21; Luke 24:21), and God's saving purpose both for his people specifically and for creation generally will be complete.[49]

Summary

Luke conceives of salvation history as God's plan to forgive the sins of his rebellious creatures, both Gentiles and Jews. Gentiles need God's forgiveness for straying into idolatry and Jews need it for rejecting God's messengers, especially the preeminent messenger, Jesus, who filled the roles of royal Messiah, Suffering Servant, and eschatological prophet. Now, with the resurrection and exaltation of Jesus, the time for repentance and forgiveness has arrived, first for God's special people Israel and then for "all the nations." Both Jews and Gentiles who repent of their sins and receive God's forgiveness will receive a place among God's people when the Messiah Jesus comes to "restore the kingdom to Israel" and to "judge the world with justice." Luke understands this entire plan, from beginning to end, to be nothing other than God's plan, as it was revealed in the law of Moses, the Prophets, and the Psalms.

THE CERTAIN TRIUMPH OF GOD'S SAVING PURPOSE

In Acts 5:34–39, rabbi Gamaliel the Elder articulates one of Luke's settled theological convictions. It is the criterion by which he wants his readers to judge the Christian movement. Speaking of the apostles who have remained defiant in the face of hostile questioning from Gamaliel's colleagues, the revered teacher says:

> Leave these men alone! Let them go! For if their purpose or activity is of human origin, it will fail. But if it is from God, you will not be able to stop these men; you will only find yourselves fighting against God.

49 Cf. Tannehill, "Story of Israel," 325–39, and Pokorný, *Theologie der lukanischen Schriften*, 49–52. Pokorný argues that in Luke–Acts the church functions as the mediator between Israel and the new humanity.

Luke believes that the work of Jesus, his apostles, and his evangelists will march relentlessly forward in the future just as it has in the past. This, he believes, is clear proof of its divine origin and should serve as assurance to readers like Theophilus that their faith, despite the suffering they are experiencing for it, is well-placed.

The Triumph of God's Purpose over Cosmic Evil Forces

Satan, the demonic world, and the powers of magic that are aligned with them play a prominent role in opposing the saving work of Jesus in both Luke's gospel and Acts.[50] Satan and his forces have the power to afflict people with debilitating illnesses (Luke 8:2; 13:11, 16; Acts 10:38), to dehumanize people (Luke 8:26–39; Acts 16:16), to pluck the word of God from their hearts (Luke 8:12; cf. Acts 13:8), and to possess people for the purpose of using them to accomplish especially evil tasks (Luke 22:3; Acts 5:3).

One of the most important elements in the vocation of Jesus, the apostles, and other evangelists is the deliverance of Satan's victims from his power (Acts 10:38; 26:18). Luke shows the vigorous opposition of Satan to this work. Before Jesus begins his ministry, "the devil" confronts him in the desert and urges him to defect from his calling as God's Son (Luke 4:1–13).[51] He enters Judas and prompts him to betray Jesus to the chief priests and temple officials (Luke 22:3–4).[52] He enters Ananias, and presumably Sapphira also, prompting them to lie to the Holy Spirit and betray the fledgling church (Acts 5:3). As with Job (Job 1:9–12; 2:4–6), Satan asks God's permission to afflict believers with hardship in the hope of shaking their faith (Luke 22:31). He uses magicians under his power to try to dissuade those interested in the word of the Lord from believing it (Acts 13:6–12), to corrupt the faith of those who already believe (8:9–24), and to place obstacles before those who "proclaim the way of salvation" (16:18a).

None of this ultimately works. In his confrontation with the devil, Jesus clings unflinchingly to God's words in the Old Testament (Luke 4:4, 8, 12). Judas, Ananias, and Sapphira all die sudden deaths (Acts 1:18; 5:5, 10), but Jesus is raised from the dead, and after the deaths of Ananias and Sapphira "more and more men and women believed in the Lord" (5:14). During his ministry, Jesus rebukes demons (Luke 4:41), heals those afflicted by evil spirits (8:2; 13:32), expels demons from those possessed by them (8:32–35), and empowers his disciples to do the same (9:1; 10:1–16). When seventy-two of his followers return from replicating Jesus' mission, they report with delight, "Lord, even the demons submit to us in your name" (10:18). Jesus responds that he has seen Satan plummet from heaven like lightning—evidently a reference to

50 See esp. Susan R. Garrett, *The Demise of the Devil: Magic and the Demonic in Luke's Writings* (Minneapolis: Fortress, 1989).

51 On the programmatic nature of the temptation scene for the struggle between God's saving purpose in Jesus and the forces of evil in Luke's gospel, see Joseph A. Fitzmyer, *Luke the Theologian: Aspects of His Teaching* (New York: Paulist, 1989), 151, 157.

52 Conzelmann, *Theology of St. Luke*, 28, believes that a comparison of Luke 4:13 and 22:3 shows that Luke believed the period of Jesus' ministry to be free of opposition from Satan. This idea is almost universally rejected now because it fails to explain adequately why most of the references to Satan and the demonic world in the gospel occur between 4:13 and 22:3 and why Jesus refers in 11:16 and 22:28 to temptations and trials during his ministry. Among the many interpreters who reject Conzelmann's view, see esp. Marshall, *Luke: Historian and Theologian*, 87–88, and Fitzmyer, *Luke the Theologian*, 161–64.

their recent exorcising activity—and tells them that they have the authority to overcome all the obstacles that "the enemy" might devise to harm them during their future ministry (10:18–19).[53]

Jesus' words find confirmation in Acts.[54] Here his followers, like Jesus himself, drive out evil spirits (Acts 8:7; 16:18; 19:12). Here too the best magician Samaria has to offer becomes a believer, is astonished at the power that accompanies the preaching of the gospel (8:13), and when caught trying to subvert the faith, fearfully submits to the authority of the apostles (8:25).[55] Another magician who tries to prevent the conversion of the proconsul of Cyprus ironically facilitates the proconsul's conversion instead when God strikes him with blindness (13:11–12). An evil spirit confesses the power of Jesus and Paul in Ephesus, a city notorious for its occult practices. As a result many Ephesians believe in Jesus, abandon their magical practices, and burn the scrolls that provided the magical formulas so essential to their former practices (19:13–20).[56]

Luke's message in this recurring theme is clear. Inimical spiritual forces are ranged against God's saving purpose. They cannot, however, ultimately frustrate God's power to heal the sick, open the hearts of people to his word, and release people from Satan's bondage.

The Triumph of God's Purpose over Opposition to Its Inclusive Character

Luke also emphasizes the triumph of God over opposition to the inclusive nature of his saving purpose as this is proclaimed in the work of Jesus, his apostles and evangelists, and his "chosen vessel," Paul. This is a prominent theme in both the gospel and Acts.

The Triumph of Inclusiveness in Luke's Gospel

At the beginning of his ministry and immediately after he has overcome the opposition of Satan to his role as Son of God, Jesus faces the opposition of the people in his hometown, Nazareth (Luke 4:16–30). He has just preached a synagogue sermon claiming that he is the fulfillment of Isaiah 61:1–2a: He will preach good news to the poor, release the captives, give sight to the blind, free the oppressed, and proclaim that the time of God's favor has come. At first his hearers greet this message with enthusiasm (Luke 4:22), but when he makes plain that, like Elijah and Elisha, he plans to extend the Lord's favor to Gentiles, a crowd hustles him to the edge of a nearby cliff to lynch him (4:29).

As with Satan's efforts to thwart Jesus at the beginning of his ministry, however, the crowd's efforts fail to hinder Jesus from including outcasts, even Gentiles, in God's

53 For this understanding of Jesus' vision of Satan's fall, see Fitzmyer, *Luke the Theologian*, 168–69.

54 Cf. Garrett, *Demise of the Devil*, 75, who, however, pinpoints Satan's fall at the time of Jesus' resurrection and ascension rather than in the exorcising activity of Jesus' disciples.

55 On the account of Simon Magus's confrontation with Peter as a caution against allowing the corruption of money and power to infest the church, see Tannehill, *Narrative Unity*, 2:106–7.

56 On the notoriety of Ephesus as a center of magical practices and writings, see Garrett, *Demise of the Devil*, 97; Clinton E. Arnold, *Ephesians, Power and Magic: The Concept of Power in Ephesians in Light of Its Historical Setting* (SNTSMS 63; Cambridge: Cambridge Univ. Press, 1989), 13–20; and Barrett, *Acts*, 2:913.

saving purpose. Jesus, we read, "walked right through the crowd and went on his way" (Luke 4:30).[57]

As he proceeds "on his way" through Galilee and eventually to Jerusalem, Jesus continues to make clear the radically inclusive nature of his ministry, and at virtually every step along the way he faces resistance from the scribes and Pharisees. Their main complaint is that Jesus consistently places the extension of healing, repentance, and forgiveness to the outcast over the observance of the Mosaic law. Thus, he extends forgiveness to a paralyzed man despite the objections of the scribes and Pharisees that only God can forgive sins (Luke 5:21). He attends a feast at the house of Levi the tax collector despite the unhappiness of the Pharisees and their scribes about his association with "tax collectors and sinners" (5:30; 15:2). Despite the criticism of the Pharisees, he places the hunger of his disciples over the observance of the Sabbath and does so because, he says, he is "Lord of the Sabbath" (6:5).

He heals the sick on the Sabbath despite infuriating the scribes and Pharisees in the process, and he justifies his action with the claim that "to save life" is an appropriate Sabbath activity (Luke 6:9; cf. 13:16; 14:5). To the astonishment of one Pharisee, he fails to wash before dinner, maintaining that inner purity is the only purity that matters and that therefore giving alms to the poor obviates the need to observe the rules of ritual purity (11:37–41). To the disdain of an expert in the Mosaic law, he tells a story that features a Samaritan who keeps the law more faithfully by aiding a stranger in need than a priest and a Levite who fail to do so (10:25–37).

Objections to his conduct, however, regularly call forth from Jesus amazing deeds and brilliant teaching that never fail to put his opponents to shame. When the Pharisees and scribes think Jesus is a blasphemer because he forgives the paralyzed man's sins, Jesus responds by healing the man of his paralysis. In comparison with his Markan source, Luke emphasizes the shock that this event gives the surrounding crowd. Mark simply says that everyone was amazed, praised God, and said that they had never seen anything like this (Mark 2:12). Luke says that amazement "gripped" everyone, that they not only glorified God but were filled with fear, and that they had seen *paradoxa*—strange, wonderful things contrary to any known rational explanation (Luke 5:26).

Similarly, after Jesus heals a crippled woman on the Sabbath—a miracle recorded only in Luke's gospel—and then skillfully defends the legitimacy of his action, Luke comments that "all his opponents were humiliated, but the people were delighted with all the wonderful things he was doing" (Luke 13:17). In another Sabbath healing—also found only in Luke—this happens again: Jesus justifies his action with such brilliance that his opponents can find no words to answer him (6:6; cf. 6:4).[58]

When the leaders of the people decide to destroy Jesus, largely because of his willingness to set aside the Mosaic law in favor of "saving" the marginalized, once again

57 The phrase "went on his way" translates the term *eporeueto*. Luke frequently uses this verb to refer to Jesus' determination to reach Jerusalem. See its use in 4:42; 9:51, 53; 13:33; 17:11; and 19:28. See also the comments of François Bovon, *Das Evangelium nach Lukas (Lk 1,1–9,50)* (EKK 3.1; Zürich: Benziger Verlag/Neukirchen-Vluyn: Neukirchener Verlag, 1989), 216, and Bock, *Luke 1:1–9:50*, 420.

58 See François Bovon, *Das Evangelium nach Lukas (Lk 9,51–14,35)* (EKK 3.2; Zürich: Benziger Verlag/Neukirchen-Vluyn: Neukirchener Verlag, 1996), 479.

Jesus' teaching frustrates their efforts. Luke tells us more explicitly than Mark that the ability of Jesus' perceptive teaching to captivate the general populace frustrates the progress of the people's leaders to destroy Jesus (19:47–48; cf. Mark 11:18).[59] Similarly, Luke alone tells us that Jesus' opponents simply cannot trick him into saying something publicly that they can then take to the governor as an accusation. They are therefore—once again—reduced to silence (Luke 20:20, 26; cf. 11:53–54; 20:40).

Finally, Jesus' opponents succeed in putting Jesus to death, and one of their most important charges against him—repeated three times in the narrative for emphasis—is that he has been misleading the people (Luke 23:2, 5, 14).[60] Luke probably intends this charge to forge a link between Jesus' death and the controversies between him and the scribes and Pharisees earlier in the gospel.[61] Since one of the most important issues in those controversies is Jesus' willingness to bring salvation to the marginalized, even when this means abandoning the Mosaic law, Luke probably intends for his readers to make a connection between precisely this issue and Jesus' death: Jesus, they claim, misleads the people by leading them to disobey the law of God.[62]

The crucifixion of Jesus, in large part based on this charge (Luke 23:14), however, only leads to the resurrection, and this in turn leads to wider extension of God's saving purpose. Far from foiling God's plan to extend "the year of the Lord's favor" to the Gentiles and the marginalized, Jesus' opponents have only succeeded in fulfilling the biblical prophecies that, beginning in Jerusalem, repentance and forgiveness of sins will be preached in the Messiah's name to all nations (24:47).

In the gospel, therefore, opposition to Jesus' inclusive ministry both from the crowd and from established authorities fails. Jesus authoritatively walks away from a premature death, and his brilliant repartee leaves the heads of his opponents spinning. When they finally seem to get their way by engineering his death, God overcomes their efforts in the resurrection and sends Jesus' teaching down a path that ends with the salvation of people from everywhere, even from the ends of the earth.

The Triumph of Inclusiveness in Acts

In Luke's second volume, opposition to the widening of the boundaries of God's people continues, and here too Luke demonstrates the inevitable triumph of God's desire to fulfill his saving purpose in all its breadth. The opposition in Acts takes two forms: Sometimes it comes from within the church, and sometimes it comes from the church's opponents.

From within the Church

Luke follows a consistent pattern in handling the theme of opposition from within the church.[63] First, the Jerusalem apostles display hesitation about or resistance to some

59 On the "much more graphic" language of Luke here, see Bock, *Luke 9:51–24:53*, 1581.

60 Tannehill, *Narrative Unity*, 1:195.

61 Ibid.

62 Cf. John 7:12, 47, where Jesus is accused of leading people astray, perhaps because he had told the lame man at the pool of Bethesda to pick up his pallet and walk on the Sabbath, thus leading him to violate the Mosaic law (5:8–9, 12). On Luke's understanding of the Mosaic law, see Frank Thielman, *The Law and the New Testament: The Question of Countinuity* (Companions to the New Testament; New York: Crossroad, 1997), 135–67.

63 Cf. Tannehill, *Narrative Unity*, 2:102–5.

form of the gospel's expansion to the Gentiles. Second, God works powerfully in the situation to demonstrate beyond any doubt that he is behind this outward movement of the gospel. Third, the apostles become aware of God's dramatic intervention and support his inclusive initiative.

This pattern appears in the advancement of the gospel to Samaria (Acts 8:4–25), in the call of the persecutor Paul to preach the gospel to the Gentiles (9:1–31), in the expansion of the gospel to a Roman centurion and his family in Caesarea (10:1–11:18), in the establishment of a church consisting of both Greeks and Jews in Antioch (11:19–30), and in the discussion at the apostolic council (15:1–21). In each case, the movement of the gospel to the Gentiles encounters resistance or hesitation from the Jerusalem apostles: They need to pass muster on Philip's evangelistic success in Samaria (8:14); they refuse to believe that Paul's conversion was genuine (9:26; cf. 9:13–14); they are reluctant to transgress the Mosaic dietary laws in order to take the word of God to the Gentiles (10:14; 11:1); they need to examine the phenomenon of Gentile belief in Antioch (11:22); and they patiently consider the thesis that Gentiles must convert to Judaism before they can be saved (15:1, 6–7a).

In each case, however, the powerful intervention of God never leaves in doubt the onward movement of his saving purpose to the Gentiles. Barnabas changes the attitudes of the Jerusalem disciples toward Saul by recounting to them how God, through an overpowering vision, instantaneously transformed this ferocious persecutor of the church into his instrument for proclaiming the gospel to the Gentiles (Acts 9:27–28). The Jewish Christian leaders in Judea become convinced that "God has even granted the Gentiles repentance unto life" (11:18) after God instructs Peter in a vision that the Mosaic dietary laws are no longer valid (10:11–16), after God pours out his eschatological Spirit on Cornelius's household (10:44–46), and after Peter recounts the whole experience to the Judean church (11:1–17).[64] Similarly, Barnabas sees in the ethnically mixed church at Antioch "the evidence of the grace of God" and, since he is a "good man," gives the church there his encouragement and support (11:23–30). Finally, at the apostolic council, the extensive debate comes to a halt when Peter, Barnabas, and Paul remind the assembly of God's powerful work among the Gentiles—how he gave to them the Holy Spirit and performed among them signs and wonders (15:6–21).

From outside the Church

Attempts to thwart the spread of the gospel to the Gentiles also come from unbelievers. These efforts are focused on the apostle Paul and originate with both Jews and Gentiles.

Two motives fuel the opposition. First, Paul's opponents resent the inroads that Paul's proclamation of God's Word has made into their own influence over various groups of people. The unbelieving Jews in Pisidian Antioch and Thessalonica, for

64 The thesis that Peter's vision implies the abrogation of the Jewish dietary laws, like Luke's understanding of the law generally, is a matter of controversy. For the opposite position to that taken here, see, e.g., Michael Pettem, "Luke's Great Omission and His View of the Law," *NTS* 42 (1996): 35–54; for a more detailed defense of the position taken here see Thielman, *Law and the New Testament*, 155–56; cf. Hübner, *Biblische Theologie*, 3:132–33.

example, become jealous when nearly the whole city turns out to hear Paul in one town (Acts 13:44–45) and in the other town when a sizable group of prominent Gentiles, who had been interested in Judaism, become persuaded that Jesus is the Messiah and join Paul's movement (17:4–5). This is matched on the Gentile side by the uproar in Ephesus over the impact of Paul's preaching on the practice of a popular religious cult in Asia. Demetrius the silversmith, worried about the decline in the sale of silver images of Artemis, thinks that Paul's success will injure the good name of his "line of business" (*meros*) and the reputation of the goddess Artemis (19:27).

Second, Paul's opponents believe that his preaching poses a threat to the established social order. The two Gentile entrepreneurs who owned the spirit-possessed slave girl in Philippi, angry that Paul has ruined their source of income, accuse him before the authorities of upsetting the city. He has, they say, advocated "customs unlawful for us Romans to accept or practice" (Acts 16:21). Similarly Paul learns from the ever-cautious church elders in Jerusalem that the unbelieving Jews there think he teaches Jews in the Diaspora to abandon their ancestral customs (21:21–22). When Paul visits the temple, he quickly finds out that the Jerusalem elders were right (21:27–28; cf. 18:13). Jews from Thessalonica sum up the fears that unbelieving Jews and Gentiles both have about the Christians when they drag a group of Christians before the city magistrates and charge them with turning "the world upside down" (17:6).

These fears about Paul's message lead his opponents, whether Jew or Gentile, to deploy an arsenal of strategies against him. They attempt to dissuade the crowds from believing his message (Acts 13:45; 14:2, 19; 17:13; 19:9). They drag him before magistrates to lodge formal charges against him (16:20–21; 18:12–13; 24:1–9; 25:7; cf. 17:6–7). They try to lynch him (14:5, 19; 21:30–31; cf. 13:49–50; 23:27). They plot against his life (20:3, 19; 23:12–15).

But none of this prevails. The opposition of the unbelieving Jews simply leads Paul to concentrate his efforts on the Gentiles (Acts 13:46; 18:6; 19:9; 28:28) and finally propels him to Rome (25:10–11; 28:14b), much as persecution in Jerusalem had earlier precipitated the proclamation of the gospel in Samaria (8:4–5) and Syrian Antioch (11:19–20). Among the Gentiles, the word of God finds resounding success (13:48; 14:1; 17:4, 12; 19:10, 26). The opposition of unbelieving Gentiles, likewise, can do nothing to impede the steady progress of God's saving purpose as everyone appointed for eternal life believes (13:48; 16:14), even if accomplishing this takes some narrow escapes from death (14:6, 19–20; 20:3; 23:16–22), the occasional intervention of a heavenly vision (16:9–10), and the persuasive power of astonishing signs and wonders (14:3; 16:25–34; 19:11–20).

Whether the opposition comes from disobedient Jewish Christians, unbelieving Jews, or unbelieving Gentiles, whether the motivation of this opposition is jealousy at Christianity's success or fear of its capacity to disrupt, resistance to the inclusive nature of God's saving purpose is futile. God's purpose will triumph—although it began in Jerusalem, it will travel to "the ends of the earth" and will eventually include "all nations" (Luke 24:47; Acts 1:8; 13:47).

Does God's Purpose Include the Salvation of Israel?

The persistent opposition of unbelieving Jews to God's saving purpose in both of Luke's volumes raises the important question of whether, in Luke's thinking, the Jews themselves have any continuing place in that purpose. One common reading of Luke understands him to exclude the Jews from God's saving purpose.[65] At first the evidence for this reading seems conclusive. The leaders of Israel and large groups of common Jews in Luke's gospel seek to destroy Jesus (Luke 4:28–29; 23:4, 13). In Acts, blame for the death of Jesus seems to fall on all the "men of Israel" (Acts 2:22–23; 3:11, 13–15; 4:27), and although Stephen's stoning happens primarily because of the opposition of a single synagogue (6:9), "the people" are also stirred up by the accusations against him (6:12) and seem to come under his final, ringing condemnation:

> You stiff-necked people, with uncircumcised hearts and ears! You are just like your fathers: You always resist the Holy Spirit! Was there ever a prophet your fathers did not persecute? They even killed those who predicted the coming of the Righteous One. And now you have betrayed and murdered him—you who have received the law that was put into effect through angels but have not obeyed it. (7:51–53)

Moreover, throughout the second half of Acts, Jewish opposition to Paul's preaching leads him repeatedly to wash his hands of the Jews and to say that he will go instead to the Gentiles (Acts 13:46; 18:6; 19:9; 28:28). In the synagogue at Pisidian Antioch, Paul implies that this turn of events is part of the determined purpose of God. The word of God "had" to go to the Jews first, he says, but since they have rejected it, he will take God's word to the Gentiles and so fulfill the role of the Servant in Isaiah 49:6, whom God would make a "light to the Gentiles" (13:46–47; cf. 3:26). Similarly, in what seems like an emphatic location at the conclusion of Luke's two-volume work, Paul tells the recalcitrant Jews of Rome, some of whom have rejected his message about Jesus, that they have fulfilled the characterization of Israel in Isaiah 6:9–10 as a people of calloused hearts. As a result, Paul says, "God's salvation has been sent to the Gentiles, and they will listen!" (28:25–28).[66]

This, however, is a biased and selective presentation of the evidence. Luke articulates an unambiguous commitment to the place of Israel in God's saving purpose at critical moments in his narrative. In the infancy narrative, for example, Luke portrays Jesus as the fulfillment of God's covenant with Israel to rescue it from oppression. For Mary, Jesus is the means through which God "has helped his servant Israel, remembering to be merciful to Abraham and his descendants forever, even as he said to our fathers" (Luke 1:55). For Zechariah, in his prayer, Jesus is the means through which "the Lord of Israel has come and redeemed his people" (1:68). For Simeon, Jesus is both a light to the Gentiles and glory for God's people Israel (2:32).

65 See esp. Jack T. Sanders, *The Jews in Luke–Acts* (Philadelphia: Fortress, 1987).

66 Such passages seem to exclude the position of Jervell, *Theology of the Acts*, 34–43. Jervell believes that for Luke Israel alone is the people of God but is divided into two groups, one that accepts Jesus as the Messiah and one that rejects him. Gentiles attach themselves to Israel in Acts only as God-fearers. His position, however, does not take adequate account of Acts 13:46–47. Here Paul implies that Jewish unbelief has opened the way for a mission to the Gentiles.

Similarly, at the end of the gospel, two disciples on the road to Emmaus express disappointment to a mysterious traveling companion that Jesus has been tragically crucified. They "had hoped that he was the one who was going to redeem Israel" (Luke 24:21). Their companion, who is Jesus himself, does not correct this hope as mistaken but instead shows them from the Scriptures that the Messiah must suffer before he enters his glory (24:26).

At the beginning of Acts, when the disciples ask if Jesus will now "restore the kingdom to Israel," Jesus replies that the date of this restoration is only for the Father to know (Acts 1:6–7). This implies that such a restoration is coming, although Christians should not calculate the timing of its arrival.

Finally, at the Jerusalem council—the most critical moment in the mission to the Gentiles—James resolves the dispute of the admission of Gentiles to the restored people of God with a quotation from Amos 9:11–12 (LXX). Here Gentiles seek the Lord not in place of Israel but as a result of God's restoration of David's fallen tent (Acts 15:16–18).[67]

In light of all this, it would be odd if Luke, who makes so much in other ways of the inevitable triumph of God's saving purpose, nevertheless intends for his readers to conclude that God has failed to accomplish the promised salvation of his people Israel. What will then become of the rejoicing in the infancy narrative over God's faithfulness to his promises?

Moreover, Luke gives the reader clear indications that he does not intend his often pessimistic description of the Jewish response to Jesus to be the final word on God's dealings with Israel. The first half of Acts offers repentance and forgiveness to Israel in spite of its complicity in Jesus' death (Acts 2:28; 3:19, 26), and multitudes accept this message and receive baptism (2:41, 47; 5:14; 6:7).

In the second half of Acts it is true that Paul repeatedly tells Jews who reject his message that they have driven him to the Gentiles; yet, despite this, he continues to preach to Jews.[68] Only a few sentences after telling the Jews in Pisidian Antioch that their rejection of his message has driven him to the Gentiles, we find him in the synagogue at Iconium "as usual" speaking to both Jews and Gentiles (Acts 14:1). Irritated by the abuse he received from Jews in Corinth, Paul promises, "from now on I will go to the Gentiles" (18:6). After he moves from the synagogue to the house of Titius Justus, however, his first convert is the ruler of the synagogue and his entire household (18:8). Since we are now used to the pattern, it is not surprising to find Paul a few paragraphs later spending three months preaching the kingdom of God in the synagogue at Ephesus (18:19–20; 19:8). Nor are we surprised when Paul leaves the synagogue because some Jews become "obstinate" only to decide, within a few paragraphs, to go to Jerusalem (19:9, 21). The purpose of his trip, it will turn out, is to bring gifts to his people (24:17).

67 Cf. Jervell, *Theology of Acts*, 25, 40, although without accepting his position that for Luke the restoration of Israel has already occurred through the conversion of massive numbers of Jews.

68 Cf. Tannehill, "Story of Israel," 334.

This is not all. Luke regularly points out that despite the intransigence of some Jews, other Jews believed Paul's message (Acts 13:43; 14:1; 17:4, 12; 18:8; 19:17; 28:24; cf. 23:9). This matches perfectly Simeon's prophecy at the beginning of Luke's opus that Jesus was destined "to cause the falling and rising of many in Israel" (Luke 2:34).[69] In the course of Paul's preaching, some within Israel fall, but others rise, and although Luke does not specifically say so, he probably understands those Jews who believe the word of God to be the true remnant within Israel.[70]

All of this makes it difficult to read Paul's words at the end of Acts as a statement of Luke's own position. By this time in the narrative, Luke has given the reader enough confidence in God's ability to triumph over any obstacle to his saving purposes, that Paul's pronouncement does not pose a threat to the fulfillment of God's promise to restore the kingdom to Israel.[71] After all, Paul was called to carry God's name not only before the Gentiles but before "the people of Israel" as well (Acts 9:15; cf. 20:21, 26:16–17).[72] Unless he is to give up on an important aspect of his calling, he cannot give up speaking the word of God to the Jews. If the prophets are to be fulfilled, as Luke firmly believes, then the word of God has to go out to the Gentiles not in place of the Jews, but from the Jews. Jews who have been persuaded to believe in Jesus as the Messiah and Gentiles who have believed that God raised him from the dead and appointed him as judge of the whole world will together comprise the fulfillment of God's promise to restore the kingdom to Israel.[73]

Summary

Luke wants his readers to know that God's saving purposes will be accomplished despite all efforts to stop them, whether invisible or visible. Satan and his minions may tempt Jesus to be unfaithful and, when that proves impossible, enter into others to block his ministry and the ministry of his disciples, but Satan will not succeed. At every turn, Jesus and his followers are found casting demons out of their victims and healing the diseases with which the demons have inflicted them. The desperate efforts of Satan to use Judas, Ananias, and Sapphira to kill Jesus and corrupt the church only end in the dramatic deaths of these three satanic tools. The foolish attempts of magicians to contest the power of the apostles and evangelists of the church similarly end in disaster for the forces of evil.

---

69 Cf. Fitzmyer, *Luke the Theologian*, 190–91; Pokorný, *Theologie der lukanischen Schriften*, 55–56.

70 Cf. Jervell, *Theology of the Acts*, 34–43.

71 Tannehill, "Story of Israel," 334–36, argues that Luke–Acts ends on a tragic note since the hopes raised for the salvation of Israel in the infancy narrative have not been realized. In evaluating the significance of the ending of Acts, however, he neglects the importance to Luke of the theme that God's saving purposes always triumph over the difficulties that they face.

72 Ibid., 336.

73 This seems to be the burden of James's quotation of Amos 9:11–12 (LXX; cf. also Jer. 12:15 and Isa. 45:21) in Acts 15:16–17. As Barrett, *Acts* 2.725–26, comments, Luke probably does not intend to outline a chronology for the influx of Gentiles but simply to show that the Scriptures legitimate a mission to "all the Gentiles" as well as to "David's fallen tent." Cf. Fitzmyer, *Luke the Theologian*, 193–94, who says that for Luke Gentiles "have ... become part of reconstituted Israel," and Pokorný, *Theologie der lukanischen Schriften*, 49–52, who sees the church as the mediator of God's saving purpose to the Gentiles. *Pace* Jervell, *Theology of the Acts*, 40, Luke probably did not think that the "restoration of the fallen house of David" had already happened. As Pokorný, *Theologie der lukanischen Schriften*, 42, says, Luke knew that "the end time, with its visible renewal of the world, had not come."

Luke lived in a world where fear of invisible cosmic forces was palpable, and many of his readers had, like the people of Ephesus in Acts 19, engaged in magical practices to hold these inimical forces at bay. Some must have been concerned that, when they embraced Christianity and refused to placate these dangerous powers any longer, they had angered them and would suffer the consequences.[74] Perhaps Luke lays such stress on Satan, the demonic, and magic in his narrative because he wants to show his readers that they have nothing to fear. God can make handy work of demonic powers, and they pose no threat to the advancement of his saving purpose for the followers of the Messiah Jesus.

In the same way, Luke wants his readers to know that God's intention to include the sick, the poor, the oppressed, Samaritans, and Gentiles within his people will advance despite the opposition that it receives from many quarters. Just as the scribes and Pharisees failed in their efforts to block the door of salvation that Jesus opened to these groups, so Gamaliel's principle (Acts 5:34–39) vindicates the proclamation of the apostles and evangelists of later years. Despite the best efforts of the opponents of inclusion—whether Jewish or Gentile, believing or unbelieving—the proclamation of God's kingdom, as the last sentence of Luke–Acts puts it, continues unhindered (Acts 28:31). Indeed, despite the best efforts of unbelieving Jews to reject "God's purpose for themselves," the triumph of God in Luke's theology leads the reader to suspect that in Luke's thought many more Israelites will one day believe and take their places with many believing Gentiles in a restored Israel.

In this way, Luke–Acts can serve as an encouragement to its beleaguered readers. Although their societies look at them as threats and outcasts, Luke tells them, they are in reality a critical part of God's purpose to bring salvation to the descendants of Abraham and, through them, to the rest of the world.

FOLLOWING JESUS

Prior to the full accomplishment of God's saving purpose, and especially in light of the suffering that they have experienced, how should Luke's readers live? Luke answers this question by showing them that they should follow Jesus along the "way" of God as the Lord Jesus taught it (Luke 20:21; Acts 9:2; 16:17; 18:25, 26; 19:9, 23; 22:4; 24:14, 22).[75] Following "the Way" apparently involved adopting a mental framework for interpreting the Scriptures so that they pointed to Jesus (Acts 18:26; 24:14); but it also involved adopting a certain way of living that Jesus himself marked out both in his teaching (Luke 20:21) and in his example of steadfastly following the difficult

---

74 That this is a possibility is clear from the evidence gathered in Arnold, *Ephesians, Power and Magic*, 18, and in Georg Petzl, *Die Beichtinschriften Westlkeinasiens* (Bonn: Rudolf Habelt, 1994). I am grateful to Dr. Arnold for bringing the Petzl volume to my attention.

75 Luke's distinctive designation of Christianity as "the Way" may have its roots in the Christian use of Isa. 40:3 (cf. Mal. 3:1) to describe the work of John the Baptist as a preparation for "the way of the Lord" (Luke 1:76; 3:4; cf. 7:27). The Qumran covenanters, who also referred to themselves as "the Way," applied Isa. 40:3 to their role of opening a "way" for God in the desert by means of their strict conformity to the law of Moses. See 1QS 8.9–16. For a comparison of the use of "the way" at Qumran and in Acts, see Joseph A. Fitzmyer, *Essays on the Semitic Background of the New Testament* (London: Chapman, 1971), 281–83.

but necessary path to Jerusalem (Luke 9:51), the geographical center of God's saving purpose. His disciples must take up their crosses "daily" and follow him along this demanding road (Luke 9:23; Acts 14:22; cf. Luke 14:27).[76] In doing so, they will find that like Jesus, they are being used of God to accomplish his saving purpose.

Luke is particularly concerned that the followers of Jesus be inclusive in their relationships with others, handle their possessions carefully, and devote themselves to persistent prayer, especially in the face of persecution. He also wants them to know, however, that God has not left them to their own resources as they follow Jesus but has given them his powerful Spirit to enable and guide them.

Inclusiveness

We have already seen that God's saving purpose in Luke–Acts is inclusive of groups that were shut out from access to power and influence within Palestinian Judaism: the poor, the infirm, tax collectors, prostitutes, Samaritans, and Gentiles. Despite resistance to its inclusiveness, God's saving purpose for Israel triumphed in the past and, Luke believes, will continue to triumph in the future. In various ways throughout both volumes of his work, Luke shows that followers of Jesus must display the inclusive nature of God's saving purpose in the way they live. Jesus' disciples must extend acceptance to three groups in particular: the physically and economically weak, sinners, and the ethnically other.

Good News to the Poor

Just as Jesus comes to fulfill Isaiah 61:1–2a (cf. 29:18; 35:5–6) by bringing good news to the poor, freedom to the captives, recovery of sight to the blind, and liberty to the oppressed (Luke 4:18–19; cf. 7:22), so his disciples must follow this example and accept the physically and economically vulnerable. Luke makes this point in Luke 14:13. A leader of the Pharisees has invited Jesus to a Sabbath dinner, but Jesus' host only wants to keep a suspicious eye on him (14:1). Jesus does not disappoint his expectations—he violates the Sabbath by healing a man in the house who is afflicted with edema (14:1–6). Jesus then begins a series of teachings on banquet conduct (14:7–14) and touches on the issue of whom to invite to a banquet (14:7, 12–14). Friends, kinfolk, and rich neighbors should not be on the list, but "the poor, the crippled, the lame, the blind" should receive invitations.

Jesus follows this instruction with his version of the parable of the great banquet (14:15–24; cf. Matt. 22:1–10), which features the host of the banquet telling his servants not simply to invite "anyone you find" (Matt. 22:9) but "the poor, the crippled, the blind and the lame." For Luke's readers the meaning is clear: Like Jesus himself at the banquet, they should help the physically and economically weak and welcome them into the church.

---

76 The term "daily" (*kath' hēmeran*) is unique to Luke's account of these words but does not mean that he has demythologized the suffering Jesus describes. Luke probably intended for disciples of Jesus to respond to their daily suffering for the faith (9:23) in the same resolute way that Jesus responded to his own destiny of suffering in Jerusalem (9:51). On this see John Nolland, *Luke 9:21–18:34*, WBC 35B (Dallas: Word, 1993), 482–83.

This actually happens in Luke's second volume. Here we find Peter and John healing a lame beggar at the Jerusalem temple (Acts 3:1–10) and Paul doing the same in Lystra (14:8–18; cf. 19:12). We also see the early church selling its possessions and giving the proceeds to the needy (2:45) with the result that no one among them was left in need (4:34–45). The church at Antioch puts this principle into effect when they learn of an imminent famine in Judea and send a gift to help alleviate the suffering of their sister church in Jerusalem (11:27–30). Paul puts it into effect when he brings alms to Judea (24:17). Here the church is living out Jesus' program of preaching good news to the poor and handicapped. As we will see below, Luke probably conceives of God accomplishing his saving purposes for the poor in part through the generosity of his people.

Acceptance of Sinners

Jesus' disciples should also extend acceptance to sinners just as Jesus accepted tax collectors and sinners. In his Sermon on the Plain Jesus tells a large crowd of his disciples and others (Luke 6:17) that they should not merely love those who love them in return but should love their enemies, defined as those who will not pay back what they owe (6:32–34). Similarly, the three parables of God's joy over the recovery of the lost among his people—the lost sheep, the lost coin, and the lost son—not only show how Jesus shamed the Pharisees and scribes over their attitude toward his acceptance of sinners but also tell Luke's readers what their attitude toward sinners should be (15:1–31).[77] If God accepts the sinner with joy, then how can Luke's readers adopt the position of Jesus' opponents and of the elder brother in the parable of the lost son and refuse to welcome graciously the sinful person who wants to belong to God's people?[78]

In Acts the dramatic conversion of the church's arch-persecutor, Saul, tests the church's willingness to follow this principle (Acts 9:1–9). At first Ananias in Damascus (9:13–14) and the disciples in Jerusalem (9:26) resist including Saul within the church, incredulous that the story of his conversion could be authentic. Eventually, however, through God's visionary intervention and with the help of Barnabas, they accept him into their fellowship (9:27–28).

Love for the Ethnically Other

Finally, in both the gospel and Acts, Luke emphasizes that followers of Jesus must, like Jesus himself, welcome into their company people from all ethnic groups. This is the primary point of the parable of the Samaritan neighbor (Luke 10:30–37), a parable unique to Luke. A Jewish legal expert prompts the story when, in an unfriendly exchange (10:29), he asks Jesus to identify the two greatest commandments and then to define the word "neighbor." In response, Jesus tells a story that compels the lawyer to identify with the plight of a man whom thieves beat senseless and leave to die in a lonely place.[79] To this lonely place, surprisingly, two travelers

77 Bock, *Luke 9:51–24:53*, 1317, 1320.

78 Nolland, *Luke 9:21–18:34*, 789, suggests that Luke may have had in mind the resistance of some to the influx of Gentiles into the church when he included 15:24–32 in his parable. If so, then this parable could also contribute to the theme of the next section, "love for the ethnically other."

79 For the following understanding of Luke 10:30–37 I am indebted to Nolland, *Luke 9:21–18:34*, 597–98.

come—first a priest and then a Levite, both members of the lawyer's own elite social group. Despite the hopes that this good fortune raises, neither traveler proves to be a neighbor to the man in his hour of desperate need; each passes by on the other side. Instead, a hated Samaritan appears, takes pity on the injured Jew, and at great trouble and expense to himself nurses him back to health.

The lawyer to whom Jesus is speaking is therefore forced to cross a great ethnic gulf and identify with the Samaritan. If the lawyer's life depended on the help of a Samaritan, he must be willing to accept him as a neighbor. The implication is obvious: If the Samaritan can become a neighbor in a time of desperate need, he should be loved as a neighbor at all times. For Luke's Christian readers, the point is equally obvious. They should show love to those as different from themselves as Samaritans are from Jews, for they qualify as neighbors.

In Acts this expectation for followers of Jesus emerges with clarity. Despite some initial reluctance, the Jerusalem church accepts the Samaritans who have believed Philip's preaching about the Messiah (Acts 8:14–17, 25). In a miracle of God's guidance, Philip tells an Ethiopian eunuch the good news about Jesus (8:26–29). In spite of the Mosaic law's unambiguous prohibitions, Peter receives unmistakable direction from God to go to Joppa, accept the hospitality of the Gentile Cornelius, and explain the good news about Jesus to him (10:1–11:18). The church decisively rejects the argument of some Christian Pharisees that Gentiles must be circumcised and must follow the Mosaic law in order to be saved (15:1–31). As a result, the extraordinary success of the word of God among Gentiles continues without hindrance (16:4–5).

Summary

Just as Jesus came "to seek and to save what was lost" (Luke 19:10), so Jesus' followers should extend salvation to the poor, the sinner, and the ethnically other. The God who is kind to the ungrateful and wicked expects those who follow his way to be merciful also (Luke 6:35–36). As the followers of Jesus imitate the inclusive work of their Lord, God will use them to accomplish his purpose of bringing salvation to the disfranchised.

Possessions

Luke is also concerned that his readers handle their possessions with care. Luke views wealth as a double-edged sword. On one hand, it can pose a threat to discipleship, but on the other hand its proper use can advance God's saving purposes.

Wealth as a Dangerous Distraction

Luke's concern that wealth not distract disciples from following Jesus appears nowhere more clearly than in the parable of the rich fool, a story unique to Luke's gospel (Luke 12:13–21).[80] Here a rich man's property produces such an abundant harvest that the man does not know what to do with it. He finally decides simply to

80 See also Jesus' blessings for the poor and woes to the rich in 6:20–26, statements that Luke placed emphatically at the beginning of Jesus' Sermon on the Plain. On this see Walter E. Pilgrim, *Good News to the Poor: Wealth and Poverty in Luke–Acts* (Minneapolis: Augsburg, 1981), 103–7.

build bigger barns and hoard his harvest, assuring himself of a good life for many years. Unfortunately, God, to whom he has not given a thought, takes the man's life that very night, and others enjoy his wealth. The problem that Jesus wants his hearers to avoid is clear both from the introduction to the parable and its conclusion. They must not think that life consists in an abundance of possessions or, put in another way, they must not store up things for themselves and fail to be "rich toward God" (12:15, 21).[81]

How can followers of Jesus avoid this pitfall? A superficial reading of Luke–Acts might give the impression that Luke believes Jesus' followers should divest themselves of all their property and in this way become rich toward God.[82] For example, after the parable of the rich fool Jesus teaches a lesson on material possessions that urges his followers not to worry even about what they will eat, drink, or wear but to "sell" their "possessions and give to the poor" (Luke 12:22–34). Later he advises the crowds traveling with him to Jerusalem to count the cost of following him just as one counts the cost of building a tower or going to war. "In the same way," he concludes, "any of you who does not give up everything he has cannot be my disciple" (14:33). In Acts, we discover the early church actually sells "their possessions and goods" and gives to those in need (Acts 2:45; 4:32, 34–35), which may explain why Peter, before healing the beggar at the temple, said to him, "I do not have silver or gold" (3:6).[83]

We should not minimize the significance of these passages by spiritualizing them: Luke believes that the danger of wealth to Christian discipleship is so great that some Christians should divest themselves of everything.[84] Still, in Luke–Acts the notion of being rich toward God is not simplistically related to selling everything and giving the proceeds to the poor.[85]

The complex nature of Luke's approach to the danger of wealth becomes clear from a careful reading of his work. For example, just before he speaks of counting the cost of discipleship, Jesus tells the parable of the great banquet (Luke 14:15–24), which also appears in Matthew 22:1–14. In Matthew's gospel, the hardhearted rejection of God's prophets is an important theme in the parable, but in Luke 14, this theme recedes into the background and the reasons for the rejection of the invitation to the banquet move to the foreground. Two types of excuses are offered: Two people reject the invitation because their possessions are more important to them than the banquet (14:18–19), and another person rejects the invitation because his recent marriage prevents him from attending the banquet (14:20).[86] In the teaching on the cost of discipleship that explains the parable, Jesus speaks not only of the need to count the economic cost of following him, but also the relational cost:

81 Cf. ibid., 110–11, 112–13.

82 As Pilgrim, *Good News to the Poor*, 87–102, and Luke Timothy Johnson, *Sharing Possessions: Mandate and Symbol of Faith* (OBT; Philadelphia: Fortress, 1981), 11–29, correctly observe.

83 Cf. Fitzmyer, *Luke I–IX*, 250.

84 This receives special emphasis in Pilgrim, *Good News to the Poor*.

85 The complexity of Luke's approach to possessions receives special emphasis in Johnson, *Sharing Possessions*. Cf. Fitzmyer, *Luke I–IX*, 249.

86 Johnson, *Sharing Possessions*, 68.

> If anyone comes to me and does not hate his father and mother, his wife and children, his brothers and sisters—yes, even his own life—he cannot be my disciple. (Luke 14:26)

The issue is not the importance of giving up one's wealth in order to follow Jesus, but refusing to be distracted by anything, whether material possessions or family relationships.[87] Jesus does not require his disciples to divest themselves of their possessions before they follow him, but they must orient their entire lives to following him and then let nothing distract them from this path.

Similarly, the problem with the rich fool is not that he owns possessions but that he has equated the abundance of life with those possessions and has therefore not been rich toward God; he has trusted his wealth rather than God to give meaning to his life. Luke tells us that this is also the problem with the Pharisees. They clean the outside of the cup but inside are full of greed (Luke 11:39). The true condition of one's life is illustrated not by the observable rituals that one follows but by an openhanded giving of alms (11:41; 16:14–15). Lot's wife fell into the same trap—the orientation of her life was toward her possessions rather than toward the God who called her to leave her possessions, and she faced destruction as a result (17:31–33).[88]

The stories of the rich ruler and Zacchaeus, which Luke places close to one another, illustrate this principle clearly. Jesus tells the rich ruler to sell everything he possesses, give to the poor, and to follow him.[89] The rich ruler becomes sad, apparently realizing that if this is the cost of following Jesus, it is too high (Luke 18:23). Jesus, in response, tells him that it is hard "for the rich to enter the kingdom of God" (18:24–25), and then clarifies that by "hard" he does not mean "impossible" (18:27).

As if to illustrate this clarification, a few paragraphs later the rich tax collector Zacchaeus appears in the narrative.[90] Zacchaeus desperately wants to see Jesus (19:3–4), welcomes him gladly into his home (19:6), and announces that his own relationship to his wealth has taken a new turn. He will give half his possessions to the poor and repay fourfold anything he has received by extortion (19:8). Zacchaeus does not give away all that he possesses, but he gives such a large amount that his action illustrates the changed orientation of his life.[91] He no longer equates life with an abundance of possessions but with following Jesus, who has come to "seek and to save what was lost" (19:10).

Read in this light, the requirement that the rich ruler give up everything is not part of an ascetic agenda for discipleship but a way of showing that this would-be disciple has succumbed to a common malady among those who fail to follow Jesus. His confidence lies in his possessions rather than in God.

What does the disciple look like who holds his possessions with a light grip because he or she is "rich toward God"? Luke provides no formulas, but he does

87 Ibid. Cf. Pokorný, *Theologie der lukanischen Schriften*, 187.

88 Johnson, *Sharing Possessions*, 66.

89 Although Mark and Matthew also have the story, Luke alone speaks of the rich ruler giving up "everything," (*panta*) (Luke 18:22; cf. Mark 10:21; Matt. 19:21).

90 See also Pilgrim, *Good News to the Poor*, 129, 132–33.

91 Cf. Pilgrim, *Good News to the Poor*, 133; Johnson, *Sharing Possessions*, 19–20.

provide portraits of people who use their possessions in a way that is consistent with a life oriented toward God. Jesus' first disciples "left everything and followed him" (Luke 5:11; 18:28), and Peter continued to be personally penniless even as he took a leading role in the early church in Jerusalem (Acts 3:6). For Peter to live this way, however, others had to support him, and so we read of some women who followed Jesus with the Twelve and used their means to provide for the group (Luke 8:2–3).

The Samaritan neighbor, similarly, did not give everything he owned to the battered and naked man he found by the road but provided ungrudgingly and generously of his money and time to restore the man to health before traveling on his way (Luke 10:34–35). Zacchaeus, as we have seen, did not give up everything, but he gave generously to the poor and generously repaid the fruit of his extortions (19:1–10). Similarly, Tabitha did not give away all she owned but helped the poor—apparently by spending significant time and money to make clothing for them (Acts 9:36, 39).[92]

The poverty of Peter, the other eleven disciples, and Jesus shows that Luke does not intend Jesus' admonitions to sell everything to be simply metaphors for giving discipleship relative priority over one's wealth. For some, the admonition means exactly what it says: They must divest themselves of their property in order to follow Jesus faithfully. Nevertheless, the consistent appearance within Luke's narrative of people who do not give away everything, but for whom life does not consist in an abundance of possessions, shows the existence of other options.

In contrast to Peter, Paul follows this alternate path. He tells the Ephesian elders:

> I have not coveted anyone's silver or gold or clothing. You yourselves know that these hands of mine have supplied my own needs and the needs of my companions. In everything I did, I showed you that by this kind of hard work we must help the weak, remembering the words the Lord Jesus himself said: "It is more blessed to give than to receive." (Acts 20:33–35)

Here Paul says that he supplied his own needs with money earned by his own labor. His own needs, however, were far from his only concern. He also supplied the needs of his companions and consistently demonstrated that the ability to share what one earns with the weak is an important reason for engaging in hard work.[93]

Luke believes that the way people handle their wealth provides an index of their spiritual condition. To handle property wisely by giving it away to the needy provides a sign of one's inner purity (Luke 11:41) and is a positive indicator of whether or not one will eventually "be welcomed into eternal dwellings" (16:9). Greed, however, goes hand in hand with a heart that is not right with God, rejects Jesus (16:15), and is destined for eternal torment (16:19–31).[94] Jesus puts the matter succinctly when he says, "You cannot serve both God and money" (16:13).

God's Saving Purposes and the Proper Use of Wealth

We have already seen that Jesus' disciples should exhibit in their lives the same quality of inclusiveness that characterized Jesus' ministry. They should bring the saving word

92 See also Pilgrim, *Good News to the Poor*, 135–36.

93 See also ibid., 159.

94 Cf. Fitzmyer, *Luke I–IX*, 250.

of the Lord especially to marginalized people, and among these people, the poor have an important place. They appear first in the programmatic passage on which Jesus preaches in the Nazareth synagogue (Luke 4:18) and in Luke's list of those invited to the great banquet (14:21).[95]

The importance of the evangelization of the poor to God's saving purposes is evident, moreover, in the prominent place that Luke gives in the gospel to the theme of economic reversal. It appears in Mary's song of praise (Luke 1:51–53), at the beginning of the Sermon on the Plain (6:20–26), in the parable of the rich fool (12:16–21), in the parable of the rich man and Lazarus (16:19–31), and in the account of the widow's offering (21:1–4).[96] God's saving purposes involve, to some extent, an economic leveling so that the disparity between rich and poor is not as great among God's people as it is among those outside his people.

How will this saving purpose be accomplished? Luke probably believes it will be accomplished, at least to some extent, through the generosity of believers toward the poor in their midst. Thus, Luke emphasizes the importance of almsgiving and the salutary effect of almsgiving on the Christian community.[97] Jesus' disciples should not merely divest themselves of wealth but should give their wealth to the poor (Luke 12:33; 18:22). Generosity toward the needy is an important element in the Samaritan neighbor's exemplary love (10:34–35) and a sign that Zacchaeus' repentance is authentic (19:8–9).

Generosity to the poor is a commendable aspect of Tabitha's character (Acts 9:36); it sets apart Cornelius as a devout Gentile (10:2); and it is part of the missionary strategy of Paul that is in turn shaped by the teaching of Jesus (20:35). As a result of this practice in the early Christian community (2:45; 4:34b–35), "there were no needy persons among them" (4:34a). Insofar as the early Christian community handled its wealth in a way that was faithful to the teaching of Jesus, the message about Jesus was truly "good news for the poor."[98]

Summary

Luke believes that because wealth demands a wholehearted commitment from those who have it, it poses a grave danger to the disciple of Jesus. Because Jesus has come to fulfill the prophecy in Isaiah that God will one day use his Servant to bring good news to the poor, the disciple of Jesus can both be free from the claim of wealth and be used of God to accomplish his saving purposes by using money to alleviate the suffering of the poor and oppressed.

Prayer

Luke also wants his readers to know that persistent prayer is the hallmark of faithfulness in the midst of persecution. Jesus and the early church prayed frequently, par-

95 The list also appears in Luke 7:22, where the poor appear not first but last. Luke 7:22 is the only one of the three lists, however, that Luke shares with Matthew. Both apparently borrowed it from Q. When Luke himself provides the list in 14:21, it follows the same order as in Isa. 61:1 and Luke 4:18.

96 Bock, *Luke 1:1–9:50*, 157.

97 Pilgrim, *Good News to the Poor*, 134–36.

98 Ibid., 162–63.

ticularly during times of duress, and Jesus taught that those who follow him along the way should also pray frequently as they experience persecution. Here too, prayer serves the additional purpose of advancing God's saving purpose in history by enabling followers of Jesus to remain faithful in the midst of hardship.

Prayer and Perseverance

In the parable of the persistent widow (Luke 18:1–8), a story unique to Luke's gospel, the primary reason for Luke's interest in prayer becomes clear. The parable follows an apocalyptic discourse on the conditions in the world at the time when the Son of Man comes (17:20–37). In that day, people in society will be as concerned with the affairs of material comfort and prosperity, and as oblivious to the things of God, as they were in the days of Noah and Lot (17:26–29), and God's people will be impatient for the Son of Man to arrive (17:22).

At that point Luke introduces the parable with the words, "Then Jesus told his disciples a parable to show them that they should always pray and not give up" (Luke 18:1). The parable features a widow who pesters a judge so persistently that, although "he neither feared God nor cared about people," he eventually gave her justice (18:1–5). In contrast to this judge, Jesus says, God will assuredly give speedy justice to his chosen ones who call out to him day and night (18:6–8a). "However," he concludes, "when the Son of Man comes, will he find faith on the earth?" (18:8b).

For Luke, the persistent prayers of God's people for vindication against their oppressors signals their faithfulness in the difficult days prior to the coming of the Son of Man. As we have seen, Luke is probably writing during a period of persecution, and in this context his admonition to "pray and not give up" must have assumed special urgency.[99] Like the widow, his readers should persevere in their prayers that God may vindicate them against their oppressors, and unlike the unjust judge, God will give his people eschatological justice "speedily" (*en tachei*).[100]

This same concern that his readers persist in prayer for divine enabling to cope with persecution also appears elsewhere in Luke's gospel. Like Matthew, Luke's rendering of the Lord's Prayer urges his readers to pray for the coming of God's kingdom (Luke 11:2; cf. Matt. 6:10), but unlike Matthew, Luke places the Lord's Prayer (Luke 11:2–4) within a context that emphasizes persistence in prayer. Luke opens his account of the Lord's Prayer with a request from one of his disciples to "teach us to pray" (11:1). He follows the prayer both with the parable of the friend at midnight (11:5–8), which commends boldness (*anaideia*) in prayer, and with a series of sayings about asking, seeking, and knocking on God's door in prayer (11:9–10).[101] The total effect is to commend an almost desperate persistence in prayer.[102]

99 Peter T. O'Brien, "Prayer in Luke–Acts," *TynB* 24 (1973), 111–27, here at 117.

100 Most commentators correctly reject the suggestion that *en tachei* in 18:8 means "suddenly" rather than "speedily." On this, see, e.g., Marshall, *Luke*, 676; Fitzmyer, *Luke X–XXIV*, 1180–81; Nolland, *Luke 9:21–18:34*, 870; and BDAG, 993.

101 On the meaning of *anaideia*, which is sometimes translated incorrectly as "persistence" (NAB, NJB, NRSV), see BDAG, 63. Matthew places the sayings on asking, seeking, and knocking in a context separate from the Lord's Prayer (Matt. 7:7–8).

102 O'Brien, "Prayer in Luke–Acts," 119, and *pace* David Crump, *Jesus the Intercessor: Prayer and Christology in Luke–Acts* (WUNT 2.49; Tübingen: J. C. B. Mohr [Paul Siebeck], 1992), 131. Crump believes that the notion of persistence is not present in the passage.

What should be the subject of these persistent prayers? Matthew simply says that those who pray should ask for "good gifts" (Matt. 7:11). Luke specifies, however, that his readers should pray for the Holy Spirit (Luke 11:13), who, Luke says a few paragraphs later, will teach Jesus' disciples what to say when they are dragged before the authorities who persecute them (12:11–12; cf. Matt. 10:20).

Both Jesus in Luke's first volume and the early church in his second volume provide examples of persistence in prayer, particularly amid persecution. Luke frequently portrays Jesus at prayer in his gospel. Jesus often withdraws from the crowds to pray (Luke 5:16; 6:12; 9:18, 28), is in prayer after his baptism (3:21), and prays during his crucifixion (23:34, 46). At least part of Luke's purpose in presenting Jesus so frequently at prayer is to provide a model for Jesus' disciples to follow in their own praying.

This becomes especially clear in two passages.[103] First, Luke prefaces his version of the Lord's Prayer with the statement that "one day Jesus was praying in a certain place." Jesus' own practice of prayer prompts one of his disciples to ask him to teach them to pray (Luke 11:1). Jesus not only teaches that prayer should be persistent, but he practices persistent prayer himself.

Second, Luke shapes his account of Jesus' agony on the Mount of Olives so that the story urges his readers to appreciate the importance of prayer in the midst of persecution. This becomes clear by comparing Luke's account with the accounts in Matthew and Mark. Both Matthew and Mark show Jesus at prayer just before his arrest (Matt. 26:36, 39, 42, 44; Mark 14:32, 35, 39). Both also record Jesus' admonition in the middle of the account to "keep watch" (Matt. 26:38; Mark 14:34) and to "watch and pray so that you will not fall into temptation" (Matt. 26:41; Mark 14:38). For Luke, however, Jesus' prayer in the midst of his trials and the disciples' need to imitate him are the primary points of the story. Both at the beginning and at the end of Luke's account, Jesus tells the disciples to pray in order to avoid falling into temptation (22:40, 46). Sandwiched between the two admonitions Luke presents a compressed description of Jesus praying in precisely these circumstances.[104]

In a similar way in his second volume, Luke portrays the early church as devoted to prayer.[105] From the first, the disciples, their wives, and Jesus' own family are constantly at prayer (Acts 1:14; 2:42, 47; 6:4).[106] They pray before selecting Judas's replacement (1:24–25), when they set apart people for special tasks (6:6; 13:2–3; 14:23), when they part from each other (20:36; 21:5), and when they ask God to raise the dead (9:40) and heal the sick (28:8). Luke also shows that they cope with persecution by means of prayer, just as Jesus admonishes his disciples to do in the parable of the persistent widow (Luke 18:1–8).

This is probably the main reason why Luke includes the long prayer of the early Christians in response to the Sanhedrin's persecution of Peter and John (Acts 4:23–31).[107] In addition, Luke portrays the church's first martyr, Stephen, following Jesus'

103 On this, see esp. Wilhelm Ott, *Gebet und Heil: Die Bedeutung der Gebetsparänese in der lukanischen Theologie* (SANT 12; München: Kösel-Verlag, 1965), 94–99.

104 O'Brien, "Prayer in Luke–Acts," 120–21.

105 Ibid., 122; Fitzmyer, *Luke I–IX*, 245–47; Luke Timothy Johnson, *The Acts of the Apostles* (SP 5; Collegeville: Michael Glazier, 1992), 34.

106 For the implications of constancy in the imperfect periphrastic phrase *ēsan proskarterountes*, see Barrett, *Acts*, 1:88.

107 Haenchen, *Acts*, 229.

example in praying that God not hold the sin of his persecutors against them (7:60) and in committing his spirit to God (7:59; cf. Luke 23:46; 23:34).[108] The church's response to the arrest of Peter by Herod Agrippa I is constant, earnest prayer on Peter's behalf (Acts 12:5).[109] Similarly, after Paul and Silas are flogged and jailed in Philippi, they begin "praying and singing hymns to God" (16:25).

It is perhaps significant that all three of these examples of prayer during persecution in Acts end with the vindication of those who have prayed. The early church prayed for continued boldness to proclaim God's Word and for confirmation of their message through signs and wonders (Acts 4:29–30). God answers their prayer immediately with the quaking of the place where the believers are meeting and with the bold, Spirit-filled proclamation of God's Word (4:31). Similarly, after Stephen commits his spirit to God's care prior to his death, he sees the Son of Man standing at God's right hand (Acts 7:56)—a symbol reminiscent of the vindication of God's persecuted people in Daniel 7:13–14, 18, and 22.[110] Peter's miraculous release from prison follows the church's prayer on his behalf (Acts 12:5, 7), and while Paul and Silas are praying and singing hymns a strong earthquake strikes, opening the prison doors and freeing the prisoners (16:26).

Is Luke giving examples in these passages of what Jesus meant when he said in the gospel that God will vindicate "speedily" his chosen ones who cry out to him day and night? If so, then Luke seems to have understood these events to be anticipations of the ultimate vindication of God's chosen people at the coming of the Son of Man.[111]

In summary, Luke wants his readers to pray frequently, especially in the midst of the persecution they are experiencing for their commitment to God's Word. This is the road that Jesus walked, and it is also the road that his disciples must walk if God is to find his chosen people faithful when the Son of Man comes.

Prayer and the Progress of Salvation History

Luke also shows his readers that God uses the prayers of his people to advance his saving purposes. In both volumes of his work, prayer marks the significant turns in the narrative.[112] Zechariah and "all the assembled worshipers" are at prayer when Gabriel appears to Zechariah to announce the birth of John the Baptist (Luke 1:10, 13). The Spirit descends on Jesus as he prays (3:21). Jesus is at prayer before he chooses the twelve (6:12). Jesus' transfiguration occurs during a trip up a mountain to pray (9:28). As we have already seen, Jesus is at prayer during his passion (22:39–46) and death (23:34, 46).

---

108 O'Brien, "Prayer in Luke–Acts," 122.

109 Luke's Greek is *proseuchē . . . ēn ektenōs ginomenē*. As in 1:14, the imperfect tense indicates constant prayer, and the notion of constancy is made more emphatic by the presence of the adverb *ektenōs*, "eagerly, fervently, constantly" (BDAG, 310).

110 Cf. C. F. D. Moule, *The Origin of Christology* (Cambridge: Cambridge Univ. Press, 1977), 17.

111 Nolland, *Luke 9:21–18:34*, 871, comments perceptively that Luke's "quickly" in Acts 18:8 "may come true in stages, through intimations already here and now, and also in ways that are not at once obvious, before ever it comes true in the fully comprehensive sense that first springs to mind."

112 O'Brien, "Prayer in Luke–Acts," 114. Cf. Fitzmyer, *Luke I–IX*, 244.

Similarly, the early Christians pray to determine who should fill Judas's role and restore the primary disciples to their proper number (Acts 1:24–25). When the gospel makes the significant step of moving beyond Jerusalem and Judea to Samaria (cf. 1:8), Peter and John pray that the Holy Spirit will come on the Samaritan believers (8:15). Prayer plays a role in Paul's commissioning to go to the Gentiles (9:11), in the critical conversion of the Gentile Cornelius (10:1, 9, 30), and in the advancement of the gospel to "the ends of the earth" (13:3; cf. 1:8).

No cause and effect relationship between prayer and salvation history is implied here. As Luke portrays him, God is completely sovereign over the course of his saving purposes.[113] Still, God seems to use the prayers of his people to move his saving work along its predetermined course, much as he uses the proclamation of his word to gather the people in a particular place who belong to him (18:10).

Summary

Luke believes that in the difficult times prior to Christ's return, God's chosen people should devote themselves to prayer. He provides Jesus and the early church as examples of those who persist faithfully in prayer amid hardship. He also believes that God uses the prayers of his people to advance his saving purposes.

The Spirit

Luke wants his readers to know that God has not left them to cope with life prior to the full accomplishment of God's saving purposes on their own. Just as God's Spirit was active in Jesus' life from the time of his conception to empower his mighty words and deeds, so God's Spirit will be present with Jesus' disciples as they shoulder their crosses and follow him. "The Spirit of the Lord" rests on Jesus, in answer to the prophecy of Isaiah 61:1–2, to empower him to preach good news to the poor, to proclaim the captives' release, to restore sight to the blind, and to free the downtrodden (Luke 4:18–19; cf. also Isa. 58:6). In a similar way, the Holy Spirit descends on the newly reconstituted twelve apostles at the festival of Pentecost, and then, in answer to the prophecy of Joel 2:28–32 that God will pour out his Spirit on all kinds of people—male and female, young and old—the Spirit comes to all who embrace the Christian message (Acts 2:1–21, 38; 8:16–17; 10:44–47; 11:15; 15:8).

The Spirit enables Christians to put God's saving plan for creation into effect. He substitutes for Jesus' physical presence with his disciples so that they are at no disadvantage because he is no longer physically with them (Luke 24:49; Acts 2:33; 16:7).[114] He enables Jesus' followers to bear effective witness to the gospel, both when preaching to crowds in the temple and, as Jesus predicted, when defending the gospel before hostile courts (Acts 2:4, 6–13; 4:8, 13; 6:5, 10; cf. Luke 12:12). The Holy Spirit also specifically guides those who preach the gospel. He guides Philip to a specific chariot containing an Ethiopian official to whom he must explain the gospel (8:29); he transports Philip to Azotus where he preaches the gospel (8:39–40); he hinders Paul and his companions from preaching in Asia and does not permit them

113 Crump, *Jesus the Intercessor*, 6.

114 Fitzmyer, *Luke I–IX*, 230.

to enter Bithynia (16:6–7); and he leads Paul to travel through Macedonia, Achaia, and on to Jerusalem (19:21; 20:22).[115]

Luke places special emphasis on the role of God's Spirit in guiding Christians to break down the traditional ethnic barriers of God's people. The Spirit brings Philip to Samaria, Peter to Cornelius, and Paul to the Gentiles because God is now widening his people to include "all who are far off" (Acts 2:39). Therefore God pours out the Holy Spirit not only on Jews but also on Samaritans and, to the amazement of Jewish Christians, on Gentiles such as Cornelius and his household (8:15–17; 10:44–48). Despite the resistance that this crossing of ethnic boundaries meets among some Jewish Christians, the presence of the Spirit among Samaritans and uncircumcised Gentiles who believe the gospel provides undeniable proof that they too are part of God's people (11:15–17; 15:8–10). As Peter says to the Jerusalem council, "God, who knows the heart, showed that he accepted them by giving the Holy Spirit to them, just as he did to us" (15:8).

Summary

Luke hopes to encourage his readers that God has not left his people to work out his saving purposes in their own strength. Just as the Spirit caused the miracle of Jesus' conception and empowered his preaching and healing ministry in answer to the prophets' predictions, so the Spirit will accompany God's newly constituted people in Jesus' physical absence. He will empower them to testify to the gospel in both friendly and hostile situations; he will give them specific guidance; and he will overcome the barriers that stand in the way of his intention to bring Samaritans and Gentiles within the boundaries of his people.

Conclusion

Luke believes that those who follow Jesus along the "way" toward Jerusalem and the cross should pursue three specific activities: inclusiveness, generosity, and prayer. By their willingness to include the socially marginalized and ethnically other in their communities of faith, they will imitate the inclusiveness of Jesus and the early church. They will also advance God's purpose of restoring the kingdom to Israel in a way that includes all the nations of the earth. By holding their wealth with a light grip, they will resist the all-consuming commitment that wealth seems to demand of those who have it and thus avoid straying onto a well-traveled side path that leads away from the cross. They will also accomplish God's intention to bring good news to the poor as they generously give of their money to those in need. By praying persistently they will remain faithful during times of testing, and God will use them to advance his saving purposes. They will not accomplish these tasks in their own strength, however, but God's Spirit will empower and guide them along the way.

115 In Acts 21:4, Luke tells us that the disciples in Tyre "through the Spirit . . . urged Paul not to go on to Jerusalem," an apparent contradiction to the claim in 20:22 that the Spirit "compelled" Paul to go to Jerusalem. The Spirit also told Paul, however, that in every city through which he would pass, "prison and hardships" awaited him (20:23). This is probably the information that the Spirit communicated to the disciples of Tyre (cf. 21:11). They probably then interpreted this information as a warning that Paul should not press forward with his travel plans. See F. F. Bruce, *The Acts of the Apostles: The Greek Text with Introduction and Commentary*, 2nd ed. (London: Tyndale, 1952), 385.

THE CERTAIN PROGRESS OF SALVATION HISTORY IN LUKE-ACTS

Luke wrote for suffering Christians who probably already longed "to see one of the days of the Son of Man" (Luke 17:22). As a people whom Greco-Roman society had moved to the margins of its social map, they needed to know where they were located in the scheme of God's purposes in history, they needed assurance that their costly commitment to the things they had been taught was right, and they needed a strategy for coping with the difficult life that faced them because of their commitment to the gospel.

By emphasizing God's saving purpose for Israel and the nations, Luke was able to show his readers that, although marginalized within Greco-Roman society, they occupied an important place in the only society that really mattered—the people of God. Through this people God was bringing the blessing of his forgiveness to all peoples, whatever their economic, social, or ethnic status. This happened first through the people of Israel, but since Israel's rejection of the Messiah, it was now happening through the Messiah's followers, the church, composed of both Jews and Gentiles. Eventually the kingdom would be restored to Israel, but only in such a way that the nations would also be included in that restoration. Jesus' resurrection from the dead provided the critical evidence that this period of restoration was under way. God had raised him from the dead as the first person to experience the general eschatological resurrection, and from his exalted position at God's right hand he dispensed the eschatological Spirit, repentance, and forgiveness.

Luke also wanted his readers to know that none of these developments was accidental. God had planned for his saving purpose to be accomplished in this way, and Luke tells his readers in many ways that these events correspond to the expectation expressed in Israel's Scriptures about the time of eschatological restoration. Providing this link between Israel's Scriptures on the one hand and the periods of Jesus and the church on the other hand lent "certainty" to the things that Luke's readers had been taught when they became Christians and provided encouragement to persevere in their commitment.

Luke used another means of providing certainty for his readers: He assured them at every turn that God's purpose would triumph despite the opposition that they inevitably encountered. Whether the opposition came from the cosmic, unseen realm, from the disobedience of believers, or the jealousy of unbelievers, it would not succeed in frustrating the saving purpose of God. God would restore the kingdom to Israel and in the process bring blessings to all nations.

Before God's work of restoration was complete, Luke wanted his readers to know that followers of Jesus should be busy with the advancement of God's saving purpose. They should model the inclusiveness of this purpose in their acceptance of the poor, sinners, and diverse ethnic groups. They should be wary of the lure that possessions offer to deviate from the way and should instead use any wealth they might possess as a tool to alleviate the suffering of the poor. Like Jesus, they should persist in prayer, particularly in the prayer that God would send the Son of Man to vindicate them speedily. God would use such prayers, as he had used the prayers of Zechariah, Jesus, and the early church, to advance his saving purpose from one stage to the next. Through the faithfulness of God's people in each of these ways and by the enabling, guiding power of his Spirit, the proclamation of God's kingdom and the teaching about the Lord Jesus Christ would continue, as it had during the time of Paul's Roman imprisonment, "boldly and without hindrance" (Acts 28:31).

Chapter 6

JOHN: FAITH IN JESUS AS THE MEANS TO ETERNAL LIFE

Like Luke, John is explicit about the purpose for which he wrote his gospel:

> Jesus did many other miraculous signs in the presence of his disciples, which are not recorded in this book. But these are written that you may believe that Jesus is the Christ, the Son of God, and that by believing you may have life in his name. (20:30–31)

Despite the reservations of some interpreters, this brief statement can account for the primary theological features of John's gospel.[1] It says that the author hopes Jesus' "signs," as they are recorded in the book, will produce or bolster the faith of its readers that Jesus is not only the "Messiah" but the "Son of God" and therefore lead the reader to "life."

Covered in this statement is John's distinctive approach

- to Jesus' identity,
- to the relationship between Jesus' signs and the belief that Jesus is the ultimate revelation of his Father,
- and to the eschatological life that comes in the present to those who have this faith.

These are arguably the principal theological themes of John's gospel.[2]

JESUS' IDENTITY

John tells his readers in his purpose statement that his book is designed to encourage in them the conviction that Jesus "is the Christ, the Son of God." In light of the close relationship between Jesus and God in the rest of the gospel, the traditional tone of this statement might at first seem surprising. After all, John began his gospel with an assertion that Jesus, as the Word, had existed with God from the beginning and was God. In addition, throughout the gospel he has emphasized Jesus' unity with God from all eternity (5:17–18; 8:58; 10:30; 17:5, 24). Moreover, only a few sentences before his purpose statement, John tells his readers that Thomas confessed Jesus as

1 In the view of some scholars, John's gospel is the product of a complex editorial history, and 20:30–31 expresses the purpose of only one of its literary levels, not the gospel as a whole. See, e.g., J. M. Thompson, "Is John XXI an Appendix?" *Expositor* 10 (1915): 144–46; Rudolf Bultmann, *The Gospel of John: A Commentary* (Philadelphia: Westminster, 1971), 697–98, esp. 698 n. 2; and Robert Tomson Fortna, *The Fourth Gospel and Its Predecessor* (Philadelphia: Fortress, 1988), 201–3.

2 See also George R. Beasley-Murray, *John* (WBC 36; Waco, Tex.: Word, 1987), 388.

"My Lord and my God" (20:28). Since John's understanding of the relationship between Jesus and God is so exalted and so unlike traditional Jewish expectations for the Messiah, why does John say that his purpose is to lead people to believe that Jesus "is the Christ, the Son of God"? As we have seen in chapter 3, the titles "Christ" and "Son of God" may refer to no more than a great Israelite king whom, according to one reading of Psalm 2, God has figuratively anointed and adopted.[3]

Throughout his gospel, John has shown that he is aware of the traditional understanding of these concepts, but he has also demonstrated that Jesus broke the boundaries of these ideas and gave new meaning to the terms "Messiah" and "Son of God."[4] As a result, by the time he articulated his purpose statement, John apparently had no fear that his readers would misunderstand him to be saying that they only needed to believe Jesus was the Messiah of traditional Jewish expectation.

John's Awareness of Traditional Expectations

John wants his readers to know that during Jesus' ministry messianic expectations were high and were basically informed by the notion that the Messiah would be either a prophet like Moses or a king like David or would combine elements of both figures. Near the beginning of the gospel a contingent of priests and Levites, sent from the Jews of Jerusalem, approach John the Baptist with the question, "Who are you?" (1:19).[5] His answer shows that he knows where their question is heading, "I am not the Christ," he tells them plainly (1:20). Near the end of Jesus' public ministry, "the Jews" have the same question for Jesus: "If you are the Christ," they say, "tell us plainly" (10:24).[6]

Between these two points, debate swirls over whether Jesus is the Messiah. The people of Jerusalem wonder if the authorities are convinced that Jesus is the Christ (7:26). Some of these people conclude that he is the Christ and believe in him (7:31). Others think that he does not fulfill the necessary criteria and reject him (7:41–44, 52). The Pharisees and Jewish leaders are convinced that Jesus is not the Messiah and that confession of him as the Messiah is politically dangerous. In their view, this volatile confession requires them to expel from the synagogue any who confess Jesus as the Messiah and engineer the death of Jesus himself (7:25–26; 9:22; 11:47–50; 12:42).

Similarly the conclusion of Jesus' ministry and the events of his passion are consumed with the issue of Jesus' status as Messiah. At his triumphal entry into Jerusalem,

3 See 4Q174 1.10–13 and 4Q246 2.1–8 and the discussion in Martin Hengel, *The Son of God* (Philadelphia: Fortress, 1976), 44–45. See also Beasley-Murray, *John*, 388; John Ashton, *Understanding the Fourth Gospel* (Oxford: Clarendon, 1991), 260–62; and Anthony Tyrrell Hanson, *The Prophetic Gospel: A Study of John and the Old Testament* (Edinburgh: T. & T. Clark, 1991), 334–35.

4 D. Moody Smith, *The Theology of the Gospel of John* (New Testament Theology; Cambridge: Cambridge Univ. Press, 1995), 86–89, 94. Cf. W. Grundmann, "χρίω (κτλ)," *TDNT*, 9:527–80, here at 567, and Marinus de Jonge, *Jesus: Stranger from Heaven and Son of God* (SBLSBS 11; Missoula, Mont.: Scholars Press, 1977), 77–85.

5 John, the herald of Jesus' coming, is never called "the Baptist" in the fourth gospel, but the term is useful nevertheless for avoiding confusion between the John to whom the gospel is traditionally ascribed and John, the herald of Jesus, who is the only person in the gospel given the name "John."

6 The meaning of the term "the Jews" is hotly debated. Among the most popular interpretations are "the Judeans," "unbelievers," and "Jewish authorities." It is probably best, however, to see the term as a reference to "the especially religious people of Judea." It is not, therefore, a reference to all Jewish people but specifically to those among the Jews of Judea who opposed Jesus on religious grounds. On the whole question see Stephen Motyer, *Your Father the Devil? A New Approach to John and "the Jews"* (Paternoster Biblical and Theological Monographs; Carlisle, U.K.: Paternoster, 1997), 46–57.

the crowds hail him as "the one who comes in the name of the Lord" and as "the King of Israel" (12:13). At Jesus' trial before Pilate, the issue becomes whether or not Jesus is "the king of the Jews," with Pilate insisting that he is (18:37, 39; 19:14–15, 19, 22) and the Jewish leaders just as emphatically insisting that he is not (19:12, 15, 21).

John tells us that Jesus' disciples believed in him because they were looking for the Messiah and believed that, in Jesus, they had found him. Thus, Andrew announces to his brother Simon, "We have found the Messiah," and to be sure that Greek speakers do not miss the significance of Andrew's identification of Jesus with this figure of traditional Jewish expectation, John supplies the gloss, "that is, the Christ" (1:41; cf. 4:25).[7] Similarly, when the Samaritan woman suspects Jesus is the Messiah, she leaves her water jug at the well in her haste and tells her Samaritan compatriots to come see Jesus. "Could this be the Christ?" she asks them (4:29).

John also wants his readers to know that the debate over Jesus' messianic identity takes place on traditional ground. A few sentences after identifying Jesus as "a prophet" (4:19), the Samaritan woman comments that the Messiah is coming and that when he arrives, he "will explain everything to us" (4:25; cf. 4:19).[8] She is perhaps echoing a belief known from much later Samaritan literature that a prophet like Moses would arise in answer to the expectations of Deuteronomy 18:18 and would speak the words of the Lord.[9]

Similarly, the Galilean crowd of 6:14–15 is convinced that the Jesus who has just fed them with bread in the wilderness "is the Prophet who is to come into the world," and they attempt to make him "king." As with the Samaritan woman, there seems to be some melding of expectations about a coming messianic king with expectations about the coming of the Prophet-like-Moses.[10] In a way analogous to the Samaritan woman's confession of Jesus as both prophet and Christ, this Jewish confession may echo first-century expectations about the Messiah in some Jewish circles, although the only clear evidence for it comes from a much later date.[11]

John also wants his readers to know that some people kept the categories of prophet and Messiah distinct and that people debated which of these two categories, if either, Jesus fit. The Jews from Jerusalem who question John the Baptist at the beginning of the gospel want to know whether he is "the Messiah," "Elijah," or "the

7 See also Smith, *Theology of the Gospel of John*, 87.

8 In 4:19 the Samaritan woman says, *kyrie, theōrō hoti prophētēs ei sy*. The word *prophētēs* does not have the article and so is often translated "a prophet." The word is a preverbal predicate nominative, however, and, if it follows the pattern of other such constructions in the New Testament, it is most likely either definite or qualitative. Daniel B. Wallace, *GGBB*, 265–66, comments that the verb *theōrō* makes an indefinite translation natural in this instance but that "the sense may be better characterized as indefinite-qualitative" ("Lord, I see that you are prophetic"). If this is what the woman is saying, then she may be gradually recognizing that Jesus is the prophet like Moses of Deut. 18:18.

9 See, e.g., the fourth century A.D. *Memar Marqah* 2.40.28; 3.6 and the discussion in Wayne A. Meeks, *The Prophet-King: Moses Traditions and the Johannine Christology* (NovTSup 14; Leiden: Brill, 1967), 246–54. James D. Purvis, "The Fourth Gospel and the Samaritans" in *The Composition of John's Gospel: Selected Studies from* Novum Testamentum, ed. David E. Orton (Leiden: Brill, 1999), 148–85, here at 175–76, cautions that "the coming of an eschatological prophet like Moses was not a *sine qua non* of early Samaritan Mosaism."

10 Meeks, *Prophet–King*, 87–98, 256–57.

11 According to *Tanchuma 'Ekeb* 7, the Messiah will "cause [the Israelites] to go in the wilderness and will make them eat leaves and straw." According to *Qoheleth Rabba* 1.8, he will cause bread to rain from heaven just as Moses brought manna to the Israelites and will bring up water just as Moses "made a well to rise." For this point and the relevant quotations, see J. Louis Martyn, *History and Theology in the Fourth Gospel*, rev. and enl. (Nashville: Abingdon, 1979), 109–10.

Prophet," with no indication that he could be more than one of these figures at the same time (1:19–28).[12] The Baptist denies he is any of these figures and points his interrogators only to "the Lord" (1:23) who "comes after" him (1:27; cf. 3:28).

Similarly, at the Feast of Booths, some people, on the basis of Jesus' claim that he could cause "living water" to flow, conclude that he is "the Prophet" like Moses, who also produced miraculous, divinely supplied water (John 7:40; cf. Ex. 17:6; Num. 20:8–11; Deut. 8:15; Neh. 9:15).[13] Others, on the basis of the signs that he works, become convinced that he is the Messiah (7:31, 41).[14] Still others, on the basis of various traditional expectations about Jesus' origins, reject him as either a prophet or the Messiah. One group follows the popular belief that the Messiah will remain hidden until his clear anointing as Israel's king and another group believes that the Messiah will come from Bethlehem, King David's ancestral home (7:27, 41–42).[15] In either case Jesus is disqualified (7:43–44) because everyone "knows" that he is from Nazareth (7:27; cf. 1:45, 46; 18:5, 7; 19:19).[16] Ironically, they reject Jesus because they assume mistakenly that his origins lie in Galilee rather than in Bethlehem (7:43–44).

The chief priests and the Pharisees also reject the notion that Jesus is a prophet on the basis that he is supposedly from Galilee. "Look into it," they say, "and you will find that a prophet does not come out of Galilee" (7:52). Much scholarly ink has flowed over the precise background to this statement. Have the Pharisees failed to notice that Jonah son of Amittai was from Galilee (2 Kings 14:25)?[17] From John's

12 Working from Mal. 3:1 and 4:5 (MT 3:23), some ancient Jews, including Jesus himself, believed that Elijah would return prior to the Lord's eschatological restoration of all things. See Matt. 11:10 (cf. Luke 7:27), 14; Mark 1:2; 9:11–13 (cf. Matt. 17:10–12); Luke 9:8; and the comments of C. K. Barrett, *The Gospel according to St. John*, 2nd ed. (Philadelphia: Westminster, 1978), 330, on 7:40.

13 Martyn, *History and Theology*, 114, 130; Raymond E. Brown, *The Gospel according to John I–XII* (AB 29; New York: Doubleday, 1966), 329.

14 Jesus' sign-working ability seems to have also played a role in bringing Nathaniel and the Samaritan woman to the conclusion that Jesus was the Messiah. Both were prompted to proclaim Jesus' messianic status after he had demonstrated miraculous insight into their personal lives (1:48–49; 4:29). Martyn, *History and Theology*, 111–18, argues that the Messiah was not expected to work "signs" and that the expectation articulated in 7:31 emerges from the mixture of traditional messianic notions with the idea that the expected prophet like Moses would, like Moses, work signs. Barrett, *Gospel according to St. John*, 323, however, wisely remarks that we do not have enough information about messianic expectation in the first century to say for certain that miracle-working was not commonly associated with the Messiah. See also Ashton, *Understanding*, 277.

15 See Justin, *Dial.* 8.4, where the Jew, Trypho, says that the Messiah, if he exists now, is unknown to anyone including himself until Elisha comes to anoint him, and 110.1, where Justin attributes to Jewish teachers the claim that the Christ remains unknown until it is obvious who he is.

16 *Pace* Meeks, *Prophet–King*, 36–41, and de Jonge, *Jesus: Stranger from Heaven*, 93–94, this is an example of Johannine irony. Meeks regards the tradition of Jesus' Galilean origins as more reliable than the tradition of his Judean origins. The birth of Jesus in Bethlehem, he argues, was developed as a polemic against precisely the kind of Jewish objections to Jesus' messianic status that appear in John 7:42 (cf. Mic. 5:1–5). John, unaware of Christian attempts to conform Jesus' origins to Jewish expectations (Matt. 2:22–23; Luke 2:1–7), maintained that Jesus was, in earthly terms, from Galilee, but that, more importantly, his real origins lay in heaven. De Jonge, 93–94, believes that John thought early Christian debate about Jesus' origins was beside the point. Writing near the end of the first century, however, John was probably not only well aware of the Christian tradition that Jesus was born in Bethlehem but accepted it as both true and important. Since his readers probably held the same convictions, he could assume that they would understand the irony implicit in 7:41–42.

17 Barrett, *St. John*, 333, for example, believes that this verse must "cast . . . doubt on John's first hand acquaintance with Judaism." Herman Ridderbos, *The Gospel of John: A Theological Commentary* (Grand Rapids: Eerdmans, 1997), 281, on the other side, comments that the present tense verb "arises" (*egeiretai*) probably refers not to a statement of precise historical fact but to a general principle: "From Galilee one expects no prophets." Brown, *John I–XII*, 325, and Beasley-Murray, *John*, 121, accept the reading "the Prophet" in the early papyrus manuscripts P66 and P75 with the result that the Pharisees deny only that Galilee will produce "the prophet like Moses."

perspective, however, the point is clear: Precisely how Jesus fit into traditional expectations for the Messiah, the Prophet, or any prophet, was the subject of intense discussion during his lifetime, and conclusions on the issue supplied grist to the mill of those who rejected him.

John wants us to know that he is familiar with a range of traditional Jewish and Samaritan expectations of a coming deliverer. Moreover, despite his detractors' skepticism, Jesus meets the qualifications for these roles.[18] He is the Prophet like Moses, as his feeding of the crowd in Galilee implies (6:1–15). He is the Messiah and King of Israel, as his signs and his Judean origins demonstrate (1:48–50; 7:31, 42; 9:17; 12:13–15). He is also the Messiah whom the Samaritans are expecting (4:25, 29). John's primary interest lies, however, in showing us that the significance of Jesus goes far beyond anything that these traditional expectations imply.

John's Redefinition of Jesus' Messiahship

When John says in his purpose statement that he intends to encourage the belief in his readers that Jesus is "the Christ, the Son of God" (20:30–31), he assumes that his readers have grasped the meaning of these terms as John has defined them throughout the gospel. We can understand much of the gospel as a pedagogical exercise in moving the reader beyond traditional categories for Jesus' identity to an understanding of Jesus' unity with God himself. John does this by means of the larger structure of his gospel and by means of the structure of several discourses within this larger framework.

The Structure of the Gospel

At the level of the gospel's larger structure, we can compare its prologue to the final narrative scene before the purpose statement.[19] In the prologue, John identifies Jesus with the "Word" (1:14) and describes the Word in the opening line as both "with God" from all eternity and as himself "God" (1:1). John then describes Jesus' being and his relationship with God in filial terms. He is the Son of God, but emphatically not the Son in some way that one might also use to describe other human beings. Rather, his sonship is "unique in kind" (*monogenēs*, 1:14).[20] Moreover, he is "God the only Son"—somehow he is both the unique Son of God and himself God (1:18).[21] By the end of the prologue, therefore, John has defined Jesus' equality with God in terms of his divine sonship.

---

18 Cf. Grundmann, "χρίω," 566.

19 de Jonge, *Jesus: Stranger from Heaven*, 6.

20 Although the term "son" does not appear in 1:14, it is implied by the reference to the Father. The rendering of *monogenēs* as "unique in kind" comes from BDAG, 658. The translation "only begotten" for this word mistakenly derives the meaning of *genēs* from the cognate verb *gennaō*, "beget." The term *genēs*, however, is more closely related to the noun *genos*, which means "kind," so that *monogenēs* means "one of a kind," rather than *unigenitus* (Vulgate) or "only begotten" (KJV). See the discussion in Brown, *John I–XII*, 13–14.

21 For the translation "God the only Son" for *monogenēs theos* see Brown, *John I–XII*, 17. In place of "only begotten God (*monogenēs theos*)," some manuscripts have "the only begotten son" (*ho monogenēs huios*). The earliest and best manuscripts (P66, P75, ℵ, B, C, among others) have the reading *monogenēs theos*, and since John uses the word *monogenēs* elsewhere with *huios* (3:16, 18; 1 John 4:9), *monogenēs theos* is also the more difficult reading. On both external and internal grounds, therefore, this reading should be considered original. See Bruce M. Metzger, et al., *A Textual Commentary on the Greek New Testament* (London: United Bible Societies, 1971), 198.

In the last scene before the gospel's purpose statement, John similarly affirms Jesus' divinity when Thomas, satisfied by his own encounter with the resurrected Jesus that Jesus has truly risen from the dead, responds to him with the words, "My Lord and my God" (20:28). When John then speaks of Jesus as "the Son of God" in the purpose statement (20:31), he leads the reader once again to consider this title in terms of Thomas' confession.

These two affirmations of Jesus' divinity in terms of his filial relationship to God, one at the beginning and one near the end of the gospel, encourage the reader to understand the whole gospel as a redefinition of traditional categories of divine sonship.[22]

The Gospel's Discourses

What John does at the level of the gospel's larger structure, he also does within the gospel itself. He repeatedly insists that although Jesus fulfills traditional expectations among Samaritans and Jews for a great future leader, these traditional boundaries cannot contain Jesus' equality and unique relationship with God.

John the Baptist's Witness to Jesus

John places an account of the Baptist's witness to Jesus immediately after the gospel's prologue (1:19–35). In the first part of this passage, various religious leaders from Jerusalem interrogate John about his identity (1:19–28). The discussion at first revolves around which category of eschatological expectation the Baptist fills: Is he Elijah, the forerunner of "the great and dreadful day of the Lord" (Mal. 4:5), the Prophet-like-Moses (Deut. 18:18), or the Messiah (2 Sam. 7:12, 16; Ps. 2)? The Baptist, however, will not leave the discussion on this level. He claims none of the traditional roles outlined for him. Isaiah certainly anticipated his role (Isa. 40:3), but his role is merely that of a voice heralding the coming of the Lord (John 1:23). Even Jesus' forerunner cannot be explained entirely within the world of traditional expectations.

The scene then shifts to the next day (John 1:29) and to the topic that the Baptist had introduced with his interrogators the day before: the identity of the one whose coming he heralds (1:29–34). Here too, traditional categories do not adequately explain who Jesus is. Jesus is certainly the innocent lamb of God described in Isaiah's fourth Servant Song, whose slaughter atones for the sins of the guilty (1:29; cf. Isa. 53:6–7, 10).[23] He is also the Servant on whom God's Spirit will come according to Isaiah's first Servant Song (John 1:32–33; cf. Isa. 42:1).[24] Jesus' significance, however, goes far beyond these descriptions, as the Baptist states: "This is the one I meant when I said, 'A man who comes after me has surpassed me because he was before me'" (1:30).

22 Cf. D. Moody Smith, *John* (ANTC; Nashville: Abingdon, 1999), 62.

23 Scholars debate the meaning of the expression "lamb of God, who takes away the sin of the world." For a description of the options and a reasonable case for seeing in the phrase an allusion to Isa. 53:7 and 10, see Brown, *John I–XII*, 58–63, and D. A. Carson, *The Gospel according to John* (PNTC; Grand Rapids: Eerdmans, 1991), 149–51.

24 Brown, *John I-XII*, 61.

John has already given us this testimony of the Baptist in the prologue (1:15), where he describes Jesus as having been "with God in the beginning" (1:2). The meaning of the words "he was before me," therefore, are not in doubt: The Baptist is claiming that Jesus existed before becoming flesh and making his dwelling with human beings. He is both God and uniquely related to God, as the prologue affirms, and these are the qualities of Jesus to which the Baptist refers when he testifies that Jesus is "the Son of God" (1:34).[25]

John will later make clear that Jesus rather than the Baptist qualifies for the roles of Messiah and Prophet. In this passage, however, the emphasis lies on the ultimate irrelevance of these categories for appreciating the full significance of Jesus. Jesus is the one who, as the prologue says, existed with God from the beginning and is himself God. The Baptist is merely the voice that announces the arrival of this one. The debate about the identities of Jesus and of the "voice" that heralded his coming simply cannot be conducted in traditional terms. That debate must take place on a different level.

The Gathering of Jesus' Disciples

In the gospel's next two scenes (1:35–42 and 43–51), which focus on the gathering of Jesus' disciples, we find a similar shift from traditional expectations to an understanding of Jesus that places him in close communion with God. Here people hail Jesus with a dizzying array of titles: "the Lamb of God" (1:36), "Rabbi (1:38, 49), "the Messiah" (1:41), "the one Moses wrote about in the Law, and about whom the prophets also wrote" (1:45), "Son of God" (1:49), and "king of Israel" (1:49).

At the conclusion of all this, John focuses on the encounter between Jesus and Nathanael and recounts how Jesus urges Nathanael to go beyond such traditional understandings of his identity. Nathanael has set aside his early skepticism about Jesus (1:46) and, on the basis of Jesus' astonishing insight into his character (1:47–48), believes that Jesus is a "rabbi," "the Son of God," and "the king of Israel." Not only is Jesus a traditional Jewish teacher, but he is the Messiah—the specially anointed king who in Psalm 2:7 is also called God's son (cf. 2 Sam. 7:14). This, however, is only a partial recognition of Jesus' true identity on the basis of a partial knowledge of Jesus' power. Thus, Jesus tells Nathanael that greater insights into his identity are in store for him: "You will see heaven open, and the angels of God ascending and descending on the Son of Man" (1:51).

The statement is difficult, and interpreters have advanced various ideas about its precise meaning, but its basic meaning is reasonably clear: Jesus, as the Son of Man, connects heaven with earth.[26] Jesus, in other words, is not merely a Jewish teacher. He is not merely the Prophet (of whom Moses wrote) or the Suffering Servant (of whom Isaiah wrote) or the messianic Son of God who is king over Israel. He is all of

25 One (א), and possibly two (P5), early Greek manuscripts, several manuscripts of the Old Latin version, and both manuscripts of the Old Syriac version, have "the elect of God" or "the elect Son of God" instead of "the Son of God" (*ho huios tou theou*) in 1:34. Despite the support that "the elect of God" has received from some learned commentators such as Brown, *John I–XII*, 57, and Carson, *John*, 152, "Son of God" has much better manuscript support and is therefore probably original. Scribes who caught the allusion to Isa. 42:1 in 1:32–33 may have been tempted to extend that allusion to include a reference to Jesus as "my elect one" (LXX *ho eklektos mou*) at this point.

26 Brown, *John I–XII*, 90–91.

these, but he is also more: He is the very means by which the heavens are opened and God is revealed to those below.[27]

Another Testimony of the Baptist

We find the same movement from an affirmation of Jesus' messiahship to a description of his unique relationship with God in a second testimony of the Baptist to Jesus. When the Baptist's disciples comment to their teacher that Jesus is imitating their master's baptizing activity and "everyone is going to him" (3:26), John makes clear to them that this is entirely appropriate. He tells them, "You yourselves can testify that I said, 'I am not the Christ [Messiah] but am sent ahead of him'" (3:28). John the evangelist and John the Baptist could hardly be any clearer about their conviction that Jesus is the Messiah. Either the evangelist or the Baptist—it is difficult to tell which—continues, however, with a description of Jesus as "the one who comes from above" (3:31), "the one who comes from heaven" (3:31), and "the one whom God has sent" (3:34). This one testifies on earth to what he has seen and heard in heaven (3:32).

The Samaritan Woman

The movement from Messiah to unity with God occurs again, albeit more subtly, in Jesus' dialogue with the Samaritan woman. The Samaritan woman first identifies Jesus as "a prophet" (4:19)—probably thinking, as we have already seen, of the prophet like Moses of Deuteronomy 18:18. Then after Jesus answers the classic problem she raises about whether the Samaritans or the Jews have the right physical location for the temple, she comments that when the Messiah comes, "he will explain everything to us" (4:25). Jesus responds to this with the simple phrase, "I am—the one who is speaking to you" (4:26, aut.).

It is possible that the two words "I am" (*egō eimi*) mean nothing more than "I am he," and that Jesus should be understood as merely saying "I am the Messiah."[28] The LXX uses precisely this phrase, however, to refer to the God of Israel.[29] "Behold! Behold! I am [*egō eimi*] and there is no God beside me" says Deuteronomy 32:39, and "I am [*egō eimi*], and there is none beside," says Isaiah 45:18. The phrase seems to be used as a personal name for God in several passages in Isaiah, echoing God's revelation of his name to Moses as "I AM" in Exodus 3:14.[30] For example, the Lord can say through the prophet, "I am 'I AM' [*egō eimi egō eimi*] who wipes away your sins" (Isa. 43:25 LXX), or "I am 'I AM' [*egō eimi egō eimi*] who speaks righteousness and proclaims the truth" (Isa. 45:19 LXX), or "I am 'I AM' [*egō eimi egō eimi*] who comforts you" (Isa. 51:12 LXX).[31]

27 Cf. Ridderbos, *John*, 92; Smith, *John*, 74–78, 80.

28 Barrett, *St. John*, 239; Carson, *John*, 227 n. 1.

29 See the full treatments of this issue in Bultmann, *John*, 225–26 n. 3; Barrett, *St. John*, 342; and Brown, *John I–XII*, 533–38.

30 Barrett, *St. John*, 342. Cf. Brevard S. Childs, *Isaiah: A Commentary* (OTL; Louisville: Westminster John Knox, 2001), 335. At Ex. 3:14, however, the LXX has *egō eimi ho ōn*, "I am the one who is" for the Hebrew "I am who I am" (*ʾehyeh ʾăšer ʾehyeh*) and *ho ōn* for the phrase "I am" (*ʾehyeh*) used as God's name later in the verse.

31 All translations from the LXX are my own. It is possible, as Brown observes, *John I–XII*, 536, that the phrase should be translated "I am he, I am he" in these passages, but the Hebrew lying beneath the Greek translation is (rendered literally) "I, I am he" (Isa. 43:25; 51:12) and "I am YHWH" (Isa. 45:19). If the translator(s) had not taken *egō eimi* to be a name in each instance, he (they) would have more naturally rendered the phrases *egō autos eimi* and *egō kyrios*. For the second expression, see Isa. 44:24; 49:23, 26; 60:16; 60:22.

In light of all this, Jesus is moving the Samaritan woman beyond merely identifying him with the Messiah to seeing him as one with the God who revealed his identity to Moses as the God of Israel.[32] In the same breath Jesus identifies himself with the Messiah of the woman's expectations and takes her beyond these expectations to identify himself with God.

The Galilean Crowds

Something similar happens in the account of the feeding of the five thousand (6:14–15, 20). Here the Galilean crowds, after Jesus has fed them miraculously supplied food, believe that he is the expected Prophet-like-Moses (6:14) and are ready to "make him king by force" (6:15). Jesus escapes by withdrawing alone to a mountain. John then tells us that Jesus' disciples set off across the lake at evening only to encounter a strong wind and rough waters (6:16–18). During this storm, Jesus comes to them "walking on the water," and the sight understandably frightens them (6:19). To comfort them, Jesus "said to them, 'It is I [*egō eimi*]; don't be afraid'" (6:20). The phrase *egō eimi* sometimes appears in frightening circumstances in the Old Testament and comes as a word of comfort, just as it does here.[33] The close match between the circumstances in which Jesus uses the phrase here and the circumstances in which God sometimes uses it in the Old Testament combine with the unusual nature of the expression to lead the reader from viewing Jesus as only the Prophet and Israel's king to viewing him as Israel's God.[34]

Dialogue at the Feast of Booths

We find this same movement from reflection on how Jesus fits the traditional categories of Messiah and Prophet to reflection on his unity with God in the discussion of Jesus' identity at the Feast of Booths (7:25–8:59). The discussion begins with the

32 Edwyn Clement Hoskyns and Francis Noel Davey, *The Fourth Gospel* (London: Faber and Faber, 1940), 244, believe that the Old Testament background of the phrase may be significant here, but go no further. Bultmann, *John*, 192, appears to believe that Jesus speaks as the "I am" here; but see 226 n. 3, where he says that "I am" in 4:26 is not used as a "sacred formula." Francis J. Moloney, *The Gospel of John* (SP 4; Collegeville: Michael Glazier, 1998), 134, understands the phrase to mean "in Jesus the revelation of the divinity takes place" but not that Jesus is the manifestation of God. Beasley-Murray, *John*, 62, agrees with the interpretation advanced here that "the formula has the overtone of the absolute being of God."

33 See, e.g., Gen. 26:24: "I am the God of your father Abraham. Do not be afraid, for I am with you"; Isa. 51:12 LXX (aut.): "I am 'I AM' who comforts you. Whom do you, being moved with fear, fear among mortal humans?" See also, closer to the time of John's composition, *Apoc. Ab.* 9.2–3. On this point see Brown, *John I–XII*, 533–34, 536, and, for a discussion of the relevance of the *Apocalypse of Abraham* to John's "I am" sayings, see Ashton, *Understanding*, 141–44.

34 Cf. Brown, *John I–XII*, 255; Moloney, *John*, 203; Smith, *John*, 150. *Pace* Barrett, *St. John*, 28, and Carson, *John*, 275, both of whom cite 9:9 as proof that the *egō eimi* formula does not always have connotations of a theophany in John. In 9:9, however, the formerly blind man is answering questions about whether he is the one who used to sit and beg (9:8). The normal way to answer such questions in Greek is *egō eimi*. In the *Vitae Aesopi* G 29.20 and the *Vita Adam et Evae* 17, for example, to the question "Are you the young man?" Aesop answers, "*egō eimi*" and to the question, "Are you Eve?" Eve answers, "*egō eimi*" (cf. Matt. 26:22, 25; Mark 14:62; Luke 22:70). In neither John 4:26 nor 6:20, however, is this the situation. In 4:26 Jesus is not responding to the question, "Are you the Messiah?" but is claiming to be the Messiah of whom the Samaritan woman has just spoken in 4:25. Had Jesus merely intended to tell the woman that he was the Messiah, he would have said "*egō eimi houtos*" ("I am this person"; cf. Andocides, *Orat. Myst.* 126.5) or "*egō eimi ho Messias*" (cf. Plato, *Phaed.* 115.c.7 where Socrates says, "*egō eimi Sōkratēs*"; cf. Luke 1:19). Similarly in 6:20, Jesus is not answering a question about his identity but simply announcing, *egō eimi*, "I am." Had he meant only "It is I," he probably would have said what he does in Luke 24:39, "*egō eimi autos*" ("It is I myself!"). The use of the phrase in Mark 6:50 (cf. Matt. 14:27; Mark 13:6; Luke 21:8) probably only means that Mark understood it in much the same way that John did. (Thanks to the *TLG* for locating these texts.)

musings of those present at the feast about whether Jesus is the Messiah (7:25–26). As we have already seen, some conclude that Jesus cannot be the Messiah or the prophet because they "know" where he is from, and his origins disqualify him from fulfilling a variety of traditional expectations about these figures (7:27, 41b–42, 52). John is not willing to concede their point, as he shows when some in the crowd ironically deny that Jesus could be the Messiah because he is not from David's family and does not come from Bethlehem (7:42). He also tells us that some, on the basis of Jesus' teaching, conclude that he is the Prophet-like-Moses (7:40; cf. 7:46) and others, apparently on the basis of his signs (7:31), conclude that he is the Messiah (7:41). From John's perspective these are correct conclusions about Jesus' identity.

John refuses, however, to leave the discussion on this level. Jesus' part in the dialogue makes clear that although on one level these opponents "know" where he is from because they know he came to Jerusalem from Nazareth (7:28), on another level they have no idea where he comes from or where he is going (8:14). Of far greater significance than the trivial debate over Jesus' geographical origins is the issue of Jesus' eternal unity with God. Thus Jesus says plainly that he is "from" God, that God "sent" him (7:29, 33; 8:29), that he is "from above" (8:23), and that he communicates to his hearers only what he has seen and heard when in the presence of his Father (8:38, 40; cf. 1:18).

Toward the end of the debate, Jesus becomes increasingly explicit about his close relationship with God. Three times he uses the absolute phrase "I am" (*egō eimi*) of himself (8:24, 28, 58), insisting that unless people believe that "I am," they will die in their sins (8:24). In a climactic ending to the entire passage, Jesus uses this unusual phrase to claim that he existed before Abraham, implying, as the prologue says explicitly, that he existed with God from all eternity (8:58; cf. 1:1–2, 14, 18). The significance of the claim is not lost on the Jews, who pick up stones to stone him in accord with the punishment mandated in the Mosaic law for those who blaspheme "the name of the LORD" (Lev. 24:16).

Once again, John has moved his readers forward from debate over Jesus' fulfillment of traditional Jewish categories for an expected deliverer to an affirmation of Jesus' eternal unity with God. Jesus is the Davidic Messiah who was born in Bethlehem of Judea, as the irony implicit in 7:41–42 acknowledges, but he is far more than Israel's king.[35]

From the Healing of the Blind Man to the Passion Narrative

The same movement happens repeatedly as the gospel progresses. In John 9, the man born blind moves from speaking of his healer simply as "the man they call Jesus" (9:11) to viewing him as "a prophet" (9:17) to confessing before the Pharisees that he is "from God" (9:33), and finally worshiping Jesus as the Son of Man (9:35–38).[36] In the course of the story, John informs us that the Pharisees had decided to put out

35 Cf. Barrett, *St. John*, 330–31; Carson, *John*, 330; and Ridderbos, *John*, 276–78. Ridderbos, however, does not think it necessary to view 7:41–42 as ironic: John, in his view, simply thinks the debate over Jesus' geographical origins unimportant.

36 As with 4:19, the preverbal predicate nominative *prophētēs* in 9:17 probably has a qualitative nuance: Jesus' actions are prophetic in nature and he may therefore qualify as a prophet. See Daniel B. Wallace, *GGBB*, 265–66.

of the synagogue anyone who confessed Jesus to be the Messiah (9:22). He then tells us that when the man born blind confesses Jesus to be from God, the Pharisees throw him out (9:34). Once again, John has subtly redefined Jesus' identity from merely that of the Messiah to the one who is from God.

In chapter 10, the Jerusalem Jews want to continue the debate over the question of Jesus' messiahship, and they want Jesus to tell them plainly whether or not he is the Messiah. Jesus responds that his "works," by which he means the signs he has performed, speak plainly about his messiahship (10:25).[37] Nevertheless, he does not come forward with the open statement that his interlocutors want. Instead he says, "I and the Father are one" (10:30), a statement that his opponents take as a claim to be God. They regard this as blasphemy and pick up stones to stone him (10:31–33). Jesus tries to explain why, even on their terms, he is not blaspheming (10:35–38), but he continues to insist on his unity with the Father. They continue to understand this as blasphemy and try to "seize him" (10:39). Here too, then, the discussion begins with the question of whether Jesus is the Messiah and ends with Jesus' claim to be one with God.

In the passion narrative this pattern happens again. Jesus' trial revolves at one level around whether or not he is "the King of the Jews," and therefore a subversive element who threatens Judea's fragile participation in the *pax romana*. John has prepared us for this concern about Jesus when he hinted that the Jewish authorities, because they concluded that Jesus was the Messiah, were trying to kill Jesus (7:25–26). The concern became clearer after Jesus raised Lazarus from the dead and "many of the Jews," having seen this astonishing event, "put their faith in him" (12:45). In response to this outpouring of support for Jesus, the leading priests and Pharisees convened a meeting of the Sanhedrin and decided that something had to be done about Jesus, or "the Romans will come and take away both our place and our nation" (11:48). Jesus must die or the whole nation will perish (11:50).

Not surprisingly, then, the Jewish leaders initiate Jesus' trial. They turn him over to Pilate as a messianic pretender—a claimant to the title "King of the Jews," whose claim threatens the right of Caesar to rule the Jews through his governor Pilate (18:29–30, 33–35; 19:15).

At another, more basic level, however, Jesus' trial revolves around the truth of the claim that has been the bone of contention between Jesus and the Jews throughout 5:1–10:42: that he is the Son of God and therefore equal to God. Four times prior to Jesus' trial the Jews tried to punish Jesus for this claim (or close approximations of it) because they considered it untrue, blasphemous, and deserving of death (5:18; 8:59; 10:31, 39). The way in which John describes the trial of Jesus before Pilate makes clear that this is also the most important reason why the Jewish leaders want Pilate to execute Jesus. When Pilate learns from Jesus that his kingdom is "not of this world" (18:36) and therefore fails to view Jesus as a credible political threat (19:4), the Jews finally divulge the deeper reason that they want to kill Jesus. "We have a law," they say, "and according to that law he must die, because he claimed to be the Son of God" (19:7).

37 Cf. 7:31 and 9:21–22, where the confession that Jesus has healed the blind man is taken to be equivalent to the confession that Jesus is the Messiah.

Ultimately they succeed in their efforts, but by their success they have unwittingly facilitated Jesus' return to his Father's presence and to the same unity with the Father that he has had from all eternity. John has prepared the reader throughout the narrative to appreciate this irony in two ways. First, he has spoken of Jesus' crucifixion as his "being lifted up" (3:14; 8:28; 12:32, 34), using a term that early Christians employed to describe Jesus' exaltation to the right hand of God after his resurrection and ascension (Acts 2:33; 5:21). Second, he has communicated to the reader that although throughout Jesus' sojourn in the world he carried the "glory" of his Father with him (1:14; 2:11; 11:4, 40; 17:4; 17:22), Jesus' death will be the means through which Jesus will return to share the same level of glory with the Father that he enjoyed before he created the world and "made his dwelling" in it (12:28; 17:5; cf. 12:23; 17:24; 21:19).[38]

As throughout the gospel, so in the passion narrative, John leads his readers to appreciate Jesus on more than the traditional levels of the expected Prophet-like-Moses or God's specially anointed king. Jesus is certainly the King of the Jews, as Pilate stubbornly insists. But as Pilate's fear when he hears it also shows, Jesus' significance goes far beyond "this world"—he is the Son of God (19:7–8; cf. 18:36). By the very death to which Pilate, despite his fear, hands him over, Jesus returns to the Father from whom he came, with his mission in the world fully accomplished (17:4; 19:30).

Summary

In the same way that the grand structure of the gospel supports the interpretation of Jesus' divine sonship as his unity with the Father, the dialogue in the gospel moves the reader from the explanation of Jesus in traditional categories to the exalted description of his unity with God in the gospel's prologue. He certainly qualifies for the roles of Messiah and Prophet-like-Moses, but he will not remain within the traditional boundaries that these roles mark out for him. He is the Son of God in a unique sense:

- He was in a close relationship with God before the world's creation (1:2, 18);
- he came to reveal God's glory and to communicate what he had seen and heard of God (1:18; 3:32; 8:40) to the world that he had created (1:14, 18); and
- through his crucifixion he has returned to God and the perfect fellowship he had with him from before the world's creation (17:5).

It is appropriate, therefore, that he should receive worship as both Lord and God from those who believe in him (9:38; 20:28).

Because John has carefully defined his terms in this way, he is confident that his readers will not take the titles "the Christ, the Son of God" (20:30–31) in his purpose statement in merely traditional terms.[39] Jesus is the Messiah, but that title cannot

38 See also 7:39; 12:16; 13:31–32.

39 Cf. Ashton, *Studying John*, 107.

describe him adequately unless it is viewed through the lens of Jesus' unique, filial relationship with his Father. Jesus is the Messiah, Son of God in the sense that he was and is "in the bosom of the Father" and therefore can make the Father known during the time of his earthly ministry (1:14, 18). One must believe this about Jesus in order to have life in his name.

SIGNS AND FAITH

The "signs" of Jesus also occupy an important place in John's purpose statement. John begins the statement with a reference to the many signs that Jesus worked and then comments that out of this large group John has selected the signs that appear in his own book so that those who read about them might believe in Jesus' identity as Messiah and Son of God, and so have life. Out of the nexus of signs and faith John hopes that life will come to his readers.

Faith as the Result of Seeing the Signs

Much within the gospel of John supports an uncomplicated reading of this purpose statement. People see Jesus work miracles and reason that since only God can give someone such power, Jesus must be from God. Throughout the gospel, by overt statement and subtle implication, John shows that this response to the signs of Jesus is appropriate.

This simple connection between signs and faith appears clearly in his first explicit reference to a sign in his gospel. John concludes his account of Jesus' changing water into wine at a wedding in Cana with the comment that this sign revealed Jesus' glory, and his disciples believed in him (2:11). A few paragraphs later, John tells us that many Jerusalemites believed in Jesus because they saw the "signs" he did during a Passover pilgrimage to Jerusalem (2:23). Only a few sentences after that statement, we learn that Nicodemus, a Jewish leader, came to interview Jesus after concluding from his "signs" that Jesus was a teacher who had come from God (3:2). The Galilean crowds decide on the basis of the "sign" of the feeding of the five thousand that Jesus is "the Prophet who is to come into the world" (6:14). Similarly, many in the crowd that gathered for the Feast of Tabernacles in Jerusalem believe that Jesus is the Messiah and comment, "When the Christ [Messiah] comes, will he do more miraculous signs than this man?" (7:31).

This connection between signs and faith among the crowds poses a dilemma for the chief priests and the Pharisees, who think that Jesus' many "signs" have led to a correspondingly large following for Jesus, and that if they allow this volatile situation to continue, the Romans will take away both their temple and their nation (11:17–19, 47–48). Near the end of what interpreters sometimes call "the book of signs" (1:19–12:50), John records his amazement at the hard-heartedness of those who, like these leaders, rejected Jesus despite seeing his signs: "Even after Jesus had done so many signs in their presence, they still would not believe in him" (12:37).[40]

40 Brown, *John I–XII*, cxxxviii, and Moloney, *John*, 23, describe 1:19–12:50 as the "book of signs." C. H. Dodd, *The Interpretation of the Fourth Gospel* (Cambridge: Cambridge Univ. Press, 1953), 290, begins the "book of signs" at 2:1. The propriety of the designation is questioned by Beasley-Murray, *John*, xc, who observes that in 20:30 John describes the entire narrative as a book of signs.

The connection between signs and faith also appears in more subtle ways. Although the word "sign" does not appear in John's account of Jesus' encounter with Nathanael, for example, something very much like a sign leads Nathanael to believe. When Jesus shows by his conversation with Nathanael that he knew his character before ever meeting him, Nathanael answers in amazement, "Rabbi, you are the Son of God; you are the king of Israel" (1:49). In the next sentence, Jesus describes this confession as faith ("you believe," 1:50).[41] Thus, Jesus' miraculous knowledge of Nathanael has led him to believe that Jesus is both Messiah and Son of God (cf. 20:31).

Something similar happens with the Samaritan woman. Jesus shows miraculous insight into her character, and she runs back to her town with the news that because Jesus told her "everything [she] ever did," he may be the Messiah (4:28–29). John tells us that as a result of precisely this testimony to Jesus' supernatural knowledge of the woman's character, "many of the Samaritans from that town believed in him" (4:39).

In the same way, after Jesus has washed his disciples' feet on the night before his crucifixion, he speaks of one of his followers who has not been chosen and who will fulfill the psalmist's complaint that one who has shared his food will betray him (13:18; Ps. 41:9). "I am telling you now, before it happens" Jesus explains, "so that when it does happen you will believe that 'I am'" (John 13:19, aut.). This is reminiscent of Jesus own prayer, shortly before calling Lazarus forth from the grave, in which he tells his Father that he has spoken his request to raise Lazarus audibly so that the crowd standing around "may believe that you sent me" (11:42; cf. 11:15). The link between the provision of a sign and belief here receives the approval of Jesus himself.

In summary, when Jesus provides signs for people during the time of his ministry, he intends that they should see them and believe that his claims about his relationship with his Father are true. By providing a written record of these signs, John hopes his readers will also "see" them and believe.

The Complex Relationship of Signs to Faith

The placement of John's purpose statement, however, immediately raises questions about this otherwise simple picture of the relationship between signs and faith. The purpose statement, with its mention of Jesus' "other" signs (20:30), directs the attention of the reader back to the account of Jesus' miraculous appearance to Thomas in the previous paragraph.[42] In this account, the link between signs and faith is anything but simple.

The appearance to Thomas occurs at the time of Jesus' second appearance to his assembled disciples. Thomas was absent at the first appearance and refused to believe the report of the others that Jesus was alive unless he saw and touched for himself the wounds of the crucified and supposedly risen Jesus (20:25). At this second appearance, therefore, Jesus insists that Thomas touch his wounds, stop doubting, and believe (20:27). After Thomas' confession, Jesus gives him a gentle rebuke: "Because you have seen me, you have believed; blessed are those who have not seen and yet have believed" (20:29).

41 This is true whether *pisteueis* is a statement or a question.

42 Cf. Raymond E. Brown, *The Gospel according to John XIII–XXI* (AB 29A; New York: Doubleday, 1970), 1058–59; Beasley-Murray, *John*, 387; Ridderbos, *John*, 650–51.

John's purpose statement, with its clear link between signs and faith, comes on the heels of this rebuke. Taken with the rebuke, the purpose statement implies that excusing unbelief with the claim that one has only read John's account of Jesus' signs and not actually seen a sign for one's self is misguided. Reading (or hearing read) without seeing should be enough to engender faith.

This is not the only place where Jesus supplies a sign to someone who refuses to believe without it and, at the same time, says that this way of coming to faith is not ideal. Jesus' second Galilean sign comes with an implicit warning that the request for a sign as a prerequisite for belief is inappropriate. When a royal official comes to Jesus in Cana to ask him to heal his son in Capernaum, Jesus responds with a rebuke both to the man and to those standing nearby, "Unless you people see miraculous signs and wonders, you will never believe" (4:48). In light of this rebuke, we are surprised to read that Jesus heals the man's son at a distance and that as a result of this healing the man and his whole family believe (4:50–53).

The same idea appears in Jesus' teaching in the gospel. At an appearance in Jerusalem during the Feast of Dedication, Jesus tells a group hostile to his claims that even though they do not believe him, they should believe his "miracles, that you may know and understand that the Father is in me, and I in the Father" (10:38). He tells his disciples something similar in the first farewell discourse, that they should believe "I am in the Father and the Father in me" on the basis of his own words. But if doubts still linger and it is absolutely necessary, he goes on to say, they should believe on the basis of the works that he has done (14:11; cf. 10:38).

Those who require a sign before they will believe will sometimes receive one, and they will sometimes, like Thomas, come to an authentic and enduring faith on this basis. John's gospel expresses reservations about faith of this kind, however, and several passages hint at why this is so.

First, such sign-based faith may not be authentic. At the Passover where Jesus cleared the temple of merchants, John tells us that "many people saw the miraculous signs he was doing and believed in his name. But Jesus would not entrust himself to them, for he knew all men" (2:23–24). By this John apparently means that Jesus recognized the insufficient nature of their faith just as he had earlier perceived that Nathanael was an Israelite in whom there was no deceit (1:47). Nicodemus, then, provides a personal example of this kind of positive, but ultimately inadequate, response to Jesus on the basis of the signs.[43] He knows from Jesus' signs that God is with him (3:2), but Jesus' talk of "being born again" (3:3–4) and spiritual birth (3:8–9) puzzles him.

Second, insistence on a sign may indicate hostility toward Jesus. In response to Jesus' ejection of the merchants from the temple (2:13–16), the Jewish leaders ask him for a "sign" to prove his authority to do what he has done (2:19). Jesus' refusal to answer them plainly (2:19) and their resulting hostility (2:20) show that the request for a sign is ill-conceived, and Jesus does not satisfy their request.

43 This is a common understanding of the relationship between 2:23–25 and 3:1–21. See, e.g., Brown, *John I–XII*, 126–27, and Beasley-Murray, *John*, 45–46; Ridderbos, *John*, 121–23.

It is probably in this same spirit that Jesus' brothers, whom John explicitly tells us "did not believe in him" (7:5), advise him to stop hiding his works and reveal himself publicly to the world by doing his works in Judea at the Feast of Tabernacles (7:4). Jesus, however, refuses to go to the Feast at the time his brothers advise him to go (7:8–9). Although he eventually does go, John tells us that "he went ... not publicly, but in secret" (7:10).[44]

Third, the request for a sign may flow from a profound misunderstanding of Jesus' significance and mission. On the basis of the "sign" that he provided when he fed them in the wilderness, the Galilean crowds similarly mistake Jesus for a prophet like Moses and a king who will satisfy their material and political needs (6:14–15; cf. 18:36). This conviction deepens when they begin to suspect that Jesus crossed the lake the following night without a boat (6:25). Jesus makes clear to them, however, that they have not really "seen" the signs that he worked because they have failed to understand him as the "food" from God that supplies eternal life (6:26–29).[45] To this they respond, "What sign then will you do that we may see it and believe you? What work will you do?" (6:30, aut.). When Jesus gives, instead of a sign, an explanation of his own death as the food and drink that gives eternal life (6:51–58), they comment that this is a hard teaching (6:60) and reject him (6:66).

In sum, the attitude expressed in John's gospel toward Jesus' signs is complex. On the one hand, John appears to understand the signs positively as the sure witness to Jesus' unity with his Father. According to his book's purpose statement and according to the way the signs often work in his gospel, they are the critical link between his readers and faith that Jesus is the Messiah and Son of God. On the other hand, John reveals some reserve toward certain connections between Jesus' signs and faith. Particularly problematic is the request for a sign as a prerequisite to faith. Such a request may flow from a positive disposition and, when the sign is supplied, result in genuine, lasting faith. Often, however, the request for a sign arises from hostility toward or misunderstanding of Jesus' claims.

A Pre-Johannine Signs Source?

What is the origin of this complicated approach to the signs in John's gospel? Interpreters sometimes claim that it arises from John's use of a "signs source" whose author placed greater weight than John himself on Jesus' signs as a means of creating faith.[46] Remnants of this source are supposedly found in several characteristics of the gospel. For example, the designation of two signs as the "first" and "second" signs of Jesus (2:11; 4:54) is supposedly an undigested remnant of the source's numbering system for Jesus' miracles.[47] The style of Greek in the source is also thought to be

44 *Pace* Fortna, *Fourth Gospel,* 240, who claims that by going to Jerusalem Jesus grants the request of his brothers.

45 Cf. Rudolf Bultmann, *Theology of the New Testament,* 2 vols. (New York: Charles Scribner's Sons, 1951–55), 2:45.

46 Representative of the many advocates of a "signs source" lying beneath the present gospel are Alexander Faure, "Die alttestamentlichen Zitate im 4. Evangelium und die Quellenscheidungshypothese," *ZNW* 21 (1922): 99–121; Bultmann, *John,* passim; Robert Tomson Fortna, *The Gospel of Signs: A Reconstruction of the Narrative Source Underlying the Fourth Gospel* (SNTSMS 11; Cambridge: Cambridge Univ. Press, 1970); idem, *Fourth Gospel;* and Ashton, *Studying John,* 90–113.

47 Bultmann, *John,* 113 and 205; Fortna, *Fourth Gospel,* 115. The correspondence between the first and second sign, however,

different from that of the gospel's final editor: It uses simple conjunctions, for example, and regularly puts the verb at the beginning of the sentence, a common feature of Semitic languages.[48]

The source is thought to be especially evident in the "aporias" of the gospel—places where the words of the source and the words of the final editor collide. For example, the presence of the source is betrayed when John speaks of Jesus' signs in passing as if he had worked many of them (2:23; 3:2; 4:45), but then incorporates into his gospel a few paragraphs later the statement of the signs source that the healing of the royal official's son was Jesus' "second" sign. Another collision between the source and John's editing is evident within the narrative of this second sign itself: Jesus scolds the people standing around the royal official for requiring a sign in order to believe, but the statement makes little sense in its present context since no one asked for a sign (4:47–48).[49]

The source's author believed that the miraculous nature of Jesus' signs could aid the reader in coming to faith in Jesus as the Messiah.[50] According to one interpreter, the author of the source thought rather simplistically that when confronted with Jesus' signs, the reader would automatically believe.[51] This simple connection between Jesus' signs and faith appears in the purpose statement in 20:30–31, which is taken to be the conclusion to the source and a clear statement of the purpose of the source's author in writing it.[52]

John's own understanding of the signs, according to these interpreters, is more nuanced than that of the signs source. One signs source advocate claims that John found the meaning of Jesus' signs not in the astonishing nature of the miracles Jesus worked but in the symbolic value of the signs as a description of Jesus' person—Jesus produced bread, healed the blind, and raised the dead because he is, symbolically speaking, food, light, and life. Far from compelling belief because of their astonishing character, John shows that the signs could be misunderstood and lead to rejection of Jesus. Thus, for John there was little difference between Jesus' signs and his words: His signs revealed who he was just as his words did, and his words, like the signs, were events that called forth faith.[53] Both Jesus' words and his signs presented Jesus as the Revealer of God, and both therefore had the same effect. The miraculous element in the signs was of little ultimate importance.[54]

is not as close as many translations make it. Whereas the Greek of 4:54 uses the adjective "second" (*deuteros*) to describe Jesus' healing of the official's son, the Greek of 2:11 literally describes the changing of water to wine not as the "first" (*prōtos*) sign but as the "beginning of the signs" (*archēn tōn sēmeiōn*).

48 Bultmann, *John*, 329 n. 2 and 395 n. 2.

49 Ibid., 113; Fortna, *Fourth Gospel*, 4–8; Ashton, *Studying John*, 91–96.

50 Bultmann, *John*, 452.

51 Fortna, *Fourth Gospel*, 220, 237.

52 Faure, "Die alttestamentlichen Zitate," 108–9; Bultmann, *John*, 698 n. 2; Fortna, *Fourth Gospel*, 201–2.

53 Bultmann, *John*, 452, 698; idem, *Theology of the New Testament*, 2:44–45, 59–60.

54 Bultmann, *Theology of the New Testament*, 2:45, comments, "The miracles may be for many the first shock that leads them to pay heed to Jesus and so begin to have faith—for this purpose, miracles are, so to speak, conceded. . . ." Cf. Faure, "Die alttestamentliche Zitate," 111–12. Fortna believes that John did not disagree with the perspective of the signs source but only found its view that the signs automatically produced faith too simple. See *Fourth Gospel*, 239–50, and cf. Ashton, *Studying John*, 107.

Interpreters who believe that John has edited a signs source have placed a helpful emphasis on the complex way in which the gospel as we have it handles the connection between Jesus' signs and faith. In the final analysis, however, the theory does not provide an adequate account of this complexity. The theory encounters two primary problems. First, it depends to a large extent on subjectively determined criteria. What to one interpreter looks like an intolerable crack in the narrative structure of the gospel—an "aporia"—to another finds a simple explanation in the wider context of the passage. In 4:54, for example, John probably does not have in mind the signs that Jesus worked while in Judea at the Passover, but only the signs that he has worked in Galilee.[55] Likewise, in 4:48 John probably intends for us to think that Jesus, who "knew all people" (2:24; cf. 1:47–48; 2:25; 4:17–19, 29, 39), also knew that the royal official and those around him were seeking a sign as a basis for belief. He therefore rebuked this hidden attitude.

In the same way, the purpose statement in 20:30–31 need not be the conclusion to a gospel of signs with which John's own attitude stands in tension.[56] As we have already seen, John's reference to "other" signs in this passage connects the statement with the immediately preceding Thomas narrative and therefore to the clearest expression in the gospel of the inadequacy of a sign-based faith. The purpose statement itself, therefore, points beyond itself to the complex connection between signs and belief as John has already expressed it in the rest of the gospel.

Second, the argument from differences in style between the source and John's editing of it is not sustainable. Careful analysis of the style of John's gospel shows the basic similarity between the supposed signs source and John's supposed redaction.[57] A comparison of John's style with ancient literary expectations for religious writing, moreover, reveals that the "aporias" in the narrative and the curiously sonorous style of the entire gospel may have been purposeful. John may have been writing with the "solemnity," "obscurity," and "sublimity" thought by some ancient literary critics to be appropriate qualities of religious discourse.[58] Whatever the explanation of the gospel's style, however, that it is both distinctive and homogenous places the theory

55 See the full and compelling discussion of Ridderbos, *John*, 178–80. Carl J. Bjerkelund, *Tauta Egeneto: Die Präzisierungssätze im Johannesevangelium* (WUNT 40; Tübingen: J.C.B. Mohr [Paul Siebeck], 1987), 55–71, has argued that 2:11 and 4:54 do not derive from a supposed "signs source" but are precise "defining statements" for which the gospel's author is responsible.

56 Faure, "Die altestamentliche Zitate," 111–12; Bultmann, *John*, 252; Ernst Haenchen, "'Der Vater, der mich gesandt hat,'" *NTS*, 9 (1962–63): 208–16, here at 208–9. To be fair, neither Fortna, *Fourth Gospel*, 239, nor Ashton, *Studying John*, 107, believes that John disagreed with the perspective of his source. Rather, he deepened its perspective. Indeed, Ashton comments perceptively on the "unlikelihood that an author will take over and adapt a document with which he wholeheartedly disagrees." In *Understanding*, 246, however, Ashton does claim that the high Christology expressed in the gospel's final redaction differs markedly from the simple messianic Christology expressed in the gospel's "signs source."

57 Eduard Schweizer, *Ego Eimi: Die religionsgeschichtliche Herkunft und theologische Bedeutung der johanneischen Bildreden, zugleich ein Beitrag zur Quellenfrage des vierten Evangeliums* (FRLANT 38; Göttingen: Vandenhoeck & Ruprecht, 1939), 82–112; Eugen Ruckstuhl, *Die literarische Einheit des Johannesevangeliums: Der gegenwärtige Stand der einschlägigen Forschungen* (Studia Friburgensia 3; Freiburg, Switzerland: Paulus, 1951); idem, "Johannine Language and Style: The Question of Their Unity," in *L'évangile de Jean*, ed. M. de Jonge (BETL 44; Leuven: Univ. Press, 1987), 125–47 (in which the two previous works are summarized). Cf. Bjerkelund, *Tauta Egeneto*, 55–71, and the more general comments of Ashton, *Understanding*, 87–88 (who nevertheless, in *Understanding*, 246, 252–53, agrees with the basic contours of Fortna's signs source theory).

58 Frank Thielman, "The Style of the Fourth Gospel and Ancient Literary Critical Concepts of Religious Discourse," in *Persuasive Artistry: Studies in New Testament Rhetoric in Honor of George A. Kennedy*, ed. Duane F. Watson (JSNTSup 50; Sheffield:

of a signs source, particularly one with which John himself stood in theological tension, on the shakiest possible footing.

Although John's handling of the link between signs and faith is complicated, it is unlikely that the complications arise from a partially digested signs source. Instead, they reflect John's own complex but coherent understanding of Jesus' signs.

The Coherence of John's Approach to Jesus' Signs

When John uses the term "sign," he means something that points allusively to a reality beyond itself—a symbol.[59] This becomes clear from the way John uses the word "signify" (*sēmainō*), the verbal form of the noun "sign" (*sēmeion*). John uses this verb three times, and in each instance it describes Jesus' allusion to the way either he himself or Peter would die. Jesus "signified" the kind of death he would die by speaking of his death as being "lifted up" (12:33; 18:32), and he "signified" the kind of death Peter would experience with the enigmatic 21:18: "When you were younger you dressed yourself and went where you wanted; but when you are old you will stretch out your hands, and someone else will dress you and lead you where you do not want to go." A sign, then, is an intimation of something beyond itself. Because it is only an intimation of this reality, it is inherently ambiguous and stands in need of interpretation—interpretation that can be accepted, misunderstood, or rejected.[60]

For John, Jesus' signs point to the reality that he is one with God. In order to see this, it is first necessary to see that John often uses the term "work" and the term "sign" interchangeably. When the Galilean crowds, for example, ask Jesus for a legitimating sign, they formulate their request with two questions that mean the same thing, but one question speaks of doing a sign and the other of doing a work: "What *sign* [*sēmeion*] will you do that we may see it and believe you? What *work* will you do [*ergazē*]?" (6:30, aut.).

The same equation appears at the beginning of the narrative about the blind man's healing. The people considered this miracle to be a sign (9:16), and Jesus refers to it as one of "the works of God" (9:3–4). When Jesus' brothers advise him to go to the Feast of Tabernacles and perform his "works" publicly so that his disciples might see them, therefore, they are probably referring to Jesus' signs (7:3–4).

After Jesus has arrived in Jerusalem for this feast, he speaks of having amazed the Jews by performing one "work" (*ergon*, 7:21), and the subsequent discussion (7:22–23) reveals that this work was the healing of the lame man at the Pool of Bethesda on the Sabbath (5:1–15). Although John nowhere calls this healing a "sign," its status both as a miracle at which people are amazed (7:21; cf. 5:20) and as a "work" demonstrate that it functions as a sign. The occurrence of this sign on the Sabbath, moreover, demonstrated that Jesus was one with God. Jesus explains that he is one

Sheffield Academic Press, 1991), 169–83. Cf. Thomas L. Brodie, *The Gospel according to John: A Literary and Theological Commentary* (New York: Oxford, 1993), 15–19, without, however, endorsing his resistance to the "Reformation insistence that scripture speaks plainly" (18), which seems to rest on a misunderstanding of the Protestant doctrine of the perspicuity of Scripture. See, e.g., the *Westminster Confession of Faith* 1.7.

59 Bultmann, *Theology of the New Testament*, 2:44.

60 Ibid., 2:44–45.

with the Father, doing whatever he sees the Father doing, and that the Father works all the time (5:17, 19). If the Father who sent him (5:36) works all the time, including the Sabbath, then Jesus can also work on the Sabbath. Not surprisingly, the Jews realize the implications of Jesus' words and try to kill him because he was "making himself equal with God" (5:18).[61]

Jesus' response to the offense they have taken only confirms the correctness of their conclusions about the significance of his claims. He says that his unity with the Father will be revealed in other, "even greater," works (5:20), one of which is the raising of the dead: ". . . just as the Father raises the dead and gives them life, even so the Son gives life to whom he is pleased to give it" (5:21). The implications of this statement are many, but among them lies an anticipation of the resurrection of Lazarus. In this sign (11:47) Jesus raises the dead Lazarus and gives him life just as the Father does. In this way, he demonstrates his unity with God.

Another of these works is executing the judgment that his Father has entrusted to him in his role as Son of Man:

> Moreover, the Father judges no one, but has entrusted all judgment to the Son, that all may honor the Son just as they honor the Father. . . . And he has given him authority to judge because he is the Son of Man. (5:22–23, 27)

This statement too has many implications, but one of its features is an anticipation of the "sign" (9:16) of the healing of the blind man. John's account of this healing ends with Jesus' urging the blind man to believe in him as the Son of Man (9:35) and with Jesus' concluding statement: "For judgment I have come into this world, so that the blind will see and those who see will become blind." Here too, then, a sign of Jesus has demonstrated his unity with the Father because through this sign he has executed a role that the Father delegated to him.[62]

As both the healing of the lame man and the healing of the blind man demonstrate, however, the signs are inherently ambiguous. It is possible to conclude from the signs alone that Jesus is wicked. Thus, in response to the healing of the lame man and the blind man, some Jews conclude that Jesus is a sinner, bent on disobeying the fourth commandment and deceiving others to do the same (5:12, 18; 7:12; 9:16).[63] It is also possible to conclude from the signs alone that Jesus is the anointed national and political liberator of Israel or, alternately, that he is a political troublemaker who will only stir up the Roman occupying force against the Jews. Thus, the Galilean crowds, on the basis of Jesus' provision of food in the wilderness, are ready to make him their king (6:15). Alternatively, the Sanhedrin worries that "everyone will believe in him, and then the Romans will come and take away both our temple and our nation" (11:48).

The signs, therefore, need the interpretive words of Jesus that accompany them in order to make their significance clear. Not surprisingly, Jesus' words are also an

61 See, e.g., Ashton, *Understanding*, 139.

62 Cf. de Jonge, *Jesus: Stranger from Heaven*, 131–36.

63 See Frank Thielman, *The Law and the New Testament: The Question of Continuity* (New York: Crossroad, 1999), 81–83.

important part of his work (8:28; 14:10; 15:22, 24).[64] Through them Jesus can explain that he and the Father are one and that therefore he, like the Father, can legitimately break the Sabbath (5:16). He can explain that he is the bread that comes down from heaven (6:32–33, 35, 50–51), the light of the world (9:4–5), and the resurrection and life (11:25).

John may have understood failure to put the signs within the context of Jesus' teaching as the reason why a signs-based faith often fell short of genuine faith. Conclusions about Jesus that people draw from the signs alone can range from the utterly perverse ("this man is not from God," 9:16) to the incomplete ("you are a teacher who has come from God," 3:2) to the fully acceptable ("my Lord and my God!" 20:28).

Conclusions about Jesus that are drawn both from Jesus' signs and from his interpretation of his signs as witnesses to his unity with the Father, however, are more reliable. They often result in either acceptance or rejection. When Jesus feeds five thousand with a child's lunch, the sign taken alone yields an unfortunate misinterpretation of his intentions. When he explains the sign by reference to his crucified flesh and blood as real food and drink, however, the meaning of the sign becomes clearer and people divide into two groups over its meaning:

> From this time many of his disciples turned back and no longer followed him.
> "You do not want to leave too, do you?" Jesus asked the Twelve.
> Simon Peter answered him, "Lord, to whom shall we go? You have the words of eternal life. We believe and know that you are the Holy One of God." (6:66–69)

Similarly, when Jesus tells the Jews gathered in Solomon's Colonnade plainly that he and the Father are one, they just as plainly reject this claim as blasphemy and pick up stones to stone him. "I have shown you many good works from the Father," Jesus responds. "For which of these do you stone me?" The issue, they tell him, is not his works but his words: "because you, a mere man, claim to be God" (10:30–33, aut.). Belief in the signs, interpreted by means of Jesus' words to refer to his unity with the Father, leads to eternal life. Left to draw their own conclusions about Jesus on the basis of the signs, people will often, although not inevitably, go astray.[65]

Why, then, in the purpose statement does John only speak of signs leading to faith, rather than to signs as interpreted through Jesus' words? Have we not simply arrived back at the original conundrum that encouraged the search for a signs source? John does not, however, speak of the signs alone but of the signs *as he has written about them*, and his record of them includes their definitive interpretation through Jesus' words.[66] John has chosen a few signs and provided extensive interpretive commentary on them because the signs by themselves are not as effective in producing the faith that leads to life as the signs interpreted through Jesus' teaching.

64 Bultmann, *Theology of the New Testament*, 2:60–61; Brown, *John I–XII*, 527.

65 That they do not always go astray explains why Jesus urges people to believe in him on the basis of the signs alone when his words do not produce belief (10:38; 14:11).

66 Cf. Bultmann, *John*, 698.

ETERNAL LIFE

The ultimate goal of John's gospel, according to his purpose statement, is that its readers may have "life" in Jesus' name. The term "life" (*zōē*) is important throughout the book. It appears thirty-six times, over one-fourth of the total occurrences of this word in the New Testament.[67] In nearly half of these instances, John pairs it with the adjective "eternal" (*aiōnios*), and the expressions "life" and "eternal life" have the same meaning.[68] What is that meaning?

"Eternal Life" in Literature Roughly Contemporaneous with John

The phrase "eternal life" is common in Jewish texts from around the time of John. The Hebrew Scriptures use the term only once, but that one use is illustrative of the way subsequent literature closer to the time of John's gospel uses it. In Daniel's final vision, a magnificent angelic being appears to the seer and describes what will happen at the end of time. After a period of great suffering, it is said, God will deliver his people and "multitudes who sleep in the dust of the earth will awake: some to everlasting life [Heb. *lᵉḥayyê ᶜôlām*; Gk. *eis zōēn aiōnion*], others to shame and everlasting contempt" (Dan. 12:2).[69]

Here eternal life comes at the end of time to those who have died but who have remained faithful, despite hardship, in life. This life will never end but, as Daniel 12:3 puts it, will continue "for ever and ever" (Heb. *lᵉᶜôlām wāᶜed*; Gk. *eis ton aiōna tou aiōnos*).

Similarly, the second of the Maccabean martyrs defies the Syrian King Antiochus IV with these dying words: "The King of the universe will raise us up to an everlasting [*aiōnion*] renewal of life [*zōēs*]" (1 Macc. 7:9). Here, too, God restores life to someone who has remained faithful in the midst of hardship and died. Time does not limit this restored life—it lasts forever. Likewise, in Mark's gospel Jesus speaks of persecution "in this present age" but of receiving in "the age to come eternal life" (Mark 10:29–30).

In the Daniel text, everlasting life for God's faithful people is contrasted with everlasting shame and contempt for those who have oppressed God's people. This same contrast reappears in the *Psalms of Solomon*, written in the first century B.C. and so closer to the time of John:

> The destruction of the sinner is forever, and he will not be remembered when (God) looks after the righteous. This is the share of sinners forever, but those who fear the Lord shall rise up to eternal life [*eis zōēn aiōnion*], and their life shall be in the Lord's light, and it shall never end. (*Pss. Sol.* 3:11–12; *OTP* 2:655)

---

67 The term appears 135 times in the New Testament, according to H. Bachmann and W. A. Slaby, eds., *Concordance to the Novum Testamentum Graece*, 3rd ed., (Berlin: Walter de Gruyter, 1987), 774–78, which means that about twenty-seven percent of its New Testament occurrences are in John's gospel.

68 Dodd, *Interpretation*, 144; W. F. Moulton and A. S. Geden, *A Concordance to the Greek New Testment*, 4th ed. (Edinburgh: T. & T. Clark, 1963), 422–23. Seventeen of the thirty-six appearances of "life" occur in the construction "eternal life" (*zōē aiōnios*). The frequent coupling of the two terms in the gospel apparently led to the reading "eternal life" at 20:31 in an impressive array of uncial manuscripts (ℵ, C, D, L, and Ψ).

69 See Dodd, *Interpretation*, 144.

This contrast also appears frequently in the New Testament. Paul contrasts those who by patient good work seek glory, honor, and immortality and so receive "eternal life" with those who, because they are selfish and wicked and reject the truth, receive "wrath and anger" (Rom. 2:7–8). Elsewhere he opposes sowing to the flesh and reaping destruction on one hand with sowing to the Spirit and reaping "eternal life" on the other (Gal. 6:8). Similarly, in Matthew 25:46 the wicked "go away to eternal punishment, but the righteous to eternal life." Eternal life, therefore, is an eschatological reality—something for which the people of God hope (Titus 1:2; 3:7; Jude 21)—and it stands in contrast to the eternal destruction that awaits the wicked.

John's Crucial Modification of Eschatological Tradition

When we turn to John's gospel, we discover not only a familiarity with and acceptance of this traditional understanding of "life" in the "age to come" but also a crucial modification to it. There Jesus says, in language that almost reproduces Daniel 12:2: ". . . all who are in their graves will hear his voice and come out—those who have done good will rise to live, and those who have done evil will rise to be condemned" (John 5:28–29).[70]

Jesus also speaks of hating one's life "in this world" and so keeping it for "eternal life" in a manner that nearly duplicates the traditional contrast between "this age" and "the age to come" (12:25; cf. Mark 10:30; Luke 18:30).[71] He likewise speaks in traditional language of the resurrection of the dead on "the last day" (John 6:39, 40b, 44b, 54b; cf. 12:48).

The crucial difference between the use of this concept in John's gospel and its use in traditional Jewish and Christian texts lies in the emphatic way John asserts that "eternal life" is realized in the present, prior to either physical death or "the last day." In 4:36, using harvest imagery that tradition connects with eschatological restoration or judgment (Isa. 27:12; Amos 9:13; Joel 3:13; Matt. 13:30, 39–42; Rev. 14:15–16), Jesus says that "*even now* the reaper draws his wages, *even now* he harvests the crop for eternal life."[72]

Similarly, in John 6:40, Jesus tells the Galilean crowds that everyone who sees and believes in the Son "shall have eternal life, and I will raise him up at the last day." Here, the traditional order of events—resurrection at the last day and subsequent eternal life—has been reversed. For John, eternal life is available in the present to those who believe in God's Son, and their resurrection from the dead will follow "on the last day." Although John affirms the final resurrection from the dead, his emphasis lies on the availability in the present, of a life that death cannot interrupt. Thus Jesus can say later in the gospel, "I tell you the truth, if anyone keeps my word, he will never see death" (8:51).

70 Nils A. Dahl, "'Do Not Wonder!' John 5:28–29 and Johannine Eschatology Once More," in *The Conversation Continues: Studies in Paul and John in Honor of J. Louis Martyn*, ed. Robert T. Fortna and Beverly R. Gaventa (Nashville: Abingdon, 1990), 322–36, here at 326.

71 Dodd, *Interpretation*, 146; Ashton, *Understanding*, 215.

72 Schnackenburg, *St. John*, 1:450–51; Brown, *John I–XII*, 182; Beasley-Murray, *John*, 63.

Similarly, in John 11:21–29 Martha expresses her disappointment that Jesus did not come more quickly when he heard that her brother Lazarus, now dead, had fallen gravely ill (11:21). When Jesus tells her that her brother will rise again (11:23), Martha understandably takes this to refer to the traditional expectation that on the last day Lazarus will be among the resurrected righteous (11:24). To this, however, Jesus responds that he is both resurrection and life. This means, he continues, that those who believe in him have already entered a state of life that physical death cannot disturb (11:25–26). This comment elicits from Martha precisely the confession that, according to John's purpose statement, expresses faith and leads to life:[73]

Martha (11:27)	**John (20:31)**
I believe that *you are the Christ, the Son of God.*	These are written that you may believe that *Jesus is the Christ, the Son of God.*

With this confession, Martha has moved into a state of life that will continue eternally and that even her own death will not interrupt. Once again, John has detached eternal life from the last day and moved it backward into the present through faith in Jesus as God's Son. Because this "life" survives physical death, even the resurrection of the dead has moved back, metaphorically speaking, into the present. As if to emphasize that a reality stands behind the metaphor, John concludes this dialogue with an account of how Jesus brought Lazarus physically back to life by his word (11:43–44).

The clearest expression of this dramatic change in traditional eschatological expectation occurs in 5:24–25, where Jesus says:

> I tell you the truth, whoever hears my word and believes him who sent me has eternal life and will not be condemned; he has crossed over from death to life. I tell you the truth, a time is coming and has now come when the dead will hear the voice of the Son of God and those who hear will live.

Here, at the same time that John affirms a future, final resurrection, he also asserts that with Jesus' appearance and teaching both eternal life and resurrection have been in some sense detached from the final day and moved into the present. It is now possible to move—in the present—out of the state of death and into the state of life by hearing and believing Jesus' word. As Jesus puts it in the prayer that concludes his farewell discourses, "This is eternal life: that they may know you, the only true God, and Jesus Christ, whom you have sent" (17:3). Since this knowledge is possible in the present, it is possible to have eternal life in the present.

It is also possible for those who do not believe to experience in the present the condemnation that, in traditional eschatology, happens in the future. In traditional thinking, the oppressor and sinner could expect a future of shame, everlasting contempt, and

73 The corresponding language appears in italics.

eternal destruction (Dan. 12:2; *Pss. Sol.* 3:11; Matt. 25:46; Rom. 2:7–8). John affirms this future condemnation at the resurrection for "those who have done evil" (5:29), but his emphasis lies on the conviction that condemnation (3:18) and the outpouring of God's wrath (3:36) already occur in the present for those who do not believe in Jesus. The positive statement in 5:24 about those who believe and cross over from death to life in the present implies, negatively, that those who fail to believe are left in a state of death. The same thought appears in 8:21, 24, where Jesus tells a hostile group of Pharisees that because they do not understand his heavenly origin they will die in their sin(s).

In summary, John claims that with the coming of Jesus, elements of the traditional expectation for eternal life, condemnation, and even resurrection from the dead have moved from the future "resurrection" and "last day" back into the present. The hour is not merely coming but "now is" when, through the voice of God's Son, God raises the dead to life (5:25; cf. 4:23).

The Theological Origin and Coherence of John's Eschatology

John's bold rearrangement of traditional eschatology raises two questions: What is the theological origin of this "realized eschatology"? Is John's dominant emphasis on eternal life and condemnation in the present theologically consistent with his occasional affirmation, in traditional language, of a future judgment and resurrection?

The Theological Origin of John's Eschatology

John's claim that major aspects of traditional eschatological expectation have been realized in the present probably originated in his conviction, discussed above, that traditional expectations for a coming deliverer could not explain Jesus' identity. As we have seen, John believes that Jesus has certainly fulfilled those expectations, but that, in addition, he is one with God (10:30). His works are the Father's works (5:17, 19, 30a; 6:38), and his words the Father's words (3:2b; 6:45; 7:16; 8:26, 28; 12:49; 14:10, 24; 15:15). He has been sent from his Father to reveal these works and words to his people (8:38a) and through his "lifting up" will return to the Father (6:62; 20:17) to resume the place of glory he occupied before creation (17:5, 24).

Therefore, to the horizontal, chronological notion that is familiar from the Synoptic Gospels—that Jesus fulfills expectations drawn from either Scripture or Jewish tradition—John adds an emphasis on the vertical, revelatory element of Jesus' appearance. Jesus is not only the Prophet-like-Moses and the King of Israel but also the Word and Son of God who was with God from before the world's creation, who descended to the world to reveal his Father, and who will ascend by means of his exaltation on the cross back to his Father. He is not only the one of whom Moses had written (1:45) but the one who passed through the open heaven to establish a direct connection between heaven and earth (1:51; cf. 3:13). He is not only the coming Prophet and King (6:14–15) but also the bread "which comes down from heaven and gives life to the world" (6:33, 38, 41, 50–51, 58). Isaiah did not merely anticipate Jesus' rejection in his own ancient call to be a prophet, but at the time of his call, he actually "saw" Jesus' glory in his vision of the exalted and enthroned Lord (12:41; cf. 8:58; see Isa. 6:1, 10).

The strength with which John asserts this claim influences his eschatological outlook.[74] If Jesus has perfectly revealed God's character and will, then God's judgment need not wait for the consummation of all things. God has no more to say than he has already said in Jesus, and so the criterion of final judgment has moved into the present. Insofar as people either finally believe or finally reject the revelation of God in Jesus, therefore, the judgment has taken place.

The Theological Coherence of John's Eschatology

If judgment takes place in the present and eternal life begins in the present, however, does John's theology have room for the traditional eschatological expectations that appear occasionally in his gospel—expectations of a "last day," of a "time . . . when all who are in their graves will . . . come out," and of Jesus' return to claim his own (5:28–29; 6:39, 40, 44, 57; 12:48; 14:3; 21:22–23)? Some interpreters of John have answered this negatively and suggested that an "ecclesiastical redactor" worked over the gospel, correcting a supposed tendency in the gospel toward docetism. Docetism emerged in the late first and early second century and denied that Jesus had come in the flesh. In addition, docetists sometimes denied any future resurrection of the dead or final judgment.[75]

Others have found in John's gospel a decided intellectual shift away from the traditional eschatological expressions of early Christianity. For these interpreters, John did not deny the truth of traditional eschatology but his emphasis lay on questions of significance for the existence of the individual that were current in the Hellenistic world with which he was in conversation: Where did I come from? Where am I going? Where can I find enduring significance for my life?[76] Some of these interpreters believe that a later editor added traditional elements to the gospel because he wanted to see explicit affirmations of traditional eschatology in it.[77] Others think that John himself included the traditional elements but constantly pointed beyond them to the significance of faith in Jesus for present existence.[78]

74 That John's distinctive eschatology originates with his high Christology is a common observation. See, e.g., Schnackenburg, *St. John*, 2:437; Beasley-Murray, *John*, 80; John T. Carroll, "Present and Future in Fourth Gospel 'Eschatology,'" *BTB* 19 (1989): 63–69, here at 65–66; Smith, *Theology of the Gospel of John*, 105–6; Stephen S. Smalley, *John: Evangelist and Interpreter*, 2nd ed. (New Testament Profiles; Downers Grove, Ill.: InterVarsity Press, 1998), 267; and Jörg Frey, *Die johanneische Eschatologie*, 3 vols. (WUNT 96, 110, 117; Tübingen: J.C.B. Mohr [Paul Siebeck], 1997–2000), 2:286–87.

75 Cf., e.g., the correction of docetic tendencies in Polycarp's *Phil.* 7:1 (early second century): "For everyone who does not confess that Jesus Christ has come in the flesh is an anti-Christ [cf. 1 John 4:2–3 and 2 John 7], and whoever does not confess the witness of the cross is from the devil. And whoever changes the sayings of the Lord according to his own desires and says that there is neither resurrection nor judgment, this person is the firstborn of Satan." See also 2 Tim. 2:18; Ignatius, *Trall.* 9:1–2; and the comments of Bultmann, *John*, 261. According to Ashton, *Understanding*, 32, Julius Wellhausen first suggested an orthodox editor of the gospel in his work *Erweiterungen und Änderungen im vierten Evangelium* (Berlin: Reimer, 1907), 7–15. See also Faure, "Die alttestamentlichen Zitate," 119–20. Faure's article appeared in 1922 and exercised an important influence on Bultmann.

76 Schnackenburg, *St. John*, 2:436–37. Cf. Dodd, *Interpretation*, 148–50, and for evidence that such questions were abroad in the first century, see Martin Hengel, *Judaism and Hellenism: Studies in Their Encounter in Palestine during the Early Hellenistic Period*, 2 vols. (Philadelphia: Fortress, 1974), 1:210–18, esp. 212.

77 Schnackenburg, *St. John*, 2:115–16. Cf. Brown, *John I–XII*, cxx–cxxi, who suggests, however, that the editor may have only been preserving older Johannine traditions that he did not want lost.

78 Dodd, *Interpretation*, 148. Cf. Barrett, *St. John*, 68–69. That the complexity of the gospel's time expressions were a result of the complex but coherent eschatology of the Johannine church and community is the burden of Frey's massive three-volume work, *Die johanneische Eschatologie*.

Something like this final position must be correct. Who can deny that John's gospel places a heavy emphasis on the encounter with Jesus' word in the present as the critical moment of judgment? It is a point on which both Rudolf Bultmann and Billy Graham can agree. At the same time, it is difficult to image an "ecclesiastical redactor" steeped well enough in the thought of the gospel to master its distinctive style nevertheless disagreeing with the gospel's theology on so critical a point.[79] Theories of a more sympathetic redactor are equally unlikely since they involve the notion that this editor worked with minute attention to detail, adding half sentences to the material before him in an extraordinarily complex way.[80]

There is no way to disprove such theories; anything is possible. But are they probable? Is it more likely that an editor who had mastered John's style added a complicated network of phrases to the gospel or that John himself wanted to affirm traditional eschatological expectations at the same time that he placed his emphasis elsewhere? Even if the two eschatological elements were contradictory, it seems more likely that John himself held incompatible eschatological convictions than that an editor worked so intricately, but ineffectively, to pull John's gospel into a more orthodox shape.

Are these elements contradictory? Interpreters of the gospel often observe that the eschatological tension expressed in it is a persistent theological tension in Christianity from its earliest days to the present. In the Synoptic Gospels, Jesus speaks frequently of the kingdom of God both as if it were present in his ministry (Matt. 12:28/Luke 11:20; Matt. 16:28–17:9/Mark 9:1–10/Luke 9:27–36) and as if he and others would enter it in the future (Mark 9:47; 10:15, 24–25; 14:25; cf. Matt. 6:10/Luke 11:2). Paul could say within the space of a few paragraphs both that "the wrath of God is being revealed from heaven against all the godlessness and wickedness of human beings" (Rom. 1:18) and that the wicked are storing up for themselves "wrath ... against the day of God's wrath, when his righteous judgment will be revealed" (2:5).

Christianity has traditionally affirmed that with the coming of Jesus the biblical promises about the restoration of creation and of God's people have largely been fulfilled but that elements of fulfillment await the future. There is nothing incoherent about affirming both that God has "already" begun to fulfill his promises for the future in Jesus and that this fulfillment is "not yet" complete.[81]

Moreover, John did not create the vertical, revelatory dimension of Jesus' ministry that appears so prominently in his gospel. The vertical dimension is implied in Paul's claim that all things came into existence through the "one Lord, Jesus Christ" (1 Cor. 8:6) and in his statement that Jesus took human form (Phil. 2:7).[82] That this

79 "The last day" is a distinctively Johannine phrase, appearing in the New Testament only in John's gospel (6:39, 40, 44, 54; 11:24; 12:48; although see, as Schnackenburg, *St. John*, 2:466–67 n. 90, points out, *Apoc. Mos.* 4.3). Other New Testament writers use the more common plural phrase "the [these] last days" (Acts 2:17; 2 Tim. 3:1; Heb. 1:2; James 5:3; 2 Peter 3:3).

80 Schnackenburg, *St. John*, 2:116, proposes that the editor of the gospel found an affirmation of the traditional view on Martha's lips (John 11:24) and then inserted this phrase into the other passages to be sure that the gospel itself affirmed traditional eschatological expectations.

81 On the frequently observed tension between the "already" and the "not yet" in New Testament theology, see, e.g., the classic statement of Oscar Cullmann, *Christ and Time: The Primitive Christian Conception of Time and History* (London: SCM, 1951), 139–43.

82 Cf. Col. 1:15–20; 1 Tim. 3:16, which assume the existence of Christ before his incarnation. Many scholars consider these texts pseudepigraphic and from a time roughly contemporaneous with

vertical dimension combined with a "horizontal," or chronological, dimension is clear from Paul's statement that "when the time had fully come, God sent his Son, born of a woman, born under the law" (Gal. 4:4), and from the Synoptic accounts of Jesus' birth in which Jesus is conceived by the Holy Spirit in answer to biblical prophecy (Matt. 1:20–23; Luke 1:32–35).[83]

The revelatory dimension of John's portrait of Jesus is also not novel. It finds an early parallel in a well known statement from the source that Matthew and Luke probably held in common ("Q"):[84]

Matt. 11:27	**Luke 10:22**
"All things have been committed to me by my Father. No one knows the Son except the Father, and no one knows the Father except the Son and those to whom the Son chooses to reveal him."	"All things have been committed to me by my Father. No one knows *who* the Son *is* except the Father, and no one knows *who* the Father *is* except the Son and those to whom the Son chooses to reveal him."

This so-called "meteorite fallen from the Johannine heaven"[85] should remind us that within early Christianity John's own theology was less unusual than scholars often think. It rested on good historical foundations and expressed an understanding of Jesus that was both known and widely accepted in early Christian circles, although John expresses it in his own, distinctive style.[86]

Having said all this, the emphasis that John places on the present significance of Jesus as the final revelation of God remains unusual within the New Testament. He has focused on the present response to Jesus' words and works as the critical moment of judgment. He has emphasized the moment of belief in Jesus as the point at which one enters unending life. By doing this, has John so weighted his gospel on the side of a realized eschatology that the scales have tipped, and there actually remains no logical need for a "last day" when the dead will be raised and Jesus returns for his disciples?

John's clear understanding and articulation of the need to persevere in faith in the midst of persecution reveal that, despite his emphasis on realized eschatology, the elements of final eschatology in his gospel are critical to his theology.[87] We have

the fourth gospel, but there are good reasons for thinking that they come from Paul's lifetime, and if so, they are early expressions of precisely the descent–ascent motif that we find in John's gospel.

83 Unlike Matthew's account, Luke's account does not quote a specific text that Jesus' birth fulfills, but the fulfillment of biblical hopes for a coming deliverer is implied in Gabriel's reference to the throne of David and to an everlasting kingdom (cf. 2 Sam. 7:11b–13). On other precedents for John's blending of "vertical" and "horizontal" elements, see Brown, *John I–XII*, cxvi.

84 The italics signal the differences between the two passages.

85 This much quoted (and misquoted) comment comes from Karl Hase, *Geschichte Jesus nach akademischen Vorlesungen* (Leipzig: Breitkopf and Härtel, 1876), 422. Hase says that the passage "macht den Eindruck wie ein Aerolith aus dem johanneischen Himmel gefallen, allenfalls auch aus dem Gesichtskreise des Paulus" ("gives the impression of a meteorite [not 'thunderbolt'] fallen from the Johannine heaven, possibly also from the conceptual world [lit. 'horizon'] of Paul").

86 Cf. Jeremias, *Theology*, 59: "Thus we may have here one of the *logia* of Jesus from which Johannine theology grew. Indeed, without such points of departure in the synoptic tradition it would be a complete puzzle how Johannine theology could have originated at all." This is also the judgment of W. D. Davies and Dale C. Allison, *A Critical and Exegetical Commentary on the Gospel according to Saint Matthew*, ICC (Edinburgh: T. & T. Clark, 1991–97), 2:282 n. 218.

87 Carroll, "Present and Future," 66–68. Cf. Barrett, *St. John*, 70, who says that John's commitment to the "primitive Christian

already seen in our study of John's purpose statement and in our study of the relationship between signs and faith that not all "faith" is authentic faith, nor are all "disciples" real disciples. While Jesus was at the Passover, John tells us, many people saw his signs and "believed in his name," but Jesus, for his part, refused to entrust himself to these "believers" because "he knew all people" (2:23–24). John seems to mean by this that Jesus knew their faith to be inauthentic.

After feeding the Galilean crowds and explaining that he is the bread who has come down from heaven whose flesh people must eat and whose blood they must drink if they are to live forever (6:51, 53), John tells us that many of Jesus' disciples took this as a hard teaching (6:60), began grumbling (6:61), and decided to follow him no longer (6:66). This did not take Jesus by surprise because he "had known from the beginning which of them did not believe" (6:64a). John adds to this that Jesus knew who, among his inner circle of twelve disciples, would betray him (6:64b), and Judas's treacherous "discipleship" holds special interest for John (6:70–71; 12:4–6; 13:2, 18–30; 17:12; 18:2, 3, 5).

By the time we reach chapter 8, we are not completely surprised to find a dialogue between Jesus and "the Jews who had believed in him" (8:31) that degenerates first into unhappiness with Jesus (8:33), then into name-calling (8:48), and finally into an attempted lynching (8:59). This dialogue begins with a statement that sums up John's approach to discipleship and faith: "To the Jews who had believed him, Jesus said, 'If you abide [*menō*] in my word, you are truly my disciples'" (8:31, aut.). As we learn by the end of the dialogue, neither the faith nor the discipleship of these opponents was "true" because they rejected Jesus' claim of eternal fellowship with his Father (8:38, 54, 58–59). In other words, they failed to "abide" in Jesus' "word."

In Jesus' farewell discourses, he tells his disciples that the world's opposition will severely test their decision to believe in him. Although he will send the Spirit of truth—the Paraclete—to help them, to teach them, and to remind them of Jesus' teaching (14:16, 26; 15:26; 16:13–15), he will be in a place that they cannot now come (13:33, 36; 17:11), and they will be left in a world that will oppose them just as it has opposed him (15:18–21; 16:1–4, 33; 17:11, 14, 15). They must, therefore, persevere in their faith—in Johannine terms, they must "abide" (*menō*) in Jesus (15:4–6) and in his love (15:9). They must not "stumble" in their discipleship as many of the "disciples" in the Galilean crowd had "stumbled" (16:1; cf. 6:61).[88] The one who does not "abide" in Jesus "is like a branch that is thrown away and withers; such branches are picked up, thrown into the fire and burned" (15:6). This is probably a reference to the final judgment, in which, like the weeds in Matthew 13:30, the offending plants are collected into bundles for burning.[89]

In this context, the expressions of unfulfilled eschatological events in John make theological sense. Those whose faith in Jesus is authentic have "eternal life" and have already "crossed over from death to life" (5:24), but in the interval between Jesus'

---

eschatology" was purposeful because he saw its value as "a constant reminder that the church lives by faith, not by sight, and that it is saved by hope."

88 In both places, John uses the verb *skandalizō*, its only two appearances in his gospel.

89 Brown, *John XII–XXI*, 678–79. Cf. Barrett, *St. John*, 475.

departure and his return, his disciples will face severe testing, equivalent to the testing that Jesus faced. They must "abide" in him during these difficult times. Even Lazarus, whose experience of realized eschatology was as vivid as anyone could hope for in the present, faced the prospect of persecution and death after Jesus had raised him from the dead (12:10–11). His resurrection was only provisional.

This makes a future, final resurrection and entry into life a theological necessity. John apparently understood this, and so the affirmation in 5:28–29 is not surprising: ". . . a time is coming when all who are in their graves will hear his voice and come out—those who have done good will rise to live, and those who have done evil will rise to be condemned."

Those whom the Father has drawn to Jesus, and whom the Father has given to Jesus, will have authentic faith and be raised on the last day (6:39–40, 44; cf. 10:27–29). Those who reject Jesus and his words in the present will be condemned on the last day (12:48). But John shows his readers throughout his gospel that it is less than clear in the present who belongs to which camp. Every believer, therefore, must abide in Jesus until the last day when he raises the dead and returns for his own.

Summary

John says more emphatically than any other voice in the New Testament that God has provided in Jesus the fullest revelation of himself that is possible in the world. Because Jesus is eternally one with the Father, he can reveal God's words and deeds more fully than anyone else. This enables eternal life and judgment to be detached from the future and to move back into the present on the basis of one's response to Jesus. It is possible to cross over from death to life—to have eternal life before the final resurrection—by believing that Jesus is the Christ and Son of God.

In the same way, it is possible to experience condemnation by finally and completely rejecting Jesus' claims. Since the last day has not arrived, however, the present remains a time in which hardship will test the faith of Jesus' disciples for its genuineness.[90] Those who abide in his word in this period of testing may experience physical death, but they will not experience death in the deepest sense. They will be resurrected on the last day and enjoy eternal fellowship with God and with his Son.

JOHN'S THEOLOGY AND THE PURPOSE OF HIS GOSPEL

John conceives of his gospel as a means by which those who read it and hear it read may believe that Jesus is both the fulfillment of biblical hopes for a coming deliverer and the perfect revelation of God, his Father. Coming to this conviction and

90 Although he places no emphasis on it, John probably also believed the converse of this—that rejection of Jesus' words and deeds at any given time did not necessarily mean eternal condemnation (as Carroll, "Present and Future," 64 col. b, 66 col. a, seems to suggest). Thus when Jesus says to the Jews, "when you have lifted up the Son of Man, then you will know that 'I am' and that I do nothing on my own but speak just what the Father has taught me" (8:28, aut.), he may be referring to the possibility that in the future at least some of them (such as Jesus' brothers? cf. 7:5) would stop rejecting him and instead believe his claims. See, e.g., Ridderbos, *John*, 303–4; *pace*, e.g., Barrett, *St. John*, 343–44.

remaining convinced of it despite persecution are so important to John because to "abide in Jesus' word" (8:31), as John puts it, is to experience life in the deepest sense of that term. It is to bring the biblical promise of unending life in the future so completely into the present that a relationship with Jesus and his Father begins that physical death cannot interrupt (5:24; 8:51; 11:25–26; 17:24–26).

John has constructed his book, therefore, to reveal the identity of Jesus by means of his signs as they are interpreted through Jesus' words. He hopes through his book to encourage the faith of those who already believe. As they face the world's hatred, persecution, and trouble, he hopes that his book will enable them to "abide" in Jesus and his word. He must also hope that his book will encourage any who have not yet believed that Jesus is the Christ, the Son of God, to follow the example of the Baptist and his disciples, of Nathanael, of the Samaritan woman and her town, of the royal official, of the man born blind, and of Martha—all of whom believed Jesus' claims. John hopes, therefore, to encourage all who read his book to believe the truth that Jesus' signs—as interpreted through his words—disclosed: Jesus is not only the fulfillment of traditional Jewish hopes but the perfect revelation of God.

Chapter 7

FOUR DIVERSE WITNESSES TO THE ONE GOSPEL OF JESUS CHRIST

Mark, Matthew, Luke–Acts, and John were written in separate settings by different authors, and each exhibits its own set of theological concerns. As we saw in chapter 2, most early Christians, despite intense pressure to harmonize these four separate gospels into a "life of Jesus" or dispense with three of the four, decided instead to keep all four—but only these four—in all their diversity. They viewed them as the only historically credible witnesses to the one gospel of Jesus Christ, and they saw them as valuable for what united them theologically as well as for their separate theological emphases. In the face of challenges from the more recent "life of Jesus" movement, we argued that the church's decision to keep all four witnesses to the one gospel of Jesus Christ was still a good decision. We have examined briefly the theology of each witness. We now need to see where the theological lines that run through the four gospels converge and where they supply separate, but valuable, theological emphases.

Four questions unite Mark, Matthew, Luke–Acts, and John:

What is the historical significance of Jesus?
What can account for his rejection?
What is the meaning of his death?
What response should he receive in the present?

WHAT IS THE HISTORICAL SIGNIFICANCE OF JESUS?

Mark, Matthew, Luke, and John each intended to proclaim the significance of Jesus within the context of God's age-old purposes. John, Mark, and Matthew emphasized that Jesus had fulfilled every expectation that Israel's Scriptures express for an eschatological deliverer, but all three were also concerned to show that Jesus exceeded these expectations and broke with the common traditions about what the Messiah should claim for himself and do for Israel. These three gospel authors, then, have a two-tiered understanding of Jesus' significance—he stands in continuity with the expectations of Israel's Scriptures, but he goes beyond the traditional understanding of those expectations. Luke does not disagree with this notion, but he accents Jesus' significance differently. He emphasizes the continuity between Jesus and the inherited tradition in order to show the central place that Jesus occupied in the progress of salvation history.

John, Matthew, and Mark: Jesus Fulfills and Exceeds Israel's Expectations

The two-tiered understanding of Jesus' relationship to Israel's traditions appears most clearly in John's gospel. John wrote his book so that his readers might "believe that Jesus is the Christ, the Son of God" (John 20:31), and yet his gospel is in part an effort to redefine these traditional terms for his readers. As we saw in the last chapter, John wants his readers to know that Jesus is the Messiah and the eschatological Prophet-like-Moses of Jewish, and even Samaritan, expectation (John 1:49; 4:19, 25–26; 6:14; 7:31, 40; 9:17). At the same time, he leads his readers beyond these traditional expectations to an appreciation of Jesus' unique relationship, even unity, with God. Somehow he is "God the only Son"—both the Son of God and one with God (1:18). Jesus existed before John the Baptist (1:15, 30), before Abraham (8:58), and before Isaiah (12:41). He was with God in the beginning (1:2; 16:28; 17:5). He is equal with God (5:18), one with God (10:30; 17:11, 21–23), and can even refer to himself with God's biblical name, "I AM" (4:26; 6:20; 8:24, 28, 58). John intends for his readers to understand the title "Son of God" in his purpose statement in 20:31 not merely in its traditional messianic sense but through the lens of Thomas's confession in 20:28 that Jesus is his God.

Mark, too, shows that Jesus both fulfilled Scriptural expectations and that traditional categories cannot contain him. Jesus fulfilled all the expectations articulated in Israel's Scriptures for a coming king, in the line of David, who would shepherd God's people Israel with justice and obtain the nations for his inheritance (Mark 1:1, 24; 8:29–30; 10:47–48; 11:10; 14:61–62; cf. Ps. 2:2, 8; Jer. 23:1–6; Ezek 34:1–6, 15–16, 23–24). Nevertheless, his divine sonship is qualitatively different from that of any other anointed sons of David. Jesus is God's uniquely beloved Son (Mark 1:11; 9:7). Like God himself, he forgave sins (Mark 2:5), rebuked the wind, and hushed the waves (Mark 4:41). Like God, he alone is good (Mark 7:37; 10:18). The traditional categories of kingship—even messianic kingship—cannot accommodate this aspect of Jesus' identity.

Mark's way of handling this theme differs from John's way in two respects. First, Mark's expression of Jesus' divinity is more muted than John's. For John the unity of Jesus with God is articulated unambiguously, from beginning (John 1:1–2, 14, 18) to end (20:28). Mark hints at Jesus' divinity with rhetorical questions: "Who can forgive sins but God alone?" (Mark 2:7); "Who therefore is this that even the wind and the waves obey him?" (4:41); and "Why do you call me good? No one is good—except God alone" (10:18). Jesus' divinity emerges forcefully, but still implicitly, in Jesus' mighty works: Jesus assumes the role of God himself as he is described in Isaiah's vision of Israel's return to Zion, conquering the enemies of his people, restoring sight to the blind, hearing to the deaf, and strength to the lame (Isa. 35:5–10; 40:10; 42:13–17; 49:24–26; 51:9–11; 52:10).

Second, for John, Jesus' revelation of his unity with God is the primary theme of Jesus' proclamation and therefore the primary theme of the gospel. In Mark, however, the theme of Jesus' unique relationship with God is a step, albeit a critical step, in a larger narrative argument about the nature of Jesus' death. Jesus, acting in the name of God, extended salvation to the outcast and forgiveness to sinners in a way that violated common messianic expectations (Mark 2:5–6, 16–17; 7:24–30; cf. *Pss. Sol.* 17:21–27). He could come in mercy rather than in wrath because he would die, as God's Son, *anti pollōn* ("in the place of many," Mark 10:45).

Like John and Mark, Matthew wants to say to his readers that Jesus both fulfilled Jewish expectations and went beyond them. His focus lies less on Jesus' unique relationship with God, however, and more on the wide variety of ways in which Jesus both met and exceeded biblical expectations. Matthew certainly affirms Jesus' divine sonship in terms that go far beyond traditional expectations for the messianic Son of David—Jesus was conceived through the Holy Spirit's power (Matt. 1:18, 20) and fulfilled Isaiah's expectation that one would come named "'Immanuel,' which means, 'God with us'" (Matt. 1:23; cf. 18:20; 20:28).[1] Matthew is chiefly interested, however, in showing how the course of Jesus' life meshed with the messianic expectations mapped out in Scripture and how the substance of Jesus' teaching brought the tendencies latent within the Mosaic law to maturity.

Matthew's fulfillment quotations often show that even seemingly unimportant details of Jesus' biography, such as his birth in Bethlehem (Matt. 2:3–6), his move with his family from Egypt to Israel (2:14–15), his family's decision to live in Nazareth (2:23), and his own decision to live in Capernaum (4:13–16), were prophesied by correspondingly obscure passages in Scripture. Matthew's point is that no one could produce even the smallest piece of evidence that Jesus had not met the qualifications for Israel's future deliverer. He met these qualifications perfectly, in every detail.

On a larger scale, Jesus' teaching, far from abolishing "the Law and the Prophets," brought the central tendencies latent in them to eschatological fulfillment (5:17–20). Jesus was himself the embodiment of Wisdom and therefore, in a Jewish context, the embodiment of God's law (11:1–30; cf. Bar. 3:32; Wisd. 9:9; Sir. 24:19–22). In addition, Jesus was like Moses: the circumstances of his birth and infancy (Matt. 1:18–21; cf. Ex. 1:15–16; 4:19–20), the significance of "the mountain" for his teaching (Matt. 5:1, 17; 4:2; 14:23; 15:29; 20:2; cf. e.g., Deut. 9:9), and Jesus' close relationship with God, visible in the shining of his face, are reminiscent of Israel's great teacher (Matt. 17:2; Ex. 34:29). Jesus was the Davidic Messiah of biblical expectation (Matt. 1:1, 6, 16–18, 20; 2:2, 5–6; 11:2–6; 9:27–31; 12:23; 15:23; 21:9, 15; cf., e.g., Jer. 23:5–6a). Jesus also filled the role of Isaiah's Servant. Like the Servant, he was more than an individual because he took the suffering of all Israel for its sins on himself, although he was personally innocent (Matt. 3:15; 8:17; 12:18–21; 17:5; cf. Isa. 42:1–4; 53:4, 11).

Just as Mark and John showed how Jesus broke through traditional expectations on the specific issue of his divine sonship, Matthew shows how Jesus broke the accepted boundaries in a number of ways. Jesus was not merely like Moses but greater

1 Cf. Marinus de Jonge, *Christology in Context: The Earliest Christian Response to Jesus* (Philadelphia: Westminster, 1988), 93–94; Hans Hübner, *Biblische Theologie des Neuen Testaments*, 3 vols. (Göttingen: Vandenhoeck & Ruprecht, 1990–95), 3:101; and Peter Stuhlmacher, *Biblische Theologie des Neuen Testaments*, 2 vols. (Göttingen: Vandenhoeck & Ruprecht, 1992–99), 2:161.

than Moses (Matt. 1:18–25; 17:4–5). Jesus did not simply explain the Mosaic law but brought it to its divinely appointed end and replaced it with his own law (5:1–7:29; 28:20). Jesus was not simply a sage who taught wisdom but was Wisdom incarnate (11:28–30). Jesus did not simply take on himself the sins of Israel but was in some more mysterious way the embodiment of God's people (2:14–23; 4:1–11; cf. Hos. 11:1; Deut. 6:13, 16; 8:2–3). On all these points, Matthew held that Jesus was a patch of unshrunk cloth only appropriate for a new garment (Matt. 9:16) and a draft of new wine that only new wineskins could contain (9:17).

For Matthew, as for Mark, the point about Jesus' continuity and discontinuity with traditional expectations is part of a larger argument. In Matthew's gospel, however, this argument takes the form of a prophetic word to the Jewish people about the gravity of the situation in which they have placed themselves through their rejection of God's anointed Son. Their position is similar to that of Israel under the prophet Jeremiah. As in Isaiah's and Jeremiah's time, so in their own day, the failure to listen to God's messenger had brought God's wrath (Matt. 8:5–13; 12:43–45; 21:33–22:14; cf. Isa. 5:1–7; Jer. 26:14–15).

Luke's Unique Perspective: Jesus as the Axis on Which Salvation History Turns

Luke's two-volume work stands apart from the other three gospels in the way he articulates Jesus' significance. Luke's primary concern was not, like that of Mark, John, and Matthew, to show how Jesus' person, teachings, and actions both fulfilled and went beyond traditional Jewish expectations. It was instead to show that if God's purpose in history was correctly distilled from the pages of the law, the prophets, and the writings, then Jesus is the axis around which this purpose revolves.

This does not mean that Luke disagrees with the exalted Christology John and Mark developed, nor does it mean that Luke fails to note the discontinuity between Jesus and Jewish tradition. Luke wants his readers to know that Jesus' conception through the Holy Spirit set him apart from John the Baptist and all others as God's unique Son (Luke 1:35).[2] In addition, the easy way in which Luke slides from speaking of Jesus as Lord to speaking of the God of Israel's Scriptures as Lord shows that Luke assumes a unity between the two (e.g. 2:11, 15).[3] Moreover, Luke's picture of Jesus' teaching in the gospel and the approach of Jesus' followers in Acts to the Mosaic law show that Luke recognizes discontinuity between Jesus and the tradition on this point.[4]

Nevertheless, Luke is not interested in developing the ontological significance of Jesus' relationship with God, nor is he interested in showing Jesus' superiority to traditional Jewish institutions.[5] Instead, he wants his readers to take away from his two

2 Cf. Joseph A. Fitzmyer, *The Gospel according to Luke I–IX* (AB 28; New York: Doubleday, 1981), 207–8.

3 Ibid., 203.

4 This statement is controversial. An argument for this perspective appears in Frank Thielman, *The Law and the New Testament: The Question of Continuity* (Crossroad Companions to the New Testament; New York: Crossroad, 1999), 135–67.

5 Cf. Ben Witherington, III, *The Many Faces of the Christ: The Christologies of the New Testament and Beyond* (Companions to the New Testament; New York: Crossroad, 1998), 158, 165. Hans

volumes, more than anything else, the conviction that Jesus is the point at which the two great lines of Israel's history converge. Israel's rebellion and God's saving purpose meet in Jesus. He is the royal Messiah who will "reign over the house of Jacob forever" (Luke 1:31–33, 69–70; 2:30; Acts 13:23; cf. 2 Sam. 7:11b–16; Isa 9:7). He is the Servant of God whom Isaiah said would be "numbered among the transgressors" and suffer "as a sheep led to the slaughter" (Luke 22:37; Acts 8:32–33; cf. Isa. 53:7–8, 12). He is the eschatological Prophet-like-Moses, about whom Moses himself spoke. He will open a new phase of salvation history with his own "exodus" brought to "fulfillment at Jerusalem" (Luke 9:31; cf. Deut. 18:15–19). This "exodus" includes Jesus' death, resurrection, ascension, and exaltation to God's right hand. It inaugurates the time of restoration that Isaiah predicted, a time when both Israel and "all flesh" would "see the salvation of God" (Isa. 40:1–5; Luke 2:31–32; 3:4–6; Acts 13:23).

Luke is therefore not as interested as the three other gospel authors in the way the titles he ascribes to Jesus speak of his nature or being. He is more interested in what these titles communicate about Jesus' crucial role in salvation history.

Summary

All four gospel authors intend to answer the question "Who is Jesus?" in their compositions, and all of them explain that question in the language of Israel's Scriptures. All of them place Jesus at the climax of Israel's biblical traditions. In the view of each author, Jesus has fulfilled every Jewish expectation legitimately held on the basis of Scripture.

Three of the four evangelists—Mark, John, and Matthew—place special stress on the inability of these traditions to fully explain the significance of Jesus. Jesus is not merely the Son of God in the sense that he is Israel's anointed king; he is God incarnate. Jesus is not merely the expected Prophet-like-Moses; he is greater than Moses and offers his own teaching as the fulfillment of the Mosaic law. The eschatological wine that he brings is new wine, and it cannot be contained in old wineskins.

Luke's primary interest lies in showing that Jesus stands at the center of God's ongoing plan of salvation. The teaching of the law and the prophets looked forward to the day of Israel's restoration, when the ultimate deliverer would come and through his work salvation would be proclaimed not only to Israel but to all nations. Luke identifies Jesus as that deliverer.

WHAT CAN ACCOUNT FOR JESUS' REJECTION?

Why would Israel reject one who so clearly fulfilled and exceeded the expectations expressed in its Scriptures for a coming deliverer? The gospel authors know that this

---

Conzelmann's brief discussion of Luke's "christological titles" in *The Theology of St. Luke* (Philadelphia: Fortress, 1961; orig. ed. 1953), 171, is correct to the extent that it emphasizes Luke's indebtedness to the tradition before him but incorrect in its claim that "we should not read any cosmological reference into the title κύριος."

puzzle cries out for a solution. All four authors agree that God's providential design is part of the solution. Scripture prophesied the rejection of the Son of Man and the suffering of God's Servant. Scripture also prophesied that Jesus' generation, like the generation of Isaiah, would reject his message as part of God's judgment on them. According to Mark, Matthew, Luke, and John, these divinely inspired prophecies had to be fulfilled.

All four gospel authors also hold those who rejected Jesus responsible for their actions. Those who failed to acknowledge him did so because they possessed and cultivated an attitude of fundamental opposition to God. The Synoptic Gospels point out that this fundamental opposition to God's deliverers had characterized Israel's relations with its God for many generations: Israel's history had too often been a story of the rejection of God's saving efforts on its behalf. John goes his own way on this point. He drops the historical argument entirely and sharpens his characterization of the inner attitude of Jesus' opponents.

The Rejection of Jesus as the Fulfillment of Prophecy

The four gospel authors all see Jesus' rejection and death as necessary events: God intended them and outlined them in advance in Israel's Scriptures. This approach to Jesus' rejection appears most prominently in the way they treat Jesus' roles as Son of Man and Suffering Servant and in the way they explain Israel's rejection of its deliverer.

Jesus Fills the Role of Daniel's Son of Man

Matthew and Luke follow Mark in placing Jesus in the role of the Son of Man described in Daniel 7:13. Like Mark, the other two Synoptic Gospels refer to Jesus in his role as Son of Man coming on the clouds of heaven, a reference that clearly echoes Daniel 7:13 (Matt. 24:30; 26:64; Luke 21:27; cf. Mark 13:26; 14:62). It is probable, therefore, that, like Mark, both Matthew and Luke also understand Jesus' death and resurrection as a fulfillment of other elements in this passage. The Son of Man, since he is "the saints of the Most High" in the vision's interpretation (Dan. 7:16b–27), suffers the oppression that the saints suffered and, like them, experiences exaltation. As we see in Mark's use of the title "Son of Man" for Jesus, Mark understands Jesus' ministry, passion, resurrection, and second coming to follow this same pattern and to be its fulfillment. The other two Synoptic Gospels follow Mark on this point (Matt. 17:22; 20:18; Luke 9:22, 44; 18:31; cf. Mark 8:31; 9:31; 10:33).

In addition, Luke may have understood Jesus' role as the suffering and vindicated Son of Man to be the fulfillment of the predetermined plan of God in a broader sense. Thus, whereas Mark and Matthew speak of Jesus' reference to his betrayal and death at the Last Supper as "the Son of Man" going "just as it is written about him," Luke refers to "the Son of Man" going "as it has been determined [*kata to hōrismenon*]" (Luke 22:22), and Luke can refer to the accomplishment of "everything written by the prophets about the Son of Man" (Luke 18:31).[6]

6 Daniel was not considered at this time to be among the prophetic books.

As with the other gospel authors, John connects the phrase "Son of Man" closely with Jesus' death (John 3:14; 6:27, 53, 62; 8:28; 12:23, 34; 13:31). John shows no interest, however, in connecting the phrase specifically to Daniel 7:13 with its mention of "the clouds of heaven."[7] The only hint of a biblical background for the phrase in John comes in John 3:14 (cf. 8:28; 12:34), where Jesus tells Nicodemus that the Son of Man must be lifted up just as Moses lifted up the serpent in the desert and so removed God's curse on Israel for their sin. There is no reference to the Son of Man in the biblical passage to which this refers (Num. 21:4–9), and John seems to see the healing effect of the uplifted serpent more as an analogy to Jesus' atoning death than as a prophecy of it. Unlike the Synoptic Gospels, therefore, John does not develop the notion of Jesus as the rejected and vindicated Son of Man of Daniel 7.

In summary, Mark, Matthew, and Luke believed that many in Israel rejected Jesus because he filled the role of the Son of Man who, according to Scripture, must suffer. Although Luke is less interested than Mark and Matthew in correlating Jesus' rejection as the Son of Man specifically with Daniel 7:13, he certainly joins the other two in seeing this text as the primary background for Jesus' Son of Man sayings. Like the other three, John speaks of Jesus' death as the death of the Son of Man, but, unlike them, he has not explored the way in which this role fulfills prophecy and therefore helps to explain the rejection of Jesus.

Jesus Fills the Role of Isaiah's Suffering Servant

All four gospel authors, including John, believe that Jesus' rejection and death fulfilled the prophecy in Isaiah of a coming Servant who would suffer for God's people. The theme is clearest in Luke but is present in allusive form in both Mark and Matthew, and to some extent in John.

Luke alone records Jesus' specific identification of himself with the vicarious suffering of Isaiah's Servant in the fourth Servant Song: "It is written, 'And he was numbered among the transgressors'; and I tell you that this must be fulfilled in me. Yes, what is written about me is reaching fulfillment" (Luke 22:36–37; Isa. 53:12). Only Luke explains Isaiah's description of the Servant's silence before his accusers and of the injustice with which he was treated as a reference to "the good news about Jesus" (Acts 8:32–35; Isa. 53:7–8). As we saw in chapter 5, this identification of Jesus with Isaiah's Suffering Servant, coupled with an identification of the Suffering Servant and the Messiah (Isa. 61:1; cf. Luke 4:18, 21), probably explains Luke's otherwise puzzling idea that the Messiah must suffer (Luke 24:26, 46; Acts 3:18; 17:3; 26:23). This suffering had to happen, says Luke, because of "all that the prophets have spoken" (Luke 24:26; cf. 24:46).

The identification of the Messiah Jesus with Isaiah's Servant also seems to lie behind Luke's frequent references in Acts to the predetermined nature of Jesus' condemnation at the hands of Israel's leaders and some of its people. Peter tells the crowd

7 In 1:51 angels ascend and descend on the Son of Man, and this is possibly a vague reference to the ascent of the Son of Man to the Ancient of Days on the clouds of heaven, but, if so, the allusion is buried very deeply.

gathered in Solomon's Portico that although they had, in their ignorance, disowned and killed the Holy and Righteous One and the author of life, "this is how God fulfilled what he had foretold through all the prophets, saying that his Christ would suffer" (Acts 3:14–18; cf. Isa. 53:11, LXX). Similarly, when the believing community summarizes in prayer the events surrounding Jesus' death, they mix language appropriate to the Suffering Servant and the royal Messiah in the context of God's predetermination of Jesus' death. The Gentile and Jewish leaders did what God "had decided beforehand should happen" when they conspired against his "holy servant [*paida*] Jesus" whom God had "anointed [*echrisas*]" (Acts 4:27; cf. Isa. 42:1; 61:1, LXX).

In light of these clear connections between the Messiah and Isaiah's Suffering Servant, it seems reasonable to think that Luke had Isaiah's Servant primarily in mind when, through Paul's speeches, he spoke of Jesus' condemnation (13:27) or of the Messiah's suffering (26:22–23, 27) as the fulfillment of what the prophets and Moses "said would happen."

As we saw in chapters 3 and 4, both Mark and Matthew interpret Jesus' suffering and death through the lens of the Suffering Servant. Mark brings out the many correspondences between the death of Jesus and the descriptions of the Servant's suffering in the third and fourth Servant Songs. These correspondences occur not only on the surface level of the events that took place—the beating, mocking, spitting, and insults, all received with silence (Mark 14:61, 65; 15:5, 27–32; cf. Isa. 50:6; 53:7)—but at the deeper level of the structure of atonement. A blameless victim identifies with his wicked people and gives up his life on their behalf (Mark 10:45; 14:24; cf. Isa 52:13–53:12). Matthew follows Mark meticulously here. He omits no aspect of Jesus' trial that corresponds with the Servant's suffering (Matt. 26:63, 67–68; 27:12, 38–43) and the atoning nature of his death (20:28; 26:28) and brings out even more clearly than Mark that Jesus' death, like that of the Servant, was "for the forgiveness of sins" (Matt. 26:28). For both Mark and Matthew, Jesus had to be rejected because he fulfilled Isaiah's expectation of a Servant who, although innocent, would suffer for the transgressions of his people.

John too considered Jesus' fulfillment of the Servant's role to be theologically important, although he does not develop the theme as extensively as the other evangelists. He says clearly that Jesus' passion was necessary because Isaiah's prophecy of the Servant's suffering described it in advance:

> Even after Jesus had done all these miraculous signs in their presence, they still would not believe in him. This was to fulfill the word of Isaiah the prophet: "Lord, who has believed our message and to whom has the arm of the Lord been revealed?" (John 12:37–38; Isa. 53:1, LXX)

John embraces the notion that Jesus is the Servant so openly here that we should probably also see the Servant behind his distinctive description of Jesus' death and ascension as his being "lifted up" (*hypsoō*, John 3:14; 8:28; 12:32) and "glorified" (*doxazō*, 7:39; 12:16; 12:23; 13:31; 17:1, 5, 24). With these expressions, John may intend for his readers to hear an echo of Isa. 52:13 (LXX),[8] where the Lord says, "My Servant shall understand and be exalted [*hypsōthēsetai*] and glorified [*doxasthēsetai*] greatly."

As with the other gospels, therefore, in John, Jesus' rejection was a necessary fulfillment of God's will as it was described long before in Isaiah's description of the Servant of the Lord. Jesus was rejected because Isaiah had said that the Servant of the Lord must be rejected, and Jesus was the Servant of the Lord.

Jesus' Rejection Fulfills the Prophecy of Isaiah's Rejection

Although all four evangelists use the call of Isaiah to explain the rejection of Jesus among his people, only John and Matthew emphasize that Jesus' rejection was the fulfillment of a prophecy contained in Isaiah's call. Isaiah received the difficult task of acting as the tool through which God, in judgment, would close the ears of his people to his message of warning:

> Go and tell this people:
> "Be ever hearing, but never understanding;
> be ever seeing, but never perceiving."
> Make the heart of this people calloused;
> make their ears dull
> and close their eyes.
> Otherwise they might see with their eyes,
> hear with their ears,
> understand with their hearts,
> and turn and be healed. (Isa. 6:9–10)

John and Matthew, the two evangelists in closest polemical contact with unbelieving Judaism, described Jesus' rejection as a specific fulfillment of this prophecy.

John explicitly states that the rejection of Jesus among his own people fulfilled this prophecy. He couples Isaiah 6:10 with Isaiah 53:1 and says that these prophecies of Isaiah's rejection and the Servant's rejection found their necessary fulfillment in Jesus' rejection. Those who rejected Jesus, therefore, "could not believe"; if they had believed, these specific Scriptures would have gone unfulfilled (John 12:39).

Matthew's reference to Isaiah 6:9–10 expands the reference to this text in Mark's gospel. In Mark, Jesus uses words that echo Isaiah's call to explain why he teaches in parables: He uses difficult terms so that those on the outside might see but not perceive and hear but not understand lest they be forgiven (Mark 4:10–12). There is no specific reference to Isaiah and no overt indication that Jesus is quoting Scripture at all.[9] In Matthew, however, after Jesus alludes to Isaiah's call, Jesus expands his comments to say that the words of Isaiah's call narrative are "fulfilled" in those who have

---

8 Raymond E. Brown, *The Gospel according to John I–XII* (AB 29; New York: Doubleday, 1966), 146, 478.

9 *Pace* frequent reference in the commentaries to Mark's "citation" or "quotation" of Isa. 6:9–10. See, e.g., William Lane, *The Gospel according to Mark* (NICNT; Grand Rapids: Eerdmans, 1974), 159; R. T. France, *The Gospel of Mark* (NIGTC; Grand Rapids: Eerdmans, 2002), 199. Vincent Taylor, *The Gospel according to Mark* (New York: Macmillan,1952), 256, says, more precisely, that "the saying is based on Isa. vi. 9 f. . . ."

rejected his teaching (Matt. 13:14a).[10] He follows this statement with a full and virtually exact quotation of Isaiah 6:9b–10 (LXX) (Matt. 13:14b–15).[11]

As we will see below, Mark and Luke use Isaiah 6:9–10 to say that in their rejection of Jesus, Israel has acted like its forbears who also rejected the ministry of Isaiah. John and Matthew, however, sharpen this role beyond what we find in Mark and Luke. For John and Matthew, Jesus was rejected as a specific fulfillment of the terms of Isaiah's call to preach to a people whom God intended to judge through hardening them against himself.

Summary

All four evangelists agree that God's design lay behind the rejection of Jesus among his own people. All four also agree that the Scriptures had recorded this startling development in advance. It was there in the Scriptures for all to see: The Son of Man in Daniel and the Servant of the Lord in Isaiah would be rejected by the people whom they represented. Jesus filled both roles and so answered these prophetic expectations. For John and Matthew, his rejection also fulfilled a prophecy embedded in the narrative of Isaiah's call. That Scripture could only be fully explained by reference to Jesus' role as a prophet who, in judgment on God's people, spoke to them in parables that they would not understand.

The Culpability of God's People

The notion that in rejecting Jesus, Israel was simply following the predetermined plan of God revealed centuries before in his Scriptures might seem to remove from Israel all responsibility for rejecting its deliverer. The problem appears with greatest clarity in John's gospel. In summarizing the Jews' rejection of Jesus' words and deeds, John says that this rejection happened "to fulfill" the prophecy of Isaiah 53:1 that God's people would neither believe his "message" nor acknowledge the revelation of his mighty "arm" (John 12:38). Then, as if to drive the point home, John says, "For this reason they could not believe" (12:39a). The reader may be tempted to respond with Paul's imaginary Jewish debating partner in Romans 9:19, "Then why does God still blame us? For who resists his will?"

The gospel authors do not formulate a philosophical answer to this question, anymore than does Paul. They simply affirm, alongside their conviction that those who rejected Jesus "could not believe," that they were nevertheless culpable for their own disbelief.

Corrupt Hearts in Mark's Gospel

Early in Mark's gospel, the scribes think that Jesus' forgiveness of the paralytic's sins is blasphemy, the penalty for which is death (Mark 2:7). A few paragraphs later,

10 In 13:13, Matthew paraphrases Mark 4:12 to stress human responsibility rather than, as in Mark, divine sovereignty. In place of Mark's "so that they may be ever seeing but never perceiving" Matthew has, "because seeing they do not see and hearing they do not hear." That Matthew did not find the two notions incompatible, however, is clear from his belief, articulated in 13:14–15, that Jesus' rejection was laid out long before in Isaiah's prophecy.

11 *Pace* W. D. Davies and Dale C. Allison, *The Gospel according to Saint Matthew*, 3 vols. (ICC; Edinburgh: T. & T. Clark, 1988–91), 2:393–94, who consider this quotation "a (very early) post-Matthean interpolation."

in response to his healing of a man's crippled hand on the Sabbath, they begin to plot his death (3:6). Soon they are attributing his power over demons to a supposed alliance between Jesus and the prince of demons (3:22). At various points, offended by his untraditional approach to the Jewish law and temple, they begin hostile debates with him over legal questions (7:5; 8:11; 10:2; 11:28; 12:13, 18; cf. 3:2), debates that climax at his trial and result in his formal condemnation (14:61–65).

Israel's leaders and many of its people respond this way to Jesus because their hearts are "hard" toward God (Mark 3:5). They are so bound to tradition that they fail to recognize the voice of God through his messenger Jesus when he insists that traditions must be changed (7:8, 9, 13). From Mark's perspective, this behavior is only what those familiar with the Scripture's account of previous generations of Israelites could expect. Both in the time of Moses (10:5) and in the time of Isaiah, Israelites were hard-hearted and rejected God's will (4:11–12; 7:6–8; cf. Isa. 6:9–10; 29:13). The only difference, according to the parable of the vineyard (Mark 12:1–12), is that now they have rejected not merely another prophet, but God's final messenger. They have rejected his beloved Son, whom he sent last of all in the hope that they would respect him (12:6).

Matthew's Intensification of the Theme

Matthew took this theme over from Mark and Q (if he used that hypothetical source) and intensified it, both emphasizing themes he found in those sources and adding other material on the same topic. Throughout Matthew's gospel, Jesus criticizes the Jewish leaders for the corruption of their hearts. This corruption, he maintains, is often hidden beneath a thin veneer of piety. They give alms, they pray, they fast, they keep the Mosaic law scrupulously, they are devoted to the temple, they speak pious words, they make proselytes, and they care for their ancestor's tombs (Matt. 6:2, 5, 16; 12:1–14; 15:3–8; 23:5, 15, 23, 25, 29). These outwardly commendable actions, however, are designed to win applause, to fill their private coffers, and to skirt their obligations (6:2, 5, 16; 15:5–6; 23:5–7, 16–22, 25). Their hearts are far from God (15:8b–9a; cf. 9:4). They are like dirty cups and bone-filled tombs (23:26–27). They might look clean outside, but inside they are corrupt and, like bad trees, they will produce bad fruit (12:33–35; cf. 15:18). This fruit appears most clearly in their rejection of Jesus (12:22–35).

Like Mark before him, but once again bolstering Mark's material with material from Q and other resources, Matthew communicated his conviction that Israel's rejection of Jesus was analogous to its rejection of its prophets in the past. The parable of the vineyard appears in Matthew 21:33–46, just as it had in Mark, with its message of Israel's rejection of a long line of God's messengers, the last of which was his Son. Matthew joins Mark in speaking both of Moses' generation and of Jesus' generation as "hard-hearted" (19:8).

In addition to these absorbed and slightly expanded references to the motif in Mark, however, Matthew expands a reference in Q to Israel's rejection and murder of the prophets with the ominous statement, "Fill up, then, the measure of the sin of your forefathers!" (Matt. 23:32; cf. 23:37; Luke 13:34). Jesus' death is only the last and worst killing of an Israelite prophet.

Matthew also contains an allusion to this motif that is unique to his gospel. In 27:25, when the crowds at Jesus' trial before Pilate say, "His blood is on us and on our children!" Matthew, as we saw in chapter 4, probably understood these words as an ironic echo of the account recorded in Jeremiah 26:1–24. There Jeremiah warned a rebellious crowd, unhappy with his prophetic message, that if they put him to death, they would "bring the guilt of innocent blood" on themselves and on Jerusalem (26:15). Matthew understands Israel's rejection of Jesus in the light of Israel's rejection both of Jeremiah and of other messengers whom God had sent to Israel.

Two Developments in Luke–Acts

Luke's understanding of the culpability of those who rejected Jesus is similar to that of Mark and Matthew, but it takes an independent path in two ways. First, Luke certainly joins Mark and Matthew in their indictment of the inner condition of those who rejected Jesus (e.g., Luke 11:37–54). At the same time, Luke recognizes in a way unique among the gospel authors that Israel's ignorance played a role in Jesus' rejection and death. In Peter's speech to the crowd that assembled after the healing of the lame man, for example, Peter holds the crowd responsible for disowning "the Holy and Righteous One" and killing "the author of life," but he also tells them that he knows they and their leaders "acted in ignorance" (Acts 3:14, 15, 17).

Jesus seems to recognize this element in his rejection when he compassionately asks his Father from the cross to forgive those who crucified him, "for they do not know what they are doing" (Luke 23:34). Paul, in his synagogue sermon at Pisidian Antioch, speaks similarly of the failure of both the people of Jerusalem and their rulers to "recognize Jesus" when they condemned him (Acts 13:27).[12] None of this excuses the actions of those who rejected Jesus, but it shows how helpless they were, in their sinfulness, to do anything but what they had done.

Second, for Luke the historical continuity between Israel's rejection of Jesus and its rejection of God's deliverers becomes, particularly in Acts, a major theme. Luke preserves in his gospel Mark's allusion to Isaiah 6:9–10 (Luke 8:10) with its implication that the Israel of Isaiah's time was as hard-hearted to the will of God as the Israel of Jesus' time is. Like Matthew, he preserves the references in Q to Israel's past abysmal record with God's prophets (Luke 11:47–48; 13:34–35; cf. Matt. 23:29–32, 37).

In his second volume, however, Luke develops this theme beyond what we find in the other gospels. He devotes the lengthy speech of Stephen to an historical review of Israel's rejection of those whom God sent to deliver his people from various desperate circumstances. The patriarchs were jealous of Joseph, whom they sold into slavery in Egypt but who nevertheless delivered Jacob and his family from famine (Acts 7:9–16). Moses, sent by God to rescue his people from slavery in Egypt, "thought that his own people would realize that God was using him to rescue them, but they did not" (Acts 7:25; cf. 7:27, 35). Not only did they push him aside when

12 C. K. Barrett, *The Acts of the Apostles*, 2 vols. (ICC; Edinburgh: T. & T. Clark, 1994–98), 1:201.

he tried to help them before the Exodus (7:27, 35), but after the Exodus, during the journey to Canaan they "refused to obey him," "rejected him," and "in their hearts turned back to Egypt" (7:39). The speech ends with a ringing indictment of Israel for its most recent, and most serious, rejection of a deliverer from God:

> You stiff-necked people, with uncircumcised hearts and ears! You are just like your fathers: You always resist the Holy Spirit! Was there ever a prophet your fathers did not persecute? They even killed those who predicted the coming of the Righteous One. And now you have betrayed and murdered him. (Acts 7:51–52)

At the end of Acts, Luke returns to Isaiah 6:9–10 in Paul's closing speech. When some of the Jews in Rome found his message unconvincing, Paul responded with these words:

> The Holy Spirit spoke the truth to your forefathers when he said through Isaiah the prophet:
>
> "Go to this people and say,
> 'You will be ever hearing but never understanding;
> you will be ever seeing but never perceiving.'
> For this people's heart has become calloused;
> they hardly hear with their ears,
> and they have closed their eyes.
> Otherwise they might see with their eyes,
> hear with their ears,
> understand with their hearts
> and turn, and I would heal them." (Acts 28:25–27)

Luke's point here is certainly consistent with what we find in John 12:39 or Matthew 13:14–15, but it is also different. The rejection of the gospel among many Jews is not simply the fulfillment of prophecy but the result of an attitude that is similar to the attitude of God's people often in its history and particularly in Isaiah's time. Israel had often rejected God's deliverers, such as Isaiah, and it is acting in a way that is consistent with this pattern when it rejects Jesus also.

As we saw in chapter 5, this does not mean that Israel's rejection of Jesus is final, but it does mean that it is not unexpected. The previous history of God's people, as it is recorded in the Jewish Scriptures, helps to explain why Israel rejected its Messiah and God's Son when he finally came in answer to God's promises.

A Dualistic Twist in John?

If Luke emphasizes the importance of historical analogy in Jesus' rejection more than Mark and Matthew, John does not emphasize this theme at all. Instead, John attributes the rejection of Jesus among the especially religious people of Judea ("the Jews")[13] to a wide range of surface causes, all of which have a single primary cause.

13 For this definition of the term "the Jews" in John's gospel, see Stephen Motyer, *Your Father the Devil? A New Approach to John and 'the Jews'* (Paternoster Biblical and Theological Monographs; Carlisle, U.K.: Paternoster, 1997), 54–56.

On the surface, "the Jews" reject Jesus for a variety of reasons. They find his tendency to testify to himself implausible (John 3:11, 32; 8:13). When he violates tradition, and particularly when he works on the Sabbath, they take offense (5:16; 9:16, 24). They view as blasphemy his claims to be one with God (5:18; 10:30–31, 38–39). His origins are too common (7:27; 9:29) or his correlation with biblical expectations too inexact (7:41–42) for him to qualify as the Messiah or a divine emissary. His popularity is too politically volatile for him to be tolerated (11:48, 50; cf. 19:12).

On the deepest level, however, all of these rejections arise from the nature of Jesus' enemies. The Jews who reject his testimony "do not have the love of God within" themselves (*en heautois*, John 5:42). Judas, who will betray Jesus, "is a devil" (6:70). The hostile Jews in the temple precincts will die in their sins and cannot follow Jesus to his Father because they are "from below" and "from this world" (8:23). Similarly, they show their unity with their murderous, deceitful father, the devil, by their own efforts to kill Jesus and spread lies about him (8:40–41, 44; cf. 5:17–18). They are blind but do not know it (9:41), and they do not listen to Jesus' voice because they do not belong to his sheep (10:26).[14] The accent here is different from what we find in the Synoptics. There, the hearts of Jesus' opponents are corrupt but statements that align them in some fundamental way with the devil are exceptional.

Does John add something more than a sharper tone to the collective voice of the other three gospels on the issue of Jesus' rejection? Has persecution driven him to the edge of the kind of dualism characteristic of Gnosticism?[15] Has a virulent "anti-Judaism" pushed him over the brink into a fully dualistic metaphysic where his own community is from above and its enemies are from below, indeed from the devil?[16]

Two considerations shed light on these questions. First, John did not invent this way of speaking. In Mark and Matthew, Jesus identifies the apostle Peter himself with "Satan" (Matt. 16:23; Mark 8:33). In Matthew, Jesus can also call inauthentic Christians "sons of the evil one" and his opponents among the Pharisees "sons of hell" (Matt. 13:38; 23:15).[17] John may have emphasized the dualistic language of the historical Jesus in his debates with his opponents, and he may have done this either to speak meaningfully to his own community in the midst of persecution or to use an idiom common in the religious world of his time or both, but he found this kind of language in the Christian tradition before him. Its roots lie in the speech of the historical Jesus and can find parallels in much Jewish literature from the second temple period.[18]

14 We should probably understand John's claims that Jesus' opponents do not know God (8:19, 55; 16:3) as grounded in the conviction that they have a nature inimical to God.

15 See, e.g., Wayne A. Meeks, "The Man from Heaven in Johannine Sectarianism," in *The Interpretation of John*, ed. John Ashton (IRT 9; London/Philadelphia: Fortress/SPCK, 1986), 141–73, here at 160–65, and C. K. Barrett, "John and Judaism" in *Anti-Judaism and the Fourth Gospel*, ed. Reimund Bieringer, Didier Pollefeyt, and Frederique Vandecasteele-Vanneuvilleb (Louisville: Westminster John Knox, 2001), 231–46, here at 235.

16 Werner H. Kelber, "Metaphysics and Marginality in John" in *What Is John? Readers and Readings of the Fourth Gospel*, ed. Fernando F. Segovia (SBLSymS 3; Atlanta: Scholars Press, 1996), 129–54.

17 Brown, *John I–XII*, 364.

18 See, among many examples, the references to the enemies of the Qumran community in the War Scroll as "the army of Belial" (1QM 1.1) or in the Temple Scroll as the "sons of Belial" (11Q19 55.3). Cf. 4Q286, frag. 7 2.6; 2 Cor. 6:15.

Second, John's understanding of the relationship between Jesus and his opponents is not dualistic in a metaphysical sense. If this were so, then the wall separating "believer" from unbeliever in John's gospel would be far firmer and more permanent than we found it to be above in chapter 6. "Disciples" of Jesus (John 6:66, 70) and "believers" (8:31) can turn against him, and a future day of judgment is necessary for John's theology precisely because perseverance is necessary. John is hopeful that even Jesus' most bitter opponents will eventually believe. In a speech delivered to "the Jews" who were trying to kill him (5:18–19), Jesus reminds his audience of John's witness to his identity and then comments, "I say these things that you may be saved" (5:33–34; cf. 1:7, 19–34).

To another hostile group of Jews, Jesus says that after they "have lifted up the Son of Man" they will "know that 'I am,' and that I do nothing on my own but speak just what the Father has taught me" (John 8:28, aut.). These are not hostile words meant to say that "the Jews" will be condemned by their own realization of what they have done but conciliatory words, extended in the hope that some believers might emerge even from the Jews who conspire to kill Jesus.[19] John makes the positive character of these words clear when he says that after hearing them, "many put their faith in him" (8:30).

In the same vein, Jesus hopes that the Jews who cannot tolerate his verbal claims to unity with his Father will at least believe in him on the basis of the signs that he does (John 10:38), and, if we take John's purpose statement seriously—that people might believe in Jesus on the basis of the signs that he does (20:31)—then we should understand Jesus' statement here as a sincere expression of hope that his opponents might believe.[20] As Caiaphas ironically but truly prophesies and as John believes, Jesus died for the Jewish people as well as for Gentiles so that they might become one people (11:51–52).

When we move from this widely neglected group of statements back to expressions that sound more dualistic than what we typically find in the Synoptic Gospels, it becomes apparent that something other than a metaphysical dualism is at issue. Jesus' opponents are not one with the devil in the same sense that Jesus is one with God, despite the truth that both Jesus and his opponents do the works of their respective fathers. Otherwise there could be no more possibility that Jesus' opponents would become his followers than there is that Jesus would transfer his loyalty to the devil. When Jesus speaks of Judas as a devil and of his opponents as children of the devil, he is making a moral point, not an ontological point. Judas and his opponents are acting like the devil when they lie about Jesus and seek to murder him (cf. 1 John 3:12, 15), but they are not fated by their nature to remain in the devil's grip.

In John's view it is not merely "the Jews" who are hostile to Jesus and whose hostility to his followers will continue, but the whole world (John 1:10; 7:7; 14:17; 15:18–19; 17:14, 25). "The Jews" participation in the world's hostility to Jesus accounts for their hostility to him (8:23). God nevertheless loves the world (3:16)

---

19 *Pace* C. K. Barrett, *The Gospel according to St. John*, 2nd ed. (Philadelphia: Westminster, 1978), 343–44.

20 Cf. Motyer, *Your Father the Devil?* 57–62, 215–16.

and sent Jesus to take away its sin (1:29), to reveal himself to the world (8:26; 9:5; 12:46), and to save the world (3:17; 4:42; 12:47). Jesus wants the world to believe in him (17:21, 23). Through faith in him, anyone in the world, whether Jew (5:33–34; 8:30; 10:38), Samaritan (4:42), or Greek (12:20–23), can become part of his people and have eternal life (12:32). John believes that Jesus died "for the [Jewish] nation, and not only for the nation but also for the scattered children of God, to bring them together and make them one" (11:51–52).

Summary

The rejection of one who seemed so clearly to fulfill the expectations in Israel's Scriptures for its deliverer cries out for an explanation in the thinking of each of the gospel authors. All four evangelists provided two basic explanations for this astonishing development. The Scriptures foretold Israel's rejection of Jesus, and therefore it was part of God's purposes. As the Son of Man and the Servant of the Lord it was necessary for Jesus to be rejected and to suffer. John and Matthew also understand Jesus' rejection as the fulfillment of a prophecy that they detect in Isaiah's call. According to this call, those to whom God's final prophet prophesied would reject him. The Son of Man must go as it has "been determined" (Luke 22:22).

At the same time, the gospel writers affirm that those who rejected Jesus were culpable for their wickedness. Their corrupt hearts gave rise to evil actions. They valued their own traditions more than the Word of God. They were greedy. They sought the approval of other people rather than God's approval. They therefore continued a lengthy history of the rejection of God's deliverers.

For all four evangelists, Jesus' rejection is attributable both to the plan of God and to the wickedness of those who rejected him. Why would God allow such wickedness to triumph, even temporarily, over his Son? Why must the Son of Man and the Servant of Yahweh "suffer many things and be rejected?" The four evangelists were also concerned with these questions.

WHAT IS THE MEANING OF JESUS' DEATH?

None of the gospels views the death of Jesus merely as a tragic miscarriage of justice or as somehow irrelevant to his mission. His death has immense theological significance for all four evangelists, and thus all four devote a large amount of space to the passion of Jesus. Of primary importance is the atoning nature of Jesus' death: Although innocent of sin himself, his death atoned for the sins of others. This understanding of Jesus' death dominates Mark and Matthew, and it is present, although less important, in John and Luke–Acts. For John and Luke, Jesus' death is primarily significant as the means by which he assumes his rightful place with God. John sees Jesus' death as the means of his exaltation—his return to the close fellowship that he had with the Father from all eternity because of his unity with him. Luke sees that death as the fulfillment of the pattern, described in Isaiah, of the suffering and vindicated Servant of the Lord who brings good news not only to Israel but to all the nations of the earth.

The Atoning Significance of Jesus' Death

Jesus' Death as Atonement in Mark and Matthew

Both Mark and Matthew emphasize the atoning significance of Jesus' death. The most prominent vehicle for communicating this concept in both authors is the description of the Suffering Servant in the fourth Servant Song (Isa. 52:13–53:12). The pattern of the Servant's suffering follows a familiar structure for atoning suffering in antiquity: One who is innocent (53:9) voluntarily (53:7b) takes on himself or herself the suffering that a guilty people deserves (53:4–6), and God accepts this person's death as a "guilt offering" for their sin (53:10–12).[21] Unlike the pattern as it is often expressed in ancient literature outside the Scriptures, however, in the biblical pattern God initiates the process of atonement and provides the sacrifice (53:10).[22]

Mark and Matthew identify Jesus' suffering with this pattern as it is expressed in Isaiah 52:13–53:12. As we have seen in chapters 3 and 4, both gospel authors describe the details of Jesus' passion—the beating, mocking, spitting, silence, and innocence—in a way that brings out the correspondence between Jesus and the Servant of the third and fourth Songs. Both also emphasize that the primary significance of Jesus' role as the Servant is found in the atoning nature of his death. He died as a ransom "for many" according to both Mark 10:45 and Matthew 20:28. In Mark's version of Jesus' words over the cup at the Last Supper, Jesus says that he "poured out" his blood "for many" (Mark 14:24). In Matthew the atoning nature of Jesus' death becomes even more explicit with the addition of the phrase "for the forgiveness of sins" (Matt. 26:28). In both Mark and Matthew, therefore, the significance of Jesus' death corresponds to that of the Servant who "poured out" his life and bore the sin of "many" (Isa. 53:12).

Mark and Matthew also bring out the atoning nature of Jesus' death by connecting it with the Day of Atonement ritual. According to the description of this ritual in Leviticus 16, only the high priest, and only on this occasion, went behind the curtain that stood in front of the tabernacle's most sacred place and sprinkled the blood of a slaughtered bull and goat on and before the "atonement cover" (*hilastērion*) that rested on top of the ark of the covenant (Lev. 16:6, 9, 11, 14–15). The high priest also, as part of the ritual, confessed the "lawlessness" and "unrighteousness" of all Israel (16:21). The purpose of the ritual was to atone for and cleanse the high priest, his family, and all Israel from their sins (16:6, 16a, 30).

21 On this pattern in Greco-Roman antiquity, see Martin Hengel, *The Atonement: The Origins of the Doctrine in the New Testament* (Philadelphia: Fortress, 1981), 1–32, and for Hengel's analysis of Isa. 52:13–53:12, which he considers unusual within the Old Testament but nevertheless critical for the formation of New Testament ideas of the atoning nature of Christ's death, see 57–60.

22 Cf. ibid., 31–32. To this difference, Hengel adds two others: (1) that in the ancient world an atoning death was typically for a particular crime among a particular people, but in Christian thinking Christ's atonement covered all the sins of the whole world, and (2) that the proclamation of Christ's atoning death took on particular urgency in light of the imminence of the day of judgment in early Christian thought.

Both Mark and Matthew tell their readers that at the moment Jesus expired, the curtain of the temple was torn in two (Matt. 27:51; Mark 15:38). It is difficult to know whether they are referring to the publicly visible curtain that separated the temple courtyard from the Holy Place (Ex. 26:36–37; Josephus, *B.J.* 5.212–214) or the more hidden curtain that divided the Holy Place from the Most Holy Place (Ex. 26:31–33; Josephus, *B. J.* 5.219).[23] Since the curtain was torn at the moment of Jesus' death and both Mark and Matthew have already shown Jesus' death to be a sacrifice, both evangelists probably understand his death to be analogous to the Day of Atonement sacrifice and so assume that their readers will understand the torn curtain to be the inner curtain. The tearing of the curtain from "top to bottom," an aspect of the event that both Mark and Matthew want their readers to notice, shows it could only have been the work of God.[24]

If this is a correct understanding of the significance of this portent in both Mark and Matthew, then both evangelists believe that God had declared through the rending of the inner Temple curtain that Jesus' death was the final atoning sacrifice, obviating the need for any future sacrificial ritual in the Most Holy Place.[25]

Jesus' Death as Atonement in Luke and John?

Do Luke and John also understand Jesus' death as an atoning sacrifice for sin? It is a commonplace in Lukan scholarship to say that Luke did not understand Jesus' death in this way. Interpreters frequently observe that Luke leaves out of his narrative Jesus' comment that the Son of Man came "to give his life as a ransom for many" (Matt. 20:28; Mark 10:45; cf. Luke 22:27), that he emphasizes the saving significance of Jesus' resurrection (Acts 2:33; 5:30–31), and that, unlike Matthew (Matt. 26:28), he never links Jesus' death explicitly with the forgiveness of sins.[26] Moreover, although Luke records the rending of the temple veil in a list of portents that occurred during the period of Jesus' suffering on the cross, the list occurs prior to, not after, Jesus expires (Luke 23:45).

It is also commonly observed that although Luke identifies Jesus with Isaiah's Servant, he stops short of using the famous fourth Servant Song to develop the idea that Jesus died "for" others.[27] In Luke 22:35–38, a passage that only appears in Luke's gospel, Jesus tells his disciples that Isaiah 53:12 must be fulfilled in the events of his passion: "And he was numbered with the transgressors" (22:37). Luke does not, however, continue the quotation into the next line—"for he bore the sin of many."

Something similar happens in Acts 8:32–33, where the Ethiopian eunuch reads Isaiah 53:7b–8a but stops just short of the crucial atonement text in v. 8b, "for the transgression of my people he was stricken." In the same way, Peter's speech in

23 See the discussion in France, *Mark*, 656.

24 Ibid., 657.

25 Hengel, *Atonement*, 42; Peter Stuhlmacher, *Reconciliation, Law and Righteousness: Essays in Biblical Theology* (Philadelphia: Fortress, 1986), 94–109, here at 99; idem, *Biblische Theologie*, 1:148.

26 See, e.g., Henry J. Cadbury, *The Making of Luke–Acts* (New York: Macmillan, 1927), 280; Conzelmann, *Theology of St. Luke*, 201; Joel B. Green, *The Theology of the Gospel of Luke* (New Testament Theology; Cambridge: Cambridge Univ. Press, 1995), 124–25; and David Ravens, *Luke and the Restoration of Israel* (JSNTSup 119; Sheffield: Sheffield Academic Press, 1995), 139–69.

27 See, e.g., Joseph A. Fitzmyer, *The Gospel according to Luke X–XXIV* (AB 28A; New York: Doubleday, 1985), 1432, and Darrell L. Bock, *Luke 9:51–24:53* (BECNT; Grand Rapids: Baker, 1996), 1747–48.

Solomon's Portico (Acts 3:12–26) calls Jesus God's "servant" twice (3:13, 26), stresses the innocence of Jesus' suffering (3:14; cf. Isa. 53:11), and says that Jesus' suffering fulfilled the prophets' words about the Messiah (3:18). The speech also calls on Peter's hearers to turn from their sins so that they may be wiped out (3:19). Nevertheless, the speech does not say, as Isaiah clearly says, that the Servant's innocent suffering provides the means by which the sins of the guilty are wiped out (Isa. 53:4–12).

Occasionally this evidence forms the basis of an argument that Luke was unsympathetic with early Christian ideas of the atonement. Scholars have advanced various reasons for this lack of sympathy. Perhaps Luke wanted to locate salvation in all of divinely ordered history, or in all of Jesus' unselfish life, not in one moment of tragic agony on the cross.[28] Perhaps as a way of assuring Jewish Christians that they were truly Jews he wanted to affirm Jewish concepts of atonement, and these had no place for a single vicarious death that covered all sins.[29]

These assessments, however, neglect Luke's account of the Last Supper.[30] There Jesus speaks, not once as in Mark and Matthew, but twice, of his death as "for" (*hyper*) others. He tells his disciples that he will give his body, like the broken bread, "for you" (Luke 22:19; cf. 1 Cor. 11:24), and pour out his blood, like the contents of the cup, "for you" (Luke 22:20).[31] This spilt blood, moreover, will establish a "new covenant" (Luke 22:20; cf. 1 Cor. 11:25) and since this is an unmistakable reference to the "new covenant" of Jeremiah 31:31–34, which God will make with his people for the forgiveness of their sins (31:34), it does not seem unlikely that Luke assumes a link between Jesus' death and the forgiveness of sins, even if, unlike Matthew, he does not express it explicitly.

Such a link explains several otherwise puzzling aspects of Luke's handling of Jesus' death both in his gospel and in Acts. First, in the gospel's crucifixion narrative, Luke unambiguously attributes saving significance to Jesus' death.[32] Jesus admits the crucified insurrectionist next to him into paradise "today," just as throughout the gospel God makes salvation available "today" because Jesus has come (Luke 23:43; cf. 2:11; 4:21; 19:9). Jesus forgives those responsible for his unjust execution (23:34). The centurion and the crowds at Jesus' crucifixion, moreover, show signs of repentance. In Luke–Acts repentance precedes forgiveness of sins and leads to life (3:3; 24:47; Acts 2:38; 3:19; 5:31; 8:22; 11:18). Without some mechanism such as a concept of the atonement, it is unclear how Jesus' death can save.

---

28 See Philipp Vielhauer, "On the 'Paulinism' of Acts," in *Studies in Luke–Acts*, ed. Leander E. Keck and J. Louis Martin (Philadelphia: Fortress, 1966), 33–50, here at 44–45, and G. B. Caird, *The Gospel of St. Luke* (Pelican Gospel Commentaries; New York: Seabury, 1963), 238.

29 Ravens, *Restoration of Israel*, 139–69, 251.

30 Vielhauer, "'Paulinism' of Acts" does not discuss it. Caird, *Luke*, 236, and Ravens, *Restoration of Israel*, 201–2, accept the improbable position that Codex Bezae and some manuscripts of the old Italian version properly omit Luke 20:19b–20 from Luke's text. Cf. Cadbury, *Making*, 280. Most commentators and editors of the New Testament text correctly believe that vv. 19b–20 should remain in the gospel not only because the passage rests on a more secure textual basis but also because it preserves the unusual order cup-bread-cup for the last supper and is therefore more likely to have given rise to other readings.

31 Cf. Hübner, *Biblische Theologie*, 3:141. Hübner believes that the reference shows that Luke wanted to emphasize the saving significance of Jesus' death but not to develop any specific theory about how Jesus' death could save.

32 Donald Senior, *The Passion of Jesus in the Gospel of Luke* (Passion Series 3; Wilmington, Del.: Michael Glazier, 1989), 135–38, 161–66.

Second, Luke's affirmation of the atoning significance of Jesus' death also explains two otherwise enigmatic expressions in Acts. In Acts 20:28, Paul tells the Ephesian elders that they should be "shepherds of the church of God, which he bought with his own blood" (Acts 20:28). It is difficult to know what this phrase means unless it refers to Jesus' death as an atoning sacrifice. Similarly, three times Luke mentions in Acts that Jesus died on a "tree" (5:30; 10:39; 13:23). The origin of this expression is probably the statement in Deuteronomy 21:22–23 that the one whose dead body is hung on a "tree" falls under the curse of God. At least from the time Paul wrote Galatians, this text was used to explain the atoning nature of Jesus' death; the curse that those who had not kept everything written in God's law deserved to receive had instead fallen on Jesus (Gal. 3:10–13).[33] Luke must assume that his readers will understand this otherwise curious description of the cross because they understand the atoning nature of Jesus' death—in his death Jesus accepted the curse that sinners deserved.

On the one hand, it is clear that Luke does not emphasize this aspect of Jesus' death. He has ample opportunity to explore its meaning in his many allusions to Isaiah's Suffering Servant, but he does not take advantage of them. On the other had, it is just as clear that Luke affirms the truth of this theological tradition and, as it came his way in the sources that he uses, wants to hand it down to his readers.

What about John? Here, too, a case has been made that John is uninterested in Jesus' death as an atonement for sin. Jesus' death is part of his "lifting up" to undisturbed fellowship with God, it is said, not the means by which God will forgive the sins of his people.[34]

This understanding of John's gospel, however, is unconvincing. The most probable meaning of the Baptist's description of Jesus as the "lamb [*amnos*] of God, who takes away the sin of the world" (John 1:29; cf. 1:36) is that Jesus is the Servant of God who suffered for the sins of others. The Servant is called both a "sheep" (*probaton*) and a "lamb" (*amnos*) in Isaiah 53:7, and although John certainly thinks of Jesus' death as the slaying of a Passover lamb (John 19:14, 29, 36; cf. Ex. 12:22, 46), the reference in John 1:29 to the removal of sin recalls most clearly the "lamb" who in Isaiah bears the sins of many and becomes a "guilt offering" for transgressors (Isa. 53:4, 10, 12).[35]

John can also speak of the atoning significance of Jesus' death by simply describing its substitutionary nature without imagery borrowed from Isaiah 52:13–53:12. Jesus speaks in 6:51, for example, of giving his "flesh ... for [*hyper*] the life of the world." As the references to his blood in the subsequent sentences show (6:52–56), he is referring here to his death. The statement is close to Jesus' words over the bread in the accounts of the Lord's Supper found in Luke 22:19 and 1 Cor. 11:24 ("This

33 I. Howard Marshall, *Luke: Historian and Theologian* (Contemporary Evangelical Perspectives; Grand Rapids: Zondervan, 1970), 173. Cf. Hengel, *Atonement*, 44.

34 See, e.g., Ernst Käsemann, *The Testament of Jesus: A Study of the Gospel of John in the Light of Chapter 17* (Philadelphia: Fortress, 1968), 17–21; cf. William Loader, *The Christology of the Fourth Gospel: Structure and Issues* (BBET 23; Frankfurt: Peter Lang, 1989), 101–2, who argues that although John acknowledges the tradition of Jesus' atoning death, it is not important to his understanding of the significance of Jesus' death.

35 Cf. Brown, *John I–XII*, 58–63.

is my body [given] for [*hyper*] you"), and just as a substitutionary significance probably lies behind the preposition *hyper* in that context, so here, Jesus means that he gives his life in the place of the life of the world.[36] When Jesus describes himself as the good shepherd who lays down his life "for" (*hyper*) the sheep (John 10:11, 15) or as the one who lays down his life "for" (*hyper*) his friends (15:13), he probably also has in mind the notion that, like a shepherd who endangers his or her own life in order to rescue an endangered sheep, Jesus dies in the place of those he loves so that they might be spared.[37]

This same understanding of Jesus' death probably lies behind Caiaphas's frustrated outburst in which he unwittingly explains the significance of Jesus' death: "You do not realize that it is better for you that one man die for [*hyper*] the people than that the whole nation perish" (John 11:50). As we saw above, John explains that although the high priest did not know it, he was prophesying that Jesus would die both "for" (*hyper*) the Jewish nation and "for" (*hyper*) other children of God who would eventually join them, creating one people of God (11:51–52). Here too Jesus' death substitutes for that of the nation: The nation will "die" if Jesus does not die, but his death will occur in its place and so the nation will be spared.[38]

Why is the nation in danger? Into what peril has God's flock strayed? The answer comes in a distinctively Johannine allusion to the reason for Jesus' death: It is necessary for him to be "lifted up" for a reason similar to that which required Moses to lift up the serpent in the wilderness (John 3:14–17). Moses lifted up the serpent as an antidote to the curse of God. God's people had grown impatient with the inconveniences of their desert wandering and had spoken against both God and Moses (Num. 21:4–5). In response, God sent poisonous snakes among them, and many died (21:6–7). But God also provided a means of removing the curse: Moses could "make a snake and put it up on a pole," and those who suffered snake bites could "look at it and live" (21:8–9). By describing Jesus' allusion to this story, John implies that God's people stand under a curse that the crucifixion of Jesus removes.

John wants to emphasize other aspects of Jesus' death, and so he does not dwell on its atoning character. The importance of the notion to him emerges, nevertheless, from a combination of considerations. His metaphor of the lamb who removes sin, with its echoes of the Suffering Servant, his frequent affirmation that Jesus died for others, and the connection that he draws between the cross and the uplifted serpent that removed God's curse all hint that John understands Jesus' death as an atoning death. In the face of gnostic challenges to the necessity for the atonement, John spells out his understanding of it in greater detail in 1 John (1 John 1:7; 2:2; 4:10; 5:6–8). Those convictions were already in place, however, when he composed the gospel.

To summarize, all four gospel authors affirm the atoning significance of Jesus' death, although they emphasize it to varying degrees. Mark and Matthew place the

---

36 Cf. Leon Morris, *The Gospel according to John* (NICNT; Grand Rapids: Eerdmans, 1971), 374 n. 116.

37 Carson, *John*, 386–87.

38 Ibid., 422.

greatest emphasis on its importance. Luke and John acknowledge its importance, but their primary interest lies elsewhere.

Jesus' Death as the Son's Exaltation in John's Gospel

John's primary interest in Jesus' death lies in its function as a means to the exaltation of Jesus. His emphasis lies on showing that Jesus' crucifixion cannot legitimately call into question Jesus' unity with God but is, instead, the means by which Jesus returned to share fully in the glory of his Father. To place the accent on this element of Jesus' crucifixion involves making both a negative and a positive point about that event.

On the negative side, John wants his readers to know that although Jesus suffered "the utterly vile death of the cross," as Origen called it, he is no less one with God for having done so.[39] This is why John emphasizes that no feature of Jesus' passion takes him by surprise, that he is in control at all times, and that he even plays a role in his own resurrection from the dead. Thus, his Jewish opponents may destroy the temple of his body, but Jesus will "raise it again in three days" (John 2:19; cf. 2:21–22). His return to the Father by means of his death can only come at the appointed "hour," an hour known only to Jesus (2:4; 7:30; 8:20; 12:23, 27; 13:1; 17:1). His death is not a tragedy initiated by others that he would have avoided if possible, but he lays down his own life at his own initiative (10:17). In the same way, he takes up his life again in accord with the authority that the Father has given him (10:18; cf. 19:11).

He takes charge of the situation at his arrest, asking his opponents whom they want. When they reply that they are looking for "Jesus of Nazareth," he identifies himself with the name of Yahweh, "I am" (*egō eimi*, John 18:4–5). Their response to this revelation is appropriate for those who find themselves unexpectedly in the presence of God—"they drew back and fell to the ground" (18:6; cf., e.g., Rev. 1:17). His betrayal (John 13:18; Ps. 41:9), the soldiers' casting lots for his garment (John 19:24; Ps. 22:18), their failure to break Jesus' legs (John 19:36; Ex. 12:46), and their stabbing him with a spear instead (John 19:37; Zech. 12:10) are all plotted beforehand in Scripture. Even the moment of Jesus' death happens as Scripture said that it would (19:28), and Jesus only dies when he voluntarily "bowed his head and gave up his spirit" (19:30).

The cross, therefore, is not a sign of Jesus' defeat. It is part of God's plan, a plan with which Jesus is in full agreement and over which, under the authority of his Father, he is in full control.

On the positive side, John understands Jesus' death to be the means by which he returns to his Father and resumes the close fellowship that he had with him prior to the time when he became flesh and dwelt among his people. Jesus "was with God in the beginning" (John 1:2; cf. 12:41), and although he was never without God's glory during the time when he walked among his own people (2:1; 8:54; 11:4, 40; 12:28),

39 Origen's phrase, from *Comm. Matt.* on 27:22, can be found in the incomparable study of Martin Hengel, *Crucifixion in the Ancient World and the Folly of the Message of the Cross* (Philadelphia: Fortress, 1977), xi.

he did not share God's glory in the same fullness with which he shared it prior to the time that he became flesh. Through his passion, resurrection, and ascension he returns to his Father (13:3, 33, 36; 16:28; 20:17), and so to "the glory that I had with you before the world began" (17:5). The events surrounding Jesus' crucifixion, therefore, are Jesus' "glorification" (7:39; 12:16; 12:23–28; 13:31), and Jesus' crucifixion itself is his "lifting up" or "exaltation" (3:14; 8:28; 12:32, 34).

This return to his primordial glory by means of his death, resurrection, and ascension, will be an advantage to his followers. It is the means by which he will gather those whom God has appointed to be his followers (John 11:51–52; 12:32). By returning to the Father, he will prepare the way for them to join him in the Father's presence (14:2–6), and once they are with him there, they will see him in the glory that God gave him before the world began (17:24). The disciples will not be able to follow Jesus into the glorious presence of God right away (13:36). Thus, in the meantime, Jesus will send the Paraclete, the Holy Spirit, to them. His presence with them will be such an advantage that Jesus can say, "It is for your good that I am going away" (16:5).

Some interpreters of John's gospel have considered John's glorification of Jesus' death to be a theological problem. John, they say, has dispensed with the scandal of the cross and turned the *via dolorosa* into a triumphal procession.[40] Under the influence of a "docetism" of a "naïve, unreflected" type, he has brought forward the glory of Christ that elsewhere in the New Testament is wisely said to be revealed only in the future and has placed it into the story of the historical Jesus.[41]

John has, without doubt, emphasized the inability of Jesus' crucifixion to call into question his unity with God. It is important, however, to set this emphasis within its historical context. John has perhaps placed such an emphasis on Jesus' exaltation on the cross because it answers a problem that was particularly acute in his own Christian community. John alone among the four gospels speaks of the ejection of Jesus' followers from the synagogue during Jesus' lifetime (John 9:22), and he joins the Synoptic Gospels in recording Jesus' prediction that his (Jewish) followers will suffer disciplinary measures in the synagogues because of their beliefs (16:2; cf. Matt. 10:17–18; 23:34; Mark 13:9; Luke 21:12–13).[42] Although it is a mistake to take these references as retrojections of John's own situation back into the life of Jesus, it nevertheless makes sense that John preserves and emphasizes these traditions if he hopes to encourage Christians for whom Jesus' prophecy of persecution has materialized.[43]

The confession that leads to ejection from the synagogue and death elsewhere in the gospel is that Jesus is the Christ—a title that John identifies with Jesus' status as Son of God and therefore equal with God (John 20:31)—and that Jesus is one with God (5:18; 8:58–59; 10:30–33; 19:7). It seems likely that to non-Christian Jews in

40 Käsemann, *Testament of Jesus*, 10, 18.

41 Ibid., 19–20, 26.

42 See Andrew T. Lincoln, *Truth on Trial: The Lawsuit Motif in the Fourth Gospel* (Peabody, Mass.: Hendrickson, 2000), 266–67.

43 The notion that John's narrative operates on two levels, that of the historical Jesus and that of John's community and that John merges the two levels in his narrative, has become popular since the monograph of J. Louis Martyn, *History and Theology in the Fourth Gospel* (Nashville: Abingdon, 1968). For a more recent and cautious statement of this view, see Lincoln, *Truth on Trial*, 263–332.

John's Christian community this confession was the most offensive element of Christian dogma. How is it possible, they may have asked, that one who was "with God in the beginning" could die the most humiliating of deaths? They may have followed the logic of the imaginary Jew whom Celsus brings forward, around A.D. 180, to expose the folly of a crucified god:

> Why, if not before, does he not at any rate now show forth something divine, and deliver himself from this shame, and take revenge on those who insult both him and his Father? . . . Do you, who are such great believers, criticize us because we do not regard this man as a god nor agree with you that he endured these sufferings for the benefit of mankind. . . ? (Origen, *Cels.* 2.35, 38)

With charges perhaps something like this ringing in his ears, John may have felt the need to emphasize an aspect of the passion of the historical Jesus that could be overlooked if Mark and Matthew were its only witnesses. There is a sense in which Jesus' passion reveals rather than conceals his divinity.

This does not mean that John fails to affirm the shameful nature of Jesus' death. He devotes an eighth of his gospel to the passion narrative. Included in his telling of the story are such grisly and humiliating details as Jesus' carrying his own cross (John 19:17), his crucifixion between two thieves (19:18), soldiers gambling for his clothes (19:24), Jesus' thirst, "quenched" with vinegar (19:29), and the sudden flow of blood and water from the expired Jesus' side when a soldier stabs him with a spear (19:34). When called on to do so, John can emphasize the theological importance of these elements, and this happens in 1 John (1 John 5:6–8). In the gospel, however, there is a need for a different emphasis, and John appropriately gives it. It is an emphasis that the church down through the ages has valued, even if the church has also wisely counterbalanced it with the witness of the Synoptic Gospels.

Jesus' Death as One Part of the Servant's Mission in Luke–Acts

The significance of Jesus' death in Luke's gospel is more difficult to trace. As we have seen, Luke affirms the atoning significance of Jesus' death, but he does not emphasize it.

What aspect of Jesus' death does Luke emphasize? Interpreters of Luke–Acts have made a variety of suggestions. For some, Luke considers Jesus' death as a martyrdom and an example to be followed, something like Eleazar in the Maccabean literature who died for his convictions and left "to the young a noble example of how to die a good death willingly and nobly" (2 Macc. 6:28; cf. 4 Macc. 5:1–7:23).[44] For others, Luke places Jesus in the role of the Righteous Sufferer described in such texts as Psalms 22, 42–43, 61, 116, and Wisdom of Solomon 2 and 5.[45] Other interpreters

44 See, e.g., Martin Dibelius, *From Tradition to Gospel* (Cambridge: James Clarke, 1971; orig. ed. 1919), 201–3.

45 Robert J. Karris, "Luke 23:47 and the Lucan View of Jesus' Death," *JBL* 105 (1986): 65–74. Senior, *Passion*, 168, views this as one motif among many. Cf. Daryl Schmidt, "Luke's 'Innocent' Jesus: A Scriptural Apologetic," in *Political Issues in Luke-Acts*, ed. Richard J. Cassidy and Philip Scharper (Maryknoll, N.Y.: Orbis, 1983), 111–21, here at 116–19, and John T. Carroll, "Luke's Crucifixion Scene," in *Reimaging the Death of the Lukan Jesus*, ed. Dennis D. Sylva (BBB 73; Frankfurt: Anton Hain, 1990), 108–24, here at 116–18.

hold that in Luke–Acts Jesus recapitulates Adam's experience of testing in the garden, but, unlike Adam, is obedient and therefore secures salvation for humanity.[46] Still others believe that although for Luke Jesus' death is both divinely ordained and important, Luke is not interested in providing an analysis of its theological significance.[47] Some scholars think that Luke finds Jesus' death to be theologically meaningful at a number of levels.[48]

The variety of suggestions about the principal meaning of Jesus' death shows that, as the last position implies, no single meaning is actually primary. Luke may have affirmed each of these meanings, but he is interested neither in focusing on any one of them in particular nor in exploring each of them in detail. Instead, Jesus' death plays one part, albeit an important part, in a crucial series of events. Although Luke acknowledges the immense theological significance of Jesus' death, he wants his readers' attention to progress from the period of Jesus' death to the segment of salvation history covered in his second volume. In this period of God's saving work, he has exalted Jesus to his right hand, and, from this exalted position, Jesus has inaugurated the time of Israel's forgiveness and restoration, an era that includes the extension of salvation to all the peoples of the earth.

This may be why, as we saw above when thinking about the rejection of Jesus in the gospels, Luke places greater emphasis than the other gospel authors on identifying Jesus with the Servant of Isaiah's four Servant Songs. Luke apparently sees that the career of Isaiah's Servant corresponded to the career of Jesus not simply in his death, but also in his exaltation and in his extension of God's salvation to the Gentiles.[49] Not only does the Servant suffer innocently in both Isaiah and Luke–Acts (Isa. 50:8; 53:9; Luke 23:4, 14–15; 23:22), but he suffers among the transgressors, a correspondence between himself and the Servant that Jesus brings out explicitly in Luke's gospel (Isa. 53:11; Luke 22:37). God vindicates both the Servant and Jesus, and this vindication leads to the justification of many (Isa. 53:11; Acts 5:31; 13:37–38). Both the Servant and Jesus—through his followers, and especially through Paul—extend God's saving work beyond Israel to the Gentiles, another correspondence that Luke brings out through explicit quotation (Isa. 42:6; cf. 49:6; Luke 2:32; Acts 13:46).

Luke, therefore, is probably less focused than the other evangelists on a single significant element of Jesus' death because he sees Jesus' death as part of a complex series of events. Through these events Jesus will carry out God's plan for Israel's restoration, a plan that the biblical description of the Servant of the Lord foreshadowed.

46 Jerome Neyrey, *The Passion according to Luke: A Redaction Study of Luke' Soteriology* (New York: Paulist, 1985), 156–92. Cf. Senior, *Passion*, 165, who thinks this theme, alongside many others, is significant for Luke. Senior is more cautious than Neyrey, however, about the extent to which this idea influenced Luke.

47 Joseph B. Tyson, *The Death of Jesus in Luke–Acts* (Columbia, S. C.: Univ. of South Carolina Press, 1986), 169–70.

48 Senior, *Passion*, 161–79, for example, thinks that Jesus' death in Luke brings salvation, demonstrates Jesus' faithfulness as both Son of God and Just One, portrays Jesus as prophet and martyr, shows how God enabled Jesus to overcome the forces of darkness, gives Jesus as an example for faithful Christian discipleship, and reveals how human death gives way to life. Cf. Carroll, "Crucifixion Scene," who finds that Luke depicts Jesus as a rejected prophet, the suffering Messiah, an innocent man, an exemplary martyr, and the giver of salvation.

49 Joel B. Green, "The Death of Jesus, God's Servant," in *Reimaging the Death of the Lukan Jesus*, ed. Dennis D. Sylva (BBB 73; Frankfurt: Anton Hain, 1990), 1–28, esp. pp. 18–28; idem, "Death of Jesus" in *Dictionary of Jesus and the Gospels*, ed. Joel B. Green, Scot McKnight, and I. Howard Marshall, (Downers Grove, Ill.: InterVarsity Press, 1992), 146–63, here at 161.

Summary and Conclusion

Why did God determine that his Son and Servant must die? All four gospels supply, in narrative form, an answer to this question. Mark and Matthew both emphasize the atoning significance of Jesus' death. Like the Servant of the Lord described by Isaiah, he died so that the sins of many might be forgiven. Although innocent himself, he voluntarily submitted to the punishment that they deserved for their iniquities and so he gave his life as a ransom for many (Mark), for the forgiveness of sins (Matthew). His sacrificial death was the Day of Atonement sacrifice to end all Day of Atonement sacrifices. There was no longer any need for the annual sacrifice performed in the most sacred place in Israel "for the whole community of Israel" (Lev. 16:17, 33), and so God rent the curtain separating the Most Holy Place from other parts of the temple at the time of Jesus' death.

John was interested in bringing out the role that Jesus' death played in revealing the divine glory of Jesus. Far from threatening his claim to unity with God, Jesus demonstrated throughout the events of the passion that he was one with the God who had determined that he should die. The major elements of that experience did not take him by surprise, nor was his death a sign of his weakness. It was the "hour" for which he was destined and the means by which he returned to the glory that he had with his Father before the world began.

Luke saw rich theological significance in Jesus' death but chose not to explore any single meaning of it in depth. Instead, Jesus' death was part of the necessary progress of salvation history, recorded in advance in Isaiah's prophecy of the Servant of the Lord. Like the Servant, Jesus had to die, but God also vindicated him and carried his saving work both to Israel and to the nations.

Contrary to some scholarly opinion, neither Luke nor John resisted the notion that Jesus died an atoning death. Both evangelists affirm this traditional way of understanding why Jesus died on the cross. They nevertheless saw other meanings that needed emphasis also. Taken together, the four gospels give special emphasis to Jesus' death as an atonement, an exaltation, and a necessary step in the inevitable progress of salvation history.

WHAT RESPONSE SHOULD JESUS RECEIVE?

All four gospels either imply or state explicitly that their narratives about Jesus require a response. Luke and John are explicit. Luke writes so that Theophilus may know with greater certainty the things that he has already believed (Luke 1:4). John writes so that those who read his book may believe—either more firmly or for the first time—that Jesus is the Christ, the Son of God (John 20:31).

Mark and Matthew are more subtle. They provide no direct statements, but they shape their narratives in a way that show they intend them to mold the convictions and actions of those who read them. Mark wants his readers to comprehend the promise of restoration to himself that God holds out even to those with the hardest hearts. Matthew issues a warning to those who have rejected Jesus and to those who claim to be Jesus' followers that they should examine their actions as a barometer of the condition of their hearts.

Faith and Love in John

We begin with John, who is most explicit about the response he desires his readers to give to his narrative: He hopes that they will believe that Jesus is the Christ, the Son of God (John 20:31). Interpreters have debated whether John hopes that his readers will come to faith for the first time through reading his gospel or whether he hopes they will continue to believe. Is his gospel intended to prompt faith or to strengthen faith?[50] If our examination in chapter 6 of the nature of belief in John's gospel is on the right track, that debate probably rests on a dichotomy John would not appreciate. Although Jesus knows those who truly believe and those who cannot fall out of the Father's hand (6:64–65; 8:31; 10:26–29; 13:18–19; cf. 13:11), some who think they believe turn out not to be believers at all (6:64a, 66, 70; 8:30, 37b; 13:10–11).

John, therefore, probably intends his gospel both to engender faith in those who do not have it and to strengthen the faith of those who are already Jesus' disciples.[51] Perhaps John writes at least in part for believing Jews who, in the face of persecution for their commitment to a Christology that the synagogue finds offensive (John 16:2; cf. 15:20–21), need encouragement to continue belief in Jesus as the Christ, the Son of God, in the untraditional way that John defines those terms. They should not be like those Galilean "disciples" who "turned back and no longer followed him" when they heard the difficult teaching that life was only available through union with Jesus' flesh and blood (6:53–62), nor should they be like Judas, who, although one of the twelve, was "a devil" (6:70; 13:10–11, 18, 27). They should remain in the vine, Jesus himself (15:1–8).

We should probably not think, however, of John's gospel—or any of the other gospels for that matter—as written simply to John's own community. John, like the other gospel authors, writes as much for anyone who will read his book as for his own "community."[52] He must have also written with the notion in mind that an unbeliever, perhaps an unbelieving Jew, might read his book (or hear it read), be chastened by it, and heed the appeal implicit in such passages as John 8:28, 10:38, and 11:49–52. As we have seen, in light of such passages, John must have held out some hope that after they had lifted up the Son of Man, even Jesus' most vocal opponents might nevertheless believe in him.

Although not a primary concern of his gospel, John also thinks that persistence in faith has an ethical dimension. Those who are really Jesus' disciples will do more

50 The gospel was written to prompt faith according to, for example, D. A. Carson, *The Gospel according to John* (Grand Rapids: Eerdmans, 1991), 87–95, 661–63. It was written primarily to deepen the faith of believers according to, for example, Raymond E. Brown, *The Gospel according to John XIII–XXI* (AB 29A; Garden City, N.Y.: Doubleday, 1970), 1059–61.

51 Cf., e.g., F. F. Bruce, *The Gospel of John* (Grand Rapids: Eerdmans, 1983), 395, and George R. Beasley-Murray, *John* (WBC 36; Waco, Tex.: Word, 1987), 387–88.

52 Richard Bauckham, ed., *The Gospels for All Christians: Rethinking the Gospel Audiences* (Grand Rapids: Eerdmans, 1998).

than fail to cave in to the pressure to drop their confession of Jesus' unity with God. They will also love one another. This is the one ethical imperative of Jesus in which John is interested. He can speak of keeping Jesus' "commands" (John 14:21), obeying his "teaching" (14:24), and bearing "much fruit" (15:8), but the only "command" that Jesus explicitly gives to his disciples is, "Love one another" (13:34–35; 15:17; cf. 13:12–14, 20; 15:11–16).

It would seem logical to find the motive for this command in a practical need for Jesus' disciples to cling together as hostility against them in the world increased. This has certainly been a popular explanation among some scholars for the prominence of the love command in the gospel. Following sociological models, they note that as groups are marginalized, they become more sectarian and more focused on cementing their bonds of unity with one another as a wall of protection against the advances of the outside world.[53] Occasionally interpreters have turned the inward focus of the command against John and criticized him for advising that his community only love its own members, neglecting in the process love for the outside world and Jesus' command—recorded elsewhere—to love one's enemy (Matt. 5:43–48; Luke 6:27, 35; 10:25–37). This position might seem to find some exegetical support in Jesus' emphasis on the hatred of the world for the disciples in the same breath that he has spoken of their need to love one another (John 15:18–16:4).[54]

As logical as all this seems at one level, it is ultimately unconvincing as an explanation of the love command in John's gospel. The text of the gospel simply fails to support it. Within the gospel itself Jesus gives a reason for the prominence of the love command that is almost diametrically opposed to the sociological model. The disciples, says Jesus, should love one another because doing so will enhance their mission to the world. Just as his Father has sent the Son into the world to proclaim the unity of Son and Father with each other, so the Son sends the disciples into the world to proclaim the same message (John 17:18; 20:21).[55] In other words, the relationship of the disciples with the world should parallel the relationship that the Father and the Son have with the world. This is a relationship not of sectarian hatred for those on the outside but of love that gives rise to mission:

> For God so loved the world that he gave his one and only Son, that whoever believes in him shall not perish but have eternal life. For God did not send his Son into the world to condemn the world, but to save the world through him. (John 3:16–17)

53 See, e.g., Stuhlmacher, *Biblische Theologie*, 2:259, who, however, views this development as understandable in light of the persecution through which the Johannine community was passing at the time.

54 See, e.g., Kelber, "Metaphysics and Marginality," 152–53, and R. Alan Culpepper, "Anti-Judaism in the Fourth Gospel as a Theological Problem for Christian Interpreters" in *Anti-Judaism and the Fourth Gospel*, ed. Reimund Bieringer, Didier Pollefeyt, and Frederique Vandecasteele-Vanneuville (Louisville: Westminster John Knox, 2001), 61–82, here at 79–81.

55 Stuhlmacher, *Biblische Theologie*, 2:259, thinks that such texts do not broaden the perspective of the love command because they still speak only of love for those to whom the Father sent the Son and who therefore will believe. God's love for the world in 3:16, however, precedes the world's response of belief, and so the outward focus of the love remains intact. Cf. 1 John 4:10, 19, and on the relationship between mission and mutual love, see François Vouga, *Une théologie du Nouveau Testament* (*MdB* 43; Genève: Labor et Fides, 2001), 208–13.

There is certainly a difference between John's love command and the command to love one's enemy in Matthew and Luke. In those gospels, Jesus' focus was on doing "good to those who hate you" (Luke 6:27) through being kind to them in practical ways—blessing them, praying for them, giving them clothing, lending to them without expecting them to repay, and generally treating them the way one would want to be treated (Matt. 5:38–48; 7:12; Luke 6:27–36; cf. 14:12–14). In John's gospel the focus is on reaching out to the world in one way only: by showing the world the unity of Father and Son and so bringing them to belief and eternal life.

This difference between John and the Synoptics does not mean, however, that John would disapprove of showing love for one's enemies. Nor does his command to love the brotherhood somehow oppose the teaching of Jesus on love for one's enemy. His focus rests on a single ethical concern: showing love for the brotherhood so that its witness to the unity between Father and Son might appear credible before the world.

For the proclamation of Jesus' disciples to be successful, however, they must cultivate two relationships: They must be one with the Son and with his Father (John 17:21; cf. 15:1–8), and they must be united with one another (17:22–23). They are, in other words, the middle link in a chain of three parts (Father/Son—disciples—world), and if the middle link disintegrates, it will be impossible to bring the world into an understanding of the unity that the Son and the Father share. Since belief in this unity leads to eternal life (3:36; 5:24; 17:3), the mission of the disciples to the world will fail if the disciples are not unified.

In summary, John believes that his gospel demands two responses: belief and mutual love. Those who have not yet come to the conviction that Jesus is God's messianic Son in the sense that he is one with his Father should embrace this truth. Those who have already committed themselves to this belief should remain in it, even in the face of the same kind of bitter persecution that the historical Jesus himself experienced. They must, moreover, love one another since this mutual love is the critical element in the fulfillment of their mission to show the world the unity between Jesus and his Father.

Perseverance in the Way in Luke–Acts

Luke is also explicit about the response that he expects his two-volume narrative to receive from Theophilus and from readers like him. He hopes that his narrative will assure them of "the certainty" of the faith to which they have committed themselves. Like John, Luke hopes to strengthen the commitment of persecuted Christians to the faith that they have embraced. Luke does this by pointing out to his readers their important location on a social map whose boundaries correspond with God's saving purposes. Luke shows his readers, as they make their way through his narrative, that they are part of a far more important people than the Greco-Roman society that has marginalized them—they are part of the people of God.

In his narrative Luke demonstrates that through this people, God is extending his saving purpose, articulated long before in the Scriptures, both to Israel and to all the nations of the earth. This saving purpose, Luke maintains, will triumph over every obstacle placed in its path, whether from a disobedient traditionalism within the church or direct opposition from unbelieving persecutors. Luke's readers have not misplaced their faith. Their faith is in a God whose purpose was planned in meticulous detail, who announced that purpose in advance in the pages of Scripture, and whose purpose would continue to advance in the future just as assuredly as it has in the past.

It is perhaps in part because he wants his readers to understand their own important location within this purpose that Luke's narrative does not limit the identification of Isaiah's Servant of the Lord with Jesus alone. As important as it is in Luke's narrative that Jesus, like the Servant, suffered, was vindicated, and from his exalted position at God's right hand oversees the extension of God's saving purpose to the nations, Luke also shows that others, especially Paul, in some sense do the work of the Servant. Just as Simeon applies to Jesus Isaiah's description of the Servant as one who will be "a light for revelation to the Gentiles" (Luke 2:32; cf. Isa. 49:6), so Paul and Barnabas turn their attention to the Gentiles in Pisidian Antioch with the words, "This is what the Lord has commanded us: 'I have made you a light for the Gentiles, that you may bring salvation to the ends of the earth'" (Acts 13:47; cf. Isa. 49:6). Both Paul (Acts 22:15; 26:16) and others (Acts 1:8; 13:31) are Jesus' "witnesses," just as the Servant and God's people are "witnesses" before the nations (Isa. 43:9–10).[56]

The work of the vindicated, exalted Servant of the Lord is not yet finished. It continues through the work of his disciples, and insofar as they are among those who "witness" to the message about Jesus, they also function as the Servant of the Lord. This important role should give them confidence as they make their way through a world that often responds to the gospel not with acceptance but with persecution.

Just as John has advice for how his readers should live as they seek to accomplish the mission that the Son has given them, so Luke has similar advice for his readers as they assume their role in the extension of God's saving purpose to Israel and the nations. As we saw in chapter 5, an important part of Luke's purpose is to show his readers how they should conduct their lives as they follow Jesus along the "Way" of God (Luke 20:21; Acts 9:2; 16:17; 18:25–26; 19:9, 23; 22:4; 24:14, 22). Luke is especially concerned that his readers extend God's saving work through three activities.

First, they should practice inclusiveness, preaching the good news of salvation to the poor, to sinners, and to various people whose culture differs from their own. Like the wounded man on the side of the road in the parable of the Samaritan neighbor (Luke 10:29–37), they should see those who are different from them as their neighbors. Unlike the lawyer who provoked the parable, they should not wait until they need the help of those different from themselves before they recognize this. The poor

56 Cf. Ernst Haenchen, *The Acts of the Apostles: A Commentary* (Philadelphia: Westminster, 1971), 143 n. 8; C. K. Barrett, *A Critical and Exegetical Commentary on the Acts of the Apostles*, 2 vols. (ICC; Edinburgh: T. & T. Clark, 1994–98), 1:291; and esp. John B. Polhill, *Acts* (NAC; Nashville: Broadman, 1992), 85.

(Luke 4:18–19; 14:13; cf. Acts 3:1–10), sinners (Luke 6:32–33; 15:1–31; Acts 9:1–31), and the ethnically other (Luke 10:29–37; Acts 8:14–7, 25, 26–29; 10:1–11:18; 15:1–31) are all objects of God's saving work.

Second, they should hold their possessions with a light grip, recognizing that wealth tends to divert its owners from the way of the Lord (Luke 12:13–21). For some this will mean divesting themselves of all wealth, like Peter (Acts 3:6). For others it will mean maintaining some wealth so that they might, like Paul (Acts 20:34–35), provide for the needs of the poor.

Third, in the midst of the hardship that they experience for their commitment to the gospel, they should "always pray and not give up" (Luke 18:1). God will use their prayers to advance his saving purposes and, in answer to them, will vindicate them against their oppressors. Often, as happens in Acts, he will provide this vindication "speedily" (18:8a; cf. Acts 4:29–30; 7:56; 12:5, 7; 16:26), but if he delays, his people should persevere in their faith, using prayer to help them cope with their suffering (Luke 18:8b; 23:34, 46; cf. Acts 4:23–31; 7:59–60).

Luke's gospel emphasizes the faithfulness of Jesus in these three activities, and his second volume shows how the early church followed his example. Luke intends that his readers, in the midst of their own suffering, should, like the early church, follow the faithfulness of Jesus in extending God's saving work to the marginalized, handling possessions with care, and praying in the midst of hardship.

Like John, therefore, Luke wants his readers to remain convinced of the faith to which they have committed themselves. This means more than simply erecting barriers against the persecution and influence of the outside world. It means following the example of Jesus and the early Christians by engaging in mission to the world and by responding to persecution not with retreat but with advancement.

The Good News of Forgiven Sin in Mark

The response that Mark wants those who read his narrative to give to it is, like so much else in his gospel, difficult to discern. Unlike John and Luke, he provides no statement of his purpose in writing. As we saw in chapter 3, however, careful attention to the narrative reveals a concern not only to identify Jesus as the Christ and Son of God but to offer the hope of Jesus' atoning death to those whose hearts have been hardened against the gospel.

Mark probably assumes that his readers will either be disciples of Jesus or people interested in what "the gospel about Jesus Christ, the Son of God" (Mark 1:1) has to offer them. He probably expects his readers to identify most naturally, therefore, with Jesus' disciples in the narrative: They will know immediately that they are not peers of the Messiah himself, or of John with his prophetic role, wild dress, and unusual diet, or of God, but peers of those in the narrative who want to obey God and so follow Jesus (1:1–20). By portraying the disciples almost entirely positively through 6:30, Mark encourages his readers to persist in this identification.[57]

57 Cf. Andrew T. Lincoln, "The Promise and the Failure: Mark 16:7, 8" in *The Interpretation of Mark*, 2nd ed., ed. William R. Telford (Studies in New Testament Interpretation; Edinburgh: T. & T. Clark, 1995), 229–51, here at 242–43.

As the hostility to Jesus among his opponents mounts in his early chapters, Mark also encourages his reader not to identify with the scribes and Pharisees. They are opposed to the one who forgives sins, heals diseases, includes outcasts, and regards compassion to the hungry as more important than obedience to the law (Mark 2:1–3:6). They have labeled the things of God as satanic (3:22) and so are "on the outside" of God's kingdom (4:11). A reader even mildly sympathetic with Mark's gospel instinctively resists identifying with Jesus' enemies.

Mark then introduces a disturbing complexity into the narrative. Beginning with the account of the feeding of the five thousand (Mark 6:30–44), he portrays the disciples in a light almost as negative as Jesus' opponents. Despite knowing from personal experience that Jesus has made his wonder-working power available to them (3:14–15; 6:7–13), they respond to Jesus' suggestion that they give the crowds something to eat with patronizing incredulity: "Should we go and buy two hundred denarii worth of bread and give them something to eat?" (6:37, aut.). Their obtuseness to Jesus' power and message continues, reaching something of a low point in 8:31–33, when Peter rebukes Jesus' claim that he must suffer and Jesus in turn rebukes him with words that could have been applied to the scribes a few chapters earlier: "Get behind me, Satan, because you do not have in mind the things of God, but the things of men" (8:33; cf. 3:20–30).

Eventually, in Jesus' hour of crisis, they cease even to be his followers and abandon him (Mark 14:10, 50, 68, 70, 71). One of Jesus' followers is so desperate to get away from him that when the mob seizes him, "he fled naked, leaving his garment behind" (14:51–52).

Mark must have hoped that this disturbing twist to his story would prompt his readers to examine their own claim to be followers of Jesus. Mark may have intended for his readers to ask of themselves the questions that Jesus poses to the disciples: "Do you still not see or understand? Are your hearts hardened? Do you have eyes but fail to see, and ears but fail to hear?" (Mark 8:17–18).

To failed disciples, Mark offers the cross of Jesus Christ, the Son of God. Jesus gave "his life as a ransom for many" (Mark 10:45). Like the Servant of the Lord, he "poured out" his blood for "many" (14:24; Isa. 53:12). His death is the ultimate Day of Atonement sacrifice (15:38). His death atones even for the sin of those whose understanding of his teaching is so clouded that they flee from him in his hour of need and deny they even know him. Thus, after Jesus' resurrection, the young man clothed in white—clearly an angelic messenger—sends a message to remind "the disciples and Peter" that Jesus awaits them in Galilee (16:7; cf. 14:28).

It is significant that the angel singles out Peter. He is the disciple Jesus identified with Satan earlier (Mark 8:33) and the disciple who, in Jesus' hour of crisis, denied three times that he knew him (14:30, 66–72). Jesus' death atoned for his sin, and, Mark seems to say, Jesus' death atones for all those who have failed to obey God but who are willing to accept in faith that Jesus died for them. As Jesus himself puts it, "I have not come to call the righteous, but sinners" (2:17).

Mark's gospel, therefore, is "gospel" in its purest sense. It is the proclamation of the same message that Jesus preached, and that message is the fulfillment of the good news described in Isaiah 40:1–5—God will offer comfort to his people because their "sin has been paid for" by the suffering of his Servant. The response that Mark desires from readers of his gospel is probably the same response that, according to his gospel, Jesus desires from his preaching of the kingdom of God: repentance and faith (1:15).

Fulfillment and Warning in Matthew

As with Mark, the response that Matthew wants from his readers emerges from a careful reading of the narrative rather than from any explicit statement. As we saw in chapter 4, Matthew is in an anguished struggle with non-Christian Jews over whether they or Jewish Christians are heirs to Israel's Scriptures. Matthew mounts a detailed argument that Jesus fulfills every biblical expectation for the Messiah and brings the ethical tendencies latent in the Mosaic law to maturity. The refusal of the Jewish leadership of Jesus' day to appreciate this arises from their corrupt, hardened hearts. God will punish their recalcitrance by destroying Jerusalem (Matt. 22:7; 23:36, 38; 24:1–2, 15–25; 21:41a) and reissuing to the Gentiles his invitation to the messianic banquet (8:11–12; 22:8–10; cf. 21:41b).

Matthew probably means this argument to fall on the ears of unbelieving Jews. As we saw in chapter 4, Matthew seems to have interpreted Jesus' role against the background of Jeremiah's troubled prophetic career. Jeremiah, like Jesus, had targeted the hypocrisy of his generation (Jer. 7:6, 9, 16–18, 22; cf. 26:1–24). Like Jesus, he had warned "this generation" that it stood "under [God's] wrath" (7:29) and that Jerusalem, with its temple, would be destroyed (7:12–15, 32–34; 26:6). Matthew probably saw himself in the same role and saw his gospel as functioning in a way similar to Jeremiah's written prophecy. If so, then Matthew may have hoped that the message of his gospel—perhaps only at second hand through the preaching of Christians whom it influenced—would lead some antagonistic Jews to repentance.

Matthew also probably intends his Christian readers to learn a salutary lesson from the negative response of so many in Israel to Jesus. As we saw in chapter 4, Matthew's denunciations of hypocrisy among the scribes and Pharisees in Matthew 6:1–18 and 23:1–39 contain imperatives that are intended for all readers of this gospel, and he probably assumes that most of them will be Christians. Matthew thinks that his Christian readers are capable of falling into the same traps of doing good deeds, praying, fasting, and coveting titles of honor merely so that others may see and praise them (6:1–6, 16–17; 23:3, 8–9). He has a realistic understanding of the church as a *corpus mixtum*, a body that includes both believers whose hearts have been changed and unbelievers who have undergone no inner change but are able to ape the words and some of the deeds of the pious (7:16–23; 13:24–30, 36–43, 47–50; 22:11–13; 24:48–51; 25:10–12).

Matthew hopes that his readers will respond to this reality not by trying to root false Christians out of the church (Matt. 13:29–30), but by working gently with those who seem to be tottering on the edge of unbelief in the hope that they may be spared. Although false Christians certainly exist in Matthew's view, only the final day will expose for certain those of genuine faith and those who have only parroted the words, "Lord! Lord!" In the meantime, the church should be slow to discipline the wayward (18:16–17), gentle toward the vulnerable (18:5–10), and eager to pursue lost sheep who have strayed from the fold (18:12–14).

In summary, Matthew hopes that the message of his gospel will benefit a wide variety of readers. For Jews who have rejected Jesus as a magician and deceiver, Matthew hopes that the message of his book—perhaps communicated through Christians who have read and learned from it—will function in the same way that Jeremiah's message functioned in the sixth century. It will warn them about their hard-heartedness and call on them to soften their attitudes toward the gospel. For those who claim to be Christians but whose inner attitudes are no different from the unbelieving Jews whom Matthew criticizes, Matthew's gospel functions in a similar way. To them, it is a salutary call to examine whether their conduct is consistent with the confession of the Lord who desires "mercy and not sacrifice" (Matt. 9:13; 12:7) and whose law places greatest weight on matters of "justice, mercy, and faith" (23:23).

What Did the Four Evangelists Expect Their Readers to Do? A Summary

Each of the four evangelists has written his work to strengthen the faith of those who have decided to follow Jesus, often in difficult circumstances. John and Luke give the clearest hints that they are writing for persecuted believers. "If they persecuted me, they will persecute you also," Jesus tells his disciples in John's gospel as he prepares them for his departure. "They will treat you this way because of my name" (John 15:20–21). He continues, "They will put you out of the synagogue," and "a time is coming when anyone who kills you will think he is offering a service to God" (16:1–2). Luke seems to expect that his readers "will long to see one of the days of the Son of Man" (Luke 17:22) and will "cry out to God for justice day and night" (18:7). He ends his narrative with the chief protagonist of his second volume—Paul—in prison (Acts 28:16, 30–31).

In light of the hardship that their Christian readers are facing for their commitment to the gospel, both John and Luke hope that those who read their works will receive encouragement to persevere in their commitment. John hopes that those who read his work will examine their faith to see if they are "really" Jesus' disciples (John 8:31), and, if not, he wants them to believe (20:31). Luke hopes that those who feel marginalized by the society around them will gain a renewed understanding of the important role they play, as God's people, in God's plan to bring salvation both to Israel and to all the nations of the earth (Acts 3:25).

Both John and Luke, moreover, have practical advice for their readers about how to live in the time before Jesus returns to take them with him to his Father's dwelling (John 14:1–4) and to restore everything as the holy prophets promised (Acts 3:21). They are to engage in the mission that Jesus has left them—showing the world the unity between Father and Son by means of their own unifying love for one another (John) and following the Way of Jesus by living lives of generosity, inclusiveness, and prayer (Luke–Acts).

The historical contexts out of which Mark and Matthew wrote are less clear. Mark may have also written in a period of persecution, perhaps in Rome under Nero.[58] Matthew's polemical engagement with unbelieving Judaism may have included the same kind of persecution that John evidently experienced. If so, each speaks from the context of suffering with a distinctive voice. Mark extends hope to those who have failed to remain faithful. He says to them that they are not the first to have buckled under the pressure of following Jesus in difficult circumstances. Jesus came to call sinners. His death has atoned for their sin, and he is awaiting them in Galilee so that they may continue to follow him.

Matthew, by contrast, recalls Israel's prophetic tradition to warn both the opponents of Christianity and inauthentic Christians of God's certain judgment. Here too, however, the ultimate hope is positive and gracious. Like Jeremiah, Matthew wants non-Christian Jews to avoid eschatological judgment by learning from the destruction of Jerusalem and from the influx of Gentiles into God's people that they must repent. He also wants Christians who read his gospel to avoid hypocrisy themselves and to rescue Christians tottering on the edge of hypocrisy. Both unbelieving Jews and hypocritical Christians will then escape the eschatological judgment reserved for those who say, "Lord, Lord" on the final day but whom the Lord himself will have to confess that he has never known.

THE GOSPEL OF JESUS CHRIST IN THE FOUR GOSPELS AND ACTS

For all their differences, the four gospels have much in common. Each evangelist addresses in his own way four questions about Jesus: Who is he? Why was he rejected? What is the significance of his death? What response does the message about him demand? As we have seen, each gospel answers each question with its own accent. Even so, the evangelists' answers to these questions occupy much common ground.

For all of them, Jesus cannot be understood apart from the background of his Jewish context. At the same time, he rises above that context to occupy ground that only God can share with him. He was with God at the beginning of creation (John), even the wind and the waves obey him (Mark), he and his teaching comprise the ultimate fulfillment of Israel's Scriptures (Matthew), and his coming has initiated the season of salvation for Israel and for all the nations of the earth (Luke–Acts).

All four evangelists understand Jesus' rejection to have stemmed from a combination of God's sovereign plan, articulated beforehand in Israel's Scriptures, and human sin. All of them believe that Jesus filled the role of Isaiah's Suffering Servant. All of them also affirm that those who reject Jesus have done so because their hearts were resistant to the things of God.

58 On this setting for Mark's gospel see, among others, Ralph P. Martin, *Mark: Evangelist and Theologian* (Exeter: Paternoster, 1972), 51–70; Martin Hengel, *Studies in the Gospel of Mark* (Philadelphia: Fortress, 1985), 1–30; idem, *The Four Gospels and the One Gospel of Jesus Christ* (Harrisburg, Penn.: Trinity Press International, 2000), 79.

All four also affirm that Jesus' crucifixion was far from the shameful end that most people in the ancient world considered any death by crucifixion to be. Because it was the suffering of God's innocent Servant, it provided full and final atonement for sin, even the sin of those who abandoned Jesus in his hour of greatest need (Mark), of those who plotted his death (Mark, Luke–Acts), and of those who, whether Jewish or Roman, placed him on the cross (Luke–Acts), if they will only repent and believe (Acts). Through Jesus' death, God exalted him to his right hand, and from there, he will send the Spirit to empower his disciples as they complete the task of preaching the gospel (Luke–Acts; John).

So each of the gospel authors hopes that his readers may respond to his narrative with strengthened faith in Jesus. In the midst of persecution, the death of Jesus atones for failure (Mark), the teaching and example of Jesus provide guidance for faithful discipleship (Matthew, Luke–Acts, and John), and the story of Jesus and the early church demonstrate that God's saving purpose for Israel and for the world will triumph (Luke–Acts).

All four gospels bear witness to the manifold ramifications of the one gospel of Jesus. In his Son and Messiah Jesus, the God of Abraham, Isaac, and Jacob has visited his people to complete his saving purpose among them and extended salvation to the Gentiles. Against all expectations, the death of Jesus on the cross and his exaltation to God's right hand has accomplished this purpose. Through Jesus' death, God has made available atonement and forgiveness of sin for all who repent. Jesus will return to bring God's saving work to a close and execute final judgment on all those who persist in their rejection of him. This means that those who have not done so must embrace the good news about him in faith, and those who have already done so must remain faithful even amid grave hardship.

Among the authors of the New Testament writings, Paul the apostle worked out the theological implications of this gospel most fully. We turn next to the theology of his letters.

Part Two

THE PAULINE LETTERS

Chapter 8

THE COHERENCE AND CENTER OF PAUL'S THEOLOGY

Within the field of New Testament theology, perhaps the most hotly disputed subtopic is Pauline theology. Part of the reason for this controversy is that Paul provides more information about his abiding theological convictions than any other New Testament author. It is true that Luke wrote more of the New Testament than Paul, but only Paul among the New Testament authors provides a number of letters written over a lengthy period, allowing us to see which theological convictions he appeals to repeatedly in diverse settings and over time. This allows us to construct what one Pauline scholar has called a "stereoscopic" picture of his theology.[1] We see it from more than one angle and are able to describe it in more than a single dimension. This large, ripe field of study naturally produces an equally large amount of fodder for interpretive disputes. As a result, a number of proposals have emerged about both the coherence of Paul's theology and what concept, if any, stands at its "center."

THE SIGNIFICANCE AND COHERENCE OF PAUL'S THEOLOGY

We can divide the major scholarly proposals about the coherence of Paul's theology into three categories: (1) claims that the theology that emerges from Paul's letters is coherent, stable, and significant, (2) claims that Paul's theology changed in significant ways as he encountered various problems in his churches, and (3) claims that Paul's theology is basically inconsistent.

Paul's Theology as Coherent and Significant

Traditionally, Christians have considered Paul the prince of theologians. From the time of Paul's own ministry, some have disputed this claim, but the orthodox church from an early date considered him to be the holy and blessed apostle Paul who, although occasionally difficult to understand (2 Peter 3:16), nevertheless wrote letters of unsurpassed sublimity. In more recent times some have continued to take a variation of this view, usually providing some historical justification for their assessment of Paul—he is the first and most influential Christian theologian—but always with a dash of admiration thrown in.

James D. G. Dunn provides a good example of this view of Paul as it is often held in modern times. Historically speaking, argues Dunn, Paul is both the first and greatest Christian theologian. This is true not because he was the first Christian to engage

1 James D. G. Dunn, *The Theology of Paul the Apostle* (Grand Rapids: Eerdmans, 1998), 13.

in theological reflection, but because he was the first to devote a considerable portion of his life to this kind of reflection, to teaching his theological convictions to others, and to writing them down. He is the greatest Christian theologian not because he is necessarily the best such theologian of all time but because of his widespread influence, particularly after the canonization of his letters in the second century. Dunn explains Paul's theology thematically, following where possible the outline of Romans in order not to impose a foreign theological system on Paul, and Dunn's study reveals a coherent, reflective, if constantly busy, pastor-theologian.[2]

Dunn believes, moreover, that Paul has something to offer the church today. Although Dunn writes with sensitivity to the historical circumstances in which Paul wrote his letters, he does not follow William Wrede's path of bracketing his commitment to the church in order to produce a purely historical portrait of Paul's theology:

> The test of a good theology of Paul will be the degree to which it enables the reader and the church not only to enter the thought world of Paul but also to engage theologically with the claims he makes and the issues he addresses.[3]

Other advocates of this approach include, from a former generation, Herman Ridderbos, and, more recently, C. K. Barrett and Thomas R. Schreiner. Ridderbos's treatment of Paul's theology differs from Dunn's on many significant points: the importance of the individual in Paul's theology, the post-Pauline origin of Ephesians and the Pastorals, and the interpretation of Paul's works-faith antithesis, to give only a representative sample.[4] Both Dunn and Ridderbos, however, hold in common the conviction that Paul's theology is basically self-consistent, can be described systematically, and has profound implications for the church.

Dunn and Ridderbos each uses the outline of Romans, Paul's most reflective and least situational letter, as the organizational structure for his theology. Dunn does this explicitly, defending his choice of organizational structure in preliminary essays and in the prologue to his full-length study.[5] Ridderbos makes no explicit appeal to Romans as the means of organizing his study of Paul's theology; but he refuses to be bound by the classic topics of the Reformed "order of salvation" (*ordo salutis*), and the core of his study, as it turns out, matches the outline of Romans. He moves from a discussion of sin (cf. Rom. 1:18–3:20) to the righteousness of God (cf. 3:21–5:21), to the new life in Christ (cf. 6:1–8:39), and to the church (cf. 12:1–15:13).

C. K. Barrett, in a volume on the nature and content of Paul's thought, views Paul from a similar perspective.[6] Barrett too takes a different road from Dunn at

2 Ibid., 1–26.

3 Ibid., 8–9. For Wrede's view, see "The Task and Methods of 'New Testament Theology,'" in *The Nature of New Testament Theology: The Contribution of William Wrede and Adolf Schlatter*, ed. Robert Morgan (SBT 2.25; London: SCM, 1973), 68–116, here at 70: "Anyone who wishes to engage scientifically in New Testament theology . . . must be guided by a pure disinterested concern for knowledge."

4 Herman Ridderbos, *Paul: An Outline of His Theology* (Grand Rapids: Eerdmans, 1975; orig. Dutch ed. 1966).

5 James D. G. Dunn, "Prolegomena to a Theology of Paul," *NTS* 40 (1994): 407–32; idem, "In Quest of Paul's Theology: Retrospect and Prospect," in *Pauline Theology. Volume IV: Looking Back, Pressing On*, ed. E. Elizabeth Johnson and David M. Hay (SBLSymS 4; Atlanta: Scholars Press, 1997), 95–115, here at 105–6; idem, *Theology of Paul*, 2–26.

6 C. K. Barrett, *Paul: An Introduction to His Thought* (Louisville: Westminster John Knox, 1994).

major exegetical intersections, such as Paul's understanding of the law and the law's relationship to both the gospel and its place in Christian ethics. Nevertheless, for Barrett, as for Dunn, Paul is not merely one of many outstanding Christian thinkers but "*the* outstanding Christian thinker."[7] Although the results of Paul's theological reflection are contained only in occasional letters, Paul was a systematic theologian; thus, the thematic treatment of his thought is an essential supplement to the occasional treatment of his thought in individual studies of each letter.[8]

Like Dunn and Ridderbos, Barrett seems to rely heavily on the outline of Romans for the arrangement of the various theological themes that he finds important in Paul. His discussion moves from "The Reign of Evil" (cf. Rom. 1:18–32) to "Law and Covenant" (cf. 2:1–3:20) to "Grace and Righteousness" and "Christ Crucified" (cf. 3:21–8:39) to "The Church" (cf. 12:1–15:13) and "The Holy Spirit and Ethics." Only in the last two sections does Barrett deviate from the outline of Romans, leaving out a discussion of Israel in Paul's theology (9:1–11:36) and covering the Holy Spirit and ethics last whereas Paul links these two issues together most prominently in the middle section of the letter (5:1–21; 8:1–39).[9]

Thomas R. Schreiner, like Dunn, Ridderbos, and Barrett, believes that Paul was a coherent and theologically consistent thinker.[10] He agrees with Dunn and Barrett that any attempt to systematize Paul's thought faces the obstacle of the occasional nature of Paul's letters. Paul was neither a systematic theologian who wrote letters with the intention that other generations would analyze the theology expressed in them, nor was he even a pastor involved in the leadership of certain churches. Schreiner believes that Paul was fundamentally a missionary who understood both his mission itself and the suffering it required in theological terms. He called people in various places to respond to the gospel in faith, and he hoped through this means to lead all peoples to give glory to God through his Son Jesus Christ. Although his letters were occasional documents intended to urge those who read them to persevere in their commitment to the gospel, the care with which he composed them and the effectiveness of Paul's missionary labors reveal the consistency and depth of his thought.

Like Dunn, Ridderbos, and Barrett, Schreiner wrote his theology of Paul after completing a major commentary on Romans.[11] Although the organization of his theology does not follow the outline of Romans, it is perhaps not insignificant that he argues for the glory that all people should give to Christ as both the leading theme of Romans and the foundation of Paul's theology generally.[12]

---

7 Ibid., ix: "If there is any question of Paul's place in a series of Outstanding Christian Thinkers it is whether he ought not to be described as *the* outstanding Christian thinker." Barrett is referring to the series "Outstanding Christian Thinkers" in which the British release of his book (London: Geoffrey Chapman, 1994) appeared.

8 Ibid., 56.

9 Ibid., 55–141.

10 Thomas R. Schreiner, *Paul: Apostle of God's Glory in Christ: A Pauline Theology* (Downers Grove, Ill.: InterVarsity Press, 2001).

11 Dunn's theology appeared ten years after the publication of his commentary on Romans. For Ridderbos the gap was seven years and for Schreiner three years. Barrett's treatment of Paul's thought appeared three years after the revision of his much earlier commentary on Romans. See James D. G. Dunn, *Romans 1–8* (WBC 38A; Dallas: Word, 1988); idem, *Romans 9–16* (WBC 38B; Dallas: Word, 1988); Herman Ridderbos, *Aan de Romeinen* (Commentaar op het Nieuwe Testament; Kampen: Kok, 1959); Thomas R. Schreiner, *Romans* (BECNT; Grand Rapids: Baker, 1998); and C. K. Barrett, *The Epistle to the Romans* (BNTC; London: A. & Black, 1957; rev. ed., Peabody, Mass.: Hendrickson, 1991).

12 See Schreiner, *Romans*, 23; idem, *Paul*, 15–35.

In sum, for these interpreters, Paul's theology is both profound and well ordered. Romans, as Paul's most reflective and least situational letter, provides access to the way in which Paul orders the major elements of his thought.[13]

Paul's Theology as a Work in Progress

The second position on Paul's status as a theologian is that he was primarily an apostle attempting to work out the implications of his gospel in the communities that his preaching had established. If his letters indicate the character of his theological thinking, then his apostolic activity often resulted in theological overstatement, misstatement, and development but also in a measure of profound theological insight. Hans Hübner, for example, agrees with Dunn and Barrett that Paul is among the greatest of early Christian thinkers, but he places special emphasis on how Paul hammered out his theology in debate with the Christian communities that he had established. Because Paul thought theologically along with these communities, his theology was in process—undergoing change and development. At the same time, it contained profound elements, such as justification by faith alone apart from works of the law, that were present from the beginning but received restatement and refinement over time.[14]

We can also place the influential treatment of J. Christiaan Beker in this category, although Beker does not believe that Paul's theology "developed" toward some goal.[15] For Beker, Paul's theological achievement lies precisely in the way that the tension between coherence and contingency was a constant feature of his thought. Beker proposes that Paul's thought cannot be separated from the circumstances in which he expressed it either for the purpose of locating its "center" or for the purpose of imposing a finished, systematic structure on it.[16] His theology can only be understood as his effort "to make the gospel a word on target for the particular needs of his churches without either compromising its basic content or reducing it to a petrified conceptuality."[17]

Beker never works out the "coherence" of Paul's thought (which he defines as "the imminent apocalyptic triumph of God") as the application of a series of propositions to particular situations.[18] It must instead, he believes, be worked out with the advice and consent of other believers in the body of Christ and under the guidance of the Spirit:

13 After a period in which many interpreters thought it necessary to deny that Romans contains a systematic presentation of Christian doctrine, the importance of the letter's place in describing at least Paul's theology in systematic terms seems to be reemerging. In addition to the work of Dunn, Ridderbos, Barrett, and Schreiner, see also Joseph Plevnik, "The Understanding of God at the Basis of Pauline Theology," *CBQ* 65 (2003): 554–67, here at 564–67.

14 Hans Hübner, *Biblische Theologie des Neuen Testaments*, 3 vols. (Göttingen: Vandenhoeck & Ruprecht, 1990–95), 2:26–29. See also idem, *Law in Paul's Thought* (Edinburgh: T. & T. Clark, 1984).

15 Beker's position appears in a number of different publications, the best known of which is *Paul the Apostle: The Triumph of God in Life and Thought* (Philadelphia: Fortress, 1980). In the wake of the scholarly response to this book, Beker clarified his position in other essays. See, for example, the preface to the 1984 paperback edition of *Paul the Apostle* and his "Recasting Pauline Theology: The Coherence-Contingency Scheme as Interpretive Model," in *Pauline Theology, Volume I: Thessalonians, Philippians, Galatians, Philemon*, ed. Jouette M. Bassler (Minneapolis: Fortress, 1991), 15–24. For Beker's resistance to the notion of "development" in Paul's theology, see *Paul the Apostle*, 39 and 94, and "Recasting Pauline Theology," 21–22.

16 Beker, *Paul the Apostle*, 15.

17 Ibid., 12.

18 Beker, "Recasting Pauline Theology," 18–20.

> Thus, [Paul's] hermeneutic of coherence-contingency is not an abstract or individualistic activity of the apostle, nor an activity of learned rabbis in a rabbinic school, but a pragmatic consensus-building activity in the body of Christ, where relevant and authentic "gospel" strategies are devised for particular problems.[19]

After Paul's death, the church failed to understand this delicate interplay between coherence and contingency in Paul's letters and transformed Paul into a "dogmatician." This process began at least as early as the composition of the Pastoral Letters in Paul's name and continued until the rise of the historical-critical method in the eighteenth century, when interpreters of Paul began to appreciate again the historically contingent nature of Paul's letters.[20]

Those who place the analysis of Paul's theology within a general account of his life and ministry, such as Jürgen Becker and Jerome Murphy-O'Connor, sometimes take a similar approach. Unlike Beker, however, these two scholars have no reservations about speaking of "development" in Paul's theology. Jürgen Becker sees Paul's theology emerging over the course of his tumultuous apostolic career, sometimes from seeds planted at his conversion but always on the anvil of the controversies that he faced.[21] Through his association with the church at Antioch Paul developed an understanding of the gospel as good news for the Gentiles, that they could be rescued from the wrath of God by faith in Christ. God chose to make this proclamation effective, and so Gentiles began to join the Antiochene community solely on the basis of God's sovereign choice and without conformity to the particularly Jewish customs found in the Mosaic law. This theology of election lies beneath Paul's Thessalonian correspondence.

Later Paul parted ways with the Antiochene church when it divided under pressure from the leadership of the Jerusalem church (Gal. 2:11–14). The Antiochene church had decided that its Gentile members must keep at least part of the law in order to ensure the Levitical purity, and therefore the ethnic distinctiveness, of the church's Jewish members (cf. Acts 15:19–20). Paul then struck out on his own, and over the next several years founded churches in Corinth and Ephesus. In his letters to the Corinthian church from Ephesus, he developed a theology of the cross as a response to the Corinthians' readiness to place the interpretation of the gospel in the hands of the economically, socially, and "spiritually" powerful. As the cross shows, said Paul, God works through weakness—through those who have nothing to offer him and who depend solely on his grace.

Finally, through his epistolary confrontation with people in Galatia and Philippi, who insisted that Gentile Christians conform to the Jewish law, Paul brought into the open and developed an insight that had been present in his thinking from the moment of his conversion: Jesus Christ brought the Mosaic law to an end so that faith in Jesus Christ is alone necessary for salvation. Paul's understanding of justification through

19 Ibid., 21.

20 Beker, *Paul the Apostle*, 1984 ed., xviii; idem, *Heirs of Paul: Their Legacy in the New Testament and the Church Today* (Grand Rapids: Eerdmans, 1991), 27–34.

21 Jürgen Becker, *Paul: Apostle to the Gentiles* (Louisville: Westminster John Knox, 1993).

faith alone developed from three sources: his conversion (in which faith in Christ replaced loyalty to the Torah), his theology of election (in which salvation is a matter of God's sovereign choice), and his theology of the cross (in which we can only offer to God what he has already given to us).

In a similar way, Jerome Murphy-O'Connor tries to show how Paul's theology developed as he responded to the often unexpected problems that he encountered in various churches, both those he had founded (in Galatia, Macedonia, Achaia, and Asia) and others established through other means (in Antioch, Colosse, and Rome).[22] In his interaction with the Thessalonian church, Paul learned that a mission church required continuous attention and that he could not simply preach the gospel, move to another location, and assume that all would be well in the previous church. Moreover, when the Thessalonians misunderstood Paul's eschatological teaching in 1 Thessalonians to mean that Jesus' second coming had already occurred secretly, Paul learned the importance of articulating his meaning carefully to avoid such misunderstandings.[23]

After Paul's defeat in his encounter with Peter in Antioch over the separation of Gentile and Jewish believers into ethnically distinct groups (Gal. 2:11–14), Paul recognized that giving the Mosaic law even the smallest place within a local church was dangerous. Eventually its influence would expand until it had taken over. This incident forced Paul to see with clarity "the fundamental incompatibility of the Law and Christ."[24]

As another example, in dealing with the Corinthians, coauthor Sosthenes probably led him to adopt an unfortunately sarcastic approach to the part of the church that was caught up in a hyper-spirituality (see, e.g., 1 Cor. 3:3–4). This only further alienated the "spirit-people" and opened them up to an otherwise unlikely alliance with the Judaizers. By the time Paul wrote 2 Corinthians 1–9, these Judaizers had arrived in Corinth from Antioch to enforce the separation of observant from nonobservant Christians. Paul used this opportunity to develop a powerful theology of suffering. Rather than viewing suffering as simply an integral part of the human condition (the typical Greco-Roman view), Paul now understood that God could use suffering as a channel of his grace. He came to this insight from dwelling on God's gracious work through the suffering of Christ and believed that this was a useful insight for all believers.

To summarize, advocates of the second approach to Paul's theology attempt to understand it either as the process of the apostle's interaction with his churches or as a body of thought that changed and matured under the pressure of his experiences. They see his letters as evidence of an active apostle, responding to some problems from the basic insight of his conversion, caught off guard by other problems and reacting to them in less thoughtful or even ignoble ways, but eventually able to articulate some

22 Jerome Murphy-O'Connor, *Paul: A Critical Life* (New York: Oxford Univ. Press, 1996).

23 Murphy-O'Connor divides 1 Thessalonians into two separate letters and believes that the problematic statements about Christ's coming (e.g., 1 Thess. 1:9b–10; and 5:2, 9–10) occurred in Paul's second letter.

24 Murphy-O'Connor, *Paul*, 153.

enduring theological insights of value to the church. In the words of Paul Meyer, for Paul, "theology is something one 'does' or produces rather than 'has.'"[25] Or, as many who adopt this approach prefer to put it, Paul did not write theology—he "theologized."[26]

Paul's Theology as Rationalization of Basic Convictions

The third approach is dominated by those who are not impressed with the quality of Paul's theological thinking. For these scholars Paul is not really a theologian but an apostle, motivated to make often inconsistent theological arguments in support of a few basic convictions, convictions that were themselves frequently not compatible with one another. His theological statements are often "contrived rationalizations" of more fundamental convictions that Paul held on the basis of his own experience.[27] E. P. Sanders is perhaps the most influential proponent of this position.[28] Sanders argues that Paul's theological thought was dominated by the dogmatically held convictions that Christ was Lord and Savior of the whole world and that God had called Paul to preach this to the Gentiles. These convictions originated in Paul's personal experience with Christ. He also held other convictions derived from his Jewish heritage, however, and these sometimes conflicted with his more recent beliefs.

For example, Paul's belief that Christ is the Savior of the whole world led to a multitude of difficulties over the nature of human sin and the purpose of the Mosaic law. Paul's prior conviction about Christ drove him to the conclusion that the whole world was under the power of sin, but this conclusion conflicted with his Jewish conviction that sin was not a power independent of God that could, like God, hold people under its sway. Paul's Jewish instincts told him that people were responsible for their own sins. Thus, in Romans, Paul's basic conviction that Christ is the Savior of the whole world leads him to argue implausibly that everyone is mired in transgression against God (Rom. 1–2 and 5). Yet that Paul himself knows this not to be true occasionally peeps through his argument (2:13–14; 5:13–14).[29]

Again, if Christ is the Savior of the whole world and not merely of Israel, then, Paul concluded, Gentiles need not conform to the Mosaic law in order to belong to

25 Paul Meyer, "Pauline Theology: A Proposal for a Pause in Its Pursuit," in *Pauline Theology, Volume IV: Looking Back, Pressing On*, ed. E. Elizabeth Johnson and David M. Hay (SBLSymS 4; Atlanta: Scholars Press, 1997), 140–60, here at 152. In the same volume, see also the essays by Victor Paul Furnish and Paul J. Achtemeier.

26 See, e.g., the chapter "The Theologizer" in Roetzel, *Paul: The Man and the Myth* (Minneapolis: Fortress, 1999), 93–134. The word appears repeatedly in *Pauline Theology*, 4 vols., ed. E. Elizabeth Johnson, David M. Hay, et al. (Minneapolis and Atlanta: Fortress and Scholars Press, 1991–97), and in Dunn's *Theology of Paul* as a way of capturing the historically contingent nature of Paul's theological reflection.

27 See Heikki Räisänen, *Paul and the Law* (WUNT 29; Tübingen: J.C.B. Mohr [Paul Siebeck], 1983), 268–69, who speaks of "the rationalizations Paul contrived in support of his intuition" that came to be seen by Protestantism as "his actual invaluable accomplishment."

28 Sanders summarizes his understanding of Paul's thought in his brief volume *Paul* (Oxford: Oxford Univ. Press, 1991). This work builds on the detailed exegesis of his two other highly influential studies of Paul, *Paul and Palestinian Judaism: A Comparison of Patterns of Religion* (Philadelphia: Fortress, 1977), and *Paul, the Law, and the Jewish People* (Philadelphia: Fortress, 1983). The position that Paul was an inconsistent thinker is not new. For a brief historical overview of this approach to Paul, see T. E. van Spanje, *Inconsistency in Paul? A Critique of the Work of Heikki Räisänen* (WUNT 2.110; Tübingen: J.C.B. Mohr [Paul Siebeck], 1999), 1–2.

29 Sanders, *Paul*, 34–39.

the people of God. But God gave the law, and if he gave it he must have done so for a reason. The varied and incompatible reasons that Paul gives (God gave the law to condemn sinners or to increase sin; sin used the law to increase sin; people have a law within them that causes them to disobey God's law) demonstrate that he had not thought through the issue systematically. The logical incompatibility of these arguments demonstrates that Paul's primary concern was not to provide a theology of the law but to maintain his instinctively held position that universal salvation is available for all through faith in Christ.[30]

Sanders has a certain admiration for the ability of Paul to pose provocative theological questions and is therefore willing to call him "a serious and compelling religious thinker," but Paul had not worked out his theological positions systematically.[31] Far from being a philosophical theologian,

> he was . . . an apostle, an *ad hoc* theologian, a proclaimer, a charismatic who saw visions and spoke in tongues—and a religious genius. Let us not put him entirely into the strait-jacket of logical arrangement.[32]

The results of this approach to Paul's theological thought are so negative that other proponents are understandably hesitant to write comprehensive books on the subject. Most, therefore, have confined themselves to examining a single theme within Paul's letters. Heikki Räisänen finds Paul's arguments on the Mosaic law to be a swirl of incompatibilities. With Sanders, he believes these inconsistencies show that Paul thought backwards from instinctively held positions to a series of incompatible arguments that these positions must be true.

To Räisänen, two convictions created special mischief for Paul's attempts to explain the impact of the coming of Christ on the Mosaic law: his belief that Christ was the exclusive Savior of the world and his belief that legal customs such as dietary observance and circumcision were not required of Gentiles. When these convictions came into conflict with Jewish unbelief and Judaizing troublemakers in his churches, Paul responded by thrashing about for reasons to justify his instinctively held positions. The specious nature of Paul's argumentation on the Jewish law and his incorrect claim that Jews believed salvation came through the law should give pause to anyone who thinks that Paul was "the Christian 'theologian par excellence.'"[33] Paul makes some thought-provoking and insightful statements, but he was

30 Ibid., 91–98.

31 Ibid., 128.

32 Ibid., 127. Cf. the similar approach of John Ashton, *The Religion of Paul the Apostle* (New Haven, Conn.: Yale Univ. Press, 2000), e.g., 121, 124, 126, 238–44, who attempts to understand Paul in what he calls "religious" rather than "theological" terms. What post-Reformation scholars have tended to identify as Paul's theology, Ashton believes, results from the imposition of a preconceived dogmatic outline on Paul's letters. Paul's religion arose not out of theological reflection but out of his mystical experiences, experiences that resemble what anthropologists call shamanism and that may have had roots in Jewish merkabah mysticism. It is not entirely clear, however, why Ashton makes such a watertight division between religious experience and theological reflection, as if Paul had to be either a mystic or a thinker. Nor is it clear that shamanism is a particularly useful heuristic category for the analysis of Paul's religion. The shaman exercises spiritual power through the unique possession of spirit, but Paul believed that the Spirit and its power were available to all believers (e.g., Gal. 3:5; Rom. 8:9). It seems more probable that Paul sometimes provided his congregations with thoughtful theological analysis of religious experience, both his and theirs.

33 Räisänen, *Paul and the Law*, 266–69.

> first and foremost a missionary, a man of practical religion who develops a line of thought to make a practical point, to influence the conduct of his readers; in the next moment he is quite capable of putting forward a statement which logically contradicts the previous one when trying to make a different point or, rather, struggling with a different problem.[34]

Similarly, Terence L. Donaldson has argued that Paul's sometimes confusing statements about the inclusion of Gentiles within the people of God derive from the convergence of two not entirely compatible convictions.[35] Paul inherited from Judaism the conviction that Gentiles must become Jewish proselytes in order to be saved from God's wrath on the final day, but after his conversion the definition of a proselyte changed for him. Now a proselyte was not a Gentile who becomes loyal to the Mosaic law but a Gentile who has faith in Jesus Christ.[36]

Nevertheless, and inconsistently, Paul's letters contain statements that show his failure fully to let go of a fundamental distinction, based on the keeping of the Jewish law, between Jews and Gentiles within the church (Rom. 9:24, 27–29; 11:1–10; 11:25–32; 15:8–9).[37] This situation is evidence that the apostle had not fully worked out the impact of his conversion on his prior Jewish convictions and that his argument for a position must be separated from his reason for holding it.[38]

To summarize, this third group of interpreters remains unconvinced that Paul is a theologian at all. He certainly exercised enormous religious influence in his own time and thereafter, but his persuasive power did not arise from the logical coherence of his thinking. To characterize him as a thinker, especially a systematic thinker, is to misunderstand him.

Paul as a Coherent but Passionate Theologian

How likely is it that Paul's theology developed and changed over the course of his letter-writing career or that he had no carefully worked out theology at all? Both of these approaches seem unlikely to be correct.

First, it is unlikely that Paul's theology developed and changed in major ways during the period covered by his letters. Paul had been a Christian between thirteen and sixteen years by the time that he wrote the first of his extant letters. At the end of this period, he had already gained such stature as a missionary to the Gentiles that the pillar apostles in Jerusalem recognized his work as equal in importance to their own (Gal. 2:9) and he was able publicly to correct Peter's conduct in Antioch (2:11–14). Moreover, Paul corrected Peter on "the truth of the gospel," implying that already at this confrontation in Antioch his basic theological convictions were firmly in place (2:14).

34 Ibid., 267.

35 Terence L. Donaldson, *Paul and the Gentiles: Remapping the Apostle's Convictional World* (Minneapolis: Fortress, 1997).

36 Ibid., 210–11.

37 Ibid., 236–47.

38 Ibid., 293–307; cf. 29–49. Cf. C. J. A. Hickling, "Centre and Periphery in the Thought of Paul" in *Studia Biblica 1978*, vol. 3, ed. E. A. Livingstone (JSNTSup 3; Sheffield: Sheffield Academic Press, 1980), 199–214, who believes that the center of Paul's thought lies at the point where the old age changes to the new age. Inconsistencies in Paul's thought are often the result of Paul's attempt to affirm both the newness of God's action in Christ and God's sovereignty over all that has happened prior to that moment.

This does not itself mean that Paul's theology had reached maturity in every area by the time he wrote his letters. Paul certainly applied his basic theological convictions in new ways to new problems, especially in the letters written during and after his imprisonment in Rome. The basic structure of his theology, however, seems to have been firm by the time he began to write the letters that we have.[39]

Second, it is also unlikely that Paul's statements on various critical theological topics are contradictory. This understanding of Paul seems unlikely to be correct from the start simply because of the profound *intellectual* influence of Paul's letters over the centuries. Augustine of Hippo, Thomas Aquinas, Martin Luther, and Karl Barth have all found in Paul's letters a primary source for their own intellectually rigorous theological systems.[40] It seems unlikely that the thought of someone whom these coherent thinkers considered seminal to the development of their ideas would itself be inconsistent in major areas.

In addition to this consideration, the claim that Paul's theological comments are only rationalizations of instinctively held convictions fails to do justice to the historical specificity in which Paul wrote his letters.[41] For example, Räisänen believes that Paul contradicts himself on the subject of whether Jewish rejection of the gospel hinders or advances the proclamation of the gospel to the Gentiles. In 1 Thessalonians 2:14–16 he says that Jewish rejection of the gospel hinders the Gentiles from hearing the gospel, but then in Romans 11:11–32 he claims that Jewish rejection of the gospel facilitates the Gentiles' acceptance of it.[42]

Close attention to the situation that Paul is addressing in each instance, however, reveals that no contradiction exists. In the 1 Thessalonians passage, the Jews are violently opposing Paul and physically preventing him from preaching the gospel to the Gentiles. Understandably, Paul calls this "hindering" the proclamation of the gospel. In the Romans passage, however, the Jews' are failing to believe the gospel, a failure that means that the gospel can go immediately to the Gentiles. The situations are as different as apples and oranges: Physically hindering the gospel's proclamation is not the same as refusing to believe the gospel, nor is it a necessary result of that refusal. In 1 Thessalonians 2:14–16 and Romans 11:11–32, therefore, Paul responds in two different ways to two different situations and his two responses are not incompatible. As T. E. van Spanje puts it, we do not consider a physician to have a contradictory medical strategy simply because in a single day he or she prescribes medicines with opposite effects. Everything depends on the condition of the patient who receives the medicine.[43]

---

39 Martin Hengel and Anna Maria Schwemer, *Paul between Damascus and Antioch: The Unknown Years* (Louisville: Westminster John Knox, 1997), 11–15. Cf. Beker, *Paul the Apostle*, 32–33, and I . H. Marshall, "Pauline Theology in the Thessalonian Correspondence" in *Paul and Paulinism: Essays in Honour of C. K. Barrett*, ed. M. D. Hooker and S. G. Wilson (London: SPCK, 1982), 173–83, here at 181.

40 See the brief survey of Paul's intellectual influence in F. F. Bruce, *Paul: Apostle of the Heart Set Free* (Grand Rapids: Eerdmans, 1977), 463–74.

41 See especially van Spanje, *Inconsistency in Paul?* 139–248.

42 Heikki Räisänen, "Römer 9–11: Analyse eines geistigen Ringens" in *ANRW* 2.25.4, 2891–939, here at 2925. Spanje summarizes Räisänen's approach to these two passages in *Inconsistency in Paul?* 100.

43 Spanje, *Inconsistency in Paul?* 157, 173–75.

As with the issue of development and change in Paul's basic theological convictions, the question of contradictions in Paul's theology is only answerable after looking at how Paul handles the same issue in different places. The burden of proof, however, lies on those who see contradictions in Paul's theology, and efforts to demonstrate contradictory theological convictions have not been convincing.

This means that of the three ways of approaching Paul's theology surveyed here, the first approach is best. Paul was both a coherent and significant theological thinker, as most of his readers in both ancient and modern times have recognized.

Still, the second and third approaches have a point that needs to be heard, particularly in the form that Beker presents it.[44] Paul's letters were unlike those of his contemporary, Seneca. Seneca was a Roman nobleman with the leisure to reflect on life's problems from the resources provided by Stoic philosophy and to record those reflections in letters to his understudy Lucilius, who had the same social privileges. Paul's calling to be an apostle to the Gentiles made the composition of such letters impossible for him. Instead, he wrote his letters to specific churches for the purpose of dealing with specific pastoral problems, and he did so in the midst of a turbulent missionary career. They were a means of extending his presence and multiplying the effectiveness of his apostolic gift—a means of being two places at once. Through a letter to Rome, for example, he could both exercise his apostolic authority to help heal a church plagued by divisiveness at the same time that he prepared in Corinth to take his collection to the famine-stricken saints in Jerusalem. Paul's letters resemble those of his kindred spirit Ignatius—like Ignatius, Paul wrote on the run and in the service of a commitment compared to which death itself paled in significance.

Paul's letters, therefore, do not easily lend themselves to theoretical analysis. The constraints of his calling meant that although he dealt with complex ideas whose full exposition required subtle and sensitive treatment, Paul had no time to give them this treatment. He often emphasized one aspect of a complex topic for pastoral purposes in one situation, only to focus on a different aspect of the same topic in a different letter.

Sometimes different perspectives on the same topic seem to occur in the same letter. This did not pose as large a problem for the original recipients as it does for us. They did not have the whole Pauline corpus before them, and if they found something difficult in their own letter or group of letters, they could sometimes write Paul a response (as did the Corinthians), appeal for help to a coworker of Paul who was with them (such as Timothy), or ask the letter's courier (such as Tychicus) to explain.[45] Those who do not have this advantage and yet who, along with Christians since at least the second century, consider the Pauline corpus of letters to be the Word of God, have to use a different strategy.

44 See especially Beker's *Paul the Apostle*, 11–19, and his *Heirs of Paul*, 19–34.

45 See, respectively, 1 Cor. 7:1 (cf. 5:9); 4:17; Col. 4:7–9 (cf. Eph. 6:21–22).

THE CENTER OF PAUL'S THEOLOGY

Locating a "center" to Paul's thought is one of the most common strategies among interpreters of Paul for making sense of his theology. These interpreters hope to find a basic concept or set of convictions that can bring some order to the apostle's inherently disorderly correspondence with its diverse theological claims, demands, and arguments.

Some scholars are not happy with the image of Paul's theology as a command center of convictions out of which he dispatches answers to various pastoral problems.[46] Dunn, for example, comments that the imagery of a "center" is too "fixed and inflexible" to do justice to the fluid, dynamic nature of Paul's theology. He prefers the image of "dialogue" to describe the way in which Paul's theology works.[47] Thus, Paul engaged in dialogue with himself over his inherited Jewish convictions, his Damascus road experience with Christ, and the impact of his gospel on his churches. His letters reveal the give and take of this dialogue.[48]

"Coherence" is the right word, says Beker, not "core," "center," or *Mitte* because these images do not capture the pliable nature of Paul's theology as he responds to the pastoral problems that his churches faced. Paul Meyer also believes that the imagery will not work since Paul's theology is never a finished product in his letters but is always in process. Even when Paul speaks of "the truth of the gospel," says Meyer, he speaks of something that "is at risk and has to survive ... or be attained" (Gal. 2:5, 14).[49]

The motive behind these reservations appears to be the desire to avoid imposing an inflexible theological system on Paul's letters that either misrepresents the apostle's real theological emphases or freezes his passionate theological activity into scholastic dogma.[50] It is true that attempts to analyze Paul's theology under the traditional *loci* of systematic theology have often been guilty of one distortion or the other, and sometimes have been guilty of both at the same time.[51] To focus on a single theme can mean excluding other important themes, and the reconfiguration of Paul's theological expressions in systematic categories has often squeezed the energy out of them. As William Wrede said, "This procedure ... forces the material into a mould which does not fit the historical reality and robs it of its living colours."[52]

To find an organizing principle for Paul's theology, however, does not necessarily involve these mistakes and may provide the heuristic key necessary for understanding what Paul means when he speaks in seemingly divergent ways on the same subject.

46 Beker uses and then criticizes this image in *Paul the Apostle*, 18.

47 Cf. Leonhard Goppelt, *Theology of the New Testament*, 2 vols. (Grand Rapids: Eerdmans, 1981–82), 2:62–63, who also speaks of Paul's theology as a "dialogue" and who, like Dunn, recommends arranging Paul's theology according to the pattern of the letter to the Romans.

48 Dunn, *Theology of Paul*, 20, 713; idem, "In Quest of Paul's Theology," 101–2.

49 Meyer, "Pauline Theology," 149. Cf. Roetzel, *Paul*, 93–94, who believes that Paul's theology was emerging as he wrote his letters.

50 Beker, *Heirs of Paul*, 28.

51 See, e.g., the arrangement of Paul's theology in Christian Friedrich Schmid, *Biblical Theology of the New Testament* (Edinburgh: T. & T. Clark, 1882), 430–513. Schmid locates the center of Paul's theology in the concept of "righteousness" and then analyzes Paul's "system of teaching" under a series of logically arranged headings that cover many of the traditional subjects of systematic theology.

52 Wrede, "Task and Methods," 76.

Even scholars who are unhappy with talk of a "center" or "core" for Paul's thought often find themselves eventually speaking of a basic principle around which Paul's theology is organized.[53] Dunn, for example, speaks of Christ as the "fulcrum" on which Paul's theology hinges.[54] Beker describes "the coherent center" of Paul's thought as the apocalyptic triumph of God through the death and resurrection of Christ.[55] Meyer describes the conviction that "controls and shapes the apostle's argument" as the authentication of "the truth of the gospel" and of Paul's apostleship through the resurrection of the crucified Jesus.[56]

The problem, then, lies not with articulating a center but in the misuse of this interpretive strategy. Those who organize Paul's theology around a single central conviction or set of convictions should make sure that their "center" arises from Paul's letters themselves and that they are not imposing it on Paul from the outside. They should also be careful not to allow the center, as important as it is, to become the sole focus in their presentation of Paul's theology.

But what is the center of Paul's theology? Is it the grace of Christ (Thomas Aquinas)?[57] Justification by faith alone apart from human effort (Martin Luther, and many Protestants since)?[58] Christ and what he has done for us (many Roman Catholic interpreters)?[59] Redemptive history (Herman Ridderbos)?[60] Reconciliation (R. P. Martin)?[61] Christ's resurrection (Paul J. Achtemeier)?[62] The apocalyptic triumph of God in the death and resurrection of Christ (J. Christiaan Beker)?[63] God's glory in Christ (Thomas R. Schreiner)?[64] The contribution of Father, Son, and Spirit to salvation (Joseph Plevnik)?[65] Something else?

The confusing variety of proposals probably results from two causes. First, interpreters of Paul who speak of a "center" for his theology have different understandings of how broad or narrow the chosen "center" ought to be. Should the "center" be some

53 This is the chief complaint about Beker's proposal in Paul J. Achtemeier, "Finding the Way to Paul's Theology: A Response to J. Christiaan Beker and J. Paul Sampley" in *Pauline Theology, Volume I: Thessalonians, Philippians, Galatians, Philemon*, ed. Jouette M. Bassler (Minneapolis: Fortress, 1991), 25–36, here at 29.

54 Dunn, *Theology of Paul*, 722–23. Cf. Beker's use of the "fulcrum" image in *Paul*, 1984 ed., xiv.

55 Beker, *Heirs of Paul*, 24–26.

56 Meyer, "Pauline Theology," 157. Cf. Achtemeier, "Finding the Way to Paul's Theology," 31 and 35, and idem, "The Continuing Quest for Coherence in St. Paul: An Experiment in Thought," in *Theology and Ethics in Paul and His Interpreters: Essays in Honor of Victor Paul Furnish*, ed. Eugene H. Lovering and Jerry L. Sumney (Nashville: Abingdon, 1996), 132–45.

57 See the prologue to his *Super epistolas S. Pauli lectura*. I am dependent upon Romano Penna, *Paul the Apostle*, 2 vols. (Collegeville: Liturgical, 1996), 1:10, for this reference.

58 See, e.g., Günther Bornkamm, *Paul* (New York: Harper & Row, 1971), 135.

59 See the surveys in Joseph Plevnik, "The Center of Pauline Theology," *CBQ* 51 (1989): 461–78, here at 462–63, and Veronica Koperski, *What Are They Saying about Paul and the Law?* (New York: Paulist, 2001), 94, 99–103.

60 Ridderbos, *Paul*, 39.

61 Ralph P. Martin, *Reconciliation: A Study of Paul's Theology* (New Foundations Theological Library; Atlanta: John Knox, 1981); idem, "Center of Paul's Theology," in *Dictionary of Paul and His Letters*, ed. Gerald F. Hawthorne, Ralph P. Martin, and Daniel G. Reid (Downers Grove, Ill.: InterVarsity Press, 1993), 92–95, here at 94.

62 Achtemeier, "Finding the Way to Paul's Theology," 35; idem, "Continuing Quest for Coherence," 138–45. Cf. Francis Watson, "The Triune Divine Identity: Reflections on Pauline God-Language, in Disagreement with J. D. G. Dunn," *JSNT* 80 (2000): 99–124.

63 Beker, *Paul the Apostle*, 355–60; idem, *Heirs of Paul*, 25.

64 Schreiner, *Paul*, 20–22. Schreiner believes that the metaphor of a house in which God in Christ forms the foundation communicates the shape of Paul's theology better than the notion of a "center."

65 Plevnik, "Understanding of God," 554–67. Plevnik, ibid., 561, prefers to speak of the "basis" or "foundation" of Paul's theology (cf. 1 Cor. 3:10–11), rather than its "center." Cf. Schreiner, *Paul*, 21–22.

theological principle from which everything else is derived—a sort of theological first cause? Or should we understand the center more narrowly to make it more useful in distinguishing Paul's theology from other Christian theologies? Second, the theological presuppositions of interpreters seem to play a hand in many assessments of Paul's "center." Lutherans tend to see "justification by faith" as the center, Roman Catholics tend to speak of something like "Christocentric soteriology," and Reformed theologians seem to favor "redemptive history."

It is possible, however, to overcome these two problems. First, if articulation of a "center" is to be useful in organizing Paul's occasional and unsystematic theological statements, it seems necessary to focus on a theological theme that is broad enough to account for other important themes, yet not so broad that it becomes useless in articulating the distinctive nature of Paul's theology. If this is right, then "justification by faith," although an important subtheme of Paul's theology, may be too specific to do justice to other elements. By contrast, "Christocentric soteriology" may be too broad to indicate Paul's distinctive concerns since much of the New Testament could fit under this heading.[66]

Second, although presuppositions are unavoidable, it is possible to resist the temptation to vindicate them by implausible readings of the text. One way to avoid the inappropriate incursion of presuppositions into the search for a center to Paul's theology is to insist that our "center" must be something that Paul explicitly says is important to him. Since Paul is a coherent theologian and we have a large corpus of theologically oriented letters from him, it seems reasonable to expect him to provide us with a "center" for his theology that will be useful in filling the gaps between his divergent theological expressions.

God's graciousness toward his weak and sinful creatures fills both these criteria. Although it is an important concern within non-Pauline New Testament texts as well, the extent to which Paul speaks of the gracious nature of God's character is distinctive. It grounds his approach to such widely differing problems as the imposition of the Jewish law on Gentile believers in Galatia (Gal. 1:6; 5:6), a divisive elitism in Corinth that arises from the church's indigenous Greco-Roman culture (1 Cor. 1:26–31), the lagging of the Corinthian contribution to Paul's collection for the poor in Jerusalem (2 Cor. 8:1, 6–7), and, at the end of Paul's life, Timothy's need for encouragement not to be ashamed of the gospel (2 Tim. 1:8–9).[67] It is, moreover, a concept that Paul himself identifies as central to his understanding of the gospel. To set God's grace aside, he says, is to imply that Christ died for nothing (Gal. 3:21).

THE ARRANGEMENT OF A PAULINE THEOLOGY

How is it possible to capture the coherent nature of Paul's theology and, at the same time, to recognize the contingent, epistolary expression of that theology? Most studies

66 See the comments of Martin, "Center," 93, on the breadth of Plevnik's suggested center.

67 God's gracious response to the plight of human sin even stands in the background of 1 Thessalonians, as Stephen Westerholm has shown in *Perspectives Old and New on Paul: The "Lutheran" Paul and His Critics* (Grand Rapids: Eerdmans, 2004), 353–61.

of Paul's theology, as we have already seen, have either arranged Paul's thought according to the loci of classic systematic theology or have used Romans as a "template," whether implicitly or explicitly.[68] These arrangements, particularly when the outline of Romans is used to organize Paul's theology, are both legitimate and necessary. They demonstrate the coherence of Paul's thought and provide a convenient summary of his thoughts on single topics. They are therefore useful in the study of Paul's thought in the same way that a concordance is useful in exegetical study. By looking at his theology in this way, we can easily compare what the apostle says on a subject in different places to see what, if any, underlying conviction supplies the origin for his statements on that subject. This is a significant gain in understanding Paul.

Still, something is lost in this kind of presentation. As we have seen, systematic presentations of Paul's convictions often fail to communicate the passion with which Paul articulated his convictions. If we were only to read the treatments of D. E. H. Whiteley or Herman Ridderbos, we would understand the coherence of Paul's thought, but we would miss the "religious affection" that accompanied his expression of his thought, or as Paul would put it, the "compulsion" behind the pursuit of his calling to be an apostle to the Gentiles (cf. 1 Cor. 9:16).[69] Yet, the passion that motivated Paul to work out his theology in his letters is itself an important element in the understanding of his theology.

Something important can be gained, therefore, by studying the theology of each Pauline letter in its historical setting and then providing a brief analysis of the whole corpus. In this format, each letter itself sets the agenda for the theological discussion, and so the pastoral nature of Paul's theology and the energy with which he pursued its articulation has a better chance of surviving the theological analysis. At the end of the process, we can summarize Paul's thoughts on the issues that arose in the course of his ministry, and the issues that he was particularly passionate about will begin to become clear. That clarity will in turn provide an entrance point for discussing the centrality of God's grace in Paul's theology.

68 Schreiner, *Paul*, is an exception. Although the theme of Romans and the foundation of Paul's theology are identical for Schreiner, he does not use the order of Paul's argument in Romans as the means for organizing his study of Paul's theology.

69 D. E. H. Whiteley, *The Theology of St. Paul* (Oxford: Basil Blackwell, 1964). Dunn, *Theology of Paul*, 2–26, and Schreiner, *Paul*, 37–40, are aware of this problem and in their studies compensate for it better than most systematic treatments of Paul's theology.

Chapter 9

FIRST THESSALONIANS: MAINTAINING FAITH, LOVE, AND HOPE IN THE MIDST OF SUFFERING

When Paul wrote to the Thessalonians, they were suffering for their commitment to the gospel. They had, Paul says, become imitators of Jesus (1 Thess. 1:6), of the Judean churches (2:14), and of Paul himself when they received the word of God amid "severe suffering" (1:6). Their hardship continued, moreover, after their initial encounter with the gospel, and Paul became so concerned about how they were faring in the midst of these difficulties that he gave up Timothy's company and sent his beloved coworker to Thessalonica to learn the state of their faith (3:1–5). Timothy's return with the good news that the Thessalonians still had fond memories of Paul and longed to see him cheered the apostle (3:6), but he wrote as if the tide of suffering was still swirling around them:

> We sent Timothy . . . to strengthen and encourage you in your faith, so that no one would be unsettled by these trials. You know quite well that we were destined for them. In fact, when we were with you, we kept telling you that we would be persecuted. And it turned out that way, as you well know. (3:2–4)

Why had their acceptance of the gospel created such turmoil in their lives? Luke's description of how the gospel first came to Thessalonica and several hints from Paul's letter itself supply a reasonably full answer.[1] Luke says that after Paul and Silas arrived in Thessalonica, Paul, as usual, found the local synagogue.[2] He attempted to show those assembled there that the Scriptures pictured a coming Messiah who would suffer and rise from the dead, and that the Jesus on whom his preaching focused was this Messiah. Some Jews believed the gospel, but Luke implies that most of those who believed came from a group of Gentiles sympathetic to Judaism and who attended the synagogue. Included among the new converts were a number of "prominent women," possibly women who played a leading role in the civic and religious affairs of the city (Acts 17:1–4).[3]

---

1 Here and elsewhere in discussions of the geography, chronology, and social setting of the Pauline letters I have used Acts as an important source of information. This is not the place to argue for the legitimacy of this method, which has been and continues to be controversial. Perhaps it is enough in this context to say that the author of Luke–Acts, where we can check him, lives up to the claims he makes for his work in Luke 1:1–4. He used Q and Mark conservatively in his gospel, and, although he apparently did not know Paul's letters, his account of Paul in Acts contains many, minute correspondences with the Paul of the letters. He seems, moreover, to have been occasionally a companion of Paul (Acts 16:10–17; 20:5–21:18; and 27:1–28:16). On the whole issue, see F. F. Bruce, "Is the Paul of Acts the Real Paul?" *BJRL* 58 (1975–76): 282–305.

2 As Acts 17:14 and 1 Thess. 1:1 hint, Timothy was also with Paul and Silas during this phase of their travels.

3 On the prominence of women in Macedonian society, see Ben Witherington III, *Friendship and Finances in Philippi: The Letter of Paul to the Philippians* (TNTC; Valley Forge, Pa.: Trinity Press International, 1994), 107–8.

Some of the Jews who had rejected Paul's message apparently viewed this response to the gospel as a threat to their own influence with people of power in Thessalonian society.[4] They therefore took steps to discredit Paul. They went to the marketplace, located some bad characters among the unemployed who were idling there, and created a riot.[5] Unable to find Paul and Silas, the mob settled for a man named Jason, who had perhaps been the Christians' host, and some other Christians in his house. Dragging them to the city magistrates, they leveled two charges against the group that they represented: that they were part of a worldwide effort to disrupt the peace and security of Rome and that by speaking of Jesus rather than Caesar as king they were violating Caesar's decrees.

These were serious charges, and although the magistrates' lenient handling of the matter shows that they doubted their validity, the magistrates were concerned enough about Paul and Silas to make Jason and his friends post bail before releasing them (Acts 17:5–9).[6] Perhaps they even received word that Paul's preaching included apocalyptic predictions about the end of the world at the very time that people were speaking of "peace and safety" (1 Thess. 5:3). If so, this news would only have confirmed their fears that this group intended to threaten the much celebrated *pax et securitas* that Caesar Augustus had supposedly bequeathed to the world.[7] Moreover, if some of the Thessalonian Christians were engaging in disruptive behavior—and this is the most likely meaning of 5:14—the attitude of the magistrates toward them may have grown considerably more severe after Paul's departure.[8]

Paul's Gentile converts in Thessalonica would have also faced problems related to their refusal to participate in their city's traditional cults now that they had become Christians. In Paul's eyes, the Thessalonian Christians stood in continuity with ancient Israel, and this meant, above all, that they would worship the God of Abraham, Isaac, and Jacob, and him alone. This was such a critical element in Paul's proclamation of the gospel that he could speak of the Thessalonian Christians' conversion as turning "to God from idols to serve the living and true God" (1:9). God-fearing Gentiles who attended the synagogue on the Sabbath may have continued to participate in the traditional cults of Thessalonica, but those who converted to Christianity could not.[9] At their conversion, they would have been suddenly unwilling to share in the cultic

4 Rainer Riesner, *Paul's Early Period: Chronology, Mission Strategy, Theology* (Grand Rapids: Eerdmans, 1998), 352.

5 On the relationship between the riot and economic conditions in Thessalonica during the early first century, see Robert Maxwell Evans, *Eschatology and Ethics: A Study of Thessalonica and Paul's Letters to the Thessalonians* (Ph.D. diss.: University of Basel, 1967), 29, 43, and 53.

6 On the nature of the charges and the plausibility of Luke's narrative at this point, see Riesner, *Paul's Early Period*, 356–58.

7 W. H. C. Frend, *Martyrdom and Persecution in the Early Church: A Study of the Conflict from the Maccabees to Donatus* (Grand Rapids: Baker, 1981; orig. ed. 1965), 96; Karl P. Donfried, "The Cults of Thessalonica and the Thessalonian Correspondence," *NTS* 31 (1985): 336–56, here at 350; and Holland L. Hendrix, "Thessalonica," *ABD*, 6:523–27, here at 524.

8 On the meaning of *ataktos* in 1 Thess. 5:14, see Ceslas Spicq, *TLNT*, 1:223–26. Paul may have intended his admonition to live quietly (4:11–12; cf. 5:15) to correct misbehavior of the Thessalonian believers toward outsiders. See John M. G. Barclay, "Conflict in Thessalonica," *CBQ* 55 (1993): 512–530, here at 520–21.

9 On the continuing participation of God-fearers in pagan cults, see Paula Fredriksen, "Judaism, the Circumcision of Gentiles, and Apocalyptic Hope: Another Look at Galatians 1 and 2," *JTS* 42 (1991): 532–64, here at 541–43. The point is important because some scholars have, without sufficient foundation, claimed that the picture in Acts of a group of converts drawn principally from the devout Gentiles in attendance at the synagogue stands in conflict with Paul's claim that his converts in Thessalonica turned to Christianity from the worship of idols. See, e.g., Ernest Best, *A Commentary on the First and Second Epistles to the Thessalonians* (HNTC; New York: Harper & Row, 1972), 5–6.

devotion heaped on the goddess Roma, the divinized Julius Caesar, and Caesar's adopted son Augustus in their city. They would have turned their backs on the mystery cults of Serapis, Dionysius, and Cabirus, all well integrated into the social world of Thessalonica.[10] This would have not only brought them under the suspicion of civic authorities, who probably viewed the prosperity of these cults as essential to social stability, but also the scorn of family and friends who may have understood the abandonment of traditional religious practices as a betrayal of blood and soil.[11]

A believing community in such dangerous waters needed Paul's pastoral help. Paul, however, was absent. When the Thessalonian lynch mob arrived at Jason's house, Paul was nowhere to be found (Acts 17:5–6), and after the magistrates had dealt with Jason and his Christian friends, Paul left, under cover of night, for Berea (Acts 17:10). Paul says that he was "torn away" from Thessalonica (1 Thess. 2:17) and wanted often to return, but that Satan hindered him from making another visit (2:18). Unable to go himself, he finally sent Timothy to strengthen the Thessalonians and encourage their faith (3:2). When Paul wrote 1 Thessalonians, probably from Corinth (Acts 17:10, 16; 18:1), Timothy had just returned from Thessalonica, and his news about the fledgling church was good: Their faith in God, love for one another, and affection for Paul were intact. Paul could breath a sigh of relief—his hope and joy, the crown in which he would boast in the presence of God at the coming of Jesus (2:19), was safe. Paul's immense sense of relief was matched by an overwhelming sense of gratitude to God for the Thessalonians' steadfastness in the faith (1:2–5; 2:13–16; 3:9).

Yet, something was amiss. Paul still prayed earnestly that he might be able to visit the Thessalonians, not only because of his affection for them (2:17–20) but also to supply what was "lacking" in their faith (3:10). What were these missing elements? At the letter's beginning Paul thanks God for the Thessalonians' faith, love, and hope (1:3), and yet it is precisely these three elements that Paul encourages in the Thessalonians throughout the letter. Paul tells the Thessalonians that he had sent Timothy to them "to find out about [their] faith" (3:5), and although Timothy has returned with a heartening report (3:6), a note of concern lingers even as Paul recounts the story of Timothy's trip. "When we were with you," he reminds them, "we kept telling you that we would be persecuted" (3:4).

In the same way, Timothy's news included an encouraging report about the Thessalonians' "love" (3:6), and so Paul says that the Thessalonians have no need for him to write them about their love for their brothers and sisters since they have been

10 Much of the evidence for these religious movements in Thessalonica comes from the second and third centuries A.D. Most scholars believe, however, that this evidence reflects conditions current at the time of Paul's mission. See Charles Edson, "Cults of Thessalonica (Macedonia III)," *HTR* 41 (1948): 153–204; Evans, *Eschatology and Ethics*, 63–87; Donfried, "The Cults of Thessalonica," 337–46; Robert Jewett, *The Thessalonian Correspondence: Pauline Rhetoric and Millenarian Piety* (FF; Philadelphia: Fortress, 1986), 126–32; Hendrix, "Thessalonica," 524–25; and Jerome Murphy-O'Connor, *Paul: A Critical Life* (New York: Oxford Univ. Press, 1996), 116.

11 On the probability that the Thessalonian believers suffered persecution because of their abandonment of traditional Greco-Roman religions, see Barclay, "Conflict in Thessalonica," 513–16. For a fascinating and well-informed description of what persecution might have looked like in the lives of a Macedonian Christian family from the service sector, see Peter Oakes, *Philippians: From People to Letter* (SNTSMS 110; Cambridge: Cambridge Univ. Press, 2001), 89–91.

taught by God how to do this (4:9). Nevertheless, he also urges them "to do so more and more" (4:10).

Paul mentions only the Thessalonians' "faith" and "love" in the same breath with the "good news" that has recently come from Timothy, and this may mean that Paul was considerably more troubled by the state of the Thessalonians' "hope." This becomes even more likely when we consider the way in which Paul introduces the topic of "hope" in the letter. In contrast to his statement that the Thessalonians do not need instruction on brotherly love (4:9; cf. 4:1), Paul begins to discuss the believer's hope with the comment, "Brothers, we do not want you to be ignorant about those who fall asleep . . ." (4:13).[12]

So Paul writes a letter that is stamped with both gratitude and concern. The gratitude is unmistakable in this letter's unusually long thanksgiving prayer report. This feature of Paul's letters normally consumes a paragraph or two, but in 1 Thessalonians it stretches over the first half of the letter.[13] Paul probably intended this lengthy description of his thankfulness to function as a commendation of the Thessalonians—he hopes that hearing of "all the joy that we feel before our God because of you" will encourage them (3:9).

At the same time, because he is concerned about the effects of the Thessalonians' suffering and of his own absence on the strength of the Thessalonians' commitment to the gospel, Paul structures the thanksgiving prayer report to encourage the Thessalonians to remain faithful. Indeed, this appears to be the primary purpose of the letter. In the thanksgiving section Paul speaks of how, when he was among them, he encouraged them as a father exhorts his children. He also describes how he sent Timothy to encourage them and how Timothy's report encouraged him. In chapters 4 and 5 Paul speaks five times of his own encouragement of the Thessalonians or of their encouragement of one another. This represents the highest concentration of the technical vocabulary for encouragement or exhortation in Paul's letters.[14]

Paul's effort to encourage the Thessalonians to remain faithful in the face of hardship takes four forms. First, he stresses their membership in a new society. Second, he assures them of the authenticity of their faith. Third, he encourages them to retain their sanctity. Fourth, he urges them to appreciate the implications of the Christian's hope.

12 Karl P. Donfried, "The Theology of 1 Thessalonians," in *The Theology of the Shorter Pauline Letters*, ed. Karl P. Donfried and I. Howard Marshall (New Testament Theology; Cambridge: Cambridge Univ. Press, 1993), 20–21.

13 The thanksgiving prayer report stretches from 1:2 to 3:13. This is clear from the appearance of expressions of thanks in 1:2–5; 2:13–16; and 3:9, and from the future-oriented petition at the end of the section (3:10–13), a feature typical of Pauline thanksgivings (cf. Rom. 1:8–10; Phil. 1:3–7; Philem. 4–6). See Peter Thomas O'Brien, *Introductory Thanksgivings in the Letters of Paul* (NovTestSupp 49; Leiden: Brill, 1977), 143–46.

14 *Parakaleō* ("encourage, exhort") appears eight times, *erōtaō* ("ask") twice, *noutheteō* ("admonish"), and *paramytheomai* ("console") twice. Exhortation was a component of consolation in much philosophically oriented Greco-Roman literature. On this see Abraham J. Malherbe, "Exhortation in First Thessalonians," *NovT* 25 (1983): 238–56, here at 254–56.

THE PRIVILEGE OF THE THESSALONIANS' SOCIAL STANDING

When the Thessalonians abandoned their idols to worship the living and true God (1:9), they stepped into the margins of their society and outside the boundaries of their families. They would have refused to participate in their city's official cults—the worship of the Julio-Claudian emperors and the Cabirii—and to carry out their family's customary acts of devotion to various deities. All of this would have made them outsiders to family and former friends.[15] This element of their suffering may explain the unusual prominence in this letter of the language of the family, of God's electing love, and of the believer's status as a member of the eschatologically restored people of God.

First Thessalonians contains the highest concentration of metaphorical references to fellow Christians as "brothers" (*adelphoi*) in the Pauline letters.[16] Whether the roots of Paul's figurative use of this term lay in the Bible (where it refers to the close alliance of God's people) or in the Greco-Roman custom of referring to a religious group with fraternal language, the frequency of its occurrence in 1 Thessalonians shows that he is not merely following convention.[17] He intends to stress the familial affection of Christians for one another.

This understanding of the language receives confirmation from Paul's use of familial metaphors and terms of affection elsewhere in the letter. He compares his demeanor during his stay among the Thessalonians to that of an infant, to that of a mother cherishing her own children, and to that of a father who exhorts, consoles, and implores his children (2:7, 11–12).[18] He reminds the Thessalonians that "we loved you so much that we were delighted to share with you not only the gospel of God but our lives as well, because you had become so dear to us" (2:8). He describes his departure from Thessalonica as being "torn away from you for a short time (in person, not in thought)" and says to the Thessalonians that "out of our intense longing we made every effort to see you" (2:17). They are his hope, joy (2x), crown of boasting, and glory (2:19–20). His concern about them during his separation from them reaches such intensity that "he could stand it no longer" (3:1, 5), and news of their spiritual well-being causes life to spring up again in the apostle (3:8). All of this seems to be saying that although their society and their families may have rejected them, they have nevertheless entered a new society where the bonds are stronger than ever.[19]

15 Cf. Wayne A. Meeks, *The Moral World of the First Christians* (LEC; Philadelphia: Westminster, 1986), 125–26, and on the importance of religion to Greek and Roman households, see John M. G. Barclay, "The Family as the Bearer of Religion in Judaism and Early Christianity" in *Constructing Early Christian Families: Family as Social Reality and Metaphor*, ed. Halvor Moxnes (London: Routledge, 1997), 66–80, here at 67–68.

16 The only letter that uses the term more often is 1 Corinthians and, as Abraham J. Malherbe, *Paul and the Thessalonians: The Philosophic Tradition of Pastoral Care* (Philadelphia: Fortress, 1987), 48, points out, it is three times longer than 1 Thessalonians.

17 For the probable biblical roots of the term's use in early Christianity, see, e.g., the quotation of Deut. 18:15 and 18 in Acts 3:22 and the discussion by Hans von Soden, "ἀδελφός (κτλ)," *TDNT*, 1:144–46. For the use of the term in papyri from the second century B.C. to refer to members of religious associations, see MM, 9.

18 Despite the enormous popularity of the reading "gentle" (*ēpioi*) for "infants" (*nēpioi*) in 2:7, the preferable reading is "infants." See Jeffrey A. D. Weima, "'But We Became Infants among You': The Case of ΝΗΠΙΟΙ in 1 Thess 2.7," *NTS* 46 (2000): 547–64 and the comments of John L. White, *The Apostle of God: Paul and the Promise of Abraham* (Peabody, Mass.: Hendrickson, 1999), 19–21.

19 Cf. Malherbe, *Thessalonians*, 36–52. Murphy-O'Connor,

Paul also sprinkles his letter with descriptions of the Thessalonian community that echo the biblical descriptions of God's affection for his people Israel.[20] Like ancient Israel, they are "the assembly of the Lord" (1 Thess. 1:1; cf. Deut. 23:1–8, LXX). God loves them and has chosen them, just as he loved and chose Israel (Deut. 7:6–8; 14:2). He has called and chosen the Thessalonian believers to be his people (1 Thess. 2:12; 4:7; 5:24), just as he called and chose Israel (Isa. 41:8–9; 42:6; 48:12). Paul probably uses this language intentionally in order to say that the Thessalonians may be outcasts from the society of "Gentiles who do not know God," but they have joined that great company of God's specially chosen, beloved, and called people, whose story is told in the Bible and who serve "the living and true God."[21] The Thessalonians, therefore, are not simply part of a new family and society, but they belong to God's specially chosen people.

THE AUTHENTICITY OF THE THESSALONIANS' FAITH

Paul also encourages the Thessalonians in the midst of their suffering for the faith by reminding them of the authenticity of their faith. Frequently in the letter he implies that the Thessalonians already know what he is telling them (1:5; 2:2, 5, 11; 3:3–4; 4:2; 5:1–2) or that they are already putting his admonitions into practice (4:1, 9–10). This has the effect not only of commending the Thessalonians and therefore of creating an atmosphere of friendliness in which his exhortations are more likely to find a receptive hearing, but also of assuring them that their response to the gospel was genuine—of reminding them that they are presently demonstrating both the knowledge and the practice that are characteristic of authentic Christian faith.

This theme also emerges in two other ways: It is present when Paul mentions his gratitude to God for the authenticity of the Thessalonians' commitment to the gospel, and it is present in Paul's defense of his own sincerity as the bearer of the gospel to the Thessalonians. Both elements figure prominently in the thanksgiving section of the letter (1:2–3:13), the second element blending almost imperceptibly with the first at the beginning of the section only to take over the section after a few sentences. In 1:4 Paul says that he is thankful to God for the Thessalonians because he knows that God has chosen them. In 1:5 he states the reason for his certainty that they belong to God's people. He is certain of God's choice of them because he and his coworkers proclaimed the gospel among the Thessalonians in a way that showed, beyond dispute, that God stood behind their message: They preached not merely with word but in power—both in the Holy Spirit and in full conviction.

Paul, 119–20, comments sensibly that Paul, having experienced conversion himself, would have understood the need among the Thessalonians to feel included in a new family.

20 On the prominence of the notion of election in 1 Thessalonians, see I. H. Marshall, "Election and Calling to Salvation in 1 and 2 Thessalonians," in *The Thessalonian Correspondence*, ed. Raymond F. Collins (BETL 87; Leuven: Leuven Univ. Press, 1990), 259–76; Donfried, "Theology of 1 Thessalonians," 28–30; and White, *Apostle of God*, 22.

21 Would the formerly idol-worshiping Gentiles in Thessalonica have understood such subtleties? Paul's original proclamation of the gospel to them would probably have included instruction on the role of believing Gentiles in the eschatological restoration of Israel. See N. T. Wright, *What Saint Paul Really Said: Was Paul of Tarsus the Real Founder of Christianity?* (Grand Rapids: Eerdmans, 1997), 80–83.

Paul will pick up the theme of his own authenticity as the messenger of the gospel again in 2:1–12 and 2:17–3:13, but for the moment he shifts his focus away from his own genuineness and that of his coworkers to the effect of God's work on the Thessalonians. From the first, the Thessalonians' faith in the gospel has been coupled with faithfulness to the gospel in the face of affliction. In 1:6 Paul says that by their willingness to suffer for their convictions, they have taken their place in a distinguished line of authentic believers—Paul, his coworkers, and Jesus himself, all of whom suffered for their faithfulness to God. Moreover, like them, the Thessalonians have provided an example for others to follow (1:7). Already believers not only in Macedonia and Achaia, but everywhere, have heard of the Thessalonians' conversion (1:9–10) and continued faithfulness (1:8).

Paul returns to this theme in his second thanksgiving prayer report in 2:13–16. Here too he describes the evidence that God is at work among the Thessalonian believers as their initial acceptance of the authenticity of Paul's message (2:13) and their imitation of the faithful suffering of other believers show. He explicitly compares the Thessalonians' faithfulness amid persecution to the faithfulness of Jewish Christians in Judea despite persecution from unbelieving Jews (2:14). In addition, his parenthetical comment that the Jews also killed the Lord Jesus (2:15a), drove Paul out of Judea (2:15b), and have continued their attempts to frustrate his proclamation of the gospel to the Gentiles (2:16a) serves as an implicit reminder that the Thessalonians' faithfulness in the midst of suffering is a characteristic of other believers and therefore a sign of the authenticity of their faith.

Paul not only wants to assure the Thessalonians that their conduct demonstrates the authenticity of their faith but also that his conduct when among them was above reproach and therefore deserves the confidence that the Thessalonians placed in it. Paul touches on this point in 1:5 and 1:9, but turns to it in earnest in 2:1–12 and in 2:17–3:13. Paul's motives for mounting this defense of his conduct have created a minor dust storm of scholarly controversy. Had critics of Paul arisen within the church to charge him with ulterior motives?[22] Were the unbelieving persecutors of the Thessalonian church accusing Paul of insincerity?[23] Was Paul only observing philosophical convention in distinguishing himself from fraudulent philosophers and, in the process, providing an example for the Thessalonians to follow?[24]

With the scanty information available to us from Paul's letter, it is impossible to decide exactly what prompts Paul's defense, but he needs only a little empathy with the Thessalonians' situation to know that the conditions are ideal for the growth of doubts about his own integrity and the authenticity of his message.[25] They are under public pressure to recant their new convictions, and Paul was absent at a time when they desperately needed his pastoral oversight.

22 Donfried, "Cults of Thessalonica," 350–51. Cf. Jewett, *Thessalonian Correspondence*, 169, and Walter Schmithals, *Paul and the Gnostics* (Nashville: Abingdon, 1972), 135–76.

23 Jeffrey A. D. Weima, "An Apology for the Apologetic Function of 1 Thessalonians 2.1–12," *JSNT* 68 (1997): 73–99.

24 See Abraham J. Malherbe, "'Gentle as a Nurse': The Cynic Background to 1 Thess ii," *NovT* 12 (1970): 203–17; *Paul and the Thessalonians*, 74–75. Cf. Barclay, "Conflict in Thessalonica," 520–24, who thinks that Paul wants to temper the Thessalonian believers' socially disruptive excesses by reminding them that his frankness was mixed with gentleness.

25 Timothy's report of the Thessalonians' "pleasant memories"

Most significant of all, orators and preachers were a common sight in major urban centers like Thessalonica, and many of them were frauds. Under the emperor Claudius, Sophistic rhetoric was rising to renewed heights, and the "entrance" (*eisodos*) of professional orators into a city as important as Thessalonica would have been a common and widely publicized occurrence. These orators made a living from attracting groups of paying disciples who wanted to imitate their skill in public speaking and who valued their advice on how to climb the ladder of civic life. The "entrance" of a prominent Sophist into a city as large as Thessalonica and the occasion of his first speech would be a widely advertised public occasion. The reception of this initial speech often decided the success or failure of the orator in that location.[26]

Itinerant Cynic philosophers, barking their criticisms of humanity, would also have been a familiar sight in Thessalonian markets and streets.[27] Ostensibly, anyway, Cynic philosophers preached not for monetary gain or to hear their audiences applaud their rhetorical ability but to convince those willing to listen of the wretchedness of the unreflective life and of the need to become independent from the cares of the world.[28] Some taught their austere philosophy under the roofs of wealthy patrons who provided room, board, and social standing. Others, hardly distinguishable from the Sophists, rented lecture halls and laid their message before people whose voluntary presence meant that the philosopher had a friendly audience.[29] But many preached their negative assessment of the lot of humanity with "frankness" (*parrēsia*) to the masses who daily passed through the marketplaces or occasionally swarmed the city for some public festival. The harsh message of these Cynics was often repaid with the unadulterated scorn of their hearers.[30]

Both Sophists and Cynic preachers spent much of their time appearing in public, and both had a distinctive way of dressing and talking. Inevitably the external message of their speech sometimes failed to match the private conduct of their lives. Sophists were sometimes accused of hypocrisy—of touting the virtues only to win public approval and earn a wage rather than from any desire to live by what they taught.[31] Cynics too were sometimes accused of preaching the harsh life of a philosopher to others and putting on a show of it in public, but in private living as indulgently as anyone else.[32] Because of their itinerant life, both Sophists and Cynics could sometimes be accused of staying in a place only as long as their public approval lasted, but at the first sign of having to endure hardship, fleeing for greener pastures.[33]

of Paul and their longing to see him (3:6) leave little room for opposition to Paul among the Thessalonian believers.

26 Bruce W. Winter, "The Entries and Ethics of Orators and Paul (1 Thessalonians 2:1–12)," *TynBul* 44 (1993):55–74. On Sophists generally, see G. W. Bowersock, *Greek Sophists in the Roman Empire* (Oxford: Oxford Univ. Press, 1969), and on Sophists in first-century Corinth, see Bruce W. Winter, *Philo and Paul among the Sophists* (SNTSMS 96; Cambridge: Cambridge Univ. Press, 1997), 116–44.

27 "Every city is filled with such upstarts," Lucian, *Fug.* 16; "It would be easier for a man to fall in a boat without hitting a plank than for your eye to miss a philosopher wherever it looks," Lucian, *Bis Acc.* 6. See Malherbe, "'Gentle as a Nurse,'" 206, n. 5, and *Paul and the Thessalonians*, 19.

28 See, e.g., Edward O'Neil, ed., *Teles (The Cynic Teacher)* (SBLTT 11; Greco-Roman Religion Series 3; Missoula, Mont.: Scholars Press, 1977).

29 See the summary of Dio Chrysostom's description of Cynic philosophers in Malherbe, "'Gentle as a Nurse,'" 204–14.

30 As in, e.g., Lucian, *Vit. Auct.* 10.

31 See Winter, "Entries and Ethics," 63.

32 See Lucian, *Peregr.* 19 and *Fug.* 19.

33 On the Sophists, see Winter, "Entries and Ethics," 72; on the Cynics, see Malherbe, "'Gentle as a Nurse,'" 208–14.

In addition, the appearance and distinctive themes of Cynic preaching were easily aped and produced a number of frauds. Lucian's dialogue *The Runaways* focuses on the tendency of common laborers to leave their workbenches and to pursue the luxury of life as a fake philosopher. According to Lucian, who is probably exaggerating, anyone could gain a following by donning the short skirt, wallet, and staff of the Cynic philosopher and spouting out a torrent of abusive language about humanity in general. With a group of disciples in place, it was then a short step to a life of private luxury—a purse full of gold, a table full of delicacies, and a promiscuous sex life.[34]

In this social context we should not be surprised that Paul wants to assure the persecuted Thessalonians of the genuineness of their faith by distinguishing his own preaching and ministry from the insincerity that so often marked those engaged in the public discourse of their culture. Paul had, after all, preached a harsh message of the future outpouring of God's wrath on unbelieving humanity at the *parousia* of Jesus (1:10), and he had left Thessalonica hurriedly in the midst of intense opposition (Acts 17:10; 1 Thess. 2:17). The Thessalonians are standing firm under the public pressure that they are still enduring (1 Thess. 3:6), but Paul wants to assure them—against any doubts that might arise—of the sincerity of his preaching and the integrity of his ministry.

In 1:5, 1:9–10, 2:1–12, and 2:17–3:13, therefore, Paul reminds the Thessalonians that at his "entrance" (*eisodos*) to their city, his preaching was not an empty show of words but arose out of deep conviction and the work of the Holy Spirit (1:5; 2:1).[35] Thus, it produced the Thessalonians' conversion from the worship of idols to the worship of the living God, ensuring their rescue from God's wrath (1:9–10). The motive of his preaching was not avarice, immorality (*akatharsia*), or public approval but the desire to share with the Thessalonians both the gospel of God and his own life as well (2:3–8, 10). The sincerity of his effort was plain in his willingness to endure opposition while among them and to labor hard and long while with them in order not to pose a financial burden to anyone (2:2, 6–10). His preaching was characterized by frankness (*eparrēsiasametha . . . lalēsai*, 2:2) but he never stooped to abuse. Instead, he was like a babe in their midst, like a nursing mother affectionately caring for her children, or like a father encouraging and exhorting his own (2:7, 11–12).

In 2:17 Paul turns from the past to the present and the future, assuring the Thessalonians of his distress at being "torn away" from them (2:17–20) and of his longing to see them again (3:10–11), a longing partially satisfied by Timothy's mission and subsequent report (3:1–9). If doubts should arise that Paul only preached the gospel, like Lucian's pseudo-Cynics, to "sheer the sheep," or if someone should think to compare Paul's coming to Thessalonica with the entrance of an insincere Sophist to their city, they should reflect on the apostle's conduct while with them, of the recent visit of Timothy, and of Paul's earnest prayer that God will prosper his way to them again.[36]

34 Lucian, *Fug.* 12–21.
35 See Winter, "Entries and Ethics," 55–74.
36 For Lucian's reference to Cynics who "shear the sheep," see *Fug.* 14.

In summary, Paul's lengthy thanksgiving prayer, with its digressions on the nature of his ministry among the Thessalonians and his longing for them, is probably intended to bolster the confidence of the Thessalonians, in the midst of their suffering, that their faith is genuine. He wants to assure them that by means of his preaching, and the preaching of his coworkers, they have experienced the transforming work of the Holy Spirit. The genuineness of their conversion is being proved in the fires of affliction. They are following the example of Jesus, the Jewish church, Paul, and Paul's coworkers.

The authenticity of the message that Paul preached and that the Thessalonians believed, moreover, is revealed in the differences between Paul and insincere Sophists on one hand and fraudulent Cynics on the other. Paul tempers his frankness with gentleness, refuses to pose a financial hardship on any Thessalonian host, and although forced to leave them in the midst of their hardship, longs to see them again. They can rest assured that the word Paul preached to them, and which they accepted, is not a human word but truly the word of God (2:13).

THE CHARACTER OF THE THESSALONIANS' LOVE

In 4:9–10 Paul commends the Thessalonians for the love they have shown to one another. The desire to show such love is not something that Paul can teach them, for, in fulfillment of Jeremiah 31:31–34, they are the eschatologically restored people of God on whose hearts God himself has written his law. Thus, Paul says, "about brotherly love we do not need to write to you, for you yourselves have been taught by God to love each other" (1 Thess. 4:9). God's transforming work has only begun, however, and they still need Paul's encouragement to show their love "more and more" (4:10). In 4:1–12, therefore, Paul reminds the Thessalonians of the traditional ethical teaching that he and his coworkers handed down to them. Two topics are particularly pressing: sexual relationships and daily labor.

First, Paul stresses in this letter the need for sexual propriety (4:1–8). The world in which the Thessalonian believers lived was replete with sexually suggestive activity and imagery. The worship of Dionysius was especially popular, and the phallus was one of his primary symbols. Images of the phallus were carried in a basket on the heads of the god's devotees at festivals, and many people decorated the grave markers of their loved ones with a phallic symbol. This symbol probably signified life and expressed the hope that those who died would enjoy the happy afterlife that the Dionysiac mystery cult promised to its adherents. But Dionysius was also the god of wine, fertility, and raw, animal maleness. As the frescoes in the Villa of the Mysteries at Pompey demonstrate, the phallus suggested more to the followers of the god than life after death.[37]

37 See Donfried, "Cults of Thessalonica," 337–38, and Marvin W. Meyer, "Mystery Religions," *ABD*, 4:941–45, here at 942–43. For a description of the Pompey frieze and a review of the controversy over its interpretation, see Mary Beard, John North, and Simon Price, *Religions of Rome*, 2 vols. (Cambridge: Cambridge Univ. Press, 1998), 1:161–63.

The Cabirus cult was also popular in Thessalonica, and although few details are available about its practices and beliefs, it too stressed the phallus and promised fertility.[38] In addition, Cynic philosophers sometimes demonstrated their independence from social convention by engaging in sexual activity in public, and, as we have already seen, the pseudo-philosophers lampooned by Lucian were known for their sexual promiscuity in private.[39]

Why should the Thessalonians not simply participate in the sexual mores of their culture? As we have already seen, Paul considers the Thessalonian Christians to be part of the eschatologically restored people of God, and since God mandated in the Mosaic law that his people were to distinguish themselves from the surrounding nations by the character of their sexual relationships, Paul believes that the Thessalonians must stand apart from the world around them in their sexual behavior also. Their "sanctification," Paul says, involves avoiding sexual immorality (4:3). It means gaining control over one's sexual urges "in a way that is holy and honorable, not in passionate lust like the heathen, who do not know God" (4:4–5).[40] Echoing the passages in Leviticus on sexual conduct (Lev. 18:1–30; cf. Ezek. 22:9b–11) and in Ezekiel that describe a time when God would cleanse the impurities of his people (Ezek. 11:19; 36:27; 37:14), Paul says that God did not call the Thessalonian believers to "impurity" but to "a holy life" and that the person who rejects this rejects God, "who gives you his Holy Spirit" (4:7–8).[41]

Although most of the Thessalonian Christians are not Jews (1:9–10), Paul believes that they are part of the eschatologically restored people of God. They have turned from idols to serve God and to await the coming of his Son, and this is enough in Paul's eyes to place them within the circle of God's people. Once there, however, he expects them to demonstrate by the way they live that they are different from "the heathen, who do not know God." In the culture of Thessalonica, this means they must stand apart from their society in their approach to sex and control their sexual urges along lines that Paul has already communicated to them (4:2, 6).

Second, Paul admonishes the Thessalonians to aspire to a "quiet life," to work with their hands, to mind their own business, and not to be dependent on anyone else (4:11–12). It is difficult to know exactly what problem lies beneath these admonitions, but the absence of an expression such as "as in fact you are living" probably means that Paul is responding to a real problem in the community and not simply underlining an important principle (cf. 4:1, 9–10). If we link these admonitions

38 Donfried, "Cults of Thessalonica," 338–39.

39 See Lucian, *Fug.* 17, and Ronald F. Hock, "Cynics," *ABD*, 1:1221–26, here at 1223.

40 The term commonly translated "wife" or "body" in 4:4 is actually "vessel" (*skeuos*). It probably refers to the male sexual organ. See Aelianus, *NA* 17.11; 1 Sam. 21:4–6; 4Q416, frag. 1, col. 4; and the discussion in J. Whitton, "A Neglected Meaning for *skeuos* in 1 Thessalonians 4.4," *NTS* 28 (1982): 142–43; Donfried, "Cults of Thessalonica," 342; Torleif Elgvin, "'To Master His Own Vessel': 1 Thess 4.4 in Light of New Qumran Evidence," *NTS* 43 (1997): 604–19; and Jay E. Smith, "Another Look at 4Q416 2 ii.21: A Critical Parallel to First Thessalonians 4:4," *CBQ* 63 (2001): 499–504.

41 See Hans Hübner, *Biblische Theologie des Neuen Testaments* (Göttingen: Vandenhoeck and Ruprecht, 1993), 2:48–50; Frank Thielman, *Paul and the Law: A Contextual Approach* (Downers Grove, Ill.: InterVarsity Press, 1994), 75–77; and Jeffrey A. D. Weima, "'How You Must Walk to Please God': Holiness and Discipleship in 1 Thessalonians," in *Patterns of Discipleship in the New Testament*, ed. Richard N. Longenecker (Grand Rapids: Eerdmans, 1996), 98–119, here at 99–103.

with Paul's later command to "warn those who are disruptive [*ataktous*]" (5:14), then it is clear that something has happened in the Thessalonian church that has added unnecessary fuel to the already burning fires of persecution.

Since the two problems of disruptive behavior and erroneous eschatological views dominate 2 Thessalonians, the disruptive behavior within the church is probably linked in some way with the eschatological fervor of the Thessalonians. Perhaps, as one scholar suggests, some of the Thessalonians left behind their occupations to preach a harsh message of God's imminent wrath on their idolatrous society.[42] Loud, rough, and direct speech coupled with a tendency to sponge off the society they so quickly criticized also characterized Cynic philosophers and made them the targets of ridicule.[43]

If the Thessalonians have fallen into this trap, Paul is concerned that they not make their own suffering worse and give the gospel a bad reputation. He advises them "to work with your own hands" and "not be dependent upon anybody" (4:11–12), and he probably intends this advice to echo his apology for his ministry while in their midst. His ministry provided an example for them: Although he had the right to be a financial burden to them, since God himself had assigned him his apostolic work, he did not take advantage of this right and "worked night and day" while he preached the gospel to them (2:6b, 9).

In summary, the Thessalonians are to stand apart from their society in their sexual conduct and love one another. The ground for both ethical characteristics is their status as a part of the eschatologically restored people of God predicted by the prophets. They are not, however, to live in a way that brings the unnecessary censure of society on them. They must behave with decorum toward those outside at the same time that they regard them as outsiders from whom God—because he has chosen the Thessalonian Christians to be part of his people—has set them apart. They are, in other words, to walk a sometimes fine line between sanctity and eccentricity.

THE IMPLICATIONS OF THE THESSALONIANS' ESCHATOLOGICAL HOPE

Both Paul's initial preaching (1:9–10) and his ongoing teaching (5:1–3) in Thessalonica emphasized the coming of God through his agent Jesus to judge the wicked and to save his people. When he and his coworkers arrived in Thessalonica, Paul preached that God would pour out his wrath on idolatrous and immoral Gentiles at Jesus' coming (1:9; 4:6), but that Gentiles found serving the living and true God and awaiting the coming of his Son Jesus would escape God's wrath (1:10; 5:9).[44] During his short stay in the city, Paul encouraged those who responded to this message "to live lives worthy of God, who calls you into his kingdom and glory" (2:12). Even as he writes 1 Thessalonians several months later, he continues to pray that they will be blameless and holy "in the presence of our God and Father when our Lord Jesus comes

42 Barclay, "Conflict in Thessalonica," 520–25.

43 Ibid., 523.

44 Cf. Rom. 1:18–32. Paul probably inherited from Judaism the belief that, apart from their repentance, idolatrous and immoral Gentiles would fall under the condemning wrath of God. See Terence L. Donaldson, *Paul and the Gentiles: Remapping the Apostle's Convictional World* (Minneapolis: Fortress, 1997), 295–96.

with all his holy ones" (3:13; 5:23). Paul has a significant investment in the Thessalonians, and in view of the certainty of Jesus' coming, he is anxious for them to see their commitment to the gospel through to the end:

> For what is our hope, our joy, or the crown in which we will glory in the presence of our Lord Jesus when he comes? Is it not you? Indeed, you are our glory and joy. (2:19–20)

Paul had taught the Thessalonians that the day of the Lord would come unexpectedly "like a thief in the night" or "as labor pains on a pregnant woman" (5:2–3)—and that they should therefore live their lives "in the presence of our God," as if the final day were arriving soon.[45] The notion that they might be alive at the coming of the Lord had turned for the Thessalonians, however, from a possibility into a certainty and then into a disappointment. Some members of the believing community had died. Had they missed out on participation in the coming kingdom? Timothy apparently has brought this question back to Paul.[46] The "faith" and "love" of the Thessalonians are both on the right track, he may have reported, but their understanding of the Christian's "hope" has derailed (3:6; 4:13).[47]

Paul attempts to address their question in 4:13–18, and then, in 5:1–11 he urges them to continue to look for the coming of Jesus. The chief point of both sections is the encouragement of the Thessalonians (4:18; 5:11). He wants to reassure them that the whole community, including those who have died, must be prepared for the day of the Lord whenever it comes, and that when that day comes God will triumph over their persecutors.

In 4:13–18 Paul assures the Thessalonians that those among their number who have died since believing the gospel will not be left out of the events surrounding the Lord's coming simply because they have died. Both the Christian conviction that Jesus died and rose again and "the Lord's own word" demonstrate that dead believers will be at no disadvantage when the Lord comes.[48] Jesus' resurrection means that believers too will be raised from death at the coming of Jesus and that Jesus will bring those resurrected into the presence of God (4:14, 16; cf. 2 Cor. 4:14).[49] Jesus' triumph over death lends such certainty to the resurrection of believers that Paul can speak of death as "sleep" and can say that the Thessalonians should not grieve over their dead like those who have no hope (1 Thess. 4:13). Paul is aware of a word of

---

45 See 2:19; 3:13. Cf. 1:3 and 3:9. Was Paul himself surprised at the delay of the Parousia? The equanimity with which he handles the problem of the deaths of Thessalonian believers prior to the Lord's coming shows that he was not. See Ben Witherington III, *Jesus, Paul and the End of the World: A Comparative Study in New Testament Eschatology* (Downers Grove, Ill.: InterVarsity Press, 1992), 25. Cf. Dunn, *Theology of Paul*, 310–13.

46 Paul introduces each of three subjects in 4:9, 13; and 5:1 with the phrase *peri de* ("now concerning"). This was a conventional way of introducing a topic of common concern to a letter's author and recipient (cf. 1 Cor. 7:1, 25; 8:1; 12:1; 16:1, 12). See Margaret M. Mitchell, "Concerning ΠΕΡΙ ΔΕ in 1 Corinthians," *NovT* 31 (1989): 229–56. In 1 Thess. 4:9–12, 13–18, and 5:1–11, Paul may be raising each topic himself, or he may be responding to concerns that the Thessalonians' communicated to him through Timothy.

47 Donfried, "The Theology of 1 Thessalonians," 20–21.

48 On the structure of 4:13–18, see Joseph Plevnik, *Paul and the Parousia: An Exegetical and Theological Investigation* (Peabody, Mass.: Hendrickson, 1997), 68.

49 Ibid., 74.

the Lord, moreover, that both the resurrected dead and those who are alive at the time of the Lord's coming will together meet the Lord in the air (4:17). God will bring the righteous—both the deceased and those alive at Jesus' coming—bodily to heaven like Enoch, Elijah, and Jesus himself.[50]

This information alone answers the Thessalonians' question about their deceased fellow believers, but Paul gives other details of the Lord's coming that stress God's victory over forces opposed to his people (4:16). The "shout" (*keleusma*) that accompanies the descent of the Lord from heaven is reminiscent of God's "rebuke" (*gāᶜar*) of the enemies of his people when he comes to deliver them in the Old Testament.[51] The "voice of the archangel," heard at the Lord's descent, similarly recalls Old Testament depictions of God, accompanied by his angels, fighting on behalf of his people (e.g., Zech. 14:1–5).[52] The sounding of God's trumpet is also reminiscent of Old Testament references to the trumpet that calls God's people into battle against their enemies, a trumpet that on the day of the Lord, the Lord himself will sound (e.g., Zech. 9:14).[53] By using this imagery, Paul probably hopes to encourage the Thessalonians as they withstand persecution that the day of the Lord will be a time of judgment for their persecutors and of rescue for the Thessalonian believers themselves.

In 5:1–11 Paul turns to the question of when the Lord will return. Although the precise problem that has prompted Paul to address this question is not clear, the purpose of his response is to encourage the Thessalonian Christians (5:11).[54] At first, he stresses the unexpected nature of the day's coming (5:1–3); then, shifting the emphasis slightly, he assures them that, as "sons of light" and "sons of the day," they are prepared for its arrival (5:4–5). Next, he comments on how they should conduct themselves as they await the day of the Lord (5:6–8). Finally he ties 5:1–8 together with 4:13–18 by assuring the Thessalonians that because of the death of Jesus, both those who sleep (the deceased) and those who are awake (the living) will experience that day not as a time of wrath but of salvation (5:9–11).[55]

Here too Paul's comments on the day of the Lord as a time of sudden destruction would come as words of encouragement to the persecuted Thessalonians. These comments are reminiscent of the teaching of Jesus, widely known in the early church, that the day of the Lord would come suddenly and would spell destruction for those who, oblivious to the sentence of doom that hung over them, treated God's call to repent with contempt.[56] This motif is common in the prophets and is often used to

50 On Paul's use of Old Testament assumption imagery here, see Charles Wanamaker, *Commentary on 1 and 2 Thessalonians* (NIGNT; Grand Rapids: Eerdmans, 1990), 175–76; Plevnik, *Paul and the Parousia*, 60–63.

51 See Ps. 18:15 [2 Sam. 22:16]; 68:30; 104:7; 106:9; Isa. 17:13; 66:15, and Plevnik, *Paul and the Parousia*, 46–47.

52 This text was probably in Paul's thoughts as he composed the letter. See 1 Thess. 3:13.

53 See the discussion in Plevnik, *Paul and the Parousia*, 58.

54 Traugott Holtz, *Der este Brief an die Thessalonicher* (EKK 13; Zurich: Benziger, 1990), 210–11, believes that Paul himself raised the issue without prompting from the Thessalonians. On the probability that the phrase "now . . . about" in 5:1 only signals the introduction of a new topic and not an answer to an inquiry from the Thessalonians, see Margaret M. Mitchell, "Concerning ΠΕΡΙ ΔΕ," 229–56.

55 This understanding of the passage follows closely Plevnik, *Paul and the Parousia*, 99–116.

56 On the unexpected nature of the Day's coming, see Matt. 25:13; 24:42–44; Mark 13:33; Luke 12:39–40; 2 Peter 3:10; Rev. 3:3; 16:15; and *Did.* 16:1. On the surprise with which destruction overtakes the unrighteous see Matt. 24:37–39; Luke 17:27–30; 21:34–36.

warn God's people, who are poised for destruction just as they are saying "peace, peace" (Jer. 6:14–15).[57] Here, however, Paul intends to encourage the Thessalonians (1 Thess. 5:11), and therefore his purpose is not to warn them but to remind them that the final day will mean destruction for their persecutors but "salvation through our Lord Jesus Christ" (5:9) for the Thessalonian believers themselves.

In 4:13–5:11, then, Paul tries both to correct misunderstanding about the coming of Christ and to underline teaching that he has already given about the day of the Lord in order to restore the confidence of the Thessalonians in the Christian hope. His primary concern here, as in other sections of the letter, has been to encourage the Thessalonians in the midst of their suffering (4:18; 5:11). Jesus will come, he has told them, and when he comes God will reverse the injustice that the Thessalonians are experiencing. He will raise dead Christians to life; living Christians will join them; and God will bring both groups into the presence of the Lord. Those who have not heeded the gospel (such as the Thessalonians' persecutors), however, will encounter the unexpected, destroying wrath of God as the Lord himself takes the battlefield against the enemies of his people.

THE SURVIVAL OF FAITH, LOVE, AND HOPE IN THESSALONICA

Twice in this letter (1:3 and 5:8) Paul combines the concepts of faith, love, and hope as a summary of Christian existence. He commends the Thessalonians in 1:3 for their "work produced by faith," for their "labor prompted by love," and for the "endurance inspired by [their] hope in our Lord Jesus Christ." In 5:8 he urges them to clothe themselves with these qualities as a warrior clothes himself with armor. The social ostracism that the Thessalonian believers have experienced because of their commitment to the gospel, along with Paul's enforced absence from them, led him to become anxious about the survival of "faith, love, and hope" in Thessalonica. This anxiety prompted Timothy's journey to Thessalonica, and Timothy's report about the condition of "faith, love, and hope" in Thessalonica prompted Paul to write this letter.

In it, he reminds them of his own authenticity as a preacher of the gospel and of the authenticity of their faith. The labor and suffering that accompanied both his preaching and their faith authenticate them both.

He urges them to distinguish themselves from the unbelieving Gentile world around them by the quality of their lives. Their relationships should not be characterized by exploitative sex but by a quality of love that signifies the eschatological work of God in their hearts, and they should live productive lives.

57 Cf. Ezek. 13:10; 38:14–16, and the discussion in Plevnik, *Paul and the Parousia*, 101–6.

He corrects their misdirected anxiety over believers who have died before the coming of Jesus. The God who raised Jesus from the dead, he argues, is not likely to allow physical death to separate his people from eternal fellowship with himself.

Throughout the letter, as Paul makes each of these points, he reminds the Thessalonians of their social standing in the eyes of one another and of God. They are brothers and sisters who stand in continuity with the people of God as the Scriptures describe this people. Moreover, they live in the age in which God is beginning to fulfill his promises to restore the fortunes of his people. The world around them may relegate them to the margins of their society, but God has chosen them to belong to his society, and, in contrast to the *polis* of Thessalonica, this society is eternal.

Chapter 10

SECOND THESSALONIANS: PERSEVERANCE DESPITE PERSECUTION AND FALSE TEACHING

UNSETTLING DEVELOPMENTS IN THESSALONICA

Sometime after Paul sent his first letter to the Thessalonians, he received an oral report on conditions there (2 Thess. 3:11), and the news was not good.[1] The situation had deteriorated on three fronts. Persecution from those ignorant of God and disobedient to the gospel was still in full swing (3:4, 6–7). Some supposedly spiritual utterance, proclamation, or "letter" ascribed to Paul had circulated to the effect that the day of the Lord had arrived, and this had shaken the believing community (2:2). As if this were not enough, some had not heeded Paul's repeated admonitions to win the respect of outsiders by living quietly and by working diligently with their own hands (3:6–16; cf. 1 Thess. 4:10–12; 5:14).

Since each of these problems corresponds to a major issue in Paul's first letter, it seems reasonable to assume that only a short period of time—perhaps a few months—had elapsed since the composition of that letter. Another letter was necessary because not only was persecution continuing but internal difficulties were mounting. Paul must have felt that if this fledgling congregation were to survive, it would need help navigating past the shoals of continued opposition from the outside and the rocks of deviation from his original teaching.

In light of this situation, it is not surprising that Paul's primary concern in 2 Thessalonians, just as in 1 Thessalonians, is for the Thessalonians' perseverance in the faith. The theme is prominent in all three major sections of the letter—when Paul commends the Thessalonians for their steadfastness in affliction (1:3–12) as well as when he admonishes them to cling to the doctrinal (2:1–17) and ethical (3:1–16) teaching that he originally gave them.[2]

1 A number of scholars believe that the less joyful tone of 2 Thessalonians and its structural similarity to 1 Thessalonians, among other peculiarities, mean that 2 Thessalonians is a pseudonymous work. This view of the letter, however, has trouble locating a plausible historical setting in a post-Pauline era for the problem of fervent eschatological expectation that the letter addresses. It also has difficulty accounting for 3:17, which, if written after Paul's time, would imply that every Pauline letter without his signature—and that includes most of the letters in the Pauline corpus—was forged. For a review of the debate and carefully reasoned arguments for the probable genuineness of the letter see, e.g., Robert Jewett, *The Thessalonian Correspondence: Pauline Rhetoric and Millenarian Piety* (FF; Philadelphia: Fortress, 1986), 3–18, and Abraham J. Malherbe, *The Letters to the Thessalonians* (AB 32B; New York: Doubleday, 2000), 364–70.

2 Cf. M. J. J. Menken, "The Structure of 2 Thessalonians," in *The Thessalonian Correspondence*, ed. Raymond F. Collins (BETL 87; Leuven: Leuven Univ. Press, 1990), 374–82.

PERSEVERANCE AMID CONTINUED PERSECUTION (1:3–12)

Paul devotes the first major section of this letter (1:3–12) to encouraging the Thessalonians to remain faithful in the midst of their suffering. He does this through a thanksgiving that becomes, at its conclusion, intercession for the Thessalonians. Paul begins his thanksgiving with a reference to the joy that the Thessalonians' progress and perseverance in the faith have given him (1:3–4; cf. 1 Thess. 1:8–10). His central concern, however, is to describe God's perspective on their faithful suffering (2 Thess. 1:5–10), and his intercessory prayer report at the end of the section (1:11–12) arises out of this concern.

Paul's description of God's perspective on the Thessalonians' perseverance begins with a thesis statement whose consequences Paul then explains. In God's eyes, Paul says, the suffering of the believers in Thessalonica is "evidence of God's righteous judgment" (1:5, aut.), and as a result of it, God will consider them worthy of his kingdom. But what does this statement mean? How could the Thessalonians' suffering somehow function as judgment from God? It is unlikely that Paul believes their suffering somehow atones for their sin and therefore makes them worthy of God's kingdom.[3] To be told that they were suffering what their sins deserved would be little comfort to the persecuted Thessalonians and, in any case, would contradict the notion that Jesus' death "for us" (1 Thess. 5:10) has already atoned for believers' sins.

Another interpretation is more satisfying. Although Paul did not believe that the day of the Lord had come (2:1–2), he did think, with many other apocalyptic writers of his time, that the suffering of God's people was part of the eschatological scenario that would come to a climax in the final day.[4] He had spoken of these appointed sufferings to the Thessalonians when he was with them and in his first letter reminded them not to be surprised by them (1 Thess. 3:3–4); they were all part of the events leading to the close of the age. The righteous judgment of God, then, was under way in the present and would climax in a future day of judgment.[5] Suffering for the gospel during this period is evidence that God's righteous judgment is already in effect, discriminating between those who will ultimately be condemned and those who, having passed safely through these troubled waters, will be "counted worthy of the kingdom of God."[6]

Paul next explains the implications of this statement. In God's righteous judgment, he says, God "will pay back trouble to those who trouble you and give relief

3 Jouette M. Bassler, "The Enigmatic Sign: 2 Thessalonians 1:5," *CBQ* 46 (1984): 496–510; Maarten J. J. Menken, *2 Thessalonians* (New Testament Readings; London and New York: Routledge, 1994), 85–86. They believe that 2 Thess. 1:4–5 parallels the theology expressed in such texts as *Gen. R.* 13.1; *Pss. Sol.* 13:9–10; 2 Macc. 6:12–16; and *2 Baruch* 13:3–10.

4 See, e.g., Dan. 12:1–3; *Jub.* 23:11–31; *2 Bar.* 25–28; 70:1–10; 2 Esdr. 4:51–5:13; 13:30–32; 14:13–18; 1QH 11:6–18; Matt. 24:9–14; Mark 13:9–13; Luke 12:11–12; 21:12–19.

5 This same eschatological pattern reappears in Romans where Paul speaks both of the outpouring of God's eschatological wrath on the ungodly and wicked in the present (Rom. 1:18) and of a future "day of God's wrath, when his righteous judgment will be revealed" (2:5).

6 Cf. Phil. 1:28; 1 Peter 4:17; the important excursus of Edward Gordon Selwyn, *The First Epistle of St. Peter* (London: Macmillan, 1946), 299–303; and the comments of I. Howard Marshall, *1 and 2 Thessalonians* (NCB; Grand Rapids: Eerdmans, 1983), 173.

to you who are troubled" (1:6–7). The "trouble" or "affliction" with which God will repay the Thessalonians' persecutors will be their just punishment (*ekdikēsin*, 1:8; *dikēn*, 1:9) and will consist of their "everlasting destruction" and banishment from the presence of the Lord and his glorious power (1:9). The "relief" that the afflicted Thessalonian believers receive will consist, correspondingly, in participation with God's people in glorifying and marveling at the Lord (1:10). All of this will happen "on that day" (1:10)—the day of the Lord, when Jesus will return (cf. 2:1–2).

Why does Paul think that this is "just"? He never explains, but appears to assume that God is just to punish those who have rejected him, disobeyed the gospel, and persecuted believers, and that he is just to reward believers with a place in the kingdom of God for their struggles at the hands of such oppressors. In adopting this position, Paul stands in continuity with a long tradition of biblical thinking that depicts God as one who, in the words of Mary, "has scattered those who are proud in their inmost thoughts," who "has brought down rulers from their thrones but has lifted up the humble," and who "has filled the hungry with good things but has sent the rich away empty" (Luke 1:51b–53; cf. 16:25).[7]

Paul also stands in continuity with a particular form of this thinking that developed in early Christian apocalyptic circles. These circles focused on the eschatological day of God's wrath as the time when God would reveal his lordship over the universe and put into effect the inexorable law of retaliation—those who rejected him would be rejected (Matt. 10:32–33; Mark 8:38; Luke 9:26; 2 Tim. 2:12), and those who harmed his people would themselves suffer harm (1 Cor. 3:17). In this sense, each will on that day be repaid according to what he or she has done (Matt. 16:27; Rom. 2:5–16).[8]

Up to this point, Paul has assumed that the Thessalonians' steadfastness will continue. He is confident that the Lord will strengthen and protect them from the evil one (3:3). Still, he refuses to presume upon this confidence, and so he concludes the first major section of his letter with an intercessory prayer that the Thessalonians will continue to persevere in the faith (1:11–12). Perhaps in anticipation of his concerns in the rest of the letter, however, the emphasis shifts subtly from the outward pressures of persecution to the inward issues of the Thessalonians' "resolve" (*eudokia*) and "work" (*ergon*). The prayer is itself an authentic request for God to take the initiative in making the Thessalonians worthy of their calling—to fulfill in them "every good resolution and deed of faith" by his power and according to his grace. It is also an effort to let the Thessalonians know that in spite of their abundant growth in faith, their multiplying mutual love, and their praiseworthy steadfastness, their progress in the faith is not complete.

7 Cf., e.g., 1 Sam. 2:2–10; Job 5:8–16; Ps. 113:7–9; 147:6; Prov. 3:34.; Sir. 10:14; Luke 16:25.

8 On this see Ernst Käsemann, *New Testament Questions of Today* (Philadelphia: Fortress, 1969), 66–81.

PERSEVERANCE AMID FALSE TEACHING (2:1–3:16)

In the second and third major sections of the letter, Paul turns to two problems internal to the Thessalonian community. First, false teaching about the timing of "the coming of our Lord Jesus Christ" has unsettled the Thessalonian believers, and Paul needs to correct these misapprehensions (2:1–12). Second, some within the Thessalonian church have continued to neglect their daily work and, living off the largesse of the community, have made themselves "busybodies" (3:6–16). This unwillingness "to settle down and earn the bread they eat" (3:12) has probably resulted from the false eschatological convictions that Paul attacks in chapter 2 and may be the trouble that he refers to when he speaks of those who have become "unsettled or alarmed" by the thought that the day of the Lord has already arrived (2:2).

Although these two problems are Paul's primary concern in this part of the letter, he does not lose sight of the theme that dominates 1:3–12, namely, the need to encourage the Thessalonians to remain faithful despite their suffering. As Paul corrects the false teaching on the coming of the Lord, he uses his reassertion of the correct apocalyptic scenario as a vehicle of encouragement for the beleaguered church. As in apocalyptic literature generally, Paul recounts the specific progress of events toward the end of the age as a way of saying that even when the righteous are suffering, God is nevertheless in control and will, at the appointed time, vindicate his chosen people.

This leads him, in 2:13–14, to thank God that in contrast to those who have "refused to love the truth and so be saved" (2:10), God has chosen and called the Thessalonians to be his people. Similarly, as Paul makes the transition from the false eschatological teaching to the disruptive behavior of some of the Thessalonians, he encourages them again by reminding them that "our Lord Jesus Christ" and "God our Father" have acted graciously in the past (2:16) and will be faithful to "protect and strengthen" them from the evil one (3:3).

Thus, even as Paul takes up the specific issues of false eschatological teaching and disruptive behavior, the concern that has been present since he was first torn away from the Thessalonians (1 Thess. 2:17) remains constant: He encourages them to remain faithful to their initial commitment to the gospel. Only in this way can he realize his overarching goal: "that the message of the Lord may spread rapidly and be honored" (3:1).

Deceptive Eschatological Teaching (2:1–17)

Paul's first concern for problems internal to the community is the possibility that some false teaching will deceive the Thessalonians about the events surrounding "the day of the Lord." He first tells what he knows about the problem and then corrects it.

Paul's knowledge of the problem is sketchy. He does not know its source, whether some spiritual utterance, authoritative word, or a letter supposedly from him. He knows only that the misinformation has to do with "the coming of our Lord Jesus Christ and our being gathered to him" (2:1) and that it has led some Thessalonian believers to think that "the day of the Lord has already come" (2:2). These statements are reminiscent of Paul's descriptions in 1 Thessalonians of "the coming of the Lord," at which, he says, Christians will be "caught up ... in the clouds to meet the Lord in the air" (1 Thess. 4:15, 17), and of "the day of the Lord," which "will come like a thief in the night" when the world looks perfectly normal to unbelievers (5:2–3).

It seems likely, therefore, that Paul's comments on the Lord's coming and the final day in 1 Thessalonians 4:13–5:11 have only added fuel to the already heated eschatological expectations of some Thessalonian believers.[9] Using elements in Paul's letter that—creatively interpreted—could lend authority to their position, they proclaimed that the final day had arrived. Their afflictions, they must have said, were the final eschatological convulsions of an evil world just prior to Jesus' coming. What else could Paul have meant when he said that God had appointed them for such suffering (1 Thess. 3:3) than that their troubles were the long-awaited messianic woes? This misunderstanding had led some "to be mentally unsettled" (*saleuthēnai apo tou noos*) and "alarmed" (*throeisthai*, 2 Thess. 2:2, aut.).

Paul corrects this notion by reminding the Thessalonian believers of the traditions he had taught them while he was still with them (2:5–6, 15). During his original ministry among them Paul had not only preached the need to abandon idols and worship God but also that believers must "wait for his Son from heaven" (1 Thess. 1:9–10).[10] In light of the broad similarities between Paul's eschatological teaching in the Thessalonian correspondence and the apocalyptic discourses in the Synoptic Gospels, he was probably familiar with some form of Jesus' teaching on the coming of the end, and this was probably the tradition he had handed on to them.[11]

Here he emphasizes the part of that tradition that speaks of signs that will precede Jesus' coming. It is true that suffering will precede the end (Matt. 24:9–14; Mark 13:9–13; Luke 21:12–19) and that the Thessalonians' persecution is related in some way to this eschatological suffering: It is a prelude to the revelation of God's justice on that final day (1:5–10) and is part of "the mystery of lawlessness" that is "already working" (2:7a). But prior to Jesus' return other critical events must take place. God will remove his hand of restraint from the lawlessness that is now at work (2:7b), the final rebellion of the evil powers against God will occur, and this rebellion will reach its horrible climax in "the man of lawlessness ... the man doomed to destruction" (2:3).[12]

9 Marshall, *1 and 2 Thessalonians*, 187; Jewett, *Thessalonian Correspondence*, 186–91; and Jerome Murphy-O'Connor, *Paul: A Critical Life* (New York: Oxford Univ. Press, 1996), 112–13, all believe that some Thessalonians misinterpreted 1 Thessalonians, but they argue the case somewhat differently from each other and from the way it is presented here.

10 Bruce, *1 & 2 Thessalonians* (WBC 45; Waco, Tex.: Word, 1982), 169.

11 See Lars Hartman, "The Eschatology of 2 Thessalonians as Included in a Communication," in *The Thessalonian Correspondence*, ed. Raymond F. Collins (BETL 87; Leuven: Leuven Univ. Press, 1990), 470–85, here at 480, and David Wenham, *Paul: Follower of Jesus or Founder of Christianity?* (Grand Rapids: Eerdmans, 1995), 305–28. Cf. also the echoes of this tradition in *Didache* 16 and Justin Martyr, *Dial.* 82:1–2.

12 Paul's references to "what is holding ... back" (*to katechon* [neuter]) and to "the one who ... holds ... back" (*ho katechōn* [masculine]) in 2:6 and 2:7 respectively are notoriously obscure. They have been explained as referring to the Roman empire and the emperor; the preaching of the gospel and Paul; God, who "delays" the coming of Christ; and an evil power and the one who exercises it. For these and other, less convincing explanations, see the survey in Charles A. Wanamaker, *Commentary on 1 and 2 Thessalonians* (NIGTC; Grand Rapids: Eerdmans, 1990), 250–52.

This man will be recognizable from his claims to be greater than any divinity or object of devotion—including seating himself in God's temple (2 Thess. 2:4; cf. Matt. 24:15; Mark 13:14), an action that Paul means probably in a symbolic sense of this man's opposition to God (cf. Isa. 14:13; Ezek. 28:2).[13] Satan will also supply him with the ability to work false signs, wonders, and other deceptions (2 Thess. 2:9–10).[14] Then, Paul says, Jesus will come (2:3) and kill this man by the mere breath of his mouth (2:8). Paul's Greek in 2:6–7 is notoriously difficult to understand, and the identification of "the man of lawlessness," "the temple" that he occupies, and "the one who now ... holds back" has generated a small library of discussion.[15] Regardless of the solution we choose to these problems, Paul's basic point is clear: The day of the Lord has not yet come because none of these events—whatever they are—has happened.[16]

Another more subtle but no less important message lies beneath this apocalyptic scenario. It is the message of virtually all Jewish and Christian apocalyptic texts, that despite the present suffering of God's chosen people, God is nevertheless in control of every detail of their lives and will one day put an end to their suffering.[17] Paul wants his readers to know that although they are not standing at the brink of history, they do live in a period of time when "the mystery of lawlessness is already at work" and that only God's restraining hand, waiting as it is for the appointed time, prevents their persecutions and afflictions from escalating into the final rebellion (2:6–7).[18] Even the apparent triumph of evil in the present, therefore, is not outside God's control, and one day, at the right moment, God will vindicate his people (2:8–12).

The primary objection to the view adopted here is that it envisions God being "taken out of the way" to make way for "the secret power of lawlessness" (2:7). If we imagine God working through an angelic agent (as he seems to work through Michael in Dan. 12:1), however, this objection loses some of its force. Cf. Marshall, *1 and 2 Thessalonians*, 199–200; Hartman, "Eschatology," 481; Menken, *2 Thessalonians*, 108–13; and Malherbe, *Letters to the Thessalonians*, 433.

13 The "temple" in 2:4 has been explained as the Jerusalem temple, a heavenly temple, the church, and, as here, a symbol of God to whom the man of lawlessness is opposed. See the survey of positions in Charles Homer Giblin, *The Threat to Faith: An Exegetical and Theological Reexamination of 2 Thessalonians 2* (AnBib 31; Rome: Pontifical Biblical Institute, 1967), 76, and Marshall, *1 and 2 Thessalonians*, 190–92. For the position taken here, see George Eldon Ladd, *A Theology of the New Testament* (Grand Rapids: Eerdmans, 1974), 559, and cf. Malherbe, *Letters to the Thessalonians*, 421.

14 The man of lawlessness has been identified with the "antichrist" (1 John 2:18, 22; 4:3; 2 John 7; cf. Matt. 24:24; Mark 13:22; Rev. 13:1–18; 19:20), with a future false prophet, and with an ill-defined figure who is a messy combination of characteristics from the Old Testament, Jewish apocalyptic speculation, and mythology. See, respectively, Best, *Thessalonians*, 289; Giblin, *The Threat to Faith*, 59–76; and William Neil, *The Epistle* [sic] *of Paul to the Thessalonians* (MNTC; London: Hodder and Stoughton, 1950), 177.

15 A couple of decades before Paul wrote 2 Thessalonians, Jesus had prophesied that prior to the coming of the Son of Man a period of rebellion would culminate in "'the abomination that causes desolation' standing where it does not belong" (Mark 13:14; cf. Matt. 24:15). This expression comes from Daniel 9:27; 11:31; 12:11, where it probably functions as a prophecy of the pagan altar that Antiochus IV Epiphanes would erect "on top of the altar of burnt offering" in an attempt to merge the worship of Yahweh with the worship of Olympian Zeus (1 Macc. 1:54, 59; 2 Macc. 6:2). Jesus seems to have used the language symbolically of the siege of Jerusalem prior to its destruction by the Romans in A.D. 70 (cf. Luke 21:20, which, instead of "the abomination that causes desolation" speaks of the "desolation" of Jerusalem). This traditional language has, therefore, already taken on a metaphorical quality by the time that Paul uses it here. In light of this, "the man of lawlessness" and "the temple" may refer more to the intensification of rebellion against God prior to the end and to the collusion of both political and religious authorities in that intensification, than to a literal man and a literal temple. Cf. the understanding of Rev. 13 in chapter 32, below.

16 For the grammatical problems in 2:6–7, see M. Barnouin, "Les problèmes de traduction concernant II Thess. II.6–7," *NTS* 23 (1976–77): 482–98.

17 Christopher Rowland, *The Open Heaven: A Study of Apocalyptic in Judaism and Early Christianity* (New York: Crossroad, 1982), 135.

18 Hartman, "Eschatology," 481, puts it well: "The present tribulations of the addressees are not the end, but nonetheless, they are eschatological."

This understanding of God's sovereign control over history, even over the suffering of his people, leads Paul in 2:13–14 to a second thanksgiving section. He and his coworkers ought always to give thanks to God, he says, because in contrast to the unbelievers Paul has just described, God "chose" the Thessalonian believers to be the "firstfruits for salvation" (2:13, aut.) and "called" (2:14) them to share in the glory of Jesus.[19] Both images recall the biblical descriptions of God's choice of and calling to ancient Israel to be his people.

When Paul says that God "chose" the Thessalonian believers to be the "firstfruits for salvation," he is echoing Deuteronomy 26. In that passage, Moses first describes the procedure that God's people should follow for bringing an offering of the firstfruits of their harvest to the Lord (26:1–11), and then, a few sentences later (26:18–19), reminds Israel that they stand apart from all other nations because God "chose" (*eilato*) them to be "a special people."[20] In 2 Thessalonians 2:13, Paul first says that, in contrast to the unbelievers described in 2:10–12, God "chose" (*eilato*) the Thessalonians to be part of his people.[21] Next, he completes the thought by changing the offering of the firstfruits into a metaphor for the Thessalonian believers—they are among the first of what will eventually be a far greater harvest as an increasing number of both Gentiles and Jews believe the gospel.[22] Paul's point is clear: Not only does God have their suffering under his sovereign control, but the Thessalonians are a first and special part of God's positive design for the many whom he will save.

In addition, Paul speaks of how God "called" the Thessalonians to membership in his people through the proclamation of the gospel (2:14). When Paul speaks of God's calling the Thessalonians, he is echoing Isaiah 40–55, where the prophet refers to God's original choice of his people from among all other peoples (Ex. 19:5–6; Deut. 7:6–8; 14:2) as a way of comforting Israel in exile. Isaiah looks back to that important moment as a way of saying to God's people that God will be faithful to his original calling and restore the fortunes of his people again. One day their vocation to be a "kingdom of priests" (Ex. 19:5–6), mediating God's gracious purposes to the nations around them, will be restored:

"I, the LORD, have called you in righteousness;
  I will take hold of your hand.
I will keep you and will make you
  to be a covenant for the people

19 Paul's use of the uncharacteristic and formal phrases "we ought always to thank God ... and rightly so" in 1:3 and "we ought always to give thanks" here in 2:13 probably reflect a customary way of praying in Judaism and early Christianity, particularly when the prayers arise from a context of suffering. See Roger D. Aus, "The Liturgical Background of the Necessity and Propriety of Giving Thanks according to 2 Thes 1:3," *JBL* 92 (1973): 432–38.

20 Cf. Deut. 7:6 and 14:2 (LXX).

21 This is the only use of *eilato* in the New Testament.

22 Paul frequently uses the firstfruits offering as a metaphor elsewhere, and he does so in various ways. See Rom. 8:23; 11:16; 16:5; 1 Cor. 15:20, 23; 16:15 (cf. James 1:18 and Rev. 14:4). Most commentators accept the reading "from the beginning" (*ap' archēs*) instead of "firstfruits" (*aparchēn*) here. NA27 and Bruce, *1 & 2 Thessalonians*, 190, however, are correct in reading "firstfruits," although not for the text-critical reasons that they give. The manuscript evidence and transcriptional probabilities are indecisive, but Paul's unmistakable echo of Deuteronomy 26 in his claim that God has chosen the Thessalonians makes it likely that he is also echoing the description of the offering of the firstfruits in that same passage.

and a light for the Gentiles,
to open eyes that are blind,
to free captives from prison
and to release from the dungeon those who sit in darkness." (Isa. 42:6)[23]

Paul's use of this language in a context where he has just stressed God's choice of the Thessalonians to be the firstfruits of a far greater harvest of salvation probably means that he understands the Thessalonians themselves to represent the beginning of the fulfillment of these promises. In contrast to the unbelievers who are persecuting them, the Thessalonians stand in continuity with God's ancient people and are the means through which the vocation of ancient Israel is completed. For Paul this is reason enough to give thanks.

Since the ability to remain faithful to their vocation until the final day lies not with the Thessalonians themselves but with God, Paul closes this section of his letter with an admonition and a prayer. He urges the Thessalonians to hold fast to the traditions he has taught them, and he prays that the God who has demonstrated his love and graciously given eternal encouragement to his people in Jesus will accomplish in the Thessalonians "every good deed and word" (2:15–17).[24] Mention of "every good ... word" perhaps looks back to Paul's concern with the false teaching present in the community, just as the phrase "every good deed" looks forward to the ethical issue that Paul raises in the next chapter.

Disruptive Behavior (3:1–16)

The second internal problem that concerns Paul in this letter is the "disruptive" or "disorderly" (*ataktōs*) behavior of some within the congregation.[25] Some of the Thessalonian believers have left productive jobs to become meddlesome "busybodies" who are disrupting the life of the church.[26]

The Background of the Problem

Apparently this problem plagued the Thessalonian community from the first, and Paul attempted to correct the situation during his Thessalonian ministry by explicit instruction and personal example. He commanded them to lead a quiet life, mind their own affairs, and keep this rule: "If anyone does not want to work, he shall not eat" (1 Thess. 4:11; 2 Thess. 3:10, aut.). Moreover, he set aside his own right as an apostle to earn his living by the proclamation of the gospel and instead toiled night and day in a workshop to earn his keep. Those who wanted to benefit from

23 Cf. Isa. 41:9; 48:12, 15; 51:2.

24 Menken, *2 Thessalonians*, 123, observes that the past tense verbs in 2:16, "loved" (*agapēsas*) and "gave" (*dous*), probably reflect the conviction that God's love came to a climax in Jesus' death on the cross.

25 Although *ataktōs* is often translated "in idleness," the link between a refusal to work and being a busybody shows that the issue is more complex than simple laziness. Not only are some refusing to work to earn their keep but they are occupying their time with matters that should not concern them. See Earl J. Richard, *First and Second Thessalonians* (SP 11; Collegeville, Minn.: Michael Glazier, 1995), 389, and, on the meaning of *ataktōs*, see Ceslas Spiq, "ἀτακτέω (κτλ)," *TLNT*, 1:223–26, and BDAG, 148.

26 R. Russell, "The Idle in 2 Thess 3.6–12: An Eschatological or a Social Problem?" *NTS* 34 (1988): 105–19, argues that the idle in Thessalonica are the urban unemployed, but this seems to conflict with Paul's implication that the problematic group does not "*want* [*thelei*] to work" (3:10).

his teaching had to visit with him or work alongside him there, much as the Cynic philosopher Crates had discussed philosophy with the shoemaker Philiscus while Philiscus stitched shoes.[27] This activity, Paul thinks, has made him a model for the Thessalonians to follow (2 Thess. 3:9).

The Thessalonians, however, have failed to get the point, and so in his first letter Paul reminded them of his previous teaching on the subject (1 Thess. 4:11) and instructed them to "admonish the disruptive" (5:14, aut.). By the time Paul wrote 2 Thessalonians, the problem not only remained firmly entrenched but Paul's willingness to devote a long passage to it in a short letter probably means that it has grown worse.

The Nature of the Problem

Why would such a problem arise? The lengthier treatment of the issue in 2 Thessalonians permits an answer to this question by implying that the problems of the timing of the Parousia and disruptive behavior are connected. Several elements of chapters 2 and 3 point toward this connection. First, Paul's discussion in the letter body only of false teaching about the day of the Lord and disruptive behavior makes it likely that these topics are connected.[28]

Second, Paul's strategy for handling each problem is similar: He appeals to his previous teaching on each subject when he was still with them (2 Thess. 2:5; 3:10), to their knowledge (2:6; 3:7), and to Christian tradition (2:15; 3:6).[29]

Third, in this letter Paul defines the disorderly nature of the activity as the desire of some not merely to cease working but to become "busybodies" (3:11). Elsewhere in his letters, Paul links busybodies who take advantage of the largesse of the Christian community specifically with false teaching (1 Tim. 5:11, 13; cf. Titus 1:10–11; 2 John 10–11). It seems likely, then, that here too the deception about the timing of the Parousia is spreading through those who would rather advance false teaching than work.[30] Moreover, structures were in place in the cultural and ecclesiastical world of the Thessalonian believers to make such an arrangement possible. Wealthy patrons often provided the basic necessities of a large clientele of poorer people, and those who merely did not want to work or who wanted to pursue the philosophical life instead of working with their hands could use the system to their advantage.[31] Early Christian communities also frequently contributed to the physical needs of poorer members through a common fund, and this system too could be abused by those who had no desire to work.[32]

27 The story is told by the Cynic philosopher Teles (fr. IVB), who prefers pursuing philosophy in such menial settings rather than in royal courts. See Ronald F. Hock, "Simon the Shoemaker as an Ideal Cynic," *Greek, Roman and Byzantine Studies* 17 (1976): 41–53, here at 47.

28 Menken, *2 Thessalonians*, 137.

29 Ibid.

30 Is it possible that they appealed to the example of Jesus, claiming that he adopted an itinerant ministry in order to preach the imminence of the kingdom of God (Mark 1:15)?

31 On the relationships between patrons and clients see Bruce W. Winter, "'If a man does not wish to work . . .'," *TynBul* 40 (1989): 303–15, and Russell, "The Idle in 2 Thess 3.6–12," 105–19. On Cynic philosophers who lived by means of the largesse of wealthy patrons, see Abraham J. Malherbe, "'Gentle as a Nurse': The Cynic Background to 1 Thess ii," *NovT* 12 (1970): 203–17, here at 205–6, and Hock, "Simon the Shoemaker," 41–53.

32 See 1 Cor. 16:1–2; Gal. 2:10; Rom. 15:25–27; cf. Acts 2:45; 4:35; 6:1–2 and the comments of Marshall, *1 and 2 Thessalonians*, 219. On the abuse of the system, see, e.g., *Did.* 12:3–4, and Lucian, *Peregr.* 13.

We can imagine, therefore, that soon after the Thessalonians' conversion some of them became so enthralled with the possibility that Jesus could return at any moment that they left their jobs and began publicly proclaiming apocalyptic doom.[33] The "frankness" (*parrēsia*) with which they preached their message may have increased the persecution they were experiencing, and soon some concluded that they were living in the time of the messianic woes, which, according to Paul, Jesus himself had predicted. In such a climate, Paul's first letter only fanned the flames of apocalyptic fervor and before long some were proclaiming that "the day of the Lord" had arrived. The end of the age was at their doorstep.

Paul's Answer to the Problem

In 1 Thessalonians Paul tried to squelch the early stages of this behavior by referring to the need to "behave decently toward outsiders" (1 Thess. 4:12), and he simply told the Thessalonians to "admonish the disorderly" (5:14, aut.). Here in 2 Thessalonians he appeals both to Christian tradition and to his own example and then gives a piece of practical advice about how to admonish those who were still refusing to comply with his teaching.

Tradition

His appeals to tradition use technical vocabulary for the handing on of a body of instruction that one has previously received from others, and Paul says that the Thessalonians received it from him when he was with them (3:6, 10).[34] The content of the tradition is straightforward: "If anyone does not want to work, he shall not eat" (3:10, aut.), or, to put it another way, those who are being disruptive ought to "work quietly and eat their own bread" (3:12, aut.). The origins of this tradition are unknown, but echoes of it appear both in Jewish and in early Christian sources (e.g., Prov. 10:4; *Did.* 12.3–4), and Paul's claim that he gives this command "in the Lord Jesus" may mean that it had been absorbed into the body of ethical teaching that those "in Christ" held in common.[35] Paul therefore knows of a rule within a body of commonly accepted Christian ethical teaching that fits the Thessalonians' situation, and he calls on the Thessalonians for at least the second time to obey it.[36]

Example

They should know how to obey this rule because Paul provided an example of its practical outworking when he was ministering among them. In 3:7–10 Paul echoes the description of his ministry among the Thessalonians in his first letter.[37]

---

33 See John M. G. Barclay, "Conflict in Thessalonica," *CBQ* 55 (1993): 512–30.

34 Paul's word for "tradition" is *paradosis* (cf. 2 Thess. 2:15). It was used in the Judaism of Paul's time to refer to traditional teaching, especially regulations for the conduct of one's life, that was handed on from one generation to another. See, e.g., Matt. 15:2, 3, 6; Mark 7:3, 5, 8, 9, 13; Gal. 1:14; Josephus, *A. J.* 10.51; 13.297, 408, and Birger Gerhardsson, *Memory and Manuscript: Oral Tradition and Written Transmission in Rabbinic Judaism and Early Christianity* (ASNU 22; Lund: Gleerup, 1961), 288–90, 293, and 304.

35 Bruce, *1 & 2 Thessalonians*, 78, 207.

36 If Paul intended 1 Thess. 4:11 to recall the rule, this would be his third attempt to correct the problem by referring to this command.

37 The statement "we worked night and day ... so that we would not be a burden to any of you" (3:8) repeats 1 Thess. 2:9 word for word. Some scholars have used this kind of detailed agreement between 1 and 2 Thessalonians to argue for the pseudonymity of 2 Thessalonians. It is likely, however, that Paul followed the custom of retaining copies of his own letters. See E. Randolph Richards, "The Codex and the Early Collection of Paul's Letters," *BBR* 8 (1998): 151–66, here at 155–60.

There his primary concern had been to distinguish himself from Sophists and charlatan philosophers, but in 2 Thessalonians he reminds the church of his original reasons for setting aside his apostolic right to earn his living by the proclamation of the gospel: "We did this ... in order to make ourselves an example for you to follow" (3:9).[38] Paul therefore has not only given them authoritative instructions relevant to their problem but he has denied his own right to support from the community in order to provide a pattern of behavior for them to follow.

Admonition

In 1 Thessalonians Paul issued a broad command to admonish the disorderly, but he provided no specific direction on what to do, perhaps hoping that the Thessalonians would find their own amicable way of solving the problem. Their lack of progress on the issue, however, meant that in the second letter stronger medicine was necessary. Paul begins and ends his comments on the problem with a command to the church generally to keep away from any of its members who ignore the teaching he has given them on the issue whether previously or in this letter (3:6, 14). The intent of this measure is not to treat the erring person as an enemy but to admonish that person as a brother (3:15). Sensing that misuse or misunderstanding of this advice could easily lead to disunity in the church, Paul concludes this section of the letter with a prayer that "the Lord of peace himself" might give them peace "at all times and in every way" (3:16).

In both 2:1–17 and in 3:6–16, therefore, Paul's concern for the steadfastness of the Thessalonians in their newfound faith remains constant. Just as he reminds them of the tradition he taught them about the Lord's coming as a way of encouraging them to "stand firm" in the faith in 2:1–17, so he reminds them of the ethical traditions he passed on to them when he was with them (3:6–16) as a way of encouraging them to "continue to do the things we command" (3:4). Paul's goal in both sections, then, is to ensure that the Thessalonians avoid falling prey to a misguided interpretation of the gospel he had preached and that they persevere in the traditions about Jesus as Paul first taught them.

PERSEVERANCE IN DEED AND WORD

The perseverance of the Thessalonians in their commitment to the gospel is the common thread that unites 2 Thessalonians. It is the dominant theme of the opening thanksgiving and intercession (1:3–12) and binds the body of the letter together (2:1–3:16). If the Thessalonians are to be Paul's crown of victory when Jesus returns (1 Thess. 2:19), part of the offering that he will give to God when his task of evangelizing the Gentiles is finished (Rom. 15:16), then they must persevere in the faith.

38 Disruptive behavior and an unwillingness to work for one's bread were apparently a problem not only after Paul left Thessalonica but already during Paul's initial ministry among the Thessalonians. In 1 Thess. 4:11 Paul says that when he was with them he "commanded" (*parēngeilamen*) them to mind their own business and work with their hands, and in 2 Thess. 3:10 he says that when he was with them he "used to command" (*parēngellomen*) them that those who did not want to work should not eat.

This means they must refuse to cave in to the social pressures of a society that rejects them, resisting the false teaching that has arisen among them, and avoiding those who, because they have embraced the false teaching, are engaged in unnecessarily disruptive social behavior. As Paul prays in 2:16–17, the Thessalonians should remain strong in both "deed" and "word"—both in the gospel as Paul has taught it to them and in the quality of life that should characterize those who believe it.

Chapter 11

GALATIANS: THE GRACE OF GOD AND THE TRUTH OF THE GOSPEL

TROUBLE IN GALATIA

After a year and a half in Corinth—the place from which he wrote both letters to the Thessalonians—Paul made his way across the Aegean Sea, touching briefly at Ephesus, and then over the eastern Mediterranean Sea, through Judea, and finally to the multiethnic church at Syrian Antioch (Acts 18:18–22). "After spending some time in Antioch" (18:23) he set out on the overland route from there to Ephesus, passing through Galatia and Phrygia on his way. Paul and Barnabas had visited this region on an earlier trip during which they preached the gospel and established churches under the auspices of the church at Antioch (Acts 13:1–14:28). Paul had visited the region again briefly with Silas and Timothy (16:6), but now he paid the young churches there a substantial visit, going, Luke says, in sequence from one place to the next "strengthening all the disciples" (18:23).[1]

During this trip he probably first became aware of the problem that would later prompt him to write to these churches in the southern part of the province that the Romans called Galatia.[2] He probably produced this letter once he reached his journey's destination in Ephesus (19:1). "Agitators" (*hoi tarassontes*; Gal. 1:7; cf. 5:10) had come to the region teaching a perverse form of the gospel, so perverse that Paul could not bring himself to use the term "gospel" of it—it "is really no gospel at all," he says (1:7).

The agitators' concerns are reasonably clear: They wanted Gentile believers to live by the Mosaic law (Gal. 4:21; 5:1) and especially to accept circumcision (5:2–3; 6:12–13; cf. 2:3). We can infer from Paul's description of his argument with Peter over table fellowship in Antioch (2:11–14) and from his mention of the Galatians' newfound fascination with the Jewish calendar (4:10) that, along with circumcision, the agitators stressed dietary and Sabbath observance as well.[3] Circumcision, food laws, and Sabbath observance were three characteristics that both Jews and their Gentile

1 BDAG, 381.

2 These were the churches of Derbe, Lystra, Iconium, and Pisidian Antioch. Usually scholars who argue that Paul wrote Galatians after the Jerusalem council of Acts 15 also assume that he wrote to churches among the Galatian tribes in the northern part of the Roman province of Galatia. See, e.g., J. B. Lightfoot, *Saint Paul's Epistle to the Galatians* (London: Macmillan, 1902), 1–56. Those who believe that Paul wrote Galatians before the Jerusalem council of Acts 15 also think that he wrote to churches in the southern part of the Roman province of Galatia. See, e.g., F. F. Bruce, *Paul: Apostle of the Heart Set Free* (Grand Rapids: Eerdmans, 1977), 178–87. On the compatibility of the south Galatian hypothesis with a late date for the letter—the position I take here—see Moisés Silva, *Explorations in Exegetical Method: Galatians as a Test Case* (Grand Rapids: Baker, 1996), 129–32.

3 James D. G. Dunn, *Jesus, Paul and the Law: Studies in Mark and Galatians* (Louisville: Westminster John Knox, 1990), 191; J. Louis Martyn, *Galatians* (AB 33A; New York: Doubleday, 1998), 305.

observers considered defining boundaries of Judaism.[4] It seems certain, then, that the agitators were trying to persuade the Gentile believers in Paul's Galatian churches to add to their faith in Jesus Christ acceptance of the Jewish way of life.[5]

Why did they want them to do this? Here our footing is less sure. Paul provides a hint of their motives in 6:12–13 where he says that by compelling the Galatians to accept circumcision his opponents hoped to avoid persecution (6:12) and to "boast about [the Galatians'] flesh" (6:13). When they became Christians, the Gentile Galatian Christians stepped out of the boundaries of their traditional religions, including the imperial cult. Rome had long tolerated the refusal of Jews to participate in worship of the emperor because of the antiquity of their traditions and because they did offer sacrifice on behalf of the emperor, if not *to* the emperor, in their temple in Jerusalem. The Gentile Christians of Galatia, however, offered no sacrifices either to or for the emperor, and they participated in none of the traditional religions of their region, including Judaism. Paul's claim that his opponents want to avoid persecution may mean that they want the Gentile Galatian Christians to adopt practices that will make them look Jewish to the society around them. Perhaps the simplicity and effectiveness of this solution to the problem of persecution lead his opponents to "boast" of their cleverness.

How the agitators have argued their case with the Galatians themselves is also difficult to discern.[6] They may have appealed to the clear statement in Genesis 17:1–14 that Abraham and his "seed" must be circumcised or face destruction.[7] They may have tried to use Genesis 21 to support a claim that only circumcised descendants of Abraham and Isaac were members of God's covenant people.[8] Perhaps they also claimed to represent the position of the authentic apostles who learned the gospel from Jesus himself. Paul, they perhaps said, was softening this authentic version of the gospel by dropping the requirement for circumcision, and he did this to make the gospel more attractive to Gentiles.[9]

Although the details of their reasoning remain dark to us, the agitators' arguments must have been compelling to Paul's Galatian churches. Paul describes his audience as those "who want to be under the law" (4:21) and who are "trying to be justified by the law" (5:4). The replacement of his customary thanksgiving prayer report with an expression of alarm ending in a curse (1:6–9) and the urgent appeals

4 E. P. Sanders, *Paul, the Law, and the Jewish People* (Philadelphia: Fortress, 1983), 102; Dunn, *Jesus, Paul and the Law*, 191–94.

5 When recounting his disagreement with Peter at Antioch, Paul speaks of Peter's attempt to force the Gentiles in Antioch "to judaize" (*ioudaizein*, 2:14). Josephus uses this term of the Roman soldier Metilius's promise to become a Jew in order to save his life after his capture by Jewish soldiers during the first Jewish war against Rome. "He alone saved his life by entreaties and promises to turn Jew (*ioudaizein*), and even to be circumcised" (*B. J.* 2.454§10).

6 There is no shortage of attempts to reconstruct their teaching as they might have given it. See, e.g., M.-J. Lagrange, *Saint Paul, Épitre aux Galates* (*Ebib*; Paris: Lecoffre, 1950), xxx–xxxii; J. Christaan Beker, *Paul the Apostle: The Triumph of God in Life and Thought* (Philadelphia: Fortress, 1980), 43–44; and Martyn, *Galatians*, 303–6.

7 Sanders, *Paul, the Law and the Jewish People*, 18; Beker, *Paul*, 48–49; John M. G. Barclay, *Obeying the Truth: Paul's Ethics in Galatians* (Minneapolis: Fortress, 1988), 52–56.

8 C. K. Barrett, *Essays on Paul* (Philadelphia: Westminster, 1982), 158; Martyn, *Galatians*, 304.

9 See, e.g., Lagrange, *Galates*, xxxi; F. F. Bruce, *Commentary on Galatians* (NIGTC; Grand Rapids: Eerdmans, 1982), 26; Jerome Murphy-O'Connor, *Paul: A Critical Life* (New York: Oxford, 1996), 195–96.

that pepper the letter (1:6, 9; 3:1, 3; 4:12–20; 5:2–4, 7–10, 12) show how grave the situation is.[10] These churches appear to be on the verge of apostasy.

Paul believes that in this battle nothing less than "the truth of the gospel" is at stake (2:5, 14). His opponents are not preaching another version of the one gospel but a different message entirely from the one Paul preached and the Galatians accepted (1:6–9). Why is the mixture of faith and "works of the law" in the teaching of Paul's opponents lethal to the "truth of the gospel"?

Paul believes that if only those who couple works of the law with faith in Christ will be acquitted in God's court on the final day, then "Christ died for nothing!" (2:21).[11] Every Jew should know, Paul says, that no one can be justified by works of the law (2:16; 6:13) and that the law pronounces a curse on all who break it (3:10). Christ died to remedy this situation; his death redeems us from the law's curse because when he died, the law's curse was turned away from us and directed toward him (3:13; cf. 2 Cor. 5:21).[12] Yet the insistence of the agitators that keeping the law is necessary for entrance into the people of God ignores this. By linking law-keeping with faith in Christ for salvation, the agitators imply that Christ's death is not adequate to the task of reversing the curse of the law and that human effort to keep the law must play some role after all.

They are denying, in other words, that the initiative in establishing a right relationship with his creatures lies entirely with God. To deny this is to set aside God's grace as it is shown in the death of Jesus, to desert "the one who called you by the grace of Christ" (1:6), and to "fall away from grace" (5:4). The only alternative for those who have set aside God's grace is to travel down the blind alley of obedience to the law (5:3). At stake, therefore, is nothing less than the central conviction of Paul's theology: God is a gracious God who takes the entire initiative in the salvation of his sinful human creation.

PAUL'S RESPONSE TO THE AGITATORS' ANTI-GOSPEL

Paul's answer to the agitators' "gospel" focuses first on the authenticity of his gospel and then on three dimensions of his gospel that make it incompatible with the agitators' teaching.

10 On the replacement of his customary thanksgiving section with a series of curses, see Luke Timothy Johnson, *Letters to Paul's Delegates: 1 Timothy, 2 Timothy, Titus* (TNTC; Valley Forge, Pa.: Trinity Press International, 1996), 114.

11 Paul's word for the status of the acquitted is "righteousness" (*dikaiosynē*). He uses the verbal form of this word, "justify" (*dikaioō*), in 2:15 to refer to God's action of acquitting those who have faith in Jesus Christ. Although J. A. Ziesler, *The Meaning of Righteousness in Paul: A Linguistic and Theological Inquiry* (SNTSMS 20; Cambridge: Cambridge Univ. Press, 1972), 172–74, and Richard N. Longenecker, *Galatians* (WBC 41; Dallas: Word, 1990), 95, argue that "righteousness" carries both ethical and forensic connotations in 2:21, it seems better to interpret the noun here by the clearly forensic use of the verb in 2:16. See Ronald Y. K. Fung, *The Epistle to the Galatians* (NICNT; Grand Rapids: Eerdmans, 1988), 125–26, and the treatment of Paul's concept of righteousness generally in Stephen Westerholm, *Perspectives Old and New on Paul: The "Lutheran" Paul and His Critics* (Grand Rapids: Eerdmans, 2004), 261–96. The righteousness in view, moreover, is a present anticipation of a final verdict. On this compare 2:16–17 and 3:6 with 5:5.

12 Christ (the Messiah) was the representative of God's sinful people and so could absorb the people's curse. On this see N. T. Wright, *The Climax of the Covenant: Christ and the Law in Pauline Theology* (Edinburgh: T. & T. Clark, 1991), 151–53.

The Authenticity of Paul's Gospel

Two "gospels" are locked in combat in Galatians: the agitators' gospel, which links faith with conformity to the Mosaic law as the means of justification, and Paul's gospel, which insists that justification comes only through faith in Jesus Christ. Judging from the amount of space Paul devotes in the letter to denying false ideas about himself—that he seeks to please people, that he still preaches circumcision, that his gospel has human origins—his opponents probably attacked his gospel first by attacking Paul himself. Paul's gospel, they likely claimed, was a truncated form of the authentic gospel. Although Paul had himself once preached the authentic message of faith in Christ and acceptance of circumcision (5:11), he realized that Gentiles balked at accepting the yoke of the law, and so he began preaching a people-pleasing message that left out the demand to follow the law (1:10).[13] The agitators probably also claimed that the Jerusalem authorities commissioned preachers of the gospel and passed muster on their message (cf. 2:12), but that Paul was a renegade. If the Jerusalem "pillars" had ever given him permission to preach the gospel, he had violated it, and he had misled those whom he had taught.[14]

Whatever the precise form of their attack on the authenticity of his gospel, Paul devotes the first major section of his letter to defending it. Paul spends most of his effort showing that he received neither the gospel he preaches nor his authority to preach it from human authorities. His message came "by revelation from Jesus Christ" (1:12), and his authority, like that of the biblical prophets, came from the call of God (1:15).[15] For many years his contact with the acknowledged leaders of the Jerusalem church was limited—they certainly did not commission him to preach—and when on one occasion he did present his gospel to them, they approved both his gospel and his call to preach it to the Gentiles (1:13–2:10).

Far from disingenuously tailoring his message to fit his audience, Paul twice stood against attempts to force the Mosaic law on Gentiles: once during his conference with the Jerusalem leaders when false brothers insisted on the circumcision of Paul's Greek coworker Titus (2:3–5) and once in Antioch when Paul was the only Jewish Christian who resisted the attempt of "men from James" to enforce Mosaic dietary restrictions on the church (2:11–14). Paul's authority to preach the gospel came from Jesus Christ, and, as the scars on his body proved (6:17; cf. 2 Cor. 11:24), he never trimmed his message to fit the desires either of his audience or of supposed representatives from Jerusalem.

13 See, e.g., Lagrange, *Galates*, 31; Heinrich Schlier, *Der Brief an die Galater*, 11th ed. (MeyerK 7; Göttingen: Vandenhoeck & Ruprecht, 1951), 15; Beker, *Paul*, 43–44; Bruce, *Galatians*, 26. Martyn, *Galatians*, 138, suggests that Paul's opponents may have compared Paul with the crowd of insincere philosophers and Sophists who frequented the urban areas of his time.

14 See, e.g., Lagrange, *Galates*, xxx–xxxi; Beker, *Paul*, 43–44; and Bruce, *Galatians*, 26.

15 See Isa. 6:1–13; 49:1–6; Jer. 1:4–5; and the comments of Franz Mussner, *Der Galaterbrief* (HTKNT 9; Freiburg: Herder, 1974), 81–83; and Hans Hübner, *Biblische Theologie des Neuen Testaments*, 3 vols. (Göttingen: Vandenhoeck & Ruprecht, 1990–95), 2:61–62.

Three Essential Dimensions of the Gospel

In the second part of the letter Paul focuses on three dimensions of the gospel that are incompatible with the agitators' "different gospel": a chronological dimension, an anthropological dimension, and an ethical dimension.

The Gospel's Chronological Dimension

Paul believes that the Galatians and their teachers have committed a serious timekeeping blunder. By turning to the Mosaic law, the Galatians are turning the clock back from the period in which God has started to fulfill his promises in Scripture to a time dominated by "weak and poverty-stricken elements" (4:9, aut.). In an effort to arrest this regression, one of Paul's most important purposes in the letter is to assert—against the agitators' teaching—the critical chronological dimensions of the gospel that he preached.

He begins with Abraham. Scripture had said that God would bless all the Gentiles in Abraham, and Paul, linking this promise with other similar ones, observes that all these promises were made not only to Abraham but to his seed. Echoing Genesis 15:18, Paul refers to God's promises to give Abraham many descendants, place them in their own land, and bless the nations in Abraham, as God's "covenant" with Abraham (4:24). This covenant, Paul emphasizes, is prior to all other covenants and is eternal; like a human will, once it has been ratified, no one can change or add to it (3:15). The covenant was provisionally fulfilled in the birth, not of Ishmael, Abraham's child by the female slave Hagar, but of Isaac, Abraham's child by his wife Sarah (4:21–23). This provisional fulfillment, however, only prefigured the future and ultimate fulfillment of this covenant.

Paul argues further that four hundred and thirty years after this covenant with Abraham, God made another covenant with his people whose stipulations were recorded in the Mosaic law. Three aspects of this later, Mosaic covenant are important to Paul.

First, the Mosaic law pronounced a curse on all who violated its stipulations, and since no one was able to keep them, God's people received the law's curse. To demonstrate this, Paul quotes from Deuteronomy 21:23 (Gal. 3:10), and with this quotation he taps into a prominent Deuteronomic theme in Scripture.[16] According to this theme, the Mosaic covenant included blessings for obedience (Deut. 28:1–14; cf. Lev. 26:3–13) and curses for disobedience (Deut. 28:15–68; cf. Lev. 26:14–39), and Israel's studied tendency had been to disobey. This is why the Babylonians captured Judah, destroyed Jerusalem, and drove many of its people into exile (Deut. 28:49–52, 64–67; cf., e.g., Ezra 9:6–15; Neh. 9:6–37; Jer. 9:12–16; Ezek. 16:1–52; Dan.

16 Beker, *Paul*, 44–58, believes Paul's logic in Gal. 3 to be tortuous. This, he says, is because Paul begins with the thought that faith in Christ and the observance of the Mosaic law are antithetical and then tries to bend the agitators' salvation-historical arguments to prove this antithesis. Cf. Sanders, *Paul, the Law, and the Jewish People*, 17–27. J. Louis Martyn, *Theological Issues in the Letters of Paul* (Nashville: Abingdon, 1997), 111–23, 169, 241 n. 14, similarly believes that Paul's opponents have used a salvation-historical scheme that is incompatible with Paul's radical disassociation of the gospel from the biblical story of God's redemptive work. Salvation history, as it is anticipated in the Deuteronomic sections of the Jewish Scriptures, served Paul's purposes nicely, however, and if we fill out his argument with this substructure, Galatians does not put law and gospel into a radical antithesis with each other.

9:4–19; Baruch 1:15–3:8). Paul's point is that Jews who knew the history of their people as it was recorded in the law and the prophets ought to know that disobedience and the law's just curse dominated the era of the Mosaic law. Anyone who paid attention to the condition of Jews under Roman rule could see the effects of that curse around them.[17]

Second, God gave the law not so that people might keep its various stipulations and be justified by keeping them, but to define sin specifically and enclose everything under sin's power.[18] Paul speaks of this period of the law's domination metaphorically as an experience of slavery (Gal. 2:4; 4:1–11; 4:21–5:1) and says that the symbol of this period is Ishmael, Abraham's child by his female slave rather than by Isaac, "his son by the free woman . . . born as a result of a promise" (4:23). Although Paul does not spell it out specifically, this identification of life under the Mosaic law with slavery probably means that when the Mosaic covenant was in effect, people were under the domination of sin and the penalty of death and exile that the law mandated for those who disobeyed its commands (cf. Deut. 28:68; Ezra 9:9; Neh. 9:36).

Third, the Mosaic law was temporary, intended to be in effect only until God fulfilled his promise to Abraham. This is the most important point Paul makes about the Mosaic law, and he emphasizes it frequently. The law was in effect, he says, "until the Seed to whom the promise referred had come" (Gal. 3:19), until "what was promised . . . might be given to those who believe" (3:22), "until faith should be revealed" (3:23), and until "the time had fully come" (4:4; cf. 4:2). The Mosaic covenant, therefore, was not an eternal covenant but a temporary step toward God's climactic act of redemption.[19]

When the law had fully completed its purposes, God sent his Son Jesus to rescue his people from "the present evil age" by his death on the cross (1:4; cf. 4:2, 4–5). Christ's death was able to accomplish this because the curse that the law pronounced on God's disobedient people was focused on Christ when he died on the cross (3:13).[20] This event split the ages in two. Before the cross, God's people lived in the age dominated by slavery under the Mosaic law. After the cross, God's people lived in the eschatological age when the curse of the law was removed from them and they

17 See Frank Thielman, *From Plight to Solution: A Jewish Framework for Understanding Paul's View of the Law in Galatians and Romans* (NovTSup 61; Leiden: Brill, 1989), 28–45, the argument of which is extended in idem, *Paul and the Law: A Contextual Approach* (Downers Grove, Ill.: InterVarsity Press, 1994), 48–68. See also Wright, *Climax*, 144–48.

18 In Galatians, the law is God's ally, used for his purposes. It is not as Martyn, *Theological Issues*, 235–49, claims, an entity inimical to the gospel. Cf. Beker, *Paul*, 54; Hyam Maccoby, *Paul and Hellenism* (London/Philadelphia: SCM/Trinity Press International, 1991), 40–43; and Hübner, *Biblische Theologie*, 2:82–83, 94. Paul's intention in saying that the law "was put into effect through angels by a mediator" (3:19) is not to dissociate God from giving the law, as Martyn, *Galatians*, 364–70, claims. Indeed, some Jews of Paul's time believed that the presence of angels at the giving of the law enhanced the law's glory (Deut. 33:2, LXX; Acts 7:53; Heb. 2:2). On this see Peter Stuhlmacher, *Biblische Theologie des Neuen Testaments*, 2 vols. (Göttingen: Vandenhoeck & Ruprecht, 1997), 1:265. The angelic and Mosaic mediation of the law in 3:19 simply emphasize the law's provisional character (cf. 2 Cor. 3:12–18).

19 Paul's emphasis on the temporal nature of the law excludes the interpretation of the letter that claims Paul is only resisting a misunderstanding of the law and that, once freed from this misunderstanding, Paul considers the law still to be in effect. See, e.g., C. E. B. Cranfield, *The Epistle to the Romans*, 2 vols. (ICC; Edinburgh: T. & T. Clark, 1975–79), 2:857–60, who believes that in Galatians Paul is opposing a legalistic misunderstanding of the law, and Dunn, *Jesus, Paul, and the Law*, 250–51, who argues that Paul is battling the law's misuse for nationalistic purposes.

20 Wright, *Climax*, 151–53.

were redeemed from slavery under the law's just penalty for sin (3:13; 4:5).[21] Everyone who hears the message of Christ crucified and believes that his death solved the problem of the law's curse receives the Spirit of God whom the prophets promised and is included among God's eschatologically restored people (3:1–5, 12, 14).

Hearing, faith, and the Spirit's work have happened among Gentiles apart from their acceptance of the Mosaic law (3:1–5), showing that faith, not the Mosaic law, is the organizing principle of the people of God. That faith in God is the basis for a relationship with him should occasion no surprise since Abraham demonstrates that God has always worked this way: "He believed God, and it was credited to him as righteousness" (3:6; cf. Gen. 15:6). That Gentiles enter God's people by faith alone should also be expected since the Scripture announced this good news beforehand to Abraham when it said, "All nations [Gentiles] will be blessed through you" (Gal. 3:8; cf. Gen. 12:3; 18:18; 22:18; 26:4; 28:14). Gentile faith in the gospel, then, represents the ultimate fulfillment of God's promises to Abraham (Gal. 3:6–9).

The manner in which Scripture describes the promises to Abraham confirm this further. Scripture says that the promises were made to Abraham, "and to his seed" (3:16). Christ is the "Seed," and those who belong to Christ are also "Abraham's seed, and heirs according to the promise" (3:29). Since people belong to Christ through faith alone, anyone can be Abraham's seed—Jew, Greek, slave, free, male, and female. Christ's involvement in the fulfillment of God's promise to Abraham, therefore, means the involvement of this diverse group of people who belong to Christ through faith (3:26–29).

By turning back to the era of the Mosaic law, however, the Galatians and their teachers have started a futile attempt to swim against the current of salvation history. They have denied the obvious—that God's inclusion of Gentiles into his people by faith in Christ is the fulfillment of his promise to bless all the Gentiles through Abraham—and have instead claimed that Abraham's inheritance can only be realized through the law, and thus through Jews and Jewish proselytes (3:18). By reintroducing the law, they have regressed in time to the period of the law's curse and have decided to live under that curse rather than under God's eschatologically provided remedy for it (3:10–12). They have preferred life under a child-minder to adult life (3:24), life under trustees and guardians to life as the grown son who has come into his inheritance (4:1–7), and life in an enslaved, earthly Jerusalem to the eschatological life of the heavenly Jerusalem (4:25–26). For the Galatians, such a life is no better than their life under the idolatrous practices of their former pagan religions (4:8–10). To regress to the Mosaic law is, in short, to desert God (1:6) and to be cut off from Christ (5:4).

21 Beker, *Paul*, 58, is correct to say that "the eschatological present dominates the letter." This does not mean, however, that "Paul bends theological tradition radically to his own purpose and comes close to a Marcionite split between law and gospel." The tension between the "already" of Christ's redemptive work on the cross and the "not yet" of life in "the present evil age" (1:4) is clear in Paul's ethical admonitions in 5:16–26.

The Gospel's Anthropological Dimension

If we were only to think of Paul as arguing in chronological terms that the period of God's curse on his people has ended, we would miss a less prominent, but nevertheless important, aspect of his argument. Paul not only believes that the nation of Israel had sinned against God and needed God's eschatological restoration but that individuals, whether Jewish or Gentile, are incapable of keeping God's commands and therefore stand individually and existentially under the curse of God. Each stands in need of Christ's gracious death on his or her behalf. From an anthropological perspective, therefore, Israel and the Gentiles are one people, for "no flesh [*sarx*]" Paul argues, can be justified by works of the law (2:15–16).[22]

This anthropological perspective is not Paul's original theological insight but was the perspective of the Jewish Scriptures and of some other Jews of the Second Temple period. When Paul says that "by works of the law no one will be justified" (2:16), he is echoing, probably consciously, the psalmist's plea to God, "Do not bring your servant into judgment, for no one living is righteous before you" (Ps. 143:2).[23] Similarly, in a liturgical confession incorporated into the book of Baruch sometime between the third and the first centuries B.C., the author mourns the transgressions of his people against the Mosaic law and bemoans the curses of the law that these transgressions have activated, but he also recognizes that the responsibility for Israel's sin lies not in a vague sense with the nation but with each Israelite:

> We did not listen to the voice of the Lord our God in all the words of the prophets whom he sent to us, but all of us followed the intent of our own wicked hearts by serving other gods and doing what is evil in the sight of the Lord our God. . . .
>
> The Lord our God is in the right, but there is open shame on us and our ancestors this very day. All those calamities with which the Lord threatened us have come upon us. Yet we have not entreated the favor of the Lord by turning away, each of us from the thoughts of our wicked hearts. (Baruch 1:21–22; 2:6–8)

Paul also recalls to the minds of the Galatians and their teachers not only that Israel has not kept the law and so stands under the law's curse as a nation but that no individual has kept the law and therefore no one can be justified by the works that it demands. This is the implication of Paul's speech to Peter at Antioch where Peter withdrew from table fellowship with Gentiles in the church in an attempt to "force Gentiles to follow Jewish customs" (Gal. 2:14). To do this, Paul claims, is to imply that the Mosaic law can justify people before God. Yet every Jew should know what Psalm

22 Paul is not saying, therefore, that even if the law could be kept, those who keep it would not be justified. For this position see Martin Luther's 1519 and 1535 lectures on Galatians in *LW* 27:218–225 and 26:122–23 and the similar positions of Rudolf Bultmann, *Theology of the New Testament*, 2 vols. (New York: Charles Scribner's Sons, 1951–55), 1:263–65, and Stuhlmacher, *Biblische Theologie*, 1:267, 278–79. Paul is instead claiming simply that the law cannot be kept. Cf. Thomas R. Schreiner, *The Law and Its Fulfillment: A Pauline Theology of Law* (Grand Rapids: Baker, 1993), 41–71.

23 On the theological similarity between Paul's assertion that no flesh will be justified by works of the law and the psalmist's plea in 143:2, see Hübner, *Biblische Theologie*, 2:64–68. Hübner aptly observes that Paul, as a former Pharisee, would have known the Psalms by heart and that his allusion to this psalm here would have arisen from a familiarity with the entire psalm as a heartfelt prayer.

143:2 affirms—that no one can keep the law well enough to be justified by it (Gal. 2:16).[24] Indeed it is this knowledge, Paul says, that has led even "we who are Jews by birth and not 'Gentile sinners'" to "put our faith in Christ Jesus" (2:15–16).

Just as Paul believes that the law's role within Israel was to define sin specifically as transgression and so to prepare for the coming of Jesus Christ and for justification by faith in him (3:19–4:7), so he can say of himself, "through the law I died to the law so that I might live to God" (2:19). For Paul individually, the law pointed to its own end—it spoke of his inability to be justified by keeping its stipulations and so prepared the way for him to "live to God" through faith in Christ, who was crucified not only so that the curse of the law might be removed from God's people generally, but from Paul individually and specifically. Thus, Paul says, the Son of God "loved me and gave himself for me" (2:20).

This set of events, whereby God through the death of his Son redeemed his people not only corporately but individually from slavery to sin, Paul calls "the grace of Christ" (1:6; 6:18) or "the grace of God" (2:21; cf. 1:15). To reintroduce the Mosaic law into the life of one whom God has called by his grace is to set aside or fall away from God's grace (2:21; 5:4). In 2:21, Paul explains why this is so. If he began keeping the Mosaic law as a means of maintaining a right relationship with God (2:18), he would imply that the law could be kept and that "Christ died for nothing." He would, in other words, be rejecting God's gracious provision for his sinful plight and be asserting what every Jew should know is untrue—that the law can be fully kept.

The Gospel's Ethical Dimension

Although we cannot be certain, it is probable that the agitators in Galatia acted the way that Peter had acted in Antioch: They attempted to coerce the Gentile believers in Paul's churches to accept circumcision by threatening to withdraw from fellowship with them if they did not accept the Mosaic law.[25] How could people trying to keep the dietary commandments of God, they might have said, eat with uncircumcised Gentiles who might serve wine or meat that was impure or tainted with idolatry? Just as Peter began to "draw back and separate himself from the Gentiles" because of such concerns (2:12), so the Galatians' new teachers, Paul says, want to exclude you "so that you may be zealous for them" (4:17).[26]

It also seems probable that the Galatian Christians were attracted to the ethical certainty that the agitators' perspective provided. When the Galatians abandoned their idolatry and accepted the gospel (4:8), they also abandoned their traditional ways of life. Their family and friends may have cut off contact with them.[27] The

24 *Pace* Sanders, *Paul, the Law, and the Jewish People*, 23, 27–29, the assumption that the law cannot be fully kept seems also to lie behind 5:3 and 6:13. In 5:3 Paul warns the Galatians that those who expect to be justified by keeping the law must keep it all, and in 6:13 he observes that not even the agitators are able to keep the whole law.

25 Cf. Barclay, *Obeying the Truth*, 59.

26 E. P. Sanders, "Jewish Association with Gentiles and Galatians 2:11–14," in *The Conversation Continues: Studies in Paul and John in Honor of J. Louis Martyn*, ed. Robert T. Fortna and Beverly R. Gaventa, (Nashville: Abingdon, 1990), 170–88, argues persuasively that the issue in Antioch was not violation of a strict rule that Jews must not associate with Gentiles. Instead, the issue was that Peter was fraternizing too extensively with Gentiles. The fear may have been that such "close association might lead to contact with idolatry or transgression of one of the biblical food laws" (186).

27 Cf. Barclay, *Obeying the Truth*, 56–60.

Mosaic law, however, provided immediate identification with a venerable social group and detailed ethical guidance.[28] To a group who may have felt that Paul's preaching of the gospel left them socially marginalized and without an ethical anchor, the agitators' message of acceptance and moral certainty must have seemed particularly appealing.

Paul believes, however, that the agitators' tactic of social coercion and the Galatians' fears that they are without an ethical anchor are inconsistent with "the truth of the gospel." Two resources answer this concern about ethics: the specific ethical teaching that the gospel itself implies and the guidance of God's Spirit.

First, Paul claims that the new era of the gospel brings with it a new law that is incompatible with the agitators' efforts to force Gentiles to accept circumcision. Paul refers to this law in 6:2, where he tells the Galatians, "Carry each other's burdens, and in this way you will fulfill the law of Christ." The "law of Christ" is probably Jesus' own summary of the Mosaic law's commands concerning human relationships. That Jesus summarized these commands in terms of love for neighbor was widely known among early Christians generally (Matt. 22:39; Mark 12:31; Luke 10:27; cf. John 13:34; 15:12, 17; 1 John 4:11), and Jesus' teaching is probably the source of Paul's own statement in Galatians, "The entire law is summed up in a single command: 'Love your neighbor as yourself'" (Gal. 5:14; cf. Lev. 19:18).[29]

Efforts to coerce Gentile Christians to accept the Mosaic law by withdrawing from fellowship with them, however, violate this new law. This may have been the sense in which Paul considered Peter a "transgressor" for trying to "force [*anankazō*] Gentiles to follow Jewish customs" (Gal. 2:14, aut.; cf. 2:18). The term "transgressor" (*parabatēs*) appears only four other times in the New Testament, and each appearance refers to transgression of a particular law (Rom. 2:25, 27; James 2:9, 11). In Galatians 2:18, therefore, Paul is saying that transgression is not a matter of violating the dietary stipulations of the Mosaic law but of refusing to eat with Gentiles. It is, in other words, a violation of the law of Christ—to love one's neighbor as one's self. Like Peter, the agitators in Galatia are trying to "force" (*anankazō*) the Gentile Galatian Christians to accept circumcision (Gal. 6:12). To accomplish this, they have threatened to "exclude" them from fellowship if they do not conform to the Mosaic law (4:17). These efforts, however, are inconsistent with the Mosaic law as Jesus taught it and made it his own when he summarized it under Leviticus 19:18, "Love your neighbor as yourself."[30]

Second, the Galatians should not fear that they are without an ethical anchor because God has fulfilled among them his promise to put his Spirit within his people during the eschatological age of their restoration.[31] He has done this apart from any requirement that they accept the yoke of the Mosaic law. Instead the Spirit came to

28 Ibid., 70–72.

29 See David Wenham, *Paul: Follower of Jesus or Founder of Christianity* (Grand Rapids: Eerdmans, 1995), 255–56.

30 See also Thielman, *Paul and the Law*, 141–42, and idem, *The Law and the New Testament: The Question of Continuity* (New York: Crossroad, 1999), 19. Cf. Barclay, *Obeying the Truth*, 223, and Jan Lambrecht, "Transgressor by Nullifying God's Grace: A Study of Gal 2,18–21," *Bib* 72 (1991): 230–36.

31 See, e.g., Ezek. 11:19; 36:26–27; 37:14; 39:29. Cf. Barclay, *Obeying the Truth*, 84–85.

them when they believed the gospel (Gal. 3:1–5, 14), and the Spirit leads believers to walk along an ethical path (5:16, 18, 25; 6:8), avoiding activities incompatible with life in the kingdom of God (5:19–21) and engaging in behavior that no law would forbid (5:22–26).

If the Galatians are concerned about ethical moorings, therefore, they will do well to reject the teaching and example of the agitators (4:30), focus on the law of Christ (5:14; 6:2), and keep in step with the Spirit who has been among them since before the agitators became interested in them (3:1–5).

A NEW INTERPRETIVE PERSPECTIVE ON GALATIANS

During the closing decades of the twentieth century, a dramatic shift took place in the scholarly interpretation of Paul's understanding of justification by faith apart from works of the law. Paul's letter to the Galatians has been at the center of this shift.[32]

Traditional exegesis of the letter considered it to be primarily a statement that only God's gift of faith in Jesus Christ, not human achievement, could effect a right standing with God.[33] More recently, many interpreters have argued that if Paul was battling a Jewish theology of salvation by human effort, he was beating the air. Second Temple Judaism did not typically claim that membership in God's people came by human effort to do what the law commands but was God's free gift to all Israelites because of his covenant with them.[34] When Paul contrasts works of the law with faith in Christ, therefore, he has perhaps misrepresented Jewish soteriology in an effort to win the argument with his opponents, or he is trying to dissociate the church from Judaism, or else he is targeting the Jewish use of the law as a national boundary for distinguishing the Jews, as God's people, from the Gentiles.[35]

This reevaluation of Galatians has often been accompanied by a complaint that since the Protestant Reformation, scholars have tended to read the letter through Lutheran-tinted spectacles. Traditionally, the argument often goes, scholars have turned Paul's comments about God's acceptance of Gentiles into statements about how the individual finds peace with God through faith rather than through human striving.[36]

32 For surveys of the rise and fall of the scholarly consensus on this issue, see Thielman, *Paul and the Law*, 14–47; Colin G. Kruse, *Paul, the Law, and Justification* (Peabody, Mass.: Hendrickson, 1996), 27–53; and esp. Westerholm, *Perspectives*, 2–258.

33 See, e.g., the comments of Martin Luther, *LW*, 26:124; John Calvin, *Commentaries on the Epistles of Paul to the Galatians and Ephesians* (Grand Rapids: Eerdmans, 1948; orig. ed. 1548), 69; and William Perkins, *A Commentary on Galatians* (New York: Pilgrim, 1989; orig. ed. 1617), 102–3, on Gal. 2:16, where "works of the law" mean human achievement and Paul's Jewish Christian opponents in Galatia are equivalent to the Papists who believe that human effort combines with God's grace to produce justification. See also the historical survey in Westerholm, *Perspectives*, 3–97.

34 E. P. Sanders, *Paul and Palestinian Judaism: A Comparison of Patterns of Religion* (Philadelphia: Fortress, 1977), 1–428, and idem, *Judaism: Practice and Belief 63 BCE–66 CE* (London/Philadelphia: SCM/Trinity Press International, 1992), 47–303.

35 For the first position, see Heikki Räisänen, *Paul and the Law* (WUNT 29; Tübingen: J.C.B. Mohr [Paul Siebeck],1983), 187–88. For the second approach, see Francis Watson, *Paul, Judaism and the Gentiles: A Sociological Approach* (SNTSMS 56; Cambridge: Cambridge Univ. Press, 1986), 69, and cf. Sanders, *Paul and Palestinian Judaism*, 551–52. For the third thesis, see James D. G. Dunn, *The Epistle to the Galatians* (BNTC; Peabody, Mass.: Hendrickson, 1993), 135–38, and, idem, *The Theology of Paul the Apostle* (Grand Rapids: Eerdmans, 1998), 334–89.

36 Dunn, *Galatians*, 135; idem, *Jesus, Paul and the Law*, 185, 246; idem, *The Theology of Paul the Apostle* (Grand Rapids: Eerdmans, 1998), 334–89; Watson, *Paul, Judaism and the Gentiles*;

The theology of Galatians, however, is rich enough to accommodate both the traditional emphasis on the justification of the sinful individual and the recent emphasis on the inclusiveness of the gospel. Paul's convictions about human sin and God's work within history to redeem his creatures from it have both social and individual implications.[37]

For Paul, sin plagues all social groups and dominates every individual within those groups. This is the burden of 2:15–21, which begins with an emphasis on the common sinfulness of Gentiles as well as Jews and ends with Paul's personal confession that through the law he died to the law that he might live for God. He believes that God has always offered faith as the solution to this all-encompassing human plight, and thus God placed Abraham in a right relationship with himself by faith. Faith looks forward to the faithfulness of the one in whom it is placed, and God showed himself faithful to Abraham in a provisional way through the birth of Isaac. He showed himself faithful in a more complete way in the birth of Jesus Christ, through whom believing Gentiles enter Abraham's family.

Between Abraham and Christ, God gave the law (through mediating angels) in order to make plain beyond any doubt the human plight of sin. The law was a temporary institution, in effect only until Christ should come and take on himself the curse that the law justly pronounced on God's people for their sin. Since this central event, God has removed the curse for all who have faith, has given the eschatological Spirit whom the prophets promised, and, as Gentiles respond to the gospel in faith, has fulfilled his promise to Abraham that all the nations of the earth will be blessed through him. Now God's people, Jews as well as Gentiles, no longer live by the law of Moses but by the law of Christ, summarized in Jesus' teaching on Leviticus 19:18.

On the surface, the error of the agitators and the Galatians is twofold. It lies, first, in their readiness to turn the clock back to the period when Abraham's promise was not yet fulfilled and the law's curse still rested on God's people. It consists, second, in failing to live by the law of Christ—to love one's neighbor as oneself. Underneath both problems, however, lies a deeper issue: an inadequate understanding of human sin. If Jews as well as Gentiles are sinners standing under the law's curse and both are alike put into a right relationship with God through faith in Christ, then God has rescued believers—both Jews and Gentiles—from the present evil age and calls on them to live in harmony with each other.

In none of this does Paul claim that all adherents of Second Temple Judaism were legalists. His argument is leveled against Jewish Christians whose imposition of the Jewish law on Gentiles implies, according to Paul, an ethnocentrism and an optimism about the human ability to keep the law that is incompatible both with Scripture and the gospel. The peculiar circumstance of the imposition of the law on

---

Wright, *Climax*, 260–61; idem, *What Saint Paul Really Said: Was Paul of Tarsus the Real Founder of Christianity?* (Grand Rapids: Eerdmans, 1997), 120–21; Barclay, *Obeying the Truth*, 82; and Bruce W. Longenecker, *The Triumph of Abraham's God: The Transformation of Identity in Galatians* (Nashville: Abingdon, 1998), 16–17.

37 Cf. Westerholm, *Perspectives*, 440–45.

Gentiles prompts Paul to draw these conclusions, not an analysis of Judaism generally. By coercing Gentiles who believed in Christ to accept the Mosaic law, the agitators implied that human social privilege and human effort had something to contribute to a right standing with God, and to say this, according to Paul, is to "set aside the grace of God" (2:21; cf. 5:4).

The "new perspective on Paul" and on Galatians, therefore, has usefully emphasized the corporate and ethnic dimensions of Paul's theology in this letter.[38] It has reminded us that Paul's argument cannot be properly understood apart from the biblical and Jewish presuppositions of both Paul and his opponents. At the same time, its advocates have been too dismissive of the traditional reading of the letter.[39] As dependent as the proper understanding of the letter is on the contingencies of its historical situation and as concerned as the letter is with the question of social identity, Paul would not have formulated his argument as we find it in Galatians had he not believed that all individuals—whatever their social location—are sinful and that no effort to keep God's requirements can win acquittal in God's court on the final day. Acquittal before that ultimate tribunal must come through faith and as God's free gift.

THE MOSAIC LAW AND THE GOSPEL OF GOD'S GRACE IN GALATIA

Paul and the agitators in Galatia have much in common. Both are Jewish; both believe that the Mosaic law is Scripture; both believe that faith in Christ is necessary for membership in the people of God; both believe that Gentiles can belong to God's people; and both believe that ethical living is important.

For Paul, however, a critical difference separates him from his opponents. In this difference lies nothing less than the truth of the gospel: To claim that Gentiles must become Jewish by shouldering the Mosaic law in addition to having faith in Christ implies that human effort is, in part, necessary for membership in God's people. If this is true, then God has not started to fulfill the promises of the prophets for the restoration of his people in Jesus' death and the Spirit's coming. The just curse of law on transgressors is still in place and evidence of the Spirit's presence among the Galatians must be some mistake. Humanity is not wholly sinful but possesses the ability to make some effort to please God and win his favor. Most important of all, God is not the gracious God that the Scriptures show him to be; rather, he is only a God who meets sinful humanity halfway toward its redemption.

Against all this, Paul insists that the Spirit's presence in Galatia shows that God's promises through the prophets are being fulfilled and that human beings are too sinful to contribute anything to their redemption. To believe this, Paul insists, is not to abandon any motivation for ethics. It is to affirm that with the power of the eschatologically given Spirit, those who are already included in God's people by his grace

38 See James D. G. Dunn, "The New Perspective on Paul," *BJRL* 65 (1983): 95–122, subsequently included in idem, *Jesus, Paul and the Law*, 183–214.

39 This is the thesis of Westerholm's book, *Perspectives Old and New on Paul*.

can and should love one another. This law of love is precisely what Paul's opponents in Galatia are violating, however, by their efforts to exclude the Galatian Christians from fellowship unless they adopt the Mosaic law.

In short, the truth of the gospel implies that God is an entirely gracious God. Adopting the manner of life that God's will requires enters the picture not as a means of joining God's people but as a response to his grace.

Chapter 12

FIRST CORINTHIANS: A PLEA FOR PEACE, HOLINESS, AND FIDELITY

CONFUSION AT CORINTH

When Paul wrote the Thessalonian letters, he was hard at work establishing a Christian community at Corinth. According to Acts, here too he earned his own bread by working with his hands alongside Aquila and Priscilla, two fellow Jews who, like Paul, were both Christians and tentmakers (Acts 18:3; 1 Cor. 4:12; 9:12, 15, 18). Each Sabbath Paul left his knife, awls, needle, and thread behind to attend the local synagogue and discuss the gospel with both Jews and Gentile sympathizers who gathered there.[1]

Soon Timothy and Silas arrived from Macedonia—presumably with monetary gifts for the support of Paul's ministry—and this permitted Paul to devote himself exclusively to his efforts in the synagogue (Acts 18:5; cf. Phil. 4:15).[2] These efforts were not, on the whole, successful. Paul's audience eventually became unreceptive, and, losing patience with this forum for his message, he proclaimed that "from now on" he would "go to the Gentiles." This change meant moving one door down the street to a house owned by a Gentile who was sympathetic to Judaism. As a result of Paul's preaching there, "many of the Corinthians who heard him believed and were baptized." Ironically this group included the synagogue ruler Crispus and his household (Acts 18:6–8), although we read of no other conversions from among Jews.[3]

Luke's account, although brief, demonstrates two aspects of the Corinthian church that receive confirmation in 1 Corinthians and aid the effort to uncover the theology of the letter. First, at least by the time Paul wrote this letter, Gentiles seem to be in the overwhelming majority. "You know," Paul says in 1 Corinthians 12:2, "that when you were Gentiles, you were led astray by dumb idols" (aut.). This impression is confirmed when we consider the nature of the problems Paul addresses in the letter. Incest (5:1–13), using prostitutes (6:12–20; cf. 2 Cor. 12:21), sexual abstinence within marriage (7:1–7), and idolatry (10:1–22) were not the vices of practicing Jews. It is

---

1 On the nature of Paul's tentmaking occupation, see Ronald F. Hock, *The Social Context of Paul's Ministry: Tentmaking and Apostleship* (Philadelphia: Fortress, 1980); Jerome Murphy-O'Connor, *St. Paul's Corinth: Texts and Archaeology* (GNS 6; Wilmington, Del.: Michael Glazier, 1983), 167–70; and idem, *Paul: A Critical Life* (Oxford: Oxford Univ. Press, 1996), 86–89.

2 Cf. also 2 Cor. 11:9; Phil. 4:15; and BDAG, 971.

3 Crispus' apparent successor, Sosthenes, was beaten by an unruly mob in the presence of the proconsul Gallio (Acts 18:17). Did he too become a Christian and later join Paul in writing 1 Corinthians from Ephesus (1 Cor. 1:1)? We cannot know since Acts 18:17 does not give an explanation for the incident. Luke's purpose in referring to the beating is simply to underline the political indifference of Gallio to Christianity since he viewed it as a Jewish concern.

unlikely, therefore, that various factions within the Corinthian congregation split along ethnic lines.[4]

Second, the congregation included people from various social classes. Paul, Aquila, and Priscilla were manual laborers, a group with low social standing. "All those workers who are paid for their labour and not for their skill have servile and demeaning employment," said Cicero, "for in their case the very wage is a contract to servitude."[5] The social standing of others within the church, however, may have been much higher. Crispus and Stephanus were householders (1 Cor. 1:16; 16:15) and therefore probably owned slaves.[6] Crispus was a synagogue ruler (Acts 18:8), and since synagogue rulers were responsible for the maintenance of the synagogue building, they were often wealthy.[7] Titius Justus owned a house that could accommodate an audience for Paul and probably occupied a prime location near the marketplace (Acts 18:7).[8] Gaius's house was large enough not only to accommodate Paul as a guest during a later visit to the city but also to serve as a meeting place for the whole Corinthian church (Rom. 16:23).

Thus, although "not many" of the Corinthian believers "were influential" or "of noble birth" (1 Cor. 1:26), some clearly were, and this must have created immediate tensions within the Corinthian Christian community.[9] Would the elite continue to attend banquets to which they were invited, although this might mean participating in idolatrous ceremonies and offense to the poor who were unaccustomed to such banquets? Would the menu and seating arrangements for the various social classes follow traditional customs when the church gathered for the Lord's Supper, or did the gospel demand different arrangements? Would the educated within the church have a different response to such Christian teachings as the bodily resurrection than that of the uneducated?

After Paul left Corinth and eventually settled in Ephesus, these and other issues led to problems.[10] He had to write a letter telling the Corinthian believers not to mix with sexually immoral people (1 Cor. 5:9). He had intended this to refer to believers who were continuing to live sexually immoral lives, but the Corinthians misunderstood him and thought that he was recommending the impractical step of dissociating from any sexually immoral person. To do that in Corinth, "you would have to leave this world" (1 Cor. 5:10)! Paul also sent Timothy to Corinth to remind the Corinthians of the apostle's "way of life in Christ Jesus" (4:17; cf. 16:10)—the

4 *Pace*, e.g., C. K. Barrett, *Essays on Paul* (Philadelphia: Westminster, 1982), 49–50, and Hans Hübner, *Biblische Theologie des Neuen Testaments*, 3 vols. (Göttingen: Vandenhoeck & Ruprecht, 1993), 2:165, who believe that the "Cephas party" at Corinth (1:12; 3:22; 9:5) was composed of Jewish Christians offended by the eating of meat offered to idols (8:1–12; 10:23–11:1).

5 *Off.* 1.150. The translation is from Cicero, *On Duties* (Cambridge Texts in the History of Political Thought; Cambridge: Cambridge Univ. Press, 1991), 58. See Murphy-O'Connor, *Paul*, 89. Similar upper class attitudes toward menial labor are found in the mid- to late-second century A.D. in Lucian (*Fug.* 13, 17) and Celsus (Origen, *Cels.* 3.55).

6 Gerd Theissen, *The Social Setting of Pauline Christianity: Essays on Corinth* (Philadelphia: Fortress, 1982), 83–87.

7 Ibid., 74–75.

8 Luke tells us that the house of Titius Justus was located next door to the synagogue. An inscription from a first-century synagogue has been found near the city's marketplace. On the location of the synagogue, see Theissen, *Social Setting*, 90.

9 Theissen, *Social Setting*, 70–73.

10 See Bruce W. Winter, *After Paul Left Corinth: The Influence of Secular Ethics and Social Change* (Grand Rapids: Eerdmans, 2001), 25–28.

manner of life he had taught them while in Corinth but that they had apparently forgotten.

Before Timothy's return, Paul received reports from various sources of a series of problems in Corinth.[11] Some of "Chloe's people" had arrived in Ephesus and told Paul that the Corinthian church was divided into factions centered on certain leaders who had at various times traveled to Corinth and worked among the Christians there—Paul, Apollos, and Cephas (1:11–12).[12] Perhaps it was also from Chloe's people that Paul "heard" of three other distressing problems: a Corinthian believer was having sexual relations with his stepmother (5:1), two believers were suing one another in a pagan court (6:1), and some Corinthian believers were using prostitutes (6:15–16).[13]

As if this were not enough, three Corinthian Christians—Stephanus, Fortunatus, and Achaicus—visited Paul and were probably the couriers of a letter from the Corinthian community asking about Paul's position on sex within marriage, divorce, and celibacy (7:1).[14] They also brought more distressing information about the condition of the congregation. The church had become confused and divided over the issue of idolatry (8:1–11:1); disorder and division plagued its corporate worship (11:1–14:40); and some Corinthian Christians had repudiated belief in the resurrection of the dead (15:1–58). To make matters worse—if that were possible—part of the community was questioning Paul's apostolic authority (9:1–3; cf. 4:3–5). All of this provided ample reason for a lengthy letter, and 1 Corinthians is the result.

Paul's letter focuses on three critical issues: peace within the church, holiness in the world, and fidelity to the gospel. First, and most important, was a peaceful resolution to the church's disunity. The Corinthian church was split into factions over who followed the most eloquent teacher and what rights a Christian was permitted to exercise, and much of the letter attempts to persuade the Corinthians that they should be unified.[15] Second, the issue of holiness, although not as dominant as unity

11 When Paul wrote 1 Corinthians, he intended to stay in Ephesus until Pentecost (1 Cor. 16:8). Luke, however, says that he left before Pentecost in order to be in Jerusalem for that festival (Acts 20:16). This probably means that Paul left Ephesus earlier than he had originally planned, but not before suffering the imprisonment from which Philippians was written (see ch. 13, below) and which may have been the culmination of the trouble that he mentions in 1 Cor. 16:9.

12 On this, see Margaret M. Mitchell, *Paul and the Rhetoric of Reconciliation* (HUT 29; Tübingen: J. C. B. Mohr [Paul Siebeck], 1991), 81–86. Mitchell argues persuasively that whereas disunity plagued the church, Paul's statement that the Corinthians are saying "I am of Paul, I of Apollos, I of Cephas, and I of Christ" (1:12) does not describe slogans that the Corinthians have adopted but Paul's assessment that they are acting childishly. "I am of Christ" is Paul's idea of what the Corinthians ought to be saying. Cf. 3:23, where Paul seems to replace this element of his characterization with "and you are of Christ."

13 This information may have come from "Chloe's people," from "Stephanus, Fortunatus, and Achaicus" (16:17), or from some other source not mentioned in the letter. Paul's use of the term "reported" (*akouetai*) in 5:1 implies that he received at least the information on which 5:1–13 is based through an oral report. Cf. 11:18, where Paul says that he "hears" (*akouō*) of divisions among the Corinthians at the Lord's Supper.

14 Scholars commonly claim that Paul uses the phrase *peri de* in 1 Corinthians (1 Cor. 7:1, 25; 8:1; 12:1; 16:1, 12) to signal those places in the letter where he is answering a specific question from the Corinthians. Margaret M. Mitchell, "Concerning ΠΕΡΙ ΔΕ in 1 Corinthians," *NovT* 31 (1989): 229–56, has now shown this to rest on a false understanding of the function of *peri de* in ancient epistolary literature. The expression was simply used to indicate the introduction of a topic well known to both author and recipient.

15 See esp. Mitchell, *Rhetoric of Reconciliation*, who argues that the letter is a piece of deliberative rhetoric whose purpose is to bring unity to a divided church and that Paul frequently uses the commonplaces of political rhetoric to accomplish this goal. As I argue in this chapter, Paul is concerned with more than unity in 1 Corinthians, and even his concern with unity is theologically rather than politically driven. Mitchell has, however, identified the

and clearly tied to it, is also a theme in its own right. As the people of God, standing in continuity with ancient Israel as described in Paul's Scriptures, the Corinthian church must avoid blurring the boundaries between itself and the wider world. Third, Paul is aware that some within the church have denied the bodily resurrection of believers. The vigor of his response shows how seriously Paul takes the problem: Without the resurrection of believers at the coming of Christ, there is no atonement for sin and no future hope for the Christian.

PEACE WITHIN THE CHURCH

Paul's chief concern in 1 Corinthians is to bring concord to a divided church. He hints at the importance of the theme already in the letter's greeting where he addresses his comments not only to the Corinthians but to "all those everywhere who call on the name of our Lord Jesus Christ—their Lord and ours" (1:2).[16] The theme breaks into the open in 1:10, where Paul begins the body of the letter with a simple statement of his thesis:

> I appeal to you, brothers, in the name of our Lord Jesus Christ, that all of you agree with one another so that there may be no divisions among you and that you may be perfectly united in mind and thought. (1:10)[17]

This statement leads directly to Paul's most vigorous description of the problem and plea for its remedy in 1:11–4:21. The Corinthians have become proud of their allegiance to one or another of various teachers who have passed through their community (1:11–16; cf. 3:21; 4:6), and the result has been division (1:10), strife (1:11; 3:3), and jealousy (3:3).

Paul's attention to the problem is not limited, however, to these chapters. Disunity comes to the fore again in 8:1–11:1, where he implicitly urges the Corinthians not to seek their "own good but the good of many, so that they may be saved" (10:33); in 11:2–16, where some have become contentious about the attire of women in public worship; in 11:17–34, where social divisions have spilled over into the celebration of the Lord's Supper; and in 12:1–14:40, where some have elevated the spiritual gift of glossolalia above all other gifts.

Why is Paul so concerned with the Corinthians' unity? Two major reasons emerge from the letter. First, Paul hopes that the Corinthians will be "strong to the end ... blameless on the day of our Lord Jesus Christ" (1:8), but their pride, with its socially destructive effects, threatens this prospect. Their haughty elevation of one Christian

letter's chief purpose and shown persuasively that Paul frequently called on common political figures of speech and strategies to persuade the Corinthians of the need for unity.

16 This is the only one of Paul's extant letters in which he qualifies a specific address in this way. Johannes Weiss, *Der erste Korintherbrief*, 9th ed. (MeyerK; Göttingen: Vandenhoeck & Ruprecht, 1910), 3–4, thought the statement so odd that he attributed it to a redactor's gloss. But compare the similar syntax of 2 Cor. 1:1 and Phil. 1:1, and see the discussion in Gordon D. Fee, *The First Epistle to the Corinthians* (NICNT; Grand Rapids: Eerdmans, 1987), 33, and Wolfgang Schrage, *Der erste Brief an die Korinther (1Kor 1,1–6,11)* (EKK 7.1; Zürich and Neukirchen-Vluyn: Benziger and Neukirchener, 1991), 105.

17 On the programmatic nature of this sentence see Mitchell, *Rhetoric of Reconciliation*, 65–183.

teacher over another threatens to deconstruct the community itself, with dire consequences on the final day both for the community as a whole and for any individual leader who might encourage such rivalry (3:15–17). Similarly, the arrogant attitude that some have taken toward their imagined freedom to participate in pagan cults threatens to encourage "weaker" members of the community to violate their own convictions, to participate in idolatry, and so to be destroyed (8:10–12).

Second, the Corinthians' discord—because it is based on personal pride—is symptomatic of a profound misunderstanding of the gospel.[18] The essence of the gospel is that God freely chose his people apart from any worthiness of their own and placed them in fellowship with Christ Jesus, who became for them "wisdom from God—that is, our righteousness, holiness and redemption." As a result of this, all boasting—except boasting in the Lord—is out of place (1:26–31). When the Corinthians boast in various leaders, pitting the rhetorical abilities of one against another (1:18–4:21), when they boast in the freedom that their knowledge gives them to engage in sexual immorality (5:1–8; 6:12–20) and idolatry (8:1–13; 10:22), when they divide into socioeconomic groups at the Lord's Supper so that the "approved" among them will be obvious (11:17–34), and when their corporate worship becomes a cacophony of tongues speakers, each merely edifying himself or herself (12:1–14:40), then the Corinthians have demonstrated a fundamental misunderstanding of who they are in God's sight and of what God has done for them in Christ Jesus.

In this letter, therefore, Paul calls the Corinthians back to the fundamental elements of the gospel as a means of urging them to live in harmony with one another. The stakes are high. If they take his pastoral counsel to heart, they will remain "strong to the end ... blameless on the day of our Lord Jesus Christ" (1:8). Otherwise, in the purging fires of the final day, the temple of God in Corinth will come crashing down with nothing left but Paul's gospel foundation and with later, more foolish builders barely escaping the fiery collapse of their shoddy work (3:10–17).

The Divisive Wisdom of the World and the Unifying Wisdom of God (1:10–4:21)

Wisdom and Division at Corinth

In 1:10–4:21 Paul responds to a report from "Chloe's people" that the church has become plagued by factions. People within the church seem to have gathered around the name of a particular leader (1:13–17), whether Paul, Apollos, or Cephas, and sorted themselves into contentious groups (1:11–12; cf. 3:3–4, 21–22), each claiming that its membership was better than the others (4:6, 19).

At the center of this factionalism lay the Corinthians' claim to "wisdom" both for themselves and for their various teachers. The clearest reference to the role that "wisdom" (*sophia*) played at Corinth appears in 3:18–21:

18 Cf. Sigurd Grindheim, "Wisdom for the Perfect: Paul's Challenge to the Corinthian Church (1 Corinthians 2:6–16)," *JBL* 121 (2002): 689–709.

> Do not deceive yourselves. If any one of you thinks he [or she] is wise by the standards of this age, he should become a "fool" so that he may become wise. For the wisdom of this world is foolishness in God's sight. As it is written: "He catches the wise in their craftiness"; and again, "The Lord knows that the thoughts of the wise are futile." So then, no more boasting about [people]!

Here Paul implies that the Corinthians think of themselves as "wise" because they follow especially "wise" teachers. The reference to boasting implies that much of the factionalism in Corinth resulted from the claim that one teacher was wiser than another.[19] Paul apparently placed last in this contest and concedes that when he came to Corinth, he did not appear to be "wise" as they defined the term (2:1).[20]

How do they define "wisdom"? Since Paul couples Greeks rather than Jews with the pursuit of wisdom (1:22), and since he ties the "worldly" and "fleshly" wisdom of the Corinthians closely with speech (1:17, 20; 2:1, 4, 6–7, 13; 4:19–20), we should probably locate the origin of their approach to wisdom in the Sophistic movement that flourished in Corinth in the first century.[21] Just as the Sophists who passed through Corinth were intensely competitive with one another and gathered around them disciples who participated in this rivalry, so the Corinthian Christians have attached themselves to their favorite leader, whether Paul, Apollos, or Cephas, and drawn invidious comparisons among them.[22]

Apollos's followers, for example, may have said that their teacher was "eloquent" (*logios*; Acts 18:24) and that he took them beyond the basics of the gospel to more sophisticated teaching (cf. 3:6).[23] Paul, by contrast, lacked "the wisdom of eloquence" (*sophia logou*; 1:17), his demeanor was weak, his focus on the cross was hardly appropriate subject matter for a winsome declamation, and he failed to use "wise and persuasive words" (2:2–4).

Grace and Eschatology in Paul's Reply

Paul's reply to all this rests on two theological foundations. First, he calls on the Corinthians to look back in time to their own entry into the people of God and to reflect on how their unity as Christians resulted from the gracious nature of the gospel. Second, he urges them to look forward to the final day when God will strip away all human pretension and only what is spiritual will remain.

---

19 Paul uses "wisdom" (*sophia*) and its adjectival form "wise" (*sophos*) twenty-six times in 1:10–4:21, far more than he uses these words in any other part of his correspondence. This probably means that the word was forced on him by the Corinthians' claim to possess wisdom and was not his own choice. See Barrett, *Essays on Paul*, 6; Birger Albert Pearson, *The Pneumatikos-Psychikos Terminology in 1 Corinthians: A Study in the Theology of the Corinthian Opponents of Paul and Its Relation to Gnosticism* (SBLDS 12; Missoula, Mont.: Scholars Press, 1973), 27; and Fee, *First Epistle to the Corinthians*, 48.

20 Such statements as 4:1–5, 18–21, and 9:1–2 reveal that the Corinthians are largely united in their opposition to Paul. Stephanus, Fortunatus, and Achaicus are not opposed to him (16:15–18), nor is the "Paul" faction; but an undercurrent of concern to reestablish his authority accompanies Paul's argument in 1:10–4:21. See Nils Alstrup Dahl, *Studies in Paul: Theology for the Early Christian Mission* (Minneapolis: Augsburg, 1997), 47–49, and Fee, *First Epistle to the Corinthians*, 8–9, and *passim*.

21 See esp. Bruce Winter, *Philo and Paul among the Sophists* (SNTSMS 96; Cambridge: Cambridge Univ. Press, 1997), 114–44, 170–76. Cf. Clement of Alexandria, *Stromata* 1.3 and Johannes Munck, *Paul and the Salvation of Mankind* (Atlanta: John Knox, 1959), 152–54.

22 On the competition among the Sophists and the rivalry among their followers, see Winter, *Paul and Philo among the Sophists*, 170–76.

23 Barrett, *Essays on Paul*, 11.

The Gracious Nature of the Gospel

The gracious nature of the gospel is revealed both in the Corinthians and in Paul. Paul calls on the Corinthians to consider who they were when God called them to belong to his people. Not many were wise, powerful, or of noble birth. They were instead foolish, weak, ignobly born, and despised—in short, nobodies (1:26–28). God graciously invested them with what they did not have in themselves: "wisdom from God—that is . . . righteousness, holiness and redemption" (1:30).[24]

Paul also reminds the Corinthians of how they heard the gospel. It did not originate with them but with God, who gave to Paul and Apollos the task of planting and nurturing the seed of the gospel in Corinth. Paul and Apollos, then, are God's coworkers and the Corinthians are God's field, God's building (3:5–9). "What do you have," Paul asks them, "that you did not receive?" (4:7). They are the church of God in Corinth because God took the initiative through the work of Paul and Apollos to call them to belong to his people. Their status as Christians, therefore, originated with God, and the gracious character of all this is inconsistent with their contentious boasting in their favorite Christian teachers (3:21; 4:7). God acted on the Corinthians' behalf through his mutually supportive servants, and "therefore, as it is written, 'Let him who boasts boast in the Lord'" (1:31; Jer. 9:24).[25]

The gracious nature of the gospel is also revealed in Paul—in the gospel he preached, in the way he preached it, and in the timing of his work among the Corinthians. First, the gracious nature of the gospel is revealed in the "foolishness" of the gospel's content. The central element of the gospel was the crucifixion of Jesus (1:23; 2:2), and yet crucifixion was universally regarded with horror as the most demeaning form of execution. It was "the worst of deaths," the "infamous stake," the "criminal wood," and the "terrible cross."[26] From the perspective of those who are perishing, therefore, "the message of the cross is foolishness" (1:18). Yet it was precisely through the preaching of the cross that God—in his own wisdom—"was pleased . . . to save those who believe" (1:21).

Why does Paul stress God's choice of a "foolish" method to accomplish his saving purposes? By showing how the experts in "the wisdom of the world" have rejected the gospel because of its foolishness or offense, Paul emphasizes the impossibility of belief in the gospel apart from God's initiative. There is only one reason that a group of people have united in Corinth around the conviction that Christ crucified is the wisdom and power of God: God has "called" them to belong to his people (1:24).

Second, Paul considers his failure to measure up to the Corinthians' standards for a successful orator to be the means through which God has demonstrated his power. Paul possessed neither eloquence nor superior wisdom when he preached among the Corinthians (2:1). He used no clever rhetorical devices (2:4). Instead his preaching exhibited weakness, fear, and trembling (2:3; cf. 4:8–13). "The spirit of

24 Behind this passage lies the theology that will eventually be expressed in Romans as "the righteousness of God." On this see Hübner, *Biblische Theologie*, 2:118, 140.

25 Cf. Rudolf Bultmann, *Theology of the New Testament*, 2 vols. (New York: Charles Scribner's Sons, 1951–55), 1:242.

26 Martin Hengel, *Crucifixion in the Ancient World and the Folly of the Message of the Cross* (Philadelphia: Fortress, 1977), 4, 7.

the world" (2:12) did not inspire it, nor did his preaching follow the canons that "human wisdom" laid down (2:13). Instead, the Spirit's power accompanied it (2:4), "the Spirit who is from God" inspired it (2:12), and the Spirit taught Paul the words to use (2:13). As a result, the Corinthians responded to Paul's message in faith (2:4).

Why did God work through the weakness of Paul's preaching? "So that your faith," Paul tells the Corinthians, "might not rest on men's wisdom, but on God's power" (2:5). Why did Paul speak words that the Spirit of God supplied? "That we may understand," Paul explains, "what God has freely given us" (2:12). God's insistence on working through weakness focused attention on God himself as the source of the Corinthians' faith; the Corinthians' membership among his people was God's gift to them, not something won through the flashy presentation of eloquent speakers or the ability of the Corinthians to rank their teachers according to the criteria of "human wisdom."

Third, God's grace was apparent in the timing of Paul's ministry among the Corinthians. Paul came to Corinth before Apollos and planted the Corinthians' faith, whereas Apollos came later and "watered" the seed that Paul had planted (3:6). Paul had laid the foundation of the Corinthian community, and another was building on it (3:10b). None of this happened, however, by human design, but according to God's own gifts: He gave to Paul and Apollos their tasks in Corinth (3:5), and Paul laid the foundation of the Corinthians' faith "by the grace" God had given him (3:10a).

Thus, Paul calls the Corinthians to unity by reminding them that everything about their incorporation into God's people points away from themselves and the teachers in whom they take pride and toward God himself. Nothing in the Corinthians prompted God to call them into his people. Nothing superficially attractive in the message Paul preached prompted them to believe. No rhetorical cleverness in Paul's presentation of the gospel compelled them to embrace the gospel. Instead, Paul tells them, "[God] is the source of your life in Christ Jesus" (1:30, NRSV). This means that they should stop boasting in themselves and—in unison—boast in the Lord.

The "Day" as the Moment of Truth

Paul's response to the Corinthians' divisive pride also focuses on "the Day" (3:13; cf. 4:3) when God will reveal the real worth of each person's work. A time is coming, Paul says, when God will reward Paul and Apollos for their own labor (3:8), and a "Day" is coming that will bring to light the worth of each person's work on "God's building" or "temple" in Corinth (3:9, 16–17). Those who have built wisely with gold, silver, and costly stones—materials appropriate for the building of God's temple—will see the survival of their work and a reward from God on that Day (3:12–14; cf. 3:8, 4:5). Those who have built with fragile materials—wood, hay, or straw—will barely escape the fiery collapse of their efforts (3:12, 15). Those who have worked to destroy God's temple, God himself will destroy (3:16–17).

Paul then turns to those in Corinth who are sitting in judgment on him and tells them that their judgment is irrelevant to him and that even his own judgment about himself is of no real importance (4:1–5). Only God can judge truly, because only he can illumine the hidden things of darkness and reveal the motives of human hearts. A time will come when he will do this, and so the Corinthians should judge no one in the present—they should await the completely just judgment of God.

To put it briefly, the nature of the final day implies that the Corinthians should stop divisive comparisons between Paul, Apollos, and Cephas for three reasons. First, by entering into these judgments they are acting prematurely. Without understanding the motives that drive the teacher to whom they cling and the others whom they despise, they cannot judge them justly. Second, by acting as judges they have assumed a role that belongs to God, who alone knows the counsels of the human heart. Third, the Corinthians' invidious comparisons are destroying God's "temple" in Corinth, and those who destroy God's temple can only expect for themselves God's destroying wrath on the final day.

Summary

In 1:10–4:21, Paul calls on the Corinthians to drop their quarrels over which Christian teacher is best by looking back to their own incorporation into God's people through his grace and by looking ahead to the final day when God will separate foolish from wise builders of his church. When they look back at God's grace, the Corinthians should see an implausible message brought by an unimpressive messenger to a group of unlikely candidates for membership in God's people. They should then realize that their membership in God's people could only be the result of God's powerful call to them and his choice of them by his Spirit. When they look ahead, the Corinthians should see a Day on which God will reveal the motives of each person's heart, will reward those who have built up his "temple" in Corinth, and will destroy those who have torn it down. Judgments about these matters before the Day, particularly when those judgments tear down the church, are therefore not merely inappropriate but eschatologically perilous.

Destructive Knowledge and Edifying Love (8:1–11:1)

In 8:1–11:1 Paul turns to the connection between eating meat and idolatry, and here too division has plagued the Corinthian community. Should the believer participate in the cultic banquets held in pagan temples? Should the believer eat meat whose origin is unknown and which might, therefore, have previously been offered in pagan sacrifice?[27] These were important issues wherever Christians and Jews worshiped the living and true God amid pagan worship of "many 'gods' and many 'lords'" (8:5). Where Jewish Christianity flourished, the answers to these questions were clear: Eating food that had been sacrificed to idols was forbidden.[28]

But Jewish Christianity was not strong in Corinth, and the Corinthian Christians prized their freedom (5:2, 6; 6:12–13). Some among the Corinthians, therefore, prided themselves on the knowledge that "an idol is nothing at all in the world" (8:4) and concluded that they had the "right" (*exousia*; 8:9) both to eat in an idol's

27 For this understanding of the issues in 8:1–11:1, see Fee, *First Epistle to the Corinthians*, 359–60.

28 See Barrett, *Essays on Paul*, 56.

temple (8:9) and to eat anything sold in the marketplace without asking questions about its origin (10:23, 25). "Everything is permissible for me" (10:23; cf. 6:12) was the watchword of this group. Not only did they claim the right to eat such food, but they claimed that their knowledge that this food was permitted to them made them superior to others who did not share this knowledge.[29] In an odd reversal of the normal Jewish and Christian posture on this issue, they apparently claimed that eating such food, because it revealed a superior knowledge, somehow brought one nearer to God—eating food offered to idols was not merely a neutral issue to them but decidedly better than abstaining (8:8).

This "knowledge," however, ran roughshod over the consciences of some within the Corinthian church who were not sure that it was right. This "weak" group was still so accustomed to idols that when they ate food in a setting where pagan religious rituals were part of the meal, they felt they were participating in idolatry. The superior attitude of the knowledgeable group put a subtle pressure on those with weak consciences and emboldened them to eat food that their convictions told them to avoid (8:10). As a result, the consciences of the weak were "defiled" (8:7), and the weak themselves were in danger of succumbing to idolatry again, of departing the church, and so of being destroyed (8:11).[30]

Paul agrees with the foundational conviction of the knowledgeable group—they are right to say that an idol is nothing and that there is only one God (8:4–6)—but he resists their conclusion that "everything" in the realm of food offered to idols "is permissible" (10:23). Later he will say that eating a meal in a pagan temple is idolatry (10:1–22). Here he argues that knowledge must submit to love, and love builds up the church (8:1; 10:23) by unselfishly setting aside its own rights so that others might be led to salvation. The knowledgeable in Corinth, however, have neglected love. By insisting on their supposed "right" (*exousia*, 8:9) to eat meals in pagan temples and by insisting further that taking advantage of this "right" made them better than those with weak consciences, they "built up" the weak to participate in such meals against their convictions. They therefore led the weak down the path of eternal destruction (8:9–11).

Paul next provides his own apostolic conduct as an example of how believers should give up their rights in order to lead others to salvation. He has the "right" (*exousia*) to receive support from the communities in which he ministers, including the Corinthian community (9:3, 12a), but he has waived this right (9:12b, 15, 18) to avoid any impediment to the gospel. He made himself a slave to all people, identifying with Jew, Greek, and weak—becoming "all things to all [people] so that by all possible means" he might bring some to salvation (9:19–22).

---

29 Cf. James Moffatt, *The First Epistle of Paul to the Corinthians* (MNTC; London: Hodder and Stoughton, 1938), 111; C. K. Barrett, *A Commentary on the First Epistle to the Corinthians* (HNTC; New York: Harper & Row, 1968); and Hans Lietzmann, *An die Korinther I/II*, 5th ed., rev. Werner Georg Kümmel (HNT 9; Tübingen: J.C.B. Mohr [Paul Siebeck], 1969), 38.

30 As Theissen, *Social Setting*, 127–28, has argued, the "weak" and the knowledgeable probably belonged to different socioeconomic classes. The knowledgeable were probably wealthy and therefore used to eating meat in a variety of settings, whereas the "weak," who were probably poor, had regular access to meat only on certain cultic occasions when it was distributed free of charge to the general population.

How, then, should the knowledgeable Corinthian believer act when faced with an invitation to participate in a temple meal or to have a meal in the home of an unbeliever? In the case of eating in a pagan temple, Paul believes that the practice is idolatrous and therefore wrong in any case (10:1–22), but here he argues that even those whose knowledge (wrongly) permits it should forego the practice since the chance is too great of sinning against weaker brothers or sisters by wounding "their conscience" and leading them to eternal destruction (8:11–12): "If what I eat causes my brother to fall into sin," he says, "I will never eat meat again, so that I will not cause him to fall" (8:13).

The same concern for the edification of another shapes Paul's advice on eating sacrificial meat in the private home of an unbeliever. The believer, Paul says, is free to eat whatever is served without discrimination—with one exception. If a well-meaning unbeliever at the meal points out that some of the food has been "devoted to a god" (*hierothyton*), the believer should not eat (10:28). Presumably this unbeliever has made a conscientious effort to prevent the believer from violating his or her religious customs, mistakenly assuming that Christians, like Jews, avoid sacrificial meat. Paul says that in such situations the believer should honor this good faith effort and avoid eating the food, not because it would be a violation of the believer's conscience to eat, but for the sake of the one who issued the reminder (10:28–30).[31]

As with 8:1–13, the point is that Christians should give up their rights to avoid causing another to stumble—whether Jewish unbeliever, Greek unbeliever, or fellow Christian—so that as many as possible might be saved. This, says Paul, is what he has done, and believers in Corinth should follow his example (10:33; cf. 9:22). In so doing, they will also be following the example of Christ (11:1; cf. 11:17–34).

We can conclude from all this that one of the primary goals of Paul's advice to the Corinthians on food offered to idols is the encouragement of those with "knowledge" to pursue the eternal welfare of their weak brothers and sisters, and the encouragement of everyone to seek the salvation of unbelievers. If the Corinthians seek to build up their church (8:1; 10:23) in this way, three consequences will follow. First, those already within the fellowship of the church will remain firm in their faith rather than be destroyed (8:11). Second, others will also be added to their number (9:22; 10:33). Third, the temple of God that the Corinthian believers and their leaders have built will survive the purifying fires of the final day (3:10–15; cf. 1:8–9).

Unity and Edification in Corporate Worship (11:2–14:40)

When the Corinthians assembled for corporate worship, their record on denying their own rights for the good of the community and the benefit of the weak was no better than when pagan rituals of worship were at issue. Here too the Corinthian believers insisted on their personal privileges to the detriment of the church's unity

31 Fee, *First Epistle to the Corinthians*, 483–85. The passage is extraordinarily difficult. For the various interpretive options, see Anthony C. Thiselton, *The First Epistle to the Corinthians* (NIGTC; Grand Rapids: Eerdmans, 2000), 788–90. Fee's reconstruction of the situation makes good sense of Paul's references to the other's conscience (10:29) and his desire to save the many (10:33).

and its witness to outsiders. Three issues proved particularly divisive: Believers were praying and prophesying without customary attire (11:2–16), the rich were eating their own well-provisioned meals at the Lord's Supper but allowing the poor to go hungry (11:17–34), and those who had the spiritual gift of speaking in tongues elevated their gift to a level of importance so lofty that they were neglecting other gifts and those who possessed them (12:1–14:40).

Disunity over Head-coverings (11:2–16)

The first issue—proper attire in worship—is notoriously obscure. What is the precise custom that Paul wants the Corinthian women to observe when praying or prophesying? Does he refer to a piece of clothing that should cover their heads or to their own hair, which they should wear on top of their heads? Why were women in Corinth not observing this custom? Were they simply following the practice of their culture, a practice that offended Paul's Jewish sensibilities, or were they following some cultural norm of Roman Corinth and so creating an unnecessary scandal? Why did Paul believe that men ought not to cover their heads? Were they violating this rule? If not, why does Paul insist that they not cover their heads?

Few scholars have answered these questions in exactly the same way, but several critical elements of the problem are clear. First, Paul concludes his advice on the issue with the statement that "if anyone wants to be contentious about this, we have no other practice—nor do the churches of God" (11:16), and this probably means that the issue has been a source of tension within the church.[32]

Second, although Paul addresses both men and women, the amount of extra attention that he devotes to women (11:6, 13–15) indicates that the primary responsibility for the problem lay with them. Moreover, the problem itself centered on the refusal of some women to cover their heads when praying and prophesying.[33]

Third, this refusal to wear a head covering, because it was a bone of contention, probably meant throwing off some customary form of attire—perhaps the head covering that seems to have been normal for married Roman women to wear in public settings.[34] If so, then these wives may have appealed as a rationale for their actions to the Corinthian Christian slogan that "everything is permissible" (6:12; 10:23), and thus they may have viewed their actions, despite the shame that it brought to their husbands (11:5–6), as within their newly found "rights" in Christ.[35]

---

32 Mitchell, *Rhetoric of Reconciliation*, 149–51.

33 See Fee, *First Epistle to the Corinthians*, 505, although Fee is perhaps too confident that Paul's comments to the men address a hypothetical situation.

34 The problem is not, therefore, a matter of hair, as some interpreters think, but of clothing. On this, see, e.g., David W. J. Gill, "The Importance of Roman Portraiture for Head-Coverings in 1 Corinthians 11:2–16," *TynBul* 41 (1990): 245–60; Winter, *After Paul Left Corinth*, 123–30; Thiselton, *First Epistle to the Corinthians*, 801, 828–29; and David E. Garland, *1 Corinthians* (BECNT; Grand Rapids: Baker, 2003), 519–21.

35 Although she is not this specific, something like this situation seems to be assumed by Judith Gundry-Volf, "Gender and Creation in 1 Corinthians 11:2–16: A Study in Paul's Theological Method," in *Evangelium, Schriftauslegung, Kirche: Festschrift für Peter Stuhlmacher zum 65. Geburtstag*, ed. Jostein Ådna, Scott J. Hafemann, and Otfried Hofius (Göttingen: Vandenhoeck & Ruprecht, 1997), 150–71, here at 164–71. Gundry-Volf helpfully emphasizes two additional elements of the situation (169): the cultural scandal that the behavior of the women would have created and the need Paul felt to curb it in order to maintain the social acceptability of the Corinthian church. To this we might add Paul's concern for the appeal of the gospel to outsiders (cf. 10:25–11:1; 14:24–25).

Paul responds that these married women should cover their heads when they pray or prophesy during the time that the church is assembled for worship. Failure to do so violates the principle built into marriage at the creation of the first wife that a wife should honor, not shame, her husband (11:7–10; cf. Gen. 2:18–22).[36] It upsets a common sense of what is fitting both in culture generally and in the church (1 Cor. 11:13–16). It therefore produces contention (11:16). Paul is quick to affirm the principle that may have led the women to dispense with their head coverings in the first place—wives and husbands are interdependent and equal to each other because God created them both (11:11–12)—but he believes that this particular manifestation of that theological principle is misguided. It is wrong because of the shame it brings to husbands and the contentiousness that it brings to the church. Christian wives in Corinth should renounce their "rights" and cover their heads when speaking in corporate worship for the sake of their husbands and the peace of the church.

Socioeconomic Divisions at the Lord's Supper (11:17–34)

The details surrounding the second issue—the humiliation of the poor at the Lord's Supper—are somewhat clearer. Paul has heard, perhaps from Chloe's people, that the Lord's Supper in Corinth has become an occasion for "divisions" (*schismata*, cf. 1:10) and for showing who within the church is "approved" (11:19, aut.). This was happening because the Lord's Supper was celebrated in connection with a full meal, and the wealthy were going ahead with their own provisions whereas "those who have nothing"—the poor—were leaving hungry and humiliated (11:21–22). The wealthy members of the Corinthian church probably sponsored these corporate worship services and provided the meal for the participants; they alone would have had homes large enough to accommodate large groups of believers, and only they would have had the means to provide bread and wine for the celebration of the Lord's Supper.[37] In harmony with the custom of the day, they may have also provided a separate, more lavish menu for themselves and their social peers as a sign of their rank in society.[38]

Paul is disgusted by this practice. Whatever they are eating, he tells them, it is not the Lord's Supper (11:20). They can eat and drink in their own houses, but the corporate worship of the church is no place for humiliating the poor (11:22, 34). To do this, he says, is to "despise the church of God" (11:22).

How does Paul support his response theologically? Paul reminds the Corinthians of the significance of the Lord's Supper, a significance that should have been apparent to them both from the traditional words of its institution that he had handed on to them (11:23) and from the single loaf—the Lord's body—that they broke as part

36 Paul bases his claim that the wife should honor her husband on the statements in Genesis that God made the woman from the man (Gen. 2:22–23; cf. 1 Cor. 11:8), and as a fitting helper for the man (Gen. 2:18; 1 Cor. 11:9). These statements probably also inform his claim that the wife's head covering is a "sign of authority" (1 Cor. 11:10a), although it is not entirely clear whether Paul means that the woman is under authority or has authority. The woman should also wear the head covering "because of the angels" (11:10b), an obscure statement that is probably related to the notion that angels were present in the worshiping community and that the women should avoid dishonoring not only their husbands but these angels by removing their head coverings.

37 I am indebted in what follows to Theissen, *Social Setting*, 145–74. Cf. also Fee, *First Epistle to the Corinthians*, 540–41.

38 See Theissen's illuminating quotations, *Social Setting*, 156–57, from Pliny, *Ep.* 2.6 and Martial, *Epigrammata* 1.20; 3.60.

of the Lord's Supper. This sacred meal, Paul says, proclaims Jesus' death until he comes, and Jesus died "for" (*hyper*) all the Corinthians (11:24; cf. 15:3).

Moreover, the Lord's Supper calls for discernment of the body of Christ (11:29), and, as Paul has already said (10:17), the one loaf of bread used in the Lord' Supper signifies the one body of believers. The Lord's Supper demands that believers come together in unity under the sacrificial death of Jesus.[39] To use this sacrament as an occasion for asserting one's social superiority to others is therefore utterly inconsistent with this demand. It is such a serious misunderstanding of the purpose of the Lord's Supper that those who engage in it, Paul says, have aligned themselves with those who put Jesus to death rather than with Jesus—they are guilty of "the body and blood of the Lord" (11:27) and are experiencing God's judgment in sickness and death (11:30).

A Divisive Emphasis on Tongues (12:1–14:40)

In 12:1–14:40 Paul turns to the third divisive practice that has plagued the corporate worship of the Corinthians: elevating the spiritual gift of speaking in tongues above all other gifts. The gist of the problem is visible in Paul's body metaphor in 12:12–27. The point of the metaphor is that the body consists not of one part but many, that it is not only an eye or only an ear or only any other single organ, but a diversity of parts working together. Some in Corinth, however, believe that everyone should have the same gift, as Paul's rhetorical questions reveal: "Are all apostles? Are all prophets? Are all teachers? Do all work miracles? Do all have gifts of healing? Do all speak in tongues? Do all interpret?" (12:29–30).

How this approach has affected those who do not possess the gift also becomes clear from the body metaphor. Some have apparently made "those parts of the body that seem to be weaker" (12:22) to feel as if they are "not a part of the body." The more "reputable" (*euschēmōn*, 12:24) wing of the church has told them that they are not needed (12:21). That the troublesome gift is speaking in tongues becomes clear not only from Paul's focus on it in 14:1–40, but by its emphatic position at the end of the lists of gifts in 12:8–10, 28, 29–30, and at the beginning of his famous digression on love (13:1).[40]

Against all this, Paul advises three courses of action. First, he counsels the reputable Corinthians to treat their weaker brothers and sisters with special honor. This will ensure that there will be no divisions, but that each member of the body receives equal care (12:24–25).

Second, he urges the Corinthians to couple their zeal for spiritual gifts with a desire to follow the high road of love (12:31b–14:1a). Unlike prophecy, tongues, and knowledge—three especially prized gifts in Corinth—love remains forever (13:8, 13).[41] The effect of love, moreover, is a unity that emerges from putting the interests of others ahead of one's own interests and rights:

39 Cf. Barrett, *First Epistle to the Corinthians*, 272–73. On the character of the Lord's Supper as demand as well as gift in Paul's theology, see Ernst Käsemann, *Essays on New Testament Themes* (Philadelphia: Fortress, 1982), 108–35.

40 See Fee, *First Epistle to the Corinthians*, 571–72. Cf. Mitchell, *Rhetoric of Reconciliation*, 270.

41 For the Corinthian emphasis on prophecy and knowledge, see 11:4–5; 14:29–33; 8:1, 4, 10–11. Cf. Mitchell, *Rhetoric of Reconciliation*, 270.

> Love is patient, love is kind. It does not envy, it does not boast, it is not proud. It is not rude, it is not self-seeking, it is not easily angered, it keeps no record of wrongs. Love does not delight in evil but rejoices with the truth. It always protects, always trusts, always hopes, always perseveres. (13:4–7)

Third, Paul instructs the Corinthians to place a higher value on intelligible speech in corporate worship than on speaking in uninterpreted tongues. The one who speaks in an uninterpreted tongue, he explains, edifies only himself, but the one who speaks an intelligible word of prophecy, an interpreted tongue, or some similarly understandable utterance, "edifies the church" (14:2–6). This edification extends, moreover, beyond the believer to the "inquirer" (*idiōtēs*) and the unbeliever who may be present when the church worships. When these outsiders hear intelligible speech, they can agree with what is said (14:16), understand that they are under God's just sentence of condemnation, and become convinced that God is really among the Christians (14:22–25).

Summary

Throughout 11:2–14:40, therefore, Paul admonishes the powerful among the Corinthians to strive for unity in the worship of the church by refusing to use their rights in ways that put weaker Christians at a disadvantage. Wives should not exercise their supposed right to uncover their heads in worship to the dishonor of their husbands. The rich should not humiliate the poor with their separate menus at the Lord's Supper. The "reputable" who possess the highly valued gift of tongues should not edify themselves with it to the neglect of others in worship. Instead, the Corinthians should restrict their rights in ways that are consistent with the sacrificial death of Jesus "for" others (11:24), with the pursuit of love (12:31b–14:1), and with the edification of the church (14:3–5, 12, 26).

Paul's Admonitions to Unity in First Corinthians: The Common Ground

Despite the varied circumstances that gave rise to Paul's admonitions to unity in 1 Corinthians and the corresponding variety in his advice, two concerns lie beneath Paul's arguments. The first is that the character of their divisiveness reveals a fundamental misunderstanding of God's grace. In Corinth, the knowledgeable, wealthy, authoritative, and respectable were busy proving that they were better than others and were engaged in the thoughtless neglect of the weak. This self-seeking approach to Christianity, however, is incompatible with the character of God as he is revealed in the gospel. The God who called the unlikely rabble of the Corinthian church to be his temple in Corinth, whose grace was shown in Christ crucified, and who communicated this good news to the Corinthians through the weak and trembling Paul is a God who, in his strength, stoops to the weak and does for them what they cannot do for themselves.

This is the burden not only of Paul's argument against Corinthian-style wisdom in 1:18–4:21 but also of his admonitions elsewhere in the letter to the strong not to neglect the needs of the weak. Thus, in 8:1–11:1, when Paul urges the knowledgeable not to trample the sensitivities of the weak brother or sister for whom Christ died, he is asking them to imitate the graciousness of God. And in 11:2–14:40, when he asks liberated wives, the wealthy, and those with impressive spiritual gifts to circumscribe their rights, he is asking them to do for husbands, the poor, and the weaker members of the body what God has graciously done for all. The grace of God, as Paul describes it in the first part of the letter, then, demands that the strong should treat the weak "with special honor" (12:23).

The second reason Paul is concerned about the disunity of the church is that it disrupts the "edification" of the church. "Edification" refers not only to harmony among established members of the church body (3:9–17), but concern for those on the fringes of the church: the weaker brother or sister who is in danger of stumbling into eternal destruction (8:1, 11) and the inquirer or unbeliever who, if present in the church's worship and edified by intelligible speech, may believe the gospel (14:16–17, 20–25, 31). "Edification" is important because the church is the temple of God—the place of God's presence among his people.[42] Paul wants God's temple in Corinth to be an integrated structure, adorned, like Solomon's temple, with gold, silver, and precious stones, and strong enough to survive the purging fires of the Day when every builder's "work will be shown for what it is" (3:12–13; cf. 1 Chron. 22:14–16; 29:2; 2 Chron. 3:6).[43]

HOLINESS BEFORE THE WORLD

Paul does not want unity, however, at the expense of sanctity. The Corinthians, he believes, are God's people, the eschatological descendants of ancient Israel as they are described in the Jewish Scriptures. Although they are not Jews, neither are they Gentiles. Like Israel in the Jewish Scriptures, they are the people "whom God has called" and "the church of God" (1:24; 10:32). The ancient Israelites who wandered in the desert are their "fathers," and the accounts of those wanderings in the Scriptures "were written down as warnings for us, on whom the fulfillment of the ages has come" (10:11; cf. 10:6). They are not Israel according to the flesh, but, by implication, Israel according to the Spirit (10:18; cf. Phil. 3:3). If all this is true, then, like Israel of old, the Corinthians need to pay careful attention to the boundaries of holiness that God prescribed for his people so that they might be separate from the peoples around them. They are "the church of God in Corinth," "sanctified in Christ Jesus," and "called to be holy" (1:2).[44]

Much to Paul's dismay, however, the Corinthians have become almost hopelessly confused about their sanctity. Some—those involved in incest, litigation, prostitution,

42 Paul probably views this Christian "temple" as the fulfillment of the promises in the prophets that in the days of Israel's restoration, God would provide a magnificent temple for his people where he would dwell (Ezek. 43:2–7). See the discussion below on 6:19 and Schrage, *Der erste Brief an die Korinther (1Kor 1,1–6,11)*, 300; Frank Thielman, *Paul and the Law: A Contextual Approach* (Downers Grove, Ill.: InterVarsity Press, 1994), 91–94; and P. W. L. Walker, *Jesus and the Holy City: New Testament Perspectives on Jerusalem* (Grand Rapids: Eerdmans, 1996), 119–22.

43 See Fee, *First Epistle to the Corinthians*, 140.

44 See T. J. Deidun, *New Covenant Morality in Paul* (AnBib 89; Rome: Pontifical Biblical Institute, 1981), 12–18, 28–32; Thielman, *Paul and the Law*, 87–91.

and idolatry—have blurred or ignored the boundaries between the church and the world. Others—those refusing to have sexual relations with unbelieving spouses—have misunderstood the boundaries or applied them inflexibly. A primary purpose of the letter, therefore, is to call the Corinthians back to a right understanding of the boundaries that should separate them, as the eschatological people of God, from the world in which they live. Even as he urges them to give the boundaries of their church a biblical shape, however, it becomes clear that in the new era these boundaries and the ways they are enforced have undergone subtle changes.

God's Eschatological Passover and the Leaven of Immorality (5:1–13)

Paul has heard a report that a young man in the Corinthian community is living in a sexual relationship with his father's wife. The way in which he expresses his dismay at this behavior, the reasons he gives for its impropriety, and the remedy he suggests for this serious breech of the boundaries of sanctity show the continuity between holiness as Paul conceives it and holiness as his Scriptures describe it. Still, a subtle difference emerges between the way in which Paul's Scriptures treat violations of sanctity and Paul's handling of them.

Paul's shocked response to the report he has heard about incest in the Corinthian church echoes Leviticus 18:1–17. In that passage Moses relays God's specific instructions to Israel on avoiding incest as a way of standing apart from the practices of the Canaanites. Sexual contact with a number of relatives was forbidden, including the wife of one's father (Lev. 18:8). Paul is horrified that a Corinthian believer has violated precisely this stipulation and is engaging in a kind of anti-holiness—he has failed even more miserably than an unbeliever to meet God's standards for sexual conduct (1 Cor. 5:1). Paul's definition of sanctification in this passage and his visceral response to the Corinthians' violation of it, therefore, arise directly from his Scriptures.

The remedy Paul proposes for the situation is also shaped by his Scriptures. He instructs the Corinthians to put into effect a judicial sentence that Paul has himself already passed on the man: In a solemn assembly they "are to hand this man over to Satan for the destruction of the flesh, so that his spirit might be saved in the day of the Lord" (5:5, NRSV). They are, in other words, to excommunicate him. Just as faithful Israelites purged their homes of leaven during the Feast of Unleavened Bread, Paul says, so Christians should keep their Passover Festival in purity and exclude from their midst those engaged in "malice and wickedness" (5:6–8). Quoting the instructions that Moses gives in Deuteronomy for flagrant violations of the Mosaic law, Paul concludes this section of his letter with the statement, "Expel the wicked man from among you" (1 Cor. 5:13).[45] This also parallels closely the instructions in Leviticus 18 for ridding Israel of those who engaged in forbidden sexual relationships: "Everyone who does any of these detestable things—such persons must be cut off from their people" (Lev. 18:29).

45 Cf. Deut. 13:5; 17:7, 12; 19:19; 21:21; 22:21–22, 24; 24:7.

Once again, the indebtedness of Paul to the Mosaic law in his understanding of Christian sanctity is unmistakable in this passage. The Corinthians are apparently in some sense Israelites, and therefore when the law's commandments against sexual immorality are violated, like Israel, they must purge their community of the violator's corrupting influence.

Yet the difference between Paul and his Scriptures at this point is also clear. The Mosaic law called for offenders in such instances to "be cut off from their people"—a permanent punishment—and the death penalty almost always accompanies the frequent refrain in Deuteronomy to "purge the evil from among you."[46] The purpose of the expulsion for Paul, however, is that the offender's "spirit" may be "saved on the day of the Lord," likely a reference to his eventual restoration to the community and salvation in the final day.[47] Whereas in the Mosaic law the offender was expelled for the good of the community, Paul's remedy has in view the spiritual well-being of both the community and the individual who has violated its sanctity.

Civil Litigation and Christian Holiness (6:1–11)

If the Corinthians are unconcerned about flagrant immorality in their midst, they are so concerned over trivial squabbles that they are taking each other to court (6:1–11). Their inability or unwillingness to grasp the most basic principles of Christian holiness has left Paul reeling: "When any of you has a grievance against another, do you dare to take it to court before the unrighteous, instead of taking it before the saints?" (6:1, NRSV).

Apparently some Corinthian believers with high social standing have continued the common Roman practice of engaging in civil litigation against others over relatively insignificant matters. The purpose of such litigation was to protect or enhance one's social position.[48] Such cases were typically tried before a judge who had favors of his own to repay, had his own reputation to enhance, or believed that the good reputation of the upper classes needed protection.[49] Paul's characterization of such judges as "unjust" (*adikēs*, 6:1) only states what anyone with experience of civil litigation in Roman society knew to be true.[50]

---

46 In Deut. 19:16–21 the false witness is to be punished in the same way that he intended his victim to be punished, "life for life, eye for eye, tooth for tooth, hand for hand, foot for foot," and in this way Israel is to "purge the evil" (19:19) from its midst.

47 As 5:11 shows, Paul's instructions to hand the man over to Satan do not refer to the death of the man but to his excommunication. See James T. South, "A Critique of the 'Curse/Death' Interpretation of 1 Corinthians 5.1–8," *NTS* 39 (1993): 539–61, here at 554–55.

48 See the compelling case of Bruce Winter, "Civil Litigation in Secular Corinth and the Church: The Forensic Background to 1 Corinthians 6.1–8," *NTS* 37 (1991): 559–72, confirmed and enhanced by Andrew D. Clarke, *Secular and Christian Leadership in Corinth: A Socio-Historical and Exegetical Study of 1 Corinthians 1–6* (AGJU 18; Leiden: Brill, 1993), 59–71. As both Winter and Clarke emphasize, Paul's reference to the legal proceedings among Corinthian Christians as "trivial cases" (6:2) implies that they are not criminal but civil cases.

49 Winter, "Civil Litigation," 562–64; Clarke, *Secular and Christian Leadership*, 62–63, 65.

50 The judges are not unjust, then, simply because they are "unbelievers" (6:6) but because they did not administer justice fairly. See Winter, "Civil Litigation," 562–64, and Alan C. Mitchell, "Rich and Poor in the Courts of Corinth: Litigiousness and Status in 1 Corinthians 6.1–11," *NTS* 39 (1993): 562–86, here at 580–81,who offer convincing evidence that equal justice was as rare in Roman Corinth as it was elsewhere. For Winter's response to Mitchell's argument that in 6:1–8 the wealthy are bringing the poor to court, see the revision of Winter's original article in *Understanding Paul's Ethics: Twentieth-Century Approaches*, ed. Brian S. Rosner (Grand Rapids: Eerdmans,1995), 101–3.

The litigants in these cases were often no more interested in justice than the judge. The chief concern for both the prosecution and the defense was not to state the truth about the circumstances that produced the legal action but to damage the reputation of their opponents in their speeches before the judge so that they would advance or protect their own reputations. Long standing enmity between litigants was a prolific by-product of this practice.[51] Paul is horrified that Christians are engaged in these brutal exercises of political one-upmanship. His comment in 6:8 probably refers not only to the injuries that led to lawsuits in the first place, but also to the tactics necessary for winning a case in court: "You yourselves do injustice [*adikeite*] and defraud, and do this to brothers!" (aut.).[52]

To remedy this problem, Paul proposes first that the Corinthian church appoint an arbitrator from their own number to adjudicate the squabbles of the wealthy (6:1–6), and second that the litigants understand their actions to be incompatible with participation in the kingdom of God (6:7–11). The focus in both sections is on the Corinthian church as God's eschatologically constituted people who, because of this status, must be holy.

In the first section (6:1–6), Paul reminds the church of a conviction commonly expressed in Jewish apocalyptic literature: The faithful remnant of God's people will participate with God in the judgment of the wicked. "God is not to destroy his people at the hand of nations," says Qumran's *Commentary on Habakkuk*, "but by means of his chosen ones God will judge all the nations" (5.4).[53] If believers will play such a critical role in the final judgment, Paul argues, then even those despised by the church are more qualified to arbitrate the mundane squabbles of the wealthy than unjust and unbelieving magistrates (6:4–5).[54]

In the second section (6:7–11) Paul turns to the litigants who, although Christians, are no more just than the judges before whom they plead their cases. One litigant practices injustice (*adikeō*) and fraud and so creates the opportunity for litigation. Then the injured party, by seeking vindication in a corrupt legal system, practices injustice (*adikeō*) and fraud in return (6:7–8).[55] But those who practice injustice (*adikoi*) in its various forms, Paul says, will not inherit the kingdom of God (6:9–10). Such wickedness is incompatible with the Corinthian church's status as a people who have been "washed ... sanctified ... justified in the name of the Lord Jesus Christ and by the Spirit of our God" (6:11; cf. 1:2).

The sanctity of the Corinthian church, then, ought to prevent the wickedness that prompts the injured party to go to court, and once an injury has occurred it ought to prevent the injured party from participating in a corrupt and corrupting

51 Winter, "Civil Litigation," 566–68; Clarke, *Secular and Christian Leadership*, 66–68.

52 Cf. Clarke, *Secular and Christian Leadership*, 68.

53 Cf. Rom. 2:27; 3:6; Wis. 3:8; Dan. 7:22 (LXX); *1 Enoch* 1:9; 38:5; 48:9; 95:3; 98:12; Jub. 1:23–25; Matt. 19:28; Luke 22:30; Rev. 3:21. See the discussion in Weiss, *Der erste Korintherbrief*, 147–48; Fee, *First Epistle to the Corinthians*, 233 n.18; and Schrage, *Der erste Brief and die Korinther (1Kor 1,1–6,11)*, 410 n. 47.

54 On the translation of *kathizete* in 6:4 as an imperative ("appoint!") rather than as an indicative ("do you appoint?"), see Clarke, *Secular and Christian Leadership*, 70, and Brent Kinman, "'Appoint the Despised as Judges!' (1 Corinthians 6:4)," *TynB* 48 (1997): 345–54.

55 Cf. Mitchell, "Rich and Poor in the Courts of Corinth," 567.

legal system. As God's holy people, the Corinthian church will participate in the judgment of the world and of angels when God fully establishes his kingdom. Therefore, believers in Corinth ought to engage in conduct compatible with life in God's kingdom. This means that when problems occur, the church ought to adjudicate them within its own boundaries rather than compound the evil by taking problems before unjust and unbelieving magistrates.

God's Eschatological Temple and the Problem of Prostitution (6:12–20)

Sexual immorality is no more compatible with life in the kingdom than civil litigation among Christians (6:9), and yet some Corinthians, citing the slogan, "Everything is permissible for me" (6:12), are consorting with prostitutes (6:13b, 15–16, 18). Since Paul never mentions adultery in 6:12–20 and distinguishes between "the sexually immoral" and "adulterers" in the vice list that immediately precedes it (6:9–10), he probably has in mind the sexual exploits of younger, unmarried men.[56]

These young men probably appealed to the common Roman convention that "everything is permitted" to upper class youth during the period of their lives between young adulthood and full maturity. Conventional wisdom among the social elite of Roman society expected such young men to attend banquets for Roman citizens of cities like Corinth, and these banquets typically combined over-indulgence in food with drunkenness and, after dinner, consorting with prostitutes.[57] Not only was this "permitted" by the custom of their culture, but it was justifiable in light of the popular notion that the body was the house of the immortal soul and that people should therefore care for the soul in the ways that Nature prompts them to care for it; cravings for food, drink, and sex were simply Nature's signals for what the body should have.[58]

The wealthier young men in the Corinthian church, therefore, were probably saying, "Everything is permissible [*exestin*] for me" (6:12). They were then justifying their claim with an argument from nature: "Food for the stomach and the stomach for food, and God will destroy both one and the other" (6:13).[59]

Paul's response to this ethical approach takes three forms. First, he argues that consorting with prostitutes is not personally advantageous (6:12a).[60] Sexual immorality, as Proverbs 6:26, 32 and Sirach 19:2–3 claim, is uniquely destructive to one's own person (1 Cor. 6:18).[61]

56 Winter, *After Paul Left Corinth*, 86–93.

57 Ibid. Winter uses and supplements the study by Alan Booth, "The Age for Reclining and Its Attendant Perils" in *Dining in a Classical Context*, ed. William J. Slater (Ann Arbor: Univ. of Michigan, 1991), 105–20.

58 Winter, *After Paul Left Corinth*, 77–80. Winter offers as evidence of this "élitist ethic" Philo's arguments against the sophistic justification of indulgence in *Det.* 33–35.

59 For this way of sorting out the Corinthian position and Paul's response to it in 6:12–13, see Barrett, *First Epistle to the Corinthians*, 146–47, and Fee, *First Epistle to the Corinthians*, 253–54. Cf. F. F. Bruce, *I & II Corinthians* (NCB; Grand Rapids: Eerdmans, 1971), 63.

60 On the common strategy in ancient political and philosophical discourse of appealing to personal advantage, see Mitchell, *Rhetoric of Reconciliation*, 25–39.

61 Cf. Prov. 5:9–11, 22; 7:22–23. Sir. 19:2–3 speaks of the personal destruction that comes to "the man who unites himself (*kollōmenos*) with prostitutes," just as Paul speaks in 6:16 of "the man who unites himself (*kollōmenos*) with a prostitute." On this see Bruce N. Fisk, "PORNEUEIN as Body Violation: The Unique Nature of Sexual Sin in 1 Corinthians 6.18," *NTS* 42 (1996): 540–58, here at 546 and 555. In addition, much of the evidence for youthful sexual indulgence in Booth, "Age for Reclining," comes from moralists who oppose these practices as destructive.

Second, Paul asserts that, contrary to the Corinthians' understanding of the body as the temporary house of the eternal soul, the body is, as Jewish tradition teaches, itself eternal (6:14).[62] The treatment of the body, therefore, has not merely temporal but eternal consequences.

Third, Paul argues that this eternal body belongs to the Lord. It is "for the Lord" (6:13b), part of Christ (6:15), and united with the Lord (6:17). God has bought believers with a price, like a buyer in the slave market would purchase a slave, and therefore believers should use their bodies to glorify their new master (6:20). The slave imagery probably also accounts for Paul's statement at the beginning of the section that as a believer he will "not be mastered by anything" (6:12b). In other words, as a slave who has been bought by a new master, Paul will not be enslaved to sexual license.

What reality within the believer does all this imagery of ownership represent? Paul gives a hint when he says that "he who unites himself with the Lord is one with him in spirit" (6:17). This probably means that the believer's human spirit is united with God's Spirit, and so the believer becomes the dwelling place of God's presence.[63] Paul makes this explicit a few sentences later when he says, "Do you not know that your body is a temple of the Holy Spirit, who is in you, whom you have received from God" (6:19).

The implication of this statement is that believers, since they are the dwelling place of God's eschatologically given Spirit, are the fulfillment of Ezekiel's promise of the restoration of God's temple on a grand scale in the eschatological age. Just as God's glorious presence will return to the temple at the time of Israel's eschatological restoration, so God's Spirit dwells within the bodies of the Corinthian believers. For Ezekiel, as for Paul, this means that God's dwelling place must be free of prostitution:

> I heard someone speaking to me from inside the temple. He said: "Son of man, this is the place of my throne and the place for the soles of my feet. This is where I will live among the Israelites forever. The house of Israel will never again defile my holy name—neither they nor their kings—by their prostitution [*porneia*, LXX] and the lifeless idols of their kings at their high places. . . . Now let them put away from me their prostitution [*porneia*, LXX] and the lifeless idols of their kings, and I will live among them forever. . . .
>
> "This is the law of the temple: All the surrounding area on top of the mountain will be most holy." (Ezek. 43:6–7, 9, 12)

Although Ezekiel probably uses "prostitution" here figuratively of idolatry (cf. Jer. 3:2, 9; 13:27; Hos. 6:10), he knew well that idolatry often went hand-in-hand with literal prostitution (Ezek. 16 and 23; cf. 1 Kings 21:1–18; 23:6–7).[64] Since in Corinth

62 See, e.g., Isa. 26:19; Dan. 12:2; *1 Enoch* 22:13; 25:6; 102:4–103:4; 2 Macc. 7:9, 11; 12:42–45; 14:46, and the discussion below of Paul's argument in 1 Cor. 15:33–34, 49, 58 that a future bodily resurrection requires avoidance of immorality.

63 Cf. Fee, *First Epistle to the Corinthians*, 260.

64 On the use of prostitution as imagery for unfaithfulness to Yahweh in Ezekiel 43:7 and 9, see Walther Zimmerli, *Ezekiel*, 2 vols. (Hermeneia; Philadelphia: Fortress, 1983), 2:418, and Daniel I. Block, *The Book of Ezekiel: Chapters 25–48* (NICOT; Grand Rapids: Eerdmans, 1998), 582.

idolatry was also linked with literal prostitution and was probably a feature of the banquets Paul has in mind in this passage (1 Cor. 8:10; 10:7–8; cf. Ex. 32:5–6; Num. 25:1–2), it is easy to see how he could understand the references to prostitution in Ezek. 43:7 and 9 literally.[65]

For Paul, then, the bodies of Corinthian believers belong to the Lord through the indwelling of God's eschatological Spirit and are temples in which God's glory dwells. Because of this, Christian youth in Corinth ought to stay away from banquets where after-dinner flings with prostitutes are the norm. Such conduct is not only personally destructive and based on false claims about the body's temporal nature, but it also violates the sanctity of the eschatological temple of God.

Idolatry and Immorality in Eschatological Israel (10:1–22)

These banquets probably also provide the background for Paul's admonitions against idolatry in 10:1–22.[66] Paul argues here that youth within the Corinthian church, and Corinthian believers generally, ought to stay away from these banquets not only because of the sexual immorality that they promote but also because a pagan "god" presides over them, and those attending them are therefore inevitably implicated in idolatry.[67]

In 10:1–22 Paul's instructions to Corinthian believers involved in these banquets arise again from his conviction that the Corinthian church stands in continuity with God's ancient people Israel, and like God's people in the Jewish Scriptures, they must distinguish themselves from the nations around them by obedience to God's commands. Paul refers to the desert generation of Israelites as "our fathers," assuming that they are the patriarchs not simply of the Jews but also of the Corinthian church (10:1). He implies, by referring casually to "Israel according to the flesh" (10:18, aut.), that the Corinthians are spiritual Israel (cf. Rom. 2:29; 9:6; Phil. 3:3). The table at which the Corinthians celebrate the Lord's Supper is analogous to the altar—"the Lord's table"—of Israel's temple (1 Cor. 10:21; cf. Mal. 1:7, 12), and the narrative of Israel's transgressions in the desert belongs to the Corinthians: "These things happened to them as examples and were written down as warnings for us, on whom the fulfillment of the ages has come" (10:11; cf. 10:6).

The correspondence between Israel's debacle in the desert and conditions in the Corinthian church is close, and Paul wants the Corinthians to benefit from the warning implicit in their ancestors' story. On two famous occasions, God's ancient people mingled banqueting with idolatry and sexual immorality during the period of their desert wandering. After Moses had been on the mountain for forty days and nights conversing with God (Ex. 24:18), the people became impatient and urged Aaron,

65 The banqueting of Roman citizens in connection with the Isthmian games in Corinth were inevitably both cultic occasions and occasions for sexual activity, although unlike cultic prostitution in ancient Israel, the two were not necessarily related. On the Roman custom, see Winter, *After Paul Left Corinth*, 93–96.

66 Ibid.

67 On the connection between feasts and idolatry in Greco-Roman culture, see, e.g., Arthur Darby Nock, *Early Gentile Christianity and Its Hellenistic Background* (New York: Harper, 1964), 73; Theissen, *Social Setting*, 127–28; and Bruce Winter, *Seek the Welfare of the City: Christians as Benefactors and Citizens* (Grand Rapids: Eerdmans, 1994), 168–74. An Asclepion with three dining rooms and couches for reclining has been excavated at the site of Roman Corinth and may date to the time of Paul. See Murphy-O'Connor, *St. Paul's Corinth*, 161–67.

"Come, make us gods who will go before us" (32:1). Aaron cast a golden calf and announced to the people, "These are your gods, O Israel, who brought you up out of Egypt" (32:4). The people then "sat down to eat and drink and got up to indulge in pagan revelry" (32:6). The verb translated "indulge in pagan revelry" has sexual connotations both in the Hebrew and Greek texts of Exodus 32:6.[68]

Later in their progress through the desert, the Israelite men indulged in sexual immorality with Moabite women. The women invited the men to offer sacrifices to their gods, and, as a result, "the people ate and bowed down before these gods" (Num. 25:1–2). God was angry with his people because of this sin and punished them with a plague that killed 24,000 (25:9).

Paul recalls both stories in 1 Corinthians 10:7–8 and emphasizes the severe punishment associated with the second story as a way of urging the Corinthians to avoid the disastrous combination of banqueting, idolatry, and sexual immorality. The Corinthian believers, he implies, are God's eschatologically constituted people. They can expect a punishment no less harsh than that of their ancestors if they break the boundaries of sanctity that God has mandated for his people and indulge in the pagan practices of the people around them.

At the same time that Paul follows the Mosaic law in forbidding idolatry, however, he permits the consumption of "anything sold in the meat market." This implies not only that the idolatrous ceremonies in which the meat has been used have not polluted it but that the food restrictions of the Mosaic law no longer apply to God's people (10:25). Just as the means of enforcing the sanctity of God's people have changed slightly (5:1–13), so some of the defining boundaries of God's people have themselves also changed.[69]

Salutary Holiness (7:12–16)

Holiness in Paul's thinking not only implies the exclusion of certain people and activities, but it also has an inclusive effect on the unbelieving family members of believers. This unexpected element of Paul's teaching on holiness becomes clear from 7:12–16, a passage in which Paul advises against the break-up of marriages between believers and unbelievers. The specific problem that prompts Paul's advice is a mystery, but probably some Corinthians have taken too far Paul's admonitions in a previous letter not to associate with immoral people (5:9). Paul intended that letter to refer to immoral believers (5:11), but the Corinthians have taken it to mean any immoral person (5:10), and since the marriage bed is the closest of all associations, they may have reasoned, surely they should divorce their unbelieving spouses.[70]

---

68 The term is *paizō* in Greek, and it normally means "play, amuse one's self" (BDAG, 750), but in the Greek text of Gen. 26:8 it refers to "sexual play," and in Gen. 39:14 and 17 a similar word (*empaizō*) has the same meaning. The Hebrew word in all four instances is *ṣāḥaq*. See Nahum M. Sarna, *Exodus* (JPSTC; Philadelphia: Jewish Publication Society, 1991), 204.

69 See also 7:19, where Paul makes the startling statement, "Circumcision is nothing and uncircumcision is nothing. Keeping God's commands is what counts." Circumcision is a commandment of the Mosaic law, but, for Paul, it is no longer a command of God.

70 This is the scenario advanced cautiously by Fee, *First Epistle to the Corinthians*, 300. Cf. Wolfgang Schrage, *Der erste Brief an die Korinther (1Kor 6,12–11,16)* (EKK 7.2; Zürich and Neukirchen-Vluyn: Benziger and Neukirchener, 1995), 103–4.

Against this idea, Paul advances the opposite principle: In the case of families, holiness is not compromised by association with unbelievers but radiates outward to encompass them:

> The unbelieving husband is made holy through his wife, and the unbelieving wife is made holy by her husband. Otherwise your children would be unclean, but as it is, they are holy. (7:14, NRSV)

The believing partner in a mixed marriage, therefore, should, if possible, keep the marriage intact, for the holiness of the believer makes both an unbelieving spouse and any children in the family holy.

What does Paul mean by this? Paul's use of a similar idea when speaking of unbelieving Israel in Romans 11:16 points to the right explanation.[71] In this verse Paul argues that the holiness of Israel's patriarchs made unbelieving Israel holy: "If the part of the dough offered as first fruits is holy, then the whole batch is holy; if the root is holy, so are the branches."[72] Israel is holy because their descent from the patriarchs has given them priority in the proclamation of the gospel (1:16), access to the oracles of God (3:2), and a host of other privileges (9:4–5), including the salvation of many Israelites on the final day (11:26). In the same way, 1 Corinthians 7:14 probably means that through their daily contact with believing family members—engaging them in conversation and observing their lives—unbelievers are more likely to be saved. This helps explain Paul's two rhetorical questions at the end of his argument: "Wife, might you not save your husband? Or husband, might you not save your wife?" (7:16, aut.).[73]

Once again, this understanding of holiness moves beyond the concept in Paul's Scriptures, and it does this in two ways. First, in the Mosaic law, only uncleanness, not holiness, is transmitted from person to person, but Paul, at least in the case of marriage, believes that holiness is communicable.[74] Second, when Ezra was faced with the problem of marriage between members of God's people and outsiders, he proposed that the marriages be dissolved (Ezra 10:10–11), fearing the commingling of Israelites with Gentiles engaged in "detestable practices" (Ezra 9:14; cf. Neh. 13:26). Paul, however, insists that in the case of the Corinthian Christians the influence runs the other way: Through association with their believing spouses, unbelievers are more likely to hear and embrace the gospel.[75]

---

71 G. R. Beasley-Murray, *Baptism in the New Testament* (Grand Rapids: Eerdmans, 1962), 192–97; Fee, *First Epistle to the Corinthians*, 300–301.

72 For this understanding of Rom. 11:16, see, e.g., Douglas Moo, *The Epistle to the Romans* (Grand Rapids: Eerdmans, 1996), 698–99.

73 For this understanding of the difficult Greek phrase (*ti . . . oidas . . . ei*), see Barrett, *First Epistle to the Corinthians*, 167; cf. Fee, *First Epistle to the Corinthians*, 301, 305–6.

74 Brian S. Rosner, *Paul, Scripture and Ethics: A Study of 1 Corinthians 5–7* (AGJU 22; Leiden: Brill, 1994), 170, observes that holiness is sometimes communicated from inanimate objects, like the altar, to those who touch them. But this common understanding of such texts as Ex. 29:37; 30:29; Lev. 6:18, 27; and Num. 16:38 probably rests on a misunderstanding of the Hebrew term *yiqdaš*. The term could mean "will become holy" (by virtue of contact with a holy object) or "must be holy" (in order to touch a holy object). The same ambiguity affects the LXX's term *hagiasthēsetai* (*hēgiasthēsan* in Num. 16:38). The priestly denial of the contagiousness of holiness in Hag. 2:12–13, however, tips the balance in favor of the second translation. See Baruch A. Levine, *Leviticus* (JPSTC; Philadelphia: Jewish Publication Society, 1989), 36–37, and Sarna, *Exodus*, 259 n. 27.

75 Cf. Thomas R. Schreiner, *Paul: Apostle of God's Glory in Christ* (Downers Grove, Ill.: InterVarsity, 2001), 428–29.

The Critical Importance of Corinthian Sanctity

Paul's rhetoric reveals how vexed he is over the Corinthians' unholy behavior:

- "It is actually reported that there is sexual immorality among you. . . ." (5:1)
- "When any of you has a grievance against another, do you dare to take it to court before the unrighteous, instead of taking it before the saints?" (6:1, NRSV)
- "Flee from sexual immorality." (6:18)
- "Flee from idolatry." (10:14)

The origin of Paul's concern lies in his conviction that the Corinthians belong to the eschatologically restored people of God. God's people had violated the covenant God made with them at Sinai and had activated the curses of that covenant.[76] The law itself and the prophets, however, looked forward to a time when God would establish a new covenant with his people and would send his Spirit to dwell within them, making them holy once again.[77] Paul believed that the death of Jesus established the new covenant (1 Cor. 11:25) and that the time of the eschatological restoration of God's people had arrived. As the dwelling place of God's presence, therefore, the Corinthians, both corporately and individually, need to be holy (3:16; 6:19).

The character of this holiness is both alike and different from the character of holiness in Paul's Scriptures. On one hand, incest, various forms of sexual immorality, and idolatry violate the boundaries of holiness for Paul, just as they do in his Scriptures (5:1–13; 6:9–20). Nevertheless, the community does not permanently exclude those who violate the boundaries of its holiness but disciplines them in the hope that they might return (5:5). Similarly, contact with unbelieving family members does not compromise the believer's holiness but extends holiness to the unbeliever (7:14). Paul sets aside food laws without comment (10:25; cf. 7:19).

A new law, then, seems to have defined the boundaries of holiness for Paul. The law of Moses no longer governs his behavior but something he calls "the law of God" (9:20) or "the law of Christ" (9:21).[78] If 1 Corinthians allows us to summarize the differences between the two laws in a single principle, it is this: The law of Christ changes the Mosaic law in the direction of greater inclusiveness. Both Jews and Gentiles viewed Jewish food laws to be distinctive practices of the Jewish people.[79] Their removal opens the doors of the people of God to many ethnic groups. Similarly, excommunication is intended to restore errant believers to full fellowship, and staying married to an

76 See, e.g., Deut. 28:1–29:1; Jer. 9:12–16, 25; 11:6–13; 16:10–13; 22:8–9; 40:2–3; and 44:2–6, 23.

77 For the new covenant theme, see Jer. 23:7–8; 24:7; 31:31–34; 32:40; 50:5. For the coming of the Spirit to God's people at the time of Israel's eschatological restoration, see, e.g., Ezek. 11:19; 36:26–27; and 37:1–14.

78 See Thielman, *Paul and the Law*, 100–118; idem, "Law and Liberty in the Ethics of Paul," *Ex Auditu* 11 (1995): 63–75; and idem, *The Law and the New Testament: The Question of Continuity* (New York: Crossroad, 1999), 40–41. Cf. Peter Stuhlmacher, *Biblische Theologie des Neuen Testaments*, 2 vols. (Göttingen: Vandenhoeck & Ruprecht, 1997), 1:256–57, 266–68. Stuhlmacher argues that parts of the Hebrew Scriptures themselves anticipate a new revelation of the law—an eschatological "Zion Torah" that replaces the Torah of Sinai. Paul's expression, the "Torah of Christ" (Gal. 6:2) refers to the eschatological fulfillment that Jesus has brought to the Sinai Torah. It also refers to Jesus' introduction of the age of the Spirit, in which the law can be kept.

79 This was also true of circumcision, which Paul excludes as a boundary marker in 7:19.

unbeliever will hopefully draw unbelievers into the company of God's people. The principle of holiness is still in effect under the new covenant, but the boundary markers have changed to include Gentiles as well as Jews.

FIDELITY TO THE GOSPEL

In a comparatively brief section near the close of the letter, Paul suddenly turns to a new subject: the bodily resurrection of believers from the dead.[80] The Corinthians are denying this Christian teaching (15:12), unable to understand its significance (15:12–9) or to conceptualize how it works (15:35).

Paul, however, is unwilling to ignore the matter. As the intensity of his rhetoric shows, he considers belief in the bodily resurrection of believers to be a cardinal tenet of the Christian faith. He calls into question whether those who doubt this teaching have really believed the gospel in the first place (15:2), ranks the teachings with which it is connected as "of first importance" (15:3), urges the Corinthians to come to their senses on this issue (15:34), and calls an imaginary interlocutor who finds a bodily resurrection difficult to conceive a "fool" (*aphrōn*, 15:36). Despite their brevity, therefore, Paul's comments on this final issue are of crucial theological importance to him. In order to understand the problem and Paul's response to it, we must understand something of the relation between body and soul in Greco-Roman anthropology.

Body and Soul in Greco-Roman Anthropology

In Greco-Roman society the belief was common that death released the soul from the shackles of the body.[81] Cicero, writing in the Latin West in the first century B.C., ridicules belief in the elaborate Greek mythology of the underworld—descent at death to a cavity in the earth where souls must cross Lake Acheron, pass by the fierce three-headed dog Cerberus, and stand before the judges Minos and Rhadamanthus (*Tusc.* 1.5.10; cf. Virgil, *Aen.*, 6). He then discusses the other more sensible options:

> Some consider death the separation of the soul from the body; some think there is no such separation, but that soul and body perish together and the soul is annihilated with the body. Of those who think that there is a separation of the soul some hold that it is at once dispersed in space, others that it survives a long time, others that it survives forever.[82]

80 On the sudden introduction of this topic, see Lietzmann, *An die Korinther I/II*, 76, although, as Fee, *First Epistle to the Corinthians*, 713–14, shows, the chapter is more closely connected to the preceding section than Lietzmann allows.

81 The view is very old. Plato in the late fifth or early fourth century B.C. refers to the common fear that the soul, stripped of the body, goes to Pluto and the underworld at death (*Crat.* 403b). Plato himself believed that the body imprisoned the soul but that philosophy could wean the soul from the body's concerns. In this way, at death, the soul could join God in the unseen world (*Phaedo* 80d–83c).

82 Cicero, *Tusc.* 1.9.18. Cicero himself seems to have held that the souls of the noble dead would ascend to the Milky Way, where they would take their places among others like them. He understood death to be an escape "from the bondage of the body as from a prison" (*Resp.* 6.14, 16).

Common to all these beliefs—even to the Greek "fables"—is that death means the shedding of the body, which dissolves and is forgotten. The notion that the body might live again was not an option worth discussing.

Lucian, writing in the Greek East about two centuries later, reveals much the same configuration of basic beliefs. He scorns the funerary practices of the masses, which show they believe in the complicated mythology found in Homer and Hesiod. They place a coin in the mouth of the deceased as fare for the ferry ride across Lake Acheron, dress them so that they will not attract Cerberus's attention, and pour wine over their tombs for their nourishment (*Luct.*, 10–12, 19). He explains that the masses believe that death sorts humanity into three groups according to their good and evil deeds. The virtuous go to the beautiful Elysian fields, the wicked to eternal torments, and the middle group, "and they are many, wander about the meadow without their bodies, in the form of shadows that vanish like smoke in your fingers" (1–9). Lucian will have none of this. Death for him leads to unconsciousness and is an enviable release from the pain and indignity of this life's physical existence (16–19).

Stories of resuscitations from the dead apparently circulated from time to time and created a stir. In Lucian's dialogue *The Lover of Lies*, a group of friends exchange the latest gossip about such accounts. At one point, Antigonus tops Cleodemus's claim that he recently toured Hades, with the following tale:

> I know a man who came to life more than twenty days after his burial, having attended the fellow both before his death and after he came to life. How was it . . . that in twenty days the body neither corrupted nor simply wasted away from inanition? (26)

More highly educated people, however, disdained such resuscitation stories. Lucian considered them popular superstition—mere ghost stories that the enlightened knew better than to believe.[83]

Many Greeks and Romans, when faced with the Jewish and Christian idea of the resurrection of the body, therefore, sympathized with Christianity's mid-second-century nemesis Celsus:

> [Christians suppose that] those . . . long dead . . . will rise up from the earth possessing the same bodies as before. This is simply the hope of worms. For what sort of human soul would have any further desire for a body that has rotted? The fact that this doctrine is not shared by some of you [Jews] and by some Christians shows its utter repulsiveness, and that it is both revolting and impossible. For what sort of body, after being entirely corrupted, could return to its original nature and that same condition which it had before it was dissolved?[84]

83 See Dale Martin, *The Corinthian Body* (New Haven, Conn.: Yale Univ. Press, 1995), 112–14. Against Martin's stress on the similarities between these beliefs and the Jewish and Christian belief, it must be said that none of these accounts contains anything like the idea that the dead bodies of an entire group would be raised to live again forever. They are instead tales of isolated resurrections of people who would presumably die again. On the uniqueness of the early Christian understanding of resurrection within the panoply of Greco-Roman views, see N. T. Wright, *The Resurrection of the Son of God* (Minneapolis, Minn.: Fortress, 2003), 32–94.

84 Origen, *Cels.* 5.14.

The Corinthian Error and Paul's Response

Like the heterodox Jews and Christians known to Celsus, some Christians at Corinth in the first century cannot swallow the notion that after their death, their corpses will breathe and walk again. "There is no resurrection of the dead," they claim (15:12). They are not denying the bodily resurrection of Jesus, since Paul assumes that he and they hold the resurrection of Jesus in common (15:1).[85] Nor are they denying, like Lucian, a conscious afterlife, since some are being baptized, by proxy, for the dead (15:29).[86] As with Celsus, they do not understand how corpses that have moldered in the tomb can live again. "How are the dead raised?" they ask. "What kind of body do they have?" (15:35).

Paul is concerned about this departure from Christian teaching because he sees an unbreakable link between the future resurrection of believers and the past resurrection of Christ on the one hand, and between the resurrection of believers and their hope for immortality on the other hand. Paul believes that the Corinthians have not thought through the theological implications of their denial of the bodily resurrection of believers in these two respects, and the purpose of 15:1–58 is to impress on them the seriousness of their error.

One aspect of his argument examines the implications of their denial of their own resurrections for their belief in the resurrection of Christ. First Paul reminds the Corinthians that he and they share in common with other Christians the belief that Jesus rose from the tomb on the third day and was seen by hundreds of witnesses, including Paul himself (15:1–8). This element of the gospel is "of first importance" (15:3).[87] Paul preaches it, the Corinthians believe it, and, insofar as they are Christians at all, they continue to stand on it (15:1–2, 11).

Next Paul postulates an unbreakable link between the resurrection of Christ from the dead and the future resurrection of believers from the dead. The resurrection of Christ is not an isolated incident as in the stories of human resuscitation or divine death and rebirth that circulated around Greek and Roman society.[88] It is the first part of an eschatological scenario by which God will triumph finally over death, and that includes, as a critical element, the bodily resurrection of believers (15:20–28, 42–57). Without the resurrection of believers, the whole plan collapses and the resurrection of Christ becomes unnecessary. Without the resurrection of Christ, however, the gospel becomes nothing but a lie. "We are then found to be false witnesses about God," Paul says, "for we have testified about God that he raised Christ from the dead."

The consequences of this are horrific: If the gospel is not true, then Christ's death has not been "for our sins," as the gospel proclaims (15:3).[89] The Corinthians are

85 Contra Lietzmann, *An die Korinther I/II*, 76. Correctly Fee, *First Epistle to the Corinthians*, 713.

86 On the significance of 15:29 for the Corinthians' understanding of immortality, see Fee, *First Epistle to the Corinthians*, 744, 767.

87 On the meaning of *en prōtois* as not merely "at the first" but "of first importance," see, e.g., Weiss, *Der erste Korintherbrief*, 347 n. 2, and Lietzmann, *An die Korinther I/II*, 76–77.

88 See Celsus' list in Origen, *Cels.* 2.55; the list in Rudolf Bultmann, *History of the Synoptic Tradition* (New York: Harper & Row, 1963), 233–34; and the detailed discussion of Wright, *Resurrection*, 32–84, who points out that the term "resurrection" is often used too loosely of such stories.

89 Cf. Fee, *First Epistle to the Corinthians*, 743–44.

consequently still living in their sins, and the grim prospect of sin's just penalty looms before them—physical death is (for them) not sleep but eternal destruction (15:17–18).

A second aspect of Paul's argument focuses on the future consequences of the Corinthians' insistence that believers will not be raised from the dead. Paul refuses to allow what the Corinthians seem to assume—that the immortality of the disembodied soul can be substituted for the notion of a bodily resurrection. Without a bodily resurrection, Paul insists there will be no immortality at all (15:18–19). Death will not be defeated (15:26, 54–55), and this life will be the sum total of Christian existence (15:19). The inscription commonly used on Roman graves will be right: *non fui, fui, non sum, non curo*—"I was not, I was, I am not, I care not."[90]

If that were true, then Paul's own apostolic labor, whether in Corinth (15:10) or in Ephesus (15:30–32), would in turn be a waste of time, and Christians would be the most pitiable of people (15:19). Death should be mourned in the way that Lucian depicts a typical father's grief over the untimely death of his son: "Never again will you roam the streets at night, or fall in love, my child, or drink deep at wine-parties with your young friends" (*Luct.* 13). By implication, life should be filled with those things of which death will deprive us: We should "eat and drink, for tomorrow we die" (15:32).

In contrast, if Christ has been raised from the dead, then he has begun to reverse the wave of death that has swept over humanity since Adam. His resurrection is the first resurrection of many others that will take place when Christ returns and God subjects all his enemies, including death, to him (15:20–28). These resurrections, moreover, are not merely the reanimation of dead bodies but the resurrection of the dead to an immortal existence (15:54). The immortality of this new existence demands a new kind of body, and even those alive at the coming of Christ will be changed so that they too might live eternally in God's kingdom. These new bodies will be imperishable, glorious, powerful, spiritual, and heavenly (15:40, 42–43, 47–49, 52).[91]

If this is the Christian hope, then how ought the Corinthians to live? The Corinthians who have consorted with prostitutes (6:12–20) and felt the freedom to attend idolatrous pagan banquets (8:10; 10:1–22) ought to realize the truth of the aphorism (from Menander's *Thais*), "Bad company corrupts good character."[92] They should come back to their senses and stop sinning (15:33–34). Paul admonishes the Corinthians, "just as we have borne the likeness of the earthly man, let us bear the image of the man from heaven" (15:49).[93] Similarly, in light of all that he has said

90 The saying was so commonly known that it was simply abbreviated NFFNSNC. See Mary Beard, John North, and Simon Price, *Religions of Rome*, 2 vols. (Cambridge: Cambridge Univ. Press, 1998), 2:236.

91 Cf. Rom. 8:23; 2 Cor. 5:1, 4; Phil. 3:21, and see the comments of Joseph Plevnik, *Paul and the Parousia: An Exegetical and Theological Investigation* (Peabody, Mass.: Hendrickson, 1997), 147–53.

92 On the link between 6:12–20, 10:1–22, and 15:33, see Winter, *After Paul Left Corinth*, 76–109. Winter observes that Paul's sentence from Menander's *Thais*, in its original context, referred to the seductions of prostitutes (ibid., 99–100).

93 Many translations, commentators, and editions of the Greek text read something like "so *shall we bear* (*phoresomen*) the likeness of the man from heaven" (NIV), but the textual witnesses to the hortatory subjunctive, "let us bear" (*phoresōmen*; cf. NIV note), are far superior to those that read the future form. See Fee, *First Epistle to the Corinthians*, 794–95, and the editions of Tischendorf, von Soden, and Vogels.

about the resurrection of Jesus and of believers in this chapter, Paul concludes with this exhortation:

> Stand firm. Let nothing move you. Always give yourselves fully to the work of the Lord, because you know that your labor in the Lord is not in vain. (15:58)

Without the resurrection, the Corinthians' labor in the Lord, like Paul's apostolic labors, will be useless. The resurrection of Christ, however, points forward to the inevitable resurrection of believers with the result that for both Paul (15:10) and the Corinthians (15:58), a life of labor in the service of the Lord, despite its hardships, is a life well spent.

UNITY, SANCTITY, AND FIDELITY IN 1 CORINTHIANS

Paul's most important task in writing 1 Corinthians is to bring the diverse and contentious Corinthian Christians together. This can only happen if they understand the gracious nature of their Christian calling and the important place that they occupy in God's plan to restore the fortunes of his people. God has incorporated them into his people at his own gracious initiative, and therefore they ought to be gracious with one another—they should replace their pride with love, the strong should protect the weak, and the whole church should work together to form an integrated edifice. This is necessary because their "edifice" is the eschatologically restored temple of God, the dwelling place of God's presence promised by the prophets.

As the restored temple, it is important for the Corinthians not only to be unified but also to be sanctified. A unity that ignores the boundaries of behavior for God's people is a useless unity, and therefore Paul devotes much of the letter to the church's sanctity. It must not tolerate sexual immorality, compromise with judicial corruption, or rationalize idolatrous practices. To do this blurs the distinction between the church and the world and means repeating the failures of the people of God during the period of the Exodus.

The unity of the church will also be meaningless if the Corinthians betray the gospel that Paul preached and on which the Corinthians claim to have taken their stand. Yet this is precisely the consequence, Paul argues, of the claim among some Corinthians that there is no resurrection of the dead. To deny the bodily resurrection of believers, he says, is to make the whole gospel a lie, and if the gospel is a lie, then the Corinthians have no remedy for their past sins and no incentive for abstaining from future sins. Without the resurrection, death has triumphed, and there is no need for the rigors of an apostle's life or for holiness within the church. Those are the most pitiful forms of existence.

Although these three themes each dominate discrete sections of the letter, they are also connected in significant ways. The themes of unity and sanctity are connected to each other both by a direct link and by a concern that runs through both like a thread.

First, Paul believes that the destruction of the church's unity is a direct violation of the church's sanctity. To divide the church over special teachers (3:3–4) and social classifications (11:19) is to destroy the temple of God and to violate its sanctity, "for God's temple is holy, and you are that temple" (3:17).

Second, into the fabric of the sections of the letter devoted to these two issues is woven a concern common to them both: to prevent believers on the borders of the faith from crossing over into its margins and to pull those on the margins of the faith into the church. Paul wants the knowledgeable to protect the fragile faith of the weak so that they will not be destroyed (8:11) and to avoid alienating the unbeliever who is trying to show good will to believers (10:28). He wants those with special gifts to make the church's worship intelligible to the inquirer and unbeliever with the hope that they too will worship God (14:16, 22–25). Similarly, he modifies the Mosaic law to avoid permanent exclusion of the sexually immoral from the community (5:5), and he makes holiness a force for the inclusion of unbelieving spouses and children rather than a reason for their exclusion (7:14, 16).

Paul's concerns for the unity and the sanctity of the church also emerge in the section of the letter devoted to fidelity to the gospel. There Paul specifies that the gospel to which the Corinthians should be faithful is not his own but the common property of the church. He passed on to them what he had received (15:3), and not only Paul but the other apostles who worked among the Corinthians preached this gospel. This is the gospel that the Corinthians believed (15:11).[94] The emphasis here is more on the unity of the Corinthians with other believers everywhere than on the unity specifically of the Corinthian church, but the effect is still to stress the adherence of the Corinthians to a common faith shared by all Christians.

Paul also connects the Christian teaching on the bodily resurrection to the issue of the Corinthians' sanctity. Without the bodily resurrection of believers in the future, believers have no hope of immortality and therefore no theological incentive to avoid "bad company" (15:33) and "stand firm" (15:58). If there is no resurrection of the dead, their labor (15:58)—and Paul's labor (15:10, 30–32)—are in vain.

The unity of the church, its holiness before the world, and its fidelity to the gospel are not, therefore, merely three theological topics that Paul discusses in separate sections of the letter. They are facets of a single prism closely connected, and each a necessary part of the whole.

94 Fee, *First Epistle to the Corinthians*, 714, 736.

Chapter 13

PHILIPPIANS: THE IMPORTANCE OF THE GOSPEL'S PROGRESS

THE REASONS FOR PHILIPPIANS

Paul's nearly three years in Ephesus ended with a period of turbulence. "A great door for effective work has opened to me," he tells the Corinthians, "and there are many who oppose me" (1 Cor. 16:9; cf. 15:32). Reflecting on this difficult phase of his work some months after he had left the city, Paul wrote that he had been

> under great pressure, far beyond our ability to endure, so that we despaired even of life. Indeed, in our hearts we felt the sentence of death. But this happened that we might not rely on ourselves but on God, who raises the dead. (2 Cor. 1:8b–9)

Although the point is not uncontroversial, these hardships probably included a period of imprisonment, and it may have been during this imprisonment that Paul's church at Philippi became so concerned about him that they commissioned one of their number, Epaphroditus, to bring Paul a monetary gift (4:18) and to stay with him to meet his needs (2:25).[1]

Probably on his way to visit Paul, Epaphroditus became ill but pressed on to complete his mission, "risking his life," as Paul tells them, "to make up for the help you could not give me" (2:30).[2] Somehow, word of Epaphroditus's condition had reached Philippi and he had become distressed about their concern for him. He longed to return (2:26), so Paul decided to send him back (2:25), and this provided the opportunity to send a letter with him. Our canonical letter to the Philippians is the result.[3]

1 Tradition, dating at least from the second century Marcionite prologue to Philippians, places Paul in a Roman imprisonment during the composition of Philippians. The record of a Roman imprisonment of Paul in Acts 28:16–31, the mention of the "praetorium" in Phil. 1:12, and the greetings from "Caesar's household" in Phil. 4:22 were probably enough to prompt ancient readers of the letter to assume a Roman imprisonment. The term "praetorium," however, can have a wide variety of meanings, including a provincial governor's headquarters (Matt. 27:27; Mark 15:16; John 18:28, 33; 19:9; Acts 23:35; Cicero, *Ver.* 4.65; 5.106), and "Caesar's household" was a large group of imperial slaves and former slaves scattered broadly across the empire. The affinity of Phil. 3:1–21 with Galatians (Phil. 3:1–11) and 1 Corinthians (Phil. 3:12–21), moreover, makes an Ephesian origin for the letter likely. On the meaning of "praetorium," see P. G. W. Glare, ed. *Oxford Latin Dictionary* (Oxford: Oxford Univ. Press, 1982), 1448. On "Caesar's household," see P. R. C. Weaver, *Familia Caesaris: A Social Study of the Emperor's Freedmen and Slaves* (Cambridge: Cambridge Univ. Press, 1972), 1–8; on this whole question, see Frank Thielman, "Ephesus and the Literary Setting of Philippians" in *New Testament Greek and Exegesis*, ed. Amy M. Donaldson and Timothy B. Sailors (Grand Rapids: Eerdmans, 2003), 205–23.

2 Paul A. Holloway, "Disce Gaudere": *Paul's Consolation of the Church at Philippi*, diss. Univ. of Chicago (1998), 26. See now idem, *Consolation in Philippians: Philosophical Sources and Rhetorical Strategy* (SNTSMS 112; Cambridge: Cambridge Univ. Press, 2001).

3 Many scholars argue that our canonical Philippians is a composite letter, fashioned from two or, more commonly, three separate letters. For a survey of the various schemes for partitioning the letter together with persuasive arguments for its unity, see David E. Garland, "The Composition and Unity of Philippians: Some Neglected Literary Factors," *NovT* 27 (1985):141–73; Holloway,

Paul's concern for the progress of the gospel among the Philippians dominates the letter. The importance of this theme is evident from 1:9–11, where he follows his customary procedure of revealing his letter's primary concerns in the intercessory prayer report:

> And this is my prayer: that your love may abound more and more in knowledge and depth of insight, so that you may be able to discern what is best and may be pure and blameless until the day of Christ, filled with the fruit of righteousness that comes through Jesus Christ—to the glory and praise of God.

Paul wants the Philippians to focus on what matters, and what matters, as Paul says in 1:12 and 25, is that the gospel progresses both in his circumstances and in theirs, whatever they may be.[4] By concentrating on the gospel's progress the Philippians will arrive at the final day pure, blameless, and filled with righteousness. Paul's labor among them will not have been in vain (2:16), and, on the day of Christ, they will be his crown of victory (4:1).

Three impediments to the gospel's progress among the Philippians loom particularly large. First, the Philippians are enduring hardship for the sake of the gospel: They are suffering political persecution and are experiencing anxiety about others who are suffering for the same reason, particularly Paul and Epaphroditus. Second, disunity within the church threatens to tarnish the church's witness. Third, with sweat still on his brow from wrestling with the Galatians and Corinthians over various deviations from the gospel, Paul wants to warn the Philippians about the kinds of errors that hindered the progress of the gospel in these other churches.

Paul addresses these problems in various ways, but two strategies for admonishing the Philippians remain consistent throughout the letter: He reminds them of the eschatological goal of their progress in the faith, and he provides examples for them to follow as they negotiate the hurdles that stand between them and this final goal.

THE PROGRESS OF THE GOSPEL AMID HARDSHIP

The Philippians are experiencing hardship in two forms. First, they are being persecuted for their faith.[5] Their church was born in the midst of persecution, as Luke's account of the flogging and imprisonment of Paul and Silas reveals (Acts 16:16–40;

"Disce Gaudere," 5–35; and, cautiously, Markus Bockmuehl, *The Epistle to the Philippians* (BNTC; Peabody, Mass.: Hendrickson, 1998), 20–25.

4 For the significance of the intercessory prayer report in determining Paul's primary concern in the letter, and for Paul's probable reliance on Stoic philosophical conventions about the importance of distinguishing between "the things that matter" (*ta diapheronta*) and the "things that do not matter" (*ta adiaphora*), see Holloway, "Disce Gaudere," 27, 52–56, and 104–12. Holloway argues persuasively that Paul's letter to the Philippians is an attempt to "console" them in the technical, philosophical sense that this term was used in ancient Latin and Greek literature. Consolation, in this sense, was "the combating of grief through rational argument" (61).

5 See esp. Peter Oakes, *Philippians: From People to Letter* (SNTSMS 110; Cambridge: Cambridge Univ. Press, 2001), 59–63, 77–96. Oakes argues that the Philippian Christians were mostly non-Romans in a city where Romans had special privileges. Few, if any, within the church would have belonged to the elite social class, and most would have been part of the service sector (bakers, etc.), slaves, farmers, and the poor. These groups would have suffered economically and physically for refusing to participate in religious rituals that conflicted with their Christian convictions.

cf. 1 Thess. 2:2), and that persecution is continuing. They are experiencing, Paul tells them, "the same struggle you saw I had, and now hear that I still have" (Phil. 1:30). Paul's admonition not to be "frightened in any way by those who oppose you" (1:28a) indicates his concern that this opposition may be a hindrance to the gospel's progress in their midst—that they will turn their eyes from what really matters (1:10a) and focus on their difficult circumstances with disastrous consequences for the final day (1:10b–11).

Second, the Philippians are anxious about the suffering of Paul and Epaphroditus. Their anxiety about Paul's "affliction" (*thlipsis*, 4:14) prompted their efforts to tend to his physical needs by sending Epaphroditus with a monetary gift (2:25; 4:18).[6] Epaphroditus is concerned because they have heard he became ill on his mission to Paul (2:26). This indicates at least that Epaphroditus knows them well enough to think that they will become anxious upon hearing this report, and possibly he has received word of their anxiety.[7] In any case, both their own suffering and the suffering of others for the sake of the gospel has left them anxious.

In the face of this hardship, Paul urges them to find joy in what matters—the progress of the gospel. As an encouragement to do this, he describes people who have themselves focused on what matters despite hardship and can serve as examples to the Philippians of how they can do the same. He also reminds the Philippians of the eschatological goal of their faith. Finally, he provides practical advice for shifting their thoughts from their anxiety-provoking circumstances to the good.

Following the Example of Others

In 3:17 Paul tells the Philippians to "join with others in following my example . . . and take note of those who live according to the pattern we gave you," and, in 4:9, "Whatever you have learned or received or heard from me, or seen in me—put it into practice." Much of the letter provides examples of those who, despite suffering, have concentrated on what matters and have found joy in the progress of the gospel.

Early in the letter, Paul begins to offer his own approach to suffering as an example for the Philippians to follow. Personal letters to friends and family in antiquity often included after the greeting and health wish a section that gave news of the person who was writing.[8] Paul follows this convention in 1:12–26 by speaking of his own circumstances, but he modifies the custom to speak less about the details of his imprisonment than about how the gospel has progressed because of it.[9]

6 Holloway, "Disce Gaudere," 48–50.

7 Cf. the early second century A.D. letter from the soldier Theonas to his mother Tetheus (POxy XII 1481) in which Theonas thanks Tetheus for a gift and says that he was very grieved that she had heard he was ill. He was not, in fact, seriously ill, he explains, and so she should not be worried. For the text, see John L. White, *Light from Ancient Letters* (FF; Philadelphia: Fortress, 1986), 158.

8 Examples of this arrangement appear in White's section on "Letters to and from Soldiers" in *Light from Ancient Letters*, 157–66. Theonas, for example, opens the body of his letter to his mother with the statement, "I want you to know that the reason I have not sent you a letter for such a long time is because I am in camp and not on account of illness" (158). Cf. Loveday Alexander, "Hellenistic Letter-Forms and the Structure of Philippians," *JSNT* 37 (1989): 87–101, here at 92 and 94–95.

9 Karl Barth, *The Epistle to the Philippians* (Richmond, Va.: John Knox, 1962), 26, observes, "To the question how it is with *him* the apostle *must* react with information as to how it is with the Gospel."

Paul does this especially here because he wants the Philippians to see that even in difficult circumstances, the believer should rejoice if the gospel is advancing. He is in prison because of the proclamation of the gospel (1:13), and some "brothers in the Lord" have added to his affliction through the insincere proclamation of the gospel (1:15a, 17). These difficulties, however, have served to advance the gospel. Because of these difficulties, people in the praetorium and beyond (1:13) have heard the gospel, and fellow believers, both friendly to Paul and otherwise, have preached the gospel more boldly. Paul's response to the insincere preaching of the gospel by his Christian opponents is also the response that he wants the Philippians to have to the hardships they are facing:

> But what does it matter? The important thing is that in every way, whether from false motives or true, Christ is preached. And because of this I rejoice. (1:18a)

Paul then turns to the future and says that although he may live or die in his imprisonment (1:20), he is confident that he will be saved in the eschatological and theological sense (1:19).[10] The prayers of the Philippians and the help of Jesus' Spirit will see him safely through the ordeal of his imprisonment with his faith intact, and whether death or life lies ahead, he will be with Christ (1:20–21; cf. 3:10–14). Because being with Christ is what matters, Paul will continue to rejoice, whatever the future holds (1:18b).

Paul also provides an example for the Philippians to follow at the end of the letter when he thanks them for their gift. This part of the letter has traditionally posed two problems for interpreters: Why does Paul wait so long to thank the Philippians for the gift they have given him, and, once he sets his hand to the task, why is he so reserved about his appreciation?[11] Both the position of Paul's appreciative comments and the way he expresses them are probably designed to model for the Philippians what it means to discern what matters.[12] Although he is appreciative of their gift

10 Paul's reference to his "salvation" (*sōtēria*) here is sometimes taken in the less theologically potent sense of his "deliverance" from prison. See, e.g., the translations in Moffatt, RSV, GNB, NIV, REB, NRSV, and, among commentators, Gerald F. Hawthorne, *Philippians* (WBC 43; Waco, Tex.: Word, 1983), 39–40. But Paul normally uses this word for eschatological salvation (see, e.g., its only other appearances in Philippians: 1:28 and 2:12), and 1:20 says that the outcome of his imprisonment may be either life or death. See J. B. Lightfoot, *Saint Paul's Epistle to the Philippians*, 4th ed. (London: Macmillan, 1896), 91; Marvin R. Vincent, *The Epistles to the Philippians and Philemon* (ICC; Edinburgh: T. & T. Clark, 1897), 23; F. F. Bruce, *Philippians* (GNC; San Francisco: Harper & Row, 1983), 24; Peter T. O'Brien, *The Epistle to the Philippians: A Commentary on the Greek Text* (NIGTC; Grand Rapids: Eerdmans, 1991), 110; Ben Witherington III, *Friendship and Finances in Philippi: The Letter of Paul to the Philippians* (NTC; Valley Forge, Pa.: Trinity Press International, 1994), 46; and Bockmuehl, *Philippians*, 83.

11 Often the first problem has been "solved" by dividing Philippians into three letters, the first of which ("Letter A") is 4:10–20. See, among many others, Jean-François Collange, *The Epistle of Saint Paul to the Philippians* (London: Epworth, 1979), 3–15, 148–54, and Jerome Murphy-O'Connor, *Paul: A Critical Life* (Oxford: Oxford Univ. Press, 1996), 216. The second problem is solved in various ways. J. Hugh Michael, *The Epistle of Paul to the Philippians* (MNTC; London: Hodder and Stoughton, 1928), 208–9, proposes that Paul is responding to a complaint from the Philippians that a previous letter was not appreciative enough of their gift to him by Epaphroditus. G. W. Peterman, *Paul's Gift from Philippi: Conventions of Gift-exchange and Christian Giving* (SNTSMS 92; Cambridge: Cambridge Univ. Press, 1997), 121–61, argues that Paul is trying to avoid the misunderstanding that the Philippians' gift to him has placed him under some social obligation to them. Gordon D. Fee, *Paul's Letter to the Philippians* (NICNT; Grand Rapids: Eerdmans, 1995), 444–45, thinks that Paul wants to elevate the significance of the mutual friendship between himself and the Philippians over the more mundane matters of giving and receiving.

12 Cf. Holloway, "Disce Gaudere," 177–82.

(4:14–16, 18) and rejoices that they have once again expressed their concern for him as they have so often done in the past (4:10), he does not want them to think that he has been discontent without it (4:11–12). The God who strengthens his people makes Paul equal to every circumstance (4:13).[13]

This is also the attitude that the Philippians should have. Like him, they should discern what is best (the progress of the gospel) and trust God to give them the strength to endure any hardship on their way to "the day of Christ Jesus" (1:6).

In addition to offering himself as an example, Paul portrays Christ Jesus (2:5–11), Timothy (2:19–24), and Epaphroditus (2:19–30) as people whom the Philippians should imitate in the midst of their suffering.[14] Since Paul describes these three people in a context where disunity in the church is his chief concern, he probably intends for them to serve primarily as examples of "having the same love, being united in spirit and purpose" (2:2). Still, each of them is also an example of staying focused on what is important in the midst of hardship. Christ Jesus endured suffering in obedience to God, and God highly exalted him (2:6–11). This is a pattern the Philippians should imitate as their own Christian convictions lead to suffering in a society that views them as a threat to social stability. If they remain faithful, God will exalt them in a way not unlike the way he exalted Christ and placed everything in subjection to him (3:20–21).[15]

Timothy and Epaphroditus have also advanced the gospel in the midst of suffering. Timothy, Paul says, is not concerned about his own interests but those of Jesus Christ and has therefore "slaved" (*douleuō*) with Paul in "the work of the gospel" (2:21–22). Epaphroditus similarly "almost died for the work of Christ" in his role as Paul's coworker and cosoldier.

Paul, Christ Jesus, Timothy, and Epaphroditus, therefore, provide examples for the Philippians to follow as they face the hardship of their own suffering for the faith and anxiety about others in the same predicament. Like them, the Philippians should respond to their circumstances neither with fear (1:28) nor with anxiety (2:26; 4:6). They should instead find joy in pondering the progress of the gospel despite, and even because of, their difficulty.

13 Paul's language of self-sufficiency in 4:12 looks superficially Stoic, since Stoicism claimed that the sage found the resources within himself to remain unperturbed by life's variable circumstances. As Peterman, *Paul's Gift from Philippi*, 142, points out, however, in 4:13 Paul reveals that "the strength he needs to encounter the vicissitudes of life does not come from his natural man but from his God in Christ."

14 Interpreters sometimes view 2:19–30 as an unfortunate but necessary deviation from Paul's primary purposes in the letter. Barth, *Philippians*, 79, complains that it contains no "direct teaching," and G. B. Caird, *Paul's Letters from Prison (Ephesians, Philippians, Colossians, Philemon)* (Oxford: Oxford Univ. Press, 1976), 130, that it contains "tiresome details" which, once "disposed of," give way "to the theme of joy which is uppermost in [Paul's] mind." These details, however, form a significant part of Paul's strategy to provide examples for the Philippians to follow in their efforts to comply with the imperative that immediately follows them—"rejoice in the Lord" (3:1), a command that urges the Philippians to focus on "the things of Jesus Christ" (2:21) rather than on the difficulties they are experiencing. This may explain why Paul, contrary to his usual practice, has not left such details for the end of the letter but places them in the midst of his argument.

15 Cf. Oakes, *Philippians*, 202.

The Believer's Eschatological Goal

Paul's effort to focus the Philippians' attention on "what is best" (1:10) or what matters (1:18) as a way of coping with their hardship also includes an eschatological component, as the intercessory prayer report with its own eschatological character (1:10b) leads us to expect. Paul says in 1:28–29 that their suffering is a gift since through it God has given them proof of their eschatological salvation. The Philippians' courageous equanimity in the face of opposition is a double-faceted sign: It shows that their persecutors stand among those who will be destroyed and that the Philippian believers stand among those who will be saved on the day of Christ.[16] Their steadfastness, therefore, is a gift because it assures them that God, in the words of 1:6, "who began a good work in you will carry it on to completion until the day of Christ Jesus."[17]

Paul also wants the Philippians to know that although the citizenry of Philippi have marginalized them, they are citizens of a heavenly city and that one day the ruler of that city will subject all other entities to himself. This is part of what Paul means when he writes in 3:20–21:

> Our citizenship is in heaven. And we eagerly await a Savior from there, the Lord Jesus Christ, who, by the power that enables him to bring everything under his control, will transform our lowly bodies so that they will be like his glorious body.

As we will see below, Paul's primary concern in this passage is to warn the Philippians against the kind of earthly-mindedness that plagued the Corinthian church (3:19), but the politically significant vocabulary that Paul uses reveals an important subsidiary purpose. The term "citizenship" (*politeuma*) recalls the significant status of Philippi as a Roman colony with the "right of Italy" (*ius Italicum*), whose citizens were enrolled on the list of the Roman *tribus Voltinia* and were therefore considered citizens of Rome.[18] Similarly, the term "savior" was commonly used for political rulers in Hellenistic and Roman society and was an especially common title for Roman emperors. Thus Julius Caesar, in an inscription from A.D. 48, is called "a visible god and political savior of human life," and another inscription from a few years later calls Nero the "savior and benefactor of the world."[19]

Clearly, in 3:20–21 Paul wants the Philippians to see their marginalization as a sign of their citizenship in another, heavenly society. On the final day, moreover, their Savior will become the sole ruler of the world and will subject their persecutors to himself (cf. 2:10–11).[20] Paul wants the Philippians to see that their salvation on the

16 In the difficult statement "which is a sign to them of destruction but of your salvation, and this from God" (1:28, aut.), the feminine singular relative pronoun "which" (*hētis*) is feminine by attraction to the gender of "sign" (*endeixis*). Its antecedent is the Philippians' refusal to be frightened by those who oppose them. For this understanding of the Greek, see Lightfoot, *Philippians*, 106; Vincent, *To the Philippians and to Philemon*, 35; and Bockmuehl, *Philippians*, 101. Cf. 2 Thess. 1:5.

17 Cf. Rom. 5:3–5.

18 On this see Peter Pilhofer, *Philippi*, 2 vols. (WUNT 87, 119; Tübingen: J.C.B. Mohr [Paul Siebeck], 1995–2000), 1:122–23, 131–32.

19 See Werner Foerster, "σωτήρ," *TDNT*, 7:1007; MM, 621–22; and Bockmuehl, *Philippians*, 235.

20 See Pilhofer, *Philippi*, 1:122–34, who points out that the same theme appears in 1:27, where Paul tells the Philippians to conduct themselves as citizens (*politeuesthe*) in a manner worthy of the gospel of Christ. It may also be present in 4:3, where Paul speaks of his coworkers as enrolled in the book of life, possibly by analogy to the roll of citizens kept in Philippi's archives.

final day—because of their faithfulness to the gospel—is, despite their suffering, "what is best" and something that "matters" (1:10; cf. 1:18). In the midst of their hardship, therefore, they should focus on this eschatological goal.

Gentleness to All, Grateful Prayer, and the Contemplation of the Good

Finally, Paul gives some practical advice about how the Philippians can rejoice in the Lord in the midst of their difficult circumstances. "Rejoice in the Lord always," he commands, "I will say it again: Rejoice!" (4:4). But how, practically speaking, can the Philippians overcome their anxiety over their own persecution, the imprisonment of Paul, and the illness of Epaphroditus?

In addition to the advice he has already given, Paul urges the Philippians to take three practical steps. First, they can remember that the Christian response to hardship for the faith is not to lash out at their enemies but to leave retribution to the Lord at his return and, in the meantime, to show gentleness (*epieikēs*) to all people. Paul knows that this is how Jesus responded to persecution (Rom. 15:3; 2 Cor. 10:1; cf. Phil. 2:8),[21] so this is how Jesus' followers should respond.

Second, Paul urges the Philippians to pray with thanksgiving, focusing less on the difficulties they face than on that for which they can be thankful. The gospel is progressing as a result of Paul's imprisonment (1:12–18a). Whatever the outcome of that imprisonment—whether life or death—Christ will be exalted in Paul's body (1:18b–26). Their own suffering is itself a gift because it assures the Philippians of their persecutors' doom and of their own salvation (1:28–29). Epaphroditus has heroically advanced the work of the gospel by his sacrificial ministry to Paul in prison (2:25–30). All of this should lead the Philippians to grateful prayer.[22]

Third, like many both before him and after his time who sought to console others in the midst of hardship, Paul advocates turning one's mind from evil to the contemplation of the good (4:8–9).[23] Epicurus advised gaining relief from the mental anguish of suffering by turning one's mind from pain to pleasurable experiences. Cicero and others modified the technique to advocate turning the distraught mind not to pleasure but to what is virtuous. Cicero's approach is also Paul's; indeed, Cicero's list of virtues for contemplation in difficult circumstances is similar to Paul's list here: "all that is lovely, honourable, of good report."[24] In addition, Paul says, the Philippians should contemplate how Paul himself has both taught them and modeled for them ways of putting these virtues into practice (4:9).

21 It is also how the righteous man of Wisd. 2:12–20 apparently responded to the persecutions of the wicked. "Let us test him with insult and torture," the wicked say as they plot their attack on the righteous man, "so that we may find out how gentle [*epieikeias*] he is" (2:19).

22 Holloway, "Disce Gaudere,"169–70, points out that in ancient consolatory literature, the consoler frequently urges his reader to focus on what they should be thankful for rather than on their difficult circumstances.

23 Paul A. Holloway, "*Bona Cogitare*: An Epicurean Consolation in Phil 4:8–9," *HTR* 91 (1998): 89–96. Cf. idem, "Disce Gaudere," 170–77.

24 Cicero, *Tusc.* 5.23.67; cf. Phil. 4:8.

Summary

In his letter, Paul provides the Philippians with resources for coping with their anxiety both about Paul's fate and about their own fate as believers in a society hostile to their commitment. They should, he says, find their joy in the progress of the gospel despite the difficulties they are experiencing. This is what really matters, and it is happening both in Paul's circumstances (1:12–26) and in the Philippians' circumstances (1:28–29). In their efforts to adopt this perspective, the Philippians should look to Paul, Christ Jesus, Timothy, and Epaphroditus as examples. They should remember the eschatological goal of their progress in the faith. They should also be gentle in the face of persecution, utter prayers of gratitude for the good that God is doing among them and those they love, and turn their minds from their difficult circumstances to the contemplation of the good. In short, they should "rejoice in the Lord" (3:1; 4:4) and not let their persecution and anxiety hinder their "progress and joy in the faith" (1:25).

THE THREAT OF DISUNITY TO THE GOSPEL'S PROGRESS

Although interpreters have occasionally questioned it, there can be little doubt that disunity plagued the Philippian church.[25] In 4:2 Paul pleads with two people, Euodia and Syntyche, "to agree with each other," and the dispute between them is so grave that Paul calls on an unnamed mediator to "help these women"—presumably to find some common ground and end their dispute. Perhaps their disagreement has spilled over into the congregation generally, or perhaps the congregation is plagued by other, unrelated problems. Whatever the cause, Paul must also tell the entire church to stop "complaining and arguing" (2:14).

The quarreling must stop because it is hindering the progress of the gospel in two respects. First, it is thwarting the Philippians' witness to the "crooked and perverse generation" in which they live and among which they should "shine like stars in the universe." The Philippians' mandate is to hold fast the word of life in this situation so that, as Daniel 12:3 says, they "might lead many to righteousness" (Dan. 12:15–16a).[26] Their disunity, however, threatens this prospect by endangering their witness.

Second, their disunity is impeding their own progress toward the final day. Paul says that they should stop complaining and arguing "in order that I may boast on the day of Christ that I did not run or labor for nothing" (2:16b). Similarly, he prefaces his appeal to Euodia and Syntyche with a reminder that the Philippians are his "crown," an athletic metaphor for the crown of victory that he will receive on the final day when his race is complete (cf. 1 Cor. 9:25; 1 Thess. 2:19; 2 Tim. 2:5; 4:8).

25 Caird, *Paul's Letters from Prison*, 117, argues that the appeals to unity in the letter do not reveal a problem in the church at Philippi but are the echoes of Paul's "unhappy dealings with the divided church at Rome."

26 Paul's statement that the Philippians "shine like stars in the universe, holding fast to the word of life" (2:15–16) echoes Dan. 12:3 where, following the resurrection, those "who lead many to righteousness" will shine "like the stars for ever and ever." See Fee, *Philippians*, 246–47, and Bockmuehl, *Philippians*, 158.

If they are to reach that day "pure and blameless" (1:11), then they must "work out" their "salvation" (2:12) by setting aside their arguments.

Paul's strategy for encouraging them to do this not only includes straightforward exhortation (2:1–18), pleading (4:2), and reminders of the final day (2:16) but, once again, as 3:17 and 4:9 lead us to expect, examples to follow. Paul, Jesus, Timothy, and Epaphroditus all provide examples not only of focusing on the progress of the gospel despite hardship, but of setting aside one's own interests in order to advance the gospel.

When Paul faces those who "preach Christ out of envy and rivalry . . . supposing that they can stir up trouble for me while I am in chains" (1:15, 17), he rejoices that Christ is nevertheless preached (1:18a). Similarly, Timothy, although surrounded by those who look out for their own interests rather than the interests of Jesus Christ, is genuinely concerned for the Philippians' welfare and willing to slave with Paul in "the work of the gospel" (2:20–21). Epaphroditus too could have turned his face toward home when he became ill, but instead he pressed on, risking his life, and he nearly died "for the work of Christ" (2:26–27, 30).[27]

Paul's most important example, however, is Jesus (2:5–11), as the exalted, almost poetic nature of Paul's prose in describing Jesus shows.[28] The rhythm of 2:6–11, its unusual vocabulary, and the journey that the passage makes from Christ's humbling of himself to God's exaltation of Christ have led most modern interpreters to view it as a piece of early Christian liturgy or as a "hymn" that Paul has taken over and perhaps modified.[29] If this is correct, then the passage provides an important piece of evidence for the Christology of the earliest Christians. As with the hypothetical source Q in studies of the Synoptic Gospels, much of the extensive literature on the passage is less interested in understanding its function in Paul's letter than with using it to reconstruct the history of earliest Christianity.[30]

There are two good reasons, however, for doubting that the passage, whether in whole or in part, is a piece of pre-Pauline liturgy. One reason is related to the style of the passage and the other is related to its context. First, although the passage does have unusual vocabulary, uses parallelism and repetition, and moves in a balanced way between Christ's self-humiliation and his exaltation, it is not exactly poetry. The sentences of the passage move from main clauses to subordinate clauses in a way typical of Paul's prose.[31] Moreover, scholars who believe the passage is a hymn are divided on how to organize it into strophes and how to scan its meter.[32]

---

27 On the connection between the example of Christ in 2:6–8 and the examples of Timothy and Epaphroditus in 2:19–30, see Holloway, "Disce Gaudere," 23–24.

28 I have borrowed the term "exalted" as a description of Paul's prose from Gordon D. Fee, "Philippians 2:5–11: Hymn or Exalted Prose?" *BBR* 2 (1992): 29–46.

29 See Ralph P. Martin, *A Hymn of Christ: Philippians 2:5–11 in Recent Interpretation and in the Setting of Early Christian Worship* (Downers Grove, Ill.: InterVarsity Press, 1997), and O'Brien, *Philippians*, 186–202. The designation of the passage as a "hymn" is anachronistic since ancient Greco-Roman hymns, and most Jewish hymns, were expressions of praise, and all were addressed to the deity. Phil. 2:6–11, however, is a statement about Christ. On this, see Stephen E. Fowl, *The Story of Christ in the Ethics of Paul: An Analysis of the Function of the Hymnic Material in the Pauline Corpus* (JSNTSup 36; Sheffield: Sheffield Academic Press, 1990), 32–33.

30 See, e.g., Martin, *Hymn of Christ*, 287–311.

31 Fee, "Philippians 2:5–11," 31–32.

32 Cf. Morna D. Hooker, "Philippians 2:6–11," in *Jesus und Paulus: Festschrift für Werner Georg Kümmel zum 70. Geburtstag*, ed. E. Earle Ellis and Erich Grässer (Göttingen: Vandenhoeck &

Second, the themes of the passage fit seamlessly into its wider context.[33] Just prior to the supposed hymn Paul counsels the Philippians to think (*phroneō*) the same way (2:2) and to consider (*hēgeomai*) others better than themselves (2:3). He then tells them to think (*phroneō*) among themselves in a way that is consistent with their status of being "in Christ" (2:5).

How did Christ think of himself? The supposed hymn answers this question. He did not consider (*hēgeomai*) his equality with God something to be exploited (2:6) but was obedient (*hypēkoos*) to God and died on a cross (2:8). "Therefore" (*hōste*), the Philippians should also be obedient (*hypakouō*), as they have been in the past, and cease their quarreling (2:12–16). It is possible that the "hymn" influenced the vocabulary of its wider context, but it seems more likely that Paul himself composed the passage in exalted prose suitable to his exalted subject, and that as he did so, he used vocabulary pertinent to the exhortation to unity that he wanted to give to the Philippians.

Jesus is the supreme example of one who set aside "self ambition" and "vain conceit" and considered "the interests of others" (2:3–4). Although he could have exploited his equality with God, Jesus made himself nothing, took the form of a slave, and, in obedience to God, suffered death on a cross (2:6–8).[34] Precisely in this self-emptying he revealed the character of God, and God recognized this by exalting him to the highest place and giving him the name above every name (2:9–11).[35] The Philippians should follow his example in their relationships with one another. If they consider one another's interests as important as their own and consider the gospel's progress as the most important interest of all, they will continue to hold fast the word of life until the day of Christ and will "shine like stars" in the crooked and perverse generation in which they live (2:15–16).

THE THREAT OF FALSE TEACHING TO THE GOSPEL'S PROGRESS

In 3:1 Paul reminds his readers of the letter's principal purpose—to urge them to rejoice in the Lord and not to be distracted by hindrances to the progress of their faith.[36] He then launches an attack on the same blind alley that the Galatians had started to travel—the notion that acquittal before God's tribunal on the final day and a right relationship with God (*dikaiosynē*, "righteousness") in the present is a

Ruprecht, 1978), 151–64, here at 157–58, who thinks that the passage may be poetry but who sees the many proposals for poetic analysis of the hymn as reason for caution.

33 Cf. ibid., 152–53 and the cautiously stated conclusion of Oakes, *Philippians*, 210–12.

34 For the translation of *harpagmos* as "something to be exploited," see the definitive study of Roy W. Hoover, "The *Harpagmos* Dilemma: A Philological Solution," *HTR* 64 (1971): 95–119. For a contrast between this attitude and that of the pagan gods, see the depiction of the acquisitiveness of pagan deities in Aristophanes, *Eccl.* 777–83, as noted by Norman H. Young, "An Aristophanic Contrast to Philippians 2.6–7," *NTS* 45 (1999): 153–55.

35 See N. T. Wright, "ἁρπαγμός and the Meaning of Philippians 2:5–11," *JTS* 37 (1986), 321–52, here at 344–51.

36 The term *to loipon* does not mean "finally" here, nor does *chairete en kyriō* mean "good-bye in the Lord," as interpreters have sometimes thought (cf. 2 Cor. 13:11). *To loipon* can mean, "as far as the rest is concerned, beyond that, in addition" as well as "finally," and therefore does not necessarily indicate the close of a letter (see BDAG, 602–3). *Chairete en kyriō,* moreover, picks up the theme of joy and rejoicing despite suffering that pervades the letter and formulates it into an imperative. See O'Brien, *Philippians*, 349, and Holloway, "Disce Gaudere," 15–19. Holloway observes that scholars have often trivialized Paul's references to joy in the letter and

matter not merely of faith in Jesus Christ but following the Mosaic law (3:1–11).[37] Elsewhere the letter is too cordial to imagine that Galatian-style "agitators" from Jerusalem had become active in Philippi.[38] Probably, then, 3:1–11 is a warning to the Philippians not to open their doors to this group, should they make their way to Philippi. Having just grappled with their "gospel" in his letter to the Galatians, he is eager to prevent their corrupting influence at Philippi.

In the same way, 3:12–21 probably reflects no serious "antinomian" threat present in Philippi at the time that Paul writes the letter but is a preventative measure, intended to warn the Philippians against the kind of error that arose indigenously at Roman Corinth and could so easily arise in Roman Philippi.[39] The Corinthians had faulted Paul for his proclamation of the cross (1 Cor. 1:18–25; 2:2), taken pride in one teacher over another, boasted of their social status, forgotten that their salvation was a gift, and claimed already to be rich (1 Cor. 4:4–8; cf. 11:19). They had also become ensnared by immorality, apparently justifying their actions by popular Greco-Roman notions of the body's mortality (1 Cor. 15:1–58). Paul is concerned that the Philippians not become entangled in a similar web, and certainly that they not do so out of some perverse response to the claim that they, like he, had already gained Christ (3:8) and experienced the power of Christ's resurrection (3:10–11).

Paul's strategy for preventing these two errors in Philippi is, once again, to provide an example for the Philippians to follow. Here he speaks only of himself as one who had personally rejected both these deviations from the path of the gospel.[40] He hopes that the Philippians will follow his example should such dangers arise in their midst.

The Threat of a Misplaced Confidence in the Mosaic Law

Paul begins his attack on placing confidence in the Mosaic law with a polemical description of the agitators. They are dogs, he says, evil workers, "the mutilation" (*katatomē*). This final epithet goes to the nub of the issue. Jews were sometimes called

his imperative here in particular. Paul is following ancient patterns of consolation in issuing a stern command to the Philippians to have the right perspective on their circumstances. When we realize this, the so-called shift in tone between 3:1 and 3:2 evaporates.

37 Two other ideas about the identity of Paul's opponents have been popular. Some believe that they are the Jews generally, not the particular group of Jewish Christians that Paul attacked in Galatians. Advocates of this position include Caird, *Paul's Letters from Prison*, 133–34; Garland, "Composition and Unity," 166–73; and Hawthorne, *Philippians*, xl–xlvii. Others claim that both in Galatians and in Philippians, Paul's opponents are Jewish gnostics who both emphasized circumcision (cf. 3:2) and had antinomian tendencies (cf. 3:19). Proponents of this position include Walter Schmithals, *Paul and the Gnostics* (New York: Abingdon, 1972), 82–83, and Willi Marxsen, *Introduction to the New Testament* (Philadelphia: Fortress, 1968), 63–64. But Rom. 9:1–5 reveals that Paul would not launch a polemical attack, such as we find in Phil. 3:2, on Jews generally, and the evidence is slight for a Jewish gnostic group that emphasized circumcision but not devotion to other aspects of the Mosaic law.

38 When Paul remembers the Philippians in prayer, he is thankful and joyful (1:3). They are his partners in the grace that God has given to him (1:5, 7; 4:14–16), his joy and crown (4:1). This stands in stark contrast to the tone of letters in which opponents are on the scene, wooing Paul's churches away from him. See, e.g., Gal. 1:6–9; 3:1; 4:11, 15–16; 5:7; 6:17; 1 Cor. 3:1–4; 4:8, 18; 6:5a; 11:17; 2 Cor. 11:19–20; 12:1, 20–21; 13:1–10.

39 For the argument that Paul speaks against a present libertinistic threat, see, e.g., Schmithals, *Paul*, 82–83; Marxsen, *Introduction*, 62–63; and Robert Jewett, "Conflicting Movements in the Early Church as Reflected in Philippians," *NovT* 12 (1970): 362–90, here at 376–82. On the Latin character of Philippi during Paul's time, see Pilhofer, *Philippi*, 1:118–22, and for the kind of error that might arise from the Roman culture in Philippi, see John L. White, *The Apostle of God: Paul and the Promise of Abraham* (Peabody, Mass.: Hendrickson, 1999), 50–51.

40 In 3:17 he also points out that others known to the Philippians could provide equally valuable examples of the kind of single-minded devotion to the gospel that has characterized his life.

"the circumcision" (*peritomē*) because this rite was one of their chief distinctives, and from their perspective it set them apart as the people of God (Eph. 2:11; Col. 4:11). From Paul's perspective, however, circumcision was not necessary for membership in God's people and for acquittal in the heavenly court on the final day. Those who circumcised Gentiles in the belief that the rite was necessary for their ultimate salvation were, therefore, only mutilating the flesh, like the frenzied prophets of Baal who were frustrated that their god would not answer their pleas (Phil. 3:2; cf. 1 Kings 18:28; also Lev. 21:5, LXX).[41]

Paul continues his argument by saying that those who insist on a literal operation in the flesh for membership in God's people are not the true "circumcision." This designation for God's people belongs instead to those who have two characteristics. First, they worship by the Spirit (3:3a). The mention of the true circumcision in the same breath with those who worship by the Spirit recalls the biblical passages in which God promises to restore the fortunes of his people after the period of their disobedience. At that time, Scripture promises, God will circumcise the hearts of his people (Deut. 30:6) and place his Spirit among them so that they might keep his commandments (Ezek. 11:19; 36:26–27; 37:14).[42] The implications of Paul's statement are clear: The presence of the Spirit in the worshiping community is the sure sign of the people of God, not the physical rite of circumcision (cf. Rom. 2:28–29; Gal. 3:1–5).

Second, the true people of God, Paul says, are those who "boast in Christ Jesus and do not put confidence in the flesh" (3:3b). Paul dwells on this second characteristic at greater length. His basic complaint against people who claim that circumcision must be added to faith in Christ as a requirement for acquittal in God's eschatological court is that their confidence is divided between Christ and a physical operation ("the flesh") rather than placed solely in Christ. Confidence placed in anything but Christ, however, is misplaced (3:4a).

To illustrate what he means, Paul next speaks autobiographically of his own experience prior to his conversion when he considered as "gains" (3:7) both his social status as a Jew (3:5a) and his zeal for the law (3:5b–6).[43] Neither of these characteristics was wrong in itself—being a Jew and pursuing the law that points toward righteousness are both commendable in Paul's eyes (Rom. 9:3–5, 31)—but Paul's attitude toward them in his earlier life was wrong. He trusted that on the final day he would be found innocent in the heavenly court on the basis of his own righteousness (3:9).[44] "To me," he says, they were "gains" (3:7).

41 See Alfred Plummer, *A Commentary on St. Paul's Epistle to the Philippians* (London: Robert Scott Roxburghe House, 1919), 69.

42 For the currency of these notions in the Second Temple period, see Scott J. Hafemann, "The Spirit of the New Covenant, the Law, and the Temple of God's Presence: Five Theses on Qumran's Self-Understanding and the Contours of Paul's Thought," in *Evangelium, Schriftauslegung, Kirche: Festschrift für Peter Stuhlmacher zum 65. Geburtstag*, ed. Jostein Ådna, Scott J. Hafemann, and Otfried Hofius, (Göttingen: Vandenhoeck & Ruprecht, 1997), 172–89.

43 White, *Apostle of God*, 24, observes that in the Mediterranean world "social identity" or "status" was determined in two ways, by "ascribed" status, determined by the family into which one was born, and by "achieved" status, which was won by one's own efforts.

44 Paul's claim to have been "blameless" with respect to the law does not mean that Paul kept the law perfectly prior to his conversion. It means instead that a human observer would have found no fault in Paul's law observance. See John Calvin, *Commentaries on the Epistles of Paul the Apostle to the Philippians, Colossians, and Thessalonians* (Grand Rapids: Eerdmans, 1948), 92–93; John M. Espy, "Paul's 'Robust Conscience' Re-examined," *NTS* 31 (1985): 161–88, here at 165–66; and Moisés Silva, *Philippians* (BECNT; Grand Rapids: Baker, 1992), 175–76.

At his conversion, however, his attitude toward his social status and law-keeping changed. Now he saw his own righteousness as inadequate for acquittal in God's tribunal. For those purposes his social status and zeal—and anything else—were a total loss (3:7–8). Paul realized that acquittal on the final day would only be his if he were found to be "in [Christ]." Only at God's initiative could anyone be in a right relationship with God on that day, and this "righteousness from God" could only come through faith in Christ (3:9). Faith in Christ, Paul continues, initiates a life of suffering in conformity to Christ's own death—and Paul's imprisonment and the Philippians' hardship are confirmation enough of this—but at the end of this road lies nothing less than conformity to Christ's resurrection from the dead (3:10–11).[45]

The Philippians, therefore, should imitate Paul's single-minded pursuit of the resurrection through faith in Christ alone. If the kind of false teaching that plagued Paul's churches in Galatia should make its way to Philippi, Paul hopes the Philippians will be able to "discern what is best" (1:10) and not allow this stumbling block to hinder the progress of the gospel in their midst.[46]

The Threat from Earthly Mindedness

If Philippians was written from an Ephesian prison during the closing months of Paul's ministry in that city, then his struggles with the Corinthian church as they are recorded in 1 Corinthians would have been fresh in his mind (1 Cor. 16:8). The Corinthians apparently thought they had achieved a higher plane of spiritual maturity than Paul with his foolish emphasis on the crucifixion of Christ. They were puffed up not only with respect to Paul (4:8, 18–19) but also with respect to those who did not follow their favorite teachers (4:6) and with respect to those who lacked their style of "knowledge" (8:1–3, 10). They looked down on the poor (11:22), and Paul was afraid that they would even despise Timothy (16:11).

To this Paul responded in 1 Corinthians that his proclamation of Christ crucified was a "message of wisdom," but that only "the mature" (*hoi teleioi*) were able to understand it (1 Cor. 2:6). The Corinthians, he said, were not among the mature, and so when Paul was among them he was not able to speak to them as spiritual people but only as fleshly people—as "mere infants in Christ." Their divisions had shown Paul that even at the time of 1 Corinthians, they were still not ready for solid food. They could only tolerate infant's milk (3:1–4).

45 In none of this does Paul claim "the basic attitude of the Jew to be one of self-confidence which seeks glory before God and which relies upon itself" (Rudolf Bultmann, "καυχάομαι [κτλ]," *TDNT*, 3:648). Paul views his own approach to the law prior to his conversion as unusual (3:4b; cf. Gal. 2:14), and it is a measure of the shock with which he views the actions of the agitators in Galatia that he equates his own preconversion trust in his social standing and zeal for the law with their zeal for circumcising Gentile believers. Certainly, the kind of self-centered approach to righteousness that we find in the preconversion Paul, in the Galatian agitators, and occasionally elsewhere in the New Testament (e.g. Luke 18:10–14) existed in first century Judaism (e.g. 4QMMT 112–118; Josephus, *C. Ap.* 2.218), just as it always has existed among Christians. This is no reason to think, however, that in either case the attitude is universal. Although E. P. Sanders has overstated his case, he has at least shown this much. See his *Paul and Palestinian Judaism: A Comparison of Patterns of Religion* (Philadelphia: Fortress, 1977), 1–428; idem, *Judaism: Practice and Belief: 63 BCE–66 CE* (London/Philadelphia: SCM/Trinity Press International, 1992), 47–303; and the balanced comments of Bockmuehl, *Philippians*, 202–3.

46 Contrast Gal. 5:7.

Other signs of their immaturity and fleshly perspective emerge from the subsequent sections of 1 Corinthians. They arrogantly permitted scandalous immorality in their midst (1 Cor. 5:1–2). They consorted with prostitutes and participated in feasts that were occasions for the worship of idols on the theory that "everything is permissible" (6:12–20; 8:10; 10:1–22). They denied the immortality of the body, possibly claiming that bodily pleasures needed to be indulged while one was in possession of his or her body (15:12, 32–33). Against all this, Paul had to assert the Christian convictions that those who engaged in flagrant immorality would not inherit the kingdom of God and that the body was both the eschatological temple of God's Spirit and the eternal possession, albeit destined for change, of the believer.[47]

It seems likely that having just grappled with these problems in Corinth, Paul attempts to forestall their emergence at Philippi in Philippians 3:12–21. After all, anywhere that the gospel clashed with traditional Roman culture, such ideas could emerge.[48] In 3:12–16, then, Paul continues to speak autobiographically but shifts the direction of the narrative to emphasize that at his conversion he did not reach the end of his progress in the faith. He has not "already been made perfect [*teteleiōmai*]" (3:12), and those who are "mature" (*teleioi*) understand this (3:15). The Philippians, he says, should imitate him and others who also have this perspective (3:17).

Paul then describes a group whom the Philippians should not imitate. Like the Corinthians who probably ridiculed Paul's proclamation of the cross, these people are "enemies of the cross of Christ" (Phil. 3:18). Like the sexually immoral in the Corinthian church they are destined for "destruction" if they do not change their behavior (cf. 1 Cor. 5:5; 6:9–10). Like some of the Corinthians, who were proud of flagrant sexual immorality in their midst (1 Cor. 5:1–2) and insisted on their right to attend banquets presided over by idols and serviced by prostitutes (6:12–20; 8:10; 10:1–22), these people worship their stomachs and glory in that of which they should be ashamed (Phil. 3:19).

Paul identifies the origin of this approach in thoughts that dwell "on earthly things" (Phil. 3:19).[49] He then contrasts this approach with the right way of thinking:

> But our citizenship is in heaven. And we eagerly await a Savior from there, the Lord Jesus Christ, who by the power that enables him to bring everything under his control, will transform our lowly bodies so that they will be like his glorious body. (3:20–21)

This statement puts into a nutshell the argument of 1 Corinthians 15:42–49. There Paul is opposing the Corinthian view that because the body will not be resurrected, it ought to be indulged (15:29–34). Against this Paul said that the mortal bodies

47 See chapter 12, above.

48 Cf. Bruce Winter, *After Paul Left Corinth: The Influence of Secular Ethics and Social Change* (Grand Rapids: Eerdmans, 2001), 27–28.

49 Cf. Paul's characterization of the Corinthians as "fleshly" (*sarkikoi*) and as people who live in a merely "human" way (*kata anthrōpon*) in 1 Cor. 3:1–4.

of believers, fashioned like Adam's body from the dust of the earth, will undergo a transformation in the future to become like the heavenly body of the resurrected Jesus. This transformation, he said, ought to be an incentive to avoid immoral behavior: "And even as we have borne the image of the man of dust, so let us bear the image of the man of heaven" (1 Cor. 15:49, aut.).

Having just fought this battle in Corinth, Paul warns the Philippians against a similar danger, one that might follow from a misreading of his talk in 3:7–11 of gaining Christ and knowing the power of his resurrection. Paul wants the Philippians to imitate him (and others who understand his approach, 3:17). Like him, he wants them to avoid mixing the gospel with popular Greco-Roman notions of immortality to produce a toxic understanding of their ethical responsibilities. In this way they can discern "what is best" and they can continue to progress in their faith.

REJOICING IN WHAT MATTERS IN PHILIPPI

In summary, Paul's letter to the Philippians is a sustained attempt to persuade believers in Philippi to rejoice in what matters (1:10, 18). What matters is the progress of the gospel, both in Paul's circumstances (1:12) and in their difficulties (1:25), and Paul argues that they should make every effort (2:12) to remove any hindrance to the progress of the gospel in their own affairs. They should not be anxious about Paul's imprisonment, Epaphroditus's illness, or their own persecution, because in all three of these instances, God has advanced the gospel either in spite of their difficulties or through them; in this, they, like Paul, should rejoice (1:18; 3:1; 4:4). They should drop their quarrels and become unified so that their witness to the gospel might be effective (2:14–16) and so that they will arrive at the day of Christ pure and blameless (1:10; 2:12). They should avoid false teaching in the forms that created such theological havoc in Galatia and Corinth (3:1–21) so that they might share in Christ's resurrection (3:10–11, 21).

In all of this they should follow the examples of Paul, his coworkers, and Jesus (3:17; 4:9). Paul rejoices when people preach the gospel, even when they preach it out of envy and rivalry (1:15, 17–18a). He remains undistracted by false teaching so that he might "attain to the resurrection from the dead" (3:11; cf. 3:21). Timothy remains faithful to "the work of the gospel" even when others are concerned only about themselves (2:21–22). Epaphroditus risks his life rather than give up on an opportunity to advance "the work of Christ" by helping the imprisoned Paul (2:30). Jesus himself refused to exploit his position of equality with God and instead became a man and died a slave's death in obedience to God (2:6–8).

These examples show what it means to rejoice in the advancement of the gospel in the midst of hardship, to drop one's personal agenda in order to work with other believers for the gospel's advancement, and to remain undistracted by false teaching so that the work of the gospel might move forward to its eschatological goal. If the

Philippians look around them at these examples of single-minded commitment to the gospel and look forward to their eschatological goal, they will be able to overcome the hindrances to their "progress and joy in the faith" (1:25) and will remain "pure and blameless until the day of Christ" (1:10). Paul is confident that the God who began a good work in them will see to it that they succeed (1:6).

Chapter 14

SECOND CORINTHIANS: POWER PERFECTED IN WEAKNESS

DEVELOPMENTS IN CORINTH

The Corinthian church experienced dramatic change during the time that separates 1 Corinthians from 2 Corinthians. Paul's assumption that the Corinthians would contribute to his collection for the famine-stricken Christians in Judea (1 Cor. 16:1–4) becomes an appeal to finish what they had been eager to start in the previous year (2 Cor. 8:10; 9:2). Paul's talk of arriving in Corinth from the north, after visiting Macedonia, and of spending the winter with the Corinthians (1 Cor. 16:5–7) becomes a defense for his decision to change these plans and visit Corinth twice, arriving once by boat from Ephesus, traveling to Macedonia, and then coming to Corinth again from there (2 Cor. 1:15–16). Apparently, however, even these plans did not materialize, for Paul says that he decided not to make "another painful visit" to Corinth (2 Cor. 1:23; 2:1), but instead composed a letter of appeal to the Corinthians (2:3–4; 7:8, 12). The letter apparently focused not on multiple factions, each promoting its favorite teacher (see 1 Cor. 1:12; 3:4, 22), but on a single opponent of Paul from within the Corinthian church who had led the church to oppose its founding apostle (2 Cor. 2:5–11; 7:11–12).[1]

Other opponents of Paul are also apparent in 2 Corinthians, but they have come from outside Corinth (2 Cor. 3:1; 11:4), and the argument that they are to be identified with "the Christ party" of 1 Corinthians or with emissaries from Cephas and other Jerusalem apostles (1 Cor. 1:12; 3:22; 9:5; 15:5) is not persuasive.[2] Paul's quarrel in 1 Corinthians is with the Corinthians themselves, who have used the names of various teachers, like Cephas, as focal points for their factions. He does not criticize the leaders, and even when he differs from them in practice, he supports their right to follow their own missionary methods (1 Cor. 9:5, 15; 16:12). In 2 Corinthians, however, intruders have been preaching another Jesus, a different spirit, and a different gospel (2 Cor. 11:4), and the problem is precisely their style of ministry.[3]

1 F. F. Bruce, *1 and 2 Corinthians* (NCBC; London: Marshall, Morgan & Scott, 1971), 168; Victor Paul Furnish, *II Corinthians* (AB 32A; Garden City, N.Y.: Doubleday, 1984), 37; and Ralph P. Martin, *2 Corinthians* (WBC 40; Dallas: Word, 1986), xlix, 237.

2 For a connection with the "Christ party" see, e.g., F. C. Baur, *Paul, The Apostle of Jesus Christ, His Life and Work, His Epistles and His Doctrine: A Contribution to a Critical History of Primitive Christianity*, 2 vols.; 2nd ed. (London: Williams & Norgate, 1876), 1:258–307, and Alfred Plummer, *A Critical and Exegetical Commentary on the Second Epistle of Paul to the Corinthians* (ICC; Edinburgh: T. & T. Clark, 1915), xxxvii. For a connection with Cephas, see C. K. Barrett, *Essays on Paul* (Philadelphia: Westminster, 1982), 14–22. Bruce W. Winter, *Philo and Paul among the Sophists* (SNTSMS 96; Cambridge: Cambridge Univ. Press, 1997), 203, claims that the same fascination with Sophistic rhetoric and with the professional class of public speakers who practiced it, which appears in 1 Cor. 1–4, also lies beneath 2 Cor. 10–13.

3 Cf. Furnish, *II Corinthians*, 53–54.

Their confidence lies in letters of recommendation, rhetorical power, and a strong bodily presence, and they have bitterly criticized Paul because, in their view, he has none of this (2 Cor. 3:1; 10:10–12; 11:6; cf. 5:12; 11:18).

What happened between the two letters to change the state of Christianity at Corinth so dramatically? In 1 Corinthians, which he wrote from Ephesus (1 Cor. 16:8), we learn that Paul was already concerned enough about the Corinthians to dispatch Timothy to "remind" them of "his way of life in Christ Jesus" (1 Cor. 4:17). His concern must have grown stronger after receiving the distressing letter and equally troubling oral reports that prompted 1 Corinthians. "If Timothy comes," he says at the end of 1 Corinthians, "see to it that he has nothing to fear while he is with you, for he is carrying on the work of the Lord, just as I am" (1 Cor. 16:10). When Timothy arrived, these concerns were probably realized—Timothy found the church firmly opposed to Paul and returned to Ephesus with this unsettling report.[4] The situation was grave enough to prompt Paul to visit Corinth immediately (2 Cor. 2:1).

When he arrived in Corinth, he met resistance led by an unknown Corinthian Christian (2 Cor. 2:5–11; 7:11). Disturbed by this painful rejection, he left Corinth, but before leaving told the Corinthians that he had decided to change his original plan of spending the winter with them after traveling through Macedonia (1 Cor. 16:5–6). Instead, he would visit them first and hopefully find the Corinthians more open to correction. He would then travel north to Macedonia and come back to the Corinthians after his trip to Macedonia. The Corinthians could then send him to Judea (2 Cor. 1:15–16), presumably with their contribution to the collection for the famine-stricken believers there.

This plan never materialized. After arriving back in Ephesus, Paul thought it wiser to spare the Corinthians what might simply be another sorrowful visit and instead sent a letter to them as a substitute.[5] He wrote to them "out of great distress and anguish of heart and with many tears," not to grieve them, he says, but to let them know the depth of his love for them (2 Cor. 2:4). Paul's coworker Titus carried this letter from Ephesus to Corinth (2 Cor. 2:13; 7:6–8, 14).

In the meantime, Paul experienced a life-threatening "affliction" (*thlipsis*) in Asia, perhaps arising out of his conflict with the many adversaries mentioned in 1 Corinthians (1 Cor. 16:8; cf. 15:32) and resulting in an imprisonment (Phil. 1:13, 17) that nearly brought a death sentence (Phil. 1:20; 2 Cor. 1:9).[6] This hardship pressed down

4 The Corinthian letter that prompted Paul to write 1 Corinthians may have already had a belligerent tone. On this, see Gordon D. Fee, *The First Epistle to the Corinthians* (NICNT; Grand Rapids: Eerdmans, 1987), 7.

5 For this reconstruction of the various itineraries implied in 1 Cor. 16:5–7; 2 Cor. 1:15–16; and 2:1, see Furnish, *II Corinthians*, 143–44, and Paul Barnett, *The Second Epistle to the Corinthians* (NICNT; Grand Rapids: Eerdmans, 1997), 11–12, 100. It is equally likely that Paul's painful visit was the first leg of the trip to Macedonia projected in 2 Cor. 1:16 and that the visit Paul decided to spare the Corinthians was his return to Corinth from Macedonia. For this scenario, see C. K. Barrett, *A Commentary on the Second Epistle to the Corinthians* (HNTC; New York: Harper & Row, 1973), 7–8, 86.

6 See Furnish, *II Corinthians*, 42, and Frank Thielman, "Ephesus and the Literary Setting of Philippians," in *New Testament Greek and Exegesis*, ed. Amy M. Donaldson and Timothy B. Sailors (Grand Rapids: Eerdmans, 2003), 205–23. A. E. Harvey, *Renewal through Suffering: A Study of 2 Corinthians* (SNTW; Edinburgh: T. & T. Clark, 1996), 19, argues that in Phil. 1:21–26 Paul appears to retain some control over whether he will live or die, whereas in 2 Cor. 1:9 he claims that he "had already received a death sentence." But Phil. 1:21–26 may have been written before the situation grew so grim that Paul "despaired even of life" (2 Cor. 1:8).

on him beyond his power to bear it, and he "despaired even of life" (2 Cor. 1:8). But just as God had raised Jesus from the dead, so he rescued Paul from the jaws of death and despair (1:9–10).

He was still deeply troubled about the church at Corinth, however, and after recovering from his nearly fatal experience, he left Ephesus and traveled north to Troas, hoping to meet Titus there and to hear how the Corinthians had responded to the tearful letter. Titus failed to appear, and although a significant opportunity for the proclamation of the gospel opened in Troas, Paul was too anxious to take advantage of it. He pressed on to Macedonia, apparently in the hope of meeting Titus (2 Cor. 2:12–13).

In Macedonia, Paul was buffeted with "every affliction, battles on the outside, fears within" (2 Cor. 7:5), but for the second time in what was probably a few weeks, the God "who comforts the downcast" (2 Cor. 7:6) comforted him, this time with the coming of Titus, and a generally favorable report about the Corinthians.[7] Paul's tearful letter had led them to sorrow and repentance (2 Cor. 7:8–9). A majority in the church had punished the leader of the opposition against Paul, and the Corinthians' desire for reconciliation was so fervent that Paul had to urge restraint in dealing with the offender (2 Cor. 2:7–8).

Still, not everything was ideal. The "majority" of the Corinthians placed the offender under church discipline (2:6), but this left a minority within the church that was presumably not on Paul's side. Jewish-Christian opponents from the outside had joined this minority (10:7; 11:22–23).[8] Although scholarly controversy swirls around the identity of these opponents, a few details are clear.[9] Paul's opponents were Jewish

7 Dieter Georgi, *Remembering the Poor: The History of Paul's Collection for Jerusalem* (Nashville: Abingdon, 1992), 68–72, argues that the "conflicts" Paul faced in Macedonia were battles among Christians (cf. Phil. 3:2). Barnett, *Second Corinthians*, 368, is more likely correct, however, when he argues that Paul refers to the persecution the Thessalonian and Philippian congregations faced. We know nothing certain about theological opposition to Paul in the churches of Macedonia, but we do know that they were experiencing persecution from unbelievers (cf. Phil. 1:28; 1 Thess. 1:6; 2:14; 3:4; 2 Thess. 1:4).

8 The arguments for the unity of the letter slightly outweigh the arguments for considering chapters 10–13 to be part of a different letter. For the now common argument that Paul wrote chapters 10–13 after chapters 1–9, see, e.g., Hans Windisch, *Der zweite Korintherbrief*, 9th ed. (MeyerK; Göttingen: Vandenhoeck & Ruprecht, 1924), 17–18; Bruce, *1 & 2 Corinthians*, 166–70; Barrett, *Second Epistle to the Corinthians*, 9–10, 12–17; Furnish, *II Corinthians*, 35–41; and Martin, *2 Corinthians*, xlv–xlvi. For the position that chapters 10–13 are the "tearful letter" referred to in 2:3–4, 9 and 7:8 see, among many others, Plummer, *Second Epistle of St. Paul to the Corinthians*, xxvii–xxxvi. The idea that 2 Corinthians is a collection of letters has gained some support but no single scheme for dividing the letter into a number of fragments has won a consensus. For a generally persuasive argument that chapters 1–9 and 10–13 belong to the same letter see Barnett, *Second Epistle to the Corinthians*, 17–23, and for a survey of the debate since Johann Salomo Semler (1725–91) see Hans Dieter Betz, *2 Corinthians 8 and 9: A Commentary on Two Administrative Letters of the Apostle Paul* (Philadelphia: Fortress, 1985), 3–36.

9 The thesis that Paul's opponents were Judaizers goes back at least as far as Theodoret of Cyrus (PG 82:434; *ACCS* 7:283). See also Plummer, *Second Epistle of St. Paul to the Corinthians*, xxxvi–xli, and Barrett, *Essays on Paul*, 65. The thesis that the opponents were Judaizers with some connection to the Jerusalem apostles appears in F. C. Baur, "Die Christus Partei in der korinthischen Gemeinde, der Gegensatz des petrinischen und paulinischen Christentum in der ältesten Kirche, der Apostel Petrus in Rom," *Tübingen Zeitschrift für Theologie* 4 (1831): 61–206, here at 102–3. See the summary of Baur's position in Jerry L. Sumney, *Identifying Paul's Opponents: The Question of Method in 2 Corinthians* (JSNTSup 40; Sheffield: Sheffield Academic Press, 1990), 15–22. Barrett, *Essays on Paul*, 20–21, 34–38, 80, also takes this position. The argument that the opponents were Jewish Gnostics appears, e.g., in Windisch, *Der zweite Korintherbrief*, 25–26, and Rudolf Bultmann, *The Second Letter to the Corinthians* (Minneapolis: Augsburg, 1985), 203–4, 214–15. Dieter Georgi, *The Opponents of Paul in Second Corinthians* (Philadelphia: Fortress, 1986) believes that Paul's opponents were Hellenized Jews claiming to be "divine men." Winter, *Philo and Paul*, 203, argues that they are Sophists whom the Corinthians recruited to teach them after Paul failed to return to Corinth. On the advisability of using only the

(11:22), claimed to belong to Christ (10:7; 11:23), and claimed to be apostles (11:13). Paul styles them, ironically, "super-apostles" (11:5; 12:11) and argues that he is not inferior to them (11:5; 12:11–12) even though he may be an amateur when it comes to rhetoric (11:6). This probably means that they prided themselves on their own superior speaking ability and charged Paul with failing to possess their level of rhetorical prowess (10:10; 11:6).[10]

These opponents also held against him his "unimpressive" and "timid" bodily presence (10:1, 10), the vacillations in his travel plans (1:15–2:4), his failure to produce letters of recommendation (3:1), and his refusal of financial support from the Corinthians (11:7–11). They probably accused him of claiming to work hard for a living among his churches while secretly dipping into the collection that he was so eager to gather from them for poor Christians in Jerusalem (12:16–18).[11] Such charges may have formed the basis for the refusal of the entire church—including the repentant majority—to follow through on their commitment during the previous year to contribute to Paul's collection (8:6, 10–12; 9:2).

Paul, for his part, accused his opponents of preaching another Jesus, a different spirit, and a different gospel (2 Cor. 11:4), and he believed that they were "false apostles, deceitful workmen, masquerading as apostles of Christ." They were Satan's servants (11:13–14). Nevertheless, his quarrel with them focused less on the content of their preaching than on their demeanor.[12] The nub of the problem for Paul was that they took "pride in what is seen rather than in what is in the heart" (5:12) and that they boasted "according to the flesh" (11:18, aut.) in such matters as their ethnic identity (11:21b–22). They put confidence in letters of recommendation from others (3:1) and in their own commendation of themselves (10:18).

Titus apparently reported all this to Paul in Macedonia, and the apostle responded with the letter we know as 2 Corinthians. The letter is a mixture of relief that the majority within the church has repented of its mistreatment of Paul during his most recent visit and concern that the church still needs to "mend [its] ways" (13:11, RSV). Paul's goal is to encourage the newly repentant majority to remain loyal to the gospel and to provide them with the theological resources for answering those who boast in outward appearance and not in the heart (5:12).

These theological resources can be summarized in one line: God's power is perfected in weakness (cf. 12:9). Paul's opponents have placed confidence in the outward trappings of "fleshly" power: letters of recommendation, rhetorical skill, and an overbearing demeanor. Paul, however, places confidence in the God who works through affliction, sorrow, and poverty to bring about life. Paul shows in 2 Corinthians how God has done this with Jesus, the Macedonian Christians, the Corinthian Christians, and, most significantly in light of the opposition that he faces, with himself. This theological principle undergirds the letter from beginning to end, giving unity to what is in other ways a difficult and disorganized argument.

clear data from 2 Corinthians to depict Paul's opponents, see Furnish, *II Corinthians*, 48–54.

10 His letters were certainly rhetorically impressive, they claimed, but his "delivery" was faulty. See Winter, *Philo and Paul*, 205–8.

11 Barrett, *Second Corinthians*, 324; Martin, *2 Corinthians*, 450; Barnett, *Second Epistle to the Corinthians*, 583; cf. Winter, *Philo and Paul*, 218.

12 Cf. Furnish, *II Corinthians*, 53.

COMFORT THROUGH DESPAIR (1:3–11)

Paul begins 2 Corinthians in an unusual way. Instead of reporting on the thanks he gives to God for his readers, Paul blesses God for delivering him from a grave peril and then reminds the Corinthians of his need for their prayers so that God may deliver him from other such perils in the future. When that deliverance happens, he says, many will give thanks for it.[13] Why does he focus in this prayer on God's work in his own circumstances? The change arises not merely because Paul has just experienced deliverance from a deadly peril, but because his experience of deliverance illustrates with clarity the theological principle that the Corinthians stand in danger of forgetting: We should not "rely on ourselves but on God, who raises the dead" (1:9).

This opening benediction can be divided into four sections: verses 3–5 praise God for the comfort that he gives to the distressed; verses 6–7 specify Christ as the means by which this happens; verses 8–10a describe how God has rescued Paul; and verses 10b–11 affirm Paul's confidence that God will continue to rescue him as the Corinthians labor with him in prayer.

Paul begins (1:3–4), as was common in Jewish prayers of gratitude for deliverance, with a benediction.[14] The point of the benediction is that because God is compassionate, he comforts people in their distress and then uses this experience in their lives to extend comfort to others who need it. There is nothing surprising in the first part of this statement; we expect a merciful God to comfort the distressed. The second part of the statement, however, is more unusual. Here we learn that God comforts the distressed so that they can in turn comfort others in their distress.

The second section (1:6–7) explains why Paul can say this. First, Jesus himself suffered in a way that brought "comfort" to others, and, in a similar way, Paul, through his suffering in the service of the gospel, extends "comfort and salvation" to others.[15] The myriad dangers that Paul has faced to bring the gospel to the Gentiles and the daily pressure of caring for his churches have extended the saving, eschatological comfort of God to many (cf. 4:7–12). Second, Paul himself has experienced the comfort of God in the midst of the dangers he has faced in completing his commission (6:5)—a theme he picks up again in 4:8–9; 6:9b–10; and 12:9–10—and in the midst of the psychological pressures that the daily care of his churches has placed on him (6:8–9; 11:28–29; cf. also 7:6–7). Paul therefore serves as an example to the Corinthians that God "comforts the downcast," and this should encourage the Corinthians to bear steadfastly the sufferings that they too must experience for their commitment to the gospel (1:6b–7).

In the third section (1:8–10a), Paul describes the specific experience of hardship that prompted the benediction of 1:3–4. The biographical details of the experience are unimportant to Paul.[16] The critical elements are the gravity of the affliction (Paul despaired of life itself), God's rescue of Paul from these desperate circumstances (God

13 Cf. Bultmann, *Second Letter to the Corinthians*, 21, 31, and Furnish, *II Corinthians*, 53.

14 See, e.g., Ps. 18:46 [17:47, LXX]; 66:20 [65:20, LXX]; Judith 13:17. In Tobit 3:11 a benediction begins a prayer for deliverance from distress.

15 Cf. Barrett, *Second Epistle to the Corinthians*, 62.

16 Harvey, *Renewal through Suffering*, 9–13.

delivered him from so deadly a peril), and, most important, Paul's theological reflection on the reason why all this happened: "But this happened that we might not rely on ourselves but on God, who raises the dead" (1:9).

In the fourth section (1:10b–11), Paul looks to his own future and to the future of the Corinthians. He trusts that God, who has delivered him in the past, will continue to deliver him as he faces physical danger and psychological pressure. He also trusts that the Corinthians will pray for him to this effect and that, when the deliverance takes place, they will offer thanks to God.

In this opening benediction Paul has laid the theological foundation for everything that he says to the Corinthians in the letter.

- In 1:12–7:16 he describes how God has brought repentance out of sorrow and life out of death in the way that he has comforted Paul both in his relationship with the Corinthians and in his difficult ministry generally. As a result of the way God has worked in the difficulties of his life, "thanksgiving [will] overflow to the glory of God" (4:15), just as Paul says in 1:11.
- In 8:1–9:15 Paul appeals to the Corinthians to renew their interest in his collection for their poor fellow believers in Jerusalem on the basis that physical poverty provides the opportunity for God's grace to work in powerful ways. The result, once again, will be "thanksgiving to God" (9:11–15).
- Throughout the letter, but especially in 10:1–13:14, Paul urges the Corinthians to abandon the view of his opponents that the essence of Christian existence is letters of recommendation, an impressive bodily presence, skillful rhetoric, and high social status. Instead, says Paul, Christian existence derives its power from the grace of God, which is most clearly seen when God produces life through the weakness of his people. "[Christ] was crucified in weakness," Paul says near the letter's conclusion, "yet he lives by God's power. Likewise, we are weak in him, yet by God's power we will live with him to serve you" (13:4).

LIFE THROUGH SORROW (1:12–2:13; 7:5–16)

Paul begins the body of his letter with an account of his recent relationship with the Corinthians that is probably designed, on the surface, to respond to two of his opponents' charges. First, they have likely claimed that the "lightness" with which he changed his plans to visit the Corinthians demonstrates his unreliability (1:12, 17). Second, they claimed that the severe letter the Corinthians recently received from Paul shows that he does not care for them (2:3–4; 7:8; 10:1; 10:9–11).[17]

In response to these charges, Paul admits the basic facts but denies the interpretation his opponents apparently placed on them. He did indeed change his plans and wrote a letter that caused sorrow for the Corinthians, but all of this, he says, arose from his love for them. He changed his travel plans once to give them the benefit of

17 Cf. Furnish, *II Corinthians*, 130.

seeing him twice (1:15), and he changed them again to spare them another painful visit (1:23). In place of another visit, he wrote them about his grief, so that when he finally came, they would be on good terms again (2:3). That letter was filled with distress, and Paul regrets it, but his motives were good—he wanted them to know that he loved them (2:4; 7:8). Beneath the surface of this defense lies Paul's principal message: God is reliable (1:18–22) and is able to use circumstances of "great distress," "anguish of heart," and "many tears" to bring repentance, life, and joy (1:23–2:13; 7:5–16).

Paul focuses on God's reliability in 1:18–22 in order to say that he, like God himself, is trustworthy. The message he preaches does not describe God as faithful to some promises and unfaithful to others, but is an account of God's fulfillment of his promises in Christ (1:18–20). Some promises await fulfillment, but in the meantime God makes believers stand firm and has anointed and sealed them with his Spirit, "a deposit, guaranteeing what is to come" (1:21–22).

In 1:23–2:13 and 7:5–16 Paul shows how the difficult circumstances surrounding his replacement of another painful visit with a severe letter brought life to the Corinthians and comfort to him. He had paid them a "painful visit" and written them an anguished, tearful letter (2:3–4) that he later regretted and that grieved the Corinthians (7:8). The situation was so bleak that Paul cut short a fruitful evangelistic ministry in Troas because Titus, the bearer of the severe letter, had not arrived there on his return trip and Paul's spirit was restless, presumably about the letter's results (2:12–13). Paul traveled to Macedonia, but there too, before the coming of Titus, he was "harassed at every turn—conflicts on the outside, fears within" (7:5).

Titus's arrival, however, turned Paul's grief into joy. Titus brought the news that Paul's letter had indeed produced sorrow among the Corinthians, but God used this sorrow to bring them to repentance and life (7:9–10).[18] The faithful God about whom Paul preaches and whose faithful character was reflected in Paul's ministry of faithfulness to the Corinthians has graciously used a skipped visit and a regrettably harsh letter to reconcile the Corinthians to Paul, to set them on the course toward salvation (7:10), and to comfort Paul (7:6, 13).

LIFE THROUGH DEATH (2:13–7:4; 10:1–13:10)

Just before Paul reaches the point in the narrative of his recent relationship with the Corinthians where God comforts him with good news from Titus, he strategically interposes an extended reflection on his understanding of apostolic, and Christian, existence.[19] "False apostles" had perhaps caused, and at least encouraged, the rift

18 Bultmann, *Second Letter to the Corinthians*, 47, points out that this statement does not contradict Paul's claim in 2:4 that he did not write the tearful letter to make the Corinthians sorry. In 2:4 Paul is not referring to the salutary sorrow that leads to repentance but to a human sorrow, produced for purposes of revenge.

19 Many scholars believe that the dramatic shift in tone and subject between 2:13 and 2:14 signals the introduction of a Pauline epistolary fragment at this point. For a survey of various theories, see R. Bieringer, "Teilungshypothesen zum 2.Korintherbrief. Ein Forschungsüberblick," in *Studies on 2 Corinthians*, ed. R. Bieringer and J. Lambrecht (BETL 112; Leuven: Leuven Univ. Press, 1994), 66–105, here at 85–98. Although a dramatic turn in the letter seems undeniable at this point (*pace* Furnish, *II Corinthians*, 186–87), the thematic links between 1:12–2:13 and

between himself and the Corinthians (11:13). These opponents of Paul valued an impressive bodily presence, sophisticated rhetorical technique (10:10; 11:6), letters of recommendation (3:1), and the Corinthians' financial support (11:7–12). Paul's understanding of apostolic and Christian existence was utterly opposed to this perspective. Thus, although the news from Titus was comforting, before Paul speaks of it, he wants to be sure that the Corinthians understand the differences between himself and his opponents.

Paul finally returns to the narrative of his relationship with the Corinthians in 7:5, and this narrative gives way in 8:1–9:15 to an appeal to the Corinthians to renew their commitment to the collection that Paul is making for the famine-stricken Jewish Christians in Judea. Then, for reasons that are not clear, he returns to a discussion of the differences between himself and his opponents in 10:1–13:10. Although Paul's argument in 10:1–13:10 is more heated, more direct, and more personal—a sign to some scholars that the situation in Corinth has progressed since he wrote chapters 1–9—both the problem and Paul's answer to it are fundamentally identical.[20]

The dispute between Paul and his opponents becomes clear from 5:13–19 and 11:1–12:13. In these two passages Paul claims that Christians think in a different way from those whose perspective is determined by the flesh. To those who think "according to the flesh" (*kata sarka*, 2:16; 10:3–4; 11:18), the life that the believer chooses to lead will appear insane (5:13). Christians, however, no longer assess people generally, or Christ in particular, "according to the flesh" (5:16). In recognizing that Christ died for them to reconcile them to God, they too have died in the sense that they no longer live for themselves but for Christ (5:14–15). They are a "new creation; the old has gone, the new has come!" (5:17–19).

This means that for the believer, boasting "according to the flesh" (11:18) can only be foolishness. Paul can only engage in such boasting ironically—to show how foolish it is—and even in the midst of his ironical boast cannot resist blurting out, "I am talking as if I were beside myself" (11:23).[21] Paul's opponents believe that he is insane (5:13) and a fool (11:16). He believes that they are fools (11:19). Their conflict with each other arises out of two utterly different views of the world and the gospel.

Throughout 2:14–7:4 and 10:1–13:10 Paul contrasts these two different approaches to apostolic and Christian existence. Those who take one approach live and fight "according to the flesh." Those who take the other approach, although living in the flesh, do not fight "according to the flesh" (10:2–3). His opponents value the visible, the powerful, and, in their sophisticated rhetoric, the deceitful. Paul argues in these two passages that the apostle and the believer should find God's power most fully present in the weakness of suffering, in telling the unadorned truth, and in the invisible human heart. The Christian should, in short, "live by faith, not by sight" (5:7).

2:14–7:4 show that the two sections belong together. Compare, e.g., 1:12–17 with 2:17; 4:2; and 6:6–10; on this see Barnett, *Second Epistle to the Corinthians*, 137 n. 1.

20 Bruce, *1 and 2 Corinthians*, 166–70; Barrett, *Second Epistle to the Corinthians*, 243–46; Furnish, *II Corinthians*, 35–41; and Martin, *2 Corinthians*, xlii and 298.

21 This is the translation of *paraphronōn lalō* in BDAG, 772.

Apostolic Weakness

Paul's opponents prided themselves on their strength. They were trained in the art of rhetoric and had a forceful bodily presence that they used to their psychological advantage in winning the Corinthians over to their side (10:10; 11:6, 20). As was customary for traveling orators in the first-century Roman world, Paul's opponents carried letters of introduction to demonstrate the web of friendships to which they were connected and as a means of gaining entry into social circles where they hoped to exercise power. They also expected the Corinthians to supply such letters for them to others (3:1). They enjoyed the patronage of the Corinthians, who paid them for their services as teachers (2:17; 11:7–11, 20; 12:13–18).

Paul, however, had none of this. His personal presence was unimpressive, his rhetoric—discounting his letters—amateurish, his letters of recommendation nonexistent, and he had no ability to win patrons. In a word, he was weak (10:10; 11:6, 7–11, 21; 12:13–18).

In his defense, Paul concedes his opponents' basic point. He is weak, he argues, but it is precisely in his weakness that God's power works. Paul begins his defense in 2:14 with a prayer of thanksgiving to the God "who always leads us to death, as a conquered slave, in a triumphal procession."[22] Paul borrowed this imagery from the custom of the Roman triumph, an elaborate procession in which the god who granted a military victory was praised and representative prisoners of war were paraded before the Roman public prior to their ceremonial execution.[23] The point of the imagery is clear: In his apostolic work Paul suffers by God's design.

Paul then shifts the imagery to make a further point. By leading him as a conquered slave, he says, God is able to spread the sacrificial fragrance of his knowledge in every place (2:14b).[24] To those who are being saved, this fragrance is the aroma of life, but to those who are perishing it is the smell of death (2:15). Paul's suffering has not been without saving purpose, therefore. God's triumphal procession has led the apostle from Jerusalem to Illyricum (Rom. 15:19), and so across the eastern Mediterranean people have responded to the gospel either with rejection, resulting in death, or with acceptance, resulting in life. God has used the apostle's proclamation of the gospel, stamped as it is with suffering, to accomplish his saving purposes (2:16a).

Several paragraphs later, Paul makes the same point. The treasure of the gospel, insofar as it is proclaimed through him, he says, is contained in a jar of clay—in his ministry of preaching the gospel he is "hard pressed on every side ... perplexed ... persecuted" and "struck down." Yet it is precisely the gospel preached through these means that God uses to discriminate between those whose minds are veiled and who are therefore perishing (4:3–4), and those who believe the gospel and in whom life

22 For this translation, see Scott J. Hafemann, *Suffering and the Spirit: An Exegetical Study of II Cor. 2:14–3:3 within the Context of the Corinthian Correspondence* (WUNT 2.19; Tübingen: J.C.B. Mohr [Paul Siebeck], 1986), 51.

23 Ibid., 7–39. On the manner in which triumphs were celebrated, see Richard C. Beacham, *Spectacle Entertainments of Early Imperial Rome* (New Haven, Conn.: Yale Univ. Press, 1999), 19–22, 39–41.

24 During a Roman triumph, the doors of the temples that lined Rome's triumphal route were opened and the fragrance of the incense that burned inside them wafted through the crowds lining the streets. See Beacham, *Spectacle Entertainments*, 20.

begins to work (4:12). "So then," Paul says to the Corinthians, "death is at work in us, but life is at work in you."

In this passage, however, Paul takes the point a step further. Glimpses of life, he says, become visible as God sustains him personally in the midst of his suffering. He is "hard pressed on every side, *but not crushed*; perplexed, *but not in despair*; persecuted, *but not abandoned*; struck down, *but not destroyed*" (4:8–9, italics added). Later he will speak of his ministry in similarly paradoxical terms:

> . . . through glory and dishonor, bad report and good report; genuine, yet regarded as imposters; known, yet regarded as unknown; dying, and yet we live on; beaten, and yet not killed; sorrowful, yet always rejoicing; poor, yet making many rich; having nothing, and yet possessing everything. (6:8–10)

Paul's ministry, therefore, is stamped with both suffering and salvation. Paul is led to his death like a captured soldier in triumphal procession as he makes his way across the eastern Mediterranean preaching the gospel. By this unlikely means, God brings salvation to those who respond to the proclamation of the gospel in faith, and God brings salvation to Paul as he sustains the apostle in the midst of hardship.

What is the origin of this strange form of ministry? The death and resurrection of Jesus. Just as Jesus died, so his apostle is "always being given over to death for Jesus' sake"; and just as Jesus rose from the dead, so "the life of Jesus" is revealed in Paul's "mortal flesh" (4:11, aut.), both in the limits that God places on his suffering (4:8–9; 6:8–10) and in the life his suffering ministry produces in the Corinthians (4:12). Near the close of the letter, Paul puts it this way: "[Christ] was crucified in weakness, yet he lives by God's power. Likewise, we are weak in him, yet by God's power we will live with him to serve you" (13:4).

Why should God's life-giving work take place in the context of such weakness? Paul answers this question in a way that 1 Corinthians 1:18–31 and 2:4–5 have led us to expect. In those passages Paul had said that God chose to work through the foolish, weak, and lowly things of the world "so that no one may boast before him" (1 Cor. 1:29). Paul had said that he did not preach to the Corinthians with wise and persuasive words so that their faith "might not rest on human wisdom, but on God's power" (1 Cor. 2:4–5). Here he says, similarly, that God has placed the treasure of the gospel in jars of clay "to show that this all-surpassing power is from God and not from us" (2 Cor. 4:7). By working in this way, God is able to show that he saves "those who are perishing" (1 Cor. 1:18; cf. 2 Cor. 2:15; 4:3) by himself and at his own initiative. This is why Paul can characterize his preaching as a message of God's grace (2 Cor. 4:15; 6:1; cf. 1:12).

Later, in the "Fool's Speech," the link between God's grace and God's use of human weakness to accomplish his purposes becomes even more explicit. There Paul only boasts "according to the flesh" ironically (11:18). If the irony drops away and he must boast sincerely, he can do so only of his weakness, whether the hardships that he suffers as an apostle or his personal thorn in the flesh (11:21b–33; 12:7–10).

Paul comments that God gave him this personally painful "thorn" to prevent him from becoming conceited, to show him that God's grace was sufficient, and to reveal that God's power is perfected in weakness (12:9). Precisely in the midst of the hardships that he endures "for Christ's sake" and in the midst of his personal suffering, the gift-character of God's power becomes evident (12:10). With no resources to accomplish the task that God has assigned him except those that God supplies, there can be no doubt that God is accomplishing the work.

Sincere Speech

Paul concludes the description of his weak and suffering ministry in 2:14–16 with the question, "And who is sufficient for these things?" (2:16b, aut.). Clearly not, he implies in 2:17, "the many who hawk [*kapēleuontes*] the word of God."[25] In this phrase, Paul is using a common philosophical complaint against Sophists who traveled from city to city promoting the virtues of their teaching, not because they knew what they were talking about but, like the merchant (*kapēlos*) in the marketplace, in order to turn a profit (Plato, *Prt.* 313.c.3–313.e.1).[26] His opponents, as was the custom among itinerant rhetoricians, charged for their services (11:7–12; 12:13–16a). The imagery also implied the use of deceit to close the sale. "A merchant can hardly keep from wrongdoing, nor is a tradesman [*kapēlos*] innocent of sin," said Ben Sira (Sir. 26:29). Paul believed that his opponents not only sold the word of God for profit but used deceitful tactics to do so (2 Cor. 2:17; 4:2; 11:3, 13–15).

What were those tactics? Among them were claims of an impressive bodily presence (10:10) and a full chest of rhetorical tools (10:10; 11:6), standard equipment for the orators of the early Second Sophistic movement and fake Cynic philosophers. Lucian described fake Cynics as common day laborers who, seeing that they could get rich quick by donning the philosopher's cloak, wallet, and staff, traveled about shouting abusively at people, occasionally beating them with their staffs, and "as they themselves express it . . . [shearing] the sheep" (*Fug.* 14). This sounds similar to Paul's description of his opponents in 11:20, where he tells the Corinthians: "You even put up with anyone who enslaves you or exploits you or takes advantage of you or pushes himself forward or slaps you in the face."

In contrast to his opponents' dishonest speech and overbearing demeanor, designed to hide their greedy motives, Paul claims to speak from sincere motives, as one sent from God who knows that he speaks in the presence of God (2:17b; cf. 1:12). God gave him his gospel on the Damascus road (4:6), and this divinely created message needs no rhetorical window-dressing. Thus, Paul claims to be unlike Moses, who veiled his face after his own vision of God so that the children of Israel

25 For the translation of *hoi . . . kapēleuontes* as "those who hawk," see Celsas Spicq, "καπηλεύω," *TLNT*, 2:254, and for the understanding of the question "Who is sufficient?" in polemical terms, see Hafemann, *Suffering and the Spirit*, 90–101.

26 Cf., e.g., Dio Chrysostom, 4.131–32; 54.1; Philostratus, *VA* 1.13; Philo, *Gig.* 39; idem, *Mos.* 2.212; Lucian, *Herm.* 59. See Windisch, *Der zweite Korintherbrief*, 100, and Spicq, "καπηλεύω," 256–57. Hafemann, *Suffering and the Spirit*, 106–26, is right to say that the merchant imagery does not necessarily imply that Paul's opponents "watered down" the gospel in the way that a dishonest wine merchant might water down his or her wine (Lucian, *Herm.* 59), but, as Hafemann recognizes, the imagery is definitely negative. As Paul's statements in 4:2; 11:3, 13–15 show, deceit was for him an important element in the imagery.

would not see that its glory was fading away. By contrast, Paul conducts his far more glorious ministry with great frankness (*pollē parrēsia chrōmetha*, 3:12).[27]

The glorious nature of this ministry means that Paul does not "shrink back" (*enkakeō*) in a cowardly way (4:1, 16), as those need to do who use deception. Instead, he has renounced secret, shameful ways, the use of deception, and distortion of God's Word. His self-commendation is found in the open presentation of the gospel to the conscience of every person (4:1–2; cf. 1:18; 6:7; 10:3–5; 11:6, 10, 31; 12:16–17; 13:8), without cost (11:7–12; 12:13–18). Those who find this gospel mysterious view it this way not because it is deceitful but because they are perishing (4:3), for Satan ("the god of this age") has blinded their minds (4:4). Those who take offense at Paul's insistence on supporting himself with manual labor as he proclaims the gospel rather than accepting the patronage of his churches are "false apostles, deceitful workmen, masquerading as apostles of Christ" (11:13).

In short, Paul presents his gospel with a candor appropriate to its divine origins and glorious nature. The clarity with which he preaches the gospel and his unwillingness to charge for preaching it allow the glory of God to shine without obscurity and thus to illumine the minds of those whom "the god of this age" has not blinded.

Things Unseen

The rhetorical techniques, imposing physical presence, and fee schedule of his opponents have in common their outward, superficial character. They derive any power they have from human ingenuity. To fight with such weapons was to wage war "according to the flesh" (*kata sarka*, 10:3–4) and to boast of them was to boast "according to the flesh" (*kata sarka*, 11:18).

A fourth weapon in the arsenal of Paul's opponents also fit this style of ministry: letters of recommendation. In Paul's time people often requested letters of recommendation from friends and gave them to friends in return, as a way of strengthening existing friendships and gaining new ones. The new friendships that these letters facilitated had utilitarian purposes such as gaining support for one's cause, receiving hospitality, and testifying to one's character in legal trials.[28] Paul's opponents had evidently brought such letters to the Corinthians and expected the Corinthians to supply such letters to others as an obligation of friendship (3:1b).[29] They had also apparently criticized Paul for having to resort to self-commendation since he produced

27 Cf. Dio Chrysostom, 4.14–15, where Dio tells the story of a meeting between Diogenes and Alexander the Great. Alexander found Diogenes in a cypress grove on the outskirts of Corinth (the Craeneion) with no pupils and no crowd about him, "as the sophists ... have." When Alexander greeted Diogenes, who was warming himself in the sun, Diogenes merely asked Alexander to step out of the sun's way. Alexander did not take offense at this, but admired Diogenes' courage, for, says Dio, the courageous admire the courageous, but cowards dislike them. "And so to the one class truth and frankness [*alētheia kai parrēsia*] are the most agreeable things in the world, to the other flattery and deceit."

28 See Peter Marshall, *Enmity in Corinth: Social Conventions in Paul's Relations with the Corinthians* (WUNT 2.23; Tübingen: J.C.B. Mohr [Paul Siebeck], 1987), 91–129, esp. 92 and 98. As Furnish, *II Corinthians*, 180, observes, Paul himself wrote such letters (e.g., Rom. 16:1–2; Phil. 2:29–30; Philemon) and so was not against using them in principle. Cf. Marshall, ibid., 128.

29 For examples of letters of recommendation from the third century B.C. to the third century A.D., see Clinton W. Keyes, "The Greek Letter of Introduction," *AJP* 56 (1935): 28–48, esp. 32–38. For an example of a letter from the third century B.C. that asks the recipient to write other letters of introduction for the person being recommended, see no. 14 on p. 34.

no such letters (3:1a; 5:12). The emphasis that his opponents placed on letters of recommendation led Paul to reflect on the inward and unseen orientation of his own apostolic ministry.

This reflection can be divided into two parts. In 3:1–18 he claims that his commendatory letter is the Corinthians themselves, who are inscribed in his heart and whose own hearts have been inscribed by the Spirit of the living God. In 4:1–7:4 he says that his gaze is fixed not on the outwardly unimpressive circumstances of his ministry but on its unseen and eternal goal.

Letters Written by the Spirit on the Human Heart (3:1–18)

Against his opponents' claims that he carries no letter of recommendation, Paul responds that he does have such a letter, albeit a metaphorical one. The Corinthians themselves are Paul's letter of recommendation, and this letter is written on Paul's heart. Paul then changes the metaphor slightly to make it conform to the covenantal language of the Mosaic law and the prophets. According to Exodus and Deuteronomy, the terms of God's covenant with Israel were recorded on "tablets of stone inscribed by the finger of God" (Ex. 31:18; Deut. 9:10–11; cf. Ex. 32:15–16, LXX). Israel violated the term of this covenant, however, and so experienced the curses of destruction and exile that the covenant had warned would come to them if they failed to keep its stipulations (Lev. 26:3–39; Deut. 28:1–31:29).[30]

The prophets, however, frequently articulate a vision of Israel's restoration. Jeremiah speaks of a time when God will make a "new covenant" with his people by writing his law on their hearts (Jer. 31:33). Ezekiel speaks of God putting a new Spirit within his people, removing their hearts of stone, and giving them hearts of flesh so that they may keep his commandments (Ezek. 11:19; 36:26). Paul recalls this biblical imagery and mixes it together when he says to the Corinthians: "You show that you are a letter from Christ, the result of our ministry, written not with ink but with the Spirit of the living God, not on tablets of stone but on tablets of human hearts" (2 Cor. 3:3).

The expression "tablets of stone" recalls the Mosaic law. The Mosaic law is, as Paul characterizes it a few sentences later, "the letter" that "kills"; it is "the ministry that brought death, which was engraved in letters on stone"; and it is "the ministry that condemns." The expression "tablets of stone" also recalls the "heart of stone" that Ezekiel says God will remove at the time of Israel's restoration (Ezek. 11:19; 36:26). According to Paul, all of this falls under the era dominated by the "old covenant," and it is passing away (2 Cor. 3:11, 13–14).[31]

The notion of "the Spirit of the living God" writing "on tablets of human hearts," by contrast, recalls the prophetic promise that God would restore Israel by changing

30 See Frank Thielman, *From Plight to Solution: A Jewish Framework for Understanding Paul's View of the Law in Galatians and Romans* (NovTSup 61; Leiden: Brill, 1989), 28–45, and the extension of the argument in idem, *Paul and the Law: A Contextual Approach* (Downers Grove, Ill.: InterVarsity Press, 1994), 48–68.

31 *To katargoumenon* ("that which is passing away") is neuter and therefore cannot refer simply to the feminine noun *doxa* ("glory"). Paul is not saying that the transitory glory of the Mosaic ministry is passing away, but that the entire Mosaic ministry—the Mosaic covenant, its sentence of condemnation, and the death that it dealt to those who disobeyed it—is passing away. See Thielman, *Paul and the Law*, 113.

the "heart" of the people and giving his Spirit to them. As one who proclaims the fulfillment of these promises, Paul is a minister of "a new covenant" that brings the life-giving Spirit (3:6, 8) and righteousness (3:9). When, under Paul's ministry, people turn to the Lord, the veil is lifted from their hearts by the work of God's Spirit, and they begin the process of transformation into the image of Christ, whose splendor they now see (3:18; cf. 4:4).

All of this is an action of God on the human heart with little physical evidence to show for it. Paul's competence (*hikanos*) as a minister is not measured, therefore, by something outward and physical, such as letters of recommendation either to or from the Corinthians. The measure of Paul's confidence as a minister is the transformed lives of those who have believed the gospel (3:4–6).

Faith, not Sight (4:1–7:4)

The emphasis of Paul's opponents on letters of recommendation, a powerful bodily presence, rhetorical skill, and speaker's fees is also symptomatic of a fundamental misunderstanding of Christian eschatology. Their gaze is fixed on the visible and transitory rather than on the invisible and eternal (5:12). God's use of Paul's suffering to unveil the hearts of believers and display his glory, and the similar way in which God brought life through the death of Jesus (4:7–12), have focused Paul's vision on the unseen and eternal:

> Because we have the same Spirit of faith as the one who wrote "I believed, and so I spoke," we also believe, and so we speak, knowing that the one who raised the Lord Jesus will raise us also with Jesus and present us with you. (4:13–14; cf. Ps. 116:10)[32]

Both the author of Psalm 116 and Paul had faith that God would deliver them from death, and this faith gave rise to speech—in the psalmist's case an honest but hopeful confession of his affliction, and in Paul's case, the faithful proclamation of the gospel in spite of the hardship he faced.[33] In both cases, hope for God's deliverance gave meaning to suffering in the present. Paul's hope was grounded in the resurrection of Jesus from the dead, an event that inaugurated the long-expected period of the restoration of God's people, a period that would climax in the resurrection of the dead (Ezek. 37:1–14; Dan. 12:2).

The period of restoration was, however, only inaugurated, and this set up an inevitable tension between what is visible in the present and the still unseen future. In the present Paul's alignment with the death of Jesus is clearly visible. He is "wasting away," afflicted with "troubles," and groaning under the burden of his "earthly tent" (2 Cor. 4:16, 17; 5:1–4; 6:4–5, 8–10). At the same time, these afflictions are both "light and momentary" in comparison to the "eternal weight of glory" that God

32 This is the translation of Furnish, *II Corinthians*, 252.

33 Paul is quoting the LXX rendering of Psalm 115:1, which differs slightly from the Hebrew: "I believed, therefore I spoke. But I was greatly humiliated." On the thematic connections between this psalm and Paul's thanksgiving for deliverance from death in 2 Cor. 1:3–11, see Harvey, *Renewal through Suffering*, 18, and on the importance of the psalm for understanding 4:13, see ibid., 61.

is producing for Paul through them (4:17, aut.; cf. 5:5).[34] Therefore only his outer person is wasting away; God is renewing his inner person each day, and he knows that if his earthly, tent-like house should be destroyed, he has an eternal house in the heavens (5:1). He also knows that if he is alive at the time of the Parousia, he will not be found naked but will put his immortal existence on over his body (5:2–4).[35] In short, Paul looks forward to the time when "what is mortal may be swallowed up by life" (5:4).

For the authentic apostle, life between the inauguration and consummation of God's purposes assumes a distinctive posture. Paul describes this posture as "not setting our eyes on what is seen, but on what is unseen" (4:18), as viewing no one from the outward, transient perspective of "the flesh" (5:16), and as living "by faith, not by sight" (5:7). Contrary to the charges of his opponents (10:1–2), Paul claims that this is not a life of discouragement—of "shrinking back" (*enkakeō*, 4:1, 16)—but of courageous confidence (*tharreō*, 5:6, 8) that the God who has given the Spirit promised by the prophets will also one day cause life to swallow up all that is mortal (5:4–5). It is a life lived in the light that the coming judgment casts back on the present, and the aspiration of those who live this way, whatever the circumstances, is to please the Lord (5:9–10).

Summary

Paul believes that the focus of his opponents on letters of recommendation, bodily presence, rhetorical technique, and speakers' fees is myopic. It has blurred and obscured from view the critical concerns of the gospel: the gracious initiative of God in salvation, the human heart as the locus of God's transforming work, and the still unseen future when God will raise his people from the dead. By taking "pride in what is seen rather than in what is in the heart" (5:12), Paul's opponents have missed the critical importance to faith of focusing on what is unseen, both in the human heart and in the future. They have apparently also led some of the Corinthians to do the same (10:7; cf. 5:20; 6:1–2; 6:11–7:4).[36] In doing this, both Paul's opponents and those Corinthians whom they have convinced of their position have hidden the gospel from view.

---

34 Paul uses the verb *katergazomai* ("accomplish, produce") in both 4:17 and 5:5. Cf. Phil. 1:12–13.

35 Bruce, *1 and 2 Corinthians*, 200, is representative of a group of interpreters who believe that between 1 Cor. 15:1–58 and 2 Cor. 5:1–5 Paul became convinced that he would probably die before Jesus' Parousia. Thus he speaks of the unappealing possibility of being "naked" between his death and the assumption of his resurrection body (5:3). It is doubtful, however, that anyone who suffered as much as Paul did prior to the composition of his first extant letter (1 Thess. 2:2; 2 Cor. 11:32) would have failed to face the possibility of his own imminent death.

36 *Ta kata prosōpon blepete* in 10:7 can mean either, "Look facts in the face" (REB; cf. NRSV and most commentators) or "You are looking only on the surface of things" (NIV; cf. NASB), depending on whether *blepete* is imperative or indicative. Bultmann, *Second Letter to the Corinthians*, 187, is probably right, however, to link 10:7 with 5:12, where Paul uses the word *prosōpon* ("face") to mean "outward appearance."

POVERTY AS AN OCCASION FOR GOD'S GRACE

The Corinthians' Failure in Generosity

At the close of 1 Corinthians, Paul had given instructions about a collection "for the saints" in Jerusalem (1 Cor. 16:1, 3). He intended that the money he collected among his predominantly Gentile churches in Galatia, Macedonia, and Achaia would help to support the poor among the Jewish Christians in Jerusalem (Rom. 15:26; cf. Acts 24:17; Gal. 2:10). In this way, he argued, the excess of necessary funds among Gentile Christians in the west would supply the needs of Jewish Christians in the east and thus produce equality among God's people (2 Cor. 8:13; cf. 9:12). Later, in his letter to the Romans, he gives an additional reason for the collection: "If the Gentiles have shared in the Jews' spiritual blessings, they owe it to the Jews to share with them their material blessings" (Rom. 15:27).

When Titus started the collection in Corinth sometime during the previous year (2 Cor. 8:6, 10; 9:2), the Corinthians were eager to contribute to it (8:10–11), and Paul had advised them in 1 Corinthians 16:1–4 to follow the procedure that he urged the Galatian churches to adopt.[37] Each week, he told them, they should set aside for the collection an amount in proportion with their income. Eventually Paul himself would come to Corinth and send representatives whom the Corinthians had chosen to Jerusalem with letters of commendation from him. Only if it seemed advisable would Paul himself go along. The recent rift between Paul and the Corinthians, however, seems to have halted the Corinthians' weekly effort to raise funds for the collection, and although Titus had brought good news to Paul about the overall effect of the severe letter on most of the Corinthians, Titus also apparently had to report that progress toward the collection continued to languish.[38]

At the same time that the Corinthians were failing in their commitment to be generous, however, the Macedonians had unexpectedly and voluntarily begged Paul for the "favor" (*charis*) of being able to participate in the offering. This request came unexpectedly since the Macedonians were themselves experiencing "the most severe trial" and "extreme poverty" (8:1–5; cf. 7:5). This display of simple generosity prompted Paul to send Titus back (8:6) with two unnamed brothers (8:18, 22–24; 9:3, 5) and the letter of 2 Corinthians in the hope that they might encourage the Corinthians to "finish the work" they had so eagerly begun.

The Central Role of Grace in Paul's Appeal

For Paul, the Corinthians' dampened enthusiasm about the collection was a serious development, not because it jeopardized the success of an errand of mercy but because it constituted evidence that God's grace had not transformed the Corinthians' hearts.[39] As Paul says to them later, on a related issue, "what I want is not your

37 For this understanding of Titus' role in the collection, see Plummer, *The Second Epistle of St. Paul to the Corinthians*, 237, and Barnett, *Second Epistle to the Corinthians*, 387.

38 Barnett, *Second Epistle to the Corinthians*, 387–88.

39 On the fundamental importance of God's grace to the development of Paul's argument in 8:1–9:15, see especially Georgi, *Remembering the Poor*, 72, 83, 89 (where, however, the argument is questionable), 96–97, 107–8, and Barnett, *Second Epistle to the Corinthians*, 388–89, and at many places in Barnett's exegesis of these chapters.

possessions but you" (12:14). Paul worries in other places in the letter that the Corinthians have not really experienced the transforming effects of the gospel. "Be reconciled to God," he begs them in 5:20. "We urge you not to receive God's grace in vain," he implores in 6:1. In 13:5, he issues this stern warning, and its position at the close of the letter renders it all the more grave:

> Examine yourselves to see whether you are in the faith; test [*dokimazete*] yourselves. Do you not realize that Christ Jesus is in you—unless, of course, you fail the test [*ei mē adokimoi este*]?

The same concern lies behind his appeal to the Corinthians in 8:1–9:15 to renew their interest in the collection. Paul stresses the need for the Corinthians to show that their faith is genuine—that God's grace is really at work in them. Thus he uses the collection "to test [*dokimazō*] the sincerity of [their] love" (8:8). He urges the Corinthians to demonstrate "the proof" (*endeixis*) of their love for Paul and the reason why he is proud of them (8:24). By contributing to the collection, they will show the "approved character" (*dokimēs*) of their service—that their obedience accompanies their confession of the gospel of Christ (9:13).[40]

The Corinthians' renewal of interest in the collection forms proof of the genuineness of their commitment to the gospel because a heartfelt willingness to give is itself a gift of God's grace. If they are willing to give cheerfully, therefore, this is evidence of God's transforming work in their hearts. The Corinthians must give the gift voluntarily, however, for a contribution that arises out of a sense of compulsion is not evidence that God's hand is at work. So throughout the passage Paul suggests that the desire to give must arise from within and that both the desire and the ability to give are themselves gifts of God.

Paul's use of the Macedonians as an example emphasizes exactly these themes. The Macedonians surprised Paul by begging him for the privilege of giving. They did this, Paul stresses, "by their own free choice" (*authairetoi*), in spite of their affliction of suffering and poverty, and after giving themselves "first to the Lord" (8:3–4). Paul wants the Corinthians to give in the same way, not because he compels them with a command to give (8:8), nor because he wants their money even if they give it grudgingly (9:5), but because they have renewed the desire to give that had been so strong in the previous year (8:10–12; 9:2–5). Paul sums up the principle this way: "Each person should give just as that person has chosen in his or her heart, not regretfully or from compulsion, for God loves a cheerful giver" (9:7, aut.). This heartfelt willingness to give arises from the prior work of God's grace. God gave to the Macedonian churches the grace to give to the collection (8:1), and the Corinthians, should they decide to give, will themselves give freely as a result of "this grace" (8:6, 7).[41]

God not only graciously gives the heartfelt desire to give, however, but he also gives the means by which giving becomes possible. Thus, the profound poverty of

40 For the translation of *dokimēs* as "approved character," see BDAG, 256.

41 Cf. A. Schlatter, *Paulus der Bote Jesu: Eine Deutung seiner Briefe an die Korinther* (Stuttgart: Calwer Verlag, 1934), 611.

the Macedonian churches only made possible the display of God's extravagant grace (cf. 9:14). God enabled them to give not merely in a way that was commensurate with their ability, but beyond their ability (8:2–3). The Lord Jesus, in the same way, revealed his grace by impoverishing himself, and precisely through this poverty he made the Corinthians rich (8:9). Paul hopes that the Corinthians will follow the example of the Macedonians and the Lord Jesus by generously "sowing" their wealth and allowing God's grace to work.

While he does not expect them to impoverish themselves (8:13–15), he tells them that as they give their money, God will "make all grace abound" to them, "so that in all things at all times, having all that you need, you will abound in every good work" (9:8). God will make them rich in every way, Paul says, so that they can give with simple generosity (9:11). This ministry of giving, he concludes, will constitute "proof" (*dokimēs*) that their confession of the gospel of Christ is genuine (9:13). It is the "obedience that arises from faith" that Paul refers to elsewhere (Rom. 1:5; 16:26).[42]

HUMAN WEAKNESS AS THE CONTEXT OF GOD'S GRACE IN 2 CORINTHIANS

Every major section of 2 Corinthians emphasizes that human weakness is the environment in which God's grace flourishes. The deadly peril that Paul faced in Asia provided the means by which Paul's life could mirror the life and death of Christ. Just as with Christ, so Paul's suffering overflowed with comfort to others (1:5). The kind of suffering that Paul had encountered in Asia was a constant feature of his ministry, yet this suffering provided the opportunity for God, as a gracious favor (*charisma*), to rescue his apostle for further service (1:10–11; 4:7–12; 6:4–10). As Paul puts it in 12:10, "When I am weak, then I am strong."

In the same way, precisely through the affliction and poverty of the Macedonians, God's "surpassing grace" (9:14) was able to effect both their willingness and their ability to give beyond anything Paul had expected (8:1–5). The Lord Jesus, too, had displayed his grace precisely through impoverishing himself (8:9). By doing this, Paul tells the Corinthians, he made others rich.

Charges from his opponents in Corinth that he lacked bodily presence (10:10), rhetorical ability (10:10; 11:6), and consistency in planning his itinerary (1:12) failed to hit the mark for Paul. Claims that he was too weak to force the Corinthians to be loyal to him by physical violence or emotional intimidation (11:20–21) or that his social pedigree failed to match theirs (3:1; 11:22) left Paul unimpressed. For Paul, God's grace did not work in such contexts.

Instead, Paul argues that God's grace expresses its full power in the weakness of suffering and in the unseen condition of the heart (3:2–3; 5:12). "My grace is sufficient for you," says the crucified and risen Lord, "for my power is made perfect in

42 Schlatter, *Paulus der Bote Jesu*, 610; Barrett, *Second Epistle to the Corinthians*, 240.

weakness" (12:9). Paul knows that God works in this way so "that we might not rely on ourselves but on God, who raises the dead" (1:9) and "to show that this all-surpassing power is from God and not from us" (4:7). Those who boast, as he had said in 1 Corinthians and repeats here, should boast in the Lord (1 Cor. 1:31; 2 Cor. 10:17).

Paul was troubled, however, by the Corinthians' failure to understand this critical theological principle. Although the sorrowful letter, in a way typical of the work of God's grace, appears to have brought repentance and life to the majority, a minority continued to cling to the apostle's opponents, and the failure of even the repentant majority to renew the grace of giving showed Paul that all was not well.

Second Corinthians, then, represents an effort to reassert in the Corinthian community a fundamental theological principle and to urge the Corinthians to embrace that principle by taking a practical step of obedience. In a variety of ways and with several confusing shifts in subject and tone, Paul argues a single thesis: God's power is perfected in human weakness. Those who have experienced the gracious work of this power have moved their focus from the face to the heart—from the seen to the unseen—and they inevitably become the instruments through which God graciously gives salvation and comfort to others.

Chapter 15

ROMANS: THE GOSPEL OF GOD'S RIGHTEOUSNESS

After Paul wrote 2 Corinthians, he traveled from Macedonia to Achaia (or "Greece," as Luke calls it), where he spent three months (Acts 20:2–3). Those three months must have been a much happier period than his last, sorrowful visit to Achaia, for during this third visit, the Achaians followed the example of the Macedonians and freely contributed (*eudokēsan*) to the collection for poor Christians in Jerusalem (Rom. 15:26); good relations between Paul and the Corinthians had been restored.[1] Paul was now poised to complete the plan that he had formulated near the end of his Ephesian ministry to journey not only to Macedonia, Achaia, and Jerusalem in the service of the needy Judean saints, but eventually to go to Rome (Acts 19:21; cf. Rom. 15:25–26). Perhaps it was during these three months that he decided to extend his journey to Spain.[2] Rome would not be the termination of his trip west but a stop along the way (Rom. 15:23–24, 28).

Rome would, however, be much more than a place to await passage to Spain. Paul had prayed ceaselessly that God might prosper his way to Rome (1:11) and had desired for many years to visit the Christians there (15:23; cf. 1:11, 13), but his commitment to preach the gospel "where Christ was not known" had delayed him (1:13; 15:20; cf. 15:22). His eagerness sprang from his obligation to preach the gospel "to Greeks and non-Greeks, both to the wise and the foolish" (1:14). God had graciously given Paul the priestly ministry of presenting the Gentiles to him as "an offering acceptable to God, sanctified by the Holy Spirit" (15:16), and so Paul hoped to strengthen the Roman Christians spiritually by preaching the gospel in Rome also (1:11, 15). He wanted to reap a harvest among them, just as he had among other Gentiles (1:13).

At first this sounds odd: Why would Paul say at the beginning of a letter to Roman Christians that he wanted to preach the gospel in their city and at its end state as his ambition to preach the gospel where Christ had not been named?[3] The

1 On the meaning of *eudokēsan* in this passage, see C. E. B. Cranfield, *A Critical and Exegetical Commentary on the Epistle to the Romans*, 2 vols. (ICC; Edinburgh: T. & T. Clark, 1975–79), 2:771. The suggestion of A. J. M. Wedderburn, *The Reasons for Romans* (SNTW; Edinburgh: T. & T. Clark, 1991), 43, that the aorist tense of this verb implies that the Achaeans *had* deemed it well to contribute to the collection but were no longer enthusiastic about it reads too much into the tense. The aorist only implies that the collection is in hand and that Paul is ready to go to Jerusalem. Had Paul intended to say that the Achaeans (and the Macedonians!) no longer looked favorably on the collection, he would have written something like *pote eudokēsan*.

2 On the other hand, Paul may have included Spain in his original plans and Luke may have decided not to mention the Spanish goal of Paul's travels in order to focus attention on Paul's journey to Rome (cf. Acts 23:11; 28:14).

3 On the exegetical seriousness of this problem see Günther Klein, "Paul's Purpose in Writing the Epistle to the Romans," in *The Romans Debate*, ed. Karl P. Donfried, rev. and exp. (Peabody, Mass.: Hendrickson, 1991), 29–43. Klein's own solution to the problem was that Paul believed the Roman church needed an apostolic foundation. The anonymous fourth-century Latin commentator on the epistle, whom Erasmus dubbed "Ambrosiaster," anticipated this theory. See *ACCS*, 6:18, 20, 23, and 25. Paul would not have spoken as he did in 1:8 and 15:14, however, if he had considered the Roman Christians' faith to be defective.

most likely explanation for this puzzle is that Paul believed the Romans needed to hear the gospel again, and that as the apostle to the Gentiles (11:13; 15:15–16), this predominantly Gentile church fell within his apostolic responsibility.[4] This only partially violated his policy of not preaching the gospel where Christ had already been named since that policy was motivated by his concern not to build on "someone else's foundation" (15: 20). Most likely even in Paul's time the origins of the Roman church were obscure, and so Paul felt free, indeed he felt obligated, to preach the gospel in Rome also.[5]

Why did Christians in Rome need to hear the gospel again? Paul's letter provides evidence for a plausible answer to this question. In 14:1–15:13 he urges two groups within the Roman churches, "the powerful" and "the powerless," to "accept one another, just as Christ accepted you" (15:1, 7; cf. 14:1, 3). The weak faith of the powerless led them to avoid meat and wine (14:1–2, 21; cf. 14:17) and to observe certain days as special (14:5–6). The powerful, however, ate "anything" (14:2) and considered every day special (14:5). Apparently, the powerful despised those who had scruples about food and days, and the powerless condemned those who did not (14:3, 10, 13). This sounds like a disagreement between Jewish Christians who observed the dietary restrictions of the Mosaic law and the Sabbath and Gentile Christians who believed that these requirements were no longer binding.[6]

Moreover, Paul's descriptions of the two groups as "the powerful" (*hoi dynatoi*) and "the powerless" (*hoi adynatoi*) probably says something about their relative power in the Christian community: Those without scruples about the Mosaic law had the upper hand.[7] This is confirmed when we consider Paul's admonition to "you Gentiles" in the community in 11:13–21. Paul tells them not to boast over unbelieving Jews who, because of their unbelief, God has pruned from the olive tree of his people. The Gentile Christians in Rome, who were in a position of power, seem to have succumbed to an anti-Jewish sentiment toward both believing and unbelieving Jews.[8]

---

4 On the relationship of Paul's apostolic responsibility to the Gentiles to his concern for the Roman Christians, see Wedderburn, *Reasons for Romans*, 98–99.

5 The first reference to Roman Christianity appears in Suetonius' statement that "since the Jews constantly made disturbances at the instigation of Chrestus, he [i.e. Claudius] expelled them from Rome" (*Claud.* 25.4; cf. Acts 18:2). On the identification of "Chrestus" with Christ, see esp. Wolfgang Wiefel, "The Jewish Community in Ancient Rome and the Origins of Roman Christianity" in *The Romans Debate*, ed. Karl P. Donfried, rev. and exp. (Peabody, Mass.: Hendrickson, 1991), 85–101, here at 92–93. "Ambrosiaster" begins his commentary on Romans with a brief historical orientation to the letter. He claims that the Roman Christians had not received the gospel from any apostle but that the church had been established through converted Jews and thus "according to a Jewish rite." See the translation of *CSEL*, 81.1, 5–6 in Wedderburn, *Reasons for Romans*, 51.

6 Although Jews did not avoid meat and wine as a matter of course, they sometimes avoided them if they were unsure about their purity, just as Daniel ate only vegetables and drank only water in Babylonian exile (Dan. 1:12), and Esther and Judith refused to eat food provided them by Gentiles (Est. 14:17, LXX; Judith 12:2). See John M. G. Barclay, "'Do We Undermine the Law?' A Study of Romans 14.1–15.6," in *Paul and the Mosaic Law*, ed. James D. G. Dunn (WUNT 89; Tübingen: J.C.B. Mohr [Paul Siebeck], 1996), 287–308, here at 291–92. Wedderburn, *Reasons*, 59–60, believes that the dispute was based more on differing attitudes toward the Mosaic law than on ethnicity. Thus some Gentile Christians may have joined Jewish Christians in advocating observance of the food laws and sacred days and some Jewish Christians may have joined some Gentile Christians in advocating freedom from the Mosaic law. Paul, however, seems to divide the two groups along ethnic lines in 15:7–13.

7 Cf. Wiefel, "Jewish Community in Ancient Rome," 96 n. 110, and Joseph A. Fitzmyer, *Romans* (AB 33; New York: Doubleday, 1993), 702.

8 Wiefel, "Jewish Community in Ancient Rome," 86–89, 97–100, demonstrates that anti-Judaism permeated Roman society in the time of Nero.

The gospel as Paul typically preached it in the synagogue provided the theological remedy to this situation by excluding every boast in social status or human achievement, whether from Jew or Gentile.[9]

How did Paul find out about the power struggle in the Roman church if he had never visited Rome? Romans 16:3–23 supplies the answer.[10] Here Paul greets twenty-six friends, all of whom he apparently met in his efforts to preach the gospel "from Jerusalem all the way around to Illyricum" (15:19), and many of whom were much more than passing acquaintances.[11] Prisca and Aquila had risked their lives for him (16:3). Epenetus was the first person in Asia to embrace the gospel under Paul's preaching (16:5). Andronicus and Junias had been in prison with Paul (16:7). Urbanus had been a coworker (16:9). Rufus's mother had been like a mother to Paul himself (16:13). Some in this list were also Jews, as Luke informs us (Prisca and Aquila), or as Paul's epithet "my compatriot" (*syngenēs*) indicates (Andronicus, Junias, Herodion; cf. 9:3).[12] It seems likely that such close friends would have kept in touch with Paul and that at least the Jews among them would have urged him to use his apostolic authority to help the Roman Christians overcome their disunity.

Paul's letter to Rome is complex and clearly had more than one purpose.[13] Paul probably meant for the letter to inform the Romans of the content of his gospel in light of his request for their support of his Spanish mission (15:24, 28–29, 32). As part of his effort to gain Roman support, he may have been answering charges of Judaizing Christians that his gospel was antinomian and anti-Jewish (3:8; 6:1, 15; 7:12; 9:1–11:36). He certainly wanted the Romans to pray for his "ministry in Jerusalem"—the offering he had taken for poor Jewish Christians as an expression of the unity of Jews and Gentiles (15:26–27; cf. 2 Cor. 8:13–15)—and perhaps he hoped that his presentation of the gospel in 1:16–15:13 would convince the Roman Christians to support this effort. In addition, he may have hoped that a clear presentation of the gospel would arm the Romans against "those who cause divisions and offenses contrary to the teaching" that the Roman Christians had learned (cf. 16:17).

If we focus on the purpose that Paul himself emphasizes, however, he wrote the letter chiefly to prepare for his arrival in Rome, where he would exercise his gift as "minister of Christ Jesus to the Gentiles" (15:16) by preaching the gospel (1:15). Since the gospel implies that every boast in social status and human achievement is out of place before God, it also implies that the Gentile majority among the Roman Christians should not please themselves but bear with the weaknesses of the Jewish minority. This is the message Paul would preach when he got to Rome, and since his

9 The synagogue setting of Paul's gospel proclamation is evident from the Jewish identity of the imaginary skeptic whom Paul occasionally uses to advance his argument. See, e.g., 2:1, 17; 3:1.

10 Cf. Wedderburn, *Reasons*, 13.

11 The number 26 excludes Aristobulus and Narcissus, whom Paul may not have known personally. They may have simply headed households that contained Christians whom Paul knew. On this see Peter Lampe, "The Roman Christians of Romans 16," in *The Romans Debate*, ed. Karl P. Donfried, rev. and exp. (Peabody, Mass.: Hendrickson, 1991), 216–30, here at 219 n. 15 and 222.

12 "Mary" (*Maria*) may not be a Jewish name but the feminine form of the Latin name "Marius." See Lampe, "Roman Christians," 225.

13 As most students of the letter recognize. See esp. Wedderburn, *Reasons for Romans*, 5–6, 140, and the comments of Cranfield, *Romans*, 2:815.

arrival there would be delayed by his trip to Jerusalem, this letter would, in the meantime, proclaim the gospel.[14]

Because Paul's letter to the Romans provides a compendium of the gospel he preaches, it simultaneously provides an unusually full statement of his theology. Paul has shaped his presentation of the gospel to meet the pastoral needs of the Roman church, and critical elements of his theology are missing or lightly treated (e.g., his understanding of the church, Christ's *parousia*, and the Lord's Supper), but Romans nevertheless offers a rare moment in the study of his theology.[15] Because Romans reveals the gospel as Paul preached it in the synagogue, it provides the apostle's fullest extant explanation of the theological convictions that fueled his missionary efforts. The discussion of its theology, therefore, should follow the outline of the letter itself. Here, we will begin with an examination of Paul's thesis statement and then follow the letter's own unfolding of this statement's emphases.

THE GOSPEL AS GOD'S RIGHTEOUSNESS FOR ALL WHO BELIEVE (1:16–17)

Paul begins his description of the gospel with a thesis statement that summarizes its three chief elements. First, the gospel is the revelation of the righteousness of God. Second, this righteousness is effective for everyone who believes. Third, the gospel stands in continuity with, not in contradiction to, the Jewish Scriptures.

The Gospel Reveals the Righteousness of God

Paul explains the significance of the gospel in 1:17 as the revelation of "the righteousness of God" (aut.). This phrase, or something close to it, appears ten times in Paul's letters, eight of them in Romans, and the eight uses of the phrase in this letter cluster around especially critical moments in Paul's argument. In addition to its appearance here in Paul's thesis statement, he uses it four times at the letter's most dramatic moment, when he describes God's response to the desperate human plight of sin (3:21–26). He also uses it twice at another critical juncture when, in answering a potentially fatal objection to his gospel, he explains why God's chosen people have not been the gospel's primary beneficiaries (10:3).[16] Clearly, then, the phrase is important; but what does it mean?

Some interpreters claim that it is a technical term of apocalyptic Judaism that the early church took over and that it consistently refers to God's righteous or saving activity on behalf of his people (understanding "of God" as a subjective genitive).[17]

14 Cf. Nils Alstrup Dahl, *Studies in Paul: Theology for the Early Christian Mission* (Minneapolis: Augsburg, 1977), 77.

15 Frank Thielman, "Paul as Jewish Christian Theologian: The Theology of Paul in the Magnum Opus of James D. G. Dunn," *PRSt* 25 (1998): 381–87, here at 383.

16 Paul also uses the phrase in 3:5 in a brief excursus that anticipates his discussion of Israel's relationship to the gospel in 9:1–11:36. On the importance of the phrase in Romans, see Arland J. Hultgren, *Paul's Gospel and Mission: The Outlook from His Letter to the Romans* (Philadelphia: Fortress, 1985), 13; Douglas Moo, *The Epistle to the Romans* (NICNT; Grand Rapids: Eerdmans, 1996), 70; and James D. G. Dunn, *The Theology of Paul the Apostle* (Grand Rapids: Eerdmans, 1998), 340–41.

17 See, e.g., Ernst Käsemann, *Commentary on Romans* (Grand Rapids: Eerdmans, 1980), 24–30. N. T. Wright, "On Becoming the Righteousness of God: 2 Corinthians 5:21" in *Pauline Theology, Volume II: 1 and 2 Corinthians*, ed. David M. Hay (Minneapolis: Fortress, 1993), 200–208, here at 203, takes the phrase as a technical term for Paul, but not one that he took over from apocalyptic Judaism.

Others believe that the phrase refers to a righteous status that God gives to those who have faith (understanding "of God" as a genitive of origin).[18]

The most satisfying understanding of the phrase recognizes, however, that Paul uses it in more than one way. He uses the phrase, or something close to it, to refer in some contexts to the righteous status that God gives to believers, in anticipation of their eschatological acquittal at his tribunal in the final day (Rom. 10:3; Phil. 3:9; 2 Cor. 5:21; cf. 1 Cor. 1:30).[19] He also uses it to refer to God's righteous character—his consistency in doing what is right and in keeping his promises (3:5, 25–26).[20] In 1:16–17, however, he uses the phrase to refer to God's powerful intervention on behalf of his people to save them. This is evident from the way the phrase explains Paul's statement that the gospel "is the power of God for the salvation of everyone who believes."[21] It is able to save those who believe, he says, because "in it a righteousness of God is revealed" (aut.).

By describing the gospel in this way, Paul links it to the biblical notion that God expresses his righteousness when he saves his people from sin and oppression (and frequently their oppression is a result of their sin) in faithfulness to his covenant with them. The expression of this idea in Psalm 97:1–3 (LXX; MT 98:1–3) is especially close to Paul's description of the gospel in 1:16–17:

> Sing to the Lord a new song because the Lord has done marvelous things. His right hand has been victorious for him, and his holy arm. The Lord has made known his salvation and revealed his righteousness [*dikaiosynēn*] before the Gentiles. He has remembered his mercy to Jacob and his truth to the house of Israel. All the ends of the earth have seen the salvation [*sōtērion*] of our God. (aut.)[22]

Here the mighty, saving acts of the Lord are celebrated as "his salvation," which is in turn equated with "his righteousness." Both God's salvation and his righteousness are defined as his remembering "his mercy to Jacob and his truth to the house of Israel." In other words, they reveal his faithfulness to the covenant that he made with his people. By using the language of God's saving righteousness, Paul establishes a link between the gospel and God's mighty acts of covenant faithfulness in the past as they are recorded in the Scriptures.[23]

18 See, e.g., Cranfield, *Romans*, 1:92–99. This interpretation is sometimes thought to be the product of the Reformers' concern with imputed righteousness. It seems to have been articulated already in the fourth century by "Ambrosiaster," however, who interprets the phrase through the lens of Phil. 3:9. See *ACCS*, 6:31.

19 Cf. Isa. 54:17 and the comments of Peter Stuhlmacher, *Reconciliation, Law, and Righteousness* (Philadelphia: Fortress, 1986), 72. Cf. idem, *Biblische Theologie des Neuen Testaments*, 2 vols. (Göttingen: Vandenhoeck & Ruprecht, 1992–99), 1:335.

20 Moo, *Romans*, 82–84, 189–90, 237–40. Thus Georg Strecker, *Theology of the New Testament* (New York: Walter de Gruyter, 2000), 151, overstates the case when he says that the term never refers to what he calls "a quality of God that resides in the divine being."

21 Ernst Käsemann, *New Testament Questions of Today* (Philadelphia: Fortress, 1969), 172–73, followed by many, including Peter Stuhlmacher, *Paul's Letter to the Romans: A Commentary* (Louisville: Westminster John Knox, 1994), 29–32; idem, *Biblische Theologie*, 327–28; and Hans Hübner, *Biblische Theologie des Neuen Testaments*, 3 vols. (Göttingen: Vandenhoeck & Ruprecht, 1990–95), 1:261.

22 See also Judg. 5:11; 1 Sam. 12:7; Ps. 71:18–19; 111:1–10; Isa. 45:8, 51:6; Dan. 9:15–19; Mic. 6:5 and the discussions in Stuhlmacher, *Romans*, 29–32, and idem, *Biblische Theologie des Neuen Testaments*, 1:327–28.

23 It seems necessary to disagree, therefore, both with Dunn, *Theology*, 341–44, and with Stephen Westerholm, *Perspectives Old and New on Paul: The "Lutheran" Paul and His Critics* (Grand Rapids: Eerdmans, 2004), 92–93. Dunn says that the debate over whether "the righteousness of God" refers to God's activity or to a gift that he gives becomes largely unnecessary when we realize that the phrase refers to God's covenant relationship with his

The Gospel Becomes Effective by Faith

The righteousness of God—his power to save—is effective for those who believe. Paul defines faith carefully in 4:18–25, using the example of Abraham and then applying this example to those who have Christian faith. Abraham's faith was a trust that God would keep his promise to give him many offspring despite the improbability, from a human perspective, that this could happen. For the purposes of bearing offspring, both he and Sarah were as good as dead, but Abraham believed, against this clear evidence, that "the God who gives life to the dead and calls things that are not as though they were ... had power to do what he promised" (4:17, 21).[24] This was more than Abraham should have hoped for from a human perspective, but because his hope was in God, he "did not waver through unbelief" (4: 20).

This willingness to trust God's promises despite appearances to the contrary is also the critical element in Christian faith.[25] Christians trust, despite appearances, that God raised Jesus from the dead, that his crucifixion and resurrection have resulted in an early acquittal in God's eschatological tribunal (4:24–25), and that we will live with Christ on that final day (6:8). The truth of this message is not at all obvious; indeed, to the very people who should have believed it first it became "a stone of stumbling and a rock of offense" (9:33). But God has promised, Paul maintains, that "the one who trusts in him will never be put to shame" (9:33; cf. 10:11). This understanding of faith probably explains why Paul begins his thesis statement with the claim that he is not "ashamed" of the gospel. As Paul had said in 1 Corinthians 1:19: "The message of the cross is foolishness to those who are perishing, but to us who are being saved it is the power of God."[26]

Paul draws two conclusions throughout Romans from the Abrahamic character of Christian faith, and those two conclusions are implied already in Romans 1:16–17. First, since the righteousness of God is effective for everyone who has faith, Gentiles who believe it become beneficiaries of the mightiest in a long line of God's mighty works that had previously benefited Israel alone, and often had benefited Israel to the detriment of the Gentiles. So in 1:16, Paul says that the gospel "is the

people. Westerholm observes that use of the term "covenant" is in short supply in Paul's letters "and—botheration!" Paul never links the notion of God's faithfulness to his promises with righteousness terminology. It is true that Paul uses the phrase "the righteousness of God" elsewhere to refer God's gift of "extraordinary righteousness" (Westerholm's phrase) to the wicked, but here in 1:17, as Westerholm admits, notions of God's saving activity are uppermost in Paul's thinking.

24 The correct reading in 4:19, on both external and internal grounds, is *kai mē asthenēsas tē pistei katenoēsen to heautou sōma* ... ("and, not weakening in faith, he considered his own body ...") rather than *kai mē asthenēsas tē pistei* ou *katenoēsen to heautou sōma* ... ("and, not weakening in faith, he did *not* consider his own body ..."). Paul's point is that Abraham stared the improbability squarely in the face that he could ever have a natural heir and still trusted that God could keep his promise. See the discussions in Cranfield, *Romans* 1:247, and Thomas R. Schreiner, *Romans* (BECNT; Grand Rapids: Baker, 1998), 239–40.

25 Cf. Adolf Schlatter, *Der Glaube im Neuen Testament*, 4th ed. (Stuttgart: Calwer Verlag, 1927), 346–48, and idem, *Romans*, 114–18.

26 This position is not uncontroversial, but the use of shame language in 9:33 and 10:11 and the close verbal parallels between 1:16 and 1 Cor. 1:18 indicate that it is the best understanding of the phrase (compare *dynamis gar theou estin eis sōtērion* with *tois de sōzomenois hēmin dynamis theou estin*). See John Murray, *The Epistle to the Romans*, 2 vols. (NICNT; Grand Rapids: Eerdmans, 1959–65), 1:26; Otto Kuss, *Der Römerbrief*, 3 vols. (Regensburg: Verlag Friedrich Pustet, 1957–78), 1: 20; and Cranfield, *Romans*, 1:86–87. There is no need, however, to think that the grandeur of Rome suggested this thought to Paul. It was an implication of the gospel wherever it was preached, as Adolf Schlatter, *Romans: The Righteousness of God* (Peabody, Mass.: Hendrickson, 1995; orig. ed. 1935), 17, saw clearly.

power of God for the salvation of everyone who believes: first for the Jew, then for the Gentile" (cf. 3:22; 10:11). This implies that the Mosaic law no longer defines the boundaries of the people of God and that Abraham is no longer the father only of the Jewish people. As Paul will say in 4:16: "The promise comes by faith, so that it may be by grace and may be guaranteed to all Abraham's offspring—not only to those who are of the law but also to those who are of the faith of Abraham. He is the father of us all."

Second, Paul emphasizes in 1:17 that the righteousness of God revealed in the gospel comes by faith and by faith alone. Paul makes this point in two ways. First, he says that righteousness comes by faith "from first to last."[27] Second, in his Scripture proof from Habakkuk, he drops the pronoun in the prophet's phrase "the righteous will live by *his* faith" and focuses the reader's attention on faith: "The righteous," he says, "will live by faith."[28] Just as God reckoned Abraham righteous by faith apart from works generally (4:1–5; cf. 3:27; 9:32), and apart from the ethnic identity marker of circumcision specifically (4:9–17; cf. 3:22, 30; 10:11–13), so the saving righteousness of God comes to those who believe, apart from any activity or ethnic association. Eschatological life, therefore, comes by faith, and by faith alone.

The Gospel Stands in Continuity with Scripture

Paul's insistence that God's climactic act of righteousness works powerfully for the salvation not only of Jews but of Gentiles as well must have come as a rude shock to some Jews. Such a gospel, they may have responded, implies not the fulfillment of God's promises in Scripture but their failure.[29] They understood Psalm 97 (98):1–3, for example, to mean that God would display his saving righteousness on behalf of his people Israel in such a way that the Gentiles who had oppressed them would come to the bitter realization of their error. As one anonymous Jewish poet of the period puts it:

> [The Messiah] will judge peoples and nations in the wisdom of his righteousness. . . . And he will have gentile nations serving him under his yoke, and he will glorify the Lord in (a place) prominent (above) the whole earth. And he will purge Jerusalem (and make it) holy as it was even from the beginning, (for) nations to come from the ends of the earth to see his glory, to bring as gifts her children who had been driven out, and to see the glory of the Lord with which God has glorified her. (*Pss. Sol.* 17.29–31)[30]

---

27 *Ek pisteōs eis pistin* should go with *dikaiosynē* rather than *apocalyptetai*, and the phrase *ek pisteōs eis pistin* should also be understood as analogous to the phrases *ek thanatou eis thanaton* and *ek zōs eis zōn* in 2 Cor. 2:16. For this understanding of the phrase, see M. J. Lagrange, *Épitre aux Romains*, 3rd ed. (*EBib*; Paris: LeCoffre, 1922), 20. Cf. Schlatter, *Romans*, 24–25; Cranfield, *Romans*, 1:99–100; and Schreiner, *Romans*, 71–72.

28 Manuscripts of the LXX disagree on the phrase, some translating "his faith" with "my faith" and others shifting the pronoun to the word "righteous" to yield, "my righteous one will live by faith" (cf. Heb. 10:38). One manuscript has the phrase as it appears in Paul's text, but the scribe probably knew Rom. 1:17 and assimilated his copy to it. An ancient Greek scroll of the Minor Prophets (8HXIIgr 17.29–30) apparently translates the Hebrew exactly. Although the first part of *dikaios* and the last part of *zēsetai* are damaged, and part of *pisteōs* is unclear, the *autou* following *pisteōs* is perfectly readable.

29 Paul's concern about his safety among unbelieving Jews and the reception of his collection from believing Jews in Jerusalem (15:30–31) show that vigorous opposition to his gospel from Jewish quarters was not a theoretical issue (cf. Acts 21:20–22).

30 *OTP*, 2:667.

Paul understood the gravity of this objection and constructed his thesis sentence to show at the beginning of his letter that he could answer it. First, although he includes believing Gentiles among those who experience God's saving power, he states unambiguously that this power comes "to the Jew first." He means by this not only that Jews were entrusted with the Scriptures (3:2; cf. 2:17–20) and were historically the recipients of many special divine gifts (9:4–5), but that God will be faithful to his promises to them as a people (11:25–29). Although the gospel implies the equality of Jew and Gentile within the people of God, it does not at the same time imply that God's promises to the Jews are no longer valid.[31]

Second, Paul's concluding quotation of Habakkuk 2:4 shows that the faith-based and universal elements of the gospel are consistent with Scripture. The quotation does this on two levels. On one level it shows that the importance of faith is not an invention of Paul but has always been the critical characteristic of the people of God. Long ago the prophet Habakkuk affirmed this when he recorded God's answer to his complaint that God's ways appeared to be unjust. "The righteous person," God had responded, "will live by his faithfulness." It was not unreasonable to take this to mean that the person who trusted God to be reliable, despite present circumstances, and so remained faithful to the covenant, would live to see his or her faith in God confirmed.[32] Paul's quotation of Habakkuk 2:4, then, anticipates his discussion of Abraham's faith in 4:18–25.

On another, and less obvious, level Paul probably considered the character of Habakkuk's complaint to God to be significant. It matched precisely the character of the complaints that Paul's gospel provoked. Habakkuk had wondered how God could punish the sins of his people by bringing the evil Babylonian hordes against them: "Why are you silent while the wicked swallow up those more righteous than themselves?" (Hab. 1:13). In a similar way a Jew might ask of Paul, "How can God be just if, as your gospel implies, Gentiles benefit from God's climactic display of his saving righteousness while Jews who have heard the gospel remain largely unconvinced?" (cf. 3:1).[33] By quoting Habakkuk here Paul hints at the answer to this question, an answer that he will develop briefly in 3:1–8 and more fully in 9:1–11:36.[34] The Scriptures show that God displays his covenant faithfulness to his people (his righteousness) in unexpected ways, and that he sometimes uses the Gentiles to

31 Cf. Moo, *Romans*, 68–69.

32 Cf. Mária Eszenyei Széles, *Wrath and Mercy: A Commentary on the Books of Habakkuk and Zephaniah* (ITC; Grand Rapids: Eerdmans, 1987), 32–33, and O. Palmer Robertson, *The Books of Nahum, Habakkuk, and Zephaniah* (NICOT; Grand Rapids: Eerdmans, 1990), 176–81; Schreiner, *Romans*, 74–75. For Paul, faith was not merely intellectual assent but was inevitably accompanied by obedience (1:5; 16:26). Significantly, although 1QpHab 8.1–3 explains "the righteous person" of Hab. 2:4 as the one who does the law, it interprets the term *beʾemûnātô* not as the righteous person's obedient deeds but as his "patient suffering and . . . steadfast faith in the Teacher of Righteousness." See William H. Brownlee, *The Midrash Pesher of Habakkuk* (SBLMS 24; Missoula, Mont.: Scholars Press, 1979), 125. *Pace*, e.g., C. H. Dodd, *The Epistle to the Romans* (MNTC; London: Hodder & Stoughton, 1932), 14.

33 Cf. Rikki E. Watts, "'For I Am Not Ashamed of the Gospel': Romans 1:16–17 and Habakkuk 2:4" in *Romans and the People of God: Essays in Honor of Gordon D. Fee on the Occasion of His 65th Birthday*, ed. Sven K. Soderlund and N. T. Wright (Grand Rapids: Eerdmans, 1999), 3–25, here at 22–24.

34 Cf. ibid., 18: "On the reading of Habakkuk proposed here, Romans 9–11 falls into place, neither as postscript nor as center, but vital nevertheless." See also Robertson, *Nahum, Habakkuk, and Zephaniah*, 183.

prompt his people to repentance. That was true of the God revealed in the pages of Habakkuk's prophecy, and it is true of the God revealed in Paul's gospel.

Summary

Paul begins the body of Romans, then, with a concise statement of the gospel's three supporting pillars. First, the gospel reveals the saving, powerful righteousness of God. Second, God's righteousness becomes effective by faith alone and therefore is available to everyone, both Jew and Gentile. Third, this way of understanding God's righteousness is consistent with the Scriptures.

Paul will unpack these statements in 1:18–11:36. His argument there takes three critical turns. First, he shows why God's saving righteousness is necessary for the Jew as well as for the Gentile, and how both Gentile and Jew avail themselves of it by faith alone, apart from human effort or wearing the national badge of circumcision (1:18–4:25). Second, he describes the quality of life that characterizes those who have been justified by faith as they live in the overlap of "this age" (12:2) and the age of Israel's restoration (5:1–8:39). This assumption that an ethnically diverse group of believers, only a minority of whom are Jews, comprise the beginnings of Israel's restoration calls into question the consistency of his gospel with God's promises in Scripture to the Jews. So third, he shows that although more Gentiles than Jews are experiencing the fulfillment of God's promises to restore his people, his gospel does not mean that God's Word has failed (9:1–11:36). In this section, Paul will often advance his argument through the questioning voice of a skeptical Jewish debating partner.

In 12:1–15:13, Paul will show the practical, pastoral implications of this gospel for the Roman church. Jewish and Gentile Christians ought to accept one another because God has accepted them as both Jews and Gentiles (1:18–4:25), because his acceptance of them has implications for the way they live (5:1–8:39), and because his acceptance of both groups is consistent with the saving plan that he announced beforehand in the Scriptures (9:1–11:36). In this way the two groups, united with each other in Christ, will fulfill God's ultimate goal in the gospel: that both Jews and Gentiles should, with one heart and voice, glorify God the Father and the Lord Jesus Christ (15:6).

WRATH FOR ALL WHO SIN, RIGHTEOUSNESS FOR ALL WHO BELIEVE (1:18–4:25)

Jews and Gentiles Alike Are All under Sin (1:18–3:20)

In 1:18–3:20 Paul's goal is to show that the need for God's saving righteousness is universal. No one, whether Jew or Gentile, will survive the day of God's wrath without it, because on that day, apart from God's saving righteousness, Jew and Gentile alike will be found "under sin" (3:9) and "the whole world held accountable to God" (3:19). As his argument moves toward this goal, however, the Jews gradually emerge as Paul's primary target. He wants to show that although the Gentiles are wicked, Jews can claim no privilege over them on the "day of God's wrath" either because of their possession or their observance of the Mosaic law. Paul's argument toward this goal takes four steps.

Gentiles Deserve God's Wrath (1:18–32)

Paul begins by describing human sin in terms that his imaginary Jewish debating partner has reserved for Gentile sin. Sinful people, he says, have no defense before the wrath of God. They know enough from creation to worship God, but instead choose to worship the creation itself, going from bad to worse as they devote themselves to people, birds, four-footed beasts, and reptiles (1:18–23). God is therefore justified in handing them over already to his punishing wrath, which takes forms appropriate to the sins it punishes: idolatry leads to social disintegration, particularly in the form of sexual confusion, as God hands people over to the consequences of their sinful desires. Although they know that God has decreed death for those who commit such crimes, Paul concludes, they have not only committed them but approved of their commission (1:24–32).

The logic of Paul's argument in this passage closely follows the approach to Gentile sin in Wisdom 11–16.[35] There too Gentiles have no excuse because although they know about God from his creation, they worship the creation rather than God (Wisd. 13:7–10; 14: 11). There too idolatry leads to social ills: "For the idea of making idols was the beginning of fornication, and the invention of them was the corruption of life" (Wisd. 14:12).

The author of Wisdom believes that God punished the Egyptians at the time of the Exodus with plagues that befitted their irrational worship. Thus the very creatures that they worshiped rose up to afflict them, "so that they might learn that one is punished by the very things by which one sins" (Wisd. 11:15–16; cf. 12:23; 15:18–16:1).

The only untraditional element in Paul's description of Gentile sin is any explicit mention of Gentiles. Those whom he describes are simply "people who suppress the truth by wickedness" (1:18). He has therefore laid a trap for the Jew who believes that Jewishness alone—symbolized by the possession of the law and circumcision—will provide exemption from the outpouring of God's wrath on the final day. In 2:1–29 he springs the trap.

Jews Also Deserve God's Wrath (2:1–29)

Paul assumes that his skeptical Jewish debating partner will find his routine description of Gentile sin unexceptionable. In 2:1–29, he advances what, at least for some Jews, is a startling claim: They will fare no better in "the day of God's wrath" (2:5) than Gentiles "because you who pass judgment do the same things" (2:1).[36] Paul's argument unfolds in three stages.

---

35 Cf., among many others, Timo Laato, *Paul and Judaism: An Anthropological Approach* (SFSHJ 115; Atlanta: Scholars Press, 1995), 86–88, 94–95, and Hübner, *Biblische Theologie*, 2:267.

36 Cf. Thomas R. Schreiner, *Paul, Apostle of God's Glory in Christ* (Downers Grove, Ill.: InterVarsity Press, 2001), 105 n. 1, who notes the similar pattern in the argument of Amos 1:3–2:3 and 2 Sam. 12:1–14.

First, Paul states that the willingness to condemn sin in others is not a qualification for escaping judgment on oneself, for on the day of his wrath God will dispense his righteousness to both Jew and Greek alike "according to ... works" (2:6). Gentiles who have only a law written on their hearts he will justly punish for their violation of that law.[37] Jews likewise he will condemn for their violation of the Mosaic law, "for God does not show favoritism" (2:1–11; cf. 2 Chron. 19:7; Sir. 35:12).

Second, Paul says that possession of the law, knowledge of its contents, and a willingness to teach it to others provides no protection against God's wrath for the Jew who fails to keep the law. Being able to teach others not to steal or commit idolatry will count for nothing on the final day, if those who teach these precepts violate the very commandments they teach. As the biblical story of their nation reveals, Jews have broken the law and been exiled as punishment, and "God's name is blasphemed among the Gentiles because of [them]" (2:17–24; cf. Isa. 52:4–5; Ezek. 36:19–20).

Third, Paul argues that circumcision provides no protection against God's wrath on the final day for those who fail to keep the law. An uncircumcised man who keeps the law, he says, can properly sit in judgment on those who possess both "the written code and circumcision" but transgress the law. Echoing the argument of Philippians 3:2–3 and 2 Corinthians 3:3–11, and anticipating Romans 7:6 and 8:1–8, Paul says that the real Jew is one who is circumcised in heart by the eschatologically given Spirit of God, not merely physically in accord with the requirement of the Mosaic law.

Paul has designed the argument from 1:18 to 2:29 to charge the Jew with sin and to deny that (1) the ability to judge Gentiles, (2) the possession and knowledge of the law, or (3) the observance of physical circumcision will exempt the Jew from condemnation on the final day. Jewish sin is as grave in God's sight as Gentile sin, and identity with the Jewish people will give no one an advantage on "the day of wrath, when his righteous judgment will be revealed" (2:5).

Is God Therefore Unfaithful? (3:1–8)

The picture of an uncircumcised Gentile condemning a circumcised Jew in God's eschatological court raises two potentially fatal objections to Paul's gospel as he has explained it so far. First, if Jews are condemned alongside Gentiles, then what becomes of God's promises through the prophets to restore the fortunes of his people?[38] Second, how can God condemn unfaithful people whom he has only used to make his own righteous character ("the righteousness of God," 3:5) shine more

37 Paul does not intend his statements that God will judge everyone impartially according to their works in 2:6–10, 13 to be understood apart from the entire sweep of his argument in 1:18–3:20, as Paul's own statement of his purpose in 3:9 demonstrates. In 2:6–16 Paul makes the hypothetical assumption that some Gentiles will be justified by their works in order to demonstrate God's impartiality. This interpretation is not uncontroversial. For full accounts of the various interpretive options see Thomas Schreiner, "Did Paul Believe in Justification by Works? Another Look at Romans 2," *BBR* 3 (1993): 131–58, here at 131–39, and Richard N. Longenecker, "The Focus of Romans: The Central Role of 5:1–8:39 in the Argument of the Letter" in *Romans and the People of God: Essays in Honor of Gordon D. Fee on the Occasion of His 65th Birthday*, ed. Sven K. Soderlund and N. T. Wright (Grand Rapids: Eerdmans, 1999), 49–69, here at 52–55.

38 Schreiner, *Romans*, 148, correctly interprets the term "advantage" (*ōpheleia*) in 3:1 to mean "saving advantage," as it does in 2:25. The question in 3:1, therefore, refers to Israel's eschatological salvation as promised in such passages as Jer. 31:31–34 and Ezek. 36:22–32.

brightly? Such an arrangement implies that the condemned are not responsible for their unfaithfulness but are only fulfilling their God-assigned role![39] Paul will answer these objections in Romans 9:1–11:36. Here, perhaps in order not to lose his Jewish audience after the first step of his argument, he simply registers his knowledge of these objections, denies their validity, and presses forward.

The Whole World Held Accountable to God (3:9–20)

The final step in Paul's argument that all—even Jews—stand condemned before God is a restatement of its major thesis in a way that shows its continuity with Scripture. Referring to the case he has made in 1:18–2:29, Paul says that he has charged everyone, Jews and Gentiles alike, with being "under sin" (3:9). He then cites a solemn litany of biblical passages that demonstrate the comprehensiveness and the gravity of human transgression (3:10–18). He concludes his case with a succinct, two-sentence statement of its primary points. First, calling the Scriptures that he has just cited "the law," he reminds his Jewish hearers that as possessors of the law, they fall under its claim that everyone without exception is liable to God's judgment. Possession of the law, in other words, so far from exempting the Jew from judgment, means certain condemnation (3:19; cf. 2:17–20). Second, because no one has succeeded in keeping the law, no one can be acquitted in God's tribunal by appeal to performance of "the works of the law" (3:20).[40]

The Saving Righteousness of God for All Who Believe (3:21–4:25)

Paul next explains how the saving righteousness of God, displayed in the atoning death of Christ Jesus, answers the plight that human sin created on one hand and maintains God's righteous character on the other (3:21–26). He then concludes from the gracious nature of God's saving righteousness that it excludes boasting in either the performance or the possession of the law (3:27–4:25).

The Righteousness of God and the Sacrifice of Christ (3:21–26)

Paul explains that God has put his saving righteousness into effect for his sinful people and has, at the same time, preserved his character as a righteous judge of the world (cf. 3:4b, 6b). He has done this through the cross of Jesus Christ. Just as in the Exodus God freely and graciously redeemed his people from slavery in Egypt, so now in the great second exodus anticipated by the prophets, he has graciously redeemed his people from their sins (3:24).[41] He has done this, says Paul, through Christ Jesus, "whom God presented as an atoning sacrifice in his blood, a sacrifice appropriated through faith" (3:25, aut.).

Here Paul shifts from the Bible's exodus imagery to its sacrificial imagery. The LXX uses the term "presented" (*protithēmi*) to refer to the presentation of offerings in the sanctuary, especially to the bread regularly "displayed" before the Lord there (Ex.

39 Thus 3:5–8 anticipates the objection of 9:14 that God is unjust in condemning those who had no choice in whether they would belong to God's people. See Schreiner, *Romans*, 151–59.

40 The judicial character of the verb *dikaioō* in 3:20 is evident from the legal terminology that surrounds it. In 3:19 the picture of mouths that cease to speak in their own defense and the use of the judicial term *hypodikos* show this. In 3:20 no one is justified "before him," just as a guilty defendant stands "before" a judge.

41 Cf. Schreiner, *Paul*, 230.

29:23; 40:23; Lev. 24:8; cf. 2 Macc. 1:8, 15).[42] The LXX also uses the term translated as "atoning sacrifice" (*hilastērion*) to refer to the cover on the ark of the covenant, the place where, on the Day of Atonement, Aaron sprinkled the blood of a bull and the blood of a goat to atone (*exilasasthai*) for the sins of the priests and the sins of the people (Lev. 16:2, 13–15).[43] Since, as in the LXX, Paul couples the term with a reference to blood, all within an explanation of God's remedy for human transgression, he is probably saying that Christ's death was the climactic and final Day of Atonement sacrifice. It was the means by which God atoned for the sins "committed beforehand," but that he had passed over, not punishing as they deserved (3:25).[44]

In the death of Christ, God's saving righteousness (1:16; 3:21) and his righteous character (3:25–26) come together.[45] He is able to remain a "just" judge who punishes sin at the same time that he "justifies," or acquits, those who deserve his punishing wrath (3:26).

Two Conclusions (3:27–4:25)

Paul draws two conclusions from this climactic event. First, its entirely gracious character (3:24) excludes boasting. Paul's argument in 1:18–3:20 targeted Jews who boasted in the possession of the law (2:17, 23) and in their assumption that they were more righteous than Gentiles (3:9–20). Now Paul says that the law with its prescription of certain works lacked the grace to exclude either kind of boast. "The law of faith" (3:27), however, eliminates both. What is the law of faith? It is probably God's climactic work of atonement "by faith in [Christ's] blood," which Paul has just described in 3:25.[46] The graciousness of this event, which Paul stressed in 3:24, makes boasting in either the possession or the doing of the Mosaic law impossible.

This was even true, Paul goes on to say, for Abraham. Some Jews of Paul's time considered Abraham to be "perfect in all his dealings with the Lord," and so "righteous" that he had no need of repentance (*Jub.* 23:10; *Pr. Man.* 8; cf. Sir. 44:19–21). If ever anyone lived who could be justified on the basis of works and therefore boast of works before God, Paul says, it was Abraham (Rom. 4:2a). But Abraham could not be justified on this basis and so had no grounds for boasting (4:2b). If considered from the perspective of his works, even he must be numbered among the ungodly (4:5; cf. 1:18). With respect to Abraham's relationship with God, his only hope was to be reckoned righteous on the basis of his faith, and, according to Genesis 15:6, this is precisely what happened (4:3).

---

42 Stuhlmacher, *Reconciliation, Law, and Righteousness*, 94–109, here at 102; Hultgren, *Paul's Gospel and Mission*, 56 and 76–77 n. 79. The term may also recall the public display of blood at the covenant ratification ceremony in Ex. 24:5–8. See James D. G. Dunn, *Romans 1–8* (WBC; Dallas: Word, 1988), 170. Lexically, the verb can also mean "foreordained," but, *pace* Cranfield, *Romans*, 1:208–10, ample reasons for the meaning "presented" in this passage appear in Christian Maurer, "προτίθημι (κτλ)," *TDNT*, 8:165–67.

43 Stuhlmacher, *Reconciliation, Law, and Righteousness*, 96–103; Hultgren, *Paul's Gospel and Mission*, 58–60.

44 Cranfield, *Romans*, 1:212. With this statement, Paul implies that the Day of Atonement sacrifices only atoned for sin because they anticipated Christ's sacrifice. Since Christ's sacrifice has now (*en tō nyn kairō*) taken place, the need for the Day of Atonement sacrifices no longer exists. See Schreiner, *Romans*, 195.

45 Schreiner, *Romans*, 176, 180–81, 195–99.

46 Cf. Moo, *Romans*, 249–50. Because sacrificial blood was used in the ratification of the Mosaic covenant (Ex. 24:1–11), Paul may have viewed Christ's sacrificial blood not only as a Day of Atonement sacrifice, but as the ratification of the new covenant as well. On this see Frank Thielman, *Paul and the Law: A Contextual Approach* (Downers Grove, Ill.: InterVarsity Press, 1994), 181.

This means that acquittal in God's court takes place not according to what one earns but as God's freely given gift (4:4–6; cf. 3:24). Paul has mixed the metaphors of the law court and the workplace, but his meaning is clear: Even the most pious person escapes God's just punishment only because of the freely given gift of Jesus' climactic sacrifice, not because of earning the right to acquittal by efforts at obedience.[47]

Abraham appropriated this free gift by having faith that God would keep his promise to make him the father of many nations, despite all appearances to the contrary (4:3, 5, 17b–22). After the death and resurrection of Jesus, God reckons Christians righteous before God through a faith of the same quality but with a different content. In the face of heckles from those who consider it folly, they believe that through the death and resurrection of Jesus, God has provided the ultimate means of atonement for transgression and has restored his people to a right relationship with himself (4:23–25; cf. 1 Cor. 1:18; 15:12, 35).

The second result of Christ's climactic sacrifice of atonement is that Gentiles as well as Jews can now belong to the people of God (Rom. 3:29–30). This is only what the student of Scripture would expect, Paul argues, for the Shema itself (Deut. 6:4) says that God is one, and this means that only one God, the God of Abraham, has rightful claim to all peoples of the earth—Jews as well as Gentiles (3:29–30). The faith of Abraham also demonstrates this point, for it was not only qualitatively similar to Christian faith because it flew in the face of common sense, but because it did not involve conformity to the ethnically specific Mosaic law.[48] Since God justified Abraham because of his faith rather than because of his conformity to the Mosaic law, Abraham's faith foreshadowed the inclusion of Gentiles into the people of God by faith apart from any requirement to keep the Mosaic law (4:9–12).

The inclusion of Gentiles into the people of God by faith rather than by conformity to the Mosaic law, moreover, supplies the fulfillment of the very promises that Abraham believed God would fulfill. If Gentiles were forced to accept the Mosaic law in order to belong to God's people, his promise to bless all the nations of the earth through him would remain unfulfilled. The Gentiles would then effectively be Jewish proselytes and would simply come under the curse that the law justly pronounced on all Israel for its disobedience to the covenant (4:13–15).[49] The promise to Abraham would remain unfulfilled, and the Gentiles, like the Jews, would only experience God's wrath. By exercising faith in the gospel apart from the Mosaic law, however, the influx of Gentiles into the people of God neatly vindicates Abraham's own faith: Abraham believed that God would make him the father of many nations; Gentiles who believe the gospel are those "nations."[50]

---

47 This stands in direct contrast to the soteriology of 4Q399, "And it will be reckoned for you as righteousness when you perform what is right and good before Him, for your own good and for that of Israel." This translation is from Geza Vermes, *The Complete Dead Sea Scrolls in English* (New York: Penguin, 1997), 228.

48 On Paul's frequent use of the term "law" (*nomos*) with specifically ethnic connotations, see esp. Michael Winger, *By What Law? The Meaning of* νόμος *in the Letters of Paul* (SBLDS 128; Atlanta: Scholars Press, 1992).

49 Thielman, *Paul and the Law*, 186; idem, *The Law and the New Testament: The Question of Continuity* (New York: Crossroad, 1999), 24.

50 The English words "Gentile" and "nation" represent the single Greek term *ethnos*.

So in 3:21–4:25 Paul has started to explain the leading notions of his thesis statement in 1:16–17. He argues that the gospel reveals God's powerful, saving righteousness, that this saving power is not limited to Jews but is for Gentiles also, that God's saving righteousness comes to those who have faith that God will, despite appearances, be faithful to his promises, and that all of this is not merely compatible with the Scriptures but fulfills them. Jesus' sacrifice is the climactic and final Day of Atonement sacrifice, the means by which a just God could leave previously committed sins unpunished and could acquit both Jews and Gentiles on the final day.

The faith that Gentiles exercise in that God uses this means of atonement to reckon them righteous is not only qualitatively similar to the faith Abraham exercised and by which he was reckoned righteous with God. It was the very means through which God showed that Abraham's faith was not misplaced, for these believing Gentiles fulfill God's promise to make Abraham the father of many nations. Paul must still describe the eschatological "life" of those who are justified by faith (5:1–8:39) and demonstrate where the biblical promises to Israel fit into his gospel (9:1–11:36), but by the end of chapter 4, the foundation of his gospel is in place.

Boasting Excluded in Rome

It is worth pausing at this point in our discussion of Paul's argument to ask what Paul's argument in 1:18–4:25 has to do with the exercise of his ministry to the Gentiles in Rome. Paul has assumed so far that he is addressing skeptical Jews, but he has done this in a letter to a mostly Gentile church. Why? Is he giving the Roman Christians a sample of the gospel that he preaches so that they might support his Gentile mission?[51] Does he use this letter as a means of reflecting on the theology that he has hammered out in the battles of the past?[52] Did he strike such a radical position on the law and the Jewish people in Galatians that he is now, prior to meeting with Christians in Jerusalem, trying to soften that position?[53]

It is more likely that Paul believes the gospel as he is explaining it has profound implications for the unity of Jewish and Gentile Christians in Rome. If some Gentiles are looking down on Jews who are scrupulous about their diet and observance of the Sabbath, and some Jews are condemning those who fail to observe the Mosaic law in these matters (14:3), then both need the reminder that the gospel excludes boasting (2:17, 23; 3:27; 4:2). Both also need to be reminded that everyone will stand before God's judgment seat to give his or her own account before God (2:5–16; 14:4, 10–12), and in that day only God himself, not anyone's scrupulosity or lack thereof, will enable him or her to stand acquitted (14:4).[54] The argument of

51 F. F. Bruce, "The Romans Debate—Continued," in *The Romans Debate*, ed. Karl P. Donfried, rev. and exp. (Peabody, Mass.: Hendrickson, 1991), 175–94, here at 193–94.

52 T. W. Manson, "St. Paul's Letter to the Romans—And Others," and Günther Bornkamm, "The Letter to the Romans as Paul's Last Will and Testament," in *The Romans Debate*, ed. Karl P. Donfried, rev. and exp. (Peabody, Mass.: Hendrickson, 1991), 3–15, 16–28, here at 15, 25–28.

53 Jacob Jervell, "The Letter to Jerusalem," in *The Romans Debate*, ed. Karl P. Donfried, rev. and exp. (Peabody, Mass.: Hendrickson, 1991), 53–64, here at 59–60. Cf. Hübner, *Biblische Theologie*, 1:232–39.

54 Cf. Luke Timothy Johnson, *Reading Romans: A Literary and Theological Commentary* (New York: Crossroad, 1997), 200.

1:18–4:25, therefore, lays the theological groundwork for the exercise of Paul's "priestly duty of proclaiming the gospel of God" in Rome. He will begin to exercise that office explicitly in 11:13–32 and 14:1–15:13, and he will continue this work when he arrives in Rome.

THE LIFE OF THOSE WHO HAVE BEEN JUSTIFIED BY FAITH (5:1–8:39)

In 5:1–8:39 Paul's argument takes a critical turn. He now surveys the character of the life to which the person justified by faith has gained access. His description of Abraham's faith in 4:17b–22 has prepared the way for this section by defining Abraham's faith as a trust in God's willingness and ability to fulfill his promises despite all appearances to the contrary. Paul makes the link between the quality of Abraham's faith and the quality of Christian faith in 4:23–25:

> The words "it was credited to him" were written not for him alone, but also for us, to whom God will credit righteousness—for us who believe in him who raised Jesus our Lord from the dead. He was delivered over to death for our sins and was raised to life for our justification.

Paul will now, in 5:1–8:39, give a description of the Christian whose acquittal at God's tribunal on the final day is so assured that it can be spoken of in the past tense (5:1), but who must live in a world that continues to be riddled with suffering itself and inflicts suffering on God's people. These chapters are dominated by the tension that prevails in the life of the person who "will be saved from God's wrath" (5:9) and whose eschatological life has been inaugurated, but who still experiences the death throws of the era of sin and condemnation.

Paul focuses on two characteristics of the believer in this difficult existence: hope and obedience. He opens and closes the section with a discussion of the believers' hope (5:1–21; 8:18–39).[55] Sandwiched between the two parts of this discussion stands a treatment of the believer's freedom from the power of sin, especially in its entanglement with the law of Moses, and of the believer's Spirit-given ability to obey the law (6:1–8:17).

The Believer's Hope (5:1–21 and 8:18–39)

In both 5:1–21 and 8:18–39, Paul describes believers as those who, in the midst of their suffering, hope for the fulfillment of God's eschatological promises.

The Character of Hope

Paul links hope closely with faith in his description of Abraham's willingness to believe that God would be faithful to his promises despite appearances to the contrary:

55 On the importance of hope in this section, see esp. Schreiner, *Romans*, 246–49. On the structure of Romans 5–8, see Dahl, *Studies in Paul*, 81–85, and Frank Thielman, "The Story of Israel and the Theology of Romans 5–8," in *Pauline Theology, Volume III: Romans*, ed. David M. Hay and E. Elizabeth Johnson (Minneapolis: Fortress, 1995), 169–95, here at 169–72.

"Against all hope, Abraham in hope believed [*pisteuō*] and so became the father of many nations" (4:18). He also links hope with faith in the letter's concluding prayer wish: "May the God of hope fill you with all joy and peace as you believe [*pisteuō*] so that you may overflow with hope by the power of the Holy Spirit" (15:13, aut.).[56] Like faith, hope is a trust in God despite appearances to the contrary, for "hope that is seen is no hope at all" (8:24; cf. 4:19; 1 Cor. 13:12; 2 Cor. 5:7).[57] But hope and faith are not identical.[58] The term "hope" places special emphasis on the perseverance of one's trust in God in the midst of continuing hardship. The believer is able to boast in suffering, because suffering provides the opportunity for perseverance, continued perseverance instills mettle in the believer, and mettle in turn produces hope (5:4; cf. 8:25). This steady hope in the face of sustained suffering defines the believer's existence between the initial exercise of faith and faith's vindication on the final day.

The Content of Hope

For what do believers hope? They hope for "the glory of God" (5:2). In 8:18–30 Paul explains what this means. He has just said in 8:14 that those whom the Spirit of God leads do not live according to the flesh (8:12) and are therefore sons of God. In 8:18–30 he describes hope as the eager expectation of the time when God will reveal the believer's status as his adopted child (8:19, 23; cf. 8:15). This means that believers share Jesus' status as Son of God presently, but will share it more fully in the future (1:3–4; 8:3, 29; cf. Gal. 4:4–7). This is "the glory that will be revealed in us" (8:18; cf. 5:2). Linked with this full revelation of the believer's status as God's child is the hope that God will liberate all creation from the futility (*mataiotēs*, 8:20) and corruption (*phthora*, 8:21) to which Adam subjected it at the Fall (cf. 1:18–32).[59] On the final day, creation itself will participate in "the glorious freedom of the children of God" (8:21).

In all of this Paul relies on traditional Jewish expectations of God's eschatological restoration of Israel. Three traditional themes are particularly important for understanding the theological significance of his argument.

First, Paul's notion that believers await the manifestation of their status as God's adopted sons uses imagery from two biblical texts: Exodus 4:22–23, which regards Israel's redemption from Egypt as a mark of its status as God's son, and Hosea 11:1–11, which describes Israel as the son whom God called out of Egypt and who subsequently rebelled. According to Hosea, this rebellion brought God's punishment, but one day the Lord will roar like a lion and "'his children will come trembling like birds from Egypt, like doves from Assyria. I will settle them in their homes,' declares the LORD" (Hos. 11:11). Paul's claim that Christians are adopted children of God who will experience their sonship more fully on the final day implies that they constitute the fulfillment of these expectations.

---

56 Rudolf Bultmann, "ἐλπίς (κτλ)," *TDNT*, 2:529–35, here at 531–32.

57 Cf. Stuhlmacher, *Romans*, 135.

58 Contra Rudolf Bultmann, *Theology of the New Testament*, 2 vols. (New York: Scribners, 1951–55), 1:319–20.

59 Cf. Paul's use of *mataioō* and *phthartos* in 1:21 and 23 and the discussion in Dunn, *Romans 1–8*, 470.

Second, Paul ties the sonship of Christians to the sonship of Christ himself, and therefore to the traditional expectation that God will one day fulfill his promise to David that his "house and kingdom" will "endure forever" (2 Sam. 7:14). Christ, as David's descendant, fulfills this promise in Paul's view (Rom. 1:2–3), and because of the presence of the eschatologically given Spirit of God within them, Christians share this sonship (8:14), for the Spirit enables them to call out to God "*Abba*, Father," just as Jesus did. They are heirs with Christ (8:17) and brothers of Christ who are destined to share the eschatological glory of Christ in the final day (8:29–30; cf. 1 Cor. 15:43, 49; 2 Cor. 4:17; Phil. 3:21).[60] Together, therefore, they and he fulfill the promise that David's house will endure forever.

Third, Paul understands the believer's hope as directed toward the restoration of all creation to its pristine condition prior to Adam's primal sin. This idea seems to stand behind Isaiah 65:17–25, where the references to the enjoyment of one's crops in peace, of not laboring in vain, and of not bearing children for disaster (65:21–23; cf. 66:22) echo God's curse on Adam and Eve for their sin (Gen. 3:16–19; 5:29). It may also stand in the background of the many references in Jewish literature of the Second Temple period to a restoration of the earth to its condition prior to Adam's sin in the eschatological era.[61] Believers hope for the time when this expectation will be fulfilled and "the creation itself will be liberated from its bondage to decay and brought into the glorious freedom of the children of God" (8:21).

The Basis of Hope

In 5:1–21 and 8:31–39 Paul speaks of three foundations for the believer's hope: the death of Christ, Christ's resurrection, and the gift of the Spirit.

First, Paul emphasizes the costliness, the undeserved nature, and the overpowering effectiveness of Christ's death as a foundation for the believer's hope. Christ's death took place at God's initiative, at great cost to God himself (8:32), and for those who had done nothing to deserve it (5:6–8). It was effective in winning acquittal for them in God's future tribunal (5:1, 9; 8:33–34a; cf. 8:1) and in reconciling them to God (5:1, 10). Moreover, it reversed the effects of Adam's disobedience (5:12–19) and the intensification of those effects in the disobedience of Israel (5:20–21).[62] This reversal came as God's free gift, and the extent of its graciousness far outpaced the effects of Adam's transgression (5:12b–18a).

Second, Paul also grounds the believer's hope in Christ's life (5:10). Because he not only died but was raised from the dead, he is at God's right hand, where he intercedes with God for us in the present (8:34). As believers suffer the final effects of Adam's disobedience and Israel's disobedience, they groan with all the fallen creation

60 James M. Scott, *Adoption as Sons of God: An Exegetical Investigation into the Background of ΥΙΟΘΕΣΙΑ in the Pauline Corpus* (WUNT 2.48; Tübingen: J.C.B. Mohr [Paul Siebeck], 1992), 244–65, and Stuhlmacher, *Romans*, 129, 136–37.

61 See, e.g., 1QS 4.23; CD 3.20; 4Q171 3.2; 1QH 4.15; *Jub.* 1:29; 4:26; *1 En.* 45:4–5; *2 Bar.* 32:6; Rev. 21:1. These links with Jewish tradition make it difficult to agree with Longenecker, "The Focus of Romans," 67, that whereas in 1:16–4:25 Paul appeals to the traditional Jewish interests of his audience, in 5:1–8:39 he summarizes the gospel as he preached it to "purely Gentile audiences."

62 The *dia touto* ("because of this," aut.) at the beginning of 5:12 probably introduces supporting evidence for the hope that Paul has just described in 5:1–11. See Otto Kuss, *Der Römerbrief*, 3 pts. (Regensburg: Verlag Friedrich Pustet, 1957–78), 1:226; Moo, *Romans*, 317; and Schreiner, *Romans*, 271.

and eagerly await their final bodily redemption (8:22–23, 35–36); but, at the same time, the risen Jesus pleads with God on their behalf (8:34). This too assures believers that God will not disappoint the hope they have placed in him.

Finally, in a similar vein, God's lavish gift of the Spirit assures believers that despite the suffering they must endure in the present, God will not disappoint their hope for future redemption (5:4–5).[63] God's gift of the Spirit in the midst of suffering is a sign of his love (5:5) and a "firstfruit," or assurance, of the complete harvest of redemption that is to come (8:23).[64] The Spirit, moreover, intercedes for believers with God and aids them in praying during the period of "weakness" that they suffer prior to the fulfillment of their hopes.[65]

In summary, the believer's hope is a steadfast trust in the faithfulness of God, despite appearances to the contrary. It is a hope that God will complete the restoration of his people that he promised in the prophets and that he has inaugurated in Jesus' life and death. It is a hope grounded on the display of God's love on the cross of his own Son, on the resurrection of his Son from the dead, and on the presence of God's eschatologically given Spirit.

The Believer's Conduct (6:1–8:17)

Before the fulfillment of the period of restoration, obedience as well as hope should characterize the believer's life. The core of 5:1–8:39, therefore, claims that Christian conduct should be consistent with the great eschatological shift that has taken place in the death of Christ.[66] Just as Adam and Christ presided over two different eras—one tragically dominated by Adam's transgression and by the increase of transgression under the Mosaic law, and the other dominated by Christ's righteous act (5:12–21)—so in the present Christians must shift their loyalty from the realm of sin, which uses the law of Moses for its own ends, to the realm of righteousness and of Spirit-led obedience to the law of God (6:1–8:17).

We can divide this central section of 5:1–8:39 into two parts. In 6:1–23 Paul focuses on the shift of the believer from the realm of sin (6:1–14) to the realm of righteousness (6:15–23). In 7:1–8:17 he focuses on the believer's transfer out of the realm of sin's entanglement with the law of Moses (7:1–25) to the realm of Spirit-led submission to the law of God (8:1–17).[67]

Dead to Sin (6:1–14) and Enslaved to Righteousness (6:15–23)

Paul first claims that believers have died to sin with Christ at his crucifixion (6:2, 6, 8, 11) and have been buried with him in their baptism (6:3–5). Although debate over precisely how Paul thinks the believer is related to Christ's death has been intense, the most reasonable explanation seems to be that the believer died to sin "with" (6:8)

63 Cf. Gordon D. Fee, *God's Empowering Presence: The Holy Spirit in the Letters of Paul* (Peabody, Mass.: Hendrickson, 1994), 494.

64 For this understanding of *aparchē*, see Fitzmyer, *Romans*, 510; Fee, *God's Empowering Presence*, 573.

65 Fee, *God's Empowering Presence*, 578–79.

66 Moo, *Romans*, 351.

67 From the perspective of the structure of Paul's argument, this part of the letter answers more fully the question of Paul's skeptical Jewish interlocutor in 3:8 ("Why not say . . . , 'Let us do evil that good may result'?"). Paul signals this link by repeating the substance of the question of 3:8 in 6:1 ("Shall we go on sinning so that grace may increase?").

or "in" (6:11) Christ in the sense that Christ atoned for the sins of the believer on the cross.[68] This is probably why Paul says that death "justified" the believer "from sin" (6:7). From the perspective of God's punishing righteousness (3:4–5), the believer has died with Christ on the cross, or, as Paul says in 2 Corinthians 5:14, "one died for all and therefore all died."[69] When Christ died, therefore, he died in the place of those who believe in him (cf. Rom. 3:25; 2 Cor. 5:21; cf. Lev. 16:20–22).

This transaction takes place when an unbeliever becomes a believer (an event that Paul describes concisely in 6:4 as baptism) and ushers those who experience it out of sin's power and into the power of righteousness. Paul uses political metaphors to describe this transfer of loyalty. Believers should not let sin "reign" (*basileuō*) in their bodies. They should not present their faculties as "weapons" (*hopla*) to sin but as "weapons of righteousness to God" (aut.). Sin will not "exercise lordship" (aut.) over them (6:12–14). In short, they have moved out of sin's realm into the realm of righteousness, and they should act as loyal citizens and soldiers of the new realm in which they live.

Paul then expands the metaphor of enslavement that he had used in 6:6 ("we should no longer be slaves to sin") to describe the believer's change from the realm of sin to the realm of righteousness in language that recalls biblical descriptions of Israel's future restoration. "You have been set free from sin," he says, "and have become slaves [*douleuō*] to righteousness" (6:18). This language is reminiscent of the biblical claim that Israel's violation of God's law led them into enslavement (LXX, *douleia*) by foreign powers (Ezra 9:8–9; cf. Neh. 9:36, LXX, *esmen sēmeron douloi*), fulfilling the Deuteronomic threat that if Israel violated the covenant, God would reverse the Exodus:

> The LORD will send you back in ships to Egypt on a journey I said you should never make again. There you will offer yourselves for sale to your enemies as male and female slaves but no one will buy you. (Deut. 28:68)[70]

The prophets envisioned a new and greater exodus, however, by which God would restore the fortunes of his people (Isa. 4:5–6; 11:16; 49:9–11; Jer. 23:7–8).[71] Paul may be echoing this biblical imagery here as a way of saying that Christians represent the fulfillment of the prophecies that God would restore his people.

This becomes likely when we consider the similarity between Ezekiel's vision of Israel's restoration and Paul's description of believers here. Paul says that believers are obedient "from the heart" to the body of Christian teaching handed down to them (6:17). He says further that they are no longer slaves to "impurity" (*akatharsia*) and

68 Cranfield, *Romans*, 1:299–300, recognizes four senses in which the believer dies to sin and with Christ, of which this is the first. The context seems to support this sense more clearly than the other senses that Cranfield mentions—Paul has just recalled the judicial significance of Christ's death (5:1–2, 6–9). See also Cranfield's *On Romans* (Edinburgh: T. & T. Clark, 1998), 23–31.

69 Cf. Cranfield, *Romans*, 1:299; idem, *On Romans*, 24.

70 Cf. Josephus, *A. J.* 4.190 where Moses predicts that God's people will be disobedient to God and, in punishment, he will cause them to "fill every land and sea with your servitude [*douleia*]."

71 See the discussion of this theme in Joseph Klausner, *The Messianic Idea in Israel from Its Beginning to the Completion of the Mishnah* (London: George Allen & Unwin, 1956), 63, 74, 97–98, 122–23, 159.

"ever-increasing wickedness" (*anomia eis tēn anomian*) but that they instead place their faculties in the service of "righteousness" for the purpose of "holiness" (6:19). In Ezekiel, God gives this account of Israel's restoration:

> "For I will take you out of the nations; I will gather you from all the countries and bring you back into your own land. I will sprinkle clean water on you, and you will be clean; I will cleanse you from all your impurities [LXX, *akatharsia*] and from all your idols. I will give you a new heart and put a new spirit in you; I will remove from you your heart of stone and give you a heart of flesh. And I will put my Spirit in you and move you to follow my decrees and be careful to keep my laws.... I will save you from all your uncleanness [LXX, *akatharsia*]." (Ezek. 36:24–29, modified)

Paul assumes in Romans 6:15–23, therefore, that believers have entered the eschatological era of which the prophets spoke. They are the restored people of God and should live in a way that is consistent with the new era that they occupy.[72]

Free from the Law's Entanglement with Sin (7:1–8:17)

This restoration was necessary because Adam had violated a specific commandment of God and plunged all humanity into sin (5:12–19), a situation that only became worse when the Mosaic law appeared in Israel with its many commands and many opportunities for rebellion against God (5:20–21; cf. 3:20; 4:15; 6:14–15). Paul will now describe more fully the role of the Mosaic law in the plight from which God has rescued his people, and he will do this in a way that exonerates the law from blame (7:1–25). He will then argue that by the power of the Spirit the believer fulfills the law (8:1–17). The law that the believer fulfills by the Spirit's power, however, is not the Mosaic law but a new law that accompanies the new covenant and that both Jews and Gentiles fulfill.

In 7:1–6 Paul states clearly what he had already implied in 6:14–15: When believers died to sin at their baptism (6:2–3), they also died to the Mosaic law, and the crucifixion of Christ made this possible (7:4; cf. 6:6). The death of Christ, he argues, has introduced a historical shift in God's saving purposes. The era dominated by the "letter" of the Mosaic law has ended. That era was a period of ever-increasing disobedience to the Mosaic law followed by God's punishing wrath, as Israel's Scriptures reveal. The era of Israel's restoration has replaced the era of disobedience and wrath, and the dwelling of God's Spirit among his people is the sure sign that this long-expected eschatological shift has happened (7:6).[73] The rest of Paul's argument

72 See also Thielman, "Story of Israel," 185–90, and N. T. Wright, "New Exodus, New Inheritance: The Narrative Substructure of Romans 3–8" in *Romans and the People of God: Essays in Honor of Gordon D. Fee on the Occasion of His 65th Birthday*, ed. Sven K. Soderlund and N. T. Wright (Grand Rapids: Eerdmans, 1999), 26–35, here at 28–29, 33.

73 The contrast between the "letter" and the "Spirit" in 7:6, therefore, is not between two ways of keeping the law (legalistic and non-legalistic), nor between two hermeneutical approaches to the law (literal and "spiritual"), but between two eras in salvation history: the era dominated by the law's entanglement with sin and its condemnation of sinners, and the era dominated by Spirit-filled fulfillment of the law's "just requirement" (8:3–4). See, e.g., Ulrich Wilckens, *Der Brief an die Römer (Röm 6–11)* (EKK 6.2; Zurich: Benziger/Neukirchen-Vluyn: Neukirchener, 1980), 69–72; Stephen Westerholm, *Israel's Law and the Church's Faith: Paul and His Recent Interpreters* (Grand Rapids: Eerdmans, 1988), 209–13; Stuhlmacher, *Romans*, 102–4; and Schreiner, *Romans*, 142–44, 353.

explains the contrast between the era of the letter (7:7–25) and the era of the Spirit (8:1–17).[74]

In 7:7–25 Paul explains why the period dominated by the Mosaic law was a time of ever-increasing sin among God's people (7:5, 7–25). The fault lay not with the law but with sin, which used the law to deceive the individual into rebellion against God's command. When God said, "Do not covet" in the Mosaic law (Ex. 20:17; Deut. 5:21), sin used the commandment to create all kinds of covetousness in the individual. The commandment itself was not sinful, therefore, but was the tool sin used to deceive the individual (7:7–12). Sin was able to do this because of the weakness of the individual's flesh. Thus, even when the individual agreed with the law that its commandments were good, sin so enslaved the flesh that the individual was still utterly unable to obey the law (7:13–25).[75]

Paul puts 7:7–25 in the first person, which has led many interpreters to believe that his focus is entirely anthropological.[76] According to this understanding of the passage, Paul is saying something about the dominion of sin over the individual and the individual's subsequent inability to fulfill God's demands. Using himself as an example, Paul says that when he became conscious of God's command, instead of obeying it, he enthusiastically disobeyed it (7:7–12), and that even when he delighted in God's law, he still discovered that sin so thoroughly ruled his flesh that he was unable to do the very thing he desired (7:13–25). According to this interpretation of the passage, the individual, mired as he or she is in sinful flesh, cannot hope to please God apart from the transforming effect of God's Spirit.

The first person singular pronouns in the passage demonstrate the element of truth in this interpretation: Whatever Paul may be saying about groups of people in general, he is also making an observation about the nature of the individual. Augustine was not remiss, therefore, in echoing the language of this passage in *Confessions* 8.5 (12) as he struggled over whether to embrace the gospel:

> In vain I "delighted in your law in respect of the inward man; but another law in my members fought against the law of my mind and led me captive in the law of sin which was in my members" (Rom. 7:22). The law of sin is the violence of habit by which even the unwilling mind is dragged down and held, as it deserves to be, since by its own choice it slipped into the habit. "Wretched man that I was, who would deliver me from this body of death other than your grace through Jesus Christ our Lord?" (Rom. 7:24–25).[77]

74 Cf. Käsemann, *Romans*, 190–91; Dunn, *Romans 1–8*, 358; Stuhlmacher, *Romans*, 104; Schreiner, *Romans*, 344, 398.

75 The identity of the "I" in this passage is a matter of intense controversy. Is it Paul (Augustine, *Propositions from the Epistle to the Romans*, 42–46; Martin Luther, *Lectures on Romans*, *LW*, 25:322–43)? "Mankind under the shadow of Adam" (Käsemann, *Romans*, 196, 200)? Israel (Moo, *Romans*, 430–31)? All three (Schreiner, *Romans*, 356)? The view that Paul speaks throughout the passage, even by means of the present tenses in 7:14–25, of the experience of Adam and Israel under the Mosaic law seems to do most justice to the rootedness of Paul's argument in salvation history, and, since Paul uses the singular first person pronoun to make his point, it seems likely that he intended to include himself personally as a member of these groups.

76 See, e.g., Augustine, *Confessions* 8.5 (12); *Propositions from the Epistle to the Romans* 42–46; *Answer to the Two Letters of the Pelagians* 1.8(13)–1.11(24); Martin Luther, *Lectures on Romans*, *LW*, 25:322–43.

77 Augustine, *Confessions*, trans. Henry Chadwick (Oxford: Oxford Univ. Press, 1991), 141. Augustine correctly understands

Paul's point is not merely anthropological, however. He is also making a statement about the dominion of sin in the era governed by Adam and the Mosaic law. The statement in 7:11 that sin "deceived me" through the commandment echoes the wiles of the serpent as Eve describes them in Genesis 3:13 (cf. Gen. 3:4–6).[78] Similarly, Paul's claim in Romans 7:13 that through the commandment sin produced death in "me" so that it might become utterly sinful parallels Paul's statement of the effect of the law on Israel in 5:20: "The law was added so that the trespass might increase. But where sin increased, grace increased all the more."[79]

Thus, the "I" of the passage was deceived by the commandment just as Adam was deceived by God's prohibition not to eat of the tree of the knowledge of good and evil. The "I" of the passage is also the place where sin increased through the law, just as Israel was the place where sin increased when God gave the Mosaic law.[80]

The passage, therefore, is not merely an anthropological statement about the utter inability of the individual to do what God requires apart from the presence of God's Spirit. Nor is it merely an analysis of the dark period of salvation history. It is both. Sin dominated the era governed by Adam's transgression not only because Adam sinned but "because all sinned" (5:12), and it dominated the era of the Mosaic law not merely because of Israel's sin as a people, but because each Israelite gave in to sin in the way that Paul explains in 7:14–25. Like Daniel, who described his confession of the nation's long history of sin against the Mosaic law as confession of "my sin and the sin of my people Israel" (Dan. 9:20), and like Baruch, who similarly admitted when confessing the sinful character of Israel's history that "all of us followed the intent of our own wicked hearts" (Bar. 1:22; cf. 2:8), Paul recognizes the role of the individual in the sin that dominated whole peoples and eras.[81]

At the death of Christ, a radical change happened both in salvation history and in the individuals who together constituted God's people. As God began to fulfill the promises of the restoration of his people through the presence of his Spirit, individuals changed masters: They were no longer slaves of sin but slaves to righteousness. As individuals made this transition from the era of the law's curse to the era of the Spirit's presence, they together formed a new, eschatologically restored people of God.

Paul describes the positive side of the movement from one era to the other in 8:1–17. Recalling the language of 3:25, he says that the death of Christ on the cross served as a sacrifice for sin (*peri hamartias*, 8:3). This sacrifice marked the division

7:14–25 as a reference to the struggle of the unbeliever with the law. Cf. his *Propositions from the Epistle to the Romans* 42–46. He later changed his mind on this issue under the pressure of his dispute with the Pelagians. See, e.g., his *Answer to the Two Letters of the Pelagians* 1.8(13)–1.11(24), and, on the reasons for Augustine's change, see Wilckens, *Der Brief an die Römer*, 2:105–6. The absence of the Spirit from the passage (in contrast to 8:1–39, where the Spirit appears nineteen times) and Paul's description of the "I" in 7:14 as "sold as a slave to sin" (cf. 6:14–15) show that Paul is speaking of the unbeliever in this passage.

78 Many commentators see a veiled reference to Adam in 7:7–13. See, e.g., the comments of Theodoret, the fifth-century bishop of Cyrrhus (*ACCS*, 6:186); Lagrange, *Romains*, 170–71; Franz J. Leenhardt, *The Epistle to the Romans* (Cleveland: World, 1961), 180–90; Cranfield, *Romans*, 1:350–53; Käsemann, *Romans*, 196; Stuhlmacher, *Reconciliation, Law, and Righteousness*, 86; and Dunn, *Romans 1–8*, 378–82, 399–402.

79 For the "I" in 7:7–13 as "Israel," see, e.g., Douglas J. Moo, "Israel and Paul in Romans 7.7–12," *NTS* 32 (1986): 122–35; idem, *Romans*, 429–31; N. T. Wright, *The Climax of the Covenant: Christ and the Law in Pauline Theology* (Edinburgh: T. & T. Clark, 1991), 197–98; Thielman, "Story of Israel," 190–94.

80 Cf. Cranfield, *Romans*, 1:352–53.

81 See also Thielman, "The Story of Israel," 193–94.

of the ages. It atoned for sin, so that believers no longer stand under condemnation (8:1; cf. 8:33–34). It also ushered in the period of God's eschatological Spirit foretold by the prophet and thus severed the link between sin, the law, and the flesh.

As a result, believers fulfill the just requirement of God's law (8:4) and are no longer in the flesh (8:9). This does not mean that they do not sin, for the resurrection still lies in the future (8:11), and Paul must still exhort his readers to live in a way that is consistent with their new position (8:12–17). Still, in the death of Jesus and the appearance of the Spirit, the critical shift has happened: God's people no longer live in the old era of sin, Mosaic law, flesh, and death but in the era of the Spirit, fulfillment of a new law, anticipation of the resurrection, and life.

Paul's shorthand for this shift is to say that "through Christ Jesus the law of the Spirit of life set me free from the law of sin and death" (8:2). The "law of sin and death" is the Mosaic law that Paul has just described in 7:1–25 as entangled with sin (7:7–10) and instrumental in the individual's death (7:11–13, 24). "The law of the Spirit of life," is, correspondingly, Paul's way of referring to the new covenant, instituted at Christ's death and sealed by the gift of the Spirit, who enables believers to keep God's law. This was the period of Israel's restoration, which Jeremiah described as a time when God will establish a new covenant with his people and write his law on their hearts (Jer. 31:31–34).

During this period, according to Ezekiel, God's Spirit will refashion the hearts of his people and breathe new life into them, making it possible for them to follow his statutes and ordinances (Ezek. 36:1–37:14).[82] This understanding of 8:2 seems to be confirmed when Paul says in 8:3–4 that God condemned sin in human flesh through the sacrificial death of Jesus so that the "just requirement of the Law" is "fulfilled" in those who "walk not according to the flesh but according to the Spirit" (8:4, aut.).

For Paul, however, the law that the believer fulfills is not the Mosaic law. The believer has been released not merely from that law's entanglement with sin, nor merely from that law's sentence of condemnation, but from that law in its entirety because it was part of the previous, sin-dominated era (7:1–6). The new covenant—the law of the Spirit of life in Christ Jesus—carries with it new obligations that intersect with the Mosaic law at critical places, such as the Decalogue and the love commandment (13:8–10), but which differ from the obligations of the Mosaic law on such matters as circumcision (Rom. 2:27), dietary observances, and festival keeping (Rom. 14:1–15:13).

Paul's rhetorical question in 2:26 confirms this perspective: "If the uncircumcised man should keep the just requirements of the law, will not his uncircumcision be counted as circumcision?" (aut.). Here Paul anticipates a situation in which circumcision does not mark the boundaries of God's people but keeping "the just requirements of the law," and he says this despite the prominence of the circumcision command in the Mosaic law (Gen. 17:1–27; Lev. 12:3). "The just requirements of

82 Cf. Hübner, *Biblische Theologie*, 2:301–3. Hübner also mentions five differences between Paul and Ezekiel. These "differences" are of varying validity. The most important of them is that whereas Paul had in view the inclusion of all ethnic groups in this eschatological restoration, Ezekiel spoke of Israel alone.

the law," therefore, must refer to the intersection of the Mosaic law with some other law that Jews and Gentiles can both observe. When we add this implication of 2:26 to Paul's statement in 2:29 that an inward Jew has experienced "circumcision of the heart, by the Spirit, not the letter" (aut.), it becomes likely that in both 2:26 and 8:4 the phrase "the just requirement(s) of the law" refers to the new law of the new covenant and implies that in many places, but not in all, this new law intersects with the law of Moses.[83]

In 8:1–17, therefore, Paul argues that the death of Christ and the coming of the Spirit have resolved the plight of all humanity since Adam, and especially of God's people Israel since the giving of the Mosaic law. Christ's death has atoned for sin with the result that the final day is one of acquittal rather than condemnation in God's court. The eschatologically given Spirit has broken the Mosaic law's unwilling alliance with sin, an alliance that the weakness of human flesh made possible. The Mosaic law, having served its purposes, has been swept away and replaced with a new law that God enables his people to keep by the provision of the Holy Spirit.

Hope and Obedience in Rome

It is again worth pausing here to ask what this general discussion of Christian existence between baptism (6:14) and resurrection (8:11) has to do with the exercise in Rome of Paul's calling to minister to the Gentiles. Although imperatives are rare in this passage, and the situation in Rome is not directly in view, the section nevertheless lays the theological groundwork for the admonitions that Paul will address to feuding Jewish and Gentile Christians in Rome in 14:1–15:13.

First, Paul prefaces those admonitions with a paragraph (13:11–14) that brings the Christian's hope directly into connection with Christian ethics and echoes his argument in 5:1–8:39.[84] He emphasizes the nearness of the consummation of God's saving purposes (13:11–12a; cf. 8:18–25), and in light of its approach encourages the Roman Christians both to "put on the weapons [*hopla*; cf. 6:13] of light" (13:12b) and not to "make provision for the flesh" (13:14, aut.; cf. 8:1–17). Then, in 14:1–15:13 he describes a specific way in which the Roman Christians can do this: They can stop passing judgment on one another and leave that to God at the final day (14:4, 10–11; cf. 14:13, 19; 15:1, 7). Paul therefore links his specific ethical advice to its theological basis in 5:1–8:39 by means of his introductory paragraph in 13:11–14.

Second, Paul's admonition to the Roman Christians to stop judging one another depends on the position on the Mosaic law articulated in 5:1–8:39. Because the Mosaic law has passed away, Paul can both agree with the "powerful" in the Roman church that "nothing is unclean in itself" (14:14a; cf. 15:1) and expect the one "whose faith is weak" to stop condemning those who eat all foods (14:3). Because "the law of the Spirit of life" has replaced the Mosaic law (8:2), and because this new law has

83 See also Thielman, *Paul and the Law*, 200–213; idem, *Law and the New Testament*, 34–41; and idem, "Law and Liberty in the Ethics of Paul," *ExAud* 11 (1995): 63–75. Cf. Stuhlmacher, *Reconciliation, Law, and Righteousness*, 87.

84 *Pace* Cranfield, *Romans,* 2:699, the *de* that begins 14:1 does not so much mark "the transition to a new section" as link 14:1–15:13 with 13:11–14. On this see Dunn, *Romans 9–16*, 797.

absorbed the Mosaic law's love commandment (13:8–10), Paul can expect the "powerful" not to take advantage of their position but to act in love toward the "weak" (14:15; cf. 14:19; 15:1).

Paul's general description of the hope and obedience in which Christians live as the restored people of God, therefore, lays a necessary foundation for his more specific exhortations later in the letter. His primarily indicative description of the character of God's people in 5:1–8:39 provides the necessary preparation for the imperatives of 14:1–15:13.

HAS THE WORD OF GOD FAILED? (9:1–11:36)

In 9:1–11:36 Paul's argument takes another critical turn. Throughout 5:1–8:39 he has assumed that the mixed group of Jews and Gentiles who have been justified by faith comprise the eschatologically restored people of God. As it turns out, however, Paul's preaching of this gospel has succeeded among the Gentiles far better than among the Jews, and this poses once again the problem that Paul's imaginary debating partner raised in 3:1. If Paul's gospel is true, then God's promises to Israel must be false. To put it another way, if the prophesied restoration of Israel as Paul has described it in 5:1–8:39 includes only a few Israelites, how can Paul's gospel be compatible with God's Word?

Paul's answer to this question has two basic parts. The first part explains that God's Word does not define membership in his people either by ethnic origin or by human effort but by God's sovereign choice (9:1–29; 11:1–10). Paul includes within this part of his answer an extensive explanation of why Israel has failed to embrace the gospel (9:30–10:21). The second part maintains that the present displacement of unbelieving Jews with large numbers of believing Gentiles in God's people is part of an eschatological scheme by which, in the end, all Israel will be saved (11:11–36).

God Decides the Membership of His People (9:1–29; 11:1–10)

In the first part of his answer to the question of God's faithfulness to Israel, Paul argues that the Scriptures offer no guarantee that Israelites, just because they are Israelites, will belong to God's people. If that were true, he says, then Ishmael as well as Isaac would be included within God's people, for Abraham was the father of both. Scripture shows, however, that Isaac, the child whom God had promised Sarah, was Abraham's true heir. Perhaps anticipating the objection that Ishmael was not chosen because his mother was the slave Hagar rather than Abraham's wife Sarah, Paul also cites the children of Rebekah and Isaac as examples. They were twins, and yet, as the prophet Malachi recognized, God loved Jacob and hated Esau.

Jacob and Esau, Paul continues, also show that one does not win inclusion among God's people by good conduct. God had decided before the birth of either child and before either had done anything good or bad that, as Genesis 25:23 puts it, "the older will serve the younger."

Although Paul does not bring it out as explicitly, this quotation from Genesis also demonstrates a theological principle that runs throughout Genesis and is prominent in Romans 9–11: God's choice is often, from a human perspective, surprising. According to the law of primogeniture, Abraham's line should have been preserved through Ishmael (the elder) rather than through Isaac (the younger) of Abraham's two sons. Isaac's heir, similarly, should have been Esau, the first of the twins to emerge from Rebekah's womb, rather than Jacob.[85] Not only does social status and human achievement fail to qualify one as a member of God's people, therefore, but God seems purposefully to choose the least likely candidates for membership within his people (cf. 1 Cor. 1:26–29).

Because the biblical God freely chooses the membership of his people, he can choose Gentiles as well as Jews, and he can exclude some Jews. As the prophet Hosea shows, he is free to call those who previously were not his people to be his people, and, as the prophet Isaiah says, he is free to limit those who belong to his people among the Jews to a remnant. He chooses this remnant, moreover, not on the basis of their works but strictly as his own free gift (9:24–29; 11:1–10).

The Nature of Israel's Present Failure (9:30–10:21)

Sandwiched between the two sections (9:1–29 and 11:1–10) of his case that God sovereignly chooses those who will belong to his people, Paul places a description of hardened Israel's unbelief (9:30–10:21). Jews who have heard the gospel and have rejected it (10:14–21), he argues, display an unwarranted optimism about their ability to keep the law and obtain the life which it promises. They pursue a law that promises righteousness (*nomon dikaiosynēs*) to those who keep it, but they are apparently oblivious to their inability apart from the gospel to reach the goal of righteousness toward which the law pointed (9:31).[86] "Christ," Paul insists, "is the goal of the law, for the righteousness of everyone who believes" (10:4, aut.).

Both the law and the gospel, in other words, pointed in the same direction—toward a right relationship between God and his people, but God has provided Christ, not the law, as the means by which this relationship will be realized. By their rejection of the gospel and their insistence on living in the era dominated by the Mosaic law, many within Israel have implied that their own works (9:32) and their own righteousness (10:3) were preferable to the righteous status that comes from God through belief in the gospel (10:3).[87]

Paul argues further that the law itself agrees with his analysis of Israel's failure. Moses, he says, describes the righteousness that comes by the law this way: "The [one] who does these things will live by them" (10:5; Lev. 18:5). This statement from the Mosaic law summarizes the law's requirement that to receive the blessings the law promises Israel, Israel must keep the law.

---

85 Robert Alter, *The Art of Biblical Narrative* (New York: Basic Books, 1981), 6. See also Frank Thielman, "Unexpected Mercy: Echoes of a Biblical Motif in Romans 9–11," *SJT* 47 (1994): 169–81, here at 177.

86 On this understanding of the phrase *nomon dikaiosynēs*, see Moo, *Romans*, 625–27.

87 Paul understood this perspective, since it had once been his own (Phil. 3:9). See also Thielman, *Paul and the Law*, 206–7, and Schreiner, *Romans*, 540.

But this statement also implies the converse proposition, that if Israel fails to keep the law, God will curse them (Deut. 27:15–28:68; 29:19–29; 30:15–20; 32:46–47; also Lev. 26:3–39). Anyone who knew the biblical account of Israel's history understood that Israel had not kept the law and received life but had violated the law and received the curse of exile and foreign domination.[88] As the prophetic nature of the blessing and curse section of Deuteronomy and Leviticus shows, the law itself predicts that life under it will be dominated by curse rather than blessing. God will hold his people responsible for failing to keep his law which, he tells them, is "very near you ... in your mouth and in your heart so you may obey it" (Deut. 30:14), and will therefore bring the curses of the law on them for their disobedience to it.

This prophetic part of the law's section of blessings and curses, however, includes, along with this pessimistic view of Israel's history, a note of hope. In Deuteronomy 30:1–10, the law also envisions a time, after Israel has experienced the curse of exile for disobedience, when God will circumcise their hearts and the hearts of their descendants so that they "may love him with all [their] heart and with all [their] soul, and live" (Deut. 30:6). Paul believes that this time had come with the death and resurrection of Jesus and the giving of God's promised Spirit. He is therefore able to make "the righteousness that is by faith" speak the words of the Mosaic law to show that the law itself points forward to the gospel:

> The righteousness that is by faith says: "Do not say in your heart, 'Who will ascend into heaven?'" [Deut. 30:10] (that is, to bring Christ down) or 'Who will descend into the deep?'" [cf. Ps. 107:26; cf. Deut. 30:13] (that is, to bring Christ up from the dead). But what does it say? "The word is near you; it is in your mouth and in your heart" [Deut. 30:14], that is, the word of faith we are proclaiming. (10:6–8)[89]

For Paul, therefore, the period dominated by the Mosaic law has ended, and in the gospel, the righteousness toward which the law pointed in its prophetic passages has been realized.

Paul argues here that unbelieving Jews, by their rejection of the gospel, have insisted on continuing to live in the era of disobedience to the law and the law's curse. By their refusal to give up the Mosaic law despite the fulfillment of its divinely appointed purposes, they imply what even the law recognizes as impossible: that a right relationship with God can be established upon obedience to the Mosaic covenant without God's eschatological intervention. They have implied that reliance on their own righteousness, without God's eschatological circumcision of their hearts, will sustain their relationship with God. They have therefore committed a massive error in timekeeping, failing to see that in the gospel God is fulfilling his purposes. They have also made a massive error about the nature of human beings, thinking that they are able, by their own efforts, to maintain a relationship of peace with God.

88 On this see Frank Thielman, *From Plight to Solution: A Jewish Framework for Understanding Paul's View of the Law in Galatians and Romans* (NovTSupp 61; Leiden: Brill, 1989), 28–45, supplemented by more evidence in idem, *Paul and the Law*, 48–68.

89 See Thielman, *Paul and the Law*, 209–10, the judicious criticism of this position in Moo, *Romans*, 652–53, and Schreiner's helpful attempt in *Romans*, 657–58, to restate the position in light of Moo's criticisms.

All Israel Will Be Saved (11:11–36)

The second major part of Paul's answer to the question of whether God has been faithful to Israel appears in 11:11–36. Paul argues that if God can sovereignly, and surprisingly, choose large numbers of Gentiles to be his people, he can also reverse the surprise at a later time and again choose large numbers of Jews. This, Paul maintains, is what God intends to do.[90] God's present choice of a large number of Gentiles and a mere remnant of Jews is only part of a larger scheme, the end result of which will be the influx of vast numbers of Jews into the believing community in the final days.[91] God has brought many Gentiles into his people in the present to make the unbelieving and hard-hearted within ethnic Israel envious so that eventually, when the full number of Gentiles has entered his people, "all Israel will be saved" (11:11–12, 25–26a). When this happens, Paul says, the hopes of Isaiah and Jeremiah for a time when God will take away the sins of his people and establish a new covenant with them will be fulfilled (11:26b–27; cf. Isa. 59:20–21; Jer. 31:31–34).

Because membership in God's people results from his sovereign and gracious choice, and because God has revealed to Paul the "mystery" that eventually he will choose "all Israel," Paul insists that any Gentile boasting over unbelieving Jews is inappropriate. Such boasting only repeats the Gentile side of the Jewish error that claimed exemption from God's wrath simply on the basis of possession of the Mosaic law (2:1–29).

This part of Paul's answer to the question of God's faithfulness to Israel, therefore, has immediate implications for the dispute between Jewish and Gentile Christians in Rome. Gentiles who may have celebrated Paul's denial of Jewish privilege on the day of God's wrath in 1:18–4:25 now discover that Paul is no more eager to support their own ethnically based boasting. As the apostle to the Gentiles (11:13), Paul wants the Gentile Christians in Rome to know that their position in God's people is only a result of God's sovereign choice and their faith (11:20). God is not only able to choose large numbers of Jews for membership in his people, but he is eager to do so (11:24), and he will do so in the end when many of them embrace the gospel (11:23, 26–32). There is, therefore, no theological basis for the ethnic superiority that probably stands behind the willingness of some Gentile Christians in Rome to "look down on" their Jewish Christian brothers and sisters (14:3). God has imprisoned both Gentiles and Jews in disobedience so that he may have mercy on both (11:32).

THE IMPLICATIONS OF THE GOSPEL FOR THE ROMAN CHURCH (12:1–15:13)

Paul begins to apply not only the insights of 11:11–36 but those of the entire argument from 1:18–11:36 specifically to the Roman Christians in 12:1–15:13. Here his argument comes full circle, and he reveals the primary reason why he is "so eager to preach the gospel also to you who are in Rome" (1:15). He prefaces this section with

90 Thielman, "Unexpected Mercy," 169–81.

91 Cf. Schreiner, *Paul*, 477–81.

a transitional paragraph that builds on everything he has said since 1:18 and foreshadows the concreteness of his admonitions in the rest of the letter (12:1–2). He then lays out a general moral vision for harmony within the church and harmony with those outside the church who sometimes violently oppose it (12:3–13:14). Finally, he applies to Jewish and Gentile believers in Rome the theology of the letter and his concern for the internal unity and the external witness of the church (14:1–15:13).

The Renewal of the Mind in the Present Age (12:1–2)

The brief paragraph that begins this section of the letter gathers the theological insights of the entire argument to this point and arranges them so that they can be unleashed as concrete commands for the Roman church in 12:3–15:13. This function of the paragraph is visible in three of its characteristics.

First, Paul here recalls his portrait of humanity's sinful plight in 1:18–32 and insists that believers in Rome reverse the way of life described in that passage.[92] In 1:18–32, sinful humanity's perverse way of thinking (1:21–22, 32) led to perverse worship (1:23, 25, 28), perverse use of the body (1:24, 26–27), and perverse relationships (1:29–31). Paul now urges the believers in Rome to present their bodies to God as an expression of "rational [*logikos*] worship" (12:1) and instructs them to be transformed by the renewing of their minds (12:2).

Second, Paul is able to issue these commands (anticipated in the imperatives of 6:11–13) because he has previously described the effect on the believer of Christ's death and resurrection and the giving of the Spirit in chapters 5–8. The body of sin has been nullified for the believer (6:6). God, through Christ, has rescued believers from the link between their bodies, sin, and death (7:24–25). Because Paul has already described these truths, he can now urge them to live in a way that is consistent with God's work on their behalf.

Third, the paragraph assumes Paul's previous position on the Mosaic law. That law has now passed away (7:1–6; 8:2; 10:4), and Christ's climactic sacrifice has obviated the need to perform the sacrificial cult described within that law (3:25). Paul can now speak of the believer's sacrifice as the devotion of the believer's body, during the overlap of the ages, to the service of God. This sacrifice, like the sacrifices of the Mosaic cult in their day, is "holy and pleasing to God" (12:1). Paul can now admonish believers to be transformed "by the renewing" of their minds, echoing the prophecy of Jeremiah that God will one day put his "laws into their minds and write them on their hearts" (Jer. 38:33, LXX; cf. 31:11, MT). A new law now governs the conduct of God's people, guiding them in the use both of their bodies and of their minds.

Harmony within the Church and Submission to the Government (12:3–13:14)

In 12:3–13:14 Paul describes the implications of this new situation for the internal harmony of the church and for its relationship with the unbelieving world, admonishing the Roman Christians in a general way to use their gifts for their mutual

92 Cf. Moo, *Romans*, 748; Brendan Byrne, *Romans* (SP 6; Collegeville: Michael Glazier, 1996), 363.

edification and to submit to the governing authorities.[93] Some scholars have argued that the general nature of this advice shows that it is detached from any specific situation within the Roman church: Paul is simply repeating traditional ethical aphorisms similar to those found in, for example, the *Didache*, Pseudo-Phocylides, and Tobit 4:5–19; 12:6–10.[94]

It is true that the twin concerns of harmony within the church and conformity to the just norms of the society are common in early Christian literature, but Paul has probably chosen to emphasize these traditional elements because they are particularly appropriate to the Roman Christians.[95] The ethnic disharmony that has already broken the surface of Paul's argument in 11:18–19 and which he will address more specifically in 14:1–15:13 probably stands behind his decision to stress the use of the gifts God has given to each believer for the common good (12:4–13), his focus on genuine love for others (12:9–11, 13; 13:8–10), and especially his appeals to his readers to turn from haughtiness and live in harmony with one another (12:3, 16).[96]

Paul's advice to the Roman Christians to live in harmony with one another leads to the admonition not to retaliate against those who do evil against them, but to let God's wrath fill that role. On the basis of Paul's comments in 1:18–32 we might imagine he would explain the wrath of God here, as he did there, as God's active handing of the wicked over to the consequences of their twisted thinking. Instead, Paul now envisions the state ruler as the agent of God's wrath on evildoers. He urges the Roman Christians, therefore, to submit to the state authorities and to pay their taxes (13:1–7).

Why does his exhortation take this direction? Paul may have in mind disturbances in Rome's Jewish community in A.D. 49, apparently over the preaching of the gospel (Suetonius *Claudius* 25.4), that led to the expulsion of Jews, including Jewish Christians such as Priscilla and Aquila (Acts 18:2). Some scholars believe, probably correctly, that these disturbances arose from the gospel's claim that Gentiles could be included within the people of God.[97] These disturbances may have occurred not only between unbelieving Jews and the church, but between Judaizing Christians and those who held to a law-free gospel within the church itself.[98]

If so, the issues of harmony within the church and submission to the governing authorities were connected in Paul's mind. Paul wanted Jewish and Gentile Roman

93 His advice is reminiscent of his charge to the Thessalonians to continue to love one another (1 Thess. 4:9–10) and to live a quiet life that will win the respect of outsiders (1 Thess. 4:11–12).

94 Martin Dibelius, *From Tradition to Gospel* (Cambridge: James Clarke, 1971; orig. ed., 1919), 238–41; idem, *James*, rev. Heinrich Greeven (Hermeneia; Philadelphia: Fortress, 1975), 3. Cf. William Sanday and Arthur Headlam, *A Critical and Exegetical Commentary on the Epistle to the Romans*, 5th ed. (ICC; Edinburgh: T. & T. Clark, 1902), 351, and Byrne, *Romans*, 362, who believe that Paul writes out of his experience as a missionary rather than out of specific knowledge of circumstances in Rome.

95 Cf. the comments of Sophie Laws, *The Epistle of James* (HNT; New York: Harper, 1980), 7, on Dibelius's classification of James as *paraenesis* and therefore unrelated to any specific pastoral situation.

96 Cf. C. K. Barrett, *The Epistle to the Romans* (HNTC; New York: Harper, 1957), 235; Dahl, *Studies in Paul*, 86; Wedderburn, *Reasons for Romans*, 78; Johnson, *Reading Romans*, 177, 181; Philip H. Towner, "Romans 13:1–7 and Paul's Missiological Perspective" in *Romans and the People of God: Essays in Honor of Gordon D. Fee on the Occasion of His 65th Birthday*, ed. Sven K. Soderlund and N. T. Wright (Grand Rapids: Eerdmans, 1999), 149–69, here at 152.

97 Wedderburn, *Reasons for Romans*, 54–59, 83.

98 Ibid., 58–59.

Christians to be united, undeterred in their common worship of God (15:7–12) either by disharmony in their midst or unnecessary persecution from the governing authorities.[99]

The Gospel and Ethnic Harmony in the Roman Church (14:1–15:13)

The pastoral goal of the entire letter reaches its climax in this section.[100] Paul has stressed throughout his presentation of the gospel in 1:16–11:36 the unity of Jews and Gentiles both in the outpouring of God's eschatological wrath and in the activation of his saving righteousness. In 1:18–3:20 he has demonstrated that the Jew could boast of no advantage over the Gentile on the day of God's judging wrath, either through the possession or the keeping of the law. In 3:21–4:25 he has demonstrated that the free gift of atonement through Christ's death and inclusion among Abraham's descendants are available to all who have faith, both Jew and Gentile. In 5:1–8:39 he has demonstrated how the prophetic promises of Israel's restoration have started to be fulfilled within an ethnically mixed group of believers whose conduct has not been defined by the Mosaic law. In 9:1–11:36 he has shown how the broad sweep of God's saving purposes excludes any Gentile counter-assertion of ethnic superiority over the Jews. "You stand by faith," Paul told the Gentiles among the Roman Christians. "Do not be arrogant, but be afraid" (11:20). As 3:23–24 puts it, "There is no difference, for all have sinned and fall short of the glory of God, and are justified freely by his grace through the redemption that came by Christ Jesus." Or, as Paul says in 11:32, "For God has bound all people over to disobedience so that he may have mercy on them all" (aut.).

Now, in 14:1–15:13, Paul applies these theological realities to the strained relationship between the "weak in faith" (14:1; cf. 14:2; 15:1) and "the powerful" (15:1) in the Roman church. In both the first and the last paragraphs of the section, Paul urges these two groups to accept each other insofar as God, through Christ, has accepted them (14:1, 3; 15:7). If while they were "weak" Christ died for the ungodly (5:6–8), then the powerful ought to be willing to accept "the weak in faith."[101] If there is no "condemnation" for those who are caught in sin's web of self, law, and death (8:1), then those who observe Jewish dietary customs should not "condemn" those who believe that all foods are clean.

How, practically speaking, should these two diverse groups work at accepting each other? Paul urges the "powerful," who are dominant because they hold the technically correct position (14:14, 19; 15:1) and are probably in the majority, neither to despise the weak (14:3a, 10b, 13) nor to flaunt their liberty from the Mosaic requirements to avoid certain foods. If they do that, they will place a stumbling block in front of the weak, perhaps leading them to act against what they believe to be right

99 Paul probably reflects the Jewish exilic tradition that God's exiled people should "seek the peace and prosperity of the city" (Jer. 29:7) to which God exiled them, because the actions of even pagan rulers are under God's sovereign authority. Cf. the strategy of 1 Peter, also written from Rome; Towner, "Romans 13:1–7," 163; Bruce W. Winter, *Seek the Welfare of the City: Christians as Benefactors and Citizens* (Grand Rapids: Eerdmans, 1994), 1; and Neil Elliott, *Liberating Paul: The Justice of God and the Politics of the Apostle* (Maryknoll, N.Y.: Orbis, 1994), 224.

100 Cf. Dunn, *Romans 1–9*, 797, and Schreiner, *Romans*, 704.

101 Cf. Johnson, *Reading Romans*, 200.

(14:13–15, 20b). The result would be grave—the one "who doubts is condemned if he eats, because his eating is not from faith, and everything that does not come from faith is sin" (14:23). The powerful should instead bear with the weaknesses of the powerless, pleasing not themselves but their "neighbor" (15:1–2; cf. 13:9).

By contrast, the weak person who eats only vegetables, avoids wine, and observes the Sabbath should not condemn those who do not follow these customs (14:3b, 10a, 13). Although the weak should not act against their convictions (14:14b, 22b–23), they should realize that God alone can rightfully sit in judgment on those whose convictions do not match their own (14:4, 10c–12).

Both parties should focus less on the debate over the issue itself (leaving judgment to God), and instead "make every effort to do what leads to peace and to mutual edification" (14:19; cf. 14:3–4, 6–12, 22). Through the Roman believers' acceptance of one another, God will accomplish his goal of assembling a group composed of Jews and Gentiles to give him praise (15:7), and the rescue of creation from the futility into which Adam plunged it will be well on its way toward completion (1:18–32; 5:12–21; 8:22).

THE GOSPEL AS THE SOURCE OF THE UNIFIED PRAISE OF GOD

The church in Rome, therefore, should, by its ethnic harmony, depict the saving purposes of God as Paul has described them in the letter. Because God's saving righteousness comes to both Jews and Gentiles by faith, Jewish and Gentile Christians in Rome should stand together in worship, giving glory to God. Paul's prayer in 15:5–6 fittingly describes the goal of both the theological argument in 1:16–11:36 and of the ethical admonitions in 12:1–15:13:

> May the God who gives endurance and encouragement give you a spirit of unity among yourselves as you follow Christ Jesus, so that with one heart and mouth you may glorify the God and Father of our Lord Jesus Christ.[102]

102 On the glory of God in Christ as the goal of Romans and of Paul's theology, see Schreiner, *Romans*, 23, and *Paul*, passim.

Chapter 16

COLOSSIANS: CHRIST PREEMINENT IN COSMOS AND HISTORY

The concern Paul expressed in Romans that when he went to Jerusalem he might meet with hostility was not unfounded. Believing Jews had heard that he taught Jews to abandon the Mosaic law, particularly circumcision, and unbelieving Jews claimed that he spoke to everyone against the Jewish people, their law, and their temple (Acts 21:21, 28). A riot at the temple broke out when word spread that Paul had brought Gentiles into areas forbidden to any but Jews. Paul was subsequently arrested and sent to Judea's administrative capital, Caesarea, where the corrupt governor Felix left him in prison for two years, hoping for a bribe (24:26). When Felix, at the secret request of Paul's opponents, suggested that Paul return to Jerusalem for trial, Paul took advantage of his right as a Roman citizen to appeal his case to Caesar in Rome (25:10–11).

While he was under house arrest in Rome awaiting his appearance before Caesar, he received a visitor named Epaphras, who had traveled from three churches clustered in the valley of the Lycus River (a tributary of the Maeander) in the south-central part of the Roman province of Asia. Epaphras was from the church at Colosse (Col. 4:12) and had probably taken the gospel to Colosse, Hierapolis, and Laodicea (4:13) after hearing it himself during Paul's long stay in Ephesus (Acts 19:10).[1] He had now come to inform Paul about the condition of Christianity at Colosse and Laodicea.[2]

Although the Spirit was at work among the Colossians and their faith was sound (1:7; 2:5), someone had started to advocate a "philosophy" within the church. Paul describes this teaching as "empty deceit" and "according to the elements of the world, and not according to Christ" (2:8, aut.). The strength of Paul's warning to the Colossians not to be ensnared by this philosophy and his implication that they are now submitting to the philosophy's special regulations (2:20) show that the threat to the Colossians' spiritual health is serious.

Despite heroic efforts from scholars to locate the philosophy within some known religious movement of the first century, its precise identity remains a mystery.[3] A few

1 A number of scholars conclude from the vocabulary, style, and theological emphases of Colossians that it is a pseudonymous letter from a post-Pauline era. This view, however, leads to significant difficulty in finding a plausible historical setting for the letter, especially for the personal details of 4:7–17. It also fails to account for the choice of Colosse as the letter's fictional setting. Colosse was a relatively insignificant city in its time, never on Paul's itinerary in Acts, and was destroyed by an earthquake in A.D. 60 or 61. For a persuasive argument that Paul supervised the production of Colossians but that Timothy (1:1) had a larger than normal role in drafting it, see James D. G. Dunn, *The Epistles to the Colossians and to Philemon* (NIGTC; Grand Rapids: Eerdmans, 1996), 35–39.

2 Paul also wrote to Laodicea (4:16), probably as a result of Epaphras's visit.

3 Jewish Gnosticism: J. B. Lightfoot, *Saint Paul's Epistles to the Colossians and to Philemon* (London: Macmillan, 1879), 73–113; Eduard Lohse, *Colossians and Philemon* (Hermeneia; Philadelphia: Fortress, 1971) 128–29; and Petr Pokorný, *Colossians: A Commentary* (Peabody, Mass.: Hendrickson, 1991), 117–20. Pythagoreanism: Eduard Schweizer, *The Letter to the Colossians: A Commentary* (Minneapolis: Augsburg, 1982). Middle Platonism:

characteristics are clear. The philosophy placed restrictions on food and drink and advocated observance of certain festivals, New Moons, and Sabbaths. Its chief advocate, similar to the Jewish Christians in Romans 14:3–4, passed judgment on those who did not conform to these observances (Col. 2:16). All of this fits comfortably within first-century Jewish dietary and calendrical customs.[4]

In addition, however, the philosophy's chief advocate delighted in "false humility" and "the worship of angels," and he also went into detail about his visionary experiences (2:18). The teaching of the philosophy also stressed the existence of cosmic "rulers and authorities" (1:16; 2:10, 15) and apparently taught the need to placate "the elements [*stoicheia*] of the world" (2:8, 20, aut.) with certain ascetic practices that Paul characterizes as "false humility" and "harsh treatment of the body" (2:23). He ironically summarizes these practices with the phrase, "Do not handle! Do not taste! Do not touch!" (2:21). The fascination of the philosophy with cosmic beings had apparently led to a corresponding lack of interest in Christ's universal preeminence and his defeat of inimical cosmic powers at his death (2:2–4; 2:19).

These further details about the philosophy allow us to pinpoint more precisely the type of Judaism to which it was indebted. Jewish apocalyptic literature from the Second Temple period usually focuses on a seer who has visions of the heavenly world, visions that often include angels. Occasionally the visions come on the heels of some ascetic exercise, and frequently the seer is so overcome with the glory of the angels that he falls down before them as if to worship them.[5] The apocalyptic literature also sometimes speaks of angels who preside over the basic "elements" of which the world was commonly thought to be composed (earth, water, air, and fire).[6]

This circle of thought produced the early second-century heretic Elchasai. He believed that Christians "ought to be circumcised and live according to the Law" (Hippolytus, *Haer.* 9). He also taught that people could find forgiveness from sins and

Richard E. DeMaris, *The Colossian Controversy: Wisdom in Dispute at Colosse* (JSNTS 96; Sheffield: Sheffield Academic Press, 1994), 98–133. A syncretistic mixture of Phrygian folk belief, local folk Judaism, and Christianity: Clinton E. Arnold, *The Colossian Syncretism: The Interface between Christianity and Folk Belief at Colosse* (WUNT 2.77; Tübingen: J.C.B. Mohr [Paul Siebeck], 1995), 228–44. Cf. Ulrich Luz, "Der Brief an die Kolosser" in *Die Briefe an die Galater, Epheser und Kolosser* by J. Becker and U. Luz (NTD 8.1; Göttingen: Vandenhoeck & Ruprecht, 1998), 218–19. Apocalyptic Judaism: Fred O. Francis, "Humility and Angelic Worship" in *Conflict at Colosse: A Problem in the Interpretation of Early Christianity Illustrated by Selected Modern Studies*, ed. Fred O. Francis and Wayne A. Meeks, rev. ed. (SBLSBS 4; Missoula, Mont.: Scholars, 1975), 163–95; Thomas J. Sappington, *Revelation and Redemption at Colosse* (JSNTSup 53; Sheffield: Sheffield Academic Press, 1991); and Walter T. Wilson, *The Hope of Glory: Education and Exhortation in the Epistle to the Colossians* (NovTSup 88; Leiden: Brill, 1997), 35. Cf. Dunn, *Epistles to the Colossians and to Philemon*, 23–35, and Peter Stuhlmacher, *Biblische Theologie des Neuen Testaments*, 2 vols. (Göttingen: Vandenhoeck & Ruprecht, 1992–1999), 2:12–13.

4 Some interpreters have wondered whether the concern about "drink" reflects the restrictions of the Mosaic law, but for a similar summary of Jewish dietary restrictions, see *Let. Arist.* 162, and for Jewish concerns about Gentile wine, see Dan. 1:5–20; Judith 10:5; Add. Est. 14:17; *Jos. and Asen.* 8.5; *m. ʿAbod. Zar.* 4.8–5.12. Cf. Rom. 14:21.

5 Tours of heaven with angelic guides appear in, e.g., *1 En.* 7–36 and *Apoc. Ab.* 9–29, and seers reverently doing obeisance before angels appear in, e.g., *Apoc. Zeph.* 6:11–15; Rev. 19:10; 22:8–9. On the connection between apocalyptic visions and fasting, see Dan. 10:2–3; *4 Ezra* 9.23–28; 12.51; and *Apoc. Ab.* 9.7. On all this, see the discussions in Sappington, *Revelation and Redemption*, 65–66, 90–94.

6 See *Jub.* 2:2 and *2 En.* 19:1–4. For the use of the phrase *stoicheia tou kosmou* to designate the four basic elements of the world's composition, see, e.g., Philo, *De aetern. mundi* 108–12; *Rer. div. her.* 134, 140, and cf. Wisd. 7:17. For the worship of earth, fire, water, and wind among the Persians, see Herodotus, 1.31 (cf. Philo, *De vit. cont.* 3). On the phrase generally, see Peter T. O'Brien, *Colossians, Philemon* (WBC 44; Waco, Tex.: Word, 1982), 129–32; Lohse, *Colossians and Philemon*, 96–98; and Luz, "Der Brief an die Kolosser," 220.

relief from physical afflictions by undergoing a second baptism or numerous washings and then using special incantations to adjure "seven witnesses," which he names as "the heaven, and the water, and the holy spirits, and the angels of prayer, and the oil, and the salt, and the earth" (ibid., 10). He believed that the moon and the stars possessed potentially inimical powers, and that harm from these could be avoided by following an intricately designed calendar (ibid., 11). Elchasai claimed to have received his religious system from an enormous angel who appeared to him (ibid., 8).[7]

From a later period, the Jewish Hekhalot literature describes a relationship between the human and the divine that bears similarities to the "philosophy" of Colosse. This literature prescribes certain ascetic rituals and specific incantations for receiving visions of the heavenly world. Often the goal of these procedures is to call a heavenly angel into one's presence in order to obtain wisdom about the content or meaning of the Torah, without, however, suffering harm from the powerful angel who might appear. Some scholars have suggested a connection between this literature and the literature of earlier, apocalyptically oriented Jewish groups, such as the Qumran covenanters and the Elchasaites.[8]

None of this provides an exact match to the Colossian philosophy, but the similarities are close enough to say that it belonged generally to this stream of Judaism. The philosophy probably demoted Christ from a position of cosmic preeminence to the level of one cosmic "ruler and authority" among many. Perhaps it then advocated a specific ascetic regimen for obtaining the wisdom necessary to placate and manipulate the cosmic powers in order to avoid the harm they could do either in this life or the next.

Against this understanding of the relationship between the human and the divine, Paul advances a case for the superiority of Christ over the universe, particularly over its inimical powers. Paul also emphasizes the sufficiency of Christ's death for the forgiveness of human sin, for inclusion within God's covenant people, and for reconciliation to God. The sufficiency of Christ's death, he argues, obviates the need for any complicated ascetic regimen as a means of placating and controlling divine powers. In place of its "harsh treatment of the body" Paul offers an ethical program that reflects Christ's defeat of the inimical cosmic powers and the reconciliation of the whole world to God through Christ's death on the cross.

7 Cf. A. J. M. Wedderburn, "The Theology of Colossians" in *The Theology of the Later Pauline Letters*, by Andrew T. Lincoln and A. J. M. Wedderburn (New Testament Theology; Cambridge: Cambridge Univ. Press, 1993), 6–12, and Wilson, *Hope of Glory*, 35–38.

8 See Rebecca Macy Lesses, *Ritual Practices to Gain Power: Angels, Incantations, and Revelation in Early Jewish Mysticism* (HTS; Harrisburg, Pa.: Trinity Press International, 1998), 64–75, 117–60. Lesses draws parallels between the ascetic practices in the Hekhalot literature and the restrictions on sexual contact at Qumran. She also cautiously suggests that the prohibition on eating vegetables in some Hekhalot adjurations may have a connection with the prohibition on certain vegetables among the Elchasaites. See ibid., 130–32, 142–44, 149–55.

CHRIST'S PREEMINENCE IN THE UNIVERSE AND IN GOD'S HISTORICAL PURPOSES

The "plausible arguments" of the philosophy implied that Christ did not have the stature that the gospel, as Epaphras originally preached it, claimed. Instead of worshiping Christ, or at least along with worshiping him, the philosophy advocated worship of "the elements of the world"—the angels who controlled the universe and who therefore governed the fate of each person. The philosophy's advocate may have claimed knowledge of incantations that could exercise control over such cosmic powers so that they would work for, rather than against, one's welfare.[9] By learning this kind of esoteric "wisdom," he presumably claimed, the Colossian Christians could gain control over their fate and gain access to a deep wisdom that was only available to those who were in touch with the heavenly world. Against these ideas Paul emphasizes the supreme authority of Christ over all cosmic powers. Those who have access to him should be confident that they have access to all necessary wisdom and knowledge.

The critical importance of this theme becomes clear from its centrality in the traditional confession that appears near the beginning of the letter as an extension of Paul's usual intercessory prayer report. The themes of this confession reverberate throughout the letter, especially its first half.[10] The confession can be divided into two strophes (1:15–18a and 1:18b–20), covering the beginning and the goal of God's purposes for his creatures.[11]

Christ's Priority over the Universe

This first part of the confession (1:15–18a) gives Christ priority, with respect to both time and rank, over the universe. He was in existence before the universe was created (1:17). All of creation, including its various "principalities and powers" (1:16; cf. 2:15), were fashioned in him, through him, and for him (1:16), and he continues to sustain them (1:17).[12]

This first strophe of this confession clothes Christ in the garments traditionally reserved for wisdom in Jewish tradition. It would have formed an apt response to any claims by the philosophy that its adherents had special access to the wisdom necessary for navigating around the dangerous powers of the cosmos or that they had need of the special wisdom such powers could reveal, especially if this wisdom was identified with the Torah. Wisdom and Torah were frequently identified in the

9 Cf. 4Q510.4–5: "And I, the Sage, declare the grandeur of his radiance in order to frighten and terr[ify] all the spirits of the ravaging angels and the bastard spirits, demons, Liliths, owls and [jackals . . .]." The second century anti-Christian polemicist Celsus also mentions Jews "who worship angels and are addicted to sorcery of which Moses was their teacher" (Origen, cont. *Cels.*, 1.26; cf. 5.6).

10 The passage is often called a hymn, but hymns in ancient Greek and Jewish contexts were songs of praise to the gods or to God. Col. 1:15–20 does not fit this category. See Stephen E. Fowl, *The Story of Christ in the Ethics of Paul: An Analysis of the Function of the Hymnic Material in the Pauline Corpus* (JSNTSup 36; Sheffield: Sheffield Academic Press, 1990), 31–34. The liturgical nature of the passage is evident in the repetition of *hos estin, prōtotokos,* and *hoti en autō* at the beginning of the first and second parts (1:15–16, 18–19). See F. F. Bruce, "The 'Christ Hymn' of Colossians 1:15–20," *BSac* 141 (1984): 99–111, here at 99–100.

11 For this bipartite division of the hymn, dictated by the relative clauses beginning 1:15 and 1:18b, see Eduard Norden, *Agnostos Theos: Untersuchungen zur Formengeschichte religiöser Rede* (Berlin: Teubner, 1923), 252. Cf. Georg Strecker, *Theology of the New Testament* (Berlin: Walter de Gruyter, 2000), 550–51, and Stuhlmacher, *Biblische Theologie*, 2:5–11.

12 O'Brien, *Colossians*, 47.

Judaism of the Second Temple period (Sir. 24:1–29, Bar. 3:9–4:4), and here Paul replaces Torah in that equation with Christ.[13]

Thus, the "riches," "wealth," and "treasuries" associated with wisdom (Prov. 8:18–21; Wisd. 7:9, 11, 14; 8:18) are found in Christ (Col. 2:2). Like wisdom, he is the visible image of the invisible God and preeminent over God's creation (1:15, 17; cf. Prov. 8:22–31; Wisd. 6:22; 7:26; 9:9; 10:1). Like wisdom, he fashioned creation himself (Col. 1:16; cf. Wisd. 7:22; cf. 7:17; Prov. 8:30). Just as kings, rulers, and princes govern by means of wisdom, so the cosmic powers and authorities only have their positions because of Christ (Col. 1:16; cf. Prov. 8:15–16).

Paul picks up these themes later in the letter to reveal the error of the philosophy's emphasis on the "elements of the world." In 2:9–10 he explains that concern with "the elements of the world" is inappropriate because all God's fullness dwells in Christ, and Christ is the head over "every power [*archē*] and authority [*exousia*]." Similarly, in 2:15 Paul says that at his crucifixion, Christ disarmed the inimical "powers" (*archē*) and "authorities" (*exousia*) and led them in triumphal procession to their execution.[14] At the same time, moreover, Christ disarmed and triumphed over the inimical principalities and powers (2:15). All such powers were created in, through, and for Christ; they only exist because his sustaining power allows it; and Christ has stripped them of their evil power at his crucifixion. There is therefore no need to worship them, but only to worship God for what he has accomplished in Christ (3:16–17).

In sum, Christ played the role traditionally assigned to "wisdom" in creation and therefore stands before and above all other cosmic powers.[15] Those who have access to him through faith (2:12), have access to all the treasures of wisdom and knowledge necessary for making their way through life.

Christ's Priority in God's Historical Purposes

The last line of the confession's first part (1:18a) introduces the theme that dominates the confession's second strophe (1:18b–20): Christ has priority in both time and rank within God's plan to reconcile all creation to himself. If God's people—the church—are conceived as a body, then Christ is its authoritative head (1:18a)

13 See W. D. Davies, *Paul and Rabbinic Judaism: Some Rabbinic Elements in Pauline Theology*, 4th ed. (Minneapolis: Fortress, 1980), 150–53, 169, 172. Cf. Stuhlmacher, *Biblische Theologie*, 2:9.

14 On the meaning of the phrase *thriambeusas autous* as "having led them in triumph to their execution," see Scott J. Hafemann, *Suffering and the Spirit: An Exegetical Study of II Cor. 2:14–3:3 within the Context of the Corinthian Correspondence* (WUNT 2.1; Tübingen: J.C.B. Mohr [Paul Siebeck], 1986), 7–39, and for a description of the Roman triumph see Richard C. Beacham, *Spectacle Entertainments of Early Imperial Rome* (New Haven, Conn.: Yale Univ. Press, 1999), 19–21, 39–41.

15 Gordon D. Fee, "Wisdom Christology in Paul: A Dissenting View," in *The Way of Wisdom: Essays in Honor of Bruce K. Waltke*, ed. J. I. Packer and Sven K. Soderlund (Grand Rapids: Zondervan, 2000), 251–79, here at 257–60, makes some persuasive observations on the differences between Christ in Col. 1:15–17 and God's wisdom as it is portrayed in such texts as Wisd. 1:6–7; 7:26; Prov. 8:22, 25; and Sir. 1:4. It is true that Paul focuses on Christ's dignity as "firstborn," with all the rights of primogeniture, rather than on any notion that God created Christ, as is the case with wisdom in Prov. 8:22, 25. Moreover, Paul focuses on Christ's preexistence rather than on his creation before anything else, as is the case with wisdom in these texts. But there is enough verbal and conceptual overlap between what Paul says about Christ in Col. 1:15–17 and what is said about wisdom in these texts, particularly in Wisd. 1:6–7 and 7:26, to make a plausible case for Paul's intentional echo of some of them.

through which the church, like creation, is sustained (2:19).[16] He is, therefore, prior to the church in rank. He is also prior temporally since he is "the firstborn from among the dead." He is the first to experience the resurrection of the dead—the event that will ultimately include all God's people and signal the completion of God's purposes to reconcile all creation to himself (1:20).

Later in the letter Paul will develop the notion of Christ's temporal preeminence. In 2:16–17 he says that Christ's position as head of his body, the church, also means that he presides over the progress of God's purposes beyond the Mosiac law to their fulfillment in the church. Against the philosophy's assertions of the continuing validity of the Mosaic law, Paul claims that the law is only a "shadow" of things to come, and that the "body" that casts the shadow is "of Christ." The meaning of Paul's phrase "the body is of Christ" (2:17b, aut.) is less than clear, but in light of his use of the term "body" elsewhere in the letter to refer to the church (1:18; 24; 2:19; 3:15), he is probably saying that the church—the body of which Christ is the head—is the eschatological goal toward which the Mosaic law pointed.[17] As the head of the church, Christ enables the church to fulfill this eschatological purpose.[18]

Paul's use of the concepts of "mystery" and "hiddenness" throughout the letter also implies that Christ is the climax of God's purposes. Just as in the Jewish apocalyptic literature a "mystery" is the knowledge about God's historical purposes that he graciously reveals to the seer or to his people (Dan. 2:17–49), so for Paul God has revealed his ultimate historical purposes in Christ (Col. 1:27).[19] These purposes were hidden for generations (1:26; cf. Dan. 2:22), but now in the proclamation of the gospel (Col. 1:27; 4:3–4) Christ is revealed as the means by which God brings his purposes to their ultimate goal with the inclusion of the Gentiles among his people. By means of the indwelling Christ, the Gentiles too share in the glory of God (1:27; cf. 3.3), bringing creation back to its condition before Adam sinned and fell short of that glory (Rom. 3:23).[20] Those who understand this mystery, as it is graciously revealed in the preaching of the gospel, possess "all the treasures of wisdom and knowledge" (2:2–3).

16 Many scholars believe that the references here to Christ as "the head of . . . the church" (1:18) and to Christ's "blood, shed on the cross" (1:20) are the additions of Paul (or the author writing under his name) to the "hymn." See, e.g., Lohse, *Colossians and Philemon*, 52–53, 60, and Schweizer, *Colossians*, 58–60. For the perspective (taken here) that Paul has added nothing to the "hymn," see Peter Stuhlmacher, "The Understanding of Christ in the Pauline School: A Sketch" in *Jews and Christians: The Parting of the Ways A.D. 70–135*, ed. James D. G. Dunn (Grand Rapids: Eerdmans, 1999), 159–74, here at 172–73, and idem, *Biblische Theologie*, 2:6–7.

17 Cf. C. F. D. Moule, *The Epistles to the Colossians and to Philemon* (CGTC; Cambridge: Cambridge Univ. Press, 1957), 103, and Lohse, *Colossians and Philemon*, 117, although Lohse denies the element of promise and fulfillment in the "shadow"–"substance" figure.

18 Luz, "Der Brief an die Kolosser," 224, claims that "shadow" and "substance" stand in direct opposition to each other as unreality and reality. See too the position of Hans Hübner, *An Philemon, an die Kilosser, an die Epheser* (HNT 12; Tübingen: J. C. B. Mohr [Paul Siebeck], 1997), 87–88. Paul's use of the phrase "things to come," however, shows that salvation history provides the framework for his thinking here.

19 Dunn, *Epistles to the Colossians and to Philemon*, 119–20.

20 R. P. Martin, *Colossians and Philemon* (NCB; London: Oliphants, 1974), 72; Dunn, *Epistles to the Colossians and to Philemon*, 123. According to Hans Hübner, *Biblische Theologie des Neuen Testaments*, 3 vols. (Göttingen: Vandenhoeck & Ruprecht, 1990–95), 2:355–56, the lack of interest in Israel here betrays a post-Pauline use of the mystery motif present in Rom. 11:25–27. It is more likely, however, that the need to assure the Colossian Christians that, although Gentiles, they belong to God's people led Paul to express himself differently here.

The message implicit in Paul's use of the traditional language of mystery and hiddenness is clear: The Colossians need not seek the esoteric wisdom that the philosophy advocates, for in the gospel God has finally revealed the goal of his purposes in history—that Christ is the means through which God includes the Gentiles among his people and returns his creation to the glory that it lost at the beginning. To use the words of the liturgical confession, "God was pleased . . . through [Christ] to reconcile to himself all things, whether things on earth or things in heaven, by making peace through his blood shed on the cross" (1:19–20; cf. 1:22).

THE SUFFICIENCY OF CHRIST'S DEATH AND RESURRECTION FOR RESCUE FROM THE AUTHORITY OF DARKNESS

The philosophy's primary proponent seems to have advocated submission both to the Mosaic law (2:16) and to special ascetic rules (2:20–23) in order to placate the inimical "elements of the world." Without such extraordinary efforts at purification and subjugation of the flesh, the Colossian believers stood in danger of angering the "dominion of darkness" (1:13) both in this world and, upon their death, in the next. Perhaps he advocated something structurally similar to what Elchasai advised concerning the Sabbath: "There exist wicked stars of impiety. . . . Honour the day of the Sabbath, since that day is one of those during which prevails (the power) of these stars" (Hippolytus, *Haer.* 9.11).

Or perhaps, like some Jewish apocalypses, he claimed that at death an individual would face an accusing angel with a "manuscript" (*cheirographon*) on which one's good and evil deeds were written.[21] Condemnation would then come to those whose good deeds failed to outnumber their evils deeds (*Apoc. Zeph.* 3.6–9; 7.1–11).[22] In either case, the philosophy seems to have advocated keeping the Mosaic law, and probably other rules of an especially ascetic character, as a way of receiving favorable treatment from the cosmic powers either in this life or the next.

Against these ideas Paul argues that God has already reconciled the Colossians to himself and included them among his people through Christ's death and apart from their conformity to special rules. Fear of what the cosmic powers will do to them either in this life or the next should not dictate their behavior. Instead, their identification with Christ's death and resurrection should govern the way they live.

The Colossians as God's People

Although the Colossian Christians are Gentiles (1:27; 2:13), Paul assures them of their place among God's people. God has qualified them, he says, "to share in the

21 In the Coptic text of *Apoc. Zeph.* 3.7, 8, 9; 7.1, 3, 4, 5, 6, 7, and 8, the term *cheirographon* ("manuscript") is transliterated from the Greek. Col. 2:14 contains the only New Testament use of this term, which LSJ, 1985, define as a "manuscript note, note of hand, bond."

22 Heavenly records of human deeds appear frequently in Jewish apocalyptic literature. See, e.g., *1 En.* 81.2, 4; 96.7; 97.5–7; 98.6–8; 104.7; 2 *En.* 44.5–7; 50.1; 52.15; 53.2–3; *Jub.* 4.23; 39.6; *Test. Ab.* 12.7, 12, 17–18 and the discussion of these texts in Sappington, *Revelation and Redemption*, 100–108. Cf. Wilson, *Hope of Glory*, 30.

inheritance [*klērou*] of the saints [*hagiōn*] in the kingdom of light" (1:12). The LXX uses the term "inheritance" (*klēros*) to refer to Israel's portion in the Promised Land (Ex. 6:8; Num. 16:14; Josh. 17:4; cf. Deut. 10:9) and then, by metaphorical extension, to the eternal destiny of God's people (Dan. 12:13, Theodotian).[23]

The term "saints" (*hagioi*) recalls Israel's status as "a kingdom of priests and a holy [LXX, *hagion*] nation" (Ex. 19:6) and is reminiscent of God's call to his people to "be holy [LXX, *hagioi*], because I am holy [*hagios*]" (Lev. 11:45). God has provided "redemption" for them, just as he redeemed his people from slavery in Egypt (Ex. 6:6), and he has provided "the forgiveness of sins" that Jeremiah claimed would be the hallmark of the era of God's new covenant with his people (Col. 1:14; cf. Jer. 31:34). They bear the sign of God's covenant people—circumcision—not in any literal sense but in the sense that fulfills God's promise to his people that he would one day circumcise their wayward hearts (Deut. 30:6). It comes as no surprise, then, that in Colossians 3:12 Paul transfers three classic designations of Israel's special status to the Gentile Colossians: They are the "God's chosen people, holy and dearly loved."[24]

God has accomplished the Colossian Christians' transference into his people by the death of Christ. Through the sacrificial blood shed in Christ's crucifixion, God has reconciled "to himself all things," including the Colossian Christians, who were once estranged from God because of their evil deeds (1:20–22).[25] If these evil deeds were recorded as a series of decrees against them in some heavenly "manuscript" (*cheirographon*), then God struck those deeds from that "manuscript," took the manuscript away, and nailed it to the cross.

In other words, when Christ was crucified, the evil deeds of Christians were crucified with him, and on that basis God forgave them (1:13–14). With this arresting metaphor Paul expresses the same understanding of Christ's death that he articulated in 2 Corinthians 5:21 and Romans 3:25. Christ's death on the cross was a sacrifice in which Christ played the role of the victim and therefore assumed the penalty for the suppliant's sins and removed the curse that fell on the suppliant for his or her transgression. In this case, however, God rather than the suppliant provided the sacrifice. As 2 Corinthians 5:21 puts it, "God made him who had no sin to be sin for us, so that in him we might become the righteousness of God."[26]

23 Cf. Wisd. 3:14 and 1QS 1:9–11, which is especially close to the language of Col. 1:12–13. See Str-B 3:625; Dunn, *Epistles to the Colossians and to Philemon*, 77–79, and J. H. Friedrich, "κλῆρος," *EDNT*, 2:199–300.

24 For "chosen" or "elect" (*eklektos*) see Ps. 105:6 and Isa. 43:20; 65:9, 15, 22 and for "beloved" (*ēgapēmenos*) see Isa. 5:1. See also Lightfoot, *Colossians and Philemon*, 221 , and O'Brien, *Colossians, Philemon*, 197–98.

25 *Pace* E. F. Scott, *The Epistles of Paul to the Colossians, to Philemon and to the Ephesians* (MNTC; London: Hodder and Stoughton, 1930), 26, and Dunn, *Epistles to the Colossians and to Philemon*, 103–4, Paul's mention of "blood" here signals the sacrificial understanding of Jesus' death that also appears in such passages as Rom. 3:25 and 1 Cor. 11:25. See Lohse, *Colossians and Philemon*, 60 n. 209, and esp. Stuhlmacher, *Biblische Theologie*, 2:10–11.

26 The Jewish background to this concept can be found, for example, in the Day of Atonement ritual in Lev. 16:1–34. On this see esp. Peter Stuhlmacher, *Reconciliation, Law, and Righteousness: Essays in Biblical Theology* (Philadelphia: Fortress, 1986), 94–109, and idem, *Biblische Theologie*, 1:196. For a persuasive case that the substitutionary and atoning nature of Jesus' death was fully intelligible in the Greco-Roman world, see Martin Hengel, *The Atonement: The Origins of the Doctrine in the New Testament* (Philadelphia: Fortress, 1981), 1–32.

The Colossians' Ethical Resources

Christ's death also provides the real antidote to the evil tendencies of "the flesh" (*sarx*, 2:23). The Colossians, who are Gentiles, were once dead in their transgressions and the uncircumcision of their flesh. But they believed in the effective power of God who raised Jesus from the dead and were baptized. In this way they became identified with Jesus' death and resurrection. Jesus' death can be compared to circumcision, since, like circumcision, it involved stripping off (*apekdyō*) his physical flesh. Similarly, the Colossians have become circumcised, not in a literal sense but metaphorically.

All this implies that the Colossians have a new identity and that their flesh has received a mortal blow. They are now alive, with Christ, to God (2:11–13; 3:3; cf. 1:22). Because of this they ought to put to death their former, sinful way of life (3:5–8), and strip off (*apekdyō*) their "old human being with its practices" (3:9, aut.). In its place, they should "put on the new human being, which is being renewed in knowledge in the image its Creator" (3:10, aut.).

The phrase "the image of its Creator" recalls the Christological confession of 1:15–20, which describes Christ as "the image of the invisible God" (1:15) and the one who created all things (1:16). Through him, and specifically though his sacrificial death on the cross, the confession affirms, God reconciled all things to himself. Paul now describes the meaning of living in the image of the one through whom God accomplished this reconciliation, namely, pursuing reconciliation and peace with others. Social barriers between people collapse; people love one another; the church lives in peace, focused on the grateful worship of God; and households live together harmoniously (3:5–4:1).[27]

Scholars customarily point out that Paul's advice on this last point—households living together harmoniously (3:18–4:1)—echoes a form of advice on household management that probably predates Aristotle and reappears in the common moral teaching of the philosophical schools current during the New Testament period. Aristotle, probably dependent on traditions in circulation before him, believed that since the household was the basic social unit of the state, its proper ordering was critical to the successful management of the state.[28] Three relationships were of particular importance: husband to wife, father to children, and master to slave. The father stood at the top of this hierarchy because he was more rational than the wife, the slave, and the children. The slave had no rationality, he said, and the children were immature.[29]

Similarly, the Stoic philosopher Epictetus believed that a good student would want to know "what is fitting with respect to the gods, to parents, to siblings, to

27 In 1:22 Paul says that Christ reconciled the Colossians to God "to present you holy in his sight, without blemish and free from accusation." The imperatives to be reconciled to one another in chapters 3 and 4 rest on this indicative of Christ's own work of reconciling God to his people.

28 Plato had already connected civic with household virtue and spoken of household virtue in terms of the duties of "child, woman, slave, free, artisan, ruler, and ruled" (*Resp.* IV 433A, C–D). See David L. Balch, *Let Wives Be Submissive: The Domestic Code in 1 Peter* (SBLMS 26; Atlanta: Scholars Press, 1981), 23–24.

29 See Aristotle, *Pol.* I 1253b 1–14 and 1260a 9–14. For these texts and the probability that the Aristotelian form of the household code was widely known in the first century, see Balch, *Let Wives Be Submissive*, 33–49.

country, to strangers" (*Diatr.* 2.17.31; cf. 2.14.8). According to Seneca, Stoic philosophy "advises how a husband should conduct himself toward his wife, or a father should bring up his children, or how a master should rule his slaves" (*Epist.* 94.1).[30] The same concern with household relationships occasionally reappears in the literature of Hellenistic Judaism, especially as an attempt to interpret the Mosaic law to a Gentile readership. Philo, for example, explained the approach of the Mosaic law to household relationships this way:

> If thou outrage either a slave or a free man, if thou keep him in bonds, if thou take him away and sell him . . . it is death. . . .
>
> There were other laws again such as that wives should be ruled by their husbands, not from any motive of insult, but with a view to obedience in all things: that parents should rule their children for safety and greater care. . . .[31]

Some link between Colossians 3:18–4:1 and these "household codes" seems likely, but the broad similarities also highlight two significant differences. First, Paul emphasizes the reciprocal nature of these relationships. Wives should be subject to their husbands, but husbands should love their wives. Children should obey their parents, but fathers should not provoke their children. Slaves should obey their masters, but masters should treat their slaves with justice and equity because they know that they too have a heavenly master.[32] It is true that reciprocity in household relationships is not a Christian innovation, but the emphasis placed on it here is unusual.[33]

Second, Paul does not legitimate his household order by finding something intrinsically inferior about its subordinate members. He refuses even to say that children are immature. The household code in Paul's letter, therefore, is integrated into the theme of social reconciliation that pervades the entire section from 3:5 to 4:1 and that is, in turn, a reflection of the reconciliation God has effected with the universe through Christ's death. In the Christian household, as in the church, a common equality undergirds the ordering of relationships because "Christ is all, and is in all" (3:11).

30 Lohse, *Colossians and Philemon*, 155, and Hübner, *An Philemon, an die Kolosser, an die Epheser*, 110. On the legal and emotional structure of the Roman family, see Andrew Wallace-Hadrill, "The Roman Family," in *The World of Rome: An Introduction to Roman Culture*, ed. Peter Jones and Keith Sidwell (Cambridge: Cambridge Univ. Press, 1997), 208–34.

31 Quoted in Eusebius, *Praep. ev.* 357d–358a. I have used the translation by Edwin Hamilton Gifford, 2 parts (Grand Rapids: Baker, 1981), 1:387–88. Cf. Josephus, *C. Ap.* 2.190–219; Pseudo-Phocylides, *Sentences* 175–227; and the discussion in Wilson, *Hope of Glory*, 45–46.

32 The mutuality of Paul's advice to slaves and masters stands in contrast to the emphasis on the *obsequium* ("obedience") of slaves in the elite literature of the period as a way of preventing slave resistance and rebellion to the oppressive conditions under which they lived. See K. R. Bradley, *Slaves and Masters in the Roman Empire: A Study in Social Control* (New York: Oxford Univ. Press, 1987), 36–37. This mutuality does not support Bradley's later statement that in Eph. 6:5 and 1 Pet. 2:18 (erroneously identified as "1 Pet. 18") "Christian leaders absorbed and indirectly supported the ideology of the slave owning classes in Roman society at large" (ibid., 114).

33 Cf. Hübner, *An Philemon, and die Kolosser, an die Epheser*, 111; Paul Achtemeier, *1 Peter* (Hermeneia; Minneapolis: Fortress, 1996), 52 n. 543; and Harold Hoehner, *Ephesians: An Exegetical Commentary* (Grand Rapids: Baker, 2002), 720–29. For the point that reciprocity in the household codes is not a Christian innovation, see John M. G. Barclay, "Ordinary but Different: Colossians and Hidden Moral Identity," *ABR* 49 (2001): 34–52, here at 41 n. 11. In addition to Philo, *De decalogo* 165–67, which Barclay cites, see the first-century A.D. Stoic Seneca (*Ben.* 2.18.1–2) and the second-century Stoic Hierocles (Stob. 4.22.24). Hierocles' work is only available in extracts from the fifth-century A.D. anthologizer Ioannes Stobeus (or Stobaeus). The relevant passages from Seneca and Hierocles appear in Balch, *Let Wives Be Submissive*, 5 and 51–52.

Paul offers an alternative to the ethical program of "the philosophy." Its leader was haughty (2:18), passing judgment on others and claiming that they were unfit to belong to his superior group unless they followed his ascetic program for placating the "elements of the world" (2:16, 18). With this fleshly attitude (2:18), Paul asserts, he has failed to hold fast to the head of the church who keeps it unified (2:19). Since Christ has triumphed over the cosmic rulers and authorities at his death (2:15), moreover, and since the Colossian Christians at their baptism have died with Christ to the "elements of the world" (2:20), they have nothing to fear from the cosmic powers as long as they hold fast to Christ.

Thus, the philosophy's claim that Christians need to placate these powers through a specific ascetic regimen dissolves, and the foundation for the haughty tendencies of the philosophy dissolves along with it (2:23). The Colossians are then free to dwell with Christ in his position of authority at God's right hand. They share his resurrection and his triumph over his enemies (3:1; cf. Ps. 110:1)—a triumph that has begun to reconcile the whole world to God. Their relationships with one another should be a reflection of this cosmic reconciliation.[34]

CHRIST'S DEFEAT OF THE COSMIC POWERS IN COLOSSIANS

Against the notions that Christ is only one among many cosmic powers, that success in this life or in the next depends on placating these powers, and that "the philosophy" is the repository of the wisdom that can placate them, Paul asserts here the preeminence of Christ. Christ is superior to the "rulers and authorities," he claims, because God created them through Christ and for Christ (1:16). He is also superior to them because through his death on the cross, he stripped them of their malevolent abilities, just as captured soldiers are stripped of their weapons, and he led them in a triumphal procession, just as a victorious general leads defeated soldiers to their execution (2:15).

When Jesus died on the cross, Christians also died with him. His defeat of these powers, therefore, is also their defeat of them. They dwell with Christ at the right hand of God and, like him, they sit next to God with these cosmic powers at their feet (3:1–3). The notion that the Colossian Christians should use ascetic practices to placate the rulers and authorities, therefore, is "hollow and deceptive" (2:8). The complicated ascetic scheme of the philosophy may resemble wisdom in some superficial way, but it is only a charade—all the treasures of wisdom and knowledge reside in Christ and the only effective means of resisting the sinful tendencies of the flesh is dying and rising with him (2:20–3:4).

The cross not only effected the defeat of the inimical cosmic powers but the reconciliation of the Colossian Christians to God (1:20, 22). Through Christ's atoning

34 On the use of Ps. 110:1 (LXX 109:1) here, see Hübner, *Biblische Theologie*, 2:360, and *An Philemon, and die Kolosser, an die Epheser*, 98.

death, God has forgiven the Colossian Christians' transgressions (2:13–14) and has included them in the beginning stages of the process by which, through Christ's atoning death on the cross, he will reconcile all things to himself and restore creation to its position of fellowship with God prior to Adam's fall (1:20). The Colossians provide evidence of the universal scope of God's plans for reconciliation because although they are Gentiles (1:27) and were dead in their sins and the uncircumcision of their flesh (2:13), God has included them among his people through the death and resurrection of Christ.

Because God has reconciled them to himself and because they form the beginning stages of God's plan to reconcile everything to himself, the Colossian Christians should reflect God's forgiving and reconciling nature in their relationships with one another. Rather than allowing a false fear of the cosmic powers and the haughty claims of the philosophy's chief advocate to dictate their behavior, the Colossian church should live in a way that reflects the peace that God has made with his creation through the blood of Jesus shed on the cross.

Chapter 17

PHILEMON: RECONCILIATION IN PRACTICE

The ethic of reconciliation that Paul advocated in his letter to the Colossians included the admonition to slaves that they should wholeheartedly obey their masters, and to slave masters that they should treat their slaves with fairness and justice.[1] In his letter to Philemon, Paul urges the reconciliation of a master to his slave because of the new relationship between the two implied by the slave's conversion to Christianity. Paul insists that Philemon (the master) set aside the brutal social conventions surrounding ancient Roman slavery and love Onesimus (the slave) as if he were his brother, indeed as if Onesimus were Paul himself, elderly and imprisoned, but no less authoritative for all that.[2] In order to understand the theology that undergirds Paul's profound transformation of Roman social conventions in Philemon, it is necessary to reconstruct, as far as possible, the circumstances that prompted this brief letter.

ONESIMUS'S FLIGHT TO PAUL AND PAUL'S LETTER TO PHILEMON

Traditionally, interpreters of the letter have thought that Onesimus stole money from his master Philemon and ran away. Somehow, he encountered his master's close friend Paul and through him became a Christian. Paul then sent the fugitive back to his master with a letter pleading for Philemon to forgive Onesimus and promising to pay back from his own funds the money that Onesimus had stolen.[3] This reconstruction depends heavily on two assumptions: that when Paul says he is sending Onesimus back (v. 12) Onesimus has run away, and that when Paul instructs Philemon to charge any injustice or debt of Onesimus to his own account (vv. 18–19), Onesimus has stolen money from his master.

1 The advice to slaves is longer than the advice to masters, which might at first seem to violate the principle of mutuality suggested in the previous chapter. This impression needs to be tempered, however, with the knowledge that probably many more slaves than slave owners were Christians. Although he writes with hostility and a century later, Celsus' social profile of Christianity in the second century is probably not too wide of the mark for the first century: "They want and are able to convince," he says, "only the foolish, dishonourable and stupid, and only slaves, women, and little children" (Origen, *Cels.* 3.44).

2 Despite the sometimes optimistic portrayal of ancient Roman chattel slavery in scholarly literature on the New Testament, the institution was brutal. On this see K. R. Bradley, *Slaves and Masters in the Roman Empire: A Study in Social Control* (New York: Oxford Univ. Press, 1987); John M. G. Barclay, "Paul, Philemon and the Dilemma of Christian Slave-Ownership," *NTS* 37 (1991): 161–86, here at 165–70; and J. Albert Harrill, *The Manumission of Slaves in Early Christianity* (HUT 32; Tübingen: J. C. B. Mohr [Paul Siebeck], 1995), 11–56.

3 See, e.g., J. B. Lightfoot, *Saint Paul's Epistles to the Colossians and to Philemon* (London: Macmillan, 1879), 310–15; C. F. D. Moule, *The Epistles to the Colossians and to Philemon* (CGTC; Cambridge: Cambridge Univ. Press, 1957), 18–21; Barclay, "Dilemma of Christian Slave-Ownership," 163–65.

This traditional scenario, however, is unnecessarily complicated. It must assume that when Onesimus fled, he did not intend to encounter Paul but that, by what seems an unlikely chance, he fell into the apostle's company.

A much simpler explanation for the letter, and one with contemporary historical precedent, holds that Onesimus has experienced a breech of relationship with his master and goes to Paul specifically to ask him to intervene on his behalf. First-century Roman law distinguished between a slave who ran away to escape his master's ownership and a slave who fled to a master's friend, to a temple, or to an image of a Roman emperor for asylum.[4] The slave who ran to such a haven to escape mistreatment was not to be considered a fugitive (*Dig.* 21.1.17.12). In a famous letter from the first decade of the second century, the younger Pliny wrote to his friend Sabinianus about a freedman in precisely this predicament (*Ep.* 9.21).[5] The freedman had come to Pliny after offending his master and, fearing some severe reprisal, asked Pliny to intercede for him with Sabinianus. Pliny appeals to Sabinianus to pardon the freedman and to renew his love for him, yet he refuses to beg Sabinianus to do this lest, he says, "I should seem rather to compel, than request you to forgive him."

Paul's letter fits this kind of situation well. Onesimus has probably made a mistake, whether intentional or not, that cost Philemon some money (v. 18). Knowing that Paul is a friend of his master, Onesimus has come to Paul to seek asylum and to ask Paul to intercede for him.[6] In his reply Paul, like Pliny, encourages Philemon to show love to Onesimus (vv. 9, 16), and, in a phrase that uncannily resembles the language of Pliny's letter, says that although he could command Philemon to do what is fitting, he prefers instead to appeal to him on the basis of love (v. 8).

These superficial similarities between the two letters, however, only highlight a striking difference. Onesimus had become a Christian during his period of asylum with Paul (vv. 10, 16), and therefore Paul's letter is not a request for Philemon to pardon his slave but a description of the radical reorientation of the relationship between Onesimus and Philemon that Onesimus's conversion entails. The two men must be reconciled to each other, but not merely as offending slave to offended master (as in Pliny's letter). They must be reconciled *as fellow believers* who have in common their conversion through Paul's faithful execution of his apostolic task and who have the common responsibility of aiding Paul in the completion of this task. Their reconciliation to each other through the gospel breaks down the social conventions by which they once only related to each other as master and slave. They now must relate to each other as Paul's children, as brothers in the flesh and in the Lord, and as coworkers with Paul in advancing the gospel.

Paul does not send Onesimus back to Philemon, therefore, in the hope that Philemon will generously overlook Onesimus's offense and accept the slave back into

4 Peter Lampe, "Keine 'Sklavenflucht' des Onesimus," *ZNW* 76 (1985): 135–37; Bradley, *Slaves and Masters*, 124–25.

5 Even after manumission, the master often retained power over a former slave. Bradley, *Slaves and Masters*, 81, explains: "As a condition of release from servile status the freedman might find himself bound to his patron by a nexus of obligations . . . as a result of which he continued to discharge various services for the patron for a certain length of time."

6 Cf. James D. G. Dunn, *The Epistles to the Colossians and to Philemon* (NIGTC; Grand Rapids: Eerdmans, 1996), 304–5, and Hans Hübner, *An Philemon, an die Kolosser, an die Epheser* (HNT 12; Tübingen: J. C. B. Mohr [Paul Siebeck], 1997), 34.

his family (as Sabinianus eventually accepted back his freedman).[7] He sends him back so that the relationship between the two men may be reoriented around their common membership in the family of God. He also sends him back so that Philemon, of his own accord, might release Onesimus to return to Paul and help him, in Philemon's place, in the work of the gospel.[8] In his letter to Philemon, therefore, the theology of cosmic reconciliation that Paul described in his letter to the Colossians takes specific expression in the radical realignment of the relationship between a Christian slave and his master.[9]

THE THEOLOGY OF PAUL'S APPEAL

Paul bases his appeal to Philemon on three theological assumptions. First, Paul assumes that God has given Philemon the desire to do what is right. Thus, Paul does not command Philemon "to do what you ought to do," although he believes that it lies within the boundary of his apostolic authority to do so, but he appeals to him on the basis of love (v. 8). Similarly, he refuses to keep Onesimus without Philemon's "consent" (*gnōmē*) and wants Philemon to send Onesimus back to him not because he is "forced" but "spontaneously" (v. 14). Paul is "confident" that Philemon will obey his wishes, but he does not want to force the issue (v. 21).

Some interpreters have understood all this to be Paul's attempt to feign magnanimity while manipulating Philemon to do exactly what he wants. After all, the letter is to be read before the church that assembles in Philemon's house (v. 2), and Paul tells Philemon that he plans to visit his home soon (v. 22). Under these circumstances, how much freedom would Philemon have to ignore Paul's wishes? Surely Paul exposes his real feelings when near the end of the letter he speaks of Philemon's "obedience" (v. 21).[10]

Elsewhere, however, Paul shows a willingness to allow his churches to make up their own minds to do what he knows is the right thing to do. In Philippians 3:12–15a, for instance, Paul offers himself as an example of one who has correctly refused to allow his confidence in the righteousness that comes from God to lead to complacency, but, he says, "if on some point you think differently, that too God will make clear to you" (3:15b). In Romans 14:1–15:13 Paul is convinced that those who do not distinguish among foods or days are correct (14:14; cf. 14:20). Nevertheless,

7 Pliny, *Ep.* 9.24.

8 Barclay's concern, "Dilemma of Christian Slave-Ownership," 170–75, over exactly what Paul is requesting of Philemon is puzzling. Paul says explicitly in vv. 13–14 that he would have liked to keep Onesimus with him, but does not want to do so without Philemon's permission. This is certainly a polite request to send Onesimus back to Paul. Moreover, the reference in v. 18 to the wrong that Onesimus has committed against Philemon, set as it is within the context of Paul's request that Philemon receive Onesimus with brotherly love, clearly shows that Paul wants Philemon and Onesimus to be reconciled.

9 Cf. Ralph P. Martin, *Reconciliation: A Study of Paul's Theology* (NFTL; Atlanta: John Knox, 1981), 231–32. The historical link between Paul's letters to the Colossians and to Philemon is clear from the common situation implied by both. Onesimus, who is said to be from Colosse, appears in Colossians, where Paul says that he is sending him back to Colosse with Tychicus, the bearer of the letter to the Colossian church (Col. 4:7–9). In addition, Epaphras, Mark, Aristarchus, Demas, and Luke are all with Paul when he writes both letters (Col. 1:7; 4:10, 12, 14, 17; Philem. 24), and Paul mentions Archippus in both (Col. 4:10; Philem. 1).

10 See esp. Barclay, "Dilemma of Christian Slave-Ownership," 171–72.

he insists that those who hold this position avoid imposing their views on others because "each one should be fully convinced in his [or her] own mind" (14:5).

Similarly, in 1 Corinthians 7, Paul allows the Corinthians the "concession" of abstaining from sexual relations with their spouses to devote themselves to prayer (7:6) and offers his "judgment" (*gnōmē*) on whether, in light of "the present crisis," marriage is advisable (7:25, 40). He does not, however, want to "throw a noose around" them, and those who do not follow his advice are not sinning (7:28, 35–36, aut.). In 2 Corinthians 8–9 he refuses to command the Corinthians to contribute to his offering for suffering Jewish Christians in Jerusalem, but he wants any contribution that they give to arise from "sincerity," "eager willingness," and the cheerful decision of one's heart (8:8, 11–12; 9:7).

If necessary, Paul could issue authoritative directives about how his churches should conduct themselves. At the same time he seems to have believed that Christian ethical behavior should arise from the individual's own inner convictions. Perhaps his understanding of the new covenant as a covenant whose stipulations are written on the heart has led him to this position (2 Cor. 3:6; cf. Isa. 54:13; Jer. 31:31–34; Ezek. 11:19; 36:26–27; 37:24).[11]

Second, Paul assumes that he and Philemon agree on the central tenet of Christian ethics: love for one's neighbor. He therefore bases his appeal to Philemon on love (v. 9)—the Christian love that Philemon has already demonstrated toward Paul and many others by his willingness to refresh their "hearts" (vv. 5, 7).[12] Because of Philemon's past demonstrations of love toward others, Paul is confident that he will act in a loving way toward Onesimus and toward Paul himself (vv. 9, 13–14, 21). Since Onesimus is Paul's "very heart" (v. 12), Paul knows that Philemon will refresh his "heart" (v. 20) both by treating Onesimus with love (v. 16) and by sending him back to work with Paul in Philemon's place (vv. 13–14, 20–21).[13]

This emphasis on love in the letter probably arises from the centrality of the love command in Paul's understanding of Christian ethics. In his letters to the Galatians and the Romans Paul had summarized the Decalogue in terms of the love command (Rom. 13:8–10; Gal. 5:14), and he had done so precisely in the context of a radical claim about the impact of the gospel on established social boundaries (Rom. 3:19, 22b, 29; 4:16–17; 9:24; 11:32; Gal. 2:11–21; 3:28). In 1 Corinthians, again, where social class distinctions were feeding the community's divisive spirit, Paul urged the "strong" in Corinth to value love above knowledge (1 Cor. 8:1–2; 13:1–13). So here too, since Philemon is a believer, to show love toward Onesimus is the right thing to do (vv. 8–9).

---

11 See Frank Thielman, "Law and Liberty in the Ethics of Paul," *ExAud* 11 (1995): 63–75. Cf. the comment of Eduard Lohse, *Colossians and Philemon* (Hermeneia; Philadelphia: Fortress, 1971), 202: "Love can only express itself concretely on the basis of a decision that is freely arrived at."

12 The "love" of v. 9, therefore, is not "love regarded as a principle that demands deferential respect," as Lightfoot, *Colossians and Philemon*, 22, and Lohse, *Colossians and Philemon*, 198, maintain. "Love" in v. 9 is instead defined by "love" in vv. 5 and 7 and is therefore Philemon's own practical demonstration of love. See Peter T. O'Brien, *Colossians, Philemon* (WBC 44; Waco, Tex.: Word, 1982), 289.

13 Lohse, *Colossians and Philemon*, 195.

Paul does not, therefore, appeal to Philemon, as Pliny seems to do, on the basis of an affection that has naturally developed between a master and his household slave, but on the basis of Jesus' own reduction of the Mosaic law's regulation of social relationships to the precept of Leviticus 19:18, "You shall love your neighbor as yourself." Like Jesus, who defined the neighbor in this command as the foreigner and enemy (Luke 10:29–37), Paul understands the love command to mean that within the newly restored people of God, the barriers between ethnic groups and social classes are leveled.[14]

Third, Paul assumes that Onesimus's conversion has radically shifted the place of Onesimus in Philemon's household.[15] In this letter and within the boundaries of the Colossian church, Onesimus is no longer Philemon's slave but, "better than a slave," he is a "beloved brother" (v. 16).[16]

Paul, moreover, takes the position of a parent to both—he has given birth to Onesimus in prison and brought Philemon into being (vv. 10, 19b). Both Onesimus and Philemon, in other words, have experienced conversion through believing the gospel Paul communicated to them. In a metaphorical sense Paul is their parent (cf. Gal. 4:19; 1 Thess. 2:7), and the two are brothers to each other. Practically speaking, this means that Paul is willing to pay Onesimus's debts, just as a parent might pay the outstanding debt of his or her child (vv. 18–19a). It also means that Philemon should be willing to overlook any injustice or debt that Onesimus has committed against him (vv. 19b–20). As if to anticipate the possibility that Philemon might leave this brotherhood in the theoretical realm without any real impact on his day-to-day interaction with Onesimus, Paul specifically says that Onesimus is Philemon's brother "both in the flesh and in the Lord" (v. 16, aut.).

In a way that is consistent with this leveling of social relationships, Paul values Onesimus as a coworker in the proclamation of the gospel (vv. 11, 13), just as he values Philemon in the same capacity (vv. 1, 13, 17). On one hand, when Onesimus arrives on Philemon's doorstep, Philemon should therefore treat Onesimus just as he would treat Paul. This is what someone who considers Paul a "partner" would do (v. 17). On the other hand, when Onesimus arrives back on Paul's doorstep, Paul will consider him to be taking the place of Philemon as he helps Paul use his imprisonment for the proclamation of the gospel (v. 13).

14 Cf. David Wenham, *Paul: Follower of Jesus or Founder of Christianity* (Grand Rapids: Eerdmans, 1995), 234–40.

15 Chris Frilingos, "'For My Child, Onesimus': Paul and Domestic Power in Philemon," *JBL* 119 (2000): 91–104. Cf. John L. White, *The Apostle of God: Paul and the Promise of Abraham* (Peabody, Mass.: Hendrickson, 1999), 52–53.

16 Cf. Norman Petersen, *Rediscovering Paul: Philemon and the Sociology of Paul's Narrative World* (Philadelphia: Fortress, 1985), 289–90, and Neil Elliott, *Liberating Paul: The Justice of God and the Politics of the Apostle* (Maryknoll, N.Y.: Orbis, 1994), 47–48. Since the letter was to be read to the whole church and within Philemon's house, Paul intends for the entire church to be aware of the realignment that has taken place in the relationship between Onesimus and Philemon. On this see Frilingos, "'For My Child, Onesimus,'" 99.

THE RADICAL SOCIAL IMPLICATIONS OF THE GOSPEL

These three theological assumptions—that God leads believers to make correct decisions, that love for the other is central to Christian ethics, and that the gospel tears down social barriers—taken together, make a social statement that, within the context of Paul's culture, is breathtakingly radical. Paul believes that the gospel reconfigures one of the most basic—and most brutal—social relationships of his day, slavery.

Slavery was deeply woven into the economic fabric of the Roman empire; without it the Romans could not have achieved political dominance of the Mediterranean region, nor would their celebrated architectural, civic, literary, and philosophical achievements have been possible. Slavery provided the wealthy classes with the leisure to develop strategies, plan buildings, debate legislation, write poetry and essays, and think about life. At the same time, slavery was unavoidably dehumanizing and oppressive—slaves, not merely their labor, were their masters' property.[17] Although "human souls," they were bought and sold like so much bronze, iron, marble, and cinnamon.[18] They had no legal rights and could be bred, raped, punished, and murdered at the whim of their masters. The institution was so brutal that it could only survive by the systematic use of fear and violence.[19]

Paul believes that the gospel transforms this social relationship so that slave and master are "beloved" brothers "both in the flesh and in the Lord" (v. 16). He also believes that brothers in the Lord should be responsible for one another's spiritual welfare (Gal. 6:1), should be slaves of one another (5:13), and should bear one another's burdens (6:2).[20] Such a radical redefinition of the relationship between master and slave removes the brutality and dehumanizing aspects of Roman chattel slavery, and with these aspects removed, the institution's demise, at least in Christian circles, awaits only the consistent application of Paul's radical social vision to be complete.

17 See esp. Bradley, *Slaves and Masters*.

18 Rev. 18:11–13.

19 Bradley, *Slaves and Masters*, 113–37.

20 Barclay, "Dilemma of Christian Slave-Ownership," 178–79, believes that Christian brotherhood and sisterhood, as Paul's theology defined it, could not be compatible with slave ownership and yet that Paul hesitated to draw these radical conclusions. This hesitation, he argues, is evident in the vague nature of Paul's request to Philemon. Paul's requests to Philemon, however, are not vague, and, as the letter's radical realignment of Philemon's household affairs shows, Paul was willing to speak the truth about the gospel's social implications, however inconvenient these may have been for the powerful.

Chapter 18

EPHESIANS: THE UNITY OF CHURCH AND COSMOS IN CHRIST

At the same time that Paul composed Colossians and Philemon, he also wrote a more general letter to Christians in the south-central part of Roman Asia.[1] Many of these churches were probably born during Paul's lengthy and far-reaching ministry in Ephesus (Acts 19:10), but not through the efforts of Paul himself. Paul may have thought of the churches in Colosse, Laodicea, and Hierapolis as part of this group, and, just as his coworker Epaphras had labored to establish churches in those places (Col. 1:7; 4:13), so other coworkers may have had similar ministries in other outlying towns.[2]

As with the gatherings of Christians in Colosse and Laodicea, Paul had likely not visited some of these churches, and thus he implies both that he does not know his readers personally and that they may not know him (1:15; 3:2; cf. 4:21–22; Col. 1:4, 9; 2:1). Paul's composition of the letter for this diverse group of readers probably accounts for its lack of references to particular problems and for the trouble that many interpreters have consequently experienced in finding a concrete life-setting for it.[3]

Ephesians, like all of Paul's letters, however, had a pastoral purpose, and, as is common with his correspondence, Paul hints at this purpose in the letter's intercessory prayer report. Paul's thanksgiving for the faith and love of his readers (1:15) turns quickly to intercession on their behalf that God will enable them to understand their hope as those whom he has called, their status as his own rich inheritance, and the immense power that belongs to them as believers (1:18–19). Paul then digresses on the blessings that have come to his readers as a result of Christ's death and resurrection (2:1–22), and on his own part in bringing these blessings to the

---

1 He probably addressed the letter to the Ephesians because Ephesus was the most important city in the region and the place of the largest Christian community. On this, see Harold W. Hoehner, *Ephesians: An Exegetical Commentary* (Grand Rapids: Baker, 2002), 79. Although *en Ephesō* ("in Ephesus") in 1:1 does not appear in several early witnesses to the text of the letter, Hoehner, *Ephesians*, 146, argues persuasively that on balance the textual evidence slightly favors the inclusion of the phrase. This produces the admittedly difficult Greek construction *tois hagiois tois ousin en Ephesō kai pistois* ("to the saints who are in Ephesus and to the faithful"). The Greek-speaking church fathers Chrysostom, Theodoret of Cyrus, and Theophylact of Achrida, however, betray no confusion about its meaning, which they take to be that the Christians in Ephesus are both saints and faithful (PG 62:9–10; 82:509; 124:1033).

2 Cf., e.g., J. Armitage Robinson, *St. Paul's Epistle to the Ephesians* (London: James Clarke, 1928), 11–13; F. F. Bruce, *The Epistles to the Colossians, to Philemon, and to the Ephesians* (NICNT; Grand Rapids: Eerdmans, 1984), 245; and Peter T. O'Brien, *The Letter to the Ephesians* (PNTC; Grand Rapids: Eerdmans, 1999), 57–58.

3 See esp. Andrew T. Lincoln, *Ephesians* (WBC 42; Dallas: Word, 1990), lxxiv, and idem, "The Theology of Ephesians" in *The Theology of the Later Pauline Letters*, by Andrew T. Lincoln and A. J. M. Wedderburn (New Testament Theology; Cambridge: Cambridge Univ. Press, 1993), 78–79. The general nature of the letter, its close relationship to Colossians, and its unusual language, style, and thought have led many scholars, including Lincoln, to conclude that the letter is pseudonymous. It seems improbable, however, that the author would copy the admonition not to lie found in Col. 3:9–10, make its language more emphatic ("each of you"), and bolster it with an allusion to Scripture (Eph. 4:25; cf. 4:15 and Zech. 8:16) all within a forgery of his own. On the genuineness of the letter, see esp. the judicious argument of O'Brien, *Ephesians*, 4–47. Cf. Hoehner, *Ephesians*, 2–61.

Gentiles (3:2–12). He concludes his digression with this statement: "I ask you, therefore, not to be discouraged because of my sufferings for you, which are your glory" (3:13).

"For this reason," Paul then explains, he prays that God will strengthen his readers by the inner working of his Spirit and that they will have the power to grasp the vast extent of his love (3:14–19).[4] Apparently, Paul believes that his readers are discouraged at least in part because of his imprisonment (3:1; 4:1; 6:20) and that they need to be reminded (2:11) of who they are as believers in the gospel and of what their new position, created by their faith, requires of them.[5]

If Paul wrote this letter during the Roman imprisonment described in Acts 28:11–31, then he had been under Roman guard between three and five years by the time of its composition—first in Caesarea (two years), then as a prisoner traveling by sea to Rome (just under a year), and finally in Rome itself (two years).[6] After such a long period of silence from the apostle most closely connected with their own commitment to the gospel, Christians in Asia may have experienced a period of discouragement, particularly if the fires of persecution to which 1 Peter and Revelation testify had started to smolder.[7] They needed an encouraging reminder of all God had done for them in Christ and that despite the assaults of the invisible powers ranged against God's purposes, the devil will not succeed in reclaiming the cosmos from the redeeming work God had already accomplished in the death, resurrection, and heavenly session of Christ Jesus. They also needed encouragement to live in a way that was consistent with their important role in God's new creation. Paul hopes to meet these needs by emphasizing two themes: (1) the eventual unification of the universe because of the death, resurrection, and heavenly session of Christ, and (2) the responsibility of the church to proclaim by its own unity this ultimate goal of God.[8]

THE UNIFICATION OF THE UNIVERSE IN THE DEATH, RESURRECTION, AND HEAVENLY SESSION OF CHRIST

Paul reveals in the extravagant blessing that begins the letter and in the letter's intercessory prayer that one of his principal goals in writing is to remind his readers of their place in God's gracious purposes. He wants them to understand that they play

---

4 The prayer in 3:14–19 has two petitions, one in v. 16 and one in v. 18, each indicated with a *hina* clause. See Petr Pokorný, *Der Brief des Paulus an die Epheser* (THKNT 10.2; Leipzig: Evangelische Verlagsanstalt, 1992), 153, and O'Brien, *Ephesians*, 256 n. 141.

5 Cf. Lincoln, *Ephesians*, lxxvi–lxxvii, and idem, "Ephesians," 82–83. Lincoln imagines a similar reason for the letter, but places it in a post-Pauline setting.

6 See Acts 24:9, 27; 28:11, 30 for the chronological notes that allow these calculations.

7 First Peter was written to churches in five provinces of Asia Minor, one of which was Asia, and was written to console Christians passing through the "fiery trial" of persecution (1 Peter 4:12). Rev. 2:3 refers to persecution in Ephesus; 2:10 to persecution in Smyrna; 2:13 to persecution in Pergamum; and 3:8–10 to persecution in Philadelphia. See chapters 30 and 32 below. A half century after Paul wrote Ephesians, Ignatius, bishop of Antioch, had to admonish churches in Ephesus, Magnesia, Philadelphia, and Smyrna to meet together more frequently and not to succumb to a heretical blend of docetic Christianity and Judaism. See, e.g., Ig. *Eph.* 5.2; 13.1; 16.1–2; *Magn.* 7.2; 8.1–11.1; *Phld.* 6.1; 8.2; *Pol.* 3.1; 4.2.

8 See Max Turner, "Mission and Meaning in Terms of 'Unity' in Ephesians," in *Mission and Meaning: Essays Presented to Peter Cotterell*, ed. Antony Billington, Tony Lane, and Max Turner (Carlisle: Paternoster, 1995), 138–66, and O'Brien, *Ephesians*, 58–65.

a critical role in God's far-reaching and merciful plan to sum up everything in Christ "for the praise of his glory." In his intercessory prayer, therefore, Paul prays that his readers may be able to comprehend the width, length, height, and depth of Christ's love, a love, he says, that surpasses knowledge (3:18–19).

In the letter's opening blessing, he describes more fully what this means. There he says that God has lavished his rich grace on Christians by revealing to them the mystery of the purpose for which Christ came (1:7–9). Christ's appearance was part of God's plan to bring the times to their fulfillment by summing up everything in heaven and on earth (1:10). This plan—to fulfill the times through gathering together things on heaven and things on earth—is the chief theological concern of the letter's first main section (1:3–3:21).[9]

God's Unification of Time in Christ

Paul says in 1:10 that God's unification of all things in Christ is part of a divine plan to bring the "times" (*kairoi*) to their fulfillment. The plural shows that Paul, like other Jewish apocalyptic thinkers of his era, divided time into discrete periods and held that God had designed these periods to progress toward a particular goal. Throughout the letter Paul reminds his readers in various ways that in Christ and in his body the church, God's historical plan has begun to reach its climax.[10] In order to understand this, we must understand the concept of history that Paul and his readers presuppose.

In the letter Paul presupposes that God possessed a plan for the universe before he created it. Thus, Paul can say that God "chose" his people "before the creation of the world" and "predestined" their adoption (1:4–5; cf. 1:11), and he can speak of God's "plan" according to which these primordial decisions took place (1:10; 3:9). In accordance with this plan, "God . . . created all things" (3:9) in both heaven and earth, and grouped both heavenly and earthly beings into units. As the Father of all these beings, he gave to each unit an appropriate family name (3:15; cf. Gen. 2:20a; Ps. 147:4; Isa. 40:25–26; 1QS 11.19).[11]

9 The critical word "to gather things together" (*anakephalaioō*) in 1:10 means to bring together a variety of items and recapitulate them in a brief, unified form, as when someone summarizes a discourse. See Heinrich Schlier, "ἀνακεφαλαιόομαι," *TDNT*, 3:681–82, and on the climactic position of this term within the blessing of 1:3–14, see Chrys C. Caragounis, *The Ephesian* Mysterion*: Meaning and Content* (ConBNT 8; Lund: CWK Gleerup, 1977), 95, and Hans Hübner, *Biblische Theologie des Neuen Testaments*, 3 vols. (Göttingen: Vandenhoeck & Ruprecht, 1990–95), 2:363–64.

10 Christ has not already accomplished the "gathering up" or "summing up" of all things as A. Lindemann, *Die Aufhebung der Zeit: Geschichtsverständnis und Eschatologie im Epheserbrief* (SNT 12; Gütersloh: Mohn, 1975), 98–99; Hübner, *Biblische Theologie*, 2:374; and Ernest Best, *A Critical and Exegetical Commentary on Ephesians* (ICC; Edinburgh: T. & T. Clark, 1998), 139, believe. Caragounis, *The Ephesian* Mysterion, 144 n. 21, points out correctly that if God had already summed up everything in Christ, it is difficult to understand how Paul could see his own preaching of this mystery as one step in its (future) accomplishment (3:8–10).

11 This interpretation presupposes that 3:15 means "every family in heaven and on earth" (NRSV; cf. NAB, REB, NJB, TNIV) rather than "his whole family in heaven and on earth" (NIV). If Paul had intended the latter translation, he probably would have placed the article before *pasa*. See O'Brien, *Ephesians*, 255–56; Best, *Ephesians*, 237–38; Hoehner, *Ephesians*, 474–75. It seems unnecessary to propose, as do Heinrich Schlier, *Die Brief an die Epheser: Ein Kommentar* (Düsseldorf: Patmos, 1957), 168, and Bruce, *The Epistles to the Colossians, to Philemon, and to Ephesians*, 325, that Paul is here undercutting gnostic concepts of the creation of the world.

God's creation, both heavenly and earthly, rebelled against him, however, and the beings that comprised the universe became alienated from their Creator.[12] On the human side, they also became alienated from one another. The devil and the cosmic powers began a struggle against the purposes of God that Paul describes in military terms. The devil rules a "kingdom of the air" that includes the rebellious cosmic powers (6:11–12), and his goal is to develop stratagems with which he can frustrate the purposes of God (6:11, 18). The devil works among God's human creatures to lead them to follow fleshly lusts, desires, and thoughts and so to disobey God (2:1, 3; 4:17–19, 27). This has led God to pour out his wrath upon his creatures (2:3) and has resulted in their spiritual death (2:1).

God did not wholly abandon his creation to "the futility of their thinking" (4:17), however, but set apart a special people whom Paul, following biblical terminology, calls both "Israel" (2:12) and "the holy ones" or "saints" (*hagioi* in 2:19). Although God's people in the Old Testament were no less sinful than the other nations (2:3), God gave them a law whose commandments and ordinances, if properly followed, would separate them from those nations so that they would become a distinct political entity (2:12, 19) and a properly pure dwelling place for God's presence (cf. Ex. 19:6; Lev. 11:44–45). If they did this, God promised, Israel would be his treasured possession out of all the other nations of the earth (Ex. 19:5).

Israel failed in this vocation. God, however, promised that he would enter into a new covenant with them and that a special king—the Messiah—would usher in this period in which he would restore his relationship with his people (2:12).[13]

God's purposes reached this climactic moment when the Messiah Jesus appeared. His death on the cross atoned for the sins of his chosen people within Israel (1:7; 2:16; 5:2, 25) and therefore fulfilled "the covenants of the promise" found in the Scriptures (2:12). Because his love and mercy are so great, however, God has not limited the reconciling effect of Christ's death to his people Israel alone, but through it abolished the Mosaic law. In this way, he reconciled Jews and Gentiles to one another and both to himself (2:11–22), creating a new, third people—the church (2:15).

In addition, the Messiah's resurrection and heavenly session sealed the defeat of the hostile powers of the heavens and unified them in subjugation beneath his feet (1:20–23). This means that those who heard and embraced the gospel have been rescued from the spiritual death to which the hostile powers, and the devil in particular, had consigned them by working among them to produce disobedience (2:5–6).

Paul recognizes that the average reader of Israel's Scriptures is not able to tell from them that God intended to admit the nations into his people on the same footing with Israel itself. It is easy to see from the Scriptures that God included the nations in his eschatological purposes (e.g., Isa. 2:2–4; 25:6–10; 55:5; 56:6–7; 66:18–23; Zech. 8:23).[14] But it is not clear that the Gentiles will have equal standing with Israel

12 This seems to be implied by the term *anakephalaioō* ("to sum up") in 1:10. See Stig Hanson, *The Unity of the Church in the New Testament: Colossians and Ephesians* (Uppsala: Almqvist & Wiksells, 1946), 126.

13 See Jer. 23:5–6; 31:31–34; Ezek. 34:23–24; 37:24–25.

14 For the clarity with which the inclusion of the Gentiles in God's eschatological purposes was understood during Paul's era see, e.g., Tob. 13:6–7; *1 En.* 90:33; *2 Bar.* 72:4.

in those days. Yet this "mystery" is precisely what God has revealed to Paul and to other Christian apostles and prophets. God will fulfill his promises to Israel in such a way that his great love (Eph. 2:4a), rich mercy (2:4b), and abundant grace (2:7) will extend beyond the boundaries of Israel itself to include all things, whether in heaven or on earth, and both Jew and Gentile on equal terms (1:10; 3:3–6, 9). Gentile Christians, he insists, are "heirs together with Israel . . . one body, and sharers" with Jewish Christians in the restored people of God (3:6).[15]

Through the death, resurrection, and heavenly session of Christ and the consequent establishment of the church, God has begun the restoration of his creation. Those who have been saved by God's gracious initiative in Christ are his "workmanship, created" through the Messiah Jesus to do good works (2:10). The Messiah abolished the law so that Jews and Gentiles could come together in one body and so that he could thus "create in himself one new human being out of the two" (2:15, aut.). This union between Christ and the church, which is his body, parallels the union of Adam and Eve in one flesh (Gen. 2:24) and is illustrated in the bodily union of husband and wife in Christian marriage (5:31).[16] In the Messiah, therefore, God has started the process by which he will eventually gather back together (*anakephalaioō*) his fragmented and alienated creation. He has, in other words, started the final and climactic phase of his plan to bring "the times" to "their fulfillment" (1:10).

When Paul says that God has placed all things under Christ's feet at his resurrection and heavenly session (1:20–23) and that believers have taken their place of victory alongside him (2:5–6), he has collapsed the beginning of this final phase and its end together. Some scholars have argued that the collapse is so complete that the eschatology of Ephesians contradicts the eschatology of the undisputed Pauline letters, where Paul resists any notion that the eschatological day has come. It is true that Ephesians emphasizes more than the undisputed Pauline letters what Christ has already done, but Christ's accomplishment is still held in tension with what is yet to be accomplished.

This becomes clear when Paul admonishes his readers in the second part of Ephesians (4:1–6:24) to "put on the new human being, created according to God's image in righteousness and holiness and truth" (4:24, aut.; cf. Col. 3:9–10), and when he instructs them to put on "the full armor" that God supplies in order to withstand the strategies of the devil (6:11). In these statements we learn that despite what Paul says in 1:20–23 and 2:5–6, God has not yet fully subdued the hostile powers or fully formed the new human being he has created (cf. 2:15). Paul must therefore instruct his readers to take off the old human creature and put on the new one (4:24).

Eventually, however, God will resolve this ambiguity between what he has already done in Christ and what he will accomplish later. On that day, God will pour out

15 See the use of the term *mysterion* ("mystery") in, e.g., Matt. 13:11/Mark 4:11/Luke 8:10; Dan. 2:47 (LXX); Rom. 11:25; 16:25; Rev. 1:20; and 17:7. On the meaning of the crucial *hōs* ("as") of 3:5, see Hoehner, *Ephesians*, 439–41; Sigurd Grindheim, "What the OT Prophets Did Not Know: The Mystery of the Church in Eph 3,2–13," *Biblica* 84 (2003): 531–53, here at 534; and Frank Thielman, "Ephesians," in *Commentary on the Use of the Old Testament in the New*, ed. Gregory D. Beale and Donald A. Carson (Grand Rapids: Baker, forthcoming).

16 Andrew T. Lincoln, "The Use of the OT in Ephesians," *JSNT* 14 (1982): 16–57, here at 35; idem, *Ephesians*, 381; and O'Brien, *Ephesians*, 432–35.

his wrath on the disobedient (5:6), Christ will present his church to himself in spotless, purified splendor (5:27), and the church will receive the inheritance of which the Holy Spirit is the down payment (1:14; 5:5). This will be the day of redemption, for which the Holy Spirit serves as a guaranteeing seal (1:13; 4:30). It will also be the day on which God's "summing up" of all things in Christ will be complete (1:10).[17]

Of the various "times" described in this plan, the most critical is that of Christ's death, resurrection, and heavenly session. These events are so important because through them God is reassembling his scattered and alienated creation, "things in heaven" and "things on earth." Paul devotes much of his letter to reminding his readers that as "the body of Christ," they share Christ's victory over the hostile heavenly powers, and by their earthly unity they both contribute to the process by which God is summing up all things in Christ and proclaim to the hostile heavenly forces that their defeat is certain.

God's Unification of the Heavenly Powers under Christ

Paul wants his readers to know that through the resurrection of Christ, God has defeated all inimical heavenly powers and, at Christ's ascension and heavenly session, he has placed them all in subjection beneath Christ's feet. He makes this point explicitly in 1:20–23 and implicitly in 4:8.

In 1:20–23 Paul alludes to Psalm 8:6 and 110:1 to show that by means of Christ's resurrection, God has placed Christ in the supreme position of kingly honor and authority at his right hand. Just as in Psalm 110:1 the Lord tells the king of his people, "Sit at my right hand until I make your enemies a footstool for your feet," so God has exalted the Messiah—the anointed King of his people—to his right hand by his resurrection and ascension (Eph. 1:20). Just as in Psalm 8:6 God made Adam the ruler of his creation and "put everything under his feet," so God has placed everything under Christ's feet (1:22). "All things," Paul makes clear, include the hostile cosmic powers: "all rule and authority, power and dominion, and every title that can be given, not only in the present age but also in the one to come" (1:21).[18]

The titles "rule," "authority," "power," and "dominion" designate heavenly forces—beings that many people, both Jewish and Gentile, feared because of the seemingly arbitrary harm they could do.[19] Two examples (one from a Jewish provenance and one from a Greek setting) will illustrate the point. In the *Testament of Solomon*, a work replete with descriptions of the horrors that demonic powers could visit on people and which probably contains magical traditions that go back to some form of Judaism in the first century A.D., "Solomon" says that he wrote his book "to the sons of Israel and ... gave (it) to them so that (they) might know the powers of the demons and

17 See the summary of the future elements of the eschatology of Ephesians in O'Brien, *Ephesians*, 30.

18 In letters prior to Ephesians, Paul frequently refers to these Old Testament texts. Cf. the similar use of Ps. 110:1 and 8:6 in 1 Cor. 15:25–27; the allusion to Ps. 110:1 in Rom. 8:34 and Col. 3:1; and the allusion to Ps. 8:6 in Phil. 3:21. The link between the use of these texts in Ephesians and 1 Corinthians is particularly close since the motif of Christ as the new Adam apparently lies beneath both. See the discussion in Lincoln, "Use of the OT," 40–42.

19 Cf. Rom. 8:38; 1 Cor. 2:8; 15:24; and, e.g., *2 En.* 20:1. See also the "detached note" on the powers in Best, *Ephesians*, 174–80, and Clinton E. Arnold, *Ephesians: Power and Magic: The Concept of Power in Ephesians in Light of Its Historical Setting* (SNTSMS 63; Cambridge: Cambridge Univ. Press, 1989), 14–20.

their forms as well as the names of the angels by which they are thwarted" (15.14).[20] The author of the book, in other words, has supplied his readers with the magical procedure necessary for guarding them against hostile heavenly powers.

Similarly Plutarch, probably writing in the late first century, devoted an entire tract to "The Dread of the Gods."[21] He comments that those who fear the gods perform a wide variety of bizarre magical rites because of their concern that, unless manipulated to do otherwise, the gods will harm them:

> They assume that the gods are rash, faithless, fickle, vengeful, cruel and easily offended; and, as a result, the one who dreads the gods is bound to hate and fear them. Why not, since he thinks that the worst of his ills are due to them, and will be due to them in the future? (*Superst.* 170 E).[22]

In the face of such notions, Paul claims that by the resurrection and heavenly session of Christ, all such powers have been defeated, and the feet of Christ rest on them just as the foot of a victorious warrior rests on the slain body of his enemy.[23]

In 2:1–6 Paul builds on this notion with his claim that before they received God's mercy, his readers "followed the ways of this world and of the ruler of the kingdom [*exousia*] of the air" (2:2). This "ruler," Paul says, is working among those who rebel against God. He keeps them dead in transgressions and sins and alive to the thoughts, lusts, and intentions of the flesh (2:1, 3). But God has transferred Paul's readers out of this realm and made them alive with Christ. He has raised them up with Christ and seated them with him in the heavenly realms (2:5–6). Although Christ occupies a unique place at God's right hand, Christians nevertheless share his victory over the hostile kingdom of heavenly powers and over their supreme "ruler."

In 3:7–13 Paul tells his readers that God has given the church the task of proclaiming to the hostile heavenly powers the "mystery" of God's reconciling work among Jews and Gentiles. God gave Paul the task of proclaiming his mystery of a racially diverse but unified church so that God might use it to make known "the manifold wisdom of God" to "the rulers and authorities in the heavenly realms."[24] Since the "wisdom of God" here stands parallel to "the mystery" of 3:9, Paul is saying that just as he has the task of preaching to the Gentiles their inclusion in God's people, so the unified church that results from his preaching has the task of showing the hostile heavenly powers that God's work of reconciliation and re-creation is "now" in progress.[25]

20 *OTP*, 1:976. In his discussion of the date of the *Testament of Solomon*, D. C. Duling says that "there is general agreement that much of the testament reflects first-century Judaism in Palestine" (*OTP*, 1:942). Some scholars have argued that in its final and much later form, the *Testament of Solomon* comes from Asia Minor. See Duling's discussion, *OTP*, 1:943.

21 The tract is commonly called *De superstitione* ("superstition"), but Plutarch's concern is with *deisidaimonia*, which is better rendered "fear [or dread] of the gods." On this see Morton Smith, "De superstitione (Moralia 164E–171F)," in *Plutarch's Theological Writings and Early Christian Literature*, ed. Hans Dieter Betz (SCHNT 3; Leiden: Brill, 1975), 1–35, here at 2–3.

22 I have slightly modified Frank Cole Babbitt's translation in the Loeb edition to reflect Smith's concern that *deisidaimonia* and its verbal cognate not be understood as referring to "superstition."

23 As the imagery of Ps. 110:1 implies.

24 The *hina* clause that begins 3:10 should be linked with the *edothē* of 3:8 to indicate the purpose for which "this grace" (i.e., the call to preach to the Gentiles) was given to Paul by God. On this see Best, *Ephesians*, 322; O'Brien, *Ephesians*, 244–45.

25 Schlier, *An die Epheser*, 157; Markus Barth, *Ephesians: Introduction, Translation, and Commentary on Chapters 1–3* (AB 34; Garden City, N. Y.: Doubleday, 1974), 363–66; Bruce, *The Epistles to the Colossians, to Philemon, and to the Ephesians*, 321–22; O'Brien, *Ephesians*, 247–48; Best, *Ephesians*, 325. Bruce's thought that the powers in view here includes friendly heavenly powers (cf.

The church, then, declares to the hostile heavenly powers the defeat of their intentions to frustrate God's purposes in creation.[26] The "evil day" in which the devil and his allies can fire their "flaming arrows" at God's people is drawing to a close, and the church, by its unity, makes this known to them.[27]

Christ's victory over hostile demonic forces probably also lies behind Paul's use of Psalm 68:18 (MT 68:19; LXX 67:19) in 4:8. In its own context, this psalm describes the triumphant ascent of the Lord to the top of Mount Zion after making captives of his enemies. Once his ascent is complete, he receives booty from his conquered enemies. Paul changes the psalm's "he received" to "he gave" and uses the resulting statement to support his claim that Christ has given to the church the gifts of people with various abilities in order to aid the church in its growth toward maturity (4:11–13).[28] Paul probably also has a secondary purpose, however, in using the language of the psalm: He wants to say subtly once again that Christ has triumphed over the hostile hosts of heaven—that he descended not merely to earth but to its lower parts (Hades, 4:9), where he triumphed over the hostile powers and took them captive as he ascended back to his position "higher than all the heavens" (4:10).[29]

Much of Ephesians, therefore, is devoted to making the emphatic statement that through Christ's resurrection, ascension, and heavenly session God has defeated the hostile forces of the heavens. By the resurrection with Christ of those who have received God's mercy and by their placement alongside him with God in the heavens, they have been transferred out of the realm that these forces control. Since through Paul's preaching those who have participated in Christ's defeat of the hostile heavenly forces are drawn from Gentiles as well as Jews, they make known to the hostile powers God's wise plan to unite all social groups in Christ by means of Christ's body, the church. Because of their unity with one another in Christ and despite both the diversity of ethnic groups from which they are drawn and the diversity of offices that God has given to them, they proclaim that the hostile powers have suffered defeat.

---

1 Peter 1:12), however, is not convincing in light of the negative view of the powers implied in 1:20–23; 4:8; and esp. 6:12.

26 In perhaps the earliest extant interpretation of Eph. 3:10, Ignatius, *Smyrn.* 6.1, says that "even things in heaven and the glory of the angels, and the rulers visible and invisible, even for them there is a judgment if they do not believe on the blood of Christ." See Peter Stuhlmacher, *Biblische Theologie des Neuen Testaments*, 2 vols. (Göttingen: Vandenhoeck & Ruprecht, 1992–99), 2:32.

27 The thought is similar to that expressed in 1 Peter 3:18–22, where Christ preaches condemnation to evil angelic powers. Cf. *1 En.* 10:11–12, where God instructs Michael to inform the evil angel Semyaza that he will die because he had illicit sexual relations with women, and *1 En.* 16:3, where God gives a similar mission to Enoch.

28 Paul's change of the verb in Ps. 68:18 has created a large body of comment. For a review of the approaches to the verse in ancient Jewish and early Christian exegesis, see W. Hall Harris, III, *The Descent of Christ: Ephesians 4:7–11 and Traditional Hebrew Imagery* (AGJU 32; Leiden: Brill, 1996), 64–122, and for a brief review of the scholarship on the passage, see Thielman, *Ephesians* (Grand Rapids: Baker, forthcoming). Probably Hoehner, *Ephesians*, 528, is correct when he says that although Paul modified the text to suit his argument at this point, his change is not arbitrary. The psalm speaks of the many gifts that God has given his people—his active presence, his care for the needy, his faithfulness to Israel throughout its history, especially in giving them victory over their enemies, his entrance into his sanctuary, and his removal of the wicked.

29 Arnold, *Ephesians: Power and Magic*, 56–58.

GOD'S UNIFICATION OF GENTILES AND JEWS IN A NEW PEOPLE THROUGH CHRIST

In 1:10 Paul blesses God not only for his plan to unite in Christ "things in heaven," but also "things on earth." The width, length, height, and depth of God's love that Paul prays his readers will comprehend reach not only the heavens but the social groups of humanity as well (3:18).[30] From Paul's perspective as a Jew, the world was divided into two social groups, Jews and "the nations" or "Gentiles" (*ta ethnē*).[31] He writes his letter as a Jew to uncircumcised Gentiles (2:11–12) and wants his readers to know that God has, by design, fashioned a new people out of both groups.

This theme is subtly present in the letter's initial blessing (1:3–14). Here Paul praises God for planning that all Christians, whether Jews or Gentiles, will receive the inheritance promised to God's people in the Scriptures (1:11–12).[32] He goes on to praise God that his Gentile readers have also been included in God's people. They received this inheritance through hearing the gospel and receiving the Holy Spirit (1:13).

Paul describes the Spirit that his Gentile readers have received both as something "promised" and as something with which they have been "sealed." Mention of the Spirit as something "promised" implies that Paul's readers are the recipients of the prophetic promise that in the last days God would pour out his Spirit on his people as part of the restoration of his covenant relationship with them.[33] Since the prophets seemed to say that only Israel would receive this eschatological blessing, the gift of it to the Gentiles came as a surprise to the early church. It was, as Paul says, the revelation of a mystery (3:9).

The activity of the Spirit among the Gentiles, however, provides the guarantee that God has, despite expectations to the contrary, included them in the blessings God promised to Israel at their eschatological restoration. Although the Spirit is a "seal" for every believer, whether Jewish or Gentile, he perhaps functions in this way especially for Gentiles; for them the Spirit serves as an authenticating mark that God himself has included them among his people (Acts 10:47; 11:17; 15:8; Gal. 3:2–5).[34] The inheritance that God promised to his people Israel is therefore theirs as well (1:14).

This theme of ethnic reconciliation among God's people rises to special prominence in 2:11–22, where Paul contrasts his readers' old status as Gentiles "excluded from citizenship in Israel" with their new status as "fellow citizens with God's people"

30 Cf. Francis Watson, "Writing the Mystery: Christ and Reality in the Letter to the Ephesians," a paper delivered to the Disputed Paulines Group of the Society of Biblical Literature, Nov. 19, 2000 in Nashville, pp. 7–9. Watson offers the attractive suggestion that the term "length" in 3:18 may refer to time conceived in spatial terms.

31 On the various ways in which Jews understood Gentiles during the Second Temple period see Terence L. Donaldson, *Paul and the Gentiles: Remapping the Apostle's Convictional World* (Minneapolis: Fortress, 1997), 51–78. Donaldson believes that prior to his conversion Paul took the relatively conservative position that Gentiles could only experience God's favor through becoming full proselytes to Judaism.

32 This interpretation assumes that the verb *eklērōthēmen* means "we have ... obtained an inheritance" (REB, NRSV, NJB, LuthB) rather than "we were ... chosen" (NAB, NIV). See Best, *Ephesians*, 145–46. The passive form of the verb could also mean that the group defined by the "we" is God's inheritance—"we were claimed by God as his portion," as O'Brien, *Ephesians*, 115, translates. But the unmistakable reference to "our inheritance" in 1:14 should probably decide the issue in favor of Best's position.

33 See, e.g., Isa. 32:15; 44:3; Ezek. 11:19; 36:26–27; 37:14; 39:29; Joel 3:1–2. Cf. Gal. 3:14.

34 That the Spirit is the seal on every believer's faith is clear from the "also" in 1:13 and the "we" in 1:14. Cf. 2 Cor. 1:22.

(2:19). Formerly, he explains, they stood apart from the Messiah, from Israel, and from the scriptural covenants containing the promises that God would fulfill among his people. They were therefore "without hope and without God in the world" (2:12). By means of the sacrificial death of Christ, however, God has abolished the Mosaic law and has overcome these vast disadvantages for them.[35] The abolition of that law was necessary because God designed it to separate Israel from other peoples as "a kingdom of priests and a holy nation" (Ex. 19:4–6). In the words of the second century B.C. author of *The Letter of Aristeas*:

> When . . . our lawgiver, equipped by God for insight into all things, had surveyed each particular, he fenced us about with impregnable palisades and with walls of iron to the end that we should mingle in no way with any of the other nations, remaining pure in body and in spirit, emancipated from vain opinions, revering the one and mighty God above the whole of creation. (139)[36]

Here the law is conceived as a wall separating Israel from the nations, and the hostility expressed toward the nations is thinly veiled—by implication they are impure in body and spirit, enslaved to "vain opinions," and they idolatrously revere God's creation rather than God himself. Now, Paul says, this "dividing wall of hostility" has been torn down (2:14–15).

Paul does not say explicitly how the death of Christ tore down the wall, but his graphic references to Christ's "blood" (2:13), his "flesh" (2:15), and his "cross" (2:16) probably mean that the sacrificial nature of Christ's death implies the law's end.[37] Christ's death on the cross was an atoning sacrifice that made possible the justification of both Gentiles and Jews "apart from the law" (Rom. 3:21–26). It was also the sacrifice through which God instituted the new covenant and thus brought the Mosaic covenant to its conclusion (1 Cor. 11:25; cf. Ex. 24:8).[38]

With the abolition of the Mosaic law, Jews and Gentiles are able to come together in Christ to form a new, third people, all of whom are at peace with God and therefore at peace with one another (Eph. 2:15, 17–18). They are a single human being—or body—created anew by God out of two disparate entities (2:15b–16). They are fellow citizens in a commonwealth that once only included Israelites (2:19a). They are members of God's household (2:19b). They are part of God's newly fashioned temple, whose foundation is the apostles and prophets and whose cornerstone is Christ. A diverse group of people function as the other, less important parts of the building, and despite their diversity, they fit tightly together to form "a holy temple in the Lord" (2:20–22).

Among this variety of metaphors, the metaphor of the body is particularly important to Paul as an expression of the unity that God has effected between Jewish and

35 Cf. O'Brien, *Ephesians*, 196–99.

36 The translation belongs to Moses Hadas's edition and translation of *Aristeas to Philocrates (Letter of Aristeas)* (New York: Harper & Brothers, 1951), 157.

37 Cf. the 1984 revision of the Lutherbibel: "durch das Opfer seines Leibes hat er abgetan das Gesetz" ("through the sacrifice of his body he has abolished the law").

38 Cf. Barth, *Ephesians 1–3*, 298–305, who does not, however, believe that the death of Christ brought the law itself to an end, but only the divisions between God and humanity and the divisions between Jews and Gentiles.

Gentile believers in one new people. He has already said in 1:22–23 that God appointed Christ as head over all things for the church, "which is his body." Now that his readers understand this body as the new human being created by God out of two formerly disparate social groups, they are prepared to understand Paul when he invents a new Greek word in 3:6 to say that Gentile Christians have joined Christians from Israel to form a "common body" (*syssōma*).[39] They are also prepared to understand the significance of his admonitions in 4:3–4, 15–16 that the various parts of this new human body should work together in unity.

THE UNITY OF THE CHURCH AS ITS VOCATION

The smooth and unified functioning of God's new human being is necessary for the completion of God's plan to restore his creation in Christ. If the church is not unified, then God's work of bringing together "all things . . . on earth" in Christ (1:10) will remain incomplete, and his plan to unite all of his creation beside Christ or beneath his feet will go unproclaimed among the hostile heavenly powers (3:10). In the second major part of his letter (4:1–6:20), therefore, Paul tells his readers how they can live in a way that is consistent with the unity toward which God is moving the universe.[40] He offers them practical admonitions on how they can avoid social discord and urges them to use the diversity of gifts that Christ has given them to enhance their unity. He speaks not only to the church generally, but also more specifically to Christian families within the church, and especially to Christian husbands and wives, whose physical unity illustrates the merger of Christ and the church into one, unified body.

At the same time that the church works toward unity, however, it must be careful not to compromise its identity as the people who reflect the character of God. For this reason, Paul weaves into his practical advice for maintaining social cohesion statements that urge the church to maintain its holiness. The church should do this, he insists, by avoiding erroneous teaching, by remaining separate from "the Gentiles," and by imitating God and Christ in its conduct.

The Unity of the Church

Paul begins this second major section of his letter with a summary of the case he has just made in the letter's first major section: There is only one God, who is over the entire universe, and he has called the church to reflect this truth (4:1–6).[41] In 4:7–6:20 he explains how, in concrete terms, the church remains unified.

39 Best's claim, *Ephesians*, 311–12, that since we do not know all of Greek literature, we should not claim that Paul has invented this word, seems too precise. Since words can be invented easily in Greek by compounding two or more other words, other Greek writers may have also "invented" the word. If it were a well-known term, however, it would probably appear somewhere else in the extant pre-Pauline literature.

40 Cf. Turner, "Mission and Meaning," 148–57; O'Brien, *Ephesians*, 63–57; and Stuhlmacher, *Biblische Theologie* 2:32.

41 Paul begins the section by saying to his readers, "Live a life worthy of the calling you have received" (4:1). The calling they have received is defined in 1:18 as the call to be God's inheritance—a united and holy people who will participate in God's final gathering together of the whole universe around and beneath Christ (1:10, 22–23; 2:6).

On one hand, the Spirit of God produces and maintains the necessary unity. The Spirit is the means through which the unified church of Jews and Gentiles gains access to the Father (2:2) and is also the presence of God that inhabits his temple once it is constructed from diverse peoples (2:18). The Spirit has revealed to the apostles and prophets the mystery that the church is a new body, comprised of both Gentiles and Israel who are in Christ Jesus (3:6). Not surprisingly, then, the unity of the church comes from the Spirit (4:3), the oneness of the church as Christ's body matches the oneness of the Spirit (4:4), and Christians grieve the Spirit when they behave in ways that disrupt the church's harmony (4:30).

On the other hand, Paul gives specific guidelines to his readers on how they can pursue social harmony.[42] They should be "completely humble and gentle . . . patient, bearing with one another in love" (4:2). They should recognize that the diversity of gifts Christ has distributed to the church is intended to foster service to one another (4:12), and that by being built up in this way the church, as Christ's body, is moving toward the eschatological goal of being entirely filled with Christ (4:13, 15–16; cf. 2:20–22). They should speak truthfully, avoid letting their anger simmer overnight, and instead of stealing should engage in productive work that will allow them to share with the needy (4:25–28). They should abstain from unwholesome speech and replace it with edifying and gracious words. They should "get rid of all bitterness, rage and anger, brawling and slander, along with every form of malice" (4:31) and instead be kind, compassionate, and forgiving (4:32).

The two notions that the Spirit produces unity and believers must act in ways that foster unity converge in 5:18–6:9. Here Paul instructs his readers to "be filled by the Spirit," describing the Spirit as the *means* by which believers are filled. With what *content* are they filled? Paul last used the language of "fullness" when he spoke of Christ's distribution of various gifts to the church for the edification of Christ's body "until we all reach unity in the faith and in the knowledge of the Son of God and become mature, attaining to the whole measure of the fullness of Christ" (4:13; cf. 1:23; 3:19; 4:10). In that statement, the church is growing toward a unity that, when finally reached, will mean that it is entirely full of Christ. In 5:18, then, we should probably understand Paul to say that the Spirit is the means by which the church grows toward this eschatological unity with Christ.[43]

Paul follows the imperative "be filled" in 5:18 with five participles that describe the results of this infilling in terms of harmonious worship within the church and harmonious relationships within the family.[44] People who are filled with the Spirit will worship God by singing and giving thanks. They will also submit to one another (5:19–21). In the family, this submission will mean that the wife submits to her husband and that the husband loves his wife. Husband and wife should do this as a way

42 The tension thus produced between the "indicative" and the "imperative" should be familiar to readers of Paul's other letters (cf. Rom. 6:1–12; 1 Cor. 6:11, 18; and esp. Gal. 5:25). In some sense Christ's death and resurrection and the gift of the Spirit have defeated the power of sin, but in another sense this victory must constantly be appropriated by the believer through faith. See Rudolf Bultmann, "The Problem of Ethics in Paul" in *Understanding Paul's Ethics: Twentieth Century Approaches*, ed. Brian S. Rosner (Grand Rapids: Eerdmans, 1995), 195–216.

43 Cf. O'Brien, *Ephesians*, 391–93.

44 Daniel B. Wallace, *GGBB*, 639.

of making known the unity between Christ and his body, the church (5:22–33). In other ways too, Paul infuses the conventional chain of command in the Greco-Roman household with a mutuality that removes its oppressive features and leaves behind a harmoniously functioning reflection of the union between Christ and the church, and of the eventual, eschatological union between God and the cosmos (6:1–9).[45]

The Identity of the Church

Since God has chosen Christians to be "holy and blameless in his sight" (1:4) and since Christ died for the church "to make her holy" (5:26), the unified church must guard its moral purity. The church could, after all, be unified around false teaching or in its willingness to tolerate sexual immorality. This situation, however, would compromise the church's identity as a company of "holy ones" (*hagioi* in 4:12; 5:3; 6:18), who, like Israel in the days of the Mosaic law, were supposed to remain separate from the world around them. Unlike ancient Israel, the new human being that God has created from both Jews and Gentiles has no ethnically specific identity but continues to have a moral identity that reflects the character of God (cf. Lev. 11:44–45; 19:2; 20:7; 20:26). The unity that Paul urges on his readers, therefore, should not come at the price of the church's identity as God's holy inheritance (1:18). This concern emerges explicitly in three passages.

In 4:14–16, Paul says that Christ has distributed to the church a variety of offices (4:11), not only so that the church will be held together in unity, but also so that by its unity it might guard against crafty false teaching. Working together in loving harmony is important, otherwise the church will fail to reveal the eschatological goal toward which God is moving the universe (1:10; 3:10); but this goal will be equally frustrated if the church does not speak the truth (4:15; cf. 4:25; 5:6–7).

In 4:17–24, Paul urges his readers to live in a way that distinguishes them from "the Gentiles." In 2:3 Paul already reminded his readers that before they became recipients of God's mercy, they followed the lusts and desires of their flesh and of their minds. They were spiritually dead and under the sway of the devil. Now Paul recalls that language in order to say explicitly what was implicit before: His readers should distance themselves from the Gentiles' way of life. Instead, their way of life should be consistent with the new creation God has been forming since the coming of Christ (4:22–24).[46]

In 4:32–5:18, Paul urges his readers to imitate God and Christ in their behavior: Just as God forgave them in Christ, so they should forgive others, and just as Christ expressed his love for them by sacrificing himself for them, so they should sacrificially love others. These general thoughts lead to more specific instructions about how a "holy people" (5:3), a people destined to inherit "the kingdom of Christ and of God" (5:5), ought to live. They should forgive others just as God forgave them

45 On the structure of the family in Roman culture see Andrew Wallace-Hadrill, "The Roman Family," in *The World of Rome: An Introduction to Roman Culture*, ed. Peter Jones and Keith Sidwell (Cambridge: Cambridge Univ. Press, 1997), 208–34, and Hoehner, *Ephesians*, 720–29.

46 The reference to the new person in 4:24 probably echoes the creation narrative. See Pokorný, *An die Epheser*, 189.

by means of Christ's atoning death (4:32; 5:2). Their conduct should be marked by love, just as Christ loved the church and gave himself as a sacrifice for it (5:2; cf. 5:25). They are "holy people" and should therefore act in a way appropriate to this identity (5:3). Thanksgiving should replace immoral speech and the actions that go with it (5:3–7), and they should live in the light of their conversion rather than in the darkness characteristic of the period before Christ's transforming light shone on them (5:8–18).

God's people should, therefore, be united as an expression of God's plan to defeat the forces of the universe that are working for its disintegration. At the same time, they should not compromise their identity as God's holy people. Like ancient Israel, the church should be holy because the Lord is holy and has set the church apart from the nations to be his own possession (cf. Ex. 19:5; Lev. 20:26).

The Armor of the Church

Paul concludes the second major section of his letter with a reminder to his readers that their efforts to remain unified and to maintain their identity as the people of God will not go unopposed. Although the triumph of Christ over the hostile heavenly powers and the share of the church in that triumph are so certain that Paul can speak of them both in the past tense (1:22; 2:6), they are not yet complete. "The days" are still "evil" and shrouded in "darkness" (5:16; 6:12–13). The devil, unwilling to surrender in the face of certain defeat, continues to fire flaming arrows at the church and, along with his supporting cosmic forces, to engage the church in a spiritual struggle (6:11–12).

In light of their historical position between God's final action for the defeat of these hostile forces in Christ and the realization of that defeat on "the day of redemption" (4:30), the church must defend the position that Christ's assault on the hostile powers has achieved for it. It must put on the armor that God has supplied to it and then take its stand (6:11, 13–14).

The church must gird itself with the truth as God has expressed it in the gospel (6:14; cf. 1:13; 4:15, 21).[47] It must put on the breastplate of the righteousness that God gives to the believer (6:14).[48] It must put on its feet the gospel—that through Christ God has made peace between Jews and Gentiles in the church and peace between himself and those within the church (6:15). It must take up the shield of the one faith that unites the church and protects it from false teaching (6:16; cf. 4:5, 13–14).[49] The church must also take the helmet of the salvation that God freely gives through faith in Christ the Savior (6:17a; cf. 2:5, 8; 5:23). Finally, it should take up

47 In Ephesians Paul speaks of truth both as a virtue that Christians should practice (4:24–25; 5:9) and as the convictions expressed in the gospel (1:13; 4:15, 21). In the context of 6:14, where a defensive struggle with the devil and his forces is in view, it seems likely that Paul has in mind the resistance of the church to the kind of cunning false teaching that he has already mentioned in 4:14 and whose antidote is "speaking the truth [presumably of the gospel] in love." Cf. Best, *Ephesians*, 599.

48 Although in Ephesians, "righteousness" is usually a virtue (4:24; 5:9), Best, *Ephesians*, 599, is correct to say that here it must be understood as something that God gives since neither the gospel of peace (6:15), nor salvation (6:17), nor the Word of God (6:17) are understood to be human activities.

49 Cf. Best, *Ephesians*, 601. Again, two options face the interpreter: "faith" as the means of salvation (1:15; 2:8; 3:12, 17; 6:23) or faith as the body of doctrine to which Christians give assent (4:5, 13). Because of the article in front of *pisteōs* and the static quality of the other pieces of armor, the second option is preferable.

the sword of the Spirit, which Paul identifies with the spoken word of God (6:17b). This is the only offensive weapon in the list of armor, and it refers to the use of the Spirit-inspired Scriptures to combat the devil's strategic attempts to knock the church off the position that God has won for it (cf. Matt. 4:1–11; Luke 4:1–13).[50]

God has given his church its position of victory over the hostile forces of the universe. He has also supplied it with the armor necessary for defending its position while it awaits the final demise of its enemies.[51] If it is not to lose the ground it has gained and if God's goal of bringing the times to fulfillment by uniting all things in heaven and on earth around Christ is to succeed, then it must take up this armor and stand firm.

A UNITED CHURCH AS A MODEL FOR A UNIFIED UNIVERSE

In an effort to encourage dispirited Christians in southern Asia, Paul has reminded them of God's plan for the universe and of the critical place of the church in that plan. His letter paints a picture of a new creation in which the invisible and hostile forces of the heavens lie conquered beneath the feet of Christ. In this picture, a church that consists of both Jews and Gentiles sits alongside the risen Christ in the heavens, sharing his triumph. This is the goal, Paul says, toward which God is moving the universe—to sum up all things in heaven and on earth in Christ.

Before "the times" reach this "fulfillment," however, the hostile cosmic powers continue to wage war against the church, and so Christians must clothe themselves in an armor that will be able to resist their onslaught—truth, righteousness, the gospel of peace, faith, and salvation. By standing united with one another in this armor, they will make "known to the rulers and authorities in the heavenly realms" God's "manifold wisdom" in reconciling Jews and Gentiles to form one new human being through the gospel. The church will therefore proclaim to these hostile powers that in the death, resurrection, and heavenly session of Christ, God has defeated their efforts to frustrate his purpose in creation.

The church plays a critical role, therefore, in God's plan to bring the times to their fulfillment by summing up everything in Christ. They are the new humanity that replaces the old, disintegrated humanity, and they are the evidence that God's plan to sum up everything in Christ is rapidly coming to its end. The church in Roman Asia should take heart that God, in his great love and rich mercy, has done so much for them. They should pursue with renewed zeal their vocation to stand strong and united against the devil and his realm as God brings his cosmic purposes to their glorious end.

50 Hoehner, *Ephesians*, 853.

51 Best, *Ephesians*, 597.

Chapter 19

FIRST TIMOTHY: THE CHURCH AS THE PILLAR AND FOUNDATION OF TRUTH

After Paul appealed to Festus to be tried before the emperor in Rome, Festus arranged for a preliminary hearing before the Jewish King Herod Agrippa II. Oblivious to the finer points of Judaism, Festus faced the unpleasant prospect of explaining to Nero why some outspoken Jews in his province wanted Paul executed. Agrippa would hopefully help him out of this potentially embarrassing situation by interpreting the Jews' grievances to Festus and giving the governor something to write to the emperor (Acts 25:13–27). Festus cannot have been too pleased with the results, for after hearing Paul's explanation of the events surrounding his arrest, Agrippa concluded, "This man could have been set free if he had not appealed to Caesar" (Acts 26:32).

In light of this, it seems likely that Nero cleared Paul of the charges against him and released him from custody. This, at least, is the nearly unanimous witness of the early church.[1] After five years under arrest, Paul's plans to visit Rome and then evangelize Spain (Rom. 15:24, 28) had changed—he did not, after all, anticipate "visiting" Rome for two years as a prisoner (Acts 28:30). In anticipation of his release, he had asked Philemon to prepare a guest room for him in Colosse (Philem. 22), and it seems probable therefore that he sailed eastward toward Asia after being cleared of the charges against him.[2]

Despite the claims of many scholars that the Pastoral Letters are not authentic letters of Paul, he probably wrote them during this period of his ministry.[3] This does not mean that the precise historical circumstances surrounding their composition are clear.[4] One likely scenario is that Paul traveled from Rome with both Timothy and Titus to Crete, where they established churches in several towns but unhappily

1 The evidence is exhaustively surveyed in J. B. Lightfoot, *Biblical Essays* (London: Macmillan, 1893), 423–27. Even Pelagius, who had doubts that Paul ever reached Spain, believed that he was released from the Roman imprisonment recorded in Acts. See Lightfoot, ibid., 427 n. 1. It is important to recognize, *pace* Luke Timothy Johnson, *Letters to Paul's Delegates: 1 Timothy, 2 Timothy, Titus* (NTC; Valley Forge, Pa.: Trinity Press International, 1996), 10, that the theory of a second Roman imprisonment does not demand a mission of Paul to Spain. On this see Herman Ridderbos, *De Pastorale Brieven* (Commentaar op het Nieuwe Testament; Kampen: Kok, 1967), 12–13.

2 For discussion of this possibility, see Ridderbos, *Pastorale Brieven*, 12–13.

3 John Ashton, *The Religion of Paul the Apostle* (New Haven, Conn.: Yale Univ. Press, 2000), 77, believes that "the so-called Pastoral Letters" are "no longer ascribed to Paul except by a handful of extreme conservatives." It would be difficult to make a case, however, that the label "extreme conservatives" fits such scholars as Luke Timothy Johnson, *Letters to Paul's Delegates*; idem, *The First and Second Letters to Timothy* (AB 35A; New York: Doubleday, 2001); Bo Reicke, *Re-examining Paul's Letters: The History of the Pauline Correspondence*, ed. David P. Moessner and Ingalisa Reicke (Harrisburg, Pa.: Trinity Press International, 2001), 52–56; and Jerome Murphy-O'Connor, *Paul: A Critical Life* (Oxford: Oxford Univ. Press, 1996), 357–59 (who denies the authenticity of 1 Timothy and Titus, but accepts the genuineness of 2 Timothy).

4 Occasionally efforts are made to account for the Pastorals within the period of Paul's ministry covered by Acts. See, e.g., Johnson, *First and Second Letters to Timothy*, 135–37, 319, and Reicke, *Re-examining Paul's Letters*, 51–59, 68–74, 85–91. For the decisive refutation of this position, see Lightfoot, *Biblical Essays*, 399–410.

also saw an unorthodox variation of their teaching begin to take root among some Jewish converts.[5] Paul left Titus on the island to preside over the appointment of leaders in these churches and to instruct them more fully in the faith.

Paul then left with Timothy for Ephesus. There they found the church in such disarray that the term "shipwreck" later came to mind (1 Tim. 1:19). "Certain people" were advocating strange teachings similar to those that Paul and his coworkers had encountered on Crete, and two Ephesians, Hymenaeus and Alexander, had fallen so seriously into error that Paul excommunicated them (1:20).

Paul left Timothy in charge of the situation and continued his travels, perhaps going first to Colosse to visit Philemon but making clear to Timothy before he left that he intended to go to Macedonia (1:3). He probably wrote 1 Timothy from Macedonia, and his primary concern in the letter is the pernicious false teaching that infected the Ephesian church.[6]

The nature of the false teaching is difficult to describe, and this is probably a direct result of Paul's intense lack of sympathy for it.[7] It is "meaningless talk" (1:6), "old wives' tales" (4:7), and "godless chatter" (6:20; 2 Tim. 2:16). Its advocates are "mere talkers" (Titus 1:10) who, despite an air of confidence, do not understand what they are talking about (1 Tim. 1:7; 6:4). In Paul's view the false teaching is so banal that it does not deserve serious intellectual engagement; indeed, to take it seriously is to be sucked into contentious and fruitless debate (6:20; 2 Tim. 2:14, 23; Titus 3:9) that seems on the one hand never to end and on the other hand never to make any progress toward the truth (3:7).[8] Unlike the misunderstanding of his own teaching that Paul faced in Thessalonica and Corinth, the intellectually challenging opposition in Galatia, or even the apocalyptically oriented philosophy that disturbed the church in Colosse, the false teaching in the Pastorals appears either to have lacked coherence or emerged from a worldview so different from Paul's that he could not make sense of it.[9]

---

5 Gordon D. Fee, *1 and 2 Timothy, Titus* (GNC; New York: Harper & Row, 1984), xviii. Lightfoot, *Biblical Essays*, 430–35, imagined that Paul traveled from Rome immediately to Asia in fulfillment of his promise to Philemon. He then evangelized Crete, went to Spain, and eventually returned to the east. This scenario is unnecessarily complicated, however, by Lightfoot's desire to incorporate a Spanish mission into Paul's travels.

6 Lightfoot, *Biblical Essays*, 434, locates the composition of First Timothy around the time that Paul was in Macedonia. As we shall see in the next chapter, Paul probably wrote Titus at the same time. Deciding which was written first is probably neither possible nor necessary, although Fee, *1 and 2 Timothy, Titus*, xxiv, speculates that Titus came after First Timothy since Titus has a less urgent tone and seems more concerned with prevention than with cure.

7 Johnson, *Letters to Paul's Delegates*, 7, 108–9, resists the claim that the error presupposed in the three Pastorals is identical. The false teaching in the three letters, however, possesses several common traits, and the best explanation of this is that the error was basically the same. In all three the error is spreading from house to house (1 Tim. 5:13; 2 Tim. 3:6; Titus 1:11), and in both 1 and 2 Timothy, the women within these houses have become especially vulnerable to it (1 Tim. 4:17; 5:13; 2 Tim. 3:6). In 1 Timothy and Titus, the false teaching involves the Mosaic law (1 Tim. 1:7; Titus 1:9). Subtle differences are present, such as identification of the heretics with "the circumcision" in Titus 1:10, the unique reference to abstinence from marriage in 1 Tim. 4:3, and the claim that the resurrection has already happened in 2 Tim. 2:18, but these differences probably represent the different emphases of the three different letters. Cf. Lightfoot, *Biblical Essays*, 412.

8 On taking seriously Paul's disparaging comments about the silly nature of the false teaching, see I. H. Marshall, *The Pastoral Epistles* (ICC; Edinburgh: T. & T. Clark, 1999), 42–43. As Johnson, *Letters to Paul's Delegates*, 109, points out, Paul does occasionally do more than just dismiss his opponents' teaching (1 Tim. 1:8–10; 4:3–5, 7–8; 6:5–10), but the brief clash of swords offered in these passages does not match the lengthy and deeply engaged argumentation present in Paul's other letters.

9 The intellectually uninteresting nature of Paul's opposition may help to account for the often observed blandness of Paul's argumentation in the letters when compared, for example, to Galatians.

Still, Paul supplies some insight into the methods that its advocates used and into its results in the lives of those embracing it. The most prominent feature of the false teaching's content that emerges from the letters is its concern with the Mosaic law. The advocates of the heresy, Paul says, "want to be teachers of the law" (1 Tim. 1:7) and engage in "quarrels about the law" (Titus 3:9). They are concerned with "Jewish myths and the commandments of people who reject the truth" (1:14). Some of the false teachers are Jewish (1:10).

Other aspects of the teaching, however, do not fit comfortably within a Jewish framework. The false teachers forbid marriage (1 Tim. 4:3) and claim that the future bodily resurrection has already happened (2 Tim. 2:18). In addition, they seem to have used magic, since Paul compares them to Jannes and Jambres, the traditional names of the magicians that Moses opposed in Pharaoh's court (2 Tim. 3:8; cf. Ex. 7:11, 22), and he cautions Timothy that "evil men and sorcerers will go from bad to worse" (2 Tim. 3:13, aut.).[10] These aberrations probably mean that their avoidance of "foods" (1 Tim. 4:3) and abstinence from "impure" things (Titus 1:15) involved something more than following the dietary and purity regulations of the Mosaic law. Paul's description of the teaching as a series of "myths and endless genealogies" (1 Tim. 1:4; cf. 2 Tim. 4:4; Titus 1:14; 3:9) may refer to speculation about the origins of the cosmos based on an exegesis of Genesis—the first book of the Mosaic law.

This kind of speculation appears in the third century in a gnostic tractate from Nag Hammadi, *On the Origin of the World.* The author of this document wove imagery from the Genesis creation narrative into his genealogical account of the gods who inhabit the cosmos. According to the author, the goddess Pistis Sophia created the god of Genesis ("the ruler") and then withdrew to her region of light, leaving "the ruler" with the impression that "[he] alone existed." The ruler's next actions look like the actions of God in Genesis 1:6–9:

> The ruler set apart the watery substance. And what was dry was divided into another place. And from matter he made for himself an abode, and he called it heaven. And from matter, the ruler made a footstool, and he called it earth. (II.101)[11]

We can work backwards from this reading of Genesis to Irenaeus's account of the early second-century heretic Saturninus, who taught that seven angels spoke the phrase "Let us make man in our image" in Genesis 1:26. These angels made the world and everything in it, including the first man, but they botched their work and their man could not stand erect. Happily, the ultimate "power above" took pity on the man and by planting a spark of his divine essence within him, enabled him to stand up and live (*Haer.* 1.24.1). Evidently since the world was an evil place and the material body the product of inferior and inept deities, the followers of Saturninus opposed marriage and procreation and refrained from eating meat (*Haer.* 1.24.2).

10 On the translation of the word *goētes* as "sorcerers" see LSJ, 356. Cf. Lightfoot, *Biblical Essays,* 412, 415, who translates the term "wizards" and "enchanters."

11 The translation is from *NHL,* 173.

If we take another step backward in Irenaeus's account, we come to Menander, successor to the Simon Magus of Acts 8:9–11 (*Haer.* 1.23.1, 5), and, according to Irenaeus, the first gnostic (*Haer.* 3.4.3).[12] Menander claimed that by his magic, "one may overcome those very angels that made the world" and that "his disciples obtain the resurrection by being baptized into him, and can die no more, but remain in the possession of immortal youth" (*Haer.* 1.23.5).[13] Here we find speculation on the world's origin (although without an explicit reference to Genesis) coupled with belief that the resurrection has already happened, at least for members of the sect. The use of magic also appears.[14]

Although none of these systems provides an exact match to the heresy behind the Pastorals, and all of them postdate the Pastorals, the false teaching in Ephesus and on Crete may have been a primitive form of such religions.[15] All three reveal a fascination with myths that trace the genealogy of the various cosmic powers downward from the ultimate power to the god or gods who created the world. All apparently believed that the created world was essentially an imperfect place, mired in the inept fabrications of the god described in the early chapters of Genesis, the first book of the Mosaic law. Menander at least used magic and thought that his followers had already been resurrected. His successor Saturninus opposed marriage, procreation, and the consumption of meat. Something like this amalgam of cosmic speculation, overrealized eschatology, magic, and asceticism probably accounts for the false teaching described in the Pastorals.[16]

The false teaching has started to spread like gangrene (2 Tim. 2:17), and its success has apparently arisen from the clever efforts of its teachers to target Christian households where the male head of the household is either absent or derelict in his familial duties. Thus Paul says that the false teachers are "ruining whole households"

12 J. Fossum, "Simon Magus," *DDD*, 781, argues persuasively that Simon's teaching was actually a nascent form of second-century gnosticism.

13 Irenaeus probably got his information from Justin Martyr, who described Menander briefly in his *Apology* (1.26; cf. 1.56). In the same paragraph Justin mentioned his work against heresies in which more information could be found (cf. Eusebius, *Hist. eccl.* 3.26). Unfortunately, Justin's work against heresies is no longer extant, but Irenaeus probably knew it and derived his more detailed account from it. On this see G. Salmon, "Menander," *DCB*, 722–23.

14 Ignatius of Antioch also provides evidence of a blend of Judaism and docetic Christianity in Asia in the early second century. On this see C. K. Barrett, "Jews and Judaizers in the Epistles of Ignatius" in *Jews, Greeks and Christians: Religious Cultures in Late Antiquity*, ed. Robert Hamerton-Kelly and Robin Scroggs (SJLA 21; Leiden: Brill, 1976), 220–44, esp. 237 and 241, where Barrett comments on the importance of Ignatius's evidence for understanding the background of the Pastoral Letters.

15 Justin Martyr mentions Saturninus in a list of heretics in his *Dialogue with Trypho* 35, apparently written shortly after the Bar Cochba war of 132–136. Saturninus must have flourished, therefore, sometime in the late first or early second century, and Menander before him. Although Saturninus lived well after the mid-60s, when the Pastorals were composed, Menander was closer to Paul. Even Simone Pétrement, *A Separate God: The Christian Origins of Gnosticism* (New York: Harper, 1984), 315, who argues that gnosticism developed from Christianity and is inclined to date its origins late, believes that Menander may have taught as early as "the last decades of the first century."

16 This does not mean that gnosticism was an independent, pre-Christian religion, as many scholars since Richard Reitzenstein (1861–1931) and Wilhelm Bousset (1865–1920), have thought. See Pétrement, *A Separate God*, 1–26. Still, it is important to take seriously the commitment of the false teaching to "myths and endless genealogies" (cf. 1 Tim. 4:7; 2 Tim. 4:4; Titus 1:14; 3:9). This element of the false teaching moves it closer ideologically (if not chronologically) to these later gnostic systems than to the problems of the Corinthian church or to the Christianity of the *Acts of Paul*. On problems of the Corinthian church and the religion reflected in the *Acts of Paul* as the background for the Pastorals, see respectively, Philip H. Towner, *The Goal of Our Instruction: The Structure of Theology and Ethics in the Pastoral Epistles* (JSNTSup 34; Sheffield: Sheffield Academic Press, 1989), 21–45, and Frances Young, *The Theology of the Pastoral Letters* (Cambridge: Cambridge Univ. Press, 1994), 13–20.

(Titus 1:11).[17] They apparently do this by insinuating themselves into homes and convincing already corrupt women of their false teaching (2 Tim. 3:6). Perhaps we can also link together Paul's claim that a desire for wealth motivated the false teachers (1 Tim. 6:5; cf. 6:6–10, 17–19), his concern that women not make ostentatious displays of their wealth (2:9), and his concern that women not teach in the church (2:11–14). Wealthy women in Ephesus may have been paying the false teachers to tutor them and then conveying the false teaching they learned to the churches that met in their houses.[18]

In 1 Timothy Paul is especially concerned about the young widows who are under the care of the Ephesian church. Some widows "live for pleasure" (1 Tim. 5:6), he writes, and apparently some widows of this type have made their way onto the list of widows that the church supports. Paul advises against placing younger widows on this list: "They get into the habit of being idle and going about from house to house. And not only do they become idlers, but also gossips and busybodies, saying things they ought not to" (5:13).

The phrase "saying things they ought not to" (*lalousai ta mē deonta*) resembles the phrase "teaching things they ought not to" (*didaskontes ha mē dei*) in Titus 1:11, where Paul describes how the teachers ruin whole households. The phrase in 1 Timothy, therefore, probably refers not simply to relatively harmless prattle but to the heretical teaching that has so disturbed the Ephesian church.[19] Because these widows receive the support of the church, they have no economic need to marry, bear children, and manage a household, and the false teaching that they hold discourages such creation-affirming domesticity. Instead of pursuing these activities, then, they can spend their time learning about the false teaching and spreading it from house to house (1 Tim. 5:13; 2 Tim. 3:7).

Here too a link with later forms of Gnosticism emerges.[20] Irenaeus mentions a woman named Marcellina who came to Rome in the mid-second century ("under Anicetus") and "led multitudes astray" with her gnostic teaching (*Haer.* 1.25.6; cf. Origen, *Cels.* 5.62). Tertullian comments on how the gnostic heretics extended privileges to women that orthodox Christianity did not give them. Among these are the privileges of teaching and disputing (*Praescr.* 41).

Whatever the details of the content of the false teaching and of its teachers' methods, Paul can hardly be clearer about its motives and results. They are motivated by greed for money (1 Tim. 6:10; Titus 1:11), their own desires (2 Tim. 4:3), depraved minds (2 Tim. 3:8; Titus 3:11), and seared consciences (1 Tim. 1:9; 4:2). The results

17 William D. Mounce, *Pastoral Epistles* (WBC 46; Nashville: Thomas Nelson, 2000), lii, observes that in Acts 20:20 Paul says that he taught the Ephesians "from house to house" (*kat' oikous*).

18 Alan Padgett, "Wealthy Women at Ephesus: 1 Timothy 2:8–15 in Context," *Interp* 41 (1987): 19–31, here at 23.

19 Fee, *1 and 2 Timothy, Titus*, 83; Lorenz Oberlinner, *Die Pastoralbriefe: Kommentar zum ersten Timotheusbrief* (HTKNT 11.2; Frieburg: Herder, 1994), 240; Marshall, *Pastoral Epistles*, 603.

20 *Pace* Towner, *The Goal of Our Instruction*, 26–27, although his suggestion is convincing (39) that a mood of women's emancipation visible in the Roman empire during the first century may have contributed to the problems in the Ephesian church. See also Bruce W. Winter, "The 'New' Roman Wife and 1 Timothy 2:9–15: The Search for a *Sitz im Leben*," *TynBul* 51 (2000): 285–94.

of their efforts are factions within the church (Titus 3:10) and shipwreck for the faith of those whom they convince (1 Tim. 1:19).

Paul wrote 1 Timothy to provide his coworker with a mandate to restore order to the Ephesian church, which had been corrupted by this teaching. Within the Pauline corpus, the letter is unusual. The salutation is not followed, as is common in Paul's letters, with a prayer or prayer report but with a description of Timothy's commission from Paul to quell the false teaching in Ephesus. The letter then continues with alternating sections of specific instructions on restoring order and personal directives to Timothy.

Letters like this were commonly sent in antiquity by a government official to a subordinate upon the subordinate's resumption of some new public responsibility. Perhaps the best extant example of such letters is the Tebtunis Papyrus 703. A government administrator sent this letter in the third century B.C. to a steward who had just taken charge of an Egyptian administrative district.[21] The letter is written as a "memorandum" (*hypomnēma*) to remind the steward of the things that the administrator had covered with him in conversation before the steward left to take his new post (ll. 258–61). The details of the letter show that the steward is to straighten out particular problems, such as the complaints of farmers against village officials (ll. 40–49) and the theft of oil revenues through smuggling (ll. 141–45). Personal admonitions are mingled with detailed practical instructions on how to administrate the nome.[22] The letter concludes with a general admonition to exemplary conduct:

> Your prime duty is to act with peculiar care, honesty, and in the best possible way ... and your next duty is to behave well and be upright in your district, to keep clear of bad company, to avoid all base collusion, to believe that, if you are without reproach in this, you will be held deserving of higher functions, to keep the instructions in your hand, and to report on everything as has been ordered. (ll. 261–80)

This letter was something like a handbook for the steward as he began the duties of his new office.[23]

Speaking of the situation under the Roman empire in the first century B.C., Dio Cassius says that "the emperor gives instructions [*entolē*] to the procurators, the pronconsuls, and the propraetors, in order that they may be under definite orders when they go out to their provinces" (*Hist.* 53.15.4). The contents of such "royal mandates" were intended for wide publication so that through them the public might know both what was expected under the new official and that the actions this new official took had the authority of the emperor behind them.[24] The emperor Trajan,

21 The text of the letter with an introduction, translation, and detailed commentary can be found in Arthur S. Hunt and J. Gilbart Smyly, *The Tebtunis Papyri*, vol. 3, part 1 (London: Oxford Univ. Press, 1933), 66–102. I am using the translation of Hunt and Smyly, and line references are to their edition of the Greek text.

22 E.g., ll. 158–63: "If you are neglectful in this ... be sure that besides the payments. . .you will fall into no ordinary contempt," and ll. 254–57: "If you act thus you will fulfill your official duty and your own safety will be assured."

23 Hunt and Smyly, *Tebtunis Papyri*, 69, describe the letter as "a kind of vade-mecum" for the steward and "his appointment charter."

24 Michael Wolter, *Die Pastoralbriefe als Paulustradition* (FRLANT 146; Göttingen: Vandenhoeck & Ruprecht, 1988), 164–70.

writing in the early second century A.D. to his governor Pliny, for example, instructs him to make his imperial mandate known to his subjects in Bithynia:

> The people of that province will understand, I believe, that I have their interests at heart. For you will take care to make it clear to them, that you were appointed specially to represent myself. (Pliny, *Ep.* 10.18)

A letter of official mandate, therefore, served as both a reminder to the subordinate of his duties and as a public commission for this subordinate.[25]

In 1 Timothy 6:14 Paul tells Timothy to "keep the commandment [*entolē*]," meaning the mandate that he has given him throughout the letter. The precise nature of this mandate emerges at several points. Timothy is to command the false teachers to stop teaching (1:18) and to enforce proper conduct within the church (3:15). Personally, he should provide an example of pious behavior (4:12, 15), making sure that neither his conduct nor his teaching slips into the pattern that the false teachers have set (4:16; 6:20). The purity of the church, both in the conduct of those who belong to it and in the teaching of its leaders, is so important because the true gospel is found in the church, and the gospel is the only means to salvation (2:1–7; 3:15; 4:7b–10, 16).

If men in the church are involved in angry disputes, they cannot lift holy hands in prayer, and if their behavior hinders their prayers, then it also hinders the advancement of the gospel (2:1–8). If women in the church are abandoning modesty and, like Eve, succumbing to Satan's offer of sinful knowledge, and then teaching this error to others (2:9–14; 5:15), then their very salvation is threatened (2:15). The church is the pillar and bulwark of the truth that everyone must know to be saved (3:15; cf. 2:4–6). For this reason Timothy must lead the church in Ephesus back to right doctrine and right conduct.

RIGHT DOCTRINE

In several places scattered about the letter Paul summarizes critical elements of Christian teaching as a way of reminding Timothy, along with the church that will hear this mandate read, of certain fundamental elements of the gospel. Timothy has received a commission to remain faithful to this "deposit" of truth when he was set apart for the work of the gospel (6:12, 20).[26] On several points the false teaching is challenging traditional Christian teaching, and Paul wants to remind Timothy—his official subordinate—and the church under his care about those fundamental places at which the gospel and the false teaching part ways.

---

25 See Hunt and Smyly, *Tebtunis Papyri*, 66–73; Ceslas Spicq, *Les Épitres Pastorales*, 2 vols., 4th ed. (Ébib; Paris: Lecoffre, 1969), 1:34–37; Benjamin Fiore, *The Function of Personal Example in the Socratic and Pastoral Epistles* (AnBib 105; Rome: Biblical Institute, 1986), 79–84; Wolter, *Die Pastoralbriefe*, 161–70; and Johnson, *Letters to Paul's Delegates*, 106–7.

26 Timothy's "good confession in the presence of many witnesses" (6:12) is therefore equivalent to "ordination." See George W. Knight III, *Commentary on the Pastoral Epistles* (NIGTC; Grand Rapids: Eerdmans, 1992), 264–65.

First, in two places Paul emphasizes that God is the only true God (1 Tim. 2:5; 6:15–16). This was a common confession in ancient Judaism (e.g., Deut. 6:4; Isa. 44:8; 45:5–6) and early Christianity (Mark 12:29; Rom. 3:30; 1 Cor. 8:1; Eph. 4:5–6; James 2:19), which served in a polytheistic context to assert the exclusive sovereignty of the God of the Jewish Scriptures over the universe. As Paul says in 1 Corinthians 8:1, "We know that an idol is nothing at all in the world and that there is no God but one."

On the one hand, it is possible that when Paul uses this language in 1 Timothy, he is only using traditional Jewish language as a reminder of God's universal sovereignty in a context where people often made similar claims about the emperor and other rulers (cf., e.g., 2 Macc. 12:15; Sir. 46:5).[27] On the other hand, Paul may be using traditional language against gnostic claims that the Jewish God is a lesser deity in a vast genealogy of deities. He may be asserting that God is not the created creator who forgot his origins and who stands beneath the unknown "power above." Rather, he is the "only potentate" (*dynastēs*), the one God above all other cosmic and earthly rulers.[28]

Second, Paul emphasizes that God is the Creator of the world and that his creation is good. Paul affirms God's creation of Adam and Eve in 2:11, and he implies that God's creation was good by placing the responsibility for transgression on Satan (who stands behind the passive voice verbs *ēpatēthē* and *exapatētheisa* in 2:14).[29] This notion appears again in 4:3–5, where Paul contrasts elements of the false teaching with his summary of the truth that the church supports in 3:15–16.

In 4:3–5, Paul refers to the Christian prophecy that in the end times some will abandon the faith for deceitful and demonically inspired teachings. He mentions two of these teachings—forbidding marriage and abstinence from foods. Since he refutes the notion that marriage is evil at other points in the letter (2:15; 3:2, 12; 5:9, 14), he focuses in chapter 4 on the idea that "foods" should be rejected.[30] Food, he argues, like everything else God has made, is good, sanctified by God's creative word and by the prayers offered by believers before they eat. God has made it, moreover, for the benefit of those who believe and recognize the truth—it was created for them to receive gratefully (cf. 1 Cor. 10:30). Here Paul echoes the Genesis account of creation, and specifically the climactic statement at the end of God's six days of creative activity: "God saw all that he had made, and it was very good" (Gen. 1:31).

Later Paul will describe God as the one "who gives life to everything" (6:13) and "who richly provides us with everything for our enjoyment" (6:17). Like 6:15–16,

27 The reference to God as the only immortal may be an allusion to the common practice, since Julius Caesar, of voting divine honors for Rome's supreme ruler. On this practice, see Mary Beard, John North, and Simon Price, *Religions of Rome*, 2 vols. (Cambridge: Cambridge Univ. Press, 1998), 206–10; for this understanding of the phrase in 2 Tim. 6:16 see, among others, J. N. D. Kelly, *The Pastoral Epistles* (BNTC 14; Peabody, Mass.: Hendrickson, 1960), 146, and Spicq, *Épitres Pastorales*, 1:573–74.

28 Cf. E. F. Scott, *The Pastoral Epistles* (MNTC; London: Hodder and Stoughton, 1936), 79, and, for 2:5, Kelly, *Pastoral Epistles*, 63. *Pace* Towner, *The Goal of Our Instruction*, 50 and 84, who connects the "one God" language with Paul's universalism (cf. Rom. 3:29–30; Gal. 3:20; Eph. 4:5–6).

29 Andreas J. Köstenberger, "Ascertaining Women's God-Ordained Roles: An Interpretation of 1 Timothy 2:15," *BBR* 7 (1997): 107–44, here at 123.

30 Knight, *Pastoral Epistles*, 190; Marshall, *Pastoral Epistles*, 542.

the description of God as the origin of life is possibly a traditional polemical thrust at a quality sometimes ascribed to the Roman emperors. Each subject supposedly considered the emperor "the origin of his life and of his existence" (*Inscr.Priene* 105.10.32).[31] Since Paul has emphasized so heavily that God created all things in 4:3–5, however, he probably means to say in 6:13, 17 that the only sovereign God is also the God who gave life to everything, and that the creation he brought into being is good. The ultimate God, in other words, is the God of Genesis 1–3, who has created and now lavishly sustains his creatures.[32]

Third, Paul emphasizes the gracious, saving work of God on behalf of his human creation through the fully human mediator between God and human beings, Christ Jesus. Paul affirms the account of the origin of human sin found in Genesis 3:1–19 (1 Tim. 2:14) and assumes that, as a result of that primal sin, everyone is in need of salvation (1 Tim. 2:4, 6; 4:10). He places special emphasis, however, on the gracious character of God and Christ, on the role of Christ as mediator between God and humanity, and on the humanity of Christ in his role as mediator. Thus, Paul gives to God the title "God our Savior" and says that God wants everyone to be saved (2:3–4). He is, therefore, "the Savior of all [people], and especially of those who believe" (4:10). God saves those who believe through Christ, and he is a merciful and gracious Savior, willing to rescue even the worst of sinners, whatever the level of their ignorance and unbelief (1:13–16).

In two traditional confessions (2:5–6 and 3:16b), Paul stresses Christ's mediatorial role between God and humanity.[33] Just as there is only one God, the first creed says, there is also only one mediator between God and humanity—Christ Jesus (2:5). The second creed also speaks of Christ as one who moves between the seen and unseen worlds—Christ was vindicated by the Spirit, seen by angels, and received up into glory, but he also was manifested in the flesh, preached among the nations, and believed on in the world (3:16). He was, in other words, "the mediator between God and humanity" (2:5).

Both creeds also emphasize the human nature of Christ as mediator. It is as "the human being Christ Jesus" that he mediates between Christ and human beings (2:5). It was also "in the flesh" that he was manifested to the world (3:16).

Why this triple stress on God's graciousness, Christ's role as mediator, and Christ's human nature? Paul is probably reminding Timothy and the church at Ephesus of precisely those points of traditional Christian teaching that most effectively rebut the claims of the false teachers. Christ is not, as heretics such as Saturninus claimed, the

31 Spicq, *Épitres Pastorales*, 1:570.

32 Cf. Walter Lock, *The Pastoral Epistles*, 3rd ed. (ICC; Edinburgh: T. & T. Clark, 1952), 71, on 6:13, and Marshall, *Pastoral Epistles*, 672, on 6:17. The participle *zōogonountos* in 6:13 is in the present tense, indicating that God presently sustains the life that he has created. On this, see Marshall, *Pastoral Epistles*, 662.

33 Commentators commonly take these two passages as quotations of previously existing, traditional material, although there is some debate about 2:5–6. For the position that 2:5–6 is a "liturgical piece" rather than a "creed" or "confession," see Martin Dibelius and Hans Conzelmann, *The Pastoral Epistles* (Hermeneia; Philadelphia: Fortress, 1972), 41, and Spicq, *Épitres Pastorales*, 366. For the idea that 2:5–6 is Paul's own composition, see Johnson, *Letters to Paul's Delegates*, 127. The balanced rhetoric of the passage probably indicates that it is a traditional statement of some kind, and, if the *Shema* (Deut. 6:4–5) on which it is based can be called a creed, surely this statement qualifies for that title also.

fleshless heavenly being who bypasses the angelic creators of the world and mediates between the unknown God and people who possess an implanted spark of the divine. He is the fully human mediator between the one God and his human creation, and his saving power is effective for all who believe in him.[34] The God who created the world, moreover, does not stand apart from the gracious "power above" who took pity on the miserable human products of the angels' creative bumblings. Instead, the God who created human beings is also the one who, through the merciful and gracious work of Jesus Christ, effected their salvation.

RIGHT CONDUCT

Most of 1 Timothy is concerned with right conduct within the church. The false teaching produces behavior that seems to flow from a seared conscience—prohibition of marriage, ascetic food restrictions, endless discussion of mumbo-jumbo based on the Genesis creation narrative, angry disputes arising from these discussions, and a lust for wealth. Women—particularly the wealthy women who may have paid the false teachers to tutor them, and the younger widows whom the church has supported from its common funds—are apparently among the chief advocates of the heresy that has led to this behavior. Wealthy women are perhaps teaching the heresy in their houses while the men spend church meetings not in prayer but in angry disputes about the heresy.[35] The younger widows, freed by the largesse of the church from the responsibilities of marriage and child-rearing, which they do not believe in anyway, can spend their time making the rounds of believers' households advocating the false teaching.[36]

The Christian households in which the church meets are therefore in doctrinal disarray, and, as a consequence, the "household of God" is in disarray. The notion that God and his people are separate from the created order threatens the biblical-theological basis of the gospel. A focus on the importance of mythic knowledge for salvation obscures the gospel's concern with salvation through God's mercy and the sacrificial mediation of Christ Jesus. The angry disputes of the men and the neglect of proper household management among both men and women are bringing on the church the justifiable censure of the outside world. As a result, the witness of the church to the gospel is seriously hindered.[37]

In the face of all this, Paul provides Timothy with a mandate to recall the Christians at Ephesus to proper conduct both in the household of God and in their own

34 This seems more likely than Towner's suggestion, *The Goal of Our Instruction*, 54, that Christ is viewed in these passages simply as the mediator of a covenant. It is true that the term *mesitēs* has covenantal overtones in its other New Testament uses (Gal. 3:20; Heb. 8:6; 9:15; 12:24), but in those passages the context makes such overtones clear.

35 Cf. Padgett, "Wealthy Women," 22.

36 This seems to be the best explanation for Paul's advice to "enroll" (*katalegō*) only widows who are advanced in age (sixty or older) and who do not have relatives to care for them (5:3–9a, 16), and to "exclude" (*paraiteō*) younger widows (5:11, aut.) since some desire to marry and others learn idleness, "going around to the houses ... saying what they should not" (5:12–13, aut.). See Marshall, *Pastoral Epistles*, 574–81, 591–92, 601–3.

37 Cf. Towner, *The Goal of Our Instruction*, 169–99. As Towner emphasizes throughout his study, this concern for mission and not the notion of *christliche Bürgerlichkeit* ("Christian citizenship"), as Dibelius and Conzelmann, *Pastoral Epistles*, 8, 39–41, describe it, accounts for the social ethic of the Pastorals.

households. He seems especially concerned about what happens when the church gathers for worship and about the need for qualified leaders in the Ephesian church. In the background of his comments on both of these issues lies the abuse among the Ephesian Christians of the complex connection between church and home.

The Church Gathered for Worship

In 2:1–15 Paul gives Timothy instructions on the conduct of the church when it gathers for worship. Apparently when the church has gathered for worship in the past, angry disputes among the men led to the neglect of prayer (2:8), and these disputes probably arose from the heavy-handed teaching of heresy by the women (2:12). Paul urges Timothy and the church to reinstate prayer as the primary focus (*prōtos*) of worship (2:1, 8), and especially urges them to pray for those in positions of government authority so that Christians may live peaceful and pious lives (2:2). Such conditions are not only desirable because they make it easier for Christians to live in a way that pleases God (2:3) but also because they facilitate the church's proclamation of the gospel to the unbelieving world (2:4–7).[38]

Paul also wants the respective roles of the sexes in the church's worship gathering to reflect positively the order of creation and negatively the experience of the Fall as they are described in Genesis 1–3. Men should stop being angry and quarreling with one another and instead should lift "holy hands" to God in prayer. Women should bring to the worship gathering lives adorned with good works rather than with ostentatious displays of wealth or immodest clothing (2:9–10). Paul probably does not mean to exclude women from praying during the church's worship gathering any more than he means to exclude men from adorning their lives with good works, but the implication of his direct command to the men about prayer is that they should at least take the initiative in this activity.[39]

In addition, Paul prohibits women from teaching or exercising inappropriate authority over a man in the church's worship (2:12a).[40] They should instead learn quietly and in "full submission" (2:11, 12b). Paul does not say who or what the women should submit to, but since he has just prohibited them from teaching, it seems likely that he intends for them to submit the church's overseers or elders, who must be men with the ability to teach (3:2; 5:17).[41]

38 On the causal nuance of the relative pronoun *hos* ("who") that begins 2:4, see Marshall, *Pastoral Epistles*, 425. Marshall draws attention to the parallel constructions in 4:10 and Titus 2:14.

39 Marshall, *Pastoral Epistles*, 447.

40 The rare verb *authenteō*, paraphrased in this sentence as "exercising inappropriate authority," has been the subject of intense debate, turning on whether it refers, in a negative sense, to the inappropriate use of authority or, in a neutral sense, to the use of authority at all. See the opposing discussions in, e.g., Andreas J. Köstenberger, "A Complex Sentence Structure in 1 Timothy 2:12," in *Women in the Church: A Fresh Analysis of 1 Timothy 2:9–15*, ed. Andreas J. Köstenberger, Thomas R. Schreiner, and H. Scott Baldwin (Grand Rapids: Baker, 1995), 81–103, and Marshall, *Pastoral Epistles*, 456–60. The unusual nature of the term indicates that Paul means to say something other than that women should not exercise authority over men (cf. Marshall, *Pastoral Epistles*, 458). Paul could have easily formulated a sentence that used a more common term, such as *proïstēmi* (cf. 3:4–5; 5:1), had he intended this meaning. He probably means, therefore, that women should not exercise inappropriate authority over men, not simply that they should never exercise authority over men.

41 The "elders" who teach in 5:17 are clearly men since Paul, who is fully capable of talking about *presbyterai* (5:2), nevertheless chooses the masculine phrase *hoi. . . presbyteroi* here.

Why this concern to separate the roles of men and women and to silence women teachers in the church's worship? At the practical level, silencing women teachers cut the false teaching off at its source—wealthy women, as we have seen, were probably financing the false teachers and spreading the false teachers' heresy themselves, and younger widows, happily released from any obligation to marry and care for children, were going about from house to house teaching the heresy.

As is already apparent from Paul's willingness to separate the roles of the sexes in worship in 2:8–9 and to silence all women teachers in 2:12, however, a deeper theological issue is at stake in this gender-specific ordering of worship. Paul states this issue explicitly in 2:13–15. God fashioned human beings in two genders, male and female, and the order in which he created them implies distinct roles in the church for each gender. Men should presumably take the initiative in prayer when the church gathers for worship, and women should submit to the authority of the church's male leadership because "Adam was formed first, then Eve" (2:13). Men, rather than women, should teach because Eve rather than Adam was Satan's first victim in the deception that led to the disobedience described in Genesis 3:6.

The implication is clear: Adam and Eve violated the divine ordering of the genders when Eve led Adam to disobey God's command. In a manner reminiscent of 1 Corinthians 11:2–16, Paul correlates activity in the church's worship with a divinely appointed ordering of the sexes at creation. Women will be saved from the satanically inspired false teaching (1 Tim. 2:15; cf. 5:15)—and therefore will be saved eschatologically—if they stop their ascetic practices and teaching and devote themselves to the creation-affirming duties of marriage, bearing children, and managing a household (2:15; 5:14).[42]

The reason for Paul's imposition of an order on the Ephesian church that reflects the order, both positive and negative, of the Genesis creation narratives is not far to seek if the false teaching at Ephesus looks something like the Gnosticism of Saturninus. A devaluation of the "Jewish god" that Genesis 1–3 describes as the Creator of the universe and therefore the Creator of Adam and Eve had led to a violation of conventions in the worship of the church, conventions that Paul believed to be rooted in that narrative. Those conventions need to be reestablished, both as a way of affirming the created order against the claims of the heresy and as a way of restoring order in the church's corporate worship.[43]

Paul hopes that if the church follows these instructions, it will experience three results. First, prayer will once again ascend for the governing authorities, thus stemming the tide of persecution and helping to preserve a social environment in which the church's witness to the gospel can flourish. Second, the primary perpetrators of

42 Cf. Mounce, *Pastoral Epistles*, 130–43. On the hotly contested meaning of Paul's statement that "women will be saved through childbearing" in 2:15, see the extensive survey of interpretations and the exegetical observations in Köstenberger, "Ascertaining Women's God-Ordained Roles," 107–44.

43 The groundwork for the heresy's appeal to women may have been laid by the "new" attitude among some wives in the late Roman Republic who sought to exercise dominance over their husbands. By the time of Augustus, this behavior was common but often viewed as scandalous. On this see Towner, *The Goal of Our Instruction*, 39, and Winter, "'New' Roman Wife," 285–94. Perhaps in 2:9–15 Paul sought to prevent the church from public scandal on this issue for evangelistic purposes, as he does with slaves in 6:1–2 (cf. Titus 2:5, 10).

the false teaching will be silenced. Third, the conduct of the church at worship will itself proclaim the God of Genesis 1–3 as the true God.

Leadership of God's Household

Leadership of the Ephesian church is in the hands of a group that Paul calls alternately "overseers" (3:1–7) and "elders" (5:17–20).[44] These leaders are probably assisted in their work by "deacons" (3:8–13). The church over which these leaders preside apparently meets in various houses, owned by individual elders or overseers. This does not mean, however, that each overseer or elder has his own house church since in 5:20 Paul instructs Timothy to rebuke sinful elders (plural) in front of the whole group.[45] It seems reasonable to think of the elder or overseer who owns a house in which the church meets as having an especially prominent role in the leadership of the church that meets in his house—a householder would be wealthy and therefore have a measure of natural social status within the church.[46]

If this understanding of church structure at Ephesus is roughly right, then the false teaching can only have gained strength if the elders in whose houses the church meets have been inattentive to both the domestic and the ecclesiastical affairs of their households. The families who live in their houses and the assemblies that meet in them are in moral and doctrinal disarray. The domestic and corporate disorder that plagues the church is giving the faith a bad name with unbelievers and hindering the proclamation of the gospel (2:1–7; 3:14–15; 6:1). An important purpose of Paul's mandate to Timothy, therefore, is to place before him and the church a list of personal qualifications for those who should serve in these offices and to urge Timothy to be an example to everyone of how to conduct domestic and ecclesiastical affairs.

Scholars frequently point out how similar Paul's list of qualifications for overseers and deacons in 3:1–13 is to the lists of qualifications found in Hellenistic philosophers and moral theorists of the period. Paul's list is similar in form and in some of the qualities mentioned, for example, to the list of qualifications for a general described in Paul's contemporary Onasander.[47] A general should be prudent and not a lover of money, preferably have children, be the right age—neither too young nor too old—and have a good reputation (along with many other good qualities); these characteristics are identical to or resemble some of the qualities in Paul's list. This is not surprising since one of Paul's chief concerns in 1 Timothy is to restore the tarnished public

44 See Titus 1:5 and 7, where the two terms seem to designate the same office. The term "overseer" (*episkopos*) is always in the singular in the Pastorals (1 Tim. 3:1, 2; Titus 1:7) and for this reason some scholars have proposed that the "overseer" and the "elders" (*presbyteroi*) fulfill different functions. R. Alastair Campbell, *The Elders: Seniority within Earliest Christianity* (SNTW; Edinburgh: T. & T. Clark, 1994), 176–205, for example, believes that the Pastorals reflect a transitional period in which a single "overseer" is chosen in each city to preside over the city's "elders" (Titus 1:5, 7). But, as Marshall, *Pastoral Epistles*, 179, observes, Titus 1:5 speaks of appointing "elders" in each city, not an "overseer" for each city. It seems better, with Marshall, ibid., 181, to view "overseer" as a title descriptive of function and "elder" as a title descriptive of status.

45 This makes Campbell's claim unlikely (*Elders*, 193) that "overseers" started out as the leaders of their own house churches.

46 See David C. Verner, *The Household of God: The Social World of the Pastoral Epistles* (SBLDS 71; Chico, Calif.: Scholars Press, 1983), 133, 152.

47 Onasander (sometimes spelled Onosander) was a Platonic philosopher who wrote during the reign of Claudius (A.D. 41–54). See the text with translation of his *De imperatoris officio* 1 in Dibelius and Conzelmann, *The Pastoral Epistles*, 158–60.

reputation of the church so that its gospel witness to those outside the church might be effective. Thus he concludes his list of qualifications for the office of "overseer" with the statement that the one who serves in this capacity must "have a good reputation with outsiders, so that he will not fall into disgrace and into the devil's trap" (3:7; cf. 2:1–6; 6:1).

In addition to these qualifications, however, Paul includes for both the overseers and deacons a number of qualities that seem particularly suited to running tranquil, just, and orderly homes, and to teaching right doctrine within the Christian assemblies that met in these homes. Both overseers and deacons should be faithful to their wives (3:2, 12), should not be prone to drunkenness (3:3, 8), and should manage their own homes, particularly their children, well (3:4, 12). Overseers should be sober, moderate, and hospitable, and rather than striking out in physical violence, should be gentle and irenic (3:2–3)—qualities especially fitting for an exemplary home.

In addition, the overseer should be skilled in teaching the faith and, together with deacons, should have a good grasp of the faith and a clear conscience about the accuracy of their beliefs (3:2, 9). Those responsible for the conduct of their homes are also responsible for the truthfulness of the teaching that takes place in them when the church meets for worship.

Why is Paul so concerned that church leaders be responsible heads of their households? The false teachers, in addition to their recruitment of younger widows (5:13), may also have targeted households where, according to Greek and Roman custom, a man held formal authority, but which were in disarray. They seem to have preyed on homes where the women were already corrupt (2 Tim. 3:6) and failed to take care of their relatives (1 Tim. 5:4, 8, 16). They were also successful in households where unorthodox teaching went unchallenged (2 Tim. 3:6; Titus 1:11).

Household heads who were also the owners of the houses in which congregations gathered for worship may have been indirectly responsible for much of this disorder by their unwillingness to take responsibility for what happened in their homes. Perhaps drunkenness (1 Tim. 3:2, 3, 8, 11), marital infidelity (3:2, 12), a lack of teaching skill (3:2), or a lack of sincerely held knowledge (3:9) hindered the exercise of their responsibilities. Perhaps the financial success of the false teachers impressed them (3:3; 3:8; cf. 6:3–10; Titus 1:11). Such people, Paul says, should not hold positions of leadership in the church, for "if anyone does not know how to manage his own family, how can he take care of God's church?" (3:5; cf. 3:12). Elders who persist in this kind of conduct are to be publicly rebuked (5:20).[48] By contrast, those who rule well deserve to receive special recognition (5:17).

Paul wants Timothy himself to provide an example not only to the leaders of the church but to everyone. "Set an example for the believers," Paul tells him, "in speech, in life, in love, in faith, and in purity" (4:12; cf. 4:15). Timothy is to view all within the Ephesian church as if they are members of his family and to treat each

48 The participle *hamartanontas* ("those who sin") is in the present tense and therefore refers to those who *persist* in sin.

metaphorical relative within this household with respect (5:1). He should avoid hasty ordinations to positions of ecclesiastical responsibility (5:22), remain free from the asceticism of the false teachers, "use a little wine" (5:23), flee the evils to which a lust for wealth gives rise, and pursue "righteousness, godliness, faith, love, endurance and gentleness" (6:3–11). Above all, he should guard "the deposit"—the "sound instruction" that Paul has entrusted to his care and which the false teachers have abandoned (1:13; 6:3).[49] In other words, like the recipients of royal mandates, he is to be an example of the kind of behavior that brought order to the world and that upheld, in Timothy's case, "the household management of God" (*oikonomian theou*, 1:4).[50]

THE MANAGEMENT OF GOD'S HOUSEHOLD IN EPHESUS

In 1 Timothy Paul is concerned to restore the evangelical witness of a church plagued by proto-gnostic teaching. This teaching advocated a disordered view of the universe, took advantage of disordered households to propagate its teaching, and left in its wake a disordered church. Those outside the church took notice of the church's chaotic state and were not favorably impressed. Despite God's desire for "all people to be saved and to come to a knowledge of the truth" (2:4), the church failed to witness effectively to the goodness of God's creation, the fallenness of humanity, and the graciousness of God's saving purposes as they have been revealed in the mediating work of Christ Jesus. Their dissent from these cardinal tenets of the faith led women to abandon the management (*oikodespoteō*, 5:14) of their homes and to exercise inappropriate teaching authority over the church's male leadership. The management of God's household, as a result, fell into disarray.[51]

But God's household—the church—is "the pillar and foundation of the truth." The truth should be evident both in what the church teaches and in the way that the church and the households who sponsor its meetings conduct their affairs. God created people male and female and assigned each gender separate roles. Paul tells Timothy that the ordering of the church's worship and the ordering of affairs in the home should reflect this work of God as Creator. If women and men in the Ephesian church align their domestic and ecclesiastical affairs with the truth that God created the world and called it good, then they will show by the way they live that the world-denying notions of the false teaching are wrong. Unbelievers will no longer slander the teaching of the church (6:1). The church will instead function as the repository for the truth about God, humanity, and God's ransom of humanity through the one mediator between God and his human creation, the man Christ Jesus (2:5–6).

49 See Ceslas Spicq, "παραθήκη," *TLNT*, 3:27.

50 For this translation of the phrase, see Johnson, *Letters to Paul's Delegates*, 112.

51 The notion of the church as God's household also appears in the earlier Pauline letters and is not a symptom of a concern for *christliche Bürgerlichkeit* ("Christian citizenship") that developed in the church after Paul's time. See Gal. 6:10; Eph. 2:19 (cf. 1 Cor. 4:1; 9:17) and the discussion in Towner, *The Goal of Our Instruction*, 133–34.

Chapter 20

TITUS: KNOWING GOD, DOING GOOD, AND MAKING SALVATION ATTRACTIVE

Around the same time that Paul wrote his mandate to Timothy in Ephesus (i.e., 1 Timothy), he also wrote a mandate to Titus. As we saw in chapter 19, the apostle had left Titus on the island of Crete to straighten out problems and appoint qualified leaders in the island's churches. Like the ancient royal mandate letters described in the last chapter, Paul's letter to Titus is written from a superior to a subordinate who is charged with the oversight of some social group. Like those documents, the letter's purpose is apparently to remind Paul's subordinate Titus of instructions he gave him orally before he embarked on his duties. Also like these "royal mandates," Paul's letter, although written to Titus himself, is a public document, intended for the whole church, as the plural "you" (*hymōn*) in its closing line shows (3:15).

Paul charges Titus with appointing leaders who can refute the false teaching that has started to corrupt the Cretan churches and replace it with "sound doctrine" (1:5, 9). As is common in such royal mandates, Titus himself is to provide a model of the belief and behavior that Paul expects of everyone in the Cretan church (2:7–8), and the public nature of the mandate shows all Cretan Christians that Titus carries with him the authoritative backing of the apostle Paul (3:15).

The false teaching that has started to disturb the churches of Crete seems virtually identical to the false teaching that had created disorder in the churches of Ephesus. It appeals to the Jewish law (Titus 3:9; cf. 1:14; 1 Tim. 1:7), has ascetic tendencies (Titus 1:14–15; cf. 1 Tim. 4:3), and emphasizes the importance of "myths" (Titus 1:14; cf. 1 Tim. 1:4; 4:7) and "genealogies" (Titus 3:9; cf. 1 Tim. 1:4). The false teachers on Crete, like those in Ephesus, have corrupt consciences (Titus 1:15; cf. 1 Tim. 4:2), crave financial gain (Titus 1:11; cf. 1 Tim. 6:10), and encourage arguments and factiousness (Titus 3:9–11; 1 Tim. 6:4). Also like their counterparts in Ephesus, they spread their teaching from house to house, upsetting the families in those houses and probably the churches that meet in them (Titus 1:11; cf. 1 Tim. 5:13).

The primary differences between the two groups lie in their ethnic and geographical origins. We know that the group on Crete was native to the island (1:12–13) and was Jewish (1:10), whereas Paul is not explicit about the origins of the group in Ephesus.[1] As in Ephesus, so on Crete, the false teaching is probably an early form

1 Crete was the largest of the Aegean islands and home to a large Jewish minority. Josephus reports that during the reign of Augustus an imposter with a superficial resemblance to Herod's son Alexander was able to convince all the Jews that he met on the island that Herod's instructions to execute his sons Alexander and Aristobulus had never been carried out and that he was Alexander (*A. J.* 17.327; cf. *B. J.* 2.103). Josephus was also married to a woman from Crete who, he says, came from a prominent family on the island (*Vit.* 427). Tacitus oddly traces the ancestry of the Jews to the people of Crete (*Hist.* 5.2), and Acts 2:11 lists Crete among the places that Jews traveled from to celebrate the festival of Pentecost in Jerusalem. All of this implies a large Jewish population on the island.

of Jewish gnosticism and probably contains some of the mythological and ascetic elements that surfaced in the later gnostic systems of Saturninus and Menander.[2]

Paul's primary concern in the letter is that this perverse teaching will continue to lead to evil behavior, which will in turn bring public discredit on the church's "trustworthy message" about God. This concern about the connection between the quality of one's knowledge about God and the quality of one's behavior dominates the letter. Deceptive teaching about God will inevitably lead to a corrupt conscience and evil deeds. The sound teaching that through Christ Jesus God saves people from evil behavior and gives them hope of eternal life, however, should lead to moral purity and good deeds. The false teaching that has infested the churches on Crete is so pernicious because its understanding of God leads to evil behavior, which in turn undermines the ability of Christians to attract outsiders to the Christian message—the message that God has offered salvation from sin and eternal hope through Jesus Christ.

In this chapter we will first examine the connection that Paul makes between belief and behavior in Titus and then discuss the origins and implications—both social and theological—of Paul's belief that evil behavior hinders the church's teaching about God as Savior.

KNOWLEDGE AND CONDUCT

The link between knowledge and conduct permeates the letter and explains the basic difference between the "sound teaching" of the Pauline gospel and the deceptive message of the false teachers. "Knowledge of the truth," as Paul says in the letter's first sentence, "leads to godliness [*eusebia*]" (1:1).[3] But the quality of the false teachers' lives belies the falsity of their claim to know God (1:16). They are insubordinate (1:10), greedy (1:11), quarrelsome (3:9), and factious (3:10). They have tainted minds coupled with corrupt consciences, and these intellectual deficiencies have led them into confusion over what is pure and what is impure (1:15).[4]

The connection Paul makes between knowledge of God and ethics explains, at least in part, his quotation from the Cretan poet Epimenides, "Cretans are always liars, evil brutes, lazy gluttons" (1:12).[5] This is not simply the insensitive repetition

2 See the comments on Saturninus and Menander in ch. 19, above.

3 In the Pastorals, the term *eusebeia* ("reverence, piety, godliness") means a knowledge of God that gives rise to right conduct. On this see Hermann von Lips, *Glaube–Gemeinde–Amt: Zum Verständnis der Ordination in den Pastoralbriefen* (FRLANT 122; Göttingen: Vandenhoeck & Ruprecht, 1979), 80–84. This understanding of the term may arise from its use in the LXX and in Hellenistic Judaism generally. See, e.g., Isa. 11:2 and 33:6, where *eusebeia* translates "the fear of the Lord" (cf. Prov. 1:7), and the discussion in Philip H. Towner, *The Goal of Our Instruction: The Structure of Theology and Ethics in the Pastoral Epistles* (JSNTSup 34; Sheffield: Sheffield Academic Press, 1989), 88, 147–54; I. H. Marshall, *The Pastoral Epistles* (ICC; Edinburgh: T. & T. Clark, 1999), 135–44, and Jerome D. Quinn, *The Letter to Titus* (AB 35; New York: Doubleday, 1990), 282–91.

4 Perhaps in a way similar to the false teachers in Colosse, the false teachers on Crete believed that God and the cosmic beings under him must be placated with ascetic practices—"commands of those who reject the truth," as Paul refers to them here (1:14; cf. Col. 2:18, 22–23).

5 Epimenides was a religious teacher who lived on Crete around 500 B.C. Nothing of his literary output has survived, but the quotation here was attributed to him as early as Clement of Alexandria (*Strom.* 1.591–2) and Jerome (*Comm. Tit.*, 707).

of a social stereotype, a failure on Paul's part to follow his own advice in 3:2 to "show every courtesy to everyone" (NRSV).[6] The Cretans were regarded by many in antiquity as lying specifically about Zeus since they claimed that he was a man divinized for his benefactions to society and whose tomb could be seen on their island. The proverb links the Cretans lie about God with their behavior. Paul's quotation of the proverb is, therefore, an effort to say that at least the false teachers fit this stereotype of Cretans because they have a false understanding of God, and this false understanding fits hand in glove with their vicious way of life.[7]

If the false teachers demonstrate the truth that a perverse understanding of God leads to perverse behavior, then the antidote to the false teaching must combine a true understanding of God with teaching about the good works to which this true understanding should lead. This link between right teaching and right conduct appears at several critical junctures in the letter. Paul says that elders should hold firmly to "the trustworthy message" and "refute those who oppose it . . . because" (*gar*, 1:9–10) there are many "rebellious people, mere talkers and deceivers." In other words, the antidote to the bad behavior of the false teachers lies in the refutation of their false teaching. Similarly, Cretan Christians of whatever age, gender, and social standing should live in sensible ways "because" (*gar*, 2:11) of what they believe about God's saving grace and their future hope (2:11–13).

Titus should remind the believers on Crete to live in submissive, honest, and peaceful ways (3:1–2) "because" (*gar*, 3:3) God has rescued all believers out of the opposite of this kind of behavior when he showed them his kindness and justified them by his grace. Cretans are not the only "liars, evil brutes, lazy gluttons," but every Christian, prior to embracing the truth about God, lived in this way: "in malice and envy, being hated and hating one another" (3:3).[8] God has rescued from this way of life everyone who has trusted him and believed the sound teaching of the orthodox gospel. Those whom he has rescued should therefore "devote themselves to doing what is good" (3:8; cf. 3:14).

MAKING THE SAVIOR ATTRACTIVE

We saw in chapter 19 that in 1 Timothy Paul took seriously the impact that the false teaching had on the ethics of those who embraced it and consequently on the witness of the church to the unbelieving public. In 1 Timothy Paul told Timothy that the peaceful and quiet lives of Christians are pleasing to "God our Savior, who wants all people to be saved and to come to a knowledge of the truth" (1 Tim. 2:4, aut.). This statement implies that God wants people within the church to live peacefully

6 The author of Titus is frequently taken to task for the comment. The remarks of Alexander Souter and Emil G. Kraeling are typical: "Such vituperation must not be taken too seriously. The ancients were much given to it, and it probably reveals as much of the taste and even character of the persons who used it as it does the nature of those they attacked." See their article, "Crete, Cretans," in *Dictionary of the Bible*, ed. James Hastings, Frederick C. Grant, and H. H. Rowley, 2nd ed. (Edinburgh, T. & T. Clark, 1963), 188.

7 Reggie M. Kidd, "Titus as *Apologia*: Grace for Liars, Beasts, and Bellies," *HBT* 21 (1999): 185–209.

8 Cf. Kidd, "Titus as *Apologia*," 200.

and quietly so that the good news of God's saving intentions for humanity might gain a hearing from those outside the church. Later, Paul told Timothy to teach the younger widows to disavow the false teaching's denigration of marriage and instead to marry, raise children, exercise responsible authority over their households, and "so give the enemy no opportunity for slander" (5:14). Slaves too should serve their masters honorably and respectfully "so that God's name and our teaching may not be slandered" (6:1–2).

Paul raises this same concern in Titus. As a result of their reformed behavior, Paul says, Christians will silence those who "malign the word of God" (Titus 2:5) and are looking for something "bad to say about us" (2:8). Christians will instead make "the teaching about God our Savior attractive" (2:10). If the younger women love their husbands and children, are self-controlled and pure, pursue their domestic responsibilities with diligence, are kind, and submit to their husbands, then no one will be able to discredit "the word of God" with the claim that it leads to domestic disorder (2:5). In a similar way, if slaves are submissive to their masters, try to please them, resist arguing with them or stealing from them, and merit their masters' trust, they will make the church's teaching about the God who saves people from their sins (cf. 3:3–5) attractive to outsiders (2:10; cf. 1 Tim. 6:2).[9]

In both 1 Timothy and Titus, Paul seems to give special attention to those whose lack of social power made them vulnerable to oppression by their superiors. Women should learn in full submission in 1 Timothy 2:11 and should submit to their husbands in Titus 2:5. Slaves should serve their masters compliantly and respectfully in 1 Timothy 6:1–2—and all the more if the masters are brothers in the faith. In Titus 2:9–10 slaves are to submit to their masters in all things without argument.

Many students of the Pastorals have understood these directives to be a capitulation on the part of the author of the Pastorals to the prevailing oppressive social structure of his time—a convenient accommodation of the church to a clear cultural evil so that the church might survive as an institution.[10] Some believe that this aspect of the Pastorals separates them from the authentic Paul, whose tendencies were much more egalitarian.[11] Others believe that they are only the later outworking of a tendency that already characterizes the earlier Pauline letters.[12]

Paul's concern, however, is not the institutional survival of the church but the survival of a hearing for the gospel. His purpose in these instructions is evangelistic.[13] This becomes clear through a close look at 1 Timothy 2:1–7. Here Paul advises the church in Ephesus to pray for everyone, especially those in positions

9 On the missionary motive for the social ethic of the Pastorals, see Towner, *The Goal of Our Instruction*, 169–99.

10 See the sympathetic portrayal of this development as a social necessity following the failure of the early church's eschatological expectations in Dibelius and Conzelmann, *Pastoral Epistles*, 40–41. For an unsympathetic reading of the Pastorals' allegedly bourgeois ethic, see Neil Elliott, *Liberating Paul: The Justice of God and the Politics of the Apostle* (Maryknoll, N.Y.: Orbis, 1994), 25–31.

11 See, e.g., Elliott, *Liberating Paul*, 25–54.

12 See, e.g., John M. G. Barclay, "Paul, Philemon and the Dilemma of Christian Slave-Ownership," *NTS* 37 (1991):161–86, and idem, "Ordinary but Different: Colossians and Hidden Moral Identity," a paper read in the "Theology of the Disputed Paulines Group" at the Annual Meeting of the Society of Biblical Literature in Boston, Mass., Nov. 20–23, 1999.

13 Cf. Luke Timothy Johnson, *Letters to Paul's Delegates: 1 Timothy, 2 Timothy, Titus* (Valley Forge, Pa.: Trinity Press International, 1996), 235–36.

of governmental authority, and to live quiet and peaceful lives. The reason for this advice is that God is the Savior and wants everyone "to be saved and to come to a knowledge of the truth." Paul then summarizes the gospel—that Jesus is the mediator between God and humanity and gave himself as the ransom that could rescue humanity from its sin (1 Tim. 2:5–6). He understands that this gospel is for everyone because God has called him to be an apostle to non-Jewish nations (2:7). The quiet and peaceful behavior of the Ephesian church, therefore, will facilitate the communication of this gospel to everyone in the hope that they might be saved.

Similarly in Titus 2:7–8, the evangelistic rather than accommodationist purposes of Paul's advice to women and slaves become clear, when Paul tells Titus, who is neither a woman nor a slave, to be an example of proper behavior and of irreproachable speech. Just as with women and slaves, the reason for this advice is so that opponents of Christianity might be put to shame and have nothing bad to say about Christians. For the Paul of the Pastorals, God is the Savior of humanity, the only hope that Cretans (1:12) or anyone else (3:3) has for living in a way that is acceptable to God (2:11–14; 3:8) and for inheriting eternal life (1:2; 3:7). Paul considers it of utmost importance that this message should gain a hearing from those outside the church. Thus, although masters of believing slaves are their "brothers" as well as masters (1 Tim. 6:2), he urges slaves to be submissive to their masters for the higher goal of bringing the gospel before the wider society.

Precisely because of its egalitarian tendencies, the gospel as Paul preached it appealed especially to society's powerless—women, children, and slaves. The censure that Christianity disrupted the social order must have been about as common in Paul's time as we know it was a century or so later in the time of Celsus, who claimed that Christianity appealed only to easily deceived women, slaves, children, stupid yokels, and the dishonorable (Origen, *Cels.* 3.44; 6.24).

The fear of religiously sanctioned social disruption that lies beneath this statement had a long history in the Roman empire, as the official suppression of the rites of Bacchus in Rome in the second century B.C. and Livy's account of it (39.8–19) about a century and a half later demonstrate.[14] In his narrative of the Roman senate's suppression of the Bacchanalia, Livy reveals an apparently common fear that secret nocturnal rites from the East promoted immorality and corrupted the young.[15] The prominent place that the cult gave to women (39.13.9; 39.15.11) and children (39.13.14) threatened the power of the father over his family and therefore the very fabric of Roman society.[16] As Livy puts it in a "speech" that the Roman consul gave to the senate on the issue:

> If you knew at what ages males were initiated, you would feel not only pity for them but also shame. Do you think, citizens, that youths initiated by this oath

14 Cf. Johnson, *Letters to Paul's Delegates*, 235.

15 If the practice of Christians in Bithynia in A.D. 117 was similar to the practice of Christians in Rome in A.D. 64, then the Roman Christians also met "on a certain fixed day before it was light" (*stato die ante lucem*). See Pliny, *Ep.* 10.96.

16 Mary Beard, John North, and Simon Price, *Religions of Rome*, 2 vols. (Cambridge: Cambridge Univ. Press, 1998), 1:93–96.

> should be made soldiers? That arms should be entrusted to men mustered from this foul shrine? Will men debased by their own debauchery and that of others fight to the death on behalf of the chastity of your wives and children? (39.15.13–14)

The large-scale persecution of Christians that broke out in Rome under Nero in A.D. 64—perhaps only a few months before Paul wrote Titus—must have found some legal foundation in the previous persecution of the mainly female followers of Bacchus.[17] We know, in any case, that Nero was able to fix the blame for Rome's great fire on "a class of men, loathed for their vices, whom the crowd styled Christians," and convicted them "not so much on the count of arson as for hatred of the human race" (Tacitus, *Ann.* 15.44.).

As we have already seen in Paul's letter to Philemon, the apostle knew that social disruptions were inevitable where the gospel was faithfully preached and believed. The apostle who proclaimed the disintegration of the barrier between Jews and Gentiles could hardly insist that the oppressive social barriers between master and slave be preserved intact. But Paul had to navigate between the Scylla of failing to honor the social implications of the gospel and the Charybdis of creating such social disruption that the message of God's saving work in Christ Jesus could not be heard.

In both 1 Timothy and Titus Paul's concern is with this second problem. If women and slaves are insubordinate, the message about God's saving work in Christ Jesus will be lost to those outside the church who will not be able to see beyond the threat that Christianity poses to their positions of power and privilege. Paul believes that Christians must look beyond their own, often subordinate, social positions, to the overriding need of everyone for the gospel.

Where does Paul get the notion that the reputation of God in the eyes of unbelievers should be a concern of God's people? The roots of this conviction probably lie in Paul's Scriptures. In Exodus 19:3–6 God entered into a covenant with his people based on his gracious rescue of them from slavery in Egypt (19:4). If Israel obeyed God's covenant with them, he said, they would be his "treasured possession" and would be for him "a kingdom of priests and a holy nation" (19:5–6).[18] The Mosaic law—the covenant that his people should obey—would separate God's people from other peoples and would show other peoples of the earth his character.[19] They should be holy, as Leviticus frequently says, because God himself is holy (Lev. 11:44–45; 19:24; 20:7, 26; 21:8).

As Paul's Scriptures revealed, however, Israel did not remain holy, and because of its sin, God used first the Assyrians and then the Babylonians to send his people into exile. In exile, God's name was profaned when those who had conquered Israel and

17 See Hugh Last, "The Study of the 'Persecutions,'" *JRS* 27 (1937): 80–92; W. H. C. Frend, *Martyrdom and Persecution in the Early Church: A Study of a Conflict from the Maccabees to Donatus* (Grand Rapids: Baker, 1981), 109–11; and Robert L. Wilken, *The Christians as the Romans Saw Them* (New Haven, Conn.: Yale Univ. Press, 1984), 17.

18 In the LXX, see, in addition, Ex. 23:22.

19 Cf., e.g., J. Philip Hyatt, *Exodus* (NCB; London: Marshall, Morgan & Scott, 1971), 200, and John I. Durham, *Exodus* (WBC 3; Waco, Tex.: Word, 1987), 262–63.

Judah assumed that their God was himself weak, like his people (Ezek. 36:20–36; cf. Isa. 52:5). This misconduct of God's people led them away from their vocation of showing the character of God to the rest of the world and instead resulted in a misunderstanding of God.

Paul seems to be echoing these biblical concerns about the vocation of God's people in 2:1–14. Here he bases his ethical teaching to various social groups on God's gracious, redeeming work in Jesus Christ. The theological pattern he follows mirrors the pattern in Exodus, where God's covenant with his people was based on his gracious rescue of his people from Egypt. The purpose for Christ's redemptive work on behalf of his people is also identical to God's purpose for rescuing Israel: "to purify for himself a people that are his very own, eager to do what is good" (2:13).[20]

In a way reminiscent of 1 Corinthians 10:1–13, the negative example of ancient Israel lies behind Paul's ethical advice in Titus 2:1–10. The Christians on Crete have failed in their vocation to be a kingdom of priests who show the world the character of God, with the result that the name of God is blasphemed. Paul, however, wants them to be faithful to their vocation. By their good works they will ensure that unbelievers will not malign the "word of God" (2:5, 8) and that the church's teaching about a God who saves people from their sins will be attractive (2:10).

KNOWLEDGE, PURITY, AND WITNESS IN TITUS

Paul's primary concern in Titus, therefore, is to prevent the false teachers on Crete from convincing the Christians there of their perverse understanding of God. Such a corrupt picture of God has already affected their consciences, confused them about the definition of purity, led them to foster unnecessary controversy within the churches, and prompted them to upset the domestic tranquility of Christian households.

For those on the outside, working backward from their observations of Christian behavior to their understanding of the Christian God, this situation spells disaster. They will see the socially disruptive effects of this perverse understanding of God and be unable to get beyond it to the message that the church should proclaim—that through the gracious gift of Christ's redeeming work, God has redeemed and is purifying a people for himself who will inherit eternal life. By his epistolary mandate to Titus, Paul has reminded his coworker of the close connection between theology, ethics, and the witness of the church, and he has instructed him to appoint leaders in the churches on Crete who understand this connection also.

20 Cf. Towner, *The Goal of Our Instruction*, 130.

Chapter 21

SECOND TIMOTHY: FAITHFULNESS TO THE GOSPEL

When Paul wrote Titus in the late summer or early autumn, he was expecting to spend the winter in Nicopolis, located in Epirus on the west side of the Greek mainland (Titus 3:12). We do not know whether he ever made it there, but when we turn to 2 Timothy, winter is at the door (2 Tim. 4:21) and Paul is not in Nicopolis with Titus but in prison in Rome (1:17). Titus has gone to Dalmatia, across the Adriatic from the Italian peninsula (4:9), and other coworkers are scattered in various places, including at least one who has deserted Paul's cause (4:10). Among his coworkers, only Luke is with him (4:11). Paul is awaiting a second judicial hearing, but he is not optimistic that it will result in acquittal since at his first hearing no one came to his defense (4:16). He believes that he will soon die (4:6–8).[1]

Out of this context, Paul turns his attention to his closest friend and coworker, Timothy (cf. Phil. 2:20–22). Timothy is apparently no longer at Ephesus (2 Tim. 4:12) but is somewhere close enough to Troas to make that town a natural stopping place on his way to Paul in Rome (4:13).[2] Paul misses Timothy and needs the cloak and books he left with a friend at Troas. He hopes to benefit from the help of Mark with whom Timothy is in contact (4:11). One purpose of the letter, therefore, is simply to ask Timothy to come to Rome with Mark as soon as possible (4:9), preferably before winter (4:21), and to bring Paul's clothing and documents with him.[3]

Paul also writes for another, more important purpose. As he approaches the end of his missionary career—and for Paul that could only be at the end of his life—he is especially conscious of the dangers that defections from the faith pose to the churches he has founded.[4] "Everyone" in the province of Asia has deserted him (1:15). Even his coworker Demas has left Paul behind in Rome and returned to Thessalonica, possibly his home (4:10).[5]

---

1 Michael Prior, *Paul the Letter-Writer and the Second Letter to Timothy* (JSNTSup 23; Sheffield: Sheffield Academic Press, 1989), 91–112, argues that 4:6–8 does not refer to the death of Paul but to Paul's fidelity to the gospel up to the point of writing. Prior believes that Paul wrote 2 Timothy during the imprisonment of Acts 28 and that, confident of his impending acquittal, he wrote 4:9–18 in order to prepare for the continuation of his mission to the Gentiles. Prior's explanation of 4:6–8, however, is unconvincing.

2 Paul's claim that he has sent Tychicus to Ephesus (4:12) implies that Timothy is not in that city, since if Timothy were also in Ephesus the comment would be unnecessary. See Jerome Murphy-O'Connor, *Paul: A Critical Life* (New York: Oxford Univ. Press, 19), 358–59, 364–65.

3 The phrase *ta biblia malista tas membranas* in 4:13 should be translated "the books, that is, the parchments." See T. C. Skeat, "'Especially the Parchments': A Note on 2 Tim 4.13," *JTS* 30 (1979): 173–77.

4 On the integration of Paul's life with his mission, the comment of Karl Barth on Phil. 1:12 is relevant: "He just would not be an apostle if he could speak objectively about his own situation in abstraction from the course of the Gospel, to which he has sacrificed his subjectivity and therewith also all objective interest in his person. To the question of how it is with *him* the apostle *must* always react with information as to how it is with the Gospel." See *The Epistle to the Philippians* (Richmond, Va.: John Knox, 1962), 26.

5 Paul mentions Demas in Philem. 24 along with Aristarchus, who was from Thessalonica (Acts 20:4; 27:2). See C. Spicq, *Les Épitres Pastorales*, 2 vols. (Ébib; Paris: LeCoffre, 1969), 2:811;

These defections seem to spring from two basic causes. In the case of Demas, the cause is love for the present age rather than, like Paul, love for the time of the Lord's appearing (4:8; cf. 4:10).[6] In the case of others, such as Hymenaeus and Philetus, the cause is wandering away from the truth into false teaching (2:17–18). Paul wants to remind Timothy of the gospel as Paul has taught it to him both by his words and by his example and to admonish Timothy to be faithful to the gospel amid the challenge of persecution and false teaching.[7]

Unlike 1 Timothy and Titus, 2 Timothy is not a "mandate." Paul is not writing to commission Timothy to restore order to a chaotic ecclesiastical situation, but to admonish him to "be strong in the grace that is in Christ Jesus" (2:1). The letter therefore follows the basic pattern of ancient paraenetic letters in which an author writes to an understudy in order to encourage him to remember and follow models of good behavior, to live according to certain moral precepts, and to avoid examples of bad behavior.[8] As Seneca tells Lucilius in a letter written at virtually the same time that Paul wrote 2 Timothy (A.D. 62–64), the written word is helpful for learning how to conduct one's life, but an experience of personal examples is better (*Ep.* 6).[9]

Timothy's grandmother, Lois, and mother, Eunice (2 Tim. 1:5), Paul's friend Onesiphorus (1:16–18), Jesus (2:2), and especially Paul himself (1:11–13; 2:9–10; 3:10–11; 4:6–8, 16–18) exemplify the kind of faithfulness to the gospel in the midst of false teaching and persecution that Paul wants to encourage in Timothy.[10] Phygelus and Hermogenes (1:15), Demas (who deserted Paul, 4:10), false teachers such as Hymenaus and Philetus (2:17), and the magicians Jannes and Jambres (3:8; cf. Ex. 7:8–11; CD 5.17–19) exemplify the waywardness and opposition to the truth that Paul instructs Timothy to avoid.[11] We can analyze the theological message of the letter under two headings: enduring hardship for the sake of the gospel and guarding the gospel against false teaching.

ENDURING HARDSHIP FOR THE SAKE OF THE GOSPEL

Paul does not want Timothy to become another Demas. Instead, Timothy needs the resolve necessary to remain true to Paul and the gospel in the midst of the suffering that will be his lot, just as assuredly as it has been Paul's (3:12). Timothy must not be ashamed either to testify about the Lord himself or to associate with Paul, the

George W. Knight, III, *The Pastoral Epistles* (NIGTC; Grand Rapids: Eerdmans, 1992), 464; and I. Howard Marshall, *The Pastoral Epistles* (ICC; Edinburgh: T. & T. Clark, 1999), 815.

6 Cf. Marshall, *Pastoral Epistles*, 815–16.

7 As Prior, *Paul the Letter-Writer*, 62, observes, the thanksgiving in 2 Timothy, like the thanksgivings in other Pauline letters, covers the primary themes of the letter. Paul's longing for Timothy appears in 1:4 and Paul's concern that Timothy remain faithful appears in 1:5–6.

8 Luke Timothy Johnson, *Letters to Paul's Delegates: 1 Timothy, 2 Timothy, Titus* (NTC; Valley Forge, Pa.: Trinity Press International, 1996), 39–41. Some scholars believe that 2 Timothy is a "farewell discourse," but Johnson argues persuasively that the genre of "paraenetic letter" matches the letter's form more closely. See also Stanley K. Stowers, *Letter Writing in Greco-Roman Antiquity* (LEC; Philadelphia: Westminster, 1986), 94–97.

9 The letter is reproduced and discussed in Stowers, *Letter Writing*, 100–101.

10 Cf. Seneca's use of himself as a moral example for Lucilius in *Ep.* 6.

11 Cf. Pliny's *Ep.* 8.23.2 (A.D. 97 or 98), in which Pliny offers his own behavior at a banquet as an example for his understudy Avitus to follow and provides the conduct of the banquet's host as an example for Avitus to avoid. See Stowers, *Letter Writing*, 101–3.

Lord's prisoner, in Paul's suffering (1:8). Instead he should suffer together with Paul (1:8; 2:3) and, despite this suffering, fulfill his commission as one to whom the gospel has been committed (4:5).

Paul grounds these admonitions in several ways. He reminds Timothy that he has received the gift of God's Spirit, which does not produce "cowardice" (*deilia*) but a "power" exhibited in both "love" and "self-control" (1:7). He reminds Timothy that God is faithful to those who have committed themselves to him and will see them safely through their trials to the final day, when they will be vindicated (1:12; 4:1, 8).

Most significantly, however, he reminds Timothy of the important role that suffering plays in the gospel itself. Timothy should not to be ashamed either of bearing testimony to the gospel or of Paul, who is imprisoned for the gospel. He should instead "join with [Paul] in suffering for the gospel, by the power of God" (1:8). Paul summarizes this gospel as the power that God has displayed in saving believers and calling them to live a holy life, "not because of anything we have done but because of his own purpose and grace . . . [which] was given us in Christ Jesus before the beginning of time" (1:9). In other words, the suffering that Paul endures, and that Timothy should join him in enduring provides the means by which God can display his power, and this way of working is consistent with the graciousness that characterizes the gospel. The God who saves people in the midst of their weakness is also the God who announces this good news to people through the suffering of his messengers.[12]

Here Paul taps into his understanding of the gospel as we know it from other letters. Because the gospel was born in the suffering of the Messiah on the cross, "a stumbling block to Jews and foolishness to Gentiles" (1 Cor. 1:23), those who are called upon to testify to it could easily find themselves ashamed of it (2 Tim. 1:8; cf. Rom. 1:16). But precisely in the suffering of the Messiah on the cross God displayed his wisdom and strength in providing righteousness, holiness, and redemption for his people (1 Cor. 1:25, 30). Through the "poverty" of Christ, God has made his people "rich" (2 Cor. 8:9). In this "foolish" gospel resides the power of God for the salvation of everyone who believes (Rom. 1:16).

The lives of those who believe this gospel also take on the foolish shape of the gospel. Thus, for example, not many wise, influential, or noble people in Corinth were part of the church (1 Cor. 1:26–28), and God worked through the poverty-stricken Macedonian Christians to produce a generous contribution to Paul's collection for the suffering Jewish Christians in Jerusalem (2 Cor. 8:2–3). Most important, however, through the suffering of Paul, God brought the gospel to many in Corinth (2 Cor. 4:7–12), to people in Asia (Eph. 3:13; Col. 1:24), and to those within the government headquarters in Ephesus (Phil. 1:12). "So then," he tells the Corinthian Christians, "death is at work in us, but life in you." Why does God work this way? He works through suffering and weakness so that no one can boast in

12 Cf. Norbert Brox, *Die Pastoralbriefe* (RNT 7; Regensburg: Verlag Friedrich Pustet, 1969), 229–30; Johnson, *Letters to Paul's Delegates*, 54–55.

himself or herself but only in God. God gives life through the gospel as a free gift, and he wants to leave no ambiguity about the graciousness of his saving work (1 Cor. 1:29, 31; 2 Cor. 1:9; 11:30; 12:5, 9–10).[13]

In four passages in 2 Timothy, Paul places himself before Timothy as an example of this kind of suffering.[14] In 1:6–18 he first summarizes the content of the gospel he was called to preach (1:9–11) and then says that because of this vocation he is presently suffering the imprisonment out of which he writes the letter (1:12). Still, he continues, "I am not ashamed" (1:12b). Just as Paul has admonished Timothy not to be ashamed to bear witness to the Lord, so Paul is not ashamed of the gospel, despite the suffering he must endure as its herald.[15] Paul intends his own faithfulness to the gospel in the midst of suffering to serve as an example to Timothy so that he too should faithfully endure the suffering to which the gospel calls him.

Paul seems to follow the same strategy in 2:8–10. Here he says that he suffers for the gospel to the point of being chained as an evildoer, but, he continues, "God's word is not chained" (2:9). Just as in 1 Corinthians 2:1–4 the power of God is at work in the weakness of his rhetorically unsophisticated apostle, just as in 2 Corinthians 4:7–12 God's apostle carries the precious treasure of the gospel in the earthen vessel of his suffering ministry, just as in Philippians 1:12–18 God advances the gospel through Paul's imprisonment and the preaching of other badly motivated Christians, so here, despite Paul's bonds, God's word remains unfettered. If his suffering is the means by which some hear the gospel and attain salvation, Paul is happy to endure it (2 Tim. 2:10; cf. 2 Cor. 4:12; Phil. 1:18a).[16] God has chosen to work through Paul's suffering. Thus for Timothy, Paul's suffering should not be the source of shame (2 Tim. 1:8) but an example to imitate.

In 3:10–12 Paul reminds Timothy of nine aspects of his life, all familiar to Timothy from his work with the apostle. He concludes the list by referring to the "persecutions" and "sufferings" he has endured—sufferings, he says, like those that happened to him in Antioch, Iconium, and Lystra and from which the Lord rescued him. Like the righteous people in Psalm 34:17, 19, and like Paul himself, "everyone who wants to live a godly life in Christ Jesus will be persecuted" (2 Tim. 3:12). This inevitably includes Timothy, but he should follow the example of faithfulness despite suffering that he has seen in Paul during the years of their common labor for the gospel.[17]

In 4:5 Paul urges Timothy to focus on his task and endure hardship as he does the work of an evangelist and fulfills his ministry. As the connecting "for" (*gar*) in 4:6 shows, Paul then offers his present, difficult situation as an example of faithful endurance of hardship in the service of the evangelical ministry:

---

13 See esp. Rudolf Bultmann, *Theology of the New Testament*, 2 vols. (New York: Scribners', 1951–55), 1:242–43.

14 On Paul's use of himself as an example for Timothy in 2 Timothy, see Philip H. Towner, "The Portrait of Paul and the Theology of 2 Timothy: The Closing Chapter of the Pauline Story," *HBT* 21 (1999): 151–70. In addition to Paul, Onesiphorus (who "was not ashamed" of Paul's chains, 1:16–18) and Jesus (whose suffering God vindicated in the resurrection, 2:8) serve as examples to Timothy.

15 Cf. Marshall, *Pastoral Epistles*, 709.

16 See also Eph. 3:1, 13; 4:1; and Col. 1:24.

17 Cf. Towner, "The Portrait of Paul," 160.

> *For* I am already being poured out like a drink offering, and the time has come for my departure. I have fought the good fight, I have finished the race, I have kept the faith. Now there is in store for me the crown of righteousness, which the Lord, the righteous Judge, will award to me on that day—and not only to me, but also to all who have longed for his appearing. (4:6–8)

A few sentences later, Paul describes how although at his first defense no one supported him, the Lord stood by his side and empowered him so that he was spared from the lion's mouth and through him the gospel was preached to the Gentiles (4:17).[18] This does not mean, as some have thought, that Paul now anticipates his release from prison for future ministry but that God's willingness to allow him to live after his first defense has provided another opportunity for him to bear witness to the gospel before his Gentile captors (cf. Phil. 1:12–13).[19] Here too Paul serves as an example for Timothy of how God uses the faithfulness of his ministers in the midst of their suffering as an opportunity to display his power to extend the gospel to the Gentiles.

GUARDING THE GOSPEL FROM FALSE TEACHING

Just as Timothy should not be ashamed of suffering for the gospel, so in his handling of "the word of truth" he should prove himself to be a skillful worker who has no cause to be ashamed of his work (2:15). The primary threat to his skill as a preacher of the Word comes from the same false teaching that had infected the churches on Crete and in Ephesus. It specializes in frivolous and corrupting talk, focuses on myths, frequently erupts in angry quarrels (2:14, 16, 23; 4:4), leads to ungodliness (2:16), and probably promotes magical practices (3:8, 13).[20]

The frequent allusions to Moses in 2 Timothy (e.g., 1:6; cf. Num. 2:19; 3:8–9; 16:5; 27:18–23; cf. also Ex. 7:11, 22) may form a subtle attack on the concern of the false teachers with the Mosaic law (cf. 1 Tim. 1:7; Titus 1:10), and the clear allusion to Korah's rebellion (2 Tim. 3:19; cf. Num. 16:5) implies that the false teachers have made serious inroads into the churches on Crete and in Ephesus. Paul has entrusted the "good deposit" of the gospel to Timothy, but Timothy must guard it from the corrupting influences of these teachers if he is to pass it on to others in its pure form (1:14; 2:2).

Paul's effort to wave Timothy away from the false teaching employs four strategies. First, he reminds Timothy of the content of the gospel. In 1:9–10 Paul uses an apparently creedal statement, reminiscent of the theology of Ephesians, to summarize this content. The statement stresses the gracious character of salvation and links this concept with God's eternal "purpose" to create, by his "call," a holy people (cf.

18 Towner, "The Portrait of Paul," 169, finds reminiscences of Ps. 22 (LXX, 21) in 4:17 and believes that Paul views his suffering here through the lens of Jesus' suffering. Just as Jesus' suffering provided an opportunity for God to show his saving power, so God follows this same pattern with Paul.

19 For the view that 4:17 refers to Paul's impending release and future ministry of preaching to the Gentiles, see Prior, *Paul the Letter-Writer*, 113–39.

20 See the description of this false teaching in ch. 19, above.

Eph. 1:4, 11, 18; 2:5–8). It also emphasizes the central place of Christ Jesus in this eternal purpose (cf. Eph. 1:10; 3:11) and the effect of the salvation in the abolition of death and the illumination of life and immortality (cf. Eph. 5:14).

Since the details of the false teaching are so sketchy, it is impossible to say for certain that this creed stresses elements of the gospel that the false teachers denied, but it seems safe to assume that the creed as a whole affirms the faith that Timothy must cling to if he is to avoid serious theological error.[21] This is the "testimony about our Lord," of which Timothy should not be ashamed and for which he should suffer (1:8).[22]

Second, Paul reminds Timothy to be faithful to his ordination to preach the gospel. Paul himself had set Timothy apart for the task of preaching by laying hands on him (1:6).[23] This commissioning confirmed that Timothy had the Spirit and that the Spirit had given him the gift of bearing "testimony about our Lord" (1:8).[24] Paul is thinking in this passage of Timothy's Spirit-endowed gift of the ability and the calling to proclaim the gospel. This is clear from the close link between Paul's instructions to Timothy to "fan into flame the gift of God," his claim that God did not give us a Spirit of timidity, and his command to Timothy not to be ashamed to testify to the Lord (1:6–8).[25]

In 4:1–2, 5, Paul specifically charges Timothy to be faithful to this vocation in light of the false teaching described in 4:3–4. Because false teaching is inevitable and caters to what people want to hear, Timothy must think clearly and "discharge all the duties" of his ministry, particularly the duty of preaching the gospel.[26] He must handle "the word of truth" correctly (2:15).

Third, Paul urges Timothy to be faithful to what he has learned from his Christian elders. Just as Paul himself had been faithful to the tradition handed down to him by his ancestors (1:3), so the memory of Timothy's forbears should kindle in him a desire to be faithful to the Scriptures they taught him from the time he was a small child (3:14–17; cf. 1:5). Timothy should also be faithful to the "sound teaching" that he received from Paul (1:13) and should "guard the good deposit" of the gospel that Paul has placed in his care, presumably at Timothy's ordination (1:14; cf. 1:6). This

21 Cf. Marshall, *Pastoral Epistles*, 702.

22 Knight, *Pastoral Epistles*, 703.

23 Brox, *Die Pastoralbriefe*, 228, believes that 1 Tim. 4:14, which speaks of Timothy's ordination by a council of elders, contradicts 2 Tim. 1:6 and that this contradiction is a sign of the pseudonymity of the two letters. With only a little goodwill, however, we can envision Paul as a member of the ordaining body described in 1 Tim. 4:14. In 2 Tim. 1:6 Paul would then be speaking of his personal participation in Timothy's ordination. See the discussion in Spicq, *Épitres Pastorales*, 2:728–29, and Philip H. Towner, *The Goal of Our Instruction: The Structure of Theology and Ethics in the Pastoral Epistles* (JSNTSup 34; Sheffield: Sheffield Academic Press, 1989), 57.

24 There is no indication here, as has sometimes been thought (e.g., Brox, *Die Pastoralbriefe*, 228), that Paul transferred the Spirit to Timothy through the laying on of his hands. Paul thought that all believers had the Spirit (1:14), and the procedure he describes here is modeled on Moses' commissioning of Joshua in Num. 27:15–23. In that passage Joshua already has the Spirit of God within him (27:18) before Moses lays his hands on him. On the significance of 2 Tim. 1:14 to this discussion, see Marshall, *Pastoral Epistles*, 699.

25 Cf. Eph. 4:11 and Paul's own frequent description of his role as an apostle and minister of the gospel to the Gentiles as a gift of God's grace (Rom. 15:15–16; Gal. 2:9; Eph. 3:6–7; Phil. 1:7).

26 "The word" that Timothy is to preach in 4:2 is the same as "the word of God" in 2:9 and "the word of truth" in 2:15. As the contexts of those phrases make clear, they refer to the Christian message. See Knight, *Pastoral Epistles*, 453, and Marshall, *Pastoral Epistles*, 800.

means that he should not only keep the gospel intact, unsullied by false teaching, but that he should hand it down to others who will themselves be able to pass it on.

Fourth, Timothy should keep clear of the false teachers and their profane babblings, since the teaching that lies at the core of all the verbiage, like gangrene, can easily infect and eat away at those who come into contact with it (2:16–17). Like Korah, Dathan, and Abiram in the days of Moses, these false teachers are mixed with the company of God's people, and although the foundation of God's house remains firm (2:19), both noble and ignoble articles exist side-by-side within its walls (2:20–21).[27] Timothy must therefore flee from these teachers and the illegitimate desires that their teaching engenders (2:22). He must keep away from their arguments (2:23) and from them (3:5).

At the same time, Timothy should not overreact to the situation. Not everyone who opposes him and takes the side of the false teachers is equally dangerous. If Timothy refuses to be sucked into their "stupid arguments" and maintains a gentle spirit toward them, he may be able to instruct some of them in "the knowledge of the truth" (2:25a). Through Timothy's gentle persuasion, God may bring them to their senses so that they escape the devil's trap (2:26).[28]

Timothy must walk a fine line between avoidance of this pernicious false teaching and those who promote it on one hand, and on the other hand attempting to persuade those whom the false teaching has infected to return to the truth. It is no wonder that Paul urges Timothy later in the letter, "keep your head in all situations" (4:5).

THE THEOLOGICAL CHARACTER OF PAUL'S FINAL LETTER

As Paul writes 2 Timothy, he believes that he is going to die in prison (4:6), and he looks back on his life and his relationship with Timothy as if both are drawing to a close (1:3–6, 13; 2:2; 3:10–11). The letter bears the marks of this difficult situation.[29] Its organizational structure is almost impossible to discern, as the widely differing attempts to analyze it show, and it does not engage in the energetic theological argumentation so characteristic of Paul's early letters.[30]

Despite these difficult circumstances, different from any under which he had previously written, Paul's fundamental theological convictions remain the same.[31] The gospel is a message of God's gracious provision for the salvation of his people apart from any effort on their part (1:9), and those who preach it faithfully will suffer for their commitment to this gospel (1:8, 12; 2:3, 9–10; 3:10–12; 4:5–6). This suffering in order to preach the gospel faithfully is the means by which God shows his power (1:8) and the means by which those whom he has chosen "obtain the salvation that is in Christ Jesus" (2:10).

27 Cf. Towner, *The Goal of Our Instruction*, 25–26.
28 Cf. ibid., 135.
29 Marshall, *Pastoral Epistles*, 40.
30 See Marshall's table of commentator's outlines, ibid., 34.
31 The circumstances of Paul's letter to the Philippians are closest to those of 2 Timothy, but in Philippians Paul suspects he will be released from his imprisonment (Phil. 1:23–26), whereas in 2 Timothy he is certain he will be executed (2 Tim. 4:6–13).

These twin emphases—the grace of God and the power of God shown through suffering—are part of the same overarching notion, so central to Paul's theology, that the gracious character of God's saving work means that God works in spite of and through human weakness to accomplish his purposes. Even here, in Paul's last and most strained letter, this conviction shines through. If Timothy is to remain faithful to the gospel of God's grace, he must not be ashamed either of Paul's suffering (1:8) or of his own (2:3; 3:12; 4:5), for it is by means of just such human weakness that God displays his saving power (1:8–10).

Chapter 22

THE COMMON EMPHASES AND CENTRAL CONVICTIONS OF PAUL'S LETTERS

The study of the theological emphases of each Pauline letter leads naturally to an examination of the themes that appear repeatedly or receive special emphasis in the whole corpus. The repetition of these themes does not in itself mean that Paul was particularly fascinated by them but only that the churches he founded often had problems related to these issues. The collection of these themes, therefore, does not look much like a systematic theology. It looks more like a first-century handbook on pastoral care for Christian churches. Once the themes themselves are collected and examined, however, it becomes clear that Paul's handling of them rests on a set of coherent and strongly held theological convictions. These convictions, logically arranged, do not in themselves form a complete systematic theology, but they do reveal the central elements of Paul's theology and the basis for his practical advice to his churches.

In this chapter we will examine the theological issues that receive repeated treatment in Paul's letters and then briefly describe the basic theological structure that supports Paul's treatment of these issues. Five issues arise repeatedly in the extant letters: perseverance in the midst of persecution, the relationship of the church to the unbelieving world, the sanctity of the church, the unity of the church, and the preservation of the church from false teaching. Paul's responses to these five issues spring from his convictions about God's saving purposes in history, the sinfulness of all people, and the graciousness of God.

THEOLOGICAL ISSUES IN THE LETTERS OF PAUL

Perseverance in Persecution

Both the Thessalonian and the Philippian Christians, because of their commitment to the gospel, faced the same kinds of social opposition from unbelievers that Paul himself frequently faced in his efforts to preach the gospel to the Gentiles. Paul had been shamefully treated in Philippi before he arrived in Thessalonica (1 Thess. 2:1), and both the Thessalonians and the Philippians had experienced the same kind of humiliation (Phil. 1:29–30; 1 Thess. 2:14–15). Luke's account of Paul's visit to Philippi reveals the kind of trouble Paul is talking about in these letters. People of influence in the community viewed Paul and Silas as a threat to the city's peace and security by advocating customs foreign to the Roman way of life (Acts 16:20–21).

In Thessalonica the charges were even more serious, for there people accused Christians of defying Caesar's decrees and giving allegiance to a rival emperor, "Jesus" (17:7).

In cities where public devotion to the Roman emperor was an important means of preserving political stability, the refusal of a new sect from the east to participate in the imperial cult would hardly have been welcome. Celsus, writing about a century after Paul, probably reveals the basic sentiment of those who from the first persecuted Christians on civic grounds:

> Even if someone tells you to take an oath by an emperor among men, that also is nothing dreadful. For earthly things have been given to him, and whatever you receive in this life you receive from him. . . . For, if you overthrow this doctrine, it is probable that the emperor will punish you. If everyone were to do the same as you, there would be nothing to prevent him from being abandoned, alone and deserted, while earthly things would come into the power of the most lawless and savage barbarians. (Origen, *Cels.* 8.67–68; cf. 8.69).

Aside from these difficulties with the authorities, Christian converts would have encountered problems in their own families as soon as they "turned to God from idols" (1 Thess. 1:9). Both Greek and Roman families typically observed domestic religious rituals that honored the gods concerned with domestic affairs—Zeus Ktesios and Zeus Herkios according to Greek custom, and the Lares according to Roman custom. The tombs of dead ancestors were decorated on the anniversary of their death. What would it have meant for a child, woman, or slave, still living under the authority of the all-powerful family father, to refuse to participate in these customs? It is hard to imagine that the consequences would have normally been anything but unpleasant.[1] Again, Celsus is instructive:

> If [Christians] are going to marry wives, and beget children, and taste of the fruits, and partake of the joys of this life, and endure the appointed evils . . . then they ought to render the due honours to the beings who have been entrusted with these things. . . . It is wrong for people who partake of what is their property to offer them nothing in return. (Origen, *Cels.* 8.55)

Although Celsus writes at a time when Christians were more numerous and widely known—and patience with them had grown thinner—than in the first century, he probably articulates the feelings of many unbelieving household fathers in Paul's time who found themselves presiding over a family with one or more Christians in it.

Paul uses three strategies to help his readers cope with this situation. First, he engages in "identity formation," reminding them that although they are ostracized by their society and their families, they are members of a new society and a new family. Second, he appeals to the eschatological elements of his gospel to remind his readers that their suffering is only part of a larger historical scheme whose ultimate

1 See John M. G. Barclay, "The Family as the Bearer of Religion in Judaism and Early Christianity," in *Constructing Early Christian Families: Family as Social Reality and Metaphor*, ed. Halvor Moxnes (London: Routledge, 1997), 66–80, here at 67–68.

outworking will mean their salvation. Third, he urges them to imitate the faithful endurance of other Christians and, in particular, to adopt his own attitude toward the role that God gives to suffering in the accomplishment of his saving purposes.

Identity Formation

In the Thessalonian letters and in Philippians, Paul reminds his readers in the midst of their suffering that they are part of a new family and a new society. As we saw in the discussion of 1 Thessalonians, Paul probably intended the intensity of his family language and of his language of election to help his readers overcome the alienation they inevitably felt from the society and from the families who had rejected them. They were part of a new family—Paul was their father, their mother, and their brother. The Thessalonian Christians were also brothers and sisters of one another. Moreover, they were part of the people of God, standing in continuity with Israel as the Jewish Scriptures describe it. Like God's people, Israel, in the Scriptures, they were God's "assembly," loved, chosen, and called by him.

Although in Philippians this theme does not rise to the prominence it has in 1 Thessalonians, it is still important, perhaps for the same reason. Not only are the Philippians Paul's "brothers" (Phil. 1:12; 3:1, 13, 17; 4:8), but they are his "brothers" whom he "loves and longs for," his "joy and crown" (4:1; cf. 1 Thess. 2:19). Paul is also surrounded by "brothers" in Ephesus (Phil. 1:14; 4:21),[2] including the Philippians' messenger, Epaphroditus (2:25). Likewise, Paul's coworker Timothy is his soulmate, a "son" who labors with him as a slave (2:20, 22) and who, like Paul, is genuinely concerned for the Philippians' welfare (2:19). Their own families may shun the Philippian Christians for not participating in the family rituals, but they have joined a tightly knit family, held together by the bond of faith in Jesus Christ. Here too, Paul uses language that identifies the Philippian Christians in terms reserved for Israel in the Scriptures. They are "the holy ones" (1:1) and "the circumcision" (3:3).

In addition to these strategies for encouragement, Paul also seems aware of the pressure that the society of Roman Philippi must have placed on believers to participate in the imperial cult. He claims that every knee in heaven and on earth will someday bow to Jesus and every tongue will confess that he is "Lord" (2:10–11). He also says that believers are citizens of a heavenly commonwealth and await a "Savior" from there, "the Lord Jesus Christ" (3:20). From the time of Claudius, people frequently used the title "lord" (*kyrios*) to refer to the universal authority of the deified emperor. From an even earlier time they used the title "savior" (*sōtēr*) to describe the deified emperor's beneficence.[3]

Augustus, for example, could be celebrated as the "savior of the common race of people" (*sōtēra tou koinou tōn anthrōpōn genous*) and Nero could be called "the lord of all the universe" (*ho tou pantos kosmou kyrios*).[4] In such a context, Paul's use of these titles to describe Jesus' authority over a particular commonwealth to which believers

2 See the introduction to ch. 13, where I argue that Philippians was written from a prison in Ephesus.

3 See BDAG, 577 and 985.

4 Werner Foerster, "σωτήρ," *TDNT*, 7:1012; idem, "κύριος (κτλ)," *TDNT*, 3:1056.

belong and to speak of the eventual acknowledgment of this Jesus as master of the entire world would have clear political connotations.[5] Although the Roman colony of Philippi marginalized the Philippian Christians because of their refusal to worship the Roman emperor, they were nevertheless citizens of the commonwealth whose ruler would one day exercise power over the entire universe.

Eschatology

Paul frequently urges his readers to remember the final Day when Christ will appear and vindicate those who are suffering for him. Paul expresses this subtly in 1 Thessalonians when he clothes the description of Christ's appearing in the biblical imagery of God's waging war on behalf of his people against those who have opposed them (1 Thess. 4:16; cf. 2:16). It becomes explicit in 2 Thessalonians and Philippians when he speaks of the persecution that his readers are enduring as a double-sided sign that God will destroy their opponents and save Christians who persevere through the hardships that their opponents inflict on them (Phil. 1:28; 2 Thess. 1:5–10). It is present in Romans when Paul urges his readers not to avenge themselves against their enemies but to await the coming wrath of God, when God will repay those who have done evil (Rom. 12:19; cf. 2 Tim. 4:14). It also lies behind Paul's own confidence that despite his present suffering, God will faithfully keep what Paul has entrusted to him "until that day" (2 Tim. 1:12). On "that day" God will award to him a crown of righteousness (4:8), rescue him from "every evil attack," and bring him "safely to his heavenly kingdom" (4:18). Because of this Paul is not ashamed to suffer, and Timothy should adopt the same perspective (1:8).

Occasionally, Paul says that the persecutions his readers are experiencing are part of the expected suffering of God's people prior to the great eschatological battle between good and evil and the final triumph of God. This idea probably stands behind Paul's reminder to the Thessalonians that he "kept telling" them when he was with them that they "would be persecuted" (1 Thess. 3:4). It probably also prompted his claim in his later letter to them that "the secret power of lawlessness is already at work" (2 Thess. 2:7). It appears explicitly in 2 Timothy when Paul describes the reckless evil that will break out in "the last days" (2 Tim. 3:1–5) and tells Timothy to avoid those involved in the evil activities he has just described (3:6–9)—clearly these evil days of the end time have to some extent already arrived (cf. 1 Tim. 4:1–4).

As in most apocalyptic literature, Paul intends this understanding of the suffering of God's people as a sign of the approaching end to comfort the victims of persecution by reminding them that their suffering does not fall outside the boundaries of God's sovereign love and ultimately his saving plan for his people.

Imitation

Paul occasionally exhorts his readers to follow the example of Jesus, of other Christians, and particularly of Paul himself in their faithfulness to the gospel despite the hardship that their commitment has entailed. Paul tells the Thessalonians that they

5 See also Markus Bockmuehl, *The Epistle to the Philippians* (BNTC; Peabody, Mass.: Hendrickson, 1998), 143–44, 147, 233–35.

are suffering in the same way that other genuine Christians, such as those in Judea, have suffered for their commitment to the gospel. Just as their unbelieving Jewish neighbors have persecuted the Judean Christians, including Paul and Jesus himself, so the Thessalonians' unbelieving Gentile neighbors are inflicting suffering on them (1 Thess. 2:14–15).

Paul compares the suffering of the Thessalonian Christians with the suffering of others chiefly to assure them of the genuineness of their faith—authentic Christians tend to suffer for their faith, and the suffering of the Thessalonians is a sign that they too are authentic Christians. This comparison, however, probably also served an important subsidiary purpose, namely, to encourage them to be faithful despite their suffering, just as other Christians had courageously endured suffering for their faith.

Similarly, in Philippians Paul reminds his readers in the midst of their suffering that they are experiencing "the same struggle" that Paul had when he ministered among them (Acts 16:16–40) and he is still experiencing (Phil. 1:12–18a). Later Paul tells the Philippians to "join others in following my example" (3:17) and to put into practice "whatever you have learned or received or heard from me, or seen in me" (4:9). One aspect of this imitation is to adopt the apostle's attitude toward suffering for the gospel. Paul believes that God is using his suffering for the advancement of the gospel (1:12); the Philippians should have this attitude as well.

As we have just seen in chapter 21 on 2 Timothy, imitation of faithful Christians as a means of coping with suffering emerges again in Paul's last letter. Timothy should join Paul in suffering for the gospel (2 Tim. 1:8). He should remember the persecutions that Paul has faced in the years of their common ministry. He should also remember that "everyone who wants to live a godly life in Christ Jesus will be persecuted" (3:11–12). As in Philippians, so here, Paul claims that God uses suffering to accomplish his purposes: Paul is "suffering for the gospel by the power of God" (1:8). His chains are one means through which God is accomplishing his saving purposes for his chosen people (2:9–10). Timothy too should take up this cause, enduring hardship alongside Paul "like a good soldier of Christ Jesus" (2:3).

The Relationship of the Church to the Unbelieving World

Paul says much more about the church's relationship with the world than simply that the world is the church's persecutor. As we saw in our study of 1 Timothy and Titus, Paul was not only concerned about the false teaching in Ephesus and on Crete because it was false but also because of the effect it had on the ability of the church to proclaim the gospel to the unbelieving world. Through corrupting the behavior of those whom it ensnared, the false teaching tarnished the reputation of the church in the eyes of unbelievers and hindered its ability to function as "God's household ... the pillar and foundation of the truth" (1 Tim. 3:15). Thus, Paul urges the believers in Ephesus to live "peaceful and quiet lives in all godliness and holiness" because God "wants all [people] to be saved and to come to the knowledge of the truth" (2:2, 4).

As the household of God and the repository of the truth about him, the households in which the church meets should operate in an exemplary manner. To be "above reproach" is the first qualification of a house church "overseer" (3:2), and the qualifications that follow, most of which are devoted to the oversight of a household (3:2–6), are elaborations of this general quality.[6] They are summarized in the concluding statement: "[The overseer] must also have a good reputation with outsiders, so that he will not fall into disgrace and into the devil's trap" (3:7). Those within the church should care for their needy relatives, particularly the elderly (5:4, 8). Likewise, "younger widows" should "marry . . . have children . . . manage their homes and . . . give the enemy no opportunity for slander" (5:14). Slaves should treat their masters respectfully so that "our teaching may not be slandered" (6:1).

The same concern appears in Paul's letter to Titus, where he exhorts slaves to behave in an exemplary way "so that in every way they will make the teaching about God our Savior attractive" (Titus 2:10), and he instructs various age and gender groups within the church to live in such a way that "those who oppose you may be ashamed because they have nothing bad to say about us" (2:8). Immediately after advising subjection to rulers, obedience, good deeds, and living in a peaceable, considerate, and humble manner "toward all people," Paul reminds Titus of the transforming effect of the gospel on those who were previously mired in evil (3:1–8). Here too Paul's concern for the exemplary behavior of Christians seems to be in part evangelistic: When unbelievers see the transformation that the gospel produces in the lives of foolish, disobedient, deceived, immoral, malicious, envious, and hateful people (3:3), they will themselves be attracted to its message.[7]

If this represents a correct understanding of these passages in the Pastoral Letters, then they are not a part of the strategy of an aging church to make peace with the surrounding world by inculcating "good Christian citizenship" (*christliche Bürgerlichkeit*).[8] They are instead attempts to ensure that the church remains an attractive source of the truth about God—a source to which unbelievers want to turn and experience for themselves what is "excellent and profitable for everyone" (Titus 3:8).[9]

Without doubt, the expression of this theme in the Pastorals differs from its expression in the undisputed letters of Paul. In the Pastorals, the theme is not only more prominent than in the undisputed letters, but it is linked to the smooth functioning of the Christian household—a link that does not appear in the undisputed letters.

Still, the theme of avoiding offense to unbelievers so that the gospel might advance is also present in Paul's earlier and undisputedly authentic correspondence. In 1 Corinthians Paul is especially concerned with the impact of the behavior of believers in the church on the church's ability to bring unbelievers under the hearing of the gospel. In 1 Corinthians 14:13–25 Paul worries that the emphasis the Corinthian church places on speaking in tongues in corporate worship could prevent an "inquirer"

6 I. H. Marshall, *The Pastoral Epistles* (ICC; Edinburgh: T. & T. Clark, 1999), 477.

7 Cf. ibid., 299.

8 See, e.g., Martin Dibelius and Hans Conzelmann, *The Pastoral Epistles* (Hermeneia; Philadelphia: Fortress, 1972), 8, 39–41; Willi Marxsen, *New Testament Foundations for Christian Ethics* (Minneapolis: Fortress, 1993), 255–60; J. Christiaan Beker, *Heirs of Paul: Their Legacy in the New Testament and the Church Today* (Grand Rapids: Eerdmans, 1991), 43–47.

9 On this, see esp. Philip H. Towner, *The Goal of Our Instruction: The Structure of Theology and Ethics in the Pastoral Epistles* (JSNTSup 34; Sheffield: Sheffield Academic Press, 1989).

(*idiōtēs*) or "unbeliever" (*apistos*) from understanding what is said and therefore from any spiritual benefit. "You may be giving thanks well enough," he comments, "but the other [person] is not being edified" (14:17). In place of uninterpreted tongues in corporate worship, Paul recommends the intelligible utterances of prophecy. If an inquirer or unbeliever hears these understandable utterances, that person may be convicted, the hidden things of his or her heart may be revealed, and he or she may be led to worship God (14:24–25).

This same concern motivates Paul's advice to Corinthian believers who might find themselves in the home of unbelievers faced with a meat dish of unknown origin (1 Cor. 10:25–11:1). Whereas a Jew might refuse to eat the meat on the grounds that it could have been part of a pagan sacrifice, Paul advises Christians to eat whatever is set before them without worrying about its origins. The only exception to this is if an unbeliever present at the meal, in a wrong-headed but well-intentioned effort to prevent the Christian from doing something against his or her religious convictions, warns the Christian that the dish consists of meat previously offered to an idol (10:28–29). To avoid giving offense, Paul says, the Christian should not eat the meat. The reason for avoiding such offenses in this and every similar setting is that many "may be saved" (10:33). Just as Paul has "become all things to all [people] so that by all possible means [he] might save some" (9:23), so the Corinthians should follow his example and avoid offending anyone unnecessarily so that as many as possible might be saved (10:33–11:1).

In the Thessalonian correspondence, Paul is likewise concerned that believers conduct themselves with decorum toward those outside the church (1 Thess. 4:11–12; cf. 5:14; 2 Thess. 3:6–15), although here the motive for the advice is not entirely clear. Paul may have been concerned that the Thessalonian Christians, by their bizarre conduct, were increasing the level of persecution directed against them. To spare them any more suffering than necessary, he may have been urging them not to give senseless offense to outsiders. Or evidence from 1 Corinthians may indicate that at least part of his concern in 1 Thessalonians is to prevent believers there from hindering the ability of the church to communicate the gospel persuasively to outsiders.

The evangelistic motivation of the household advice in the Pastorals, therefore, is consistent with expressions of Paul's theology in the undisputed letters. The notion that the church's conduct ought to commend the gospel to those outside is present in the apostle's correspondence at least from the period of 1 Corinthians, and probably earlier.

The Holiness of the Church

As we have seen throughout our study of Paul's letters, Paul assumes that his churches, despite their predominantly Gentile composition, represent the beginning stages of the promised restoration of God's people. According to the prophets, an important element in that event would be the restoration of Israel's holiness. When God constituted his people as a nation at Mount Sinai, he promised them that if they kept the covenant he was about to make with them, they would be "a kingdom of priests and a holy nation" (Ex. 19:5–6). The laws of the Sinai covenant were supposed to separate Israel from other nations so that, as a kingdom of priests, they might reveal God's character to all the nations of the earth. The people of Israel were to "consecrate" themselves and to "be holy" because God is holy (Lev. 11:44–45; 19:2; 20:7).

In Leviticus, for example, the sexual conduct of God's people and the kinds of foods that they should avoid are explicitly linked to the separation of Israel from the other nations as God's chosen people. The preface to the list of unlawful sexual relations in Leviticus reads this way:

> The LORD said to Moses, "Speak to the Israelites and say to them: 'I am the LORD your God. You must not do as they do in Egypt, where you used to live, and you must not do as they do in the land of Canaan, where I am bringing you. Do not follow their practices. You must obey my laws and be careful to follow my decrees. I am the LORD your God. Keep my decrees and laws, for the man who obeys them will live by them. I am the LORD.'" (Lev. 18:1–5)

The dietary regulations have a similar explanation:

> "I am the LORD your God, who has set you apart from the nations.
>
> "'You must therefore make a distinction between clean and unclean animals and between unclean and clean birds. Do not defile yourselves by any animal or bird or anything that moves along the ground—those which I have set apart as unclean for you. You are to be holy to me because I, the LORD, am holy, and I have set you apart from the nations to be my own.'" (Lev. 20:24b–26)

At least from the perspective of the prophets, however, Israel did not keep the terms of the covenant. Instead of separating itself from the nations as a witness to them of God's character, Israel participated in the idolatry of the nations. Ezekiel, for example, echoes the "holiness code" of Leviticus 17–26 when he charges Israel with idolatry, adultery, and usury (Ezek. 18:5–18; cf. Lev. 19:4; 20:10; 25:35–37). The penalty for violating these, and other, covenant stipulations was exile (Lev. 26:17, 27–39). Ezekiel explains to the Israelites, whom the Babylonians have defeated and driven into exile, that their own sin in these areas, not the sins of their ancestors, have brought God's wrath justly upon their heads (Ezek. 18:1–32).

Nevertheless, Israel should not despair, says Ezekiel, because God has not abandoned his people. One day he will restore their fortunes, and in that day he will also restore their holiness. They will be a holy people and therefore a proper place for his Spirit to dwell. God will dwell both in their hearts (Ezek. 11:19; 36:26) and in a magnificent, newly constructed sanctuary (37:26–28).

Paul believed that with the death and resurrection of Christ and the establishment of assemblies of those who believed in him, this day had dawned. The churches that he and other Christians had founded comprised the beginnings of God's eschatologically restored people. These churches and the individuals who belonged to them were God's eschatological sanctuary, the dwelling place of his Spirit. Paul was naturally concerned, therefore, that his churches demonstrate their status as God's restored people by living holy lives. As Paul puts it, "God's temple is sacred, and you are that temple" (1 Cor. 3:17).

In a way reminiscent of both Leviticus and Ezekiel, Paul was especially concerned that the newly restored people of God avoid sexual immorality (1 Cor. 5:1–13; 6:12–20; 2 Cor. 12:21; Eph. 5:3; 1 Thess. 4:3–8) and idolatry (1 Cor. 10:1–22; cf. 2 Cor. 6:14–7:1). For example, in an astonished rebuke to the Corinthians for their flippant attitude toward sexual immorality, Paul asks, "Do you not know that your body is a temple of the Holy Spirit, who is in you, whom you have received from God?" (1 Cor. 6:19). In another place he combines quotations both from the holiness code of Leviticus and from a passage in Ezekiel that speaks of God's eschatological dwelling place with his people to remind his readers of the importance of their holiness:

> What agreement is there between the temple of God and idols? For we are the temple of the living God. As God has said: "I will live with them and walk among them, and I will be their God, and they will be my people." (2 Cor. 6:16; cf. Lev. 26:12; Ezek. 37:27)

Neither Leviticus nor Ezekiel, however, anticipated Paul's conviction that the Mosaic law has ceased to set the boundaries of sanctity for God's people. Paul replaces literal circumcision with a spiritual circumcision of the heart (Rom. 2:25–29; 1 Cor. 7:19; Phil. 3:3; cf. Col. 2:11–12). He considers the dietary restrictions no longer in force (Rom. 14:14a; 1 Cor. 10:25). Although he reaffirms the Decalogue (Rom. 13:8–9), he summarizes it, following Jesus' teaching, in terms of Leviticus 19:18, "Love your neighbor as yourself" (Rom. 13:10; Gal. 5:14). He apparently calls that teaching "the law of Christ" (Gal. 6:2; cf. 1 Cor. 9:21) by analogy to the designation, "the law of Moses."

The Decalogue itself, moreover, has changed slightly: Paul no longer attaches the Sabbath commandment to a particular day and instead deems every day as special (Rom. 14:5; 15:1). He changes the promise attached to the commandment to honor father and mother so that it refers not to a long life within the literal geographical boundaries of Israel (Ex. 20:12; Deut. 5:16) but to a "long life on the earth" (Eph. 6:2–3).

A literal temple with its sacrifices and priesthood is no longer necessary. God's people are his temple, the dwelling place of his eschatologically bestowed Spirit (1 Cor. 6:19; 2 Cor. 6:16). Christ's death on the cross was the climactic and, by implication, final Day of Atonement sacrifice (Rom. 3:25–26). The believer's ethical conduct is his or her "spiritual sacrifice" (Rom. 12:1; cf. Phil. 3:3). Paul himself is a priest who offers the sacrifice of believing Gentiles to God (Rom. 15:16), and, in the process, he himself is poured out as a sacrifice to God (Phil. 2:17; 2 Tim. 4:6). Thus, there is no more need to observe the vast body of laws regulating the temple cult.

In addition to these discontinuities between Paul's understanding of sanctity and the understanding of sanctity found in Leviticus and Ezekiel, we should recall the apostle's new understanding of how holiness is communicated or tainted. As in the

Mosaic law, the sin of the community's members can taint the holiness of God's people. Thus, Paul warns the Corinthians that their disputes over which leader is the greatest, because they are dividing the church, are a threat to the sanctity of God's temple (1 Cor. 3:17). He also urges them, echoing a refrain employed in Deuteronomy for similar purposes, that when sexual immorality arises among them, they must "expel the wicked person from [their] midst" (1 Cor. 5:13; cf., e.g., Deut. 13:5; 17:7, 12; 19:19; 21:21; 22:21–24:7).

Nevertheless, unbelievers who have a family connection to the church or who are interested in the church's worship do not pollute either the individual believer or the worshiping community. Since they might be saved or led to worship God by these affiliations, Paul encourages the preservation of such relationships—the wife married to an unbelieving husband or the husband married to an unbelieving wife should remain married since the unbelieving spouse, and any children in the home, are "sanctified" through the believing member of the family (1 Cor. 7:12–16). Similarly, the church should conduct its corporate worship in a way that will "edify" the inquirer or unbeliever in its midst (1 Cor. 14:16–17, 22–25).

The most obvious consequence of Paul's changes to the Mosaic boundaries of sanctity is the inclusion of Gentiles as Gentiles into the people of God. People cross the boundary into the new "Israel of God" (Gal. 6:16) simply by faith that God has graciously reckoned them to be in a right relationship to himself because of the death of Jesus Christ. The sign of this faith is the presence of God's Spirit within them, and God's Spirit bears in their lives ethical "fruit" (Gal. 5:16–24) that conforms to "the law of Christ." The "law of Christ" is a body of ethical teaching that at least includes Jesus' summary of the Mosaic law in terms of Leviticus 19:18 and probably includes a slightly modified form of the Decalogue, but it does not include any of the recognizably "Jewish" elements of the Mosaic law (1 Cor. 9:21; Gal. 6:2; cf. 1 Cor. 7:19).

Faith in Christ and the presence of the Spirit, who leads Christians to obey this new body of ethical teaching, distinguish God's people from the Gentiles, "who do not know God" (1 Thess. 4:5; cf. 1 Cor. 5:1; 10:32). This new people of God do not need to practice circumcision, nor do they need to keep the Sabbath or observe the Mosaic law's dietary restrictions. These signal marks of Judaism are unnecessary because God's people consists of all those, from whatever ethnic background, who have faith in Christ and the Spirit of God.

To use the language of Ephesians, Christ "destroyed the barrier, the dividing wall of hostility" between Jews and Gentiles "by abolishing in his flesh the law with its commandments and regulations" (Eph. 2:14–15). In other words, God has set aside the Mosaic law with the coming of Christ (Rom. 7:6; Gal. 3:19). As a result, God now defines the sanctity of his people in a way that is not specifically Jewish.[10]

10 On this see Frank Thielman, *Paul and the Law: A Contextual Approach* (Downers Grove, Ill.: InterVarsity, 1994); idem, *The Law and the New Testament: The Question of Continuity* (New York: Crossroad, 1999), 7–43.

The Unity of the Church

The restored, sanctified people of God should be a united people, and Paul works hard to preserve the unity of his churches despite powerful tendencies toward disintegration that are sometimes at work within them. The problem of disunity is most visible in the Corinthian letters, but Paul also addresses it in Romans, Galatians, and Philippians. His efforts to persuade his churches to live together harmoniously seem to come from two theological convictions. Paul believes that the gracious nature of salvation excludes haughtiness. He also believes that in view of the coming final Day, the church should work together for the extension of the gospel to unbelievers and the perseverance of believers in their faith.

The Problem of Disunity

In the Corinthian letters, as we have seen, disunity has resulted from many different issues. The elitist elevation of one teacher over another, using standards of measurement apparently set by the Second Sophistic movement, led to the fragmentation of the church into groups following Paul, Apollos, Cephas, and Christ (1 Cor. 1:10–4:13). Eventually, when opponents of Paul arrived in Corinth, they made use of this tendency among the Corinthians to alienate the church from Paul himself (2 Cor. 10–13). In addition, some Corinthian Christians had come to the conclusion that their "knowledge" about participating in pagan cultic meals brought them closer to God than the "weak," who did not have this knowledge. The "weak" in the congregation were therefore pressured to violate their consciences, opening the possibility that they could fall away from the fellowship of the church and be eternally destroyed. Knowledge in this situation had replaced love and promoted the fragmentation of the church (1 Cor. 8:1–13).

In addition, a focus on personal liberation from societal conventions in matters of dress was disrupting worship (and perhaps Christian families as well), and the observance of class distinctions during the Lord's Supper had encouraged, in an inappropriate way, the discord among social classes that prevailed outside the church's boundaries (1 Cor. 11:1–34). A single gift—glossolalia—was thought to be the only "reputable" (*euschēmōn*) gift, and those who did not possess it were effectively told by those who had it, "I don't need you!" (12:12–26).

In Romans, Galatians, and Philippians Paul also addresses Christians who need to be reconciled to one another. A Gentile Christian majority in Rome was apparently boasting over their majority status in the church and looking down on Jewish Christians in their midst who were insisting on observing a Jewish calendar and diet (Rom. 11:18–19; 14:3). Jewish Christians, on their side, were condemning those who failed to keep the Mosaic laws concerning diet and special days (14:3).

In Galatia, the Judaizing "agitators" apparently wanted "to exclude" Gentile Galatian believers who refused to conform to the Jewish law in order to shame them into being "zealous" for the Judaizers and their cause (Gal. 4:17).[11] The result of this tactic may have been that the law-observant part of the congregation was unwilling to

11 Cf. John M. G. Barclay, *Obeying the Truth: Paul's Ethics in Galatians* (Minneapolis: Fortress, 1991), 59–60.

associate with the nonobservant part, much as Peter withdrew from table fellowship with Gentile Christians in Antioch under pressure from "the circumcision group" (2:12). This is perhaps why Paul warns the Galatians that if they continue "biting" and "devouring" one another, they will destroy one another (5:15).

In Philippi the disagreement between Euodia and Syntyche (Phil. 4:2) was apparently only one of several failures to heed Paul's message to "do nothing out of selfish ambition or vain conceit" (2:3).

Common to each of these situations was an elitist mentality or haughtiness on the part of at least one party, prompting it to look down on the other party. The Corinthians were "boasting" (1 Cor. 3:21; 4:7; 5:6; 2 Cor. 11:18, 21) and "puffed up" (1 Cor. 4:6; cf. 8:1; 13:4; 2 Cor. 12:20), thinking that they were "different" from (and better than) others (1 Cor. 4:7; cf. 11:19). At least some believed they had already arrived at spiritual perfection (1 Cor. 4:8). Their haughtiness led them to abandon Paul because of his physical and rhetorical weaknesses and to cling instead to Paul's power-wielding opponents (2 Cor. 10:1–12:21).

Both sides of the rift between Jews and Gentiles in the Roman church adopted a haughty attitude toward their opponents, either despising or condemning them (Rom. 14:3–4). The dissension among the Galatian churches was likewise based on an exclusivist attitude (Gal. 4:17; 5:15; 6:12–13), and although the details of the Philippian disunity are unclear, an element of haughtiness likely prompted Paul's concern throughout the letter that the Philippians had not considered others better than themselves (Phil. 1:23–25; 2:3–4; 2:19–30).

The Gracious Nature of Salvation, Which Excludes Haughtiness

The main theological conviction that fuels Paul's responses to these problems is the gracious nature of salvation, which he emphasizes as an antidote to elitism especially in 1 Corinthians, Galatians, and Romans. The divisiveness in Corinth can be healed if the Corinthian Christians recognize what most of them were when God called them—neither wise nor influential nor noble—and understand that they are only "in Christ Jesus" because God himself took the initiative to include them among his people (1 Cor. 1:26–30). "Who makes you different from anyone else?" he asks rhetorically. "What do you have that you did not receive? And if you did receive it, why do you boast as though you did not?" (4:7). The attempt of Paul's opponents in Corinth to drive a wedge between him and the Corinthians is likewise wrong because confidence in human strength fuels it. It fails to recognize that God is gracious and works powerfully through human weakness (2 Cor. 11:30; 12:9).

In Galatians too Paul resists the exclusivism of the Judaizing "agitators" by appealing to God's grace. When Peter withdrew from fellowship with Gentile Christians in Antioch, Paul reminded him of the implications of his behavior. By excluding believing Gentiles from fellowship, he implied that keeping the Mosaic law—a form of human effort—was necessary for inclusion among God's people. This Paul insisted was false, because a right standing with God comes from faith in Christ, and to claim otherwise is to "set aside the grace of God" made available in Christ (Gal. 2:21).

Galatian Christians who insisted on observing the law of Moses as an entrance requirement to the people of God, therefore, had "fallen away from grace" (5:4).

The argument of Romans is also carefully crafted to lay stress on how the gospel excludes all boasting, either in one's ethnic affiliation or in one's efforts to do what the Mosaic law requires. Paul silences "every mouth" with his argument that all are, without exception, under sin and therefore under God's just condemnation (Rom. 1:18–3:20). He structures his argument that God has solved this plight through Christ's atoning death to lead to the conclusion that all "boasting," especially Jewish boasting in the possession of or accomplishment of the Mosaic law, "is excluded" (3:27). The stress on God's sovereign grace in election, apart from ethnic affiliation (9:6b–9) or human effort (9:11; cf. 4:16; 11:5–6), facilitates Paul's case that God shows his mercy in surprising ways and that any boasting from Gentile Christians of their majority status in the people of God is therefore premature and inappropriate (11:17–24). Paul's appeal to unity at the end of the letter (14:1–15:13), therefore, rests on the foundation of God's grace in salvation that Paul has already laid.

In all three of these letters Paul tackles divisiveness by emphasizing the unity of people in their need for God to act on their behalf, and the unity of all Christians in their experience of God's freely given gift of salvation or justification. Elitism and haughtiness are inappropriate within the church because everyone—whatever their social standing or "knowledge"—needs God's gracious saving action, and no one within the church has merited God's gift of salvation by any personal qualification.

The Church's Responsibility to Edify Others

Another important theological conviction that undergirds Paul's desire for unified churches is his concern that believers "edify" others. The verb "to edify" (*oikodomeō*) seems to refer both to the encouragement of unbelievers to accept the gospel and to the encouragement of believers to persevere in the faith until the final Day. In 1 Corinthians Paul urges the Corinthian Christians to avoid divisively asserting their rights in order to edify unbelievers with whom they come into contact. Although believers have the right to eat anything offered for sale in the market place, they should abstain from eating meat previously offered in a pagan sacrifice if abstaining would "edify" the unbeliever (1 Cor. 10:23, 28).

In the same way, in corporate worship the Corinthians should place higher value on prophecy than on the "reputable" gift of speaking in tongues so that unbeliever and believer alike might be "edified" (14:3–5, 12, 17, 26). Similarly, believers who have "knowledge" should not exercise their freedom at the expense of those whose consciences are weak. They should instead act in love, to "edify" the weak (8:1). Otherwise, the reverse of edification might take place—the weak believer might be pressured through the example of the knowledgeable believer to violate his or her conscience and so to be destroyed (8:10–11). This destruction is not a psychological concept but an eschatological idea, and Paul does not want the weak to experience destruction on the final Day because they have failed to persevere in their faith.[12]

12 Paul uses the term *apollymi* to refer to this destruction, a term that nearly always in his letters refers to eschatological destruction (1 Cor. 1:18–19; 10:9–10; 15:18; cf. 2 Cor. 2:15; 4:3; cf. Rom. 2:12; 14:15; 2 Thess. 2:10). The one possible exception is 2 Cor. 4:9.

In Romans Paul uses language that closely echoes what he had previously written in 1 Corinthians on this issue. He advises the Gentile Christian majority in Rome to tread lightly on the sensitive consciences of the Jewish Christian minority. Here too Paul says that exercising one's right to eat anything may "destroy [a] brother for whom Christ died" (Rom. 14:15b, 20). Instead, the Gentile majority in the church should act in love, which may mean giving up the exercise of their right, in order to pursue "peace" and "mutual edification" (14:19).

Summary

In advising his churches to work for unity, therefore, Paul has his eye on two events in salvation history—the cross, where God graciously provided atonement for sinners, and the final Day, when God will destroy the unfaithful and save those who have persevered in their faith in the gospel. The cross excludes all boasting because it implies that all are sinners, and the final Day demands that believers "edify" one another and unbelievers so that, when that Day arrives, they might be saved.

The Preservation of the Church from Theological Error

Many of what are commonly considered the most important elements of Paul's theology appear in letters that seek to correct a misunderstanding of his theology, to set right some indigenous disagreement with Paul, or to refute the false teaching of theological opponents who have come to Paul's churches from elsewhere. These moments in Paul's letters are especially useful for constructing the apostle's theology for two reasons.

First, when Paul corrects an error, we can assume that he does so against some theological standard. In the course of the correction this standard often becomes clear. Some interpreters of Paul have disputed this, claiming that at least some of Paul's "theological" corrections are really sociologically motivated—Paul is simply attempting to keep his churches together under his authority and uses theological rhetoric as a convenient way of doing this. When Paul's specific handling of different problems in different churches seems to arise from the same core conviction or when a conviction emerges in both a polemical and a nonpolemical setting, however, it seems safe to assume that this conviction is a settled element of his theology and not a theological expedient only lightly held (or not held at all) because it was developed under the pressure of the moment.

Second, Paul's desire to correct the errors in the first place shows that they represent deviations from convictions that he believes are worth the fight. As we have just seen, the unity of his churches was important to Paul, and he did not lightly risk dividing them. On even important issues that were nevertheless not central to his theological convictions he consistently practiced and advised tolerance: He was willing to concede a point (1 Cor. 7:6–7), to make appeals rather than to command (Philem. 8–10), to restrain acting on his own convictions out of deference for those with "weak" faith (Rom. 14:14a; 15:1; cf. 1 Cor. 8:9–13; 9:12, 19–23; 10:27–11:1), and to leave to God the task of convincing those who disagreed with him (Phil.

3:15).[13] All of this means that when we do find Paul engaged in vigorous debate over a particular theological issue, that issue is likely to be crucial to his theology.

Paul corrects false teaching at many points in his letters. In his early letters he often had to correct erroneous views of the final Day, of the resurrection, of the afterlife, and of the imminence of the end. In the middle of his letter-writing career, at least as we have plotted it, he was especially concerned with the false gospel of Judaizing Christians and particularly with the issue of who will stand acquitted before God on the Day that he appears to judge all people. His latest letters frequently address false teaching on the relationship between the seen and unseen worlds: What is the nature of the Creator of the world, of the world he created, and of the invisible cosmic forces that inhabit that world?

The Nature of the Final Day

Early in Paul's letter writing career, at least as we know it, the issue of the final Day posed a problem that prompted several vigorous responses from the apostle. In 1 Thessalonians, misunderstanding of the bodily resurrection of believers, and in 1 Corinthians outright rejection of it, caused Paul to express his thoughts on this topic at length. In 2 Thessalonians, confusion over the timing of the coming of the Lord prompted a substantial corrective from Paul. When we add to the lengthy treatments in these letters passing references to the final Day from other letters, a reasonably full picture of his eschatological convictions comes into focus.

The Resurrection and the Afterlife

In 1 Thessalonians Paul addresses a situation in which new converts to Christianity, deprived of Paul's full teaching on the gospel, assumed the common conviction of their Greco-Roman culture that those who died have "no hope" (1 Thess. 4:13). To them, this meant that although living believers would escape "the coming wrath" and participate in God's kingdom, believers who died would be unable to participate. Their costly decision to turn from their idols to the living and true God had placed such believers at no advantage over deceased unbelievers. In their view, death had simply snuffed deceased believers out of existence.[14]

As we have seen in the discussion of 1 Thessalonians, Paul tells the Thessalonian Christians that their perspective on the death of believers and the coming of God's kingdom rests on a serious misunderstanding of the events of the final Day. Death is not the end of the believer's existence, he says, any more than it was the end of Christ's existence. Just as God raised Jesus from the dead, so he will "bring with Jesus those who have fallen asleep in him" (1 Thess. 4:14). Paul then backs up and describes the apocalyptic scenario from the first: Jesus will descend from heaven ready to do battle against the enemies of God; deceased believers will rise from the dead; believers who are alive at the time will join resurrected believers, and together they will

13 See Frank Thielman, "Law and Liberty in the Ethics of Paul," *ExAud* 11 (1995): 63–75.

14 The issue is not, therefore, merely whether the deceased believer will be resurrected after the Parousia and therefore miss participation in that glorious event, as many commentators believe. For the position adopted here and above in the chapter on 1 Thessalonians, see I. Howard Marshall, *1 and 2 Thessalonians* (NCB; Grand Rapids: Eerdmans, 1983), 122.

meet Jesus in the air; all believers, both those who died before Jesus' coming and those alive at the time of his coming, will be with the Lord always (4:16–18).

What does Paul mean, however, when he says both that Jesus will bring deceased believers with him at his coming (1 Thess. 4:14) and that these believers will rise from the dead and meet him in the air (1 Thess. 4:16–17)?[15] Does he mean that deceased believers, in some unembodied form, will come with the Lord from heaven to earth where they will be united with their bodies?[16] Dogmatism is unwise here, but it seems more likely that when Paul says Jesus will bring with him those who have fallen asleep, he means that at Jesus' coming God will raise the bodies of the Christian dead and that Jesus will then bring these resurrected believers with him into the presence of God. Jesus "brings" deceased believers, therefore, not from heaven to earth but from earth into the presence of God. According to 4:17, believers who are alive at the Lord's coming will also "be caught up with them" and spend eternity in the Lord's presence.

This way of understanding 1 Thessalonians 4:14–17 receives confirmation in 2 Corinthians 4:14. There Paul assumes for the moment that he will be dead and the Corinthians alive at Christ's return. If this happens, then "the one who raised the Lord Jesus from the dead will also raise us with Jesus and present us with you in his presence." Here too, God will raise the Christian dead and bring them into his presence along with those who were alive at the time of the resurrection.[17]

To those like the Thessalonians and the Corinthians whose preconversion religious convictions clashed with the notion of a bodily resurrection, another question clamored for an answer: How can physical bodies, subject to corruption, participate in the immortal existence of heaven? The Corinthians found this question so difficult that some of them had completely rejected Paul's teaching on the resurrection of believers. In response Paul tells them that every believer, both those who have been resurrected and those who are alive at the coming of Jesus, "will be changed" at the time of Christ's Parousia (1 Cor. 15:52).

This change will happen instantly; it will not involve sloughing off the present body, but "clothing" the perishable, "mortal" body with a body that is imperishable and immortal (15:53–54). This new body will stand in contrast to Adam's body made from "dust" and returned to "dust" (15: 21–22, 45–49; cf. Gen. 2:7; 3:19). The new body will instead be like the resurrected body of Christ, the second man, whose origins lay not in the "dust" but in "heaven" (1 Cor. 15:42–53). As a result of this change, death will be "swallowed up" and finally defeated (15:54; cf. Isa. 25:8).

This understanding of the nature of the resurrected body is confirmed in 2 Corinthians 5:1–5 and Romans 8:18–27. In the former passage, Paul describes his present existence as one in which he suffers as he seeks to fulfill his apostolic commission. It is a time of "groaning" and "longing" for the resurrection that lies ahead (2 Cor.

15 "Quite how the two are to be correlated remains unclear"—James D. G. Dunn, *The Theology of Paul the Apostle* (Grand Rapids: Eerdmans, 1998), 300.

16 Ben Witherington, *Jesus, Paul and the End of the World: A Comparative Study in New Testament Eschatology* (Downers Grove, Ill.: InterVarsity Press, 1992), 157.

17 Joseph Plevnik, *Paul and the Parousia: An Exegetical and Theological Investigation* (Peabody, Mass.: Hendrickson, 1997), 71–76.

5:2). Here too the resurrection will mean not the sloughing off of his present body but being "clothed" with a "heavenly" body (5:2, 4), and when this happens what is "mortal" will be "swallowed up by life" (2 Cor. 5:4; cf. Isa 25:8). This unseen, future reality, whose certainty the Spirit's presence guarantees (2 Cor. 5:5), gives Paul the courage to persist in his missionary labors despite the opposition and physical suffering that these labors inevitably entail (5:6–8a).

The same perspective emerges in Romans 8:18–26, where Paul joins all creation in "groaning" as he awaits being "liberated from . . . bondage to decay" (8:21), which for Paul and other believers will mean "the redemption of our bodies" (8:23). Here too this reality lies in a future that is the object of Paul's hope and is confirmed by the presence of the Spirit (8:23), but which cannot be "seen" (8:24–25).[18]

In a brief statement in Philippians Paul brings together his understanding of Christ's return as articulated in 1 Thessalonians 4:14–17 and the transformation of the body as explained in Romans 8:18–26; 1 Corinthians 15:50–57; 2 Corinthians 5:5–10:

> But our citizenship is in heaven. And we eagerly await a Savior from there, the Lord Jesus Christ, who, by the power that enables him to bring everything under his control, will transform our lowly bodies so that they will be like his glorious body. (Phil. 3:20–21)

Here Paul puts in a nutshell what the other texts, taken together, explain more fully—that at the Parousia of Christ the bodies of all believers will be transformed so that they will be like the glorious, resurrected body of Jesus himself.[19]

The occasional scholarly claims that Paul's thinking on the nature of existence after death underwent a shift from a materialistic to a spiritual conception, from a Jewish to a Hellenistic understanding, or, at least in the Corinthian letters, developed ad hoc to accommodate his audience and counter his opponents, have little plausibility in light of this evidence.[20] Since the language Paul uses of the resurrection in these passages is similar and the pieces can easily fit together into a consistent pattern, these theories introduce more problems than they solve.

In 1 Thessalonians Paul speaks of the resurrection of deceased believers and their gathering with living believers to be with the Lord "always." It seems natural that Paul would have some idea in mind about how the dead bodies of deceased believers and the mortal bodies of living believers could assume an eternal existence. Some change seems required, and we learn how Paul conceives of that change in 1 Corinthians 15:50–57—the "physical body" becomes a "spiritual body," or, to put it another way, the mortal is "clothed" with the "immortal."

Although Paul does not use the term "body" of the resurrected individual in 2 Corinthians 5:1–10, he speaks, in a famously mixed metaphor, of the present "tent"

18 See the discussion of Paul's concept of "hope" in Plevnik, *Paul and the Parousia*, 197–220, esp. 210–12.

19 Dunn, *Theology*, 307.

20 See respectively, C. F. D. Moule, *Essays in New Testament Interpretation* (Cambridge: Cambridge Univ. Press, 1982), 200–221; Jacques Dupont, *ΣΥΝ ΧΡΙΣΤΩΙ: L'union avec le Christ suivant Saint Paul* (Paris: Éditions de l'Abbaye de Saint-André, 1952), 153–58, 170–71; and Wilfred L. Knox, *St. Paul and the Church of the Gentiles* (Cambridge: Cambridge Univ. Press, 1939), 128, 142.

being "further clothed" (NRSV; the verb is *ependyomai*) with a "heavenly dwelling" (5:1–4).[21] Paul has not shifted from thinking of the transformation of the body in 1 Corinthians 15 to the replacement of the body in 2 Corinthians 5.[22] Both texts speak of putting a set of clothing on over something that already exists.[23] The lack of any shift is confirmed in Philippians 3:20–21, where Paul speaks again of the body's transformation at the coming of the Lord Jesus Christ, and in Romans 8:23, which speaks of the redemption of our bodies. Paul therefore describes the resurrection in similar language in several letters written over several years while addressing widely divergent situations. This is not the strategy of someone who quickly changes his theological convictions in mid-stream to conform them to the theological convictions of his readers.[24]

Did Paul's eschatological thinking endure another kind of shift, however, a shift from the assumption at the time he wrote 1 Thessalonians that he would be alive at the time of the Lord's return to the belief by the time he penned 2 Corinthians that he might die before that event? Has he also developed the corresponding view that at his death he will be immediately and consciously with the Lord?[25] This thesis at first seems to describe the relevant texts accurately. In 1 Thessalonians 4:15 he speaks of "*we* who are still alive, who are left till the coming of the Lord," as if he will be alive at that time. By the time we reach 1 Corinthians 15:51 we can imagine some doubt that the majority of Christians alive now will still be alive at Jesus' coming when Paul says, "We will not *all* sleep, but we will all be changed."[26] Finally, in 2 Corinthians 5:1–10, having passed through the near-death experience recounted in 1:8–11 and faced squarely the deadly implications of his ministry as described in 4:10–12, Paul believes that he might die before the Parousia. This, then, leads him to ponder what existence will be like between his own death and the time when he is clothed with his heavenly dwelling.[27]

Even this shift is implausible, however. It seems unlikely that someone who was lowered in a basket from a city wall window to escape arrest by the governor of Damascus (2 Cor. 11:32–33) and who had suffered affliction and rejection in Philippi before ever arriving in Thessalonica (1 Thess. 2:2) had not faced the possibility that he might die before the Parousia. And all this happened before Paul wrote his first extant letter. Some Jews of Paul's time, moreover, believed that a person could leave his or her body and have esoteric experiences in heaven prior to death, and Paul seems to have been one of them (2 Cor. 11:32–33).[28] If Paul held this belief even before he became a Christian (and there is no reason to think it is

21 On the meaning of *ependyomai*, see BDAG, 361.

22 As Moule, *Essays*, 212–21, argues. Cf. Dupont, *ΣΥΝ ΧΡΙΣΤΩΙ*, 153–58, who argues that Paul's view oscillates between a Jewish and Hellenistic perspective within the space of 2 Cor. 5:1–10.

23 John Gillman, "A Thematic Comparison: 1 Cor 15:50–57 and 2 Cor 5:1–5," *JBL* 107 (1988): 439–54.

24 As Knox, *St. Paul*, 128, 142, believes.

25 C. H. Dodd, *New Testament Studies* (Manchester: Manchester Univ. Press, 1953), 109–18. Cf. F. F. Bruce, *1 & 2 Corinthians* (NCB; Grand Rapids: Eerdmans, 1971), 200.

26 Dodd, *Essays*, 110.

27 Bruce, *1 & 2 Corinthians*, 200. Cf. Dodd, *Essays*, 113, 118, and 127.

28 Paul Hoffmann, *Die Toten in Christus: Eine religionsgeschichtliche und exegetische Untersuchung zur paulinischen Eschatologie* (NTAbh 2; Münster: Verlag Aschendorf, 1966), 325.

a postconversion development), then he would have been able at any time in his letter-writing career to conceive of dying and going immediately to be with the Lord.

In his later correspondence he expresses these convictions explicitly.[29] Although the prospect of being "unclothed" is not appealing (2 Cor. 5:3–4), he says that to depart the body in death is to be with the Lord (2 Cor. 5:8–9) and that is "better by far" (Phil. 1:23; cf. 2 Cor. 5:8). Nevertheless, even in his final letter Paul assumes that he is living in "the last days" (2 Tim. 3:1) and counts himself among those who have "longed" for the Lord's appearing (4:8), a conclusion that remains firm even on the presupposition that Philippians or Romans is Paul's final letter (Rom. 13:11–12; Phil. 3:20; 4:5). From his first to his last extant letter Paul reveals the convictions both that the Lord might come within his lifetime and that he could die before that moment. In either case, he believes, he will immediately be in the presence of the Lord. As he puts it in 1 Thessalonians 5:10, "He died for us so that, whether we are awake or asleep, we may live together with him."

The Imminence of the End

As we have seen, when Paul wrote 1 Thessalonians, his primary objective was to encourage a persecuted and struggling Christian community to remain faithful to their commitment to the gospel. An important element in this effort was Paul's reminder of the eschatological nature of their existence. Paul believed they were living in the period of intense suffering that many Jews expected to precede the "day of the Lord." He refers to this when he tells the Thessalonians not to be "unsettled" by the trials they are facing since, as they know, they are "destined for them" (3:3). Paul had predicted their suffering when he was among them, and he reminds them of his prophecy now (3:4). As is true of apocalyptic literature generally, Paul intends this concept to comfort the Thessalonians with the knowledge that their suffering is not out of God's sovereign control but is part of an orderly plan.

This understanding of Christian suffering, both Paul's own and that of Christians generally, remains constant in the apostle's letters.

- In 2 Thessalonians the swirling tide of persecution that the Thessalonians continue to experience (2 Thess. 1:4) is part of the final eschatological scenario. Their suffering will get worse in the future, when the restraining hand of God is removed and "the man of lawlessness" appears (2:6), but even now the "secret power of lawlessness is already at work" (2:7).
- In Romans 1:17–18, the wrath of God that is presently being revealed (*apokalyptō*) from heaven against human impiety stands parallel to the eschatologically revealed (*apokalyptō*) righteousness of God, demonstrating that it too is one of the expected events of the end times. Romans 8:18 claims that the "present sufferings" are not worthy to be compared with the coming glory that will be revealed (*apokalyptō*) in believers.

29 Cf. Plevnik, *Paul and the Parousia*, 276.

- In Colossians 1:24, Paul rejoices that his suffering is filling up the lack in the suffering of the Messiah—an enigmatic statement that is most intelligible against the apocalyptic background of a predetermined amount of suffering whose completion will usher in the final day.[30]
- Finally, in 2 Timothy 3:1–5a Paul describes the "terrible times" of the "last days," but then reveals in 3:5b–9 that the havoc false teachers have created in the church at Ephesus is among these terrible events (cf. 1 Tim. 4:1–5).

Since Paul understood believers to be living in the last days, it is not surprising that he frequently stresses the imminence of the "day of the Lord" as a motive for steadfast commitment to the gospel and blameless behavior. In 1 Thessalonians 5:1–11 Paul reminds the believers of the suddenness with which that day will come and of the necessity, therefore, of alertness, self-control, and standing ready with the defensive armor of faith, love, and hope (5:4–6, 8). For believers, who are "sons of the light and sons of the day" (5:5), that day will mean salvation (5:9), but for the unprepared, who blithely speak of "peace and security" (5:3) and who live in darkness (5:4–5), it will be a day of sudden destruction (5:3) and wrath (5:9; cf. 1:10).

In a similar way, in 1 Corinthians 7:17–40 Paul urges his readers to consider the eschatological urgency of the time in which they live as they make decisions whether to remain circumcised, seek freedom from slavery, or marry a betrothed. The "present crisis" (7:26) has relativized the importance of each of these long-standing customs. "The time has been shortened" (7:29),[31] and it is evident that "this world in its present form is passing away" (7:31). Because of the critical nature of their present existence, believers should make decisions about these transitory matters that will foster "undivided devotion to the Lord" (7:35). Paul may be responding in this passage to people in Corinth who imbibed the notion that the world is eternal whereas people are ephemeral and that they should "eat, drink, and be merry" while the opportunity presents itself.[32] Paul is saying that the truth is actually the reverse of this: People are eternal whereas the world as we know it is ephemeral, and the closing days of the world are upon us. Believers, he says, should live in a way that shows their awareness of this truth.

He says this again in Philippians 3:18–4:1, where he urges his readers to live in a way that is different from "the enemies of the cross of Christ," whose "mind is on earthly things." Believers should instead live in the awareness that they are citizens of another city, and that they are awaiting the arrival from heaven of their Savior and Lord, who will transform their humble existence in the present so that it conforms to his glorious existence. In light of this truth, Paul says, the Philippian Christians should "stand firm."

30 See Dale C. Allison Jr., *The End of the Ages Has Come: An Early Interpretation of the Passion and Resurrection of Jesus* (Philadelphia: Fortress, 1985), 62–65.

31 On the translation of the phrase *ho kairos synestalmenos estin* as "the time has been shortened," see Ben Witherington III, "Transcending Imminence: The Gordion Knot of Pauline Eschatology," in *Eschatology in Bible and Theology: Evangelical Essays at the Dawn of a New Millennium*, ed. Kent E. Brower and Mark W. Elliott (Downers Grove, Ill.: InterVarsity Press, 1997), 171–86, here at 173–74.

32 See Bruce W. Winter, "'The Seasons' of This Life and Eschatology in 1 Corinthians 7:29–31" in *Eschatology in Bible and Theology: Evangelical Essays at the Dawn of a New Millennium*, ed. Kent E. Brower and Mark W. Elliott (Downers Grove, Ill.: InterVarsity Press, 1997), 323–34.

The same concern reemerges in Romans 13:11–14. Here too Paul stresses the imminence of the final Day and uses it to urge his readers to live in light of its approach. They should love one another (13:8–10), "and do this, understanding the present time" (13:11). Paul uses the night–day, dark–light imagery that he had used in 1 Thessalonians 5:5 and 7 (Rom. 13:12–13) to draw a sharp contrast between the moral behavior that believers should embrace and "the deeds of darkness" (Rom. 13:12). He also uses the imagery of donning armor, just as he did in 1 Thessalonians 5:8, to describe the necessity of standing against the onslaught of evil (13:12). They should do this because "the night is nearly over; the day is almost here" (13:12).

In two of Paul's later letters—Colossians and Ephesians—the link between the imminence of Christ's coming and ethics is not as prominent. In Colossians the note of eschatological imminence is muted and the emphasis falls instead on the believer's existence in the present with Christ—the believer has been raised with Christ (2:12) and made alive with him (2:13), and now sits with him in the realms "above" (3:1). The ethical imperative flows out of this status that the believer has already attained (3:2–3, 5). Spatial concepts come to the fore while temporal concepts recede into the background. Some have concluded from this that Paul did not write the letter and that the change in eschatological emphasis is evidence of a later time when eschatological expectation was beginning to wane.[33]

The link between eschatology and ethics is not absent from Colossians, however. Thus, Paul instructs his readers not only to "put to death" immoral behavior because their lives are "now hidden with Christ in God" (Col. 3:3) but because "the wrath of God is coming" (3:6). Why did Paul not sound this note more often or more clearly in Colossians? As we saw in the chapter on Colossians, Paul was opposing a false teaching that questioned whether the Colossian believers' commitment to Paul's gospel was sufficient for their survival on the Day of Judgment. Against such a notion, the Colossians needed to hear that their place in the people of God was secure—their rescue from the dominion of darkness, their redemption, and their forgiveness stood firm because on the cross Christ had triumphed over their sins and over the cosmic powers (1:13–14; 2:13–15).

The situation is similar in Ephesians. Here Paul advances a realized eschatology that is startling when placed alongside the emphasis on the imminent expectation of Christ's coming in his earlier correspondence. God has raised Christ from the dead and seated him at his right hand in the upper heavens (*epouraniois*, Eph. 1:20). God has likewise made believers alive, raised them from the dead, and seated them in these upper heavens (*epouraniois*) with Christ (2:5–6). God has already saved them by grace through faith (2:5, 8).

Just as in Colossians, however, this shift arises from the situation Paul addresses, so that it turns out to be more a matter of emphasis than a deviation from the substance of Paul's eschatological convictions as they are expressed in his earlier correspondence. As we have seen in the chapter on Ephesians, Paul wrote the letter to Christians who

33 Eduard Lohse, *Colossians and Philemon* (Hermeneia; Philadelphia: Fortress, 1971), 180.

lived in an environment that stressed the existence of invisible powers whose ability to help or hurt people could be controlled through magic.[34] In this context, for Paul to speak of believers having been saved and of sharing Christ's position of victory over "all rule and authority, power and dominion, and every title that can be given" (Eph. 1:21) made good practical sense.[35]

Even so, the existential tension that marks Paul's eschatological expectations in his earlier letters is not absent from Ephesians. Paul still awaits the summing up of all things in Christ (Eph. 1:10) and the redemption of his inheritance as a believer (1:14; 4:30). He understands the division between the present age and the age to come (1:21; 2:7). He knows both that the present age is a time of suffering for believers (5:16), in which they must arm themselves for struggle against "the devil's schemes" (6:11, 16), and that in the age to come God will pour out his wrath on the disobedient (5:6). Paul certainly emphasizes the realized aspects of his eschatological convictions in this letter, but he does not do this so completely that the letter's eschatology is fundamentally out of harmony with his earlier correspondence.

We can go even further and say that the way in which Paul applies his eschatology in Colossians and Ephesians matches its application in Galatians. As in Colossians and Ephesians, so in Galatians, Paul opposes the position that God's work in Christ was somehow insufficient to effect a right standing between human beings on one hand and God or the cosmic powers on the other. Here too eschatology, although not absent, recedes into the background.[36] Believers live in "the present evil age," but the death of Christ has rescued them from it (Gal. 1:4) and "redeemed" them "from the curse of the law" (3:13–14) in the fullness of time (4:4–5). They are already sons and heirs (4:7), which makes it odd that any of them would turn the clock back to a time before their maturity when they placed their confidence in something other than Christ (4:7–10). The declaration "not guilty" in God's court still lies in the future (2:16–17; 5:5), but if "faith has come" and people are justified by faith (3:24–25), then at least for those who have faith, justification must in some sense be a present reality. It is true that "at the proper time" believers "will reap a harvest," but this may happen only after a long period of perseverance in doing good (6:9).[37]

Much the same pattern emerges in Romans. The part of the letter that summarizes Paul's convictions about the criterion for survival on the final Day (Rom. 1:16–4:25) lays no stress on the imminent expectation of "the Day." Instead, God's righteousness and saving power, as well as his eschatological wrath, is being revealed in the present (1:17–18; 3:26). When Paul shifts his concern in the letter to the concrete ethical behavior that the gospel entails, however, he speaks unambiguously of the eager expectation of believers for their eschatological redemption (8:23) and of the nearness of God's eschatological salvation (13:11).

34 See esp. Clinton E. Arnold, *Power and Magic: The Concept of Power in Ephesians* (SNTSMS 63; Cambridge: Cambridge Univ. Press, 1989).

35 Ibid., 153–55.

36 See the discussions of this characteristic of Galatians in F. F. Bruce, *Commentary on Galatians* (NIGTC; Grand Rapids: Eerdmans, 1982), 54, and J. L. Martyn, *Galatians: A New Translation with Introduction and Commentary* (AB 33A; New York: Doubleday, 1997), 97–105, esp. 102–3, 105.

37 James D. G. Dunn, *The Epistle to the Galatians* (BNTC 9; Peabody, Mass.: Hendrickson, 1993), 332, comments on 4:9, "Imminent expectation is hardly marked here."

Therefore, in both early and late letters the imminent expectation of the Parousia receives less emphasis where the challenge to the sufficiency of faith in Christ for justification or salvation is strong. In such contexts Paul considers it necessary to remind his readers of what God has already accomplished for them in the death of Christ (Galatians, Colossians, and Ephesians) and in his resurrection and heavenly session (Colossians and Ephesians). In one letter (Romans), both emphases appear—the stress on Christ's accomplishment in the first part, where the criterion for entry to the people of God is an issue (Rom. 1–4), and the stress on eschatological redemption in later sections, where ethics become especially important (chs. 8 and 13).

The Criterion for Acquittal in God's Court

In his letters to the Galatian, Philippian, and Roman Christians Paul argues against the idea that access to God's people can only be gained through Judaism and observance of its law (cf. Gal. 5:1; cf. Acts 15:10). In all three letters the debate revolves around the law's command that all male Jews be circumcised (e.g., Rom. 2:25–29; Gal. 6:13; Phil. 3:2–3), a command that, in the wake of the persecution of Jews by the Seleucid kingdom in the second century B.C., had become a defining characteristic of the Jewish people. Circumcision, however, was just a first step; for the Judaizers, the observance of Jewish festivals (Gal. 4:10; cf. Rom. 14:5–6), of its dietary requirements (Gal. 2:12; cf. Rom. 14:2, 14–15, 21, 23), and of its other commandments (cf. Rom. 13:10; Gal. 5:14) was also necessary for the Gentile Christian who wanted to be included within the boundaries of God's people.

Against this notion, Paul insists that the only criterion for entry to the people of God is faith in Jesus Christ. Faith in Christ, Paul argues, makes the believer a member of Abraham's family (Rom. 4:11; Gal. 3:7), and the inner work of God's Spirit, not circumcision, makes one a true Jew (Rom. 2:25–29; Phil. 3:3).

Most often, Paul focuses the debate more narrowly on the question of the basis on which God "justifies" people.[38] Is a person justified because he or she does the works of the law or because of faith in Christ? Paul argues emphatically that people are "not justified by observing the law, but by faith in Jesus Christ" (Gal. 2:16). This thesis, repeated in various ways throughout Galatians and Romans and articulated again in Philippians 3:2–11, has sparked a massive debate over two principle questions: What does Paul mean when he speaks of justification by faith? How central is justification by faith to Paul's theology?

What Does Justification by Faith Mean?

When Paul uses the verb "justify" (*dikaioō*), he most often seems to evoke the image of a courtroom in which a judge declares the defendant innocent.[39] "Who will bring any charge against those whom God has chosen," Paul asks in Rom. 8:33a, "It

38 Cf. Stephen Westerholm, *Perspectives Old and New on Paul: The "Lutheran" Paul and His Critics* (Grand Rapids: Eerdmans, 2004), 442.

39 The language of justification is notoriously confusing in English where the verb "justify," the adjectives "righteous" and "just," and the nouns "righteousness" and "justice" are all used to translate words that in Greek have a common root: *dikaioō*, *dikaios*, and *dikaiosynē*. Paul uses the noun "justification" (*dikaiōsis*) only twice (Rom. 4:25; 5:18).

is God who justifies, who is he that condemns?" (8:33b–34a; cf. 2:13; 3:19–20).[40] Sometimes Paul speaks of this verdict as something God will render in the future, on the final Day (e.g., Rom. 2:13), and sometimes he speaks as if God has already rendered it (e.g., Rom. 5:1, 9; 8:30; 1 Cor. 6:11).[41]

Paul's use of the noun "righteousness" (*dikaiosynē*) is even more complex. Sometimes it recalls biblical texts where God's righteousness is displayed in the "marvelous things" he has done to save his people and to show them his love (Rom. 1:17; cf. Ps. 98:1–3). At other times it refers to an authority that now rules believers in place of sin and leads to sanctification (Rom. 6:12–23). At times Paul uses it in a forensic sense that stands in sharp contrast to its ethical use, such as his statement that God reckoned Abraham's faith to him as "righteousness" even though he was "ungodly" (Rom. 4:3–8).[42] Since here it is precisely the ungodly person who is nevertheless declared right with God (contrast Rom. 2:13), this "righteousness" must come as a gift from God (Rom. 5:17; cf. 2 Cor. 5:21; Phil. 3:9). Here too, the timing of the arrival of this righteousness is complex. Has righteousness already been reckoned to us in the past (Rom. 4:3)? Is it being revealed in the present (Rom. 1:17)? Or do we hope for its future coming (Gal. 5:5)?

This varied usage has prompted a debate over which facet of righteousness is most basic to Paul's theology. Is it the idea that God declares believers to be righteous (the classic Protestant perspective)?[43] Is it that God not only acquits but also transforms people so that they become righteous (the classic Roman Catholic perspective)?[44] Is it, as some scholars have argued, that God is being faithful to the covenant he has made with his people?[45] Or is it, as still others have emphasized, that God works powerfully to save and to transform his creatures?[46]

The last perspective seems to be most faithful both to Paul's own use of righteousness language and to the biblical background that informed it. As we saw in the chapter on Romans, Paul's use of the phrase "the righteousness of God" in Romans 1:17

---

40 See the discussion in Douglas Moo, *The Epistle to the Romans* (NICNT; Grand Rapids: Eerdmans, 1996), 86–87.

41 Bultmann, *Theology*, 1:273–74; Herman Ridderbos, *Paul: An Outline of His Theology* (Grand Rapids: Eerdmans, 1975), 161–68.

42 Westerholm, *Perspectives*, 263–84, distinguishes helpfully between "ordinary" and "extraordinary" righteousness and points to Rom. 5:7–8 as a good place to see the difference clearly.

43 See, e.g., Bultmann, *Theology*, 270–85; Mark A. Seifrid, *Justification by Faith: The Origin and Development of a Central Pauline Theme* (NovTSup 68; Leiden: Brill, 1992); C. K. Barrett, *Paul: An Introduction to His Thought* (Louisville: Westminster John Knox, 1994), 87–103; Moo, *Romans*, 79–90; Westerholm, *Perspectives*, 273–84, with the careful qualification of n. 39 on 277–78.

44 See, e.g., M.-J. Lagrange, *Épitre aux Romains*, 3rd ed. (Paris: LeCoffre, 1922), 119–41; Otto Kuss, *Der Römerbrief*, 3 vols. (Regensburg: Pustet, 1959–78), 1:121–31.

45 See esp. N. T. Wright, "On Becoming the Righteousness of God" in *Pauline Theology, Volume II: 1 and 2 Corinthians*, ed. David M. Hay (Minneapolis: Fortress, 1993), 200–208; idem, "Romans and the Theology of Paul," in *Pauline Theology, Volume III: Romans*, ed. David M. Hay and E. Elizabeth Johnson, (Minneapolis: Fortress, 1995), 33–34, 38–39; and idem, "New Exodus, New Inheritance: The Narrative Substructure of Romans 3–8," in *Romans and the People of God: Essays in Honor of Gordon D. Fee on the Occasion of His 65th Birthday*, ed. Sven K. Soderlund and N. T. Wright (Grand Rapids: Eerdmans, 1999), 26–35.

46 Credit for formulating this position usually goes to Ernst Käsemann, "Gottesgerechtigkeit bei Paulus," *ZTK* 58 (1961): 367–78, translated in idem, *New Testament Questions of Today* (Philadelphia: Fortress, 1969), 168–82. Gottlob Schrenk had already adopted something close to this position, however, in his 1935 article "δικη (κτλ)," *TDNT*, 2:178–225, here at 203–4. For more recent advocates of this position, see, among others, Karl Kertelge, *"Rechtfertigung" bei Paulus: Studien zur Struktur und zum Dedeutungsgehalt des paulinischen Rechtfertigungsbegriffs* (NTAbh 3; Münster: Aschendorff, 1967), 107–9; Peter Stuhlmacher, *Biblische Theologie des Neuen Testaments*, 2 vols. (Göttingen: Vandenhoeck & Ruprecht, 1992–99), 1:335–37.

with such clear allusions to the biblical notions of God's powerful saving activity on behalf of his people shows that Paul does not conceive of righteousness in static terms. It is not merely the verdict of innocence that God pronounces over the one who has faith in Christ, but it is also a saving power by which God rescues those who have faith in Christ. Thus, Paul's use of righteousness terminology in 1:17 overlaps with his use of this terminology in 6:12–23. In both places, righteousness is not an inert status but an activity that God performs (1:16–17) or an authority that demands service (6:12–23). In both places, in other words, God's righteousness is a power that radically changes believers—it both saves them and demands their obedience.[47]

This does not mean, however, that the Reformation emphasis on God's declaration of righteousness for the believer was wrong. To the contrary, Paul himself emphasizes that God counted Abraham's faith as righteousness (Rom. 4:3, 5, 6, 9, 11; Gal. 3:6) and did so because he justifies the ungodly simply on the basis of their faith in Christ (Rom. 4:5; 5:6–9) and as a gift (Rom. 3:24; 5:17; 1 Cor. 1:30; 2 Cor. 5:21). This is a forensic declaration of innocence in God's sight—"before God," as Paul puts it (Rom. 2:13; 3:20)—and is so final that no one can bring further charges against or condemn those whom God has justified (Rom. 8:33).[48] On the final Day, neither possession of nor doing the Mosaic law will exempt one from the condemnation of God, for God is impartial, rewarding only the doing, not merely the possession of the law, and no one can keep the law fully (1:18–3:20). Only faith that God, in the death of Christ, has atoned for the sins of his people can rescue one from God's judgment on that Day. For the believer, God has already rendered his eschatological judgment, and he has judged in the believer's favor because the death of Christ has made this acquittal possible (Rom. 3:9–5:21; Gal. 2:15–16; 3:10–14; Phil. 3:2–11).[49]

To the question of whether this makes God an unjust judge (cf. Deut. 25:1), Paul would answer that God's willingness to deliver his own Son to death as an atoning sacrifice for the sins of the ungodly allows him both to be righteous and to declare that the ungodly are righteous as a free gift on the basis of their faith alone (Rom. 3:25–26; 5:10; 8:32). To the objection that all this is merely a legal fiction whereby God closes his eyes to sin, Paul might well respond that at some point the legal metaphor breaks down. The judge has entered into a covenant with those whom he acquits—they are his people and he is their God. His acquittal of them on the basis of the death of his Son shows that he does not take their sin lightly, that he does not pretend that they have not sinned when he pronounces them innocent. They are righteous in the sense that God now declares them to be in a right relationship with him.[50]

---

47 See esp. Käsemann, "'The Righteousness of God,'" 171.

48 Moo, *Romans*, 86–87.

49 Cf. Bultmann, *Theology of the New Testament*, 1:274–79; Moo, *Romans*, 87; and esp. Westerholm, *Perspectives*, 273–84.

50 Cf. Bultmann, *Theology of the New Testament*, 1:276; Moo, *Romans*, 87. *Pace* Westerholm, *Perspectives*, 286–96.

How Central Is Justification by Faith to Paul's Theology?

Since the Protestant Reformation, justification by faith has often been considered the central feature of Paul's theology. In the words of one influential Pauline scholar, "For Paul, as for the Reformers after him, the gospel of justification by faith alone was the article by which the church stood or fell."[51]

Some scholars, however, have dissented from this view. According to one group, Paul's claim that faith justifies the believer apart from works of the law arose not because he held this notion as a settled conviction but because his opponents were trying to impose the Mosaic law on his Gentile churches. Prior to this unhappy conflict with Jewish Christianity Paul had not puzzled through the relationship between his pre-Christian convictions about the Mosaic law and his present mission to the Gentiles. He only knew that God had extended salvation to the Gentiles—as Gentiles—through the gospel of Jesus Christ. But when faced with the claim from his Jewish Christian opponents that these Gentiles had to accept the Mosaic law in order to be saved, he developed the counter-thesis that justification before God on the final Day came not by works of the law but through faith in Christ and as a free gift of God. "Theory was the child, not the parent, of practice."[52] The result, according to some scholars, was a distorted portrait of Judaism as a legalistic, graceless religion when, in reality, it emphasized God's grace.[53]

According to many other scholars, the distortion of Judaism belonged not to Paul but to his interpreters who misunderstood his contrast between faith in Christ and works of the law as a contrast between trust in God for salvation on one hand and human effort that seeks to win God's acceptance through good deeds on the other hand.[54] Paul, however, intended "works of the law" to refer to the observance of the Mosaic law that sets one apart from the rest of the world as a Jew, not to refer to human effort abstractly conceived.[55] When Paul is read in this way, the need to paint Judaism as a legalistic religion evaporates.

According to scholars who adopt this "new perspective on Paul," the soteriological pattern in Paul and Judaism actually begins to look similar: Both presuppose that

51 Günther Bornkamm, *Paul* (New York: Harper & Row, 1971), 135. Bornkamm is alluding to the Lutheran dictum that justification is the "*articulus stantis et cadentis ecclesiae*" ("the article by which the church stands or falls"). Although Luther did not speak in precisely these terms, he says something close to this in *Smalcald Articles* 1. The later dictum dates at least to the early seventeenth century, on which see Alister E. McGrath, *Iustitia Dei: A History of the Christian Doctrine of Justification*, 2nd ed. (Cambridge: Cambridge Univ. Press, 1998), 188, 450 n. 3.

52 William Wrede, *Paul* (London: Philip Green, 1907), 146. See also Heikki Räisänen, *Paul and the Law* (WUNT 29; Tübingen: J.C.B. Mohr [Paul Siebeck], 1983), 251–63; Terence L. Donaldson, *Paul and the Gentiles: Remapping the Apostle's Convictional World* (Minneapolis: Fortress, 1997), 111–13. Cf. E. P. Sanders, *Paul and Palestinian Judaism: A Comparison of Patterns of Religion* (Philadelphia: Fortress, 1977), 442–51; idem, *Paul, the Law, and the Jewish People* (Philadelphia: Fortress, 1983), 47. Sanders argues that Paul worked backward from his Christological conviction that Christ was the Savior of the world to the notion that all the world, both Gentiles and Jews, needed the salvation that Christ provides.

53 Wrede, *Paul*, 127. Cf. Räisänen, *Paul and the Law*, 177–91, who believes that the distortion lay not in a claim that Judaism was a graceless religion but in the implication that the Torah was the way of salvation in Judaism just as Christ was the way of salvation in Christianity.

54 See esp. Sanders, *Paul and Palestinian Judaism*, 1–428.

55 Sanders, *Paul, the Law, and the Jewish People*, 20, 47, 147, 152–53, 160; Dunn, *Jesus, Paul and the Law: Studies in Mark and Galatians* (Louisville: Westminster John Knox, 1990), 183–214; idem, *Theology*, 335–40, 354–71; Donaldson, *Paul and the Gentiles*, 171–72. The notion that the phrase "works of the law" in Paul refers to such specifically Jewish commandments as circumcision, Sabbath keeping, and dietary restrictions goes back at least as far as "Ambrosiaster" and Pelagius. See the collection of their comments on Rom. 3:20 in *ACCS*, 6:95, 97, and on Rom. 3:28 in *ACCS*, 6:104–5.

God freely gives salvation to his people not because they have earned it but simply on the basis of his own mercy, and both argue that good works are the necessary means of remaining within God's people.[56] Within the context of Judaism, this pattern of religion has been dubbed "covenantal nomism," since Jews experienced God's mercy as inclusion within his covenant people and the provision of means of atonement for transgression.[57] The difference between Paul and his Jewish opponents, whether Christian or non-Christian, lies in the central place Paul gives in his thinking to Christ. For Paul, unlike his opponents, entrance into the church through identification with Christ in baptism is the only necessary requirement for membership in God's people. Judaizing Christians, therefore, cannot impose observance of the Mosaic law on Gentiles as an entrance requirement.

It is possible to hold to this new understanding of the faith–works antithesis and still to consider justification by faith to be a fundamental element in Paul's theology.[58] Even if the problem is understood as a contrast between trust in God and trust in one's national affiliation rather than as a contrast between trust in God and trust in human effort abstractly conceived, the problem is still a lack of trust in God, and its symptom is still human boasting. On this reading, the basic structure of justification by faith and the possibility that it is central to Paul's theology remains undisturbed.

Most interpreters who adopt the "new perspective," however, accept as a corollary of it the notion that justification by faith is a polemical doctrine that was not fundamental to Paul's theology.[59] They commonly cite two reasons for their position. First, they claim that "justification by faith" occupies an important position in the argument of only those letters in which Paul is attacking Judaizers.[60] Second, they argue that Paul's notion of participation in Christ is more fundamental to his theology than his teaching on justification by faith.[61]

Is justification by faith only a polemical doctrine? It is true that Paul develops the claim that righteousness comes by faith in Christ apart from works of the Mosaic law only in Romans, Galatians, Philippians, and Titus.[62] It is also true that

56 Morna D. Hooker, "Paul and Covenantal Nomism," in *Paul and Paulinism: Essays in Honour of C. K. Barrett*, ed. Morna D. Hooker and S. G. Wilson (London: SPCK, 1982), 47–56; Donaldson, *Paul and the Gentiles*, 172; Kent L. Yinger, *Paul, Judaism, and Judgment according to Deeds* (SNTSMS 105; Cambridge: Cambridge Univ. Press, 1999), 288–90. Cf. Sanders, *Paul and Palestinian Judaism*, 513–14, who believes that although Paul's religion is similar to "covenantal nomism," the idea of repentance is too infrequently expressed in Paul's letters and the notion of participation in Christ is too common in them for Paul's Christianity and Judaism's covenantal nomism to represent the same "pattern of religion."

57 Sanders, *Paul and Palestinian Judaism*, 75, 236; idem, *Judaism: Practice and Belief 63 BCE–66 CE* (Philadelphia: Trinity Press International, 1992), 262–75.

58 This seems to be the case with Dunn, *Theology*, 379, who comments that even when interpreted without the Reformation polemic against human effort, the doctrine is "a profound conception of the relation between God and humankind—a relation of utter dependence, of unconditional trust."

59 See, e.g., Sanders, *Paul and Palestinian Judaism*, 434–42; Donaldson, *Paul and the Gentiles*, 111–13, who both echo the older concerns of Wrede, *Paul*, 122–37; Albert Schweitzer, *The Mysticism of Paul the Apostle* (New York: Henry Holt, 1931), 205–26; and W. D. Davies, *Paul and Rabbinic Judaism: Some Rabbinic Elements in Pauline Theology*, 4th ed. (Philadelphia: Fortress, 1980), 221–23.

60 See, e.g., Wrede, *Paul*, 123; Schweitzer, *Mysticism*, 220; Donaldson, *Paul and the Gentiles*, 112–13.

61 See, e.g., Sanders, *Paul and Palestinian Judaism*, 434–42, 502–8; and Donaldson, *Paul and the Gentiles*, 112. Cf. Schweitzer, *Mysticism*, 205–26, 294–95.

62 The concept seems to appear in 1 Cor. 1:30; 6:11; 2 Cor. 5:21, but it is not developed there. It appears briefly but in a fully developed form in Titus 3:5–7, a passage treated below.

Titus is often immediately sidelined in discussions of Paul's theology because its Pauline authorship is disputed and that in the remaining letters Paul is engaged in a polemical exchange with Judaism over what a right relationship with God entails.[63] If the debate is strictly over where the Paul of the undisputed letters uses certain terms, then it is difficult to deny that he uses the language of justification by faith in contexts where his opponents are Jewish or at least take Jewish positions.

If the debate is broadened, however, to include the theological principle behind Paul's justification language, it becomes equally difficult to deny that this principle held immense importance for Paul.[64] To speak of justification by faith apart from the Mosaic law within a Jewish context was fundamentally to assert that God's people stand in a right relationship with him not on the basis of their ethnic origin or on the basis of their efforts to do what God requires (efforts that must always end in failure), but because God has graciously put them in a right relationship with himself. Those who have faith that God has done this through the death of Christ are the recipients of this gift. Paul can articulate this fundamental theological conviction without using the language of justification apart from the Mosaic law, and he does so often.[65]

The Corinthian correspondence provides a good example of this.[66] As we have seen in chapters 12 and 14, Paul answers the Corinthian insistence on creating divisions through emphasizing social distinctions with a reminder that the Corinthians themselves show that God accomplishes his purposes not through strong people but through those who are weak (1 Cor. 1:26–31), nor through eloquence and wisdom but through the preaching of the cross (1:27–2:16). The antidote to the Corinthians' proud preference for one teacher over another is the humbling realization that they have received from God every spiritual gift that they claim to possess (4:7).

Similarly, Paul answers the Corinthians' objections to his suffering with a sustained argument that God works through weakness. The death of Jesus and the suffering of the apostle provided the means through which God brought the Corinthians to life (2 Cor. 4:7–12). In the same way, Jesus' self-imposed poverty and Paul's willing suffering have made the Corinthians rich (8:9; cf. 6:3–10). Paul himself boasts in his weakness because God works powerfully "in weaknesses, in insults, in hardships, in persecutions, in difficulties" to accomplish his redemptive purposes (11:30; 12:9–10).

The problem with the Corinthians in both letters is their insistence on making judgments within the church on the basis of outward appearances according to the common standards of Roman society (2 Cor. 5:12; 10:7) and then boasting in the results. They must follow the teacher with the most impressive rhetorical credentials (1 Cor. 1:12; 2:1–5); they are proud of sexual sin (5:2); they must best one another

63 Even Titus contains polemic against "those from the circumcision" (1:10).

64 Cf. Moo, *Romans*, 90.

65 Cf. John L. White, *The Apostle of God: Paul and the Promise of Abraham* (Peabody, Mass.: Hendrickson, 1999), xxii, "Paul was not opposed just to the law as a way of defining the Jewish relationship with God. He was equally opposed to analogous Gentile principles and emphases within his own communities." Cf. Seifrid, *Justification by Faith*, 249, 257.

66 Cf. Bultmann, *Theology of the New Testament*, 283–84; idem, "πιστεύω (κτλ)," *TDNT*, 6:174–228, here at 220.

in legal battles (6:1–11); they display their "knowledge" by participating in idolatry (8:1–2, 10); they must discriminate between social classes at the Lord's Supper (11:19); and they must use the most flamboyant of spiritual gifts (12:1–14:40). They are attracted to those who boast in their social credentials (2 Cor. 11:21b–23), to those who provide impressive letters of recommendation (3:1), and to those who openly display their rhetorical and physical strength (10:10; 11:6). As a result of this attitude among the Corinthians, praise in their churches goes to the people who meet their criteria for superiority, not to God. Against all this Paul says in both letters to Corinth, "Let him who boasts boast in the Lord" (1 Cor. 1:31; 2 Cor. 10:17; cf. Jer. 9:23–24).

But this is also the problem that Paul addresses in his letters to the Romans, Galatians, and Philippians. In Galatians one group boasts that they are promoting circumcision (Gal. 5:13) and is excluding the other group as a way of coercing them to accept circumcision (4:17; cf. 2:12–13). Paul's remedy is to stress the leveling effect of the gospel of God's grace (2:14–16, 21)—all are sinners, whether circumcised or not, and all need God's intervention on their behalf through the cross of Christ if they are to belong to his people (2:20–21; 3:10–14). As a result, the cross alone is worth the believer's boast (6:14).

In Philippians Paul counters the same group with an autobiographical statement about boasting in Christ Jesus and placing no confidence in (circumcised) flesh (Phil. 3:3–9).

In Romans, a group of Jews is passing judgment on a group of Gentiles (Rom. 2:1; 14:1–4, 10, 13), and both groups are boasting in their own resources: the Jews in the possession of and keeping of the Mosaic law (2:17, 25–29; 3:27–4:8), and the Gentiles in their majority status in the eschatologically restored people of God (11:18).[67] Here too the remedy is to understand the gospel—that sin has captured all human beings without exception, enslaved them to its power, and placed them under the just condemnation of God's law (1:18–3:20), but that God has graciously intervened in this disastrous situation with the atoning sacrifice of Christ on the cross (3:21–26). As a result, all boasting in human accomplishments or in social status is excluded (3:27–4:25). Just as in the Corinthian correspondence, the object of the believer's boasting is transformed. The believer now boasts in suffering because God uses suffering and weakness to accomplish his saving purposes (5:3, 6–8), and the believer boasts in God who uses Christ's atoning suffering to reconcile sinners to himself (5:11).

Although the issue of boasting in human effort is more prominent in the correspondence that targets Judaizing Christianity than it is in the Corinthian correspondence, the fundamental principle remains the same: God, in his grace, takes the initiative in reconciling sinners to himself, and he makes his gracious initiative clearly visible by working through human weakness.

67 Cf. Seifrid, *Justification by Faith*, 249, 257.

This fundamental conviction that the basis for inclusion in God's people is God's grace rather than anything originating from his people themselves reappears in the later Pauline letters. Here human effort is just as prominently the object of Paul's polemic as it was in the earlier letters devoted to the Judaizing controversy, but now human effort itself is not linked with observance of the Mosaic law. Paul's letter to the Colossians assures its readers that God has already incorporated them within his people (Col. 1:12; 2:11–12), has already raised them from spiritual death (2:13), and has already raised them with Christ (3:1) on the basis of his death. Because his death on the cross effected the forgiveness of sins (1:13–14; 2:13–14; 3:13), the Colossian believers need not pursue the false teachers' ascetic regimen for placating the heavenly powers.

In Ephesians, Paul likewise affirms that God made Christians alive in Christ when they were dead in transgressions and that God saved them by his grace through faith, not because of any "works." Just as in Romans, Galatians, Philippians, and the Corinthian letters, God saves people in this way "so that no one can boast" (Eph. 2:4, 8–9).

Similarly, 1 Timothy recounts Paul's conversion from a life of blasphemy, persecution, violence, ignorance, and unbelief as a result of God's willingness to pour out the grace of the Lord on him (1 Tim. 1:12–14). Paul then follows this statement with a "faithful saying" that epitomizes this element of his theology: "Christ Jesus came into the world to save sinners—of whom I am the worst" (1:15). The book of Titus speaks of God's saving desperate sinners not because of the "righteous things" they have done but because of his "mercy" (Titus 3:5) and summarizes the effect of this saving work of God as "having been justified by his grace" (3:7).

If these statements originate with Paul himself, they provide clear evidence of the importance of the principle that lies beneath the justification language of Romans, Galatians, and Philippians. Even if they do not come from Paul but from someone writing at a later time in Paul's name, as many advocates of the "new perspective" believe, they still show that long before the Protestant Reformation interpreters of Paul understood the grace-works or faith-works antithesis to be of fundamental importance to his theology.[68]

Justification by faith apart from the law can only be marginalized as a polemical doctrine, therefore, if it is separated from the fundamental theological conviction of which it is an expression—that God takes the initiative in salvation. If we understand the phrase "justification by faith" to be a summary of this notion, then it is legitimate to consider it one of Paul's most important theological principles.

Is justification by faith secondary to participation in Christ? Those who claim that Paul's teaching on justification by faith is not central to his theology often claim that Paul's understanding of the believer's union with Christ is more fundamental to his theology than justification by faith. Paul's juridical language, it is said, is a particular way of expressing his concept of being "in Christ" when he is in debate with Jewish opponents.[69]

68 On this see I. H. Marshall, "Salvation, Grace and Works in the Later Writings in the Pauline Corpus," *NTS* 42 (1996): 339–58.

69 Schweitzer, *Mysticism*, 220; Sanders, *Paul and Palestinian Judaism*, 505–6.

These interpreters advance several reasons for their position, but three arguments are particularly strong. First, Paul does not derive his ethical teaching from his understanding of justification by faith but from his notion of the believer's unity with Christ or infilling with the Spirit. Thus, for example, when Paul develops a basis for ethics in Romans 6:1–11, he appeals not to the juristic concepts expressed in 1:18–5:21 but to the believer's death with Christ in baptism.[70] Similarly, in 1 Corinthians 6:15–17 and 10:19–21 he admonishes the Corinthians to avoid sexual immorality or idolatry not on the basis of any juridical notion about the death of Christ as an atonement for sin but on the basis that these sins set up unions that are incompatible with union with Christ.[71]

Second, if justification by faith were fundamental to Paul's theology, his references to the death of Christ would serve more often than they do as the basis for the juridical notion that Christ died an atoning death for transgressions. Instead of this, Paul uses the death of Christ most often as a basis for his conviction that believers are united with Christ.[72] To put it another way, the argument of Romans 6:1–11 is more typical of Paul's handling of Christ's death than the argument of 3:21–26.

Third, if a juristic understanding of salvation were fundamental to Paul's theology, he would have developed a concept of repentance to cope with the transgressions of believers after their justification. As is well known, however, Paul rarely uses the terminology of repentance, forgiveness, or guilt. In Romans 3:9, for example, Paul's conclusion to his argument in 1:18–2:29 that both Jews and Gentiles have committed sins is not that they are guilty of transgression from which they need to repent but that they are "under [the power of] sin."[73]

Paul's dominant understanding of the human plight, therefore, is that people are under the power of sin, not that they have committed transgressions. The solution to this plight is identification with Christ's death through baptism, not forgiveness of guilt or a declaration of innocence on the basis of the atoning sacrifice of Christ's crucifixion. That Paul could sometimes describe the human plight as transgression (Rom. 2–3) and sometimes describe it as being under sin's power (3:9; 6:1–11) without ever explaining how—or if—the two concepts were related only shows that he thought backward from his conviction that all people must come under Christ's lordship to various reasons why this must be so.[74]

These are strong arguments, but they are ultimately unconvincing. First, it is true that the theological foundation of Paul's ethical teaching is the presence of the Spirit and union with Christ, but Paul sometimes connects notions of participation in Christ and the Spirit with the language of righteousness. In Romans 6:7, for example, Paul hints that participation in Christ's death originates in God's juridical declaration of the believer's innocence:

---

70 Donaldson, *Paul and the Gentiles*, 112. Cf. Schweitzer, *Mysticism*, 225–26, 294–95, and the more nuanced argument of Sanders, *Paul and Palestinian Judaism*, 339–41.

71 Sanders, *Paul and Palestinian Judaism*, 503.

72 Ibid., 502–3.

73 Ibid., 503.

74 Ibid., 497–502.

> Our old self was crucified with him so that the body of sin might be made powerless in order that we might no longer be slaves to sin, for the one who has died has been justified [*dedikaiōtai*] from sin. (Rom. 6:6–7, aut.)

The first part of this statement describes the believer's "mystical" participation in Christ's death and claims that this participation has freed the believer from the grip of sin. The second part of the statement, however, grounds this freedom in God's declaration that the believer is innocent.[75] In the second half of Romans 6 Paul uses the term "righteousness" in an ethical sense to describe the believer's new "lord" to whom he or she is enslaved (6:13–20). This suggests that the declaration of the believer's righteous status was the beginning point of the participation.[76]

A similar link between justification by faith and the indwelling of God's Spirit appears in Galatians 3. Here Paul reminds the Galatian Christians that God has included them within his eschatologically restored people and justified them apart from any observance of the Mosaic law, simply on the basis of their faith in the gospel: "Does God supply you with his Spirit and work miracles among you by works of the law or by hearing with faith? Just as Abraham believed God and he credited it to him as righteousness" (Gal. 3:5–6).[77]

The presence of God's Spirit among Gentile Galatians is the sign of their inclusion in God's eschatologically restored people. This Spirit is also, however, the sign that God has, on the basis of their faith, declared them righteous in his sight, just as he declared Abraham to be righteous on the basis of his faith. Paul does not explain the connection between their reception of the Spirit, their faith, and their justification, but that some connection exists is clear. Justification by faith and life in the Spirit, therefore, are closely related in his thinking. It seems reasonable to think of the Spirit as coming among people whom God has declared righteous on the basis of their faith and who, by virtue of this declaration, constituted the fulfillment of his promises in the prophets to restore the fortunes of his people.

Second, it is again true that Paul's references to the death of Christ more often support his notion of participation in Christ's death than they support explanations of God's justification of the sinner. This may have to do more with the circumstances that prompted Paul's letters, however, than with the structure of Paul's theology. Both in 1 Corinthians and in Romans, where Paul uses the death of Christ to support his

75 C. E. B. Cranfield, *A Critical and Exegetical Commentary on the Epistle to the Romans*, 2 vols. (ICC; Edinburgh: T. & T. Clark, 1975–79), 1:310–11. Cf. J. A. Ziesler, *The Meaning of Righteousness in Paul: A Linguistic and Theological Inquiry* (Cambridge: Cambridge Univ. Press, 1972), 200–201. Sanders, *Paul and Palestinian Judaism*, 503, 506, argues that because Paul speaks of justification from "sin" rather than from "sins" in Rom. 6:7, he is pressing justification language into the service of the notion that by union with Christ's death one is freed from the power of sin. He then takes this as evidence that justification is not the means by which one enters union with Christ. But Paul thought that one manifestation of being under the power of sin was the tendency to commit sins (Rom. 5:12, 16, 19). Thus, the notion that God declares the believer innocent despite the power that sin exercises over the believer is intelligible. The NAB seems to capture this understanding of the verse when it translates *dedikaiōtai apo tēs amartias* as "has been absolved from sin."

76 Both concepts together are summarized in the phrase "the righteousness of God," which, as I have argued above, should be understood in both a juridical and a transformative sense. See Schreiner, *Romans*, 66–67.

77 Many commentators begin a new division of the letter at 3:6, but for the close relationship between 3:5 and 3:6; see Bruce, *Galatians*, 152–53, who comments insightfully, "The connexion implied in καθώς would be lost unless there were the closest possible link between receiving the Spirit and being justified."

ethical teaching, ethics are a primary concern. The problems that prompted 1 Corinthians were ethical problems, perhaps related to a misunderstanding of Paul's teaching on justification by faith as a license to sin. Similarly, rumors had circulated in Rome that Paul's teaching on justification by faith supported the notion that people should sin all the more, and these concerns apparently prompted Paul to address the issue of ethics in Romans 6. In neither context is the issue of justification by faith on the basis of Christ's death in dispute.

Third, it is also true, as interpreters have often noticed, that Paul does not develop a doctrine of repentance.[78] He seems to ignore the existence of this teaching in Judaism and seldom refers to the repentance of Christians.[79] This is understandable, however, on the basis of the link that Paul makes between the atoning death of Christ and justification by faith. In Romans 3:25–26 Paul says that God has justified sinners on the basis of Christ's atoning death and implies that this death was the climactic and final sacrifice of atonement for sin. Because of it, God was able to let "sins committed beforehand [go] unpunished [*paresin*]" and still remain just. In other words, repentance from sin and sacrifice for sin were only effective in the past because of the future atoning sacrifice of Christ on the cross.

In the same way, as Romans 8:1–4 and 33–34 show, sins that Christians might commit after believing the gospel are also covered proleptically by this sacrifice. By his death "for sin" Christ Jesus condemned sin in the flesh (8:3), and because God has justified sinners in this way, they need not fear condemnation in the future (8:33–34). Believers who commit sins will continue to be justified, therefore, not because of any process of repentance for these sins but because of the atoning sacrifice of Christ.

In the new situation that the atoning death of Christ created, Paul apparently found the term "faith" more serviceable than the term "repentance" to describe the appropriate response to sin. From the time of Christ's death, the proper response to sin was faith that this death was the climactic and final sacrifice of atonement for sin and had ended God's justified wrath against the sinner, enabling God to be both just and the justifier of the ungodly. The notion that justification came by means of faith rather than by means of repentance is exactly what we would expect of one who believed that Christ's death atoned for every believer's every sin, whether past or future. The scanty use of repentance language in Paul and the frequent use of faith language, therefore, so far from constituting evidence that justification by faith was not a fundamental theological conviction for Paul, is a sign that it was basic to his theology.

78 See, e.g., Claude G. Montefiore, *Judaism and St. Paul: Two Essays* (London: M. Goschen, 1914), 75–76; John Knox, *Chapters in A Life of Paul* (New York: Abingdon, 1950), 149–55; Sanders, *Paul and Palestinian Judaism*, 499–501, 503, 507, 449–50; John Ziesler, *Pauline Christianity*, rev. ed. (Oxford Bible Series; Oxford: Oxford Univ. Press, 1990), 76.

79 Paul uses the language of repentance in Rom. 2:4; 2 Cor. 7:9–10; 12:21; and 2 Tim. 2:25, and the concept of repentance lies beneath his description of the Thessalonians as people who "turned to God from idols to serve the living and true God, and to wait for his Son from heaven" (1 Thess. 1:9–10).

This teaching, by itself, could easily leave Paul open to the charge that he promoted sin by failing to provide any incentive for turning from it to a "righteous" way of life, and it is indicative of the important place that justification by faith held in Paul's teaching that he has been widely misunderstood in precisely this direction, both in ancient (Rom. 3:8; Gal. 2:17; cf. Rom. 6:1, 15) and in more recent times.[80] For Paul, however, faith entails the same kind of turning toward God and steady commitment to the way of life that God desires that the term "repentance" was commonly thought to describe in Judaism.[81] The importance of this aspect of faith appears clearly in Paul's description of Abraham's faith:

> Against all hope, Abraham in hope believed and so became the father of many nations, just as it had been said to him, "So shall your offspring be." Without weakening in his faith, he faced the fact that his body was as good as dead—since he was about a hundred years old—and that Sarah's womb was also dead. Yet he did not waver through unbelief regarding the promise of God, but was strengthened in his faith and gave glory to God, being fully persuaded that God had power to do what he had promised. This is why "it was credited to him as righteousness." (Rom. 4:18–22)

Faith, then, is a steady trust in God that shapes the entire life of the one who has it. This is why Paul can speak naturally of "faith expressing itself through love" (Gal. 5:6) and of "the obedience that comes from faith" (Rom. 1:5; 16:26). This is why he can speak simultaneously of "obeying" the gospel and of "believing" it (10:16), of confessing Jesus as "Lord" and "believing" that God had raised him from the dead (10:9).[82] It is also why he could visualize a judgment according to works for believers—while their salvation was certain, God would distribute rewards and punishments according to deeds.

This judgment according to works sometimes takes place in the present (1 Cor. 11:30), but Paul most often speaks of it as something that will happen on the final Day (3:15; cf. 4:4–5; 2 Cor. 5:10; Rom. 14:10).[83] For Paul, therefore, faith is not as far removed from repentance as has sometimes been thought. Succinctly put, "faith" for Paul is "repentance" viewed from the eschatological perspective provided by Christ's climactic and final sacrifice of atonement.

Summary. Paul's understanding of justification by faith apart from works of the law, therefore, is one manifestation of his fundamental conviction about human weakness and God's initiative in salvation. Since it is derivative of that notion, it cannot

80 For a modern example of this criticism of Paul's doctrine of justification, see Knox, *Chapters in a Life of Paul*, 153–54.

81 On the concept of repentance in Judaism, see George Foot Moore, *Judaism in the First Centuries of the Christian Era: The Age of the Tannaim*, 3 vols. (Cambridge, Mass.: Harvard Univ. Press, 1927–30), 1:497–534, and Sanders, *Judaism*, 252–53, 271. On the overlap of Paul's concept of faith with the Jewish concept of repentance, see Adolf Schlatter, *The Theology of the Apostles: The Development of New Testament Theology* (Grand Rapids: Baker, 1998; orig. ed., 1922), 239–41, and Johannes Behm, "μετανοέω (κτλ)," *TDNT*, 4:989–1022, here at 1005.

82 Kertelge, *"Rechtfertigung" bei Paulus*, 174–75.

83 Ridderbos, *Paul*, 178–81; Judith Gundry-Volf, *Paul and Perseverance: Staying in and Falling Away* (WUNT 2.37; Tübingen: J. C. B. Mohr [Paul Siebeck], 1990), 131–57; Sanders, *Judaism*, 273–74. *Pace* Yinger, *Paul, Judaism, and Judgment*, 259, 279, and 287–88, who believes that judgment according to works in Paul, even when applied to believers, refers to their eternal salvation.

qualify as the center of Paul's theology according to the criteria discussed in chapter 8, but it is nevertheless close to the center of his theology. Paul believes that no human quality or activity contributes to God's decision to include one within his people or to find one innocent on "the day of God's wrath." Membership in God's people and acquittal in his eschatological court come solely through faith in Christ.

The Relationship between the Visible and the Invisible Worlds

In Colossians, Ephesians, 1 Timothy, and Titus, Paul responds to people who are teaching a false notion of the relationship between the visible, material world and the invisible beings who inhabit the unseen world. The error appears most clearly in Colossians, where Paul responds to a false teacher who apparently claimed that various invisible beings must be placated by an ascetic regimen ("human tradition," as Paul calls it in Col. 2:8). The regimen involved restrictions on eating and drinking and insisted on the observance of particular festivals (2:16). Paul summarizes its ascetic requirements ironically in the phrase, "Do not handle! Do not taste! Do not touch!" (2:21), and says that this regimen involves "harsh treatment of the body" (2:23).

Beneath these teachings lies a perverse understanding of creation, both visible and invisible (cf. Col. 1:16). The false teachers seem to have elevated angelic beings to such a status that they believe these beings pose a threat even to Christians. They also seem to think that an ascetic discipline that denies the body food, drink, and other sensory pleasures is the means by which these beings can be placated and their threat neutralized. The invisible world provides much to fear, and rejecting aspects of the visible, created world provides the solution to that fear.

Against this teaching, Paul asserts that Christ's death has effectively reconciled God's earthly and heavenly creation to their creator. God has created the universe through Christ and has used the death of Christ on the cross to gain victory over all inimical cosmic elements (Col. 2:15) and to provide forgiveness for the sins of his people (2:13)—in short, "to reconcile to himself all things, whether things on earth or things in heaven" (1:20). Ascetic discipline as a means of placating supposedly hostile angelic beings is therefore useless. This approach to the invisible and visible worlds fails to recognize that the death of Christ on the cross has defeated the hostile invisible powers and provided forgiveness for human sins.

In Ephesians too Paul asserts that believers have nothing to fear from the invisible world. The notion that one must placate inimical cosmic powers through ascetic discipline is absent, but here also Paul claims that God, through the resurrection and heavenly session of Christ, has defeated the cosmic powers. Although believers are still subjected to the devil's offensive assaults (Eph. 6:10–18), they share Christ's position in the heavens (1:20–23; 2:5–6) and therefore to some extent share his victory over "all rule and authority, power and dominion, and every title that can be given" (1:21).

The problem Paul faces in the Pastoral Letters is similar to the problem he encountered in Colosse. Here the false teachers seem to have numbered Christ as one among many invisible powers that mediated between God and humanity. Such a teaching at least accounts for Paul's concern to emphasize the unity of God (1 Tim. 2:5; 6:15–16), Christ's unique role as mediator between God and humanity (2:5; 3:16), and Christ's human nature (2:5; 3:16). Perhaps here too it was thought that magical practices (2 Tim. 3:13) and an ascetic approach to life (1 Tim. 4:3–5; Titus 1:15) somehow placate these powers or provide access to knowledge about them. This appears all the more likely since Paul designates the ascetic practices that the false teachers advocate as "things taught by demons" (1 Tim. 4:1). Paul responds not only by affirming the unity of God, the uniqueness of Christ's mediatorial role, and Christ's human nature, but with a reaffirmation of marriage (1 Tim. 3:2, 12; 5:9), motherhood (2:15; 5:14), the family (5:5, 8), and the enjoyment of food and drink (4:3–5; 5:23).

These problems and Paul's responses to them are collected in the later Pauline letters, but they are consistent with Paul's theology of creation as we find it in his earlier correspondence, particularly in 1 Corinthians. In 1 Corinthians 8:1–11:1, where he addresses the issue of eating meat offered in sacrifice to pagan gods, Paul argues against any intrinsic connection between food and the divine; whether one eats or does not eat certain foods has nothing to do with his or her relationship to God (8:8). The elitists in Corinth who think their "knowledge" that they can eat such meat brings them closer to God are wrong, and so, by implication, are any who imagine that abstinence from such meat brings them closer to God. Christians are free to "eat anything sold in the meat market without raising questions of conscience" (10:25). God created the animals who supply the meat and therefore no pagan sacrificial ritual can interfere with the inherent propriety of eating it (10:26).

Paul does prohibit participation in cultic meals "in an idol's temple," however, both on the basis that those who eat such meals may cause a Christian with a weak conscience to stumble into idolatry (1 Cor. 8:11–12) and because to participate in these meals is to participate in demonic activity (10:14–22).[84] Paul is referring here to attendance at meals where a pagan god was thought either to be the sponsor or at least to be present. One such invitation from the second century A.D. runs, "Chairemon invites you to sup at the table of the Lord Serapis in the Serapion, tommorrow, that is the 15th, at the ninth hour."[85] One of the benefits of attending such meals was apparently the appeasement of demons who might otherwise prove harmful. As Porphyry says (albeit in the third century A.D.), Serapis was identified with Pluto, who was thought to rule over the demons, and therefore sacrifices to Serapis were made for "propitiating or averting their influence" (Eusebius, *Praep. ev.* 174 b–c).[86]

84 Here I follow Gordon D. Fee, *The First Epistle to the Corinthians* (Grand Rapids: Eerdmans, 1987), 357–63.

85 The Greek text and a German translation, along with a full note on cultic meals in antiquity can be found in Hans Lietzmann and Werner Georg Kümmel, *An die Korinther I–II*, 5th ed. (HNT; Tübingen: J. C. B. Mohr [Paul Siebeck], 1969), 49–51.

86 I have used the translation of *Preparation for the Gospel* by Edwin Hamilton Gifford, 2 vols. (Oxford: Clarendon, 1903), 1:191. Eusebius is quoting from Porphyry's work, *Of the Philosophy to Be Derived from Oracles*, which is no longer extant. I am indebted to Lietzmann, *An die Korinther*, 50, for bringing this text to my attention.

Paul wants his readers to know that he does not accept the reality of gods like Serapis, nor does he accept the idea that the sacrifices offered at the meals where these gods supposedly preside have the desired propitiatory effects. Even though people make reference to "many gods" and "many lords," there is only one creator God and one Lord Jesus Christ, through whom God created all things (1 Cor. 8:5–6). In the same way, although participation in meals over which a pagan god presides is idolatry, the prohibition against it is not an admission that these pagan gods actually exist or that the sacrifices offered to these gods actually work in the way unbelievers think they work (10:19–20). Nor is the meat used in these pagan ceremonies somehow tainted by them, making it unfit to eat—God created the animals from whom the meat comes, and no idolatrous ritual can interfere with God's ownership of this meat (10:25–26).

Paul acknowledges the existence of demons, however, and claims that these demons are present at meals sponsored by Gentile gods, just as the Lord is present at the Lord's Supper (1 Cor. 10:20–21). Those who eat these meals are "participants with demons" in the meal (10:20), and those who eat the Lord's Supper are participants with fellow Christians in the benefits of Christ's death (10:16–17). Each of these invisible spheres of participation is incompatible with the other (10:21).

Paul does not explain why they are incompatible, but a reasonable inference is possible. If participants in meals sponsored, for example, by Serapis thought that they were exercising control over the demonic world or over Serapis, or both, by participating in the sacrifices that accompanied the meal, then Christian participation in these meals implied that God was not in full control of the demonic world. It implied that these invisible forces had some power independent of the one God who created and sustains the universe. Perhaps this is why Paul calls such participation "idolatry"—when the demons take on a power independent of God, they become "gods" and "lords" and therefore, from Paul's perspective, they become idols. Thus Paul places his discussion of this issue in the context of a command to "flee from idolatry" (10:14).

Paul's approach to the relationship between the visible and invisible worlds is therefore consistent in the letters that address the issue, despite the years that intervened between the composition of 1 Corinthians and the composition of his later letters. God created all things through Jesus Christ. He has sovereign control over this creation, even over the demonic powers who are no longer aligned with him. These powers have suffered a defeat from which they will not recover when Christ disarmed them at his crucifixion, and Christ is now seated in heaven at God's right hand with these inimical powers beneath his feet. Christians share this victory. For this reason, and also because God created them and ultimately owns them, the special use or abstinence from food, drink, and marriage as a means of controlling the demonic world is unnecessary. It is also idolatry, since it implies that these demonic beings have some standing and power independent of their creator.

This understanding of the demonic world does not mean that demons are unable to frustrate the worship of God by leading Christians astray, nor does it mean that the devil is unable to plot against and attack believers. It does mean, however, that the assaults of these powers can be defeated in the present by the well-armed and strategically positioned Christian. It also means that the complete defeat of these powers in the future is secure, so secure that Paul can already speak of them as lying slain beneath the feet of the victorious Christ.

THE BASIC STRUCTURE OF PAUL'S THEOLOGY

Beneath Paul's pastoral responses to persecution, ethics, disunity, and false teaching lie several basic convictions about the nature of history, the character of humanity, and the character of God.

The Nature of History

For Paul, history moves along a continuum from Adam to Christ to the final Day, and God's purpose in history is to assemble a people from all the nations of the earth who will glorify him. This purpose was seemingly hindered when Adam sinned against God, bringing the curse of death on himself and all his descendants. Death came on them not only because Adam sinned but also because they have all sinned, and their fundamental error is a failure to glorify God as God (Rom. 5:12–14, 17; 1 Cor. 15:22).

God did not leave people in this state of rebellion against him, however, but selected Abraham and his family as the means through which he would eventually bless all nations by reconciling them to himself (Rom. 4:13, 17; Gal. 3:8). God promised Abraham that he would bless all the nations of the earth through his family. The patriarch believed this promise, despite his own childlessness and the apparent impossibility that it could be fulfilled (Rom. 4:18–22; Gal. 3:6, 8, 17). As a result, God placed Abraham into a right relationship with himself (Rom. 4:3, 22; Gal. 3:6).

Abraham's descendants, however, did not keep faith with God. God gave them a law through the mediation of Moses to instruct them in knowledge and truth and to enable them to instruct others (Rom. 2:17–20). The law stipulated that if God's people Israel obeyed all that the law required, they would live, whereas if they disobeyed the law, they would die and go into exile. But as soon as they received the law they sinned against it—the command, "You shall not covet," for example, only produced in them all manner of coveting (Rom. 7:7–8; cf. 5:20; Gal. 3:19, 22–24). The result was the outpouring of God's wrath, which, in accord with the curses of the Mosaic law, meant exile and death (Rom. 2:24; 4:15; 5:20–21; 7:7–25; 1 Cor. 15:56).

At this extraordinarily bleak moment in history God sent his Son, the Messiah, to "redeem" his people from the law's curse (Rom. 3:24; 5:6, 20; Gal. 3:13; 3:19, 23; 4:4–5). Christ put this redemption into effect through his death on the cross, which was the climactic and final sacrifice of atonement for sin (Rom. 3:25; cf. 2 Cor. 3:6). It also instituted the "new covenant" that Jeremiah had said God would make with his people to rescue them from their sin (1 Cor. 11:25). God graciously and freely acquits everyone who believes this good news of wrongdoing (Rom. 3:22–24). Justification, in other words, comes solely by faith and as a result of God's grace.

This means that it is available on the same terms to Gentiles as well as Jews and that through assembling a new people—the church of God—whose boundaries are not delimited by the possession of the Jewish law but only by faith in Christ and the sanctifying work of God's eschatologically given Spirit, God is able to begin fulfilling his promise to Abraham. All the nations of the earth are being blessed through him as they imitate his faith and believe "the God who gives life to the dead and calls things that are not as though they were" (Rom. 4:17).

Through the death and resurrection of Christ, God is not merely fulfilling his promise to Abraham but he is also beginning to restore all creation to fellowship with himself. Adam disobeyed God's command and brought sin and death to everyone after him; but Christ was obedient to the point of death and so brought many into righteousness and life (Rom. 5:15, 17–19; 1 Cor. 15:22; Phil. 2:8). Those whom God has saved by his gracious initiative in Christ are the beginning of his "new creation"—they are his "handiwork," "created" by him (Gal. 6:15; 2 Cor. 5:17; Eph. 2:10). They are the beginning of a new humanity, neither divided from one another by socially driven hostility, nor divided from God by God's justified hostility against their sin (Rom. 8:21–22).

Eventually, after the full number of Gentiles has embraced the gospel and entered God's people, a large number of Jews will join their ranks, and God will fulfill the prophecy of Jeremiah that he would take away the sins of his people Israel by establishing a new covenant with them (Rom. 11:25–27). When this plan is complete, God's creation will be liberated from its "bondage to decay" and its "groaning" under the consequences of sin (Rom. 8:21–22). Instead, all things in heaven and on earth will be united under the headship of Christ (Eph. 1:10).

In the end his people, drawn from both Jews and Gentiles, will "with one mind and voice glorify the God and Father of our Lord Jesus Christ" (Rom. 15:6). God's purposes in creation will then be fulfilled. A creation united under the headship of Christ will finally give to God the glory that Adam, and everyone after him, failed to give, and God "will be all in all" (1 Cor. 15:28).

The Sinful Character of Humanity

Essential to this understanding of God's purposes in history is the notion that all people are helplessly mired in sin. Adam's sin infected all of humanity, with the result that everyone after Adam is born into a state of spiritual death and sin (Rom. 5:12–14, 17; Eph. 2:1, 3). Paul believes that, other than Christ ("who had no sin"), there are no exceptions to this common human plight (2 Cor. 5:21). All people sin as Adam sinned, and all are born into the state of spiritual death that Adam initiated when he sinned (Rom. 5:12; 1 Cor. 15:22). Because of Adam's sin, "'There is no one righteous, not even one . . . no one who does good, not even one'" (Rom. 3:10, 12).[87]

87 Verse 10 paraphrases Ps. 14:1 and 3, and verse 12 quotes them exactly (from the LXX).

This means that no one can claim exemption from God's judgment on the basis of his or her own good works, ethnic or national affiliation, family ties, or social standing (Rom. 3:9–20; 1 Cor. 1:26–29; Gal. 2:15–16; 3:10–12; Eph. 2:8–9; Titus 3:5). "There is no difference," says Paul, "for all have sinned and fall short of the glory of God" (Rom. 3:22–23). Gentiles are "dead in [their] transgressions and sins," and Jews, such as the pre-Christian Paul, are "also . . . gratifying the cravings of [their] sinful nature and following its desires and thoughts" (Eph. 2:1, 3). Jews are "like the rest . . . by nature objects of wrath" (Eph. 2:3; cf. Rom. 1:18–3:20). Without God's Spirit, Paul—and everyone else—is "sold under sin," and "nothing good lives in [him]" (Rom. 7:14, 18).

God has therefore justly pronounced a sentence of condemnation on Adam and everyone who lives after him (Rom. 5:16–17). He had already started punishing his sinful creatures by handing them over to the consequences of their sin (Rom. 1:18, 24, 26, 28; 5:16–17; Eph. 1:3). Still, a final "day of wrath" looms on the horizon, and on this Day God, through Jesus Christ, will execute the full measure of his punishing wrath against the disobedient (Rom. 2:5, 8; 5:9; 9:22; 1 Thess. 1:10; 2 Thess. 1:5–10).

The Gracious Character of God

Perhaps the most characteristic element of Paul's understanding of God is God's graciousness to his creatures in their common plight of sin, a plight that, apart from God's intervention, inevitably doomed them to destruction on "the day of God's wrath" (Rom. 2:5). Even in 1 Thessalonians, Paul says that God took the initiative, through his Son, to rescue believers "from the coming wrath," and he affirms that God did this through the death of the Lord Jesus Christ "for us"—a death that will enable believers to live together with Christ at his coming rather than experience the "blazing fire" to be visited on those "who do not know God and do not obey the gospel" (1 Thess. 1:10; 5:10; 2 Thess. 1:7–8).

In Galatians Paul says that to maintain the position that righteousness comes through accepting the law—and therefore by some human initiative—is to "set aside the grace of God" and to fall "away from grace" (Gal. 2:21; 5:4).

In the Corinthian correspondence, God takes the initiative in Christ Jesus to substitute for the human lack of "righteousness, holiness, and redemption" Christ Jesus' own ability to fill these necessary requirements for a restored relationship with God (1 Cor. 1:30). God reconciles the world to himself in Christ by not counting the sins of people against them and instead exchanging human sinfulness for the righteousness of Christ (2 Cor. 5:19, 21). Paul's own experience of God's grace, despite his former persecution of the church of God and his present weakness, provides a personal illustration of this aspect of God's character (1 Cor. 15:10).

In Romans Paul affirms constantly that believers have a right relationship with God because of the atoning death of Christ and that this comes "by his grace as a gift" (Rom. 3:24, NRSV; cf. 4:4; 5:2, 15–17, 20–21; 6:23; 8:32; 11:5–6). God had to take the initiative in rescuing his people from sin and punishment, he says, because they were themselves "powerless" (*asthenōn*) to do anything about their plight (Rom. 5:6).

Paul reaffirms this theme in his later letters. In Ephesians he praises God's glorious, lavish, and freely given grace demonstrated in Christ's atoning death for sinners who were "dead in [their] transgressions and sins" and utterly incapable of doing anything to bring about their own salvation (Eph. 1:6–7; 2:1, 8–9). In the Pastorals, Paul again speaks autobiographically of how God took the initiative in overcoming his "ignorance and unbelief" and by "the grace of our Lord Jesus Christ" appointed him to the service of the gospel (1 Tim. 1:12–14). Here too, salvation is by God's mercy and grace—at his initiative—and does not come in response to any human effort (2 Tim. 1:9; Titus 3:5).

Paul sees God's gracious response to human weakness as not only applicable to entry into the people of God, however, but relevant to the character of the believer's existence within the people of God. Believers, Paul says, "now stand" in God's grace (Rom. 5:2). They exist "under grace" (6:14–15). Although that grace, by definition, cannot be earned, it does not remain passive in those who receive it. If it did that, Paul says, it would be "without effect" (*kenē*). Instead, it empowers its recipients to labor hard in the service of the gospel—to become "God's fellow workers" (1 Cor. 15:10; 2 Cor. 6:1; cf. Eph. 2:8–10; 2 Tim. 2:1). Thus, it empowered the Macedonian churches to give of their meager resources to help the famine-stricken Jewish Christians in Judea, and Paul is hopeful that it will prompt the Corinthians to renew their interest in the collection and to give generously to it also (2 Cor. 8:1–15; 9:13–14). In the same way, Christ apportions "grace" to each believer for the edification of the church, its unity, and its protection from false teaching (Eph. 4:7–16).

Human Sinfulness and God's Grace in Paul's Letters

Paul believes that the solution for many of the problems he addresses in his letters is a clearer understanding of human sinfulness and God's gracious response to it in history through Jesus Christ. A failure to realize the common human sinfulness of both Jews and Gentiles and their common need for justification by faith in Jesus Christ lies beneath the distinctions that Peter, Barnabas, and the people from James made in Antioch and that the Judaizers made in Galatia. Paul counters his opponents in Galatia, therefore, in the same way that he resisted Peter in Antioch, namely, by reminding them that no Jew can keep the law and that both Jew and Gentile enter a right relationship with God on the basis of faith and as a result of God's grace (Gal. 2:15–16, 21; 3:10–14; 5:4).

The Corinthians, similarly, will be more unified if they only understand who they are before God and all that God has done for them in spite of their inabilities. They are foolish, weak, and lowly, but Christ Jesus has become for them wisdom, righteousness, holiness, and redemption (1 Cor. 1:26–31). The creation of distinctions among themselves for the purpose of boasting is inappropriate because all that they possess, they have received from God's hand (1 Cor. 4:7; cf. 11:19).

Paul tackles his opponents in 2 Corinthians in the same way. Their haughty rejection of Paul because he does not meet their standards of rhetorical sophistication and fails to command a powerful presence rests on a misunderstanding of who they are and of how God works. God graciously chooses to accomplish his purposes through "jars of clay" and to perfect his power in weakness (2 Cor. 4:7; 12:7–10).

In Romans too Paul attempts to bring healing to a divided church by reminding both Jews and Gentiles of their common plight of sin and of their common experience of God's grace through their faith in the atoning death of Christ. "Where, then, is boasting?" Paul asks. "It is excluded" (Rom. 3:27).

Later in his career, as Paul faced other problems, he continued to regard the grace of God as a central concept within the expression of the gospel. When faced with an argument that Christ's death was not sufficient to deal with sin on the final day in Colossians, Paul asserted that through Christ's death God had freely forgiven Christians. When faced with discouragement among the predominantly Gentile churches in Asia, Paul reminded them in Ephesians of the crippling effects of their sin and of God's lavish supply of grace in spite of their sin. When faced with an obscure form of gnosticism in the Pastorals, Paul summarized the gospel in terms of human sinfulness and inability, and of God's gracious response to this plight in Christ.

GOD'S GRACE: THE CENTER OF PAUL'S THEOLOGY

If one theological theme is more basic than others in Paul's letters, therefore, it is this notion that God is a gracious God and that he has shown his grace preeminently in his arrangement of history to answer the problem of human sinfulness in the death and resurrection of his Son, Jesus Christ.

This is "the truth of the gospel" that Paul passionately defended against those who threatened it in Jerusalem and Antioch. When false brothers at the Jerusalem council tried to insist that a right relationship with God was defined not only by faith in Christ but by conformity to the Mosaic law, Paul "did not submit to them even for a moment, so that the truth of the gospel might remain intact" (Gal. 2:5, NAB). When Peter, under pressure from Jewish believers from Jerusalem, tried to force Gentile Christians in Antioch to conform to the Mosaic law, Paul told him that he was out of line with "the truth of the gospel" (Gal. 2:14).

The problem in both instances was that by insisting on conformity to the Mosaic law as a means—however partial—of bringing people into a right relationship with God, both the false brothers and Peter had "set aside the grace of God" and implied that "Christ died for nothing" (Gal. 2:21). Here, then, Paul answers for us the question of the "center" of his theology. It is an answer given in the passion of the moment, but as the importance of this concept throughout the Pauline corpus demonstrates, it was an answer that arose from Paul's deepest convictions.

Part Three

THE NON-PAULINE LETTERS AND THE REVELATION OF JOHN

Chapter 23

FINDING UNITY IN THE NON-PAULINE LETTERS AND REVELATION

The New Testament letters that make no claim to Pauline authorship together with the Revelation of John comprise the least tidy part of the New Testament canon.[1] The narrative form of the gospels and Acts bind the first part of the canon together naturally. The common claim to Paul's authorship and an epistolary genre do the same for the thirteen Pauline letters. The nine texts that comprise the rest of the New Testament, by comparison, present the reader with a variety of authorial claims and wide variations on the epistolary genre. Some claim an apostolic author (1 Peter, 2 Peter, and James), some name an author who is not an apostle (Jude and probably Revelation), and some name no author at all (Hebrews and the Johannine letters).

All nine texts certainly have epistolary features, but they often mix these features with other generic characteristics in surprising ways. First Peter, 2 Peter, 2 John, 3 John, and Jude faithfully follow common epistolary conventions. Hebrews, however, has no epistolary introduction and looks more like a homily until its conclusion, where typical epistolary conventions suddenly emerge. James begins with an epistolary salutation but then continues to the end in the form of sage ethical advice or "wisdom paraenesis." First John neither begins nor ends with conventions typical of ancient letters, yet the author frequently speaks of "writing" to his readers as if he is composing a letter to them. Similarly, Revelation has both an epistolary salutation and an epistolary conclusion, but it blends these generic features with apocalyptic and prophetic elements in an unusual way.

In the first editions of the New Testament, the organizational problems that these disparate writings posed were solved by taking the gospels as one unit, placing Acts with the non-Pauline letters after them, putting the Pauline letters (including Hebrews) together as a third unit, and allowing Revelation to stand by itself at the end. The order of the units sometimes varied, as did the order of the texts within each unit, but the four-unit organizational scheme was remarkably stable through the fifth century.[2] This scheme had the merit of using Acts as a historical orientation to the people who had written the letters and of honoring both the peculiar and the eschatological nature of Revelation by putting it in its own category at the end.

1 Cf. Luke Timothy Johnson, *The Writings of the New Testament: An Interpretation*, rev. ed. (Philadelphia: Fortress, 1999), 410.

2 On this, see David Trobisch, *The First Edition of the New Testament* (Oxford: Oxford Univ. Press, 2000), 24–28, who comments that the order of the New Testament canon in modern editions originated with a late Byzantine organizational scheme that Erasmus adopted in his first printed edition of the New Testament Greek text. Printers have adopted this now familiar scheme since his time.

If we want to understand each New Testament writing on its own terms, however, this arrangement has at least three problems. First, it divides Acts from its narrative companion, Luke. Second, it assumes that Hebrews is a Pauline epistle. Third, it ignores the epistolary features of Revelation that bind it, however loosely, to the non-Pauline letters of the canon.

Where, then, should we place these documents in a theological analysis of the New Testament writings? One of the most influential answers to this question in modern times claims that we should think of them together as witnesses to "early catholicism."

"EARLY CATHOLICISM"

The expression "early catholicism" refers to the emergence in the postapostolic church of authoritative structures, clearly defined doctrines, specific ethical teaching, and a canon of sacred writings. Those who use the term to describe a trend in early Christian history usually think of the church of the first two centuries as gradually evolving from a primitive community with a relatively simple belief structure into a complex organization with highly refined teachings and discipline. One of the champions of this conceptual paradigm in modern times, Ernst Käsemann, defined "early catholicism" as "a characteristic movement toward that great Church which understands itself as the *Una Sancta Apostolica*."[3]

The Development of the "Early Catholic" Approach

Ferdinand Christian Baur

This way of understanding early Christian history goes back at least to the early nineteenth-century scholar Ferdinand Christian Baur and his students, who called themselves "the Tübingen School" (after the town and university where Baur taught from 1826 until his death in 1860).[4] Baur was profoundly influenced by Georg Wilhelm Friedrich Hegel's "idealistic" philosophy of history. Hegel believed that history was the unfolding of a series of conflicts (antitheses) between the abstractly conceived Absolute Spirit or "Ideal" Rational Principle and individual expressions of this principle in history. Each antithesis eventually produced a synthesis between the two, which in turn produced further antitheses and further syntheses. The goal of this historical process, Hegel believed, was human freedom.[5]

Although Baur differed from Hegel in important ways, he adopted the basic structure of Hegel's philosophical approach for his description of early Christian history.[6] During its first two centuries, Baur believed, the church was engaged in an all-consuming

3 Ernst Käsemann, *New Testament Questions of Today* (Philadelphia: Fortress, 1969), 237.

4 On the history of the "early catholic" paradigm, see esp. François Vouga, *Geschichte des frühen Christentums* (Tübingen: Francke Verlag, 1994), 236–39; on Baur, see Horton Harris, *The Tübingen School: A Historical and Theological Investigation of the School of F. C. Baur*, rev. ed. (Grand Rapids: Baker, 1990), 11–54.

5 See, e.g., Hegel's *Philosophy of History* (New York: Dover, 1956), 22–29, particularly his helpful analogy between the forces of history and the construction of a house (27). This book is a translation of a compilation of student lecture notes on Hegel's course on the philosophy of history at the University of Berlin in the winter term of 1830–1831, shortly before his death in November of 1831.

6 On this, William Baird, *History of New Testament Research*, 3 vols. (Minneapolis: Fortress, 1992–), 1:269, says, "Had Baur been an uncritical devotee of Hegel, he would have affirmed the synthesis of the Jewish thesis and the Pauline antithesis in the

struggle between two tendencies. On one side stood Paulinism with its emphasis on justification by faith, its focus on the Spirit, and its universal appeal. On the other side stood Jewish Christianity, embodied in the apostle Peter, with its emphasis on the necessity of keeping the Mosaic law and its "Jewish particularism."[7] By the time of Irenaeus in the late second century, the catholic church had emerged from the struggle between these two great forces and represented a compromise or synthesis between them.[8]

Having plotted the course of early Christian history in this way, Baur then assigned each New Testament writing an appropriate place on the resulting trajectory. Only four New Testament letters and Revelation were authentic apostolic documents because only they gave clear evidence of the antithesis between Paul and the "older apostles." The four letters were all from Paul (Romans, 1 Corinthians, 2 Corinthians, and Galatians), and Revelation came from the apostle John.[9] To the rest of the New Testament he assigned a mediating tendency, which meant that the composition of these documents often had to be pushed into the postapostolic period. Most of them had to fall in the second century when this tendency began to take hold.[10]

Other than Revelation, Bauer saw the nine texts that conclude the modern New Testament canon as products of the postapostolic age and as evidence of the move toward the catholic synthesis of earliest Christianity's two conflicting impulses. The author of Hebrews, for example, wanted his readers to understand his work within the context of Pauline Christianity, as his reference to Timothy at the conclusion of the work shows (Heb. 13:23). Hebrews also reveals a universal tendency in which everything that comes before Christ is merely a shadow and preparation for Christ, who transcends all previous religious movements. The Jewish tendency in the letter, however, is equally clear in the author's concern at the surface level with Judaism alone as the preparation for Christ.[11]

The letter of James, which Baur considered pseudonymous, is not a simple polemical tractate against Paul's teaching on justification by faith. Its author instead wants to blend a Jewish Christian interest in practical morality with the valuable insights of Paulinism. Like Paul, therefore, he emphasizes inward concerns and liberty, but does this in a distinctively Jewish Christian way—speaking, for example, of "the perfect law that gives freedom" (James 1:25) and of "the word planted in you" (1:21).[12]

First Peter, similarly, is an attempt to bring Jewish Christianity (embodied in the reference to Peter in 1 Peter 1:1) and Pauline Christianity (embodied in the reference to Paul's companion Silvanus/Silas in 5:12) together. Here too, the author combines distinctively Pauline ideas (e.g., on the death of Christ) with a distinctively Jewish Christian concern for practical morality.[13]

---

accommodation of the second century. In actuality, Baur's own theological sympathies are solidly on the side of Paul."

7 F. C. Baur, *The Church History of the First Three Centuries*, 2 vols. (London: Williams and Norgate, 1878–79; orig. German ed., 1853), 1:44–76. For the phrase "Jewish particularism," see p. 54.

8 Ibid., 1:76–114, 148–49.

9 Ibid., 1:53–74, 84–87. Cf. F. C. Baur, *Paul, the Apostle of Jesus Christ*, 2 vols. (London: Williams and Norgate, 1875; orig. German ed., 1845), 1:245–49. Baur found a polemic against Paul in John's reference to those who said they were apostles but were not in Rev. 2:2, in John's opposition to eating meat offered to idols in Rev. 2:14–20, and in his omission of Paul from the number of the apostles in Rev. 21:14.

10 See the helpful chart of Baur's conclusions on the date and tendency of each New Testament book in Harris, *Tübingen School*, 237.

11 Baur, *Church History*, 1:114–21.

12 Ibid., 1:128–30.

13 Ibid., 1:131, 150–51.

In 2 Peter, the process of reconciliation between Pauline and Petrine Christianity reaches a climax. Here the author makes the apostle Peter embrace the apostle Paul as a brother, rebukes Paul's nay-sayers as misinterpreters of his letters, and describes Paul's letters as canonical Scripture.[14]

Each of these late canonical documents, therefore, bears witness to a time in the late first and early second century when Pauline Christianity and Jewish Christianity were merging into the synthesis that soon became "catholic" Christianity. In this synthesis, elements of order and discipline borrowed from Judaism tempered the spiritual impulses of Pauline Christianity toward human freedom.

The "Early Catholic" Approach at the Turn of the Nineteenth Century

Although the details of Baur's understanding of early Christian history never gained a foothold outside the "Tübingen School," the basic structure of the approach endured.[15] It reappears, for example, at the end of the nineteenth century in Heinrich Julius Holtzmann's widely used *Textbook on New Testament Theology*, originally published between 1896 and 1897. This book is the fruit of Holtzmann's research and teaching at the University of Strassburg from 1874 until the time of its publication.[16] As Christianity evolved into "the old Catholic church," said Holtzmann, it became more legalistic and concerned with the basis for church authority, both apostolic and canonical. It also began to develop both a structure and confessional statements in response to the reality that the world, contrary to initial Christian expectations, might not end any time soon. The books of 1 John, James, 1 Peter, Jude, 2 Peter, and Revelation were part of this development.[17]

The basic approach appears again at the turn of the century in Adolf von Harnack's popular book on "the essence of Christianity," published in 1900 and based on a series of lectures he gave in Berlin in the winter term of 1899–1900.[18] Seventy-seven thousand copies of this book were in print in fourteen languages at the time of its fiftieth anniversary edition.[19] Here Harnack maintains that by the end of the second century, Christianity had evolved from a series of communities with a living faith, a fervent hope in the coming of God's kingdom, a concern with the Spirit, an experience of the miraculous, and a commitment to fervent prayer into an institution comprised of interconnected congregations with a homogenous organizational structure, a "law of doctrine," and a liturgy.[20]

Gone from Harnack's analysis is Baur's Hegelianism—there is no inevitable movement from conflict between two antithetical principles to a synthesis that

14 Ibid., 1:150.

15 For the development of Baur's basic approach among his students, see the work of Baur's student and friend Albert Schwegler, *Das nachapostolische Zeitalter in den Hauptmomenten seiner Entwicklung*, 2 vols. (Tübingen: Ludwig Friedrich Fues, 1846), summarized in Harris, *Tübingen School*, 198–207.

16 Heinrich J. Holtzmann, *Lehrbuch der neutestamentlichen Theologie*, ed. by A. Jülicher and W. Bauer, 2 vols. (Tübingen: J. C. B. Mohr [Paul Siebeck], 1911; orig. German ed. 1896–97).

17 Ibid., 1:562–80.

18 Adolf von Harnack, *Das Wesen des Christentums: Sechzehn Vorlesungen vor Studierenden aller Facultäten im Wintersemester 1899/1900 an der Universität Berlin* (Leipzig: Hinrichs, 1900).

19 See Adolf von Harnack, *Das Wesen des Christentums: Neuauflage zum fünfzigsten Jahrestag des ersten Erscheinens mit einem Geleitwort von Rudolf Bultmann* (Stuttgart: Ehrenfried Klotz Verlag, 1950), iv. The book's English title is *What Is Christianity?* References below are to the English edition published in Gloucester, Mass. by Peter Smith in 1978.

20 Adolf von Harnack, *What Is Christianity?* 192–93.

incorporates both. Harnack is instead interested, among other things, in the sociological principle that Spirit-led communities inevitably give way to structured communities. Still, Baur's conviction about the institutionalization of Christianity lives on—that Christian history proceeded from a period of spiritual freedom, embodied in Paul, to a period in which this freedom was domesticated by the moral and political concerns of the developing church. Just as with Baur and Holtzmann, Harnack believed all of this represented "the Christian religion in its development toward Catholicism."[21]

A few years later, Ernst Troeltsch followed the same path in his treatise on *The Social Teaching of the Christian Churches*.[22] He claimed that the second major development of Christianity after Paul occurred when the church created a set tradition, the office of bishop, and a regular clergy charged with administering the sacrament of the Lord's Supper.[23] All this came in response to the need to tame the excesses of enthusiasm prompted by the feeling that the Spirit of the exalted Christ was present in the midst of the Christian community. Troeltsch called this development "early Catholicism."[24]

Rudolf Bultmann

This approach received a detailed exposition in Rudolf Bultmann's enormously influential *Theology of the New Testament*, published between 1948 and 1951.[25] Just as idealistic philosophy formed the fulcrum from which Baur's description of early Christian history gained its leverage, and just as sociological concerns were important to Harnack and Troeltsch, so Bultmann's description of the "early catholic" phase of Christian history hinged on his understanding of early Christian eschatology.

The development of church structure and church law, said Bultmann, came with the waning expectation within the church that the end of the world would come soon. As the eschatological fervor of the earliest Christians died out with the passing of time, Christians began to worry about the maintenance of the church within the ongoing world. This not only meant the institutionalization of the church but a transformation in the church's self-understanding. It now conceived of itself not as the eschatological people of God, separated from the world and awaiting God's imminent eschatological intervention, but as an institution that mediates salvation to a bourgeois people continuing to live and function within the world.[26]

In the same way, as time passed, Christians developed a "special knowledge" beyond the self-knowledge that the eschatologically driven decision of faith provided to the believer. Although the seeds of concern with this special knowledge were already present in Paul's time and in Corinth were even highly developed, the desire

21 Harnack, *Das Wesen des Christentums* (1950 ed.), 113; cf. Baur, *Church History*, 1:112–13.

22 Ernst Troeltsch, *The Social Teaching of the Christian Churches*, 2 vols. (Chicago: Univ. of Chicago Press, 1981; orig. German ed. 1911). Much of the material for this study appeared in piecemeal form in the *Archiv für Socialwissenschaften und Sozialpolitik* between 1908 and 1910. On this see the "Introduction" by H. Richard Niebuhr to the University of Chicago Press translation, p. 8.

23 Ibid., 1:91–92; cf. Harnack, *What Is Christianity?*, 191–92.

24 Troeltsch, *The Social Teaching*, 1:91.

25 Rudolf Bultmann, *Theology of the New Testament*, 2 vols. (New York: Charles Scribner's Sons, 1951–55; orig. German ed. 1948–51), 2:95–236

26 Ibid., 2:111–18.

for knowledge that went beyond faith intensified as the decades passed and led to the perversion of the Christian proclamation. This perversion, in turn, produced strategies among the orthodox for keeping intact "the faith that was once for all entrusted to the saints" (Jude 3).[27]

The last nine documents of the modern New Testament canon fit neatly into this development. The earliest Christians, says Bultmann, had lived in a period of eschatological tension between God's decisive act of sweeping the past away in Christ Jesus and the imminent consummation of God's purposes in the future. This led them to live in faith in the present, refusing to place their security in anything but God.[28] As the imminent expectation of the consummation of God's purposes began to fade, however, this eschatological tension grew slack, and in its place, legalism began to develop.

Revelation falls into this pattern. This text looks back to the apostles as the founders of the church, and although it certainly looks forward to the final Day, it is interested more in what that Day holds for the individual rather than, as with the earliest expectation, the completion of God's purposes in history and the transformation of the universe.[29]

Hebrews is so far from the primitive eschatology that it makes following the Christian way of life a necessary condition for the achievement of salvation in the future.[30] The same is true of James, 2 Peter, and Jude, all three of which have lost the early Christian sense of "betweenness" and in its place have put a doctrine of self-effort, whereby salvation on the final Day is guaranteed to the individual who has, after baptism, maintained a pure life.[31]

As it settled down in the world and adopted this legalistic frame of reference, Bultmann believed, the Christianity of these late New Testament documents absorbed a bourgeois morality derived from Judaism (James) or from Greco-Roman philosophy (1 Peter).[32] With this development, he says, "the Church is on the way to straying into a religious moralism."[33]

Since many Christians during this period were interested in esoteric knowledge, the latest books of the New Testament also struggle against gnosticizing tendencies. The author of 1 John tries to make clear to his readers what it means to know God in response to gnostic false teaching (1 John 2:3–6). The author of Revelation resists those who boast that they know "the deep things of Satan" (Rev. 2:24). Second Peter and Jude attempt to defeat gnostic opponents not by engaging their arguments intellectually but by accusing them of immorality.[34]

The meaning of the word "faith" now shifts from a life-changing decision based on a personal encounter with the proclaimed word to a set body of doctrines regarded by church authorities to be correct teaching. It is now "the faith" that has been entrusted once for all to the saints (Jude 3), and "faith as precious as ours," which orthodox Christians share with one another but not with heretics (2 Peter 1:1).[35]

27 Ibid., 2:127–42.

28 Bultmann explains Paul's understanding of "existence in faith" in ibid., 1:322.

29 Ibid., 2:105–6, 112.

30 Ibid., 2:113, 166–68.

31 Ibid., 2:161–69, 212.

32 Ibid., 2:163, 182, 213, 225–27.

33 Ibid., 2:215.

34 Ibid., 2:132–33.

35 Ibid., 2:136, 211.

These circumstances explain why the authors of these later texts begin to use words with the "pseudo–" prefix, such as "pseudo-prophets" and "pseudo-teachers" (1 John 4:1; 2 Peter 2:1). A concern develops for the orthodox interpretation of Christianity's sacred writings, whether the Old Testament (2 Peter 1:20–21) or the developing New Testament canon (James 2:14–26; 2 Peter 3:16).[36] A similar concern develops to trace orthodox doctrine back to the original apostles and through them to Jesus himself (Jude 17; 2 Peter 3:2).[37]

The Continuity between Baur and His Successors

The basic similarity between this approach and that of Baur appears clearly in the use to which Bultmann's student Ernst Käsemann put this understanding of early Christian history. Reflecting on the concept of "early Catholicism," Käsemann writes this:

> Ever since the eschatological understanding of the New Testament replaced the idealistic interpretation, we can and must determine the various phases of earliest Christian history by means of the original imminent expectation of the parousia, its modifications and its final extinction. Early catholicism means that transition from earliest Christianity to the so-called ancient Church, which is completed with the disappearance of the imminent expectation.[38]

Käsemann suggests here that the idealistic notion, derived ultimately from Hegel, that Christian history moves forward by means of a series of conflicts and syntheses was replaced in his own time with the notion that Christian history moved in stages from a period of fervent eschatological expectation to a period of bourgeois accommodation to the on-going world. That is certainly an important difference between the Tübingen School and more recent historians of early Christianity.[39]

Käsemann's comment also implies, however, an important similarity between Baur's reading of early Christian history and more recent readings, such as those of Käsemann's teacher, Bultmann. He tells us that under the new eschatological paradigm, Christianity moves forward in a neat sequence from one developmental phase to the next; the fervent eschatological expectation of the earliest community gives way to a period when this expectation undergoes modification, and this in turn yields to a period in which the fervent expectation disappears.

The reason for the increased institutionalization of Christianity is different in the Tübingen historical trajectory from that in the Bultmann–Käsemann trajectory, but the notion of a neat evolution of the church from simple, "enthusiastic" communities into structured organizations is the same in both schemes. For Käsemann, as for many other early Christian historians from Baur to Bultmann, the authentic Pauline letters reveal the first phase of this development whereas Luke–Acts, Ephesians, the Pastorals, and the final third of the New Testament canon reveal its second phase.

36 Ibid., 2:131–32.

37 Ibid., 2:138.

38 Käsemann, *New Testament Questions*, 237.

39 Harnack, *What Is Christianity?* 193, and Holtzmann, *Neutestamentlichen Theologie*, 1:562, 578, also comment on the delay of the Parousia as an impetus in the development of the early catholic church.

Weaknesses and Strengths of the "Early Catholic" Paradigm

This influential way of understanding early Christian history is riddled with weaknesses, as a wide range of scholars in more recent years has realized.[40] At the same time, it has produced undeniable insights into the nature of early Christianity. Three aspects of the method show both its value and its limitations.

First, the early proponents of this perspective were aware of the unavoidability and importance of *theological presuppositions* in the task of reconstructing early Christian history. The scholars who advocated the "early catholic" paradigm were often explicit about the philosophical and theological commitments that drove them to see early Christianity in the way they described it.[41] The investigation of early Christian history was for them not merely a descriptive exercise but an effort to discover God at work in early Christianity. They recognized that from the beginning their concept of God and his relationship to the world would determine the way they went about their work, whether, as with Baur, they viewed God as the Absolute Spirit that advanced its purposes through conflict, synthesis, and human reflection on this process, or, as with Bultmann, Harnack, and Käsemann, they understood themselves as Protestants attempting to interpret Luther's great insight of justification by faith in critical but appreciative ways for the modern world.

Not surprisingly, however, these philosophical and theological presuppositions sometimes distorted their historical analyses. Advocates of the "early catholic" paradigm, for example, tended to correlate the emphases of the early catholic period of Christian history with the emphases of Judaism or with Jewish Christianity. This correlation was not plausible historically but fit an underlying notion of the way history should have happened. For Baur, the early catholic church found the building blocks for its institutions "ready to her hand" in Judaism.[42] For Harnack, Marcion looked at the church around him in the mid-second century and "perceived with distress" that "everything had been crystallized in legalistic forms"—that "Christianity had once again become a version of Judaism."[43] For Bultmann, James is so moralistic that he may have taken "over a Jewish document and only lightly retouched it."[44] Revelation, similarly, represents "a weakly Christianized Judaism" in which Christian existence is deprived of the eschatological tension that Paul gave to it and is reduced to waiting for the end, as in the Jewish apocalypses.[45]

40 See the criticisms of, e.g., Martin Hengel, *Acts and the History of Earliest Christianity* (London: SCM, 1979), 121–22; Vouga, *Geschichte*, 455–56, 495; and Richard J. Bauckham, *Jude, 2 Peter* (WBC 50; Waco, Tex.: Word, 1983), 8.

41 See, e.g., Ferdinand Christian Baur, *Die ignatianischen Briefe und ihr neuester Kritiker* (Tübingen: Ludwig Friedrich Fues, 1848), 119–20, quoted and discussed in Harris, *Tübingen School*, 158–59, and Harnack, *What Is Christianity?* 282–301. See also Bultmann, "Is Exegesis without Presuppositions Possible?" in *Existence and Faith: Shorter Writings of Rudolf Bultmann*, ed. Schubert M. Ogden (Cleveland: World Publishing, 1960), 289–96, and his own comments on Baur in *Theology*, 2:244–45. Käsemann is everywhere aware of his Protestant pre-suppositions, as, for example, in the closing comments of his essays "Paul and Early Catholicism" and "An Apologia for Primitive Christian Eschatology" (see *New Testament Questions*, 250–51, and *Essays on New Testament Themes* [Philadelphia: Fortress, 1982], 194–95). Troeltsch is the clear exception. He seems to have imagined that he evaluated the history of the Christian church without presuppositions. See his 1898 essay on "Historical and Dogmatic Method in Theology," in *Religion in History* (Edinburgh: T. & T. Clark, 1991), 11–32.

42 Baur, *Church History*, 1:112. Cf. Holtzmann, *Neutestamentlichen Theologie*, 1:564.

43 Adolf von Harnack, *Marcion: The Gospel of the Alien God* (Durham, N.C.: Labyrinth, 1990; orig. German ed., 1922), 128.

44 Bultmann, *New Testament Theology*, 2:163.

45 Ibid., 2:175.

It is difficult not to see at work here peculiarly German Protestant presuppositions. Paul, it is supposed, appeared within a particularistic, works-oriented Judaism, supplied an incisive critique of Judaism, and developed his own liberating and universalizing refinement of it. In the development of the church, however, Paul's insight soon became clouded with more pedestrian notions of institutional survival, and the church lapsed back into a "Jewish" concern with practical morality and institutional boundaries. Paul's insight remained lost to the church only to be rediscovered periodically prior to Luther by, for example, John (Bultmann) and Marcion (Harnack).[46] The question here is not whether Baur and Bultmann were correct to analyze early Christian history on the basis of their philosophical and theological presuppositions, but the extent to which their presuppositions were philosophically and theologically correct, and the extent to which they refused to revise their presuppositions when the historical evidence made it necessary to do so.

Second, Baur's conviction that early Christianity was marked by conflict between distinct theological tendencies, although driven by his Hegelian presuppositions, is surely correct historically and helps to explain the character of several of the letters that we study in the following chapters. One need look no further than the tension latent in Paul's comment that the Jerusalem apostles are "those who seemed to be important" (Gal. 2:6), his irritation at the "people from James" in 2:12, or the Corinthian division into groups loyal to Paul, Apollos, and Cephas in 1 Corinthians 1:12 (cf. 3:4, 22) to see that early Christian leaders did not always agree. The different concerns and emphases of the various leaders within the early Christian movement—Paul, James, Jude, Peter, John, and others—may have eventually produced theological disputes within early Christianity, and Baur's emphasis on conflict in the early church brings this out clearly.

It is equally clear from the relevant texts, however, that the tensions between these early Christian leaders were not, as Baur thought, fundamentally theological. Baur's map of early Christian history had two poles, a Jewish Christian party that was particularistic and devoted to the law and a Pauline Christian party that was universalistic and devoted to freedom. The two parties represented two gospels—two antithetical principles at loggerheads with each other. When Paul met with the pillar apostles in Jerusalem, Baur believed, they parted company as theological enemies to preach two different gospels, one for the circumcised and one for the uncircumcised.[47]

Despite the continuing popularity of this model of basic theological conflict between Jewish and Pauline Christianity, it is not a probable reading of the relevant texts.[48] Paul and the Jerusalem apostles parted company after agreeing that they preached the same gospel and after agreeing on a strategy by which they might most

46 See Bultmann, *New Testament Theology*, 2:3–14, 70–92; Harnack, *Marcion*, 131, 139. Harnack also believed that John, like Paul, Marcion, and Luther, had rejected Jewish legalism and emphasized freedom.

47 Baur, *Church History*, 1:53–54.

48 See, e.g., Gerd Luedemann, *Opposition to Paul in Jewish Christianity* (Minneapolis: Fortress, 1989), 35–115; Michael Goulder, *St. Paul versus St. Peter: A Tale of Two Missions* (Louisville: Westminster John Knox, 1994); Bart Ehrman, *Lost Christianities: The Battles for Scripture and the Faiths We Never Knew* (New York: Oxford Univ. Press, 2003), 172.

effectively spread the gospel to both Jews and Gentiles (Gal. 2:9). This does not mean that James had no particularly Jewish Christian interests that he wanted to protect, or that Paul's Gentile mission presented James with no complications. As we will see in the next chapter, Acts 21:17–26 reveals the kind of difficulty Paul's mission presented for James and the Jerusalem church. That passage also reveals, however, that Paul and James had no fundamental theological differences (cf. Gal. 2:1–10). The "brotherly handshake" between Peter and Paul that Baur's student Albert Schwegler believed only took place in 2 Peter, and therefore in the second century, actually happened prior to the composition of what, on Baur's reckoning, is the earliest extant Christian document—Galatians.[49]

Third, the conviction that runs through the "early catholic" paradigm from Baur to Käsemann that Christianity developed from a period of conflict to a period of synthesis or from a period of spiritual enthusiasm and freedom to a period of structure, creed, and discipline is correct in general terms. Since the work of the sociologist Max Weber (1864–1920), it has seemed natural to think of movements that begin with charismatic leaders eventually developing structures and doctrines—"routinization," as Weber called it.[50] The history of the Christian movement follows this same general pattern in that the further the church is removed from Jesus chronologically, generally speaking, the more complex its institutions and the more refined its doctrines.[51]

Whatever the general trend may be, however, the evidence of early Christian texts does not reveal that a simple correlation exists between the structural or doctrinal complexity in an early Christian text and its relative date.[52] In what is perhaps the earliest Christian text (1 Thessalonians), Paul already counsels his readers to hold in high esteem those who "lead" (*proïstamai*) the congregation. He uses a term that also appears in connection with elders who "lead" the church (*hoi kalōs proestōtes presbyteroi*) in the supposedly pseudonymous and "early catholic" Pastoral Letters (see 1 Thess. 5:12–13; 1 Tim. 5:17). In Galatians he advises his readers that "anyone who receives instruction in the word must share all good things with his instructor" (Gal. 6:6). Such a comment presupposes both paid teachers and a set body of instruction that they communicate.

Much the same can be said about the supposed development from an eager expectation for the end of the world in early Christian communities to the development

49 Schwegler, *Nachapostolische Zeitalter*, 1:490: "The keystone of the Ebionite line of development is the second epistle of Peter. In this letter the two opposing viewpoints celebrate their peace-treaty and the two apostles, Peter and Paul, the names formerly the rallying-call of the two contending parties, give each other a brotherly handshake [*den brüderlichen Händedruck*]. Ebionism has now attained the standpoint of catholicity." The translation is from Harris, *Tübingen School*, 203. For Baur's dating of Galatians, see *Paul*, 1:256–57.

50 See S. N. Eisenstadt, ed., *Max Weber on Charisma and Institution Building: Selected Papers* (The Heritage of Sociology Series; Chicago: Univ. of Chicago Press, 1968), 54–61. Weber had a significant influence on his friend Ernst Troeltsch. On this see Niebuhr, "Introduction," 10–11.

51 Weber applies his idea to religious communities in *The Sociology of Religion* (Boston: Beacon, 1963; orig. German ed. 1922), 60–79.

52 Weber recognized that routinization often begins during the lifetime of the charismatic leader. See his comments on "The Nature of Charismatic Authority and Its Routinization," in *Max Weber on Charisma and Institution Building*, 54. Vouga, *Geschichte*, 241–42, points out that "early catholic" features also cannot be used to distinguish between orthodox and heretical writings since some of the Nag Hammadi documents also have "early catholic" features.

of a bourgeois ethic as this expectation faded. Such a development surely happened in some quarters in early Christianity, but the notion that it evolved slowly over decades and that it happened at much the same pace everywhere is, with equal certainty, mistaken.

Again, 1 Thessalonians is instructive. Here the entire development is visible within a few months. Eschatological expectation among the Thessalonians was at a fever pitch, as their distress at the death of community members prior to the coming of the Lord reveals (1 Thess. 4:13–18). Paul responds with a reminder that the Lord's coming will be like a thief in the night (5:2)—at any time, not necessarily when we want it to happen—and that in the meantime the Thessalonian Christians need to pursue a "bourgeois" ethic of minding their own affairs and working with their hands (4:11–12).

When we find a concern in Jude and 2 Peter that false prophets and teachers are resisting established authority (2 Peter 2:1, 10; Jude 8) or threatening "the faith that was once for all entrusted to the saints" (Jude 3; cf. 2 Peter 2:1–3, 15), or when we discover in James and 1 Peter a concern to give guidance on how Christians should live in the world, we should not assume that these documents come from a postapostolic age—a time late enough for such concerns to develop. For the same reason, we should not be surprised to find in James, Jude, 1 Peter, 2 Peter, 1 John, and Revelation the continuing conviction that Christ could appear at any time.

Moreover, 2 Peter, which both Baur and Käsemann believed to be "one of the latest books of the canon," maintains not only that ages could pass before the day of the Lord (2 Peter 3:8) but, like 1 Thessalonians, that "the day of the Lord will come like a thief" (2 Peter 3:10; cf. 1 Thess. 5:2). Earliest Christianity was a complex and diverse movement, and therefore analyzing its history on the basis of a smooth developmental scheme that runs from the simple to the complex is not likely to yield accurate results.[53]

Despite its occasional insights, the "early catholic" understanding of the non-narrative, non-Pauline parts of the New Testament fails as a unifying historical framework for these nine texts. The philosophical presuppositions that undergird it have driven its advocates to implausible readings of these texts—readings that exaggerate the conflict between the texts and Pauline Christianity, and readings that impose on these nine documents an unlikely correlation between concern with order and chronological lateness.

PERSECUTION AND HERESY

It is possible that the failure of the "early catholic" paradigm for understanding the last third of the modern New Testament canon should serve as a warning that any organizational scheme for these texts is inappropriate. Apart from the obvious groups such as the Johannine letters and the Petrine letters and Jude, perhaps these texts

53 Cf. Johnson, *Writings*, 455–56.

should be left to testify, each in its own way, to the wide variety of early Christian religious and social experiences. It may be appropriate, following Luke Timothy Johnson, simply to treat at least the non-Johannine texts in this part of the canon under the broad rubric "Other Canonical Witnesses."[54]

Although we should be careful not to burden these nine texts with unifying schemes that they will not bear, they do seem to fall into two broad categories defined by the primary problems they address. The first of these categories echoes a major emphasis of the "early catholic" approach. Six of these nine texts address problems of doctrinal deviation from two main theological streams in early Christianity: the Pauline tradition and the Johannine tradition. The authors of James, Jude, and 2 Peter all seem to have been aware that some Christians who rallied around Paul's name had taken the apostle's teaching on justification by faith apart from works of the law and on the centrality of God's grace in decidedly heretical directions. Each of them probably targeted a form of Christian teaching that excused and even advocated immoral behavior on theological grounds, and this foundation, they may have believed, was laid by Paul.

The ties the authors of these texts have with the Jerusalem church are not accidental. That church was understandably concerned with the ethical consequences that the influx of Gentiles, as a result of the Pauline mission, would have on the eschatological people of God.

As we have already said, however, and as we will see in the chapters that follow, this does not mean that these texts arise from "anti-Paulinism." Paul did not fight against himself when he charged with slander those who perverted his teaching to mean that we should "do evil that good may result" (Rom. 3:8). The appearance of a perversion of Pauline teaching already in Paul's own lifetime also shows that the correction of similar perversions in James, Jude, and 2 Peter need not push the date of these compositions into the postapostolic era.

In a similar way, the three Johannine letters all arise from a situation in which a group within Johannine Christianity has "progressed" beyond the teaching of the gospel on the identity of Jesus and the necessity of his death. Here too, this deviation from orthodoxy has produced ethical consequences.

Second, three of the nine texts that we will study next are concerned primarily with the Christian response to persecution. As we have already seen in the preceding chapters on Paul and as we will see in the chapters that follow, the marginalization of early Christians in Greco-Roman society was motivated to a large extent by the popular notion that Christians had rejected the moral framework that held society together. Because they seemed untethered from both Judaism on one hand and traditional pagan religions on the other, it was easy for unbelievers to imagine that Christians were a threat to social stability. Matters became even more complicated when Christians failed to live up to the moral standards that their traditions advocated, or when they seemed to justify socially offensive behavior theologically.

54 Ibid.

In this situation, the argument of 1 Peter, Hebrews, and Revelation that Christians should persevere in their faith despite the hardship they are enduring takes on an understandably moral character. The final Day will not merely be a time when God brings the oppressors of Christians to justice but also a day on which he will call on his people to account for their own conduct.

In the chapters that follow we will examine each of these nine texts as compositions that address the themes of heresy and persecution. As we do so, however, we will also try to honor the untidy nature of the final third of the New Testament canon.

Chapter 24

JAMES: THE WISDOM OF THE UNDIVIDED LIFE

The letter of James has puzzled students of the New Testament for centuries. At the level of its form and genre, interpreters have wondered why it begins as if it were a letter but, following this introduction, contains no other epistolary characteristics. They have also wondered why the author seems to follow no clearly discernable plan or argument, sometimes jumping from topic to topic for no apparent reason and sometimes arranging his material by means of catch-word rather than any logical progression of thought.

At the level of content, students of the letter have frequently criticized it for having no theology, for having a shallow theology, or for having a wrong theology. There is no discussion of Christology, nor are there any references to the death of Christ, his resurrection, or God's Spirit.[1] In perhaps the most famous passage in the letter (2:14–26), the author seems to oppose Paul's complex and perceptive theological insight that because of the profound effect of sin on the human plight, justification must come entirely by God's grace.[2] Some scholars believe that James replaces this idea with the unperceptive claim that faith and works can cooperate to produce salvation.

This puzzlement and dissatisfaction with the letter, however, spring from a misunderstanding both of its historical setting and its literary genre. Before examining its theological contribution, therefore, it is necessary to address briefly both of these issues.

THE SETTING AND GENRE OF JAMES

Despite the general nature of its admonitions, a close look at James yields a surprising amount of information about its historical setting. The letter's character meshes well with what we know from other early sources of the role that James, the brother of the Lord, played in the history of the early Jerusalem church.

The letter's introduction identifies its author as "James, a servant of God and of the Lord Jesus Christ" and its addressees as "the twelve tribes in the Diaspora" (1:1). Both the scholars who think the letter is genuine and those who think it is pseudepigraphic agree that of the five people called James in the New Testament, this "James" must be the one who was the Lord's brother and the leader of the Jerusalem

1 James 4:5 probably refers to the human spirit, which God breathed into the first man at creation (Gen. 2:7), rather than to God's Spirit. On this see Peter Davids, *Commentary on James* (NIGTC; Grand Rapids: Eerdmans, 1982), 164.

2 See ch. 22 above.

church. Any other James would need to identify himself more specifically if he expected the large audience he addresses to recognize him.[3]

Although this James, like Jesus, must have originally lived in Galilee, he settled in Jerusalem after seeing the risen Lord.[4] Whenever we meet James in the New Testament, he is in Jerusalem and in a position of leadership, sometimes alongside Peter and John (Gal. 1:18–19; 2:9). He seems to be a sort of first-among-equals in the church there.[5] When Paul lists the "pillars" of the Jerusalem church, he puts James first (Gal. 2:9), and in the Acts narrative, although the church appears to be governed by a group of elders (Acts 11:30; 21:18), some of whom were apostles (15:2, 4, 6, 22, 23; 16:4), James moves to the forefront as their spokesperson (15:13; 21:18–20).[6] He seems to replace Peter as the principal authority in the Jerusalem church after Peter departed Jerusalem for "another place" (12:17).[7] Unlike Peter, whose missionary work took him abroad, James seems to have stayed in Jerusalem until his martyrdom either at the hands of "the scribes and the Pharisees" (Hegesippus) or, as is more likely, at the hands of the Sadducean high priest Ananus (Josephus) in A.D. 62.[8]

Despite his long tenure as leader of the Jewish Christians in Jerusalem, the Acts narrative portrays James as deeply concerned about the state of Jewish Christianity in the Diaspora. When Jewish Christians from Judea tried to impose the Mosaic law on Gentile Christians in the Diaspora and the Antiochean Christians brought the matter before "the apostles and elders" in Jerusalem, James proposed a compromise. He agreed in principle that Gentiles should not have to follow the Mosaic law in order to be considered members of God's people (Acts 15:14–19), but he was also concerned that

3 Although many critical scholars believe the letter is pseudepigraphic, a growing number accept its authenticity. See, e.g., Franz Mussner, *Der Jakobusbrief* (HTKNT 13.1; Freiburg: Herder, 1964), 1–59; Luke Timothy Johnson, *James* (AB 37A; New York: Doubleday, 1995), 108–21; Richard Bauckham, *James: Wisdom of James, Disciple of Jesus the Sage* (New Testament Readings; London: Routledge, 1999), 11–25; Martin Hengel, *Paulus und Jakobus* (WUNT 141; Tübingen: J.C.B. Mohr [Paul Siebeck], 2002), 511–48.

4 *Pace* John Painter, *Just James: The Brother of Jesus in History and Tradition* (Studies on Personalities of the New Testament; Minneapolis: Fortress, 1999), 11–41. The weight of the New Testament evidence is against seeing James and other members of Jesus' family (except perhaps Mary, John 19:25) as followers of Jesus during his lifetime (see Mark 3:21, 31–35; 6:4; John 7:5). Perhaps James was in Jerusalem for the Passover with other members of Jesus' family such as Mary (John 19:25) when his brother was crucified, and perhaps it was there that he joined Jesus' disciples after seeing the risen Lord (1 Cor. 15:7).

5 In the Acts narrative he does not appear to be the first "bishop" of Jerusalem, as later tradition made him (Eusebius, *Hist. eccl.* 2.1.2, 3.5.2). Instead, he emerges from the group of "apostles and elders" as their spokesperson (Acts 15:13–21, 23; 21:18–25). The picture in Acts meshes well with the egalitarian character of James's letter.

6 Luke uses the phrase "the apostles and elders" only when covering the Jerusalem council and its decree. The phrase probably means that although some of the original Twelve had scattered by this time in the narrative, some also remained in Jerusalem, where they served together with "elders" as leaders of the church. Perhaps some of the apostles returned to Jerusalem for the council. On this see Richard Bauckham, "James and the Jerusalem Church," in *The Book of Acts in Its Palestinian Setting*, ed. Richard Bauckham (Grand Rapids: Eerdmans, 1995), 415–80, here at 437.

7 This phrase may refer to another place within Jerusalem, or, as Oscar Cullmann, *Peter: Disciple, Apostle, Martyr: A Historical and Theological Essay* (Philadelphia: Westminster, 1953), 37–38, suggests, to another city (such as Rome or Antioch). Bauckham, "James and the Jerusalem Church," 434–35, argues convincingly that Luke's silence about the city is a narrative indicator that Peter's significance for Jerusalem and within the narrative fades from view at this point.

8 On the missionary travels of Peter, see Acts 8:14; 9:32–10:48; 12:17; Gal. 2:11; 1 Cor. 1:12; 3:22; 9:5. On the death of James in Jerusalem, see Eusebius, *Hist. eccl.* 2.23, who quotes both Hegesippus and Josephus, *A. J.* 20.197.199–203. On the likelihood that Josephus has the more reliable account of James's death, see Craig C. Hill, *Hellenists and Hebrews: Reappraising Division within the Earliest Church* (Minneapolis: Fortress, 1992), 185.

these Gentile Christians not behave in ways that made it difficult for law observant Jews to eat with them (Acts 15:20–29). James seems concerned here to preserve the rights of both groups—Gentile Christians should be free not to observe the Mosaic law, but no one should suggest that Jewish Christians abandon observance of that law in order to associate with their fellow Gentile Christian believers.

This, at least, is James's concern in Acts 21:20–25 when the apostolic decree came up again. Paul arrived in Jerusalem with his offering for the needy Jewish believers there after a vigorous and successful effort to preach the gospel to the Gentiles (24:17). James joined the elders of the Jerusalem church in praise to God for his work through Paul among the Gentiles, but he also joined them (and was probably their spokesperson) in concern that Paul scotch a rumor circulating among Jewish believers in Jerusalem.

According to that rumor, Paul had encouraged Jewish believers in the Diaspora to abandon observance of the Mosaic law. The elders made clear to Paul that they believed Jewish Christians should not only be free to observe such Jewish customs as the taking of a Nazarite vow (Acts 21:23–24), but that Gentile believers should remember the terms of the compromise in Jerusalem—to avoid the consumption of meat offered to idols, blood, strangled animals, and sexual immorality, so that Jewish Christians might be able to eat with them without fear of compromising basic Jewish dietary restrictions or becoming tainted with idolatry (21:25).[9]

James may have understood his own role with respect to Jewish Christianity in a way that is analogous to the responsibility Paul felt for Gentile Christians. Paul believed he had some pastoral responsibility even for Gentile Christians whom he had not met, such as those at Rome (Rom. 1:13–15; 11:13; 15:15–16), Colosse, and Laodicea (Col. 2:1). God had given him the task of ministering among the Gentiles (Rom. 15:16; cf. Eph. 3:1–2, 6–8), and as long as he did not interfere in another person's territory (Rom. 15:20; 2 Cor. 10:13–16), he had the responsibility, if possible, to give Gentile Christians everywhere pastoral oversight. Perhaps James, although located in Jerusalem, felt a similar pastoral responsibility for Jewish Christians abroad.

If this is so, then we should take the reference in James 1:1 to "the twelve tribes in the Diaspora" not as a figurative reference to all Christians everywhere (cf. 1 Peter 1:1) but as a literal reference to Jewish Christians living outside the land of Israel.[10] There was certainly ample precedent for letters on religious practice from Jewish authorities in Jerusalem to Jews of the Diaspora (e.g. Jer. 29:1–23; 2 Macc. 1:1–2:18).[11]

9 For this understanding of the "apostolic decree," see Frank Thielman, *The Law and the New Testament: The Question of Continuity* (Companions to the New Testament; New York: Crossroad, 1999), 157–58. Bauckham, "James and the Jerusalem Church," 459, offers the interesting alternative proposal that the four elements of the decree match the four commandments of Lev. 17–18 that "the alien who sojourns in your/their midst" is required to keep: (1) Lev. 17:8–9; (2) 17:10, (3) 12; 17:13; and (4)18:26.

10 Bauckham, *James*, 14–16.

11 Ibid., 19–20, and "James and the Jerusalem Church," 423–25. Some scholars, e.g., Jonathan A. Goldstein, *II Maccabees* (AB 41A; New York: Doubleday, 1983), 157–68, deny the authenticity of the letter contained in 2 Macc. 1:10b–2:18. Cf. the definitely inauthentic letters in Baruch 6:1–72 and 2 Baruch 78–86. Even if fictional, such "correspondence" demonstrates the currency of the idea that Jews in Jerusalem should write authoritative letters on Jewish practice to their compatriots in the Diaspora.

Is there any precedent, however, for sending such a loosely organized, aphoristic collection of religious teachings to Jews of the Diaspora as an authentic letter? Some scholars have argued that James is actually not a letter but "paraenesis," or a "text which strings together admonitions of general ethical content" such as *The Sentences of Pseudo-Phocylides* or Isocrates' orations *To Nicocles* and *Nicocles*. For these scholars, the epistolary introduction of James is a fiction.[12]

The paraenetic nature of James is clear. Like other paraenetic literature, it is eclectic, often lacks continuity of thought, repeats identical motifs in different places, and contains material applicable to a wide variety of circumstances and readers.[13] It is not for this reason, however, a fictional letter, and a more precise identification of its genre shows why.

Apart from its ascription, James fits into a genre of Jewish aphoristic literature for which the books of Proverbs and Sirach serve as the best ancient examples.[14] Here loosely arranged aphorisms on a variety of topics alternate with longer "treatises" on various themes, all of them designed to encourage the reader to live wisely—to live under the fear of the Lord and therefore according to God's law.[15] Although Sirach is not a letter, was originally composed in Hebrew, and is much longer than James, in its Greek form it provides a loose parallel to James's letter. The original Hebrew edition of the book originated in Jerusalem with a sage known as Jesus son of Eleazar son of Sirach (Sir. 50:27). Jesus' grandson translated the book into Greek in Egypt sometime around 132 B.C. ("the thirty-eighth year of the reign of Euergetes"), and did so "for those living abroad who wished to gain learning and are disposed to live according to the law" (Prologue). Here we find a book that, like James, frequently speaks in loosely organized aphorisms and brief essays and was published for Jews of the Diaspora to provide them with religious instruction. One scholar aptly calls this literature "wisdom paraenesis."[16]

James probably decided to mix the epistolary genre with "wisdom paraenesis" to provide a format for the publication of his wisdom collection. If so, he followed a procedure not unlike that of John the seer in the publication of his Apocalypse. Although both an apocalypse (Rev. 1:1) and a prophecy (1:3; 22:18), John put his book in the form of a letter to the seven churches in Asia (Rev. 1:4–5).[17]

James may have written his letter shortly before his martyrdom in A.D. 62 out of a concern similar to that of Ben Sira's grandson—he wanted to pass on his wisdom to Jewish Christians of the Diaspora. In light of what we know from Acts of James's concern for Jewish Christians in the Diaspora, moreover, it does not seem unlikely that he included in his letter aphorisms and treatises that he felt especially

12 Martin Dibelius, *James*, rev. by Heinrich Greeven (Hermeneia; Philadelphia: Fortress, 1975), 1–11.

13 Ibid., 5–11.

14 On this, see Bauckham, *James*, 29–35.

15 See, e.g., Sir. 1:28–2:6, which consists first of a series of disparate admonitions not to "disobey the fear of the Lord" (1:28a), not to "approach him with a divided mind" (1:28b), not to "be a hypocrite before others" (1:29a), to "keep watch over your lips" (1:29b), and not to be proud (1:30), followed by a sustained treatment of trusting in the Lord even during times of hardship (2:1–11). For the identification of wisdom with the fear of the Lord, see, e.g., Prov. 1:7; 2:1–5; 9:10; 15:33; Sir. 1:11–27. For the identification of wisdom with the fear of the Lord and the instruction found in the Mosaic law, see, e.g., Sir. 19:20; 21:11; cf. 23:27.

16 This is Bauckham's term in *James*, 29–35.

17 Ibid., 11–14.

appropriate to their situation.[18] The publication of his letter for a wide audience necessarily meant that he would frame his wisdom in general terms and cover a wide spectrum of social settings. Thus, he addresses the merchant class (4:13–16), field hands (5:4, 7–11), and those in between the two groups (2:3).[19] This is nevertheless a real letter from an important Jewish Christian leader within the early church, and a real pastoral situation stands behind it.

THE UNDIVIDED LIFE

Into the eclectic collection of wise aphorisms and treatises that comprise his letter, James has woven a unifying theme.[20] James wanted his Jewish Christian readers to devote themselves anew to a life of undivided commitment to God and to the Lord Jesus Christ.[21] He expresses this theme primarily through the notion of perfection that runs through the letter. His readers should be "perfect [*teleios*] and complete" (1:4). They should remember that "every good and perfect [*teleios*] gift" comes from an unvarying, unchanging God (1:17). They should look into "the perfect [*teleios*] law that gives freedom" and do the task it assigns them (1:25). They should "keep" (*teleō*) the royal law (2:8). Like Abraham, their faith should be perfected (*teleō*) by their works (2:22). Each one should strive to be "perfect" (*teleios*, 3:2).

In contrast to perfect people stand those who are "double-minded" (*dipsychos*, 1:6–8; 4:8) and "shallow" (*kenē*, 2:20, RSV). These people cannot make up their minds to do what is right (1:6), and they act insincerely (3:17). They are quick to boast of "understanding" and "wisdom," but their deeds tell the true story—the story of a corrupt heart (3:14; 4:8). These are divided people, boasting of heavenly wisdom but acting in agreement with its earthly, unspiritual opposite (3:13–17).

James wants his readers to know that "friendship with the world is hatred toward God" (4:4).[22] He wants them to live lives of integrity, lives that single-mindedly pursue the wisdom that comes as a gift from God himself (1:17; 3:17). He is especially hopeful they will live undivided lives in three areas. First, he wants them to cultivate perseverance; their faith should remain unwavering in the midst of testing. Second, he wants them to live in simplicity; wealth should not distract them from doing what God requires. Third, he wants them to live in sincerity; the good words they speak should find fulfillment in good deeds.

Perseverance: A Life Undivided by Hardship

James begins his letter with an admonition to his readers to understand that "trials of many kinds" can have a positive outcome for their faith if the believer endures

18 Cf. Sophie Laws, *The Epistle of James* (HNTC; San Francisco: Harper & Row, 1980), 8–9, who deduces from what the author says about wealth that he and his intended audience are at odds with one another on this subject.

19 Cf. Johnson, *James*, 24.

20 *Pace* Dibelius-Greeven, *James*, 1–11.

21 Cf. Johnson, *James*, 20–21, who makes a plausible case for a connection between James and the philosophical "protreptic" literature of antiquity. This literature encouraged people to follow a life of undivided dedication to virtue. See also Douglas Moo, *The Letter of James* (PNTC; Grand Rapids: Eerdmans, 2000), 45–46.

22 On the centrality of this statement to James's concern throughout the letter, see Johnson, *James*, 84.

without compromise (1:2). Among these various trials, the problem of persecution for the Christian faith is probably uppermost in James's mind—for two reasons. First, his admonition to ask God for wisdom in 1:5 comes directly after his admonition to persevere under trial. Although James provides no clear logical link between the two ideas, in some first-century Jewish wisdom literature, wisdom is the means by which the persecuted righteous person endures persecution (4 Macc. 7:17–18).[23] The close proximity of the themes of perseverance under trial and the need for wisdom in James 1:4–5 probably means that James is indebted to this tradition. If so, then when he speaks of "trials of many kinds," the trial of persecution is uppermost in his mind.

Second, James knows that Jewish Christians in the Diaspora sometimes faced judicial punishment for their faith and that this persecution often originated with the wealthy:

> Is it not the rich who are exploiting you? Are they not the ones who are dragging you into court? Are they not the ones who are slandering the noble name of him to whom you belong? (2:6–7)[24]

James seems to have the same situation in mind in his prophetic denunciation of wealthy oppressors in 5:1–6. Among the accusations he levels at them is that they "have condemned [*katedikasate*] and murdered the innocent person" (5:5). This is judicial language. James seems to say that the wealthy have managed to gain convictions of Christians in court and, despite their innocence, see them executed. Immediately after this blast against unjust rich people, James advises his readers to persevere in their faith (5:7–11). Once again, he seems to link persecution and perseverance.[25]

James offers two admonitions to help his readers remain firm in their faith despite various trials, especially the trial of persecution. First, he urges them to lift their eyes from the hardship itself to its good result, for when believers encounter various trials and refuse to cave in to their pressures, they become more "perfect" and "complete" (1:2–4). In other words, they become more single-minded in their commitment to the wisdom that is from above (3:17) and less prone to the double-mindedness and instability characteristic of those whose wisdom is earthly, unspiritual, and demonic (3:15). If they have the end result of their testing thus in view, they will be able to consider (*ēgēsasthe*) their trials a cause for joy.

James seems to understand that the joyful perspective he advocates toward suffering is impossible to develop apart from God's intervention.[26] He therefore tells those

23 Donald E. Gowan, "Wisdom and Endurance in James," *HBT* 15 (1993): 145–53.

24 Cf. Paul in Acts, who sometimes lands in front of a magistrate after clashes with the merchant class (Acts 16:16–40; 19:23–41). Cf. also the situation presupposed in Pliny, *Ep.* 10.96, where judicial action seeks to curb the economic impact of Christian conversions. Now that a few Christians have been executed, Pliny reports, "There is a general demand for sacrificial animals, which for some time past have met with but few purchasers."

25 James links 5:7 to 5:6 with the inferential particle *oun* ("therefore"), which is evidence that he saw a logical connection between his criticism of the wealthy oppressors in 5:1–6 and his advice to his readers to persevere in 5:7–11. Dibelius–Greeven, *James*, 241–42, see the section as an isolated "series of sayings on various themes," but they do not even comment on the *oun*. For the perspective taken here, see esp. Mussner, *Der Jakobusbrief*, 199–201.

26 Dibelius-Greeven, *James*, 77, believe that the thought of 1:2–4 and the thought of 1:5–8 are not linked by any logical sequence of ideas but only by the mneumonic device of "catchword," common in paraensis, for joining disparate admonitions to each other. On this reading, *leipomenoi* ("lacking") links 1:4 to

who lack this "wisdom" to pray for it, and God will graciously grant their request (1:5). Later James will describe God as the giver of "every good and perfect gift ... from above" (1:16) and will also describe the wisdom of which he speaks as the "wisdom from above" (3:17). Those who lack a joyful perspective on their trials should pray to their gracious God, who grants his wisdom to those who ask for it. The only condition he attaches to his gift is that the request for it be sincere—the prayer for wisdom should arise out of a wholehearted desire for the wisdom it seeks (1:6–8).

Second, James reminds his readers that their perseverance in faith will have an eschatological outcome in their favor. Those who condemn and kill the innocent (5:6), James says, "have fattened [themselves] for the day of slaughter" (5:5). In light of this future judgment (*oun*, 5:7) on those who oppress them, James urges his readers to persevere in their faith in the knowledge that "the Lord's coming is near" (5:8).[27] Eventually, the Lord will fulfill his purposes (5:11). Just as the farmer waits patiently for his crops to grow (5:7), and just as the prophets and Job waited patiently for God to vindicate them (5:10–11), so the Lord will come to rescue his suffering people.

James's reference to "trials of many kinds" in 1:2 shows that, in addition to the trial of persecution, he is also concerned about other forms of testing. In 1:12–15 he seems to turn to testing of a more general kind: the temptation to do evil. Certainly the temptation to cave in to the pressure of persecution is a temptation to follow one's evil desires (as in 4 Macc. 7:17–18).[28] This, however, is far from his only concern. He probably also has in mind at least the temptations to show favoritism to the rich (2:1–12), to drive a wedge between faith and obedience (2:14–26), to curse people with the same tongue that blesses God (3:9–10), to envy, to promote one's own interests at the expense of others, to boast (3:14; 4:16), to covet, quarrel, and even kill (4:1–2), to slander a fellow believer (4:11–12), or to grumble against one another (5:9).

These sinful actions arise from "the desires that battle within you" (4:1), and in 1:12–15 James warns his readers not to take the bait these desires offer or to be dragged away by them (1:14–15). As with perseverance under persecution (1:3), such temptations result in perseverance and "approvedness" (1:12).[29] In addition, as with perseverance under persecution, perseverance under temptation also results in eschatological blessing. Just before describing the specific trial of enticement by one's evil desires, James issues this beatitude: "Blessed is the one who perseveres under trial, because after standing the test that person will receive the crown of life God has promised to those who love him" (1:12, aut.).[30]

---

leipetai ("lacks") in 1:5. In 1:5–8, therefore, James speaks only of praying in faith and not of praying for wisdom. As Johnson, *James*, 182, suggests, however, the imperative "consider" in 1:2 urges on the readers a certain perspective on their trials, and this forms a natural conceptual link to the prayer for "wisdom" in 1:5, since wisdom for James is a matter of one's world-and-life view.

27 On the connection between 5:1–6 and 5:7–11, see Johnson, *James*, 311–12.

28 On this, see Gowan, "Wisdom and Endurance in James," 150–51.

29 In 1:3 the "testing" (*dokimion*) of one's faith produces "perseverance" (*hypomonē*), and in 1:12 the one who "perseveres" (*hypomonei*) becomes "approved" (*dokimos*; NIV, "stood the test").

30 *Pace* Dibelius-Greeven, *James*, 71, 88, who see 1:12 as "an isolated saying which is connected neither with what follows nor with what precedes."

To summarize, James recognizes that faithfulness to God entails hardship of various kinds, and he wants "the wisdom from above" to shape his readers' perspective on this hardship. Although trials will come in many different kinds, James speaks especially of the hardship that persecution and the temptation to follow one's evil desires impose on the believer. Perseverance through these hardships, he says, tests the believer's mettle and eventually makes the believer "perfect" (*teleios*) and "complete" (*holoklēros*)—undivided by a compromised loyalty to God. Because perseverance has this result, the trials bound up with it will, for the wise person, bring joy. They are also the source of eschatological blessing since, at the time of the Lord's Parousia, he will vindicate the righteous against their oppressors and bestow the crown of life on those who have persevered.

Wealth: A Life Undivided by the Lure of Riches

As we saw above, James thinks in terms of two utterly incompatible perspectives: earthly wisdom (3:15) and friendship with the world (4:4) on one hand and wisdom from above (3:17) and friendship with God (2:23) on the other. James urges his readers toward "perfection" and "completeness"—toward lives informed entirely by the wisdom from above and friendship with God. They must avoid becoming "double-minded" (*dipsychos*), mouthing a commitment to God's wisdom while giving in to the allurements of earthly wisdom (1:8; 4:8).

For James, material wealth is the great symbol of earthly wisdom with all its allurements. One's attitude toward wealth is the touchstone for one's ultimate loyalties, for the world views those who have faith as poor if they have no wealth, but God views them as rich heirs of his kingdom (2:5).[31] James sees three basic problems with wealth.

First, wealth dupes people into regarding it as of ultimate importance and therefore leads them to neglect God. Wealth, James says, deceives people into thinking that worldly existence and the affairs of this life are more permanent than they really are, and as a result, the wealthy tend to forget God. The wealthy person is as ephemeral as a wild flower at the break of a hot day (1:10–11), as transitory as a vapor (4:14), but the business of making a profit so dominates the thinking of the wealthy that they forget this, and thus they forget that the Lord decides what will happen from day to day (4:14–15). This twisted view of reality fuels an attitude of pride in the wealthy as they neglect God and focus on their own accomplishments (4:16).

Second, wealth infects even the believing community with neglect of the poor. This happens, for example, when Christians join the world in showing favoritism to the rich (2:1–6). To seat the rich person in comfortable accommodations in the Christian assembly while shooing the poor to the margins where they can stand or, worse, seating them on the floor beneath the feet of their social superiors, is to take the world's perspective on poverty and riches (2:1–5). It is to violate one of two

31 Cf. the comments of Johnson, *James*, 190, on the correlation between 1:9–11 and 2:5.

commandments that Jesus identified as most important: Leviticus 19:18, "Love your neighbor as yourself" (2:8–9).[32] It is therefore to become guilty of breaking the whole law (2:10–11) and to stand in danger of the merciless judgment that God has reserved for those who refuse to show mercy to others (2:12).

Third, wealth can lead the rich to violence against those who stand in the way of their desire for it. This violence can take both active and passive forms. On the active side, James probably has the desire for wealth in mind when he says that quarrelling and physical violence often arise from wanting something that one cannot have. Killing and coveting—violating the sixth and tenth commandments—originate with wanting something but failing to get it (4:1–2; cf. 3:16).

On the passive side, the wealthy abuse the poor simply by hoarding their riches rather than giving the excess to those in need.[33] This is probably what James means when he says, in his prophetic denunciation of the oppressive rich (5:1–6), that their "wealth has rotted" and that "moths have eaten" their clothes (5:5). Rather than sharing their hordes of money and clothing with the poor to alleviate their suffering, the wealthy have let their wealth rust and molder in storage.

Condemnation of hoarding wealth was a familiar thought to James both from the Mosaic law and from Israel's wisdom tradition. The law forbade reaping a field greedily up to its edges or going back over a harvested field to gather every last bit of grain. The leavings, it says, are "for the poor and the alien" (Lev. 19:9–10). The wisdom tradition of Second Temple Judaism also picked up this thought and formulated it in a way close to James's expression of it. Sirach 29:9–11, for example, says,

> Help the poor for the commandment's sake,
>   and in their need do not send them away empty-handed.
> Lose your silver for the sake of a brother or a friend
>   and do not let it rust under a stone and be lost.
> Lay up your treasure according to the commandments of the Most High,
>   and it will profit you more than gold.

The passive greed of the wealthy takes a more sinister turn in James 5:4, where he indicts them for withholding the wages of the poor laborers who have harvested their grain fields. Here too James echoes the law, which urges Israelites not to "take advantage of a hired man who is poor and needy" but to "pay him his wages each day before sunset, because he is poor and is counting on it" (Deut. 24:14–15; cf. Lev. 19:13). Here too, Israel's wisdom tradition picks up this commandment and repeats it (Job 31:38–40; Tobit 4:14a).

As with those who claim to be believers but continue to neglect the poor in favor of the rich (James 2:13), however, a time of judgment is coming for wealthy unbe-

32 James's description of Lev. 19:18 as the "royal law" may arise from his knowledge of Jesus' teaching on how life in the kingdom of God should be structured. On this, see, e.g., Davids, *James*, 114, and Moo, *James*, 111–12. That James is also aware of the original biblical context of Lev. 19:18, however, emerges from his echoes of Lev. 19:15 in James 2:1, 9; of Lev. 19:16 in James 4:11; and of Lev. 19:13 in James 5:4.

33 Mussner, *Der Jakobusbrief*, 194.

lievers who oppress the poor. Like the blood of Abel that cried out to God from the ground (Gen. 4:10), like the poor field worker who, defrauded of his wages, cries out to the Lord in Deuteronomy 24:15, and like the cries of the oppressed Israelites laboring under the heavy hand of Pharaoh (Ex. 3:7), the unpaid wages of those who harvested the fields of the wealthy (James 5:4a) and the voices of the poor themselves (5:4b) have cried out to God for justice and deliverance.[34]

Those who hoard their wealth, oblivious to the needs of the poor around them, and those who greedily withhold the wages of the poor who have labored in their fields, James says, will one day—and it is coming soon (5:8, 9b)—receive just punishment from the Lord for their misdeeds. Far from helping them in that day, their horde of wealth, spoiled from unuse, will serve as a witness against them. On that day, the corrosion of their wealth will spread to the wealthy themselves and "eat [their] flesh like fire" (5:3). They are like livestock fattening themselves for the day of slaughter (5:5).

In sum, James wants his readers to be wary of the dangers that wealth poses to the believing community. It is often the goal of the bitter envy and selfish ambition of those whose wisdom is earthly, unspiritual, and of the devil. Pursing wealth to the neglect of God and at the expense of others, particularly the poor, takes one down the path that ends in God's eschatological condemnation. The lure of wealth can infect the Christian community, leading to a division between one's verbal commitment to the well-being of the poor and one's actions on their behalf. This is the division of soul that James wants his Jewish readers in the Diaspora to avoid as they face the temptation to ease the difficulties of their own lives by showing favoritism to the rich.

Speech: A Life Undivided by Duplicity

If we count James's instructions on prayer, his criticism of boasting, and his blast against those who claim to have faith but produce no deeds to back it up, then James says more about speech than any other single topic in his letter. It is, he assures his readers, an inherently dangerous activity. The tongue is full of deadly poison, it can set the world ablaze, and teachers, as professional speakers, engage in a hazardous profession (3:1–12).

The problem with speech is that it is so often false: boasting, slander, and empty claims have in common their failure to match reality. When this falsity takes the form of pious claims that remain unfulfilled in pious deeds, a division is set up in one's soul. The result is as incoherent as a spring that spouts both fresh and salt water or a fruit tree that yields the wrong crop.

James does not simply warn his readers of the danger of speech. He also shows them that, when it comes from God and is directed to God in faith, it can be both active and transforming.

34 According to Josephus in *A. J.* 1.53, Cain was motivated by monetary gain (*pros kerdainein*). Cf. James 4:13, where merchants say, "We will make money (*kerdēsomen*)."

The Problem: A Division between Word and Deed

James has something to say about angry words (1:20–21), about boasting (3:5, 14; 4:16), about cursing others (3:9), about slander (4:11), and about grumbling against fellow believers (5:9), but his greatest concern on the subject of speech is the division that it often sets up in the individual between claims and reality. It is a division that is visible when the same tongue praises the Lord and curses the people whom he has created (3:9). This arises from a divided soul—one that yields both sweet and bitter water and produces the wrong kind of fruit (3:10–12). It is a division that is visible in a somewhat different way when people hear the word of God in his law but forget what they have heard and fail to obey it (1:22–24).

This unhealthy division between word and deed is the burden of 2:14–26, James's best known, and most controversial, passage. The passage has drawn so much attention because many students of the text believe it contradicts Paul's teaching on the relationship between faith, works, and justification.

The problem can be clearly understood if we look at a synopsis of the evidence. James is making the point that "faith by itself, if it is not accompanied by action, is dead" (2:17), and he brings in Abraham to illustrate the point. Paul, in Romans 4:1–4, makes the point that the works the Mosaic law prescribes, such as circumcision, do not place one within the people of God and therefore justify one in God's sight—only faith can do that:[35]

James 2:21–24	**Rom. 4:1–4**
Was not *Abraham our father justified by works* when he offered Isaac his son upon the altar? You see that faith was working together with his works, and by works faith was made perfect. And the *Scripture* was fulfilled which says, "*And* Abraham *believed God and it was reckoned to him for righteousness,*" and he was called the friend of God. You see that a person is justified by works and not by faith alone.	What therefore shall we say *Abraham our* fore*father* according to the flesh found? For if Abraham was *justified by works,* he has ground for boasting, but not before God. For what does the *Scripture* say? "*And Abraham believed God and it was reckoned to him for righteousness.*" But to the one who works, the wage is not reckoned as a gracious gift but as something owed, but to the one who does not work and believes in the one who justifies the ungodly, his faith is reckoned for righteousness.

The verbal similarity between James and Paul here is extremely close, rising to the level of word for word agreement in places. This terminological overlap makes unlikely the otherwise plausible claim that James and Paul are not concerned with

35 Author's trans. in both cols. Italics show word-for-word agreement. Cf. Rom. 3:28; Gal. 2:16; Eph. 2:8–9; 2 Tim. 1:8–9; Titus 3:5.

each other at all but are both working independently with a Jewish tradition about Abraham. This tradition, it is supposed, tried to puzzle out how the text of Genesis could both say that Abraham was justified by his faith (Gen. 15:6) and that God made his promises to him of many descendents and the land because of his works (Gen. 22:16–17; 26:4–5).[36] If the terminological agreement between Paul and James makes this explanation unlikely, however, then what is the relationship between them? Is James, or the pseudonymous author, attacking Paul?[37] Is James, or the pseudonymous author, attacking a misunderstanding of Paul's teaching—either a misunderstanding of his own or of others?[38]

The account of the relationship between James and Paul that emerges from both Paul's letter to the Galatians and the Acts narrative makes unlikely the theory that James either misunderstood Paul's position or disagreed with it.[39] Paul, by his own account, laid his gospel before James at the Jerusalem council, and James responded with the right hand of fellowship (Gal. 2:2, 9). The picture in Acts of James's agreement with the mission to the Gentiles at the Jerusalem council (Acts 15:12–19) and of his positive response, along with the other elders, to the account of Paul's work among the Gentiles when Paul visited Jerusalem with his collection (21:18–20), is consistent with Paul's account in Galatians. The venerable scholarly tradition that finds Paul and James at odds with each other over the substance of the gospel, therefore, is unlikely to be correct.[40]

The accounts in Galatians and Acts do support the notion, however, that James accented the gospel differently from Paul. James was concerned to preserve the right of Jewish Christians to continue observance of the Mosaic law. He was also concerned that Gentile Christians, while not obligated to the Mosaic law themselves, avoid sexual immorality and limit their diet when they shared a meal with observant Jewish Christians. If he had heard rumors that Paul taught Jewish Christians to abandon the law, even if he did not believe them, it would do no harm to remind Jewish Christians scattered abroad, many of them in the lands where Paul had ministered and in the churches he had founded, that Paul's gospel should not be misconstrued as a license to sin. Paul himself certainly encountered this kind of misunderstanding of his gospel (Rom. 3:8; 6:1, 15). It is possible that worsening problems with it stand behind the articulations of justification by faith alongside expressions of the necessity for works in his later letters (Eph. 2:8–10; Titus 3:1–8).

Perhaps because he is aware of such problems, James weaves into his treatment of the dangers of speech a warning not to reduce justification to the inevitable result

36 Bauckham, *James*, 130–31; cf. Johnson, *James*, 64.

37 See, e.g., Hengel, *Paulus und Jakobus*, 526–29.

38 See, e.g., James Hardy Ropes, *A Critical and Exegetical Commentary on the Epistle of James* (ICC; Edinburgh: T. & T. Clark, 1916), 204–6.

39 See Bauckham, "James and the Jerusalem Church," 471–75, and Johnson, *James*, 92–108, who reach the same conclusions independently of each other and in publications released in the same year (1995). See also Bauckham, *James*, 148–49.

40 As we saw in chapter 23, this position appears in the work of Ferdinand Christian Baur, e.g., *The Church History of the First Three Centuries*, 2 vols. (London: Williams and Norgate, 1878–79; orig. German ed., 1853), 1:44–76. More recent examples include James D. G. Dunn, *Unity and Diversity in the New Testament: An Inquiry into the Character of Earliest Christianity* (Philadelphia: Westminster, 1977), 252–57, and Michael Goulder, *St. Paul versus St. Peter: A Tale of Two Missions* (Louisville: Westminster John Knox, 1994). On the inadequacy of this approach to the relationship between James and Paul, see Hill, *Hellenists and Hebrews*, esp. 183–91.

of verbal assent to a certain creed, however correct that creed may be. James defines "faith" in 2:14–26 as mere verbal and intellectual assent. This is clear from three elements of the passage. First, the context of the passage expects us to read the discussion in light of a division between speech and action. James's criticism of Christians who show favoritism to the rich and therefore disobey the command to love one's neighbor as one's self ends with the admonition to "speak and act as those who are going to be judged by the law that gives freedom" (2:12).

Second, the introduction to the passage formulates the problem in terms of a division between what one says and what one does with "faith" serving as a shorthand expression for "what one says." Faith, as this passage defines it, is happy to talk, but it does nothing more. "What good is it, my brothers," says James, "if a man claims [*legō*] to have faith but has no deeds?" (2:14). James follows this introductory statement immediately with a vivid illustration of just the kind of empty claim he has in mind. In this illustration, someone verbalizes a commitment to the well-being of the needy, but this verbiage turns out to be nothing more substantive than a cheery send-off, "Go, I wish you well; keep warm and well fed." These words replace the more important activity of giving the needy "the things necessary for the body" (2:16, aut.). Such faith is both profitless and dead because it involves a division between words and deeds, between what one claims to believe and what one's actions reveal about one's real commitments.

Third, the reference in 2:19 to the classic Jewish confession that "God is one" (Deut. 6:4) implies that James is concerned with mouthing creeds but failing to back up these affirmations with action. The demons, James says, have faith of this kind; they give intellectual assent to the truth that God is one, but this intellectual assent hardly saves them or justifies them in God's sight (2:19).[41]

Against such empty verbiage from the "shallow person" (2:20, cf. RSV) James proposes that one's actions reveal whether or not one is really headed for salvation or is right with God. Speech is fine and even necessary (2:12), as long as it is controlled (1:26; 3:3–7a), but more important than how one talks for determining whether one is really religious is how one acts. "Religion that God our Father accepts as pure and faultless is this," says James, "to look after orphans and widows in their distress and to keep one's self from being polluted by the world" (1:27).

James places Genesis 22:2–10 (the story of Abraham's obedience to God's command to sacrifice his only son) before Genesis 15:6 in his discussion of justification. Abraham's obedience in Genesis 22 made his faith in Genesis 15 "complete" (*teleioō*). The message to his readers is clear: The proof is in the pudding. Intellectual assent expressed in speech is useless without obedience, and true religion involves doing what God requires.

If so, however, has not James flatly contradicted the priority of God's grace in salvation, which occupies such an important place in Paul's teaching?[42] Does he not

41 Bauckham, *James*, 121.

42 Laws, *James*, 133; Andrew Chester, "The Theology of James," in *The Theology of the Letters of James, Peter, and Jude*, ed. Andrew Chester and Ralph P. Martin (New Testament Theology; Cambridge: Cambridge Univ. Press, 1994), 46–53.

teach the opposite of what Paul says in Romans 4—that God justifies the ungodly on the basis of faith apart from obedience, and that he specifically justified Abraham in Genesis 15:6 on the basis of his faith before Abraham obeyed God in the matter of circumcision in Genesis 17?

This would certainly be true if James in this passage defined "faith" in the same way that Paul defines it in Romans 4. As it turns out, however, Paul's understanding of Abraham's faith in Romans 4 is not too far distant from James's understanding of "works" or of "pure and faultless religion" or of being "perfect" and "complete." Paul describes Abraham's faith as an unwavering trust in God (4:19), free of doubt (4:20), and full of conviction that, as improbable as it seemed that God could keep his promises, he would keep them nevertheless (4:21).[43] This was a faith that determined the course of Abraham's life. Paul assumed that it incorporates obedience within it, and so he spoke naturally of "the obedience of faith" elsewhere in Romans (Rom. 1:5; 16:26), spoke equally naturally in Galatians of living in the flesh "by faith" (Gal. 2:20), and in Philippians, with one breath, spoke of "working out" one's "salvation with fear and trembling" (Phil. 2:12) and in the next of "the righteousness that comes from God and is by faith" (3:9).[44]

It is true that Paul regularly speaks of the priority of God's grace in salvation and so makes it clear that righteousness is credited to believers by faith as a free gift of God apart from anything they do to earn it (Rom. 3:24; 4:4–8; 11:5–6; Gal. 2:15–16; Eph. 2:8–9; 2 Tim. 1:9–10; Titus 3:3–7). Obedience to God arises from the shift in loyalties that faith entails—a shift from service to sin to service to righteousness (Rom. 6:1–23)—and God makes this obedience possible by the gift of his Spirit (Rom. 8:1–17; Gal. 5:16–26).

James also knows, however, that God's action is prior to human action in forgiveness, salvation, and obedience.[45] He differs from Paul in the way he articulates this principle, but the theological principle undergirding his language is the same. Rather than contrasting a gift with a wage or using the language of the Spirit, James speaks instead of the right kind of speech: speech that comes from God to people (his Word) and speech that people direct to God (prayer). By means of this speech God gives birth to his people, shows them how to live, and forgives them when they fail.

The Antidote to Poison Speech

Although not a major topic in his letter, James wants his readers to know about more positive kinds of speech—the Word of God, which transforms those to whom it comes and provides them wisdom to guide their lives, and prayer, by which the believer can ask God for wisdom and appeal to him for forgiveness, healing, and rescue.

43 See ch. 15 above.

44 Paul comes close to James's use of the word "faith" in 1 Cor. 13:2 where he says that having a faith "that can move mountains" amounts to nothing unless "love" accompanies it. Paul then defines love in practical terms (13:4–7). Here, therefore, Paul divides faith from loving works in a way that is virtually identical to James.

45 *Pace* Laws, *James*, 133.

The Word of God

In 1:17–18 James tells his readers that among the good gifts the Father gives from above is birth by "the word of truth." This may refer to God's use of his word in creation to bear human beings the way a woman bears a child (Gen. 1:26), an idea that has a close parallel in Philo, who speaks of God's begetting creation by having union with his knowledge (*Ebr.* 30).[46] Since elsewhere in the New Testament "the word of truth" refers to the gospel (Eph. 1:13; Col. 1:5; 2 Tim. 2:15), however, it probably refers to the gospel here, and therefore to the effect of the gospel in re-creating or giving new birth to those who embrace it.[47] This happens by God's will (*boulomai*) and therefore at his initiative.

James also identifies the word of God with "the perfect law that gives freedom" (James 1:22–25). The law instructs people how to live, just as a mirror tells them how they look, and this opens the possibility of duplicity—that people will merely hear the words of the law and turn away from them, unwilling to do what they say. An encounter with the law, however, also brings with it the possibility of obedience and blessing.

Prayer

James opens and closes his letter with a reference to prayer and connects prayer closely with faith (1:5–7; 5:13–20). Unlike the "faith" of those who merely give verbal assent to correct belief in 2:14–26, in these passages faith has wholly positive connotations. James defines it by contrast with "wavering" or "doubting" (*diakrinō*), and so it has connotations not unlike those that Paul gives to faith when he uses Abraham as an example of faith in Romans 4:17–22. Prayer with this kind of faith brings the wisdom that enables one to view both persecution and temptation as opportunities for the development of perseverance and completeness (James 1:2–8, 13–15). Prayer with this kind of faith brings rescue from trouble, affirmation of happiness, healing from illness, and forgiveness for sin (5:13–16).

"Faith" in these contexts is different than the "faith" of 2:14–26, which is divorced from works and shared with the demons. In 1:2–8, 13–15; 5:13–16, James comes close to Paul's understanding of faith and shows, whether intentionally or not, that he and Paul are in substantial agreement on the role of faith in the Christian life. Although James does not put his thinking together in the way Paul does and never refers to the Spirit, as Paul does so frequently in similar contexts, James's letter reveals the raw material for constructing an understanding of Christian existence not unlike Paul's own. It might look something like this:

God re-creates or regenerates people by the word of truth (1:18), which is the gospel, with the result that both their speech and their action match each other (2:12)—their good words find fulfillment in their good deeds, and their intellectually held beliefs

46 Johnson, *James*, 197.

47 Here I follow the instincts of Mussner, *Der Jakobusbrief*, 95–96, and Davids, *James*, 89, without, however, following the details of their exegesis. Mussner adopts the improbable position that "the word of truth" was used in baptismal practice, and Davids, *James*, 89, mistakenly includes 2 Cor. 6:7 (cf. also Mussner, *Der Jakobusbrief*, 94) and 1 Peter 1:25 in his list of places where the phrase refers to the gospel. The phrase means "true speech" in 2 Cor. 6:7 and does not appear at all in 1 Peter 1:25.

express themselves in obedience (2:14–26). James anticipates failures, for he knows that "we all stumble in many ways" (3:2), but he also knows that God is gracious to those who pray with faith (1:5–6, 16; 3:17). In response to their prayers, God gives his people the wisdom necessary for the right perspective on their hardships and temptations (1:2–6, 13–15) and gives them forgiveness for their sins (5:16).

JAMES AND THE UNDIVIDED LIFE

In his letter, James assembles and recasts wisdom from the Jewish and Jewish Christian tradition in order to urge Diaspora Christians, wherever they might be, to live a "perfect" or "complete" life. James does not mean by this that they can attain sinlessness but that their commitment to the wisdom that comes from above should be as unalloyed as possible. His readers should not be in turmoil, like a storm-tossed sea, nor should their souls be split—like a grapevine that bears figs—about whether to take the path of friendship with the world or the path that Abraham followed to friendship with God. The pursuit of the wisdom from above, he makes clear, involves hardship, temptation, poverty in the eyes of the world, and care that one's actions match one's claim to worship God and to follow his law.

Paradoxically, James maintains, such a life is marked by joy. God graciously provides the wisdom necessary both for pursuing it successfully and for realizing why the hardship involved is worth the "completeness" it yields. In this missive the leader of the Jerusalem church urges the Jewish Christians of the Diaspora, over whom he has pastoral responsibility, to turn their backs on the world and to pursue with wholehearted devotion "the wisdom that comes from heaven."

Chapter 25

JUDE: CONTENDING FOR THE FAITH AGAINST A PERVERSION OF GOD'S GRACE

If James provides a general response to the possible antinomian misunderstanding of Paul, his brother Jude has a more specific instance of such false teaching in mind.[1] Although eager to write about the salvation he shared with his "beloved" readers, he felt compelled, instead, to encourage them "to contend for the faith that was once for all entrusted to the saints" (v. 3).

This urgent admonition is necessary because a group of impious people have invaded the community to which he is writing (v. 4). Unless they are resisted, this group will corrupt both the faith (v. 3) and the morals (vv. 4, 12) of the community, dividing its fellowship (v. 19) and leading them down a path that ends in eschatological destruction (vv. 4, 7, 13, 14–15). The substance of the letter falls into two parts: a relatively lengthy description of the false teachers (vv. 4–19), and a brief strategy for coping with them (vv. 3, 20–22).

JUDE'S OPPONENTS: CORINTHIANESQUE ANTINOMIANS

Jude provides several hints about his opponents' tactics and beliefs. On their tactics, he says that they have "slipped in" or "infiltrated" the community (v. 4). Here he uses a term (*pareisdyō*) that implies both invasion from the outside and secrecy about their full range of beliefs.[2] In addition, Jude implies that his opponents have assumed the role of authoritative teachers in the community to which he writes. He refers to them as "shepherds who feed only themselves" (v. 12), alluding to Ezekiel's attack on the wicked "shepherds" (kings) of Israel who led their "sheep" (the nation) astray into idolatry, with disastrous consequences (Ezek. 34:1–31).[3] Perhaps Jude calls them

1 Many scholars assume that Jude's letter is pseudonymous. As we will see below, however, the letter fits well within the world of the missionary labors of Paul, Peter, and the Lord's brothers. Cf. Richard Bauckham, Jude, 2 Peter (WBC 50; Waco, Tex.: Word, 1983), 14–16; idem, Jude and the Relatives of Jesus in the Early Church (Edinburgh: T. & T. Clark, 1990), 171–78.

2 Paul uses the related term *pareisaktos* in a similar setting where he accuses "false brothers"—specifically Judaizing Christians—of slipping secretly into Christian communities where the observance of the Mosaic law was not a prerequisite for fellowship. These false believers, he says, intended "to spy on the freedom we have in Christ Jesus" (Gal. 2:4). That the false teachers of Jude's letter were itinerant prophets is a common position among commentators. P. H. R. van Houwelingen, *2 Petrus en Judas: Testament in tweevoud* (Commentaar op het Nieuwe Testament; Kampen: Kok, 1993), 117–20, offers a well-reasoned if ultimately unconvincing case that Jude's opponents were "dissident freebooters" who arose from within the community itself (cf. Acts 20:30; 2 Peter 2:1).

3 "Woe to the shepherds of Israel who only take care of themselves!" Ezekiel prophesies, "Should not shepherds take care of the flock?" (Ezek. 34:2).

"dreamers" because, like those who advocated the "hollow and deceptive philosophy" in Colosse, they base their teaching on visions (Col. 2:8, 18).[4]

Jude comments that hope of monetary gain motivates these teachers and that their teaching style is designed both to flatter themselves and those whom they teach (vv. 11, 16). They are concerned with worldly, not spiritual matters (v. 19). Jude's opponents, therefore, are a group of false teachers who claim that their teaching is heaven-inspired and who are motivated not by any altruistic concerns but by their greed.

Hand in hand with the claim of Jude's opponents to give authoritative teaching seems to have gone a resistance to the previously established structure of authority in the community to which Jude writes. Here the evidence is more ambiguous, but Jude's comparison of the false teachers with Enoch's "angels who did not keep their positions of authority" (v. 6; cf. *1 En.* 12.4) and with those "destroyed in Korah's rebellion" (Jude 11; Num. 16:1–50) hints that they skirt or undermine the recognized authority structure of the community. This notion may also be in Jude's mind when he characterizes the false teachers as "discontented murmurers [*gongystai mempsimoiroi*]"[5] The wilderness generation of Israelites "grumbled" against their leaders, Moses and Aaron, not least in their expression of unbelief in Kadesh and in Korah's rebellion, two events to which Jude explicitly refers (Jude 5, 11; cf. Num. 14:2, 27, 29, 36; 16:7–9, 11).[6] Apparently this refusal to abide by established structures of authority had already started to divide the community to which Jude writes (v. 19).

What do these infiltrators teach? Jude cites two specific problems. First, they pervert the grace of God into behavior that violates recognized norms of decency (*aselgeia*).[7] Apparently they claim that because God is graciously disposed toward them, they need not worry about the eschatological consequences of their conduct. Specifically, Jude charges them with behaving like the fallen angels of *1 Enoch* 6–7, who "took wives unto themselves, and everyone (respectively) chose one woman for himself, and they began to go unto them" (*1 En.* 7.1; cf. Gen. 6:1–2; Jude 6, 8).

Similarly, they have acted like the people of "Sodom and Gomorrah and the surrounding towns," who engaged in sexual immorality and, in particular, went "after flesh other than their own" (v. 7).[8] It does not seem necessary to think that Jude's opponents are teaching that human beings should mingle sexually with angels. His concern seems to be more generally with the violation of commonly observed sexual boundaries and with using God's gracious character as a reason for doing so without fear of God's punishment.[9]

4 Bauckham, *Jude, 2 Peter*, 55, translates the participle *enypniazomenoi*, "on the strength of their dreams" and observes that the verb *enypniazesthai* often appears in the LXX to describe false prophecy. See Deut. 13:2, 4, 6; Isa. 56:10; Jer. 23:25; 36:8.

5 This is Bauckham's translation in *Jude, 2 Peter*, 93, 98.

6 The LXX uses the verb *diagongyzō* in Ex. 15:24; 16:2; Num. 14:2, 36; 16:11; the verb *gongyzō* in 14:27, 29; and the noun *gongysmos* in Ex. 16:12; Num. 16:7–9; 17:20, 25.

7 BDAG, 141, explains the term *aselgeia* as "lack of self-constraint which involves one in conduct that violates all bounds of what is socially acceptable."

8 BDAG, 102.

9 Commentators are divided over whether Jude is thinking of the homosexuality of the inhabitants of Sodom and Gomorrah when he says that they acted immorally and went after "other flesh." For the case that he does not have homosexuality in view, see, e.g., Henning Paulsen, *Der zweite Petrusbrief und der Judasbrief* (MeyerK 12/2; Göttingen: Vandenhoeck & Ruprecht, 1992),

It is possible that the false teachers are trying to turn the Christian community's "love feasts" into opportunities for sexual debauchery. Jude charges his opponents with using these Christian meals to engage in immoral behavior: They feast together with believers "shamelessly" (*aphobōs*), he says, and they are *spilades*—either "rocks" or "stains"—on these occasions (v. 12).[10] Since banqueting in Greek and Roman antiquity commonly involved gluttony, drunkenness and sexual liaisons, it seems likely that Jude's opponents are trying to transform Christian cultic meals into just this kind of symposium or convivium.[11] The first-century Roman educational theorist Quintillian, for example, bemoans the unsuitable environment for the education of children to be found in many Roman homes of the elite classes. Among other problems, "every dinner party is loud with foul songs, and things are presented to [the children's] eyes of which we should blush to speak" (*Inst.* 1.2.8).[12]

By the late second century, Christian feasting had developed a bad reputation within Roman society generally. "You . . . abuse our humble feasts," says Tertullian to detractors of Christianity in his *Apology* (sec. 39), "on the ground that they are extravagant as well as infamously wicked." Pagan feasting is both lavish and debauched, he complains, but it is about the "modest supper-room of the Christians alone" that "a great ado is made."[13]

Jude, therefore, may be concerned with people who have entered the Christian community and begun to teach that since they are covered by God's grace, Christians should use their *agapē* feasts as occasions to indulge their appetites for food, drink, and sex. Although certain heretical groups of the early third century (specifically the Carpocratians) taught something similar to this, there is no indication that, like gnostic groups, Jude's opponents justify their teaching with complex philosophical or cosmological speculation.[14] They seem simply to have excused their bad behavior by appealing to the gospel of God's grace.

64, and Anton Vögtle, *Der Judasbrief, der Zweite Petrusbrief* (EKK 22; Solothurn: Benziger/Neukirchen-Vluyn: Neukirchener, 1994), 43. For the case that he was thinking at least in part of homosexual behavior, see J. N. D. Kelly, *A Commentary on the Epistles of Peter and Jude* (BNTC; London: A. and C. Black, 1969), 259, 261; Jerome Neyrey, *2 Peter, Jude* (AB 37C; New York: Doubleday, 1993), 61; and Robert A. J. Gagnon, *The Bible and Homosexual Practice: Texts and Hermeneutics* (Nashville: Abingdon, 2001), 87–88.

10 BDAG, 938, do not try to decide between the two options. For "rocks" see, e.g., Bauckham, *Jude, 2 Peter*, 86–87, and Vögtle, *Das Judasbrief/Der zweite Petrusbrief*, 67 ("Felsriffe" or "Klippen"); cf. Kelly, *Epistles of Peter and Jude*, 270, who, however, believes that the rocks are "hidden." For "stains" see, e.g., Paulsen, *Der zweite Petrusbrief und der Judasbrief*, 69, 71 ("Flecken" or "Schandflecken"), and Neyrey, *2 Peter, Jude*, 74–75.

11 On customs of Greek and Roman banqueting in antiquity, see Alan Booth, "The Age for Reclining and Its Attendant Perils," in *Dining in a Classical Context*, ed. William J. Slater (Ann Arbor: Univ. of Michigan Press, 1991), 105–20.

12 I am indebted to Booth, "Age for Reclining," 112–13, for drawing this passage to my attention.

13 Like Jude (12), Tertullian calls this feast specifically the *agapē*. For similar charges against Christians, see the paraphrase of Celsus in Origen, *Cels.* 6.40, and the quotation of Marcus Aurelius's tutor, Marcus Cornelius Fronto, in Minucius Felix, *Oct.* 9. Clement of Alexandria laments that the gnostic Carpocratians have brought the name of Christ under censure by their behavior and then later charges them with gluttony and sexual promiscuity at a feast that Clement refuses to dignify with the Christian name of "love feast" (*Strom.* 3.2.5.1; 3.2.10.1). Cf. Justin, *1 Apol.* 26, who suggests that the Marcionites may be responsible for the unfortunate rumors that circulate about Christian feasting.

14 On the beliefs of the Carpocratians, see Clement, *Strom.* 3.2. Clement saw so much similarity between what the Carpocratians taught and the false teaching described in Jude that he believed Jude had prophesied the emergence of "these and similar sects in his letter" (3.2.11.2). I have used the translation by John Ferguson, *Clement of Alexandria* (FC 85; Washington, D.C.: Catholic Univ. of America Press, 1991), 263.

Second, Jude claims that his opponents "slander celestial beings" (*doxas*; lit., "glories"). At first this statement may seem to support the idea that Jude is opposing at least incipient gnostic cosmological speculation, and it has sometimes been taken this way.[15] According to Irenaeus, the Carpocratians claimed that evil angels, led by the devil himself, created the world, and this would certainly count as slandering celestial beings.[16] Still, if something like this lies behind the error that Jude attacks, it is difficult to see why Jude focuses his counterargument on the slandering of angels rather than on the more serious error that these angels rather than God created the world.[17]

Some scholars hold that the author of Jude is promoting a theology that was opposed by the writer of Colossians, who championed Christ as supreme over all angelic beings and thus taught that angels should not be worshiped. Jude, so it seems to these scholars, is concerned that certain human beings are slandering angels instead of giving them the honor that is their due (Jude 8)—which is precisely what Paul wrote against.[18] It is a large jump, however, from Jude's concern that angelic beings not be blasphemed to the idea that they should actually be worshiped. The text of Colossians, moreover, speaks disparagingly not of all angelic beings, but of inimical angelic beings and of the attempt to placate them through worship.

Is it possible, then, that the false teachers in Jude are slandering the angels who, according to Jewish and early Christian tradition, were present at the giving of the law?[19] Perhaps such a view went hand-in-glove with their antinomianism.[20] This is a reasonable idea, but, if correct, it seems strange that Jude omits any mention of the law here.

The most plausible suggestion may be that the false teachers laugh off the notion that they will face a future judgment for their actions—a judgment that both the Lord Jesus Christ and the angels will execute.[21] They scoff at the significant place that angels occupy in the eschatology of Jude's camp. Notions that angels who sinned sexually in primordial times are actually being held for judgment in the final day (v. 6; *1 En.* 10.6) and that God will bring countless thousands of his angels with him when he comes to execute judgment on the wicked (vv. 14–15; *1 En.* 1.9) are to them worthy of scorn (v. 18).

The false teaching that Jude faces, therefore, claims that God's grace excludes the future judgment of sinful acts. They use this notion as a theoretical support for their permissive attitude toward immorality, and they use Christian *agapē* feasts as an opportunity to act on this false teaching. Jude, however, does not consider them

15 See, e.g., James Moffatt, *The General Epistles: James, Peter and Judas* (MNTC; London: Hodder & Stoughton, 1928), 235, and Kelly, *Epistles of Peter and Jude*, 264.

16 Irenaeus, *Haer.* 1.25.

17 Bauckham, *Jude, 2 Peter*, 12, 58.

18 Roman Heiligenthal, *Zwischen Henoch und Paulus: Studien zum theologiegeschichtlichen Ort des Judasbriefes* (TANZ 6; Tübingen: A. Francke, 1992), 95–127. Cf. Gerhard Sellin, "Die Häretiker des Judasbriefes," *ZNW* 77 (1986): 206–25, here at 214–17.

19 See, e.g., Acts 7:38, 53; Heb. 2:2. In *Jubilees* God commands the angel of the presence to "write for Moses from the first creation until my sanctuary is built in their midst forever and ever," and this angel then tells Moses to "write the whole account of the creation" (*Jub.* 1.27–2.1; *OTP* 2.54–55). Josephus says, similarly, that Jews "have learned the noblest of our doctrines and the holiest of our laws from the messengers [*angelōn*] sent by God" (*A. J.* 15.136). I am indebted for these references to Bauckham, *Jude, 2 Peter*, 58.

20 Bauckham, *Jude, 2 Peter*, 58–59.

21 Vögtle, *Das Judasbrief/Der zweite Petrusbrief*, 57–58. Vögtle believes that the "lordship" the false teachers "reject" according to v. 8 is the role of Christ the Lord in the judgment.

Christians at all—they are "worldly" (*psychikoi*), he says, and do not have the Spirit (v. 19b). Their worldliness manifests itself not only in their behavior but in the divisiveness that their false teaching has brought to the community (v. 19a).

All this is not unlike the mixture of Christianity and Greco-Roman culture that Paul encountered in Corinth.[22] In his letters to the Corinthians he had to confront the notion that Christians could freely indulge their sexual appetites and participate in idolatrous feasts (1 Cor. 6:12–20; 8:1–10:22; 2 Cor. 12:21). "Everything is permissible for me" (1 Cor. 6:12; 10:35) and "food for the stomach and the stomach for food" (6:13) were popular Corinthian slogans.

Paul saw such notions as both "worldly" (*psychikos*, 1 Cor. 2:14–16) and "fleshly" (*sarkinos*, 3:1–4), and he identified these attitudes as a source of Corinthian divisiveness (3:3–4).[23] He urged the Corinthians to take seriously both the belief in a final judgment (3:13–15; 6:13) and the belief that angels were present in the Christian community's corporate worship of God (11:10). He tried to persuade them to reject teachers who charged speaking fees (2 Cor. 11:7; cf. 12:14) and boasted of their rhetorical prowess (10:9, 12; 11:6, 18). Paul says in Romans (written from Corinth) that some people concluded from his teaching that they should "do evil that good may result" (Rom. 3:8; cf. 6:1, 15). Perhaps the Corinthians justified their own sinful behavior from a perverse understanding of Paul's teaching on God's grace.

Paul's own response to this distortion of his teaching appears throughout the Corinthian letters and in Romans 6–8. In his own letter, Jude, the "brother of James," provides a glimpse of how the circle of Christians who identified primarily with James, the Lord's brother, responded to a similar error.[24]

JUDE'S RESPONSE: ESCHATOLOGICAL JUDGMENT AND PRESENT HOPE

Jude wants his readers to understand who his opponents are, the eschatological judgment toward which they are moving, and, by implication, what will happen to Christians who fall prey to their deceptions. He also gives his readers a strategy for coping with the false teachers in the present. Jude builds this strategy on the hope that not only can his readers avoid falling prey to the false teaching but that they can rescue others—including the false teachers themselves—who are already in its grasp.

Jude's Opponents as the Eschatological Opponents of God's People

Through a series of allusions to Scripture and traditional Jewish interpretations of it, Jude exposes the false teachers as the opponents of God who will arise in the

22 Cf. Rainer Riesner, "Der zweite Petrus-brief und die Eschatologie," in *Zukunftserwartung in biblischer Sicht: Beiträge zur Eschatologie*, ed. Gerhard Maier (MStud 313; Wuppertal: R. Brockhaus Verlag, 1984), 124–43, here at 135.

23 Cf. Sellin, "Die Häretiker," 218.

24 Sellin, "Die Häretiker," 209–11, argues that the author is alluding to Rom. 3:8 when he says in v. 4 that the false teachers' condemnation "was written about in those days." Sellin also proposes that when the author speaks of "this condemnation" (*touto to krima*) he means the "condemnation" (*to krima*) that Paul pronounces on those who have slandered his teaching. This proposal, although interesting, is less likely than the notion that Jude refers in v. 4 to the prophecies recorded in vv. 5–19. See Bauckham, *Jude, 2 Peter*, 35–37.

last days.[25] They fulfill both prophecies and typological pointers that their kind of rebellion against God would plague the final era of God's dealings with his people. Some of these prophesies and types were written down "long ago" (v. 4) in Scripture and in traditional interpretations of Scripture, and some of them were spoken more recently by "the apostles of our Lord Jesus Christ" (v. 17), but both predicted that from among God's people a group would emerge who advocated faithlessness, rebellion, and shameless conduct and, in so doing, would seek to lead God's people astray.

The false teachers, therefore, do not simply act like the faithless generation of Israelites in Numbers 14:1–45, the fallen angels of Genesis 6:2 (interpreted through the lens of *1 En.* 6–7), and the Sodomites of Genesis 19:1–9 (Jude 5–7, 12, 13). These passages actually describe the false teachers of Jude's time typologically.[26] The same is true of the passages in the Scriptures that describe Cain, Balaam, and Korah as Jude's comment in verse 11 shows (cf. Gen. 4:8; Num. 31:15–16; 16:1–40). The false teachers, he says there, "have been destroyed in Korah's rebellion." The future judgment of the false teachers in some sense took place when Korah and his followers were destroyed during the days of the Exodus. Korah and his rebels are the type of which Jude's opponents are the corresponding, eschatological antitype.

Similarly, Jude believes that the wicked kings of Israel, identified metaphorically in Ezekiel 34 as shepherds, are biblical types to which the false teachers correspond as antitypes. Just as Ezekiel's shepherds "have cared for themselves rather than for my flock" (Ezek. 34:8; cf. 34:2), so Jude's opponents appear at the Christian *agapē* meal "as shepherds who feed only themselves" (Jude 12). They also correspond to Isaiah's description of those who refuse to respond to God's mercy with repentance. "The wicked," says Isaiah, "are like the tossing sea, which cannot rest, whose waves cast up mire and mud" (Isa. 57:20). Jude, echoing these words, calls his opponents "wild waves of the sea, foaming up their shame" (Jude 13).

In addition to these prior records of the false teachers in Scripture, more recent prophecy from "the apostles of our Lord Jesus Christ" has indicated that in the last times "scoffers" would arise (Jude 17–18). Jude views his opponents as these scoffers. Their appearance within the Christian community to whom Jude writes, therefore, is an expected, if troublesome, development of the world's final age (v. 18; cf. 1 Tim. 4:1; 2 Tim. 3:1–5).

The Destiny of Jude's Opponents

If the appearance of these false teachers in the present reveals that they are the expected end-time enemies of God's people, then their judgment in the future, unless they repent, is certain. Those whom God delivered from slavery in Egypt afterward "did not believe," and God "destroyed" them (v. 5). Jude alludes here to Numbers 14, which speaks of God's displeasure with the Israelites' refusal "to believe" in him (14:11) and of God's promise to punish this disbelief by barring all those over nineteen years

25 Bauckham, *Jude and the Relatives of Jesus*, 216–21.

26 See esp. the exegesis of vv. 5–10 in Bauckham, *Jude, 2 Peter*, 42–64, and idem, *Jude and the Relatives of Jesus*, 187–88.

old from entering the land (14:26–35). "Your bodies," God tells them, "will fall in this desert" (14:32). The implication for Jude's opponents is clear: They are on a path that leads to eschatological destruction.

Similarly, God consigned the rebellious angels of Genesis 6:2, 4 to a dark imprisonment, where they await their final judgment (Jude 6). Here Jude adopts the interpretation of Genesis 6:1–8 found in *1 Enoch*, where the "sons of God" are identified as angels whose desire for beautiful human women led them to "abandon the high heaven," which was their assigned dwelling place (*1 En.* 12.4; cf. 15.3, 10) and intermarry with human beings (6.1–7.6). Like Jude's false teachers, these rebellious angels "taught" their wives evil practices (7.1; 9.6). God instructed the good angel Raphael to execute judgment on the leader of these rebellious angels. "Bind Azazʾel hand and foot," God tells Raphael, "(and) throw him into the darkness!" Raphael then made a hole in the desert, threw Azazʾel into it, and covered him with rocks to keep him in darkness until he is "sent into fire on the great day of judgment" (10.4–6). Somewhat later, it becomes clear that the other rebellious angels shared Azazʾel's fate (19; 21.10).

Apparently, after the "great day of judgment," the lot of these angels will not improve. They will join "the stars of heaven which have transgressed the commandments of the Lord" in a "terrible opening," a "prison house" where "they are detained forever" (*1 En.* 21.7–10; cf. 18.9–19.3; cf. 88.1–3).

Jude wants his readers to know that the false teachers in their midst are moving toward something like this fearful fate. He reminds them of the temporary imprisonment of the rebellious angels in darkness (Jude 6). He quotes Enoch to show his readers that the Lord Jesus will come, accompanied by angels, to judge and convict the ungodly (v. 14; *1 En.* 1.9). He also recalls the ultimate fate of Enoch's transgressing stars and rebellious angels when he describes the false teachers as "wandering stars, for whom blackest darkness has been reserved forever" (Jude 13).[27]

In addition, Jude reminds his readers of the judgment that God visited on Sodom and its environs (v. 7). Like the false teachers, the people of Sodom had mixed sexual immorality with scorn for angelic beings (Gen. 19:1–9). God met this wickedness with a rain of "burning sulfur" (19:24) that destroyed the area, including its vegetation. The destruction was so complete that "smoke" rose "from the land, like smoke from a furnace" (19:28). Jude's present tense comment that the destroyed cities "are exhibited as an example" (*prokeintai*) of those who suffer eternal punishment probably means that he understands the site of the "cities of the plain" to be the southern Dead Sea region, a barren wasteland that continues to testify to the destruction God had long ago brought to the wicked people who once lived there.[28]

27 Bauckham, *Jude, 2 Peter*, 89–90; Paulsen, *Der zweite Petrusbrief und der Judasbrief*, 72–73; and Vögtle, *Der Judasbrief/Der zweite Petrusbrief*, 69. Bauckham observes that Jude may also have *1 En.* 80 in mind since in that text erring stars lead sinners astray.

28 Bauckham, *Jude, 2 Peter*, 54–55; idem, *Jude and the Relatives of Jesus*, 187; Vögtle, *Der Judasbrief, der zweite Petrusbrief*, 45–46. Josephus, *B. J.* 4.476–85, says that next to the Dead Sea is "the land of Sodom, in days of old a country blest in its produce and in the wealth of its various cities, but now all burnt up. It is said that, owing to the impiety of its inhabitants, it was consumed by thunderbolts; and in fact vestiges of the divine fire and faint traces of five cities are still visible" (4.483–84). Cf. Wisd. 10:7: "Evidence of their wickedness still remains: a continually smoking wasteland, plants bearing fruit that does not ripen, and a pillar of salt standing as a monument to an unbelieving soul."

His claim that the false teachers have taken Cain's way and rushed for profit into Balaam's error (Jude 11) probably also intends to remind his readers of the punishment that these figures received for their impiety and false teaching. God punished Cain with a curse, condemning him to the status of "a restless wanderer on the earth" (Gen. 4:12). Similarly Balaam, who advised the Midianites to entice Israel into sexual immorality and idolatry, was killed along with the Midianites when God commanded his people to take vengeance on them (Num. 31:8, 16; cf. Josh. 13:22). Jude's reminder becomes explicit with the third figure, Korah, who led a rebellion against the priesthood of Moses and Aaron. God punished Korah and his band by opening the earth so that it swallowed them, and "they went down alive into the grave" (Num. 16:33). Unless they repent, Jude is so certain that the false teachers will suffer a similar fate that he can speak of them as if they too were "destroyed in Korah's rebellion."

A Strategy for Coping with the False Teachers

Why does Jude place such emphasis on the eschatological punishment of these false teachers? He does this to lay the ground work for the strategy that he commends to his readers for resisting them. The goal of this strategy is both to guard the readers themselves from plunging into the pit of eschatological destruction (Jude 20–21, 23) and to suggest a method for rescuing those who stand on the brink of this final disaster, including the false teachers themselves (vv. 22–23).

How Jude's Readers Can Avoid Falling into Error

In Jude 20–21, Jude advises his readers on how they can avoid succumbing to the false teaching and suffering the fearsome fate he has just described for the false teachers. He does this in four admonitions, the last of which lays an eschatological foundation for the other three.[29] In this last admonition, Jude tells his readers to await the mercy of their Lord Jesus Christ, who will bring them into eternal life (v. 21b). What are they to do while they wait? The first three admonitions in verses 20–21 tell them.

First, they should "build [themselves] up in [their] most holy faith" (v. 20a). This way of speaking of the faith is reminiscent of the letter's beginning, where Jude announces that he intends to provide a strategy by which his readers can "contend for the faith that was once for all entrusted to the saints" (v. 3).[30] "The faith" here seems to refer to a standard body of teaching from which Jude's opponents have deviated,

29 Vögtle, *Der Judasbrief, der zweite Petrusbrief,* 99, believes that the participles in v. 20 (*epoikodomountes* and *proseuchomenoi*) are dependent upon the imperative (*tērēsate*) in v. 21, but Bauckham, *Jude, 2 Peter,* 111–12, is correct to view all four verbal forms in vv. 20 and 21 (including *prosdechomenoi* in v. 21) as having imperative force.

30 This way of speaking is not a sign of "early catholicism," as, for example, Werner Georg Kümmel, *Introduction to the New Testament,* rev. ed. (Nashville: Abingdon, 1975), 426–27, claims with specific reference to Jude 3: "The letter does not contain any real message of Christ at all, and its 'early Catholic' concept of faith stands in unrelieved tension with the understanding of faith in the chief witnesses of the NT." How then can we explain Paul's positive summary of the Judean Christians' reference to his preaching as the proclamation of "the faith [*tēn pistin*] he once tried to destroy" (Gal. 1:23)? Evidently this was the way the earliest Jewish Christian community in Palestine summarized the content of the gospel that they and others preached. It is not unnatural, therefore, for Jude, as a member of this community, to refer to the faith in this way.

and now Jude tells his readers that they must build on the foundation of this body of teaching, not on the unstable foundation that the false teachers have advocated.

Second, they should "pray in the Holy Spirit" (v. 20b). Jude's description of the false teachers as relying on their dreams (v. 8) and "not having the Spirit" (v. 19) may reflect their own claims that their teaching included Spirit-inspired prophecy.[31] Perhaps in this second admonition, Jude takes the emphasis off proclaiming what the Spirit teaches—a notion that the false teachers have used to their own advantage—and places it on the Spirit's role in assisting the believers' prayers.

Third, Jude's readers should "keep [themselves] in God's love" (v. 21a). This is probably an ethical admonition, designed to counter the unethical behavior of the false teachers. The initiative that God has taken to show us love implies that we must "keep" ourselves in that love by living in the way that God requires.[32]

If Jude's readers follow his advice and persevere until the time when "Jesus Christ" brings them "to eternal life" (v. 21), then they will avoid the fate of Israel's wilderness generation, the rebellious angels, the cities of the plain, Cain, Balaam, Korah's followers, Ezekiel's wicked shepherds, Isaiah's unrepentant wicked—and the false teachers in their midst. Jude is confident that God will enable his readers to avoid "falling" and that they will appear before him on the final day "without fault" (v. 24).

How Jude's Readers Can Help Those under the False Teaching's Influence

Jude is also concerned, however, about the rescue of those who have fallen under the spell of the false teaching. Probably the short, "two-clause" form of verses 22–23, preserved in a third-century papyrus manuscript (P^{72}), represents what Jude originally wrote at this point in his letter. If so, then these lines read, "Snatch some from the fire, but on those who dispute have mercy with fear, hating even the clothing that has been soiled by the flesh."[33] Jude advocates separate approaches to those who have fallen under the influence of the false teachers and to the false teachers themselves. The community should not give up on those who are sympathetic with the false teachers. They should snatch them from the "eternal fire" that the cities of the plain are already experiencing (v. 7).

A different approach is necessary for the false teachers themselves, since here rescue from the fire involves the dangerous possibility of deceit and destruction for the rescuers themselves. Jude says that his readers should show mercy to "those who dispute"—that is, the false teachers themselves. He is not explicit about what he hopes this mercy will accomplish, but he probably has in mind something similar to Paul's advice to Timothy:

> Those who oppose [the Lord's servant] he must gently instruct, in the hope that God will grant them repentance leading them to a knowledge of the truth, and that they will come to their senses and escape from the trap of the devil, who has taken them captive to do his will. (2 Tim. 2:25–26)

31 Bauckham, *Jude, 2 Peter*, 11, 55–56, 106–7, 113.
32 Ibid., 113–14.
33 Ibid.,108–11. Cf. Neyrey, *2 Peter, Jude*, 85–86.

Jude wants his readers to pursue this course with caution, however. They should "fear" what will become of them if the influence should run the other way. They should, moreover, avoid the merest taint from the false teachers' immoral behavior.

DEVIATION, JUDGMENT, AND MERCY IN JUDE

Jude takes the appearance of false teachers among his readers to be a sign that he and other Christians are living in "the last age." This conviction lends special urgency to his letter. The last chapter in God's dealings with his creatures, he says, has begun, and the final judgment of the wicked may come at any time. In light of this, Jude warns his readers of the eschatological consequences that will come to those whose teaching deviates from "the faith once for all delivered to the saints" if they do not repent. He implies that if his readers fall prey to their teaching, they too will experience these consequences.

The false teachers have argued that God's grace exempts Christians from moral responsibility and that final judgment is a figment of fertile apocalyptic imaginations. In response, Jude claims that one need only survey the Scriptures as Jewish tradition has interpreted them to know that these two tenets of the false teaching are foolish and perilous ideas. Indeed, one need only look at the smoking wasteland south of the Dead Sea to know that those who act like the inhabitants of the cities of the plain—showing disrespect for moral norms and for angelic beings—cannot escape the judgment of God.

It is not too late, however, for anyone—from sympathetic readers of Jude's letter, to the followers of the false teachers, to the false teachers themselves—to turn away from the brink of destruction. Jude's readers should focus on faith, love, and hope—the faith, unchanged from its traditional form, the love that originates with God and overflows into true love for others, and the hope that Jesus Christ will show mercy on the final day to those who have been faithful to him. Jude's readers should also reach out in mercy to rescue those tottering on the edge of the fiery abyss of judgment through their flirtations with the false teaching, and should even—albeit cautiously—show mercy to the false teachers themselves in the hope that they too may be saved.

Chapter 26

SECOND PETER: ETHICS AND ESCHATOLOGY

Second Peter is sometimes considered the one real embarrassment in the New Testament canon. It is said to have an affected and ostentatious literary style, to stoop to name-calling, to restrict the Spirit to the safety of church authority, and to exchange the Christological orientation of traditional Christian eschatology for an anthropological orientation.[1] This modern evaluation of the book stands in contrast to the value that the ancient church placed on it, for although it struggled to rise to the level of a canonical writing, it was widely read and valued even before it found a place in the canonical lists of all major Christian traditions.[2] A sympathetic hearing of the book, however, requires an understanding of the literary genre that it fills and of the historical problems that prompted its composition.[3]

PETER'S TESTAMENT AND ITS HISTORICAL SETTING

Just as James is both a letter and "wisdom paraenesis," so 2 Peter is both a letter and a testament. The beginning of the document, which follows the standard form for the opening of ancient letters, and the conclusion of the document, which also contains standard epistolary features, mark 2 Peter clearly as a letter. Just as clearly, however, this text is a "testament." In this literary genre, common in both Hellenistic Judaism and early Christianity, a person on the verge of death gives a set of ethical instructions and prophecies to relatives or followers who are gathered in his presence. Often, although not always, the setting is fictional, and the one giving the speech is a great luminary from the past (e.g., Abraham, one of Jacob's sons, Moses, Job).

1 Peter Müller, "Der 2. Petrusbrief," *TRu* 66 (2001): 310–37, here at 310, 315, 322–23, provides an overview of such criticisms. See esp. Ernst Käsemann, *Essays on New Testament Themes* (Philadelphia: Fortress, 1964), 169–95; Günther Klein, *Ärgernisse: Konfrontationen mit dem Neuen Testament* (München: Chr. Kaiser Verlag, 1970), 109–14; James D. G. Dunn, *Unity and Diversity in the New Testament: An Inquiry into the Character of Earliest Christianity* (Philadelphia: Westminster, 1977), 350–51; and Ralph P. Martin, "The Theology of Jude, 1 Peter, and 2 Peter" in *The Theology of the Letters of James, Peter, and Jude*, by Andrew Chester and Ralph P. Martin (New Testament Theology; Cambridge: Cambridge Univ. Press, 1994), 163.

2 Although the evidence is disputed, Clement of Rome and the authors of *2 Clement*, *Barnabas*, and the *Shepherd of Hermas* may have used 2 Peter around the end of the first century. M. Minucius Felix, Justin, and Irenaeus may also refer to it in the second century. Second Peter appears in P72 from the early third century. Although Origen knows that it is a disputed work, he uses it often and considers it to be one of Peter's "two trumpets" (*Hom. Jes. Nav.* 7.1). Eusebius, *Hist. eccl.* 3.3.1, although he does not consider 2 Peter canonical, says that it "nevertheless . . . has appeared useful to many, and has been studied with other Scriptures." Later he counts it among "the Disputed Books which are nevertheless known to most" (3.25.3). On all this see Carsten Peter Thiede, "A Pagan Reader of 2 Peter: Cosmic Conflagration in 2 Peter 3 and the *Octavius* of Minucius Felix," *JSNT* 26 (1986): 79–96; Robert E. Picirilli, "Allusions to 2 Peter in the Apostolic Fathers," *JSNT* 33 (1988): 57–83; and P. H. R. van Houwelingen, *De tweede trompet: de authenticiteit van de tweede brief van Petrus* (Kampen: Kok, 1988), 21–35, 299.

3 Cf. Jerome Neyrey, "The Form and Background of the Polemic in 2 Peter," *JBL* 99 (1980): 407–31, here at 407 and 430–31.

In 2 Peter, Peter is close to death (1:14–15). He wants to remind his readers of the ethical responsibilities that "the way of truth" (2:2), which leads to the "eternal kingdom of our Lord and Savior Jesus Christ" (1:11), entails (cf. 3:11–14). He also speaks prophetically of the emergence of false teachers in the church (2:1) who have deviated from "the straight way" (2:15) and therefore face eschatological judgment (2:3b–10, 17b).[4] Although Peter says that these false teachers will come in the future in accord with the dictates of the testament genre (2:1–3a; 3:3), he makes clear by his use of the present and aorist tenses that they are already in the churches he addresses (2:4–22; 3:5, 16).[5]

These false teachers have precipitated the crisis that prompts the letter, and in order to understand Peter's response to them we must first understand what they teach. They were at one time themselves "cleansed from past sins" (1:9) and "escaped the corruption of the world by knowing our Lord and Savior Jesus Christ" (2:20). Now, however, they have brought "the way of truth into disrepute" (2:2), have "left the straight way" (2:15), and have abandoned "the way of righteousness" (2:21). They have also introduced destructive teachings into the churches (2:1).

These false teachings have two chief characteristics. First, they deny that God will, in the future, judge people for their wickedness. Not only does this understanding of their teaching seem likely from Peter's frequent insistence on the certainty of eschatological judgment, but, as we found in our study of Jude's letter, it seems to be the best understanding of the claim that the opponents are not afraid to "slander celestial beings" (2:10b; *doxas*, lit., "glories"). As in Jude 8, the "glories" are probably the angels who will be present at the final judgment.

The false teachers are attacking the traditional Christian position on an eschatological day of judgment in two ways. On one hand, they claim that the idea of Jesus' glorious return (at which the judgment will take place) is a fabrication both of the Old Testament prophets and of the apostles. The prophets may have had visions and dreams of some sort, but their writings are a product of their own imaginations (1:20–21).[6] Something more sinister has happened in the case of the apostles; they have followed cleverly devised tales to dupe people about "the power and coming" of Jesus Christ (1:16).[7] By contrast, the false teachers appear to claim that the idea of such a "final" day is unreasonable. God, they say, has not intruded on creation from its beginning (3:4b), and all the claims that Jesus Christ will return have remained unfulfilled too long for them to carry conviction (3:4a, 9a).[8]

Second, the false teachers deduce from their denial of any future judgment that they can break the boundaries of decency. According to Peter, they promote "shameful ways" (*aselgeiais*, 2:2; cf. Jude 4) and "follow the flesh in defiling lust" (2:10a). They have adulterous eyes and are ceaseless sinners (2:14). They have ensnared

4 Richard Bauckham, *Jude, 2 Peter* (WBC 50; Waco, Tex.: Word, 1983), 131. Robert A. Kugler, *The Testaments of the Twelve Patriarchs* (Guides to the Apocrypha and Pseudepigrapha; Sheffield: Sheffield Academic Press, 2001), 16, points out that although there is disagreement among scholars about the precise content of the testamentary genre, the literary form of death-bed instruction is widely accepted as the genre's dominant characteristic.

5 Cf. 1 Tim. 4:1–5, 7; 2 Tim. 3:1–9.

6 Bauckham, *Jude, 2 Peter*, 235.

7 Ibid., 155, 221.

8 Ibid., 154–56, 294.

recent converts to Christianity with empty promises of fleshly debauchery and moral freedom (2:18–19). They apparently make good on these promises at Christian feasts, probably the "love feasts" familiar from Jude 12. According to 2 Peter 2:13, "their idea of pleasure is to carouse in broad daylight. They are blots and blemishes, reveling in their pleasures while they feast with you."

Peter accuses these false teachers of being motivated by greed (2:3, 15), and he is concerned that their behavior "will bring the way of truth into disrepute" (2:2). From what we have seen of the worries that many Romans had about the socially disruptive nature of Christianity, and particularly of Christian feasting, in this period, this is a valid concern.[9]

Can we locate these opponents more specifically? Although some commentators are impressed by the differences between this letter's opponents and those in Jude, there are many similarities.[10] Jude's opponents changed "the grace of our God into a license for immorality," a probable reference to the misinterpretation of Paul's teaching on God's grace (Jude 4). Peter's opponents similarly "distort" Paul's letters to their own destruction (2 Peter 3:16). The two characteristics of Peter's opponents that seem most prominent—the denial of a coming judgment and advocacy of debauchery, particularly at Christian feasts—are also prominent features of Jude's opponents (Jude 8, 12, 14–15). Both sets of opponents are teachers (2 Peter 2:1; Jude 8, 12), both upset the established structure of church authority (2 Peter 2:10; Jude 6, 8, 11, 16), and both adopt an attitude of scorn toward orthodox teachings with which they disagree (2 Peter 2:10b–12; 3:3–4, 9; Jude 8–10, 18).

It is true that Jude implies his opponents have infiltrated the community from outside geographically (Jude 4) whereas Peter implies no more than that his opponents are outside the doctrinal boundaries of the faith (2:1), but there is no reason to think that Peter's opponents themselves have not also come from outside the area.[11] It seems likely, therefore, that the opponents of Jude and Peter are at least similar to each other and are possibly the same group.

Second Peter, however, focuses more effort than Jude on the theoretical dimension of the false teaching. Peter's rebuttal of the false teachers implies that they have thought about the Scriptures, and in particular about Paul's letters, and offered their own alternative to the orthodox interpretation of them (2 Peter 3:16). It is perhaps their appeal to the minds of Peter's readers that leads him to characterize them, in response, as "ignorant" (*amathēs*, 3:16) people with "fabricated arguments" (2:3).[12] Peter's emphasis on knowledge in his letter (1:2, 3, 5, 6, 8, 12; 3:18) and the description of his objective in writing as the stimulation of his readers to "wholesome thinking" (3:1; cf. 1:12–13,

9 See chapter 25, above.

10 Bauckham, *Jude, 2 Peter*, 143, 155–56, argues that the opponents in 2 Peter differ from those in Jude because (1) when the author of 2 Peter uses Jude's letter he omits Jude's references to his opponents' claim to have the Spirit and to receive prophetic revelation (cf. Jude 8 and 19 with 2 Peter 2:10); (2) the author omits any reference to the opponents' perversion of God's grace (cf. Jude 4 with 2 Peter 2:1–3); (3) the opponents in 2 Peter claim to be teachers rather than prophets (2 Peter 2:1), but Jude's opponents probably claimed to be prophets under the influence of the Spirit (Jude 8 and 19); and (4) Jude's opponents blasphemed the angels who gave the law (Jude 8–9), whereas the opponents in 2 Peter laugh at the idea that they could be under the power of the devil (2 Peter 2:10).

11 *Pace* Bauckham, *Jude, 2 Peter*, 239.

12 For this translation of *plastois logois*, see Bauckham, *Jude, 2 Peter*, 243.

15) make most sense as a response to a situation in which his opponents have appealed to his readers' understanding.

Peter may have therefore known information about the false teaching that we cannot glean from Jude, or he may have theorized from what he read in Jude the kinds of arguments that the false teachers were using.[13] They not only deny a future judgment but use the delay of Christ's coming as an argument against it. If the Lord promised to return, they say, he is certainly being slow about it (3:9). In addition, they use the argument that the world has, since creation, ticked along in the same orderly way with no cataclysmic intervention on God's part. "Ever since our fathers died," they say, "everything goes on as it has since the beginning of creation" (3:4).[14]

This second argument sounds like something that people under the influence of Epicurean philosophy would say.[15] Epicureans viewed God in the way they liked to view themselves, as untroubled by pain or fear. Epicurus argued that "the blessed and eternal being has no trouble himself and brings no trouble upon any other being; hence he is exempt from movements of anger and kindness" (Diogenes Laertius, *Vitae philosophorum*, 10.139).[16]

One implication of this teaching, an implication that the Epicureans drew and for which they were criticized, was that one's conduct in the present life had no implications for what happened after death. The view appears in the first line of Epicurus's *Tetrapharmakos*, or "four-fold remedy," a summary of his basic beliefs: "God presents no fears, death no cause for alarm; it is easy to procure what is good; it is also easy to endure what is evil" (Philodemus, *Ad contubernales* in *Papyri Herculanenses* 11005, cols. 4.9–14).[17]

Although Epicurus did not conclude from this belief that one should live to gratify bodily pleasures, he was popularly thought to have advocated such a life and was charged with advocating a philosophy that inevitably led to immorality.[18] The Christian apologist Lactantius (ca. 240–ca. 320), for example, complains that Epicurean theology leads people inevitably into wickedness:

> If any chieftain of pirates or leader of robbers were exhorting his men to acts of violence, what other language could he employ than to say the same things which Epicurus says: that the gods take no notice; that they are not affected with anger or kind feeling; that the punishment of a future state is not to be dreaded, because the souls die after death, and there is no future state of punishment at all.[19]

13 On the close literary relationship between Jude and 2 Peter and the probability that the author of 2 Peter used Jude in the composition of his work, see Bauckham, *2 Peter, Jude*, 141–43.

14 Commentators regularly claim that the "fathers" here are the first Christian generation and that therefore 2 Peter is a late first-century or early second-century document. The term "fathers," however, wherever it appears elsewhere in the New Testament, always means the patriarchs of the Old Testament, never the first generation of Christians. It likely means the Old Testament patriarchs here also. On this, see esp. Thomas R. Schreiner, *1, 2 Peter, and Jude* (NAC 37; Nashville: Broadman & Holman, 2003), 373–74.

15 Bauckham, *Jude, 2 Peter*, 294, following Neyrey, "Form and Background."

16 I have taken this quotation from Neyrey, *2 Peter, Jude*, 123. Cf. idem, "Form and Background," 408, and Michael Erler and Malcolm Schofield, "Epicurean Ethics," in *The Cambridge History of Hellenistic Philosophy*, ed. Keimpe Algra, Jonathan Barnes, Jaap Mansfeld, and Malcolm Schofield (Cambridge: Cambridge Univ. Press, 1999), 642–74, here at 646.

17 I have taken this quotation from Erler and Schofield, "Epicurean Ethics," 645.

18 Ibid., 642–43.

19 *Inst.* 3.17, as quoted in Neyrey, *2 Peter, Jude*, 123–24. Cf. idem, "Form and Background," 418.

Peter's opponents may be motivated primarily by a desire to satisfy their animal instincts (2:12), but they are also thinkers who have come up with a theoretical justification for their actions. Theirs is a considered approach to pleasure (2:13).[20] Although any connection between the opponents and Epicureanism must remain speculative, something like this philosophy may be providing Peter's opponents with the theoretical framework that they need for their false teaching.[21] If so, it probably does not trouble them in the least that Epicurus would not have approved of the conclusions they have drawn from his philosophy.

As a working hypothesis, we can imagine Jude's opponents, who took their teaching from place to place, eventually arriving in some of the churches to which Peter addressed his first letter. In that letter Peter had expressed a concern for the good reputation of Christians within the wider pagan culture (see ch. 30, below).[22] This newly arrived group, claiming Paul as their authority and mixing a perverse understanding of his emphasis on God's grace with something like Epicurean philosophy, has enticed some among these churches to follow them into debauchery. Because of their flagrant violation of commonly accepted norms (*aselgeia*), these false teachers are bringing "the way of truth into disrepute" (2:2) and are therefore not only damaging the gospel's appeal to outsiders but increasing the likelihood that outsiders will actively persecute Christians. More importantly, these false teachers are interfering with the growth of Christians in "the grace and knowledge of our Lord Jesus Christ" (3:18) and increasing the likelihood that on the Day of the Lord, they will not be "found spotless, blameless and at peace with him" (3:14).

Such a situation may have developed just prior to Peter's own martyrdom, perhaps while he was awaiting execution under Nero in Rome around A.D. 65. If so, then Peter may have committed the composition of his response to someone else who appropriately framed it in terms of the apostle's last will and testament. If something like this understanding of the letter is correct, then a forger did not attempt to rescue "the way of truth" from deceptive teaching with a deception of his own. Instead, Peter's authorized representative composes 2 Peter in his own grammatical and theological idiom.[23] He may have relied heavily for his understanding of the false

20 Peter describes his opponents in 2:13 as *ēdonēn hēgoumenoi tēn en hēmera tryphēn*, "considering self-indulgence in broad daylight to be pleasure." The term *hēgoumenoi* may have a somewhat technical sense here of "thinking through" the reasons for an action. Cf. BDAG, 434, who define *hēgeomai* as "to engage in an intellectual process, *think, consider, regard*."

21 Schreiner, *1, 2 Peter, and Jude*, 280, is correct to be cautious about Neyrey's Epicurean hypothesis. If the opponents have been influenced by Epicurean thinking, they are certainly not typical followers of Epicurus either in their theology (unlike Epicurean philosophy, they probably maintain some involvement of God in the world) or their ethics (their licentious tendencies would not have pleased Epicurus). The overlap, however, between the opponents and Epicurean thinking on the absence of eschatological judgment and the constancy of the universe render some influence of that philosophy on Peter's opponents plausible.

22 As I mention in the preface and at the end of ch. 23 above, I have not attempted to follow a chronological order for the New Testament texts treated in this third part of the book. I have placed the treatment of 2 Peter before that of 1 Peter because it seemed best to group it with the other texts that address heretical developments of the Pauline theological tradition (James and Jude) rather than with texts that address primarily the problem of persecution (1 Peter, Hebrews, and Revelation).

23 This understanding of the authorship of 2 Peter comes close to the position of John Calvin, *The Epistle of Paul the Apostle to the Hebrews and the First and Second Epistles of St. Peter* (Calvin's Commentaries; Grand Rapids: Eerdmans, 1963; orig. ed. 1551), 325. Most scholars assume that 2 Peter is a pseudepigraphical letter. Bauckham, *Jude, 2 Peter*, 158–62, offers the most compelling case for this position with his thesis that the testamentary genre of the letter would have alerted ancient readers that the letter itself was

teaching on both the letter of Jude and on his own familiarity with Epicurean philosophy. He writes to remind (1:12; 3:2) his readers of the certainty of judgment and, by this reminder, to rekindle their commitment to the Christian tradition as it had been handed down by prophets and apostles (1:1–13, 16–21; 3:1–2).[24]

THE WAY OF TRUTH AND THE DANGER OF DEVIATION FROM IT

Peter, through his commissioned representative, responds to the false teaching with both a positive presentation of the "way" that Christians should follow and a vigorous rebuttal of the false teachers' accusations. His positive presentation is concentrated in the letter's beginning (1:3–11) and conclusion (3:11–18); his refutation of the false teachers' position is in the letter's central section (1:12–3:10).

The Way of Truth and Righteousness

Peter conceives of the Christian life as a "road" or "way" (*hodos*) from which the false teachers have deviated. It is the "way of truth" (2:2), the "straight way" (2:15), or "the way of righteousness" (2:21). It is the way whose final steps Peter himself is about to tread, for his "departure" (*exodos*) is near (1:15). It is also the way that Peter wants his readers to tread faithfully so that they might "receive a rich welcome [*eisodos*] into the eternal kingdom of our Lord and Savior Jesus Christ" (1:11).

The end of this road is of critical theological importance for Peter. The "eternal kingdom of our Lord and Savior Jesus Christ" is the goal of Jesus' "very great and precious promises" (1:4; cf. 3:4, 9, 13). Entry to it will mean participation "in the divine nature and escape [from] the corruption in the world caused by evil desires" (1:4; cf. 2:20). It will also mean escape from the destruction that will come to the heavens and the earth (3:7, 10) and from the punishment that will come to the wicked (2:9–10, 12–13, 17, 21; 3:14) on "the day of the Lord" (3:10; cf. 2:9, 3:7, 12).

In his positive presentation of Christian existence, Peter emphasizes that virtuous living must characterize the Christian journey toward this day. Because Peter's readers are progressing toward a destination that will end in final escape from the world's corruption (1:4), they should "make every effort" to cultivate faith, goodness, knowledge, self-control, perseverance, godliness, brotherly kindness, and love (1:5–7).[25] Because the heavens and earth will be destroyed with a fiery roar (3:7, 10),

a transparent fiction. See, however, the comments of Brevard S. Childs on Bauckham's thesis in *The New Testament as Canon: An Introduction* (Philadelphia: Fortress, 1984), 468, and of Schreiner, *1, 2 Peter, and Jude*, 274–76. Perhaps the most sophisticated defense of the letter's authenticity in modern times appears in van Houwelingen, *Tweede trompet*, summarized in English on pp. 299–305. Cf. idem, *2 Petrus, Judas: Testament in tweevoud* (Commentaar op het Nieuwe Testament; Kampen: Kok, 1993), 11–27. In English, see the careful defense of Petrine authorship in Schreiner, *1, 2 Peter, and Jude*, 255–76.

24 Since on this theory the letter was written with Peter's authorization and during his lifetime, I will continue to refer to Peter as the author.

25 There is some debate over whether the participation in divine nature and escape from the world's lustful corruption occur eschatologically or in the present. James M. Starr, *Sharers in Divine Nature: 2 Peter 1:4 in Its Hellenistic Context* (ConBNT 33; Stockholm: Almqvist & Wiksell, 2000), 47–48, argues against an eschatological interpretation, citing 2:18–19 as evidence that the escape from lusts and corruption happens at conversion. The reference to Christ's "promises" in 1:4, however, is clearly eschatological (cf. 3:4, 9, 13) and orients the entire sentence to the last day.

Peter's readers should "live holy and godly lives" (3:11). Righteousness will find a home in the "new heavens and new earth" of God's biblical promises (3:13; cf. Isa. 65:17; 66:22).

This conception of Christian existence has sometimes come under harsh criticism. Some have seen it as fundamentally incompatible with the important theological conception articulated elsewhere in the New Testament of God's justification of the impious on the basis of his grace.[26] Second Peter, it is said, replaces that idea with "a doctrine of rewards and punishments" supposedly typical of Hellenistic Judaism and of "early catholicism." The Christian now becomes a gladiator who struggles for virtue and at the end of the process makes his "entry" (*eisodos*) into the kingdom "with full pomp and circumstance, with God himself as the master of ceremonies."[27] The author, it is said, has replaced the notion that the sinner can flee for refuge to the grace of God with an atmosphere of panic intended to frighten people into pious behavior.[28]

In addition, some believe that the author has conceded too much to Hellenistic conceptions of the world in these passages and painted a thoroughly dualistic picture of two worlds, one corrupt and evil and the other immortal and divine. The author urges his readers, it is said, to move from one realm to the other by cultivating a fairly typical list of Hellenistic virtues in 1:5–7. He has placed before them the Hellenistic ideal of escape from the corrupt world of sensory perception into union with God himself.[29]

These criticisms represent a misreading of both Peter's letter and the challenge that the false teaching posed to him. First, when considering the emphasis that Peter places on the Christian's pursuit of virtue, it is necessary to remember that even here, in the positive presentation of his message, he already has in mind the false teaching that has wreaked such havoc in the churches to which he writes, both at the level of leading Christians to destruction (2:18–19) and at the level of bringing Christianity itself into disrepute in the wider society (2:2). The virtues that Peter advocates serve as a barrier to becoming "ineffective and unproductive" in the "knowledge of our Lord Jesus Christ" not in some abstract sense, therefore, but in light of these practical problems that the false teachers have introduced. Peter probably has the false teachers specifically in mind when he says that "if anyone does not have" these virtues, "he is nearsighted and blind, and has forgotten that he has been cleansed from his past sins" (1:9; cf. 2:20–22). In this polemical situation, we should not expect a balanced presentation of Peter's soteriology but a presentation that emphasizes the need for Christians to live godly lives (1:3).

Second, even with this emphasis, Peter does not abandon the notion that salvation is God's gift and that the Christian's virtuous life is the outworking of that gift.

26 See, e.g., Rom. 4:5; Eph. 2:4–5.

27 Käsemann, "Apologia," 179, 184.

28 Klein, *Ärgernisse*, 110–12.

29 Käsemann, *Essays on New Testament Themes*, 179–80. Paulsen, *Der zweite Petrusbrief und der Judasbrief*, 109–10, believes that Käsemann's analysis is justified because, in an effort to enter into dialogue with the syncretistic mood of the times, the author has fundamentally changed the Christian foundation on the basis of which he intended to argue.

Jesus, whom Peter identifies with God, is the source of the Christian's precious faith (1:1) and has used his divine power to give believers everything necessary for living godly lives (1:3). Peter's readers are Christians because God has called and chosen them (1:10), concepts that imply God's initiative in salvation.

The list of godly qualities that the Christian should zealously cultivate, moreover, begins with faith (1:5) rather than, as so often in lists from Hellenistic philosophy, with "virtue." This is probably because "faith" here is not conceived as "faithfulness" and therefore as another virtue, but as a quality that is itself the gift of God (1:1) and the foundation from which the ethical characteristics in the list arise. Moreover, Peter puts "love" at the end of the list, a position that probably arises from its status as the sum of the other virtues in the list.[30] The biblical concepts of "faith" and "love," therefore, stand like bookends around the more Hellenistic virtues in the rest of the list. This shows that Peter conceives of these items in the list as most important.

Third, it is certainly true that Peter speaks in a Hellenistic idiom throughout the letter both rhetorically and conceptually. The structure of his list of virtues, for example, recalls similar lists from Hellenistic philosophy and uses terms as common in that literature as they are rare in the rest of the New Testament.[31] Escape from the corruptibility of the world into union with the divine certainly sounds like something from Plato or one of his Neoplatonic followers.[32] The notion of the destruction of the "elements" of the universe in a great conflagration (3:7, 10, 12) is also redolent of Hellenistic cosmology, which, at least in Stoicism, anticipated the dissolution and renewal of the universe by its reduction to its most basic element, fire.[33] All of this probably means that the person whom Peter commissioned to compose this letter studiedly tries to answer the philosophically inclined false teachers in an idiom that matches their philosophical claims.

30 This again demonstrates the indebtedness of the ethical list to traditional Christian teaching about the importance of love. See Bauckham, *Jude, 2 Peter*, 187.

31 "Virtue" (*aretē*), "self-control" (*egkrateia*), and "godliness" (*eusebeia*) are all common in pagan lists of virtues but appear only once each in New Testament ethical lists (Gal. 5:23; Phil. 4:8; 1 Tim. 6:11). On this see Adolf Deissmann, *Light from the Ancient East* (London: Hodder & Stoughton, 1927), 317–18, who refers to a first-century B.C. inscription from Asia Minor with an ethical list that "mentions successively the *faith, virtue*, righteousness, *godliness*, and *diligence* of the person to be honored," and Bauckham, *Jude, 2 Peter*, 174. The form of Peter's list, in which each term but the last is repeated, is also especially common in Hellenistic philosophical writers and finds a place in the literature of Hellenistic Judaism. See, e.g., Wisd. 6:17–20, and Cicero, *Rosc. Amer.* 75. Cicero uses the device in a list of vices rather than virtues. In the New Testament, see Rom. 5:3–5 and James 1:3–5, 14–15. On "the concatenation as a rhetorical form" see esp. Martin Dibelius, *James*, rev. by Heinrich Greeven (Hermeneia; Philadelphia: Fortress, 1975), 94–99, and the discussion in Bauckham, *Jude, 2 Peter*, 175–76.

32 See, e.g., Plato, *Theaet.* 167ab: "It is impossible that evils should be done away with . . . for there must always be something opposed to the good; and they cannot have their place among the gods, but must inevitably hover about mortal nature and this earth. Therefore we ought to try to escape [*pheugein*] from earth to the dwelling of the gods as quickly as we can; and to escape [*phygē*] is to become like God [*homoiōsis theō*], so far as this is possible; and to become like God is to become righteous and holy and wise" (*Theaet.* 176ab). Cf. 4 Macc. 18:3, which says of the Maccabean martyrs that those who "gave over their bodies in suffering for the sake of religion were not only admired by mortals, but also were deemed worthy to share in a divine inheritance."

33 See, e.g., Cicero, *Nat. d.* 2.118: "Our Stoic spokesmen (they used to concede that Panaetius registered doubts about this) believe that the ultimate outcome will be that the entire universe will go up in flames; for once the moisture has evaporated, the earth cannot obtain nourishment, and the air cannot circulate, since it cannot rise when all the water has dried up, with the result that nothing is left but fire. Then the universe will be restored from this living and divine element of fire; it will come into being embellished as before." I have used the translation of P. G. Walsh, *Cicero: The Nature of the Gods* (Oxford: Clarendon, 1997), 90. See also the discussion of Bauckham, *Jude, 2 Peter*, 300, who drew my attention to this text.

In doing so, however, he does not compromise the fundamental convictions of most Jews and early Christians about God's relationship to his creation. "Evil desire" is characteristic of the world not because, as in Plato, the world is indelibly stained by its very nature with corruption. Instead, the world's corruption is a result of sin (1:4), and escape from it comes in answer to the promises of God.[34] Peter defines these promises in terms familiar from biblical and early Christian eschatology as the "promise" of Christ's Parousia (3:4) and the "promise" of "new heavens and a new earth" (3:13, NRSV).[35] Participation "in the divine nature," which is the object of these promises, probably refers to participation in the moral perfection, immortality, and incorruptibility of God, something similar to Paul's concept of the eschatological change that will transform people from "perishable" to "imperishable" and from "mortal" to "immortal" (1 Cor. 15:50, 53–54; cf. 2 Cor. 5:1–5).[36]

Similarly, the language of the earth's destruction in fire and subsequent renewal is fundamentally biblical, not Stoic in nature. When the Stoics spoke of the reduction of the universe to fire, they were concerned with cosmology—the natural structure of the world—but Peter is concerned with God's use of fire to punish the wicked on the day of judgment (2 Peter 3:7, 10–12). This was a typically biblical, Jewish, and early Christian concern (e.g., Isa. 66:14–16; *Sib. Or.* 3.53–60, 71–74, 79–92; Rev. 20:10).[37] Peter's understanding of the emergence of "new heavens and a new earth" from this conflagration (3:13), moreover, is borrowed not from Stoicism, but from Isaiah, or from early Christian traditions indebted to Isaiah (Isa. 65:17; 66:22; Rev. 21:1).[38]

In summary, Peter's positive presentation of "the way" that Christians should travel emphasizes the necessity of living a life that is consistent with the Christian's eschatological destiny. Christians will one day experience the fulfillment of Christ's promises and a rich welcome into his kingdom. That will be a place, however, free of the world's sinful desires and corruption. In light of their destiny, Christians should pursue virtuous lives, marked especially by faith, the source of the virtues, and love, the summary of them all. To deviate from this path is to move toward the fiery doom that awaits the wicked on the Day of Judgment.

When we place Peter's letter in its context—the threat of a false teaching that appeals to philosophical concepts to support a flagrantly immoral way of life—we

34 Cf. Bauckham, *Jude, 2 Peter*, 183.

35 On the promise of "new heavens and a new earth" see Isa. 65:17; 66:22; and Rev. 21:1.

36 Bauckham, *Jude, 2 Peter*, 181; Anton Vögtle, *Der Judasbrief, Der zweite Petrusbriefe* (EKK 22; Solothurn: Benziger Verlag/Neukirchen-Vluyn: Neukirchener Verlag, 1994), 141. *Pace* Starr, *Sharers in Divine Nature*, 47–48, 226–36, who seems to place insufficient weight on the eschatological connotations of Christ's promises in 1:4.

37 Cf. Bauckham, *Jude, 2 Peter*, 300–301, and Schreiner, *1, 2 Peter, and Jude*, 378. *Sib. Or.* 79–92 seems to combine language reminiscent of Stoicism with the Jewish notion of the eschatological punishment of the wicked in fire in a way similar to Peter.

38 Cf. Rainer Riesner, "Der zweite Petrus-brief und die Eschatologie," in *Zukunftserwartung in biblischer Sicht: Beiträge zur Eschatologie*, ed. Gerhard Maier (MStud 313; Wuppertal: R. Brockhaus Verlag, 1984), 124–43, here at 140: "The Stoics expected a restored world, that is a *neos kosmos*, but Second Peter expects a wholly new creation, a *kainos ouranos kai gē kainē* (2:13)." It is perhaps not insignificant that Peter's reference to "new heavens and a new earth" (*kainous . . . ouranous kai gēn kainēn*) is closer to the Hebrew text of Isa. 65:17 and 66:22, which has "heavens" in the plural, than to either the LXX or Rev. 21:1, both of which have the singular: Peter is thinking in biblical, not Stoic, terms.

can see that he has not fallen prey to a dualistic understanding of the universe or to a soteriology based on works. His stress on the necessity of the virtuous life and the philosophical tone of his work answer the stress on immorality and the philosophical pretensions of his opponents. Even after casting his letter in such a mold, however, Peter retains the priority of God's grace in salvation and the goodness of God's creation, which, after the purifying fire of God's judgment, will remain forever as "new heavens and a new earth."

The Certainty of Final Judgment

Peter cannot merely present his convictions positively with the false teachers in mind. In addition, he must answer their specific arguments. He seems to respond to two basic accusations that the false teachers have leveled at the traditional Christian understanding of final judgment. First, they claim that the apostles and prophets have invented the notion of Jesus' second coming (1:16, 21; cf. 3:2). Second, they say that the continuing, orderly function of the universe from time immemorial proves that, contrary to the claims of the prophets and apostles, "the day of the Lord" will never come (3:4b).[39]

Cleverly Invented Tales

The false teachers apparently claim that the notion of Jesus' coming arose from slyly concocted myths (*sesophismenois mythois*) with which Peter and his fellow apostles have duped others (1:16). In addition, they seem to maintain that the Old Testament prophets misinterpreted their own visions and therefore cannot be trusted when they speak of coming judgment (1:20–21).[40] Peter replies to the first accusation with a reminder to his readers that he personally witnessed the transfiguration of Jesus and heard God the Father say of Jesus, "This is my Son, whom I love; with him I am well pleased" (1:17–18). It is not entirely clear how this reminder of the transfiguration supports the truthfulness of the apostolic witness to Jesus' second coming, but Peter presumably assumes that his readers will understand the event to be a foreshadowing of the coming day. At Jesus' transfiguration, Peter seems to say, Jesus appeared with the majesty and divine approval that will again be evident at his Parousia.

The false teachers not only claim that the apostles concocted the notion of Jesus' Parousia but that when the prophecies contained in the Scriptures speak of a coming

39 Bauckham, *Jude, 2 Peter*, 221, 255, 235, and 301–2, describes four objections that the false teachers have to traditional Christian teaching on the Parousia, and Neyrey, *2 Peter, Jude*, 107–10, 112, 170, 175, 183, 189, 226, 232, and 237, speaks of five. Both of these schemes, however, can be collapsed into two general arguments, one that targets the integrity of those who bore witness to divine judgment (Bauckham, nos. 1–3; Neyrey, nos. 1–4) and the other that argues against the idea of divine judgment itself (Bauckham, no. 4; Neyrey, no. 5).

40 Cf. 3:2, where the author, in summarizing what he has written so far, says that he wants to remind his readers of "the words spoken in the past by the holy prophets and the command given by our Lord and Savior through your apostles." This understanding of 1:20–21 follows Bauckham, *Jude, 2 Peter*, 228–35, but it is not uncontroversial. Some interpreters believe that the passage replies to the false teachers' misinterpretation of Old Testament prophecy. For this understanding of the passage, see, e.g., Kelly, *Epistles of Peter and Jude*, 323–25, and Paulsen, *Der Zweite Petrusbrief und der Judasbrief*, 122–24, who agrees with Käsemann, *Essays on New Testament Themes*, 190, that the author is concerned to regulate the interpretation of Scripture "by tying it to the Church's teaching office."

judgment, they are merely the product of the prophet's own imagination. Unless the false teachers have said something like this, it is difficult to know why Peter insists that "no prophecy had its origin in human will" (1:21). In response, Peter says that neither the record of the prophets' visions nor the record of their interpretations of those visions originated with the prophets themselves. God's Holy Spirit inspired both (1:20–21). If this is true, then Peter can claim that in addition to the evidence supplied by his personal witness to the transfiguration of Jesus, the belief that Christ will come in judgment rests on the "very certain" (*bebaioteron*) "word of the prophets" (1:19a).[41]

These prophecies, he tells his readers, also provide a beacon of light that will illumine and guide their own thinking "until the day dawns and the morning star rises in your hearts" (1:19). With this attractive metaphor, Peter urges his readers not to scoff at the biblical prophets, as the false teachers are evidently doing, but to view the prophetic Scriptures as a valuable and necessary beacon to guide them out of the darkness that shrouds the thinking of the false teachers.

An Idea to Be Mocked

As we saw above, Peter's opponents do not simply impugn the integrity of the apostles but attempt to support with an appeal to the mind their claim that there is no future divine judgment for the wicked. They scoff at the idea (3:3), claiming that it has no basis in the world of human experience: "Where is this 'coming' he promised? Ever since our fathers died, everything goes on as it has since the beginning of creation" (3:4; cf. 3:9).[42] If the promise of the Lord's coming is true, they have apparently said, he is certainly slow in keeping it.

Peter responds to this point in basically two ways. First, he reasserts for his readers the certainty and the gravity of God's judgment on the wicked, and particularly on the false teachers. He follows the lead of Jude's letter in the way he demonstrates the certainty of the false teachers' judgment. Jude understood various biblical descriptions of apostate groups that emerged from within God's people as types, and therefore latent prophesies, of the false teachers who had arisen within the community to which he wrote (Jude 5–7, 11–12).[43] In addition, Jude claimed that "the apostles of our Lord Jesus Christ" foretold the coming of eschatological "scoffers" who would "follow their own ungodly desires" and implied that the false teachers among his readers were these scoffers (Jude 18).

Peter borrows this theme from Jude and enhances it. The wicked angels of Noah's generation and the ungodly people of Sodom and Gomorrah, prominent in Jude 6–7, both reappear in Peter's letter (2 Peter 2:4, 6), and Peter probably intends for his readers to see them as prophetic types of the false teachers in their midst. To this set

41 For this understanding of 1:19a, see Bauckham, *Jude, 2 Peter*, 223.

42 The form of this taunt resembles the form that the taunts of God's enemies commonly take in Scripture (Ps. 42:3 [LXX 41:4], 10 [LXX 11]; 79 [LXX 78]:10; 115:2 [LXX 113:10]; Jer. 17:15; Joel 2:17; Mic. 7:10; Mal. 2:17). The taunt in 2 Peter 3:4, therefore, probably represents Peter's own paraphrase of his opponents' words in a common biblical idiom. On this, see Bauckham, *Jude, 2 Peter*, 289.

43 See Bauckham, *Jude, 2 Peter*, 44–45, 78 and ch. 25 above.

of evil types, however, Peter adds a set of corresponding references to righteous people who remained faithful despite the wickedness around them. He therefore extends Jude's reminder of the wicked angels of Genesis 6:1–4 with a reminder of the wickedness of Noah's own generation and, in contrast, of the righteous Noah and his family (2 Peter 2:5). In the same way, he balances Jude's reference to the wickedness of Sodom and Gomorrah (2:6; cf. Jude 7) with a reminder of Lot's revulsion at the evil of his compatriots (2 Peter 2:7–8).

The precise conditions that have arisen with the coming of Peter's opponents, therefore, have been anticipated in the Scriptures. The very Scriptures that the false teachers reject (1:21) or distort (3:16) have predicted their arrival and the resistance of righteous people to them, and this is proof that the judgment also predicted in those Scriptures is certain (2:9–10).

In addition, in accord with the well-understood characteristics of testamentary literature, Peter predicts the coming of the very false teachers who have already arrived among his readers (2:1–3a; 3:3–4; cf. 2 Tim. 3:1–9). Thus, Peter himself provides an apostolic "prophecy" of the false teachers' coming that is reminiscent of other such early Christian prophesies (Mark 13:6; 2 Thess. 2:3–4, 9–10; 1 Tim. 4:1–3; 2 Tim. 3:1–9; 1 John 2:18–19). This is perhaps his way of saying what Jude put more explicitly when he told his readers to remember that the apostles had foretold the arrival of scoffers in the last days (Jude 18). Here too, if the false teachers themselves provide vindication of the truthfulness of the apostolic witness that scoffers will come in the last days, then they, and those under their influence, should also heed the apostolic witness that God will punish the wicked (2 Peter 2:12–13, 17, 21; 3:16).

Both the Scriptures and the apostles, therefore, witness to the arrival and impending judgment of the false teachers. If they are right about their arrival, Peter seems to imply, they are also likely to be right about their swift destruction.

Second, Peter also responds to the rationalistic mockery of "the day of the Lord" with a brief biblical theology of history. The false teachers have claimed that the world has, from its beginning and from the time of the biblical patriarchs, continued on a regular, predictable path without dramatic interference from God.[44] They have also claimed that if Christ really gave the promise of his Parousia, then he is certainly slow about keeping it (3:9). Peter's answer shows that God's involvement in the world stretches from its beginning to its end and that the present delay in the coming of the final day has a clear theological rationale.

His response unfolds in four chronologically arranged stages. First, he states that the false teachers ignore God's involvement at the beginning of creation, when he made the world by his word (3:5). Second, he reminds his readers that, contrary to the false teachers' claim that "everything goes on as it has since the beginning of creation," God has been involved in world history—indeed, in the judgment of the world—as the flood that destroyed Noah's generation proves (3:6; cf. 2:5). Third, if the heavens and the earth have continued intact from that time to this, they have

44 On the interpretation of "the fathers" as the biblical patriarchs, see note 14, above.

done so again by God's word and in anticipation of their eventual destruction (3:7). Fourth, that day will come. "The heavens will disappear with a roar," says Peter, "the elements will be destroyed by fire, and the earth and everything in it will be laid bare" (3:10). At each stage in cosmic history, God is actively involved by means of his word (stages 1 and 3) and occasionally by means of dramatic actions (stages 2 and 4).

The author spends most of his energy in this part of his argument on stage 3—the period between the distant past and the future coming of the day. Here too God is active, but active in preventing the destruction of the world until the time is ripe. The present heavens and earth are being "reserved" for fire and "kept" for destruction (3:6).

Why this delay? Peter gives two reasons. First, he maintains that God reckons time differently from human beings. Here Peter alludes to Psalm 90:4 with its statement that "a thousand years in [God's] sight are like a day that has just gone by." The meaning of Peter's allusion becomes clear from the broader context of this psalm. God exists from "everlasting to everlasting" (90:2), but people are like the grass—new in the morning and withered by the close of day (90:5–6). The eternality of God and the transitory nature of the human life span mean that when people fail to take God's eternal nature into account, they inevitably become impatient with his timing (2 Peter 3:9a).[45]

Second, God's delay of the destruction of the heavens and the earth has a merciful purpose. It provides time for the wicked to repent before they too are destroyed. God wants no one to perish but all to repent and escape the final disaster that will befall the wicked (3:9b). Here Peter echoes a common theme in Jewish and early Christian literature. The prophet Joel, for example, after describing the "great" and "dreadful" day of the Lord, which no one can endure, appeals to his hearers: "Even now . . . return to the LORD your God, for he is gracious and compassionate, slow to anger and abounding in love, and he relents from sending calamity" (Joel 2:12–13).

In summary, Peter responds in two ways to his opponents' claims that God will never trouble the rhythm of the world with a day of judgment. The opponents themselves provide fulfillment of the prophecy, both biblical and apostolic, that in the last days false teachers will come. Ironically, they themselves are proof that the final day whose coming they deny is actually near. In addition, the pattern of history outlined in the Scriptures shows that God has been actively involved in the world from the beginning: His word both created and sustains it, and even now only his compassion for sinners like the false teachers and their followers prevents him from putting into action his plan to destroy the present heavens and earth and make them anew.

MORAL PREPARATION FOR THE PAROUSIA

In 2 Peter, the apostle Peter responds around the time of his martyrdom, and perhaps through a coworker, to the threat of false teachers in Asia Minor who claim that

45 Bauckham, *Jude, 2 Peter*, 310.

Christians are free from moral constraint because Christ will never return in judgment. They appeal to Paul's letters, and specifically to his central convictions about God's grace, to support their ideas, and they advance these ideas on the basis of specious theological and philosophical arguments. Peter's situation and the arguments of the false teachers profoundly influenced the form and the content of this text. Peter's coworker writes within a genre that he has found appropriate for the actual circumstances at the end of Peter's life, composing his response as both a testament and a letter. Following the requirements of the testamentary genre, he prophesies the coming of the false teachers themselves. They are part of the apostasy of the final days that they deny will ever come.

Adopting a philosophical mode of expression appropriate to the philosophical pretensions of the false teachers, Peter argues that judgment is certain, and, in light of its certainty, Christians must continue their pilgrimage on "the way of truth" and "righteousness." This pilgrimage is one of moral virtue, but virtue that originates in God's grace and human faith and can be summarized as love. Those who persevere on this pilgrimage will receive a welcome to Christ's kingdom at the end of their journey. Those who deviate from it and those who lead them to these deviations can only expect destruction in the roaring fire of judgment on the day of the Lord. In light of these truths, Peter urges his readers to repudiate the false teachers and to "grow in the grace and in the knowledge of our Lord and Savior Jesus Christ" (3:18).

This is certainly not everything that must be said about the theological basis for Christian ethics, but Peter does not pretend to write a complete treatise on the subject. He writes in the face of a moral crisis and, in light of this crisis, emphasizes the need for moral transformation. The theological strain that forms the leitmotif of 2 Peter—the Day of Judgment as an incentive to moral behavior—is not an aberration within the New Testament. Paul himself emphasized it repeatedly (Rom. 13:11–14; 14:10–12; 1 Cor. 3:10–17; 2 Cor. 5:10; 1 Thess. 4:6).

Second Peter's philosophical idiom, moreover, represents not a capitulation to the dualism of Neoplatonism but a creative attempt to speak a language that those who have fallen under the pretensions of the false teachers can understand. Second Peter is, therefore, far from an embarrassment to the New Testament canon. It provides an exemplary attempt to emphasize an important theological principle in the face of specific attacks on it, and to do so in a way that is sensitive to the culture of those whom it addresses.

Chapter 27

FIRST JOHN: THE TRUTH ABOUT JESUS, HIS DEATH, AND HIS LOVE COMMAND

Some Christians interpreted the Johannine stream of Christian tradition in unfaithful directions in much the same way that others misinterpreted the Pauline tradition. In three letters, an early Christian leader who identifies himself only as "the Elder" (2 John 1; 3 John 1) and who is probably himself the author of the fourth gospel addresses a deviation from Johannine Christianity as the fourth gospel articulates it.[1] Near the end of his first letter, the Elder tells his readers exactly why he writes to them.[2] Both the position of this statement in the letter and the language that the statement uses parallel the purpose statement of John's gospel:

1 John 5:13	**John 20:31**
I write these things to you who believe in the name of the Son of God so that you may know that you have eternal life.	But these are written that you may believe that Jesus is the Christ, the Son of God, and that by believing you may have life in his name.

Like the purpose statement in the gospel, the purpose statement in 1 John comes near, but not quite at the end.[3] The content of both statements, moreover, is similar: the concept of belief, the identity of Jesus as Son of God, the mention of his "name," and the goal of eternal life.[4]

1 Scholars debate whether the letters were composed by the same person and whether that person composed the gospel, or perhaps parts of the gospel. The style of the letters is so homogenous, and so much like the peculiar style of the fourth gospel, that all four documents probably came either from the same person or from the gospel's primary author and a close associate (who may have also written John 19:35 and 21:24). In the chapters on the Johannine letters, I will follow the convention of referring to the fourth gospel as John's gospel and identify the author of the letters as "the Elder," using the title that the author uses for himself in 2 and 3 John (cf. Raymond E. Brown, *The Community of the Beloved Disciple* [New York: Paulist, 1979], 94).

2 Nothing in the opening or closing of 1 John indicates that it is a letter, although the Elder frequently refers to writing to his readers (1:4; 2:1, 7, 8, 12, 13 [3x], 14 [2x], 21, 26; 5:13). Scholars have often called the document a "tractate" or "sermon," as in the commentaries of Hans Windisch, *Die katholischen Briefe*, 3rd ed., rev. Herbert Preisker (HNT 15; Tübingen: J. C. B. Mohr, 1951; orig. ed. 1911), 107–8, 136, and C. H. Dodd, *The Johannine Epistles* (MNTC; London: Hodder & Stoughton, 1946), xxi. It is probably best, however, to think of the composition as an unusual letter (similar to Hebrews), written for the Elder's own community and therefore stripped of the normal epistolary introduction and conclusion. On this see Georg Strecker, *The Johannine Letters* (Hermeneia; Minneapolis: Fortress, 1996), 3, and Judith Lieu, *The Theology of the Johannine Epistles* (New Testament Theology; Cambridge: Cambridge Univ. Press, 1991), 3.

3 First John 5:13 is followed by 5:14–21 just as John 20:30–31 is followed by 21:1–25. The Elder speaks of his purpose for writing in five other places: 1 John 1:4; 2:1, 12–14, 21, 26. The purpose statement in 5:13, however, encompasses these other, more specific, purpose statements.

4 On the parallelism between John 20:31 and 1 John 5:13, see Raymond E. Brown, *The Epistles of John* (AB 30; Garden City, N.Y.: Doubleday, 1982), 91, 605, 631, 634, and Hans-Josef Klauck, *Der erste Johannesbrief* (EKK 23.1; Zürich and Neukirchen-Vluyn: Benziger and Neukirchener, 1991), 318–21. The view of Lieu, *Theology of the Johannine Epistles*, 7, 101, that the Elder's knowledge of John's gospel cannot be taken for granted seems too skeptical in light of the many structural, conceptual, and verbal similarities between the two works.

There is, however, an important difference. In the gospel, John wrote to encourage faith in Jesus not merely as the traditional Messiah or prophet of Jewish and Samaritan expectation but as the unique Son of God, whose eternal fellowship with his Father permitted him to be the perfect revelation of God himself within the world.[5] "Life" was the goal of this faith. In 1 John, the Elder has moved a step beyond this purpose. He assumes that his readers believe Jesus to be the Son of God, and he writes instead to assure them that the faith they have already embraced will lead them to eternal life.[6]

THE REASON FOR 1 JOHN

The rest of 1 John makes reasonably clear what has happened to prompt this change in emphasis. A group of people have left the fellowship of the Elder's church over their understanding of Jesus' identity (2:19). Despite their departure from the Elder's community, they are still in contact with it and are attempting to "teach" that the grasp of the truth about Christ among the Elder's community is inadequate (2:20, 26–27). The Elder calls these secessionists "antichrists" (2:18), and this name provides a window onto their teaching. A couple of sentences after he speaks of their secession, he says:

> Who is the liar but the one who denies that Jesus is the Christ [the Messiah]? This person is the antichrist, the one who denies the Father and the Son. No one who denies the Son has the Father; everyone who confesses the Son has the Father also. (2:22–23, NRSV)

It seems reasonable to take this as a description of the primary difference between the secessionists and the main group: The secessionists have stopped identifying Jesus as the Messiah, the Son of God—precisely the critical confession that leads to eternal life according to John's gospel (John 11:27; 20:31). This receives confirmation from the warning against false teaching in 2 John 9: "Anyone who runs ahead and does not continue in the teaching of Christ does not have God; whoever continues in the teaching has both the Father and the Son."

In other words, some have "run ahead" or, from their own perspective, "progressed" (*proagōn*) beyond the traditional teaching of the main group about the Messiah, and in doing so they have left behind the crucial connection between the Father and the Son.[7] The false teachers have introduced a pernicious complication into the confession that Jesus is the Messiah and the Son of God. In what direction have they "progressed"?

We have already seen in chapter 6 that in the gospel, John took trouble to define the term "Messiah" to mean that Jesus was God's unique, eternal Son. The Elder assumes this redefinition and moves beyond it slightly to use the terms "Messiah"

5 See chapter 6, above.

6 Brown, *Epistles of John*, 634.

7 Ibid., 673–74. Brown points out (673) that the phrase *ho proagōn* means "the one who progresses" and has no necessarily pejorative connotations. It may represent the Elder's use of a word that the secessionists favored.

and "Son of God" interchangeably with no discernable difference in meaning. Thus, immediately after saying that the secessionists deny Jesus to be "the Christ," he says that they deny "the Son" (2:22–23; cf. 2 John 9), and later he can speak in the same breath of believing "that Jesus is the Christ" and believing "that Jesus is the Son of God" (5:1, 5).[8] Calling Jesus either the Christ or the Son is a way of referring to the divinity of the human Jesus.

This means that the secessionists have stopped identifying the human person Jesus with the divine being described in John's gospel, the one whom John calls "God the only Son, who is at the Father's side" (John 1:18, aut.). This understanding of the situation receives support from the contrast the Elder draws between "every spirit that acknowledges that Jesus Christ has come in the flesh" on one hand and, on the other hand, "every spirit that does not acknowledge Jesus."[9] Some people acknowledge that the man named Jesus is also the divine Messiah. Others deny this. The first group, the Elder says, is "from God," while the other is "the spirit of the antichrist" (4:2–3). Any lingering doubts that this is the main tenet of the false teaching disappear when we find that in 2 John 7 the same issue reappears but is explicitly connected with "deceivers" (*planoi*)—precisely the term the Elder uses of the secessionists in 1 John 2:26 (*tōn planōntōn*)—and anyone who teaches this idea is called an "antichrist":

> Many deceivers, who do not acknowledge Jesus Christ as coming in the flesh, have gone out into the world. Any such person is the deceiver and the antichrist.[10]

If we can take some of the Elder's admonitions to his readers as attempts to strengthen traditional beliefs that the secessionists have denied, then we can provide even more details about their convictions. They apparently claim to be without sin (1:8, 10).[11] Paradoxically, however, they continue to sin (3:6, 9; 5:18) in obvious ways—they walk in darkness (1:6; cf. 2:11), hate others (2:9, 11; 3:15–18; 4:20), and love the world (2:15).[12] In one of the Elder's more enigmatic statements, he says

8 M. de Jonge, "The Use of the Word ΧΡΙΣΤΟΣ in the Johannine Letters," in *Studies in John Presented to Professor Dr. J. N. Sevenster* (Leiden: E. J. Brill, 1970), 66–74, here at 67–68; Martin Hengel, *The Johannine Question* (London: SCM/Philadelphia: Trinity Press International, 1989), 59.

9 Hengel, *Johannine Question*, 59, points out that the Elder "introduces the single word Jesus in connection with confessional formulations" five times (2:22; 4:3, 15; 5:1, 5). This is consistent with the theory that the secessionists refuse to assign religious significance to the human Jesus and that the Elder wants to reassert this significance.

10 Judith Lieu, *The Second and Third Epistles of John* SNTW (Edinburgh: T. & T. Clark, 1986), 81–87, believes that it is "both impossible and misguided to attempt to identify the false teachers" by means of the confession in 1 John 4:2. If the Elder were opposing docetism, she claims, he would have used an accusative and infinitive construction to describe the confession, not the more ambiguous participial construction (*elēlythota*) that actually appears in the text. The change of this perfect participle to the present participle (*erchomenon*) in 2 John 7, moreover, demonstrates that no specific false teaching is in mind in this later letter by a different author. Lieu is not clear, however, about why these grammatical subtleties prevent either text from referring to the beliefs of docetic heretics. Both Lieu (ibid., 83) and Strecker, *Johannine Letters*, 70, puzzlingly claim that 2 John differs from 1 John in designating the opponents as "deceivers" (*planoi*). In 1 John 2:26, however, the Elder refers to his opponents as "those who deceive you" (*tōn planōntōn hymas*). It is difficult to see the difference.

11 See, e.g., Dodd, *Johannine Epistles*, 21–22, and I. H. Marshall, *The Epistles of John* (NICNT; Grand Rapids: Eerdmans, 1978), 112–13. *Pace* Strecker, *Johannine Letters*, 75, who believes that 1:8–10 cannot be used as evidence that the false teachers considered themselves to be without sin and who thinks (33–34) that false teaching is only one of the Elder's concerns in the letter.

12 Strecker, *Johannine Letters*, 75, claims that the Elder's polemic against the false teachers as sinners simply derives from their break with the community—they hate their brothers and love the world

that Jesus Christ "came by water and blood . . . not . . . in water only, but in water and blood" (5:6, aut.). The Elder's concern to say that Jesus did not come only "in water" probably reflects an emphasis of the secessionists on the baptism of Jesus and their corresponding unwillingness to admit the significance of Jesus' death. Against this, the Elder recalls the only other passage in the Johannine literature where blood and water are closely linked—the eyewitness description in John's gospel of the aftermath of Jesus' death:

> One of the soldiers pierced Jesus' side with a spear, bringing a sudden flow of blood and water. The man who saw it has given testimony, and his testimony is true. He knows that he tells the truth, and he testifies so that you also may believe. (John 19:34–35)

In 1 John 5:6, therefore, the Elder is probably affirming, against the secessionists' denials, that Jesus' ministry is marked not by one, but by two critical events—his baptism at the beginning of his ministry and his crucifixion at the end. It is not enough to speak of his baptism (the second mention of "water" in 5:6), but it is theologically necessary also to speak of the moment in his life when water was mixed with blood—the time of his death on the cross.[13]

This portrait of the secessionists' theology looks like a less elaborate form of certain heretical movements that troubled the orthodox church in the second century. Ignatius, writing in A.D. 117, warned Christians in western Asia Minor of "unbelievers" who thought that Jesus' suffering was only an appearance and failed to confess that he was a "flesh-bearing" person (*Smyrn.* 2.1; 5.2; *Trall.* 10:1). In addition, they apparently did not believe "in the blood of Christ" (*Smyrn.* 6.1) and abstained from the Eucharist and prayer because they did not confess that the Eucharist is the flesh of our Savior Jesus Christ—the flesh that suffered for our sins, which in kindness the Father raised up" (*Smyrn.* 7.1). Their deviant doctrines were accompanied by a lack of love toward those in need: "They take no care for love, whether for widow, for orphan, for the afflicted, for the imprisoned or released, or for the hungry or thirsty" (*Smyrn.* 6.2).

Irenaeus, writing in the late second century, attributes to an Ephesian named Cerinthus the belief that Jesus was an ordinary, if unusually wise, man on whom a spiritual "Christ" descended after his baptism and from whom this same "Christ" departed prior to his crucifixion and resurrection (*Haer.* 1.26.1).[14] Irenaeus also speaks of a tradition that "John, the disciple of the Lord" fled from Cerinthus when he came

in the Elder's opinion simply because they have severed ties with the original group. Brown, *Epistles of John*, 325–27, believes the charge of love for the world reflects the secessionists' missionary concern. These understandings of the Elder's polemic, however, do not adequately account for his concern that his readers not become entrapped (presumably like the secessionists) in the "lust of the flesh and the lust of the eyes and the pride of life" (2:15–16).

13 For this understanding of 5:6, see Brown, *Epistles of John*, 577–78.

14 Cf. the belief of some Valentinians that "Christ" passed through Mary like water through a tube and descended on the Savior at his baptism. The Savior "continued free from all suffering, since indeed it was not possible that He should suffer who was at once incomprehensible and invisible." For the same reason, "the Spirit of Christ" was removed from the Savior when he was brought before Pilate (Irenaeus, *Haer.* 1.7).

across him in the baths at Ephesus, crying as he rushed out that Cerinthus was "the enemy of the truth" (*Haer.* 3.3.4).

There are important differences between the teachings of Cerinthus, those of the "unbelievers" whom Ignatius describes, and those of the secessionists in 1 John, and these differences make it unlikely that any of these three sets of teachings can be identified with each other. Ignatius' false teachers "practiced Judaism" (*Magn.* 10.3; cf. 8–9) whereas the followers of Cerinthus have no discernibly Jewish characteristics. Similarly, the secessionists of the Johannine letters show no proclivities toward either Jewish practices or the complex cosmology of Cerinthus, who "taught that the world was not made by the primary God, but by a Power far separated from him" (Irenaeus, *Haer.* 1.26.1).[15]

Still, an ample measure of common ground lies beneath the three movements. Adherents of all three movements regarded the fleshly nature of Jesus as a hindrance to his role as a revealer of God. None of the three found a place for the crucifixion of Jesus. Ignatius' "unbelievers" and the Johannine secessionists could both be criticized for failing to show love toward others, particularly those in need, and saw no significance in Christ's death as an atonement for sin. Followers of Cerinthus, like the secessionists, distinguished between the human Jesus and the divine Christ. They too could agree with the orthodox church that Jesus' baptism was important, but they failed to see any theological significance in his crucifixion. In light of this common ground, it seems prudent to understand the secessionists of the Johannine letters as a nascent form of heresies that developed more fully and in these various directions throughout the second century.[16]

One critical element found among the secessionists of 1 John that appears neither among the "unbelievers" in Ignatius nor among the followers of Cerinthus in Irenaeus' *Against Heresies* is the claim to be without sin (1:8, 10). This claim may arise, however, from something similar to the Valentinian gnostic belief that the roadblock between people and salvation is not transgression of the moral law of God but possession of a "material" nature. Irenaeus tells us:

> They hold that they shall be entirely and undoubtedly saved, not by means of conduct, but because they are spiritual by nature. For, just as it is impossible that material substance should partake of salvation (since, indeed, they maintain that it is incapable of receiving it), so again it is impossible that spiritual substance (by which they mean themselves) should ever come under the power of corruption, whatever the sort of actions in which they indulged. For even as gold, when submersed in filth, loses not on that account its beauty, but retains its own native qualities, the filth having no power to injure the gold, so they affirm that they cannot in any measure suffer hurt, or lose their spiritual substance, whatever the material actions in which they may be involved. (*Haer.* 1.6.2)

15 Rudolf Schnackenburg, *The Johannine Epistles: Introduction and Commentary* (New York: Crossroad, 1992), 21, 23.

16 Cf. ibid., 23.

If we allow the gnostics to speak for themselves, we find this understanding of sin confirmed by "Jesus," supposedly speaking to his disciples, in the late second-century *Gospel of Mary*:

> There is no sin, but it is you who make sin when you do the things that are like the nature of adultery, which is called "sin." That is why the Good came into your midst, to the essence of every nature, in order to restore it to its root.[17]

Later Jesus warns his disciples not to "lay down any rules beyond what I appointed for you" or to "give a law like the lawgiver [Moses] lest you be constrained by it."[18]

Here too the human problem that needs resolution from another world is not transgression of commandments, such as, "You shall not commit adultery," but the identification of those who have a spiritual nature and the restoration of these people to their basic nature. One's nature, whether material or spiritual, determines whether one is saved.

Since an atoning sacrifice is a remedy for transgression against God's law, it has no place in a system where the problem is formulated differently, in terms of one's essential nature. For gnostics such as these, therefore, the atoning death of Christ was hardly necessary for salvation. If anything, such a death was an offense because it implied that the "material" powers had conquered the gnostic Savior who was supposed to save spiritual people from these very powers.

The secessionists in 1 John cannot be identified as Valentinian gnostics any more than they can be identified with Ignatius' opponents or the Cerinthians, but they may have held to a Christology and a soteriology that resembled these later forms of gnostic teaching. Thus they may have dismissed the theological significance of Christ's crucifixion not only because they felt he could not suffer but also because, for them, "sin" in the traditional sense of violating God's law did not exist.

In summary, those who have seceded from the group to which 1 John is written attempt to detach the historical Jesus from the eternally existent Christ. This spiritual Christ is God's Son and has made his Father known. The secessionists probably sever the human "Jesus" from the spiritual "Christ" because they understand the material world to be inherently evil. As the divine revealer of the Father, Christ is free from this evil. Because of this, he only appears to take the form of Jesus and is not subject to the normal physical troubles of a human being, such as birth, suffering, and death. He came on Jesus in spiritual form at baptism and departed from Jesus prior to his crucifixion. They may also identify their own problem not as estrangement from God because of their violation of God's law but as the need for reorientation to their intrinsically spiritual natures.

Because 1 John is often not explicit about the beliefs of the secessionists, this picture is necessarily speculative, but it has the merit of bringing both explicit statements and more ambiguous hints about the false teachers into a coherent portrait.

17 *NHL*, 471–72. Cf. Irenaeus, *Haer.* 1.7, who says that the Valentinians believe that "some are by nature good, and others by nature evil. The good are those who become capable of receiving the [spiritual] seed; the evil by nature are those who are never able to receive that seed."

18 *NHL*, 472

This portrait, moreover, matches in its broad outlines several known religious movements that arose less than a century after the composition of this letter.

Although the Elder is not explicit about the activities of the secessionists after they left the original group, they seem to have tried to influence those they left behind to join them in their new beliefs (2:27). In their view, they have "progressed" beyond the old traditions of the original group (2 John 9). Perhaps they view themselves as prophets in touch with "the Spirit of truth" that Jesus said would come to his disciples to teach them about himself and to lead them into all truth (4:1, 6; John 15:26; 16:13). Evidently their efforts have been successful in undermining the confidence of some in the original group about Jesus. The Elder writes, therefore, in order to assure this group that what they have heard from the beginning is the truth and that they should "remain" or "abide" in it (2:24). He wants to bolster their confidence that the truth he and his associates taught is the means to eternal life (2:21; 5:13).

THE ELDER'S RESPONSE

Although 1 John has no obviously traceable argument, the Elder nevertheless returns again and again to five themes: the authority and truthfulness of the early traditions, the witness of those traditions to Jesus' humanity, their witness to the relationship between the Christian and sin, their witness to the significance of Jesus' death, and their witness to love as proof of claims to have a relationship with God.[19]

The Authority and Truthfulness of the Early Traditions

Since the false teachers who have seceded from the community believe that their teaching has "progressed" beyond the elementary traditions about Jesus of the group they left behind, the Elder is at pains throughout his composition to stress the authority and adequacy of precisely those early traditions. His readers have an anointing from the Holy One, the Elder assures them, and this anointing teaches them what they need to know (2:20). They have no need, in other words, for further, "progressive" teaching beyond what they have received in the traditions handed on to them when they became Christians and which the Holy Spirit, with whom they have been anointed, has prompted them to embrace.[20]

Although the Elder often speaks directly to his audience in the first person singular, when he emphasizes the authority of the original traditions he uses the first person plural (1:2–5). It is likely that this plural is not meant merely rhetorically

19 Commentators diverge sharply on how to divide 1 John, some choosing two, some three, and some seven divisions. See the list in Brown, *Epistles of John*, 764. The division that seems to attract the largest following is 1:5–2:17; 2:18–3:24, and 4:1–5:12, although even here only seven of the forty-three scholars and versions in Brown's list agree on this structure. The genre of the document is also difficult to discern.

20 For this understanding of 2:20, 27, see Brown, *Epistles of John*, 341–48, and Klauck, *Erste Johannesbrief*, 156–58. This passage in 1 John contains the only three appearances of the term *charisma* ("anointing") in the New Testament. Occasionally scholars have taken it to refer to something other than the Holy Spirit, such as the gospel or the teaching that the Elder's readers have heard. A reference to the Holy Spirit is more likely, as most commentators recognize, since in the New Testament the Holy Spirit is the object of the related verb *chriō* in three out of its five occurrences (Luke 4:18; Acts 10:37–38; 2 Cor. 1:21–22).

(otherwise why use the singular at all?), but includes other authoritative keepers of the original traditions about Jesus. The Elder communicates to his audience, therefore, that he does not merely speak on his own authority but with the authority that others share.[21]

In contrast to the apparent emphasis of the secessionists on the progressive nature of their teaching, the Elder points his audience back to two traditional "beginnings" from which they should not stray: the beginning that God effected through his Word and their own beginning as Christians. The prologue of John's gospel affirms that precisely the Jesus who "became flesh and made his dwelling among us" was with God "in the beginning." Echoing this statement, the Elder opens his composition by telling his audience that he proclaims to them "that which was from the beginning [*ap' archēs*]" (1:1; cf. 2:13a, 14a). Then throughout the rest of his composition he recalls to his audience their "beginning" as Christians. They heard the commandment to love their brothers and sisters "from the beginning" (*ap' archēs*, 2:7; 3:11), and they should abide in the teaching that they heard "from the beginning" (*ap' archēs*, 2:24).

The Elder and his circle comprise the authentic connection between these two beginnings because they are firsthand witnesses to Jesus' life and teaching. This is the significance of the references to sense perception in the first sentence of the Elder's composition. The one whom John's gospel describes as both "the Word" and "the life" is the one whom the Elder and his circle of authoritative witnesses saw, touched with their hands, and heard (1:1–3). At least one person within this circle saw the water and the blood come from Jesus' side after his death on the cross (5:6–9; cf. John 19:34–35). The message that they heard from Jesus is also what they have communicated to the Elder's audience. Thus, what they have seen is the basis of their testimony (1 John 1:5; 2:7; 3:11; 4:14), and this testimony is confirmed by the witness of the Spirit of truth whom Jesus promised to send (John 14:17; 15:26; 16:13) and with whom the Elder's readers have been anointed (1 John 2:20, 26–27; 5:7–8).

Because the Elder and his circle of witnesses connect the Elder's audience with the historical Jesus, their witness functions as the touchstone for the authenticity of all claims about Jesus' identity and significance. Their teaching is what the Elder calls "our faith" (5:4). By means of this body of teaching the Elder's audience can discriminate between theological friends and enemies, between truth and error: "We are from God, and whoever knows God listens to us; but whoever is not from God does not listen to us. This is how we recognize the Spirit of truth and the spirit of falsehood" (4:6).

Much is at stake here because only by abiding in the proclamation of the Elder's circle of witnesses can the audience continue to have fellowship with the Father and his Son Jesus Christ (1:3). Only by remaining in fellowship with the Father and his Son, moreover, is it possible to have eternal life (1:2; 2:24–25; 5:20).[22]

---

21 Samuel Byrskog, *Story as History—History as Story: The Gospel Tradition in the Context of Ancient Oral History* (WUNT 123; Tübingen: J. C. B. Mohr [Paul Siebeck], 2000), 241–42.

22 Cf. Hengel, *Johannine Question*, 58.

The Witness of the Traditions to Jesus' Humanity

Against the conviction of the secessionists that Jesus Christ has not come in the flesh (1 John 4:2; 2 John 7), the Elder places special emphasis on Jesus' humanity. The importance of this theme is evident from the Elder's extensive treatment of it at the opening of his composition (1 John 1:1–4). This opening is modeled on the prologue of John's gospel. Like John 1:1–4, 14, it begins with a reference to the "beginning," speaks of Jesus as the "Word," identifies the Word with "life," and says this life was both "with" God and was manifested, and that "we beheld" him.[23]

Unlike the gospel prologue, where the emphasis lies on the eternal unity between the unique Son and his Father, here the Elder emphasizes the humanity of the "Word of life" by speaking graphically of Jesus' physical reality. Those within the Elder's circle of authority heard, saw, and touched the "Word of life." The emphasis in this description lies on precisely the elements of Jesus' nature that are in dispute between the Elder and those who have broken fellowship with his community. Both the Elder and his opponents seem to agree that the Word, who recently appeared in history, revealed God through his teaching, but the physical nature of the Word's recent appearance is another matter. The Elder says four times within the space of a single Greek sentence (1:1–3a) that he and his circle of witnesses "saw" Jesus. They saw him, moreover, not merely in some intellectual or spiritual sense but with their eyes. In the same way, they touched him, not metaphorically, but with their hands (1:1).

The Elder may have emphasized his personal, sensory connection with Jesus at the beginning of the letter because he intends later in the letter to assert again and again that "the Christ, the Son of God" is none other than the fully human Jesus, and in one critically important passage, that he was a man of flesh and blood who really died the violent death described in the Johannine gospel (John 19:34–35; 1 John 5:6–9). The secessionists may have been happy to speak, like the Johannine Christians from whom they have separated, of the coming of "the Christ, the Son of God" (John 11:27; 20:31), but they are unwilling to identify this figure with the man Jesus. If so, then the Elder, who uses "Christ" and "Son of God" interchangeably, insists against this notion that the one who denies that Jesus is the Christ is a liar (1 John 2:22). Later, he claims that "every spirit that does not confess Jesus is not from God" (4:3). He emphasizes that belief in Jesus as the Son of God (4:15; 5:5, 20) and the Christ (5:1, 20) is essential for those who want to align themselves with God. Without the "Son"—defined as the human Jesus—it is impossible to have the Father (2:22b–23).

The failure to confess Jesus as the Son of God not only violates Christian tradition about the past, but also confirms Christian tradition about the emergence of false teaching in the future. According to the Elder, those who refuse to confess the fleshly Jesus align themselves with "the antichrist" (2:22; 4:3). The parallels here with the language of the Synoptic apocalyptic discourses seem too close not to have some relevance for the problem that the Elder addresses.

23 See the useful chart of parallels in Schnackenburg, *Johannine Epistles*, 50 n. 3.

In those passages Jesus issues warnings against the coming at "the end of the age" (Matt. 24:3; cf. Mark 13:3) of many who will say, "I am the Christ," and, by this claim, will "deceive" (*planēsousin*) many (Matt. 24:5; cf. Mark 13:5; Luke 21:8). He warns further against the rise of "false prophets" (*pseudoprophētai*), who will also "deceive" (*planēsousin*) many (Matt. 24:11). Finally, he speaks in one breath of "false Christs" (*pseudochristoi*) and "false prophets" (*pseudoprophētai*), who will produce signs and wonders in order to "deceive" (Mark 13:22, *apoplanan*; Matt. 24:24, *planēsai*) even the elect. The Elder seems to be familiar with this tradition and borrows its language to describe the secessionists as "many antichrists" (*antichristoi*, 1 John 2:18), "many false prophets," (*pseudoprophētai*, 4:1), and "those who are deceiving [*planōntōn*] you" (2:26).[24] Their appearance he takes, in agreement with the Synoptic discourses, to signal the arrival of the "last hour" (2:18).[25]

Why does the Elder do this? He follows this strategy not because the secessionists are themselves claiming to be messianic figures like the false prophets in the Synoptic discourses, but probably because, from the Elder's perspective, they have substituted their own understanding of the Messiah's identity for the traditional Johannine understanding. In their view the Messiah has come, but he cannot be identified with the man Jesus in any simple way. Theirs is a substitute Christ, and insofar as they persuade others that he is the correct Christ, they are themselves antichrists, similar to the Antichrist who will, in traditional Christian eschatology, arise in the last times (2:18).[26] Perhaps it is with this false Christ in mind that the Elder, in a famously puzzling command at the end of the letter, urges his readers to keep themselves from idols (5:21).[27] The Elder's readers should not substitute for the Jesus of the Johannine tradition, who "became flesh and made his dwelling among us" (John 1:14), a Christ who was only loosely affiliated with the fleshly Jesus. To do so, warns the Elder, is idolatry.[28]

The Witness of the Traditions to the Relationship between the Christian and Sin

The Elder believes that those who have seceded from his community have failed to take sin seriously. They seem to have been happy to speak of their fellowship with

24 Strecker, *Johannine Letters*, 241, asserts, plausibly, that the "false Christs" and "false prophets" of Mark 13:6 and 22 are comparable to the "antichrists" of 1 John 2:18.

25 See also 1 Tim. 4:1; 2 Tim. 3:1; 2 Peter 3:3; Jude 18, and the comments of Gregory C. Jenks, *The Origins and Early Development of the Antichrist Myth* (BZNW 59; Berlin: Walter de Gruyter, 1991), 339.

26 The term "antichrist" is used only in 1 John 2:18 (2 x), 22; 4:3; and 2 John 7 within the New Testament. *Pace*, e.g., Richard Chenevix Trench, *Synonyms of the New Testament*, rev. ed. (London: Macmillan, 1865), 101–5, it probably does not refer to a figure who is "against" Christ but to one who replaces the authentic Christ (although Trench is correct that this case cannot be made by appeal to the meaning of the preposition *anti*). For the concept elsewhere in early Christianity, without the term, see in addition to the Synoptic passages mentioned above, 2 Thess. 2:3–12; Rev. 11:7; 12:1–13:18; 14:8–11; 17:1–18; 19:17–20:10; and *Did.* 16.4. In these passages and in the Synoptic apocalyptic discourses, the false prophet tradition of Deut. 13:1–5 mingles with the tradition of a political ruler fiercely opposed to God and his people in the last days from Dan. 11:36. The Elder is more interested in the false prophet side of the tradition because the opposition of which he speaks arises from false teachers rather than from political persecution. See Jenks, *Antichrist Myth*, 340, 339–44; Schnackenburg, *Johannine Epistles*, 135–39; and Strecker, *Johannine Letters*, 236–41.

27 Cf. Brown, *Epistles of John*, 628–29.

28 To do so is therefore to violate precisely the warning in Deut. 13:1–11 against anyone, whether false prophet or family member, who tries to lead God's people astray into the worship of other gods.

God at the same time that, from the Elder's perspective, they "walk in the darkness" (1:6). This traffic in "darkness" has shown itself chiefly in hatred for others (2:9), a hatred demonstrated pre-eminently in the actual secession of the Elder's opponents from fellowship with him and his group (2:19).[29]

Although this hate-motivated separation is the primary example of his opponents' sinfulness, their sins are certainly not limited to this one event. In addition to Jesus' "new command" to "love one another," they ignore his "commands" and his "word" generally (2:3–4, 7–8) and fail to "walk" as Jesus himself "walked" (*peripateō* in 2:6, aut.). When the Elder warns his readers not to love the world and the things associated with it—illicit desires, whether fleshly or visual, and the arrogance of opulent living (2:16)—and when he describes the failure to love one's brother as refusing to meet the needs of the believing poor (3:17), he is probably thinking of the seceders. They claim to have fellowship with God but do not believe that their claim must prove itself in righteous conduct (1:5, 7).

Although it is impossible to identify with certainty the origins of this careless attitude toward sin, the secessionists themselves perhaps appeal for justification to John's gospel. They may have reasoned that if they are abiding in Jesus, then, like Jesus, they cannot be convicted of sin (John 8:46). Like the blind man in the gospel, they worship Jesus as their Lord (9:38), and therefore like him they are not "guilty of sin" (9:41; cf. 15:22, 24). Thus they can claim that since they have decided to believe in Jesus, they have stepped outside the sphere in which sin matters: They are not now sinning nor have they sinned (1:8, 10). Sin is simply not an issue that need trouble them for they have advanced to a higher level of spiritual existence than the one on which people wring their hands over committing this or that transgression against the law.[30]

Against this notion, or something like it, the Elder insists that sin is a serious issue. He maintains that it is impossible to say truthfully either that one has not sinned in the past (1 John 1:10) or that one is currently not susceptible to sin (1:8). At the same time, it is impossible to treat the sin that one inevitably commits flippantly, as if one can have fellowship with the God of light (1:5) but blithely walk in darkness (1:6), carelessly disobey Christ's commands (2:4), and without a thought for his instruction to love one another, hate the brotherhood (2:9, 11; 3:10, 17).

In maintaining this position, the Elder is asserting the traditional understanding of the Christian's relationship to sin as it appears both in John's gospel and elsewhere in early Christianity. It is true that in the gospel the quintessential sin is failure to believe that Jesus Christ is the revelation of his Father and that Christians have therefore avoided this sin, but Jesus' encouragement of his disciples throughout the farewell discourses to love one another (13:34; 15:12, 17) and to keep his commands (14:15, 21, 23–24; 15:10, 14) assumes the possibility of sinning by breaking these commands. Why, otherwise, would such encouragement be necessary?

29 In addition to the section below on "The Witness of the Traditions to the Necessity of Love," see esp. the discussion in Brown, *Community*, 131.

30 This is basically the position of Brown, *Epistles of John*, 81–83, 230–42, although it does not follow Brown in drawing what appear to be oversubtle distinctions between the Elder's descriptions of the secessionists' position in 1:6, 8, and 10.

The same tension, as is well known, appears throughout Paul's letters. On one hand, Paul can say that "those who belong to Christ Jesus have crucified the sinful nature with its passions and desires" (Gal. 5:24), and, "We died to sin; how can we live in it any longer?" (Rom. 6:4). On the other hand, these very statements are ethical admonitions to live in a way that is consistent with the truth they express. In other words, by making such statements, Paul reveals his assumption that believers will sometimes sin and therefore need to be admonished to "keep in step with the Spirit" (Gal. 5:25) and to avoid obeying the body's "evil desires" (Rom. 6:12).

Where this tension appears in early Christianity, it is best explained eschatologically.[31] The final age will be characterized by the sinlessness of God's people (e.g., Jer. 31:31–34; Ezek. 11:19b–20; 36:25–27), and early Christians believed that this age had broken into the present in the coming of Jesus. Yet they still lived in "the present evil age" (Gal. 1:4) and still awaited the full transformation of themselves (e.g., Rom. 8:19–23; Phil. 3:21). Because the present age overlaps with the age to come, sin is still a possibility for believers.

As elsewhere in orthodox Christianity, therefore, the Elder asserts that Christians should not engage in sin because such "lawlessness" (1 John 3:4) is incompatible with fellowship with God, in whom there is no sin (3:5). Nevertheless, Christians should be alert to the possibility of sinning and, when they do sin, they should admit it (1:9; 2:1b). Both activities—avoiding sin as incompatible with one's fellowship with God and acknowledging sin when it happens—arise from taking sin seriously. They result from refusing to believe that one has been translated to a higher level, above the plane of existence on which sin can affect fellowship with God.

If this is the Elder's understanding, however, what could he mean by the following statements?

- Everyone who abides in him does not sin. (3:6a; aut. in all cases)
- Everyone who sins has neither seen nor known him. (3:6b)
- The one who does sin is from the devil because the devil sinned from the beginning. (3:8a)
- Everyone born from God does not do sin because his seed abides in him, and he is not able to sin because he is born from God. (3:9)
- In this are the children of God and the children of the devil evident: everyone who does not do righteousness is not from God, and the one who does not love his brother is not from God. (3:10)
- We know that everyone born from God does not sin, and the One who was born from God keeps him, and the evil one does not touch him. (5:18)

In these passages the Elder states clearly that those who abide in Christ, who are born from God, and who are his children do not sin, whereas those who have neither seen nor known God and who are children of the devil reveal their evil alliance with the devil by sinning. How can these straightforward statements possibly cohere

31 See also Lieu, *Theology of the Johannine Epistles*, 59.

with the criticism earlier of liars who refuse to acknowledge their sin (1:8, 10), or with the Elder's efforts to encourage his readers to confess their sins (1:9; 2:1–2)?

The interpretive literature on 1 John contains a mosaic of answers to this difficult question. Some scholars bring in an editor to account for the claims that believers do not sin or argue that the Elder is quoting statements of his opponents.[32] Often subtle differences between the aorist and the present tenses in Greek come to the rescue—the present tenses in 3:6 and 3:9 speak, it is said, of a studied, habitual way of life, not of occasional, regrettable lapses.[33] Perhaps the Elder was attacking two different groups of people, one that claims they do not sin (1:8, 10) and one that claims their sins do not matter (3:6, 9).[34] Perhaps the Elder has two different kinds of sin in mind—common sins in 1:8, 10 and rebellion (*anomia*) against God in 3:1–10.[35] Or perhaps the Elder simply contradicts himself.[36]

Each of these explanations is unnecessarily complicated. It seems likely that the Elder has instead expressed two sides of a single truth with a simplicity typical of his style elsewhere.[37] Fellowship with God and the claim to be without sin are incompatible. At the same time, everyone who abides in God does not, indeed cannot, sin. The Elder apparently expects his readers to allow each statement to qualify the other. He thus leaves the total impression with his readers that the one who knows God will want to keep his commands and yet will sometimes sin. Because sin is still a possibility, confession and forgiveness are also necessary.

Two pieces of evidence point to this as the right explanation of the seeming contradiction. First, in 2:1–6 the Elder expresses both convictions in the same paragraph. On one hand, he says in several different ways that sinning is incompatible with the claim to know God (2:1, 3–5, 6). On the other hand, he makes clear his belief that those who know God do sometimes sin and that God has made merciful provision to atone for these sins through Jesus' death (2:1b–2). Here the Elder's two convictions about the relationship of the believer to sin appear side by side. It seems unlikely that the Elder has never pondered how they both can be true. Both he and his readers probably have a standard way of reconciling them that remains unexpressed in the letter, perhaps because both the Elder and his readers know it well.

Second, the Elder uses this same approach to other issues in the letter, making it likely that this is simply a constant feature of his style. In 2:7–8, for example, he insists that the same command is both old and new, with no explanation of how it

32 For the editor theory, see Windisch, *Katholischen Briefe*, 136, who believes that the idea of Christian sinlessness expressed in 3:9–10 and 5:18 was added to the original composition, perhaps by the Presbyter who penned 2 and 3 John.

33 Among translations, see, e.g., the NIV and ESV; among commentators, see, e.g., John R. W. Stott, *The Epistles of John* (TNTC; Grand Rapids: Eerdmans, 1964), 126–27, 130–36. Colin G. Kruse, *The Letters of John* (PNTC; Grand Rapids: Eerdmans, 2000) 120, 124, appears to support this position, but then, ibid., 131–32, argues against it and suggests that in 3:6 and 3:9 the Elder is thinking of the special sin of rebellion.

34 Both Dodd, *Johannine Epistles*, 80, and Stott, *Epistles of John*, 126, suggest this explanation.

35 Colin G. Kruse, *The Letters of John*, (PNTC; Grand Rapids: Eerdmans, 2000) 128–29, 131–32.

36 Klauck, *Erst Johannesbrief*, 198, who, however, claims that the contradiction "reflects nothing other than the contradiction of Christian existence." But if the Elder is faithfully reflecting Christian experience, why complain of his lack of precision, weak arguments, and logical gaps? More complete lists of the various positions on this problem appear in Brown, *Epistles of John*, 413–15; Klauck, *Erste Johannesbrief*, 195–97; and Kruse, *Letters of John*, 129–31.

37 Cf. A. E. Brooke, *A Critical and Exegetical Commentary on the Johannine Epistles* (ICC; New York: Scribner's, 1928), 86.

can be both. Evidently the Elder expects his readers to understand that the command is old in the sense that it dates back to Jesus and new in the sense that Jesus originally gave it as a "new" commandment. Similarly, in 2:13–14 the Elder tells both youths and fathers that they have overcome the world, but in the next sentence urges them, "Do not love the world or anything in the world" (2:15). The same pattern appears: Youths and fathers are victors over the world in one sense but not in another. Precisely how both statements can be true the Elder does not tell us.

Against the secessionists, therefore, who probably believe that sin is irrelevant to their fellowship with the God of light, John insists that sin is a serious matter. To deny its presence in one's life or to view it flippantly is to align one's self with deceit and darkness. To regard sin as incompatible with abiding in God and therefore to be dissatisfied with its presence in one's life and confess it, however, is to receive forgiveness and cleansing and to continue to have fellowship with the God of light. The Elder expresses this perspective in his own distinctive style: Christians must admit that they sin, and Christians must not sin. There is a tension here, but it is ultimately the same tension that lies beneath the ethical teaching of much of the New Testament. It is to this traditional understanding of the relationship between the Christian and sin that the Elder calls his readers.

The Witness of the Traditions to the Significance of Jesus' Death

If the secessionists think that their fundamentally spiritual existence means either that sin is impossible for them or that sin, should they commit it, does not matter, then the death of Christ has no logical significance in their system. Christ's death would only mean that he too succumbed to the mire of the material world; it would certainly do nothing to cleanse them of their own material entanglements. Therefore, along with the Elder's need to refute the secessionists' faulty understanding of sin goes the need to refute their refusal to accept the theological significance of Christ's death.

The Elder does this by reminding his readers of the early Christian conviction that Jesus' death was the fulfillment of the Day of Atonement ritual, the most solemn and important rite in Israel's sacrificial system. In it, the high priest alone, and on only this occasion, went behind the curtain that stands in front of the temple's most sacred place and sprinkled the blood of a slaughtered bull and goat on and before the "atonement cover" (*hilastērion*) that rested on top of the ark of the covenant (Lev. 16:6, 9, 11, 14–15). The high priest also, as part of the ritual, confessed the "lawlessness" and "unrighteousness" of all Israel (16:21). The purpose of the ritual was to atone for and cleanse the high priest, his family, and all Israel from their sins (16:6, 16a, 30). It was the blood, we are told, that effected this atonement (17:11).[38]

Only a few decades after Jesus' death, Paul echoed this passage in Romans 3:25, when he spoke of Christ's death as an "atoning sacrifice [*hilastērion*] by his blood." His unusual vocabulary in this passage, and other stylistic oddities, may mean that

38 Cf. Klauck, *Erste Johannesbrief*, 91.

he was using a still earlier Christian tradition about Jesus' death at this point. The same understanding of Christ' death permeates the letter to the Hebrews (e.g., Heb. 2:17; 9:5–7, 11–12) and is probably why, in the view of the authors of the Synoptic Gospels, God tore the temple veil in two at the time of Jesus' death (Matt. 27:51; Mark 15:38; Luke 23:45).[39] John was probably aware of some form of this tradition when, in his gospel, he spoke of Jesus' blood as that which gave believers life (John 6:51, 53–56) and when he observed that blood and water flowed from Jesus' wounded side at the time of his death (John 19:34).[40]

It is to this tradition that the Elder wants to recall his readers in the face of the secessionists' false teaching.[41] The secessionists are quite happy to speak of the redemptive significance of Christ's coming, perhaps focusing, as we have seen, on his baptism as the moment at which he assumed his redemptive mission, but they fail to find any significance in Jesus' death. Against this, the Elder reminds his readers that John had seen Jesus die and had himself understood the sacrificial significance of his shed blood (1 John 5:6–8; cf. John 19:34–35). Elsewhere, the Elder alludes to the Greek text of Leviticus to explain Jesus' death, and these allusions place him within the mainstream of the early Christian interpretation of Jesus' death as the climactic and final Day of Atonement sacrifice.

For the Elder, the shedding of Jesus' blood "cleanses" (*katharizei*) us "from all sin" (*apo pasēs hamartias*, 1 John 1:7), just as the purpose for the Day of Atonement ritual, according to the LXX's rendering, was to "cleanse" (*katharisai*) Israel "from all . . . sins" (*apo pasōn tōn hamartiōn*, Lev. 16:30).[42] For the Elder sin is clearly defined as "lawlessness" (*anomia*, 1 John 3:4) and "unrighteousness" (*adikia*, 5:17), and the "cleansing" (*katharisē*) of people from "all unrighteousness" (*pasōs adikias*) occurs when they "confess" their sin (1:9).

At first this notion may seem to be at odds with the conviction that an atoning sacrifice is necessary as a remedy for sin. If confession brings forgiveness, why is atonement necessary? The instructions to the high priest in Leviticus 16:21 may answer this question. He was to "confess . . . the lawlessness (*pasas tas anomias*) of the Israelites, and all their unrighteousness (*pasas tas adikias autōn*)" on the Day of Atonement. Just as the Day of Atonement ritual held together the two concepts of confession and atoning sacrifice, so the Elder holds them together.[43] Not surprisingly in light of these many verbal correspondences, the Elder considers Jesus to be the "atonement" (*hilasmos*) for our sins (1 John 2:2; 4:10), the precise term that the Greek rendering of Leviticus uses to describe the Day of "Atonement" (*hilasmou*, Lev. 25:9).[44]

39 The temple veil tore "from top to bottom" (Matt. 27:51; Mark 15:38), signaling that God had torn it. On the pervasive nature of the interpretation of Jesus' death as the climactic Day of Atonement sacrifice in earliest Christianity, see Peter Stuhlmacher, *Reconciliation, Law and Righteousness: Essays in Biblical Theology* (Philadelphia: Fortress, 1986), 94–109, esp. 99.

40 Cf. Brown, *Epistles of John*, 202–3, who, however, takes the blood in 6:53–56 as a reference to eucharistic blood rather than to the blood shed on the cross. It is puzzling that Brown does not take it to refer to both.

41 Brown, *Epistles of John*, 239–40.

42 Cf. Klauck, *Erste Johannesbrief*, 91.

43 The two concepts also appear together in Lev. 5:5–6.

44 Cf. Klauck, *Erste Johannesbrief*, 107. In light of the central role that blood played in the meaning of the Day of Atonement ritual (Lev. 17:11) and in the Elder's understanding of atonement (1 John 1:7), the occasional attempts to play down the role of blood sacrifice in the Elder's understanding of the atonement are not helpful for understanding the letter. See, e.g., Dodd, *Johannine Epistles*, 27.

There can be little doubt that the Elder understands Jesus' death in traditional terms as analogous to the Day of Atonement sacrifice of a bull and a goat to "cleanse" all Israel of its "lawlessness" and "unrighteousness."[45] If he follows the common understanding of atoning sacrifice in Near Eastern and Greco-Roman antiquity, he would also understand this atonement according to the logic of substitutionary sacrifice. Greco-Roman literature that touches on the subject usually assumes that certain sins against the gods required the death of the offender and brought the wrath of the gods on the offender's people until this requirement was satisfied. Often a substitution of another's death for that of the offender was acceptable, whether this substitute was a willing and courageous member of the nobility, as so often in Greek tragedy, or an unwilling criminal or outcast.[46]

This understanding of substitutionary atonement also emerges in the Old Testament. It is present, for example, when Moses offered to forfeit himself to "make atonement" for the sin of Israel after they worshiped the golden calf (Ex. 32:30, 32) or when David gave up seven of Saul's sons to the Gibeonites to "make atonement" for Saul's unfaithfulness to them (2 Sam. 21:1–14, esp. v. 3; cf. Josh. 9:16).[47] The blood of the bull and the goat made atonement for sinful Israel because it represented the lives of these animals (Lev. 17:11), and they, in turn, died in the place of sinful Israel. Although the Elder is nowhere explicit about how Christ's death effects atonement, it seems highly likely that he believes Jesus took the role of the goats and the bulls in the Day of Atonement ritual, and died, as they did, in the place of sinners (1 John 2:2).

The Elder, therefore, opposes the secessionists' dismissal of Jesus' death with a clear case for its importance. He formulates this case in terms familiar to other early Christians and, in harmony with widespread views of the need for atoning sacrifice in antiquity, reminds his readers that John himself, the primary source of their own tradition, embraces this view of Jesus' death. When Jesus died, he atoned for sin because his death substituted for the death that sinners deserved. He was the climactic and final Day of Atonement sacrifice.

The Witness of the Traditions to Love as the Proof of a Relationship with God

The secessionists' lack of love for their fellow Christians is, in the Elder's view, the most telling of their various sins. This is clear from the increasingly specific discussion of sin in 2:15–3:24. Here the Elder moves from a general description of sin

45 Judith M. Lieu, "What Was from the Beginning: Scripture and Tradition in the Johannine Epistles," *NTS* 39 (1993): 458–77, here at 461–67, argues that Ex. 34:6, and the interpretive traditions surrounding it, is the primary background for the Elder's use of *hilasmos*. The mention of the cleansing significance of Jesus' blood in 1:7, however, and the close verbal correspondences between the Old Testament descriptions of the Day of Atonement and the Elder's language in 1 John stand against her thesis.

46 *Pace* Joel B. Green and Mark D. Baker, *Recovering the Scandal of the Cross: Atonement in New Testament and Contemporary Contexts* (Downers Grove, Ill.: InterVarsity Press, 2000), 104. For the historical evidence, see esp. Martin Hengel, *The Atonement: The Origin of the Doctrine in the New Testament* (Philadelphia: Fortress, 1981), 19–32, and for a sensitive reflection on the relationship between atoning sacrifice and love, see C. S. Lewis's retelling of the myth of Cupid and Psyche in his novel *Till We Have Faces* (San Diego: Harcourt, 1956), esp. 45–47, 295.

47 Cf. Jonah 1:11–16.

(2:15–17), to mention of the secessionists and their withdrawal from the community (2:18–23), to the incompatibility of sinning with abiding in God (2:24–3:10a), and finally to a detailed discussion of the need for believers to love one another (3:10b–24; 4:7–12). For the Elder, therefore, his opponents' secession from the community is the most serious sign of their lack of love, and their lack of love is a symptom of lives given over to sin. Lives spent in this way cannot, at the same time, be lived in fellowship with God. Much of the Elder's composition is devoted to making this connection between knowledge of God and love for other members of the Christian community.

Here too the Elder reminds his readers of what they have "heard from the beginning" (2:24, 27; 3:11). If they are to "abide" or "remain" in God (3:24), then what this tradition teaches about love needs to "abide" in them (3:11). Accordingly, the Elder's treatment of the need for love contains many links to John's gospel, especially to Jesus' farewell discourses.

As he treats this theme, the Elder is chiefly concerned to show that love for one's brothers and sisters in the faith is the proof of the authenticity of one's claims to have fellowship with God (1:6), to know him (2:4; 4:7–8), to abide in him (2:6; 4:16), and to love him (4:19, 21; 5:1–3). The Elder follows two paths of reasoning throughout the letter as he makes this case.

First, he insists that the actions of people reveal their basic loyalties and that only two options are possible. Either one walks in the light with God and loves fellow believers, or one walks in darkness and stumbles around blind (1:5–7; 2:8–11). Either one loves fellow believers and is a child of God—indwelt by God's seed—or one fails to love and is a child of the devil (3:9–10; 4:7–8). Either one abides in life and loves fellow believers, or one abides in death and does not love (3:14–15). Cain illustrates the principle: He was of the evil one and murdered his brother—his deeds matched his fundamental loyalties (3:12).

In reasoning this way, the Elder is drawing on traditions found in John's gospel.[48] There, Jesus calls Judas, the one who broke away from the twelve disciples and proved disloyal, "a devil" (John 6:7). Later, when Judas set out to put his plan of betrayal into action, John comments that "it was night" (13:30). The one who broke away from the twelve walked in darkness, just as the secessionists, who have failed to show love to their brothers and sisters in the faith, also walk in darkness (2:9–11).

Similarly, one of Jesus' sharpest debates in the gospel is with a group identified as "the Jews who had believed in him." Like Judas and like the secessionists in 1 John, these inauthentic believers failed to "hold" to Jesus' teaching and had "no room" for his "word." Instead, they tried to kill Jesus, and this impulse, Jesus insists, arose from their tendency to "do the works of your father." A few sentences later we learn that their father is "the devil," who from the beginning has been a murderer (8:31–47). For the Elder of 1 John, those once aligned with the Jesus of John's gospel but who now hate their brothers are showing their true colors in a way that John's gospel has

48 Cf. Brown, *Epistles of John*, 468–69.

anticipated. "If you were really Abraham's children," Jesus tells them, "then you would do the things Abraham did" (8:39). One's actions reveal the family from which one springs.[49]

Second, and more positively, the Elder maintains that those who know God and seek to abide in him should imitate his loving actions, as well as those of his Son, Jesus Christ. John emphasizes that God took the initiative in loving us despite our sinful condition by sending his Son to die in our place as an atoning sacrifice for our sin (4:10, 19b). This powerful demonstration of what it means to love those who do not merit love should, in the Elder's view, provide an incentive for believers to love one another (4:11, 19a). The same can be said of God's Son, who by laying down his life "for us"—as a sacrifice of atonement, in our place—provides a concrete illustration of the meaning of love (3:16a) and a concrete example of the kind of love that believers should demonstrate toward one another (3:16b). This kind of love serves as the sure mark of the authentic believer. "This is how we know we are in him," says the Elder, "whoever claims to live in him must walk as Jesus did" (2:5–6).

Specifically what does this love entail? The Elder describes two practical examples of this self-giving love. Believers demonstrate this love by remaining in fellowship with the Elder, his community, its authentic tradition, and the Father and Son to whom the tradition points. The Elder says that he has written his composition so that its readers might remain in fellowship with these manifestations of the truth (1:3–5, 7), for it is only within this circle of fellowship that sin is forgiven (1:7–9), shame at his coming is avoided (2:28), and eternal life is found (5:13). The secessionists have broken this fellowship (2:19) and thereby demonstrated their lack of love.

Believers also demonstrate this love by sharing their wealth with other believers who need practical forms of assistance. The Elder says that it is impossible for God's love to "abide" or "remain" in a person who has worldly wealth but closes down his or her feelings of compassion and refuses to share with a believing brother or sister in need (3:17).[50] Love, the Elder insists, is not an empty claim but an active, practical assistance of those in need, which arises from one's knowledge of the truth (3:18).

In his conviction that love means the imitation of God's action in Christ, the Elder is again tapping Johannine tradition, especially as it appears in the gospel's farewell discourses. There Jesus washes the feet of his disciples and urges them to follow the pattern of unselfish love that he has given them in this action: "I have set you an example that you should do as I have done for you" (John 13:15). Similarly, after commanding his disciples to love one another (15:12), Jesus defines love as laying down one's life for one's friends (15:13), a clear allusion to his death for his disciples, who, as he says in the next sentence, are his friends (15:14; cf. 10:11).[51]

49 Ibid., 431.

50 Cf. Deut. 15:7 and the comments of Brown, *Epistles of John*, 474.

51 Cf. Brown, *Epistles of John*, 474.

That believers should love one another in the unselfish way that Christ has first loved them is the essence of the "new command" as Jesus explains it in the gospel: "A new command I give to you: Love one another. As I have loved you, so you must love one another. By this all will know that you are my disciples, if you love one another" (John 13:34–35). This is the "new command" that the Elder also regards as an "old command" because it is part of the tradition that he and his readers share and it goes back to "the beginning" (1 John 2:7; 3:11).[52]

Like John in the gospel, the Elder speaks frequently of the need to keep God's (or Jesus') "commands" (1 John 2:3–4; 3:24; 5:2–3; cf. John 14:15, 21; 15:10, 14) or "word" (1 John 2:5; cf. John 14:23–24; cf. 15:20), but he focuses on one command: to love one another (1 John 2:10; 3:23; 4:21; cf. John 13:34; 15:12, 17).[53] In addition, he takes Jesus' willingness to lay down his life for believers as both love's defining moment and the chief example that those who believe in Jesus should follow (1 John 3:16; cf. John 15:13–14).

In the Elder's view, the secessionists' departure from the community signals their lack of love for their brothers and sisters in the faith, and this lack of love belies their claims to a close relationship with God (2:4, 6; 4:7–8, 16, 19, 21; 5:1–3) and to knowledge of the truth (2:9, 21). Jesus made it clear in John's gospel that the mark of an authentic disciple is love for fellow disciples (John 13:35), and the secessionists' withdrawal from fellowship with the Elder and his community is a miserable failure of this critical test. Probably to counteract the attempts of the secessionists to influence his community, the Elder urges them to show love for their brothers and sisters by remaining in fellowship with them.

FIRST JOHN AS A REAFFIRMATION OF TRADITIONAL CHRISTIAN CONVICTIONS

The group that seceded from the Elder's community and the Elder himself each had a different understanding of the human plight, and this led them to embrace incompatible understandings of everything else. Although our picture of the secessionists' precise beliefs is necessarily speculative, it is likely that they believed human nature was material and therefore evil. The problem that existence posed for them was how to engineer the escape of their eternal spirits from the prison of their material bodies and the material world that they inhabited. In response to this problem, they fashioned from language they found in John's gospel a "Christ" who was wholly spiritual and so without the "taint" of human flesh. He was not himself subject to the material world—certainly not to death by crucifixion—but was a pure revelation of his spiritual Father, able to lead them out of the world and into the realm of light. Ethical conduct was of no importance. Spiritual escape from the material world was the goal of existence.

52 Cf. ibid., 286.

53 Both the gospel and 1 John mention other commands, such as believing that Jesus Christ is God's Son (1 John 3:23; cf. John 14:11; 16:26–27), but the command to love is the chief concern of the author of this letter, just as it is of Jesus in the gospel.

For the Elder, the human plight was framed in terms familiar from the Old Testament and early Christian tradition and in terms that he knew undergirded John's gospel. The inability and unwillingness of human beings to obey God's law and their determination instead to follow "the cravings of the flesh" have alienated human beings from God. Because of their disobedience to God, they deserve God's wrath rather than eternal life. Jesus Christ answered this problem when he came in the flesh and, although himself righteous, died in the place of sinners as the climactic and final Day of Atonement sacrifice. This sacrifice for sin implied, by its unselfish character, that Christians should lay down their own lives in love for one another. Those who claim to have fellowship with, know, abide in, and love God should prove the genuineness of their claim by engaging in such sacrificial love.

The secessionists had encouraged doubts within the Elder's community about the validity of these traditional truths. In the face of this crisis, the Elder calls his community back to these fundamental convictions of early Christian traditions—traditions that go back to Jesus himself and that the Elder's readers embraced when they became Christians. By continuing to hold to these convictions, he believes, they can avoid the error of Judas, of other inauthentic believers during Jesus' ministry, and of the secessionists themselves. By believing and living out these convictions they can know that they have eternal life.

Chapter 28

SECOND JOHN: AVOIDING THOSE WHO HAVE ABANDONED TRUTH AND LOVE

It was not enough for the author of 1 John to warn his own community against the influence of those who left their group and "progressed" beyond the community's traditions. He also has pastoral responsibility for churches in outlying areas. Traveling advocates of the secessionists' faulty Christology and ethics, he fears, may have reached one of these churches also. This concern prompts him to write a letter to a church that seems to be an especially likely stop for these missionaries. In this letter, known from antiquity as "the second [letter] of John," the author adopts his widely recognized title of authority—"the Elder"—and urges this church to test anyone who might visit them. If the teaching of the visitors fails to conform to the traditions about Christ that the church has heard from the beginning (vv. 6, 9–10a), they should reject them (v. 10b).[1]

A portrait of the false teachers in miniature appears in verse 7, and it is a picture already familiar from 1 John: "Many deceivers, who do not acknowledge Jesus Christ as coming in the flesh, have gone out into the world. Any such person is the deceiver and the antichrist." The "many deceivers" act in the spirit of the "antichrist," replacing the flesh and blood Jesus of John's gospel with a fleshless Christ. They have, moreover, not only gone out into the world literally as missionaries in the cause of their error, but, as 1 John made clear, they went out into the world metaphorically also—embracing the ways of the world (1 John 2:15–17), breaking the fellowship of the Elder's community (2:19), and demonstrating their hatred for their brothers and sisters (2:9; 3:13, 15; 4:20). The problem is one of "truth and love" (2 John 3)—the itinerant false teachers fail to teach the truth about the Messiah and they fail to love their brothers and sisters in the community.

LOVE, TRUTH, AND REJECTION IN THE ELDER'S RESPONSE

The elder responds to the possible spread of the false teaching by encouraging the members of the community to which he writes to love one another, to measure all teaching by the tradition about Christ that they have already received, and to reject

1 Scholars have proposed widely differing possibilities for the order, occasion, and authorship of the three Johannine letters. The proposal suggested here follows the broad outlines of the theory developed by Raymond E. Brown, *The Community of the Beloved Disciple* (New York: Paulist, 1979), 98–99; idem, *The Epistles of John* (AB 30; New York: Doubleday, 1982), 69–71, 750–51.

those who fail the test. The consequences are grave, he warns, for failing to evaluate critically teachers who may visit their community.

The Necessity of Love

If the divisiveness of the secessionists is the primary fruit of their false teaching, then the community to whom the Elder writes in 2 John can brace itself against the attack of the false teachers by placing special emphasis on their love for one another.[2] Already in the first line of his letter's greeting, the author says that those who know the truth must cling to one another in love. He loves the community to which he writes (v. 1a), and "all who know the truth" love them also (v. 1b). This mutual love among those committed to the truth is "because of the truth, which lives in us and will be with us forever" (v. 2). Those who know the truth, in other words, reinforce their commitment to the truth through their love for one another.

The Elder devotes the first part of his letter's body (vv. 4–6) to the premise that Jesus' command to his disciples to love one another (John 13:34; 15:12, 17) is an important part of the truth to which they should cling. This command came from the Father through Jesus and is present in the tradition that the Elder's readers embraced when they became Christians. It is, therefore, not a "new command" but one they have had "from the beginning"—both the beginning of their tradition in Jesus' own teaching and the beginning of their commitment to that tradition when they became believers (v. 5).[3]

The author's next statement is confusing. A literal translation looks like this:

> And this is love, that we should walk according to his commandments. This is the commandment, even as you heard from the beginning, that in it you should walk. (v. 6)

Is the Elder defining love for God in this statement? Is he defining love for neighbor? Is he perhaps referring to both? Why, moreover, is the statement so redundant, saying in effect, "This is the commandment: to live by the commandment"?

Interpreters sometimes say that the Elder speaks of love for God, which one shows by keeping God's commands, as in 1 John 5:3 ("For this is the love *of God*: that we should keep his commandments," aut.).[4] Others point out, however, that at the end of the preceding sentence the Elder spoke of love for one another ("I ask that we love one another," 2 John 5) and that he is unlikely to have swiveled so quickly from the notion of loving others to the idea of loving God.[5] The problem is occasionally found to be the result of an attempt by an unskilled imitator of 1 John to copy 1 John 5:3, an attempt that unfortunately left out the crucial phrase "of God."[6]

2 That this is the motive for the author's stress on love within the community is evident from the *hoti* ("because") that begins v. 7. His readers should walk in love (v. 6) "because" many deceivers are abroad.

3 *Pace* Judith Lieu, *The Second and Third Epistles of John* (SNTW; Edinburgh: T. & T. Clark, 1986), 75, who believes that throughout the Johannine correspondence the phrase refers to the "beginning of the church's life." For the interpretation of the phrase adopted here, see Brown, *Epistles of John*, 664.

4 See, e.g., Bernard Weiss, *Die drei Briefe des Apostel Johannes* (MeyerK 14; 6th ed.; Göttingen: Vandenhoeck & Ruprecht, 1899), 177.

5 See, e.g., Brown, *Epistles of John*, 665.

6 See, e.g., Lieu, *Second and Third Epistles*, 76.

The Elder's statement is certainly puzzling, but this kind of ambiguity is a stylistic characteristic of the Johannine literature generally and is abundantly present in 1 John.[7] Moreover, if we do not feel compelled to read the statement in light of 1 John 5:3, the puzzle is reasonably easy to solve. The "it" in the second half of the statement refers not to "commandment" but to "love" in the first half.[8] The statement as a whole roughly follows an A B B′ A′ pattern:

A Love
  B is walking according to his commandments;
  B′ the commandment
A′ is to walk in love.

This is a playful way of repeating two common themes in John's gospel and 1 John: the single command to love summarizes all the commandments, and love should show itself in loving actions toward the fellowship of believers.[9]

The Elder, then, hopes to avoid in the outlying church to which he writes the same kind of fracture in fellowship that his own community has experienced (1 John 2:19) and that the secessionists encouraged by their false Christology. His letter stresses the need for the community to which he writes to "walk" in Jesus' original command to his disciples, the command that summarizes all others: They should show their love for one another in practical ways.

The Teaching about Christ as the Criterion for All Teaching

In the second major part of the letter's body, the author turns to the possibility that the community to which he writes will be visited by traveling false teachers from the secessionists who broke fellowship with his own local community. His readers will recognize these deceivers, should they arrive, by their departure from traditional Johannine "teaching," especially from one particular element of that teaching—that when Jesus appeared in the world, he came as a person of real flesh and blood.

From what we have already seen of the author's style, it is not surprising that in this section also, he states this warning with a measure of ambiguity. Two interpretive problems are particularly significant. First, the author warns his readers that the deceivers will fail to confess "Jesus Christ as coming in the flesh," using the present participle (*erchomenon*, v. 7). Does this mean that the false teachers refuse to recognize that when Jesus returns in the future, he will come in the flesh?[10] Does the present participle refer to the "timeless" nature of Christ's incarnation—that he was and

7 See the section "The Witness of the Traditions to the Relationship between the Christian and Sin" in chapter 26 above, and Frank Thielman, "The Style of the Fourth Gospel and Ancient Literary Critical Concepts of Religious Discourse" in *Persuasive Artistry: Studies in New Testament Rhetoric in Honor of George A. Kennedy*, ed. Duane F. Watson (JSNTSup 50; Sheffield: Sheffield Academic Press, 1991), 169–83.

8 *Autē* ("it") is feminine and could refer either to *agapē* ("love") in the first half of the sentence or to *entolē* ("commandment") in the second half. In ambiguous cases like this, the antecedent is admittedly most often the closest possible noun, as Lieu, *Second and Third Epistles*, 76–77, points out. Here, however, the rhetoric of the passage, revealed in the A B B′A′ pattern, must override this grammatical consideration. Cf. the NIV; Rudolf Schnackenburg, *The Johannine Epistles: Introduction and Commentary* (New York: Crossroad, 1992), 283; and Colin G. Kruse, *The Letters of John* (PNTC; Grand Rapids: Eerdmans, 2000), 208–9.

9 For the command to love as the summary of the commandments, see John 13:34; 14:15, 21; 15:10, 12, 14, 17 and 1 John 2:3–4, 20; 3:23–24; 4:21; 5:2–3. For the need to show love by practical action, see John 13:12–17 and 1 John 3:17–18; 4:20–21.

10 Strecker, *Johannine Letters*, 233–36.

is in the flesh?[11] Or does the present participle somehow refer to Jesus' past incarnation in a way reminiscent of 1 John 4:2, which, however, uses the perfect participle *elēlythota* ("has come") and thus makes a reference to the past explicit?[12] Is this once again a sign that 2 John is using material from 1 John but introducing confusing changes along the way?[13]

The solution to the conundrum is found in remembering that John's gospel frequently refers to Jesus as "the one who comes" (John 1:15, 27; 3:31; 6:14; 11:27). In 2 John 7, then, the elder is probably borrowing this expression to say that "the one who comes" in John's gospel "comes" in the flesh, and that those who deny this precept are out of accord with traditional teaching.[14]

Second, the author warns his readers against succumbing to the notion that they should "progress" beyond "the teaching of Christ [*tou Christou*]" (vv. 9–10a). Does this mean "the teaching that Christ gave" (taking *tou Christou* as a subjective genitive)?[15] Or does it mean "the teaching of the Johannine tradition about Christ" (taking *tou Christou* as an objective genitive)?[16] If we see the confession of verse 7 as in some way parallel to the teaching of verses 9–10, then it seems likely that we should understand Christ to be the object of the teaching just as he was the object of the confession.[17]

In the second part of his letter, therefore, the author urges his readers to measure the ideas of any visiting teachers by the traditions about Jesus that they know from John's gospel. In particular, they should remember that John's gospel affirms Jesus to be not merely "the one who comes" but the one who "became flesh" (John 1:14). Anyone who deviates from this element of the Johannine tradition about Christ has substituted a false Christ for the true one and is therefore both an "antichrist" and a "deceiver" (v. 7).

The Necessary Response and The Consequences of Failing to Give It

The second major part of the letter's body speaks of what will happen to the community if it imbibes the deception of the false teachers. It also describes the response that the Elder wants the community to give to the false teachers in order to avoid falling prey to their deceit. If the Elder's readers fail to remain in traditional Johannine teaching about Christ and instead "progress" to other understandings of him, then the pastoral work of the Elder will be lost and his readers will fail to receive their reward (v. 8).[18] This reward is probably "eternal life," which is the goal of their belief about Jesus, the Messiah and Son of God (John 20:31; 1 John 2:25; 5:13).[19]

11 A. E. Brooke, *A Critical and Exegetical Commentary on the Johannine Epistles* (ICC; New York: Scribner's, 1928), 175; Rudolf Bultmann, *The Johannine Epistles* (Hermeneia; Philadelphia: Fortress, 1973; orig. German ed., 1967), 112; Schnackenburg, *Johannine Epistles*, 284.

12 Kruse, *Letters of John*, 210, who believes the present tense in 2 John 7 emphasizes the "process" of Jesus' coming in the flesh.

13 Lieu, *Second and Third Epistles*, 86–87.

14 See, e.g., Schnackenburg, *Johannine Epistles*, 284, and Brown, *Epistles of John*, 670.

15 See, e.g., Schnackenburg, *Johannine Epistles*, 286, and Brown, *Epistles of John*, 674–75

16 Georg Strecker, *The Johannine Letters* (Hermeneia; Minneapolis: Fortress, 1996; orig. German ed. 1989), 242 n. 53.

17 Ibid.

18 This assumes with N-A27 that the reading *eirgasametha* ("we worked") in v. 8 rather than the reading *eirgasasthe* ("you worked"), adopted in N-A25, is correct.

19 Cf. Bultmann, *Johannine Epistles*, 113.

The sentiment is similar to Paul's frequent expressions of warning to the churches he has founded that if they do not change their convictions or their conduct, then his apostolic labor and their faith will have been "in vain" (1 Cor. 15:2; 2 Cor. 6:1; Gal. 3:4; 4:11; Phil. 2:16; 1 Thess. 3:5).[20]

The consequences of falling prey to the false teachers are so grave that the Elder advises taking extreme measures to avoid contact with them. His readers should not welcome them into their houses and should not even say hello to them, for anyone who says hello to them will share in their evil deeds (vv. 10–11). This approach by the Elder has encountered heavy criticism from those who feel that it is uncharitable and hypocritical. How can he accuse those who withdraw from his own community (1 John 2:19) of hating the brotherhood (1 John 2:9, 11; 3:15; 4:20) when he urges his own readers not even to greet traveling secessionists? What has happened to the much-touted love command?[21]

Such chastisements, however, seem oddly out of touch with the actual historical situation of this text.[22] Three issues are particularly important to consider in evaluating this response. First, the Elder is not concerned in verses 10–11 about showing hospitality to rank and file members of the secessionist group who may be traveling for a variety of reasons unrelated to their theological convictions, but about the group's teachers sent out especially for the purpose of deceiving unwary Christians. To provide hospitality for them is to facilitate their efforts to deceive.

Second, as we have already seen in our study of the Pastoral Letters, first-century churches relied on the few wealthy people in their midst who owned homes to supply meeting places for their regular times of worship. For Christians to welcome false teachers into their homes, therefore, must have often meant supplying these teachers with ready-made audiences inclined to view whatever they said as authoritative. This situation probably accounts for the spread of the false teaching opposed in the Pastorals (1 Tim. 3:15; 2 Tim. 3:6; Titus 1:11), and it is probably the problem that the Elder has in view in 2 John 10–11.[23]

Third, as v. 11 shows, we should not understand the Elder's admonition to refuse a greeting to the false teachers as a curious reluctance even to extend a common formal courtesy to them. Instead, the Elder is referring here to optimistic, verbal encouragement of the false teachers' "evil deeds."[24] A warm welcome to the false teachers

20 On this see Martin Hengel, *Johannine Question* (London: SCM/Philadelphia: Trinity Press International, 1989), 44, 174.

21 See C. H. Dodd, *The Johannine Epistles* (MNTC; London: Hodder and Stoughton, 1946), 150–52, esp. the comment on p. 152: "If the norm of charity, as the First Epistle so eloquently sets forth . . . is the love of Christ, who died for our sins . . . is it possible to exclude from its operation even the most obdurate heretic?" See also C.K. Barrett, "The Centre of the New Testament and the Canon," in *Die Mitte des Neuen Testaments: Einheit und Vielfalt neutestamentlicher Theologie: Festschrift für Eduard Schweizer zum siebzigsten Geburtstag*, ed. Ulrich Luz and Hans Weder (Göttingen: Vandenhoeck & Ruprecht, 1983), 5–21, here at 8: "'This is how all men will know that you are my disciples, if you have love among yourselves' ([John] 13, 35). One wonders if the Elder or Diotrephes qualified"; and Brown, *Community*, 131–35, esp. the comment on p. 135: "In [the Elder's] attitude toward the secessionists in a passage like II John 10–11 he supplied fuel for those Christians of all times who feel justified in hating other Christians for the love of God."

22 Cf. Hengel, *The Johannine Question*, 45.

23 Cf. Lieu, *Second and Third Epistles*, 97.

24 I. Howard Marshall, *The Epistles of John* (NICNT; Grand Rapids: Eerdmans, 1978), 74. Cf. Hengel, *Johannine Question*, 43, who comments that the greeting in this context is part of the offer of hospitality.

would indicate a positive disposition toward their teaching and therefore would encourage their work.

The Elder is convinced that the "many deceivers" who have left his own community and sought followers elsewhere are capable of destroying his pastoral work and leading people away from eternal life. In the face of such a threat, the leader of this beleaguered community understandably counsels his readers not to provide traveling false teachers with a ready-made platform for their message, practical support for their mission, and verbal encouragement to engage in their work.[25]

TRUTH, LOVE, AND REJECTION IN 2 JOHN

The Elder believes that the only path to eternal life lies in the conviction, which all faithful Johannine Christians share, that Jesus is the Christ, the Son of God, and that he came in the flesh. The missionaries of whom he speaks in 2 John have distorted these traditions by claiming Jesus Christ was not a fleshly human being. They also refuse fellowship with Johannine Christians who do not share their views. From the Elder's perspective, deceit and division are the hallmarks of their movement.

Against the threat that these missionaries pose to one of the churches under his pastoral care, the Elder encourages a renewed commitment to truth and love. The community to which he writes should love one another in practical ways as Jesus, in John's gospel, instructed his disciples. They should also measure every visiting teacher by the traditional teaching about Christ. If missionaries arrive on their doorstep renouncing the fleshly existence of Jesus Christ, they should not encourage their deceptive work. The community should not admit them to their houses, where worship and teaching take place, nor should they offer practical or emotional support to their efforts. To do so would be to participate in their evil deeds of deceit and division and to join them in their wrong-headed journey away from eternal life.

25 The situation is perhaps not unlike that faced by the Confessing Church in Germany during World War II. Dodd, in a commentary published in 1946, seems to have recognized this and to have drawn the appropriate analogy only then to criticize the Elder for not realizing that a policy such as the author recommends fails to serve "the cause of 'truth and love,' upon which [the Elder] lays such stress." See Dodd, *Johannine Epistles*, 151–52.

Chapter 29

THIRD JOHN: WORKING TOGETHER WITH THE TRUTH

If the secessionists of 1 John 2:19 had broken fellowship with the Elder's community, and if some of them had gone to outlying Johannine churches to spread their divisive, erroneous teaching, then the Elder probably found it necessary to send out counter-missionaries of his own to refute the teaching of these deceivers.[1] The person or persons who carried 2 John to its destination must have been on just such a mission.[2]

When we turn to 3 John, we discover that a surprising complication has arisen in the Elder's efforts to oppose the secessionists and their false teachers. A leader in one of the outlying churches to which the Elder's missionaries have traveled—a man named Diotrephes—has refused them hospitality, following a procedure not unlike that recommended by the Elder himself in 2 John for the secessionist false teachers (v. 9b; cf. 2 John 10–11). Diotrephes may have rejected a letter of introduction that the Elder had written to commend the missionaries to the churches to which they have traveled (3 John 9a).[3] He has definitely made outrageous and disparaging comments about the Elder (v. 10a) and has added injury to insult by expelling from his church anyone who wanted to extend hospitality to the Elder's missionaries (v. 10b).

Why does Diotrephes take such extreme measures? It is improbable that he holds heretical convictions and rejects the Elder's orthodoxy.[4] It is equally improbable that he holds orthodox convictions and rejects the Elder's missionaries as heretics.[5] If the dispute between the two leaders were rooted in theological issues, the Elder would

1 For this understanding of the circumstances that prompted 3 John, see Raymond E. Brown, *The Epistles of John: A New Translation and Commentary* (AB 30; New York: Doubleday, 1982), 708, 742.

2 The Elder's interest in mission does not place him in tension with a supposedly inward-looking perspective in the Fourth Gospel as Judith Lieu, *The Second and Third Epistles of John* (SNTW; Edinburgh: T. & T. Clark, 1986), 106–7, 109, 163, believes. Such passages as John 1:41–42, 45; 4:35–42; 10:16; 12:20–22 demonstrate that Johannine Christianity generally was not opposed or indifferent to mission.

3 For the theory that the letter to which the Elder refers in v. 9a was a letter of commendation, see, e.g., Hans Windisch, *Die katholischen Briefe*, rev. Herbert Preisker, 3rd ed. (HNT 15; Tübingen: J. C. B. Mohr [Paul Siebeck], 1951; orig. ed. 1911), 142. Brown, *Epistles of John*, 744, advances this idea as a possibility but is prudently cautious about filling in this detail on the basis of so little evidence.

4 This was the view of Walter Bauer, *Orthodoxy and Heresy in Earliest Christianity* (London: SCM, 1972; 1st German ed., 1934), 93, and it has been taken up more recently by Gerd Lüdemann, *Heretics: The Other Side of Christianity* (Louisville: Westminster John Knox, 1996), 182–83.

5 This was the view of Ernst Käsemann, "Ketzer und Zeuge," *ZTK* 48 (1951): 292–311, esp. 297–99. The thesis has been advanced more recently by Georg Strecker, *The Johannine Letters* (Hermeneia; Philadelphia: Fortress, 1996), 262–63. Käsemann and Strecker differed, however, on the kind of heresy that the Elder supposedly advocated. Käsemann believed that the Elder was a gnostic heretic who penned the equally gnostic fourth gospel. Strecker argued that the Elder represented a chiliastic apocalypticism that stood on the margins of orthodox developments. Both Diotrephes and the author of the fourth gospel, in Strecker's view, represented the "spiritualizing" or "gnosticizing" tendency in the Johannine tradition.

not fail to air them as explicitly in this letter as he does in 1 and 2 John.[6] Diotrephes is not an evildoer because of his theological convictions but because of his conduct: He loves to be first, slanders the Elder, and, most serious of all, opposes the Elder's missionary efforts.

The one bright spot on this bleak landscape is the man to whom the Elder writes: Gaius (v. 1). He is evidently the host of a church not too distant from Diotrephes's house, but he has not followed Diotrephes's lead in rejecting the Elder's missionaries.[7] According to the report of the missionaries after their return, Gaius took the missionaries in (vv. 5–6a) and gave them reason to believe that he would be willing to continue to support their work in spite of Diotrephes's opposition (v. 6b).

This practical encouragement from Gaius prompts the Elder to write 3 John. The letter seems to have one purpose, expressed in vv. 6b and 12: The Elder urges Gaius to continue to support his mission by continuing to extend hospitality to his missionaries, especially Demetrius (who is perhaps their leader).[8] The Elder hopes to persuade Gaius to do this by commending Gaius's past generosity (vv. 3–6a), by reminding him why such generosity is necessary (vv. 7–8), and by holding up Diotrephes's ungenerous behavior as a negative example (vv. 9–11). We can examine these three persuasive elements, and the theology that informs them, by looking at the author's appeal to Gaius (vv. 3–8) and then at his description of Diotrephes (vv. 9–11).

TRUTH AND LOVE AT WORK IN GAIUS

The Elder uses a twofold strategy to persuade Gaius to fulfill his request "to send" the missionaries "on their way in a manner worthy of God" (v. 6b). First, he commends Gaius for the hospitality that he has already shown to the missionaries. When they returned, the missionaries told not only the Elder but the entire church under his oversight that Gaius was committed to the truth and had demonstrated this commitment in practical ways; he both possessed the truth and walked in it (v. 3; v. 6a). This assessment of Gaius, the Elder continues, is based on concrete evidence of his faithfulness. He worked for the benefit of the missionaries although they were strangers to him (v. 5). This commendation of Gaius is not only a sincere expression of thanks but confirms that his conduct was the right course of action, despite the efforts of Diotrephes to oppose it. It is therefore a way of urging Gaius to continue to show hospitality to the missionaries when they return to his region.

Second, the Elder supplies an explicit reason why Gaius should continue to show hospitality to the missionaries. These missionaries left their homes for the sake of

6 Strecker, *Johannine Letters*, xl, believes that the Elder wrote both 2 and 3 John but not 1 John, and this would, to some extent, answer this objection. Even the author of 2 John 7–11, however, would not have been likely to withhold criticism from Diotrephes if he had held "spiritualizing" views. See C. H. Dodd, *The Johannine Epistles*, MNTC (London: Hodder & Stoughton, 1946), 165, who comments memorably that the Elder "is not wont to be mealy-mouthed when heresy is concerned." See also the comments of Brown, *Epistles of John*, 737.

7 Brown, *Epistles of John*, 731.

8 As Brown, ibid., 721–22, comments, we should not think of Demetrius as known to Gaius. The Elder himself knows Demetrius well and commends him to Gaius with the apparent assumption that Gaius does not know him.

"the Name" (v. 7)—probably a reference to the correct identity of Jesus as the Christ and Son of God in whom alone is eternal life (John 20:31; cf. 6:68; 14:6). They followed a strategy in their missionary labors, moreover, of not accepting hospitality from unbelievers. All Christians, says the Elder, are obligated to support such itinerant teachers (3 John 8a) because by doing so, they become coworkers "with the truth" (v. 8b). They become, in other words, what Gaius has already demonstrated himself to be: people whose commitment to the truth shows itself in supporting the advancement of the truth in practical ways.

This two-pronged persuasive strategy appears to arise from a mixture of both distinctively Johannine theological elements and theological emphases that are characteristic of broader Christian, and especially, Pauline concerns.[9] The Elder's emphasis on loving behavior as an extension of one's commitment to the truth and as a witness to the authenticity of this commitment is thoroughly Johannine. The Elder takes Gaius's generosity to be precisely the kind of practical aid to a needy brother or sister that the Elder commended in 1 John as the very definition of love (1 John 3:16). It is a practical test of whether or not "we belong to the truth" (3:19; cf. 1:6). "If anyone has material possessions and sees his brother in need but has no pity on him," says the Elder, "how can the love of God be in him?" (3:17). Or, to state the principle positively, "We know that we have passed from death to life, because we love our brothers" (3:14). This is similar to Jesus' claim in John's gospel that his disciples' love for one another demonstrates the validity of their discipleship (John 13:35). Gaius's willingness to show hospitality to unfamiliar but theologically sound Christians is credible evidence that he possesses the truth (3 John 3).

The obligation that the Elder lays on all Christians, and by implication on Gaius also, to show hospitality to itinerant teachers is also phrased in a distinctively Johannine way: "We ought [*opheilō*] therefore to show hospitality to such people" (v. 8). The term "ought" is important in Johannine theology, for it links the behavior of the Christian with the conduct of Jesus himself, or, in this case, of those who serve him. Thus, Jesus' disciples "ought" to wash one another's feet because Jesus has washed their feet (John 13:14). Christ has laid down his life for Christians, so Christians "ought" to lay down their lives for one another (1 John 4:11). The missionaries left home to safeguard the proper understanding of Jesus' identity, and Christians who do not themselves engage in itinerant teaching "ought" to follow their sacrificial example by lending them practical support.[10]

The Elder's comment that the brothers left on their mission "for the sake of the Name" (v. 7a) strikes another Johannine cord. We have already seen in our study of both the gospel and 1 John that the correct understanding of Jesus' identity as not only Messiah but Son of God was considered critical to receiving eternal life. In the

9 The connections between Paul's letters and 3 John help to substantiate the intuition of Martin Hengel, *The Johannine Question* (London: SCM/Philadelphia: Trinity Press International, 1989), 50, that Pauline and Johannine theology—especially as it is expressed in 1 John—have close, if somewhat puzzling, connections.

10 Cf. Brown, *Epistles of John*, 262, 713, 741, and Hans Josef Klauck, *Der zweite und dritte Johannesbrief* (EKK 23.2; Zürich/Neukirchen-Vluyn: Benziger/Neukirchener, 1992), 93.

purpose statement of both the gospel and the first letter, this correct understanding of Jesus is called his "name" (John 20:31; 1 John 5:13).

In the gospel, Christians needed to be strengthened in their conviction that as Son of God Jesus shared the divine being of his Father. In 1 John, Christians needed to be reassured that their traditional understanding of Jesus as not only one with God but as a true, flesh-and-blood human being was correct. The "name" of Jesus seems to be in some way connected in both cases with these correct understandings of Jesus' person. Now, in his letter to Gaius, the Elder speaks of brothers who have left home for the sake of the proper understanding of Jesus—his "name." They believe, as Johannine Christianity has affirmed from the first, that eternal life is connected with faith in the right understanding of Jesus' nature.

On the Pauline side, the Elder's request that Gaius send the itinerating brothers, when they return, "on their way in a manner worthy of God" (v. 6) is reminiscent of Paul's request "to be sent on my way" to Spain by the Roman church (Rom. 15:24). The relevant Greek term in both instances is *propempō*. Paul seems to have first given this word the technical meaning of providing practical material support for traveling Christian teachers, a meaning that it continued to have in later Christian literature.[11]

The Elder's statement that the missionaries, as a matter of strategy, should receive "no help from the pagans" (v. 7) is also reminiscent of a Pauline concern: The itinerant work of an apostle of the gospel of God should not be confused with the work of traveling Cynic philosophers and Sophists, some of whom engaged in their trade disingenuously as a way of making easy money.[12] For this reason, Paul plied a trade in the course of his apostolic labors (1 Cor. 9:12, 18; 1 Thess. 2:1–12; 2 Thess. 3:7–9) and encouraged other Christians to live by the rule, "If a man will not work, he shall not eat" (2 Thess. 3:10).[13]

Here too, a strategy that began with Paul seems to have become common currency by the turn of the first century. Thus, *Didache* 12, probably composed in the late first or early second century, provides a detailed procedure for the support of traveling teachers. One who comes in the Lord's name should be received and shown hospitality for two or three days. If he wants to settle down, however, he must be willing to ply a trade for his own support: "He should work and he should eat" (*Did.* 12.3). If he refuses to follow this rule, he is "one who carries on a cheap trade in the teachings of Christ" (*Did.* 12.5; cf. 11.6).[14]

The Elder may be working within this conceptual world; if so, he brings the basic outline of this common early Christian policy to Gaius's attention. Unlike Cynic philosophers and Sophists, his group of counter-missionaries cannot appeal

11 The term is used in 1 Macc. 12:4 and 1 Esdras 4:47 of people who are given letters of recommendation to facilitate their journeys. Paul seems to use it in a similar way (but without reference to accompanying letters) in 1 Cor. 16:6, 11 (cf. esp. 1 Macc. 12:4). He uses it in the sense of supplying practical support in Rom. 15:24; 1 Cor. 16:6; 2 Cor. 1:16; and Titus 3:13. After Paul's time, this second meaning continues in Polycarp, *Phil.* 1.1, and, according to BDAG, 873, in Acts 15:3. See also Lieu, *Second and Third Epistles*, 106.

12 Cf. Lieu, *Second and Third Epistles*, 126.

13 This concern is also evident in the precautions that Paul took to avoid any misunderstanding of his collection for the Jerusalem church (1 Cor. 16:1–4; 2 Cor. 8:20–21) and in his response to his sophistically inclined opponents in Corinth (2 Cor. 4:21).

14 For this translation, see BDAG, 1090.

for support to a common public who may misunderstand their motives. They must depend on believers who understand the missionaries' need for support and have guidelines in place for preventing abuses of Christian generosity. Christians such as Gaius, therefore, are obligated to show hospitality to traveling Christian teachers not only because (as the Johannine tradition emphasizes) they ought to participate in the advocacy of the truth but also because (as Paul and the wider Christian tradition might say) Christians must not tarnish the gospel by appealing to pagans for support in a way that the pagans can easily misinterpret.

In summary, the Elder bases his request to Gaius "to send" the missionaries "on their way in a manner worthy of God" (v. 6b) in part on a positive appeal. This positive approach has two facets. He commends Gaius for demonstrating his commitment to the truth in the practical support that he has offered to the missionaries. He also reminds Gaius that hospitality to traveling teachers is a fundamental ethical responsibility of Christians generally and that Gaius should therefore continue to support the missionaries. This appeal emerges not only from distinctively Johannine concerns about the relationship between Christology and eternal life and between truth and love but also from widely recognized early Christian concerns that seem to have their roots in Paul's letters.

DIOTREPHES AS A NEGATIVE EXAMPLE

The Elder also advances his appeal along negative lines. Diotrephes supplies an example of the kind of behavior that arises from not having seen God (v. 11b), and therefore Gaius should avoid imitating Diotrephes's handling of the Elder and the Elder's missionaries. Diotrephes refused to extend a friendly reception either to the Elder's letter of commendation for the missionaries or (depending on how we take v. 9) to the missionaries themselves (vv. 9–10). In addition, he slandered the Elder, and, as if this were not enough, he ejected from the fellowship of the church anyone who gave the missionaries a friendly welcome (v. 10).

Scholars frequently speculate about the reasons for Diotrephes's resistance to the Elder and his missionaries, floating the possibility that the Elder is at least partly at fault. Perhaps, say some, the Elder has failed to accept gracefully a natural change of church structure. As time has advanced, the authority once concentrated in the apostles and their immediate successors has begun to dissipate, and younger ministers, leaders in their own congregations, have started to govern their own affairs. Diotrephes, an example of the younger generation, has perhaps been impatient and ungracious in taking the reins, and the Elder has been unwilling to accept change and give them up.[15]

Perhaps, say others, Diotrephes is simply trying to be a responsible pastor and protect his church against heresy in much the same way that the Elder recommends in 2 John 10–11. Rather than take the trouble to examine each traveling visitor only

15 Dodd, *Johannine Epistles*, 164, cautiously offers this scenario as a possibility.

to discover too late that a false teacher is in his midst, he has refused hospitality to all visitors regardless of their claims. The Elder's attitude toward Diotrephes, therefore, is somewhat hypocritical: He has been as intolerant of the secessionists and Diotrephes as Diotrephes and the secessionists have been of him. A dualistic outlook that hampers his ability to consider the nuances of a situation has left him with this blind spot.[16]

It is precisely here, however, that the connections the Elder has made in the first part of the letter to the broader, non-Johannine, Christian tradition become important. The Elder knows that whereas it is important not to entertain traveling teachers who are both deceptive and divisive (2 John 7–11), simply refusing hospitality to all teachers without first testing them is not an option. This is perhaps why the Elder never recommends this much simpler course of action in 2 John. Instead, he urges that the "elect lady" measure visiting teachers by the standard of the traditional "teaching about Christ" (2 John 9–10).

Similarly, the *Didache* could easily have advocated keeping away those who "carry on a cheap trade in the teachings of Christ" by refusing to show hospitality to any visiting teachers. Instead, it recommends examining visitors to see whether their teachings are right or wrong (*Did.* 12.1). The virtue of showing hospitality to strangers was widely and highly valued in early Christianity, and church leaders in particular were expected to be hospitable. The Elder has adopted this tradition, expressing it in typical Johannine terms of truth and love (3 John 3–5).[17]

The would-be church leader Diotrephes, however, has abandoned this virtue. Unable or unwilling to trouble himself with any doctrinal distinctions between visiting missionaries, he seems to have repudiated them all. He has exercised this inflexible policy, moreover, with a heavy hand, not merely rejecting the missionaries themselves but all who do not agree with his approach to them. Genuine astonishment lies behind the Elder's comment that Diotrephes not only "refuses to welcome the brothers" but "even prevents those who want to do so and expels them from the church" (v. 10).[18]

The Elder makes clear to Gaius, who is perhaps an emerging church leader himself, that he should not imitate such evil behavior. Just as Gaius has proved his affiliation with the truth by the hospitality that he has shown to the missionaries, so Diotrephes has revealed his own alliance with evil by his evil deeds (v. 11a). It is therefore critical for Gaius not to cross over to the side of evil by wavering in his commitment to supply hospitality for the traveling missionaries on their return to his area. This would be inconsistent with his status as one who has seen God in Jesus Christ (v. 11b; cf. John 12:45; 14:9; 1 John 3:6).[19]

16 Brown, *Epistles of John*, 747–48. Brown is not as openly critical of the Elder as this summary of his position indicates, but this criticism is certainly implied by the scenario that Brown suggests. Cf. Windisch, *Die katholischen Briefe*, 141–42.

17 See, e.g., Rom. 12:13; 1 Tim. 3:2; Titus 1:8; Heb. 13:2; 1 Peter 4:9; *1 Clem.* 10.7; 11:1; 12:1, 3; Herm. *Mand.* 8.10; Herm. *Sim.* 9.27.2.

18 NRSV, which, unlike most translations, correctly captures this element of surprise by rendering the second of the three *kai's* in v. 10 with "even" rather than "also."

19 *Pace*, e.g., Windisch, *Die katholischen Briefe*, 142, the Elder is not referring in v. 11b to a mystical vision of God but to the revelation of God in Jesus Christ, and *pace* Lieu, *Second and Third Epistles*, 116, the reference to seeing God is not a pale imitation of 1 John 3:6 by an author who has forgotten that in the Johannine tradition no one can see God (John 1:18; 6:46; 1 John 4:12,

HOSPITALITY AS PROOF OF A COMMITMENT TO THE TRUTH

According to John's gospel, Jesus left his disciples with the singularly important command that they should love one another (John 13:34; 15:12, 17). He also left them with an enacted parable whose point was that their love for one another should take practical form: Although he was their master, he took the role of a slave and washed their feet (13:1–17). Such practical expressions of love, even for the most authoritative members of the community, were essential to membership within the church (13:6–9). These loving actions were the sure mark of authentic discipleship (13:35).

This theme became a major concern in 1 John, where, as we have seen, the secessionists revealed their lack of concern for the truth not only in their faulty confession of Christ but in their unloving withdrawal from the orthodox community (1 John 2:19). Their commitment to the truth was only skin deep because they failed to "do the truth" by loving their brothers and sisters (1:6). Their love was only a matter of word and tongue rather than of deed and truth (3:18).

The theme reemerged in 2 John when the Elder reminded the church to which he wrote of the central place that Jesus' command to love one another occupied in Johannine ethics (2 John 4–6). Against the onslaught of secessionist false teaching, this command must bind the church together through prompting practical expressions of love. It is a command in which Christians must "walk" (v. 6).

In 3 John the general nature of these statements suddenly becomes concrete and specific.[20] A crisis in the church has arisen because a church leader named Diotrephes has not only instituted a heavy-handed and unloving policy of refusing to show hospitality to itinerant missionaries but of rebuffing any dissent from this ill-considered plan. In defiance of these evil actions, however, a householder named Gaius has provided hospitality to the missionaries.

From the perspective of the Elder, Gaius has put his commitment to the truth into practice and has shown the genuineness of his love. He has washed the feet of brothers in Christ, although they were strangers, by courageously giving them the practical help they needed to carry out their assignment. The Elder's letter to Gaius is an effort to encourage him to continue down this path of practical love for his brothers and sisters in Christ, a path that both John's gospel and the other two letters commend at a more theoretical level. The gospel and the other two letters provide moving expressions of the importance of the love command. Third John provides an example of this command at work.

20). In the Johannine literature there is a sense in which Jesus is the only one who has ever seen God (John 1:18; 6:46; 1 John 4:12, 20) and a sense in which all who believe that Jesus is the Christ, the Son of God, have seen God through the revelation that Jesus provides (John 12:45; 14:9). In a way typical of Johannine style, these two sides of a complex notion are simply stated and the underlying logic that connects them is left unexpressed. See the section in ch. 27 titled "The Witness of the Traditions to the Relationship between the Christian and Sin"; see also the discussion of Klauck, *Zweite und dritte Johannesbrief*, 113–14.

20 This happens to some extent in 1 John 2:19 and 3:16–19, where love seems to be defined respectively as not breaking fellowship and as giving to the poor. Third John, however, is more concrete than either of these two statements, the first of which is not explicit about disunity as failure to love and the second of which refers to a common topos of ethical paraenesis (as in, e.g., Tobit 4:7; James 2:15–16).

Chapter 30

FIRST PETER: ON SUFFERING AS A CHRISTIAN

First Peter was written for a large audience—all the Christians in the regions of Pontus, Galatia, Cappadocia, Asia, and Bithynia, an area that covered 300,000 square miles and thus nearly all of the Anatolian peninsula.[1] We should not expect, therefore, that Peter will give us a detailed account of the conditions of his audience.[2] He must speak in terms that cover many people, living in various cultural conditions, and he may speak more from his own experiences in Rome (5:13) than on the basis of any reports he has heard from Anatolia.[3] As he says toward the letter's conclusion, he speaks about experiences that Christians "throughout the world are undergoing" (5:9). Even so, he is clear about the crisis that prompts him to write: The Christians in these regions are suffering for their commitment to "the word" preached to them (1:25).

Peter assumes that when his audience first heard this word, they were pagans.[4] Note 4:3, where he reminds them not to return to their former way of life because

1 Paul J. Achtemeier, *1 Peter* (Hermeneia; Philadelphia: Fortress, 1996), 83. John H. Elliott, *1 Peter: A New Translation and Commentary* (AB 37B; New York: Doubleday, 2000), 84, estimates the size of the area differently at "129,000 square miles, about the size of the state of Montana" but still "larger . . . than any other letter of the NT," except perhaps for the letter of James.

2 Achtemeier, *1 Peter*, 50. Many scholars assume that 1 Peter is pseudonymous and that the persecutions of which it speaks come from the late first century, well after Peter's death under Nero in Rome around A.D. 65. The literary Greek of the letter, presumably impossible for a Galilean fisherman, and the letter's Paulinisms figure prominently in this judgment. The persecution that the letter assumes, however, is not official action from the emperor or governors (1:13–14) but the kind of mob violence for which 1 Thessalonians provides evidence already in the early 50s. The literary sophistication of the letter and the connection with Paul could easily have originated with Silvanus, "through" (*dia*) whom Peter wrote the letter (5:12; cf. 1 Thess. 1:1; 2 Thess. 1:1; 2 Cor. 1:19). These features of the letter could also come from Peter himself, who had significant theological contact with Paul (Gal. 1:18; 2:9) and who lived in Bethsaida (John 1:44) and Capernaum (Mark 1:29), both on important international trade routes and both in an area where Greek was freely spoken. Indeed, Peter's brother Andrew bore a Greek name (Matt. 4:18; 10:2; John 1:40, 44).

3 "Babylon" in 5:13 is a symbolic reference to Rome. Cf. Rev. 14:8; 16:19; 17:5; 18:2, 21. In Revelation, Babylon sits on "seven hills" (Rev. 17:9) and is "the great city that rules over the kings of the earth" (17:18)—clearly references to Rome. In first-century Jewish literature, see *Sib. Or.* 5:159; *2 Bar.* 11:1; 16:7; *4 Ezra* 3:1, 28, 31. Since these non-Petrine references occur in literature composed after the destruction of Jerusalem and thus after the probable date of Peter's death, many scholars believe that they are evidence for the pseudonymous nature of 1 Peter. The name Babylon might have become attached to Rome in the mind of any Christian or Jew, however, who appreciated the similarities between the wickedness of the two empires and their often oppressive policies toward God's people.

4 *Pace* P. H. R. van Houwelingen, *1 Petrus: Rondzendbrief uit Babylon* (Commentaar op het Nieuwe Testament; Kampen: Kok, 1991), 32–34, who believes that Peter writes to Jewish Christians of the Jewish Diaspora. Most commentators believe that 1 Peter was written to a group that included both Jews and Gentiles. See, e.g., Edward Gordon Selwyn, *The First Epistle of Peter*, 2nd ed. (London: Macmillan, 1947), 42–44; Achtemeier, *1 Peter*, 50–51; and John H. Elliott, *A Home for the Homeless: A Sociological Exegesis of 1 Peter, Its Situation and Strategy* (Philadelphia: Fortress, 1981), 65–67; idem, *1 Peter*, 95–97. Among the Christians in the vast area to which Peter writes there are certainly some Jewish Christians, but 1:18 and 4:3 show that he is thinking of Gentiles when he writes. Like Paul, he considers these Gentiles to be heirs to the traditions of Israel. See, e.g., 1 Cor. 10:1–22, where Paul, speaking to Christians who are attending feasts in idolatrous settings, can nevertheless admonish them not to imitate the sin of their Israelite ancestors.

they "have spent enough time in the past doing what the Gentiles choose to do—living in debauchery, lust, drunkenness, orgies, carousing and detestable idolatry." In 1:18 he tells his audience, similarly, that they were "redeemed from the empty way of life handed down to [them] from [their] forefathers." The adjective "empty" in this phrase was commonly used in the LXX and in early Christianity to refer to the futility of worshiping idols (Lev. 17:7; Jer. 8:19; 10:15; Acts 14:15).[5] He also seems to assume his audience's former paganism in 1:14 when he says that their previous way of life was characterized by lust and ignorance.

Many people who came into contact with Christians, however, rejected their message (2:8) and were offended by the Christian claim that traditional pagan ways of life were futile. In response, they made life difficult for people in their societies who converted to Christianity. Peter says that those to whom he writes "suffer grief in all kinds of trials" (1:6). These trials are so severe that he can describe them as a "burning" (*pyrōsis*)—an ordeal by fire (4:12). He suggests that much of the abuse is verbal; that is, he envisions opponents of Christians slandering (*katalaleō*, 3:16), reviling (*blasphēmeō*, 4:4), and mocking (*oneidizō*, 4:14) them because they bear the name "Christian" (4:14, 16).

Verbal abuse of Christians was common in the earliest years of Christianity's existence. According to Luke, during Paul's time the Jewish leaders of Rome informed him that Christianity "is spoken against everywhere" (Acts 28:22). A few decades later, but writing of the same general time period, the Roman historians Tacitus (ca 115) and Suetonius (ca 120) both confirm this bad reputation. Tacitus had to explain Christianity to his audience because Nero had attempted to fix the blame for the great fire of Rome in A.D. 64 on them. Christians, he says, are followers of a "pernicious superstition," affecting "vast numbers" and originating from an executed criminal named Christus. They are "loathed for their vices," although the only vice he mentions is "hatred of the human race," slander that elsewhere he levels at the Jews (*Ann.* 15.44; cf. *Hist.* 5.5.1).[6] Suetonius similarly claims that Christians are "a class of people given to a new and mischievous superstition" (*Nero* 16).

In subsequent years the claim became common that Christians met in secret to engage in bizarre and immoral behavior bound to undermine the stability of the empire. The origins of this fear are probably complex, but memory of the mayhem that followers of Bacchus caused in Rome in 186 B.C. undoubtedly had something to do with it.[7] Here too a foreign religion from the east had invaded Rome and, in a series of secret meetings marked by sexual immorality, murderous plots, and fraud, created much trouble among a number of prominent families.

Writing a full century later, the incident still sent chills down Livy's spine as he recounted the events and imagined that the social fabric of Rome had nearly come unraveled (39.8–18). Nero's persecution of Christians was probably rationalized in

5 Achtemeier, *1 Peter*, 127.

6 See the discussion of Tacitus's comments in W. H. C. Frend, *Martyrdom and Persecution in the Early Church: A Study of a Conflict from the Maccabees to Donatus* (Oxford: Basil Blackwell, 1965), 162–63.

7 On the connection, see Hugh Last, "The Study of the 'Persecutions,'" *JRS* 27 (1937): 80–92; cf. ch. 20, above.

part by the collective memory of this incident.[8] Even Pliny's famous letter to Trajan—written nearly three and a half centuries after the Bacchanal conspiracy—betrays some fear that the Christians were engaged in the kind of fanatical, immoral, and superstitious behavior that nearly undermined the Roman republic long ago.[9] By the mid-second century the idea was current that Christian families met at night for secret banquets. At the signal of an overturned, lighted lamp, these secret meetings supposedly devolved into drunken orgies.[10]

As we have seen in our study of Jude and 2 Peter, it is also possible that rumors of immoral behavior had some factual basis. Jude spoke of "godless people, who change the grace of God into a license for immorality [*aselgeia*]" and have slipped into Christian communities with their teaching (Jude 4). Second Peter describes the false teachers it opposes as those who "follow . . . shameful ways [*tais aselgeiais*] and . . . bring the way of truth into disrepute" (2 Peter 2:2). These teachers were heterodox, but the existence of documents like Jude and 2 Peter shows that the boundaries between orthodox and heterodox communities were sometimes blurred. Pagans already suspicious of Christians could hardly be expected to make the necessary theological distinctions, and apparently in later years detractors of Christianity were only too happy to lump orthodox Christians with heterodox groups and to claim that they were all busy undermining the social and moral fabric of the empire.[11]

From the second century B.C. until well after the time of 1 Peter, therefore, Rome feared foreign religions from the east that corrupted family life and plotted secret mayhem. For many who lived within the empire and for the educated elite who governed them, Christianity seemed to fall into this category.

Peter writes to console Christians living in these circumstances.[12] He has three dominant concerns. First, he does not want his audience to fold under the pressure their various societies are exerting on them. These societies have marginalized Christians, and Christians know that they can move out of the margins and back into the center by returning to their traditional, pre-Christian way of life (1:14, 18; 4:3). They can do this either by renouncing their faith or by compromising with prevailing religious practice.[13]

Second, he wants to be sure that the Christians to whom he writes provide no fodder for pagan slander by unnecessarily violating pagan social mores. They should submit to the various civil authorities (2:13–14). They should not use their "freedom as a cover-up for evil" (2:16). Slaves should submit to masters; wives should

8 Last, "'Persecutions,'"

9 Cf. Robert L. Wilken, *The Christians as the Romans Saw Them* (New Haven, Conn.: Yale Univ. Press, 1984), 16–17.

10 Justin, *1 Apol.* 26, and Minucius Felix, *Oct.* 9, quoting an earlier anti-Christian speech of Marcus Aurelius's tutor, Marcus Cornelius Fronto. Cf. Wilken, *Christians*, 17–21.

11 This would explain Justin's concern to separate the behavior of orthodox Christians from the behavior of those who lay false claim to the name Christian in *1 Apol.* 4 and 26. Cf. Minucius Felix, *Oct.* 5–13. The evidentiary basis is not clear, however, for Joseph Hoffmann's claim that Christians began to define the boundaries of their doctrine chiefly in an effort to dissociate themselves from pagan charges of scandalous behavior. See his "General Introduction" to Clesus, *On the True Doctrine: A Discourse against the Christians* (New York: Oxford Univ. Press, 1987), 18.

12 On the overlap between 1 Peter and ancient philosophical approaches to consolation, see Paul Holloway, "*Nihil inopinati accidisse*—'Nothing unexpected has happened': A Cyrenaic Consolatory *Topos* in 1 Pet 4.12ff.," *NTS* 48 (2002): 433–48, here at 433 and 441–48.

13 Cf. those reclining for meals in idol temples in 1 Cor. 8:10 and "Jezebel" and her followers in Rev. 2:20; cf. 2:14.

submit to husbands (2:18; 3:1, 5); husbands should be considerate of their wives (3:7); and young men within the church should submit to their elders (5:5). Christians should not receive punishment for sinning against those in authority over them (2:20; 3:13, 17), and no one should suffer "as a murderer or thief or any other kind of criminal, or even as a meddler" (4:15). To the contrary, Christians should shame their neighbors by their impeccable conduct (2:15; 3:16) and attract them to the worship of God (2:12; 3:1–2).

Third, Peter wants to take his readers off the defensive and encourage them to engage in active witness both through their conduct and through reasoned speech to their detractors. They should not follow the accepted social structures in ways that cause them to melt into the fabric of their societies and become invisible. Instead, they should follow these widely accepted behaviors in ways that are both distinctively Christian and attractive to unbelievers. As a result, Peter hopes, some will "be won over" (3:1) and led to "glorify God" (2:12).

Peter addresses these concerns with a twofold strategy that he explicitly describes in 5:12. "I have written to you briefly," he says, "exhorting and testifying that this is the true grace of God."[14] His letter both testifies to God's grace and exhorts his readers to remain faithful to their vocation as the people of God, despite the persecution this entails. By testifying to God's grace and exhorting his readers on the basis of this grace, he hopes to move them from a defensive to an offensive posture. He wants to take them from a point where their suffering threatens to push them back to their ancestral way of life to a position from which they can shame their accusers—and even win some of them over—by their exemplary conduct.

TESTIMONIES TO GOD'S GRACE

Throughout his letter, Peter places special emphasis both on God's grace and on the joyful response it produces in Christians who have experienced it. Christians have already received the eschatological gift of a new life (1:10; 3:7), and they will receive the eschatological gift of final salvation when Jesus Christ is revealed (1:13; 5:5). They serve a wholly gracious God (5:10, 12). Despite their suffering, therefore, they should be filled with joy (1:6, 8; 4:13).

Two aspects of God's grace are particularly important to Peter. First, he wants his readers to understand that they have adopted all that is good about the identity of Israel in the Scriptures. God chose them out of all the peoples of the earth for a special purpose, and despite the ostracism that they are experiencing in their own societies, they are therefore part of the most important of all societies—the people of God.

Second, Peter wants his readers to understand that the redemptive action of Christ's death, together with his subsequent resurrection and ascension to God's right hand, have completely reoriented their existence for the good. Despite the suffering

14 Achtemeier, *1 Peter*, 352, calls this statement, "an admirable summary of the entire letter." Cf. Ernest Best, *1 Peter* (NCB; Grand Rapids: Eerdmans, 1971), 13, 177. Cf. Leonhard Goppelt, *A Commentary on 1 Peter* (Grand Rapids: Eerdmans, 1993), 372–73; Elliott, *1 Peter*, 877.

they must endure for their commitment, God has rescued them from the past, positioned them to receive an immensely valuable inheritance in the future, and has given significance to their present existence.

The Privileged Status of Christians as the People of God

In various ways throughout the letter but especially in 1:1–2:10, Peter tells his audience that they belong to a group of people, scattered throughout the world, whom God has chosen to be his special people. They are newborn babies (2:2; cf. 1:3, 23), but their new birth has given them membership within Israel, God's graciously chosen people, as described in the Scriptures. Just as God both "chose" and "called" Israel to be his people (e.g., Deut. 7:6–8; 14:2; Isa. 41:8–9; 42:6; 43:20; 48:12), so God "chose" (1 Peter 1:1; 2:9; 5:13) and "called" (1:15; 2:9, 21; 3:9; 5:10) Peter's audience to be his people. They belong to his "family" (4:17).

Israel had been formally constituted as God's people after God had carried them "on eagle's wings" out of slavery in Egypt and initiated a covenant with them. The terms of that covenant are stated succinctly in Exodus 19:5–6, where God says to Israel through his mediator Moses:

> Now if you obey me fully and keep my covenant, then out of all nations you will be my treasured possession. Although the whole earth is mine, you will be for me a kingdom of priests and a holy nation.

Later, after the details of the people's covenant obligations were spelled out, the covenant was ratified by sacrifices in which blood was "sprinkled" on the altar and on the people (Ex. 24:3–8). Eventually God supplied Israel with a priesthood, a tabernacle, and a system of sacrifices (chs. 25–40). When Israel strayed so far from its covenant obligations that God could call them "not my people," he nevertheless refused to renounce his commitment to them and promised that one day, once again, he would show them mercy and say to them, "You are my people" (Hos. 2:23).

Why did God do all this? According to the prophet Isaiah, he "chose" his people, "formed" them for himself, and remained committed to them despite their sin so "that they may proclaim my praise" (Isa. 43:20–21).

Peter echoes all these passages in his description of his Christian audience. He transfers the notion of Israel's unfaithfulness after entering into a covenant with the Lord to a time prior to his audience's Christian commitment. At that time, when they were pagans, living in ignorance according to the empty traditions handed down to them by their ancestors (1 Peter 1:14, 18; 4:3), they were "no people" (2:10). Now, however, like ancient Israel, they have entered into a covenant with God, at his initiative. He has constituted them as "a royal priesthood, a holy nation, a people belonging to God" (2:9; cf. 2:5, "holy priesthood"). This covenant, moreover, has been ratified by the "sprinkling" of Jesus Christ's blood (1:2).[15] Just as God gave ancient

15 See, e.g., Norbert Brox, *Der erste Petrusbrief*, 3rd ed. (EKK; Zürich: Benziger/Neukirchen-Vluyn: Neukirchener Verlag, 1989), 57–58, and Achtemeier, *1 Peter*, 88–89. Goppelt, *1 Peter*, 74–75, argues against this view. He claims that the author's mention of "sprinkling by his blood" merely appropriates a common Christian expression for coming under the influence of Christ's death. He does not give appropriate weight, however, to the author's development of the covenant theme in 2:9.

Israel a priesthood, a tabernacle, and sacrifices, so Christians, in Peter's view, have all three of these. The Christian community is both a "spiritual house" and a "holy priesthood," and it offers "spiritual sacrifices acceptable to God through Jesus Christ" (2:5).

Why has God done all this for Peter's audience? God chose them and constituted them as his people so that they might "declare the praises of him who called [them] out of darkness into his wonderful light" (2:9).

In summary, although Peter's audience lives among people who "heap abuse" on them (4:4) because they stand apart from traditional societal norms (1:18; 4:3), they are "a chosen people, a royal priesthood, a holy nation, a people belonging to God" (2:9). They may suffer rejection from the world around them, but God has freely chosen to consider them his special people.

The Value of Christian Redemption

Peter also reminds his readers of the inestimably valuable nature of the salvation that God, in his "great mercy" (1:3) and immensely gracious (5:10) character, has freely given to them. It is so valuable primarily for two reasons.

First, it came at great cost. In 1:18–19 Peter says that his audience was redeemed from their futile way of life "not with perishable things such as silver or gold" but "with the precious blood of Christ, a lamb without blemish or defect." Interpreters are divided about whether the author means that redemption came at a high price (more valuable than gold) or that redemption is imperishable (unlike perishable silver and gold).[16] Since the blood of Christ is explained as coming from an unblemished (and therefore valuable) lamb, and since the notion that Christ's blood is the high price of Christian redemption is common in Christian literature from this period (Acts 20:28; Eph. 1:7; Rev. 1:5; 5:9; 14:4), Peter probably intends to describe the immense cost of his audience's rescue from their former way of life. Their redemption is possible only through the sacrificial death of a sinless Messiah, God's choice and precious cornerstone (2:4–7).

Second, the salvation of Peter's readers is immensely valuable because it has redefined their existence in new and better terms. God has conceived them anew (1:3) through the proclamation of the gospel (1:23–25).[17] They are like newborn babies (2:3). This merciful action has rescued them from the past, assures them of a bright future, and because of that assurance, gives them joy in their troubled present.

They have been redeemed "from the empty way of life handed down" to them from their ancestors (1:18). This life was characterized by "ignorance" (1:14), "debauchery, lusts, drunkenness, orgies, carousing and detestable idolatry" (4:3). Because God has rescued them from this evil way of life, they will not suffer God's wrath when it breaks out in the future against human wickedness (1:5, 9, 13; 4:3–5, 17–18). Rather than the condemnation of God (4:5, 17), they will receive an

16 For the first position see, e.g., Selwyn, *First Epistle of St. Peter*, 145; Francis Wright Beare, *The First Epistle of Peter* (Oxford: Blackwell, 1947), 79–80; Best, *1 Peter*, 90; and van Houwelingen, *1 Petrus*, 66. For the second position, see Achtemeier, *1 Peter*, 128, and Elliott, *1 Peter*, 373; cf. *1 Clem*. 7.4 (which Elliott cites).

17 This understanding of 1:3 follows Actemeier, *1 Peter*, 94, 138–39. *Pace* Brox, *Der erste Petrusbrief*, 63, the emphasis in 1:3 is probably not on baptism but on the creative power of God's word (cf. 1:23–25).

inheritance "that can never perish, spoil or fade" (1:4; cf. 1:23). This inheritance is the "salvation" of their "souls" and will come to them as God's free gift (1:10, 13).

Since this inheritance lies in the future, as the present suffering of Peter's audience makes painfully clear, the present is a life of "faith and hope . . . in God" (1:21). Despite the hardship that the life of faith and hope entails, it is nevertheless "of greater worth than gold" (1:7). It is not an anxious existence (5:7) but is "filled with an inexpressible and glorious joy" (1:8; cf. 1:6; 4:13). Why is this so? Several reasons emerge from the letter.

For one thing, the hope in which Christians live is not a desperate desire that the future might be brighter than the present; rather, it is a "living hope"—a settled assurance that they will one day inherit salvation and that it will be both valuable and eternal (1:4, 9). This assurance rests on the Christian conviction that Jesus rose from the dead (1:3, 21), ascended into heaven, and is presently seated at God's right hand with all inimical powers in submission to him (1:21; 3:19, 22). The prophets had long awaited these events, and now they have happened, placing Christians at an eschatological advantage over all the faithful who lived before them. The author's audience is living during a time in which God has put his final purposes—outlined in advance in his Word—into motion.

For another thing, Christians know from their own experience that the Lord is kind (2:3). Although they have never seen Jesus themselves (1:8), their response to the gospel has resulted in palpable changes in their lives—they have "tasted" the Lord's kindness.[18] In particular, the word of God has effected an ethical transformation in them (1:18–25); rather than living in ignorance (1:14), futility (1:18), and debauchery (4:3), they have started to show a sincere and profound love for one another (1:22).

In addition, despite their present suffering and the location of "the goal of their faith" in the future, God is with them to protect them so that they can be assured of reaching this goal. God's power shields them from any ultimate harm, preserving their faith despite their persecutors' attacks (1:5). Because they trust in the chosen and precious stone that God has laid in Zion, they "will never be put to shame" (2:6).

Although they suffer, therefore, Peter's audience should lead joyful lives. God has done much for them. Through his effective, eternal word he has radically changed their lives for the better. They once lived in futility and in a manner that could only end in eschatological destruction. Now they live in loving fellowship with one another, protected by God's power and by their precious faith from any ultimate harm. They are, moreover, poised to receive an eternal inheritance of salvation when Jesus Christ is revealed.

---

18 Interpreters have sometimes thought that the quotation of Ps. 33:9 (LXX) in 2:3 refers to the Eucharist. Peter would then be saying that his audience has experienced the goodness of the Lord when they participated in eucharistic fellowship. See, e.g., Selwyn, *First Epistle of St. Peter*, 157, and Peter H. Davids, *The First Epistle of Peter* (NICNT; Grand Rapids: Eerdmans, 1990), 84, both of whom advance the suggestion tentatively. It is far more likely that Peter refers to tasting the blessing of redemption generally, although foremost in his thinking is the blessing of ethical reformation that has dominated the context since 1:22. Cf. Best, *1 Peter*, 98–99.

In summary, God has given Peter's readers a new start. They have been conceived again and transformed into newborn babies. Now they are God's people, members of God's family. All this is testimony to God's mercy and grace and should be cause for great rejoicing. It should lead Peter's audience to live in a way that sets them apart from the world around them. As we will see below, it should also lead them both to persevere through their suffering and to adopt an active, attractive witness to those outside the people of God.

LIVING AS RESIDENT ALIENS

Peter is especially concerned that his readers avoid inappropriate ways of coping with their suffering and instead adopt the perspective of "resident aliens" toward the world around them. As the heirs of ancient Israel, especially Israel of the Diaspora, they must continue to live according to the distinctive manner of life required of God's people, refusing to accommodate themselves to the futile way of life dominant in their various societies. At the same time, they should not withdraw from these various societies but they should live under the scrutiny of unbelievers—and live in such a way that they both shame their accusers and lead them to conversion. As they seek to maintain this delicate balance between accommodation and withdrawal, they should place their complex existence in eschatological perspective.

Holiness and Accommodation

Peter reminds his readers that as God's specially chosen people, they are "holy"—separated from the societies in which they live by their manner of life. Their former way of life, handed down to them in the traditions of the societies in which they lived (1:18) was characterized by ignorance (1:14), futility (1:18), and various forms of debauchery (4:3). Now, however, God's Spirit (1:2; 4:14) has separated them from these societies, not physically, but by means of their behavior. They are obedient to Jesus Christ (1:2, 14), and this obedience makes them "holy"—the quality that, according to the Mosaic law, characterizes God himself and should therefore also characterize God's people (1:15–16; cf. Lev. 11:44–45; 19:2; 20:7, 26). Their behavior should separate them from other societies as God's distinct possession.

If they are faithful to the call to live holy lives, they will inevitably suffer the ostracism of "resident aliens and sojourners in the world" (2:11, aut.). They will adopt the identity of Israel during the exile—living as sojourners of the Diaspora (1:1) and forced to spend the time of their sojourning (1:17) in a pagan and hostile "Babylon" (5:13). Some scholars have argued that Peter's portrayal of his audience as resident aliens has a literal basis to it: Either they are Jewish Christians living among the Jewish Diaspora, or they are dislocated immigrants, or they are Jewish Christians tossed out of Rome under the Emperor Claudius.[19] It is best, however, to see these descrip-

19 See, respectively, van Houwelingen, *1 Petrus*, 32–34; Elliott, *A Home for the Homeless*, 21–49, 67–73; Karen Jobes, *1 Peter* (BECNT; Grand Rapids: Baker, forthcoming).

tions as metaphorical—as part of Peter's effort to identify his audience as the new Israel. With this metaphor he shows that his audience is not only the object of God's gracious choice but also, like biblical Israel, of Israel's fate as a people scattered from its homeland and forced to live as foreigners among the Gentiles.[20]

Despite the problems that such an existence has caused, Peter urges his audience not to respond to their alienation by returning to their former worldview. "Slander" is to be expected (4:4), but Peter's audience should not cope with this slander by reverting to their preconversion way of life (4:3). "Do not conform to the evil desires you had when you lived in ignorance," he tells them (1:14). Instead they should "be holy" (1:15–16) and "live [their] lives as strangers here" in the fear of the Lord (1:17).

Their holy behavior arises from two sources. First, the preaching of the gospel has radically reoriented the lives of Peter's audience. Because the gospel is the word of God, it is also "imperishable," "living," and "enduring" (1:23). It is capable of "reconceiving" people (1:23), of making them "newborn babies" (2:2). The behavior of Peter's audience will, therefore, emerge from this inner transformation (2:1–3). They will love one another "without pretense" (1:22), and their concrete behavior will arise from their "conscience" (2:19; 3:16), the "inner self" (3:4), or the "quiet spirit" (3:4; cf. 2:6; 4:6). Peter can therefore tell them to do good as "free people," using their freedom not as a cover for evil but in the service of God (2:16). He can instruct leaders in the various congregations of Anatolia to serve as overseers "not because you must, but because you are willing" (5:2).

Second, Peter appeals to Jesus' death as both a source and a pattern for Christian behavior. He makes this point through a series of allusions to Isaiah 52:13–53:12, first in 1 Peter 1:19 and then in 2:21–24.[21] In 1:19, the mention of Jesus' blood and the description of him as an unblemished lamb recalls the imagery of atoning sacrifice in Isaiah 53:7 and 10. The costly nature of Jesus' atoning death implies that Christians should "live out the time of" their "sojourning in reverent fear" (1 Peter 1:17, aut.). Similarly, in 2:21–24, Jesus' atoning death as Isaiah's Servant empowers Christians to avoid future sins. In his role as servant, Jesus "bore" (2:24; Isa. 53:12) the sins of Christians when he died on the cross so that they themselves "might die to sins and live for righteousness" (1 Peter 2:24a). His bruises have healed them, therefore, not only by atoning for sins but by enabling Christians to avoid sinning (2:24b).

Isaiah 52:13–53:12 also offers help with the specific sin of retaliating against one's persecutors in kind. Viewed through the lens of this passage, Jesus' conduct during his trial and death provides a "pattern" for Christians to follow when they suffer unjustly. Jesus traces the "steps" in which they should walk (1 Peter 2:21). As Isaiah

20 The metaphor of alien residency was redolent with connotations of suffering in both Jewish and Greco-Roman thinking. On the Jewish side, see Ps. 137:1–3; Dan. 1:15; 3:8, 24–27; 6:13–14, 24. In the Greco-Roman world generally, the terms "foreigner" (*xenos*), "immigrant" (*metoikos*), and "exile" (*phygas*) were sometimes used as insults, and exile was considered a tragedy. For specific literary evidence from the Greco-Roman world, see Achtemeier, *1 Peter*, 174, and Holloway, "*Nihil inopinati accidisse*," 433–48, here at 434.

21 In light of its importance throughout the letter, Peter is probably thinking primarily of Isa. 52:13–53:12 when he speaks in 1 Peter 1:11 of the Spirit predicting through the prophets "the sufferings of Christ" (Isa. 52:13–53:10a) and "the glories that would follow" (53:10b–12a).

prophesied, Jesus did not sin by reviling those who beat him. He "did not open his mouth" (Isa. 53:7) and so no "deceit was found in his mouth" (1 Peter 2:22; cf. Isa. 53:9). When reviled, he did not revile in return (1 Peter 2:23). Slaves who suffer for doing good should endure their suffering in the same way (2:20). As the alteration between the second person plural and the first person plural in 2:21–25 shows, however, Peter's advice is intended for his whole readership, whether slaves or not.[22]

To summarize, Peter underlines the need for his audience to respond to the suffering that they must endure as Christians by living in a way that is consistent with their status as God's holy people. This means refusing to accommodate themselves to many of the norms of the societies in which they live and accepting their role as "resident aliens" within those societies. God has, however, given them resources for this difficult task. His word, in the form of the gospel, has powerfully transformed them. Jesus' atoning death has released them from the futile manner of life they once lived and empowered them to live in ways that are pleasing to God. The way in which Jesus died, moreover, provides them with a pattern to follow in their own response to the unjust treatment they are receiving at the hands of the hostile societies surrounding them.

Holiness and Withdrawal

At the same time that Peter urges his audience not to accommodate themselves to the debauchery and idolatry in the societies around them, he also exhorts them not to withdraw from these societies. Instead, they are to live out their lives under the close scrutiny (*epopteuō*) of unbelievers (2:12; 3:2). Verbal abuse (4:4, 14) should not prompt a retreat from the world but a renewed determination to do what is good (2:14–15; 3:15–16) and, in particular, to adopt an ethic of nonretaliation: Although victims of verbal violence themselves, Christians should not repay their abusers in kind (2:23; 3:9). When reviled, like Jesus, they should not revile in return (2:23; 3:9; cf. 3:1, 16).

Peter gives two reasons why Christians should live in this way under the gaze of their persecutors. First, by engaging their persecutors with their good conduct and reasoned speech, Christians will shame them. "It is God's will," he says, "that by doing good you should silence the ignorant talk of foolish people" (2:15, aut.). Similarly, he says that by giving a reasoned defense of their faith "with gentleness and respect," all the while "keeping a clear conscience," Christians will shame "those who speak maliciously against [their] good behavior in Christ" (3:15–16).

Second, Peter hopes that as Christians live good lives under the scrutiny of their detractors, their persecutors will be attracted to the God whom the Christians worship and become Christians themselves. Wives should submit to their husbands, says Peter, "so that, if any of them do not believe the word, they may be won over without words by the behavior of their wives, when they see [*epopteuō*] the purity and reverence" of their wives' behavior (3:1–2). Similarly, all Christians are to "live such

22 Goppelt, *1 Peter*, 207. Peter uses the first person plural in the first part of v. 24 and the second person plural everywhere else.

good lives among the pagans that, though they accuse you of doing wrong, they may see [*epopteuō*] your good deeds and glorify God on the day he visits us" (2:12).

Peter's "household code" (2:13–3:7) should be understood in light of these two purposes for engaging the culture. Similar outlines of the family's authority structure were common currency in discussions of ancient political philosophy and were used by ancient Jewish apologists to show that Judaism upheld these widely recognized social structures.[23] Peter's concern that all Christians should submit to the political authorities, that slaves should submit to masters, that wives should submit to husbands, and that husbands should be considerate of their wives probably also has an apologetic concern. Christians are to follow the expected social pattern in these areas so faithfully that they do not come under society's censure for violating these norms (2:20a; 3:13; 4:15). They should not provide any grist for the pagan rumor mill by allowing their behavior to fall below the standards of decency expected within an orderly society (2:15; cf. 3:17; 4:15). This apologetic concern may stand behind Peter's exhortation to Christians to shame their detractors with their good behavior (3:16; cf. 2:15).[24]

For Peter, however, Christian support of the social structures undergirding Greco-Roman society is not simply intended to "silence the ignorant talk of foolish people" (2:15) but also, and even primarily, to prompt them to join the people of God in declaring the praises of God (2:9, 12).[25] This is clear from Peter's use of his comment in 2:12 to introduce the household code: The good conduct of Christians should lead unbelievers to glorify God "on the day he visits us"—either the Day of Judgment or the day of conversion.[26] Peter's evangelistic concern is also clear from the unusual nature of the code. He is not simply counseling his audience to conform to the social structures of authority and subordination common in the Greco-Roman world of the first century, but he is advising them to adopt an unusual ethic of nonretaliation patterned specifically after the conduct of Jesus before his accusers (2:21–24).

Certainly Peter wants the good conduct of his audience to demonstrate that Christians are good citizens of their various societies, but he also wants their conduct to stand out as different from and superior to that of their detractors. He hopes that in this way, those who persecute Christians might not only become ashamed of their conduct but also be "won over" by Christian "behavior" (3:1).

---

23 See ch. 16, above, and the extraordinarily useful collection of and commentary on ancient household codes in David L. Balch, *Let Wives Be Submissive: The Domestic Code in 1 Peter* (SBLMS 26; Atlanta: Scholars, 1981), 1–80.

24 Ibid., 81–116.

25 *Pace* Balch, *Let Wives Be Submissive*, 87, 108, 119, 132–36.

26 If the phrase refers to the Day of Judgment, then Peter conceives of unbelievers converted in the present giving glory to God on the final Day (cf. Goppelt, *1 Peter*, 160). Elliott, *1 Peter*, 470–71, believes that the expression refers to the time of the individual's conversion. Achtemeier, *1 Peter*, 178, thinks that the use of the phrase in the Bible and in early Jewish and Christian literature generally supports a reference to the final Day of Judgment, and that this, in turn, diminishes the probability that Peter sees a missionary purpose in Christian good works. Cf. Balch, *Let Wives Be Submissive*, 87, 111 n. 27, who argues that 2:12 speaks of a "doxology of judgment" in which pagans will glorify God on the final Day just before their condemnation. Neither Balch nor Achtemeier, however, adequately explains the parallel between 3:1–2, which must be understood evangelistically, and 2:12. Both texts use the rare verb *epopteuō* ("watch, observe, see") to describe the scrutiny that unbelievers will give to their believing neighbors and householders. This scrutiny "will win over" husbands (*kerdēthēsontai*) in 3:1–2 and prompt pagans to "glorify God" in 2:12.

Peter's understanding of Christian alien residency, therefore, does not imply that present Christian existence involves slogging through life on earth until one can finally live as a citizen of heaven. Christians must live out their time as resident aliens in such a way that they engage the societies of which they are a part. They live under the scrutiny of non-Christians and, in doing so, should conduct themselves with such surprising equanimity and gentleness that some of their detractors become ashamed and themselves join the people of God.

Suffering and Hope

Throughout his letter, Peter urges his readers to put their suffering in eschatological perspective. He considers three elements of this perspective especially important. First, he shows his readers that their suffering provides proof of the genuineness of their faith and of their future acquittal in God's eschatological court. Second, he reminds his readers that their suffering leads to eschatological blessing. Third, he tells them that their persecutors will not escape God's eschatological wrath.

Suffering as a Sign of Faith's Genuineness

In one group of statements, Peter reminds his audience that their suffering is proof of the genuineness of their faith. Their suffering should therefore assure them that they are destined for eschatological glory (1:6–7; 4:1; 4:14). He says this most explicitly in 1:6–7, where he tells his readers that the suffering they are presently enduring for their faith is part of a refining process necessary to prepare God's people for the revelation of Jesus Christ. If their faith is to receive "praise, glory and honor" from God on that Day, then it must be tested by suffering. From the proverbial wisdom that repeated exposure to fiery heat improves the quality of gold, Peter draws the analogy that suffering refines faith and gives it a quality that brings praise from God on the final Day.[27] For this reason, although the suffering is difficult, it should not dampen the joy of Peter's audience.

Peter probably intends to say something akin to this when he comments in 4:1, "since Christ suffered in his body, arm yourselves also with the same attitude—that [*hoti*] the one who has suffered in his body has ceased from sin" (aut.). This statement is burdened with ambiguities. Does the *hoti* mean "that," as translated here, or, as most translations and commentators render it, "because"?[28] Does suffering make sin cease by purging it from the body, by disciplining the person who suffers, by leading to the suffering person's death, or by some other way?[29]

The most probable reading of the statement takes it as an echo of what Peter has already said of Christ's suffering in 2:21–23.[30] When he suffered unjustly, he did not give in to the temptation to sin by reviling his persecutors in return. Instead, when he took the role of the Servant of Isaiah 53:9, he remained innocent through the

27 Here I closely follow the explanation of 1:7 found in Achtemeier, *1 Peter*, 101–2.

28 Although see, e.g., the 1599 Geneva Bible; NJB; J. N. D. Kelly, *A Commentary on Epistles of Peter and Jude* (HNTC; New York: Harper & Row, 1969), 166; and Achtemeier, *1 Peter*, 278.

29 For the first position, see Selwyn, *First Epistle of Peter*, 209–10; for the second position, see Elliott, *1 Peter*, 716–18; and for the third position, see Goppelt, *1 Peter*, 282.

30 Achtemeier, *1 Peter*, 280.

whole ordeal. Undergirding this attitude, says Peter, was Jesus' knowledge that one day God would render a just judgment against his persecutors. If we read 1 Peter 4:1 in these terms, then Peter says that those who suffer in this way demonstrate their desire to please God rather than to sin, through refusing to retaliate against those who make them suffer. They have armed "themselves with the same attitude" that Jesus had toward his unjust suffering.

The willingness of believers to suffer is, therefore, an expression of a far-reaching commitment to a worldview different from that of the societies around them. They are focused not on present pleasures but on the end of the present period of time, when their sojourning will be complete (4:2–3; cf. 1:17, 20) and God will bring justice to their oppressors (2:23; 4:5, 17–18). They are "done with sin" in the sense that they know that a life dedicated to the pursuit of "debauchery, lust, drunkenness, orgies, carousing . . . detestable idolatry," and retaliation ends in disaster on the Day of Judgment (4:4–5). As with 1:7, their suffering implies that they have invested their lives in the gospel and its eschatological perspective. It therefore implies that their commitment is genuine.

In 4:14, similarly, the author takes the verbal reproach Christians receive from the surrounding society as a blessing because it is evidence that "the Spirit of glory and of God rests on" them. Although the precise meaning of the phrase is difficult, the mention of "glory" points to the final day when Christ's "glory" will be revealed (4:13).[31] Peter says, therefore, that the suffering of his audience carries with it the benefit of the assurance that God's Spirit rests on them and that in some paradoxical way, the final Day, when Christ will be gloriously revealed, has broken into the present in their suffering.[32]

Faithfulness in Suffering Leads to Eschatological Blessing

In another series of statements, Peter reminds his audience that the eschatological blessing awaiting God's people comes to those who, despite their suffering, remain faithful to him. Peter's audience, as God's "called" people, must not repay their persecutors with evil and insult "but with blessing" because by this means they will "inherit a blessing" (3:9). Similarly, participating in the sufferings of Christ leads to rejoicing on the final Day when "his glory is revealed" (4:13). Through accepting the humiliation to which their surrounding societies subject them, Christians submit themselves to the path of suffering that God has marked out for them in the present.[33] This path, however, will lead to exaltation at the right time (5:6). They may have to suffer for a little while, but in the end God will "restore" them and "make [them] strong, firm and steadfast" (5:10).

We should probably also understand the statement in 4:6 this way: "For this is the reason the gospel was preached even to those who are dead, so that they might be judged, from the human perspective, in the flesh, but that they might live, from

31 Kelly, *Epistles of Peter and Jude*, 186–87; Brox, *Erste Petrusbrief*, 215–16; Goppelt, *1 Peter*, 323; Achtemeier, *1 Peter*, 309.

32 On this, see esp. Brox, *Erste Petrusbrief*, 215–16.

33 This is why Peter uses the passive imperative *tapeinōthēte*, "be humbled." God is the agent of the passive action. On this see Achtemeier, *1 Peter*, 338, and Elliott, *1 Peter*, 850.

God's perspective, in the Spirit" (aut.). The statement is a notorious crux, plagued with exegetical difficulties. Who are "the dead" here? Who preached to them? How could this preaching lead to judgment on one hand and life on the other? Discussion of these issues is vast, but the best resolution to the problems lies in understanding the statement as a reference to Christians who heard the gospel while living but have since died. Their commitment to the gospel led to condemnation from their unbelieving neighbors but to God's gift of life, through the Spirit. Their faithfulness to the gospel, despite the suffering that such faithfulness entailed, was not a futile existence finally extinguished in the grave but an existence approved by God and that led to life.[34]

God Will Bring the Persecutors of His People to Justice

In still another group of statements, Peter urges his readers to view their persecutors from the perspective of the final Day, when God judges the wicked. Like Jesus, Christians can refuse to retaliate against their persecutors with equanimity because they know that God will one day judge their oppressors with justice (2:23; cf. 4:3–4, 19). They should not be ashamed if they suffer as Christians because this suffering is insignificant compared to the condemnation that comes to those "who do not obey the gospel of God" (4:16–19).

Peter's especially difficult statements in 3:18–22 should probably also be placed within this context. Here Peter says that during the period of time surrounding Jesus' death and resurrection, he not only atoned for sins by his death but "went and preached to the spirits in prison who disobeyed long ago when God waited patiently in the days of Noah while the ark was being built" (3:19–20). A long tradition of interpretation has held that Peter refers here either to Christ's preaching through Noah to those who eventually perished in the flood or to Christ's own preaching around the time of his death and resurrection to the departed spirits of those who perished in the flood.[35]

Probably neither of these approaches is correct. Peter clearly indicates that Christ's preaching occurred neither prior to his death nor between his death and resurrection but after he was "made alive in the Spirit"—that is, after his resurrection (3:19). Moreover, Peter's use of the verb "went" (*poreuomai*) both at the beginning of the passage when he speaks of Christ going to the spirits in prison (3:19) and at the end of the passage when he speaks of Christ going into heaven (3:22) shows that Jesus preached to these spirits at his ascension.[36] The "spirits in prison" in 3:19 are, therefore, identical to the "angels, authorities, and powers" that were forced into submission when he ascended to heaven and took his place at God's right hand. This means that Christ's proclamation to the spirits in 3:19 is the announcement of defeat and

34 This is a common understanding of the verse. See, e.g., Selwyn, *First Epistle of St. Peter*, 337–39; Achtemeier, *1 Peter*, 286–91; and Elliott, *1 Peter*, 730–42.

35 For the first position, see, e.g., Wayne Grudem, *1 Peter* (TynNTC; Leicester, Eng.: InterVarsity Press, 1988), 203–39, basically following Augustine, *Ep.* 164.14–18. For the second position, see, e.g., Beare, *First Epistle of Peter*, 146, and Goppelt, *1 Peter*, 255–56.

36 Many commentators make this point, but see the esp. clear presentation in Elliott, *1 Peter*, 653.

condemnation not to the spirits of dead human beings but to malevolent spirits.[37] They are demonic powers that, like the persecutors of God's people (3:16–17), stand opposed to God.[38]

Peter's point is that God's eschatological defeat of the powers of evil that stand behind the oppression of God's people has already been put into motion with the resurrection, ascension, and heavenly session of Christ. Christians can take heart that the final cataclysm that will ultimately sweep away their oppressors has already started in Christ's defeat of the demonic powers. Faithful Christians will survive this latter day "flood," but their detractors will experience the fate of Noah's generation (3:20–21).[39]

The notion that Peter's readers should look forward to the justice of God on the final Day has an important ramification that Peter does not want his audience to miss: The prospect of God's coming judgment means that Christians themselves dare not abandon their commitment to the gospel and rejoin their persecutors in their debauched way of life. To do so would be to leave the only haven of safety from the future outpouring of God's wrath on the wicked. They should live out the time of their alien residency in fear (1:17; 2:17; 3:2), but they should not fear their persecutors (3:14). Instead, in their "hearts" they should "set apart Christ as Lord" (3:14–15). If Peter's audience turns back to the sins of their former way of life, they will experience the same judgment that the wicked around them will receive if they continue to reject the gospel (4:3–4, 17). The thought that "the end of all things is near" should instead lead Peter's audience to clear thinking, self-control, prayer, love, hospitality, and the efficient use of God's gifts (4:7–11).

GOD'S GRACE AND CHRISTIAN SUFFERING

Peter is writing to people suffering the plight of "aliens and strangers." Conversion to Christianity has separated them from their traditional ways of life and placed them on the margins of their societies. Like literal exiles, they need consolation, in the ancient philosophical sense of that word.[40] They need a mental map on which they can place their suffering in order both to make sense of it and to move beyond it.

37 In Jewish and early Christian literature the term "spirits" refers far more often to angelic beings than to human beings. The only unambiguous use of the term to refer to human beings in the New Testament appears in Heb. 12:23, where the author speaks of "the spirits of righteous people made perfect." On this, see Achtemeier, *1 Peter*, 255; Elliott, *1 Peter*, 657.

38 For this same basic position, see, e.g., Kelly, *Epistles of Peter and Jude*, 152–57; R. T. France, "Exegesis in Practice: Two Examples," in *New Testament Interpretation: Essays on Principles and Methods*, ed. I. Howard Marshall (Grand Rapids: Eerdmans, 1977), 252–81, here at 264–78; Brox, *Der erste Petrusbrief*, 169–75; William Joseph Dalton, *Christ's Proclamation to the Spirits: A Study of 1 Peter 3:18–4:6*, 2nd ed. (AnBib 23; Rome: Editrice Pontificio Istituto Biblico, 1989); Achtemeier, *1 Peter*, 239–74; and Elliott, *1 Peter*, 651–64.

39 Cf. *1 Enoch* 6–16, which incorporates the myth of the fallen angels, or Watchers, into the interpretation of Gen. 6:1–9:17. The author of this passage in *1 Enoch* interprets the "sons of God" who mingle with the "daughters of men" (Gen. 6:2) as fallen angels who introduced a long list of vices to humanity and brought evil and mayhem to earth through their gigantic progeny. God imprisoned these angels in the earth, where they await the eschatological judgment, and Enoch was sent to proclaim to them their condemnation. Cf. Sir. 16:7; *1 En.* 64–69; 85–89; 106; *Jub.* 4.21–22; 7.20–33; 10.1–6; 2 Peter 2:4–5; and Jude 6, 13–15. There is no reason to think that Peter embraces every element of Enoch's interpretation of Gen. 6:1–9:17, but he has apparently found in the basic structure of this myth an apt description of Christ's defeat of all invisible, malevolent powers. On this, see Brox, *Erste Petrusbrief*, 173.

40 Holloway, "*Nihil inopinati accidisse*," 434.

Peter provides this map in his letter.[41] He reminds his readers that God has been both gracious and merciful to them. He has rescued them from his certain and imminent judgment against the wicked and made them his people. Although estranged from the societies in which they live, the mantle of biblical Israel has fallen on them. They are, therefore, "a chosen people, a royal priesthood, a holy nation, a people belonging to God."

This transformation has been both costly and effective and therefore immensely valuable. It has come only through the sacrificial death of the righteous Messiah and resulted in the transformation of Peter's readers from debauched pagans into people whose lives are now filled with sincere love and gentleness, even in the face of wholly unjustified brutality. Because of this present transformation, they have hope for the future—a heavenly "inheritance" that can "never perish, spoil or fade" (1:4).

Their status as God's people also implies, however, that with respect to the pagan societies in which they live, they are "resident aliens." Their conduct must differentiate them from the societies in which they live, as "holy" people, and such conduct will inevitably lead to suffering. This suffering, however, should not lead them to accommodate themselves to the low moral standards of their societies or to withdraw themselves from engagement with these societies. They certainly should not confirm the slander that Christians are engaged in evil practices by violating widely recognized norms of political and moral order or engaging in criminal behavior. Instead, they ought to respond to their detractors with reasoned speech and gentle behavior, taking Christ's refusal to retaliate against his enemies as their example.

Peter recognizes that this refusal to retaliate against injustice is only tolerable if one is assured of justice eventually. For this reason, his letter frequently reminds his audience of their eschatological hope. For those who persevere through the fires of persecution, there waits an eschatological blessing. Their persecutors, by contrast, will succumb to the same defeat that Christ has already dealt—after his own experience of oppression—to the rebellious and malevolent spiritual powers in the invisible world.

41 For Peter's concern with the inner, esp. the mental, resources of his readers, see 1:13–14; 3:15; 4:1.

Chapter 31

HEBREWS: JESUS AS PERFECTER OF THE FAITH AND LEADER OF THE FAITHFUL

This anonymous homily, known since ancient times as "the letter to the Hebrews," offers a sustained argument of exceptional rhetorical sophistication for the eschatological superiority of the Christian message of salvation to the system of atonement described in the Mosaic law.[1] An understanding of their privileged eschatological position, the author argues, ought to encourage Christians to be faithful to the message of salvation they have heard.

The author's argument focuses on a complex and highly original portrait of Jesus' significance.[2] Jesus is God's final word of revelation and offers both clarity and unity to God's diverse and piecemeal revelation of himself in the past in the Scriptures. Jesus stands both above the angels in his deity and beneath the angels in his humanity, enabling him to lead human beings into the presence of God. He has pioneered the way into God's presence by becoming the perfect high priest and offering the perfect atoning sacrifice for sin in the true, heavenly tabernacle. By this means, he leads "many sons to glory," enabling God's people to become all that God intended for them to be.

For God's people to reach this eschatological goal, however, they must persevere in the faith, following the example of those among his people who have endured hardship in the past, especially Jesus.[3] Throughout his argument the author engages in detailed exegesis of Scripture and thus demonstrates how Jesus brings clarity and unity to what the prophets spoke previously "at many times and in various ways."

In this chapter we will look first at the circumstances that prompted the author to produce this complex argument and then at the argument itself. Our review of the letter's argument will fall into two parts. In the first and longest section we will look at the author's case that Jesus is God's final and complete revelation of himself and, as high priest, has pioneered the way for humanity to enter God's presence. In

1 Generically, the document is a hybrid, taking on the appearance both of a sermon, written to be delivered orally, and of a letter, sent to a distant congregation. Thus it refers to its own argument in oral and aural terms (2:5; 5:11; 6:9; 8:1; 9:5; 11:32; 13:22), as if the recipients would hear the text read or "preached" aloud, and it opens with a line of such rhetorical sophistication (1:1) that it is difficult to imagine the author ever intended anything else to precede it, such as an epistolary introduction. At the same time, the document's conclusion fits squarely within expectations for the ending of an ancient letter: it refers to the author having "written" (*epesteila*) to the recipients, mentions news of a mutual acquaintance, forecasts the author's travel plans, and sends greetings (13:22–24). Probably the text is a homily that the author sent as a letter and intended to be read aloud to the gathered church. On all this, see William L. Lane, *Hebrews 1–8* (WBC 47A; Dallas: Word, 1991), lxix–lxxx, and Barnabas Lindars, *The Theology of the Letter to the Hebrews* (New Testament Theology; Cambridge: Cambridge Univ. Press, 1991), 6–7.

2 On the uniqueness of the author's portrait of Jesus as high priest, see Albert Vanhoye, *Structure and Message of the Epistle to the Hebrews* (*SubBi* 12; Roma: Editrice Pontificio Istituto Biblico, 1989), 7.

3 Harold W. Attridge, *Hebrews* (Hermeneia; Philadelphia: Fortress, 1989), 21, and Lane, *Hebrews 1–8*, xcix–ci, emphasize appropriately that the author developed his sophisticated Christology not for speculative but for pastoral reasons.

the second, shorter section we will examine the author's pastoral encouragement of his readers to remain faithful to their Christian commitment in light of the privileged position that they occupy on the timeline of redemptive history.

THE CIRCUMSTANCES THAT PROMPTED HEBREWS

Although much about this homily is mysterious—who wrote it, where he was located, when he wrote—the author supplies a relatively large amount of evidence about the circumstances of his audience. His frequent use of the first person plural when referring to them shows that the author considers himself part of his audience's community, although, as the conclusion of his composition demonstrates, he is now in a different geographical location (13:19, 23–24).

He and his audience belong to the second Christian generation—they have heard the message of salvation not from Jesus himself but from those who first heard Jesus declare it (2:3; cf. 4:2). Not long after their conversion, they endured severe persecution for their commitment to the gospel—public shaming, imprisonment, and confiscation of their property (10:32–34), although no one had died as a result (12:4). The community endured these hardships bravely, standing by those most deeply affected (10:33) and continuing to demonstrate their commitment to the faith by their hard work, particularly by their practical demonstrations of love toward others (6:10).

Now, however, their commitment to the faith is beginning to soften. As the author writes his homily, persecution and maltreatment continue their suffering (13:3). Although many in his audience also continue to do good and show love in the midst of it (6:10), the author feels that his audience needs encouragement not to give up on their commitment to the gospel. They need someone to remind them of "the elementary truths of God's word" (5:12), to encourage them not to give up meeting together (10:25), and to warn them not to take sin, especially sexual sin, lightly (3:12–13; 10:24–27; 12:1, 16; 13:4).

Over and over the author urges them to remain faithful to their original commitment to the message of salvation contained in the gospel. They must "pay more careful attention" to what they have heard (2:1), not ignore "such a great salvation" (2:3), avoid turning away from the living God (3:12), not fall away from (6:6) or waver (10:23) in their original commitment, maintain their former diligence to the end (6:11), have perseverance (10:36; 12:7), and not grow weary or give out (12:3).

The author uses a rich set of images to provide for his audience a vivid picture of his concern. They should not drift away (*pararreō*) like unmoored boats. They should hold firmly (*katechō, krateō*) to the faith (3:6; 3:14; 4:14). Like those following a road to its end, they should not fall short of their goal (4:1, 11), throw off all hindrances, run the race with perseverance (12:1), and keep their eyes fixed on Jesus (12:2). They should continue their journey with strengthened arms and knees (12:12) and on level paths (12:13).

It seems reasonably clear that the author's audience has grown weary of the social ostracism and physical violence of persecution for their faith. Life "outside the camp," bearing the disgrace of Jesus, has taken its toll (13:11–13), and at least some of the author's audience are in grave danger of turning their backs on their commitment to the message of "salvation" that they earlier embraced (2:2–3; 4:2).[4]

Can we also say with confidence that these people are Christian Jews who are tempted to revert specifically to the synagogue? Many interpreters have thought this, and with good reason.[5] The text of the homily demands a sophisticated knowledge of the Jewish Scriptures in Greek translation and provides a sustained argument for the superiority of Jesus to such popular Jewish figures as angels, Moses, and the high priest. In addition, it makes a lengthy case for the superiority of Jesus' atoning sacrifice to that of the Day of Atonement ritual. This rhetorical strategy would fit snugly a situation in which societal ostracism, perhaps from non-Christian Jewish friends and neighbors, is pushing Christian Jews back into the widely known and respected boundaries of their former religion.[6]

The homily, then, becomes an urgent plea not to step over this brink. Doing this would be "crucifying the Son of God all over again and subjecting him to public disgrace" (6:6). It would be trampling "the Son of God under foot" (10:29). Most seriously, it would mean turning back the eschatological clock and settling for the shadowy outline of atonement when the substance that the outline describes has already arrived and Christ has already provided the ultimate atonement (1:3; 7:27; 9:11–14, 25–28; 10:1–17, 29).

A number of interpreters, however, believe that this portrait of the recipients and of the letter's purpose is distorted. Since all early Christians, whether Jewish or not, claimed the Jewish Scriptures as their own Scriptures, all of them had to gain familiarity with these Scriptures.[7] The recipients of Hebrews have themselves been taught "the elementary truths of God's word" (5:12), and so nothing about their ethnic origins can be determined by the author's assumption of their detailed knowledge of Scripture. The author's argument for the superiority of Christianity to Judaism, both because Christianity is more advanced eschatologically and because it succeeds where Judaism has failed, is a common theme in Christian literature of the first three centuries. New sects constantly need to define themselves as superior to their parent bodies and alternative religions, and so the argument of Hebrews would have met with approval from Christians whatever their ethnic background and former religious

4 Cf. David A. deSilva, *Perseverance in Gratitude: A Socio-Rhetorical Commentary on the Epistle "to the Hebrews"* (Grand Rapids: Eerdmans, 2000), 16–20, although in light of 13:3, it is difficult to agree with deSilva's claim (19) that the audience was not experiencing violent persecution.

5 See, e.g., Brooke Foss Westcott, *The Epistle to the Hebrews*, 3rd ed. (London: Macmillan, 1909), xxxv–xlii; F. F. Bruce, *The Epistle to the Hebrews*, rev. ed. (NICNT; Grand Rapids: Eerdmans, 1990), 3–9; and Lane, *Hebrews 1–8*, liii–lv.

6 This approach accounts for references to persecution in the letter better than Lindars's idea, *Theology of the Letter to the Hebrews*, 10, 14, and *passim*, that the homily's audience was attracted to the synagogue because Jewish ritual seemed to relieve the guilt that they felt over their sins more effectively than Christian teaching. On the wide attraction of Judaism in the ancient Roman world, see John G. Gager, *The Origins of Anti-Semitism: Attitudes toward Judaism in Pagan and Christian Antiquity* (New York: Oxford Univ. Press, 1985), 35–112.

7 See, e.g., Hans-Friedrich Weiss, *Der Brief an die Hebräer*, 15th ed. (MeyerK 13; Göttingen: Vandenhoeck & Ruprecht, 1991), 70–72; Attridge, *Hebrews*, 12; deSilva, *Perseverance*, 2–7.

commitments.[8] There is therefore no need to think of the recipients as Jewish Christians or to think of them as people tempted to abandon Christianity for Judaism.

The truth may lie somewhere between these two common approaches to the letter's recipients. It should be conceded that the sophisticated use of Scripture in Hebrews tells us nothing about whether the recipients of the letter are Jews or Gentiles. Gentile Christians quickly appropriated the Jewish Scriptures for themselves, and their teachers presupposed this knowledge when instructing Gentile converts to Christianity. This is clear from Paul's subtle use of Scripture in letters directed to principally Gentile audiences a few decades before Hebrews and from Clement's sophisticated use of Scripture in his letter to the Corinthians a decade or so after Hebrews.[9]

At the same time, the argument of Hebrews works best if at least some within the author's audience, whether Christian Jews or Christian Gentiles, are contemplating adherence to the synagogue as a means of avoiding the social ostracism, imprisonment, theft, and violence that went with their commitment to an unpopular and novel eastern cult. The author's tandem concerns to exhort his audience to persevere in the faith and to show them the superiority of Christianity to Judaism is fully understandable within such a situation.[10]

Paul's letter to the Galatians provides an analogy. Paul explicitly states that Gentiles within the Galatian churches are contemplating conversion to Judaism, albeit a Christian form of Judaism. In a couple of famously enigmatic comments, he also implies that promoting conversion to Judaism is a way of avoiding persecution (Gal. 5:11; 6:12).[11] The Judaizing missionaries who have come to Galatia to promote circumcision among Paul's converts have themselves practiced a form of social ostracism as a way of advancing their agenda (4:17). Paul's readers, it seems, are both attracted to Judaism in itself and experiencing pressure to convert. Paul's response, like the argument of Hebrews, is largely an effort to show the eschatological superiority of faith in Jesus Christ over adherence to the Mosaic law.[12] The situation that prompts Hebrews a few decades later is probably similar, although the lack of specific references in Hebrews to pressuring believers to convert to Judaism will always make this reconstruction of the situation tentative.

In summary, the author writes this homily and sends it to his home church to encourage the Christians there to remain faithful to the message of salvation they have received, despite the social ostracism and violence they have long experienced for their convictions. Since at least some members are casting an envious eye at the tranquil existence of the Jewish community in their midst and are thinking about seeking refuge there, the author develops a sophisticated argument to show the eschatological superiority of Christianity to Judaism and the corresponding gravity of rejecting God's final revelation of himself in Jesus Christ.

8 deSilva, *Perseverance*, 5–6.
9 Weiss, *Hebräer*, 71.
10 Cf. Bruce, *Hebrews*, 6.
11 On this understanding of Gal. 6:12, see ch. 11, above.
12 See ch. 12, above.

JESUS AS GOD'S CLIMACTIC REVELATION

The author argues that Jesus' message, Jesus himself, and Jesus' work supply God's complete and final revelation of salvation, and he builds this argument gradually. He begins with a brief statement that the message that came through God's Son is superior to the message that came through the biblical prophets (1:1–3a). He continues with a longer statement that God's Son is superior to the angels described in Scripture (1:4–2:16). He then explains at even greater length, and climactically, that Jesus is a high priest superior to the high priests that the Mosaic law appointed and that his atoning sacrifice is superior to the Day of Atonement sacrifice described in Leviticus 16 (Heb. 1:3b; 2:17–18; 4:14–5:10; 6:19b–10:17; 12:24; 13:10–12, 20).

God's Word Given through Jesus Is Superior to His Word Given through the Scriptures

The author reveals the strategy of his argument throughout his homily in the first line when he compares the way God spoke in the past to the way in which he has spoken "in these last days" (1:1–3:a). Previously, he says, God spoke "through the prophets." Since he rarely mentions the classical prophets in his argument, he probably includes, in addition to the prophets, all others through whom God spoke in Scripture.[13] This would include Moses (7:14; 9:19; 10:28; 12:21), Joshua (4:8), and David (4:7), all of whom spoke in Scripture and were popularly known as prophets in the author's time.[14] The first member of the author's contrasting pair, therefore, is the vast body of people through whom God spoke the words of Scripture.[15] The author ascribes three characteristics to these Scriptures: They are piecemeal (*polymerōs*); they take diverse forms (*polytropōs*); and they are from the past (*palai*). With these terms he intends to stress both the diversity of the Scriptures and their provisional nature.

In contrast to this old and diverse way of speaking, however, stands God's speech through his Son. His speech excels that of the Scriptures in quality because it comes from one source, and the "word" that serves as its vehicle is the powerful word that made and sustains the universe (1:2–3a). This Son, the author will later say, is the Lord, who spoke the message of salvation to his first followers and, through these first followers, to the author's audience (2:3). The message was so powerful that, when it was spoken, "signs, wonders and various miracles" accompanied it (2:4).

None of this means that the author believes the Scriptures are now a dead letter confined to the past and no longer useful. He will quickly show through detailed exegetical work in the Scriptures themselves that they are, quite to the contrary, "living and active, sharper than any double-edged sword" (4:12) when viewed through the lens of God's latest revelation in his Son, Jesus.[16] Nevertheless, the author wants his readers to

13 The author quotes the prophets only twice (2:13; 8:8–12; 10:16–17; cf. Isa. 8:17–18; Jer. 31:31–34) and refers to them explicitly only here and in 11:32.

14 See Attridge, *Hebrews*, 38–39, who points to Philo, *Vit. Mos.* 2.187–91; Sir. 46:1; and Philo. *Agric.* 50 as examples of the ancient notion that Moses, Joshua, and David, respectively, were prophets.

15 Why speak then of "prophets" rather than of "the Scriptures"? Perhaps the author was trying to preserve the highly valued rhetorical device of alliteration in "p" for his opening line: *polymerōs kai polytropōs palai ho theos lalēsas tois patrasin en tois prophētais.*

16 Lane, *Hebrews 1–8*, 103, and Weiss, *Hebräer*, 284, correctly resist the interpretation of "the word of God" in 4:12–13 as something other than the Scriptures. *Pace*, e.g., Westcott, *Hebrews*, 102,

understand that apart from the clarity that Jesus brings, the Scriptures of Israel leave those who read them with a diverse and obscure picture of God's saving work.

The Son of God is Superior to the Angels

In his contrast between God's speech through the Scriptures and his speech through his Son, the author has already described that Son as the one through whom he made and sustained the universe. He is the "reflection" or "radiance" (*apaugasma*) of God's glory and has the "imprint" (*charaktēr*) of his essential nature (1:2–3). The author now engages in an exegesis of a series of biblical passages, primarily from the Psalms, to show that this close connection between God and his Son makes the Son superior to the angels (1:4–14). After an hortatory intermezzo (2:1–4), he continues his comparison between the Son and the angels, but now focuses on the humanity of the Son, whom he appropriately calls "Jesus" for the first time (2:5–16).[17]

The Different Relationships of Son and Angels to God (1:5–14)

The author first demonstrates from the Scriptures the vast difference between the relationship that the Son has with God and the relationship that the angels have with God. The author makes this clear by punctuating this paragraph with three explicit statements of contrast between the Son and the angels:

- "For to which of the angels did God ever say . . ." (1:5)
- "In speaking of the angels he says . . ." (1:7)
- "But to which of the angels did God ever say . . ." (1:13).[18]

Between these explicit statements of contrast the author weaves seven biblical quotations that together demonstrate the superiority of the Son to the angels in two basic ways.

Jesus as Royal and Exalted Son

The author shows first that Jesus is superior to the angels because, as he stated in his opening line (1:2–3), he is God's Son and has assumed an exalted position at God's right hand (1:2–3). He is, in other words, God's anointed king. To make this point, the author begins and ends his series of citations with texts commonly used in early Christianity to show that Jesus is God's royal Son. He begins with a combined citation of Psalm 2:7 and 2 Samuel 7:14 (1 Chron. 17:13), texts that speak of the king as God's Son and that first-century Jews, both Christian and non-Christian, often took as references to the Messiah.[19] He ends with a reference to Psalm 110:1 (LXX 109:1), another royal psalm that Jesus himself explained in terms of the Messiah (Matt.

who believes that it means "the word spoken by the Son," and James Moffatt, *A Critical and Exegetical Commentary on the Epistle to the Hebrews* (ICC; Edinburgh: T. & T. Clark, 1924), 54–55, who believes that it means "the Christian gospel."

17 On the balance between attention to Jesus' divine and human natures in this section of the homily, see Vanhoye, *Structure and Message*, 23–25.

18 Lane, *Hebrews 1–8*, 22.

19 On the Christian side, see the gospel narratives of Jesus' baptism (Mark 1:11; cf. Matt. 3:17; Luke 3:22) and transfiguration (Mark 9:7; cf. Matt. 17:5; Luke 9:35) and the explicit quotation of "the second Psalm" in Acts 13:33. On the non-Christian side, see the comment about "David's seed" of the skeptical crowd at the Feast of Booths in John 7:42 and the use of 2 Sam. 7:12–14 in 4QFlor, frag. 1, col. 1, line 10. I am indebted to Lane, *Hebrews 1–8*, 25, for calling these texts to my attention.

22:41–46; Mark 12:35–37a; Luke 20:41–44). Early Christians also frequently quoted and echoed this text to show that Jesus, having conquered his enemies, presently reigns from a position at God's right hand.[20]

Immediately after both citations, the author contrasts the angels' position with that of Jesus. After the first citation (Heb. 1:6–7), he describes the angels as beings who "worship" God's Son (Ps. 97:7 [LXX 96:7]) and do his bidding, like the created elements of wind and fire (104:4 [LXX 103:4]). After the last citation (Heb. 1:14), he speaks again of the angels as "ministering spirits," although now, as a way of introducing his second major contrast between Jesus and the angels, the author says that the angels serve those who benefit from the Son's saving work. The author has therefore skillfully constructed his series of biblical citations to open and close with the thought that Jesus' position as God's royal and exalted Son is unique and that therefore no angel can share with him this special office.

Jesus as the Divine and Eternal Agent of Creation

The Son's relationship with God also differs from that of the angels because of its eternal quality. The author has already stated in his homily's first line that God created and sustains the universe through the Son and that the Son is the reflection and very imprint of God's own nature (1:2–3). Here he borrows language from the description of Wisdom in Proverbs 8:22–31, where it is stated that Wisdom existed before the world was made (8:22–29) and was the "craftsman" at God's side when God made the world (8:30). He also seems to have borrowed language from the description of Wisdom in Wisdom of Solomon 7:1–8:1 as the "fashioner of all things" (7:21) and the "reflection [or radiance] of eternal light, a spotless mirror of the working of God" (7:26).[21]

Now in the center of his series of biblical quotations, he cites Psalm 45:7–8 (LXX 44:7–8) and 102:25–28 (LXX 101:25–28) to show that the Son is not merely God's anointed king but is in some sense God himself and occupies a "throne" that "will last for ever and ever" (Heb. 1:8). Since he "laid the foundations of the earth" (1:10), he is himself eternal and unchanging (1:11), whereas his creation "will be changed" (1:12).

In contrast to the divine and unchanging nature of the Son stand the lowly angels. The author has already said that the angels offer worship to the Son (1:6) and that they resemble the changeable elements, such as wind and fire, of the Son's creation (1:7). In addition, he probably thinks of the angels as filling the role of the "companions" of the Son mentioned in Psalm 45:7 (LXX 44:7), and that psalm states explicitly that God has set the Son above these "companions" (Heb. 1:9). Once again, the Son stands in contrast to the angels, this time because he has assumed the role of Wisdom and in that role is divine, eternal, and the fashioner of all things, including the angels themselves.

20 The text is quoted in Acts 2:34 and 1 Cor. 15:25. Allusions to it appear in Acts 5:31; Rom. 8:34; Eph. 1:20; Col. 3:1; and 1 Peter 3:22. See Attridge, *Hebrews*, 62 n. 140, whose reference to Rev. 3:4, however, appears to be a mistake.

21 Lindars, *Theology of the Letter to the Hebrews*, 31–32.

The Different Relationships of Son and Angels to Human Beings (2:5–16)

The author is not content to speak only of the contrast between Jesus' royal and divine dignity and the angels' roles as Jesus' worshipers and servants, but he also draws a contrast between the angels' inability to help human beings reach their God-given destiny and the help that Jesus, as a human being, can give. He begins in 2:5 with a statement about something that is not true of the angels and follows the same rhetorical strategy he has used in 1:13:

Heb. 1:13	**Heb. 2:5**
To which of the angels did God ever say, "Sit at my right hand until I make your enemies a footstool for your feet"?	It is not to angels that he has subjected the world to come, about which we are speaking.

This rhetorical strategy, common to the author's arguments in 1:13 and 2:5, has led many interpreters to claim that just as the contrast in 1:13 is between the angels and the Son, so the contrast in 2:5 must be between the angels and the Son.[22] In 1:14, however, the author has already progressed to another thought—the notion that the angels have a lower status than the human beneficiaries of salvation: "Are not all angels ministering spirits," he asks, "sent to serve *those who will inherit salvation*?" (italics added). In 2:5, therefore, his audience is prepared to think not of the Son but of human beings as filling the other side of the contrast: The world to come is not subjected to angels but to human beings.[23]

This understanding of the text seems confirmed when the author goes on to support his argument from Psalm 8:4–6 (LXX 8:5–7). The author's citation speaks specifically of God's care for human beings, of his making them "a little lower than the angels." It speaks also of the "glory and honor" that God gave to human beings and of his putting all things under their feet.[24] In Hebrews 2:8 the author then supplies his comment on this psalm: "In putting everything under him [humanity], God left nothing that is not subject to him. Yet at present we do not see everything subject to him." In other words, although the "world to come" has begun to break into the present age (2:4), humanity is a long way from having the sovereignty over creation that God intended to give to it.

It is at this low point that Jesus enters the picture. The author uses the name given to him at his birth for the first time in his homily (2:9) and shows his audience that, by Jesus' incarnation and death, he assumed the role that God intended for humanity and was able to begin the process whereby humanity itself also assumed this role (2:9–16). Jesus was also made "a little lower than the angels" at his incarnation and

22 See, e.g., Moffatt, *Hebrews*, 21; Lane, *Hebrews 1–8*, 45–46; and Weiss, *Hebräer*, 192.

23 See Westcott, *Hebrews*, 41, and G. B. Caird, *New Testament Theology*, ed. L. D. Hurst (Oxford: Oxford Univ. Press, 1994), 64, 96. Cf. deSilva, *Perseverence*, 108–12, and Craig R. Koester, "Hebrews, Rhetoric, and the Future of Humanity," *CBQ* 64 (2002): 103–23, here at 110–11, who believe that the author tries to encourage a double reading of Psalm 8 so that it becomes applicable both to humanity and to Christ.

24 It is true that this last element seems to echo Ps. 110:1 (LXX 109:1), which is applied in Heb. 1:13 to Christ, but the words that the author cites are part of Ps. 8 (v. 6 [7]) and so are best understood in this instance as a reference to human beings rather than to Christ.

through his death destroyed the power of death over humanity (2:9, 14–15). God rewarded his unselfish death for others with glorification (2:9).

His death, therefore, opened the way for human beings to join him in glory and so attain the glorified state of authority over the world that God intended they should have all along (2:9–10). Because Jesus became part of the human "family" and became a brother to human beings through his suffering, he is able to bring "many sons to glory" (2:10–11). He is able, in other words, to lead those who follow him faithfully to the eschatological destiny that God intended for humanity from the beginning.[25]

The author closes this part of his argument with the statement, "For surely it is not angels he helps, but Abraham's descendants" (2:16). In other words, Jesus is superior to the angels because, unlike the angels, he assumed the human condition, experiencing, like his human family, suffering and death. He can therefore accomplish something that no angel can do: He can become the human "leader" (*archēgon*, 2:10; cf. 12:2) of the way out of death's domain and so bring "many sons" to the "glory" God intended for humanity to have over the world to come.[26]

Summary

After the author briefly shows in the opening to his homily the superiority of the message of God's Son to that of the prophets, he argues at greater length that Jesus is superior to the angels in two ways. First, his status as God's royal Son and immutable agent in creation is superior to their status as changeable, created servants. Second, his human nature enabled him to identify with human beings in their suffering, to conquer death on their behalf, and to open the way for them to receive the glory that God created them to enjoy.

But exactly how does he do this? The means by which Jesus, as a human being, leads "many sons to glory" is the central doctrinal concern of the author's homily.

Jesus' High Priesthood Is Superior to the Levitical High Priesthood

In his homily's opening statement, the author said that Jesus took his position of exaltation at God's right hand only after providing "purification of sins" (1:3). He anticipated with this comment the primary concern of his discourse (8:1a): Jesus' high priesthood is superior to the Levitical high priesthood and has provided the final satisfaction for sins to which the Levitical high priesthood pointed. By assuming the position of high priest, Jesus leads human beings into the glory that God intended for them when he created them.

25 For this way of understanding the author's point in 2:5–18, see L. D. Hurst, "The Christology of Hebrews 1 and 2," in *The Glory of Christ in the New Testament: Studies in Christology*, ed. L. D. Hurst and N. T. Wright (Oxford: Clarendon, 1987), 151–64, here at 151–53, where Hurst describes the undeveloped thesis of George B. Caird. It is not necessary to accept Hurst's unconvincing attempt to read 1:5–14 without reference to the Son's preexistence in order to appreciate his and Caird's understanding of 2:5–18.

26 The translation of the term *archēgon* as "leader" is not uncontroversial. BDAG, 138, renders the term in this passage "originator, founder." Lane, *Hebrews 1–8*, prefers "champion" since he believes the author is echoing the Greek tradition about Hercules, who, like Jesus in 2:14–16, wrestled with and overcame Death (Euripides, *Alcestis*, ll. 843–44). The translation "leader," however, brings out more fully the author's play on the term *agagonta* ("leading") and is more consistent with the pervasive motif of pilgrimage in the homily. Cf. Attridge, *Hebrews*, 87–88, and Weiss, *Hebräer*, 209–11.

This high priesthood, says the author, is both like and unlike the high priesthood mandated in the Mosaic law under the first covenant. Like the best high priests under the first covenant and because of his humanity (2:5–16), Jesus is both faithful and merciful (2:17–3:6a; 4:15; 5:1–8). He is, therefore, able both to provide an example of faithfulness to people (3:6b–4:11, 14) and to offer them sympathetic help in their own difficult circumstances (4:15–16). Unlike the Levitical high priests, however, Jesus' high priesthood is of the superior "order of Melchizedek" (5:10; 6:20b–7:28); he was made perfect through his climactic and final sacrifice (5:9; 7:28–9:25), and through this sacrifice he became the source of eternal salvation (5:9; 9:26–10:17).[27]

Jesus' Similarity to the Levitical High Priests (2:17–3:6a; 4:15; 5:1–8)

On the heels of his argument that Jesus is superior to the angels because he became human and is therefore able to lead human beings to the glory that God intends for them, the author now describes specifically the kind of human being that Christ became: a high priest. The author makes the transition to this section of his argument with the statement that Jesus became "a merciful and faithful high priest in the service of God" (2:17). He then explores these two qualities of Jesus' priesthood, qualities that any priest should have and qualities that allowed Jesus to benefit humanity in the same way that the Levitical high priests benefited humanity. Even here, where the author's primary point is the similarity between Jesus and the Levitical high priests, however, he brings out in each case the superiority of Jesus.

Jesus, the Faithful High Priest (3:1–6)

First, the author says that Jesus, as high priest, was faithful to God who appointed him to be high priest (3:1). In his faithfulness, he stands parallel to Moses, who was "faithful in all God's house" (3:2). The author's language echoes Numbers 12:6–8, a passage in which God praises Moses and contrasts him with the prophets. Speaking to Aaron and Miriam, who questioned whether Moses was the only mouthpiece of God, the Lord said:

> Listen to my words:
>
> "When a prophet of the LORD is among you,
> I reveal myself to him in visions,
> I speak to him in dreams.
> But this is not true of my servant Moses;
> *he is faithful in all my house.*
> With him I speak face to face,
> clearly and not in riddles;
> he sees the form of the LORD.
> Why then were you not afraid
> to speak against my servant Moses?" (italics added)

27 On the structure of this section of Hebrews, see Vanhoye, *Structure and Message*, 24–29.

The author of Hebrews knows that the term "house" (*oikos*) here refers to Israel, the people of God, and he interprets the term in much the same way in 3:6 to refer to his audience as the eschatological people of God. At the same time, however, the author may intend for his readers to think of the tabernacles in which both Moses and Jesus faithfully served as priests. Moses was a Levite, and such passages as Exodus 24:4–8 and Psalm 99:6 picture him in a priestly role.[28] The term "house," moreover, refers to Solomon's temple in 1 Chronicles 17:14 (LXX, *oikos*), a passage that the author echoes when he says that Jesus "was faithful to the one who appointed him" (Heb. 3:2). The author, therefore, seems to think of Moses as a faithful priest, and he compares Jesus' own faithfulness as a priest to that of Moses.[29]

The author cannot rest with a simple comparison, however. He must also point out Jesus' superiority to his priestly counterpart, and to do this he continues to play on the multiple meanings of the term "house." Moses is both like a house (3:3) and like a servant in a house (3:5), but Jesus is both like the house's builder (3:3) and like the builder's Son whom he has appointed over his house (3:6). This means, as the author has already argued in 1:2–3 and 10, that Jesus is like God, "the builder of everything" (3:4), and, as the author has argued in 1:2–3, 5–6, and 13, is God's royal Son, who, in answer to the prophecy of 2 Samuel 7:13–14 (2 Chron. 17:13–14), will preside over God's temple.[30] "House," therefore, means both the sanctuary where the high priest serves and the world itself, and in both these houses, Jesus is superior to Moses as creator, Son, and priest.

Jesus, the Merciful High Priest (4:15; 5:1–8)

Jesus is also like other high priests because he participated in the human condition. Like other high priests, he knew from his own experience what both subjection to authority and suffering meant.[31] Other high priests, the author says, are selected and appointed to their task by God (5:1, 4). Jesus too was appointed to his high priesthood by God (5:5) and had to obey God, just as other high priests do (5:8).

Just as they are beset by weakness (5:2), moreover, so Jesus was subject to human weakness (4:15). The form of his human suffering was not unlike that of the author's audience. Just as their faithfulness to the message of salvation is being tested by persecution, so Jesus' faithfulness to the mission and appointment that God had given him (3:1–2) had to be worked out in the midst of hardship and the temptation to give up. This is probably what the author means when he says that Jesus was "tested in every way, just as we are" (4:15).[32] To demonstrate his point, the author recalls Jesus' struggle in Gethsemane with the cup of death that God had given him to drink:

28 Lane, *Hebrews 1–8*, 74. See also the picture of Moses in the author's near contemporary, Philo of Alexandria. In *Mos.*, 2.66 and 2.71 Philo portrays Moses as a priest, and in 2.75 as a high priest.

29 *Pace* William L. Lane, *Hebrews 9–13* (WBC 47B; Dallas: Word, 1991), 285, the author probably also has this dual reference in mind in 10:21 where he uses the phrase "great high priest over the house of God" to refer not only to Jesus' authority over the people of God but also his sacrifice, described in detail in 9:1–10:18, in the heavenly sanctuary.

30 For the notion that the world God has created is the "house" that he has built and oversees, see Philo, *Sobr.* 62–64. I am indebted to Attridge, *Hebrews*, 109 n. 60, for drawing my attention to this passage.

31 On this way of structuring 5:1–8, see Vanhoye, *Structure and Message*, 56; cf. Lane, *Hebrews 1–8*, 117, on v. 4.

32 On this, see esp. Weiss, *Hebräer*, 295–96.

> During the days of Jesus' life on earth, he offered up prayers and petitions with loud cries and tears to the one who could save him from death, and he was heard because of his reverent submission. (Heb. 5:7; cf. Matt. 26:38–39; Mark 14:34–36; Luke 22:42; also John 12:27)

Participation in the human condition gives to other high priests the advantage of being able to sympathize with those whom they represent before God (5:1–2). Because they know from their own experience what it is like to wander into sin as a result of ignorance and weakness, they are able to show compassion to those whose human condition, in the same way, leads them into sin (5:2). Because Jesus was also a high priest and therefore fully human, his experience of testing has enabled him to be sympathetic with and therefore merciful to those who are subject to similar trials (2:17–18; 4:15; 5:8).

Just as he did when comparing Jesus' priesthood to that of Moses, so here the author brings out a difference between Jesus and other high priests. Unlike other high priests, he says, Jesus' suffering and testing did not result in sin (4:15). It drove him not to unfaithfulness but to obedience (5:8).

Summary

In the first two sections of his argument that Jesus is God's perfect high priest, the author emphasizes the similarity between Jesus and the high priests of Israel's Scriptures. Like their best representatives, such as Moses, he was faithful to his appointment and therefore could serve as an example of faithfulness to the many sons whom he leads to glory. Also like other high priests, he can be merciful because he has experienced for himself the human condition: He was subject to God's authority and beset with human suffering.

Even as the author emphasizes these similarities, however, he also points out the differences between Jesus and other Israelite high priests. Jesus is not merely a high priest but God's eternal, royal Son, his agent in creation and his anointed ruler. Unlike other high priests, moreover, he committed no sin but was wholly obedient to God, even in the midst of his suffering.

Jesus' Differences from the Levitical High Priests (5:1, 4–6, 10; 6:20b–10:17)

Although it is important to the author that Jesus' humanity took the form of a high priest, he is most interested in demonstrating that Jesus' high priesthood is superior to that of the Levitical high priests. Both his high priestly office and his sacrificial work within that office perfected the old Levitical system, fulfilling its ultimate purpose and bringing it to an end. The author shows this eschatological superiority of Jesus' high priesthood in three ways, outlined at the end of his argument that Jesus is like other high priests in his faithfulness and mercy (5:9–10).[33] He brought the priesthood to perfection (5:9a), was the source of eternal salvation for those who obey him (5:9b), and belonged to the priestly order of Melchizedek (5:10). The author tackles the last item in his list first.

33 Vanhoye, *Structure and Message*, 27–29.

Jesus is a Priest of Melchizedek's Order (7:1–28)

As we have just seen, in 5:1, 4–6 the author shows that Jesus is like other high priests because both he and they are appointed to their offices by God. To make this point, the author quotes Psalm 110:4 (LXX 109:4):

> Every high priest is selected from among human beings and is appointed to represent human beings in matters related to God. . . .
>
> No one takes this honor upon himself; he must be called by God, just as Aaron was. So Christ also did not take upon himself the glory of becoming a high priest. But God said to him . . . "You are a priest forever, in the order of Melchizedek." (aut.)

The author does not stop to explain why he can place Jesus in the priestly order of Melchizedek or claim that Psalm 110:4 applies to him. In a way typical of his argumentation throughout the letter, he simply states this astonishing claim and awaits the right opportunity to explain it. That opportunity comes in Hebrews 6:20b–7:28, where the author focuses on the ways in which Jesus' special priestly order makes him superior to priests of the Levitical order.[34] The author makes this argument not only on the basis of Psalm 110:4 but also from Genesis 14:18–20, the source for the reference to the priestly order of Melchizedek in Psalm 110:4.

Jesus' order, says the author, makes him superior in four ways to the high priests described in the Mosaic law. First, his priesthood is eternal. Two passages imply this for the author: Genesis 14:18–20 and Psalm 110:4. In the Genesis passage, Melchizedek, king of Salem and "priest of God Most High," appears without any introduction in the story of Abraham's defeat of Kedorlaomer and the kings allied with him (Gen. 14:1–24). The absence of any information about Melchizedek's origins or eventual fate implies to the author of Hebrews that he prefigured the eternal duration of Jesus' high priesthood: "Without father or mother, without genealogy, without beginning of days or end of life, like the Son of God he remains a priest forever" (Heb. 7:3).

Psalm 110:4 implies the same idea when it declares to the king that he is a priest of Melchizedek's order "forever." The author, together with Jesus himself (Matt. 22:41–46; Mark 12:35–37a; Luke 20:41–44) and early Christian tradition (Acts 13:33), believed that the "Son" to whom the Lord speaks in this psalm is in some sense Jesus (Heb. 1:5; 5:5). If so, reasons the author of Hebrews, then Jesus is not only the "Son" of Psalm 110:1 but also the "priest" of 110:4. This is confirmed by Jesus' resurrection from the dead, which fits perfectly the description of this person as a "priest forever" (Heb. 7:8, 16; cf. 13:20). Because his high priesthood is permanent, his intercession for "those who come to God through him" is also eternal, and therefore he is able to save them completely (7:24–25).

The Levitical priests, by contrast, all die (7:8). Because they die, many of them must serve in succession, and any measure of salvation they provide, the author implies, is necessarily incomplete (7:23).

34 Ibid., 60.

Second, the interaction between Melchizedek and Abraham in the Genesis narrative demonstrates the superiority of Jesus' priestly order to that of the Levitical priests. Melchizedek gave Abraham a blessing in the name of "God Most High, Creator of heaven and earth" (Gen. 14:19), and since "the lesser person is blessed by the greater," Melchizedek is greater than Abraham (Heb. 7:7). Although left unstated, the implication is clear: Jesus, whose priesthood follows the pattern laid down by Melchizedek, is greater than the Levitical priests, who are descended from Abraham.

Abraham's willingness to give a tenth of the booty that he took from the kings he had routed also demonstrates the superiority of Melchizedek's priestly line to that of Levi. The Levitical priests, the author recalls, did not work the ground but lived on the tithes that Israelites from other tribes paid to them (Num. 18:20–24; cf. Deut. 18:1–2; Neh. 13:10–11).[35] Through his ancestor Abraham, however, Levi himself had paid a tithe to Melchizedek (7:5–6, 9–10). The author leaves the implications of this unexpressed, but they are reasonably clear: If Levi paid a priestly tithe to Melchizedek through his ancestor Abraham, and if Jesus is of the priestly order of Melchizedek, then even the Levitical priests themselves must acknowledge that Jesus' priestly order is superior to their own.

Third, Jesus' high priesthood results from God's own change in the regulations that govern priestly service, and this change implies that the new situation is an improvement over its predecessor. The change is evident both from Jesus' own origins in the tribe of Judah and from the chronological relationship between the Mosaic law and God's oath in Psalm 110:4 (LXX 109:4).

Jesus was not from the tribe of Levi, says the author, and yet, according to the Mosaic law, only Levites may serve as priests (Heb. 7:6, 14). The solution to this problem cannot be that Jesus is not a priest, since his "indestructible life," demonstrated in his resurrection, has shown him to be the "priest forever" of Psalm 110:4 (Heb. 7:16–19). The only solution to the problem is that a new priestly order has been established, regulated by a "better covenant" (7:22).

In addition, a psalm of David, written after the Mosaic law, established this new order (7:28b). The establishment of a priesthood in the order of Melchizedek, therefore, is God's latest word on the subject and shows that this new priestly order is an improvement over its predecessor.

Fourth, the author argues that a divine oath confirmed Jesus' priesthood in Psalm 110:4. That passage speaks not only of the king as God's Son and as an eternal priest, but it also says that God appointed the king to be his priest with an oath. The author points this out with a full quotation: "The Lord has sworn and will not change his mind: 'You are a priest forever, in the order of Melchizedek.'" In a previous passage the author already argued that when God utters an oath, what he says is more emphatic than ever. God's word alone is certain, says the author, but it becomes doubly certain to the hearer when God confirms what he says with an oath (Heb. 6:13–18). Unlike

35 In the first century, dutiful priests still refrained from working the ground and lived on the tithes of the people. On this, see E. P. Sanders, *Judaism: Practice and Belief 63 BCE–66 CE* (London/Philadelphia: SCM/Trinity Press International, 1992), 146–69.

Levitical priests, God established Jesus' high priesthood with such an oath. In light of this, his priesthood is better than the priesthood regulated by the Mosaic law (7:22).

In summary, the author argues that since Jesus belongs to the priestly order of Melchizedek, his high priesthood is eternal, receives the homage of Abraham and Levi, is a later and more perfect institution of God, and was established with an emphatic divine oath. In all these ways it is superior to the Levitical high priesthood.

Jesus' Sacrifice Makes Him a Perfect High Priest (8:1–9:28)

The author announced in 5:9 that in his discussion of Jesus' high priesthood, he intended to show how Jesus' suffering made him perfect. In 7:28 he tells his audience that he will now take up this point: "For the law appoints as high priests men who are weak; but the oath, which came after the law, appointed the Son, who has been made perfect forever" (7:28).[36]

In order to understand the author's argument, it is necessary first to appreciate the special meaning he gives to the terms that mean "perfection" when he applies them to Jesus' suffering (*teleioō* in 2:10 and 5:9; *teleiōtēs* in 12:2). When applied to Jesus, such terms do not refer to his moral perfection, as if in order to be the ultimate high priest he first had to learn to be virtuous by his suffering.[37] The author is clear that Jesus never sinned (4:15; 7:27).[38] If he had sinned, his death would have been a blemished sacrifice in violation of the expectations in the Mosaic law that guilt offerings should be "unblemished" (*amōmos*, 9:14; cf. Lev. 4:22–35; 9:1–15 in LXX). Rather, Jesus is made perfect by his suffering because through it he performs the ritual that brings the Day of Atonement mandated in the Mosaic law to its appointed goal. By means of his suffering, he became the high priest who offered the "perfect" and therefore final sacrifice for sin. In 8:1–9:25, the author shows how Jesus' suffering resulted in his perfection in this sense.

The author grounds his thinking about Jesus' perfection in Scripture. Two passages are particularly important. First, he quotes at length the prophecy of Jeremiah 31:31–34 (LXX 38:31–34) that God will establish a new covenant with his people (Heb. 8:7–13). This passage demonstrates that God intended to make two covenants with his people, and this in turn implies that the first one was not faultless (8:8). Jeremiah's talk of a second covenant shows that even in his time the first covenant was becoming obsolete (8:13).[39] This second and better covenant, legally regulated through better promises, has now come (8:6), obviating the need for the old, imperfect priesthood and the law bound up with it (7:11).

Second, the author appeals to the biblical description of Israel's desert tabernacle to demonstrate that it required perfection through a later tabernacle. He first focuses on God's comment to Moses at several places in Exodus and Numbers to make the tabernacle and its furnishings "according to the pattern" he had shown him "on the mountain" (Heb. 8:5b; cf. Ex. 25:9, 39–40; Num. 8:4). Mention of a pattern that

36 Vanhoye, *Structure and Message*, 27–28.

37 The association of perfection with moral virtue was common in Stoicism. On this see Attridge, *Hebrews*, 84.

38 On this see esp., Lindars, *Theology of the Letter to the Hebrews*, 44–45.

39 Westcott, *Hebrews*, 227–28; Attridge, *Hebrews*, 229.

Moses should follow implies to the author the existence of a "true" tabernacle "in heaven" after which Moses' tabernacle was patterned (Heb. 8:2) and of which that tabernacle was a pale imitation (8:5a). Since Jesus is a high priest and has "sat down at the right hand of the Majesty in heaven" (8:1; cf. 1:3), the author reasons that his high priestly service must also be located in heaven and therefore in this "greater and more perfect tabernacle that is not man-made, that is to say, not a part of this creation" (9:11; cf. 4:14).

The author then focuses on the structure of the earthly tabernacle and explains that its two-part design corresponds to the two ages of God's dealings with his people: the present age and the age to come. He observes that the Mosaic tabernacle comprised two sections, a "first" or "outer" tent (9:2, 6, 8) and a "second" or "inner" tent (9:3, 6).[40] Priests commonly entered the first tent to preside over the daily sacrifices (9:6), but entry into the second tent, the author notes, was reserved for the high priest alone, and even he entered that most holy sanctuary (9:3, 8) only once yearly on the Day of Atonement (9:7).

The author takes these two parts of the earthy tabernacle as illustrations of the two parts of salvation history.[41] While the first tent still had some cultic standing, access to the place of atonement for sin was limited. This, says the author, symbolizes the inability of the sacrifices offered under the Mosaic system "to perfect [*teleioō*] the conscience of the worshiper" (9:9) and signals that some other, better means of atonement had to come. Christ, as high priest of "the greater and more perfect tabernacle" (9:11), supplied this perfect means of atonement.

For this "perfect" situation to materialize, however, God's royal Son and eschatological high priest had to die and, by his death, establish a new covenant. Playing on the ambiguity of the Greek term *diathēkē*, which is used in Jeremiah 31:31–34 (LXX 38:31–34) to mean "covenant" but can also mean "will," the author comments that for a will to take effect a death must take place (Heb. 9:16–21). Thus, when the first covenant was established, Moses sacrificed calves (9:19). When the second and final covenant was established, Christ had to die (9:15). He also had to die so that he might enter heaven where the greater and more perfect tabernacle is located (8:1–4; 9:12, 24–25; cf. 4:14) and so that he might have a sacrifice to offer in the true, heavenly tabernacle (8:3; 9:12; 9:26).

By the end of chapter 9, therefore, the author has made clear why Christ had to be perfected through suffering. His suffering was the only path by which he could become the final high priest who would offer the final and completely effective sacrifice of atonement for sin, thereby bringing the system of atonement provided in the Mosaic law to its divinely appointed end. This perfection through suffering, qualifying him to serve as high priest in the heavenly tabernacle and then to sit down at God's right hand in heaven, sets the high priestly work of Jesus apart from the provisional work of other, previous high priests.

40 The author uses the Greek term *skēnē* to refer both to the tabernacle in its entirety (8:5; 9:21) and to the two "tabernacles" of which it is composed (9:2, 6–8). To avoid confusion, I use "tabernacle" for the entire structure and "tent" for its two constituent parts.

41 Lane, *Hebrews 9–13*, 223.

Jesus Is the Source of Eternal Salvation (10:1–18)

The only one of the three elements mentioned in 5:9–10 that remains for the author to explain is how Jesus "became the source of eternal salvation for all who obey him." In the course of his discussion of Christ's perfection through suffering, the author has already introduced the main elements of his argument on this final point. He now turns to them in earnest with the claim that Christ will one day appear "to bring to salvation those who are waiting for him" (9:28).[42]

Salvation will be available on that final day because Christ's high priestly work of atonement was far more effective than that of the Levitical high priests. Their "gifts and sacrifices . . . were not able to clear the conscience of the worshiper" (9:9) and only provided outward cleansing (9:10, 23). As a result, they did not really cleanse those who worshiped or erase their guilt (10:2, 11). The author seems to have traced the inadequacy of these efforts at atonement to three causes, each of which, he says, Christ's sacrifice has remedied.

First, the Levitical priests who offered these sacrifices were themselves sinful. Because of their sinfulness, they had to make atonement first for their own sins before they could offer sacrifices to atone for the sins of the people (7:27). Christ, however, was sinless (7:27; 9:14), and his sacrifice involved the offering not of animals but of the holy, blameless, and pure priest himself (7:26–27; 9:12, 14, 23, 26; 10:5, 10).[43]

Second, the Levitical priests had to repeat their sacrifices again and again (9:25; 10:1–3, 11), and this indicates to the author the imperfection of their efforts. If such sacrifices had been effective, the author asks rhetorically, "would they not have stopped being offered?" (10:2). As it is, their repetition only serves to remind worshipers of the problem that sin presents without providing them with any solution for it (10:1, 3, 11). Christ, however, only sacrificed once (7:27; 9:12, 25–26, 28; 10:10, 12, 14). This one sacrifice was sufficient to perfect its beneficiaries forever (10:13) and to forgive their sins for all time (10:18).

Third, theirs were animal sacrifices—goats, calves, bulls, and heifers (9:12–13), and he believes that "it is impossible for the blood of bulls and goats to take away sins" (10:4). Why is this impossible? The author's answer to this question has two elements that are woven together in a complex relationship. One element is simply that the Scriptures prophesy the replacement of the Mosaic system of sacrifices with another system and so, the author reasons, this must mean that the previous system was inadequate for the completion of God's saving purposes. The author believes that two passages of Scripture show this: Jeremiah 31:31–34 (LXX 38:31–34) and Psalm 40:6–8 (LXX 39:7–9). In the first passage a new covenant replaces the first covenant; in the second, the willing, bodily sacrifice of God's king replaces the Mosaic system of sacrifices with which God is not pleased. God sets aside one system in order to replace it with the other, says the author (Heb. 10:9), and this implies that the first system was inadequate.

42 Vanhoye, *Structure and Message*, 27–29.

43 Why did Christ's sinlessness make his atoning work more effective than that of the Levitical high priests? The author does not explain, but he may have thought that it would be impossible for ordinary high priests to offer themselves in sacrifice since their offering would then be blemished. For reasons we will examine shortly, a willing human sacrifice was necessary to provide complete atonement for sin.

The other element of the author's answer uses both biblical passages to explore more deeply the reasons why the previous system was inadequate. The author seems to take Jeremiah 31:31–34 as support for his idea that animal sacrifices only provide cleansing for the flesh (Heb. 9:13–14; cf. 9:23), not the inner cleansing of the conscience necessary for full ransom from sin (9:15; cf. 10:2, 22). Under the new covenant, in contrast to the first covenant, God will both "remember the sins and lawless acts" of his people "no more" (10:17) and give them changed hearts and minds so that they may "serve the living God" (9:15; 10:16). In this new situation, therefore, there will be no need for the sacrifices mandated by the Mosaic law.

In the same way, Psalm 40:6–8 speaks of Christ's willing sacrifice of his body as the eschatological replacement of the Mosaic system of sacrifices (10:7, 9).[44] By the emphasis that the author places on the willingness of Christ's sacrifice, he sets up an implicit contrast between it and the external nature of the sacrifices under the Mosaic system.[45] As with his reading of Jeremiah 31:31–34, the author's reading of Psalm 40:6–8 implies that Christ's sacrifice is superior because it deals with interior rather than exterior concerns and therefore addresses the ultimate source of sin.

Summary

The author argues not only that Jesus is like the best Levitical high priests in his faithfulness to God and mercy toward sinners but that he is different from the Levitical high priests in three critical ways. He announces these differences in 5:9–10 and then explains them each in detail in 6:20b–7:28; 7:28–9:28; and 10:1–17.[46]

First, Jesus is a priest not in the order of Levi but in the order of Melchizedek. Unlike the Levitical priests who died, therefore, Jesus lives forever and is able to provide eternal salvation to his people.

Second, unlike the Levitical priests, Jesus' high priesthood was perfected through suffering. This enabled him to establish a new covenant, to enter heaven where he could sacrifice in the true tabernacle, and to offer himself there as a superior sacrifice.

Third, unlike the sacrifices of the Levitical priests, Jesus' high priestly service secured final and fully effective salvation for his people. It was able to do this because it was the sacrifice of God's willing and sinless King himself rather than of animals, and it was a one-time event intended to end sacrifice forever by cleansing the consciences of God's people. It therefore abolished the need for any further sacrifice.

Jesus' High Priesthood as the Means by Which He Leads Many Sons to Glory: A Summary

The author began his homily with an extended comparison between God's Son and the angels, a comparison that emphasized both the Son's elevation above the angels in his unique relationship with God (1:2–3, 5–14) and Jesus' identification

44 The author emphasizes this point by making the phrase "to do your will, O God" dependent on the verb "I have come" (*ēkō*) rather than, as in the LXX, on the verb "I have desired" (*eboulēthēn*). See Attridge, *Hebrews*, 274, and Lane, *Hebrews 9–13*, 263.

45 Cf. Attridge, *Hebrews*, 274.

46 As we have seen, however, he neither explains these points in the order that he lists them in 5:9–10, nor does he explain them in tightly defined units.

with the human condition through his incarnation (2:5–18). Because Jesus stood both above and below the angels, he could become the "leader" of human salvation, bringing many sons into the glory he shared with God by identifying with their human plight and conducting them out of it to heaven (2:10; 12:2).

It is precisely in his capacity as high priest that Jesus was able to do this (2:17). As a human high priest, he could identify with the human need for faithfulness in the midst of suffering (2:18) and could deal gently with those tempted by persecution to deviate from the path to God's glory (4:15–16; 5:2, 7–8). Through his death on the cross and subsequent resurrection and ascension, he proved to have an "indestructible life," and therefore God appointed him to be a high priest in the eternal order of Melchizedek (7:16–17, 24). This enabled his death to serve as his high priestly, Day of Atonement sacrifice, and enabled this sacrifice to take place in the heavenly sanctuary where God is present (9:11–12). By thus going through the heavens and into God's presence with his own sacrificial blood, Jesus has provided eternal forgiveness for human sins and therefore eternal access to God for God's people (6:19–20; 9:11–14; 10:19–24). His priesthood, therefore, has provided the means by which he can lead "many sons to glory" (2:10).

The completion of Jesus' priestly service in heaven through his death on the cross brought him back, full circle, to the proper position for God's royal Son: seated at God's right hand (1:3, 13; 8:1; 10:12; 12:2). From that position he continues to function as a merciful priest, who both helps sinners in their time of need and intercedes for them with God (4:16; 7:25). From that position he will one day "appear a second time, not to bear sin, but to bring salvation to those who are waiting for him" (9:28). At that time, faithful followers of Jesus will inherit the salvation he has secured for them (1:14).

THE PRACTICAL IMPLICATIONS OF BELIEF IN GOD'S CLIMACTIC REVELATION

The author of Hebrews has developed these complex theological ideas for pastoral reasons. All of them are designed to encourage his audience to remain faithful to their initial commitment to the message of salvation despite the prolonged oppression they have had to endure for it. Just as the author has focused on the eschatological superiority of the message of salvation to God's previous revelation in the Scriptures, so his exhortations describe how the new eschatological situation of Christians should encourage them to remain faithful.

On this eschatological foundation, the author builds three kinds of admonitions. First, he says that if God's previous, provisional revelation of himself in the Mosaic law demanded a measure of faithfulness, then his final revelation of himself through his Son demands faithfulness in even greater measure. Second, he argues that his audience should follow the examples of Jesus, Moses, Abraham, and many others throughout redemptive history who have been faithful to God despite the invisible nature of God's being and purpose and despite the hardship that their faithfulness entailed. Third, he argues that they should avoid following the example of unfaithful Israel during its period of wilderness wandering when they rebelled against God and so failed to reach their destination of God's eschatological "rest."

Faithfulness under the Mosaic Law Implies Even Greater Faithfulness in the Era of Salvation

Near the beginning and end of his homily, the author draws a comparison between the Mosaic law and the message of salvation spoken by Jesus. The comparison assumes a positive stance toward the Mosaic law but also suggests that the message of salvation through Jesus has transformed this law. Rather than something that dictates the conduct of God's people, it has now become a witness to God's latest and final revelation of himself in his Son.

In 2:1–4, the author assumes, along with other first-century Jews, that God used angels to give the law to Moses, who then gave it to the people.[47] That law, he says, was firm and exact in handing out just punishments for all transgressions. The message of salvation through Jesus has some formal correspondence to this law handed down through the angels—it is also firmly established, having been confirmed both by the witness of Jesus' followers and, like the Mosaic law (Num. 14:11), by astonishing signs of God's power.

Nevertheless, the message of salvation that comes through Jesus is far greater. As the author has just argued (1:4–14), Jesus is superior to the angels—they are mere servants, created, like wind and fire, to do God's bidding—but Jesus is God's royal Son and agent in creation who receives the angels' worship. The message of salvation that in these last days has come through God's Son is correspondingly greater than the Mosaic law. If it is greater, the author implies, then it demands even more careful attention than the Mosaic law demanded, and those who ignore it will not be able to escape eschatological punishment.

In 12:18–29, the author's exhortation to persevere in God's grace follows the same strategy. He first describes the terror-inspiring scene at Mount Sinai when God gave the law to his people (12:18–21). The mountain was made so holy by God's presence that even an animal that touched it had to die, and it was swathed in darkness, gloom, storm, and fire. Trumpet blasts could be heard, and the command not to touch the mountain was so fearsome to the people that they "begged that no further word be spoken to them." Even Moses trembled with fear.[48] Again, the author wants his audience to see a formal correspondence between this scene and the eschatological scene that comes at the end of the Christian pilgrimage. Both feature God's fiery presence, a mountain, a covenant made with blood, a warning, and the human response of "reverence and awe."

47 See, e.g., Deut 33:2, LXX; Ps. 68:17; *Jub.* 1.27–2.1; Acts 7:30, 38, 53; Gal. 3:19; and the comments of Lane, *Hebrews 1–8*, 37; Attridge, *Hebrews*, 65 n. 28; and Weiss, *Hebräer*, 185 n. 13. Weiss correctly rejects the idea that the angels of 2:2 are to be identified with the prophets of 1:1.

48 Cf. Exod. 19:12–13, 16–22; 20:18–21; Deut. 4:11–12; 5:22–27; 9:19.

Here too, however, the eschatological reality is far superior to its predecessor (12:22–29). In place of the fear that Mount Sinai inspired in God's people, repelling them by its holiness, Mount Zion is an inviting place of joy where "the spirits of righteous [people] made perfect" assemble at the end of their pilgrimage. In place of the accusing blood of Abel is the forgiveness that comes through the blood of Jesus, the mediator of the prophesied new covenant in which God will forgive the wickedness of his people and remember their sins no more (8:12; 10:17). This forgiveness makes the joyful experience of the presence of God possible. In place of a shakable earthly world, God provides "a kingdom that cannot be shaken" (12:28).

As in 2:1–4, so here, the author draws from the eschatological privileges that his readers will inherit the conclusion that they should be much more faithful to the salvation God has provided them: "If they did not escape when they refused him who warned them on earth, how much less will we, if we turn away from him who warns us from heaven?" (12:25b; cf. 2:2–3)[49] The author finds both the similarities and the differences between his audience's situation under the new covenant and their spiritual ancestors' situation under the first covenant to be significant. Like their ancestors, they have received a revelation from God, and as in their situation, that revelation calls for obedience and includes sanctions against those who disobey. Unlike their ancestors' revelation, however, God's revelation to them is his final and saving word. To ignore it is to incur a correspondingly final condemnation.

The difficult exhortations at the beginning and end of the homily's great central section on Jesus' high priesthood (5:11–6:12; 10:19–39) should be understood within the context of this same strategy. As we have seen, the burden of this section is the argument that Jesus is the perfect high priest who offers the perfect sacrifice in the holiest part of the perfect, heavenly sanctuary. He has shown all the Mosaic provisions for atonement to be copies (8:5; 9:23–24) and shadows (8:5; 10:1) of these realities.[50] Jesus has made atonement for sin in such a perfect way that no further atonement is ever necessary.

To turn one's back on this is, correspondingly, an act of ultimate rejection of God's provision for salvation. The author says at the beginning of his argument that Jesus is the perfect high priest and that it is impossible for those who have participated in the eschatological blessings of God's people to repent again if they fall away (6:4–6; cf. 12:16b–17). He concludes his argument with an equally sobering word of warning that if the Mosaic law punished those who rejected it without mercy, those who deliberately continue to sin after receiving "the knowledge of the truth" can only expect to face the eschatological judgment of "raging fire that will consume the enemies of God" (10:26–27).[51]

49 Many commentators note the similarity between 2:2–3 and 12:25b. See, e.g., Bruce, *Hebrews*, 363; deSilva, *Perseverance*, 470; Weiss, *Hebräer*, 685; and esp. Lane, *Hebrews 9–13*, 477.

50 The language is Platonic, but, as Lindars, *Theology of the Letter to the Hebrews*, 51, observes, "the idea is strictly temporal in accordance with Jewish and Christian eschatology." This is clear, Lindars says, from the eschatological notion of perfection that is developed in the homily.

51 The Greek phrase describing those who "deliberately continue to sin" is *hekousiōs. . .hamartanontōn*. The term *ekousiōs* is an adverb that describes an action as undertaken "willingly . . . without compulsion . . . deliberately, intentionally" (BDAG, 307), and the term *hamartanontōn* is a present participle, indicating action that persists. Together, the two terms speak of a deliberate choice to live one's life in a sinful manner.

These warnings have created much consternation among interpreters of Hebrews down through the centuries for two reasons. First, some have understood them to mean that for a Christian to commit any "mortal" sin brings eternal damnation. Many in the first centuries of the church thought this. Tertullian, for example, quoted Hebrews 6:4–8 to support his notion that there was no second repentance for the Christian who became an "adulterer and fornicator" (*Pud.* 20.3–5). Speaking of the author of Hebrews, he says, "He who learnt from the apostles and taught with the apostles never knew any second repentance promised by the apostles to the adulterer and fornicator."[52] Some modern commentators believe that this is basically a correct understanding of the passage.[53]

Second, among those who believe that this passage refers to apostasy rather than to particular "mortal" sins, the worries still linger. Does it imply that an authentic member of God's people, in whom God's Spirit has done a transforming work, can still turn from the faith and be eternally condemned? Some claim that the passage implies this.[54] Others claim that the enlightened, who have tasted the gift of heaven, shared in the Holy Spirit, and experienced the benefits of God's word and work (6:4–5) never were genuine Christians.[55]

These passages, however, do not speak directly to either of these issues. The author is concerned not with certain "mortal" sins but with the one sin of apostasy from the faith. This is clear from the author's talk in the first passage of falling away from various experiences that attend membership in the people of God (6:4–5). It is equally clear in the second passage when the author speaks of those who abandon the general meeting of believers (10:25) and trample the "Son of God under foot" (10:29). These are descriptions of people who have chosen to leave behind their initial commitment to the message of salvation.

Moreover, the author does not have the harsh approach to sinners that commentators sometimes attribute to him on the basis of these passages alone.[56] He is not surprised that the Mosaic high priests had to offer sacrifices for their own sin (5:3; 7:27), and he is fully aware of human frailty (2:14–18; 4:15). It is precisely the tendency for Christians to sin that makes so valuable Jesus' ability, as a fellow human being, to identify with "those who are ignorant and are going astray" (5:2). It is this same tendency that makes the continuing intercession of Christ on their behalf so valuable (4:16; 7:25).[57]

Were these people "saved" in the first place? Since the author speaks of salvation as a future experience toward which all believers are traveling on the pilgrim way,

52 This quotation comes from Lindars, *Theology of the Letter to the Hebrews*, 69, who points out that the phrase "he who learnt from the apostles and taught with the apostles" is an echo of Heb. 2:3. It might be added that the references to adultery and fornication echo 12:16 and 13:4. Cf. the review of patristic attitudes toward repentance after baptism in Philip E. Hughes, *A Commentary on the Epistle to the Hebrews* (Grand Rapids: Eerdmans, 1977), 214–15.

53 Hugh Montefiore, *A Commentary on the Epistle to the Hebrews* (BNTC; London: Adam & Charles Black, 1964), 107–10.

54 See, e.g., Paul Ellingworth, *The Epistle to the Hebrews* (Epworth Commentaries; London: Epworth, 1991), 47. Cf. idem, *The Epistle to the Hebrews: A Commentary on the Greek Text* (NIGTC; Grand Rapids: Eerdmans, 1993), 317–25.

55 See, e.g., Hughes, *Hebrews*, 206–22.

56 Both Montefiore, *Hebrews*, 108, and Ellingworth, *Hebrews* (Epworth edition), 47, compare the supposed harshness of the author unfavorably with Paul's gentler approach to sinners.

57 Cf. Lindars, *Theology of the Letter to the Hebrews*, 60–61.

this question is not in his field of vision.[58] He is simply concerned to warn his audience against turning back or turning aside from the path that leads to Mount Zion and to the heavenly Jerusalem. To do so—especially if it involves turning back to the temporary and now obsolete provisions for approaching God found in the sacrificial ritual of the Mosaic law—is to abandon God's final and perfect means of atonement for sin.[59] It is to refuse the forgiveness that God has graciously offered through the atoning death of his Son and therefore to experience the condemnation of all those who, in God's eschatological court, have refused the offer of his mercy.

Following the Example of Faithful Pilgrims toward the Eschatological Zion

The author depicts Christian existence in the present as a pilgrimage toward an eschatological destination. He uses six images to describe this destination: the rest into which God entered on the seventh day of creation (4:3b–11), the presence of God (7:19, 25; 12:23), a city (11:10, 16; 13:14)—identified as the heavenly Jerusalem (12:22), a better, heavenly country (11:14–16), the goal post at the end of a foot race (12:1), and Mount Zion—the hill in Jerusalem on which the temple was located (12:22).[60] Most of these images are traditional symbols for the future existence of God's people in a recreated world.[61]

The journey toward this future existence is fraught with peril. The author's audience can drift from the right direction of travel, like a ship whose anchor fails to hold (2:1). They can give up the journey and fall short of their goal (4:1). They can become lazy (6:12; cf. 5:11). They may swerve from the path (10:23). Encumbrances can weigh them down or trip them up (12:1). Their path can grow rough, their arms tired, and their knees lame (12:12–13). They may grow ashamed of their leader as their journey with him outside society's boundaries brings them into disgrace (13:13).

In light of these dangers, the author urges his audience to follow the example of those who have made the journey before them, or, in one case, to avoid the example of a group who fell short of the eschatological goal. "We do not want you to become lazy," he tells his audience, "but to imitate those who through faith and patience inherit what has been promised" (6:12).

Jesus himself is the most important example of faithfulness in the pilgrim journey. God used suffering to perfect him in his role as high priest (2:10, 17; 5:8–9), and his suffering was great, as his "loud cries and tears to the one who could save him from death" (5:7) reveal. Like the author's readers, who know the "reproach" (*oneidismos*) of society (10:33), Jesus bore "disgrace" (*oneidismos*, 13:13; cf. 12:2) when he died on the cross. He was, nevertheless, faithful in his suffering and so

58 On this see Thomas R. Schreiner and Ardel B. Caneday, *The Race Set Before Us: A Biblical Theology of Perseverance and Assurance* (Downers Grove, Ill.: InterVarsity Press, 2001), 193–204.

59 Cf. Lane, *Hebrews 1–8*, 142.

60 Ernst Käsemann, *The Wandering People of God: An Investigation of the Letter to the Hebrews* (Minneapolis: Augsburg, 1984; orig. ed., 1939), 23, observes that the many verbs of motion in 10:19–13:25 also betray the importance of this motif.

61 For the notion of eschatological rest, see, e.g., *T. Dan.* 5:12; *1 En.* 45.3; of the heavenly Jerusalem, e.g., *2 Bar.* 4.1–7; *4 Ezra* 7.26; 8.52 (which also mentions "rest" in Paradise); of the eschatological Zion, e.g., Joel 3:16–17; *Jub.* 1.28. For these and other references, see Attridge, *Hebrews*, 126 n. 52, 324 n. 38; and 374 n. 50.

entered the joy of God's presence (12:2). His faithful suffering has opened the way for us also to enter God's presence and, at the completion of our own course, to participate in the joyful assembly of angels and "righteous people made perfect" (12:23).

Jesus therefore becomes the "leader" of a pilgrim people whom he brings to glory (2:10), fulfilling God's purpose for his human creatures (2:5–8).[62] Because of this, the author's readers must "fix" their gaze on Jesus, the "leader and perfecter" (aut.) of their faith. In the midst of the ostracism they experience for their commitment, they must follow his example of faithfulness (12:2–3). If they remain faithful on their pilgrimage, as he was on his, they will, like him, experience the joy of God's presence.

Other figures from redemptive history also provide examples of faith (10:39; 11:1) and endurance (10:36; 12:1).[63] Moses and Abraham are the most important of these examples. Although Jesus was greater than Moses, just as the builder of a house is greater than the house itself, "Moses" was, nevertheless, "a faithful servant in all God's house" (3:3, 5). His faithfulness was revealed when he left the physical comfort and social prestige of his position in Pharaoh's family to identify with God's people despite their "disgrace" (*oneidismos*, 11:24–26a). He did this in response not to anything visible in the present, moreover, but in obedience to an invisible God and in view of a future reward (11:26b–27). Although he could see neither his reward nor the God who promised it, he was willing to endure hardship because he was sure that his hope was not misplaced (11:1).

Abraham's life also had this quality. He trusted that God would be faithful to his promises although he could not see how, humanly speaking, this could happen. Thus, although he and Sarah were too old to have children, Abraham believed that God would fulfill his promise to give him many descendants, and so he waited patiently for God to give him a child (6:13–15; 11:11–12).[64] In the same way, he made preparations to sacrifice the child that God had given him in obedience to God's command, believing that God would raise the child from the dead if necessary to fulfill his promise (11:17–19).

Abraham maintained this faith in God, moreover, despite the hardship it entailed. He obeyed the call of God to leave his homeland although he had no clear vision of his destination (11:8) and lived as a wanderer and alien because he "was looking forward to the city with foundations, whose architect and builder is God" (11:9–10; cf. 11:13–16). Like Moses, he was certain that this hope would not be disappointed, although he could not see how God would make it real (11:1). As a result of this certainty, he was willing to endure the hardship of social ostracism—to be "a stranger in a foreign country."

62 For the connection between Jesus suffering, the suffering of his followers, and his role as "leader" in Hebrews, see Weiss, *Hebräer*, 209–11.

63 "Endurance" (*hypomonē*) and "faith" (*pistis*) are the two themes of 11:1–12:13. Following his normal procedure, the author announces his new subjects at the end of the previous section (10:36–39), and then takes them up in reverse order ("faith" in 11:1–40 and "endurance" in 12:1–13). On this, see Vanhoye, *Structure and Message*, 29–30, and Lane, *Hebrews 9–13*, 312–14.

64 Lane, *Hebrews 9–13*, 315, notes perceptively that the author's reference to Abraham in 6:13–15 foreshadows the review of faithful witnesses in 11:1–40.

Jesus, Moses, and Abraham are only the most important examples of faithfulness in a long list of faithful figures throughout redemptive history. The author devotes a sizeable section of his homily to a review of these exemplary members of God's society. He briefly tells the stories of Abel, Enoch, Noah, Isaac, Jacob, Joseph, Moses' parents, the people of Israel during the Exodus and Conquest, and Rahab (11:4–7, 20–23, 29–31), stressing the faithfulness of each. He makes clear to his audience that he could also tell other, similar stories (11:32–38). These people too responded in obedience to the call of one they could not see. They also often endured hardship, including society's rejection, in order to be faithful.

With "such a great a cloud of witnesses" surrounding them (12:1), the author's readers should also be willing to cast off sin and endure the hardship of society's reproach as they make their way toward the joyful assembly at Mount Zion in the heavenly Jerusalem. Although they cannot see either God or the outcome of his promises to them in any concrete sense, they can see Jesus (2:9; 12:2), and this puts them at an advantage over the faithful elders of ancient times (11:39–40). They should, therefore, look back to the faithful figures of biblical history and look ahead to Jesus their leader. Following those examples, they can endure their present hardship as they continue their journey toward the city with foundations, whose builder and maker is God.

Heeding the Warning of Those Who Failed to Enter God's Eschatological Rest

The author also presents to his audience the negative example of Israel's wilderness generation as a warning of what can happen to those who set out on the pilgrimage toward the presence of God but whose hearts become unbelieving and rebellious along the way. His warning takes the form of an exegesis of Psalm 95:7b–11 (LXX 94:7b–11), which, in the author's view, alludes to Genesis 2:2 and Numbers 13:1–14:45.[65] The logic of the argument depends on the author's understanding of Psalm 95:7b–11 as cited in Hebrew 3:7—11:

> So, as the Holy Spirit says:
>
> "Today, if you hear his voice,
>   do not harden your hearts
> as you did in the rebellion,
>   during the time of testing in the desert,
> where your fathers tested and tried me
>   and for forty years saw what I did.

65 The author quotes Gen. 2:2 in his exegesis of Ps. 95:7b–11. His connection of this psalm with Num. 13:1–14:45 is less obvious but is implied in his reference to the unbelief of the wilderness generation (Num. 14:11) and his mention that the Israelites' bodies "fell" in the "desert" (Num. 14:29, 32–33). The Hebrew text of Ps. 95:8 refers to Massah ("dispute") and Meribah ("testing"), the names given to the place where Israel quarreled with Moses about a lack of water in Ex. 17:1–7 (cf. Num. 20:2–13, where only the name Meribah appears). In Ps. 95:11, however, the MT also echoes the reference in Num. 14:20–23, 28–35 to God's oath that this generation of Israelites would not enter Canaan. On this, see Lane, *Hebrews 1–8*, 85.

That is why I was angry with that generation,
and I said, 'Their hearts are always going astray,
and they have not known my ways.'
So I declared on oath in my anger,
'They shall never enter my rest.'"

The author accepts the LXX's ascription of this psalm to David and draws several conclusions from the date for the psalm that this attribution implies. First, this psalm's last line, "They shall never enter my rest" implies that God was at "rest" at the time David wrote the psalm and presumably is still at rest. The author reasons that this "rest" of God must refer to his Sabbath rest, which, according to Genesis 2:2, he entered after his six days of creative activity (Heb. 4:3–4).

Second, the author concludes from the middle section of his text that the wilderness generation of Israelites were on a pilgrimage toward this eschatological presence of God when their progress was interrupted and they failed to reach their goal (Heb. 4:6b).

Third, the author takes David's admonition to those in his own day ("today") to mean that even the subsequent generation of Israelites who did enter Canaan under Joshua did not, by their arrival there, enter God's eschatological rest. If they had, then David would not have spoken in his own, later time as if God's people had not yet entered his rest (4:7–8). The author deduces from this that "there remains . . . a Sabbath-rest for the people of God" (4:9) and that "we who have believed are entering that rest" (4:3, aut.; cf. 4:6a).

These three premises lay the foundation for the author's primary point. He observes that according to Psalm 95, which itself summarizes Numbers 13:1–14:45, the Israelites failed to enter God's rest because of their sinful, unbelieving, and hardened hearts (Heb. 3:12–13, 17, 19). They failed to trust God's ability to lead them to victory over the Canaanites and wanted instead to stone Moses, Aaron, Joshua, and Caleb, choose a leader of their own, and go back to Egypt (Num. 13:26–14:10). As a result, God declared with an oath that they would not enter his rest (Heb. 3:11; 4:3, 5; cf. Ps. 95:11 (94:11 in LXX); their bodies would fall in the desert (Heb. 3:17; Num. 14:32–33).

This condemned wilderness generation, the author says, stands parallel in important ways to his audience. They heard the gospel message (Heb. 4:2), just as the author and his audience heard it in its most recent edition from the followers of Jesus (2:1, 3b–4). They were on a pilgrimage toward the Sabbath rest of God, just as those "who have believed are entering that rest" (4:3). The author does not say so explicitly, but he probably assumes that his audience will remember that the Israelites faced battle with a large foe (Num. 13:31–33), just as the author's audience forms a disenfranchised and persecuted minority in their own society (Heb. 10:32–35; 13:13).[66]

66 From the author's detailed exegesis of Num. 13:1–14:45, Lane, *Hebrews 1–8*, 90, concludes that "the writer had the Book of Numbers opened before him when he composed this section of the sermon."

In light of this similar situation, it is critical for the author's audience not to imitate the disobedience of the earlier generation of God's people. Ancient Israel lost its courage, failed to trust God, and abandoned its pilgrimage toward his Sabbath rest. The author's audience, in contrast, must "hold on to" its "courage" and its "hope" (3:6b). "Let us, therefore, make every effort to enter that rest," he says, "so that no one will fall by following their example of disobedience" (4:11).[67]

In summary, the wilderness generation should serve as a cautionary example of what happens to those who begin the pilgrimage toward the eschatological presence of God but who, through fear of hardship, decide to return to the land of slavery from which they have come. Those who turn back from the path that the leader Jesus has cut through the heavens and into the presence of God (4:14) will, like Israel's wilderness generation, face God's judgment.

JESUS AS THE LEADER AND PERFECTER OF CHRISTIAN FAITH

The author of Hebrews has probably written his homily to encourage a group of Christians not to seek refuge from persecution in the synagogue's shadow and copy of Christian faith. To do this would be to make a prodigious error in time-keeping. It would turn the clock back from atonement itself to the blueprint for atonement found in the Mosaic law. It would be to come within sight of the heavenly Jerusalem and Mount Zion but then turn back and retrace one's steps to a place where no atonement for sin can be found.

Jesus, says the author, is God's final revelation, the one who brings coherence to the diverse and piecemeal witness of Israel's Scriptures. He stands both above the angels with God and below the angels with humanity. He is, therefore, able to function as the leader of the faith—the one who clears the path that leads from humanity to the presence of God. In this role, he leads "many sons to glory." He is able to do this as the perfect high priest, whose human suffering has allowed him to become the example of faithfulness to the many sons who follow him, to sympathize with them in their persecution, and to serve as their perfect atoning sacrifice.

The pressures that society has placed on the author's audience for their unpopular commitment to this message of salvation has caused some among them to ponder whether the eschatological reward at the end of their pilgrimage is worth the suffering that the journey entails. The author not only warns them of the dangers of giving up the journey, but he places before them a compelling description of the eschatological joy that awaits them at journey's end and an attractive portrait of Jesus as the merciful and faithful high priest who has opened for them the way into God's presence.

67 This statement calls into question the conclusion of Lane, *Hebrews 1–8*, 99, that in the author's view believers presently enjoy God's rest. Instead, the author seems to depict believers as engaged in an often difficult pilgrimage toward the eschatological rest of God. The verb *eiserchometha* ("we are entering") in 4:3, on which Lane bases his view, is a progressive present (on which, see Daniel B. Wallace, *GGBB*, 518–19) indicating that the action is not yet completed but is ongoing. Cf. Attridge, *Hebrews*, 126, and the perceptive discussion of deSilva, *Perseverance*, 153–56.

Chapter 32

REVELATION: MEANING AMID OPPRESSION

Revelation is the source of endless puzzlement among students of the New Testament—"the paradise of fanatics and sectarians," according to one erudite interpreter.[1] Even established scholars, however, show signs of confusion. One insists that John wrote to stir up Christian discontent with Rome during peaceful times for the church.[2] Another says that John wrote to persecuted and embattled Christians.[3] Still another believes that the book contains secret teachings of the historical Jesus so radical that they sparked the Jewish revolt against Rome in A.D. 66–70.[4] Perhaps most unusual of all is the view that Revelation explains current first-century events by describing the movements of stars and comets.[5] It seems safe to say that the book's complex literary structure and unusually rich symbolism have made it something of a Rorschach blot on which both lay and professional readers have freely exercised their imaginations.

This state of affairs has often led Christians to avoid the book altogether or to approach it with a sense of despair. Many would agree with Luther's assessment:

> They are supposed to be blessed who keep what is written in this book; and yet no one knows what that is, to say nothing of keeping it. This is just the same as if we did not have the book at all.[6]

When we place the book in its first-century context in Roman Asia, however, and when its rich network of biblical allusions is given appropriate weight, its basic message emerges with surprising clarity. John wrote to Christians who were suffering under the heavy hand of Roman imperial authority. At least one member of the churches to which he wrote had died and others were impoverished. Perhaps everyone was tempted to listen to those who advised keeping a low profile and compromising when necessary.

Into this situation John introduces his prophetic vision from the throne room of God. From the perspective of God's throne, Rome is far from the divine and eternal

1 G. B. Caird, *A Commentary on the Revelation of St. John the Divine* (HNTC; New York: Harper & Row, 1966), 2.

2 Leonard L. Thompson, *The Book of Revelation: Apocalypse and Empire* (New York: Oxford, 1990), 171–85. Cf. Richard Bauckham, *The Theology of the Book of Revelation* (New Testament Theology; Cambridge: Cambridge Univ. Press, 1993), 4, 15; idem, *The Climax of Prophecy: Studies on the Book of Revelation* (Edinburgh: T. & T. Clark, 1993), 349–50.

3 Helmut Koester, *Introduction to the New Testament*, 2 vols. (Berlin: Walter de Gruyter, 1982), 2:248–57.

4 Margaret Barker, *The Revelation of Jesus Christ Which God Gave to Him to Show to His Servants What Must Soon Take Place (Revelation 1.1)* (Edinburgh: T. & T. Clark, 2000).

5 Bruce J. Malina, *On the Genre and Message of Revelation: Star Visions and Sky Journeys* (Peabody, Mass.: Hendrickson, 1995).

6 "Preface to the Revelation of St. John [I]" (1522), in *LW*, 35:398–99. Luther is alluding to Rev. 22:7: "Blessed is the one who keeps the words of the prophecy of this book." Luther assessed the book more positively in his 1530 preface, but he was still uncertain of its meaning.

power that it claimed to be in all the glittering pomp it exhibited on the many festal days that dotted the ancient Asian calendar. Rome is a prostitute and a satanically inspired beast. Its destiny is a lake of fire.

John insists that no compromise with this beast is possible and that the suffering through which God's people must pass at the hands of the beast is both laden with meaning and limited. Those who faithfully endure the hardship that their refusal to compromise imposes on them will become citizens of a new and truly eternal city, where they will live forever in the presence of God.

In this chapter we will first place Revelation and the seven messages with which it opens into their first-century setting. We will then examine the two primary sections of John's throne vision, one organized around a series of three sets of judgments and the other organized around two cities—one a beast and a prostitute and the other the place where God and humankind dwell together.

REVELATION IN ITS FIRST-CENTURY SETTING

Roman Empire and Religion in the First and Early Second Centuries

By the first century A.D., Rome had conquered a multitude of ethnic groups from Britain in the north to North Africa in the south and from Spain in the west to the border of Parthia in the east. Rome in its imperial period provided many benefactions for its subject peoples. If the sentiments of the provincial assembly of Asia in 9 B.C. signal the feelings of other subject peoples, many were grateful to the Roman emperor for purging the high seas of pirates and providing a period of peace that led to economic prosperity for the region.[7]

Ultimately, however, Rome's rule over the diverse ethnic groups that comprised its extensive empire was conducted not for the advantage of the groups themselves but for the economic advantage of Rome's elite social classes. First-century moralists, themselves members of Rome's elite, sometimes wrung their hands over these excesses. Petronius Arbiter, writing in the late first century, has his fictional character Eumolpus describe the situation this way:

> The conquering Roman now held the whole world, sea and land and the course of sun and moon. But he was not satisfied. Now the waters were stirred and troubled by his loaded ships; if there were any hidden bay beyond, or any land that promised a yield of yellow gold, that place was Rome's enemy, fate stood ready for the sorrows of war, and the quest for wealth went on. There was no happiness in familiar joys, or in pleasures dulled by the common man's use. The soldier out at sea would praise the bronze of Corinth; bright colours dug from the earth rivaled the purple; here the African curses Rome, here the Chinaman

7 S. R. F. Price, *Rituals and Power: The Roman Imperial Cult in Asia Minor* (Cambridge: Cambridge Univ. Press, 1984), 54–57. The provincial assembly of Asia issued a statement in 9 B.C. that described Augustus as, among other things, "a savior who put an end to war and established all things." As Price points out, these were genuine expressions of gratitude. Such expressions became less glowing as emperor succeeded emperor, but, Price argues, this is due to a predictable "routinization" of the emperor cult after Augustus rather than any necessary loss of the sentiment behind it.

> plunders his marvellous silks, and the Arabian hordes have stripped their own fields bare. (*Sat.* 119)[8]

The late first-century British chieftain Calgacus, at least as Tacitus imagines him speaking, is even less sanguine:

> Harriers of the world, now that earth fails their all-devastating hands, they probe even the sea: if their enemy have wealth, they have greed; if he be poor, they are ambitious; East nor West has glutted them; alone of mankind they behold with the same passion of concupiscence waste alike and want. To plunder, butcher, steal, these things they misname empire: they make a desolation and they call it peace. (*Agr.* 30)[9]

Although there is evidence that the level of ostentation in the lifestyle of Rome's upper classes waxed and waned in the first century, even under the best circumstances the self-serving nature of Rome's imperialism remained in place.[10]

To maintain its advantageous position of power over its subject peoples, Rome used, among other strategies, a combination of military strength, promotion of the idea that its hegemony was divinely sanctioned, and selective granting of privileges to indigenous supporters. Roman officials and the Roman army were placed across the empire to ensure that any disturbance of the *pax Romana* would meet a swift and violent response. With them went traditional Roman religion. The military observed a standard form of the Roman religious calendar wherever in the world it was posted, just as that calendar was observed in Rome itself.

Sacrifices marked major Roman festivals, and the calendar called for celebrations on the birthdays of deified emperors. On January 3, Rome worshiped its traditional gods Jupiter, Juno, and Minerva, and the army, wherever it found itself in the world, vowed its support of the emperor's well-being and pledged the eternal existence of the Roman empire.[11] The army brought with it specialists in Roman sacrificial practice, who knew the traditional method of slaughtering sacrificial victims and the customary method of reading the omens supposedly provided by the victim's entrails.[12]

Since Asia was a proconsular rather than an imperial province, the army was not present there in large numbers, but Roman provincial governors also vigorously promoted traditional Roman religion in their conquered territories.[13] They too retained

8 Cf., e.g., Lucan 9.426–430; Seneca, *Ep.* 87.41; Tacitus, *Ann.* 3.53–54. I am grateful to Bauckham, *Climax of Prophecy*, 367–68, for bringing these passages and the passage in Petronius to my attention.

9 I am grateful to David A. deSilva, *The Hope of Glory: Honor Discourse and New Testament Interpretation* (Collegeville, Minn.: Liturgical, 1999), 201 n. 22, for bringing this passage to my attention.

10 For Tiberius's encouragement of restraint in Rome and its effects, see Tacitus, *Ann.* 3.53–55.

11 Mary Beard, John North, and Simon Price, *Religions of Rome*, 2 vols. (Cambridge: Cambridge Univ. Press, 1998), 1:325–26. See also idem, 2:71–74, 87–88, where a religious calendar for the military stationed at Dura Europas from the third century A.D. can be compared with a Roman religious calendar from the grove of the Arval brothers that dates to the late first century A.D. The two calendars are similar.

12 Ibid., 1:326–27.

13 From the time of Augustus, Asia was considered a senatorial province, governed by a proconsul who was theoretically chosen by the senate, although under the Flavians there was a tendency to bring this wealthy province more and more under imperial control. The Roman army tended to be concentrated in imperial provinces, governed by legates who were given command of the legions quartered in their territory. Even in senatorial provinces, however, the military had a small "police" presence. On this "police"

specialists in Roman sacrifice on their staffs.[14] The local population that they governed was required, probably through the regular assembly of their representatives, to perform a sacrificial ritual that indicated their loyalty to the Roman emperor.[15]

The Romans also often insisted on certain changes in the religious customs of conquered peoples: They sometimes required local deities to take Roman names in addition to their traditional names; they sometimes placed a traditional Roman god, like Jupiter, in the indigenous pantheon; they often revised the structure of the priesthood in territories where the priest had political power.[16] The purpose of all this could hardly have been in doubt among those whose indigenous religious customs the Romans changed: The gods themselves had determined that Rome should rule over its empire forever.

Two specific cultic expressions of loyalty to Rome were of particular importance for advancing this message. First was the link that Rome encouraged in various ways between certain emperors and the gods. The senate declared certain deserving, deceased emperors to be gods by a vote. Rome then encouraged the worship of these former emperors along with Rome's other gods both in Rome and throughout the empire. Rome even connected the living emperor with the divine in various ways, and often, especially in the Greek east, subject peoples worshiped him as a god.

Second, Rome also encouraged cults devoted to Roma—the personification of the city of Rome as a goddess. There is no evidence that this cult was practiced in Rome itself before the early second century A.D., but it was widely practiced throughout the empire from the early second century B.C., and its popularity in the provinces increased as Rome's power spread outward.[17] It was especially popular in the province of Asia, where it was established as early as 195 B.C. in Smyrna and by A.D. 29 in Pergamum.[18] We do not know why the cult was so common in the Greek east, but it seems safe to say that it was linked in the minds of those who participated in it with the notion that Rome's rule over its many subject peoples was divinely sanctioned.[19]

For people who lived in Rome's provinces, lending religious support to the notion that Rome's authority was divinely decreed could carry with it enormous economic, social, and political advantages.[20] Cities in Asia competed energetically with one another for the privilege of erecting a temple to the emperor within their boundaries. A city granted this permission from the senate took on a status above other cities in

force, see John Richardson, "Governing Rome," in *The World of Rome: An Introduction to Roman Culture*. ed. Peter Jones and Keith Sidwell (Cambridge: Cambridge Univ. Press, 1997), 112–39, here at 135. On Flavian control of Asia, see David Magie, *Roman Rule in Asia Minor to the End of the Third Century after Christ*, 2 vols. (Princeton, N.J.: Princeton Univ. Press, 1950), 1:566–69.

14 Beard, North, and Price, *Religions of Rome*, 1:320.

15 Ibid.

16 Ibid., 1:339–40, 345–46. Cf. Peter Garnsey, "Religious Toleration in Classical Antiquity," in *Persecution and Toleration*, ed. W. J. Sheils (Studies in Church History 21; Oxford: Blackwell, 1984), 1–27, here at 6–7, who describes the Roman practice of *evocatio*. In this ritual, the gods of a city under Roman siege were called out of the city they supposedly protected and offered worship of the same or better quality among the Romans.

17 Beard, North, and Price, *Religions of Rome*, 1:160.

18 Ibid., 1:158–59.

19 Beard, North, and Price speculate that perhaps the cult of Roma offered a way of honoring Rome without having to establish a new cult every time one of the many emperors that reigned in rapid succession during this period ascended the throne. See ibid., 1:160.

20 Ibid., 1:352, 358–59, 362. See also Price, *Rituals and Power*, 62–65.

the area.[21] Influential and wealthy provincials eagerly sought to be priests of these imperial cults and often found this office to be a stepping-stone to more important and prestigious positions.[22] Not surprisingly, epigraphic evidence reveals that the social elites in particular locations were more supportive of Roman religious innovations and practices than the lower classes.[23]

From the time of Augustus, cultic veneration of the emperor formed an important expression of the unity of the empire under Rome's hegemony and benefactions.[24] Imperial festivals were frequent and were important, city-wide events, as this first-century decree of the provincial assembly of Asia reveals:

> Since one should each year make clear display of one's piety and of all holy, fitting intentions towards the imperial house, the choir of all Asia, gathering at Pergamum on the most holy birthday of Sebastos Tiberius Caesar god, performs a task that contributes greatly to the glory of Sebastos in hymning the imperial house and performing sacrifices to the Sebastan gods and conducting festivals and feasts. . . .[25]

The festivals themselves frequently featured release from work, parties, and processions.[26] Residents whose houses lined the parade route were expected to place small altars outside their doors on which they would offer sacrifices as the festal procession passed.[27] Any clearly noticeable failure to participate in such activities would have been considered not merely odd but socially dangerous and a threat to the divinely ordained *pax Romana*.[28]

The one exception to this pattern was the tolerance normally given to Jewish aversion to the veneration of images. Prior to the destruction of their temple in A.D. 70, however, the twice-daily sacrifice that Jews offered God for the emperor's well-being demonstrated their acknowledgment of Rome's authority. After the Romans destroyed the Jewish temple, a two-drachma tax imposed on the Jews for repairs to Rome's principal temple accomplished the same goal.[29]

The Consequences of Religious Dissent

If support of Roman religion in its various forms in the provinces signaled support of Rome, Roman authorities sometimes interpreted a group's assertion of its own religion against that of Rome or resistance to Roman interference in religious matters as affronts to its authority.[30] When a German priest of the imperial cult ripped

21 Price, *Rituals and Power*, 64–65.

22 Ibid., 62–64.

23 Beard, North, and Price, *Religions of Rome*, 1:338, 361–62.

24 Price, *Rituals and Power*, 54–57.

25 I have taken this quotation from Price, *Rituals and Powers*, 105.

26 Ibid., 107–11.

27 Ibid., 112.

28 Ibid., 122–26; cf. Thompson, *Book of Revelation*, 161–62. Price's evidence is drawn from a later period, but there is no reason to think that the response to Christian failure to offer sacrifice to the gods and to the living emperor would have been any different in the late first century.

29 For the imposition of the tax, see Josephus, *B. J.* 7.218, and on the probable use of the tax to finance the rebuilding of the temple on the Capitoline hill in Rome, which had burned the previous year, see E. Mary Smallwood, *The Jews under Roman Rule from Pompey to Diocletian: A Study in Political Relations* (SJLA 20; Leiden: Brill, 1981), 374. On the significance of Jewish sacrifice on behalf of the emperor, see Price, *Rituals and Power*, 220–21.

30 *Pace* Hugh Last, "The Study of the 'Persecutions,'" *JRS* 27 (1937): 80–92, here at 87–88.

the symbols of that cult off his clothing and left his post in the early first century, he signaled his intention to join the local uprising against Rome (Tacitus, *Ann.* 1.39, 57).[31] Several decades later, when revolt against Rome broke out in Britain, the rebels regarded the temple devoted to the worship of Claudius as "a citadel of an eternal tyranny" and destroyed it when they gained the upper hand (Tacitus, *Ann.* 14.31–32).[32] A few years later still, the Jews stopped offering the twice-daily sacrifices to God on behalf of the emperor—sacrifices that had been in place since the time of Augustus—and everyone knew this was a serious sign of revolt that would not escape the wrath of the Roman legions (Josephus, *B. J.*, 2.409, 416).[33]

During the last years of Emperor Domitian's reign (A.D. 81–96), devotion to the living emperor as a god seems to have taken a particularly authoritarian turn. Even if we take into account the bias against Domitian in the ancient descriptions of his reign, it seems that Domitian at least encouraged recognition of himself as "lord and god" both in Rome and elsewhere in the empire, especially in the province of Asia.[34] Temples for the worship of Domitian were built during his reign at both Ephesus and Laodicea.[35] Coinage from the same period also confirms his interest in promoting the notion of his divinity.

This interest probably lies behind his stepped-up enforcement of the two-drachma tax on Jews (Suetonius, *Dom.* 12.2).[36] It may also lie behind the executions of Domitian's cousin Flavius Clemens, the consul Manius Acilius Glabrio, and others; the exile of his niece and Clemens' wife, Flavia Domitilla; and the confiscation of some of the property of certain other people (Dio Cassius 67.14.1–3). All had apparently adopted the Jewish way of life, and the emperor seems to have interpreted this as treason.[37] This treason may have consisted of their refusal to acknowledge him in cultic expressions as "lord and god." Such a refusal posed no threat when it came from ethnic Jews, but evidently Domitian took it as an insult to his honor for people among Rome's ruling classes to refuse to worship him on the grounds that they wanted to follow the teachings of this foreign religion.[38]

About two decades later when the emperor Trajan was on the throne, someone accused certain people under the jurisdiction of Pliny the Younger, then governor of Bithynia, of being "Christians" (*Ep. Tra.* 10.96). Pliny had only the vaguest idea of what "Christians" taught and did, but he did know stubbornness in a subject people

31 Beard, North, and Price, *Religions of Rome*, 1:347.

32 Ibid.

33 Ibid.

34 On Domitian's desire to be hailed as "lord and god," see, e.g., Suetonius, *Dom.* 13; Dio Chrysostom, *Or.* 45.1; Pliny, *Pan.* 33.4; 52; Dio Cassius, 67.4.7; 67.13.4. Thompson, *Book of Revelation*, 95–115, 159, claims that Suetonius, Dio Chrysostom, Tacitus, and Pliny have exaggerated the atrocities of Domitian's reign, and in particular his attachment to the titles "lord and god," as a means of providing a foil for their flattery of Trajan, who followed Domitian after Nerva's brief reign. Although these authors probably exaggerated what they considered to be Domitian's faults, both the frequency of their claim that he was especially interested in his own divinity and the confirmation of this claim in nonliterary sources indicate that it had some substance. See the balanced response to Thompson in G. K. Beale, *The Book of Revelation* (NIGTC; Grand Rapids: Eerdmans, 1999), 9–12; cf. Grant R. Osborne, *Revelation* (BECNT; Grand Rapids: Baker, 2002), 6–7.

35 Price, *Rituals and Power*, 139–40, 183, 255, 264.

36 Smallwood, *Jews under Roman Rule*, 376–78, believes that Domitian's strict collection of the tax was simply an attempt to raise extra revenue, but this seems unlikely since it follows the pattern of Domitian's later suppression of Judaism for political reasons.

37 Dio Cassius says that under Domitian's successor Nerva, "no one was allowed to accuse other people of treason or Jewish life" (68.1.2). See Smallwood, *Jews under Roman Rule*, 378.

38 Ibid., 378–85.

when he saw it, and that was enough to seal the fate of those whom he had summoned for interrogation. He had them executed when they refused to denounce their loyalty to this strange group. The affair mushroomed, and more suspects were summoned, some of whom claimed that they had never been Christians and some of whom said they had once been Christians but were Christians no longer. As proof of their sincerity, Pliny required them to worship both the statues of the gods and the image of the emperor.[39] Here, the worship of the local gods and of the living emperor was taken to be an important test of one's willingness to preserve social stability as Rome defined and enforced it.

Revelation and the Religious Hegemony of Rome

John wrote his "revelation of Jesus Christ" for the benefit of Christians in the western part of the Roman province of Asia who were suffering persecution, probably during the time of Domitian's reign.[40] Like Pliny's Christians, some of them at least refused to worship either the local deities or participate in the various religious practices, such as emperor worship, that honored Rome specifically. Pagan cults were ubiquitous in the cities to which John addressed his seven letters, and, as we have seen, worship of Roman emperors and of the deified personification of Rome itself had taken root throughout the province's urban areas with the encouragement of the provincial assembly.[41] Many Christians, however, would have avoided public displays of devotion to the emperor, such as sacrificing to his bust as religious processions passed their houses on festival days.

The consequences of this kind of nonconformity would be particularly high for Christians who belonged to society's elite classes. For such people, failure to participate in the thoroughly religious and public celebrations of Rome's hegemony that dotted the annual calendar or refusal to participate in the worship of the patron deities of one's trade guild could easily spell economic disaster, or worse.[42] The temptation to compromise must have been great.

The messages that John conveys from Jesus to the seven churches reveal the difficulty of living faithfully in this complex cultural and religious situation. The two

39 Price, *Rituals and Power*, 221–22, distinguishes between the worship of the gods' "statues" (*simulacra*) and Trajan's "image" (*imago*), arguing that the worship of the gods would have been more important to the authorities than worship of the emperor's image. This is certainly plausible, but the distinction would have mattered little to the Christian.

40 At the end of a lengthy discussion of the meaning of the number 666, Irenaeus (writing in the 180s) says that John wrote "almost in our day, towards the end of Domitian's reign" (*Haer.* 5.30.3). Clement of Alexandria and Origen do not name Domitian but seem to imply that John wrote under his rule. Clement says that John wrote "after the tyrant's death" (*Quis div.* 42), and Origen, that "the Roman emperor, as tradition teaches, condemned John" (*Comm. Matt.* 16.6). For these texts, see Henry Barclay Swete, *The Apocalypse of St. John*, 3rd ed. (London: Macmillan, 1909), 2.

41 For Ephesus, there is evidence of a temple of Roma and Julius Caesar, a temple of Augustus on the grounds of the temple to Artemis, a separate temple of Augustus elsewhere within the city, and a temple of Domitian. For Smyrna, a temple to Tiberius, Livia, and the senate. For Pergamum, a temple of Roma and Augustus. For Sardis, a temple of Augustus. For Laodicea, a temple of Domitian. The imperial cult temple in Philadelphia dates to the time of the third-century emperor Caracalla. The specific evidence available demonstrates the far-reaching character of the imperial cult, which must have been present from the time of Augustus in all the urban centers of Asia. See the comments of Price, *Rituals and Power*, 80, and his catalogue, 249–74.

42 On the presence and religious practice of trade guilds in Asia, esp. in Thyratira, see Swete, *Apocalypse*, lxiii–lxiv, and Colin Hemer, *The Letters to the Seven Churches of Asia in Their Local Setting* (JSNTSup 11; Sheffield: Sheffield Academic Press, 1986), 107–9, 120–21.

churches that receive no criticism but only praise are poverty-stricken (Smyrna, 2:9) and weak (Philadelphia, 3:8). Both experienced opposition from the synagogue (2:9; 3:9). At least in Smyrna (2:9) and probably in Philadelphia as well (3:9), Jewish opposition has taken the form of "slander" against the Christians. This is probably a reference to Jewish denunciation of Christians before the authorities in order to avoid confusion with a despised group who claimed the Jewish Scriptures and the Jewish God as its own but failed to keep the Mosaic law.[43]

Jesus commends the churches in Ephesus, Pergamum, and Thyratira for their steadfastness, evidently in the midst of persecution (2:2, 13–14, 19). He is also pleased that at least a few Christians in Sardis "have not soiled their clothes" (3:4). The phrase is obscure, but it probably means that these Christians have not caved in to the pressure to "soil" themselves with the idolatry that permeated their culture.[44]

Other Christians among the seven churches, however, are more eager to accommodate themselves to the prevailing culture. They have discovered ways both to participate in the worship of the local gods and of the emperor and to retain their commitment to the church. If John considered himself a prophet (1:3; 22:18–19), the churches at Pergamum and Thyatira have their own prophets who think John's approach is too severe (2:14, 20; cf. 2:2).[45] If the church at Smyrna has accepted economic deprivation as the necessary price to pay for spiritual riches in the times in which it lives (2:9), the church at Laodicea spurns suffering and embraces economic prosperity (3:17–18).[46] If some at Sardis have not "soiled their garments" by participating in various activities where the emperor or various local deities are venerated, many within the church have compromised with the prevailing culture and engaged in such practices (3:1–2, 4).[47]

The composite picture that emerges from John's messages is of a situation in which the pressure is intense to compromise with both the traditional religious customs of these cities and with imperial cultic celebrations. Failure to conform to society's religious expectations—whether worship of the trade guild's patron deity or religious support of Rome's authority over its subjects—often entailed economic impoverishment. Sometimes, as in the case of Antipas in Pergamum, it meant death (2:13).

Into this situation, John brings a prophet's spiritual perception. In the first major section of his book (1:9–3:22), he peals back the layers of the visible world to show the seven churches of Asia both a picture of Jesus as he presently exists and a picture of the seven churches as Jesus sees them.[48] The exalted Jesus in all his divinity and

43 Cf. Justin, *Dial.* 10.

44 Beale, *Revelation*, 276, observes that in 14:4, the only other appearance of the verb "soil" (*molynō*) in Revelation, the term appears to have this meaning. The verb is also connected with idolatry in 1 Cor. 8:7, the only other occurrence of the word in the New Testament.

45 Hemer, *Letters to the Seven Churches*, 119–21.

46 Jesus advises the church at Laodicea to "buy" from him "gold refined in fire," probably a reference to the church's need to repudiate compromise and face the economic consequences (cf. Ps. 66:10; Zech. 13:9; 1 Peter 1:7). See Beale, *Revelation*, 305–6, and Osborne, *Revelation*, 209.

47 On the link between the metaphor of soiled garments and sexual promiscuity, see 14:4 and the comments of Beale, *Revelation*, 276, 740.

48 The structure of Revelation is the subject of much learned debate. Here I follow with some minor adjustment the detailed and perceptive analysis of Bauckham, *Climax of Prophecy*, 2–22. Bauckham points out the importance for the book's structure of the phrase "in the Spirit" (1:10; 4:2; 17:3; and 21:10) and the parallels between the visions of Rome as a harlot (17:1; 19:9–10) and of Jerusalem as

glory walks among these churches, says John, and has them in his hand (1:10–16). Nothing is hidden from him; he "knows" the spiritual condition of each church (2:2, 3, 9, 13, 19; 3:1, 8, 15). He is able to "search minds and hearts" and is therefore able to judge each person justly, according to his or her works (2:23). He is standing at the door, knocking in the hope that those who have been blind to his presence will open the door, see him as he is, and renew their fellowship with him (3:20).[49]

In the book's second major section (4:1–16:21), another door—the door to heaven—is flung open, and John is admitted to the throne room of God (4:1–2). From his vantage, John can again give his readers a vision of reality otherwise inaccessible to them. He shows them the Roman empire as God sees it in all its military, religious, political, and economic brutality. He shows them God's purpose for the church's suffering under this brutal regime. He also shows them the destiny of the unrepentant persecutors of God's people and of those people themselves.

In the book's third major section (17:1–22:5), John provides his readers with a portrait of two cities—Rome, pictured as a prostitute, and the new Jerusalem, pictured as the bride of Christ. The prostitute's destiny is not eternal rule over its subjects, as its soldiers vowed every January 3, but eternal torment.[50] The bride of Christ, not the Roman prostitute, endures forever as a city of peace for God's creation—a place where God's people, drawn from all nations, will dwell in God's presence and give him glory and honor. It will also be a place free from wickedness and its curse.

For all its difficulty in other ways, the basic message of the book for its original audience seems reasonably clear. Those who compromise with the brutal authoritarianism of Rome's military and religious policies will share the prostitute's fate of eternal destruction in the lake of fire. Those who remain faithful to Jesus, despite the intense suffering that God's rebellious creatures heap on them, will live in eternal peace in the enjoyment and worship of God. John expresses this message through a symbol-laden vision that takes up the second and third major sections of his book.

SUFFERING AS THE MERCY AND JUSTICE OF GOD (4:1–16:21)

The View of the Church's Suffering from the Throne Room of God

After conveying the seven messages from Jesus to the churches for which they are intended, John opens the great central section of his book with a vision of the throne room of God (4:1–5:14). The judgments John describes in the three series of seven

a bride (21:9–10; 22:6–9), esp. between the introductions and conclusions to those two visions. Arguments for a redactional history for the book such as those in David E. Aune, *Revelation 1–5* (WBC 52; Dallas: Word, 1997), cv–cxxxiv, do not seem to outweigh arguments, such as those articulated in Bauckham, *Climax of Prophecy*, 1–37, that the book is a tightly woven unity.

49 The comments of Christopher Rowland, *The Open Heaven: A Study of Apocalyptic in Judaism and Early Christianity* (New York: Crossroad, 1982), 439–41, while not specifically intended to explain 3:20, neatly sum up the verse's perspective.

50 On the annual vow "for the well being and eternity of the empire," see Beard, North, and Price, *Religions of Rome*, 1:326. Perhaps the Briton's view (Tacitus, *Ann.* 14.31) that the local temple to the deified Claudius was "the citadel of an eternal tyranny" also reflects a negative response to the notion of Rome's eternal authority.

seals, seven trumpets, and seven bowls come from this throne room and thus from God himself.[51] John shows this by linking the imagery of this initial vision to the imagery of the judgments in these three series.

The slain Lamb who stands before the throne (5:6) opens each of the seven seals (5:9). The events that accompany the opening of the first four of the seven seals each come at the command of one of the four living creatures before God's throne (4:6; 6:1, 3, 5, 7). The "flashes of lightening, rumblings and peals of thunder" that come from the throne in the original vision (4:5) reappear with slight variations at the beginning and at the end of the trumpet plagues (8:5; 11:19) and at the end of the bowl plague sequence, which concludes the series (16:18–21). By returning the reader in this way to the original vision of God's throne in 4:1–5:14, John shows that all he describes in 6:1–16:21 comes from God's hand in order to accomplish his purposes.

What are those purposes? The initial throne vision summarizes them for John's audience. The twenty-four elders who are seated around God's throne, crowned, wearing white garments, and occupying their own thrones symbolize God's people down through the ages.[52] Twenty-four is a multiple of twelve, and twelve was both the number of the tribes of Israel and the number of the apostles, a point John emphasizes elsewhere (21:12–14). Multiples of twelve, therefore, were particularly apt numerical symbols for God's people.[53] John uses white throughout his book as a symbol of faithfulness to Jesus and resistance to compromise with the idolatry and sexual promiscuity of the prevailing culture (2:17; 3:4–5, 18; 6:11; 7:9, 13–14; 19:14). According to the throne vision, therefore, God's people will remain faithful to him and will worship him forever (4:10–11; 5:14).

All creation has the same destiny, as the worship that the four living creatures give to God demonstrates. Four is the number that John gives to the created world consistently throughout Revelation.[54] The earth has four corners (7:1; 20:8) and four areas (5:13; 14:7), and the first four judgments in each series of seven bring suffering to the world (6:8; 8:7–12; 16:2–9).[55] All creation will therefore one day worship God as the eternal one (4:8–9), who created everything and sustains what he has created (4:11; 5:13–14; cf. 10:6).

For John's first audience, however, there is an obvious gap between this reality as John's heavenly vision describes it and the existence of the church as they experience it. The pomp, pageantry, and worship in the society around them seem to go to the local deities and to Rome. Those who expect to flourish economically must compromise with Rome's religious hegemony. Those who fail to compromise experience increasing hardship for their dissent from society's expected norms. How can the vision portrayed in 4:1–11 ever materialize?

---

51 Bauckham, *Theology of the Book of Revelation*, 40–41.

52 The identity of the twenty-four elders has been hotly contested. Many commentators (e.g., Osborne, *Revelation*, 228–29) believe that they are angelic rather than human beings. For the position taken here (which is also common among commentators), see the exhaustive survey of the relevant data in Aune's excursus in his *Revelation 1–5*, 287–92, and his conclusion on p. 314.

53 John was presumably aware that Jesus had described his twelve key disciples as one day sitting on "twelve thrones, judging the twelve tribes of Israel" (Matt. 19:28; Luke 22:30).

54 Bauckham, *Theology of the Book of Revelation*, 66–67.

55 Ibid., 66.

The second part of John's initial throne vision answers this question.[56] In 5:1–14 John sees a scroll with seven seals in the hand of God. Only Jesus is found worthy to open the seals of the scroll and reveal its contents. He is worthy to do this because he has "conquered" by means of his suffering (5:5, 9–10). He is the Lamb who was slain (5:6) and whose shed blood purchased God's church from "every tribe and language and people and nation" (5:9; cf. 1:5). We learn elsewhere that through his shed blood he has nullified the accusations of Satan against God's people and that in this way he enables God's people to "conquer" Satan (12:10–11).[57] The Lamb, in other words, has conquered the forces of rebellion against God through first being conquered by those forces himself.

Each of the letters to the seven churches concluded with a blessing for those who "conquer" (2:7, 11, 17, 26; 3:5, 12, 21). It now becomes clear what this means: Like Jesus, God's people will conquer the forces of rebellion around them through suffering. This understanding of the victory of God's people is confirmed when the contents of the scroll with seven seals are revealed (10:1–11:13).[58] God's people will be "conquered" by their godless persecutors (11:7). This suffering, however, will be the means through which God's purposes both to punish the wicked and to save his people will be accomplished. The suffering of his people will usher them into the presence of God (11:11–12), where their victory will be complete (3:21; 12:11).

The wickedness of those who have caused them to suffer will become the basis for their just condemnation (11:13, 18). As God brings his wrath on the wicked among the nations, many will perish (8:11; 9:15, 18; 11:13a), but their fear will lead some to give "glory to the God of heaven" (11:13b). The faithfulness of God's people in the midst of their suffering and the outpouring of his wrath on the wicked will therefore be the means through which God accomplishes his final purpose of effecting justice and bringing a people from all nations and from all creation into his presence to worship him eternally.

Suffering as Punishment and Warning

John devotes most of his vision at God's throne to a symbolic representation of the suffering that God will bring on the wicked as a result of their rebellion against him. This portrayal of God's punishment of the wicked is organized around three sets of plagues (6:1–17; 8:1, 7–9:21; 11:15–19; 16:2–21). These plagues break loose as the scroll's seals are opened, as a series of trumpets sounds, and as the contents of bowls are poured out in succession.

As with much else in Revelation, interpretations of the significance of these three sets of judgments diverge widely. It is probably best, however, to see these judgments

56 In the following two paragraphs I am heavily indebted to the interpretation of Revelation 4–16 found in Bauckham, *Theology of the Book of Revelation*, 66–108. Cf. idem, *Climax of Prophecy*, 238–337.

57 Swete, *Apocalypse*, 156; Beale, *Revelation*, 664; Osborne, *Revelation*, 476.

58 The contents of the scroll are revealed only after the last seal is opened and the scroll can be unrolled. The events that occur at the time of the opening of each seal, therefore, are not contained within the scroll. Instead, the "scroll" (*biblion*) of 5:1–14 is identical with the "little scroll" (*biblaridion*) of 10:2, 9, 10. (In 10:8 it is again called a "scroll" [*biblion*].) The contents of this scroll are revealed in 11:1–13. On this, see Bauckham, *Climax of Prophecy*, 243–57; idem, *Theology*, 80–84.

as a symbolic portrayal of the increasing level of suffering that will come to the wicked as the time for God's final judgment draws closer. Although the wicked are responsible for much of the suffering described in the plagues, none of it lies outside God's sovereign purposes, a point that John makes clear by showing that all the plagues come from the throne room of God and of the Lamb. With respect to the plagues, the purpose seems to be twofold: to punish the wicked and to warn them to repent.

Suffering as Punishment

The purpose of the plagues as a punishment for the persecutors of God's people is evident from two considerations. First, the four plagues that accompany the opening of the first four of the seven seals describe the horrors that military regimes like the Roman empire perpetrated against those whom they conquered: setting out to conquer (6:1–2) leads to war (6:3–4), famine (6:5–6), and death (6:7–8).[59] As the messages to the seven churches in chapters 2 and 3 have revealed, faithful Christians have become victims of this wicked will to dominate others through violence.

At the opening of the fifth seal, therefore, Christians who have suffered under such violence ask the Lord how long they will have to wait before their unjust deaths are vindicated (6:9–10). The reason for the delay, they are told, is that others must join them in martyrdom before the final judgment of the wicked (6:11). After the number of persecuted Christians is complete, the sixth seal is opened, and the wrath of God and of the Lamb breaks forth against the wicked, beginning with "the princes, the generals, the rich, the mighty" (6:15). One clear purpose of these calamities is to punish those who have wreaked havoc in the world, and especially against Christians, through their military, political, and economic tyranny.

Second, the trumpet and the bowl plagues are modeled on the plagues with which God troubled the Egyptians just prior to Israel's exodus from Egypt, plagues whose primary purpose was to punish the Egyptians for their disobedience (Ex. 7:8–11:10).[60] This is clear from the echoes of the Egyptian plagues that John plants in his descriptions of the trumpet and bowl plagues. Hail, fire, blood, painful sores, locusts, and darkness, all of which appear in the ten plagues visited on Egypt, now reappear in the trumpet and bowl plagues.[61]

If the specific description of the trumpet and bowl plagues in Revelation recalls the plagues visited on the Egyptians, then it seems probable that the theology underlying the narrative of the plagues in Exodus is also fundamental to John's description

59 As Ernst Lohmeyer, *Die Offenbarung des Johannes*, 2nd ed (HNT 16; Tübingen: J.C.B. Mohr [Paul Siebeck], 1953), 58, points out, John is also dependent on traditional biblical conceptions of the ravages of war. See, e.g., Jer. 15:2–3 (cf. 21:7; 24:10), where the effects of war are described as death, sword, starvation, and captivity, and God sends out "four destroyers" to punish his sinful people. John's four horses, as interpreters frequently observe, seem to be inspired by the four horse-drawn chariots of Zech. 6:1–8, each distinguished by a different color. Cf. also Joel 2:4–5.

60 Many interpreters take this position, beginning as early as Irenaeus, *Haer.* 4.30. See the esp. thorough discussions of David E. Aune, *Revelation 6–16* (WBC 52B; Nashville: Nelson, 1998), 495, 499–506, who argues that there was a strong tendency in ancient Jewish literature to renumber the ten plagues in Exodus as seven plagues, and Beale, *Revelation*, 465, 809–10, who believes that the theological tendencies lying beneath Ex. 7–12 informed John's own theological perspective as it is expressed in the plagues of the seven trumpets and seven bowls.

61 These elements recall the first (blood), sixth (boils), seventh (hail and fire), eighth (locusts), and ninth (darkness) plagues on the Egyptians. Joel 2:1–14 lies more prominently than the Egyptian locust plague in the background of the events that accompanying the sounding of the fifth trumpet, but the Egyptian locust plague was probably also in John's mind.

of the trumpet and bowl plagues. The Egyptian plagues were designed in part to punish the idolatry of the Egyptians, who worshiped the objects affected by them.[62] In addition, the Exodus narrative stresses the recalcitrance of Pharaoh who, despite the warning of the plagues, refused to obey God. In the same way, the trumpet and bowl plagues in Revelation are designed to punish the idolatrous persecutors of God's people and to reveal their recalcitrance since the victims of the plagues, despite their suffering, refuse to repent of their idolatry (9:20–21; 16:2, 11).[63] Moreover, just as God sent the plagues to the Egyptians to punish Pharaoh's persecution of his people, so John's plagues demonstrate that God will similarly punish the persecutors of the new Israel for their idolatry, murder, sorcery, sexual immorality, and theft (9:21).[64]

Suffering as a Summons to Repentance

In addition, John seems to intend that the plague sequences reveal God's mercy in delaying judgment in the hope that the wicked might repent.[65] The notion that God is slow to anger and mercifully delays punishment to provide ample opportunity for repentance is a common biblical and early Christian theme.[66] The theme appears clearly in Joel 2:1–14, the passage that provides the primary model for the locust plague of the fifth trumpet (9:1–12). Joel ends his terrifying description of the invading locust army on a note of hope. It is still possible, he says, for God's people to repent before the final disaster of the "day of the Lord" breaks out:

> "Even now," declares the LORD,
> "return to me with all your heart,
> with fasting and weeping and mourning."
> Rend your heart
> and not your garments.
> Return to the LORD your God,
> for he is gracious and compassionate,
> slow to anger and abounding in love,
> and he relents from sending calamity.
> Who knows? He may turn and have pity
> and leave behind a blessing—
> grain offerings and drink offerings
> for the LORD your God. (Joel 2:12–14)[67]

Even the Egyptian plagues evidently prompted some Egyptians to attach themselves to Israel and follow them out of Egypt. This at least is the way in which Philo of Alexandria, writing, like John, in the first century, interpreted the enigmatic notice in Exodus 12:38 that "many other people went up with them [the Israelites]." Philo writes:

62 Wisd. 12:23–27 provides an example from the second temple period of this understanding of the plagues' purpose.

63 Beale, *Revelation*, 465–67, 808–12.

64 For the idea that John portrays the plagues of 8:6–12 as the start of a new exodus for God's people, see Caird, *Revelation*, 112–16.

65 Cf. Osborne, *Revelation*, 271, and *pace* Aune, *Revelation 6–16*, 495–96, 499, who sees the plagues as entirely punitive.

66 See, e.g., Ex. 34:6; Num. 14:18; Ps. 86:15; Jonah 4:2; Rom. 2:4; 2 Peter 3:9.

67 Cf. Jonah 4:2.

> These were . . . those who, reverencing the divine favour shewn to the people, had come over to them, and such as were converted and brought to a wiser mind by the magnitude and the number of the successive punishments. (*Mos.* 1.147)[68]

The importance of this theme to John appears both in three explicit statements that he makes about the response of the wicked to the plagues and in the way he structures the three sequences of plagues. Three times John says that the wicked victims of the trumpet and bowl plagues fail to learn from them and repent:

> The rest of humankind, who were not killed by these plagues, did not repent of the works of their hands or give up worshiping demons and idols of gold and silver and bronze and stone and wood, which cannot see or hear or walk. And they did not repent of their murders or their sorceries or their fornication or their thefts. (9:20–21, NRSV)
>
> [People] cursed the name of God, who had authority over these plagues, and they did not repent and give him glory. (16:9b, NRSV)
>
> [People] gnawed their tongues in agony, and cursed the God of heaven because of their pains and sores, and they did not repent of their deeds. (16:10b–11, NRSV)

John wants his readers to know that up until the final condemnation of the wicked, the plagues have a pedagogical intention—through them God is urging his rebellious creatures to learn from their punishments, come to their senses, and abandon their idols.

In addition, John structures the plagues so that they show an increase in severity, hinting that God is encouraging the wicked to see the destructive tendency of their idolatry, immorality, and greed before he punishes them finally and completely. The suffering that comes from the opening of the first four seals is a seemingly natural result of the human desire to dominate others and is, compared with later plagues, relatively mild. Similarly, when John describes the last three trumpet blasts as three woes (8:13; 9:12) and solemnly warns the reader against them, it becomes clear that they are more severe than the plagues of the first four trumpet blasts. Even among these last three woes there is an increase in the severity of the punishment from the first woe, in which the locusts are only allowed to torment but not to kill people (9:5), and the second woe in which a third of humanity is killed (9:15, 18).

The bowl plagues, which symbolize the rapid outpouring of God's wrath on the wicked at the final day, are also more severe than the trumpet plagues. In the trumpet sequence, the punishments of the first six trumpets affect the heavens, earth, and humanity in thirds (8:7–9:21). In the bowl sequence, however, judgment is handed

68 See Beale, *Revelation*, 466, who does not, however, understand this to be a major concern of the trumpet and bowl sequence.

out in complete units—all who have the mark of the beast are afflicted with sores, the whole sea becomes blood, all fresh water becomes blood, all people are scorched with fire, complete darkness descends on the beast, and the whole world is swept up into war at Armageddon (16:2–21).[69]

The structure of the plague sequences also brings out the willingness of God to delay the final outpouring of his wrath in the hope that the victims of his preliminary judgments might learn from them and repent. The reader expects the completion of God's punishment of the wicked with the opening of the seventh seal and the sounding of the seventh trumpet, but John interrupts each sequence just before its conclusion with two long sections that fall outside the sequence of sevens (7:1–17; 10:1–11:14).[70]

In addition, John interposes a long passage between the first two sets of plagues and the last set. In this last set, angels pour out a series of plague-filled bowls in rapid succession with no intervening delay, signifying that as the Day of Judgment approaches, the pace of suffering will quicken. John's placement of digressions before the seventh seal, the seventh trumpet, and the outpouring of the final bowl plagues provided for his original audience a sense of merciful delay prior to the final judgment of God.

In summary, John's picture of the suffering of the wicked in the symbolic events accompanying the seven seals, seven trumpets, and seven bowls provides an important part of God's perspective on the suffering that John's first audience is experiencing. Prior to the end of all things, the steadily increasing level of suffering does not lie outside God's control—it is both a punishment on the wicked for their evil, particularly for their persecution of God's people, and a merciful pedagogical effort designed to extend to them every possible opportunity to repent prior to the final outpouring of God's wrath on them.

Suffering as the Path to the Salvation of God's People and the Condemnation of Their Enemies (7:1–17; 10:1–11:14)

Before the opening of the seventh seal and the blast of the seventh trumpet, John interposes two passages that, as we have seen, create a sense of merciful delay before the judgment of the wicked in the blast of the seventh trumpet and the outpouring of the seven bowls. These two interludes, however, are self-contained units that describe two purposes for the suffering of the church. In the first of these passages (7:1–17) John demonstrates that the path the Christian must walk to arrive in the presence of God and the Lamb leads through suffering. In the second interlude (10:1–11:14), John shows that the suffering of God's people also provides the necessary legal basis for the just condemnation of the wicked.

The Church Reaches God's Presence by Its Perseverance (7:1–17)

The horrors that accompany the opening of the sixth seal and bring the reader to the brink of the final judgment conclude with an anguished statement from the

69 Bauckham, *Climax of Prophecy*, 12–15; idem, *Theology of the Book of Revelation*, 40–41, 82–83.

70 Bauckham, *Climax of Prophecy*, 12–13.

suffering wicked that turns into a question, "The great day of . . . wrath has come, and who can stand?" (6:17). Chapter 7 provides the answer to this question with its description in 7:1–8 of a group of 144,000—twelve thousand from each of the twelve Israelite tribes who are sealed as servants of God and protected from the outpouring of his final judgment (7:1–8).

Interpreters have hotly contested the identity of this group. Are they the faithful remnant of Jews? Are they Jewish Christians? Are they all Christians? Are they Christians who have survived the calamitous period just prior to the end of all things because God has specially protected them from these dangers? Should they be identified with the "great multitude that no one could count" that stands "before the throne and in front of the Lamb" in 7:9–17?[71]

The solution to this conundrum lies in understanding the significance of the number 144,000, and the key to the meaning of this number is its relationship to the number twelve. The number twelve, as we have already seen, signifies the people of God. Just as the number of elders before God's throne—twenty-four—signified the people of God down through the ages because it was the sum of twelve (tribes) plus twelve (apostles), so the number one hundred forty-four is the quotient of twelve (tribes) times twelve (apostles).[72] This quotient is multiplied by a thousand to indicate the vastness of the number of the people of God (cf. Gen. 13:16; 15:5; 32:12).[73] Like the number twenty-four, therefore, it signifies God's people, but with a special emphasis on the large size of that company.

The emphasis on size provides a link between the 144,000 and the "great multitude" of 7:9–17 and means that the vast throng who worship God and the Lamb in the heavenly throne room are the glorified people of God. Chapter 7 in its entirety, therefore, describes all Christians as some already are, and all will eventually be, when they stand in God's presence. They are his people who survive the outpouring of his wrath on the ungodly, who are exalted to the throne room of God, and who worship God and the Lamb forever, free of suffering and sorrow.

How did they get there? John tells us that they endured "the great tribulation" and that they "washed their robes and made them white in the blood of the lamb" (7:14). Although this second phrase has often been understood as a reference to the atoning death of Jesus, a teaching that John fully embraces elsewhere (1:5; 5:9), his mention of the great tribulation in this passage means that here robes washed in the Lamb's blood probably refers to the martyrdom of Christians.[74] Their faithfulness to Jesus to the point of death, just as Jesus was faithful to the point of death, has brought them into God's presence. As 14:4 puts it, the 144,000 are those who "follow the Lamb wherever he goes"—even, John seems to imply, to the point of death.[75]

71 See the lengthy discussion of the various options in Aune, *Revelation 6–16*, 440–45.

72 Beale, *Revelation*, 417; Osborne, *Revelation*, 310–12. In addition, as commentators frequently point out, John assumes elsewhere that Christians are the true Israel (2:9; 3:9), and here (7:3) he describes the 144,000 as "the servants of our God," a title that John would probably not apply to only one group of Christians. See Swete, *Apocalypse*, 99; Lohmeyer, *Offenbarung*, 69; and Caird, *Revelation*, 95. *Pace* Aune, *Revelation 6–16*, 440–45.

73 Cf. Bauckham, *Theology of the Book of Revelation*, 77.

74 Ibid.

75 Ibid., 78.

This interpretation seems to be confirmed by a careful examination of 7:1–3 and 14:1–5. In 7:1–3, four angels stand at the four corners of the earth, poised to unleash winds of destruction. Another angel seals the 144,000 before the four destroying angels begin to "harm the land and the sea" (7:3). These four angels are reminiscent of the four horsemen who wreaked havoc on the earth at the opening of the first four seals (6:1–8).[76] In 7:1–3, therefore, John moves back in time to a point prior to the unleashing of the military conquest, war, famine, and death symbolized by the four horsemen at the opening of the first four seals.[77] According to 7:1–3, God seals the 144,000 to protect them from the ravages of these four horsemen.

We have already said that those four horsemen depict the mayhem and destruction unleashed by the sinful human desire to dominate others through military might, something that John understands firsthand through his experience of the military power and religious authoritarianism of the Roman empire. Here he seems to be saying that the Christians to whom he writes, and Christians generally, will be preserved from the ravages of such regimes. Since his messages to the persecuted Christians of Asia reveal that he knows about the economic (2:9; 3:8) and physical (2:13) harm that had come to Christians through the violence of such regimes, what could he mean when he says that Christians are sealed against such violence?

He means that they are immune from the attack of Rome's authoritarian regime on their faith. Despite intense pressure to compromise with the idolatry that Rome has imposed on its subjects as part of its strategy to keep them under its control, the people of God will remain faithful. Their faith will not collapse under the pressure to compromise by participating in idolatrous celebrations, festivals, and banqueting with its "after dinner" liaisons with prostitutes for those among society's elite who had attained their majority.[78] They will refuse to keep a deceitfully low profile about their faith.

This may well result in martyrdom, as it had for the "faithful witness" Antipas of Pergamum (3:13) and as it will for increasing numbers of Christians as history grinds toward Armageddon. It is, however, precisely by washing their robes in the blood of the Lamb—by remaining faithful, if necessary, to the death—that they will enter God's presence and worship him and the Lamb in God's heavenly throne room. Paradoxically, through suffering hardship for the faith Christians will persevere in the faith and come to no ultimate harm.

This understanding of chapter 7 also receives confirmation from 14:4–5. Here John says that the 144,000 "did not defile themselves with women, for they are virgins" and that "no lie was found in their mouths." Although it is difficult to know what John means by the virginity of the 144,000, his explanatory gloss that they are not sexually "defiled" (*molynō*, 14:4) may refer to the refusal of Christians to

76 The four horses and the four angels that hold back the wind both derive from Zech. 6:1–8, where four chariots, drawn by horses of various colors, are interpreted as "the four winds of heaven." This common origin of the two images shows that we are on the right track in interpreting the two images together.

77 Caird, *Revelation*, 94.

78 On the sexual promiscuity, esp. after banquets, among Roman elites who had attained the *toga virilis* (or, in Greek, *to andreion himation*), see Bruce W. Winter, *After Paul Left Corinth: The Influence of Secular Ethics and Social Change* (Grand Rapids: Eerdmans, 2001), 86–93.

participate in the idolatry so prominent in their culture.[79] Like the minority of the church in Sardis, they have not "defiled" (*molynō*) their clothes and so will walk with Jesus, "dressed in white" (3:4–5).

None of this means that John believes all Christians will suffer martyrdom. John only expects some in Smyrna to be thrown into prison and face death (2:10).[80] The faithful minority in Sardis who have refused to compromise "will walk with" Jesus "dressed in white" not because their faithfulness has ended in martyrdom but simply because they have been unwilling to "soil their clothes" by compromising with the prevailing idolatry and sexual immorality of their culture.[81] John takes martyrdom—the most extreme example of Christian faithfulness—as a cipher for all Christian perseverance. His point is that Christians must persevere in their faith through hardship if they are to arrive finally in the presence of God. They must "conquer," even if that means, like Jesus, being "conquered" by God's enemies. "To him who conquers," says Jesus, "I will give the right to sit with me on my throne, just as I conquered and sat down with my Father on his throne" (3:21).

By Its Faithful Suffering the Church Testifies against the Wicked (10:1–11:14)

The second passage that John interposes before describing the final judgment of the wicked functions like the first passage to create a sense of merciful delay before that final Day of Judgment comes. In this passage too John describes God's perspective on the suffering of the church, but here the focus is different: Rather than describing the role that the church's suffering plays in its salvation, as he did in the first passage, John describes the role that the church's suffering plays in the final condemnation of the wicked.

The opening of the passage takes John's audience back to the second half of his initial vision of the throne room. There John had seen a scroll with seven seals in God's right hand and a "mighty angel" had asked aloud who was worthy to open the scroll's seals. The slain Lamb was found to be worthy because he had suffered just as his people would be required to suffer according to the events that accompanied the opening of the seven seals. By the time we reach chapter 10, all seven seals that held the scroll closed have been broken, and the scroll can be opened and read. This is the scroll that "another mighty angel" who bestrides creation now gives to John. As the angel gives John the now unsealed scroll, he commissions him to prophesy.

The whole scene is redolent of Ezekiel's prophetic call. Just prior to that call, Ezekiel received a vision of the throne room of God and of God himself. God was as bright as "glowing metal, as if full of fire," was encompassed by brilliant light, and had the appearance of "a rainbow in the clouds on a rainy day" (Ezek. 1:26–28).

79 See Beale, *Revelation*, 740, who points out that the Old Testament often refers to Israel's idolatry as sexual defilement and that the LXX sometimes uses the terms *molynō*, *molysmos*, and *molynsis* to refer to Israel's idolatry. See esp. Isa. 65:4; Jer. 23:15; 51:4

80 Ibid., 177.

81 Cf. Osborne, *Revelation*, 179–80. The phrase *ho nikōn houtōs peribaleitai en imatiois leukois* (3:5) should not be translated as "Like them, the Conqueror shall be robed in white" (Caird, *Revelation*, 47, 49; cf. NIV, NRSV, NJB), as if the Conqueror belongs to a special class of Christians who suffer martyrdom. The phrase should instead be rendered something like, "the one who conquers *in this way* shall be clothed in white garments." See, e.g., Beale, *Revelation*, 278; Aune, *Revelation 1–5*, 223, and, among translations, the RSV, NAB, and ESV.

Similarly the angel who gives the scroll to John is, among other things, wrapped in a cloud, has a rainbow over his head, and has a face as bright as the sun (10:1). Like Ezekiel, John is given a scroll that he is commanded to eat and that has a sweet taste (Ezek. 2:9–3:3; Rev. 10:9–10). In Ezekiel, the scroll was sweet because it was the word of God (cf. Ps. 19:10; 119:103; Jer. 15:16). It symbolized, therefore, the message from God that Ezekiel was to prophesy, a message that plotted the way of restoration for God's people through the path of suffering. In the same way, for John, the scroll is God's prophetic word to him that he is to pass along to his readers (10:11). It too speaks of suffering and so, after its initially sweet taste, it becomes bitter in his stomach (10:10).

Although cast specifically as a prophecy rather than as a heavenly vision and using different symbolism, the scroll in Revelation holds a message similar to that of the seven seals, seven trumpets, and seven bowls and to the interlude between the sixth and seventh seal. As the three series of sevens indicate, suffering will increase as history progresses toward the final judgment, and, as the first interlude indicates, the church will be caught up in that suffering. In this second interlude, however, the church's suffering becomes the basis for the final judgment of the wicked.

At the beginning of his prophecy, John is told, as Ezekiel was often told, to engage in a symbolic action.[82] He is to measure the temple, its altar, and those who worship around the altar but not the temple's outer court, which is left exposed to the ravages of "the nations" (11:1–2). Although the finer nuances of this action's meaning are obscure, its basic significance becomes clear if we remember that even the outer court of the temple was part of the temple complex and therefore sacred. The action then follows a pattern with which we are familiar from the first interlude: The wicked damage something sacred but are not allowed to do it any ultimate harm. Just as in the first interlude the great multitude experienced the great tribulation (7:14) and yet entered the throne room of God because God had sealed them against any ultimate harm (7:3–4), so here the nations trample the outer precincts of the temple (11:2), but the place of God's presence comes to no ultimate harm (11:1).

John is probably, therefore, following the common Christian custom of identifying God's people with God's temple.[83] Here too, although his people suffer, God protects them from ultimate harm. Indeed, as the rest of the passage demonstrates, he uses their suffering as a basis for his sovereign purposes; it provides the evidence for the just condemnation of the wicked.

The story of this purpose employs a series of enigmatic metaphors. Two witnesses become two olive trees and two lampstands. These two—or four—witnesses work astonishing deeds and are supernaturally kept from harm for 1,260 days. At the end of this period a beast ascends from a bottomless pit, kills these witnesses and leaves

82 Bauckham, *Climax of Prophecy,* 266–67. Symbolic action is more characteristic of Ezekiel than of any other biblical prophet. See Ezek. 4:1–5:17; 12:1–28; 21:1–22; 24:15–27; 37:15–28, and the comments of J. Lindblom, *Prophecy in Ancient Israel* (Philadelphia: Fortress, 1962), 170–71. The measurement of the eschatological temple is a prominent theme in Ezekiel 40–48, although rather than making the measurements himself, Ezekiel only watches as measurements are made.

83 John uses the Greek term *naos* for the part of the temple complex that John is to measure. This is precisely the term used metaphorically for God's people in 1 Cor. 3:16–17; 2 Cor. 6:16; Eph. 2:21.

their bodies exposed to the derision of the earth's inhabitants. After three and a half days of this, the breath of God enters the witnesses, who then come to life and ascend to heaven in a cloud. At that moment a great earthquake rocks the city where all this has taken place, killing many and leading others to glorify God (11:3–13).

Understandably, this confusing whirlwind of images has been the subject of vigorous interpretive debate. Much becomes clear, however, when we see that John alludes in these few sentences to a wide range of biblical passages. The two witnesses are the minimum number required in the Mosaic law to convict the guilty (Deut. 19:15).[84] They prophesy for precisely the same length of time that Daniel had said God's enemies would persecute his people—for "a time, times, and half a time," a figure that can be understood as "a year, two years, and half a year" (Dan. 7:25; 12:7), or 1,260 days. John's description of them as two olive trees and two lampstands recalls Zechariah's vision of a lampstand flanked by two olive trees that supply it with oil. This vision turned out to be a word of encouragement to Zerubbabel and Joshua, the two anointed representatives of God's people (the two olive trees).

This encouraging message explained that, despite great obstacles, God's Spirit (the oil) would empower them to rebuild the temple (the lampstand) that Nebuchadnezzar had so ruthlessly destroyed (Zech. 4:1–14).[85] The miraculous powers of John's two witnesses echo the powers that Elijah and Moses exercised against the wicked on God's behalf. The two witnesses will fulfill the expectation that in the days of the restoration of God's people, Moses (Deut. 18:15) and Elijah (Mal. 4:5–6) will return, and their testimony, like the great punishing miracles of these two prophets, will seal the doom of many of their persecutors.[86]

The beast that ascends from the abyss and wages a successful war against the two witnesses is reminiscent of the fourth beast described in Daniel 7:13 and interpreted in Daniel 7:23. There, just as here in Revelation 11:7, the beast wreaks havoc among God's people.[87] John then switches his attention to Ezekiel 37:1–14, where the prophet describes the restoration of God's people as the resurrection of a vast army of dried bones that the breath of God brings to life.[88] In the same way, in Revelation 11:11–12, the persecuted, derided, and martyred people of God are restored to life and enter God's presence. John says that they travel to heaven "in a cloud," which is reminiscent of the cloud that receives the vindicated Son of Man—the symbol of God's faithful, persecuted people—in Daniel 7:13 and 18.

84 Bauckham, *Theology of the Book of Revelation*, 85.

85 Cf. Beale, *Revelation*, 576–78.

86 Ibid., 582–85. Caird, *Revelation*, 136, perceptively comments that the metaphorical nature of these references is revealed in the statement that "fire comes from their mouths" (11:5). This stands in contrast to the literal fire that Elijah called down from heaven on the emissaries of King Ahaziah (2 Kings 1:10, 12).

87 In Daniel, the most immediate referent of the beast was the infamous persecutor of the Jews, Antiochus IV Epiphanes, who outlawed the possession or keeping of the Mosaic law and insisted that the chief deity of the Hellenistic pantheon—Zeus—be worshiped in the precincts of the Jewish temple. John appropriately borrowed Daniel's metaphor to describe the authoritarian regime under which he lived and saw it as an example, just as Daniel saw Antiochus IV Epiphanes as an example, of the intensification of wickedness that will characterize the world just prior to the final judgment of the wicked.

88 As Beale, *Revelation*, 597, points out, John's clear echo of this biblical text demonstrates that he did not conceive of the two witnesses in 11:3–13 as two individuals but as symbols for the people of God.

When we put all this together, John seems to be saying that God's people will endure hardship from God's enemies for a predetermined period of time but that this suffering is not outside God's purposes. It will serve as evidence in God's eschatological court to convict the persecutors of God's people of injustice. They will experience a destruction so severe that those who are not killed as a result of it will be gripped with fear and glorify God.[89] Those who have suffered faithfully for their commitment to the gospel, however, will be resurrected, and God will bring them, vindicated, into his presence.

Summary

In his two interludes that mercifully delay the final judgment of the wicked, John provides two further statements about the purpose of his readers' suffering. Their suffering gives God an opportunity to display his mercy to the wicked by punishing them in such a way that he calls them to repent. This is the point of the plagues.

The suffering of John's readers also has two other purposes. First, their suffering is an integral part of following the slain Lamb. Just as Jesus sat down at God's right hand only after "conquering" through being "conquered," so those who will reign with him from his throne must also come into God's presence after persevering in their faith. The suffering and martyrdom depicted in the two interludes are the most vivid examples of this necessary perseverance.

Second, the suffering of God's people testifies to the wickedness of those whom God will eventually condemn at the final judgment. Their treatment of God's people demonstrates the justice of God's condemnation of them on the final day. Rather than responding to the testimony of God's suffering people by embracing the gospel, they have only received it as an insult and rejoice whenever God's people are silenced by death.

Christian Victory over Rome Expressed in Myth (12:1–15:4)

Just before the final, terrible outpouring of God's wrath in the bowl judgments (16:2–21), John once again gives his readers the impression of a merciful delay. Rather than focusing on God's purpose for the suffering of his people at the hands of his wicked foes, however, in this interlude John describes in mythological terms the victory of God over Satan, and thus the ultimate victory of first-century Christians over the forces of evil that Rome has unleashed on them. Here John translates into symbolic language the story of the struggle between God, his Messiah, and his people on one side and Satan, the Roman empire, and the imperial priesthood on the other side. John shows his readers the "beastly" nature of Roman imperial power

89 Does this mean that the persecutors of God's people who are not among those killed in the earthquake will repent of their wickedness and escape eternal punishment? Commentators are divided on this issue. Some, notably, Bauckham, *Climax of Prophecy*, 278–80; idem, *Theology of the Book of Revelation*, 86–87, think so. Others, such as Beale, *Revelation*, 603–8, believe that the glory that those who survived the earthquake give to God falls short of repentance and conversion. Since John has emphasized God's hope that the punishment of the wicked will lead to the repentance of some, Bauckham is probably correct on this. The theme does not, however, rise to the level of significance that Bauckham gives to it. See also Osborne, *Revelation*, 433–35, who emphasizes correctly that this conclusion does not imply the repentance of all previously unrepentant humanity. Cf. 1 Peter 2:12, on which commentators are also divided.

and those who advocate religious devotion to it. He also shows that although they will suffer under Rome's satanically inspired oppression, God will nevertheless protect them and eventually bring them to victory.

The Woman, the Child, and the Dragon (12:1–17)

In this passage, John tells again the story of the oppression of God's people and of God's protection of his people in the midst of that oppression. He also shows that God will one day bring this oppression to an end, establish his kingdom, and destroy Satan. The faithful suffering of his Messiah and of his people has meanwhile already begun to seal Satan's doom.

John tells the basic story in highly symbolic language in 12:1–6. He then repeats in greater detail, and again with a complex use of symbolism, two elements of the story in 12:7–12 and 12:13–17. In 12:1–6 a woman and a dragon appear in heaven.[90] The woman is clothed beautifully in the heavenly cosmos—she is robed with the sun, her feet rest on the moon, and she wears a crown of twelve stars. She is in the throes of childbirth. The dragon is a fearsome red beast with seven heads and ten horns. He creates chaos in the heavens by swiping his tail through them and smashing to earth a third of the stars. He then prepares to devour the woman's child when she gives birth. Once born, however, her child ascends to the throne room of God and the woman flees to the desert for 1,260 days.

John has clearly borrowed elements of a myth that circulated for centuries in the Mediterranean world of the conflict between a monster and a pregnant woman. The monster receives intelligence that the woman's son will be his undoing and so he pursues the woman to kill her. The woman, however, receives divine protection, is saved from the monster, and gives birth to a son who then slays the monster.[91]

A common form of the myth in the Greco-Roman world explained how the dragon Python pursued Latona, the mother of the god Apollo, in an attempt to kill her and her unborn son. Zeus and Neptune aided Latona, one summoning a wind to blow her to the island of Delos and the other submerging Delos to hide Latona from Python. When the danger passed, Neptune brought Delos to the surface, Latona gave birth to Apollo (and Diana), and a very precocious four-day-old Apollo tracked down Python and killed him.[92]

John has not merely borrowed the myth but also infused it with elements drawn from the Scriptures. It is in these elements that the theological message of John's retelling of this old story lies. The woman who is in the midst of labor pains (12:1) is reminiscent of the use of labor pains to describe the trouble that exile inflicted on God's people. According to the prophets, God will shortly remove these labor pains

90 The relationship of 12:7–12 and 12:13–17 to 12:1–6 is not entirely clear, but of the several proposals, the outline given here seems to make the most sense. See Osborne, *Revelation*, 467, 481, although I have not adopted his view that the battle between the forces of God and Satan described in 12:7–12 occurred in the past.

91 See the description of the basic myth in, e.g., Caird, *Revelation*, 147–48; Adela Yarbro Collins, *The Apocalypse* (New Testament Message 22; Wilmington, Del.: Michael Glazier, 1979), 84–85; and esp. Aune, *Revelation 6–16*, 667–74, who offers an incisive critique of Yarbro Collins' claim that John has closely followed the "combat myth" in 12:1–17.

92 This is the form of the myth found in the obscure second century A.D. Latin author Hyginus. The part of his *Genealogiae* (often cited as *Fabulae*) that recounts the myth can be found in Aune, *Revelation 6–16*, 670.

(Isa. 26:17 [LXX]; 66:7–9; Mic. 4:9–10; 5:3).[93] Confirmation that the woman represents the people of God comes from the woman's crown with its twelve stars—for John, twelve is the symbolic number of God's people.[94]

The dragon has become "that ancient serpent called the devil, or Satan, who leads the whole world astray" (12:9)—an allusion to the serpent who deceived Eve in the garden with terrible consequences for all creation (Gen. 3:1–24). The pregnant woman's child is the Messiah of Psalm 2, who will "rule" the nations "with an iron scepter" and whom the "rulers of the earth" should serve (Ps. 2:9–12; cf. Rev. 2:5). The woman finds refuge from the dragon not on a submerged island but in the desert, the place where God provided refuge for his people from their slave-masters in Egypt (Ex. 13:17–22). She stays there 1,260 days (12:6), a time period that, as we have already seen, is drawn from Daniel's "time, times, and half a time" (Dan. 7:25; 12:7; cf. Rev. 12:14). John has also modified the standard myth with elements drawn from his knowledge of the historical Messiah, Jesus. Thus, the woman flees from the dragon not before but after giving birth, and her son is protected from the dragon not because he is hidden but because he ascends from the earth to the throne of God (Rev. 12:5; cf. 3:21; 5:6; 7:9–10, 17; 22:1, 3).[95]

These biblical allusions hold the key to the story's message. John is telling the account of God's people from creation to the present. From the time of the woman's encounter with the deceitful serpent in the garden, Satan has been on the rampage against God's people. He even tried to kill God's anointed ruler who would assure Satan's demise and lead God's people to victory. This only resulted, however, in Christ's ascension and heavenly enthronement. God, moreover, has always protected his people from ultimate harm, just as he protected Israel from Pharaoh in the desert. This protection did not mean that God's people were exempt from suffering. Rather, just as in Daniel, so here John reminds his readers that this period of suffering at the hands of God's enemies is both real and of limited duration.

In the next paragraph (12:7–12), John focuses the attack of the dragon on the stars of heaven that he had mentioned briefly in 12:4. He explains this statement in terms of a war that the dragon wages against Michael and his angels in heaven. Here too John echoes elements of a common myth, this time from Jewish tradition. It tells of a heavenly encounter between Satan and God's angels that ends in the expulsion of Satan from heaven. In ancient Jewish literature, this encounter sometimes takes place at the beginning of time (*Vit. Ad.* 12–16), sometimes just prior to the flood (*1 En.* 9–10; 86:1, 3; cf. Gen. 6:4), and sometimes in the final, terrible days before the end of all things (Dan. 12:1). Scripture occasionally uses this myth, not to describe something that happened in primordial times but to illustrate the demise of God's enemies (Isa. 14:12–15; Dan. 12:1; cf. Luke 10:18).[96] John uses the story in the same way and takes it, like Daniel (who also mentions Michael), to refer to something that happens in the last days (Dan. 12:1).

93 Beale, *Revelation*, 630.

94 Ibid., 626–27.

95 On these and other differences between John's story and Yarbro Collins' "combat myth," see Aune, *Revelation 6–16*, 671–72.

96 Cf. Caird, *Revelation*, 153, "The Bible knows nothing of the premundane fall of Satan, familiar to readers of *Paradise Lost*." *Pace* Osborne, *Revelation*, 467–73.

The loud voice in heaven (12:10–12a) tells us how we should understand the story. John's description of Satan's defeat in heaven is simply a retelling of the story of the dragon's pursuit of the woman on earth, but it takes the story a step further to speak both of the purpose of the suffering of God's people and of the final establishment of God's kingdom. The Roman empire is presently doing the will of Satan on earth by its oppressive military, religious, and economic policies, policies that have already resulted in the deaths of people like Jesus himself (5:6) and the faithful witness Antipas in Pergamum (3:13). Just as God's angelic forces won the war that John describes in heaven, however, so God will defeat the attempts of the Roman empire, and other regimes like it, who have joined forces with Satan through their oppression of God's people. This defeat of Satan will happen both through the atoning death of Jesus on the cross—"the blood of the Lamb"—and through the faithful suffering of God's people.[97] This faithful suffering often means, as it meant for the Lamb himself, opting for death rather than compromising with evil.

In the final paragraph of this section (12:13–17), John provides a more detailed explanation of his brief statement in 12:6 that the woman fled to the desert. We now learn for certain what the reference to the 1,260 days in 12:6 led us to suspect—that just as that time period in Daniel refers to the time of the suffering of God's people (Dan. 7:25; 12:7), so the woman in the desert, although protected from any ultimate harm, is still suffering attack from the dragon. God enabled her flight to the desert, we now learn, by giving her eagle's wings, just as he had brought Israel out of slavery in Egypt "on eagle's wings" (Ex. 19:4) and just as those who hoped in his faithfulness would "soar on wings like eagles" (Isa. 40:31).

Satan has not given up, for the dragon attacked the woman even in her safe desert haven, hoping to drown her in a flood just as Pharaoh had tried to drown Israelite boys in the Nile (Ex. 1:22). This attack on God's people cannot ultimately succeed, however. The water is swallowed by the earth, just as Pharaoh's army and Korah's allies were swallowed by the earth when they rebelled against God and his people (Ex. 15:12; Num. 16:33).[98]

The Dragon, the Two Beasts, and the Eschatological Judgment (13:1–16:21)

John next describes the triumph of Christians over their persecutors by means of a second myth, which he connects to the first through the dragon, who, according to the first myth, was hurled to earth (12:13) and who symbolizes Satan. In this second myth, the dragon inspires two beasts, a sea beast (13:1–2) and an earth beast (13:11), both of whom are enemies of God and his people (13:7, 15–17). The basic identity of both beasts is reasonably clear.

The "beast coming out of the sea" is Roman imperial power as it is concentrated in the emperor. Several characteristics of this beast point to this identity. First, the beast rises from the sea, just as, looking west from the coast of Asia Minor, the Roman

97 Swete, *Apocalypse*, 156; Bauckham, *Theology of the Book of Revelation*, 75–76; idem, *Climax of Prophecy*, 228–29.

98 Caird, *Revelation*, 158–60, and Beale, *Revelation*, 671–76.

proconsul always arrived from the sea, seeming to emerge slowly from the ocean depths as his ships approached.[99]

Second, the number of the sea beast (666) points to the emperor Nero (13:18). Although the meaning of 666 has been the subject of much learned (and unlearned) debate, the explanation that makes the most sense within John's circumstances is that John has employed the ancient technique of gematria to symbolize the name "Nero Caesar." Hebrew and Greek, like many ancient languages, used letters to designate numbers, and thus any word could be given a number simply by adding together the individual numbers for which each letter stood. When "Nero Caesar" is transliterated from Greek (Νέρων Καῖσαρ) into Hebrew (נרון קסר), the Hebrew letters add up to 666. When the Greek word for "beast" (θηρίον) is put into Hebrew characters (תריון), it yields the same sum.[100]

Third, John says that the beast from the sea suffers a fatal head wound from a sword and then recovers (13:3, 14), and this again seems to refer to Nero. Nero killed himself by driving a dagger into his throat (Suetonius, *Nero* 49.3), but for decades after his death, rumors circulated that instead of killing himself, Nero had fled to the east where he was mustering support for a return to power. Nero was popular with the people of Rome, with subjects in the Greek east, and with the Parthians. Many within these groups apparently hoped that the rumors of his return would come true.[101]

None of this means that John also believes the rumors and thinks that Nero will return as the Antichrist.[102] John could hardly have escaped knowing that Nero had cruelly persecuted Christians and that the apostles Paul and Peter had both lost their lives to his craven effort to blame the Roman church for a great fire that broke out in the city.[103] John probably sees Nero, therefore, as a fitting symbol for Roman imperial opposition to God's people whenever it occurs, and he probably sees the returning Nero myth as a convenient parable for the phoenix-like reemergence of order in the empire after the chaos that followed Nero's death in A.D. 68.

By mid-January of A.D. 69, the Praetorian guard had lynched Nero's successor, Galba; Otho had secured the imperial throne, and civil war had broken out between forces loyal to Otho and Vitellius. Within a few more months Vitellius had been proclaimed emperor and then himself faced civil war instigated by troops loyal to Vespasian.[104] As if all this were not enough, the small but strategically located province of Judea on the Parthian frontier was aflame with rebellion and war.

99 Cf. W. M. Ramsay, *The Letters to the Seven Churches of Asia and Their Place in the Plan of the Apocalypse* (New York: Hodder & Stoughton, 1904), 103–5; Caird, *Revelation*, 162; Beale, *Revelation*, 682.

100 See the full discussion in Bauckham, *Climax of Prophecy*, 384–407.

101 Suetonius, *Nero* 57; Tacitus, *Hist.* 1.2; 2.8–9; Dio Cassius 64.9; *Sib. Or.* 4.137–39, 145–48.

102 Richard Holland, *Nero: The Man behind the Myth* (Thrupp, England: Sutton, 2000), 236–39, suggests that John, crazed with a desire to avenge Nero's persecution of Christians, predicted the emperor's return so that he could be thrown into the lake of fire and tortured eternally. If not John's view, he says, it was certainly a common interpretation of John in early Christianity.

103 Tacitus, *Ann.* 15.44.2–8; Suetonius, *Nero* 16.2; *1 Clem.* 5–6; Eusebius, *Hist. eccl.* 2.25.5–8.

104 This summary is dependent upon the account of these events in M. Cary, *A History of Rome down to the Reign of Constantine*, 2nd ed. (London: Macmillan, 1957), 594–606.

Into what must have seemed to many like the collapse of the empire walked Vespasian and the Flavian family. Vespasian and his son Titus pacified Judea, and their rule restored a stability to the empire that continued, under Titus's brother Domitian, into John's own time. From John's perspective, the fatally wounded beast of Roman imperial power had recovered.[105]

To many unbelievers both in Rome and abroad, the coming of the Flavian dynasty after the chaotic "year of the four emperors" must have appeared to be divine confirmation that Rome's claim to eternal rule over its subjects was valid. This was certainly a notion that the Flavians themselves were eager to promote.[106] In John's words, "the whole world was astonished and followed the beast" (13:3), and people "worshiped the beast and asked, 'Who is like the beast? Who can make war against him?'" (13:4). The events of A.D. 68–69, in other words, bolstered religious devotion to Rome, whether expressed through the cult of Roma, sacrifice to various local deities on behalf of Rome, worship of deceased emperors, or participation in the cult of the living emperor.

For believers, such success could only mean conflict and suffering. Like the "little horn" in Daniel's vision, Rome adopted and encouraged the blasphemous view that it was divine (13:5, 8; Dan. 7:8, 11, 20, 25), and like the fourth of Daniel's terrible beasts, Rome, in its renewed confidence, would oppress the people of God (Rev. 13:7, 10; cf. Dan. 7:21, 25).[107]

The "beast coming out of the earth" refers to the local assemblies and priests in Asia itself who encouraged cultic devotion to Rome. This beast comes from the earth because, although these authorities encouraged religious devotion to Roman power, they were located in Asia.[108] John envisions them as compelling people to worship the first beast by a combination of both specious persuasion and oppressive dissuasion. Fake miracles, probably in the form of the magical arts so prevalent in Roman Asia, are provided for the gullible to urge them to acknowledge Rome's divine pretensions (13:13–15).[109]

For those inclined to dissent, the earth beast forbids anyone who is without the beast's mark to buy or sell. This may refer to the economic pressure put on those who refused to participate in the numerous cultic festivals that dotted the Roman and provincial calendars, or to pressure from trade guilds to participate in the imperial cult. This kind of pressure seems to have deeply affected John's readers, impoverishing the faithful, such as those at Smyrna (2:9), and making attractive to others "the

105 Bauckham, *Theology of the Book of Revelation*, 37; idem, *Climax of Prophecy*, 444–45.

106 Giancarlo Biguzzi, "Ephesus, Its Artemision, Its Temple to the Flavian Emperors, and Idolatry in Revelation," *NovT* 40 (1998): 227–90, here at 282.

107 It is possible that the reference of Pliny the Younger, writing from Bithynia under the reign of Trajan, to Christians who had abandoned their faith "as much as twenty-five years ago" (A.D. 85–90, *Ep.* 10.96) refers to people who abandoned their commitment to Christianity under the pressures that John describes in Rev. 13.

108 Ramsay, *Letters*, 104–5. Caird, *Revelation*, 171, identifies the beast from the earth with the provincial assembly of Asia. Bauckham, *Theology of the Book of Revelation*, 38, prefers the idea that the earth beast is the Asian imperial priesthood. Beale, *Revelation*, 707–8, believes that the earth beast refers to Christian false prophets who encourage compromise with idolatrous practices. It is difficult to imagine Christian false prophets persecuting other Christians, however, as 13:16–17 seems to envision, and it seems prudent not to identify the beast too specifically with either the provincial assembly or the imperial priesthood.

109 Swete, *Apocalypse*, xci–xcii, 170; Caird, *Revelation*, 172.

teaching of Balaam" and of "that woman Jezebel," which advocated sexual immorality and participation in the banquets where idols were honored (2:14, 20).

In contrast to "Balaam" and "Jezebel," John believes that Christians cannot compromise with these beasts. Involvement in any form of religious devotion to Rome is incompatible with Christian worship. He shows this by describing both the beast from the sea and the beast from the earth as parodies of God and the Lamb.

The sea beast wears diadems on each of its ten horns (13:1), a symbol of its claim to the kingship that belongs to Christ alone (19:16).[110] Satan gives his power, throne, and authority to the beast (13:2), parodying the power, kingdom, and authority that God shares with Christ (12:10). The beast seems to have been "slaughtered" (*hos esphagmenēn*, 13:3) and then comes back "to life" (*ezēsen*, 13:14), just as Jesus seemed to have been "slaughtered" (*hos esphagmenon*, 5:6) and then "came to life" (*ezēsen*, 2:8).[111] Every tribe, people, tongue, and nation worship the beast, a parody of the worship of the true God and of the Lamb by the great multitude drawn from every nation, all tribes, peoples, and tongues (7:9; cf. 5:10).

The earth beast's parody of Jesus is less developed but is nevertheless clear. He has "two horns like a lamb" (13:11), an echo of the description of Jesus as the Lamb who stands before God's throne (5:6–13). In addition, the earth beast works "signs" in an effort to show the divinity of the sea beast (13:13–14), just as, in the Johannine tradition, Jesus worked "signs" that pointed people to the truth of his divine sonship (John 20:30).

John intends by all this a straightforward message. The two beasts and the dragon on one side and God and the Lamb on the other side make the same, totalistic claims. No one, therefore, can legitimately worship both at the same time.

In light of this situation, John makes clear to his readers what their commitment to God and the Lamb requires. They must suffer the oppression of the two beasts for the same period of time that in the myth of the dragon and the woman God will protect his people from ultimate harm: "1,260 days" (12:6) or "time, times and half a time" (12:14), expressed here as "forty-two months" (13:5). As we have seen, this is the same period of time that Daniel had called on God's people to suffer the oppression of a similar beast (Dan. 7:7–12, 25; 12:14).

As always, this number is figurative, indicating that God's people will suffer but that God has put specific limits on the amount of suffering they must endure. Some will become prisoners, some will die by the sword, and some will become poor (13:9–10, 17), but God calls on all to endure these trials faithfully, without compromise (13:10). In the story of the dragon and the woman, John emphasized that God would protect his people from ultimate harm during this period. In the present story of the dragon and the two beasts, John's emphasis lies on the responsibility of God's people to remain faithful during this period of hardship.

If they do so, then at the end of their trials, they will join the genuine Lamb, whom they have followed through faithful suffering (14:1–5). They will gather with

110 Caird, *Revelation*, 163.

111 Bauckham, *Climax of Prophecy*, 432–33.

him on Mount Zion, the biblical gathering place of the remnant of God's people whom he has brought safely through the time of testing (2 Kings 19:31; Isa 4:2–3; 10:20; Joel 2:32; Obad. 17; Mic. 4:7–8).[112] In this way they will "conquer" the beast (Rev. 15:2) who had first "conquered" them (13:7), and so, like the Lamb, they will conquer by being conquered. They will, therefore, sing the victory song of the Lamb, modeled on the song of Moses, in which God's people celebrated their rescue from the pursuing Egyptians by God's power (15:3–4; cf. 14:3; Ex. 15:11).

If the wicked who oppress God's people continue to reject the gospel (14:6–7) and the clear warning of the beast's coming judgment (14:8), however, they will experience the outpouring of God's wrath (15:9–11, 14–20). The echoes in the bowl judgments of the ten plagues that God brought on the Egyptians mean that God will not spare the unrepentant oppressors of his people any more than he spared the Egyptians (16:1–21). God will give to Rome and to those who support her oppressive authority "the cup filled with the wine of the fury of his wrath" (16:19).

Summary

The two mythological stories that separate the seven seals and seven trumpets from the rapid outpouring of God's wrath on the wicked in the seven bowls communicate several layers of meaning. At one level, since these two stories interrupt the series of three sets of plagues, they demonstrate God's merciful desire to delay judgment so that the wicked might be given more time to repent.

At another level, they offer both an encouragement and a challenge to God's people as they suffer under the oppression of the wicked during this allotted "time, times, and half a time." The encouragement comes in the form of the story of the dragon and the woman. This story shows that despite Satan's attempts to destroy God's people, God will protect them from ultimate harm and bring his purposes to completion. The challenge comes in the form of the story of the dragon and the two beasts, where John shows that the church must remain faithful during the difficult days of Roman oppression prior to the final outpouring of God's wrath on the wicked.

God's Perspective on the Suffering of His People: A Summary

In the central section of his book, John has tried to show his readers how God calls on them to live in the times that he has given them. He has done this by entering the throne room of God and supplying his readers with a vision of their suffering from God's perspective. His readers live during a time when God is pouring out his fully justified wrath on his rebellious creatures. Like the Egyptians whom God "tormented through their own abominations" (Wisd. 12:23), God is pouring out his wrath on the wicked by causing them to experience the suffering that comes with the lust for power. As time progresses, God will increase their suffering until he finally pours out the full force of his wrath on them.

112 Beale, *Revelation*, 731–32.

The present, however, is a time of delay, and this delay is of great importance both for the wicked and for God's people. For the wicked, the delay had a twofold significance. First, it mercifully allows them time to repent of their rebellion against God. John hints in 11:13 that, especially as God begins to increase their suffering, some of the wicked will do just that. Second, and paradoxically, the delay allows God to assemble his judicial case against the unrepentant wicked as they continue to reject the witness of his people.

For God's people, the delay also has a twofold significance. First, as they continue to experience suffering and oppression at the hands of the wicked, they should remember that this suffering is part of God's predetermined plan and that he will protect them from apostasy during this difficult time. Just as assuredly as the earth beast exercises the authority of the dragon for forty-two months, so God protects the woman from the dragon for 1,260 days, or for a "time, times, and half a time." Second, this comforting truth nevertheless does not release them from the responsibility of remaining faithful to God and the Lamb during the period allotted to the oppressive beast. As the sealed people of God, they must keep themselves pure, and, after they do, they will join the ultimately victorious Lamb on Mount Zion. There they will sing the new song of the victory of God's people.

TWO CITIES AND THEIR SEPARATE DESTINIES (17:1–22:5)

Two of the same angels who poured out the bowls of judgments now introduce the final section of Revelation (17:1; 21:9). This indicates that the visions in this final section, like the visions in the previous section, appear in the throne room of God. These visions too give God's perspective on the oppression of his people.

Each of the angels shows John a vision of a city. The first angel shows him the city of Rome, conceived from two different perspectives both as a beast and a prostitute (17:1–20:15). The second angel shows him the new Jerusalem, described as the bride of the Lamb (21:1–22:5). Both visions are designed to demonstrate the character and the destiny of these two cities. Just as in the great central section, John both encourages and warns Christians who must live in the wicked but seductive atmosphere of the *pax Romana*. John wants to encourage the suffering faithful that one day the evil system that oppresses them will be destroyed. He also wants to warn Christians against Rome's promise of power and luxury to those willing to compromise with its system. The end of this system, he says in this passage, is destruction.

Rome as Prostitute and Beast (17:1–20:15)

Rome as Prostitute

The city of Rome, personified as a richly robed woman, had been worshiped as a goddess in many of Roman Asia's urban centers since at least the early second century B.C. Smyrna had erected a temple for the worship of *Dea Roma* in 195 B.C. In the second half of the first century B.C. Augustus allowed both Ephesus and Pergamum to do the same.[113]

In contrast to this dignified conception of Rome, John portrays the city as a prostitute (17:9, 18). The image captures much of what John found wrong with Roman power. Just as the prostitute corrupts both herself and those she seduces in order to enrich herself, so Rome lures "the kings of the earth" and "the inhabitants of the earth" into participation in her idolatrous, authoritarian regime with promises that they too will be rich if they help Rome satisfy her craving for luxury (17:1–2; 18:3, 7, 9; 19:2).[114]

This is why the prostitute is richly adorned with the classic symbols of Roman luxury. She wears purple and scarlet clothes, is adorned with gold, jewels, and pearls, and carries a golden cup (17:4; 18:6). This is also why, when God destroys the prostitute, "the merchants of the earth will weep and mourn over her" (18:11a). As John puts it, "no one buys their cargoes any more" (18:11b). He then lists these cargoes in detail, and they turn out to be the luxury items that Rome imported from its provinces to maintain the comfortable way of life of its elite classes (18:12–13).[115]

The prostitute's enticements are also reminiscent for John of the Bible's frequent coupling of idolatry with sexual immorality, both in a literal and a metaphorical sense. When Israel worshiped the golden calf while Moses lingered on Mount Sinai, they organized a festival at which "they sat down to eat and drink and got up to indulge in revelry" (Ex. 32:6). Later, God warned Israel not to enter into treaties with the peoples who lived in the land to which he was leading them, "for when they prostitute themselves to their gods and sacrifice to them, they will invite you and you will eat their sacrifices," and when Israelite men intermarry with the women of these peoples, God says, these women will lead the men to "prostitute themselves to their gods" (Ex. 34:15–16).

This very thing happened in Moab just before Israel crossed the Jordan into the land of promise: Moabite women, apparently with the promise of sexual rewards, enticed Israelite men to worship their gods (Num. 25:1–2). Israel's willingness to worship other gods and its other departures from its "marriage contract" with Yahweh often appear in the prophets as metaphorical adultery (e.g., Isa. 1:21; 57:3; Jer. 2:20; Hos. 1–3).[116] Perhaps most significantly for understanding Revelation, the biblical Jezebel, wife of Israel's King Ahab, was not only viewed as an idolater (1 Kings 16:31–33; 18:19) but also as a prostitute (2 Kings 9:22). John's description of Rome as a prostitute, therefore, also serves as an implicit warning to God's newly constituted people not to succumb to her enticements as God's ancient people had done.

113 Beard, North, and Price, *Religions of Rome*, 1:158–59; Steven J. Friesen, *Imperial Cults and the Apocalypse of John: Reading Revelation in the Ruins* (Oxford: Oxford Univ. Press, 2001), 25–27. See Tacitus, *Ann.* 4.56, and Dio Cassius 51.20.6–9. For the rich robes of Roma, see the photograph of the late second century B.C. statue of the goddess on the island of Delos in Beard, North, and Price, *Religions of Rome*, 1:159.

114 John found precedent for describing the commercial exploits of a large city as the activity of a prostitute in such biblical passages as Isa. 23:15–18 (Tyre); Nah. 3:1–7 (Nineveh); Isa. 47:10, LXX (Babylon). See Friedrich Hauck and Siegfried Schulz, "πόρνη (κτλ)," *TDNT* 6:579–95, here at 587.

115 Bauckham, *Climax of Prophecy*, 338–83.

116 For the persistence of the link between sexual immorality and idolatry in Second Temple Judaism, see, e.g., Wisd. 14:12; *T. Reu.* 4:6, 11; *T. Sim.* 5.3.

Rome is not only the great prostitute but "the mother of prostitutes" (17:5), and John wants his Christian readers to avoid her corrupting influence.

The prostitute is also a wicked woman, and therefore this image can serve as a link to one of John's most important themes: Rome is like Babylon (14:8; 16:19; 17:5; 18:2, 10, 21), the classic biblical opponent of God and his people. The importance of the theme for John can perhaps best be seen by a comparison of his description of the prostitute and her fate with the descriptions of Babylon and her fate in Isaiah 47 and Jeremiah 51. In Isaiah 47:1–15, the prophet describes Babylon as a haughty queen, "the queen of kingdoms" (47:5), who thinks that she will last forever (47:7) and who arrogates to herself titles that only belong to God: "I am," she says, "and there is none besides me" (47:8, 10; cf. 45:6). John similarly describes the prostitute as glorifying herself (Rev. 18:17a) and thinking of herself as a queen who will never mourn the loss of either husband or children (18:7b). In Isaiah, Babylon is a "wanton creature," "lounging in . . . security" (Isa. 47:8), and, at least in the LXX's rendering of Isaiah 47:10, she engages in "sexual immorality." This is reminiscent of John's description of Rome as a prostitute who lived sensually (Rev. 18:7a).

Similarly, in Jeremiah 51:1–64, Babylon is a woman (Jer. 51:6–8) who, like John's prostitute (Rev. 17:2, 4; 18:3), carries a gold cup with which she makes the nations drunk (Jer. 51:7). She lives "by many waters," like John's prostitute who sits "on many waters" (Rev. 17:1, 15), and she is a "destroying mountain (Jer. 51:25), just as Rome sits on "seven mountains" (Rev. 17:9). Babylon, like the prostitute Rome (Rev. 17:4), is also "rich in treasures" (Jer. 51:13).

Two elements of the biblical picture of Babylon are particularly important for John. First, Babylon was utterly destroyed, just as Rome will be utterly destroyed. The great queen of kingdoms who thought she would never experience loss of children or widowhood would be overtaken by both of these tragedies "in a moment" (Isa. 47:9). She who poured out the cup of God's wrath on his people would "suddenly fall" (Jer. 51:8). Rome too, although she said, "I am not a widow, and I will never mourn," will be destroyed "in one day," indeed "in one hour" (Rev. 18:7–8, 10, 17, 19).

Babylon's destruction will be measured out in accord with the destruction that she measured out to God's people (Jer. 51:35). Similarly, Rome will receive a double portion of the violence that she has visited on others (Rev. 18:6–8). Just as Babylon became "a heap of ruins, a haunt of jackals . . . a place where no one lives" (Jer. 51:37), so Rome will be "a home for demons and a haunt for every evil spirit, a haunt for every unclean and detestable bird" (Rev. 18:2; cf. 18:21–23). Just as Babylon, which once controlled various surrounding nations, was attacked by various nations (51:27), so surrounding nations will turn on Rome and destroy her power (17:16).

Second, just as Jeremiah warned God's people to flee from Babylon lest they be caught in its sudden destruction (Jer. 51:6, 9, 45, 50), so John urges his readers to "come out" of Rome so that they "will not share in her sins" and "will not receive any of her plagues" (Rev. 18:4). For Jeremiah this refrain reflects a concern that God's people not experience the terrors that will come to Babylon when it falls and a concern that they return to the land of Israel to participate in the fulfillment of Israel's promised restoration. It is, in other words, a literal command to flee from one geographical region to another.[117]

For John, however, the command is metaphorical, for he hopes his Christian readers will flee from the wiles of the Roman prostitute.[118] They should not succumb to society's pressure to participate in the idolatrous practices with which Rome supports its hegemony over its vast empire. They should not support the oppressive regime that builds wealth and stability, but does so on the backs of the socially disfranchised. To participate in this ungodly and unjust system is to follow the teaching of Balaam and Jezebel (2:14, 20). It is to soil one's clothes with the immorality of a society doomed to destruction (3:4; cf. 16:15).

Rome as Beast

If the picture of Rome as a prostitute warns John's readers against the tendency of the government under which they live to lure them into idolatry with promises of wealth, John's picture of Rome as a beast warns them that institutionalized idolatry will only grow worse until God himself intervenes to rescue his people and exact retribution for their oppression. In chapter 13, John's portrayal of Rome and those who supported her as two beasts was, as we have just seen, intended to provide comfort to God's people that their present suffering is under God's control and that they should be faithful during this time of trial. Although they are being conquered by the beast (13:7), their suffering will one day end. Now John turns to the future and describes the fate of the beast.

As in chapter 13, so here in chapter 17, John describes the beast in terms reminiscent both of Daniel 7 and of the popular myth of Nero's return. The beast of chapter 17, like its counterpart in chapter 13 and the fourth beast of Daniel 7, has ten horns and makes blasphemous claims for itself (Rev. 17:3; cf. 13:1, 5–6; Dan. 7:7, 8, 11, 20, 25). Like its counterpart in chapter 13 and like Nero in the myth, the beast of chapter 17 disappears and then eventually reappears to the astonishment of the world (17:8, 11).

Now, however, the beast becomes a future "eighth king." He "now is not" but his coming will be a parody of Christ's Parousia—he will ascend from the Abyss and go to destruction (17:8), just as Jesus will descend from heaven (19:11) and reign forever (11:15).[119] John's purpose in projecting the returning Nero myth into the future is to show that although the suffering of God's people will grow worse under rebellious institutions such as Rome's authoritarian rule, God will use the very wickedness of Rome to destroy Rome itself and will eventually bring all such wickedness to an end.

John shows that Rome's wickedness will lead to its own demise by merging the returning Nero myth with the imagery of the ten-horned beast of Daniel 7:7, 20, and 24, and then giving the ten horns a function within the myth.[120] They now

117 J. A. Thompson, *The Book of Jeremiah* (NICOT; Grand Rapids: Eerdmans, 1980), 750, 765.

118 Cf. Osborne, *Revelation*, 638–39.

119 Cf. Bauckham, *Climax of Prophecy*, 436.

120 In Rev. 12:3 and 13:1 John only mentions the ten horns without assigning them a specific function.

become the kings from the east who, in the returning Nero myth, will join Nero to wage war on Rome. They "give their power and authority to the beast" and "hate the prostitute," whom they bring to ruin (17:13, 16). Just as in some Jewish forms of the returning Nero myth, God uses the wicked beast and his allies to punish those who had mistreated his people (cf. *Sib. Or.* 4.145–48), so, in John's retelling of the myth, Rome's blasphemous abuse of its military might leads to its own destruction by God's design (17:17).[121]

For John, the returning Nero is also a symbol of Rome's vicious, if sporadic, persecution of Christians. The returning Nero and his allies will act no differently toward Christians than the historical Nero; like Daniel's little horn, Rome will "make war against the Lamb" and oppress the saints of the Most High (17:14; cf. Dan. 7:8, 21, 25).

Here, too, God will intervene. In contrast to the picture of the beast in chapter 13, where he conquers Christians (13:7), now the Lamb—the true Lord of lords and King of kings—will ride forth with the army of his faithful followers and conquer the beast and his allies (17:14). Together with the beast from the sea of 13:11–17, now identified simply as the false prophet (19:20; 20:10; cf. 16:13), they will experience "the fury of the wrath of God Almighty" (19:11–21). The allies of the beast and his prophet will be killed, and the beast and prophet themselves will be thrown into "a fiery lake of burning sulfur" (19:20).

John takes the returning Nero myth as expressed in chapter 17 no more literally than he took it in chapter 13. His description of the beast shows that institutionalized rebellion against God will only grow worse as history progresses and that Christians will frequently suffer under these worsening conditions. It also shows, however, that God uses the self-destructive nature of such rebellion to punish those who promote it and compromise with it, and that eventually he will bring all such rebellion against him and persecution of his people to an end.

The Millennium

John shows next that after the destruction of the beast and his prophet, the tables will be turned. Rather than Rome and its allies ruling the nations, Christ and his faithful followers will rule the nations. Unlike Rome whose rule will only span a few centuries, Christ and his people will rule for a thousand years. Rather than experiencing, like the beast and false prophet, the "second death" of the lake of fire, those who have died under Rome's persecutions will experience the "first resurrection" so that they might reign with Christ (20:4–5). Just as Satan once gave his authority to the Roman beast so that the beast might persecute God's people (12:3, 9, 13, 17; 13:1, 2, 4, 11; 16:13), so he will be bound and rendered impotent to resist the rule of the Messiah and his people (20:2).

To prove both the unyielding nature of Satan's opposition to God and his impotence in the face of God's power, God releases Satan at the end of the thousand years, like some wild animal whose viciousness goes briefly on display before its keepers

121 On *Sib. Or.* 4.145–48, see Bauckham, *Climax of Prophecy*, 415–16.

handily dispatch it. Once again Satan deceives the nations and inspires an army to attack God's people (20:7–9a), but his effort turns out to be a tempest in a teapot, a mere mockery of his stubborn but doomed attempt to resist God's power. Finally, God consigns him to the lake of fire (20:10), and, along with him, go death and Hades (20:14).

Just as with his use of the returning Nero myth, so here John speaks symbolically. Although the concept of a period during which God's people will rule the nations before final judgment is common in apocalyptic literature from John's period, John shows by the way that he handles this tradition that he does not intend for his readers to understand it literally.[122] For John, the Millennium becomes a symbol of God's determination to correct the abuses that Christians have experienced at the hands of Satan, the Roman political and military authorities, and those who promoted religious devotion to Rome in its various idolatrous forms.

The Roman empire existed for a short time; Christ's sovereignty over the nations exists for a thousand years. Satan used Rome to kill Christians with relative abandon; Satan is bound for a thousand years. Satan waged a lengthy war against Christians in which he conquered them; Satan wages a brief war against Christians in which he is quickly squashed. Christians were executed for resisting Roman religious authority; Christians are raised from the dead to exercise authority. The second death is the fate of Satan and his allies; Christians are immune from the second death and instead experience the first resurrection.[123]

For John, this symbol of the millennial reign of Christians demonstrates the impotence of Satan to gain the ultimate victory over God and his people. It shows that as strong as Satan may have looked in the form of the vicious red dragon that inspired the Roman beast to do his bidding, he was never an equal opposite to God. He is nothing more than God's own creature, who will continue to insist to the bitter end on rebelling against God but whom God will one day, when all his purposes are accomplished, effortlessly destroy.

The New Jerusalem, the Bride of Christ (21:1–22:5)

In contrast to Rome the gaudy prostitute, now wiped from the face of the earth, stands the eternal new Jerusalem, the bejeweled bride of Christ, "beautifully dressed for her husband" (21:2, 11, 18–21).[124] Here the purposes of God in history reach their goal. As the many references to the number twelve in John's description of the city indicate (21:12, 14, 21; 22:2), the city is the final dwelling place of God's people. Here they have unmediated access to God's presence because no evil can intrude between God and his people. Here people from all nations assemble to give their glory and honor to God because Adam's curse is reversed and all creation has returned to the condition it had before sin distorted its shape.

122 John alone makes the intermediary period of the rule of God's people over the earth last for a thousand years, but the idea of such an intermediary rule appears in *1 En.* 91:12–17; 4 Ezra 7:26–30; *2 Bar.* 29.3–30.1; 40.1–4; 72.2–74.3, all of which were written prior to or at roughly the same time as Revelation. See David E. Aune, *Revelation 17–22* (WBC 52C; Nashville: Nelson, 1998), 1104–8.

123 Cf. Bauckham, *Theology of the Book of Revelation*, 106–8.

124 Cf. Caird, *Revelation*, 262.

The Presence of God with His People

John pictures the new Jerusalem as the place where God's people have constant, unmediated access to his presence. The new Jerusalem is the fulfillment of prophetic expectations that one day, when God restores the fortunes of his people, he will be fully present in their midst. In Ezekiel, God puts the promise this way: "I will put my sanctuary among them forever. My dwelling place will be with them; I will be their God, and they will be my people" (Ezek. 37:26–27). John borrows this language to formulate God's announcement of the descending holy city: "Behold! The tabernacle [*skēnē*] of God is with humankind, and he will dwell [*skēnōsei*] with them, and they themselves will be his peoples, and he himself will be with them" (Rev. 21:3, aut.).

John's reference to the "tabernacle" of God recalls the use of the term *skēnē* in the LXX to refer to the "Tent of Meeting," the tent that God instructed Moses to build in the desert after the exodus from Egypt. God's presence with his restored people would be analogous to, but greater than, that period of God's presence and provision for his people in the wilderness.

No literal tabernacle or sanctuary will be required, however, for "the Lord God Almighty and the Lamb are [the city's] temple" (21:22). The tabernacle and temple were not only symbolic of God's presence with his people but, because purity regulations strictly limited access to them and because in them priests offered atoning sacrifices, they also spoke of the separation between God and humankind. Since there will be no sin in the new Jerusalem, however, there will be no need for a temple to symbolize the distance that sin placed between God and his people.

Because God and the Lamb are present with their people in the holy city, moreover, their glory supplies the light that would normally come from the moon and the sun. Their luminous presence fulfills the expectation expressed throughout Isaiah that when God restored his people, he would dispel the darkness and himself supply the light for his people to see, making the sun and moon unnecessary (21:23; 22:5; cf. Isa. 9:2; 30:26; 42:16; 58:8; 60:1–2, 19).[125]

The Absence of Evil

God's presence is able to dwell among his people in the holy city because all evil is banished from it. Again using imagery from Isaiah, John says that God "will wipe every tear from" the "eyes" of his people and that "there will be . . . no more death or mourning or crying or pain, for the old order of things has passed away" (21:4; cf. Isa. 25:8).[126] "The cowardly, the unbelieving, the vile, the murderers, the sexually immoral, those who practice magic arts, the idolaters and all liars"—in other words, all those who have followed the path that Rome's idolatrous regime cut for them—will go into the lake of fire (21:8).[127] Nothing "impure . . . shameful . . . or deceitful"

125 John may also intend to echo the language of Zech. 14:6–7, which describes "the day of the LORD" this way: "On that day there will be no light, no cold or frost. It will be a unique day, without daytime or nighttime—a day known to the LORD. When evening comes, there will be light."

126 Caird, *Revelation*, 265.

127 Ibid., 267.

will enter the city (21:27). The world will return to its condition prior to Adam's fall and God's subsequent, justified curse. "The river of the water of life" and "the tree of life" will be there, and "no longer will there be any curse" (22:1–3; cf. Gen. 3:17).[128]

This concept probably lies behind the list of twelve jewels that comprise the material for the city's twelve foundations (21:19–21). John's list roughly matches the list of jewels on the high priest's breastpiece according to Exodus 28:17–20 and 39:10–12.[129] Since the city is the habitation of God's people, as the numbering of its many features in twelves and multiples of twelve indicates, John probably intends by his list of jewels that all who live in the city are priests, indeed high priests, something he says explicitly in 20:6.[130] The city and its people, therefore, are entirely holy, and God can dwell among his people without compromising his own holiness.[131]

A Place from Which God Exercises Sovereignty over All Creation

The twelve different kinds of fruit from the tree of life hint that God's people will be composed of people from all nations, a hint made more explicit when John goes on to say, "the leaves of the tree are for the healing of the nations" (22:2). Much of John's imagery for the heavenly city has come from Ezekiel, who speaks similarly of a future city of certain dimensions (Ezek. 45:6), a river flowing from the place of God's presence (in Ezek. 47:1–6, the temple), and trees "of all kinds" growing on either side of the river, which will bear fruit every month (47:12).

The leaves of Ezekiel's trees also contain healing power, but there is no mention in Ezekiel of the healing of the nations.[132] John makes this explicit because his city is a place where "the nations will walk by" the light that the glory of God and the Lamb gives to the city (21:24). John sees the city as a place to which the nations will bring not their impurities, as had happened so often in the past history of the historical Jerusalem, but their own glory and honor (21:26). The names of those from the nations who pass into the perpetually opened gates of the city are all "written in the Lamb's book of life" (21:27). These people, therefore, are all part of the people of God.

The significance of the opening announcement of the presence of the heavenly city can now be fully appreciated. In that announcement, a voice from God's throne had said that "the tabernacle of God is with humankind" and that "they themselves will be his peoples" (21:3). It now becomes clear that this means all humankind in its various ethnic expressions throughout God's creation. There is now "no longer

128 Ibid., 280.

129 The differences can be reasonably explained if John made his own translation of the list from Hebrew to Greek and did not rely on previous Greek translations, such as those expressed or implied by the LXX, by Philo (who takes the biblical list to be identical with the twelve stones associated with the zodiac, *Vit. Mos.* 2.124), or by Josephus (who gives the list in two different orders, *B. J.* 5.234 and *A. J.* 3.168). See Caird, *Revelation*, 274–77.

130 Cf. Beale, *Revelation*, 1081, who draws attention to the similar idea expressed in 1 Peter 2:5.

131 Beale, ibid., 1082–85, argues that in addition to suggesting the holiness of God's people, the list of jewels of which the city's foundation is composed also suggests the security of God's people and the glory of God himself. The notion of safety from any danger of future oppression, he says, is suggested by the echoes of Isa. 54:11–12 in Rev. 21:18–19 and 21, and the use of precious jewels to express God's glory is present not only in 21:11 (cf. 4:3) but in early Jewish literature (such as Wisd. 18:24–25).

132 Osborne, *Revelation*, 772.

133 Bauckham, *Climax of Prophecy*, 310–13; idem, *Theology of the Book of Revelation*, 136–40.

... any curse" (22:3), and so humanity in its various kinds can enjoy unmediated access to the full presence of God (22:4).[133]

John therefore brings to a climax a leitmotif of his work. Despite the alliance of many nations with the Roman beast in its oppressive policies, particularly its persecution of God's people (17:2, 12–14; 18:3, 9–20), and the necessary destruction of those among the nations who have refused to acknowledge him (8:11; 11:13a; 9:15, 18; 19:15, 17–18, 21), God has nevertheless continued to proclaim the gospel to the nations (14:6–7). Many among the nations have responded to God's merciful overtures with repentance (5:9; 7:9; 11:13b; cf. 15:4), and now their participation in the joy of God's presence demonstrates the full triumph of God over the wickedness that formerly ravaged his creation and his people.[134]

In this John sees the fulfillment of the prophetic hope that one day the nations will join Israel in bringing homage to God. John's description of the holy city as on "a mountain great and high" (21:10) recalls Isaiah's expectation that "in the last days the mountain of the LORD's temple will be established as chief among the mountains; it will be raised above the hills, and all nations will stream to it" (Isa. 2:2).

John's claim that "the nations will walk by" the "light" that God and the Lamb supply and will bring their glory through perpetually opened gates (21:24–25) similarly recalls Isaiah's hope that one day "nations will come to [Israel's] light and kings to the brightness of [Israel's] dawn" (Isa. 60:3). At that time, says Isaiah, the gates in the walls of security surrounding his people "will always stand open, they will never be shut, day or night, so that people may bring [Israel] the wealth of the nations" (60:11; cf. Rev. 21:10, 24). John clarifies this vision, however, to show that the wealth the nations bring is their "glory" and "honor" (Rev. 21:24, 26) and that the focus within the holy city is on service to God (22:3).[135] In the new Jerusalem, the prophetic expectation of the restoration of God's people and of God's unquestioned sovereignty over all creation is fulfilled.

THE DESTINY OF GOD'S PEOPLE AND THE MEANING OF THEIR SUFFERING

The Christians in the Roman province of Asia for whom John writes Revelation are facing a crisis. A Roman procurator had crucified Jesus, a host of Roman Christians had died violently at the whim of the emperor Nero, and a certain Antipas, known to John, had died in Pergamum for his faithful witness to Jesus. Many who had escaped physical violence had nevertheless suffered economically because of their refusal to support Rome's claim that its imperial authority was divinely sanctioned. John's heavenly vision had shown him, moreover, that conditions would become much worse.

What is the meaning of all this suffering—past, present, and future—and what will be its outcome? Will Rome, with its immense power, succeed in quashing the

134 Cf. Osborne, *Revelation*, 772.

135 Cf. Bauckham, *Climax of Prophecy*, 313–16.

tiny, despised group of Christians—"a class loathed for their vices," as Tacitus called them (*Ann.* 15.44.3)? Or will the prophets be vindicated so that God will restore the fortunes of his people as he promised to do after Babylon had oppressed them? To people asking questions like these, John hopes to provide both an encouragement and a challenge.

He does this by describing, like prophets and seers before him, a vision of the throne room of God. From the perspective of God's throne, the might of Rome and the suffering of Christians look different than they do from the perspective of Asia. In Asia, Rome claims divine status and eternal sovereignty over its empire. Frequent festivals celebrating these claims provide lavish displays of Rome's wealth and its political and military might. Those who support these claims prosper, and there is no shortage of Christian attempts to accommodate them. From God's throne, Rome looks like a satanically inspired beast bent on false claims to divinity and the persecution of those who say otherwise. It looks like a gaudily dressed and drunken prostitute, seducing the nations of the earth to support wicked schemes—including the oppression of God's people—for its own enrichment.

Rome and those who support her power will not succeed, however, in their scheme to snatch God's crown and destroy his people. They will experience the outpouring of God's wrath in various plagues. They will feel the sword of the rider on the white horse. They will plunge headlong into a fiery lake. God's people will rule in Rome's place and inherit a beautiful city where there is "no more death or mourning or crying or pain." Here, God's people will be so safe that the city's gates can remain perpetually open to receive the nations, who will come through them to pay homage to God.

What, then, is the purpose of all the suffering? John views the suffering of the wicked and the suffering of God's people from different perspectives. The wicked suffer for two reasons. First, through their suffering, God punishes them for their sins. Both the first four horsemen and the attack of the beast and his ten horns on the prostitute show that God will use Rome's lust for military and political dominion as the instruments of her own destruction. Second, through the suffering he brings to them, God calls the wicked to repent. Often the punishing hand of God only hardens their opposition to him, but sometimes it succeeds in leading them to conversion.

God's people likewise suffer for two reasons. First, as in the case of Jesus, the Lamb who was slain, their suffering is the means by which they show their faithfulness and enter God's presence. Their faithful suffering in the face of pressure to compromise with Rome's religious claims is an indication of the genuineness of their commitment to God's sole sovereignty. Second, through their suffering at the hands of the wicked, they are providing evidence for God's just sentence of condemnation against the wicked. In addition, John offers to the suffering among God's people the comforting message that God has limited their affliction and that, although the dragon will assault them, God will protect them from any ultimate, eternal harm.

John therefore offers a word of both challenge and comfort to his readers. He challenges them not to compromise with the beast. Whatever "Balaam" and "Jezebel" may say, the beast usurps the authority of God and lays total claim to the loyalties of its subjects. The destiny of the beast, the false prophet, and those who compromise with them lies in the lake of fire. John also offers a word of comfort that God has sealed from ultimate harm those who follow the Lamb wherever he goes. Although, like the Lamb whom they follow, they may have to suffer death for their faithfulness, they will inherit the new Jerusalem. In that place "there will be no more death or mourning or crying or pain," and they will join a vast company "from every nation, tribe, people and language" in the presence of the eternal God.

Chapter 33

THE CLASH OF WORLDVIEWS IN HEBREWS TO REVELATION

The nine texts that stretch from Hebrews to Revelation in modern editions of the New Testament comprise a diverse group. They come from at least six different authors. They have a wide variety of affinities with other ancient literature, from Jewish wisdom traditions (James), to Jewish apocalyptic traditions (Jude and Revelation), to the traditions of Hellenistic philosophy (2 Peter). They also come from various streams of early Christian tradition. First Peter and Hebrews breathe a Pauline atmosphere. Second Peter, although aware of and friendly to Paul, has little overlap with his theology. It is instead deeply indebted to the Jewish Christian tradition out of which Jude arose. James knows Paul and is leery of misinterpretations of his theology. The Johannine letters speak a singular idiom that they share with the gospel of John. Revelation seems to have arisen within a type of Jewish Christianity that valued symbol-laden apocalyptic themes, but the lavishness of its symbolism even sets it apart from this tradition.[1]

Despite these differences, these nine texts also overlap theologically with one another in significant ways. In this chapter we will examine several areas of overlap, first among the texts that devote the most energy to attacking heresy and then among the texts that encourage Christians in the midst of persecution. Both sets of texts share a concern to provide their readers with a worldview or vision of reality different from that of their opponents.

One set of texts responds to false teachers that intellectualized the gospel. These false teachers have interpreted Jesus' teaching and Paul's understanding of grace and faith in ways that take the emphasis off ethics and place it on verbal affirmation and progressive knowledge. The canonical writers respond to this problem by emphasizing three aspects of the Christian tradition: eyewitness testimony about Jesus, ethics as a proving ground of one's theological authenticity, and the need to heed the warning of Christian eschatological teaching.

The other group of texts responds to persecutors who see Jesus' followers as a threat to the stability of society. These texts provide a biblical vision of God's Messiah, his people, their oppressors, their suffering, and the future.

Beneath the considerable diversity of these texts lies the attempt of all of them to present their readers with a picture of the world as it exists to the eyes of God, his Son, and the first witnesses to the Christian faith.

---

1 Richard Bauckham, *The Theology of the Book of Revelation* (New Testament Theology; Cambridge: Cambridge Univ. Press, 1993), 9.

FALSE INTELLECTUAL PROGRESS AND ORTHODOX RESPONSES

The Problem of Intellectual "Progress"

Several of these nine texts have focused on problems that teachers created who claim to have progressed beyond traditional Christian doctrine. This problem is clearest in the three Johannine letters. Here a group has split from the Johannine community (1 John 2:19), claiming that they have moved beyond the teaching that Jesus Christ had come in the flesh (2 John 7, 9; cf. 1 John 4:2–3). They have not been content, however, simply to remove themselves from their parent group, but they hope to convince those whom they have left behind that their "progressive" teaching is correct.[2] Their teachers, therefore, have apparently shaken the confidence of many who remain in the original group, causing them to wonder if the old traditions about Jesus to which they cling are really sufficient for eternal life.

Something like this strategy probably lies behind the Elder's assurances to his readers in 1 John that they have "an anointing from the Holy One," that they already "know" what is necessary for eternal life (1 John 2:20–21, 24–25), and that they have no need for anyone to "teach" them (2:27). These "progressives" have also "gone out into the world," attempting to convince other communities founded on the beloved disciple's teaching that they too must move beyond that teaching to more advanced knowledge (2 John 7–11; cf. 1 John 4:1).

A similar problem plagues the communities to which both Jude and Peter (in 2 Peter) write. Jude's opponents have "slipped in" the community he addresses, indicating that they too are itinerant teachers. Like the Elder's opponents, these teachers are "people who create divisions" (Jude 19). Like Korah, they have rebelled against established ecclesiastical authority and the traditions that this authority guarded (vv. 3, 8, 11). Several elements of Jude's description hint that, like the Elder's opponents, these teachers also consider themselves to be progressives who have advanced beyond the outmoded teaching of traditional Christianity. They are, he says, "grumblers and faultfinders," and they "boast about themselves" (v. 16). They not only "slander" traditional teaching (vv. 8, 10) but ridicule it as well (v. 18).

Peter adopts much of Jude's descriptive language in his attack on false teachers—possibly the same false teachers that concerned Jude. They "despise authority" (2 Peter 2:10a), including that of the apostles (1:16; 3:15–16) and the prophets (1:19–21). They are "bold and arrogant" (2:10b), blaspheme traditional teaching (2:10b, 12), and "mouth empty, boastful words" (2:18). They are "scoffers" who ridicule the idea that God will intervene in the future in a world he has allowed to continue on its way from the beginning of time (3:3–4). They too target those who follow traditional Christian teaching, focusing their efforts on recent converts (2:18). Here again a picture emerges of teachers who ridicule traditional doctrine, claiming it is irrational. The elements of ridicule and scorn in their persuasive strategies probably mean

2 Raymond E. Brown, *The Epistles of John* (AB 30; Garden City, N.Y.: Doubleday, 1982), 645, 673, translates 2 John 9, "Anyone who is so 'progressive' that he does not remain rooted in the teaching of Christ does not possess God."

that they too consider themselves progressives. They probably view those who cling to the ancient Christian traditions as intellectually backward.[3]

The progressives' abandonment of traditional Christian ethics is of special concern to the Elder, Jude, and Peter. The Elder addresses the distinction his opponents make between knowledge and practical expressions of love. "The [one] who says, 'I know [Jesus],'" writes the Elder, "but does not do what he commands is a liar, and the truth is not in him" (1 John 2:4). These commands can be summarized in Jesus' single mandate to "love one another" (3:23–24), and in the expression of that love through sharing one's material possessions with needy fellow Christians (3:17). Practical expressions of love for others, therefore, prove one's claim to "know God" (4:7–8). The Elder admonishes his "children" not to "love with word or tongue but with actions and in truth" (3:18), and he rejoices when his children are "walking in the truth" (2 John 4; 3 John 3). The Elder's opponents seem to have thought that since knowledge is the key to salvation, love for others is unimportant.

The false teachers who stand behind Jude and 2 Peter have apparently taken a similar approach to the relationship between their teaching and ethics. Jude says that they pervert God's grace into debauchery (Jude 4). He also seems to say that they deny the reality of a final judgment (vv. 8, 14). Apparently this implies for them that God will not punish sinful behavior, permitting them to follow their own impious desires and to use Christian *agapē* meals as occasions for doing so (vv. 12, 16). Jude never clearly says that his opponents are particularly interested in knowledge, although he does accuse them of ignorance of orthodox doctrine and of acting in irrational, animal-like ways (v. 10).[4] Perhaps this is a counterblast to their claims to possess special knowledge, and if so, perhaps they claim that their visions (v. 8) and special relationship with the Spirit (v. 19) provide the basis for this knowledge.

If Jude's opponents are identical with the group that Peter attacks, then the case becomes weightier that they claim some special knowledge and insist that their knowledge permits their scandalous behavior. Peter is careful to link "the knowledge of God and of Jesus our Lord" (2 Peter 1:2) to ethical behavior. The knowledge of God, he says, leads to piety (1:3; cf. 2:20–21). Knowledge should be accompanied by self-control, the opposite of the vice of moral abandonment that the false teachers cultivate (2:2, 7). Peter writes to keep his readers, who are in danger from the deceptions of these teachers, from being "ineffective and unproductive" in their

3 Richard Bauckham, *Jude, 2 Peter* (WBC 50; Waco, Tex.: Word, 1983), 156, says that "perhaps they saw themselves as rather daring young radicals trying to clear a lot of traditional nonsense out of the church."

4 Some scholars believe that the use of the word "orthodox" to describe Christian texts of the first and early second century is anachronistic. At this period, they reason, a wide variety of understandings of Jesus competed for followers, and what we now call "orthodox" Christianity—the Christianity defined by the great ecumenical councils—only gradually emerged as dominant. See, e.g., Walter Bauer, *Orthodoxy and Heresy in Earliest Christianity* (Philadelphia: Fortress, 1971; orig. German ed., 1934), and, more recently, Bart D. Ehrman, *Lost Christianities: The Battles for Scripture and the Faiths We Never Knew* (Oxford: Oxford Univ. Press, 2003). Ehrman uses the term "proto-orthodox" to describe the eventually dominant group. A plausible case can be made, however, that what eventually becomes orthodox teaching represents more faithfully than other competing ideas the historical and theological significance of Jesus. It does not seem inappropriate, therefore, to use the term "orthodox" at this stage of early Christian history. On the overemphasis in some scholarly circles on the variety in earliest Christianity, see Rudolf Schnackenburg, *The Church in the New Testament* (New York: Seabury, 1965), 14–15.

"knowledge of our Lord Jesus Christ" (1:8; cf. 3:18). It seems reasonable, in light of this emphasis, to think of Peter's opponents as coupling their immoral behavior, which is Peter's chief concern (2:2–22), with a claim to special knowledge.[5]

Like the Elder, therefore, Jude and Peter attack opponents whose teaching departs from Christian orthodoxy not only in its understanding of God and what he has done in Christ Jesus, but also in its claims about the ethical implications of their new, "progressive" teaching. All these false teachers are alike in espousing a deviation from Christian orthodoxy that also means a deviation from Christian ethics.

The two kinds of false teaching, however, are also different from each another in one important respect. On the one hand, John's opponents seem to have separated their theology and Christology entirely from ethics; one's behavior, they claim, is irrelevant to salvation. This idea seems to stand behind their concept of sin. They probably claim to be sinless, not because they have kept Jesus' command to love one another, but because they regard it as irrelevant (1 John 1:9–10; 3:4, 23).

In the same way, they may have denied the atoning significance of Jesus' death because they believe that no such mechanism is necessary for their salvation. If transgression of God's command is irrelevant to salvation, any atonement for breaking that command is also irrelevant (1 John 2:2; 4:10). They do not, therefore, advocate unethical behavior but seem instead to be morally indifferent.[6]

On the other hand, the opponents of Jude and Peter seem to link their understanding of God's grace specifically to their scandalous behavior. Debauched behavior is actually implied as a result of their understanding of God's grace. Their thinking is close to that of the Corinthians, who were "puffed up" because a man was living in a sexual relationship with his father's wife. This, Paul says, is a type of immorality "that does not occur even among pagans" (1 Cor. 5:1). It was therefore similar to the scandalous moral "self-abandonment" (*aselgeia*) in which the opponents of Jude and Peter engage (2 Peter 2:2, 18; Jude 4).[7] The pride of the Corinthians over socially scandalous behavior implies that, from the Corinthian perspective, their behavior had some theoretical justification. Similarly, the opponents of Jude and Peter have found theoretical justification for their scandalous behavior in their perverse teaching on God's grace and their denial of coming judgment (2 Peter 3:3–16; Jude 4, 8, 14–15).

In summary, both the Johannine letters and Jude and 2 Peter attack false teachers who think they have progressed beyond traditional Christian doctrine. The Elder describes the false teachers among his churches this way explicitly when he says that anyone who follows them "runs ahead" (*ho proagōn*) and does not remain in the teaching of Christ (2 John 9). These "progressives" seem to claim that they possess an advanced body of knowledge and to emphasize the importance of knowledge over ethics. These elements reappear in Jude and 2 Peter where the false teachers employ

5 *Pace* Bauckham, *Jude, 2 Peter*, 150, 170, who believes that since Peter does not use the term "knowledge" (whether *epignōsis* or *gnōsis*) in an explicitly polemical way, his opponents probably made no appeal to it.

6 Cf. Brown, *Epistles of John*, 54–55, 80–81.

7 For this translation of *aselgeia*, see BDAG, 141.

a strategy of ridicule toward traditional Christian teaching and use their knowledge to justify morally scandalous behavior.

Wisdom and Ethics in James

Should we include James in this group of letters that attack intellectually "progressive" false teaching? It is difficult to know whether James had any false teaching of a reflective type in mind when he wrote his tractate. He seems to attack a misunderstanding of Paul's thinking on justification by faith in 2:14–26, and that misunderstanding elevated the importance of one's intellectual assent to Christian doctrine above the conduct of one's life. The problem James addresses, however, may be nothing more than a superficial argument that as long as one adopts a basic Christian confession intellectually, one's behavior does not matter. James' target may not be a thoughtful person who attempts to explain either indifference to ethics or unethical behavior theoretically, but a person who, as he puts it in 4:17, "knows the good he ought to do and does not do it."

One passage may indicate, however, that James has in his sights a group similar to the opponents that the Elder, Jude, and Peter attack. In 3:13–18 James contrasts two types of wisdom:

> Who is wise and understanding among you? Let him show it by his good life, by deeds done in the humility that comes from wisdom. But if you harbor bitter envy and selfish ambition in your hearts, do not boast about it or deny the truth. Such "wisdom" [*sophia*] does not come down from heaven but is earthly [*epigeios*], unspiritual [*psychikē*], of the devil [*daimoniōdēs*]. For where you have envy and selfish ambition, there you find disorder and every evil practice.
>
> But the wisdom that comes from heaven is first of all pure; then peace-loving, considerate, submissive, full of mercy and good fruit, impartial and sincere. Peacemakers who sow in peace raise a harvest of righteousness.

Like the opponents of the Elder, Jude, and Peter, those against whom James speaks in this passage claim to have wisdom, but the fruit of this "wisdom" betrays it as merely "earthly" and "unspiritual" in nature—the wrong kind of wisdom entirely. As with the Elder's opponents, the claim to knowledge is nothing but empty words and breaks up the fellowship of believers (James 14, 16, 18; cf. 1 John 2:4, 19; 3:18). As with Jude's opponents, this "wisdom" yields division and is "unspiritual" (*psychikos*, James 3:15; cf. Jude 19).

James' language also sounds like the language Paul used to refute Corinthian claims to wisdom—claims that the Corinthians' divisiveness and immorality proved to be false. In answering these claims, Paul distinguished between "the wisdom [*sophia*] of the world" and "the wisdom of God" (1 Cor. 1:20–21, 23–24). He also contrasted the "unspiritual [*psychikos*] person" with the "spiritual person" who discerns all things (2:14–15).

When we couple these connections with James' polemic against the misuse of Paul's language of faith and justification in 2:14–26, it becomes easy to think that

James is concerned with people who have some connection with Pauline theology but who, from the first, have adopted Paul's gospel in a truncated form. They are happy to use Paul's language of God's grace and human faith as the means of justification but fail to link these concepts with the notion of the ethical holiness of the people of God that is also important to Paul.

If something like this misuse of Paul's theology lies beneath James' concerns with a "good life" and "deeds done in the humility that comes from wisdom" (James 3:13; cf. 2:14, 24, 26), then those whom James attacks stand conceptually close to the opponents of Jude and Peter. Those opponents also seem to have a connection to Paul's theology of grace (2 Peter 3:16; Jude 4), however attenuated. If some conceptual connection exists, then James appears to address the problem at a primitive stage of its development when people are simply using God's grace as an excuse for their failure to do what they know to be right (2:16; 4:17). They have not yet developed reasoned arguments that ethical behavior is not actually "right" at all. This does not mean that the problem James attacks occurs chronologically earlier than the problems that the other authors address, only that we find it in a less developed form.

Summary

The Johannine letters on one side and Jude and 2 Peter on the other side bear witness to two movements toward the intellectualization of the apostolic traditions from which they sprang. One arose within churches under the leadership of the beloved disciple, and the other arose within churches with some connection to Paul. It is impossible to know whether they had any relationship to each other, and the evidence that James knew of either movement remains ambiguous.

Still, the broad similarity of these two movements is remarkable: Both excuse or justify unethical behavior on the basis of their progressive knowledge. The false teachers that wreak such havoc in the Elder's churches claim to have "progressed" beyond the traditions the Elder has taught. The false teachers that Jude and Peter oppose specialize in ridiculing the implausible idea that God will judge the world. Both sets of false teachers, therefore, cultivate the notion that they have access to higher knowledge than traditional Christians possess. This knowledge provides them with a view of reality different from the traditionalists whom they have left behind and sets them free from the ethical standards of orthodox Christianity.

The Orthodox Response to Intellectual "Progress"

With all their differences from one another, James, Jude, Peter, and the Elder also share a similar strategy for coping with the intellectualizing of the Christian tradition. Each author emphasizes against the "progressives" a vision of reality built on tradition, ethics, and eschatology.

Apostolic Tradition as the Bridge to the Historical Jesus

Among these four authors, the Elder is most concerned with tradition, perhaps because both he and his opponents lay claim to precisely the same tradition—that enshrined in the beloved disciple's gospel. Whereas the Elder's opponents seem to both claim the tradition and "progress" beyond it, however, the Elder insists that to progress beyond the community's tradition is to depart from the one bridge that links his community's present Christian existence with the historical Jesus. The Elder himself is one of the pillars that support this bridge.

Against the claims of the progressives that Jesus did not assume a fleshly body (1 John 4:2–3; 2 John 7), the Elder emphasizes his status as an eyewitness to the physical existence of Jesus. Along with others, he saw and touched him (1 John 1:1b). He can confirm the eyewitness testimony of the gospel that at Jesus' death water and blood poured from his wounded torso (1 John 5:6–7; cf. John 1:14; 19:34–35). When the Elder claims to have heard the historical Jesus (1 John 1:1, 3), he may have thought especially of his opponents' indifference to ethics and his own ability to say with authority that the commandments to love one another came from Jesus himself (1 John 3:23; cf. John 13:34–35; 15:12, 17).

He and other eyewitnesses to Jesus are the critical link between Jesus himself, who "was from the beginning" (1 John 1:1; 2:13, 14), and the "beginning" of his readers' Christian commitment (2:7, 24; 3:11). Only by remaining in the tradition that the Elder has communicated to them at the beginning of their Christian commitment will his readers "remain in the Son and in the Father" and have "eternal life" (2:24–25). Only by remaining connected to this tradition will the Elder's readers be able to discriminate between truth and error: "We are from God, and whoever knows God listens to us; but whoever is not from God does not listen to us. This is how we recognize the Spirit of truth and the spirit of falsehood" (1 John 4:6).

Jude and Peter also grapple with opponents who try to wrest the Christian tradition from their grasp and then progress beyond it. Apparently they are doing so in the name of Paul (2 Peter 3:15–16), making capital out of Paul's central concern with God's grace (Jude 4). If this is a correct understanding of the opponents' strategy, then it is significant that neither Jude nor Peter attacks Paul himself. Jude affirms "the grace of our God" and calls the false teachers' attempt to turn it into a foundation for scandalous behavior a perversion (v. 4). Peter considers Paul "our dear brother" and views his opponents' attempts to justify their false teaching from Paul's letters and the rest of Scripture to be a distortion of them (2 Peter 3:15–16).

Instead of attacking the Pauline tradition, Jude and Peter appeal to their own connection with the apostolic tradition. Jude begins his letter with a comment on his personal relationship with James (Jude 1), the Lord's own brother (Gal. 1:19), a witness to Jesus' resurrection (1 Cor. 15:7), and a pillar of the Jerusalem church (Gal. 2:9). The implication of Jude's claim to be "a brother of James" would not be lost on his readers: Jude, the brother of James, was also the brother of Jesus. Such a close associate of the apostles and of Jesus himself, therefore, possesses the authority to remind his readers of the words of the apostles (Jude 17).

Jude also understands his letter as a struggle with his opponents for "the faith that was once for all entrusted to the saints" (Jude 3). This implies that the majority of Christians ("the saints") will accept the "faith" Jude defends in his letter and that it is an unchangeable body of tradition carefully handed from one generation of believers to the next. It is "most holy"—set apart as pure—and the foundation on which Jude's readers should build (Jude 20). Jude conceives of his own role as a bridge between his readers and "what the apostles of our Lord Jesus Christ foretold" (v. 17). He stands among those to whom the apostles have handed the tradition, and his letter is an effort to be sure that this tradition emerges intact from the assault of the false teachers.

Peter too considers the apostles to be the conduit of reliable tradition about the teaching of Jesus. The apostles are eyewitnesses to the events of Jesus' ministry (2 Peter 1:16) and have heard the commands he taught (3:2). Their testimony to Jesus takes a place equal to that of "the holy prophets" in authority (3:2; cf. 3:16). As an apostle himself (1:1), Peter is therefore highly qualified to refute the "destructive heresies" (2:1) of the false teachers and to assure his readers that their faith is of "equal value" (1:1) to those who saw the events of Jesus' ministry and heard him teach.[8]

Peter claims, moreover, that he was an eyewitness not merely of Jesus' ministry generally but of the specific event in Jesus' ministry (the transfiguration) that shows the error of the false teachers' refusal to believe in Jesus' second coming (2 Peter 1:16–18). He is well qualified, therefore, not only to remind his readers of the truth (1:12–15), but also to state that the false teachers have deviated from Jesus' teaching (1:16–18).

Like the Elder and Jude, Peter stands as a supporting pillar beneath the bridge of tradition that connects the faith of his readers with the historical Jesus. Peter regards the attempt of the false teachers to appeal to tradition through Paul's letters and "the other Scriptures" to be a distortion and a failure. His own connection with the events of Jesus' ministry and the commands that Jesus taught gives Peter the authority to make this judgment.

Once again, James does not fit neatly into the same category with the letters of the Elder, Jude, and Peter, although several similarities emerge. When James, at the end of his letter, urges his readers to rescue those who wander from the truth and to turn sinners from the error of their way, he probably has in mind something similar to what he has himself tried to do in James 2:14–26 and perhaps 3:13–18.[9] In these passages, as we have seen, James may be responding to a misunderstanding of Paul's theology similar to the permutation of Paul's teaching that Paul himself occasionally encountered (Rom. 3:8). The "superficial person" (*anthrōpos kenos*) whom James attacks in 2:14–26 and the "wise" person of 3:13–18 probably claim Paul as an apostolic authority.

If so, however, James shows no interest in asserting his own apostolic authority against Paul. He is remarkably egalitarian in his approach to authority, appealing not to any office or eyewitness status but calling himself merely "a servant of God and of the Lord Jesus Christ" (James 1:1).[10] He mentions teachers, but only to say that since they will be judged more strictly than others, not many should seek that office

8 Cf. Bauckham, *Jude, 2 Peter*, 167.

9 Luke Timothy Johnson, *The Letter of James* (AB 37A; New York: Doubleday, 1995), 346.

10 On James' egalitarianism, see Johnson, *James*, 82, to which this paragraph is indebted.

(3:1). He speaks of elders, but they are servants of others whom the sick summon for prayer (5:14). His readers are "brothers and sisters" both of James and of one another and should be treated with compassion even if they are poor (2:14). James appeals not to his apostolic status for authority but only to "the word of truth" (1:18, 21–23) and "the perfect law" (1:25; 2:8–12; 4:11), and his test of genuineness is conducted in accord with these repositories of God's will (1:22–23, 2:12).

It is difficult to say why James's letter differs in this way from the Johannine letters, Jude, and 2 Peter. Probably the origin of the difference lies in the different situation that James addresses, and again there are signs that the problem James tackles is not as advanced as the problem in the other letters. The "intellectualizing" of the Christian tradition that James attacks has not yet evolved into a thoughtful effort to elevate knowledge over behavior or to say that one's progressive knowledge legitimates scandalous behavior. James's opponents also seem to have appealed more to the language of Paul than specifically to his apostolic authority for support of their relatively superficial thinking on justification by faith.

Ethics as a Test of Authenticity

Each of the six letters that is primarily concerned with false teaching uses behavior as a test of authenticity. For the Elder, sinful behavior, particularly unloving behavior manifested in an unwillingness to show compassion to the needy, is a clear sign of falsehood. The Elder could hardly be clearer on this point:

> This is how we know who the children of God are and who the children of the devil are: Anyone who does not do what is right is not a child of God; nor is anyone who does not love his brother. (1 John 3:10; cf. 3:8, 14–15; 4:19)

A few sentences later he becomes specific about how this lack of love manifests itself: "If anyone has material possessions and sees his brother in need but has no pity on him, how can the love of God be in him?" (3:17).

This is true even if the claims of the false teacher in question seem at first to be orthodox. People may claim to have fellowship with God's Son, Jesus, and to know and love God, but if they walk in darkness and do not keep his commands—particularly the command to love their fellow believers—they are liars (1 John 1:6; 2:4; 4:19). This is why the Elder can become just as exercised about Diotrephes's failure to show orthodox missionaries hospitality as he was about those who denied that Jesus came in the flesh (1 John 4:2; 2 John 7). Although Diotrephes's Christology is apparently thoroughly orthodox, his imitation of evil rather than good shows that he has "not seen God" (3 John 11).

Similarly, Jude and Peter claim that the immoral activity of the teachers they oppose reveals the true, evil nature of these teachers and is therefore a sure sign that their teaching is false. Jude is deeply concerned about the sexual immorality of the false teachers against whom he writes and carefully shows how their sexual debauchery aligns them with those whom, in Jewish tradition, God opposed. Whatever their claims to special revelation from God via dreams and access to the Spirit (Jude 8,

19), their conduct places them with the grumblers of Israel's wilderness generation (v. 5), the wicked angels of Noah's time (v. 6), the citizens of Sodom and Gomorrah (v. 7), and Cain, Balaam, and Korah (v. 11). Their sexual immorality arises, says Jude, from their affinity with animals whose sexual instincts come naturally and are untempered by reason (v. 10). Thus, the true nature of the false teachers becomes visible in their conduct.

Peter takes the same position and expands it. Knowledge of God and of the Lord Jesus Christ leads to godliness and to the cultivation of the virtues. It does not remain idle and unfruitful (2 Peter 1:3, 8), and the virtues to which it leads provide the means by which Christians can make their "calling and election sure" (1:10). "If anyone does not have" these virtues, says Peter, "he is nearsighted and blind, and has forgotten that he has been cleansed from his past sins" (1:9)—a clear reference to the false teachers whom Peter describes later as becoming entangled once again in the world's corruption after initially escaping it "by knowing our Lord and Savior Jesus Christ" (2:21). Their reversion, through their conduct, to "the corruption of the world" reveals their true nature, just as a dog or pig inevitably leaves its filth behind only to return to it (2:21–22).

Like Jude, Peter aligns the false teachers with the conduct of those in Jewish tradition whom God destroyed or imprisoned for future destruction: the wicked angels and ungodly people of Noah's time, the cities of Sodom and Gomorrah, and Balaam (2 Peter 2:4–16). Like Jude, the falsity of the false teachers in Peter's letter is visible in the way they behave.

The Elder, Jude, and Peter are certainly concerned with the deviations from orthodox doctrine of the false teachers whom they have targeted, whether from the teaching that Christ came in the flesh or from the doctrine of a final judgment. The behavior of the false teachers, however, is of equal concern to these three authors. Their falsehood lies not merely in the content of their Christology and eschatology but in their lack of compassion for fellow Christians, their divisiveness, and their sexual immorality.

On this point, James is close to the other three. Like John who urges his readers not to "love with words or tongue but with actions and in truth" (1 John 3:18), and who is suspicious of Diotrephes on the basis of his conduct alone (3 John 9–11), James tells his readers, "Do not merely listen to the word, and so deceive yourselves. Do what it says" (James 1:22). Both John and James know that their opponents can use language that sounds orthodox—"I have fellowship with him," "I know him," "I love God," "Go . . . keep warm and well fed," "There is one God"—but that the conduct of their opponents betrays the reality behind this pious façade.

Like Jude and Peter, James believes that people act in a way consistent with their basic commitments, whatever they may say. After all, a salt spring cannot produce fresh water any more than a fig tree bears olives or a grapevine bears figs (3:11–12). Envy, selfish ambition, disorder, and every evil practice are the fruits of those who possess the wrong kind of wisdom—the wisdom that is earthy, unspiritual, and demonic (3:13–16). The historical context in which James makes these and other similar remarks about the divide between claims and action appears, moreover, to be one in which some Christians were beginning to ground their claim that behavior did not matter in Paul's teaching on justification by faith (2:14–26). Here too, as we have seen, James resembles Jude and 2 Peter.

Once again, though, there is an important difference between James and the other three. James's opponents are just beginning to argue their case on theological grounds and are doing a poor job of it (2:18). The superficiality of their commitment to their ideology is clear (2:20). The sentiments that they express at this point are often orthodox enough; the doctrinal problems arise only when they attempt to define justifying "faith" as mere intellectual assent (2:24).

Eschatology as Revelation and Warning

The Elder, Jude, and Peter all use eschatological themes in their letters in two ways. First, they identify the false teachers that they attack with the eschatological enemies of God's people who, according to a common theme in Jewish apocalyptic literature, will emerge in the period of time leading up to the final Day of Judgment. Second, they warn their readers of the fate that will come to these false teachers at that time and, by implication, to any who follow their teaching.

The Elder tells his readers that he is writing in "the last hour" and that the presence of the eschatological Antichrist has been foreshadowed by the appearance of "many antichrists" (1 John 2:18). These antichrists turn out to be those who have seceded from the Elder's community (2:19) and have substituted for the Christ of the fourth gospel their own fleshless Christ (2:22; 4:2–3). The Elder also calls them "deceivers" (2:26; 2 John 7) and "false prophets" (1 John 4:1). He probably considers their emergence at least a partial fulfillment of Jesus' prophecy, found in the Synoptic apocalyptic discourses, that at "the end of the age" "false Christs," "false prophets," and "deceivers" will arise (Matt. 24:3, 5, 11, 24; cf. Mark 13:3, 5, 22; Luke 21:8). With this motif, the Elder offers both comfort and warning to his readers: comfort that the troubling appearance of deviation from apostolic teaching is not an unexpected development, and warning that his readers should "continue" in the Son "so that when he appears we may be confident and unashamed before him at his coming" (1 John 2:28).

The same dual emphasis appears in Jude and 2 Peter. Jude describes the false teachers against whom he writes as "certain men whose condemnation was written about long ago" (Jude 4). He then gives three examples of this written prophetic tradition: a series of biblical types to which the false teachers correspond (vv. 5–7, 11), a citation from *1 Enoch* (Jude 14–15; cf. *1 En.* 1:9), and a quotation from "what the apostles of our Lord Jesus Christ foretold" (Jude 17–18).[11]

When Jude mentions the prophecies of the apostles, he may have in mind some of the same warnings of Jesus that the Elder has in mind, for although Jesus spoke

11 Cf. Bauckham, *Jude, 2 Peter,* who argues convincingly both that Jude 5–19 explain v. 4 and that the reference to apostolic prophecy in vv. 17–18 need not "bear the full weight" of *palai* ("long ago") in v. 4.

them, the apostles handed them down.[12] Also like the Elder, Jude's description of the eschatological fate of these false teachers in the "judgment of the great Day" (Jude 6) probably implies a warning to his readers not to be deceived by them and so suffer their fate. Just as the false teachers are moving toward the "eternal fire" depicted in the smoking ruins of Sodom and Gomorrah (v. 7), Jude is concerned that his readers snatch "from the fire" any among their number who are presently following the false teachers but might be saved (v. 22).

Peter, relying partially on Jude, follows the same pattern. The "condemnation" (*krima*) of the false teachers, he says, "is not idle from of old [*ekpalai*], and their destruction is not sleeping" (2 Peter 2:3, pers. trans.). This echoes Jude's statement (Jude 4) that his opponents' "condemnation" (*krima*) was described "long ago" (*palai*). Also like Jude, Peter considers his biblical examples of the wicked to be more than examples: They are typological prophecies of the false teachers and their fate.[13] This becomes clear from 2 Peter 2:5 and 3:6–7, where Peter takes the waters of the flood in Noah's time to be prototypical of the destruction that will come on the world "in the day of judgment" (3:7).

If so, then Peter probably takes the wicked angels, whom he assumes are described in Genesis 6:1–4, to be prototypical of the false teachers in the communities to which he writes (2 Peter 2:1–4). In the same way, Peter seems to have seen the destruction of Sodom and Gomorrah by fire as a type of the destruction of the world by fire on the Day of Judgment. He therefore probably also views the "filthy" people (2:7) of these towns as prophetic types of the false teachers. Just as destruction of the people of Sodom and Gomorrah provides an example of what will happen to the "ungodly" (*asebesin*, 2:6), so the Day of Judgment will bring destruction to "ungodly" people (*asebōn*, 3:7) like the false teachers.

This implies that the false teachers' presence is a sign of the "last days," and Peter says this explicitly in 2 Peter 3:3: "You must understand that in the last days scoffers will come, scoffing and following their own evil desires." At first this looks like a prophecy of false teachers to come, but when Peter begins in 3:5 to refute the ridicule that the eschatological false teachers have aimed at his readers, it becomes clear that the prophecy has been fulfilled and Peter considers the false teachers to be a sign that the last days have already come (cf. 2:1, 10b).

As with the Elder and Jude, Peter's eschatology also serves to warn his readers against falling prey to the false teachers' deceptions. Although the context of his comments shows that he has the false teachers primarily in mind when he speaks of the eschatological punishment of the unrighteous (2 Peter 2:6, 9; 3:7), his descriptions of the objects of God's punishment are general enough that they can encompass not only the false teachers but anyone to whom the words "ungodly" and "unrighteous" might apply.

12 It is possible that he also has in mind such prophecies of the apostle Paul as Acts 20:29–30; 1 Tim. 4:1–3; 2 Tim. 3:1–9. Like Jude, these passages do not mention false prophets, and they focus on the unscrupulous nature of the false teachers who will arise in later times.

13 Here I depend on the detailed discussion of the relevant passages in Bauckham, *Jude, 2 Peter*, 248–52.

Peter makes this implication of his eschatology clear toward the end of his letter. There he tells his readers that since they await both the destruction of the universe and its recreation on "the day of the Lord"—a day that will come with the suddenness of a thief—they should be eager to be found at that time "spotless, blameless and at peace" (2 Peter 3:10–14). He especially has in mind the possibility that his readers may fall from their secure position by succumbing to the enticing promises of the false teachers (3:17; cf. 2:2–3, 18–19).

Once again, James stands apart from the other authors. He does not even hint that those who separate faith from works or who claim to possess "wisdom" are the eschatological enemies of God. Instead, he calls on rich oppressors to recognize that it is already the "day of slaughter" and that, by their greed, they are fattening themselves for the kill (James 5:1–6). To the righteous victims of the rich, James urges patience and speaks the comforting words that "the Lord's coming is near" and "the Judge is standing at the door" (5:7–11).

These would certainly be sobering words to rich oppressors of Christians. They would also give pause to rich "Christians" who mistreat the poor (2 Peter 2:14–15). In neither case, however, do such people rise to the level of eschatological opponents of God. Perhaps James would have assessed them differently if the wealthy Christians had been actively teaching their position, like the opponents of Jude and Peter. As it is, they seem only to have justified their own comfortable but harmful way of life with a superficial appeal to their orthodoxy.

The Apostolic Call for a Return to Right Belief and Right Behavior

Both the Pauline and the Johannine streams of Christian tradition produced aberrations that are addressed within the New Testament itself. Although there is little evidence of a historical connection between these two kinds of error, they share two basic characteristics. First, both were interested in intellectual "progress" beyond the old traditions. Those who deviated from the Johannine tradition stressed the need to move beyond the knowledge that was available "from the beginning." Those who deviated from the Pauline tradition may also have emphasized knowledge—although this is less clear. In any case, they certainly scoffed at the traditional idea of a coming judgment.

Second, both heretical movements separated religious knowledge from traditional Christian ethics. Those who deviated from the Johannine tradition did this through indifference to moral behavior, particularly to Jesus' command to love one another. Those who deviated from the Pauline tradition did this through justifying immoral behavior theologically.

On both points, James seems to attack a primitive form of the error. His opponents give intellectual assent to orthodox confessions, but they have started to separate these confessions from any ethical implications. Intellectual assent and the claim to wisdom is enough for them. They refuse to be bothered with the sort of radical obedience that James insists is necessary for justification.

In response, the Elder, Jude, and Peter call their readers back to an understanding of spiritual reality rooted in Christian tradition. They remind their readers of their own connection, through the apostolic tradition, to the historical Jesus. James makes no use of this argument, perhaps because the false teaching he refutes is less developed. His opponents may have borrowed Paul's language but without explicit claims that the mantle of Paul's apostolic authority has fallen on them.

All the authors, including James, also remind their readers of the connection that tradition makes between ethics and claims to religious knowledge. Real wisdom and knowledge tends to produce obedience to the law (James), to Jesus' love command (the Elder), or Christian virtues (2 Peter and, to some extent, Jude).

The Elder, Jude, and Peter also connect the rise of false teachers and the coming Day of Judgment. This eschatological point serves two purposes: It comforts the readers of these texts that the rise of opponents to orthodoxy is not unexpected, and it warns any who might follow the false teachers that judgment for the wicked, such as the false teachers and any who might imitate them, is coming. Perhaps because the false teaching that James resists was little interested in concocting and teaching some theological justification for its claims, James has no interest in portraying its advocates as antichrists or as the fulfillment of prophecy. They are simply people who know the good they ought to do but make no effort to do it.

It is important to say at this point that the stress on apostolic authority, the link between knowledge and ethics, and the presence of judgment according to works in the six letters that we have surveyed in this section are marks neither of late composition nor of "early catholicism." All three characteristics appear in the indisputably genuine Corinthian correspondence of Paul. There Paul responds to people who think that wisdom is a matter of rhetorical eloquence and that knowledge is more important than love (1 Cor. 1:18–2:16; 8:1–3). As part of this response, he admonishes the Corinthians that they should love one another (8:1–3; 13:1–13), reminds them of a coming judgment according to works (3:13; 2 Cor. 5:10), and points out where their thinking diverges from apostolic tradition (1 Cor. 15:1–8).

It is true that Paul also applies to the problems in Corinth his profound theology of the cross and of God's grace. It is likewise true that the six letters we have studied in this section do not develop the notion of God's grace to the same depth. Some of them (Jude, 2 Peter, James) do not even mention the cross. This does not mean, however, that they are later than Paul—only that their authors are not Paul.

This also does not mean that the authors of these letters betray a growing comfort with the structures of the ongoing world. Second Peter counsels patience in light of the delay of the Parousia, possibly for thousands of years (2 Peter 3:8–9), but he also recognizes that "the day of the Lord will come like a thief" (3:10). James similarly speaks of waiting patiently for eschatological vindication (James 5:7), but in the same breath can say that the Lord's coming is near and that the judge is standing at the door (5:8–9). Jude views himself as living "in the last times" (Jude 18), and the Elder urges his readers to continue in Christ "so that when he appears we may be confident and unashamed before him at his coming" (1 John 2:28). The eschatological awareness revealed in these comments does not fit snugly with the theory that those who composed them want to adapt the church's structure and doctrine to a world that will last for generations.

PERSECUTION AND THE CALL TO FAITHFULNESS

Three of the texts that we have studied in this final section focus primarily on the problem that opponents from outside the church have posed for Christians. When piety, reverence, and religion are gone, wrote Cicero, "life soon becomes a welter of disorder and confusion" (*Nat. d.* 1.4).[14] The disappearance of piety, he continued, entails the disappearance of loyalty, social union, and justice itself. The governing elite in the societies where Christians first flourished outside Palestine took this viewpoint and regarded Christianity as a threat to social stability. They believed that its exclusive claims for its God and his Son Jesus, along with its insistence that its followers not participate in the many expressions of public piety that were woven into civic affairs, resulted from stubborn impiety and dangerously superstitious convictions.[15]

Left unchecked, these writers believed that such ingratitude toward the traditional gods would surely anger them, and the prosperity and peace of the Roman empire depended on their good favor. As Celsus put it, if everyone worshiped the God of the Jews and the Christians, neglecting, as they did, the "customary honours to both gods and men," the Roman world would end up like the Jewish nation and the Christian people:

> Instead of being masters of the whole world, [the Jews] have been left no land or home of any kind. While in [the Christians'] case, if anyone does still wander about in secret, yet he is sought out and condemned to death. (Origen, *Cels.* 8.69)

In the face of the ostracism, deprivation, imprisonment, and even death to which neighbors and magistrates with this worldview subjected Christians, the urge of Christians to respond to their persecutors in inappropriate ways seems to have been strong. Some were tempted simply to leave their faith and return to their former lives. Others cherished the desire to lash back at their persecutors. Some sought refuge in the relatively peaceful haven of the synagogue. Still others thought that they could engage in pagan cultic rituals and still hold their basic Christian convictions.

First Peter, Hebrews, and Revelation reject these responses to persecution and urge their readers to remain faithful. They do this by offering their readers an alternate vision of reality to that of the societies in which they live.[16] We can summarize

14 Robert Wilken, *The Christians as the Romans Saw Them* (New Haven, Conn.: Yale Univ. Press, 1984), 59, brought this passage to my attention.

15 Ibid., 48–67.

16 Cf. David Arthur deSilva, *Despising Shame: Honor Discourse and Community Maintenance in the Epistle to the Hebrews* (SBLMS 152; Atlanta, Ga.: Scholars Press, 1995), 276–79. DeSilva speaks of an "alternate court of reputation." He means by this that the author of Hebrews constructs for his readers an alternative to the court of public opinion. In this court, God decides matters of honor and shame for his people according to his own standards. Cf. idem, *The Hope of Glory: Honor Discourse and New Testament Interpretation* (Collegeville, Minn.: Liturgical Press, 1999), 4–7.

this vision by asking these texts five questions: Who is Jesus? Who are Christians? Who are the opponents of God's people? What is the significance of Christian suffering? What does the future hold?

Who Is Jesus?

The unbelieving Roman elite viewed Jesus as an executed man around whom a vulgar eastern cult had arisen. The Judean procurator Porcius Festus called Jesus "a dead man . . . who Paul claimed was alive" (Acts 25:19). Tacitus knew him as the judicially executed "founder" of a pernicious sect (*Ann.* 15.44.4).

In contrast to this assessment, 1 Peter, Hebrews, and Revelation paint the very different picture of Jesus as the Messiah whose crucifixion led to his resurrection, his victory over the malevolent powers that opposed him, his ascension to heaven, and his session at God's right hand. The authors of all three texts understand this set of events to be a fulfillment of Psalm 110:1 (LXX 109:1):

> The LORD says to my Lord:
> "Sit at my right hand
> until I make your enemies
> a footstool for your feet."

Peter comforts his persecuted readers with the reminder that although Christ himself "was put to death"—a fate that they too may have to endure—God raised him from the dead. After this, he went to heaven, where he has taken his place at the right hand of God, "with angels, authorities and powers in submission to him" (1 Peter 3:18–22; cf. also Ps. 8:7). Although Peter refers primarily here to the subjection of the fallen angels of Genesis 6:1–4 to Christ (1 Peter 3:19–20), his readers can hardly fail to identify the magistrates before whom they must be ready to give a gentle and respectful defense (1 Peter 3:15) with the "authorities and powers" who are now in submission to Christ.[17]

To outside observers, it may seem that the Roman authorities hold Christians under their power, but Peter insists that the reality is quite different. Christ sits at the right hand of God's heavenly throne in fulfillment of the prophecy of Psalm 110:1. The spiritual powers are subject to him, and soon the political powers will be subject to him as well.

The author of Hebrews also uses Psalm 110:1 as an encouragement to his persecuted audience, but in a different way. He is fully aware of the affront that Jesus' crucifixion and the Christian proclamation of it present to Roman society. Jesus, he says, "endured the cross, scorning its shame" (Heb. 12:2). He was crucified outside the city walls, a symbol of the disgrace he bore when he endured this shameful death (13:13). He insists, however, that this suffering was the necessary path to his exaltation to "the right hand of the throne of God" (12:2).

17 On this see G. B. Caird, *New Testament Theology* (Oxford: Oxford Univ. Press, 1994), 102–7, esp. p. 105, and Ernest Best, *1 Peter* (NCB; Grand Rapids: Eerdmans, 1971), 148; *pace* Leonard Goppelt, *A Commentary on 1 Peter* (Grand Rapids: Eerdmans, 1993), 272–73.

Only by means of Jesus' own death could he fulfill the second main part of Psalm 110 and become the eternal priest in the order of Melchizedek (Heb. 5:6; 7:17, 27; 8:1; cf. Ps. 110:4). Only by means of his willing and obedient death could he offer "for all time one sacrifice for sins." After doing this, the author says, "he sat down at the right hand of God" (Heb. 10:9–14; cf. 1:3). As with Peter, therefore, the author of Hebrews wants his readers to understand the heavenly perspective on Christ: His suffering led him not merely to death but through death to exaltation at God's right hand.

Unlike Peter, however, the author of Hebrews does not focus on the subjection of angels, authorities, and powers to the exalted Jesus after his obedient death. Emphasizing the still incomplete state of Jesus' victory, he says that since the time of his exaltation to God's right hand, Jesus has been waiting "for his enemies to be made his footstool" (Heb. 10:13; cf. 1 Cor. 15:25–26, 28). The author of Hebrews uses Christ's suffering and exaltation instead to urge his readers to follow Jesus' example. They should travel the path of suffering that Jesus their exalted "leader" (*archēgon*) has marked out for them. Fixing their eyes on him, seated at God's right hand, they should consider that he arrived at his goal by "enduring the cross" and "scorning its shame" (Heb. 12:2–3).

John the seer, in Revelation, like Peter and the author of Hebrews, wants to give his readers a vision of Jesus that will counter the image of him painted by their persecutors. Jesus Christ, says John, is with God in his throne room, and from that location he is "the ruler of the kings of the earth" (Rev. 1:4–5; cf. 12:5). Like the author of Hebrews, John emphasizes that Jesus' path to this position of authority led through suffering. He too calls on his readers to endure the same kind of suffering that Jesus endured and to receive a similar reward: "To the one who conquers I will give a place with me on my throne, just as I myself conquered and sat with my Father on his throne" (3:21, NRSV).

In Revelation, "the one who conquers" is the person who remains faithful to Jesus despite the pressure of persecution to compromise (Rev. 2:10–11; 2:20–27; 3:4–5, 8–12; 12:11).[18] Faithful Christians, says John, have conquered Satan "by the blood of the Lamb and by the word of their testimony; they did not love their lives so much as to shrink from death" (12:11). In 3:21, therefore, Jesus promises that those who suffer for their faithfulness as Jesus suffered for his faithfulness will share his kingly rule from God's throne.

This same pattern appears elsewhere in Revelation. In 2:26–27 the Christians in Thyatira have not compromised their faith by worshiping the local gods (2:20), and they receive the same authority to rule the nations that Jesus himself received according to Psalm 2:9 (cf. Rev. 12:5; 19:5). Similarly, when the heavens are opened and John receives a vision of God's throne room, the Lamb appears in the center of God's throne, but he is the "Lamb, looking as if it had been slain, standing in the center of the throne" (5:6; cf. 5:12). This Lamb shepherds those who have washed their robes

18 Bauckham, *Theology of the Book of Revelation*, 14, 75–76.

in his blood (7:14), and just as this Lamb is at the center of God's throne (7:17), so they are before his throne (7:15). Likewise, the 144,000 who stand with the Lamb on Mount Zion are those who have not compromised their faith and who "follow the Lamb wherever he goes" (14:4–5; cf. 2:20), probably a reference to their suffering like the Lamb.

In answer to the question, "Who is Jesus," therefore, 1 Peter, Hebrews, and Revelation encourage and challenge their readers with a vision of Jesus as the kingly Messiah of Psalm 110:1 (LXX 109:1), who now reigns at God's right hand. Although his victory over the powers that oppress God's people is not yet complete (Heb. 10:13), it is certain (1 Peter 3:22). To those who remain faithful amid often violent pressure to compromise their faith, Hebrews and Revelation extend the promise that they will share the reign of the enthroned Christ.

Who Are Christians?

The Greco-Roman elite thought no better of Christians than of their "founder." According to Acts, a group of Epicurean and Stoic philosophers who gathered around Paul in the Athenian marketplace viewed him as a "babbler" or an advocate of "foreign gods" and "sneered" at his ideas (Acts 17:18, 32). Tacitus, Pliny, and Suetonius all thought of Christians as adherents of a "superstition"—a word that Romans used of religions that were foreign, irrational, and fanatical. By their desire for access to the gods outside the normal societal boundaries, superstitions threatened the stability of society.[19] Tacitus calls Christian superstition "deadly" (*Ann.* 15.44.4). Pliny calls it "depraved and excessive" (*Ep.* 10.96), and Suetonius describes it as "new" and "mischievous" (*Nero* 16). The Christians themselves, says Pliny, are prone to "stubbornness and inflexible obstinacy" (*Ep.* 10.96). To Tacitus, they are "loathed for their vices" (*Ann.* 15.44.3) and take their place among the "horrible" and "shameful" things that tend to "collect" and "find a vogue" in Rome (*Ann.* 15.44.4).

We have already seen in chapter 30 that Peter provides his readers with a vision of themselves different from these negative assessments. He describes Christians with the biblical language of Israel's temple and of Israel's constitution as God's special people. Their persecutors heap verbal abuse on them (1 Peter 4:4), but Peter reminds them that they are "living stones . . . being built into a spiritual house to be a holy priesthood" (2:5). Echoing Exodus 19:6 (LXX) a few sentences later, he calls them "a chosen people, a royal priesthood, a holy nation, a people belonging to God" (1 Peter 2:9). They have taken over the vocation of Israel to serve as priests of God's character to the world around them and so to "declare the praises of him who called you out of darkness into his wonderful light" (2:9).[20]

John the seer, in Revelation, also speaks of Christians as God's temple. In heaven the presence of God and of the Lamb serves as the temple (Rev. 21:22; cf. 14:15, 17; 16:17), and Jesus promises that he will make the Christians who remain faithful

19 Wilken, *Christians*, 50–51, 61; Mary Beard, John North, and Simon Price, *Religions of Rome*, 2 vols. (Cambridge: Cambridge Univ. Press, 1998), 1:217–18.

20 G. K. Beale, *The Book of Revelation* (NIGTC; Grand Rapids: Eerdmans, 1999), 193.

despite the pressures of persecution "a pillar in the temple of my God" (3:12; cf. 7:15). According to the most probable interpretation of 11:1–2, John also conceives of Christians in the present as "the outer court" of the temple. John's angelic companion who interprets his heavenly vision for him tells him not to measure this outer part of the temple "because it has been given to the Gentiles. They will trample on the holy city for 42 months" (11:2). Here the church seems to be conceived as an extension of the heavenly presence of God. When the "Gentiles" persecute the church, therefore, they are trampling on the place where God's presence in the world is most clearly visible.

John follows this same pattern in 13:5–6, where the beast from the sea—John's symbol for Roman imperial power—is "given a mouth to utter proud words and blasphemies and to exercise his authority for forty-two months" (13:5). This blasphemy involves the slander of God's "dwelling place . . . those who dwell in heaven." Here John identifies God's people ("those who dwell in heaven") with God's "dwelling place," using a term that appears frequently in the LXX and elsewhere in early Christian literature to refer to the "tabernacle" of Israel's wilderness wanderings (*skēnē*).[21] Once again John implies that the church is the place on earth where God's presence is most clearly visible and is therefore an extension of God's heavenly presence.

Like Peter, John also conceives of Christians in terms drawn from Exodus 19:6 as "a kingdom of priests" (Rev. 1:6; cf. 5:10; 20:6). They have inherited the vocation of Israel as a nation of priests who both enjoy the presence of God and mediate the character of God to the rest of his creation.[22] As a kingdom, they both "reign" in the present (1:6; 5:10) and "will reign" in the future (20:6).[23] Although the world around them loathes them for their refusal to participate in the indigenous cults that honor the power of Rome and lend stability to society, John assures them that they live in the presence of God, serve as his priests, and are a critical element in the exercise of his reign over the world he has created.

Who Are the Opponents of God's People?

The Roman elite of the first century B.C. and first century A.D. often claimed to be the most pious of peoples. Livy said that King Numa, who established the city of Rome, brought its people out of ignorance and prevented them from extravagance and idleness by instilling in them "the fear of Heaven" (1.19.4).[24] Cicero believed that although the Romans might be equal, or even inferior, to other peoples in many respects, "yet in the sense of religion, that is in reverence for the gods, we are far superior" (*Nat. d.* 2.8).[25] Dionysius of Halicarnassus, an Asian-born advocate for the Roman way of life, wrote that "among the Romans . . . all reverence is shown to the gods, both in words and actions, beyond what is practiced among either Greeks or

21 See, e.g., Ex. 27:21; 29:4; Lev. 1:1; Num. 1:1; Acts 7:44; and BDAG, 928. Cf. Rev. 21:3.

22 G. B. Caird, *A Commentary on the Revelation of St. John the Divine* (HNTC; New York: Harper & Row, 1966), 17; Beale, *Revelation*, 193–94.

23 On the likelihood that the present rather than the future tense of *basileuō* ("reign") should be read at 5:10, see Beale, *Revelation*, 362–64.

24 Wilken, *Christians*, 57–58, brought this passage to my attention.

25 Ibid., 57. Cf. Hugh Last, "The Study of the 'Persecutions,'" *JRS*, 27 (1937): 80–92, here at 84.

Barbarians" (*Ant. rom.* 2.19, 3).[26] Pliny said that the Roman state is "devoted to *religiones* and always earning by piety the favour of the gods" (*Pan.* 74.5).[27]

Such piety went hand-in-glove with virtuous behavior, and the Romans worried about religions and philosophies that might undermine their commitment, at least officially, to the virtues. Livy believed that the Bacchanalia threatened this societal commitment (39.8–14). Pliny, Tacitus, and Celsus believed that Christians threatened it too (*Ep.* 10.96; *Ann.* 15.44.2–8; Origen, *Cels.* 8.55, 68–69, respectively).[28]

Peter and John both provide a different understanding of Roman religiosity. Peter tells his Christian readers that "you were redeemed from the empty way of life handed down to you from your forefathers" (1 Peter 1:18). Far from staying within the boundaries of tradition and propriety, their Gentile way of life, prior to their conversion, led them to live "in debauchery, lust, drunkenness, orgies, carousing, and wanton idolatry" (4:3, aut.). The term "wanton" (*athemitos*) refers not to illegal activity but precisely to violation of tradition or of commonly recognized norms for decency and propriety.[29] In other words, Gentiles, prior to their entry into the people of God through faith in the gospel, did not participate in a pious and virtuous society but were awash in a "flood of debauchery" (4:4, aut.).

Revelation has an equally negative and more thorough critique of Roman piety. John depicts both Roman religion and the military might with which it is allied as two beasts, one from the sea and one from the land (Rev. 13:1–18; 19:20). The land beast, representing the imperial priesthood, is one means through which the military might of Rome exercises its power over its subjects (13:12). By economic oppression of those who refuse to worship the beast, Rome quashes religious dissent and keeps its power intact (13:17; 14:9; 19:20). Rome and its prophets, however, are allied with the unclean spirits (16:13), and Satan inspires their oppression of Christians (12:3–4, 7–9, 13, 15, 17–18).

Rather than being virtuous, Rome is "the great prostitute" with whom "the kings of the earth committed adultery," and, John says, "the inhabitants of the earth were intoxicated with the wine of her adulteries" (Rev. 17:1–2, 5). Rome and her allies have lived in luxury at the expense of others, including Christians. She has trafficked in a lengthy list of luxury items, including, John says climactically, the "bodies and souls of [human beings]" (18:12–13). She has "corrupted the earth by her adulteries" (19:2; cf. 11:18).

Both Peter and John, therefore, offer a picture of those who persecute Christians far different from the picture that the persecutors paint of themselves. The Romans and the societies in Asia Minor allied with them are neither pious nor virtuous but confederates of Satan himself and perpetrators of an empty way of life that leads to human misery.

26 Wilken, *Christians*, 58. Cf. Donald A. F. M. Russell, "Dionysius," in *The Oxford Classical Dictionary*, 2nd ed., ed. N. G. L. Hammond and H. H. Scullard (Oxford: Oxford Univ. Press, 1970), 351.

27 Beard, North, and Price, *Religions of Rome*, 1:216.

28 See esp. Last, "Study of the 'Persecutions,'" 84–92, who seems, however, to overstate the role that concern with morality played in the persecution of strange religions and to understate the role that Roman fear of "superstition" played. For the correct balance, see G. E. M. de Ste. Croix, "Why Were the Early Christians Persecuted?" *Past & Present* 26 (1963): 6–38, and "Why Were the Early Christians Persecuted? A Rejoinder [to A. N. Sherwin-White]," *Past & Present* 27 (1964): 28–33.

29 BDAG, 24.

What Is the Significance of Christian Suffering?

Pliny the Younger wrote his letters to Trajan in the early second century, several decades after the composition of 1 Peter, Hebrews, and Revelation. His perspective on the suffering that he inflicted on Christians, however, probably reflects the thinking of Roman magistrates generally in the late first and early second centuries. For Pliny, Christians who refused to recant their faith "deserved chastisement" because their very refusal to recant, apart from any problems that their creed itself might raise, was a sign of "contumacy and inflexible obstinacy" (*Ep.* 10.96). In his reply, the emperor Trajan agreed with this approach: Those found guilty of being Christians should be punished, but those willing to deny it and offer proof of doing so should "be pardoned on the ground of repentance" (*Ep.* 10.97).

Once again, our three texts construct a different understanding of reality for their readers. First Peter, Hebrews, and Revelation all attribute value to the suffering that Christians must endure from their persecutors, but a different value than their persecutors gave to their punishment of Christians. Peter, the author of Hebrews, and John understand Christian suffering as a means of assuring Christians that their faith is genuine and even as an opportunity for winning their detractors over to their worldview.

As we saw in chapter 30 above, Peter considers the suffering that his readers must endure for their faith to be part of a necessary refining process that their faith must undergo to show its genuineness (1 Peter 1:6–7). It reveals that they have set aside the life of sin in which they were once enmeshed (4:1, 4) and have adopted a new, eschatological perspective from which they value their suffering as preparation for receiving "praise, glory and honor when Jesus Christ is revealed" (1:7). The verbal abuse that they must endure for their faith, says Peter, is a sign that "the Spirit of glory and of God rests on you" (4:14).

Hebrews describes the willingness of persecuted Christians to endure their suffering as a sign that they are on the pilgrim path that Abel, Enoch, Noah, Abraham, Sarah, Isaac, Jacob, and, above all, Jesus, walked before them. The patriarchs and matriarchs of Israel's tradition "admitted that they were aliens and strangers on earth," and, the author continues, "people who say such things show that they are looking for a country of their own" (Heb. 11:13–14). Although they had the opportunity to return to the land from which God had called them, they did not do so because "they were longing for a better country—a heavenly one" (11:16). The implication is clear for the author's audience: Their willingness to follow this "great cloud of witnesses" on their difficult pilgrimage, throwing off "everything that hinders and the sin that so easily entangles" and running "with perseverance the race marked out" (12:1), demonstrates that they too "are looking for a country of their own," the city that God has prepared for them (11:14, 16). Their commitment is genuine.

By their perseverance in suffering they also show that they are children of God and brothers and sisters of Jesus. Jesus is preeminently God's Son (Heb. 1:2, 5–13). His suffering entailed becoming part of the human family, a brother of his fellow human beings (2:11, 17). Just as Jesus, God's Son, learned obedience through suffering (5:8), so God calls on Christians to "endure hardship as discipline," for "God is treating you as sons" (12:7). This, he says, is proof that those who endure hardship are genuine, not illegitimate children (12:9).[30]

The theme that perseverance through persecution is the mark of genuine Christian faith dominates Revelation. As we have just seen in chapter 32, "the one who conquers" is the one who endures persecution without compromise (Rev. 2:26; 3:5, 12; 21:7). The 144,000, who represent the vast multitude of God's people, are sealed to keep their faith in tact during the time of tribulation that God's people must experience (7:2–4, 5, 12). They have been "redeemed from the earth" and kept themselves pure from the sexual immorality and deceit practiced among disingenuous and compromising Christians, such as the followers of "Balaam" and "Jezebel" (14:1–5; cf. 2:14, 20).

Similarly, the "great multitude . . . wearing white robes," who also represent God's people, are "they who have come out of the great tribulation" (Rev. 7:9, 14). The woman who gives birth to the child represents God's people, and she is pursued by the dragon, which represents both Satan and the Roman empire allied with him (12:1–6, 9, 13, 17; 13:1). For John, willingness to stand firm despite the flood of oppression that refusal to compromise required of Christians provided the stamp of authenticity on Christian faith.

In addition to their understanding of Christian suffering as a sign of genuineness, Peter and John develop the notion that Christian suffering serves as a witness to the truth of the gospel to those persecuting Christians. It opens the possibility that these enemies may also repent and be saved from God's eschatological wrath. As we saw in chapter 30, this is probably how we should understand 1 Peter 2:12. Peter says that Christians should live such good lives among "the pagans" that the Gentile slander of Christians as evildoers might be transformed into praise of God "on the day he visits us" (2:12). Suffering for the faith without succumbing to the temptation to abuse one's accusers in return can lead one's persecutors to be ashamed of their unwarranted attacks. Although he does not say so explicitly, Peter probably implies that such nonviolent responses may even lead those who persecute Christians to embrace the Christian perspective (cf. 3:1, 15–16).

John develops this theme more fully and in a more complex way in Revelation. Christians are caught up, along with everyone else, in the gradual disintegration of Rome's empire: "In her was found the blood of prophets and of the saints, and of all who have been killed on the earth" (Rev. 18:24). Like others, Christians suffer bitterly as victims of Rome's desire to dominate the world and accrue wealth and luxury for herself. The tribulation that afflicts the church is part of a tribulation that afflicts the world dominated by Rome (6:1–17; 8:6–21).

John insists, however, that the disintegration of the Roman system is not merely self-inflicted. God is behind it, and although part of its purpose is the punishment of the wicked and the gathering of evidence for their judgment, God also intends

30 Cf. deSilva, *Despising Shame*, 296; idem, *Hope of Glory*, 8.

this suffering to lead at least some among the wicked to repent before the great, final Day of Judgment. As we saw in the previous chapter, this is clear from the way John structures the seal and trumpet plague sequences to incorporate the principle of increasing severity and a merciful delay before the outpouring of final judgment. It is probably also implied in the response of those who survived the great earthquake after the resurrection and ascension to heaven of the two witnesses: "The survivors were terrified and gave glory to the God of heaven" (Rev. 11:13).[31]

For Peter, John, and the author of Hebrews, therefore, Christian suffering under persecution is far from a means of maintaining Roman hegemony in the face of the Christian threat to Roman stability and economic prosperity. Christian suffering under the hand of persecution both provides a seal of authenticity to one's Christian faith and prompts one's persecutors to see the truth of the gospel's claims.

What Does the Future Hold?

The Romans thought of their system of government, especially after Augustus, as the eternal government of the world.[32] Augustus's reforms had saved the world from destruction. His birthday marked "the beginning of good tidings," according to the statement of the provincial assembly of Asia in 29 B.C., and according to the provincial governor of the same year, "people would be right to consider this to have been the beginning of the breath of life for them."[33] He had, in a sense, made the world anew, and the Roman empire would be eternal.[34] Thus, John records the boast of the great prostitute: "I sit as queen; I am not a widow, and I will never mourn" (Rev. 18:7).[35] Roman soldiers stationed in Dura Europas in the early third century A.D., although far from Rome, sacrificed to the traditional gods of Rome on January 3 and vowed "the eternity of the empire and of the Roman people."[36] Even Tertullian, writing at about the same time, believed that Rome would remain as "long as the world shall stand" (*Scap.* 2).

Peter and John disagreed. Peter, repeating the sentiment of Isaiah 40:6–8, tells his readers that "all flesh is like grass and all its glory like the flower of the field; the grass withers and the flower falls" (1 Peter 1:24–25). Even now, the malevolent angels, authorities, and powers of the invisible world are in submission to the risen and ascended Christ (3:22). Even now, the time of God's judgment has begun (4:17). The unbelieving persecutors of God's people have failed to believe because all along they "were destined for" this judgment (2:7–8). One day God will require them to render an account to him for their actions (4:5), and he will judge them both justly and severely (2:23; 4:17–18).

31 Cf. Bauckham, *Theology of the Book of Revelation*, 86.

32 On this see esp. Bruce W. Winter, "'The Seasons' of This Life and Eschatology in 1 Corinthians 7:29–31," in *Eschatology in Bible and Theology: Evangelical Essays at the Dawn of a New Millennium*, ed. Kent E. Brower and Mark W. Elliott (Downers Grove, Ill.: InterVarsity Press, 1997), 323–34, here at 324–29.

33 See the translation in S. R. F. Price, *Rituals and Power: The Roman Imperial Cult in Asia Minor* (Cambridge: Cambridge Univ. Press, 1984), 54–55.

34 Winter, "'Seasons' of This Life," 326. Cf. deSilva, *Hope of Glory*, 190–91.

35 DeSilva, *Hope of Glory*, 190.

36 A translation of this use-worn papyrus roll appears in Beard, North, and Price, *Religions of Rome*, 2:71–74.

John is more explicit. Rome's economic and political exploitation of the earth and its peoples will go from bad to worse (Rev. 6:1–8), and Christians will be caught up in Rome's evil machinations (6:9–11; 7:1–8) until finally God puts a stop to it all and brings a devastating judgment on Rome and its allies (6:12–17). At that time, Rome and its imperial cult will totter and crash (14:8). The Lamb will defeat them in battle (17:14; 19:11–21), and God will both judge them justly and punish them eternally (14:9–11; 16:1–21; 17:8, 16; 18:1–24; 19:2–3; 20:10, 11–15; 21:8).

The future for Christians who remain faithful, by contrast, is bright. Peter says that they have an unfading inheritance awaiting them (1 Peter 1:4), an eternal and joyful experience of the glory of Christ and of God (4:13; 5:10). He goes even further to suggest that just as the time of judgment has already begun (4:17), so the period of eschatological joy has also already started for Christians. They already rejoice that their salvation is ready to be revealed in the last time (1:5). They also rejoice in their suffering because they know it is the prelude to the overwhelming joy they will experience at the revelation of his glory (4:13).

Their location on the cusp of the eschaton, Peter says, is a privileged position. The prophets carefully described the future time of Christ's coming but did not experience it. Instead those who heard the preaching of the gospel experienced the fulfillment of these prophecies (1 Peter 1:10–12).

The author of Hebrews develops the same thought. The "Day," he says, is "approaching" (Heb. 10:25). Christians who are faithful to complete their pilgrim journey will enter God's eschatological rest (3:7–4:11). Because they live in the age when Jesus has pioneered the way into God's presence and sat down at God's right hand (12:2), they have, in a sense, already come to Mount Zion and started to experience the joyful worship of God with the angels and the spirits of those who have died and been perfected (12:22–24). This means that they possess an enormous historical advantage over faithful pilgrims who lived before Christ:

> All these people were still living by faith when they died. They did not receive the things promised; they only saw them and welcomed them from a distance.... God had planned something better for us so that only together with us would they be made perfect. (Heb. 11:13, 40)

John does not emphasize the present joy that Christians experience in the midst of suffering but describes at length the many privileges that they will inherit once God has finished waging war against the forces of evil. They will gain the right denied to the disobedient Adam "to eat from the tree of life, which is in the paradise of God" (Rev. 2:7; 22:2, 14). They will receive the "crown of life" (2:10), a sign of victory and honor. Christ will give them "hidden manna" and "a white stone" (2:17), both probably symbolic of the eschatological banquet to which victorious Christians will gain entrance. Like the Messiah himself, they will have "authority over the nations" (2:26–28; cf. 3:21). They will be "dressed in white" (3:4–5), indicating their purity, and will stand in God's presence eternally (3:12; 21:3).

In God's presence Christians will experience "no more death or mourning or crying or pain" (21:4). There they will dwell in safety in a city whose gates never need to be shut, to which the nations come to bring their glory to God, and where the glorious splendor emanating from God and the Lamb supplies an eternal light (21:1–27; 22:5).

All three texts emphasize, however, that this bright reality belongs to those who remain faithful to their commitment to the gospel, refusing to give their persecutors cause for alarm by socially destructive behavior and refusing to compromise with the idolatry that their persecutors want them to practice. Peter tells his readers to be self-controlled (1 Peter 1:13), to be holy in all they do (1:15; cf. 2:1, 11), and to live such good lives among their unbelieving opponents that they may be won over (2:12; 3:1). No one should deserve the beating that he or she gets (2:20; 3:13), nor should anyone retaliate against unjust treatment (2:23; cf. 3:9, 15), but Christians should shame those who slander them by their good behavior (3:16).

Peter seems to be concerned in such texts that Christians not behave immorally and lend truth to the claims of their persecutors. Perhaps this same concern lies beneath the admonitions that conclude Hebrews that God will judge the sexually immoral (Heb. 13:4), that Christians should be free from greed (13:5–6), and that they should follow the example of their leaders (13:7).

John the seer is more concerned that his readers not compromise with the idolatrous and sexually immoral customs woven into the fabric of Roman society as a way of relieving the pressure put on them to compromise their faith. This concern probably stands behind his polemic against "the teaching of Balaam" and the prophetess "Jezebel," who seems to have found a way to accommodate her Christian beliefs to participation in cultic banquets sponsored by the local temples (Rev. 2:14, 20; cf. 3:4). For those tempted to alleviate the pressure of alienation from Roman society by compromise or to profit from alliances with its evils, John records the appeal of God: "Come out of her, my people, so that you will not share in her sins, so that you will not receive any of her plagues" (18:4).

Peter, the author of Hebrews, and John, therefore, urge their readers to live their difficult lives in the light of the future realities they describe. Although the power of Rome must have often seemed invincible and its grandeur unfading to its subjects—even to Christians—these three authors insist that eternal power and glory belong to God alone.[37] Those who remain faithful to him, even at the cost of suffering, will experience the joy of his eternal splendor forever.

An Alternative Vision of the World

In summary, 1 Peter, Hebrews, and Revelation offer their readers an alternative worldview to that which dominated the wider society in which they lived. Jesus was

37 From the time of Augustus, cities throughout the empire were filled with lavish visual images of Rome's divine right to rule its provinces. On this see Paul Zanker, *The Power of Images in the Age of Augustus* (Jerome Lectures 16; Ann Arbor, Mich.: Univ. of Michigan Press, 1988), esp. ch. 8, "The Roman Empire of Augustus: Imperial Myth and Cult in East and West." The imagery that Zanker describes must have served as a constant reminder to Christians of the clash between their own convictions and the claims of Rome.

not a troublemaker whose annoyance to the governing authorities somehow failed to end at his death. He presently reigns as King at God's right hand, with all invisible, malevolent forces conquered beneath his feet. In due course, unbelieving Roman magistrates will join these invisible cosmic enemies of God in submission to God's Messiah. Christians are not a group of unhinged fanatics, so stubbornly un-Roman in their religious convictions that they pose a threat to the stability of society. They are a kingdom of priests, the place in the world where God focuses his presence most intensely. If the people of the world want to know God, they must find him in the church.

The traditional piety of Roman society, therefore, is not piety at all but an instrument of corruption and oppression. The oppression that Christians experience under Rome's heavy hand is not the needed discipline of an obstinate rabble but the seal of genuineness on the Christian confession of those who suffer and a witness to their persecutors of the gospel's truth. Rome will not remain, as even Tertullian seems to have thought, as long as the world should stand. Instead, a Day is drawing ever nearer when Rome and its allies will plummet into the lake of fire, and those who have refused to compromise their faith under societal pressure will enter the new Jerusalem to live forever.

Here again it seems important to say that the responses of 1 Peter, Hebrews, and Revelation to persecution do not neatly fit the trajectory of the historical framework of a so-called "early catholicism." None of these three texts shows a tendency to negotiate a settlement with the society around them. Hebrews and Revelation insist that Christians remain on the margins of society and be faithful to Jesus. Hebrews urges its readers to "go to him outside the camp" (Heb. 13:13), and Revelation exhorts them to "come out" of Roman society (Rev. 18:4).

Even 1 Peter's household code is not advice on living "a decent and clean bourgeois life" but on living in a way that will win over unbelieving opponents so that they may survive the final Judgment (1 Peter 2:12; cf. 3:1).[38] The way in which Peter uses his admonitions to submit to governing and household authorities (2:12–3:7) is similar to Paul's advice to the Thessalonians in an early Christian text whose eschatological fervor is lively:

> Make it your ambition to lead a quiet life, to mind your own business and to work with your hands, just as we told you, so that your daily life may win the respect of outsiders and so that you will not be dependent on anybody. (1 Thess. 4:11–12)

First Peter, Hebrews, and Revelation all display an energetic engagement with the idea that the enthroned Christ can return at any moment. "The end of all things is

38 The quotation comes from Rudolf Bultmann, *Theology of the New Testament*, 2 vols. (New York: Charles Scribner's Sons, 1951–55), 2:182.

near," announces Peter (1 Peter 4:7). "Let us encourage one another—and all the more as you see the Day approaching," urges the author of Hebrews (Heb. 10:25). In Revelation, Jesus says again and again, like the tolling of a bell: "I am coming soon"; "Behold, I am coming soon"; "Yes, I am coming soon" (Rev. 3:11; 22:7, 12, 20). This is not the perspective of authors and communities who are becoming comfortable with the structures of the world.

HERESY, PERSECUTION, AND THE TRUTH CLAIMS OF THE EARLY CHURCH

The nine texts that comprise the final third of the modern New Testament canon, although widely diverse, are all concerned to assert the church's vision of reality against attacks on that vision from different directions. One set of texts opposes a vision that has intellectualized spiritual reality. The Johannine letters, 2 Peter, Jude, and probably James fall into this category. Against a vision of the gospel that implies an indifference to ethics or permits unethical behavior, these texts assert a vision of spiritual reality defined by Christian tradition. An indifference to the love of one's Christian brothers and sisters or a speciously argued link between God's grace and sinful behavior deviates from the path that leads from the present to the historical Jesus. It also betrays an affinity with the eschatological enemies of God's people.

The other set of texts opposes a vision of social reality that claims the divine and eternal right of Rome to rule the peoples she has conquered for her own benefit. Those who support the imperial cult and the numerous indigenous religions that in various ways legitimate Rome's rule view Jesus and his followers as superstitious troublers of the peace and a threat to societal prosperity. Left unchecked, their movement will eat away at the fabric of society, carefully woven of an alliance between Rome's military power and the will of the gods. "Our empire," said Cicero, "was won by those commanders who obeyed the dictates of religion" (*Nat. d.* 2.8).

Against this idea, 1 Peter, Hebrews, and Revelation provide their readers with a vision of the world from the perspective of the one true God, enthroned in the heavens, and of Jesus the Messiah, enthroned with him. The "gods" of Rome and of the societies that support her hegemony lie prostrate at the feet of Christ Jesus. The victory of God and his Messiah over evil has begun, and when it is complete, all those who have oppressed Christians and refused to repent will experience the judgment and wrath of God. All God's people, however, will begin an untroubled and eternal enjoyment of his presence.

CONCLUSION

Chapter 34

THE THEOLOGICAL UNITY OF THE NEW TESTAMENT

William Wrede had a point when he insisted that a theology of the New Testament should describe the living, breathing world of the earliest Christians. It should be something more, he complained, than the arrangement of material from the New Testament under various doctrinal headings. In the preceding chapters I have tried to allow each of the New Testament's twenty-seven books to speak theologically within the specific situations of their composition. Wrede hardly had this in mind—he envisioned an "objective" history of early Christianity unencumbered either by the canon or by Christian faith, a vision that in the first chapter we found both unattainable and undesirable.

Nevertheless, Wrede was right to insist that a New Testament theology should provide a window on the world in which early Christians lived. Such an exercise is important not because, as Wrede imagined, it would prevent a Christian interpreter's theological convictions from disabling his or her historical acumen, but because it shows the Christian reader an important theological truth: God revealed himself in the day-to-day affairs of his people. His word not only became flesh and dwelt among us through his Son Jesus Christ but also in the divine speech that most Christians, over many centuries, have identified with the New Testament Scriptures.

Because the Scriptures are the Word of God, however, it is not enough in a description of New Testament theology to discuss only the discrete theological message of each writing or group of writings. It is necessary also to indicate, even if only briefly, how these writings comprise a theological unity. Where do the New Testament Scriptures converge? What issues emerge as most important from reading them together as a single unit? In the interpretation of the New Testament writings proposed here, five issues occupy an especially important place: the significance of Jesus, faith as a response to Jesus, the outpouring of God's Spirit, the church as the people of God, and the consummation of all things.

THE CONVERGENCE OF THE HUMAN PROBLEM AND GOD'S ANSWER TO IT IN JESUS

Jesus as More than the Messiah

The New Testament writers often insist that Jesus fulfilled traditional expectations, based ultimately on the Jewish Scriptures, of a coming Messiah. He is, for example, the Son of God and anointed King of Psalm 2 and the kingly Lord of Psalm 110, whom God would appoint to rule his people and whose enemies God would subdue. As we saw in our study of the gospels in chapters 3 through 7, however, the authors of these texts are not content to describe Jesus only in such traditional language. In the Synoptic Gospels, Jesus interprets Psalm 110 to mean that the Messiah is not only David's Son but, like God himself, David's Lord (Matt. 22:45; Mark 12:37; Luke 20:44; cf. Acts 2:34–35). John is even more explicit. He says that those who believe Jesus to be the Messiah and Son of God will have life (John 20:31), but under John's definition of these terms, Jesus and God are one (10:30; 17:11, 22).

A chorus of other New Testament voices joins this affirmation of the gospels. For Paul, Jesus is not merely declared Son of God at the resurrection (Rom. 1:4; cf. Acts 2:36), but somehow is God's preexistent Son whom God sent into the world (Rom. 8:3; Gal. 4:4) and the very means through which the world itself came into existence (1 Cor. 8:6; Col. 1:15–17).[1] For the author of Hebrews, Jesus is not simply the royal son of Psalm 2:7 and 2 Samuel 7:14 (Heb. 1:5), nor merely the ultimate high priest who perfected the Mosaic sacrificial system (Heb. 9:11–12), but the full expression of God's nature (1:3), the one through whom God created the universe (1:2, 10), and the one who sustains it (1:3). Similarly, for John the seer, Jesus is not merely the king to whom God, according to Psalm 2:8–9, would give the authority to rule the nations with a rod of iron (Rev. 2:26–27), but somehow also the Lamb who occupies the throne of God himself (7:17; 22:1, 3; cf. 3:21; 5:13; 6:16; 7:9–10).

Universal Rebellion as the Reason for Jesus' Rejection

The New Testament writers frequently also affirm that despite Jesus' fulfillment of scriptural expectations for God's anointed King and the evidence from both his teaching and his mighty deeds or signs that he is one with God, many people have rejected him. This paradox emerges time and again. Within the first few paragraphs of Mark's narrative, leaders from both the religious and political parties of Judea have conspired to kill him (3:6). John tells us, almost in the same breath, both that Jesus created the world and that, when he became flesh, the world rejected him (John 1:9–11). Paul insists that he must preach the paradoxical notion of "Christ crucified" (1 Cor. 1:23)—that the expected Davidic king who came to subdue God's enemies himself suffered rejection and crucifixion. In the same way, John the seer tells us that the Lamb at the center of God's throne in Revelation looks as if he was slaughtered (Rev. 5:6, 9, 12; 13:8).

The explanation of this paradox—the rejection of the Messiah and the Son of God, indeed of God himself—is a major New Testament concern. Many New Testament writers imply that if we understand Israel's Scriptures correctly, there is nothing surprising about this act of rebellion. God's people Israel frequently rejected God's word, whether it came from God himself in his Scriptures (Mark 7:9, 9, 13) or from his messengers the prophets (Mark 4:11–12; 7:6–8; 12:1–5). This the Synoptic Gospels, Acts, and Paul all affirm, so it comes as no surprise that God's people also

1 *Pace* James D. G. Dunn, *Christology in the Making*, 2nd ed. (Grand Rapids: Eerdmans, 1996), 38–46, 179–83, and idem, *The Theology of Paul the Apostle* (Grand Rapids: Eerdmans, 1998), 267–79, it does not seem possible to contain Pauline notions of Christ's preexistence solely within the framework of Jewish concepts of the sending of a prophet or the preexistence of wisdom.

rejected God's Son (12:6–8; Acts 28:25–27; 1 Thess. 2:14–16). In the words of Stephen to Judea's Sanhedrin:

> "You stiff-necked people, with uncircumcised hearts and ears! You are just like your fathers: You always resist the Holy Spirit! Was there ever a prophet your fathers did not persecute? They even killed those who predicted the coming of the Righteous One. And now you have betrayed and murdered him—you who have received the law that was put into effect through angels but have not obeyed it." (Acts 7:51–53)

The New Testament does not, however, lay either the spirit of rebellion against God generally or the rejection of Jesus specifically solely at the door of the Jews who rejected Jesus. The Jews' rejection of God's word, whether it came through his prophets or his Son, is only one manifestation of a rebellion against God that has permeated humanity from the beginning.

Paul is clearest on this. When Adam transgressed God's command, sin entered the world and everyone after Adam has sinned also, bringing God's just condemnation of all humanity (Rom. 5:12, 15–19; 1 Cor. 15:22).[2] This conviction about the sinfulness of all humanity, both Gentile and Jewish, is an important driving force behind Paul's missionary labors. In what is probably the earliest extant Christian text (1 Thessalonians), Paul implies both that the Jews who have rejected Jesus deserve the wrath of God (1 Thess. 2:16) and that Gentiles who have responded to the gospel have, by their response, escaped the "coming wrath" (1:10; 5:9). Apart from faith in the gospel, in other words, both Jews and Gentiles will experience God's wrath for their rebellion against him.

In his letter to the Romans, the conviction that "Jews and Gentiles alike are all under sin" (Rom. 3:9) and that "the whole world [is] accountable to God" (3:19) forms the first critical step in Paul's explanation of the gospel (1:18–3:20). Most of this first part of Romans is concerned with proving that the Jew, despite possession of God's will in the Mosaic law, is no more exempt than the Gentile from God's justified condemnation of the sinful (1:18–4:25). Toward the end of the letter, however, Paul turns the tables and addresses Gentiles. They too can claim no special privilege over the Jews by reasoning that they, unlike most Jews, have believed the gospel (11:11–32).

"As for you," he tells the Gentile audience of his letter to the Ephesians, "you were dead in your transgressions and sins, in which you used to live when you followed the ways of this world and the ruler of the kingdom of the air, the spirit who is now at work in those who are disobedient" (Eph. 2:1–2). "All of us also," he continues, now speaking as a Jew, "lived among them at one time, gratifying the cravings of our sinful nature and following its desires and thoughts" (2:3). Paul is studiedly even-handed in his condemnation of all humanity.[3]

2 Paul acknowledges the role of Eve in the primal sin (2 Cor. 11:3; 1 Tim. 2:13–14), but when he speaks of the effect of this sin on all humanity, he identifies it as Adam's responsibility.

3 The antecedents of the pronouns here are not entirely clear. Many commentators believe that Paul is speaking of all Christians, whether Jewish or Gentile, in 2:3. See, e.g., Ernest Best, *Ephesians*

Early Christian tradition both inside the New Testament and elsewhere reveals the same conviction. As we saw in chapter 3, Mark's portrait of Jesus' disciples is nearly as unflattering as his portrait of the scribes, Pharisees, Sadducees, and the Jewish high priest. Both Jesus' disciples and his enemies have, at different points in the narrative, hard hearts, and if the Jewish leadership engineers Jesus' death, the disciples flee from him in cowardly fear when the leadership's plot reaches its climax.

Matthew certainly constructs a searing indictment of the scribes and Pharisees as blind hypocrites, white-washed tombs, and hell-bound serpents (Matt. 23:1–36), but, as we saw in chapter 4, he is also unsparing in his criticism of hypocrisy among people who call Jesus "Lord" (7:21–22; 25:11). Luke makes clear that those who conspire against Jesus in Jerusalem include not only Herod Antipas and the people of Israel but Pontius Pilate and the Gentiles as well (Acts 4:27). In John it is not merely the Jewish leadership that "do not have the love of God" within themselves (John 5:42), are "from below" (8:23), and have the devil as their father (8:44), but one of Jesus' own disciples also turns out to be "a devil" (6:70). Jesus' own people do not receive him (1:11), but neither does the world of which his people are only a part (1:10; 8:23).[4]

The importance of this teaching about the universality of sin in early Christian theology is also evident from its reemergence in charges against Christians during the second century. Celsus scores Christians for their claim that everyone, without exception, is a sinner, a charge that Origen, in his third-century reply, has to admit is true:

> We say it is impossible for any man to look up to God with virtue from the beginning. For of necessity evil must exist among men from the first, as Paul says: "But when the commandment came sin revived and I died." (*Cels.* 3.62)

Part of the reason for the frequent charge against Christians that they encourage "hatred of the human race," as Tacitus puts it, may be this conviction that all people, without distinction, are sinners and subject to the eschatological wrath of God.[5]

In summary, when God himself entered the world in human flesh, as an Israelite, the world did not know him and his own people rejected him. As paradoxical as this seems, the New Testament affirms that this is only the climactic expression of human rebellion against God that began with the first human being and continued both in Israel specifically and among the peoples of the world generally.

Although a less prominent theme, various New Testament writers also imply that this problem of human rebellion mirrors the rebellion of invisible cosmic powers

(ICC; Edinburgh: T. & T. Clark, 1998), 207–8, and Harold Hoehner, *Ephesians: An Exegetical Commentary* (Grand Rapids: Baker, 2002), 317–18. For the reading I adopt here, see, e.g., Peter T. O'Brien, *The Letter to the Ephesians* (PNTC; Grand Rapids: Eerdmans, 1999), 161–62.

4 Cf. 1 Peter 2:4, where Jesus is rejected by human beings generally, not simply by Israel. On this see Leonhard Goppelt, *A Commentary on First Peter* (Grand Rapids: Eerdmans, 1993), 137.

5 Tacitus, *Ann.* 15.44.5. Tacitus and others also level this charge at the Jews (e.g., Tacitus, *Hist.* 5.5; Diodorus Siculus 34.1.1). Jewish observance of the Sabbath, avoidance of pork, and practice of circumcision, and the Jewish and Christian refusal to participate in the cultic rituals that were so prominent in Greco-Roman culture were probably also among the reasons for this slander.

against God. Here too, the problems go back to the primal days not long, relatively speaking, after the creation of the world. The New Testament writers most closely associated with the Jerusalem church affirm, in general outline, an understanding of this primal rebellion that was common among Jews of the Second Temple period. At the time of Noah, they say, a group of angels rebelled against the position in the cosmos that God assigned to them, and God banished them to a dark prison, where they presently await judgment (1 Peter 3:19–20; 2 Peter 2:4; Jude 6).[6] Although they are imprisoned there, their evil designs continue in the form of false teachers within the church (2 Peter 2:9; Jude 8) and those who persecute Christians (1 Peter 4:4–5).

John the seer creates a powerful version of this story in his account of the cosmic battle in heaven between Michael and his angels on one side and the dragon, whom John identifies as Satan, with his angels on the other side (Rev. 12:7–9). Michael and his angelic forces defeat the dragon and his angelic forces and cast them down from heaven to the earth (12:9). From there, however, they are able to persecute God's people (12:13). This is why, after Michael casts him out of heaven, the dragon stands on the beach to preside over the emergence of the sea beast (Roman imperial power) and the land beast (the Asian supporters of the Roman imperial cult). Both beasts then persecute those who refuse to engage in the idolatrous worship that the sea beast demands (13:7, 12, 17).

The thinking of these New Testament writers on the fall of Satan may go back to the emphasis that Jesus himself places on a traditional Jewish understanding of the struggle between God and Satan, a struggle in which God will inevitably be victorious.[7] The gospels and Acts frequently describe the power of Jesus and his first followers over the demonic world during the time of Jesus' earthly ministry and shortly thereafter. After hearing from a group of his followers that "even the demons" have submitted to them in his name, Jesus says that he saw Satan fall like lightening from heaven (Luke 10:17–18; cf. John 12:31). This fall, however, did not spell the end of Satan's malevolence against the people of God—Luke will show in many places in Acts that, although God ultimately triumphs over these powers, skirmishes between God's power and the malevolent forces of the universe continue.[8]

At least in his extant correspondence, Paul does not delve into the origins of the cosmic rebellion, but he too believes that the universe is populated with "rulers," "authorities," and "powers" aligned with darkness and wickedness (Eph. 6:12). These powers, he maintains, seek to frustrate God's purposes by encouraging people to rebel against him (2:1–3; cf. Gal. 1:4) and separating them from the love that he has shown to his creatures in the gospel (Rom. 8:38–39).

It is possible that Paul understands the crucifixion of Christ to be the work of these cosmic "rulers." In 1 Corinthians 2:6 he explains to the Corinthians that their

6 Cf., e.g., *1 En.* 6–19; *2 En.* 4; *Jub.* 5.6; 10.5–6; *2 Bar.* 56.13; cf. Sir. 16:7; CD 2.18–20.

7 See. e.g., *Jub.* 23.29; *T. Levi* 18.12; *T. Jud.* 25.3; *T. Dan* 5.10; *As. Mos.* 10.1 and the discussion in I. Howard Marshall, *Commentary on Luke* (NIGTC; Grand Rapids: Eerdmans, 1978), 428–29.

8 Cf. Rev. 12:13, where the fall of Satan from heaven to earth both portends his ultimate defeat and is also the opportunity for him to persecute the earthly church.

fascination with human wisdom is misguided, since it is also the concern of "the rulers of this age," and these rulers crucified the Lord of glory. Paul's primary reference here is probably to people like Pontius Pilate (1 Tim. 6:13), who crucified Jesus as a matter of political expediency, but he may also have in mind the cosmic rulers whose will Pilate unwittingly accomplished.[9]

In summary, since the time of Adam all human beings have been in a state of rebellion against God, who created them. This rebellion reaches its climax when both Jewish and Gentile rulers crucify God's Son, who existed in unity with God from the beginning and was the means through whom he created the world. This human rebellion finds a parallel in a cosmic rebellion of angelic powers against God. These powers refused to stay within the boundaries that God created them to occupy and instead warred against their Creator. In punishment God cast them from heaven and sealed their fate, but they continue to encourage rebellion against God in the human sphere and insist on attempting to frustrate God's purposes. If Paul is thinking, at least partially, of these powers in 1 Corinthians 2:6 and 8, then he implies that they too expressed their rebellion by engineering the crucifixion of "the Lord of glory."

The Death of Jesus as the Defeat of Rebellion against God

Paradoxically, the New Testament writers affirm that precisely in the crucifixion of Jesus God has provided the remedy to the universal plight of sin. In Jesus' death, God has given the means both for restoring his rebellious human creatures to a relationship with himself and for sealing the fate of the malevolent cosmic forces bent on frustrating his gracious, loving purposes.

Jesus' Death Atones for Human Sin

All four gospels, in various ways, describe Jesus' death as an atoning sacrifice for sin, wherever sin occurs and regardless of how serious it is. In Matthew and Mark, Jesus takes the role of Isaiah's Suffering Servant and dies as a ransom for many (Matt. 20:28; Mark 10:45). His blood is poured out for many (Mark 14:24), and Matthew tells us explicitly that this is for the forgiveness of sins (Matt. 26:28). In these two gospels, the inner curtain of the temple, separating the Holy Place from the Most Holy Place, splits at Jesus' death from top to bottom, indicating that God has accepted Jesus' death as the atoning sacrifice to end all atoning sacrifices (Mark 15:38; 27:51). Luke is less explicit, but also says that Jesus' death was "for" his disciples (Luke 22:19–20) and that Jesus "bought" the church "with his own blood" (Acts 20:28). Although not a major emphasis in John, Jesus nevertheless describes his death as "for the life of the world" (John 6:51–56); he gives his life "for the sheep" and "for [his] friends" (10:11, 15; 15:13).

The gospels also make clear that the atoning effects of Jesus' death are open to everyone, whether Jew or Gentile—even to those who put Jesus on the cross. John makes this especially clear in his interpretive comment on Caiaphas's statement that

9 See the discussion in Anthony C. Thiselton, *The First Epistle to the Corinthians* (NIGTC; Grand Rapids, Eerdmans, 2000), 233–39.

Jesus' death is expedient since it involves only one person and will spare the nation (John 11:49–50; cf. 18:14):

> He did not say this on his own, but as high priest that year he prophesied that Jesus would die for the Jewish nation, and not only for that nation but also for the scattered children of God, to bring them together and make them one. (11:51–52)

Luke implies that Jesus' death has opened the way for forgiveness even of those most closely involved in his crucifixion. "Father, forgive them," Jesus says from the cross, "for they do not know what they are doing" (Luke 23:34).[10]

Paul also frequently affirms this understanding of Jesus' death. "God did not appoint us to suffer wrath," he tells the Thessalonians, "but to receive salvation through the Lord Jesus Christ. He died for us" (1 Thess. 5:9–10a). Jesus has given his body and his blood "for you," he tells the Corinthians, quoting the tradition he received containing Jesus' own interpretation of his death (1 Cor. 11:24). When he preached the gospel to the Galatians, he clearly portrayed Jesus the Messiah as crucified (Gal. 3:1), and if his comments a few sentences later are a reliable guide to why he did this, he speaks of Jesus' death as a substitutionary, atoning sacrifice: "Christ redeemed us from the curse of the law by becoming a curse for us, for it is written: 'Cursed is everyone who is hung on a tree'" (Gal. 3:13).

Jesus absorbed the curse that God justly placed on those, whether Jew or Gentile, who fail to do what he requires (Gal. 2:15–16; 3:10). He became a curse "for us" (*hyper hēmōn*)—that is, in our place. Paul makes this understanding of Jesus' death even more explicit in 2 Corinthians and Romans. In 2 Corinthians he says that "God made him who had no sin to be sin for us, so that in him we might become the righteousness of God" (2 Cor. 5:21). There is no difference between Jew and Gentile, he says in Romans, "for all have sinned and fall short of the glory of God" and all "are justified freely" by the "sacrifice of atonement" (*hilastērion*) of Christ's death (Rom. 3:21–25; cf. Eph. 2:11–17).

Other New Testament writers express the same idea in their own way. The Elder says that Jesus "is the atoning sacrifice [*hilasmos*] for our sins, and not only for ours but also for the sins of the whole world" (1 John 2:2; cf. 4:10; Heb. 2:17). Peter says that "Christ died for sins once for all, the righteous for the unrighteous, to bring you to God" (1 Peter 3:18).

How does Jesus' death substitute for the punishment of sinners and bring us to God? Why was it necessary? For most New Testament writers, the mechanism of atoning sacrifice apparently is too familiar to need much explanation. Throughout

10 This saying does not appear in an impressive list of Alexandrian and Western manuscripts, and some commentators think that Luke's original text did not include it. The manuscript evidence for the inclusion of the saying, however, is not insignificant. In addition, the saying fits well with Luke's literary concerns to show the parallels between the death of Jesus and the death of Stephen (Acts 7:60), to emphasize the ignorance of those responsible for Jesus' death (Acts 3:17; 13:27; 17:30), and to conclude the narrative divisions of his description of the crucifixion with a saying of Jesus (Luke 23:31, 43, 46). On all this see Marshall, *Luke*, 867–68, and Darrell L. Bock, *Luke 9:51–24:53* (BECNT 3b; Grand Rapids: Baker, 1996), 1867–68.

their various cultures, the death of an innocent victim was thought to atone for sin against the gods.[11] Paul spells out what others assume:

> God presented him as a sacrifice of atonement, through faith in his blood. He did this to demonstrate his justice, because in his forbearance he had left the sins committed beforehand unpunished—he did it to demonstrate his justice at the present time, so as to be just and the one who justifies those who have faith in Jesus. (Rom. 3:25–26)

God, in his mercy, left sins unpunished for generations. This raised the question, however, of God's justice. How could he be a righteous God and leave sin unpunished? Christ's sacrificial death solves the problem. It recognizes the gravity of sin but allows the guilty to escape God's wrath.

Perhaps Paul wants to explain the mechanism of atonement here because he also wants to bring out an important difference between the way Christ's death has effected atonement and the way the death of an innocent person was often thought to bring atonement in the Greco-Roman world. In the common way of thinking, human beings initiate an atoning sacrifice at great cost to themselves in order to stave off the worse fate of the gods' continuing wrath.[12] This was not, however, the way atonement worked in the Old Testament. There, God provided the sacrificial system as a gift to deal with human sin. In the words of Leviticus 17:11: "The life of a creature is the blood, and I have given it to you to make atonement for yourselves on the altar; it is the blood that makes atonement for one's life."

For Paul too, the ultimate sacrifice of atonement comes at God's initiative and at great cost to himself to people whose sinfulness makes any attempt to propitiate God impossible. God justified us "freely by his grace" when he put forward Christ Jesus as a sacrifice of atonement (Rom. 3:24–25). He justifies the wicked "according to grace" (4:4–5). He "demonstrates his own love for us in this: While we were still sinners, Christ died for us" (Rom. 5:8–9). In 1 John, the Elder describes the same idea in his own idiom: "This is love: not that we loved God, but that he loved us and sent his Son as an atoning sacrifice for our sins" (1 John 4:10). The New Testament, like the Old Testament, insists that the solution to God's wrath against human rebellion has come not from human beings—who are, because of their rebellious hearts, utterly incapable of providing it—but as a free gift from God himself.

The New Testament writers also often emphasize the willing nature of Christ's participation in this free gift of atonement. They do not portray Christ's death as an act of God the Father against his Son for sinful human beings but as the willing collusion of Father and Son together in the loving and costly rescue of undeserving,

11 For two examples from the first century, see, e.g., Lucan, *Pharsalia* 2.304–9 and 4 Macc. 6:28–29, and for a careful investigation of the whole subject, see Martin Hengel, *Atonement: The Origins of the Doctrine in the New Testament* (Philadelphia: Fortress, 1981).

12 See, for example, the attempts to propitiate the local gods in the numerous "Lydian-Phrygian confession inscriptions" catalogued in Georg Petzl, *Die Beichtinschriften Westlkeinasiens* (Bonn: Rudolf Habelt, 1994). I am indebted to Clinton E. Arnold, "'I Am Astonished That You Are So Quickly Turning Away!' (Gal 1:6): Paul and Anatolian Folk Belief," Institute for Biblical Research Annual New Testament Lecture (Nov. 22, 2003), for drawing my attention to these inscriptions.

rebellious creatures. The Synoptic Gospels describe Jesus' death on the cross for others as the willing obedience of the Son to the Father's will (Matt. 20:28; 26:39; Mark 10:45; 14:36; Luke 22:42).

The apostle John makes clear that Jesus did not merely submit passively to the Father's will that he should go to the cross but that he actively desired to fulfill his mission of bringing glory to his Father and bringing those who believe in him into the unity that he shares with his Father—a mission that involved his being "lifted up" on the cross (John 12:27–28, 32; 17:24). Similarly, the author of Hebrews emphasizes the willing nature of Jesus' sacrificial death. He imagines Jesus saying to the Father at his incarnation, "Here I am, I have come to do your will" (Heb. 10:7, 9; paraphrasing Ps. 40:7–8 [LXX 39:8–9]).

In sum, God himself has solved the problem of human rebellion against the Creator by transforming the worst act of rebellion against him, the crucifixion of his unique Son, who is eternally one with him, into the means of human redemption. God's Son was not a passive or unwilling participant in this plan but obeyed it willingly. Through that willing death, God maintained his own commitment to moral order at the same time that he acquitted the guilty. He did this at great cost to himself when humanity was helpless to do anything other than continue its rebellion. Why would he do this? Because he is a gracious and loving God.

Jesus' Death and the Defeat of the Malevolent Powers

The death of Christ has not only provided the remedy for human rebellion, however. It is also the critical step in the defeat of the malevolent cosmic powers. Paul says this most explicitly in Colossians 2:15, where he tries to assure his readers that they have nothing to fear from such powers: "Having disarmed the powers and authorities, [Christ] made a public spectacle of them, triumphing over them by the cross." John also ties the crucifixion of Jesus closely to the defeat of "the ruler of this world." At the close of Jesus' public ministry in which both his signs and his teaching have demonstrated his equality and union with the Father and just prior to his suffering and death, Jesus seems to interpret his passion as the moment of Satan's defeat: "Now is the time for judgment on this world; now the prince of this world will be driven out. But I, when I am lifted up from the earth, will draw all [people] to myself" (John 12:31–32).

John goes on to comment that Jesus "said this to show the kind of death he was going to die" (John 12:33). Despite the involvement of Satan in orchestrating the practical details of Jesus' betrayal and crucifixion (13:27), according to this passage, Jesus' being "lifted up" on the cross is the means by which he will return to undisturbed unity with his Father and draw people from the whole world to them both. Later we learn that those whom he draws to himself will share the unity that Father and Son have with each other (17:20–23).

In other passages the focus shifts from the death of Jesus as the moment of the defeat of the invisible evil powers to the resurrection, ascension, or heavenly session of Christ as the sign of their certain defeat. Even here, however, the death of Jesus is present by implication as the bridge to the position of heavenly authority that he now occupies. In Ephesians 1:20–22 Paul says that Christ's resurrection and heavenly session at God's right hand placed Jesus "far above all rule and authority, power and dominion, and every title that can be given." By means of his resurrection and heavenly session, God has also "placed all things under his feet." There is no mention of the death of Christ here, but the reference to his resurrection implies it, and a few sentences later Paul says specifically that Christ's death has reconciled Jews and Gentiles to each other and both groups to God (2:13–18).

Similarly, Peter speaks in the same breath of the atoning effect of Christ's death for the unrighteous (1 Peter 3:18a) and Christ's proclamation of condemnation to the "the spirits in prison who disobeyed long ago." These spirits are now, after his ascension, in submission to him (3:18b–22). Hebrews also connects the heavenly session of Christ and the subjugation of his enemies with his accomplishment of atonement through his death: "After he had provided purification for sins, he sat down at the right hand of the Majesty in heaven" (Heb. 1:3; 8:1; 10:12; 12:2). In Revelation, Jesus conquers his enemies and then sits with his Father on his throne (Rev. 3:21), but Jesus' means of conquering his enemies is his sacrificial death (5:5–6, 9–10, 12–13).[13]

The New Testament writers are uninterested in the precise time of the defeat of the malevolent cosmic powers. In one sense they were already defeated when God imprisoned them in "ancient" times (2 Peter 2:5). In another sense they were defeated when Jesus sent out the seventy-two with authority over the demonic world (Luke 10:17–18). Jesus defeated them at the beginning of his passion (John 12:31), at the time of his crucifixion (Col. 2:15; Rev. 3:21), at his ascension (1 Peter 3:18–22), and after he sat down at God's right hand (Eph. 1:20–22).

Some New Testament writers say that although the defeat of these powers is certain, their full subjugation still lies in the future (Heb. 10:13; cf. Eph. 6:11–12, 16). The critical point is not the timing of their defeat, but that at the death of Christ God's victory over them was sealed. Although they can still unleash their flaming arrows, particularly of heresy and persecution, their defeat is certain.

Summary

In the death of Christ, both human and cosmic rebellion against God was unleashed with full force. God used this moment of extreme rebellion, however, to accomplish his saving purposes. Through that death and the accompanying events of Jesus' resurrection, ascension, and heavenly session at God's right hand, God both began to reconcile his people to himself and sealed the fate of all demonic forces. God did all this, moreover, at his own initiative and as an act of grace and love.

---

13 Richard Bauckham, *The Theology of the Book of Revelation* (New Testament Theology; Cambridge: Cambridge Univ. Press, 1993), 74.

FAITH AS RESPONSE TO GOD'S GRACIOUS INITIATIVE

The application of the restoring and reconciling work of God to his people begins, from their perspective, when they respond to his gracious initiative in Christ with faith. Faith is the defining quality of Christian existence, present not only at the beginning of a person's reconciliation with God but throughout that person's life. It stares the visible, surface realities of life in "this present evil age" (Gal. 1:4; cf. Eph. 6:12) full in the face and denies that they tell the whole truth about either the world itself or the God who created it. Faith has three primary qualities in the New Testament: It is centered on God, it has an eschatological character, and it goes hand in hand with obedience.

Faith's Focus on God

Christian faith in the New Testament characteristically has a theological focus. It is specifically trust in the healing, justifying, saving work of God through his Son Jesus Christ rather than trust in one's own strength or in the structures of the present world. God declared Abraham to be righteous not because he performed works in which he could boast, but as a free gift and in spite of his wickedness. Abraham received this gift through faith (Rom. 4:1–5). In other words, Abraham did not trust in his own works for salvation but in God, whom he knew to be gracious (cf. Rom. 11:6).

Paul insists that God uses the matrix of weakness "to save those who believe" (1 Cor. 1:18–31). He uses the seemingly foolish proclamation of a crucified Messiah to do this, and those whom he calls to be his people in this way are neither wise, nor powerful, nor of noble birth. Rather, they are foolish, weak, lowly, and despised—the nothings. In Christ Jesus, however, God gives them everything they need to be his people: "righteousness, holiness and redemption." God works in this way so that no one can boast in his presence and so that the only boasting will be in the Lord. Faith is born in the midst of a weakness that acknowledges one's only hope is in God.

This same quality appears in the record in the Synoptic Gospels of Jesus' ministry. Jesus forgives the sins of a paralytic after seeing the faith of the four men who dug through the roof to get their friend through the crowd to him. This faith is not merely a belief that Jesus can heal the paralyzed man but an acknowledgment that the man's only hope lies in Jesus (Mark 2:3–5; cf. Matt. 9:2; Luke 5:20).[14]

Similarly, the woman with the flow of blood does not simply believe that Jesus can heal her but that after twelve years of only growing worse physically and poorer financially under the care of many physicians, Jesus is her only hope.[15] "Daughter," Jesus tells her, "your faith has saved you" (Mark 5:25–34, aut.; cf. Matt. 9:22; Luke 8:48). Jesus tells the synagogue ruler Jairus, whose only hope for his dead daughter lies in Jesus, "Do not fear; only believe" (Mark 5:36; cf. Luke 8:50).[16]

14 Cf. Christopher D. Marshall, *Faith as a Theme in Mark's Narrative* (SNTSMS 64; Cambridge: Cambridge Univ. Press, 1989), 78–90.

15 Cf. ibid., 103–4.

16 Cf. ibid., 90–100.

Blind Bartimaeus is so desperate to get to Jesus that he casts his possessions aside and ignores attempts to silence him in order to attract Jesus' attention to his plight.[17] Again, Jesus responds, "Your faith has saved you" (Mark 10:46–52; cf. Matt. 9:29; Luke 18:42).

In the New Testament, Christian faith focuses on God because those who believe recognize that their only hope lies in him. On their own and in their weakness, they have nothing in which to boast, and they have no hope for survival. They must go to God, through his Son Jesus Christ, for mercy and help.

Faith's Eschatological Character

New Testament writers also characteristically give to faith an eschatological quality. Abraham's faith reached far beyond the time of Isaac's birth and the span of his own life to an era when God would make him the father of many nations. His faith was marked by "hope"—the settled assurance that the God who raises the dead would in the future do what he promised (Rom. 4:13–18; cf. Heb. 11:12). For Paul, the resurrection of Jesus from the dead signals the beginning of this final era and means that God's people should live in light of this truth. God will count them righteous, just as he counted Abraham righteous, if they have faith that the God who raised Jesus from the dead has also atoned for their transgressions (Rom. 4:24–25; cf. 4:17).

Paul conducts his own ministry in this kind of faith. He tells the Corinthians that he is able to continue to preach, despite the hardship that this entails, because he is confident that "the one who raised the Lord Jesus from the dead will also raise us with Jesus" and bring us, together with those who have responded to his message, into the presence of God. Paul calls this "the spirit of faith" (2 Cor. 4:13–14; cf. 1 Cor. 15:12–34).[18]

Throughout the Synoptic Gospels, Jesus calls for this kind of faith—the trust that in him God has brought the final Day into the present. The theme is especially clear in Mark, where, in a programmatic statement at the beginning of this gospel, Jesus calls everyone to "repent and believe the good news" that in Jesus' words and deeds, "the time has come ... and the kingdom of God is near" (Mark 1:14–15).[19] As we saw in chapter 3, this summary of Jesus' proclamation echoes God's promise to Isaiah that he will one day restore the fortunes of his people. The faith that Jesus desires from those who come to him for help is trust that in him God has brought into the present the eschatological era that Isaiah described.[20] He fulfills the prophets' hopes that in the era of Israel's restoration, the blind will see, the deaf hear, and the lame grow strong (Isa. 35:5–10).

This is also the understanding of faith that emerges from Hebrews 11. This faith focuses on the reward that God gives to those who seek him (Heb. 11:6; cf. 10:35). It looks "forward to the city with foundations, whose architect and builder is God"

17 Cf. ibid., 131–32.

18 On the important theological foundation that hope provides for faith, see Jürgen Moltmann, *Theology of Hope* (New York: Harper & Row, 1967), 19–22.

19 Marshall, *Faith*, 38–39.

20 Cf. ibid., 34, 47, 50.

(11:10). It welcomes the fulfillment of God's promises from afar (11:13) and looks for a country of its own, a better and heavenly country (11:14–16).

The New Testament writers often emphasize that the eschatological element of faith, like its theological element, grows out of weakness. Now, however, the focus is not on the weakness of those who come to God in faith but on the means God uses to reveal his eschatological power. Jesus often did not look like the Messiah, and Christians often do not look like the restored people of God. The people in Jesus' hometown took offense at the idea that this local carpenter whose family everyone in the village knew spoke with wisdom and performed mighty deeds (Mark 6:1–6). Surely some other explanation—perhaps insanity—accounted for his unusual behavior (Mark 3:21). Jesus, we read, marveled at their "unbelief" (Mark 6:6).

For the chief priests and teachers of the law to believe that Jesus is the Messiah and King of Israel he must first "come down from the cross" (Mark 15:31–32). Behind this comment probably lies not merely the sentiment that some grand magical display is necessary for Jesus to prove his claims but also the notion that the cross is no place for the Messiah, the leader of God's eschatological restoration. Such an idea is, as Paul says, "a stumbling block to Jews" (1 Cor. 1:23).

Similarly Christians in the New Testament, particularly apostles, often do not look like the eschatologically restored people of God. Just as God worked through the unlikely means of Jesus' crucifixion to accomplish the eschatological redemption of his people, so Paul's life, as an apostle of this message, looks more like an extended death (2 Cor. 4:7–12; Gal. 2:19). The gospel he preaches focuses on the cross—not a suitable subject for a public declamation (1 Cor. 1:23). His own speaking abilities and his own physical suffering, moreover, do not project a convincing image of power and wisdom to the unbelieving world (1 Cor. 2:1–5; 4:9–13; 2 Cor. 11:16–33; 12:7–10).

Paul's Greek and Roman opponents in Corinth, like Jesus' Jewish opponents during his ministry and his crucifixion, find such a message and such a messenger incredible (2 Cor. 5:12; 10:10; 11:6). The word of the cross is folly to the Gentiles as much as it is a stumbling block to the Jews (1 Cor. 1:18, 22–23). Paul insists, however, that through his cruciform ministry God is bringing eschatological life to people and glory to himself (2 Cor. 4:12, 15). God's choice to show his eschatological power through the weakness of Jesus and his followers means that people only benefit from it if they have eyes to see and ears to hear the in-breaking of the final Day in the gospel—if they have, in other words, faith that God's work of eschatological restoration involves these elements of weakness and suffering.

John develops this idea in his subtle treatment of the relationship between signs and faith. Jesus' signs are laden with so much ambiguity that although some believe on the basis of them (John 2:11, 23; 4:50, 53; 6:14; 11:45–48; 12:10–11; 20:28–29), others see them and draw distorted conclusions from them about the nature of Jesus' identity (3:2; 6:14) or reject him altogether (12:37). Some see Jesus' signs and conclude that he is both Lord and God (20:28; 9:38), but Jesus' signs lead others to conclude that he is a political powerbroker (6:14), a sinner (9:24), a blasphemer

(5:18), or a threat to the nation (11:48). As we saw in chapter 6, Jesus' discourses must interpret the signs for the reader of John's gospel if they are to lead to lasting faith. In these discourses we learn that Jesus brings the final Day into the present as people either accept or reject his claim to be one with God (5:24–27; cf. 11:25–26).

Even here, therefore, where the stress lies on the realized element of the eschatological tension, faith has an eschatological quality. People who encounter Jesus' signs and his explanation of their significance in John's gospel face a critical decision: Will they accept the presence of God's eschatological power in the weakness of obscurity and ambiguity, or will they reject Jesus' testimony and await some other, more convincing demonstration?[21]

In summary, the New Testament writers often give to faith an eschatological orientation. It is not merely the affirmation of an otherwise implausible claim, but the settled conviction that in Christ's words and deeds God has started to fulfill the promises he made through the prophets to restore his people to fellowship with himself. This eschatological event, however, occurs in the context of weakness and ambiguity. Embracing it as true calls for faith that, like Abraham's faith (Rom. 4:18–22), carefully considers all the evidence to the contrary and nevertheless concludes that God has begun the consummation of all things in Jesus, a consummation that he will surely bring to completion in due time.

Faith as Obedience

The New Testament writers also frequently affirm that Christian faith involves a life of obedience. This obedience has a cognitive element, visible when New Testament writers use the expression "the faith" to refer to a body of doctrines that the Christian acknowledges to be true. "The faith" is equivalent to "the knowledge of the truth" (Titus 1:1). All believers hold it in common (1 Cor. 16:13; Gal. 6:10; 1 Tim. 1:2; Titus 1:4; 2 Peter 1:1), and it is especially important that people in positions of authority in the church should hold to "the faith" with sincerity (1 Tim. 3:9). They should "fight" for it (1 Tim. 6:12; 2 Tim. 4:7; Jude 3) and should be nurtured in its "words" (1 Tim. 4:6). "The faith" is a deposit of truth—a deposit that false teachers have abandoned (1 Tim. 4:1) and from which they have strayed (1 Tim. 6:10, 21; cf. 2 Tim. 2:18).

This definition of faith is, therefore, the touchstone for separating those who preach the gospel from enemies of the gospel (Gal. 1:23), for detecting and rejecting heresy (2 Tim. 3:8; cf. 1 Cor. 15:11; 2 Cor. 13:5), and for religious health generally (Titus 1:13; cf. 1 Tim. 5:8). The Elder tells his readers that they should not "believe every spirit, but test the spirits" against the standard of his eyewitness testimony that Jesus Christ has come in the flesh (1 John 4:1–2; cf. 1:1–3; 5:1, 5, 10–13).

"Faith" as mere intellectual assent to various propositions, however, is worthless for salvation or justification, and saving faith is more than simply an entry point to

21 Cf. Rudolf Bultmann, *Theology of the New Testament*, 2 vols. (New York: Charles Scribner's Sons, 1951–55), 2:75–92, and Mark's similar emphasis on the link between the ambiguity of Jesus' miracles and faith as described in Marshall, *Faith*, 57–74.

the people of God.[22] The command of God that we must obey, says the Elder, is not only to "believe in the name of his Son, Jesus Christ," but also "to love one another" (1 John 3:23). Even faith that can move mountains, says Paul, has no benefit without love (1 Cor. 13:2), and faith implies obedience (Rom. 1:5; 16:26). As James points out, faith without works is dead (James 2:26).

Faith, therefore, is not primarily acknowledgment of a body of doctrine but a conviction about the truth of the gospel so strong that it radically reorients one's life toward dependence on God even in the most difficult circumstances. This dependence leads to following God's commands even when, from the unbeliever's perspective, these make no sense. An apostle, Paul says, lives by faith and not by sight (2 Cor. 5:7). He fixes his eyes not on the visible and temporal but on what is presently unseen but eternal (4:18).

Living by faith means renouncing efforts to gain success through clever but deceitful strategies. It means becoming an example of the eschatological tension between the cross and the resurrection—between the reconciliation that God has already accomplished through the cross of Christ and the reception on the final Day of "an eternal glory that far outweighs" any human suffering (2 Cor. 4:17). For an apostle, this life of faith involves enduring suffering and hardship as the means through which God brings eschatological life to others. It entails being "hard pressed on every side, but not crushed," "always carrying around in [the] body the death of Jesus, so that the life of Jesus may also be revealed in [the] body" (2 Cor. 4:1–18). What is true for an apostle in his special calling is also true for the believer generally (5:1–10).[23]

In the Synoptic Gospels also, the faith that saves leads those who have it to follow Jesus single-mindedly even to crucifixion. Blind Bartimaeus refuses to let his possessions or the objections of bystanders hinder him from coming to Jesus in faith, and his faith leads him to follow Jesus "on the road" to the cross (Mark 10:46–52).[24] For many early Christians, following the Lamb slain on the cross was more than a metaphor for living the Christian life. It meant social ostracism, economic deprivation, and even death, and much of the New Testament is devoted to urging Christians to maintain their faith in God in the face of such hardship.

The threat that persecution poses to the faith of the Thessalonian Christians worries Paul so much that he sends Timothy both to discover the condition of their faith and to place it on a firmer footing (1 Thess. 3:2, 5, 10). At the opposite end of his letter writing career, the imprisoned Paul awaits execution with the confidence that he has "fought the good fight ... finished the race ... kept the faith" (2 Tim. 4:7). Keeping the faith for him has meant, among other things, enduring hardship for the sake of the gospel (1:15–18; 3:10–12; 4:6, 16–18).

This concern rises to special prominence in the third part of the New Testament canon where 1 Peter, Hebrews, and Revelation are all devoted to encouraging perseverance among Christians as they face the social ostracism that their commitment

22 Cf. Thomas R. Schreiner, *Romans* (BECNT; Grand Rapids: Baker, 1998), 61.

23 In 2 Cor. 5:1 Paul's first person plurals begin to refer not merely to himself but to his readers also.

24 Marshall, *Faith*, 129–31, 237.

to the gospel entails. Peter understands faith as a life of obedience to truths that are unseen because, either like Jesus' earthly ministry, they happened in the past (1 Peter 1:8), or, like Jesus' triumph over the demonic powers, they happened in the invisible world (1:21; 3:18–22), or, like his readers' salvation, they have not yet fully happened (1:9; cf. 1:4).

A commitment to such truths is the watershed that separates "unbelievers" from "believers" (1 Peter 2:7), those who obey the gospel from those who disobey it (2:8; 3:1, 20; 4:17). Unlike their unbelieving and disobedient persecutors, Christians have a steady hope that in the future God will give them their inheritance of an eternal, heavenly, and gracious salvation (1:3–5, 13; cf. 1:21; 3:5, 15). They have entrusted themselves to the care of their Creator in the belief that he is a "faithful" God (4:19), who will in the future fulfill the promises of salvation that he makes in the gospel (1:9). This trust in God is the means by which his power protects Christians from betraying their commitment to the gospel in the face of persecution (1:5), and persecution itself has the value of showing that this faith, like fire-purified gold, is "unalloyed"—"genuine" (1:7).[25]

In 1 Peter, therefore, Peter sees faith as an enduring commitment to trust that the historical claims and especially the eschatological promises offered in the gospel are true, and to live out the gospel's implications. For Peter, Christian faith means shaping one's life by such truths despite their invisible nature and despite intense social pressure to abandon them.

The understanding of faith in the letter to the Hebrews is similar. Here too, the author describes faith within a context of persecution where unbelievers do not merely think that what Christians claim about Jesus and God is incredible but also that it is shameful (Heb. 12:2; 13:13). Like Peter, this author thinks of faith as a settled confidence in what the word of God affirms, despite its invisibility to believers and the social pressure put on them to abandon their commitment to it.

As with Peter's readers (1 Peter 1:8), the first readers of Hebrews had no exposure to Jesus himself. The author says that his readers believed the word of salvation because those who had seen Jesus proclaimed this word to them and because God himself confirmed its truth with "signs, wonders and various miracles" (Heb. 2:3–4). Also like Peter, the author of Hebrews emphasizes the unseen nature of the truths in which the Christian believes, whether the creation of the world through the word of God in the past (11:3) or the conviction that in the future they will inhabit a heavenly city that they, along with God's faithful people of all ages, can call their own (11:10, 14–15; cf. 11:7, 27).

With Peter, the author of Hebrews places heavy emphasis on the need for persistent obedience to the faith in the face of social pressure to abandon it. He urges his readers not to imitate the wilderness generation of Israelites who failed to unite their hearing of the gospel with faith (Heb. 4:2), or, as the author says a few sentences later, with obedience (4:6, 11). Their lack of obedient faith cost them their

25 BDAG, 256.

inheritance in God's promised rest (4:3, 5–6). Christians must be careful not to follow this example and also fail to enter God's eschatological rest (4:1–3, 11).

In Hebrews, therefore, faith has much in common with "steadfastness" and involves persistence in the "work" and "love" of "serving the saints" (Heb. 6:10–12). Having the "full assurance of faith" means holding "unswervingly to the hope" that Christians profess (10:22–23), not abandoning the "confidence" in God that leads to a rich reward (10:35), and persevering until God's promise reaches its fulfillment (10:36). It means trusting in the coming salvation of God and not succumbing to the temptation to "shrink back" (10:37–39; paraphrasing Hab. 2:3–4). It means following the example of "the ancients" in persevering toward a future "not yet seen" (Heb. 11:7; cf. 11:10, 13, 14, 27), and especially of Jesus "the author and perfecter of our faith, who for the joy set before him endured the cross, scorning its shame, and sat down at the right hand of the throne of God" (12:2).

In Hebrews as with 1 Peter, therefore, the context of persecution leads the author to emphasize obedience and the future orientation of Christian faith. Despite visible evidence to the contrary, Christians must continue to trust that God will be faithful to the promise of eschatological salvation offered in the gospel. They must also live in a way that is consistent with this trust.

In Revelation, the context of persecution leads John to view faith in Christ almost entirely in terms of the refusal to crack under the social pressure to participate in the military and religious structures of Roman might and oppression. John tells his readers that God will give to Rome, for a limited time, the power to war against the saints and conquer them (Rev. 13:7)—to take them captive and execute them (13:10a). This difficult period, looming on the horizon, calls, he says, for the "patient endurance and faithfulness on the part of the saints" (13:10b). A few paragraphs later, John uses similar language to describe the need for Christians to avoid the temptation to "worship the beast and its image" (14:9–11): "This calls for patient endurance on the part of the saints who obey God's commandments and remain faithful to Jesus" (14:12).

Remaining faithful to Jesus goes together with obedience to God's commandments—particularly the first commandment of the Decalogue—and involves steadfastness in the face of Roman displeasure with those who fail to acknowledge the superiority of its gods (cf. Rev. 12:17).[26] It is "faithfulness" to Jesus in the same way that Jesus himself and God's Word are "faithful and true" (3:14; 19:11; 21:5; 22:6; cf. 1:5).[27] It is equivalent to holding fast to Jesus' name, and its opposite is denying what Jesus calls "my faith" (*tēn pistin mou*), something that the Christians in Pergamum, particularly the slain Antipas, refused to do (2:13).

Faith, therefore, involves both a willingness to embrace the understanding of the world articulated in the Christian gospel and obedience to that understanding. The

26 David E. Aune, *Revelation 6–16* (WBC 52B; Nashville: Nelson, 1998), 837–38, points out the close parallel to Rev. 14:12 in 1QpHab 8.1–3, which speaks of obedience to the Torah and faithfulness to the Teacher of Righteousness. Aune also shows that the phrase *pistin tērein* was idiomatic in Hellenistic Greek for "keeping faith" or "remaining loyal." Cf. Grant Osborne, *Revelation* (BECNT; Grand Rapids; Baker, 2002), 543–44.

27 Cf. Osborne, *Revelation*, 204, 680.

New Testament writers insist that faith implies commitment to an often difficult pilgrimage toward its ultimate goal. Faith and obedience go hand in hand.

Summary

God's human creatures appropriate their Creator's gracious offer of reconciliation through the death and resurrection of Jesus and join him in his triumph over all evil cosmic forces, by faith. Faith entails a candid admission of weakness—that peace with God comes not through one's own efforts to propitiate his wrath or to earn some payment from him but through embracing the initiative that God has taken in his Son Jesus Christ to restore his fallen human creatures to himself. Faith also involves an eschatological focus—keeping one's gaze firmly fixed on Jesus, who has gone before the believer into God's heavenly presence and sits at God's right hand. The believer is a pilgrim toward this same goal, faithfully moving forward toward an eternal existence in the presence of God.

Faith, therefore, means trusting that God and his promise of living in his presence eternally because of Christ's death and resurrection, although they are now invisible, are nevertheless real. These commitments, moreover, are far more than intellectual affirmations; they are convictions that entail the radical reorientation of one's life. Repentance and faith in the gospel, as Jesus says in Mark 1:15, go hand in hand.[28]

THE SPIRIT AS THE ESCHATOLOGICAL PRESENCE OF GOD

God has not left his people to slog their way over the difficult terrain of the pilgrim pathway by themselves. Their journey is not grim but joyful, and this is because God's powerful presence—his Spirit—goes with them. According to the New Testament writers, the prophets foretold that in the time of Israel's eschatological restoration God would pour out his Spirit on his people to an extent previously unknown. The Spirit's power would be focused on God's special, anointed king, God's servant, but God would also pour out his Spirit on all his people.

The Spirit's Presence in the Life of Jesus

Luke and Matthew both make explicit what the other New Testament writers probably assume—that the Spirit's presence in Jesus' life answers the expectations expressed in Isaiah that God's Spirit would rest on his specially anointed Servant. In Luke's gospel Jesus quotes Isaiah 61:1–2 at the beginning of his ministry and claims that in him this Scripture is fulfilled (Luke 4:18–19). This passage speaks of the Lord's Anointed, who proclaims the restoration of God's favor to his people, as one on whom "the Spirit of the Sovereign LORD" rests (Isa. 61:1).

28 See Adolf Schlatter, *Der Glaube im Neuen Testament*, 4th ed. (Stuttgart: Calwer Verlag, 1927), 99, "The creator of the formula, 'by faith alone' is Jesus—he says 'only believe' (Mark 5:36)—but we do not understand his call to faith correctly if we think that in it he has sought nothing from people, and produces nothing in them, but mere faith."

Similarly, Matthew claims that Jesus' ministry of healing fulfills Isaiah 42:1–4, a passage closely related to Isaiah 61:1–2 (Matt. 11:17–21). Like that passage, Isaiah 42:1–4 speaks of the agent of God's eschatological restoration as one on whom God will put his Spirit. Both Luke and Matthew, therefore, understand the Spirit's presence in Jesus' ministry as a sign that the days of eschatological restoration have arrived and that Jesus is the anointed Servant of God who has introduced this new era.

In Luke's gospel, the Spirit radiates his presence backward into the period of the conception and birth of Jesus and his forerunner, John.[29] The Spirit's presence here seems to anticipate the great outpouring of the Spirit later in the ministry of Jesus. The angel of the Lord tells Zechariah that his son John "will be filled with the Holy Spirit even from birth" (Luke 1:15). Elizabeth is "filled with the Holy Spirit" when she greets Mary, who is pregnant with Jesus (1:41). The Holy Spirit is on the "righteous and devout" Simeon. He has given this man special revelations and moves him to praise God when he sees the infant Jesus and his parents in the temple (2:25–27). Luke and Matthew agree that the Holy Spirit miraculously causes the conception of Jesus (Matt. 1:18, 20; Luke 1:35).

The four gospels and Acts are united in portraying the Spirit as the divine power that enables Jesus to bring in the eschatological age. John the Baptist prophesies the coming of Jesus as one who baptizes not with water, as did John, but with the Holy Spirit (Matt. 3:11; Mark 1:8; Luke 3:16; cf. John 1:33; Acts 1:5; 11:16). At Jesus' baptism, the Spirit descends on him in the form of a dove (Matt. 3:16; Mark 1:10; Luke 3:22; cf. John 1:32–33) and then leads Jesus into the desert, where the devil unsuccessfully puts him to the test (Matt. 4:1; Mark 1:12; Luke 4:1).

Although references to the Spirit in the gospels—even in Luke—become sparser after this point, where they do appear they make clear that the gospel writers assume that the Spirit empowers the mighty words and deeds of Jesus' ministry. As we have just seen, in Luke and Matthew Jesus' ministry fulfills the expectation of Isaiah that God's Spirit will rest on the Servant and king who will bring Israel's restoration.

In addition, in the Synoptic Gospels Jesus understands hardened opposition to his ministry, particularly to his ministry of exorcism, to be blasphemy against the Holy Spirit (Matt. 12:31–32; Mark 3:29; Luke 12:10). John links Jesus' life-giving words with the Spirit (John 3:34; 6:63), which finds an echo in Luke's gospel where Luke prefaces a brief—and very Johannine—speech of Jesus to his disciples with the statement that he spoke "full of joy through the Holy Spirit" (Luke 10:21–22; cf. Acts 1:2). As Peter puts it in his speech to Cornelius's household, "God anointed Jesus of Nazareth with the Holy Spirit and power, and ... he went around doing

29 I refer to the Spirit as "him" here because, although the Spirit can function in the New Testament metaphorically like breath, fire, or water, the New Testament writers view him as a person, not as an impersonal force. This is especially clear in Paul and John. In Paul, the Spirit acts as a person would act: He "searches," "teaches," "leads," "bears witness," "helps," "intercedes," "strengthens," and is "grieved." On this see Gordon D. Fee, *God's Empowering Presence: The Holy Spirit in the Letters of Paul* (Peabody, Mass.: Hendrickson, 1994), 829–31. John speaks of the Spirit as "another advocate," similar to Jesus (John 14:16), and pointedly defines him in personal terms as "the Advocate" (*ho. . .paraklētos, to pneuma to hagion*, 14:26) rather than with a more impersonal expression such as "the Spirit that advocates" (*to paraklēton pneuma*). For this point, see H. B. Swete, *The Holy Spirit in the New Testament* (London: Macmillan, 1909), 291–92.

good and healing all who were under the power of the devil, because God was with him" (Acts 10:38).

The gospels, therefore, depict Jesus as the bearer of God's Spirit. The Spirit was unusually active among God's people from the time just prior to his birth, and both his miracles and his teaching during his ministry are Spirit-empowered. All of this fulfills prophetic expectations that God's Spirit will rest on the anointed Servant whom God sends to his people to open blind eyes, free captives, preach good news to the poor, and proclaim the year of the Lord's favor (Isa. 42:7; 61:1–2).

The Spirit's Presence with God's People

After Jesus' death, resurrection, and ascension, the Spirit now remains with his followers as the substitute, until his return, for his physical presence. Luke hints at this when he describes Jesus' telling his disciples, just before his ascension, that he will send to them what the Father promised and when he speaks of the Spirit as "the Spirit of Jesus" (Luke 24:49; Acts 16:7).[30]

John's gospel raises this function of the Spirit to the level of an important theme. There Jesus tells his disciples that in his absence the Father will send them the Advocate (*paraklētos*)—the Holy Spirit—in Jesus' name (John 14:26). He is the Spirit of truth and will help them, teach them, and remind them of his teaching (John 14:16, 26; 15:26; 16:13–15). Later, after his death and resurrection, he fulfills this promise when he gives the Spirit to his disciples (20:22; cf. 7:38–39).[31]

Luke (and probably John as well) understands this continuing presence of the Spirit with the church to be another fulfillment of prophecies concerning the Spirit's presence in the age of Israel's eschatological restoration.[32] Just as Isaiah said that the presence of God's Spirit would rest on God's anointed Servant during this period, so Ezekiel and Joel spoke of the presence of God's Spirit with all God's people. Ezekiel told the exiles in Babylon that one day God would gather them from the countries into which he scattered them because of their sins against his law and bring them into their own land (Ezek. 36:24; cf. 11:16–18). At that time, the Lord said through the prophet:

> I will give you a new heart and put a new spirit in you; I will remove from you your heart of stone and give you a heart of flesh. And I will put my Spirit in you and move you to follow my decrees and be careful to keep my laws. (Ezek. 36:26–27; cf. 11:17–20; 36:24–30; 37:6, 11–14)

30 Cf. Rom. 8:9; 2 Cor. 3:17–18; Gal. 4:6; Phil. 1:19; 1 Peter 1:11; Joseph A. Fitzmyer, *The Gospel according to Luke I–IX* (AB 28; Garden City, N.Y.: Doubleday, 1981), 230; and BDAG, 834.

31 How the gift of the Spirit prior to Jesus' ascension in John 20:22 correlates with the outpouring of the Spirit on the twelve apostles in Acts 2:4 is not clear. D. A. Carson, *The Gospel according to John* (PNTC; Grand Rapids: Eerdmans, 1991), 649–55, discusses the options thoroughly and offers a plausible solution: John, who surely knew the widespread tradition that the Holy Spirit came at the first Jewish Pentecost after Jesus' resurrection, describes a symbolic action of Jesus, later fulfilled at Pentecost. The solution to the puzzle, however, is not as important as the main point of both texts: The same Spirit that empowered Jesus' words and deeds would remain with the followers of Jesus to continue his astonishing work.

32 Cf. Fitzmyer, *Luke I–IX*, 229.

Similarly, Joel prophesied a time when God would "restore the fortunes of Judah" (Joel 3:1) and "pour out" (LXX, *ekcheō*) his "Spirit on all people" and work "wonders" and signs (2:28–32). On the day of Pentecost, this prophecy is fulfilled when the Spirit comes on the apostles visibly, like flames of fire, and they begin declaring the wonders of God in the widely diverse languages of the large crowd that has gathered. Peter explains to the astonished crowd what has happened with a quotation of Joel 2:28–32 (Acts 2:17–21), and he insists that Jesus, who now sits at God's right hand, has "poured out" (*ekcheō*) the Holy Spirit and the accompanying miracles in fulfillment of this prophecy (Acts 2:33; cf. 2:17–18; 10:45).[33]

This perspective also emerges from Paul's letters. After reminding the Thessalonian Christians that they should avoid sexual immorality and be holy (1 Thess. 4:3, 7), he writes that those who reject this instruction are not rejecting some human advice "but God, who gives to you his Holy Spirit" (4:8). This language echoes Ezekiel 11:19; 36:26; 37:6 and 37:14, which speak of the eschatological gift of the Holy Spirit that God would give to his people to purify them, to equip them to obey his commandments, and to restore them to life. Paul understands the Thessalonian Christians to be the fulfillment of this prophecy—God has placed his Spirit into them, just as he said he would place his Spirit into his people in the day of their restoration.[34]

Paul takes the same approach in 2 Corinthians, where, challenged to provide letters of recommendation for his ministry, he offers as his "letter" the Corinthians themselves: "You show that you are a letter from Christ, the result of our ministry, written not with ink but with the Spirit of the living God, not on tablets of stone but on tablets of human hearts" (2 Cor. 3:3). Here again, Paul alludes to Ezekiel's prophetic promises of the Spirit's coming and advances an implicit claim that such texts find fulfillment in the Corinthians who have responded to his ministry among them with faith in Christ. As a result of his ministry, God has written on their hearts with the metaphorical ink of his Spirit.[35] These prophetic promises of the coming of God's Spirit to his people also probably stand behind Paul's comment in Galatians 3:14 that those who have faith "receive the promise of the Spirit" (cf. Eph. 1:13).[36]

This does not mean that the eschatological age has fully arrived. The Spirit is a "deposit" of what is to come in all its fullness later. As a deposit, he is both a part of the inheritance that is to come (Eph. 1:14; cf. 2 Cor. 5:5) and an assurance that those who have the Spirit will participate in that future (2 Cor. 1:22). But he is not everything.[37] The same eschatological tension that surrounded the presence of the Spirit in Jesus' ministry, therefore, is present in the life of the church. Where Jesus went,

33 Paul also speaks of the outpouring of the Spirit in Rom. 5:5 and Titus 3:5–6.

34 Cf. esp. Paul's *didonta to pneuma autou to hagion eis hymas* in 1 Thess. 4:8 with the Septuagint's *dōsō to pneuma mou eis hymas* in Ezek. 37:14 (cf. 37:6); see the discussion in Fee, *God's Empowering Presence*, 52.

35 T. J. Deidun, *New Covenant Morality in Paul* (AnBib 89; Rome: Pontifical Biblical Institute, 1981), 33–35; Frank Thielman, *Paul and the Law: A Contextual Approach* (Downers Grove, Ill.: InterVarsity Press, 1994), 109–10; Fee, *God's Empowering Presence*, 302–4.

36 Deidun, *New Covenant Morality*, 49; Thielman, *Paul and the Law*, 135; Fee, *God's Empowering Presence*, 395.

37 Cf. the discussion of the term *arrabōn* ("deposit") in Andrew T. Lincoln, *Ephesians* (WBC 42; Dallas: Word, 1990), 40–41; Fee, *God's Empowering Presence*, 293; and Hoehner, *Ephesians*, 241–42.

the power of the Spirit brought the kingdom of God out of the future and into the present, but these were anticipations of the full coming of the kingdom at a later time. In the same way, in the life of the church, the Spirit brings the "righteousness, peace and joy" that characterize the eschatological age (Rom. 14:17), but the full and eternal experience of those gifts awaits the age to come.[38]

The New Testament writers assign to the Spirit a number of roles in the life of the church prior to this coming age, but five functions stand out as especially important. The Spirit aids the church in its witness to the gospel; he gives direction to the church; he teaches the church; he ensures the church's inclusiveness; and he preserves the church's holiness.

The Spirit Empowers the Church's Witness

The Synoptic Gospels each say that Jesus predicts a role for the Spirit in aiding Jesus' followers to bear witness to the gospel, especially in contexts of persecution. When his followers appear before councils, synagogues, governors, and kings to give an account for their witness to the gospel, Jesus says, they should not worry about what to say because the Holy Spirit will supply them with the right words (Matt. 10:20; Mark 13:11; Luke 12:12). Acts emphasizes the Spirit's role in supplying the twelve apostles and Paul with power for the proclamation of the gospel and then aiding them to bear witness before the authorities when arrested for doing so.

The Twelve declared the wonders of God in the languages of the crowd gathered to celebrate Pentecost "as the Spirit enabled them" (Acts 2:4, 11). Despite the harassment of the Sanhedrin, the Christians in Jerusalem "were all filled with the Holy Spirit and spoke the word of God boldly" (4:31). Just before Peter made an astonishing defense before a hostile Sanhedrin, he was "filled with the Holy Spirit" (4:8). Similarly, shortly before Stephen's brilliant speech to the inflamed Synagogue of the Freedman that he was "full . . . of the Holy Spirit" (6:5), and his accusers were not able to counter "the Spirit by whom he spoke" (6:10; cf. 7:55).

The author of Hebrews confirms the widespread nature of this early Christian conviction about the Spirit. He writes that when his readers heard the message of salvation from the followers of Jesus himself, "God also testified to it by signs, wonders and various miracles, and gifts of the Holy Spirit distributed according to his will" (Heb. 2:4).[39]

The Spirit Directs the Church

The Spirit not only aids the first preachers of the gospel in their verbal testimony to it but also gives them direction about where and to whom they should preach. This theme is especially prominent in Acts. The Spirit directs Philip to explain the gospel to the Ethiopian official on the road from Jerusalem to Gaza (Acts 8:29) and then transports him to the coast to preach the gospel in the cities between Azotus

38 For the understanding of Rom. 14:17 presupposed here, see Ulrich Wilckens, *Der Brief an die Römer (Röm 12–16)* (EKK VI/3; Zürich/Neukirchen-Vluyn: Benziger/Neukirchener, 1982), 93–94.

39 Perhaps 1 Cor. 14:23–25 gives an example of such miraculous testimony. Here prophecy, a gift of the Spirit (14:1), miraculously convinces an unbeliever that God is really among Christians when they gather.

and Caesarea (8:39). The Spirit guides Peter to the Roman centurion Cornelius (10:19; 11:12). He tells the Christian prophet Agabus about an impending famine in Judea so that the Christians of Antioch can send relief to them (11:28–29). He tells the church at Antioch to commission Paul and Barnabas to take the gospel elsewhere (13:2) and then sends them to the port city of Seleucia and on to the island of Cyprus (13:4). The Spirit hinders Paul and his companions from speaking the word in Asia and Bithynia (16:6–7), but leads Paul to Macedonia, to Achaia, and to Jerusalem (19:21; 20:22).

The Spirit Teaches the Church

Closely related to his role in directing the church is the Spirit's role in teaching the church. In John's gospel, one of the Holy Spirit's primary functions is to teach Jesus' disciples "all things" and to "remind" them "of everything" Jesus has said to them (John 14:26). He will "guide" them "into all truth" (16:13). Something like this seems to happen in Acts when the "apostles and elders" in the Jerusalem church send a letter to the church at Antioch recording the decision of the Jerusalem council on whether Gentiles should keep the Mosaic law. Their decision, they write, "seemed good to the Holy Spirit and to us" (Acts 15:28). The Holy Spirit, in other words, has led them to the position they eventually adopted on this important doctrinal matter.

In a similar way, Paul assumes in his letters that the Holy Spirit teaches the church through the gifts of prophecy and interpreted glossolalia (1 Cor. 14:1–40), and he especially values prophecy as a means both of edifying the church and bearing witness to unbelievers (14:1–5). He is anxious that believers not "put out the Spirit's fire," "treat prophecies with contempt" (1 Thess. 5:19–20), or "forbid speaking in tongues" (1 Cor. 14:39). Jude views the absence of the Spirit as a hallmark of false teaching (Jude 19–20). In Revelation, John the seer provides a complex written example of the kind of instruction that the Spirit can give to the churches by means of prophecy (Rev. 2:7, 11, 17, 29; 3:6, 13, 22; 22:6).

Yet the concept of Spirit-inspired instruction comes with problems. Simply because someone can act as if he or she is inspired does not mean that God's Spirit has inspired them. Evil spirits can inspire people also and so lead the church astray (1 Tim. 4:1; 1 John 4:1, 6; cf. James 3:15; Rev. 16:14).[40] The false teaching that arose in the Johannine community and that the Elder addresses in 1 and 2 John apparently came from teachers claiming that the Spirit inspired their "progressive" notions. Most likely they appeal to Jesus' teaching in John's gospel that the Spirit will lead their community "into all truth" (John 16:13). The Elder counters these claims with an admonition to his community not to "believe every spirit, but test the spirits to see whether they are from God, because many false prophets have gone out into the world" (1 John 4:1).

Paul has to follow a similar procedure. Only a few months after telling the Thessalonians not to quench the Spirit or despise prophesying, he must write again and

40 Cf. *Did.* 11.7–12, where the author says that not everyone who speaks "in a spirit" (*en pneumati*) is a prophet and that those who claim to be Spirit-inspired prophets should be tested by the truthfulness of their teaching and the integrity of their actions.

correct false teaching that originated with a fabricated source of authority not entirely clear to Paul. One possibility for its origin, however, is "a spirit" (2 Thess. 2:2), and this probably refers to the "spirit-inspired" utterance of a prophet.[41] Similarly, in Corinth, someone claiming the Spirit's inspiration had produced the odd outburst, "Jesus is accursed!" (1 Cor. 12:3). Despite Paul's advice to the Corinthians that the church should weigh their prophets' utterances carefully (14:29, 32), Paul later has to write in exasperation that they are willing to tolerate the preaching of "a different spirit from the one" they received when he preached to them (2 Cor. 11:4).[42]

Even with all the trouble the concept generates, however, the writers of the New Testament do not abandon the concept that the Holy Spirit can teach the church through speech he inspires. In one of his last letters, Paul urges Timothy not to neglect the gift that he has received "through a prophetic message" when he was set apart for his work by the laying on of hands (1 Tim. 4:14). In his final letter, Paul sees the Holy Spirit as an aid to guarding the deposit of orthodox belief from false teaching (2 Tim. 1:14).

Similarly, John the seer, although well aware of the dangers of false prophecy (Rev. 2:20; 16:13; 19:20; 20:10), nevertheless claims the inspiration of the Spirit for his own prophetic book (1:10; 4:2; 17:3; 21:10; 22:6). The Elder too does not forbid claims of Spirit-inspired teaching, but in light of the challenge that false prophets have presented to his community, he urges more careful attention to "the Spirit he gave us" (1 John 3:24).

From an early time, the solution to the problem of false spirit-inspired teaching is the development of criteria for distinguishing between true and false claims of the Spirit's inspiration. In his first letter to them, Paul urges the Thessalonian Christians to test supposedly Spirit-inspired prophecy by separating the good from the evil (1 Thess. 5:19–22).[43] Since in his second letter he seems to be applying this procedure himself to false prophecy, we can legitimately look there for more specific information about what separating good from evil involves. In 2 Thessalonians, Paul argues that the false eschatological teaching circulating around Thessalonica fails on both doctrinal and ethical grounds. It is inconsistent with the accepted Christian teaching that a rebellion and a man of lawlessness will precede the end (2 Thess. 2:3), and that the church should not subsidize those who are unwilling to work (3:10). When Paul tells the Corinthians to weigh the words of their prophets, perhaps he has such doctrinal and ethical criteria in mind (1 Cor. 14:29, 32).

The Elder addresses the problem of false prophetic teaching in his community in the same way. The Spirit God has given to the community, he writes, will acknowledge

41 Cf. David E. Aune, *Prophecy in Early Christianity and the Ancient Mediterranean World* (Grand Rapids: Eerdmans, 1983), 219–20; Fee, *God's Empowering Presence*, 59, 74.

42 Not every conflict over Spirit-inspired speech, however, was understood as a conflict between God and the devil. It was apparently possible for information actually revealed by the Spirit to be incorrectly interpreted, as seems to have happened with the disciples of Tyre in Acts 21:4. On the frequent ambiguity of early Christian prophecy, see Ben Witherington III, *The Acts of the Apostles: A Socio-Rhetorical Commentary* (Grand Rapids: Eerdmans, 1998), 630–31; idem, *Jesus the Seer: The Progress of Prophecy* (Peabody, Mass.: Hendrickson, 1999), 341–42, 343–48.

43 On the connection between 1 Thess. 5:19–20 and 21–22, see Aune, *Prophecy in Early Christianity*, 219, and Fee, *God's Empowering Presence*, 57.

the physical existence of Jesus (1 John 3:24; 4:2–3), not depart from the eyewitness tradition of which the Elder and others in his circle are guardians (4:6; 5:6–8), and encourage love for others (4:8, 12–13). Truly Spirit-inspired teaching, in other words, is consistent with the traditions received from eyewitnesses about what Christians should believe and how they should behave.

The Spirit Dissolves Ethnic Barriers

Both Luke and Paul emphasize that the Spirit breaks down the traditional ethnic boundaries of God's people and encourages the proclamation of the gospel to everyone without regard for ethnicity. The Spirit brought Philip to Samaria, Peter to Cornelius, and Paul to the Gentiles precisely because the promise of the Holy Spirit is not only for Jews but "for all who are far off—for all whom the Lord our God will call" (Acts 2:39). In Acts the Holy Spirit falls not only on Jewish believers but also on Samaritans (8:15–17), and, to the astonishment of the circumcised believers, on Gentiles like the Roman centurion Cornelius and his household (10:44–48). Despite the dismay this causes to some Jewish Christians (11:1–3; 15:1–2), the church cannot deny that God has included Gentiles within his eschatologically formed people because he has poured out his Spirit on them just as obviously as he poured the Spirit out on the apostles at Pentecost (11:15; 15:8–9). To deny that uncircumcised but believing Gentiles are now part of the people of God is to "oppose God" (11:17; 15:10).

The same theme rises to prominence in Paul's letters. The presence of God's promised Spirit among the Galatian Christians is one of Paul's most forceful arguments that they should not shoulder the yoke of the Mosaic law as a way of completing their transition into the people of God. They received the Spirit when they heard and believed the gospel (Gal. 3:2), and the Spirit provided miraculous evidence of his presence among them (3:5). With this evidence that God has included them fully within his people, they have no need to "complete" their conversion through doing such "works of the law" as circumcision. The fulfillment of the "promise" that the prophets made concerning the coming of God's eschatological Spirit is received "by faith" and therefore is available to Gentiles as Gentiles (3:14). Similarly, the seal of the "promised Holy Spirit" reveals that the Gentile Christians to whom Paul writes in Ephesians have the same status "in Christ" as Jewish Christians (Eph. 1:13).

The Spirit Sanctifies God's People

If Gentiles are to come into God's people, however, a radical transformation must begin in their lives to make them appropriate dwelling places for God's Holy Spirit—they need to be holy. Among the New Testament writers, Paul especially emphasizes the role of the Spirit in effecting this transformation. He tells the mainly Gentile Thessalonian Christians that their "holiness" (*hagiasmos*) is God's will and that they must, therefore, exercise sexual self-control "in holiness" (*en hagiasmō*, 1 Thess. 4:3–6). God has called them "in holiness" (*en hagiasmō*, 4:7), and the person who rejects this instruction rejects the God who has given to his people his "Holy [*hagion*] Spirit"

(4:8). The holiness of God's Spirit, therefore, demands moral holiness from those among whom he dwells.[44]

Similarly, Paul reminds the predominantly Gentile Corinthian Christians that since the Spirit of God has washed, sanctified, and justified them, they should avoid the kind of immorality that characterized their lives prior to their conversion (1 Cor. 6:9–11). Since their body is the temple of the Holy Spirit, they should flee sexual immorality (6:18–20).

He instructs the Gentile Galatians to "live by the Spirit" and tells them that by doing this they will "not gratify the desires of the sinful nature" (Gal. 5:16). He then provides a detailed list of exemplary acts of "the flesh" (NIV, "sinful nature") and contrasts with it an equally detailed list of examples of the ethical "fruit of the Spirit" (5:19–23).[45]

Paul follows much the same pattern in Titus, addressed to a coworker in charge of the predominantly Gentile churches newly established on Crete. Prior to their conversion the new Cretan Christians were "foolish, disobedient, deceived and enslaved by all kinds of passions and pleasures," including malice, envy, and mutual hatred (Titus 3:3). When God kindly provided the Holy Spirit to wash and renew them, however, he transformed them so that they might devote themselves to good works (3:4–8).

In brief, Paul, as an apostle to the Gentiles, is one instrument through whom God brings Gentiles within the boundaries of his eschatologically renewed people. As the Spirit works among them, it prompts them to respond to the gospel in faith and begins the transforming work that will make them an acceptable habitation for God's spiritual presence. Paul puts this succinctly in Rom. 15:16 when he says that he is

> a minister of Christ Jesus to the Gentiles with the priestly duty of proclaiming the gospel of God, so that the Gentiles might become an offering acceptable to God, sanctified by the Holy Spirit.[46]

Neither the Spirit's presence at conversion nor the ethical change that the Spirit works in believers, however, is limited to Gentile converts. Ezekiel, speaking to Israelites, described the eschatological era of the Spirit as a time when God would purify Israel and transform the hearts of Jews so that they would obey his law (Ezek. 11:18–20; 36:25–27). The Spirit would animate Israel's dead bones, and they would live (37:6, 14). For Paul, too, ethnic Jews need more than fleshly circumcision—they need the true circumcision of the heart that comes only through God's Spirit (Rom. 2:29; cf. Phil. 3:3). Jews as well as Gentiles have access to the Father through one Spirit (Eph. 2:18). Jews who once lived under the Mosaic law and therefore under the condemnation and death it brings to those who disobey its statutes (Rom. 7:6; 8:2, 6, 10–11) need to experience "new life in the Spirit" (7:6; 8:2).

44 Cf. Fee, *God's Empowering Presence*, 880–81.

45 As Fee observes, ibid., 882, the representative rather than exhaustive nature of these lists is clear from Paul's expression "such things" (*ta toiauta*) at the conclusion of each list (5:21, 23).

46 Cf. 1 Peter 2:5, where Peter calls his readers "a spiritual house" and "a holy priesthood." These identities, he says, should prompt them to offer "spiritual sacrifices acceptable to God through Jesus Christ."

In other words, the Spirit allows all Christians, whether Jewish or Gentile, to fulfill the righteous requirement of the law (Rom. 8:4a), to avoid walking according to the flesh (8:4b), to put to death the (mis-)deeds of the body (8:13), and to live, both now (8:10) and at the time of the final resurrection of the dead (8:11).

The Spirit, then, breaks down social boundaries and brings unity to the church. The church as a social group has taken the place of Israel's temple as the symbol of the dwelling place of God's Spirit (1 Cor. 3:16). In this role, the individual Christians who comprise the church need to work for the "edification" of one another (3:14; Eph. 2:18–22) and use their spiritual gifts to this end (1 Cor. 14:1–5, 12; cf. 12:1–11). They should work against divisiveness since it threatens to bring God's temple crashing to the ground (3:14–16). Christians must "make every effort to maintain the unity of the Spirit through the bond of peace" (Eph. 4:3).

Summary

The New Testament claims that the coming of Jesus has ushered in the eschatological period, anticipated in the biblical prophets, when God will be present by means of his Spirit with all of his people. The Spirit fills those associated with the births of Jesus' forerunner, John the Baptist, and of Jesus. This activity of the Spirit anticipates the much fuller evidence of the Spirit's presence in the words and deeds of Jesus himself during his ministry. The Spirit's presence does not dissipate after Jesus' ascension, however, but from his position at God's right hand Jesus pours on his apostles the same Spirit that empowered his own ministry, and through their ministry he pours the Spirit on all Christians.

Among his many other functions, the Spirit enables the apostles and other Christians to bear effective witness to the gospel, even in situations of persecution. He gives the church strategic direction about where to preach the gospel and to whom. He provides the church with teaching, insists that it tear down social and ethnic barriers, and empowers Christians to live holy lives. In these ways, the Spirit enables the church to become an appropriate place for God's presence to dwell.

THE CHURCH AS THE PEOPLE OF GOD

God has poured out his Spirit on his eschatologically restored people, and the nature of that people itself is a subject on which the New Testament frequently reflects. Three aspects of the identity of the people of God are particularly important to the New Testament writers: the status of the church as the restored Israel, the church as the dwelling place of God's presence, and the church as the repository of the truth.

The Church as the Restored Israel

Many New Testament witnesses describe the "assembly" (*ekklēsia*; NIV, "church") of Christians, whether conceived as a local group or an invisible worldwide fellowship, as standing in continuity with "the assembly of the Lord" in Israel's Scriptures.

The four gospels and Acts emphasize the importance of the number of Jesus' inner circle of disciples as twelve, a number that corresponds to the twelve tribes of Israel (Matt. 10:1–2; Mark 3:14; Luke 6:13; cf. Matt. 19:28; 1 Cor. 15:5).[47] They imply that the church, which arose from these twelve apostles, constitutes God's people in the same way that the twelve tribes of Israel constituted Israel.

Luke takes special pains to show that the promised Spirit of the eschatological restoration of God's people came only after God had led the apostles to fill the gap in their number left when Judas defected (Acts 1:12–26). John the seer uses the symbolism latent in the number twelve repeatedly in Revelation to show that Christians are the people of God in the same way that biblical Israel was the people of God (e.g., Rev. 4:4; 7:4–8; 21:14). For Paul, Christians are "the assembly of God" (1 Cor. 10:32; cf. 1:2; 11:22; 15:9; 2 Cor. 1:1), language that echoes the repeated references to "the assembly of the LORD" (*ekklēsia kyriou*) in Deuteronomy 23:1–8 (LXX). They are the true "circumcision" (Phil. 3:3; cf. Rom. 2:28–29; Eph. 2:11; Col. 2:11–13) and "the Israel of God" (Gal. 6:16).[48] Peter can call the Gentile Christians of Asia Minor "the exiles of the Dispersion ... chosen and destined by God" (1 Peter 1:1, NRSV) and apply to them a whole series of terms that the Scriptures use of Israel—"chosen people, a royal priesthood, a holy nation, a people belonging to God" (2:9).[49]

The most astonishing aspect of this common theme in the New Testament texts is its inclusive nature. A broad spectrum of New Testament texts claim or assume that Gentiles as Gentiles are included in the group that they identify with the eschatologically restored Israel. Israel's Scriptures hinted at this when, for example, God promised Abraham that he would be the father of many nations (Gen. 17:5; cf. 12:3) or Isaiah spoke of a surviving remnant of faithful Israel proclaiming to the nations the fame and glory of the Lord (Isa. 66:18–19; cf. 2:1–5; Zech 8:20–23). Some Second Temple Jews who lived before Christ understood this hope and kept it alive (Tobit 14:6–7).[50]

Many early Christians, however, raised this biblical theme to special prominence, taking such texts to mean that Gentiles would join Jews on an equal footing—and as Gentiles—to form the eschatologically restored people of God.[51] They even took

47 On the link between twelve disciples, twelve tribes, and the eschatological restoration of Israel, see, e.g., E. P. Sanders, *Jesus and Judaism* (Philadelphia: Fortress, 1985), 95–106; N. T. Wright, *Jesus and the Victory of God* (Minneapolis: Fortress, 1996), 300; and John P. Meier, "Jesus, the Twelve and the Restoration of Israel," in *Restoration: Old Testament, Jewish, and Christian Perspectives*, ed. James M. Scott (JSJSup 72; Leiden: Brill, 2001), 365–404.

48 A spirited debate focuses on whether "Israel of God" in Gal. 6:16 refers to ethnic Israel or to the multi-ethnic group of those who believe in Jesus. Thomas R. Schreiner, *Paul: Apostle of God's Glory in Christ* (Downers Grove, Ill.: InterVarsity Press, 2001), 482–83, correctly observes that if this phrase carried ethnic connotations, then it would undercut the letter's argument that Gentile believers belong to the family of Abraham. It is more likely to be a crowning rhetorical flourish to Paul's argument about the inclusion of Gentiles in the people of God than an enigmatic concession to the claims of Paul's opponents that Israel's ethnic identity carries with it some special status.

49 See the LXX renderings of Ex. 19:4–5; 23:22; Isa. 43:20–21.

50 See also *1 En.* 10.21; 90.27–33; *2 Bar.* 72–73; *T. Levi* 18.3, 9; *T. Naph.* 8.3–4; *T. Jud.* 24.6; 25.5; *T. Zeb.* 9.8; *T. Ben.* 3.9; *Sib. Or.* 3.702–4, 716–20, 767–75; Philo, *Mos.* 2.43–44; *Praem.* 164–72, and the discussion of these texts in Terence L. Donaldson, *Paul and the Gentiles: Remapping the Apostle's Convictional World* (Minneapolis: Fortress, 1997), 70–73. Cf. G. B. Caird, *Jesus and the Jewish Nation* (London: Athlone, 1965), 14–15; Sanders, *Jesus and Judaism*, 213–18.

51 See, e.g., the use of Isa. 66:1–2 among Hellenistic Jewish Christians such as Stephen in Acts 7:49–50 and Paul's use of Gen. 12:3 in Gal. 3:8 and of Gen. 17:5 in Rom. 4:17. Other Jewish Christians, such as Paul's opponents in Galatia and those whose

texts that originally referred to the restoration of a disobedient Israel and applied them to the influx of formerly excluded Gentiles into the boundaries of God's people. Both Paul and Peter use the language of Hosea 2:23 (MT; LXX 2:25) and 1:10 (MT; LXX 2:1), originally a description of Israel's northern kingdom, to Gentile Christians:

> "I will call them 'my people' who are not my people;
> and I will call her 'my loved one' who is not my loved one. . . .
> It will happen that in the very place where it was said to them,
> 'You are not my people,'
> they will be called the 'sons of the living God.'" (Rom. 9:25–26; cf. 1 Peter 2:10).

The phrases "my people" and "not my people" no longer describe the transfer of Israel from a disobedient to an obedient people but the transfer of Gentiles, who were never God's people, into the people of God.

The contrast between the large numbers of Gentiles who have joined the eschatologically restored people of God and the comparatively small numbers of Jews who have done so raises a theological problem for several New Testament writers. Paul senses the irony especially sharply:

> The Gentiles, who did not pursue righteousness, have obtained it, a righteousness that is by faith; but Israel, who pursued a law of righteousness, has not attained it. Why not? (Rom. 9:30–32a)

Has God's Word, in which he promises to be faithful to his people, failed (cf. Rom. 9:6)? Did God reject his people, Israel (11:1)?

The dominant answer to this dilemma in the New Testament is that the fault lies not with God but with Israel, which opted out of God's work of restoration by rejecting the Messiah Jesus, who ushered it in. Immediately after Jesus comments that he has not found "anyone" in Israel with faith as great as that of the Roman centurion in Capernaum, Matthew places Jesus' comment that "many will come from east and west, and will take their places at the feast with Abraham, Isaac and Jacob in the kingdom of heaven. But the subjects of the kingdom will be thrown outside" (Matt. 8:10–12). Their rejection of Jesus means that God has transferred their status as his vineyard (Isa. 5:1–7) to others (Matt. 21:41)—he has taken his kingdom from them and "given [it] to a people who will produce its fruit" (21:43).

Paul agrees. Many Gentiles have obtained righteousness by faith whereas most within Israel have not, Paul says, because Israel is so blinded by zeal for the works of the law that when they hear the gospel, they reject it (Rom. 9:30–10:21). In Acts, Luke tells us that Paul articulates this reasoning to Jews who reject his message. By rejecting Jesus, they are acting like their forefathers who rejected the prophets, and now "God's salvation has been sent to the Gentiles," who "will listen" (Acts 28:25–28; cf. 13:46; 18:6; 19:9).

---

insistence on the circumcision of Gentile Christians sparked the Jerusalem council of Acts 15:1–35, where willing to admit Gentiles into the eschatologically restored people of God, but only as proselytes to Judaism.

The dominant answer to the question of why Gentiles outnumber Jews in the eschatologically restored people of God, therefore, is that most Jews have rejected the Messiah who brought in the period of restoration. In response, God has replaced the Jews with a new people comprised primarily of Gentiles.

The New Testament supplements this answer, however, with other perspectives on the problem of Jewish rejection of the gospel. Paul points out that the existence of some Jewish Christians, including himself, reveals that God has not been unfaithful to his people (Rom. 11:1–2). As in the days of Elijah, "there is a remnant chosen by grace" that stands as a sign of God's faithfulness to his former promises (11:3–6).

James the Lord's brother and leader of the Jerusalem church may have understood his own status in much the same way. Along with Peter and John, James was engaged in a mission to the Jews (Gal. 2:9). He never articulates the reason for this special concentration on the Jews, but he may have agreed with Paul both that unbelieving Jews should hear the gospel first (Rom. 1:16) and that believing Jews retain a special status within the people of God as the ethnic group in whose spiritual blessings Gentile Christians share (15:27). If the argument in our discussion of James is correct (see ch. 24), James addresses his letter to Jewish Christians of the Diaspora, and they retain the ancient title "the twelve tribes" (James 1:1). So even in the eschatological people of God, where everyone is on the same footing, Jewish Christians retain some special status, not because they are more deserving than others but because God has chosen them as the conduit of his blessings to the world (Rom. 15:27; cf. Gen. 12:2–3; Rom. 4:16–17; Gal. 3:8–9).

Paul even goes further in Romans 11:11–32. When faced with the conceit of certain Gentile Christians over their belief that they have replaced the Jews as God's people, Paul explains a "mystery"—a truth that would have remained unknown had God not graciously revealed it.[52] The hardening of Israel and the flood of Gentiles into the church, he explains, is part of God's grand historical design. Contrary to traditional expectations, the Gentiles will not turn to God after the restoration of ethnic Israel; instead, Gentiles will first flood into the restored people of God (11:11, 25, 28, 31). After this influx, ethnic Israel will become jealous of the Gentiles' inheritance of God's saving work and will themselves embrace the gospel (11:11–12, 23–24, 26, 31). God's purposes will then move swiftly toward their consummation in the resurrection of the dead (11:12, 15). In this way, all of ethnic Israel alive during these final days will be saved (11:26a); once again, God is found faithful to his scriptural promises (11:26b–29).

Does this claim that God will eventually prove faithful to his promises to ethnic Israel stand in tension with Paul's claim elsewhere, and the claim of other New Testament writers, that the church, comprised of both Jewish and Gentile believers, is the restored Israel of prophetic expectation? Paul never explains how these two understandings of the prophetic promises fit together, but his easy movement from one to the other shows that he does not believe them to be incompatible.[53]

52 For this understanding of the term *mystērion* ("mystery"), see its use in Dan. 2 and the helpful excursus in Hoehner, *Ephesians*, 428–34.

53 Cf. Schreiner, *Paul*, 482–83, and idem, "The Church as the New Israel and the Future of Ethnic Israel in Paul," *StudBib* 13 (1983): 17–38, here at 24–37.

Paul probably conceives of eschatologically restored Israel in two ways. On the one hand, it is the multiethnic group of those who believe in Christ Jesus in the present. This multiethnic group includes Jewish Christians, who form a faithful remnant analogous to the seven thousand who did not bow to Baal in Elijah's time (Rom. 11:1–10). On the other hand, this restored Israel comprises those Jews whose hardened hearts will be softened just prior to the resurrection of the dead, all of whom will be saved and whose salvation will fulfill Isaiah's expectations for the eschatological deliverance of Zion (11:26–29; cf. Isa. 59:20–21, LXX). Although Paul never says so explicitly, he probably thinks the two groups will merge with one another as God's purpose to show mercy to all draws to its magnificent conclusion in the resurrection of the dead (Rom. 11:15, 32).

Christians, in summary, form the eschatologically restored people of God in fulfillment of the promises of the prophets. As the Scriptures hinted, moreover, this group of people includes Gentiles; indeed, Gentiles far outnumber Jews. The primary reason for this surprising turn of events is that most Jews have rejected the gospel. Nevertheless, God's faithfulness to the Jewish people is revealed in the present in the Jewish remnant, whom he has called by his grace to be part of his people. God's faithfulness to his people will be even clearer in the future when "the full number of the Gentiles has come in" and "all Israel will be saved" (Rom. 11:25–26).

The Church as the Dwelling Place of God's Presence

Several New Testament writers speak of the church as the dwelling place of God's eschatologically given Spirit and therefore as the metaphorical temple of God. As with the idea that God's eschatologically restored people will include Gentiles, the origins of this notion lie in Israel's Scriptures, particularly Ezekiel's prophecy. Ezekiel prophesied that eventually God would build a magnificent temple to which his glory, presently absent because of Israel's sin (Ezek. 8:6; 9:3; 10:18; 11:22–23), would return and live forever (43:6–12). This return would take place after God had purified his people (36:25–27) and they had renounced the "detestable practices" that had led to their destruction and to the destruction of the Jerusalem temple by the Babylonians (43:8–9; cf. 6:9; 16:61; 20:43; 36:31).

Not everyone believed that the temple built after the return from exile met Ezekiel's expectations.[54] The author of Tobit, for example, anticipated a time when "the temple of God would be rebuilt, just as the prophets of Israel have said concerning it" (Tobit 14:5). The author of *1 Enoch*, similarly, thought that in the future "a house" would be "built for the Great King in glory forevermore" (*1 En.* 91.13; cf. *Jub.* 1.17, 27–28; 2 Macc. 2:4–8; 11Q19 29.8–9).

Early Christians not only opt out of the idea that the second temple is a permanent structure but out of the notion that the eschatological temple is a structure at all. They emphasize Isaiah's notion that no physical structure can contain the

54 See the discussions of Otto Michel, "ναός," *TDNT*, 4:880–90, here at 886; Bertil Gärtner, *The Temple and the Community in Qumran and in the New Testament* (SNTSMS 1; Cambridge: Cambridge Univ. Press, 1965), 16–17; and Stephen Westerholm, "Temple," *ISBE*, 4:759–76, here at 768.

presence of God. Recalling Isaiah 66:1–2, Stephen says, "The Most High does not dwell [*katoikeō*] in houses made by hand [*cheiropoiētois*]" (Acts 7:48–50). Mark makes the same point when he phrases the false testimony at Jesus' trial before the Sanhedrin this way: "We heard him saying, 'I will destroy this made-by-hand [*cheiropoiēton*] temple and within three days will build another, not made by hand [*acheiropoiēton*]" (Mark 14:58). The parallel sentence in Matthew 26:61 does not describe the two temples as made and not made by hand respectively, and it is likely, therefore, that this addition represents Mark's effort to show that the false witnesses are speaking more truthfully than they intend.[55] The body of Jesus—resurrected after three days—fulfills the expectation for an eschatological temple, not a literal structure (cf. John 2:19–21).[56]

Several New Testament texts identify the eschatological temple not with the body of the resurrected Christ but with the church. Both Christians individually (1 Cor. 6:19) and Christians corporately (3:16–17) comprise God's "temple" (2 Cor. 6:16) or "house" (1 Peter 4:17). The church represents the fulfillment of Ezekiel's vision that God will build a splendid temple in which his glory dwells (Rev. 11:1–2). God's Spirit dwells in this house (1 Cor. 3:16; 6:19), and it is spiritual in nature (1 Peter 2:5). This characteristic of the Christian church fulfills the prophetic expectation that God will one day live and walk among his people by establishing his sanctuary in their midst (2 Cor. 6:14–7:1; cf. Ezek. 37:27–28; *Jub.* 1:17–18).

In a way reminiscent of the idea that the resurrected body of Jesus is the eschatological temple, both Paul and Peter can describe him as the "cornerstone" in this temple (Eph. 2:20; 1 Peter 2:6) or as the foundation (1 Cor. 3:11). The apostles and prophets, Paul says in Ephesians, form the foundation of this temple, and it is presently being built of the united group of believers (Eph. 2:20). Peter, similarly, speaks of Jesus as the "living Stone" who is "chosen" and "precious" to God, terms drawn from Isaiah 28:16, and Christians are also "living stones" in God's "spiritual house" (1 Peter 2:4–5). Jesus, therefore, joins Christians as part of God's eschatological temple. Like those who comprise his church, he is one of the stones that make up the dwelling place of God (*katoikētērion*), although he is the cornerstone that holds the whole building together (Eph. 2:21–22).

John makes an equally subtle, but more profound, connection between the temple of Jesus' resurrected body and the community of believers. When the Word became flesh, he "tabernacled [*eskēnōsen*] among us" (John 1:14), and his resurrection from the dead replaces Judaism's second temple with a newly "raised" one (2:19). Jesus, particularly the resurrected Jesus, therefore, is this new temple.

John takes this a step further in his record of the discussion between Jesus and the Samaritan woman on true worship (John 4:19–24). There Jesus speaks of a time when all true worshipers, including Samaritans, will worship God neither in

55 Cf. John 11:50, where the high priest Caiaphas unwittingly articulates a Christian understanding of the atonement.

56 R. T. France, *The Gospel of Mark* (Grand Rapids: Eerdmans, 2002), 605–7. Some scholars, e.g., P. W. L. Walker, *Jesus and the Holy City: New Testament Perspectives* (Grand Rapids: Eerdmans, 1996), 10–11, see a reference to the establishment of the Christian community in this temple "not built by hand," but the reference to "three days" makes this unlikely.

Jerusalem nor on Mount Gerazim (the locations of each people's temple), but in Spirit and in truth. In the context of John's gospel, this means that Jesus is the replacement of the Jerusalem temple and the gathering place for a multiethnic body of people who worship God in the way he desires.[57]

The New Testament writers who use temple imagery for the church draw from such imagery three conclusions about the character of the church. First, since as the temple of God the church is his dwelling place, it must be holy. Individual Christians must avoid sexual immorality because their "body is the temple of the Holy Spirit" (1 Cor. 6:19). They should move away from the influence of false apostles because they are the "temple of the living God" (2 Cor. 6:14–7:1). They should abstain from "sinful desires" and live "good lives among the pagans" (1 Peter 2:11–12; cf. 2:1) because they have come to the living Stone and are, like him, living stones in God's "spiritual house" (2:4–5).

Second, they should be unified with one another. The divisiveness in Corinth, based in pride over comparisons between the rhetorical skills of various teachers, is a way of building God's temple with cheap materials. Those who build God's temple, however, must do so with care (1 Cor. 3:10). Disunity will destroy God's temple, and those who foster this disunity God will in turn destroy (3:17). Similarly, the faith of the Gentile readers of Paul's letter to the Ephesians has brought them into a closely knit unity with Jewish believers, and together they are growing into "a holy temple in the Lord ... a dwelling in which God lives by the Spirit" (Eph. 2:21–22; cf. 4:12). The unity of Christians from various ethnic backgrounds, as we have just seen, also lies behind John's use of the image (John 4:19–24; cf. 7:35; 10:16; 11:51–52; 12:20–22, 32).

Third, Christians should take courage that God will protect their faith in the midst of persecution just as God guards his temple. Behind the principle that "if anyone destroys God's temple, God will destroy him" (1 Cor. 3:17) lies the assumption that God will protect his temple. John the seer uses this motif to encourage those who are experiencing hardship for their witness to Jesus that their faith, if genuine, can come to no ultimate harm. Conceiving of God's people as occupants of the inner court of God's temple, John is told to "measure" it as a symbol of its protection not against suffering, but against being driven by suffering to apostasy (Rev. 11:1–2). God may allow attacks on it both to gather evidence for the judgment of the wicked and to call some of them to repentance, but he has limited the duration of these attacks so that no ultimate harm befalls the faith of his people (11:2–3).[58] Those who remain faithful despite the hardship they experience for their witness will eventually be established as "pillars" in God's temple (3:12)—a symbol of God's eternal presence (7:15; 11:19; 14:15, 17; 15:5–8; 16:1, 17; 21:22).

In summary, the church fulfills the expectation of Ezekiel that in the era of Israel's eschatological restoration, God will rebuild his temple and dwell there among his

57 Frank Thielman, *The Law and the New Testament: The Question of Continuity* (Companions to the New Testament; New York: Crossroad, 1999), 94–96; N. T. Wright, *The Resurrection of the Son of God* (Minneapolis: Fortress, 2003), 440–41; cf. F.-M. Braun, *Jean le théologien: Le grandes traditions d'Israël l'accord des Écritures d'après le Quatrième Évangile*, EBib (Paris: Librairie Lecoffre, 1964), 91.

58 On this, see chapter 32.

people. Because the church is the dwelling place of God's eschatologically given Spirit, it must be holy and unified. Although God may allow attacks on his people for a time in accord with his intentions both for the punishment of some of the wicked and the salvation of others, he will protect his people against any ultimate harm.

The Church as a Repository of the Truth

Many New Testament writers portray the church as the trustee of the truth about God, his human creatures, and the reconciliation between the two that has come through Jesus Christ. It is "the pillar and foundation" of the truth that God is the only God, and Jesus Christ, who offered himself as a ransom for people, is the "one mediator" between God and his human creation (1 Tim. 2:4–5; 3:15). The church has received "the faith" that was "once for all entrusted" to them (Jude 3). It is the recipient of "a faith as precious as ours," "the sacred command," that all Christians hold in common (2 Peter 1:1; 2:21). The church possesses the knowledge of "the way of righteousness" that leads to "the eternal kingdom of our Lord (1:10–11; 2:21).

These are the terms in which to understand Jesus' otherwise enigmatic statement to Peter and to the other apostles in the gospels that they have the power to bind and loose, to forgive sins or leave them unforgiven (Matt. 16:19; John 20:23).[59] The beloved disciple of John's gospel, similarly, passes on his eyewitness testimony to the identity and significance of Jesus, and so is the conduit of eternal life to others (John 19:35; 20:8, 30–31; 21:24; 1 John 1:1–4; 4:14; 5:8, 13).

Because the church is the one place where the truth of the gospel can be found, it is important that this truth remain free of false teaching. Because heresy threatens the church at Ephesus, Timothy must "guard the good deposit that was entrusted" to him (2 Tim. 1:14; cf. 1 Tim. 6:20) and must resist anyone who teaches what is contrary to "sound doctrine" (1 Tim. 1:10; cf. 1:3; 6:3). When Titus trains overseers to govern the newly established churches on Crete, he should be sure that they can teach "sound doctrine" and refute any who contradict it (Titus 1:9). Titus should be able to do the same (2:1).

Jude finds it necessary "to contend" for the faith with which the church has been entrusted, since false teachers have attacked it (Jude 3). Peter labors to resist the disaster that false prophets have created by leading new converts off "the way of righteousness" and encouraging them to retreat from "the sacred command" (2 Peter 2:21). The Elder, similarly, refutes the docetic false teaching that has invaded his community by recalling the community to his status as a keeper of the apostolic eyewitness tradition about Jesus:

59 Scholars frequently bring forward evidence that "binding" and "loosing" in an ancient Jewish context referred to enforcing or making exceptions to the rules of the sages. They then connect Matt. 16:19 with 18:18 and claim that Peter here is a sort of first-among-equals in a newly established "apostolic college." See, e.g., Michael Goulder, "Matthew's Vision for the Church," in *A Vision for the Church: Studies in Early Christian Ecclesiology in Honour of J. P. M. Sweet*, ed. Markus Bockmuehl and Michael B. Thompson (Edinburgh: T. & T. Clark, 1997), 19–32, here at 22–23. Peter, however, is given keys, whose function is to lock and unlock, to permit or prohibit entry. Since entry into the kingdom of heaven is an important theme in Matthew (Matt. 5:20; 7:21; 18:3; 19:23; 19:24), this is the lens through which we should interpret Peter's authority to "bind" and "loose." He will take the lead in the church's witness to the gospel, a role that he fulfills in Acts 2:14–39; 3:6, 11–26; 4:8–12; 10:1–11:18; 15:6–11.

> We are from God, and whoever knows God listens to us; but whoever is not from God does not listen to us. This is how we recognize the Spirit of truth and the spirit of falsehood. (1 John 4:6)

Of equal importance to preserving the orthodoxy of the church's witness is preserving its attractiveness. Paul expresses this concern in 1 Corinthians when he advises Christians in Corinth to be sensitive to the feelings of unbelievers in whose homes they are eating (1 Cor. 10:23–30). They should conduct themselves in the way that Paul conducts his own ministry (9:19–23; 10:31–11:1)—avoiding offense to Jews, Greeks, and to weaker Christian brothers and sisters (cf. 8:1–13) "so that they may be saved" (10:33). The same concern should govern the use of tongues and prophecy when the church gathers for worship (14:23–25).

This is an important theme in 1 Timothy and Titus. Paul's claim that the church is "the pillar and foundation of the truth" in 1 Timothy 3:15 comes on the heels of his comment that he writes so that Timothy may know how Christians should conduct themselves in the church. Why is the conduct of the church as important as the soundness of its doctrine? Because God is a "Savior who wants all [people] to be saved and to come to a knowledge of the truth" (2:5). This is why it is so important that the Christians in Ephesus "live peaceful and quiet lives in all godliness and holiness" (2:2). Avoiding the slander of God's name is, similarly, the reason why slaves should be considerate and respectful of their masters (6:1).

In his letter to Titus, Paul urges Titus to set an example to the new Cretan Christians in order for them to learn to do "what is good . . . so that those who oppose you may be ashamed because they have nothing bad to say about us" (Titus 2:7–8). Slaves should be subject to their masters "so that in every way they will make the teaching about God our Savior attractive" (2:10).

The same concern emerges from 1 Peter, where Peter tells Christians to "live such good lives among the pagans that, though they accuse you of doing wrong, they may see your good deeds and glorify God on the day he visits us" (1 Peter 2:12). Similarly, Christian wives married to unbelieving husbands should let the "purity and reverence" of their behavior speak for them and win their husbands over to faith in the Word (3:1–2).

In sum, the church is the repository of the truth of the gospel. Because of this, it must both "guard" this "good deposit" and, at the same time, make "the household of God" a hospitable, attractive place for unbelievers.

THE CONSUMMATION OF ALL THINGS

The main lines of New Testament theology converge in the hope that God will bring his saving purposes to their consummation in a new creation. These purposes have taken their most important step forward in the incarnation, ministry, death, and resurrection of Christ. The faith that characterizes Christian existence rests on the hope for eternal enjoyment of God's glory forever in a new heaven and a new earth. The multiethnic people of God that constitute the church are the prototype of this new creation. It is the place where God's Spirit begins to fulfill the hope that God will live among his people forever, a people not restricted to one ethnic group but representative of all God's human creatures.

What can be said of Christianity generally is also true of the New Testament specifically: "The eschatological is not one element *of* Christianity, but it is the medium of Christian faith as such, the key in which everything in it is set."[60] The New Testament focuses on three characteristics of this hope, each of which we can describe in a question: What will the new creation be? When will the new creation come? How should hope for the new creation influence Christian behavior?

What Will the New Creation Be?

The new creation will be a place where the effects of Adam's transgression against God's command are reversed. Adam's one transgression brought sin to everyone (Rom. 5:12, 14–19). From the moment they come into existence, people are sinners, deserving the wrath of God (Eph. 2:3), and every person decides to rebel against God in the same way that Adam rebelled (Rom. 5:12). The just penalty for this rebellion both in Adam's case and for everyone else is death (1:32; 5:12, 14, 17, 21; 6:23; 8:2, 6, 13; 1 Cor. 15:21–22).

God originally created people to give him glory and to share in that glory themselves (Rom. 1:23; 3:23; Heb. 2:7, quoting Ps. 8:5), to experience the intimacy of marriage (Matt. 19:4–6; Mark 10:6–8; Eph. 5:31), and to rule over his creation (Heb. 2:8, quoting Ps. 8:6), but sin has twisted these purposes into cruel parodies of God's intentions. People worship the creatures God made rather than God himself (Rom. 1:21–23, 25) and transform intimacy with one another in the marriage of male and female into sexual immorality, including homoerotic liaisons (1:24, 26–27). In short, everyone has fallen from the glory of God (3:23). The effects of human sin reach to the creation generally as it has been "subjected to frustration" and put "in bondage to decay" so that "all creation lets out a groan in common pain" (8:20–22).[61]

In the coming new creation, however, all these "first things" will pass away, yielding to a new order in which God will make "everything new" (Rev. 21:4–5; cf. 2 Peter 3:13). God's people will regain the glory they lost after Adam sinned, and all of creation, now liberated from its bondage to decay, will enjoy that glory (Rom. 8:21). Jesus is the "last Adam" and has begun the process by which Adam's error and its effects are reversed. Just as Adam disobeyed God's command, so Christ was obedient. Just as Adam brought physical death to everyone, so Christ's resurrection will bring immortal life to everyone in a "spiritual body" that will never experience decay (1 Cor. 15:44; Rev. 21:4).

60 Moltmann, *Theology of Hope*, 16. On the importance of New Testament eschatology to New Testament theology see Greg K. Beale, "The Eschatological Conception of New Testament Theology" in *Eschatology in Bible and Theology: Evangelical Essays at the Dawn of a New Millenium*, ed. Kent E. Brower and Mark W. Elliott (Downers Grove, Ill.: InterVarsity Press, 1997), 11–52, here at 12–18.

61 For the translations here, see BDAG, 977.

"Death," in other words, "will be swallowed up in victory" (1 Cor. 15:54). All of God's creatures will give him praise, whether angelic, human, or animal (Rev. 4:4–11; 7:11–12; 19:4). All rebellious creatures, whether spiritual or human, are banished from this new creation, and so there will be no oppression or persecution there (1 Cor. 15:24; Heb. 10:13; Rev. 7:16–17; 21:4, 6, 8, 27; 22:15). God's people will have matured into "the new human being, created to be like God in true righteousness and holiness" (Eph. 4:24, aut.).

In addition to their bodily immortality and ethical perfection, God's people will be unified with one another across all ethnic and national boundaries. Jews will join Gentiles in glorifying God (Rom. 15:8–12). God's people will include "every tribe and language and people and nation" (Rev. 5:9), and together they will bring praise to God and serve him unceasingly (7:9–10, 15). Isaiah's grand vision for the pilgrimage of the nations to the Messiah and for geo-political harmony in a new heavens and a new earth (Isa. 11; cf. 2:1–5; 65:17–25; 66:19–23) will find fulfillment (Rev. 21:1, 24–26; 22:2).

In summary, the new creation will return the earth to a condition qualitatively like its condition prior to Adam's sin. Death and rebellion against God will disappear, and God's creatures will live together in peace, united by their worship of God.

When Will the New Creation Come?

The tone of eschatological urgency and hope that runs through the New Testament comes from the conviction, expressed with remarkable consistency and frequency, that the consummation of God's saving purposes for his people can happen at any time. Even among the authors who stress the delay or the realization of eschatological events there is often a parallel affirmation that Christ may return suddenly. Luke tells his readers that no matter how long they must wait for their master to come home, they should be dressed and keep their lamps lit so that when he comes, they will be ready; it may be at any time, and he will come quickly (Luke 12:35–48; cf. 18:8).[62] In John's gospel, the hour "now is," but it also "is coming" (John 4:23; 5:25, 28–29). Second Peter, similarly, not only warns that the final day could be thousands of years away (2 Peter 3:8) but, almost in the same breath, that it will "come like a thief" (3:10).

The very texts that place greatest emphasis on transmitting the traditions of the faith intact to other generations (1 Tim. 3:9; 4:6; 6:3; 2 Tim. 1:14; 2:11–14; 4:2, 5; Jude 3) often emphasize the possibility that the final day could come within the lifetime of the readers (1 Tim. 6:14), that the Day of Judgment is certain (2 Tim. 4:1; Jude 14–15), and that Christians should long for Christ's appearing (2 Tim. 4:8). The false teachers whom these texts often attack are evidence that Christians are living in "the last days" (2 Tim. 3:1–5; 2 Peter 3:3; cf. 1 Tim. 4:1–2; Jude 18).

62 Darrell L. Bock, *Luke 1:1–9:50* (BECNT; Grand Rapids: Baker, 1994), 42. Cf. Georg Strecker, *Theology of the New Testament* (Berlin: Walter de Gruyter, 2000), 336.

Alongside this sense of living at the dawn of the new creation, however, stands a concern that believers not be deceived into thinking that, as Paul puts it, "the day of the Lord has already come" (2 Thess. 2:2). "Watch out that no one deceives you," Jesus tells his disciples (Mark 13:5; cf. Matt. 24:4; Luke 17:22–23; 21:8), and Paul similarly warns the Thessalonian Christians not to let "anyone deceive you in any way" (2 Thess. 2:3). Not only can such overheated eschatological fervor lead Christians to follow false messianic claimants (Matt. 24:5; Mark 13:6; Luke 17:23; 21:8), but also to stop working, sponge off the Christian community, and create a public scandal (2 Thess. 3:6–15; cf. 1 Thess. 4:11–12; 5:14).

Both Jesus and Paul seek to forestall these problems by sketching in broad strokes the course of world history down to the time of Jesus' Parousia. Jesus tells his disciples that three developments must take place before the end, but that, within these parameters, the end could come at any time.

First, sin and mayhem will continue and grow worse. People will use Jesus' name to make false religious claims, some of them accompanied by miracles; among them, according to Luke, will be the claim that "the time is near" (Luke 21:8; cf. Matt. 24:4–5, 11, 23–24; Mark 13:5–6, 21–23). Geopolitical strife, natural disaster, and persecution of God's people will continue unabated (Matt. 24:6–13; Mark 13:7–13; Luke 21:9–19). Some Christians, according to Matthew, will fall away (Matt. 24:10).

Second, "the gospel must first be preached to all nations" before the end (Mark 13:10; Matt. 24:14; cf. Matt. 10:18). This task will face the obstacle of extreme persecution not only from councils, synagogues, governors, and kings (Matt. 24:17–18; Mark 13:9; Luke 21:12–13), but also from family members (Mark 13:12; Luke 21:16; cf. Matt. 10:21), indeed from everyone (Matt. 24:9b; Mark 13:13; Luke 21:17).

Third, Jerusalem must fall to the Gentiles, and this means that the "abomination that causes desolation" will be set up in the temple, just as happened under Antiochus IV Epiphanes two centuries earlier in fulfillment of Daniel's prophecy. Jesus borrows this language to prophesy the Roman destruction of Jerusalem and the temple in A.D. 70, a point that Luke brings out clearly (Matt. 24:15; Mark 13:14; Luke 21:20, 24).[63]

This destruction and the chaos that follows it will bring such a radical realignment of the political and social world of Judea that one can only speak of it in terms that Isaiah, Ezekiel, and Joel used for the destruction of the Babylonians, Egyptians, and other wicked nations—the sun and moon will be darkened, the stars will fall, and the heavenly powers will be shaken (Matt. 24:29; Mark 13:24–25; Luke 21:11, 25).[64] Then, Jesus says, the Son of Man will come in the clouds of heaven, and his

63 Compare Dan. 9:27; 11:31; 12:11 with 1 Macc. 1:54, 59. That Luke interpreted "the abomination that causes desolation" as the Roman sack of Jerusalem is clear from his substitution of the "desolation" of Jerusalem for Mark's reference to "the abomination that causes desolation." For the same general perspective on these texts, see H. B. Swete, *The Gospel according to St. Mark* (London: Macmillan, 1898), 285–86; Wright, *Jesus and the Victory of God*, 349–54; and France, *Mark*, 522–26.

64 See, e.g., Isa. 13:6, 9–11, 19; 14:4, 12–15; Ezek. 32:5–8; Joel 2:10–11, 30–32; 3:14–15. Swete, *St. Mark*, 292, remarks aptly: "Physical phenomena are used to describe the upheaval of dynasties, or great moral and spiritual changes; and it is unnecessary to exact any other meaning from the words when they are adopted by Christ. The centuries which followed the fall of Jerusalem were destined to witness dynastic and social revolutions greater and wider than any which swept over Babylon and Egypt, and to these portents of Christian history the Lord's words may reasonably be referred." See also the discussion of these, and other similar texts, in Caird, *Jesus*, 18–19; Wright, *Jesus and the Victory of God*, 354–56; and France, *Mark*, 532–33.

angels will gather his chosen people from all corners of the earth (Matt. 24:30–31; Mark 13:26–27; Luke 27). Here Jesus uses symbolic language drawn again from Daniel 7:13, and Matthew identifies the meaning of this language clearly as a reference to Jesus' Parousia at the end of the age (Matt. 24:3, 27, 37, 39).[65]

In summary, Jesus' survey of history up to its end, as the Synoptic Gospels preserve it, strikes a balance between eschatological watchfulness and the sobering possibility of a long delay before his coming. The effects of sin, in the form of false religious claims, wars, natural disaster, persecution, and apostasy, will grow worse. One of the worst of these events will come when the Romans lay siege to Jerusalem and its temple and then trample them underfoot. This will result in a radical realignment of the political and social situation in Judea. Such "birth pangs" will place immense obstacles in the way of those who proclaim the gospel to the nations, but this proclamation will succeed. Eventually, at the end of all the turmoil, Jesus will return.

These same basic elements also emerge from Paul's attempt to correct the overzealous eschatological expectations of the Thessalonians in his second letter to them.[66] In response to erroneous teaching, supposedly with Paul's authority behind it, the Thessalonians have concluded that "the day of the Lord has already come" (2 Thess. 2:2). Paul throws a bucket of cold water on this idea by outlining events up to that day in a brief apocalypse (2:3–12). If we arrange his description of Jesus' Parousia and the events leading up to it chronologically, the correspondence with Jesus' own teaching is close.

First, at present, the eschatological power of lawlessness is already at work, although it is only visible to those to whom God has given the power to see it (2 Thess. 2:7a).[67] Paul maintains that God's restraining hand presently prevents this lawlessness from devolving into the chaos of evil that it will eventually become (2:6–7). This corresponds roughly to Jesus' claim that political strife and religious error—including false teaching connected with the idea that "the time is near" (Luke 21:8)—will continue as they have in the past (Matt. 24:3–8; Mark 13:3–8; Luke 21:7–11).

Second, God will remove the restraint he has placed on evil, and the forces of rebellion will gather together in a single figure, "the man of lawlessness," who will set "himself up in God's temple, proclaiming himself to be God" (2 Thess. 2:3–4). Satan will empower him to perform miracles and deceive people into thinking that

65 *Parousia* is the early Christian technical term for the coming of Jesus at the time of the general resurrection of the dead (1 Cor. 15:23; cf. 1 Thess. 2:19; 3:13; 4:15; 5:23; 2 Thess. 2:1, 8; James 5:7–8; 2 Peter 1:16; 3:4, 12; 1 John 2:28; BDAG, 780–81). For this reason it is necessary to part company at this point with Caird, *Jesus*, 20–22; Wright, *Jesus and the Victory of God*, 360–65, and France, *Mark*, 530–31, and to follow instead the century-old but perceptive exegesis of Swete, *St. Mark*, 293. Caird, Wright, and France believe that since Dan. 7:27 interprets 7:13 as "the saints, the people of the Most High," the reference in Mark 13:26 also has a corporate dimension. In their view, the coming of the Son of Man refers to Jesus and his people as the replacement of the destroyed Jerusalem temple. If this is correct, then Mark 13:27 ("and he will send his angels and gather his elect from the four winds") refers to the proclamation of the gospel after the destruction of Jerusalem but before the end as the means by which God will gather his multinational people from the four corners of the earth. This scenario, however, seems to contradict Matthew's interpretation of Mark's apocalyptic discourse.

66 Cf. David Wenham, *Paul: Follower of Jesus or Founder of Christianity?* (Grand Rapids: Eerdmans, 1995), 302.

67 This is probably the significance of Paul's reference to the "mystery" of lawlessness. See Abraham J. Malherbe, *The Letters to the Thessalonians* (AB 32B; New York: Doubleday, 2000), 423.

his claims are true (2:9–10). This figure seems to sum up in himself both the significance of the "abomination that causes desolation" to which Jesus referred (Matt. 24:15; Mark 13:14; Luke 21:20) and the significance of the miracle-working "false Christs and false prophets" who Jesus says will come prior to the advent of the Son of Man (Mark 13:21–22; Matt. 24:23–24; cf. Luke 17:23).

Like the "abomination," this person will insist on false worship in God's temple, and like the false teachers his miracles will deceive people into believing in him. Just as in Jesus' teaching the time of political and social chaos that the abomination's appearance unleashes yields eventually to the coming of the Son of Man (Matt. 24:30–31; Mark 13:26–27; Luke 21:27), so in 2 Thessalonians Jesus' appearance stops the frenzy of wickedness that "the man of lawlessness" put in motion (2 Thess. 2:8).

When we move from Jesus and Paul to the rest of the New Testament, we find the same general approach to the timing of the end. Evil will grow increasingly worse in the political and religious realm, so that oppression and heresy will plague the church. Eventually, however, God will bring all of this to an end with the coming of Christ. The Elder is aware of the tradition that this continuous uptick in evil will come to expression in an individual, and he, alone among the New Testament writers, calls this individual the "antichrist" (1 John 2:18). He is interested not in the political side of this figure but in his religiously deceptive side, and he identifies the advocates of a fleshless Christ who have split his community with the spirit of the antichrist. Their activity is a sign that Christians are living in the age of increased evil prior to the end:

> Dear children, this is the last hour; and as you have heard that the antichrist is coming, even now many antichrists have come. This is how we know it is the last hour. (1 John 2:18, 22; 4:3; 2 John 7)

John the seer brings both the political oppression and the religious deceptions of the Roman empire together in the figures of the two beasts who conspire to oppress the world, especially God's people. They derive their authority from Satan and arrogate to themselves the symbols of divinity (Rev. 13:2–4, 7, 11–12). The wickedness of Rome, however, will reach such maniacal proportions that it will implode as its former allies in oppression fight against it (17:1–18:24). Eventually the rider on the white horse, the King of kings and Lord of lords, will enter the fray, defeat Rome and its allies, and throw them all, together with Satan himself, into "the fiery lake of burning sulfur" (19:1–21).

The New Testament writers who speak of the timing of the end, therefore, give only a general outline of world history up to the Parousia of Christ. Evil will grow worse in both the political and religious realm. Jerusalem will suffer destruction and the temple will suffer desecration in a way reminiscent of the attempt of Antiochus IV Epiphanes to exercise political control through religious oppression. After that time, a radical realignment of the political and social world of the Jews will take place. The world will continue to suffer bitterly under the ravages of wickedness, and the church will experience special hardship at the hands both of governments and false teachers. Near the end, evil and suffering will reach almost unimaginable proportions, and the conspiracy between political and religious forces will lead even some within the church to fall away. It is then, according to Jesus, Paul, and John the seer, that Jesus will come, bringing relief to his people and judgment to the wicked.

According to the New Testament authors who use it, this outline of events has two implications. Its measure of specificity should prevent Christians from believing any deceptive claims that the end is nearer than it really is. At the same time, its latent ambiguity means that Christians must remain wakeful. The closing paragraphs of the book of Revelation ring out this truth: "Behold, I am coming soon! . . . Behold, I am coming soon! . . . Yes, I am coming soon!" (Rev. 22:7, 12, 20).

How Should Hope for the New Creation Influence Christian Behavior?

When New Testament authors speak of the certainty and imminence of the end and of the events that will precede the coming of the end, they are not engaged in academic speculation. Inevitably they describe the timing of Jesus' Parousia, the resurrection of the dead, and the eschatological judgment for pastoral reasons.[68] Sometimes they emphasize the imminence of the end in order to assure their readers that God will bring justice to the oppressors of his people. This is a primary concern of 2 Thessalonians, 1 Peter, and Revelation (2 Thess. 1:5–10; 1 Peter 4:5; Rev. 6:10; cf. James 5:1–8). Most often, however, when the writers of the New Testament texts remind their readers of the imminence of the end, they hope to encourage Christians to remain faithful. As Jesus puts it in Luke's gospel, "When the Son of Man comes, will he find faith on earth?" (Luke 18:8).

That the unknown time of Jesus' Parousia should provide an incentive for his followers to remain faithful appears frequently in Jesus' teaching in the Synoptic Gospels. This is an especially common theme in his parables. Here a number of metaphors contrast the disastrous consequences of being oblivious to the coming eschatological crisis with the reward that comes to those who live in the light of its impending arrival. Indifference to the reality of judgment, sleep through the night, drunkenness and drunken behavior, and irresponsible use of the time before the end characterize the unprepared, whereas wakefulness, sobriety, and faithful service mark those who are ready for its arrival.

Jesus says that his followers should not imitate Noah's generation, going about business as usual only to be surprised by the catastrophe of the flood (Matt. 24:37–42; Luke 17:26–35). They should not be like a man peacefully sleeping, unaware of the thief trying to break into his house (Matt. 24:43–44; Luke 12:39–40). They should avoid the example of the servant who, in the long interval before his master's return, beats his fellow servants and feasts with drunkards, only to fall under the master's wrath and be assigned a lot with the unfaithful at the master's return (Matt. 24:45–51; Luke 12:41–46; cf. Mark 13:35). They should not be like virgins, waiting far into the night

68 Malherbe, *Thessalonians*, 427–34, correctly emphasizes this element of Paul's apocalyptic survey in 2 Thess. 2:3–12.

for the bridegroom to appear, who fall asleep and let their lamps die out, only to be caught unprepared for the groom when he appears (Matt. 25:1–13; cf. Mark 13:35–37; Luke 12:35–38). Nor should they imitate a servant who makes no use of the money his master has given him to invest while gone on a long trip and who, in consequence, is thrown into the darkness when his master returns (Matt. 25:14–30; Luke 19:11–27; cf. Mark 13:34).

Probably under Jesus' influence, these metaphors of warning against complacency frequently reemerge elsewhere in the New Testament. Paul warns against investing in the façade of "peace and safety" that the structures of society provide or being a person of the night who sleeps and gets drunk (1 Thess. 5:3). "The day of the Lord," he says, "will come like a thief in the night" (5:2). Christians should therefore be awake and sober (5:4–8; cf. Rom. 13:11–12). Similarly, Peter recalls the judgment that came on Noah's generation in the sudden flood and reminds his readers that the Lord will come "like a thief" (2 Peter 2:5; 3:6).

What is involved in being ready for the coming of that Day? The New Testament authors tie the answer to this question closely to the nature of the Day itself. First, it will be a day on which God will judge people according to their response to the gospel. This response, as we saw in the section on faith, entails more than simply intellectual assent to the gospel or acknowledging that it is true; rather, it involves a radical reorientation of one's life. Matthew brings this out when he concludes Jesus' apocalyptic discourse with a section describing how the Son of Man, at the time of his coming, will gather the nations before him for judgment (Matt. 25:31–33). The criterion for judgment will be the way people from the nations have treated the messengers of the gospel (25:34–46; cf. 16:27). Have they given them food and clothing and sought to alleviate their suffering in times of persecution? In other words, have they responded positively to the gospel and acted on that response?[69]

Paul, similarly, reminds the Christians to whom he writes that the day of the Lord will entail judgment of their behavior. Some will discover that they will escape the purging fires of that Day only barely, with the scent of smoke still clinging to their clothes, because, although genuine Christians, their pride divided the church (1 Cor. 3:12–15). Others, whose conduct belies their claim to be part of God's kingdom, will not inherit that kingdom on the final Day (1 Cor. 6:9–10; Gal. 5:21; Eph. 5:5). Every believer will face a judgment according to works (Rom. 14:9–10; 2 Cor. 5:10).

On this, Paul speaks with the same voice as James, Peter, and John the seer. James insists that faith consisting merely of verbal assent, unmatched by any transformation of life, is dead (James 2:17, 26), and this conviction is consistent with his understanding of the final judgment. It will certainly be a time when God will judge the wealthy and influential persecutors of Christians (5:1–8; cf. 2:7), but it will also be a day on which Christians must give account for grumbling against one another (5:9).

Similarly, for Peter, persecutors of Christians within the church will face judgment (1 Peter 4:5), but the nearness of the end means that Christians too should be

69 For this understanding of the passage, see Craig L. Blomberg, *Matthew* (NAC; Nashville: Broadman, 1992), 375–80.

clear-minded, self-controlled, loving, hospitable, and, as in James, avoid grumbling (4:7–9; cf. 4:17–18). God will destroy false teachers among his people in the final cataclysm that establishes the new heavens and the new earth (2 Peter 2:4–10, 13, 17). "Since everything will be destroyed in this way," Peter asks his readers, "what kind of people ought you to be?"

John's lengthy and complicated prophecy also stands as a warning to Christians against compromise with the Roman beast and its oppressive, boastful policies, because both Rome and all who compromise with her will meet their end in the lake of fire (Rev. 20:9–10, 14–15). As in Paul, so here, the dead, whether believers or unbelievers, will be judged according to what they have done (20:12–13; cf. 2:23; 14:13; 20:12).

Second, that day will involve the resurrection of the dead. Jesus' resurrection marked the dawning of the general resurrection of the dead, an event that will take place on the final Day. This is a resurrection of the bodies of those who have died. Although transformed to make them immortal like Jesus' resurrected body, therefore, there will be continuity between the body that died and the body that is raised (1 Cor. 15:35–55).

According to Paul, this continuity has implications for the way people should use their bodies in the present. "The body is not meant for sexual immorality," he tells the Corinthians, "but for the Lord, and the Lord for the body. By his power God raised the Lord from the dead, and he will raise us also" (1 Cor. 6:13b–14). Here Paul assumes that the future resurrection of believers involves giving them bodies like the resurrected body of Jesus, and he draws from this the conclusion that the bodies of believers are "for the Lord" and not, therefore, for sexual immorality. The continuity of the resurrected body with the presently existing body implies that Christians must use their bodies in ways that are pleasing to the Lord, not to satisfy any bodily appetite in whatever way one may find convenient (6:12–13a).

Paul makes the same point later in the letter when he tells the skeptical Corinthians that if there is no resurrection of the dead, we might as well enjoy the pleasures of life in whatever way our whim desires and associate even with people who lead us into immorality (1 Cor. 15:32–33). Since Jesus' resurrection will find completion in a general resurrection, however, the bodily existence of Christians in the present should anticipate its immortal existence in the future. "Just as we have borne the likeness of the earthly man [i.e., Adam], so let us bear the likeness of the man from heaven [i.e., the resurrected and returning Jesus]" (15:49).[70] Even now we need to act in a way that is consistent with the immortality of our bodies.[71]

The same idea emerges in Philippians and Ephesians. In Philippians, Paul contrasts the way of life of the immoral people whom he wants the Philippians to avoid with the way Christians should live in light of the future that awaits them (Phil.

70 Some editions of the Greek New Testament and many translations read *phoresomen* ("we shall bear") here rather than *phoresōmen* ("let us bear"), but the textual evidence for *phoresōmen* is superior to the evidence for the alternative reading. On this, see Gordon D. Fee, *The First Epistle to the Corinthians* (NICNT; Grand Rapids: Eerdmans, 1987), 794–95, and ch. 12 above (on 1 Corinthians).

71 Cf. Wright, *Resurrection*, 290.

3:18–21). We should not indulge in gluttony and sexual immorality, says Paul, because we await the coming of our Savior from heaven and the transformation of "our lowly bodies so that they will be like his glorious body" (3:20–21). In Ephesians Paul substitutes the language of new creation for resurrection, but the idea is the same. His readers should "put on the new human being, created to be like God in true righteousness and holiness" (Eph. 4:22–23, aut.). They should live in a way that is consistent with the new creation God is establishing through his people.

The coming Day of Judgment, the resurrection, and the establishment of a new creation, therefore, are critically important in guiding the lives of believers in the present. Since that Day can come at any moment, they must be prepared for its arrival. This preparation will involve working out the ethical implications of two theological truths: God will judge all people according to their response to the gospel, and the response of faith will bring with it faithful service to God. God will also raise everyone from the dead, and believers will inhabit immortal bodies that will form part of God's new creation. Believers should begin to live in the ways that God has instructed his created beings to live. Their bodily existence is neither irrelevant nor momentary, but eternal. Christians should therefore treat their bodies and the bodies of others in light of the truth that they, in their bodily existence, belong to the Lord for eternity.

Summary

The New Testament writings are united in the conviction that the eschatological restoration both of Israel and of all things has dawned with the coming of Christ Jesus. The faith that people place in Jesus when they become his followers and that sustains them on the way is in part a settled conviction, or hope, that God will one day, through Christ, bring the day that has dawned to a glorious conclusion. At that time Adam's rebellion and its effects on all God's creatures will disappear. God will wipe every tear from the eyes of his people—death and bereavement will be banished. In short, the old order of things will pass away.

Christians must beware of two pitfalls: of thinking that this day will certainly come soon and of failing to be wakeful and ready for its coming. They can rest assured, however, that prior to its arrival, rebellion against God and the harmful effects of this rebellion on his creatures will only go from bad to worse. Being wakeful in the meantime means living in a way that recognizes that all God's people, although rescued from God's wrath by his gracious initiative in Christ Jesus, will nevertheless stand before his judgment seat to account for their actions. It also means recognizing that eternal existence is still embodied existence, and that Christians should use their bodies in ways that are consistent with the splendid and immortal form they will one day take.

THE CENTRALITY OF CHRIST TO THE THEOLOGICAL VISION OF THE NEW TESTAMENT

Although 1 Thessalonians is probably its earliest writing, the New Testament begins logically with Jesus. It makes the astonishing claim that in this rabbi from Nazareth and Capernaum, the God who created the universe lived among human beings. He lived specifically among his chosen and beloved people Israel as the Messiah. Because God's creation, both human and angelic, was in a state of rebellion against him, however, God's people Israel, and the world God created, rejected and killed Jesus. Surprisingly, this death was the very means through which God began to reconcile his rebellious human creation to himself and to defeat the malevolent demonic powers. Jesus' death served as an atoning sacrifice for human sin, and, in Jesus' death, resurrection, and heavenly session at God's right hand, God defeated the invisible, cosmic forces of rebellion against him. Since his resurrection, Jesus, who has always been God's Son, reigns in power as the victorious Messiah.

Through his Spirit, God has assembled a people who believe that Jesus is Israel's Messiah and that through him, God has begun to restore his rebellious and devastated creation to the glory it had before Adam sinned. This people live by faith—the steady trust that, through Christ, God has begun to mend his weak and sinful creatures and the disastrous results of their sin. Since faith in Christ is the hallmark of this people, they need not come merely from Israel but from all the nations of the earth. They form the new temple of God, the dwelling place of his Spirit, who assures them of their future inheritance and gives them guidance, both in their proclamation of the gospel to others and in how they should live in the often oppressive societies that surround them.

One day the risen Christ will return. That Day of the Lord will bring God's purposes to their glorious climax. Evil and death will be banished, God's creation will be restored to its former glory, and a vast multitude of God's human, angelic, and even animal creation will give united praise to God and share his glory for eternity. Before that Day, which can come at any point, Christians must continue to be faithful, remembering that they will stand before God one day and will live with him in an immortal but bodily existence.

All of this—from the coming of the Messiah to his rejection among God's chosen people, to his resurrection and heavenly session, the outpouring of God's Spirit, the assembling of a multiethnic people, and the Messiah's return—was anticipated in Israel's Scriptures. The New Testament articulates the final chapter of a story that begins there.

For all the distinctiveness of its discrete textual witnesses, the New Testament is remarkably homogenous in its commitment to these basic themes. It offers a compelling vision of reality, both the horrific and the beautiful, and it invites those who read its various texts sympathetically to adopt its Christ-centered vision of the universe as their own.

WORKS CITED

Aalen, Sverre. *Guds Sønn og Guds Rike: Nytestamentlige Studier*. Oslo: Universitetsforlaget, 1973.

Achtemeier, Paul J. *1 Peter*. Hermeneia. Minneapolis: Fortress, 1996.

_____. "The Continuing Quest for Coherence in St. Paul: An Experiment in Thought." Pages 132–45 in *Theology and Ethics in Paul and His Interpreters: Essays in Honor of Victor Paul Furnish*. Edited by Eugene H. Lovering and Jerry L. Sumney. Nashville: Abingdon, 1996.

_____. "Finding the Way to Paul's Theology: A Response to J. Christiaan Beker and J. Paul Sampley." Pages 25–36 in *Pauline Theology, Volume I: Thessalonians, Philippians, Galatians, Philemon*. Edited by Jouette M. Bassler. Minneapolis: Fortress, 1991.

Aland, Barbara, Kurt Aland, et al. *Novum Testamentum Graece*. 27th ed. Stuttgart: Deutsche Bibelgesellschaft, 1993.

Aland, Kurt. *The Problem of the New Testament Canon*. Contemporary Studies in Theology 2. London: A. R. Mowbray, 1962.

Alexander, Loveday. "Ancient Book Production and the Circulation of the Gospels." Pages 71–111 in *The Gospels for All Christians: Rethinking the Gospel Audiences*. Edited by Richard Bauckham. Grand Rapids: Eerdmans, 1998.

_____. "Hellenistic Letter-Forms and the Structure of Philippians." *Journal for the Study of the New Testament* 37 (1989): 87–101.

Allison, Dale C. *The End of the Ages Has Come: An Early Interpretation of the Passion and Resurrection of Jesus*. Philadelphia: Fortress, 1985.

_____. *The New Moses: A Matthean Typology*. Minneapolis: Fortress, 1993.

Alter, Robert. *The Art of Biblical Narrative*. New York: Basic Books, 1981.

(Pseudo-)Aristeas. *To Philocrates*. New York: Harper & Brothers, 1951.

Arnold, Clinton E. *The Colossian Syncretism: The Interface between Christianity and Folk Belief at Colossae*. Wissenschaftliche Untersuchungen zum Alten und Neuen Testament 2.77. Tübingen: J. C. B. Mohr (Paul Siebeck), 1995.

_____. *Ephesians, Power and Magic: The Concept of Power in Ephesians in Light of Its Historical Setting*. Society for the Study of the New Testament Monograph Series 63. Cambridge: Cambridge University Press, 1989.

Ashton, John. *The Religion of Paul the Apostle*. New Haven, Conn.: Yale University Press, 2000.

_____. *Understanding the Fourth Gospel*. Oxford: Clarendon, 1991.

Attridge, Harold W. *Hebrews*. Hermeneia. Philadelphia: Fortress, 1989.

Augustine. *Confessions*. Oxford: Oxford University Press, 1991.

Aune, David E. *Prophecy in Early Christianity and the Ancient Mediterranean World*. Grand Rapids: Eerdmans, 1983.

_____. *Revelation 1–5*. Word Biblical Commentary 52A. Dallas: Word, 1997.

_____. *Revelation 6–16*. Word Biblical Commentary 52B. Nashville: Nelson, 1998.

_____. *Revelation 17–22*. Word Biblical Commentary 52C. Nashville: Nelson, 1998.

Aus, Roger D. "The Liturgical Background of the Necessity and Propriety of Giving Thanks according to 2 Thes 1:3." *Journal of Biblical Literature* 92 (1973): 432–38.

Baarda, Tjitze. "ΔΙΑΦΩΝΙΑ—ΣΥΜΦΩΝΙΑ: Factors in the Harmonization of the Gospels, Especially in the Diatessaron of Tatian." Pages 133–54 in *Gospel Traditions in the Second Century, Origins, Recensions, Text, and Transmission*. Edited by William L. Petersen. Christianity and Judaism in Antiquity 3. Notre Dame, Ind.: University of Notre Dame Press, 1989.

Bachmann, H., and W. A. Slaby, eds. *Concordance to the Novum Testamentum Graece.* 3rd ed. Berlin: Walter de Gruyter, 1987.

Baird, William. *History of New Testament Research.* 3 vols. Minneapolis: Fortress, 1992–.

Balch, David L. *Let Wives Be Submissive: The Domestic Code in 1 Peter.* Society of Biblical Literature Monograph Series 26. Atlanta: Scholars, 1981.

Balla, Peter. *Challenges to New Testament Theology: An Attempt to Justify the Enterprise,* Wissenschaftliche Untersuchungen zum Alten und Neuen Testament 2.95. Tübingen: Mohr, 1997.

Balz, Horst, and Gerhard Schneider, eds. *Exegetical Dictionary of the New Testament.* 3 vols. Grand Rapids: Eerdmans, 1990–93.

Barclay, John M. G. "Conflict in Thessalonica." *Catholic Biblical Quarterly* 55 (1993): 512–30.

_____. "'Do We Undermine the Law?' A Study of Romans 14.1–15.6." Pages 287–308 in *Paul and the Mosaic Law.* Edited by James D. G. Dunn. Wissenschaftliche Untersuchungen zum Alten und Neuen Testament 89. Tübingen: J. C. B. Mohr (Paul Siebeck), 1996.

_____. "The Family as the Bearer of Religion in Judaism and Early Christianity." Pages 66–80 in *Constructing Early Christian Families: Family as Social Reality and Metaphor.* Edited by Halvor Moxnes. London: Routledge, 1997.

_____. *Obeying the Truth: Paul's Ethics in Galatians.* Minneapolis: Fortress, 1988.

_____. "Ordinary but Different: Colossians and Hidden Moral Identity," *Australian Biblical Review* 49 (2001): 34–52.

_____. "Paul, Philemon and the Dilemma of Christian Slave-Ownership." *New Testament Studies* 37 (1991): 161–86.

Barker, Margaret. *The Revelation of Jesus Christ Which God Gave to Him to Show to His Servants What Must Soon Take Place (Revelation 1.1).* Edinburgh: T. & T. Clark, 2000.

Barnett, Paul. *The Second Epistle to the Corinthians.* New International Commentary on the New Testament. Grand Rapids: Eerdmans, 1997.

Barnouin, M. "Les problèmes de traduction concernant II Thess. II.6–7." *New Testament Studies* 23 (1976–77): 482–98.

Barr, James. *The Scope and Authority of the Bible.* Philadelphia: Westminster, 1980.

Barrett, C. K. *The Acts of the Apostles.* International Critical Commentary. 2 vols. Edinburgh: T. & T. Clark, 1994–98.

_____. "The Centre of the New Testament and the Canon." Pages 5–21 in *Die Mitte des Neuen Testaments: Einheit und Vielfalt neutestamentlicher Theologie: Festschrift für Eduard Schweizer zum siebzigsten Geburtstag.* Edited by Ulrich Luz and Hans Weder. Göttingen: Vandenhoeck & Ruprecht, 1983.

_____. *A Commentary on the First Epistle to the Corinthians.* Harper's New Testament Commentaries. New York: Harper & Row, 1968.

_____. *A Commentary on the Second Epistle to the Corinthians.* Harper's New Testament Commentaries. New York: Harper & Row, 1973.

_____. *The Epistle to the Romans.* Black's New Testament Commentaries. London: A. C. Black, 1957.

_____. *The Epistle to the Romans.* Rev. ed. Peabody, Mass.: Hendrickson, 1991.

_____. *Essays on Paul.* Philadelphia: Westminster, 1982.

_____. *The Gospel according to St. John.* 2nd ed. Philadelphia: Westminster, 1978.

_____. "Jews and Judaizers in the Epistles of Ignatius." Pages 220–44 in *Jews, Greeks and Christians: Religious Cultures in Late Antiquity*. Edited by Robert Hamerton-Kelly and Robin Scroggs. Studies in Judaism and Late Antiquity 21. Leiden: E. J. Brill, 1976.

_____. "John and Judaism." Pages 231–46 in *Anti-Judaism and the Fourth Gospel*. Edited by Reimund Bieringer, Didier Pollefeyt, and Frederique Vandecasteele-Vanneuville. Louisville: Westminster John Knox, 2001.

_____. *Paul: An Introduction to His Thought*. Louisville: Westminster John Knox, 1994.

Barth, Karl. *The Epistle to the Philippians*. Richmond: John Knox, 1962.

Barth, Markus. *Ephesians: Introduction, Translation, and Commentary on Chapters 1–3*. Anchor Bible 34. Garden City, N.Y.: Doubleday, 1974.

Barton, John. *Holy Writings, Sacred Text: The Canon in Early Christianity*. Louisville: Westminster John Knox, 1997.

Bassler, Jouette M. "The Enigmatic Sign: 2 Thessalonians 1:5." *Catholic Biblical Quarterly* 46 (1984): 496–510.

Bauckham, Richard. The Climax of Prophecy: Studies on the Book of Revelation. Edinburgh: T. & T. Clark, 1993.

_____. "James and the Jerusalem Church." Pages 415–80 in *The Book of Acts in Its Palestinian Setting*. Edited by Richard Bauckham. Grand Rapids: Eerdmans, 1995.

_____. *James: Wisdom of James, Disciple of Jesus the Sage*. New Testament Readings. London: Routledge, 1999.

_____. *Jude, 2 Peter*. Word Biblical Commentary 50. Waco, Tex.: Word, 1983.

_____. *Jude and the Relatives of Jesus in the Early Church*. Edinburgh: T. & T. Clark, 1990.

_____. *The Theology of the Book of Revelation*. New Testament Theology. Cambridge: Cambridge University Press, 1993.

Bauckham, Richard, ed. *The Gospels for All Christians: Rethinking the Gospel Audiences*. Grand Rapids: Eerdmans, 1998.

Bauer, Walter. *A Greek-English Lexicon of the New Testament and Other Early Christian Literature*. 3rd ed. Revised and edited by Frederick William Danker. Chicago: University of Chicago Press, 2000.

_____. *Orthodoxy and Heresy in Earliest Christianity*. London: SCM, 1972.

Baur, Ferdinand Christian. *The Church History of the First Three Centuries*. 2 vols. London: Williams and Norgate, 1878–79.

_____. "Die Christuspartei in der korinthischen Gemeinde, der Gegensatz des petrinischen und paulinischen Christentum in der ältesten Kirche, der Apostel Petrus in Rom." *Tübingen Zeitschrift für Theologie* 4 (1831): 61–206.

_____. *Die ignatianischen Briefe und ihr neuester Kritiker*. Tübingen: Ludwig Friedrich Fues, 1848.

_____. *Paul, The Apostle of Jesus Christ, His Life and Work, His Epistles and His Doctrine: A Contribution to a Critical History of Primitive Christianity*. 2 vols. 2nd ed. London: Williams & Norgate, 1876.

_____. *Vorlesungen über neutestamentliche Theologie*. Edited by F. F. Baur. Darmstadt: Wissenschaftliche Buchgesellschaft, 1973.

Beacham, Richard C. *Spectacle Entertainments of Early Imperial Rome*. New Haven, Conn.: Yale University Press, 1999.

Beale, G. K. "The Eschatological Conception of New Testament Theology." Pages 11–52 in *Eschatology in Bible and Theology: Evangelical Essays at the Dawn of a New Millenium*. Edited by Kent E. Brower and Mark W. Elliott. Downers Grove, Ill.: InterVarsity Press, 1997.

_____. *The Book of Revelation*. New International Greek Testament Commentary. Grand Rapids: Eerdmans, 1999.

Beard, Mary, John North, and Simon Price. *Religions of Rome*. 2 vols. Cambridge: Cambridge University Press, 1998.

Beare, Francis Wright. *The First Epistle of Peter*. Oxford: Blackwell, 1947.

Beasley-Murray, George R. *Jesus and the Kingdom of God*. Grand Rapids: Eerdmans, 1986.

_____. *John*. Word Biblical Commentary 36. Waco, Tex.: Word, 1987.

_____. *Baptism in the New Testament*. Grand Rapids: Eerdmans, 1962.

Becker, Jürgen. *Paul: Apostle to the Gentiles*. Louisville: Westminster John Knox, 1993.

Beker, J. Christiaan. *Heirs of Paul: Their Legacy in the New Testament and the Church Today*. Grand Rapids: Eerdmans, 1991.

_____. *Paul the Apostle: The Triumph of God in Life and Thought*. Philadelphia: Fortress, 1980.

_____. "Recasting Pauline Theology: The Coherence-Contingency Scheme as Interpretive Model." Pages 15–24 in *Pauline Theology, Volume I: Thessalonians, Philippians, Galatians, Philemon*. Edited by Jouette M. Bassler. Minneapolis: Fortress, 1991.

Berger, Klaus. *Theologiegeschichte des Urchristentums: Theologie des Neuen Testaments*. 2nd ed. Tübingen: Francke, 1995.

Berkowitz, L. and K. A. Squitier. *Thesaurus linguae graecae: Canon of Greek Authors and Works*. 3rd ed. Oxford: Oxford University Press, 1990.

Best, Ernest. *1 Peter*. New Century Bible. Grand Rapids: Eerdmans, 1971.

_____. *A Commentary on the First and Second Epistles to the Thessalonians*. Harper's New Testament Commentaries. New York: Harper & Row, 1972.

_____. *A Critical and Exegetical Commentary on Ephesians*. International Critical Commentary. Edinburgh: T. & T. Clark, 1998.

_____. *Essays on Ephesians*. Edinburgh: T. & T. Clark, 1997.

Betz, Hans Dieter. *2 Corinthians 8 and 9: A Commentary on Two Administrative Letters of the Apostle Paul*. Hermeneia. Philadelphia: Fortress , 1985.

_____. *The Sermon on the Mount*. Hermeneia. Minneapolis: Fortress, 1995.

Bieringer, R. "Teilungshypothesen zum 2.Korintherbrief: Ein Forschungsüberblick." Pages 66–105 in *Studies on 2 Corinthians*. Bibliotheca ephemeridum theologicarum lovaniensium 112. Edited by R. Bieringer and J. Lambrecht. Leuven: Leuven University Press, 1994.

Biguzzi, Giancarlo. "Ephesus, Its Artemision, Its Temple to the Flavian Emperors, and Idolatry in Revelation." *Novum Testamentum* 40 (1998): 227–90.

Bjerkelund, Carl J. *Tauta Egeneto: die Präzisierungssätze im Johannesevangelium*. Wissenschaftliche Untersuchungen zum Alten und Neuen Testament 40. Tübingen: J. C. B. Mohr (Paul Siebeck), 1987.

Black, C. Clifton. "Christ Crucified in Paul and in Mark: Reflections on an Intracanonical Conversation." Pages 184–206 in *Theology and Ethics in Paul and His Interpreters: Essays in Honor of Victor Paul Furnish*. Edited by Eugene H. Lovering and Jerry L. Sumney. Nashville: Abingdon, 1996.

Block, Daniel I. *The Book of Ezekiel: Chapters 25–48*. New International Commentary on the Old Testament. Grand Rapids: Eerdmans, 1998.

Bock, Darrell L. *Jesus according to Scripture: Restoring the Portrait from the Gospels*. Grand Rapids: Baker, 2002.

_____. *Luke 1:1–9:50*. Baker Exegetical Commentary on the New Testament 3A. Grand Rapids: Baker, 1994.

_____. *Luke 9:21–24:53*. Baker Exegetical Commentary on the New Testament 3B. Grand Rapids: Eerdmans, 1996.

Bockmuehl, Markus. *The Epistle to the Philippians.* Black's New Testament Commentary. Peabody, Mass.: Hendrickson, 1998.

Boers, Hendrikus. *What Is New Testament Theology: The Rise of Criticism and the Problem of a Theology of the New Testament.* Philadelphia: Fortress, 1979.

Bonz, Marianne Palmer. *The Past as Legacy: Luke–Acts and Ancient Epic.* Minneapolis: Fortress, 2000.

Boobyer, G. H. "The Secrecy Motif in St. Mark's Gospel." *New Testament Studies* 6 (1959–60): 225–35.

Booth, Alan. "The Age for Reclining and Its Attendant Perils." Pages 105–20 in *Dining in a Classical Context.* Edited by William J. Slater. Ann Arbor: University of Michigan, 1991.

Bornkamm, Günther. "End-expectation and Church in Matthew." Pages 15–51 in *Tradition and Interpretation in Matthew.* Edited by Günther Bornkamm, Gerhard Barth, and Heinz Joachim Held. New Testament Library. Philadelphia: Westminster, 1963.

_____. "The Letter to the Romans as Paul's Last Will and Testament." Pages 16–28 in *The Romans Debate.* Edited by Karl P. Donfried. Rev. and exp. ed. Peabody, Mass.: Hendrickson, 1991.

_____. *Paul.* New York: Harper & Row, 1971.

Bovon, François. *Das Evangelium nach Lukas (Lk 1,1–9,50).* Evangelisch-katholischer Kommentar zum Neuen Testament 3.1. Zürich: Benziger Verlag/Neukirchen-Vluyn: Neukirchener Verlag, 1989.

_____. *Das Evangelium nach Lukas (Lk 9,51–14,35).* Evangelisch-katholischer Kommentar zum Neuen Testament 3.2. Zürich: Benziger Verlag/Neukirchen-Vluyn: Neukirchener Verlag, 1996.

Bowersock, G. W. *Greek Sophists in the Roman Empire.* Oxford: Oxford University Press, 1969.

Braaten, Carl E. *Mother Church: Ecclesiology and Ecumenism.* Minneapolis: Fortress, 1998.

Bradley, K. R. *Slaves and Masters in the Roman Empire: A Study in Social Control.* New York: Oxford University Press, 1987.

Braun, F.-M. *Jean le théologien: Le grandes traditions d'Israël l'accord des Écritures d'après le Quatrième Évangile.* Études bibliques. Paris: Librairie Lecoffre, 1964.

Braun, Herbert. "Hebt die heutige neutestamentliche-exegetische Forschung den Kanon auf?" *Fuldaer Hefte* 12 (1960): 9–24.

Brecht, Martin. *Martin Luther.* 2 vols. Minneapolis: Fortress, 1990.

Brodie, Thomas L. *The Gospel according to John: A Literary and Theological Commentary.* New York: Oxford, 1993.

Brooke, A. E. *A Critical and Exegetical Commentary on the Johannine Epistles.* International Critical Commentary. New York: Scribner's, 1928.

Brown, Raymond E. *The Birth of the Messiah.* 2nd ed. Anchor Bible Reference Library. New York: Doubleday, 1997.

_____. *The Community of the Beloved Disciple.* New York: Paulist, 1979.

_____. *The Epistles of John.* Anchor Bible 30. Garden City, N.Y.: Doubleday, 1982.

_____. *The Gospel according to John I–XII.* Anchor Bible 29. New York: Doubleday, 1966.

_____. *The Gospel according to John XIII–XXI.* Anchor Bible 29A. New York: Doubleday, 1970.

_____. "The Gospel of Peter and Canonical Gospel Priority." *New Testament Studies* 33 (1987): 321–43.

Brownlee, William H. *The Midrash Pesher of Habakkuk.* Society of Biblical Literature Monograph Series 24. Missoula, Mont.: Scholars, 1979.

Brox, Norbert. *Der erste Petrusbrief.* 3rd ed. Evangelisch-katholischer Kommentar zum Neuen Testament. Zürich: Benziger/ Neukirchen-Vluyn: Neukirchener Verlag, 1989.

_____. *Die Pastoralbriefe.* Regensburger Neues Testament 7. Regensburg: Verlag Friedrich Pustet, 1969.

Bruce, F. F. *I & II Corinthians.* New Century Bible. Grand Rapids: Eerdmans, 1971.

_____. *1 & 2 Thessalonians.* Word Biblical Commentary 45. Waco, Tex.: Word, 1982.

_____. *The Acts of the Apostles: The Greek Text with Introduction and Commentary.* 2nd ed. London: Tyndale, 1952.

_____. "The 'Christ Hymn' of Colossians 1:15–20." *Bibliotheca sacra* 141 (1984): 99–111.

_____. *Commentary on Galatians.* New International Greek Testament Commentary. Grand Rapids: Eerdmans, 1982.

_____. *The Epistles to the Colossians, to Philemon, and to the Ephesians.* New International Commentary on the New Testament. Grand Rapids: Eerdmans, 1984.

_____. *The Epistle to the Hebrews.* Rev. ed. New International Commentary on the New Testament. Grand Rapids: Eerdmans, 1990.

_____. *The Gospel of John.* Grand Rapids: Eerdmans, 1983.

_____. *Paul: Apostle of the Heart Set Free.* Grand Rapids: Eerdmans, 1977.

_____. *Philippians.* Good News Commentary. San Francisco: Harper & Row, 1983.

_____. "The Romans Debate—Continued." Pages 175–94 in *The Romans Debate.* Edited by Karl P. Donfried. Rev. and exp. ed. Peabody, Mass.: Hendrickson, 1991.

Bultmann, Rudolf. *Faith and Understanding.* Edited by Robert W. Funk. Philadelphia: Fortress, 1987.

_____. *The Gospel of John: A Commentary.* Philadelphia: Westminster, 1971.

_____. *The History of the Synoptic Tradition.* New York: Harper & Row, 1963.

_____. "Is Exegesis without Presuppositions Possible?" Pages 289–96 in *Existence and Faith: Shorter Writings of Rudolf Bultmann.* Edited by Schubert M. Ogden. Cleveland, Ohio: World, 1960.

_____. *The Johannine Epistles.* Hermeneia. Philadelphia: Fortress, 1973.

_____. "The Problem of Ethics in Paul." Pages 195–216 in *Understanding Paul's Ethics: Twentieth Century Approaches.* Edited by Brian S. Rosner. Grand Rapids: Eerdmans, 1995.

_____. *The Second Letter to the Corinthians.* Minneapolis: Augsburg, 1985.

_____. *Theology of the New Testament.* 2 vols. New York: Charles Scribner's Sons, 1951–1955.

Büsching, Friderich. *Gedanken von der Beschaffenheit und dem Vorzug der biblisch-dogmatischen Theologie vor der alten und neuen Scholastichen, und von theologischen Aufgaben.* Lemod: Meyerschen Buchhandlung, 1758.

Byrne, Brendan. *Romans.* Sacra Pagina 6. Collegeville, Minn.: Liturgical, 1996.

Byrskog, Samuel. *Story as History—History as Story: The Gospel Tradition in the Context of Ancient Oral History.* Wissenschaftliche Untersuchungen zum Alten und Neuen Testament 123. Tübingen: J. C. B. Mohr (Paul Siebeck), 2000.

Cadbury, Henry J. *The Making of Luke–Acts.* New York: Macmillan, 1927.

Caird, G. B. *A Commentary on the Revelation of St. John the Divine.* Harper's New Testament Commentaries. New York: Harper & Row, 1966.

_____. *Jesus and the Jewish Nation.* London: Athlone, 1965.

_____. *New Testament Theology.* Edited by L. D. Hurst. Oxford: Oxford University Press, 1994.

_____. *Paul's Letters from Prison (Ephesians, Philippians, Colossians, Philemon).* Oxford: Oxford University Press, 1976.

Calvin, John. *Commentaries on the Epistles of Paul to the Galatians and Ephesians.* Grand Rapids: Eerdmans, 1948.

_____. *The Epistle of Paul the Apostle to the Hebrews and the First and Second Epistles of St. Peter.* Grand Rapids: Eerdmans, 1963.

_____. *Commentaries on the Epistles of Paul the Apostle to the Philippians, Colossians, and Thessalonians.* Grand Rapids: Eerdmans, 1948.

Cameron, Ron. *The Other Gospels: Non-Canonical Gospel Texts.* Philadelphia: Westminster, 1982.

Campbell, R. Alastair. *The Elders: Seniority within Earliest Christianity.* Studies of the New Testament and Its World. Edinburgh: T. & T. Clark, 1994.

Caragounis, Chrys C. *The Ephesian* Mysterion*: Meaning and Content.* Coniectanea neotestamentica 8. Lund: CWK Gleerup, 1977.

Carroll, John T. "Present and Future in Fourth Gospel 'Eschatology.'" *Biblical Theology Bulletin* 19 (1989): 63–69.

_____. "Luke's Crucifixion Scene." Pages 108–24 in *Reimagining the Death of the Lukan Jesus.* Edited by Dennis D. Sylva. Bonner biblische Beiträge 73. Frankfurt am Main: Anton Hain, 1990.

Carson, D. A. *The Gospel according to John.* Pillar New Testament Commentaries. Grand Rapids: Eerdmans, 1991.

_____. "Matthew." Pages 3–599 in vol. 8 of *The Expositor's Bible Commentary.* Edited by Frank E. Gaebelein. 12 vols. Grand Rapids: Zondervan, 1976–1992.

_____. "Unity and Diversity in the New Testament: The Possibility of Systematic Theology." Pages 65–95 in *Scripture and Truth.* Edited by D. A. Carson and John D. Woodbridge. Grand Rapids: Zondervan, 1983.

Cary, M. *A History of Rome Down to the Reign of Constantine.* 2nd ed. London: Macmillan, 1957.

Chadwick, Henry. *Introduction to Origen: Contra Celsum.* Cambridge: Cambridge University Press, 1953.

Charlesworth, James H. *The Old Testament Pseudepigrapha.* 2 vols. New York: Doubleday, 1983–85.

Chester, Andrew. "The Theology of James." Pages 1–62 in *The Theology of the Letters of James, Peter, and Jude.* Edited by Andrew Chester and Ralph P. Martin. New Testament Theology. Cambridge: Cambridge University Press, 1994.

Childs, Brevard S. *Isaiah.* Old Testament Library. Louisville: Westminster John Knox, 2001.

_____. *The New Testament as Canon: An Introduction.* Philadelphia: Fortress, 1985.

Chilton, Bruce D. "Assessing Progress in the Third Quest." Pages 15–25 in *Authenticating the Words of Jesus.* Edited by Bruce Chilton and Craig A. Evans. New Testament Tools and Studies 28. Leiden: E. J. Brill, 1999.

Cicero, *On Duties.* Cambridge Texts in the History of Political Thought. Cambridge: Cambridge University Press, 1991.

_____. *Cicero: The Nature of the Gods.* Oxford: Clarendon, 1997.

Collange, Jean-François. *The Epistle of Saint Paul to the Philippians.* London: Epworth, 1979.

Conzelmann, Hans. *The Theology of St. Luke.* Philadelphia: Fortress, 1961.

Crossan, John Dominic. *Four Other Gospels: Shadows on the Contours of Canon.* Minneapolis: Winston, 1985.

_____. *The Historical Jesus: The Life of a Mediterranean Jewish Peasant.* San Francisco: HarperSanFrancisco, 1991.

_____. *Jesus: A Revolutionary Biography.* New York: HarperCollins, 1994.

Cranfield, C. E. B. *The Epistle to the Romans.* 2 vols. International Critical Commentary. Edinburgh: T. & T. Clark, 1975–79.

_____. *The Gospel according to Saint Mark.* Cambridge Greek Testament Commentary. Cambridge: Cambridge University Press, 1959.

_____. *On Romans.* Edinburgh: T. & T. Clark, 1998.

Cullmann, Oscar. *The Early Church.* Edited by A. J. B. Higgins. London: SCM, 1956.

_____. *Christ and Time.* London: SCM, 1951.

_____. *Peter: Disciple, Apostle, Martyr: A Historical and Theological Essay.* Philadelphia: Westminster, 1953.

_____. "Die Pluralität der Evangelien als theologisches Problem im Altertum." *Theologische Zeitschrift* 1 (1945): 23–42.

Culpepper, R. Alan. "Anti-Judaism in the Fourth Gospel as a Theological Problem for Christian Interpreters." Pages 61–82 in *Anti-Judaism and the Fourth Gospel.* Edited by Reimund Bieringer, Didier Pollefeyt, and Frederique Vandecasteele-Vanneuville. Louisville: Westminster John Knox, 2001.

Dahl, Nils A. "'Do Not Wonder!' John 5:28–29 and Johannine Eschatology Once More." Pages 322–36 in *The Conversation Continues: Studies in Paul and John in Honor of J. Louis Martyn.* Edited by Robert T. Fortna and Beverly R. Gaventa. Nashville: Abingdon, 1990.

_____. *Studies in Paul: Theology for the Early Christian Mission.* Minneapolis: Augsburg, 1997.

Dalton, William Joseph. *Christ's Proclamation to the Spirits: A Study of 1 Peter 3:18–4:6.* 2nd ed. Analecta biblica 23. Rome: Editrice Pontificio Istituto Biblico, 1989.

Davids, Peter. *Commentary on James.* New International Greek Testament Commentary. Grand Rapids: Eerdmans, 1982.

_____. *The First Epistle of Peter.* New International Commentary on the New Testament. Grand Rapids: Eerdmans, 1990.

Davies, W. D. *Paul and Rabbinic Judaism: Some Rabbinic Elements in Pauline Theology.* 4th ed. Philadelphia: Fortress, 1980.

_____. *The Setting of the Sermon on the Mount.* Cambridge: Cambridge University Press, 1964.

Davies, W. D., and Dale C. Allison. *The Gospel according to Matthew.* 3 vols. International Critical Commentary. Edinburgh: T. & T. Clark, 1988–1997.

Deidun, T. J. *New Covenant Morality in Paul.* Analecta biblica 89. Rome: Biblical Institute Press, 1981.

Deissmann, Adolf. *Light from the Ancient East: The New Testament Illustrated by Recently Discovered Texts of the Graeco-Roman World.* London: Hodder & Stoughton, 1927.

DeMaris, Richard E. *The Colossian Controversy: Wisdom in Dispute at Colossae.* Journal for the Study of the New Testament Supplement 96. Sheffield: Sheffield Academic Press, 1994.

Dibelius, Martin. *From Tradition to Gospel.* Cambridge: James Clarke, 1971.

_____. *James.* Revised by Heinrich Greeven. Hermeneia. Philadelphia: Fortress, 1975.

Dibelius, Martin, and Hans Conzelmann. *The Pastoral Epistles.* Hermeneia. Philadelphia: Fortress, 1972.

Dodd, C. H. *According to the Scriptures: The Substructure of New Testament Theology.* London: Nisbet, 1952.

_____. *The Epistle to the Romans.* Moffatt New Testament Commentary. London: Hodder & Stoughton, 1932.

_____. *The Interpretation of the Fourth Gospel.* Cambridge: Cambridge University Press, 1953.

_____. *The Johannine Epistles.* Moffatt New Testament Commentary. London: Hodder and Stoughton, 1946.

_____. *New Testament Studies.* Manchester: Manchester University Press, 1953.

Donaldson, Terence L. *Paul and the Gentiles: Remapping the Apostle's Convictional World.* Minneapolis: Fortress, 1997.
Donfried, Karl P. "The Cults of Thessalonica and the Thessalonian Correspondence." *New Testament Studies* 31 (1985): 336–56.
_____. "The Theology of 1 Thessalonians." Pages 3–79 in *The Theology of the Shorter Pauline Letters.* Edited by Karl P. Donfried and I. Howard Marshall. New Testament Theology. Cambridge: Cambridge University Press, 1993.
Duhm, Bernard. *Das Buch Jesaia.* 4th ed. Göttingen: Vandenhoeck & Ruprecht, 1922.
Dunn, James D. G. *Christology in the Making.* 2nd ed. Grand Rapids: Eerdmans, 1996.
_____. *The Epistle to the Galatians.* Black's New Testament Commentary. Peabody, Mass.: Hendrickson, 1993.
_____. *The Epistles to the Colossians and to Philemon.* New International Greek Testament Commentary. Grand Rapids: Eerdmans, 1996.
_____. *Jesus, Paul and the Law: Studies in Mark and Galatians.* Louisville: Westminster John Knox, 1990.
_____. *Jesus Remembered.* Grand Rapids: Eerdmans, 2003.
_____. "Prolegomena to a Theology of Paul." *New Testament Studies* 40 (1994): 407–32.
_____. "In Quest of Paul's Theology: Retrospect and Prospect." Pages 95–115 in *Pauline Theology Volume IV: Looking Back, Pressing On.* Edited by E. Elizabeth Johnson and David M. Hay. Society of Biblical Literature Symposium Series 4. Atlanta: Scholars, 1997.
_____. *Romans 1–8.* Word Biblical Commentary 38A. Dallas: Word, 1988.
_____. *Romans 9–16.* Word Biblical Commentary 38B. Dallas: Word, 1988.
_____. *The Theology of Paul the Apostle.* Grand Rapids: Eerdmans, 1998.
_____. *Unity and Diversity in the New Testament: An Inquiry into the Character of Earliest Christianity.* Philadelphia: Westminster, 1977.
Dupont, Jacques. *ΣΥΝ ΧΡΙΣΤΩΙ: L'union avec le Christ suivant Saint Paul.* Paris: Éditions de l'Abbaye de Saint-André, 1952.
Durham, John I. *Exodus.* Word Biblical Commentary 3. Waco, Tex.: Word, 1987.
Ebling, Hans Jürgen. *Das Messiasgeheimnis und die Botschaft des Marcus-Evangelisten.* Beihefte zur Zeitschrift für die neutestamentliche Wissenschaft 19. Berlin: A. Töpelmann, 1939.
Edson, Charles. "Cults of Thessalonica (Macedonia III)." *Harvard Theological Review* 41 (1948): 153–204.
Ehrman, Bart. *Lost Christianities: The Battles for Scripture and the Faiths We Never Knew.* New York: Oxford University Press, 2003.
Eisenstadt, S. N., ed. *Max Weber on Charisma and Institution Building: Selected Papers.* The Heritage of Sociology Series. Chicago: University of Chicago Press, 1968.
Elgvin, Torleif. "'To Master His Own Vessel.' 1 Thess 4.4 in Light of New Qumran Evidence." *New Testament Studies* 43 (1997): 604–19.
Ellingworth, Paul. *The Epistle to the Hebrews.* Epworth Commentaries. London: Epworth, 1991.
_____. *The Epistle to the Hebrews: A Commentary on the Greek Text.* New International Greek Testament Commentary. Grand Rapids: Eerdmans, 1993.
Elliott, J. K. *The Apocryphal New Testament.* Oxford: Oxford University Press, 1993.
Elliott, John H. *1 Peter.* Anchor Bible 37B. New York: Doubleday, 2000.
_____. *A Home for the Homeless: A Sociological Exegesis of 1 Peter, Its Situation and Strategy.* Philadelphia: Fortress, 1981.
Elliott, Neil. *Liberating Paul: The Justice of God and the Politics of the Apostle.* Maryknoll, N.Y.: Orbis, 1994.

Erler, Michael, and Malcolm Schofield. "Epicurean Ethics." Pages 642–74 in *The Cambridge History of Hellenistic Philosophy*. Edited by Keimpe Algra, Jonathan Barnes, Jaap Mansfeld, and Malcolm Schofield. Cambridge: Cambridge University Press, 1999.

Espy, John M. "Paul's 'Robust Conscience' Re-examined." *New Testament Studies* 31 (1985): 161–88.

Eusebius. *Preparation for the Gospel*. 2 pts. Grand Rapids: Baker, 1981.

Evans, C. Stephen. *The Historical Christ and the Jesus of Faith: The Incarnational Narrative as History*. Oxford: Oxford University Press, 1996.

_____. *Faith beyond Reason: A Kierkegaardian Account*. Reason & Religion. Grand Rapids: Eerdmans, 1998.

Evans, Robert Maxwell. *Eschatology and Ethics: A Study of Thessalonica and Paul's Letters to the Thessalonians*. D.Theol. diss., University of Basel, 1967.

Faure, Alexander. "Die alttestamentlichen Zitate im 4. Evangelium und die Quellenscheidungshypothese." *Zeitschrift für die neutestamentliche Wissenschaft und die Kunde der älteren Kirche* 21 (1922): 99–121.

Fee, Gordon D. *1 and 2 Timothy, Titus*. Good News Commentaries. New York: Harper & Row, 1984.

_____. *The First Epistle to the Corinthians*. New International Commentary on the New Testament. Grand Rapids: Eerdmans, 1987.

_____. *God's Empowering Presence: The Holy Spirit in the Letters of Paul*. Peabody, Mass.: Hendrickson, 1994.

_____. *Paul's Letter to the Philippians*. New International Commentary on the New Testament. Grand Rapids: Eerdmans, 1995.

_____. "Philippians 2:5–11: Hymn or Exalted Prose?" *Bulletin for Biblical Research* 2 (1992): 29–46.

_____. "Wisdom Christology in Paul: A Dissenting View." Pages 251–79 in *The Way of Wisdom: Essays in Honor of Bruce K. Waltke*. Edited by J. I. Packer and Sven K. Soderlund. Grand Rapids: Zondervan, 2000.

Fieger, Michael. *Das Thomasevangelium: Einleitung, Kommentar, und Systematik*. Neutestamentliche Abhandlungen 22. Münster: Aschendorffsche Verlagsbuchhandlung, 1991.

Fiore, Benjamin. *The Function of Personal Example in the Socratic and Pastoral Epistles*. Analecta biblica 105. Rome: Biblical Institute, 1986.

Fisk, Bruce N. "ΠΟΡΝΕΥΕΙΝ as Body Violation: The Unique Nature of Sexual Sin in 1 Corinthians 6.18." *New Testament Studies* 42 (1996): 540–58.

Fitzmyer, Joseph A. *A Wandering Aramean: Collected Aramaic Essays*. Chico, Calif.: Scholars, 1979.

_____. *Essays on the Semitic Background of the New Testament*. London: G. Chapman, 1971.

_____. *The Gospel according to Luke I–IX*. Anchor Bible 28. Garden City, N.Y.: Doubleday, 1981.

_____. *Luke the Theologian: Aspects of His Teaching*. New York: Paulist, 1989.

_____. *Romans*. Anchor Bible 33. New York: Doubleday, 1993.

Fortna, Robert Tomson. *The Fourth Gospel and Its Predecessor*. Philadelphia: Fortress, 1988.

_____. *The Gospel of Signs: A Reconstruction of the Narrative Source Underlying the Fourth Gospel*. Society for New Testament Studies Monograph Series 11. Cambridge: Cambridge University Press, 1970.

Fowl, Stephen E. *The Story of Christ in the Ethics of Paul: An Analysis of the Function of the Hymnic Material in the Pauline Corpus*. Journal for the Study of the New Testament Supplement 36. Sheffield: Sheffield Academic Press, 1990.

France, R. T. "Exegesis in Practice: Two Examples." Pages 252–81 in *New Testament Interpretation: Essays on Principles and Methods*. Edited by I. Howard Marshall. Grand Rapids: Eerdmans, 1977.

_____. *The Gospel of Mark*. Grand Rapids: Eerdmans, 2002.

_____. *Matthew: Evangelist and Teacher*. Grand Rapids: Zondervan, 1989.

Francis, Fred O. "Humility and Angelic Worship." Pages 163–95 in *Conflict at Colossae: A Problem in the Interpretation of Early Christianity Illustrated by Selected Modern Studies*. Edited by Fred O. Francis and Wayne A. Meeks. Rev. ed. Society of Biblical Literature Sources for Biblical Study 4. Missoula, Mont.: Scholars, 1975.

Fredriksen, Paula. "Judaism, the Circumcision of Gentiles, and Apocalyptic Hope: Another Look at Galatians 1 and 2." *Journal of Theological Studies* 42 (1991): 532–64.

Freedman, David Noel, ed. *Anchor Bible Dictionary*. 6 vols. New York: Doubleday, 1992.

Frend, W. H. C. *Martyrdom and Persecution in the Early Church: A Study of the Conflict from the Maccabees to Donatus*. Grand Rapids: Baker, 1981.

Friesen, Steven J. *Imperial Cults and the Apocalypse of John: Reading Revelation in the Ruins*. Oxford: Oxford University Press, 2001.

Frilingos, Chris. "'For My Child, Onesimus': Paul and Domestic Power in Philemon." *Journal of Biblical Literature* 119 (2000): 91–104.

Fung, Ronald Y. K. *The Epistle to the Galatians*. New International Commentary on the New Testament. Grand Rapids: Eerdmans, 1988.

Funk, Robert W. *Honest to Jesus: Jesus for a New Millennium*. New York: HarperCollins, 1996.

Furnish, Victor Paul. *II Corinthians*. Anchor Bible 32A. Garden City, N.Y.: Doubleday, 1984.

Gager, John G. *The Origins of Anti-Semitism: Attitudes toward Judaism in Pagan and Christian Antiquity*. New York: Oxford University Press, 1985.

Gagnon, Robert A. J. *The Bible and Homosexual Practice: Texts and Hermeneutics*. Nashville: Abingdon, 2001.

Garland, David E. *1 Corinthians*. Baker Exegetical Commentary on the New Testament. Grand Rapids: Baker, 2003.

_____. "The Composition and Unity of Philippians: Some Neglected Literary Factors." *Novum Testamentum* 27 (1985): 141–73.

Garnsey, Peter. "Religious Toleration in Classical Antiquity." Pages 1–27 in *Persecution and Toleration*. Edited by W. J. Sheils. Studies in Church History 21. Oxford: Blackwell, 1984.

Garrett, Susan R. *The Demise of the Devil: Magic and the Demonic in Luke's Writings*. Minneapolis: Fortress, 1989.

Gärtner, Bertil. *The Temple and the Community in Qumran and in the New Testament*. Society for New Testament Studies Monograph Series 1. Cambridge: Cambridge University Press, 1965.

Gaston, Lloyd. "The Messiah of Israel as Teacher of the Gentiles: The Setting of Matthew's Christology." *Interpretation* 29 (1975): 24–40.

Georgi, Dieter. *The Opponents of Paul in Second Corinthians*. Philadelphia: Fortress, 1986.

_____. *Remembering the Poor: The History of Paul's Collection for Jerusalem*. Nashville: Abingdon, 1992.

Gerhardsson, Birger. *Memory and Manuscript: Oral Tradition and Written Transmission in Rabbinic Judaism and Early Christianity*. Acta seminarii neotestamentici upsaliensis 22. Lund: Gleerup, 1961.

Giblin, Homer. *The Threat to Faith: An Exegetical and Theological Reexamination of 2 Thessalonians 2*. Analecta biblica 31. Rome: Pontifical Biblical Institute, 1967.

Gill, David W. J. "The Importance of Roman Portraiture for Head-Coverings in 1 Corinthians 11:2–16." *Tyndale Bulletin* 41 (1990): 245–60.

Gillman, John. "A Thematic Comparison: 1 Cor 15:50–57 and 2 Cor 5:1–5." *Journal of Biblical Literature* 107 (1988): 439–54.

Glare, P. G. W., ed. *Oxford Latin Dictionary*. Oxford: Oxford University Press, 1982.

Gnilka, Joachim. *Das Evangelium nach Markus*. 2 vols. 3rd ed. Evangelisch-katholischer Kommentar zum Neuen Testament 2. Zürich/Neukirchen-Vluyn: Benziger/Neukirchener, 1989.

_____. *Das Matthäusevangelium*. 2 vols. Herders theologischer Kommentar zum Neuen Testament. Freiburg: Herder, 1988.

Goldingay, John E. *Daniel*. Word Biblical Commentary 30. Dallas: Word, 1989.

Goldstein, Jonathan A. *II Maccabees*. Anchor Bible 41A. New York: Doubleday, 1983.

Goppelt, Leonard. *A Commentary on 1 Peter*. Grand Rapids: Eerdmans, 1993.

_____. *Theology of the New Testament*. 2 vols. Grand Rapids: Eerdmans, 1981–82.

Goulder, Michael. "Matthew's Vision for the Church." Pages 19–32 in *A Vision for the Church: Studies in Early Christian Ecclesiology in Honour of J. P. M. Sweet*. Edited by Markus Bockmuehl and Michael B. Thompson. Edinburgh: T. & T. Clark, 1997.

_____. *St. Paul versus St. Peter: A Tale of Two Missions*. Louisville: Westminster John Knox, 1994.

Gowan, Donald E. "Wisdom and Endurance in James." *Horizons in Biblical Theology* 15 (1993): 145–53.

Grässer, Erich. "Der Schatz in irdenen Gefässen (2 Kor 4,7): Existentiale Interpretation im 2. Korintherbrief." *Zeitschrift für Theologie und Kirche* 97 (2000): 300–316.

Green, Joel B. "The Death of Jesus, God's Servant." Pages 1–28 in *Reimaging the Death of the Lukan Jesus*. Edited by Dennis D. Sylva. Bonner biblische Beiträge 73. Frankfurt am Main: Anton Hain, 1990.

_____. "Death of Jesus." Pages 146–63 in the *Dictionary of Jesus and the Gospels*. Edited by Joel B. Green, Scot McKnight, and I. Howard Marshall. Downers Grove, Ill.: InterVarsity Press, 1992.

_____. *The Theology of the Gospel of Luke*. New Testament Theology. Cambridge: Cambridge University Press, 1995.

Green, Joel B., and Mark D. Barker. *Recovering the Scandal of the Cross: Atonement in New Testament and Contemporary Contexts*. Downers Grove, Ill.: InterVarsity Press, 2000.

Grindheim, Sigurd. "What the OT Prophets Did Not Know: The Mystery of the Church in Eph 3,2–13." *Biblica* 84 (2003): 531–53.

Grudem, Wayne. *1 Peter*. TynNTC. Leicester, Eng.: InterVarsity Press, 1988.

Guelich, Robert A. *Mark 1–8:26*. Word Biblical Commentary 34A. Dallas: Word, 1989.

_____. *The Sermon on the Mount: A Foundation for Understanding*. Waco, Tex.: Word, 1982.

Gundry, Robert H. "In Defense of the Church in Matthew as a Corpus Mixtum." *Zeitschrift für neutestamentliche Wissenschaft und die Kunde der älteren Kirche* 91 (2000): 153–65.

_____. *Mark: A Commentary on His Apology for the Cross*. Grand Rapids: Eerdmans, 1993.

Gundry-Volf, Judith. "Gender and Creation in 1 Corinthians 11:2–16: A Study in Paul's Theological Method." Pages 150–71 in *Evangelium, Schriftauslegung, Kirche: Festschrift für Peter Stuhlmacher zum 65. Geburtstag*. Edited by Jostein Ådna, Scott J. Hafemann, and Otfried Hofius. Göttingen: Vandenhoeck & Ruprecht, 1997.

_____. *Paul and Perseverance: Staying in and Falling Away*. Wissenschaftliche Untersuchungen zum Alten und Neuen Testament 2.37. Tübingen: J. C. B. Mohr (Paul Siebeck), 1990.

Haenchen, Ernst. *The Acts of the Apostles: A Commentary*. Philadelphia: Westminster, 1971.

Hafemann, Scott J. "The Spirit of the New Covenant, the Law, and the Temple of God's Presence: Five Theses on Qumran's Self-Understanding and the Contours of Paul's

Thought." Pages 172–89 in *Evangelium, Schriftauslegung, Kirche: Festschrift für Peter Stuhlmacher zum 65. Geburtstag*. Edited by Jostein Ådna, Scott J. Hafemann, and Otfried Hofius. Göttingen: Vandenhoeck & Ruprecht, 1997.

_____. *Suffering and the Spirit: An Exegetical Study of II Cor. 2:14–3:3 within the Context of the Corinthian Correspondence*. Wissenschaftliche Untersuchungen zum Alten und Neuen Testament 2.19. Tübingen: J. C. B. Mohr (Paul Siebeck), 1986.

Hagner, Donald A. *Matthew 1–13*. Word Biblical Commentary 33A. Dallas: Word, 1993.

Hanson, Anthony Tyrrell. *The Prophetic Gospel: A Study of John and the Old Testament*. Edinburgh: T. & T. Clark, 1991.

Hanson, Stig. *The Unity of the Church in the New Testament: Colossians and Ephesians*. Uppsala: Almqvist & Wiksells, 1946.

Hare, Douglas R. A. *The Son of Man Tradition*. Minneapolis: Fortress, 1990.

von Harnack, Adolf. *Marcion: The Gospel of the Alien God*. Durham, N.C.: Labyrinth, 1990.

_____. *Das Wesen des Christentums: Sechzehn Vorlesungen vor Studierenden aller Facultäten im Wintersemester 1899/1900 an der Universität Berlin*. Leipzig: Hinrichs, 1900.

_____. *Das Wesen des Christentums: Neuauflage zum fünfzigsten Jahrestag des ersten Erscheinens mit einem Geleitwort von Rudolf Bultmann*. Stuttgart: Ehrenfried Klotz Verlag, 1950.

_____. *What Is Christianity?* Gloucester, Mass.: Peter Smith, 1978.

Harrill, J. Albert. *The Manumission of Slaves in Early Christianity*. Hermeneutische Untersuchungen zur Theologie 32. Tübingen: J. C. B. Mohr (Paul Siebeck), 1995.

Harris, Horton. *The Tübingen School: A Historical and Theological Investigation of the School of F. C. Baur*. Rev. ed. Grand Rapids: Baker, 1990.

Harris, W. Hall III. *The Descent of Christ: Ephesians 4:7–11 and Traditional Hebrew Imagery*. Arbeiten zur Geschichte des antiken Judentums und des Urchristentums 32. Leiden: Brill, 1996.

Hartman, Lars. "The Eschatology of 2 Thessalonians as Included in a Communication." Pages 470–85 in *The Thessalonian Correspondence*. Edited by Raymond F. Collins. Bibliotheca ephemeridum theologicarum lovaniensium 87. Leuven: University Press, 1990.

Harvey, A. E. *Renewal through Suffering: A Study of 2 Corinthians*. Studies of the New Testament and Its World. Edinburgh: T. & T. Clark, 1996.

Hase, Karl. *Geschichte Jesus nach akademischen Vorlesungen*. Leipzig: Breitkopf and Härtel, 1876.

Hasel, Gerhard. *New Testament Theology: Basic Issues in the Current Debate*. Grand Rapids: Eerdmans, 1978.

Hawthorne, Gerald F. *Philippians*, Word Biblical Commentary 43. Waco, Tex.: Word, 1983.

Hays, Richard B. *Echoes of Scripture in the Letters of Paul*. New Haven, Conn.: Yale University Press, 1989.

Heckel, Theo K. *Vom Evangelium des Markus zum viergestaltigen Evangelium*. Wissenschaftliche Untersuchungen zum Alten und Neuen Testament 120. Tübingen: J. C. B. Mohr (Paul Siebeck), 1999.

Hegel, G. W. F. *Philosophy of History*. New York: Dover, 1956.

Hemer, Colin. *The Letters to the Seven Churches of Asia in Their Local Setting*. Journal for the Study of the New Testament Supplement 11. Sheffield: Sheffield Academic Press, 1986.

Hengel, Martin. *Acts and the History of Earliest Christianity*. London: SCM, 1979.

_____. *The Atonement: The Origins of the Doctrine in the New Testament*. Philadelphia: Fortress, 1981.

_____. *Crucifixion in the Ancient World and the Folly of the Message of the Cross*. Philadelphia: Fortress, 1977.

_____. *The Four Gospels and the One Gospel of Jesus Christ.* Harrisburg, Penn.: Trinity Press International, 2000.

_____. *The Johannine Question.* London: SCM/Philadelphia: Trinity Press International, 1989.

_____. *Judaism and Hellenism: Studies in Their Encounter in Palestine during the Early Hellenistic Period.* 2 vols. Philadelphia: Fortress, 1974.

_____. *Paulus und Jakobus.* Wissenschaftliche Untersuchungen zum Alten und Neuen Testament 141. Tübingen: J. C. B. Mohr (Paul Siebeck), 2002.

_____. *The Son of God: The Origin of Christology and the History of Jewish–Hellenistic Religion.* Philadelphia: Fortress, 1976.

_____. *Studies in Early Christology.* Edinburgh: T. & T. Clark, 1995.

_____. *Studies in the Gospel of Mark.* Philadelphia: Fortress, 1985.

Hengel, Martin, and Anna Maria Schwemer. *Paul between Damascus and Antioch: The Unknown Years.* Louisville: Westminster John Knox, 1997.

Henke, E. L. T. "Gabler, Johann Philipp." Pages 720–22 in vol. 4 of *Realencyklopädie für protestantische Theologie und Kirche.* 24 vols. 3rd ed. Leipzig: J. C. Hinrichs'sche Buchhandlung, 1896–1913.

Hickling, C. J. A. "Centre and Periphery in the Thought of Paul." Pages 199–214 in *Studia Biblica 1978.* Edited by E. A. Livingstone. Journal for the Study of the New Testament Supplement 3. Sheffield: Sheffield Academic Press, 1980.

Hill, Craig C. *Hellenists and Hebrews: Reappraising Division within the Earliest Church.* Minneapolis: Fortress, 1992.

Hill, David. "Son and Servant: An Essay on Matthean Christology." *Journal for the Study of the New Testament* 6 (1980): 2–16.

Heiligenthal, Roman. *Zwischen Henoch und Paulus: Studien zum theologiegeschichtlichen Ort des Judasbriefes.* Texte und Arbeiten zum neutestamentlichen Zeitalter 6. Tübingen: A. Francke, 1992.

Hendrix, Holland L. "Thessalonica." Pages 523–27 in vol. 6 of the *Anchor Bible Dictionary.* Edited by David Noel Freedman. 6 vols. New York: Doubleday, 1992.

Hock, Ronald F. "Simon the Shoemaker as an Ideal Cynic." *Greek, Roman and Byzantine Studies* 17 (1976): 41–53.

_____. *The Social Context of Paul's Ministry: Tentmaking and Apostleship.* Philadelphia: Fortress, 1980.

Hoehner, Harold. *Ephesians: An Exegetical Commentary.* Grand Rapids: Baker, 2002.

Hoffmann, Heinrich. "Zachariae, Gotthilf Traugott." Pages 587–88 in vol. 21 of *Realencyklopädie für protestantische Theologie und Kirche.* 24 vols. 3rd ed. Leipzig: J. C. Hinrichs'sche Buchhandlung, 1896–1913.

Hoffmann, Paul. *Die Toten in Christus: Eine religionsgeschichtliche und exegetische Untersuchung zur paulinischen Eschatologie.* Neutestamentliche Abhandlungen 2. Münster: Verlag Aschendorf, 1966.

Holladay, William L. *Jeremiah.* 2 vols. Hermeneia. Philadelphia: Fortress, 1986–89.

Holland, Richard. *Nero: The Man behind the Myth.* Thrupp, Eng.: Sutton, 2000.

Hollander, John. *The Figure of Echo: A Mode of Allusion in Milton and After.* Berkeley: University of California Press, 1981.

Holloway, Paul A. "*Bona Cogitare*: An Epicurean Consolation in Phil 4:8–9." *Harvard Theological Review* 91 (1998): 89–96.

_____. Disce Gaudere: *Paul's Consolation of the Church at Philippi.* Ph.D. diss., University of Chicago, 1998.

_____. *Consolation in Philippians: Philosophical Sources and Rhetorical Strategy.* Society for New Testament Studies Monograph Series 112. Cambridge: Cambridge University Press, 2001.

_____. "*Nihil inopinati accidisse*—'Nothing unexpected has happened': A Cyrenaic Consolatory *Topos* in 1 Pet 4.12ff." *New Testament Studies* 48 (2002): 433–48.

Holtz, Traugott. *Der erste Brief an die Thessalonicher.* Evangelisch-katholischer Kommentar zum Neuen Testament 13. Zürich: Benziger/Neukirchen-Vluyn: Neukirchener, 1990.

Holtzmann, Heinrich Julius. *Lehrbuch der neutestamentlichen Theologie.* Edited by A. Jülicher and W. Bauer. 2 vols. Tübingen: J. C. B. Mohr (Paul Siebeck), 1911.

Hooker, Morna D. *Jesus and the Servant.* London: SPCK, 1959.

_____. "Paul and Covenantal Nomism." Pages 47–56 in *Paul and Paulinism: Essays in Honour of C. K. Barrett.* Edited by Morna D. Hooker and S. G. Wilson. London: SPCK, 1982.

_____. "Philippians 2:6–11." Pages 151–64 in *Jesus und Paulus: Festschrift für Werner Georg Kümmel zum 70. Geburtstag.* Edited by E. Earle Ellis and Erich Grässer. 2nd ed. Göttingen: Vandenhoeck & Ruprecht, 1978.

_____. *The Son of Man in Mark.* Montreal: McGill University Press, 1967.

Hoover, Roy W. "The Harpagmos Dilemma: A Philological Solution." *Harvard Theological Review* 64 (1971): 95–119.

Hornig, G. "Semler, Johann Salomo." Pages 246–57 in *Dictionary of Biblical Interpretation.* Edited by John H. Hayes. 2 vols. Nashville: Abingdon, 1999.

Hoskyns, Edwyn Clement, and Francis Noel Davey. *The Fourth Gospel.* London: Faber and Faber, 1940.

van Houwelingen, P. H. R. *1 Petrus: Rondzendbrief uit Babylon.* Commentaar op het Nieuwe Testament. Kampen: Kok, 1991.

_____. *2 Petrus en Judas: Testament in tweevoud.* Commentaar op het Nieuwe Testament. Kampen: Kok, 1993.

_____. *De tweede trompet: De authenticiteit van de tweede brief van Petrus.* Kampen: Kok, 1988.

Hübner, Hans. *Biblische Theologie des Neuen Testaments.* 3 vols. Göttingen: Vandenhoeck & Ruprecht, 1990–95.

_____. *An Philemon, an die Kolosser, an die Epheser.* Handbuch zum Neuen Testament 12. Tübingen: J. C. B. Mohr (Paul Siebeck), 1997.

Hughes, Philip Edgcumbe. *A Commentary on the Epistle to the Hebrews.* Grand Rapids: Eerdmans, 1977.

Hultgren, Arland J. *Paul's Gospel and Mission: The Outlook from His Letter to the Romans.* Philadelphia: Fortress, 1985.

Hummel, Reinhart. *Die Auseinandersetzung zwischen Kirche und Judentum im Matthäusevangelium.* Beiträge zur evangelischen Theologie 33. München: Kaiser, 1966.

Hunt, Arthur S., and J. Gilbart Smyly. *The Tebtunis Papyri.* Vol. 3, pt. 1. London: Oxford University Press, 1933.

Hurst, L. D. "The Christology of Hebrews 1 and 2." Pages 151–64 in *The Glory of Christ in the New Testament: Studies in Christology.* Edited by L. D. Hurst and N. T. Wright. Oxford: Clarendon, 1987.

Hyatt, J. Philip. *Exodus.* New Century Bible. London: Marshall, Morgan & Scott, 1971.

James, William. "The Will to Believe." Pages 457–79 in *William James: Writings: 1878—1899.* Library of America. New York: Library Classics of the United States, 1992.

Jenks, Gregory C. *The Origins and Early Development of the Antichrist Myth*. Beihefte zur Zeitschrift für die neutestamentliche Wissenschaft 59. Berlin: Walter de Gruyter, 1991.

Jervell, Jacob. "The Letter to Jerusalem." Pages 53–64 in *The Romans Debate*. Edited by Karl P. Donfried. Rev. and exp. ed. Peabody, Mass.: Hendrickson, 1991.

_____. *The Theology of the Acts of the Apostles*. New Testament Theology. Cambridge: Cambridge University Press, 1996.

Jeremias, Joachim. *New Testament Theology*. Vol. 1. London: SCM, 1971.

Jewett, Robert. "Conflicting Movements in the Early Church as Reflected in Philippians." *Novum Testamentum* 12 (1970): 362–90.

_____. *The Thessalonian Correspondence: Pauline Rhetoric and Millenarian Piety*. Foundations and Facets. Philadelphia: Fortress, 1986.

Jobes, Karen. *1 Peter*. Baker Exegetical Commentary on the New Testament. Grand Rapids: Baker, 2005.

Johnson, Luke Timothy. *The Acts of the Apostles*. Sacra Pagina 5. Collegeville, Minn.: Michael Glazier, 1992.

_____. *The First and Second Letters to Timothy*. Anchor Bible 35A. New York: Doubleday, 2001.

_____. *James*. Anchor Bible 37A. New York: Doubleday, 1995.

_____. *Letters to Paul's Delegates: 1 Timothy, 2 Timothy, Titus*. The New Testament in Context. Valley Forge, Pa.: Trinity Press International, 1996.

_____. *The Real Jesus: The Misguided Quest for the Historical Jesus and the Truth of the Traditional Gospels*. San Francisco: HarperCollins, 1996.

_____. *Reading Romans: A Literary and Theological Commentary*. New York: Crossroad, 1997.

_____. *Sharing Possessions: Mandate and Symbol of Faith*. Overtures to Biblical Theology. Philadelphia: Fortress, 1981.

_____. *The Writings of the New Testament: An Interpretation*. Philadelphia: Fortress, 1986.

de Jonge, Marinus. *Christology in Context: The Earliest Christian Response to Jesus*. Philadelphia: Westminster, 1988.

_____. *Jesus: Stranger from Heaven and Son of God*. Society of Biblical Literature Sources for Biblical Study 11. Missoula, Mont.: Scholars, 1977.

_____. "The Use of the Word ΧΡΙΣΤΟΣ in the Johannine Letters." Pages 66–74 in *Studies in John Presented to Professor Dr. J. N. Sevenster*. Leiden: Brill, 1970.

Kähler, Martin. "Biblische Theologie." Pages 192–200 in vol. 3 of *Realencyklopädie für protestantische Theologie und Kirche*. 24 vols. 3rd ed. Leipzig: J. C. Hinrichs'sche Buchhandlung, 1896–1913.

_____. *The So-called Historical Jesus and the Historic Biblical Christ*. Philadelphia: Fortress, 1988.

Karris, Robert J. "Luke 23:47 and the Lucan View of Jesus' Death." *Journal of Biblical Literature* 105 (1986): 65–74.

Käsemann, Ernst. *Commentary on Romans*. Grand Rapids: Eerdmans, 1980.

_____. *Essays on New Testament Themes*. Philadelphia: Fortress, 1982.

_____. "Gottesgerechtigkeit bei Paulus." *Zeitschrift für Theologie und Kirche* 58 (1961): 367–78.

_____. "Ketzer und Zeuge," *Zeitschrift für Theologie und Kirche* 48 (1951): 292–311.

_____. *New Testament Questions of Today*. Philadelphia: Fortress, 1969.

_____. "The Problem of a New Testament Theology." *New Testament Studies* 19 (1972–73): 235–45.

_____. *The Testament of Jesus: A Study of the Gospel of John in the Light of Chapter 17*. Philadelphia: Fortress, 1968.

_____. *The Wandering People of God: An Investigation of the Letter to the Hebrews.* Minneapolis: Augsburg, 1984.

Kee, Howard Clark. "The Function of Scriptural Quotations and Allusions in Mark 11–16." Pages 165–88 in *Jesus und Paulus: Festschrift für Werner Georg Kümmel zum 70. Geburtstag.* Edited by E. Earle Ellis and Erich Gässer. Göttingen: Vandenhoeck & Ruprecht, 1975.

Keener, Craig. A. *A Commentary on the Gospel of Matthew.* Grand Rapids: Eerdmans, 1999.

Kelber, Werner H. "Metaphysics and Marginality in John." Pages 129–54 in *What Is John? Readers and Readings of the Fourth Gospel.* Edited by Fernando F. Segovia. Society of Biblical Literature Symposium Series 3. Atlanta: Scholars, 1996.

Kelly, J. N. D. *A Commentary on the Epistles of Peter and Jude.* Black's New Testament Commentary. London: A. and C. Black, 1969.

_____. *The Pastoral Epistles.* Black's New Testament Commentaries. Peabody, Mass.: Hendrickson, 1960.

Kermode, Frank. *The Genesis of Secrecy: On the Interpretation of Narrative.* Cambridge, Mass.: Harvard University Press, 1979.

Kertelge, Karl. "The Epiphany of Jesus in the Gospel (Mark)." Pages 105–23 in *The Interpretation of Mark.* Edited by William R. Telford. 2nd ed. Studies in New Testament Interpretation. Edinburgh: T. & T. Clark, 1995.

_____. *"Rechtfertigung" bei Paulus: Studien zur Struktur und zum Dedeutungsgehalt des paulinischen Rechtfertigungsbegriffs.* Neutestamentliche Abhandlungen 3. Münster: Aschendorff, 1967.

Keyes, Clinton W. "The Greek Letter of Introduction." *American Journal of Philology* 56 (1935): 28–48.

Kidd, Reggie M. "Titus as *Apologia*: Grace for Liars, Beasts, and Bellies." *Horizons in Biblical Theology* 21 (1999): 185–209.

Kingsbury, Jack Dean. *The Christology of Mark's Gospel.* Philadelphia: Fortress, 1983.

_____. *Matthew: Structure, Christology, Kingdom.* 2nd ed. Minneapolis: Fortress, 1989.

Kinman, Brent. "'Appoint the Despised as Judges!' (1 Corinthians 6:4)." *Tyndale Bulletin* 48 (1997): 345–54.

Kittel, G., and G. Friedrich, eds. *Theological Dictionary of the New Testament.* 10 vols. Translated by Geoffrey Bromiley. Grand Rapids: Eerdmans, 1964–76.

Klauck, Hans-Josef. *Der erste Johannesbrief.* Evangelisch-katholischer Kommentar zum Neuen Testament 23.1. Zürich:Benziger/Neukirchen-Vluyn: Neukirchener, 1991.

Klausner, Joseph. *The Messianic Idea in Israel from Its Beginning to the Completion of the Mishnah.* London: George Allen & Unwin, 1956.

Klein, Günther. *Ärgernisse: Konfrontationen mit dem Neuen Testament.* München: Chr. Kaiser Verlag, 1970.

_____. "Paul's Purpose in Writing the Epistle to the Romans." Pages 29–43 in *The Romans Debate.* Edited by Karl P. Donfried. Rev. and exp. ed. Peabody, Mass.: Hendrickson, 1991.

Knight, George W., III. *Commentary on the Pastoral Epistles.* New International Greek Testament Commentary. Grand Rapids: Eerdmans, 1992.

Knowles, Michael. *Jeremiah in Matthew's Gospel: The Rejected Prophet Motif in Matthaean* (sic) *Redaction.* Journal for the Study of the New Testament Supplement 68. Sheffield: Sheffield Academic Press, 1993.

Knox, John. *Chapters in a Life of Paul.* New York: Abingdon, 1950.

Knox, Wilfred L. *St. Paul and the Church of the Gentiles.* Cambridge: Cambridge University Press, 1939.

Köstenberger, Andreas J. "Ascertaining Women's God-Ordained Roles: An Interpretation of 1 Timothy 2:15." *Bulletin for Biblical Research* 7 (1997): 107–44.

_____. "A Complex Sentence Structure in 1 Timothy 2:12." Pages 81–103 in *Women in the Church: A Fresh Analysis of 1 Timothy 2:9–15*. Edited by Andreas J. Köstenberger, Thomas R. Schreiner, and H. Scott Baldwin. Grand Rapids: Baker, 1995.

Koester, Craig R. "Hebrews, Rhetoric, and the Future of Humanity." *Catholic Biblical Quarterly* 64 (2002): 103–23.

Koester, Helmut. *Introduction to the New Testament*. 2 vols. Berlin: Walter de Gruyter, 1982.

Koperski, Veronica. *What Are They Saying about Paul and the Law?* New York: Paulist, 2001.

Kraftchick, Steven J. "Facing Janus: Reviewing the Biblical Theology Movement." Pages 54–77 in *Biblical Theology: Problems and Perspectives: In Honor of J. Christiaan Beker*. Edited by Steven J. Kraftchick, Charles D. Myers Jr., and Ben C. Ollenburger. Nashville: Abingdon, 1995.

Kruse, Colin G. *The Letters of John*. Pillar New Testament Commentary. Grand Rapids: Eerdmans, 2000.

_____. *Paul, the Law, and Justification*. Peabody, Mass.: Hendrickson, 1996.

Kugler, Robert A. *The Testaments of the Twelve Patriarchs*. Guides to the Apocrypha and Pseudepigrapha. Sheffield: Sheffield Academic Press, 2001.

Kümmel, Werner Georg. "Current Theological Accusations against Luke." *Andover Newton Quarterly* 16 (1975): 131–45.

_____. *Introduction to the New Testament*. Rev. ed. Nashville: Abingdon, 1975.

_____. *The New Testament: The History of the Investigation of Its Problems*. Nashville: Abingdon, 1972.

_____. "Notwendigkeit und Grenze des neutestamentlichen Kanons." *Zeitschrift für Theologie und Kirche* 47 (1950): 227–313.

_____. *The Theology of the New Testament*. Nashville: Abingdon, 1973.

Küng, Hans. *Structures of the Church*. New York: T. Nelson, 1964.

Kuss, Otto. *Der Römerbrief*. 3 vols. Regensburg: Verlag Friedrich Pustet, 1957–78.

Laato, Timo. *Paul and Judaism: An Anthropological Approach*. South Florida Studies in the History of Judaism 115. Atlanta: Scholars, 1995.

Ladd, George Eldon. *A Theology of the New Testament*. Grand Rapids: Eerdmans, 1974.

Lagrange, M.-J. *Épitre aux Galates*. Études bibliques. Paris: Lecoffre, 1950.

_____. *Épitre aux Romains*. 3rd ed. Études bibliques. Paris: LeCoffre, 1922.

Lambrecht, Jan. "Transgressor by Nullifying God's Grace: A Study of Gal 2,18–21." *Biblica* 72 (1991): 230–36.

Lampe, Peter. "Keine 'Sklavenflucht' des Onesimus." *Zeitschrift für die neutestamentliche Wissenschaft und die Kunde der älteren Kirche* 76 (1985): 135–37.

_____. "The Roman Christians of Romans 16." Pages 216–30 in *The Romans Debate*. Edited by Karl P. Donfried. Rev. and exp. ed. Peabody, Mass.: Hendrickson, 1991.

Lane, William L. *The Gospel according to Mark*. New International Commentary on the New Testament. Grand Rapids: Eerdmans, 1974.

_____. *Hebrews 1–8*. Word Biblical Commentary 47A. Dallas: Word, 1991.

_____. *Hebrews 9–13*. Word Biblical Commentary 47B. Dallas: Word, 1991.

Last, Hugh. "The Study of the 'Persecutions.'" *Journal of Roman Studies* 27 (1937): 80–92.

Laws, Sophie. *The Epistle of James*. Harper's New Testament Commentaries. San Francisco: Harper & Row, 1980.

Leenhardt, Franz J. *The Epistle to the Romans*. Cleveland: World, 1961.

Léon-Dufour, Xavier. *The Gospels and the Jesus of History*. London: Collins, 1968.

Lesses, Rebecca Macy. *Ritual Practices to Gain Power: Angels, Incantations, and Revelation in Early Jewish Mysticism*. Harvard Theological Studies. Harrisburg, Pa.: Trinity Press International, 1998.

Lessing, Gotthold Ephraim. "On the Proof of the Spirit and of Power." Pages 51–56 in *Lessing's Theological Writings*. Edited by Henry Chadwick. Library of Modern Religious Thought. London: Adam & Charles Black, 1956.

Levine, Amy-Jill. *The Social and Ethnic Dimensions of Matthean Salvation History: "Go Nowhere among the Gentiles" (Matt. 10:5b)*. Studies in the Bible and Early Christianity 14. Lewiston, N.Y.: Mellen, 1988.

Levine, Baruch A. *Leviticus*. Jewish Publication Society Torah Commentary. Philadelphia: Jewish Publication Society, 1989.

Lewis, C. S. *Till We Have Faces*. San Diego: Harcourt, 1956.

Lietzmann, Hans. *An die Korinther I/II*. 5th ed. Rev. by Werner Georg Kümmel. Handbuch zum Neuen Testament 9. Tübingen: J. C. B. Mohr (Paul Siebeck), 1969.

Lieu, Judith. *The Second and Third Epistles of John*. Studies of the New Testament and Its World. Edinburgh: T. & T. Clark, 1986.

_____. *The Theology of the Johannine Epistles*. New Testament Theology. Cambridge: Cambridge University Press, 1991.

_____. "What Was from the Beginning: Scripture and Tradition in the Johannine Epistles." *New Testament Studies* 39 (1993): 458–77.

Lightfoot, J. B. *Biblical Essays*. London: Macmillan, 1893.

_____. *Saint Paul's Epistle to the Galatians*. London: Macmillan, 1902.

_____. *Saint Paul's Epistle to the Philippians*. 4th ed. London: Macmillan, 1896.

_____. *Saint Paul's Epistles to the Colossians and to Philemon*. London: Macmillan, 1879.

Lindars, Barnabas. *The Theology of the Letter to the Hebrews*. New Testament Theology. Cambridge: Cambridge University Press, 1991.

Lincoln, Andrew T. *Ephesians*. Word Biblical Commentary 42. Dallas: Word, 1990.

_____. "The Promise and the Failure: Mark 16:7, 8." Pages 229–51 in *The Interpretation of Mark*. Edited by William R. Telford. 2nd ed. Studies in New Testament Interpretation. Edinburgh: T. & T. Clark, 1995.

_____. "The Theology of Ephesians." Pages 73–166 in *The Theology of the Later Pauline Letters*. By Andrew T. Lincoln and A. J. M. Wedderburn. New Testament Theology. Cambridge: Cambridge University Press, 1993.

_____. *Truth on Trial: The Lawsuit Motif in the Fourth Gospel*. Peabody, Mass.: Hendrickson, 2000.

_____. "The Use of the OT in Ephesians." *Journal for the Study of the New Testament* 14 (1982): 16–57.

Lindblom, J. *Prophecy in Ancient Israel*. Philadelphia: Fortress, 1962.

Lindemann, A. *Die Aufhebung der Zeit: Geschichtsverständnis und Eschatologie im Epheserbrief*. Studien zum Neuen Testament 12. Gütersloh: Mohn, 1975.

von Lips, Hermann. *Glaube–Gemeinde–Amt: Zum Verständnis der Ordination in den Pastoralbriefen*. Forschungen zur Religion und Literatur des Alten und Neuen Testaments 122. Göttingen: Vandenhoeck & Ruprecht, 1979.

Loader, William R. G. *The Christology of the Fourth Gospel: Structure and Issues*. Beiträge zur biblischen Exegese und Theologie 23. Frankfurt am Main: Peter Lang, 1989.

_____. *Jesus' Attitude towards the Law: A Study of the Gospels*. Wissenschaftliche Untersuchungen zum Alten und Neuen Testament 2.97. Tübingen: J. C. B. Mohr (Paul Siebeck), 1997.

Lock, Walter. *The Pastoral Epistles*. 3rd ed. International Critical Commentary. Edinburgh: T. & T. Clark, 1952.

Lohmeyer, Ernst. *Die Offenbarung des Johannes*. 2nd ed. Handbuch zum Neuen Testament 16. Tübingen: J. C. B. Mohr (Paul Siebeck), 1953.

Lohse, Eduard. *Colossians and Philemon.* Hermeneia. Philadelphia: Fortress, 1971.

Longenecker, Bruce W. *The Triumph of Abraham's God: The Transformation of Identity in Galatians.* Nashville: Abingdon, 1998.

Longenecker, Richard N. "The Focus of Romans: The Central Role of 5:1–8:39 in the Argument of the Letter." Pages 49–69 in *Romans and the People of God: Essays in Honor of Gordon D. Fee on the Occasion of His 65th Birthday.* Edited by Sven K. Soderlund and N. T. Wright. Grand Rapids: Eerdmans, 1999.

_____. *Galatians.* Word Biblical Commentary 41. Dallas: Word, 1990.

Lossius, F. A. *Biblische Theologie des Neuen Testaments; oder die Lehren des Christenthums aus einzelnen Schriften des N. T. entwickelt.* Leipzig: C. G. Kayser, 1825.

Lüdemann, Gerd. *Heretics: The Other Side of Christianity.* Louisville: Westminster John Knox, 1996.

_____. *Opposition to Paul in Jewish Christianity.* Minneapolis: Fortress, 1989.

Luomanen, Petri. "*Corpus Mixtum*—An Appropriate Description of Matthew's Community?" *Journal of Biblical Literature* 117 (1998): 469–80.

Luz, Ulrich. "Der Brief an die Kolosser." Pages 181–244 in *Die Briefe an die Galater, Epheser und Kolosser.* By J. Becker and U. Luz. Das Neue Testament Deutsch 8.1. Göttingen: Vandenhoeck & Ruprecht, 1998.

_____. *Das Evangelium nach Matthäus (Mt 18–25).* Evangelisch-katholischer Kommentar zum Neuen Testament 1.3. Zürich/Neukirchen–Vluyn: Benziger Verlag/Neukirchener Verlag, 1997.

_____. *Matthew 8–20: A Commentary.* Hermeneia. Minneapolis: Fortress, 2001.

Maccoby, Hyam. *Paul and Hellenism.* London/Philadelphia: SCM/Trinity Press International, 1991.

Mack, Burton L. *The Lost Gospel: The Book of Q and Christian Origins.* Shaftesbury, Dorset, U.K.: Element, 1993.

Magie, David. *Roman Rule in Asia Minor to the End of the Third Century after Christ.* 2 vols. Princeton, N.J.: Princeton University Press, 1950.

Malherbe, Abraham J. "Exhortation in First Thessalonians." *Novum Testamentum* 25 (1983): 238–56.

_____. "'Gentle as a Nurse': The Cynic Background to 1 Thess ii." *Novum Testamentum* 12 (1970): 203–17.

_____. *The Letters to the Thessalonians.* Anchor Bible 32B. New York: Doubleday, 2000.

_____. *Paul and the Thessalonians: The Philosophic Tradition of Pastoral Care.* Philadelphia: Fortress, 1987.

Malina, Bruce J. *On the Genre and Message of Revelation: Star Visions and Sky Journeys.* Peabody, Mass.: Hendrickson, 1995.

Manson, T. W. "St. Paul's Letter to the Romans—And Others." Pages 3–15 in *The Romans Debate.* Edited by Karl P. Donfried. Rev. and exp. ed. Peabody, Mass.: Hendrickson, 1991.

Marcus, Joel. *Mark 1–8: A New Translation and Commentary.* Anchor Bible 27. New York: Doubleday, 2000.

_____. "Mark—Interpreter of Paul." *New Testament Studies* 46 (2000): 473–87.

_____. *The Way of the Lord: Christological Exegesis of the Old Testament in the Gospel of Mark.* Louisville: Westminster John Knox, 1992.

Marguerat, Daniel. *Le jugement dans l'évangile de Matthieu.* Le Monde de la Bible 6. 2nd ed. Geneva: Labor et Fides, 1995.

Marshall, Christopher D. *Faith as a Theme in Mark's Narrative.* Society for the Study of the New Testament Monograph Series 64. Cambridge: Cambridge University Press, 1989.

Marshall, I. Howard. *1 and 2 Thessalonians*. New Century Bible. Grand Rapids: Eerdmans, 1983.

_____. *Commentary on Luke*. New International Greek Testament Commentary. Grand Rapids: Eerdmans, 1978.

_____. "Election and Calling to Salvation in 1 and 2 Thessalonians." Pages 259–76 in *The Thessalonian Correspondence*. Edited by Raymond F. Collins. Bibliotheca ephemeridum theologicarum lovaniensium 87. Leuven: Leuven University Press, 1990.

_____. *The Epistles of John*. New International Commentary on the New Testament. Grand Rapids: Eerdmans, 1978.

_____. *Luke: Historian and Theologian*. Grand Rapids: Zondervan, 1970.

_____. *The Pastoral Epistles*. International Critical Commentary. Edinburgh: T. & T. Clark, 1999.

_____. "Pauline Theology in the Thessalonian Correspondence." Pages 173–83 in *Paul and Paulinism: Essays in Honour of C. K. Barrett*. Edited by M. D. Hooker and S. G. Wilson. London: SPCK, 1982.

_____. "Salvation, Grace and Works in the Later Writings in the Pauline Corpus." *New Testament Studies* 42 (1996): 339–58.

Marshall, Peter. *Enmity in Corinth: Social Conventions in Paul's Relations with the Corinthians*. Wissenschaftliche Untersuchungen zum Alten und Neuen Testament 2.23. Tübingen: J. C. B. Mohr (Paul Siebeck), 1987.

Martin, Dale. *The Corinthian Body*. New Haven, Conn.: Yale University Press, 1995.

Martin, Ralph P. *2 Corinthians*. Word Biblical Commentary 40. Dallas: Word, 1986.

_____. "Center of Paul's Theology." Pages 92–95 in the *Dictionary of Paul and His Letters*. Edited by Gerald F. Hawthorne, Ralph P. Martin, and Daniel G. Reid. Downers Grove, Ill.: InterVarsity Press, 1993.

_____. *Colossians and Philemon*. New Century Bible. London: Oliphants, 1974.

_____. *A Hymn of Christ: Philippians 2:5–11 in Recent Interpretation and in the Setting of Early Christian Worship*. Downers Grove, Ill.: InterVarsity Press, 1997.

_____. *Mark: Evangelist and Theologian*. Grand Rapids: Zondervan, 1973.

_____. *Reconciliation: A Study of Paul's Theology*. New Foundations Theological Library. Atlanta: John Knox, 1981.

_____. "The Theology of Jude, 1 Peter, and 2 Peter." Pages 63–163 in *The Theology of the Letters of James, Peter, and Jude*. By Andrew Chester and Ralph P. Martin. New Testament Theology. Camridge: Cambridge University Press, 1994.

Martyn, J. Louis. *Galatians*. Anchor Bible 33A. New York: Doubleday, 1998.

_____. *History and Theology in the Fourth Gospel*. Rev. and enlarged ed. Nashville: Abingdon, 1979.

____. *Theological Issues in the Letters of Paul*. Nashville: Abingdon, 1997.

Marxen, Willi. *Introduction to the New Testament*. Philadelphia: Fortress, 1968.

_____. *New Testament Foundations for Christian Ethics*. Minneapolis: Fortress, 1993.

McGrath, Alister E. *Iustitia Dei: A History of the Christian Doctrine of Justification*. 2nd ed. Cambridge: Cambridge University Press, 1998.

McKnight, Scot. "A Loyal Critic: Matthew's Polemic with Judaism in Theological Perspective." Pages 55–79 in *Anti-Semitism and Early Christianity: Issues of Polemic and Faith*. Edited by Craig A. Evans and Donald A. Hagner. Minneapolis: Fortress, 1993.

Meadors, Edward P. "The Orthodoxy of the 'Q' Sayings of Jesus." *Tyndale Bulletin* 43 (1992): 233–57.

Meeks, Wayne A. "The 'Haustafeln' and American Slavery: A Hermeneutical Challenge." Pages 232–53 in *Theology and Ethics in Paul and His Interpreters: Essays in Honor of Victor Paul Furnish*. Edited by Eugene H. Lovering, Jr. and Jerry L. Sumney. Nashville: Abingdon, 1996.

_____. "The Man from Heaven in Johannine Sectarianism." Pages 141–73 in *The Interpretation of John*. Edited by John Ashton. Issues in Religion and Theology 9. London/Philadelphia: Fortress/SPCK, 1986.

_____. *The Moral World of the First Christians*. Library of Early Christianity. Philadelphia: Westminster, 1986.

_____. *The Prophet-King: Moses Traditions and the Johannine Christology*. Novum Testamentum Supplement 14. Leiden: Brill, 1967.

Meier, John P. "Jesus, the Twelve and the Restoration of Israel." Pages 365–404 in *Restoration: Old Testament, Jewish, and Christian Perspectives*. Edited by James M. Scott. Journal for the Study of Judaism in the Persian, Hellenistic, and Roman Periods, Supplement 72. Leiden: Brill, 2001.

_____. *Law and History in Matthew's Gospel*. Analecta biblica 71. Rome: Biblical Institute Press, 1976.

_____. *A Marginal Jew: Rethinking the Historical Jesus*. 3 vols. Anchor Bible Reference Library. New York: Doubleday, 1991–2001.

_____. *The Vision of Matthew: Christ, Church, and Morality in the First Gospel*. New York: Paulist, 1979.

Menken, M. J. J. *2 Thessalonians*. New Testament Readings. London and New York: Routledge, 1994.

_____. "The Structure of 2 Thessalonians." Pages 374–82 in *The Thessalonian Correspondence*. Edited by Raymond F. Collins. Bibliotheca ephemeridum theologicarum lovaniensium 87. Leuven: University Press, 1990.

Merk, Otto. *Biblische Theologie des Neuen Testaments in ihrer Anfangszeit*. Marburger theologische Studien 9. Marburg: N. G. Elwert Verlag, 1972.

Merkel, Helmut. *Die Widersprüche zwischen den Evangelien: Ihre polemische und apologetische Behandlung in der Alten Kirche bis zu Augustin*. Wissenschaftliche Untersuchungen zum Alten und Neuen Testament 13. Tübingen: J. C. B. Mohr (Paul Siebeck): 1971.

Metzger, Bruce M. *A Textual Commentary on the Greek New Testament*. London: United Bible Societies, 1971.

Meyer, Marvin W. "Mystery Religions." Pages 941–45 in the *Anchor Bible Dictionary*. 6 vols. Edited by David Noel Freedman. New York: Doubleday, 1992.

Meyer, Paul. "Pauline Theology: A Proposal for a Pause in Its Pursuit." Pages 140–60 in *Pauline Theology, Volume IV: Looking Back, Pressing On*. Edited by E. Elizabeth Johnson and David M. Hay. Society of Biblical Literature Symposium Series 4. Atlanta: Scholars, 1997.

Michael, J. Hugh. *The Epistle of Paul to the Philippians*. Moffatt New Testament Commentary. London: Hodder and Stoughton, 1928.

Migne, J.-P. *Patrologia graeca*. 162 vols. Paris, 1857–86.

_____. *Patrologia latina*. 217 vols. Paris, 1844–64.

Mitchell, Alan C. "Rich and Poor in the Courts of Corinth: Litigiousness and Status in 1 Corinthians 6.1–11." *New Testament Studies* 39 (1993): 562–86.

Mitchell, Margaret M. "Concerning ΠΕΡΙ ΔΕ in 1 Corinthians." *Novum Testamentum* 31 (1989): 229–56.

_____. *Paul and the Rhetoric of Reconciliation*. Hermeneutische Untersuchungen zur Theologie 29. Tübingen: J. C. B. Mohr (Paul Siebeck), 1991.

Moessner, David P. *The Lord of the Banquet: The Literary and Theological Significance of the Lukan Travel Narrative.* Minneapolis: Fortress, 1989.

Moffatt, James. *A Critical and Exegetical Commentary on the Epistle to the Hebrews.* International Critical Commentary. Edinburgh: T. & T. Clark, 1924.

_____. *The First Epistle of Paul to the Corinthians.* Moffat New Testament Commentary. London: Hodder and Stoughton, 1938.

_____. *The General Epistles: James, Peter and Judas.* Moffatt New Testament Commentary. London: Hodder and Stoughton, 1928.

Moloney, Francis J. *The Gospel of John.* Sacra Pagina 4. Collegeville, Minn.: Michael Glazier, 1998.

Moltmann, Jürgen. *Theology of Hope.* New York: Harper & Row, 1967.

Montefiore, Claude G. *Judaism and St. Paul: Two Essays.* London: M. Goschen, 1914.

Montefiore, Hugh. *A Commentary on the Epistle to the Hebrews.* Black's New Testament Commentary. London: A. and C. Black, 1964.

Moo, Douglas. *The Epistle to the Romans.* Grand Rapids: Eerdmans, 1996.

_____. "Israel and Paul in Romans 7.7–12." *New Testament Studies* 32 (1986): 122–35.

_____. *The Letter of James.* Pillar New Testament Commentary. Grand Rapids: Eerdmans, 2000.

Moore, George Foot. *Judaism in the First Centuries of the Christian Era: The Age of the Tannaim.* 3 vols. Cambridge, Mass.: Harvard University Press, 1927–30.

Morris, Leon. *The Gospel according to John.* New International Commentary on the New Testament. Grand Rapids: Eerdmans, 1971.

Motyer, Stephen. *Your Father the Devil? A New Approach to John and 'the Jews'.* Paternoster Biblical and Theological Monographs. Carlisle, U.K.: Paternoster, 1997.

Moule, C. F. D. *The Epistles to the Colossians and to Philemon.* Cambridge Greek Testament Commentary. Cambridge: Cambridge University Press, 1957.

_____. *Essays in New Testament Interpretation.* Cambridge: Cambridge University Press, 1982.

_____. *The Origin of Christology.* Cambridge: Cambridge University Press, 1977.

Moulton, James Hope, and George Milligan. *The Vocabulary of the Greek Testament Illustrated from the Papyri and Other Non-Literary Sources.* Grand Rapids: Eerdmans, 1959.

Moulton, W. F., and A. S. Geden. *A Concordance to the Greek New Testament.* 4th ed. Edinburgh: T. & T. Clark, 1963.

Mounce, William D. *Pastoral Epistles.* Word Biblical Commentary 46. Nashville: Nelson, 2000.

Morgan, Robert. "Can the Critical Study of Scripture Provide a Doctrinal Norm?" *Journal of Religion* 76 (1996): 206–32.

Müller, Peter. "Der 2. Petrusbrief." *Theologische Rundschau* 66 (2001): 310–37.

Munck, Johannes. *Paul and the Salvation of Mankind.* Atlanta: John Knox, 1959.

Murphy-O'Connor, Jerome. *Paul: A Critical Life.* New York: Oxford University Press, 1996.

_____. *St. Paul's Corinth: Texts and Archaeology.* Good News Studies 6. Wilmington, Del.: Michael Glazier, 1983.

Murray, John. *The Epistle to the Romans.* 2 vols. New International Commentary on the New Testament. Grand Rapids: Eerdmans, 1959–65.

Mussner, Franz. *Der Galaterbrief.* Herders theologischer Kommentar zum Neuen Testament 9. Freiburg: Herder, 1974.

_____. *Der Jakobusbrief.* Herders theologischer Kommentar zum Neuen Testament 13.1. Freiburg: Herder, 1964.

Neill, Stephen, and Tom Wright. *The Interpretation of the New Testament 1861–1986.* 2nd ed. New York: Oxford University Press, 1988.

Neil, William. "The Criticism and Theological Use of the Bible, 1700–1950." Pages 238–93 in *The Cambridge History of the Bible.* Edited by S. L. Greenslade, G. W. H. Lampe, P. R. Ackroyd, and C. F. Evans. 3 vols. Cambridge: Cambridge University Press, 1963–70.

_____. *The Epistle* (sic) *of Paul to the Thessalonians.* Moffat New Testament Commentaries. London: Hodder and Stoughton, 1950.

Nestle, Erwin, and Kurt Aland. *Novum Testamentum Graece.* 25th ed. London: United Bible Societies, 1975.

Neyrey, Jerome. *2 Peter, Jude.* AB 37C. New York: Doubleday, 1993.

_____. "The Form and Background of the Polemic in 2 Peter." *Journal of Biblical Literature* 99 (1980): 407–31.

_____. *The Passion according to Luke: A Redaction Study of Luke's Soteriology.* New York: Paulist, 1985.

Niebuhr, H. Richard. "Introduction" to *The Social Teaching of the Christian Churches,* by Ernst Troeltsch. 2 vols. Chicago: University of Chicago Press, 1981.

Nock, Arthur Darby. *Early Gentile Christianity and Its Hellenistic Background.* New York: Harper, 1964.

Nodet, Étienne. *Histoire de Jésus? Nécessité et limites d'une enquête.* Lire la Bible. Paris: Cerf, 2003.

Nolland, John. *Luke 9:21–18:34.* Word Biblical Commentary 35B. Dallas: Word, 1993.

Norden, Eduard. *Agnostos Theos: Untersuchungen zur Formengeschichte religiöser Rede.* Berlin: Teubner, 1923.

Oakes, Peter. *Philippians: From People to Letter.* Society for the Study of the New Testament Monograph Series 110. Cambridge: Cambridge University Press, 2001.

Oberlinner, Lorenz. *Die Pastoralbriefe: Kommentar zum ersten Timotheusbrief.* Herders theologischer Kommentar zum Neuen Testament 11.2. Frieburg: Herder, 1994.

Oden, Thomas C., ed. *Ancient Christian Commentary on Scripture.* Downers Grove, Ill.: InterVarsity Press, 1998–.

O'Brien, Peter T. *Colossians, Philemon.* Word Biblical Commentary 44. Waco, Tex.: Word, 1982.

_____. *The Epistle to the Philippians: A Commentary on the Greek Text.* New International Greek Testament Commentary. Grand Rapids: Eerdmans, 1991.

_____. *Introductory Thanksgivings in the Letters of Paul.* Novum Testamentum Supplement 49. Leiden: Brill, 1977.

_____. *The Letter to the Ephesians.* Pillar New Testament Commentary. Grand Rapids: Eerdmans, 1999.

_____. "Prayer in Luke–Acts." *Tyndale Bulletin* 24 (1973): 111–27.

O'Neil, Edward, ed. *Teles (The Cynic Teacher).* Society of Biblical Literature Texts and Translations 11. Greco-Roman Religion Series 3. Missoula, Mont.: Scholars, 1977.

Osborne, Grant R. *Revelation.* Baker Exegetical Commentary on the New Testament. Grand Rapids: Baker, 2002.

Oswalt, John N. *The Book of Isaiah: Chapters 40–66.* New International Commentary on the Old Testament. Grand Rapids: Eerdmans, 1998.

Ott, Wilhelm. *Gebet und Heil: Die Bedeutung der Gebetsparänese in der lukanischen Theologie.* Studien zum Alten und Neuen Testaments 12. München: Kösel-Verlag, 1965.

Overman, Andrew. *Matthew's Gospel and Formative Judaism: The Social World of the Matthean Community.* Minneapolis: Fortress, 1990.

Padgett, Alan. "Wealthy Women at Ephesus: 1 Timothy 2:8–15 in Context." *Interpretation* 41 (1987): 19–31.

Painter, John. *Just James: The Brother of Jesus in History and Tradition*. Studies on Personalities of the New Testament. Minneapolis: Fortress, 1999.

Pao, David W. *Acts and the Isaianic New Exodus*. Wissenschaftliche Untersuchungen zum Alten und Neuen Testament 2.130. Tübingen: J. C. B. Mohr (Paul Siebeck), 2000.

Pauck, Wilhelm, ed. and trans. *Melanchthon and Bucer*. Library of Christian Classics 19. Philadelphia: Westminster, 1969.

Paulsen, Henning. *Der zweite Petrusbrief und der Judasbrief*. Meyers kritisch-exegetischer Kommentar über das Neue Testament 12/2. Göttingen: Vandenhoeck & Ruprecht, 1992.

Pearson, Birger Albert. *The Pneumatikos-Psychikos Terminology in 1 Corinthians: A Study in the Theology of the Corinthian Opponents of Paul and Its Relation to Gnosticism*. Society of Biblical Literature Dissertation Series 12. Missoula, Mont.: Scholars, 1973.

Pelikan, Jaroslav, et al., ed. *Luther's Works*. 55 vols. Saint Louis, Mo.: Concordia/Philadelphia: Fortress, 1955–86.

Penna, Romano. *Paul the Apostle*. 2 vols. Collegeville, Minn.: Liturgical, 1996.

Perkins, William. *A Commentary on Galatians*. New York: Pilgrim, 1989.

Peterman, G. W. *Paul's Gift from Philippi: Conventions of Gift-exchange and Christian Giving*. Society for the Study of the New Testament Monograph Series 92. Cambridge: Cambridge University Press, 1997.

Petersen, Norman. *Rediscovering Paul: Philemon and the Sociology of Paul's Narrative World*. Philadelphia: Fortress, 1985.

Petersen, William L. *Tatian's Diatessaron: Its Creation, Dissemination, Significance, and History in Scholarship*. Vigiliae christianae Supplements 25. Leiden: Brill, 1994.

_____. "Textual Evidence of Tatian's Dependence upon Justin's ΑΠΟΜΝΗΜΟΝΕΥΜΑΤΙΑ." *New Testament Studies* 36 (1990): 512–34.

Pétrement, Simone. *A Separate God: The Christian Origins of Gnosticism*. New York: Harper, 1984.

Petzl, Georg. *Die Beichtinschriften Westkleinasiens*. Bonn: Rudolf Habelt, 1994.

Picirilli, Robert E. "Allusions to 2 Peter in the Apostolic Fathers." *Journal for the Study of the New Testament* 33 (1988): 57–83.

Pilgrim, Walter E. *Good News to the Poor: Wealth and Poverty in Luke–Acts*. Minneapolis: Augsburg, 1981.

Pilhofer, Peter. *Philippi*. 2 vols. Wissenschaftliche Untersuchungen zum Alten und Neuen Testament 87. Tübingen: J. C. B. Mohr (Paul Siebeck), 1995–2000.

Plevnik, Joseph. "The Center of Pauline Theology." *Catholic Biblical Quarterly* 51 (1989): 461–78.

_____. *Paul and the Parousia: An Exegetical and Theological Investigation*. Peabody, Mass.: Hendrickson, 1997.

_____. "The Understanding of God at the Basis of Pauline Theology." *Catholic Biblical Quarterly* 65 (2003): 554–67.

Plummer, Alfred. *A Commentary on St. Paul's Epistle to the Philippians*. London: Robert Scott Roxburghe House, 1919.

_____. *A Critical and Exegetical Commentary on the Second Epistle of Paul to the Corinthians*. International Critical Commentary. Edinburgh: T. & T. Clark, 1915.

Plymale, Stephen F. "Luke's Theology of Prayer." Pages 529–51 in the *Society of Biblical Literature 1990 Seminar Papers*. Atlanta: Scholars, 1990.

Pokorný, Petr. *Der Brief des Paulus an die Epheser*. Theologischer Handkommentar zum Neuen Testament 10.2. Leipzig: Evangelische Verlagsanstalt, 1992.

_____. *Colossians: A Commentary*. Peabody, Mass.: Hendrickson, 1991.

_____. *Theologie der lukanischen Schriften*. Forschungen zur Religion und Literatur des Alten und Neuen Testaments 174. Göttingen: Vandenhoeck & Ruprecht, 1998.

Polhill, John B. *Acts*. New American Commentary. Nashville: Broadman, 1992.

Porter, Stanley. *Idioms of the Greek New Testament*. Biblical Languages: Greek Series, 2. Sheffield: Sheffield Academic Press, 1992.

Prior, Michael. *Paul the Letter-Writer and the Second Letter to Timothy*. Journal for the Study of the New Testament Supplement 23. Sheffield: Sheffield Academic Press, 1989.

Price, S. R. F. *Rituals and Power: The Roman Imperial Cult in Asia Minor*. Cambridge: Cambridge University Press, 1984.

Purvis, James D. "The Fourth Gospel and the Samaritans." Pages 145–85 in *The Composition of John's Gospel: Selected Studies from* Novum Testamentum. Edited by David E. Orton. Leiden: Brill, 1999.

Quinn, Jerome D. *The Letter to Titus*. Anchor Bible 35. New York: Doubleday, 1990.

Räisänen, Heikki. *Beyond New Testament Theology: A Story and a Programme*. 2nd ed. London and Philadelphia: SCM and Trinity Press International, 2000.

_____. "Liberating Exegesis." *Bulletin of the John Rylands Papyrus Library* 78 (1996): 193–204.

_____. *The 'Messianic Secret' in Mark*. Edinburgh: T. & T. Clark, 1990.

_____. *Paul and the Law*. Wissenschaftliche Untersuchungen zum Alten und Neuen Testament 29. Tübingen: J. C. B. Mohr (Paul Siebeck), 1983.

_____. "Römer 9–11: Analyse eines geistigen Ringens." *Aufstief und Niedergang der Römischen Welt* 2.25.4 (1987): 2891–939.

Ramsay, W. M. *The Letters to the Seven Churches of Asia and Their Place in the Plan of the Apocalypse*. New York: Hodder & Stoughton, 1904.

Ravens, David. *Luke and the Restoration of Israel*. Journal for the Study of the New Testament Supplement 119. Sheffield: Sheffield Academic Press, 1995.

Reicke, Bo. *Re-examining Paul's Letters: The History of the Pauline Correspondence*. Edited by David P. Moessner and Ingalisa Reicke. Harrisburg, Pa.: Trinity Press International, 2001.

Reimarus, Hermann Samuel. *The Goal of Jesus and His Disciples*. Leiden: Brill, 1970.

Richard, Earl J. *First and Second Thessalonians*, Sacra Pagina 11. Collegeville, Minn.: Michael Glazier, 1995.

Richards, E. Randolph. "The Codex and the Early Collection of Paul's Letters." *Bulletin for Biblical Research* (1998): 151–66.

Richardson, John. "Governing Rome." Pages 112–39 in *The World of Rome: An Introduction to Roman Culture*. Edited by Peter Jones and Keith Sidwell. Cambridge: Cambridge University Press, 1997.

Riches, John. *A Century of New Testament Study*. Valley Forge, Pa.: Trinity Press International, 1993.

Ridderbos, Herman. *Aan de Romeinen*. Commentaar op het Nieuwe Testament. Kampen: Kok, 1959.

_____. *The Gospel of John: A Theological Commentary*. Grand Rapids: Eerdmans, 1997.

_____. *De Pastorale Brieven*. Commentaar op het Nieuwe Testament. Kampen: Kok, 1967.

_____. *Paul: An Outline of His Theology*. Grand Rapids: Eerdmans, 1975.

_____. *Redemptive History and the New Testament Scriptures*. Phillipsburg, N.J.: Presbyterian & Reformed, 1963.

Riesner, Rainer. *Paul's Early Period: Chronology, Mission Strategy, Theology*. Grand Rapids: Eerdmans, 1998.

_____. "Sollen wir das Neue Testament unhistorisch-unkritisch auslegen?" Pages 22–41 in *Gotteswort im Menschenwort? Zum Verstehen und Auslegen der Bibel.* Edited by Sven Grosse and Jochen Walldorf. Porta-Studien 30. Marburg: Studentenmission in Deutschland, 1999.

_____. "Der zweite Petrus-brief und die Eschatologie." Pages 124–43 in *Zukunftserwartung in biblischer Sicht: Beiträge zur Eschatologie.* Edited by Gerhard Maier. Monographien und Studienbücher 313. Wuppertal: R. Brockhaus Verlag, 1984.

Robertson, O. Palmer. *The Books of Nahum, Habakkuk, and Zephaniah.* New International Commentary on the Old Testament. Grand Rapids: Eerdmans, 1990.

Robinson, J. Armitage. *St. Paul's Epistle to the Ephesians.* London: James Clarke, 1928.

Robinson, James M., ed. *The Nag Hammadi Library in English.* 3rd ed. New York: Harper & Row, 1988.

Roetzel, Calvin J. *Paul: The Man and the Myth.* Minneapolis: Fortress, 1999.

Ropes, James Hardy. *A Critical and Exegetical Commentary on the Epistle of James.* International Critical Commentary. Edinburgh: T. & T. Clark, 1916.

Rosner, Brian S., ed. *Understanding Paul's Ethics: Twentieth-Century Approaches.* Grand Rapids: Eerdmans, 1995.

_____. *Paul, Scripture and Ethics: A Study of 1 Corinthians 5–7.* Arbeiten zur Geschichte des antiken Judentums und des Urchristentums 22. Leiden: Brill, 1994.

Rowland, Christopher. *The Open Heaven: A Study of Apocalyptic in Judaism and Early Christianity.* New York: Crossroad, 1982.

Rowley, Harold Henry. *The Servant of the Lord and Other Essays on the Old Testament.* London: Lutterworth, 1952.

Russell, Donald A. F. M. "Dionysius." Page 351 in *The Oxford Classical Dictionary.* 2nd ed. Edited by N. G. L. Hammond and H. H. Scullard. Oxford: Oxford University Press, 1970.

Russell, R. "The Idle in 2 Thess 3.6–12: An Eschatological or a Social Problem?" *New Testament Studies* 34 (1988): 105–19.

Saldarini, Anthony J. *Matthew's Christian-Jewish Community.* Chicago Studies in the History of Judaism. Chicago: University of Chicago Press, 1994.

Sanders, E. P. *Jesus and Judaism.* Philadelphia: Fortress, 1985.

_____. "Jewish Association with Gentiles and Galatians 2:11–14." Pages 170–88 in *The Conversation Continues: Studies in Paul and John in Honor of J. Louis Martyn.* Edited by Robert T. Fortna and Beverly R. Gaventa. Nashville: Abingdon, 1990.

_____. *Judaism: Practice and Belief 63 BCE–66 CE.* London/Philadelphia: SCM/Trinity Press International, 1992.

_____. *Paul.* Oxford: Oxford University Press, 1991.

_____. *Paul and Palestinian Judaism: A Comparison of Patterns of Religion.* Philadelphia: Fortress, 1977.

_____. *Paul, the Law, and the Jewish People.* Philadelphia: Fortress, 1983.

Sanday, William, and Arthur Headlam. *A Critical and Exegetical Commentary on the Epistle to the Romans.* 5th ed. International Critical Commentary. Edinburgh: T. & T. Clark, 1902.

Sandys-Wunsch, John, and Laurence Eldredge. "J. P. Gabler and the Distinction between Biblical and Dogmatic Theology: Translation, Commentary, and Discussion of His Originality." *Scottish Journal of Theology* 33 (1980): 133–58.

Sappington, Thomas J. *Revelation and Redemption at Colossae.* Journal for the Study of the New Testament Supplement 53. Sheffield: Sheffield Academic Press, 1991.

Sarna, Nahum M. *Exodus*. Jewish Publication Society Torah Commentary. Philadelphia: Jewish Publication Society, 1991.

Schaff, Philip. *The Creeds of Christendom*. 3 vols. New York: Harper & Brothers, 1877.

Schlatter, Adolf. *Der Glaube im Neuen Testament*. 4th ed. Stuttgart: Calwer Verlag, 1927.

_____. *Romans: The Righteousness of God*. Peabody, Mass.: Hendrickson, 1995.

_____. *The Theology of the Apostles: The Development of New Testament Theology*. Grand Rapids: Baker, 1998.

_____. "The Theology of the New Testament and Dogmatics." Pages 117–66 in *The Nature of New Testament Theology: The Contribution of William Wrede and Adolf Schlatter*. Edited by Robert Morgan. Studies in Biblical Theology. London: SCM, 1973.

Schlier, Heinrich. *Die Brief an die Epheser: Ein Kommentar*. Düsseldorf: Patmos, 1957.

_____. *Der Brief an die Galater*. 11th ed. Meyers kritisch-exegetischer Kommentar über das Neue Testament 7. Göttingen: Vandenhoeck & Ruprecht, 1951.

Schmid, Christian Friedrich. *Biblical Theology of the New Testament*. Edinburgh: T. & T. Clark, 1882.

Schmidt, Daryl. "Luke's 'Innocent' Jesus: A Scriptural Apologetic." Pages 111–21 in *Political Issues in Luke-Acts*. Edited by Richard J. Cassidy and Philip Scharper. Maryknoll, N.Y.: Orbis, 1983.

Schnackenburg, Rudolf. *The Church in the New Testament*. New York: Seabury, 1965.

_____. *Jesus in the Gospels: A Biblical Christology*. Louisville: Westminster John Knox, 1995.

_____. *The Johannine Epistles: Introduction and Commentary*. New York: Crossroad, 1992.

Schrage, Wolfgang. *Der erste Brief an die Korinther (1Kor 1,1–6,11)*. Evangelisch-katholischer Kommentar zum Neuen Testament 7.1. Zürich: Benziger/Neukirchen-Vluyn: Neukirchener, 1991.

_____. *Der erste Brief an die Korinther (1Kor 6,12–11,16)*. Evangelisch-katholischer Kommentar zum Neuen Testament 7.2. Zürich: Benziger/Neukirchen-Vluyn: Neukirchener, 1995.

Schreiner, Thomas R. *1, 2 Peter, and Jude*. New American Commentary 37. Nashville: Broadman & Holman, 2003.

_____. "The Church as the New Israel and the Future of Ethnic Israel in Paul." *Studia Biblica* 13 (1983): 17–38.

_____. "Did Paul Believe in Justification by Works? Another Look at Romans 2." *Bulletin for Biblical Research* 3 (1993): 131–58.

_____. *The Law and Its Fulfillment: A Pauline Theology of Law*. Grand Rapids: Baker, 1993.

_____. *Paul: Apostle of God's Glory in Christ: A Pauline Theology*. Downers Grove, Ill.: InterVarsity Press, 2001.

_____. *Romans*. Baker Exegetical Commentary on the New Testament. Grand Rapids: Baker, 1998.

Schreiner, Thomas R., and Ardel B. Caneday. *The Race Set Before Us: A Biblical Theology of Perseverance and Assurance*. Downers Grove, Ill.: InterVarsity Press, 2001.

Schwegler, Albert. *Das nachapostolische Zeitalter in den Hauptmomenten seiner Entwicklung*. 2 vols. Tübingen: Ludwig Friedrich Fues, 1846.

Schweitzer, Albert. *Geschichte der Leben-Jesu-Forschung*. 2nd ed. Tübingen: J. C. B. Mohr (Paul Siebeck), 1913.

_____. *The Mysticism of Paul the Apostle*. New York: Henry Holt, 1931.

_____. *The Quest of the Historical Jesus*. New York: Macmillan, 1968.

Schweizer, Eduard. *Ego Eimi: Die religionsgeschichtliche Herkunft und theologische Bedeutung der johanneischen Bildreden, zugleich ein Beitrag zur Quellenfrage des vierten Evangeliums*. Forschungen zur Religion und Literatur des Alten und Neuen Testaments 38. Göttingen: Vandenhoeck & Ruprecht, 1939.

_____. "Johannine Language and Style: The Question of Their Unity." Pages 125–47 in *L'évangile de Jean*. Edited by M. de Jonge. Bibliotheca ephemeridum theologicarum lovaniensium 44. Leuven: University Press, 1987.

_____. *The Letter to the Colossians: A Commentary*. Minneapolis: Augsburg, 1982.

_____. "Matthew's Church." Pages 149–77 in *The Interpretation of Matthew*. Edited by Graham N. Stanton. 2nd ed. Edinburgh: T. & T. Clark, 1995.

Scott, E. F. *The Epistles of Paul to the Colossians, to Philemon and to the Ephesians*. Moffatt New Testament Commentary. London: Hodder & Stoughton, 1930.

_____. *The Pastoral Epistles*. Moffatt New Testament Commentary. London: Hodder & Stoughton, 1936.

Scott, James M. *Adoption as Sons of God: An Exegetical Investigation into the Background of ΥΙΟΘΕΣΙΑ in the Pauline Corpus*. Wissenschaftliche Untersuchungen zum Alten und Neuen Testament 2.48. Tübingen: J. C. B. Mohr (Paul Siebeck), 1992.

Seifrid, Mark A. *Justification by Faith: The Origin and Development of a Central Pauline Theme*. Novum Testamentum Supplement 68. Leiden: Brill, 1992.

Sellin, Gerhard. "Die Häretiker des Judasbriefes." *Zeitschrift für die neutestamentliche Wissenschaft und die Kunde der älteren Kirche* 77 (1986): 206–25.

Selwyn, Edward Gordon. *The First Epistle of St. Peter*. London: Macmillan, 1946.

Senior, Donald. *The Passion of Jesus in the Gospel of Luke*. Passion Series 3. Wilmington, Del.: Michael Glazier, 1989.

deSilva, David A. *Despising Shame: Honor Discourse and Community Maintenance in the Epistle to the Hebrews*. Society of Biblical Literature Monograph Series 152. Atlanta: Scholars, 1995.

_____. *The Hope of Glory: Honor Discourse and New Testament Interpretation*. Collegeville, Minn.: Liturgical, 1999.

_____. *Perseverance in Gratitude: A Socio-Rhetorical Commentary on the Epistle "to the Hebrews."* Grand Rapids: Eerdmans, 2000.

Silva, Moisés. *Explorations in Exegetical Method: Galatians as a Test Case*. Grand Rapids: Baker, 1996.

_____. *Philippians*. Baker Exegetical Commentary on the New Testament. Grand Rapids: Baker, 1992.

Sim, David C. *The Gospel of Matthew and Christian Judaism: The History and Social Setting of the Matthean Community*. Studies of the New Testament and Its World. Edinburgh: T. & T. Clark, 1998.

_____. "Matthew's Anti-Paulinism: A Neglected Feature of Matthean Studies." Paper presented at the annual meeting of the Studiorum Novi Testamenti Societas. Montreal, Quebec, August 2, 2001.

Skeat, T. C. "'Especially the Parchments': A Note on 2 Tim 4.13." *Journal of Theological Studies* 30 (1979): 173–77.

Smalley, Stephen S. *John: Evangelist and Interpreter*. 2nd ed. New Testament Profiles. Downers Grove, Ill.: InterVarsity Press, 1998.

Smallwood, E. Mary. *The Jews under Roman Rule from Pompey to Diocletian: A Study in Political Relations*. Studies in Judaism in Late Antiquity 20. Leiden: Brill, 1981.

Smith, D. Moody. *John*. Abingdon New Testament Commentaries. Nashville: Abingdon, 1999.

_____. *The Theology of the Gospel of John*. New Testament Theology. Cambridge: Cambridge University Press, 1995.

Smith, Morton. "De Superstitione (Moralia 164E–171F)." Pages 1–35 in *Plutarch's Theological Writings and Early Christian Literature*. Edited by Hans Dieter Betz. Studia ad corpus hellenisticum Novi Testamenti 3. Leiden: E. J. Brill, 1975.

Smith, Jay E. "Another Look at 4Q416 2 ii.21, a Critical Parallel to First Thessalonians 4:4." *Catholic Biblical Quarterly* 63 (2001): 499–504.

Schmithals, Walter. *Paul and the Gnostics*. Nashville: Abingdon, 1972.

Souter, Alexander, and Emil G. Kraeling. "Crete, Cretans." Page 188 in the *Dictionary of the Bible*. 2nd ed. Edited by James Hastings. Revised by Frederick C. Grant and H. H. Rowley. Edinburgh: T. & T. Clark, 1963.

South, James T. "A Critique of the 'Curse/Death' Interpretation of 1 Corinthians 5.1–8." *New Testament Studies* 39 (1993): 539–61.

Spanje, T. E. *Inconsistency in Paul? A Critique of the Work of Heikki Räisänen*, Wissenschaftliche Untersuchungen zum Alten und Neuen Testament 2.110. Tübingen: J. C. B. Mohr (Paul Siebeck), 1999.

Spener, Philipp Jacob. *Pia desideria*. Edited by Kurt Aland. Kleine Texte für Vorlesungen und Übungen 170. Berlin: Walter de Gruyter, 1964.

Spicq, Ceslas. *Les Épitres Pastorales*. Études bibliques. 4th ed. 2 vols. Paris: Lecoffre, 1969.

_____. *Theological Lexicon of the New Testament*. 3 vols. Peabody, Mass.: Hendrickson, 1994.

Stanton, Graham. "The Fourfold Gospel." *New Testament Studies* 43 (1997): 317–46.

_____. *A Gospel for a New People: Studies in Matthew*. Edinburgh: T. & T. Clark, 1992.

Starr, James M. *Sharers in Divine Nature: 2 Peter 1:4 in Its Hellenistic Context*. Coniectanea neotestamentica 33. Stockholm: Almqvist & Wiksell, 2000.

de Ste. Croix, G. E. M. "Why Were the Early Christians Persecuted?" *Past & Present* 26 (1963): 6–38.

_____. "Why Were the Early Christians Persecuted? A Rejoinder [to A. N. Sherwin-White]." *Past & Present* 27 (1964): 28–33.

Stendahl, Krister. *Meanings: The Bible as Document and as Guide*. Philadelphia: Fortress, 1984.

Sterling, Gregory. *Historiography and Self-Definition: Josephos, Luke–Acts and Apologetic Historiography*. Novum Testamentum Supplement 64. Leiden: Brill, 1992.

Stott, John R. W. *The Epistles of John*. Tyndale New Testament Commentaries. Grand Rapids: Eerdmans, 1964.

Stowers, Stanley K. *Letter Writing in Greco-Roman Antiquity*. Library of Early Christianity. Philadelphia: Westminster, 1986.

Strack, Hermann Leberecht, and Paul Billerbeck. *Kommentar zum Neuen Testament aus Talmud und Midrasch*. 4 vols. München: C. H. Beck, 1924–89.

Strauss, Mark L. *The Davidic Messiah in Luke–Acts: The Promise and Its Fulfillment in Lukan Christology*. Journal for the Study of the New Testament Supplement 110. Sheffield: Sheffield Academic Press, 1995.

Strecker, Georg. *The Johannine Letters*. Hermeneia. Minneapolis: Fortress, 1996.

_____. *Theology of the New Testament*. Berlin: Walter de Gruyter, 2000.

Stuhlhofer, Franz. *Der Gebrauch der Bibel von Jesus bis Euseb: eine statistische Untersuchung zur Kanonsgeschichte*. Monographien und Studienbücher 335. Wuppertal: Brockhaus, 1988.

Stuhlmacher, Peter. *Biblische Theologie des Neuen Testaments*. 2 vols. Göttingen: Vandenhoeck & Ruprecht, 1992–99.

_____. *Paul's Letter to the Romans: A Commentary*. Louisville: Westminster John Knox, 1994.

_____. *Reconciliation, Law and Righteousness: Essays in Biblical Theology*. Philadelphia: Fortress, 1986.

_____. "The Understanding of Christ in the Pauline School: A Sketch." Pages 159–74 in *Jews and Christians: The Parting of the Ways A.D. 70–135*. Edited by James D. G. Dunn. Grand Rapids: Eerdmans, 1999.

Sumney, Jerry L. *Identifying Paul's Opponents: The Question of Method in 2 Corinthians*, Journal for the Study of the New Testament Supplement 40. Sheffield: Sheffield Academic Press, 1990.

Swete, Henry Barclay. *The Apocalypse of St. John*. 3rd ed. London: Macmillan, 1909.

_____. *The Gospel according to St. Mark*. London: Macmillan, 1898.

_____. *The Holy Spirit in the New Testament*. London: Macmillan, 1909.

Széles, Mária Eszenyei. *Wrath and Mercy: A Commentary on the Books of Habakkuk and Zephaniah*. International Theological Commentary. Grand Rapids: Eerdmans, 1987.

Tannehill, Robert C. "The Disciples in Mark: The Function of a Narrative Role." Pages 169–95 in *The Interpretation of Mark*. 2nd ed. Edited by William R. Telford. Studies in New Testament Interpretation. Edinburgh: T. & T. Clark, 1995.

_____. "The Story of Israel within the Lukan Narrative." Pages 325–39 in *Jesus and the Heritage of Israel: Luke's Narrative Claim upon Israel's Legacy*. Edited by David P. Moessner. Luke the Interpreter of Israel 1. Harrisburg, Pa.: Trinity Press International, 1999.

Taylor, Vincent. *The Gospel according to St. Mark*. London: Macmillan, 1957.

Theissen, Gerd. *The Social Setting of Pauline Christianity: Essays on Corinth*. Philadelphia: Fortress, 1982.

Thiede, Carsten Peter. "A Pagan Reader of 2 Peter: Cosmic Conflagration in 2 Peter 3 and the *Octavius* of Minucius Felix." *Journal for the Study of the New Testament* 26 (1986): 79–96.

Thielman, Frank. "Ephesians." In *Commentary on the Use of the Old Testament in the New*. Edited by Gregory D. Beale and D. A. Carson. Grand Rapids: Baker, forthcoming.

_____. "Ephesus and the Literary Setting of Philippians." Pages 205–23 in *New Testament Greek and Exegesis*. Edited by Amy M. Donaldson and Timothy B. Sailors. Grand Rapids: Eerdmans, 2003.

_____. *From Plight to Solution: A Jewish Framework for Understanding Paul's View of the Law in Galatians and Romans*. Novum Testamentum Supplement 61. Leiden: Brill, 1989.

_____. "Law and Liberty in the Ethics of Paul." *Ex Auditu* 11 (1995): 63–75.

_____. *The Law and the New Testament: The Question of Continuity*. Companions to the New Testament. New York: Crossroad, 1999.

_____. *Paul and the Law: A Contextual Approach*. Downers Grove, Ill.: InterVarsity Press, 1994.

_____. "Paul as Jewish Christian Theologian: The Theology of Paul in the Magnum Opus of James D. G. Dunn." *PRSt* 25 (1998): 381–87.

_____. "The Story of Israel and the Theology of Romans 5–8." Pages 169–95 in *Pauline Theology, Volume III: Romans*. Edited by David M. Hay and E. Elizabeth Johnson. Minneapolis: Fortress, 1995.

_____. "The Style of the Fourth Gospel and Ancient Literary Critical Concepts of Religious Discourse." Pages 169–83 in *Persuasive Artistry: Studies in New Testament Rhetoric in Honor of George A. Kennedy*. Edited by Duane F. Watson. Journal for the Study of the New Testament Supplement 50. Sheffield: Sheffield Academic Press, 1991.

_____. "Unexpected Mercy: Echoes of a Biblical Motif in Romans 9–11." *Scottish Journal of Theology* 47 (1994): 169–81.

Thiselton, Anthony C. *The First Epistle to the Corinthians*. New International Greek Testament Commentary. Grand Rapids: Eerdmans, 2000.

Thompson, J. A. *The Book of Jeremiah*. New International Commentary on the Old Testament. Grand Rapids: Eerdmans, 1980.

Thompson, J. M. "Is John XXI an Appendix?" *Expositor* 10 (1915): 144–46.

Thompson, Leonard L. *The Book of Revelation: Apocalypse and Empire*. New York: Oxford, 1990.

Thompson, William G. *Matthew's Advice to a Divided Community: Mt. 17,22–18,35*. Analecta biblica 44. Rome: Biblical Institute Press, 1970.

van der Toorn, Karel, Bob Becking, and Pieter W. van der Horst. *Dictionary of Deities and Demons in the Bible*. 2nd ed. Leiden: Brill/Grand Rapids: Eerdmans, 1999.

Towner, Philip H. *The Goal of Our Instruction: The Structure of Theology and Ethics in the Pastoral Epistles*. Journal for the Study of the New Testament Supplement 34. Sheffield: Sheffield Academic Press, 1989.

_____. "The Portrait of Paul and the Theology of 2 Timothy: The Closing Chapter of the Pauline Story." *Horizons of Biblical Theology* 21 (1999): 151–70.

Trench, Richard Chenevix. *Synonyms of the New Testament*. Rev. ed. London: Macmillan, 1865.

Trobisch, David. *The First Edition of the New Testament*. Oxford: Oxford University Press, 2000.

Troeltsch, Ernst. *Religion in History*. Edinburgh: T. & T. Clark, 1991.

_____. *The Social Teaching of the Christian Churches*. 2 vols. Chicago: University of Chicago Press, 1981.

Tuckett, Christopher. "Introduction." Pages 1–28 in *The Messianic Secret*. Edited by Christopher Tuckett. Philadelphia: Fortress, 1983.

_____. *Nag Hammadi and the Gospel Tradition: Synoptic Tradition in the Nag Hammadi Library*. Studies in the New Testament and Its World. Edinburgh: T. & T. Clark, 1986.

_____. "Thomas and the Synoptics." *Novum Testamentum* 30 (1988): 132–57.

Turner, Max. "Mission and Meaning in Terms of 'Unity' in Ephesians." Pages 138–66 in *Mission and Meaning: Essays Presented to Peter Cotterell*. Edited by Antony Billington, Tony Lane, and Max Turner. Carlisle, U.K.: Paternoster, 1995.

Tyson, Joseph B. *The Death of Jesus in Luke–Acts*. Columbia, S. C.: University of South Carolina Press, 1986.

Valantasis, Richard. *The Gospel of Thomas*. London: Routledge, 1997.

Vanhoye, Albert. *Structure and Message of the Epistle to the Hebrews*. Subsidia biblica 12. Roma: Editrice Pontificio Istituto Biblico, 1989.

Vermes, Geza. *The Complete Dead Sea Scrolls in English*. New York: Penguin, 1997.

Verner, David C. *The Household of God: The Social World of the Pastoral Epistles*. Society of Biblical Literature Dissertation Series 71. Chico, Calif.: Scholars, 1983.

Vielhauer, Philipp. "On the 'Paulinism' of Acts." Pages 33–50 in *Studies in Luke–Acts*. Edited by Leander E. Keck and J. Louis Martin. Philadelphia: Fortress, 1966.

Vincent, Marvin R. *The Epistles to the Philippians and Philemon*. International Critical Commentary. Edinburgh: T. & T. Clark, 1897.

Vögtle, Anton. *Der Judasbrief, der Zweite Petrusbrief*. Evangelisch-katholischer Kommentar zum Neuen Testament 22. Solothurn: Benziger/Neukirchen-Vluyn: Neukirchener, 1994.

Vouga, François. *Geschichte des frühen Christentums*. Tübingen: Francke Verlag, 1994.

_____. *Une théologie du Nouveau Testament*. Le Monde de la Bible 43. Geneva: Éditions Labor et Fides, 2001.

Wace, Henry, and William C. Piercy. *A Dictionary of Christian Biography and Literature to the End of the Sixth Century A. D. with an Account of the Principal Sects and Heresies*. Peabody, Mass.: Hendrickson, 1994.

Walasky, Paul W. *'And So We Came to Rome': The Political Perspective of St. Luke*. Society for New Testament Studies Monograph Series 49. Cambridge: Cambridge University Press, 1983.

Walker, P. W. L. *Jesus and the Holy City: New Testament Perspectives on Jerusalem.* Grand Rapids: Eerdmans, 1996.

Wallace, Daniel B. *Greek Grammar beyond the Basics: An Exegetical Syntax of the New Testament.* Grand Rapids: Zondervan, 1996.

Wallace-Hadrill, Andrew. "The Roman Family." Pages 208–34 in *The World of Rome: An Introduction to Roman Culture.* Edited by Peter Jones and Keith Sidwell. Cambridge: Cambridge University Press, 1997.

Wanamaker, Charles A. *Commentary on 1 and 2 Thessalonians.* New International Greek Testament Commentary. Grand Rapids: Eerdmans, 1990.

Watson, Francis. *Paul, Judaism and the Gentiles: A Sociological Approach.* Society for the New Testament Monograph Series 56. Cambridge: Cambridge University Press, 1986.

_____. "The Social Function of Mark's Secrecy Theme." *Journal for the Study of the New Testament* 24 (1985): 49–69.

_____. *Text and Truth: Redefining Biblical Theology.* Grand Rapids: Eerdmans, 1997.

_____. "The Triune Divine Identity: Reflections on Pauline God-Language, in Disagreement with J. D. G. Dunn." *Journal for the Study of the New Testament* 80 (2000): 99–124.

_____. "Writing the Mystery: Christ and Reality in the Letter to the Ephesians." Paper presented at the annual meeting of the Society of Biblical Literature, Nov. 19, 2000, Nashville.

Watts, Rikki E. "'For I Am Not Ashamed of the Gospel': Romans 1:16–17 and Habakkuk 2:4." Pages 3–25 in *Romans and the People of God: Essays in Honor of Gordon D. Fee on the Occasion of His 65th Birthday.* Edited by Sven K. Soderlund and N. T. Wright. Grand Rapids: Eerdmans, 1999.

_____. *Isaiah's New Exodus in Mark.* Wissenschaftliche Untersuchungen zum Alten und Neuen Testament 2.88. Tübingen: J. C. B. Mohr (Paul Siebeck): 1997.

Weaver, P. R. C. *Familia Caesaris: A Social Study of the Emperor's Freedmen and Slaves.* Cambridge: Cambridge University Press, 1972.

Weber, Max. *The Sociology of Religion.* Boston: Beacon, 1963.

Wedderburn, A. J. M. *The Reasons for Romans.* Studies of the New Testament and Its World. Edinburgh: T. & T. Clark, 1991.

_____. "The Theology of Colossians." Pages 1–71 in *The Theology of the Later Pauline Letters.* By Andrew T. Lincoln and A. J. M. Wedderburn. New Testament Theology. Cambridge: Cambridge University Press, 1993,

Weeden, Theodore J. *Mark: Traditions in Conflict.* Philadelphia: Fortress, 1971.

Weima, Jeffrey A. D. "An Apology for the Apologetic Function of 1 Thessalonians 2.1–12." *Journal for the Study of the New Testament* 68 (1997): 73–99.

_____. "'But We Became Infants among You': The Case of ΝΗΠΙΟΙ in 1 Thess 2.7." *New Testament Studies* 46 (2000): 547–64.

_____. "'How You Must Walk to Please God': Holiness and Discipleship in 1 Thessalonians." Pages 98–119 in *Patterns of Discipleship in the New Testament.* Edited by Richard N. Longenecker. Grand Rapids: Eerdmans, 1996.

Weiss, Bernard. *Die drei Briefe des Apostel Johannes.* Meyers kritisch-exegetischer Kommentar über das Neue Testament 14. 6th ed. Göttingen: Vandenhoeck & Ruprecht, 1899.

Weisse, Christian Hermann. *Die evangelische Geschichte Kritische und philosophisch bearbeitet.* 2 vols. Leipzig: Breitkopf & Härtel, 1838.

Weiss, Hans-Friedrich. *Der Brief an die Hebräer.* 15th ed. Meyers kritisch-exegetischer Kommentar über das Neue Testament 13. Göttingen: Vandenhoeck & Ruprecht, 1991.

Weiss, Johannes. *Das älteste Evangelium: Ein Beitrag zum Verständnis des Markus-Evangeliums und der ältesten evangelischen Überlieferung.* Göttingen: Vandenhoeck & Ruprecht, 1903.

_____. *Der erste Korintherbrief.* Meyers kritisch-exegetischer Kommentar über das Neue Testament. 9th ed. Vandenhoeck & Ruprecht, 1910.

Wellhausen, Julius. *Erweiterungen und Änderungen im vierten Evangelium.* Berlin: Reimer, 1907.

Wenham, David. *Paul: Follower of Jesus or Founder of Christianity?* Grand Rapids: Eerdmans, 1995.

Westcott, Brooke Foss. *The Epistle to the Hebrews.* 3rd ed. London: Macmillan, 1909.

Westerholm, Stephen. *Israel's Law and the Church's Faith: Paul and His Recent Interpreters.* Grand Rapids: Eerdmans, 1988.

_____. *Perspectives Old and New on Paul: The "Lutheran" Paul and His Critics.* Grand Rapids: Eerdmans, 2004.

_____. "Temple." Pages 759–76 in vol. 4 of *The International Standard Bible Encyclopedia.* Edited by Geoffrey Bromiley, et al. Rev. ed. 4 vols. Grand Rapids: Eerdmans, 1979–88.

White, John L. *The Apostle of God: Paul and the Promise of Abraham.* Peabody, Mass.: Hendrickson, 1999.

_____. *Light from Ancient Letters.* Foundations and Facets. Philadelphia: Fortress, 1986.

Whiteley, D. E. H. *The Theology of St. Paul.* Oxford: Basil Blackwell, 1964.

Whitton, J. "A Neglected Meaning for *skeuos* in 1 Thessalonians 4.4." *New Testament Studies* 28 (1982): 142–43.

Wiefel, Wolfgang. "The Jewish Community in Ancient Rome and the Origins of Roman Christianity." Pages 85–101 in *The Romans Debate.* Edited by Karl P. Donfried. Rev. and exp. ed. Peabody, Mass.: Hendrickson, 1991.

Wilckens, Ulrich. *Der Brief an die Römer (6–11).* Evangelisch-katholischer Kommentar zum Neuen Testament 6.2. Zürich: Benziger/Neukirchen-Vluyn: Neukirchener, 1980.

_____. *Der Brief an die Römer (Röm 12–16).* Evangelisch-katholischer Kommentar zum Neuen Testament 6.3. Zürich: Benziger/Neukirchen-Vluyn: Neukirchener, 1982.

Wilken, Robert L. *The Christians as the Romans Saw Them.* New Haven, Conn.: Yale University Press, 1984.

Wilson, Walter T. *The Hope of Glory: Education and Exhortation in the Epistle to the Colossians.* Novum Testamentum Supplement 88. Leiden: Brill, 1997.

Windsch, Hans. *Die katholischen Briefe.* 2nd ed. Rev. by Herbert Preisker. Handbuch zum Neuen Testament 15. Tübingen: Mohr, 1951.

_____. *Der zweite Korintherbrief.* 9th ed. Meyers kritisch-exegetischer Kommentar über das Neue Testament. Göttingen: Vandenhoeck & Ruprecht, 1924.

Winger, Michael. *By What Law? The Meaning of Νόμος in the Letters of Paul.* Society of Biblical Literature Dissertation Series 128. Atlanta: Scholars, 1992.

Winter, Bruce W. *After Paul Left Corinth: The Influence of Secular Ethics and Social Change.* Grand Rapids: Eerdmans, 2001.

_____. "The Entries and Ethics of Orators and Paul (1 Thessalonians 2:1–12)." *TynBul* 44 (1993): 55–74.

_____. "'If a man does not wish to work....'" *Tyndale Bulletin* 40 (1989): 303–15.

_____. *Philo and Paul among the Sophists.* Society for New Testament Studies Monograph Series 96. Cambridge: Cambridge University Press, 1997.

_____. "The 'New' Roman Wife and 1 Timothy 2:9–15: The Search for a *Sitz im Leben.*" *Tyndale Bulletin* 51 (2000): 285–94.

_____. "'The Seasons' of this Life and Eschatology in 1 Corinthians 7:29–31." Pages 323–34 in *Eschatology in Bible and Theology: Evangelical Essays at the Dawn of a New Millennium.* Edited by Kent E. Brower and Mark W. Elliott. Downers Grove, Ill.: InterVarsity Press, 1997.

_____. *Seek the Welfare of the City: Christians as Benefactors and Citizens.* Grand Rapids: Eerdmans, 1994.

Witherington, Ben, III. *The Acts of the Apostles: A Socio-Rhetorical Commentary.* Grand Rapids: Eerdmans, 1998.

_____. *Friendship and Finances in Philippi: The Letter of Paul to the Philippians.* The New Testament in Context. Valley Forge, Pa.: Trinity Press International, 1994.

_____. *Jesus, Paul and the End of the World: A Comparative Study in New Testament Eschatology.* Downers Grove, Ill.: InterVarsity Press, 1992.

_____. *Jesus the Sage: The Pilgrimage of Wisdom.* Minneapolis: Fortress, 1994.

_____. *Jesus the Seer: The Progress of Prophecy.* Peabody, Mass.: Hendrickson, 1999.

_____. *The Many Faces of the Christ: The Christologies of the New Testament and Beyond.* Companions to the New Testament. New York: Crossroad, 1998.

_____. "Transcending Imminence: The Gordion Knot of Pauline Eschatology." Pages 171–86 in *Eschatology in Bible and Theology: Evangelical Essays at the Dawn of a New Millennium.* Edited by Kent E. Brower and Mark W. Elliott. Downers Grove, Ill.: InterVarsity Press, 1997.

Wolter, Michael. *Die Pastoralbriefe als Paulustradition.* Forschungen zur Religion und Literatur des Alten und Neuen Testaments 146. Göttingen: Vandenhoeck & Ruprecht, 1988.

Wrede, William. *The Messianic Secret.* Cambridge: James Clarke, 1971.

_____. *Paul.* London: Philip Green, 1907.

_____. "The Task and Methods of 'New Testament Theology.'" Pages 68–116 in *The Nature of New Testament Theology: The Contribution of William Wrede and Adolf Schlatter.* Edited by Robert Morgan. Studies in Biblical Theology 25. London: SCM, 1973.

_____. *Über Aufgabe und Methode der sogenannten neutestamentlichen Theologie.* Göttingen: Vandenhoeck & Ruprecht, 1897.

Wright, N. T. "ἁρπαγμός and the Meaning of Philippians 2:5–11." *Journal of Theological Studies* 37 (1986): 321–52.

_____. *The Climax of the Covenant: Christ and the Law in Pauline Theology.* Edinburgh: T. & T. Clark, 1991.

_____. *Jesus and the Victory of God.* Minneapolis: Fortress, 1996.

_____. "New Exodus, New Inheritance: The Narrative Substructure of Romans 3–8." Pages 26–35 in *Romans and the People of God: Essays in Honor of Gordon D. Fee on the Occasion of His 65th Birthday.* Edited by Sven K. Soderlund and N. T. Wright. Grand Rapids: Eerdmans, 1999.

_____. "On Becoming the Righteousness of God: 2 Corinthians 5:21." Pages 200–208 in *Pauline Theology, Volume II: 1 and 2 Corinthians.* Edited by David M. Hay. Minneapolis: Fortress, 1993.

_____. *The Resurrection of the Son of God.* Minneapolis: Fortress, 2003.

_____. *What Saint Paul Really Said: Was Paul of Tarsus the Real Founder of Christianity?* Grand Rapids: Eerdmans, 1997.

Yarbro Collins, Adela. *The Apocalypse.* New Testament Message 22. Wilmington, Del.: Michael Glazier, 1979.

Yinger, Kent L. *Paul, Judaism, and Judgment according to Deeds.* Society for the Study of the New Testament Monograph Series 105. Cambridge: Cambridge University Press, 1999.

Young, Edward J. *The Prophecy of Daniel: An Introduction and Commentary*. Grand Rapids: Eerdmans, 1949.

Young, Frances. *The Theology of the Pastoral Letters*. Cambridge: Cambridge University Press, 1994.

Young, Norman H. "An Aristophanic Contrast to Philippians 2.6–7." *New Testament Studies* 45 (1999): 153–55.

Zachariä, Gotthilf Traugott. *Biblischer Theologie, oder Untersuchung des biblischen Grundes der vornehmsten theologischen Lehren*. 4 pts. Göttingen und Kiel: Verlage Victorinus Bospiegel und Sohn, 1771–75.

Zanker, Paul. *The Power of Images in the Age of Augustus*. Jerome Lectures 16. Ann Arbor, Mich.: University of Michigan Press, 1988.

Ziesler, J. A. *The Meaning of Righteousness in Paul: A Linguistic and Theological Inquiry*. Society for New Testament Studies Monograph Series 20. Cambridge: Cambridge University Press, 1972.

_____. *Pauline Christianity*. Rev. ed. Oxford Bible Series. Oxford: Oxford University Press, 1990.

Zimmerli, Walther. *Ezekiel*. 2 vols. Hermeneia. Philadelphia: Fortress, 1983.

SCRIPTURE AND APOCRYPHA INDEX

Jeremiah

Mark

Luke

John

1 Corinthians

2 Corinthians

Galatians

Ephesians

Philippians

OTHER ANCIENT LITERATURE INDEX

SUBJECT INDEX

MODERN AUTHOR INDEX

We want to hear from you. Please send your comments about this book to us in care of zreview@zondervan.com. Thank you.

GRAND RAPIDS, MICHIGAN 49530 USA

WWW.ZONDERVAN.COM